THE DRAMA
OF THE
MEDIEVAL CHURCH

Oxford University Press, Ely House, London W. 1

GLASGOW NEW YORK TORONTO MELBOURNE WELLINGTON
CAPE TOWN SALISBURY IBADAN NAIROBI LUSAKA ADDIS ABABA
BOMBAY CALCUTTA MADRAS KARACHI LAHORE DACCA
KUALA LUMPUR HONG KONG TOKYO

FIRST PUBLISHED 1933

REPRINTED LITHOGRAPHICALLY IN GREAT BRITAIN
AT THE UNIVERSITY PRESS, OXFORD
FROM CORRECTED SHEETS OF THE FIRST EDITION
1962, 1967

1. The Three Marys at the Tomb, from Hartker's *Liber responsalis*,
St Gall, Stiftsbibliothek, MS 391, p. 33

THE DRAMA

OF THE

MEDIEVAL CHURCH

BY

KARL YOUNG

Professor of English in Yale University

VOLUME I

OXFORD
AT THE CLARENDON PRESS

TO
FRANCES BERKELEY YOUNG

PREFACE

THE essential purpose of the present treatise is to assemble, in their authentic forms, the dramatic compositions which were employed by the medieval Church in Western Europe as a part of public worship, and which are commonly regarded as the origins of modern drama. This undertaking began, years ago, in a modest desire to clarify some of the ecclesiastical circumstances under which these early plays were written and performed. Since it had appeared that a good many persons concerned with dramatic history would welcome instruction in a few matters of Church custom, I projected a slight volume which should offer something in the way of an exposition of the Roman liturgical system, accompanied by a few of the relevant dramatic pieces. In the course of preparing what had been intended as a mere introductory handbook, however, I conceived a plan for presenting, instead of a few specimens of Church plays, the whole body of them. The printed texts were found to be not only widely scattered or inaccessible, but often defectively edited as well; and it became clear also that a substantial amount of fresh material, unknown to the established historians of the subject, must be adequately considered. Yet, in spite of its growing proportions, the total collection of extant examples of Church drama seemed not to exceed the possibility of inclusion in a single treatise of generous dimensions.

Hence what was undertaken as an introductory manual has become primarily a *corpus*. The expository element, however, remains, and from being a mere preliminary guide, has persistently developed into a continuing commentary upon all the dramatic texts. At one time I assumed that the plays themselves might occupy one volume, and the discussion, another; but experience proved that the matters requiring elucidation were often so technical that explanations could be effectual only when attached directly to the texts themselves. Although, then, the originals and the commentary are intermingled, the reader is invited to centre his attention upon the plays themselves, and to assign to the accompanying exposition only such secondary importance as may seem to him appropriate. He is urged to remember that my comments are not intended to provide merely another general account of the subject. The descriptive and explanatory element, therefore, along with such literary appraisals as I have interjected, may or may not seem to have a continuity and serviceableness apart from the texts. My chief obligation, in any case, has been to present the actual writings of the ecclesiastical playwrights, accompanied by the means for interpreting them. Thus if I fail to gratify Thomas Warton's 'reader of taste' by what I have written myself, I may, perhaps, still hope to 'merit the thanks of the antiquarian' through putting into his hands a considerable body of originals either freshly verified, or now brought forward for the first time.

Concerning one part of the exposition I venture a further word of clarification. The opening chapters treating the Roman Mass and the Canonical Office—a grasp of which is indispensable to the present study—are designed solely for those concerned with dramatic literature. Inspired by masters such as the late Edmund Bishop and the venerable Dom Cabrol, one would be most happily occupied in writing of aesthetic and spiritual aspects of the liturgy—its majesty, its charm, and its significance; or guided by a comfortable supply of approved manuals, one might readily reproduce the liturgical rubrics appropriate for those who officiate in public worship. It happens, however, that for our present secular purpose comment of these two sorts would not be useful. Our requirement here is a simplified statement of commonplaces, many of which are inevitably and properly omitted both from practical manuals and from works of erudition, and are, therefore, not easily obtained by the uninitiated. An explanation of the Roman liturgical system which shall avoid confusing the uninstructed student of the drama must steadfastly disregard innumerable matters of ceremonial and calendar important for officiants, and must nevertheless supply other details which to the expert would seem superfluous. Whether or not the opening chapters succeed in their purpose, therefore, it may be understood that their unadorned austerity is intentional.

The general method employed throughout the treatise is primarily descriptive, rather than historical. Since certain of the Easter plays are the earliest of the extant dramatic pieces, and served as models for some of the Christmas plays, the dramatizations of the theme of Easter Day are treated first; but the distribution of the later chapters is governed merely by convenience of description. Within a single chapter the several versions of the same play are arranged in what may be called the *logical*

order of development, from the simplest to the most complex
and elaborate. Presumably this is, in general, also the *historical*
order, but from the dates of the manuscripts a demonstration
is usually impossible. The simplest forms are not always found
in the earliest manuscripts, and they sometimes appear in the
latest. I have therefore attempted to describe and interpret the
texts rather than to implicate them in a web of theorizing as to
Urformen and cross-influences. Speculative investigation of this
sort is undoubtedly important, as will be suggested again below,
but it hardly provides a humane or lucid scheme for a comprehensive display of dramatic pieces such as is attempted here.
The descriptive method, moreover, has the advantage of being
less liable to invalidation through the inevitable discovery of
fresh material. Whereas a newly-found text may often discredit
a genealogical construction, it can usually take its appropriate
place in a descriptive plan without general disturbance.

I am conscious of the fact that the space devoted to the various
groups of plays is not always proportionate to their intrinsic
merit. The first volume, for example, is dominated by dramatic
texts associated with Easter, considerable numbers of which
differ from one another only slightly, and none of which has the
literary interest found in certain plays treated more briefly in
the second volume. The *Visitatio Sepulchri* of Easter is not only
preserved in an astonishing number of examples, but it also
presents an unusual variety of small dramatic considerations
requiring explanation. The *Officium Pastorum* of Christmas, on
the other hand, seems to have been cultivated very little during
the Middle Ages, and the extant examples are few and relatively
simple in content. Some of the longer plays, such as those presenting the story of Daniel, far exceed the productions of Easter
and Christmas in literary interest, but are often free from liturgical technicalities needing elucidation. It is to be hoped, therefore, that what might seem to be a disproportion among the
treatments of the several groups of plays may be justified by the
varying numbers and peculiarities of the examples at hand.

It is sufficiently apparent, presumably, that a determined
effort has been made to remove from the body of the treatise a
mass of relevant information, by no means unimportant, which
might easily have encumbered the general movement of the
exposition, and have distracted attention from the essential
dramatic texts. The footnotes are intended to contain only brief

references or explanations which apply directly to the matter under discussion, and which the reader is assumed to desire immediately, without the inconvenience of searching in other parts of the treatise. Bibliographical lists, however, along with illustrative quotations, controversial discussion and additional dramatic texts, are relegated to the Notes assembled at the end of each volume. In some instances the dramatic material in the Notes approaches in extent and importance the chapter to which it applies, and the decision as to whether a particular text should be included in the main discussion or given the less conspicuous position was sometimes difficult. In general, however, the Notes need be consulted only by readers who desire exhaustive information. If such inquirers choose to regard certain parts of the Notes as more significant than what is offered in the formal chapters, I shall be neither astonished nor offended.

Since the essential part of these volumes is the texts of the plays themselves, it is desirable that I define the editorial principles according to which they have been printed.

(1) As a whole, the dramatic texts have been edited anew from the original sources in manuscripts or early printed service-books. This statement absolves me, I hope, from the necessity of reaffirming this fact in connexion with each of the several hundred separate pieces. Each text is accompanied by a reference to its source, and to previous editions when there are such; and it may be understood that, unless the contrary is declared, my text is based not upon the editions, but upon the original. In general, I have recorded my departures from the editions only when such annotations might be useful to the reader. Several of the early editors—and a few of the later ones—were obviously inexperienced in palaeography, and free from a restraining sense for exactitude. Although the listing of their misreadings and omissions might gratify the vanity of a new editor, it could be only a useless distraction to the reader. In dealing with a few particularly significant texts, the difficulty of which has inspired much emendation, I have adopted the more spacious policy of recording virtually all the editorial proposals of others. This is especially true of my treatment of the plays from the *Carmina Burana*.

(2) With the slight exceptions mentioned below, all my departures from the exact spelling of the manuscripts are recorded in the footnotes. The number of my rectifications is, perhaps,

smaller than some readers might desire, and a good many of the spellings left intact in my texts can hardly fail to offend persons who know Latin only through purified editions of classical authors. It seems desirable, however, that those who care to familiarize themselves with writings from medieval service-books should accustom themselves to the forms repeatedly found there. In such editorial changes as I have made, and declared, I cannot claim to have been rigidly consistent. I have, no doubt, altered my treatment somewhat in accordance with the varying standards of the scribes themselves. In a text generally normal in spelling, I have usually rectified an exceptional wayward form; but when the spelling is barbarous throughout the piece, I have felt inclined to let it convey its full original flavour, without the tempering effect of suggested substitutions. I have, however, tried to avoid confronting the reader with vagaries which might deceive him as to the meaning. No such difficulty, I assume, arises from such spellings as *aput* (*apud*), *set* (*sed*), *capud* (*caput*), *mendatium* (*mendacium*), *inditium* (*indicium*), or *suplicium* (*supplicium*). I have made no attempt to reproduce all the scribal forms of the words *Christus*, *Jesus*, and *alleluia*. I print *Ihc* and *Ihs* as *Ihesus*, *Xpc* and *Xps* as *Christus*, and *aevia*, *all*, and *allel* as *alleluia*. When a text is accompanied by variants from another manuscript, these do not include unimportant differences in spelling such as *gratia—gracia*, *nova—noua*, and *quaero—quero*.

(3) In the syntax of the originals I have suggested very few emendations. Occasionally a verb is supplied, to elucidate the relation of a rubric to a spoken passage, and verbs are sometimes brought into agreement with their subjects in number. Some of the syntax is so defective as to defy correction except through radical revision; again the defects, though obvious, are not such as to obscure the meaning, and need not be tampered with; and sometimes what might be mistaken for a solecism is merely a medievally acceptable departure from classical usage, such as the 'nominative absolute'. Editorial additions are enclosed within pointed brackets. These appear most conspicuously in the completions of well-known liturgical sentences. In the parts supplied editorially I have used normalized spellings.

(4) Since the purpose of the treatise is literary, I have not attempted to report palaeographical details exhaustively. The amount of such information that can be conveyed successfully otherwise than through photography is, at best, very limited.

The end of a manuscript page is indicated by a vertical bar. In expanding abbreviations I have used italics (or in passages wholly in italics, roman type) only when the scribe's or author's intention could be doubted. In a rubric, for example, *canī* and *dīc* might represent *cantat* or *cantet*, *dicit* or *dicat*; hence I have used printed forms such as cant*at* or cant*et*, dic*it* or dic*at*. Scribal corrections are reported whenever they might conceivably throw direct or indirect light upon interpretation, but the scribe's use of expunction, for example, is often passed over in silence. Thus the correction of *nescis* into *nescio* is recorded, but such writings as *maŋgnus* and *Mariịa* are merely printed as *magnus* and *Maria*, without comment. For ampersand in print, and for numerals and abbreviations of *et* in manuscripts, I usually give the words represented, rather than the symbols.

(5) In order that the dramatic texts may be as readily intelligible as possible, the descriptive rubrics are printed in roman type, and the speeches in italics. The punctuation is modernized throughout. Considerable variation has been admitted in the division of the speeches into lines. Sometimes a prose sentence has been broken into separate units in order to indicate a parallelism in rhythm or an attempted rhyme. A particular metrical form may be presented in varying ways, in accordance with internal rhyme or the conveniences of printing. Thus a verse of fifteen syllables $(8+7)$ may appear as a single long line, or as two short lines. In the body of the treatise I have, in general, tried to avoid the distraction that would arise from appending to the texts variants from additional manuscripts. When such textual apparatus is required, it is usually relegated to the Notes at the end of each volume. In a treatise such as the present one, however, the use of variants in footnotes is found to be less profitable than is usual in editions of literary pieces. Most of the texts are brief, and the speeches are commonly accompanied by rubrics, which are often more important and more subject to variation than the speeches are. Hence if the variants are worth considering at all, they can often be presented effectually and comfortably only through printing the piece straight through.

In labouring for a considerable time upon a task concerned with hundreds of separate dramatic pieces written during a period of five or six centuries and produced in scores of churches all over Western Europe, one inevitably becomes aware of a host of associated problems left only half-solved or neglected

altogether. Even though the editor and commentator may dare
to hope that he has not shirked his essential task, he cannot
avoid a feeling of regret over what he has failed to accomplish,
either through sheer lack of time or through incompetence. Of
such omissions from the present treatise I briefly mention a few
that seem to me especially conspicuous, in the expectation that
they will eventually be supplied by others.

Of the cultural background from which the plays emerge, or,
more precisely, of the local conditions under which they were
produced, our knowledge is very inadequate. We have, to be
sure, the general satisfaction of associating the invention of
tropes and of the primal Easter play with the Carolingian
Renaissance and with a few specific literary centres; and we can
be fairly certain of the political and ecclesiastical situation which
explains the existence of the so-called *Ludus de Antichristo*. But
it is humbling to record one's ignorance of the dramatic traditions at St-Benoît-sur-Loire which made possible the Fleury
play-book in its thirteenth-century form, and at the cathedral
school of Beauvais which produced the highly wrought play of
Daniel. Unquestionably there was much inter-borrowing of
dramatic texts among literary centres all over the West. The
Roman liturgy was international, the dramatic pieces were
largely conventionalized, and the dates and provenance of the
manuscripts seldom assure us as to where and when their con-
tents were first written. For large groups of dramatic texts, no
doubt, a *Stammbaum* is for ever impossible. But not all investigation of interrelationships can be so comfortably set aside.
Chapter XII below, for example, sets a simplified problem
that cries out for a solution—the presence in a large group of
German texts of a single alien example, that from Dublin. It
is to be hoped that scholars who find use for these volumes will
be able to establish numerous points of contact which I have
had no opportunity to investigate or which I have failed to
discern.

Another aspect of these plays which has been generally un-
explored is their melodies. I do not feel called upon to apologize
for having treated these pieces from an exclusively literary point
of view, and were a defence required, one could cite eminent
precedents. It is an obvious fact, however, that since the plays
of the Church were actually sung, our knowledge of them cannot
be complete until such of their music as exists has been published,

elucidated and heard.[1] I am not a specialist in the theory of plain-song or in musical palaeography, and the slight incursions into musicology of even eminent amateurs, such as Meyer and Pfeiffer, are not very reassuring. Resemblances or differences between the melodies of parallel passages of separate plays, or between those of the plays and those of the service-books, are often easily discerned, and I have occasionally ventured to record them. For my observations in this direction, however, I candidly disclaim any large significance. The adequate editing and exposition of the music associated with the dramatic texts might well require a separate treatise equal to the present one in extent. Such a study would undoubtedly aid in the interpretation of certain texts, would assist a demonstration of relationships, and would probably disclose unsuspected traditionalisms or originalities throughout the body of plays. Its chief contribution, however, would consist, I think, in opening to us the full charm of these dramatic pieces, and in making possible a larger number of moving performances such as the recent ones of Mrs. Justine B. Ward and the chorus of the Pius X School of Liturgical Music, in New York. The sensitive auditor will then discover that certain dramatic utterances of no great distinction in their words are magically touching in their melodies.

Among the ungrasped opportunities suggested by the present study I would mention, finally, those associated with the physical background of the performances. Of costumes and 'stage-properties' we can hardly hope to learn much more than is disclosed in the rubrics in the texts of the plays themselves, but of the exact location of the 'stage' for certain performances, and of the surrounding fabric of the buildings, a good deal could undoubtedly be learned through further archaeological investigations similar to those of Arens, Dalman, and Lanckoronski. Although I have written at some length concerning the Easter Sepulchre and the Christmas *præsepe*, I am conscious of having neglected numerous clues. Probably the position of the *sepulchrum*, for example, could be accurately determined in many additional instances through combining hints in the rubrics of the plays with known facts concerning the church buildings. The final comprehensive study of *mise en scène* in liturgical drama,

---

[1] A large proportion of the extant texts lack music in the MSS; but, fortunately, most of the longer and more significant plays have it. The melodies of a generous number of plays have been published by Coussemaker. For further bibliography see below, p. 542.

indeed, has not yet been made. For such an undertaking this treatise, and the monographs mentioned incidentally throughout, may perhaps serve as a convenient point of departure.

The pleasure which I feel in recording my obligations to generous helpers is tempered by the reflection that my dependence upon others greatly exceeds any indications which appear in the course of these volumes, or any estimate which I can formulate here.

My interest in the drama of the Church was first aroused by the enthusiastic expositions of Professor George P. Baker when I was a pupil of his at Harvard University, and since that time I have had a friend's privilege of drawing upon his counsel. My closer study of the subject began under the instruction of Professor John M. Manly, of the University of Chicago, without whose encouragement I could hardly have begun or completed the present undertaking. At an early stage in my studies I had the advantage also of occasional conferences with that master of dramatic history, Sir Edmund Chambers. I cherish my memory of his courtesy, years ago, to a youthful investigator, and I take pleasure in pointing to my use of his *Mediaeval Stage* in most of the chapters that follow.

I wish to pay especial homage to the group of learned men who have given me whatever understanding I possess of the liturgy of the Church. Never to be forgotten are the skill, patience, and goodwill of my first teacher in liturgiology, the Very Reverend James Barron, C.SS.R. At a later time the resources for a study of liturgical palaeography were opened to me through the traditional hospitality of the Order of Saint Benedict. To the Abbot of Solesmes, and to the late Prior, the Reverend Dom André Mocquereau, I express my gratitude for charming courtesies received during my several sojourns as their guest. For detailed instruction I am particularly indebted to my friend, the Reverend Dom G. M. Beyssac, O.S.B., who for two decades has continuously guided my steps and enlarged my collectanea. Almost equally numerous are my obligations to the late Reverend H. M. Bannister, of Oxford. At various times I have been graciously aided also by the late Edmund Bishop, the Reverend Dom Fernand Cabrol, O.S.B., the Right Reverend James H. Ryan, Mr. Charlton B. Walker, and the Reverend Dom André Wilmart, O.S.B. The Reverend T. Lawrason Riggs and the Reverend Speer Strahan, of New Haven, have generously criticized several chapters in manuscript, and Father Riggs has given me painstaking guidance in many particulars.

From my more immediate professional colleagues I have had help in abundance. Ever since my student days Professor E. K. Rand, of Harvard University, has been an indispensable resource for information and correction. Year after year Professor Neil C. Brooks, of the University of Illinois, has freely shared with me his private collectanea and his special knowledge of the subjects treated here. Professor Alfons Hilka, of Göttingen, and Professor Otto Schumann, of Hamburg, have given me generous information about matters associated with their monumental edition of *Carmina Burana*, now in process of publication. Both editors have sent me valuable textual notes on the plays in the Benediktbeuern manuscript, and Professor Hilka, as literary executor of the late Wilhelm Meyer, has allowed me to draw upon the unpublished notes of that eminent *savant*. Professor T. Atkinson Jenkins, of the University of Chicago, and Professor Raymond T. Hill, of Yale University, have given me lavishly of their time and learning in the interpretation of substantial passages in Romance dialects. For courteous aid in a variety of matters I am indebted also to Dr. Otto E. Albrecht, of the University of Pennsylvania, Dr. Oskar Eberle, of Schwyz, Dr. E. A. Lowe, of Oxford, Professor W. O. Sypherd, of the University of Delaware, Professor L.-P. Thomas, of Brussels, and the following friends at Yale University: G. L. Hendrickson, Angelo Lipari, Mary H. Marshall, Eduard Prokosch, C. R. Schreiber, E. T. Silk, and D. V. Thompson.

The favours shown to me by librarians in England, France, Germany, Austria, Switzerland, and Italy are far too numerous for detailed acknowledgement. A mere list of them would be portentous. I must, however, be allowed to refer to the extraordinary kindness of the following: Dr. Otto Clemen, of Zwickau; Reverend Hippolyte Delehaye, of Brussels; Reverend Dr. Bonaventura Egger, of Engelberg; Mr. A. A. Ellis, of London; Reverend Pius Fank, of Vorau; Dr. A. Fäh, of St Gall; Mr. Strickland Gibson, of Oxford; Reverend Luigi Guidaldi, of Padua; Reverend Berthold Haydrich, of Herzogenburg; Reverend Beda Lehner, of Kremsmünster; Dr. G. Leidinger, of Munich; Dr. Karl Löffler, of Stuttgart; M. Henri Omont, of Paris; Dr. Wilhelm Schier, of Melk; Reverend Damiano Sciore, of Sulmona; Sig. Ruggiero della Torre, of

Cividale; Dr. F. Trenkler, of Graz; and Reverend G. Vale, of Udine. At home, the staff of the Yale University Library have served me with flawless courtesy and skill.

In the latest stages of my work I have been effectually assisted by the staff of the Clarendon Press. At every stage along the way I have owed most to the comrade whose name appears in the dedication.

In offering my thanks to those who have helped me, however, I must insist that none of the persons named above be reproached for errors of fact or opinion which may appear in the subsequent pages. For any defects I alone am responsible. *In prævaricatione qua prævaricatus est, et in peccato suo quod peccavit, in ipsis morietur.*

K. Y.

New Haven,
  June, 1932.

CONTENTS
VOLUME I

PLAYS UPON OTHER SUBJECTS FROM THE BIBLE AND FROM LEGENDS

LIST OF ILLUSTRATIONS
VOLUME I

VOLUME II

ABBREVIATIONS

Brev. = Breviarium
Grad. = Graduale
Lib. resp. = Liber responsalis
Miss. = Missale
Ordin. = Ordinarium
Process. = Processionale
sæc. = sæculum
Trop. = Troparium

INTRODUCTION

THE dramatic manifestations to be considered in these volumes were the independent creation and possession of the medieval Church in Western Europe.[1] They are to be regarded not as a continuation of an ancient tradition, and not as a worldly importation from outside, but as a spontaneous new birth and growth within the confines of Christian worship. From the date of its beginning, in the tenth century, throughout the Middle Ages and into modern times, this drama remained essentially free from the contamination of alien forms. The vernacular drama which emerged from the Church during the later Middle Ages, to be sure, was freely modified under secular influences; but the germinal plays of the Church itself, written in Latin, and worshipfully performed by ecclesiastics within the Church walls, persisted in their independence until they were gradually removed from the service-books altogether, during the generations following the Reformation. With a readiness which is perhaps unparalleled, therefore, the Latin drama of the Church lends itself to a treatment in isolation. No other dramatic tradition engendered it, or dictated its form or content.

It should be fairly remembered, however, that in all their reverent self-sufficiency, the plays invented by the Church, and later resigned to literary craftsmen in the European vernaculars, do not represent the entire dramatic activity of the Middle Ages. There was continuous, and sometimes lively, competition outside. Our view of the productions of Church playwrights will be more enlightened, therefore, if we approach them through a brief survey of the three other dramatic traditions which maintained themselves, more or less persistently, throughout the medieval period.

I

Of these the most appealing, and most noteworthy in its written remains, is the dwindled legacy from the literary drama of pagan antiquity.[2] With the fall of the Roman Empire the greater part of the dramatic achievement of the ancient world

---

[1] For general bibliography see Notes, p. 541.
[2] See especially Chambers, i, chapters i– iv; Creizenach, i, 1–42; Cloetta, *Beiträge*, i; Jacobsen, pp. 1–66.

passed into obscurity. By the tenth century, the tragedy and comedy of Greece were, at least in Western Europe, virtually forgotten.[1] Of the Roman drama, however, a limited though still substantial amount survived. Seneca's ten tragedies— probably never acted in antiquity—were adequately preserved. There is evidence of their being known during the ninth century and the tenth, but no indication of a considerable reading of them before the fourteenth. They seem to have been esteemed chiefly for their *sententiæ*, which were gathered into anthologies. Of the reading of Plautus little is recorded. Of his twenty plays, twelve seem to have been generally forgotten; and when he is mentioned, it is usually as the supposed author of the anonymous comedy called *Querolus*, of the fourth century. The neglect of this author, it is surmised, was due, at least in part, to the difficulty of his language.

The one ancient dramatist who retained something like his full fame throughout the medieval period was Terence.[2] This distinction he won, no doubt, through the clarity and finish of his style and his terse 'sentences'—the presence of ethical nuggets which could be readily extracted from his writing. These characteristics established his plays, or selections from them, as text-books for schools. Our present interest in this author, however, arises not from his pervasive influence in education, but from his artistic services to a justly celebrated dramatic disciple, Hrotsvitha of Gandersheim.[3]

It is safe to say that this delightful person was born about the year 935, that she was of gentle birth, and that she entered the nunnery of Gandersheim in her younger years—probably in her early twenties. Her early education, which must have been considerable, was continued in the cultivated atmosphere of the cloister under the tutelage of such capable women as Riccardis and the abbess, Geberga, a highly instructed niece of the Emperor Otto I. The single complete manuscript of Hrotsvitha's writings divides them into three *libri*, the first containing chiefly saints' legends versified in hexameters or distichs, the second comprising her six plays in prose, and the third presenting, in hexameters, a panegyric of the reign of Otto I, and a history of her own monastery. Of these evidences of her piety and literary

---

[1] See Notes, p. 543.
[2] See M. Manitius, in *Philologus*, lii (1894), 546–52; Creizenach, i, 1–8; Jacobsen, pp. 2–5.
[3] For bibliography concerning Hrotsvitha see Notes, p. 543.

gift we can consider here only the plays. These are introduced
by a preface of irresistible charm and candour:[1]

Plures inveniuntur catholici, cuius nos penitus expurgare nequimus
facti, qui pro cultioris facundia sermonis gentilium vanitatem librorum
utilitati præferunt sacrarum scripturarum. Sunt etiam alii, sacris in-
hærentes paginis, qui licet alia gentilium spernant, Terentii tamen
fingmenta frequentius lectitant et, dum dulcedine sermonis delectantur,
nefandarum notitia rerum maculantur. Unde ego, Clamor Validus
Gandeshemensis, non recusavi illum imitari dictando, dum alii colunt
legendo, quo eodem dictationis genere, quo turpia lascivarum incesta
feminarum recitabantur, laudabilis sacrarum castimonia virginum iuxta
mei facultatem ingenioli celebraretur. Hoc tamen facit non raro vere-
cundari gravique rubore perfundi, quod, huiusmodi specie dictationis
cogente detestabilem inlicite amantium dementiam et male dulcia col-
loquia eorum, quæ nec nostro auditui permittuntur accommodari,
dictando mente tractavi et stili officio designavi. Sed ⟨si⟩ hæc erube-
scendo neglegerem, nec proposito satisfacerem nec innocentium laudem
adeo plene iuxta meum posse exponerem, quia, quanto blanditiæ
amentium promptiores ad illiciendum, tanto et superni adiutoris gloria
sublimior et triumphantium victoria probatur gloriosior, præsertim
cum feminea fragilitas vinceret et virilis robur confusioni subiaceret.
Non enim dubito, mihi ab aliquibus obici, quod huius vilitas dictationis
multo inferior, multo contractior penitusque dissimilis eius, quem pro-
ponebam imitari, sit sententiis. Concedo; ipsis tamen denuntio, me in
hoc iure reprehendi non posse, quasi his vellem abusive assimilari, qui
mei inertiam longe præcesserunt in scientia sublimiori. Nec enim tantæ
sum iactantiæ, ut vel extremis me præsumam conferre auctorum
alumnis; sed hoc solum nitor, ut, licet nullatenus valeam apte, supplici
tamen mentis devotione acceptum in datorem retorqueam ingenium.
Ideoque non sum adeo amatrix mei, ut pro vitanda reprehensione
Christi, qui in sanctis operatur, virtutem, quocumque ipse dabit posse,
cessem prædicare. Si enim alicui placet mea devotio, gaudebo; si autem
vel pro mei abiectione vel pro vitiosi sermonis rusticitate placet nulli,
memet ipsam tamen iuvat, quod feci, quia, dum proprii vilitatem
laboris, in aliis meæ inscientiæ opusculis heroico ligatam strophio, in
hoc dramatica vinctam serie colo, perniciosas gentilium delicias ab-
stinendo devito.

Of the touching disclosures in this passage we need examine
here only what is said of her model and of her literary intention.
Clearly Hrotsvitha was one of the many whom Terence's style
had enticed into reading salacious stories. Hence she purposed
to employ his dramatic form for bringing before her readers not

[1] Strecker, pp. 113–4.

shameful themes such as his, but accounts of the laudable chastity of holy virgins.[1] Her plays were to be an anti-Terence! She confesses that, even in the legends which she treats, the amorous blandishments of evil men caused her to blush; but she adhered to her purpose in the conviction that the greater the temptation of her heroines, the greater their glory. Of her own lack of stylistic polish Hrotsvitha is fully conscious, and she declares that she forgoes the use of verse, such as she had used in her metrical legends, in the intention of avoiding the pernicious attractiveness of pagan writings.[2]

The plays themselves are, in general, relatively brief, simple and faithful treatments of traditional legends. *Gallicanus* dramatizes the story of the pagan military commander who demanded marriage with the consecrated virgin, Constantia, but was converted to Christianity, received into a state of celibacy, and eventually martyrized. *Dulcitius* portrays the lust of the governor of that name for the three Christian maidens, Agapes, Chionia, and Hirena, and recounts the comic thwarting of his intentions through divine intervention. *Calimachus* culminates in scenes of resurrection. The hero is guilty of a passion for the married Christian, Drusiana, and she, after a violent amorous scene with her suitor, prays successfully for escape through death. Calimachus goes to her tomb with the purpose of violating her body, but is killed by a serpent. Through the prayers of St John the Apostle he and Drusiana are restored to life. *Abraham* and *Paphnutius* dramatize stories of harlots reclaimed by holy hermits disguised as lovers. In the former play the erring one is Abraham's niece, Maria; in the latter, she is the courtesan, Thaïs. In *Sapientia* the holy virgins, Fides, Spes, and Caritas, are tortured and murdered before their mother's eyes. She recovers the three bodies, and buries them with honour outside Rome. Forty days later Sapientia herself dies while praying at the grave of her children.

Although Terence was Hrotsvitha's inspiration, she did not imitate him slavishly. Whether she grasped his metrical form or not, she used rhymed prose. There is no evidence that she intended her plays for actual representation upon a stage, and

---

[1] Since four of her plays embody episodes of illicit love, Hrotsvitha may have conformed consciously to the medieval notion that this element was a characteristic of comedy as a type. See below, p. 6. In regard to the ethical objections to Terence sometimes raised during the Middle Ages see Creizenach, i, 2–3; Jacobsen, pp. 2–3.

[2] We are left in doubt as to how much she understood of Terence's metrical forms.

probably she did not know that Terence's plays themselves were so acted. Certainly her freedom with the unities of time and place would have made impossible a performance after the manner of her master.[1] Her product differs from his most essentially in the extent of the comic element. Only *Dulcitius* evokes laughter. In this play Hrotsvitha shows a mastery in mingling the serious and the ludicrous: the terror and suffering of the holy virgins, and the insane antics of the lustful official as he begrimes himself with embracing pots and pans. In this one instance she adopts almost completely the technique and temper of her model.

But whether she is faithfully Terentian or not, she is, in general, successfully dramatic. She selects for presentation the critical moments in her stories, skilfully excludes narration, and develops the action directly through dialogue. At the opening of *Paphnutius*, to be sure, the hero and his adherents retard the action by an irrelevant discussion of the *quadrivium*; and in an early scene of *Sapientia* the emperor betrays an unfortunate curiosity concerning the properties of numbers. These passages, however, are exceptional. In the plays as a whole the exposition is deft, the heart of the action is reached promptly, and the movement is continuous.

Hrotsvitha's rarest gift is in characterization. Sometimes the disclosures seem to arise from her own monastic experience, as when she shows the penitent Thaïs shrinking from the confinement and prospectively loathsome state of her narrow cell.[2] This skill appears even more strikingly in love-scenes, in which, as a vivacious critic has recently remarked, certain phrases 'cry out from the printed page'.[3] Such an effect is seen in the passage in which Drusiana senses the passion of Calimachus, and in terror appeals to Christ for deliverance.[4] It appears again in the passage presenting the parting of Gallicanus and Constantia. Although these two have renounced earthly love, the embers of passion still glow; and when Constantia's father invites the penitent Gallicanus to take up residence in the palace, the former suitor exclaims at the danger in his having always before his eyes the one whom he loved beyond kin or life or soul:[5]

> Gallicanus. *Unde non expedit me frequentius virginem intueri, quam præ parentibus, præ vita, præ anima a me scis amari!*

---

[1] The prevailing opinion now is that her plays were not intended for acting. See Cloetta, *op. cit.*, i, 127; Creizenach, i, 17–8; Chambers, ii, 207.

[2] See Strecker, pp. 193, l. 30–194, l. 9.
[3] See Waddell, p. 76.
[4] See Strecker, pp. 150–1.
[5] Strecker, p. 131.

In the presence of such talent and literary zest as Hrotsvitha's, one is at a loss to explain the isolation of her achievement. Her plays, never acted and probably little read, seem to have been generally neglected for centuries. No medieval writer mentions them, and to the modern world they became known only when a single complete manuscript was rediscovered at the end of the fifteenth century, and edited by Conrad Celtes in 1501. Why had this talented nun no followers? Why was she the only one to imitate the admired and famous Terence?[1] Why were neither his plays nor those of his enchanted disciple ever put into action upon a stage?

Possibly this neglect becomes somewhat more intelligible in the light of certain medieval misconceptions as to the nature of drama in general.[2] It is clear, for example, that the littérateurs of the Middle Ages were ignorant of the fact that Terence's plays were written for delivery through dialogue. It was commonly supposed, indeed, that in ancient times a comedy was recited by a single reader, while actors merely accompanied the reading with silent gesticulation. Still more perversive were the notions attached to the terms *tragœdia* and *comœdia*, both popularly and in the formal definitions of the erudite. These two words ceased to denote either scenic representation or the exclusive use of dialogue. Tragedy and comedy were regarded, rather, as forms of narrative, in which dialogue was hardly required. It might predominate, or it might be reduced almost to the point of vanishing. The essential criteria of the two dramatic types were thought to be these:[3]

(1) That tragedy should begin happily, but end with misfortune, whereas in comedy the sequence should be the reverse;

(2) That tragedy should be written in an elevated style, and comedy, in the colloquial speech of ordinary life;

(3) That tragedy should treat weighty events in the lives of eminent persons, whereas comedy should be concerned with the lower ranks of society, and, characteristically, with illicit love.

In these senses the words *tragœdia* and *comœdia* were applied to literature in general. Thus the epics of Lucan and Statius and

---

[1] For evidence that Terence was being read in another nunnery about the time of Hrotsvitha see E. Dümmler, in *Z.f.d.A.*, xix (1876), 466–7. For conjectures as to the possibility that Hrotsvitha's plays had some influence upon the acted drama of the Church see Coffman, *New Approach*, pp. 256–64. In regard to recently discovered copies and fragments of some of her plays see below, p. 543.

[2] See especially Cloetta, *op. cit.*, i, 16–54; Creizenach, i, 9–16; Chambers, ii, 208–11; Mantzius, ii, 1–2.

[3] See Cloetta, *op. cit.*, i, 28.

the elegies of Ovid were regarded as 'tragedies', the eclogues of Virgil, as 'comedies', and the satires of Horace, Persius, and Juvenal, as either the one or the other, according to their varying content and to the point of view of the interpreter.[1] Dante's epic becomes a *commedia*, and Chaucer's monk narrates short 'tragedies'.

Of particular interest in dramatic history is the embodiment of these misconceptions in the so-called elegiac comedies, or *comœdiæ elegiacæ*, of which a score or more have been preserved from the period between the eleventh century and the thirteenth.[2] These are sophisticated, and usually brief, compositions in Latin, drawing their comic subject-matter partly from Terence and partly from contemporary life, but modelling their form more or less directly upon the poems of Ovid. A typical example is the *Geta*, or *Amphitryon*, of a certain Vitalis, a *comœdia* of 530 lines in elegiac distichs, written before the middle of the twelfth century.[3] This piece, quite obviously inspired by Plautus's *Amphitryon*, is notable chiefly for its ridiculing of metaphysical dialectic and its centring the action in the two servants, the airy-minded Geta and the grossly stolid Birria. The 'comedy' was widely known throughout the later Middle Ages, was used in schools, was frequently quoted, and in the personages of the servants furnished two highly esteemed comic types. As a characteristic *comœdia elegiaca* it takes the form not of a drama but of a narrative. Although the speeches appear as direct discourse, they are introduced or interrupted by *ait, inquit, clamat, dixit*, and the like, and are sometimes separated by substantial narrative passages in the third person.

In the proportion of narrative included, the elegiac comedies vary considerably. In the well-known *Paulinus et Polla*, for example, the interruptions of the narrator are relatively inconspicuous.[4] A few pieces—the so-called Horatian comedies, or *comœdiæ Horatianæ*—are essentially monologues, in which the speaker recounts the action as if it had happened to himself, but

[1] See Creizenach, i, 12; Chambers, ii, 210.

[2] These are fully discussed by Cloetta, *op. cit.*, i, 68–106, with references to editions. See also Creizenach, i, 19–41; Chambers, ii, 212–3; Jacobsen, pp. 7–32; Manitius, iii, 1015–40. Because of the narrative element in these compositions they are sometimes called ' epic ' comedies. As to a few ' tragedies ' in the same literary form see Cloetta, i, 109–27. I have not seen G. Cohen's *Comédie latine en France au xiie siècle*, announced by him in *Revue des Études latines*, vi (1928), 270, as ready for publication in 1929.

[3] See Cloetta, *op. cit.*, i, 68–75. Modern writers often name the author Vitalis Blessensis, but there seems to be no evidence of his association with Blois. *Geta* is edited by Wright, pp. 79 sqq.

[4] For the text see Du Méril, *Poésies inédites*, pp. 374 sqq.

reports the remarks of his interlocutors in direct discourse.[1] Several comedies of substantial length eliminate the narrative element altogether, and thus become true dramas. Of this sort are the celebrated twelfth-century plays *Babio* and *Pamphilus*. The author of the former shows an acquaintance with the *Geta* of Vitalis, but draws his action largely from medieval life. *Pamphilus* treats a story of seduction conducted under medieval circumstances in the full spirit of Ovid's *Ars Amatoria*.[2]

As to the manner in which the elegiac comedies were spoken we have no positive evidence. Presumably they were commonly recited in a semi-dramatic way by minstrels or other performers. Possibly the speeches provided for the several characters were sometimes delivered by separate persons,[3] and probably the persons engaged in the recital sometimes used gestures and changes of voice by way of suggesting impersonation; but we have no assurance that even such compositions as *Pamphilus* and *Babio* were performed as plays, with complete use of impersonation and scenery.[4] Nor can we be sure that the elegiac 'comedies' and 'tragedies' as a group are precisely the antecedents from which developed the secular literary comedy of the later Middle Ages.[5]

II

Alongside the tradition deriving from the literary drama of classical antiquity there persisted, more or less continuously throughout the Middle Ages, two other dramatic impulses, less elevated in their appeal and less tangible in their evidences: that from the popular entertainers of antiquity, and that from the ritualistic observances of the folk. For our knowledge of these we cannot resort to a succession of written examples, but only to isolated references of uncertain interpretation.

[1] The chief examples are conveniently surveyed by Creizenach, i, 38–9; Jacobsen, pp. 14–6.

[2] The text of *Babio* is edited by Wright, pp. 65 sqq.; that of *Pamphilus*, by A. Baudouin, *Pamphile, ou l'Art d'être aimé*, Paris, 1874. See Cloetta, *op. cit.*, i, 86–93; Creizenach, i, 32–4; Jacobsen, pp. 18–21.

[3] In the MSS the names of the several characters were often entered in the margins, opposite their utterances. See Cloetta, *op. cit.*, i, 130–3. Cf. the manner in which the liturgical *Passiones* of Holy Week were sung at the end of the Middle Ages, as explained below, p. 101; and consider also the marginal entries in texts of the pseudo-Augustinian sermon, below, ii, 126 sqq.

[4] Jacobsen (pp. 28–32) contends that these plays were so acted. For a more cautious opinion see Cloetta, *op. cit.*, i, 100–6, 130–8. As to the reciting of the French 'mimes' of the thirteenth century see Faral, *Mimes*, pp. xii–xv.

[5] This represents the opinion of Creizenach, i, 41. Jacobsen (p. 32) presents a more positive view thus: ' Les comédies élégiaques ont donc pour le développement du théâtre comique populaire la même importance que le drame liturgique et biblique latin pour le développement du théâtre religieux en langue française.'

Even during the early years of the Roman Empire literary drama began to yield ground in popular estimation before theatrical entertainments of a lower order.[1] Comedy and tragedy were gradually overshadowed by farce and pantomime. The type of farce particularly in favour seems to have descended from the Greek mime (μῖμος) which had arisen in Sicily and Magna Græcia centuries before the Christian era.[2] The mime combined the coarsest forms of farcical action with a certain amount of ethical portrayal and comment. Indecency was mingled with morality, and both arose from direct observation of contemporary life. The mimes that flourished under the Empire seem to have been of a particularly degraded order, sacrificing the ethical element to a shamelessly realistic representation of human depravity; and these theatrical skits were accompanied by crude dancing and buffoonery. Sometimes such pieces contained satire of so offensive a sort as to bring legal retribution upon the performers themselves.

The Roman pantomime differed from the mime in its origin, and was patronized by a higher class of society. It arose especially from the declining literary drama, and consisted in the effort of a single *pantomimus* to represent, by means of dancing and dumb show, the whole development of a dramatic action. In the course of his performance he often assumed the roles of several separate personages, and his means of impersonation were often lascivious. The action was commonly accompanied by music.

The profession of the *scenici*, including *mimi*, *pantomimi*, and other types of public and private entertainers, was never legally honourable, and its ranks were usually recruited from the class of slaves. The whole body of such performers was reprobated with vehemence by the growing Christian Church.[3]

When the Empire disintegrated, and the Roman theatres were abandoned, the *mimi* and *pantomimi* survived. Since they had long been largely independent of the regular stage, they could find occupation, throughout the provinces, in private entertainments and in popular gatherings. The art of the pantomime, being more fragile and subtle, maintained itself, presumably, with some difficulty; but the coarser offerings of the mimes were

---

[1] For bibliography see Notes, p. 543.
[2] See Reich, i, chap. vi; Chambers, i, 1–5. The term *mime*, or *mimus*, designates either the actor or the piece acted.
[3] See Chambers, i, 10–9.

readily marketed. It is generally believed that the *mimi* were absorbed into the great body of medieval nomadic entertainers who, in small groups, wandered along the routes of trade and pilgrimage, offering amusement at tavern, castle, or cross-roads along the way. Such groups might be known as minstrels, *jongleurs*, or *joculatores*, and among their activities might be included those of that ancient narrative poet and reciter, the Germanic *scôp*.[1]

Our immediate interest in the fraternity of minstrels centres in the question as to how far their entertainments went in the direction of drama. That their *chansons à personnages, aubes, tensons, contes,* and *débats* included the element of dialogue is certain, and that in such recitals the separate roles were taken by separate speakers, with some sort of impersonation, is conceivable, but unproved. In spite of all the dramatic possibilities here, none of these particular literary diversions can be called a play. If there was genuine drama in the repertory of the minstrels, it was probably a survival from the old farce of the mimes. As to whether there was such a survival, opinions have been sharply divided. There is no positive reason why the mimes could not have persisted throughout the centuries, and have achieved literary permanence ultimately in such forms as Rutebeuf's *Dit de l'Erberie* of the thirteenth century, and the farces of the end of the Middle Ages. But if there was a continuous tradition of this sort, it left no examples, and the external evidences cited in support of it have not been universally accepted as unequivocal. Some critics regard such a continuous development as an established fact, some accept it as an unproved possibility, and others dismiss it as an extravagant fancy.[2]

III

Similar to the vagueness which surrounds the traditions of the *mimi* throughout the Middle Ages is that which obscures the dramatic activities of the folk.[3] The ultimate origin of these, we know, was certain pagan ceremonies of a quasi-religious nature, the purpose of which was to secure the fertility of the earth, of animals, and of human beings through the use of sympathetic magic. It was assumed that man could bring about the natural phenomena on which his life depended by imitating them. Thus

---

[1] See Chambers, i, 23 sqq.; Reich, i, 807 sqq.; Faral, *Jongleurs*, pp. 2 sqq.

[2] For bibliography see below, p. 543.

[3] For bibliography see Notes, p. 544.

the primitive worshipper fancied that by dressing himself in leaves and flowers, and by hanging such objects on trees, he could encourage the earth to reclothe herself with verdure; or that by putting to death some representative of the principle of life and subsequently reviving him, he could bring about a repetition of this act on a comprehensive scale by the mighty forces which govern the physical world. The outward manifestations of these beliefs have been, from very early times to the present, a variety of festivals, games, processions and dances which centred in acts imitating or symbolizing the departure and return of life, and particularly the death of vegetation in winter and the revival of it in the spring. All of these ritualistic observances contained dramatic elements, many of which are remote from the general subject now before us. Some of them, however, developed out of folk festival, through symbolic dances, into independent spoken drama.

Of these last the most conspicuous is the one called in English the mummers' play, which was particularly appropriate to the season of spring, but which, through the influence of Christianity, was attracted, in the course of time, to the season of Christmas.[1] Although the examples of this play recorded in writing are comparatively modern, the essentials are unquestionably very old, their origins being lost in the haze of pagan antiquity. The typical performance falls into three successive parts, which may be called the presentation, the action, and the *quête*. In the first, one of the performers speaks a prologue, requesting room for the actors, introducing the chief characters, and promising a pleasurable entertainment. The second part consists of a fight between the two principal protagonists, in the course of which one of them is slain. The doctor is summoned, boasts of his professional proficiency, and promptly revives the fallen hero. The third part is a sort of epilogue, in which various minor personages appear, one of whom collects money. The performance ends with a song.

Obviously the essential element of the play is the duel, resulting in a death and a resurrection. The chief fighter is commonly St George, and his antagonist is usually either the 'Turkish Knight' (or 'Prince of Paradise') or a person called 'Slasher' (or 'Captain Slasher', 'Bold Slasher'). In these contests, curiously enough, St George is not always victorious. In about half of the recorded examples, indeed, it is he who is slain. This

[1] See especially Chambers, i, chap. x; Tiddy, pp. 70 sqq.; Beatty, pp. 275 sqq.

indifference to the success or failure of a particular hero lends emphasis to the fact that the germ of the play is not the romance or realism of the story, but the symbolism of death and revival in themselves. Although personages and themes from medieval life and literature easily crept into the mummers' play from time to time, it successfully preserved its essential character as a product of pagan religious ritual.

With the three dramatic traditions that have now been briefly reviewed the plays of the Church had no direct association. As has already been said, organized Christianity originated and fostered a drama of its own. Unlike its religious daughter, Hrotsvitha, the Church did not borrow the technique of its worldly predecessors and undertake to reform their morals; and for any rivals who appeared during the course of the Middle Ages it expressed its aversion. Having denounced the plays of others, the Church spontaneously, independently and gropingly invented a new theatrical product, thus becoming the youthful and unskilled competitor of seasoned practitioners. As the generations passed, it did not entirely avoid reflecting the influence of its rivals, but in general it advanced with slow deliberation upon its own path.[1] So modest were its beginnings, so measured were its innovations, and so ample are the records of its falterings, that the drama of the medieval Church presents to the historian a unique opportunity for isolating a literary form and observing its development from almost inarticulate origins, through centuries of earnest experiment, into firmly conceived results. Of this process a detailed survey is undertaken in the pages that follow.

[1] As to alleged alien influences upon Church drama see Notes, p. 544.

THE LITURGY OF THE CHURCH OF ROME

CHAPTER I

THE ROMAN MASS

THE liturgy, or plan of public worship, in the midst of which the Christian drama of the Middle Ages arose is that of the Church of Rome. From the date of the earliest genuine dramatic manifestations, in the tenth century, to the period when the plays abandoned the precincts of the Church, Roman liturgical forms dominated Western Europe. The plays, to be sure, seem never to have been sanctioned or performed at Rome itself; but wherever they appeared, in France, England, Germany, Spain, or Northern Italy, they were associated with a liturgical design over which the Roman See formally presided.[1] This ecclesiastical control, it appears, was not exercised with uniform vigour in all quarters, and certainly it was not applied with equal rigidity to all parts of the liturgy. Some of the reasons for these discrepancies will appear presently, when we touch upon certain matters of origin and ecclesiastical organization. Meanwhile, we shall best serve the purposes of our particular literary inquiry by ignoring many peculiarities of locality and of detail, and by giving our attention chiefly to what might be called a generalized survey of the structure and content of the Roman system of daily collective worship.[2]

This liturgical scheme falls naturally into two distinct parts: a single sacrificial observance called the Mass, and a succession of eight separate devotional services which, as a group, are called the Canonical Office, *Cursus*, or *Horæ*. The several *horæ* are distributed throughout the day of twenty-four hours, and in the interval between the fourth and fifth of these services occurs the Mass. The complete liturgical day, therefore, has the following nine separate offices: Matins (*Matutinum*), Lauds (*Laudes*), Prime (*Prima*), Terce (*Tertia*), Mass (*Missa*), Sext (*Sexta*), None (*Nona*), Vespers (*Vesperæ*), and Compline (*Completorium*). The Mass differs greatly from the eight services of the Canonical Office both in external form and in essential significance; and since it is much the older, and incomparably the more hallowed, it may appropriately be considered first.

[1] Concerning the attitude of the Roman hierarchy toward the drama see below, ii, 410 sqq.

[2] For general bibliography see Notes, p. 544.

The Mass was instituted and first performed by Christ Himself at the Last Supper, through certain acts of which St Matthew, for example, gives the following record:[1]

Cœnantibus autem eis, accepit Jesus panem, et benedixit, ac fregit, deditque discipulis suis, et ait: Accipite, et comedite: hoc est corpus meum. Et accipiens calicem gratias egit: et dedit illis, dicens: Bibite ex hoc omnes. Hic est enim sanguis meus novi testamenti, qui pro multis effundetur in remissionem peccatorum.

The words and acts of Christ on this occasion, which He commanded His disciples to repeat in memory of Him, formed the nucleus of the liturgical observance which eventually acquired the name *Missa*.[2] From the earliest Christian centuries the service seems to have consisted of two parts: an introduction, and the commemorative sacrificial and sacramental act itself. The introduction, modelled on the ordinary services of the Synagogue, was devotional in character, comprising readings, prayers, preaching, and the singing of psalms.[3] In the second, and essential, part were repeated the acts and words of Christ Himself. Bread and wine were brought to the officiating person, and placed upon a table or altar. Standing before the table in an attitude of prayer, the officiant took the bread and wine in his hands, gave thanks,[4] and recited the words used by Christ in instituting the observance. He then broke the bread thus consecrated, and gave it to the people in communion. The contrast between these two parts, as we shall see, is clearly discernible in the Mass of to-day.[5]

We may assume that, at first, certain prayers and other parts in the service were spoken extemporaneously; hence when, in the course of time, forms were set down in writing in the various Christian communities, the results inevitably differed somewhat, although all agreed in including Christ's own words, and in providing that His acts should be repeated. By the fourth century

---

[1] Matt. xxvi, 26–8. See also Mark xiv, 17–26; Luke xxii, 14–20; 1 Corinthians xi, 23 sqq. The edition of the Vulgate regularly cited is that of Hetzenauer. In quotations, however, I do not always follow this editor's conventions of punctuation and spelling. For general bibliography relating to the Mass, see Notes, p. 545.

[2] The origin of this designation is indicated below, p. 42.

[3] See Cabrol, *Origines*, pp. 133–5.

[4] Hence the name 'Eucharist' (εὐχαριστία, thanksgiving) applied both to the service of the Mass and to the elements consecrated from bread and wine. See below, p. 34.

[5] The first part is, in general, represented by the first main division (I. The Preparation) in the outline of the Mass below. For comprehensive observations on the origins of the two parts of the Mass see, for example, Cabrol, *Origines*, pp. 130–41.

there existed some four clearly differentiated types of observance: those of Antioch, Alexandria, Rome, and Gaul.[1] In the West, the Roman form, after having been palpably influenced by the Gallican, came to be regarded as the norm in most communities. By the tenth century, or thereabouts, it had taken complete possession of Western churches, except at Milan and Toledo. The form of Roman Mass which achieved this ascendancy was essentially that of to-day.[2]

The aim of the pages immediately following is to present a liturgical norm such as will enable the reader to comprehend the context and performance of the Roman Mass as they existed from about the tenth century onwards—the period during which the plays of the Church arose. The exposition undertakes to set forth the full text of the Mass, in order that its scope and structure may be completely apparent, and also to indicate the general assignment of responsibilities among those who officiate. The details of ceremonial—that is, the minutiæ of external movement and gesture—will be noticed only in part, since these matters are not, in general, essential for our present purpose, and a complete treatment of them would require the reprinting of many chapters from the official rubrics and liturgical commentaries. The present exposition, then, aims to serve not as a manual of liturgical practice, but merely as a guide to liturgical intelligence such as will effectually elucidate the relations between the drama of the Church and the forms of worship to which it was attached.

One would be glad to construct a norm for the Mass from a full array of facts of the tenth century, or thereabouts, from a community such as St Gall, Limoges, or Winchester, in which dramatic manifestations appeared at an early date. For even so simplified a description as I am attempting, however, the necessary liturgical details for the year 900, and the succeeding centuries, are not forthcoming, either from these communities or from Rome itself.[3] It appears, therefore, that our soundest and most convenient approach is through the service-books and rubrics of our own time. In form and content the Mass of the tenth century and that of to-day are, as has been said, virtually identical; and in points at which the two are known to differ in

---

[1] See Fortescue, *Mass*, pp. 76–109.
[2] For a brilliant discussion of the Roman and Gallican elements in the Roman Mass see Bishop, pp. 1–19. See also Stapper, *Feier*, pp. 8–9.
[3] See Notes, p. 546.

content or manner of performance, the differences can conveniently be mentioned in appropriate places.

The general form of the Roman Mass is shown in the outline on the opposite page. For convenience of exposition, the liturgical pieces are grouped into five divisions. The first of these (I. The Preparation) may be described as merely devotional or instructional, for the psalms, readings, and prayers in it are not essential to the sacrificial observance which follows. The other four divisions are composed of prayers and formulæ grouped round the central act of consecrating the bread and wine as the body and blood of Christ. It will be noticed that almost half of the liturgical subdivisions are marked as 'proper', that is, as variable from day to day in their texts, in accordance with the nature of the feast. It is because of this variation in a substantial part of the liturgical text that we can regard each separate day, or feast (*festum*), as having its own Mass. Although the forms and words used for the central act of consecration, for example, are always the same, the textual changes in other parts of the observance permit us to use such designations as 'Mass of Easter', or 'Mass of Palm Sunday'.[1]

The observance to be described as our norm is a solemn Mass (*Missa solemnis*) sung on Easter Day in a well-appointed church which provides an adequate liturgical chorus—a chorus, that is to say, which takes its full prescribed part in the service, and sings nothing extraneous.[2] It is assumed that the chorus occupies stalls arranged along the two sides of the choir, or eastern division of the church building.

Among the persons who officiate at the Mass the most important is the celebrant (*celebrans*), who utters the formulæ of consecration, and is the agent through whom the sacrificial act is accomplished.[3] He is immediately assisted by two ministers (*ministri*),

[1] As we shall see below (p. 547; ii, 137), Christmas is exceptional in having three Masses.

[2] A *solemn* Mass—sometimes called ' high Mass ', or ' solemn high Mass '—and a *low* Mass have the same liturgical text, but differ fundamentally in ceremonial. In a solemn Mass, the celebrant is supported by a chorus, is served by a deacon, subdeacon, thurifer, acolytes, and torch-bearers, and sings those of his utterances for which music is provided. In a low Mass the celebrant has only a server to assist him, and employs no music. Historically the solemn Mass is the only complete and correct form of this observance. The low Mass is a permitted simplification, or make-shift. In my exposition I assume a Mass celebrated in a parish church, rather than in a cathedral or a monastery, in order to avoid the numerous, but unimportant, variations in ceremonial entailed by the presence of a bishop or an abbot.

[3] The celebrant also reads, in a low voice, everything sung by the chorus, and the more important passages uttered by the ministers, such as the epistle and the gospel. This reading entails certain elements of ceremonial which I omit from the present survey. See,

THE MASS (MISSA)

I. The Preparation

1. Introit (*Introitus*. Chorus. Proper).
2. Kyrie eleïson. (Chorus.)
3. Gloria in excelsis. (Chorus.)
4. Prayer, or Collect (*Oratio*, or *Collecta*. Celebrant. Proper).
5. Epistle (*Epistola*. Subdeacon. Proper).
6. Gradual (*Graduale*. Chorus. Proper).
7. Alleluia. (Chorus. Proper) or
   Tract (*Tractus*. Chorus. Proper).
8. Sequence (*Sequentia*. Chorus. Proper).
9. Gospel (*Evangelium*. Deacon. Proper).
10. Creed (*Credo*, or *Symbolum*. Chorus).

II. The Oblation

11. Offertory (*Offertorium*. Chorus. Proper).
12. Prayers at the Offering of Bread and Wine (*Orationes*. Celebrant).
13. Prayers at the General Censing (*Orationes*. Celebrant).
14. Psalm xxv (Washing of hands. Celebrant).
15. Prayer of Oblation (*Oratio*. Celebrant).
16. Prayer for Acceptance (*Oratio*. Celebrant, and Deacon and Subdeacon).
17. Secret (*Secreta*. Celebrant. Proper).

III. The Consecration

18. Preface (*Præfatio*. Celebrant. Proper).
19. Sanctus. (Chorus.)
20. The Canon (*Canon Missæ*).
    a. Prayers preceding the Consecration (*Orationes*. Celebrant).[1]
    b. The Consecration. (Celebrant.)
    c. Prayers following the Consecration (*Orationes*. Celebrant).

IV. The Communion

21. Pater Noster. (Celebrant.)
22. Prayers at the Fraction and the Commingling (*Orationes*. Celebrant).
23. Agnus Dei. (Chorus.)
24. Kiss of Peace (*Pax*. Celebrant).
25. Prayers at the Communion of the Celebrant (*Orationes*. Celebrant).
26. Ablution (*Ablutio*. Celebrant).
27. Communion (*Communio*. Chorus. Proper).
28. Postcommunion (*Postcommunio*. Celebrant. Proper).

V. The Dismissal

29. Ite, missa est. (Deacon.)

---

for example, Fortescue, *Ceremonies*, pp. 108, 115.

[1] Two of these prayers vary somewhat in content with the liturgical season. See below, pp. 35, 36.

the deacon (*diaconus*) and subdeacon (*subdiaconus*), and, less directly, by a master of ceremonies (*cæremoniarius*), who directs the movements of the several officiants, by a thurifer who carries the thurible for censing, and by acolytes and torch-bearers. The celebrant is further supported by the liturgical chorus already mentioned. Four singers of this chorus, called cantors, assume the special duty of leading, and of singing certain passages separately.

The extent to which different parts of the liturgical text are distributed into separate volumes for the use of the officiants and chorus is dictated by the convenience of those who are to use them. The following are the service-books normally used in singing Mass in the Middle Ages:[1]

(1) A sacramentary (*sacramentarium*), containing the parts said by the celebrant.

(2) A gradual (*graduale*), containing the parts sung by the chorus, with the music.

(3) A gospel-book (*evangeliarium*), containing the liturgical gospels read by the deacon.

(4) An epistle-book (*epistolarium*), providing the epistles read by the subdeacon.

As a guide to the use of these books in choir, and for ceremonial in general, a church required a fifth volume containing rubrics, or directions, called the ordinary (*ordinarium*). Usually this service-book contained no complete part of the liturgical text itself, but merely the *incipit*, or opening words, of each liturgical piece. If a particular church so desired, two or more of the books named above might be united in one volume. Thus the gospel-book and the epistle-book might be brought together in a lectionary (*lectionarium*). The modern missal (*missale*) combines all four of the volumes enumerated above, along with substantial parts of the ordinary.[2] It does not, however, contain the music used by the chorus. Missals approaching the modern book in fullness began to be used as early as the eleventh century. Such a volume may conveniently be called *missale plenum*.

From these preliminary explanations we pass to the text of the Mass itself.

---

[1] See Wordsworth and Littlehales, pp. 170 sqq.

[2] In the usual modern missal these parts of the ordinary are found chiefly in the *Ordo Missæ*, in the middle of the volume, between the text proper to Holy Saturday and that proper to Easter. The *Ordo Missæ* describes the general procedure of Mass, and gives in full most of the parts which do not change from day to day.

I. The Preparation

1. Introit (*Introitus*).

The introit is sung by the chorus after the celebrant and his ministers have entered the church from the sacristy and have approached the altar at the east end of the choir.[1] The text is as follows:

> *Resurrexi, et adhuc tecum sum, alleluia; posuisti super me manum tuam, alleluia; mirabilis facta est scientia tua, alleluia, alleluia.* Psalmus: *Domine, probasti me, et cognovisti me; tu cognovisti sessionem meam, et resurrectionem meam.* Versus: *Gloria Patri, et Filio, et Spiritui Sancto; sicut erat in principio, et nunc, et semper, et in sæcula sæculorum. Amen.*

This piece is sung according to the following arrangement of parts:[2]

Antiphona: *Resurrexi . . . alleluia, alleluia.* (First word sung by the cantors; remainder sung by the chorus.)

Psalmus: *Domine . . . resurrectionem meam.* (Opening words sung by the cantors; remainder sung by the chorus.)

Versus: *Gloria . . . sæculorum. Amen.* (Opening words sung by the cantors; remainder sung by the chorus.)

Antiphona: *Resurrexi . . . alleluia, alleluia.* (Chorus.)

The introit consists essentially, then, of a so-called antiphon[3] and a single psalm-verse, these being followed by the traditional doxology and a repetition of the antiphon. Since the introit was designed for occupying time while certain liturgical acts were being performed, it must often have been of considerable length. The single psalm-verse of the introit before us may represent a whole psalm originally sung in this place, the antiphon being repeated after each verse, or along with a doxology at the end.[4]

During the singing of the introit, the celebrant and his ministers, standing at the foot of the altar steps, recite certain prayers and forms in preparation for their liturgical offices. Since these forms were not an essential part of the Mass during the Middle Ages, and were fixed in their present state only in the sixteenth century, we need mention them only summarily, as follows:[5]

---

[1] It must have been intended originally that the introit should be sung *during the entrance* of the celebrant and his ministers. See Fortescue, *Mass*, pp. 216-7.

[2] See *Graduale*, p. xiv.

[3] For the meaning of the word antiphon see Notes, p. 546.

[4] See Wagner, pp. 68-78; Fortescue, *Mass*, pp. 217-8.

[5] See Fortescue, *Mass*, pp. 225-30.

In nomine Patris, et Filii, et Spiritus Sancti. Amen. (Celebrant.)
Judica me, Deus. (This is Psalm xlii, which, with its antiphon *Introibo ad altare Dei,* is said antiphonally by the celebrant and his ministers.)[1]

Versus: *Adjutorium nostrum in nomine Domini.* (Celebrant.)
Responsio: *Qui fecit cœlum et terram.* (Ministers.)

Confiteor Deo omnipotenti, beatæ Mariæ semper virgini, beato Michaëli Archangelo, beato Joanni Baptistæ, sanctis Apostolis Petro et Paulo, omnibus Sanctis, et vobis, fratres, quia peccavi nimis cogitatione, verbo, et opere, mea culpa, mea culpa, mea maxima culpa. Ideo precor beatam Mariam semper virginem, beatum Michaëlem Archangelum, beatum Joannem Baptistam, sanctos Apostolos Petrum et Paulum, omnes Sanctos, et vos fratres, orare pro me ad Dominum Deum nostrum. (Celebrant.)

Misereatur tui omnipotens Deus, et dimissis peccatis tuis, perducat te ad vitam æternam. (Ministers.)

Amen. (Celebrant.)

Confiteor Deo omnipotenti, beatæ Mariæ semper virgini, beato Michaëli Archangelo, beato Joanni Baptistæ, sanctis Apostolis Petro et Paulo, omnibus Sanctis, et tibi, pater, quia peccavi nimis cogitatione, verbo, et opere, mea culpa, mea culpa, mea maxima culpa. Ideo precor beatam Mariam semper virginem, beatum Michaëlem Archangelum, beatum Joannem Baptistam, sanctos Apostolos Petrum et Paulum, omnes Sanctos, et te, pater, orare pro me ad Dominum Deum nostrum. (Ministers.)

Misereatur vestri omnipotens Deus, et dimissis peccatis vestris, perducat vos ad vitam æternam. (Celebrant.)

Amen. (Ministers.)

Indulgentiam, absolutionem, et remissionem peccatorum nostrorum, tribuat nobis omnipotens et misericors Dominus. (Celebrant.)

Amen. (Ministers.)

Versus: *Deus, tu conversus vivificabis nos.* (Celebrant.)
Responsio: *Et plebs tua lætabitur in te.* (Ministers.)
Versus: *Ostende nobis, Domine, misericordiam tuam.* (Celebrant.)
Responsio: *Et salutare tuum da nobis.* (Ministers.)
Versus: *Domine, exaudi orationem meam.* (Celebrant.)
Responsio: *Et clamor meus ad te veniat.* (Ministers.)
Versus: *Dominus vobiscum.* (Celebrant.)

---

[1] As to antiphonal singing of a psalm see   also below, p. 51.
what is said above concerning the introit, and

Responsio: *Et cum spiritu tuo.* (Ministers.)

Oremus. (Celebrant.)

Aufer a nobis, quæsumus, Domine, iniquitates nostras, ut ad Sancta Sanctorum puris mereamur mentibus introire. Per Christum Dominum nostrum. Amen. (Celebrant, silently, as he ascends to the altar.)

Oramus te, Domine, per merita Sanctorum tuorum, quorum reliquiæ hic sunt, et omnium Sanctorum, ut indulgere digneris omnia peccata mea. Amen. (Celebrant, silently, at the altar.)

Ab illo benedicaris, in cujus honore cremaberis, Amen. (Celebrant, blessing the incense.)

At the conclusion of this last prayer the celebrant takes the thurible and censes the altar, and then is himself censed by the deacon.

2. Kyrie eleïson.

In the modern missal the *Kyrie eleïson* stands as follows:

Kyrie eleïson. Kyrie eleïson. Kyrie eleïson.
Christe eleïson. Christe eleïson. Christe eleïson.
Kyrie eleïson. Kyrie eleïson. Kyrie eleïson.

This choral piece appears to have been sung originally, as a sort of litany, between the chorus and the congregation. Later the singing was left to the chorus alone, each of the expressions *Kyrie eleïson* and *Christe eleïson* being repeated an indefinite number of times, until a signal was given to cease. The melodies for certain of the vowels were often very long and elaborate.[1] In modern practice the singing is arranged thus:[2]

Kyrie eleïson (Chorus or semi-chorus).
Kyrie eleïson (Cantors or semi-chorus).
Kyrie eleïson (Chorus or semi-chorus).
Christe eleïson (Cantors or semi-chorus).
Christe eleïson (Chorus or semi-chorus).
Christe eleïson (Cantors or semi-chorus).
Kyrie eleïson (Chorus or semi-chorus).
Kyrie eleïson (Cantors or semi-chorus).
Kyrie eleïson (*Kyrie* by cantors or semi-chorus; *eleïson* by chorus).

The general alternation, then, is between the chorus and the cantors, or between the two semi-choruses.

[1] See Wagner, pp. 78–82.

[2] See *Graduale*, pp. xiv–xv. The authorized *Graduale* allows a certain liberty in the assignment of details. In the first *Kyrie eleïson*, for example, *Kyrie* may be sung by cantors, and *eleïson* by the chorus or a semi-chorus.

3. Gloria in excelsis.

The text of this liturgical piece is as follows:

Gloria in excelsis Deo. Et in terra pax hominibus bonæ voluntatis. Laudamus te, Benedicimus te, Adoramus te, Glorificamus te. Gratias agimus tibi propter magnam gloriam tuam. Domine Deus, Rex cælestis, Deus Pater omnipotens. Domine Fili unigenite, Jesu Christe. Domine Deus, Agnus Dei, Filius Patris. Qui tollis peccata mundi, miserere nobis. Qui tollis peccata mundi, suscipe deprecationem nostram. Qui sedes ad dexteram Patris, miserere nobis. Quoniam tu solus sanctus, Tu solus Dominus, Tu solus Altissimus, Jesu Christe, Cum Sancto Spiritu, in gloria Dei Patris, Amen.

The words *Gloria in excelsis Deo* are sung by the celebrant, and then the succeeding phrases are sung alternately between two semi-choruses, or between the cantors and the chorus.[1]

4. Prayer, or Collect (*Oratio*, or *Collecta*).

At the conclusion of the *Gloria in excelsis*, the celebrant recites the special prayer proper to the day, introducing it as follows:

Versus: *Dominus vobiscum.* (Celebrant.)

Responsio: *Et cum spiritu tuo.* (Chorus.)

Oremus. Deus, qui hodierna die per Unigenitum tuum, æternitatis nobis aditum, devicta morte, reserasti, vota nostra quæ præveniendo aspiras, etiam adjuvando prosequere. Per eumdem Dominum nostrum, Jesum Christum, Filium tuum, qui tecum vivit et regnat in unitate Spiritus Sancti Deus, per omnia sæcula sæculorum. (Celebrant.)

Amen. (Chorus.)

This prayer is a collect: a petition uttered upon behalf of a whole congregation.

5. Epistle (*Epistola*).

After the prayer, the subdeacon, facing the altar, reads the following epistle (1 Cor. v, 7–8):

Lectio Epistolæ beati Pauli Apostoli ad Corinthios.

Fratres: Expurgate vetus fermentum, ut sitis nova conspersio, sicut estis azymi. Etenim Pascha nostrum immolatus est Christus. Itaque epulemur, non in fermento veteri, neque in fermento malitiæ et nequitiæ; sed in azymis sinceritatis et veritatis.

6. Gradual (*Graduale*).

Immediately after the epistle follows the gradual, of which the text for Easter is the following:

---

[1] See *Graduale*, p. xv. In the Middle Ages the whole chorus, taking up the words *Et in terra pax*, may have sung the piece straight through to the end. See Wagner, pp. 82–5.

Hæc dies quam fecit Dominus; exultemus et lætemur in ea. Versus: *Confitemini Domino, quoniam bonus, quoniam in sæculum misericordia ejus.*

The modern arrangement for singing this liturgical piece is the following:

Responsorium:[1] *Hæc dies . . . in ea.* (The first two words sung by one or two cantors; the remainder by the chorus.)

Versus: *Confitemini Domino . . . misericordia ejus.* (Two cantors, the chorus joining in singing the last word.)

Responsorium: *Hæc dies . . . in ea.* (Chorus.)

As a typical medieval arrangement we may take the following:[2]

Responsorium: *Hæc dies . . . in ea.* (Cantor.)

Responsorium: *Hæc dies . . . in ea.* (Chorus.)

Versus: *Confitemini Domino . . . misericordia ejus.* (Cantor.)

Responsorium: *Hæc dies . . . in ea.* (Chorus.)

These two forms illustrate adequately enough the principle of *responsorial* singing, in which the alternation occurs not between two choruses or semi-choruses, but between an individual cantor (or a selected group of two or four cantors) and the chorus. In this form of psalmody the cantor sings the verses, after each of which the chorus sings a refrain. In the gradual before us the psalm is represented by only a single verse.

7. Alleluia, or Tract (*Tractus*).

Exept on a very few occasions, the gradual is followed either by an *Alleluia* and its verse, on days of rejoicing, or by a chant called the tract, on days of mourning and penitence. The text of the *Alleluia* for Easter is this:

Alleluia. Alleluia. Versus: *Pascha nostrum immolatus est Christus.*

The medieval arrangement of it was as follows:[3]

Alleluia. (Cantors.)

Alleluia. (Chorus.)

Versus: *Pascha nostrum immolatus est Christus.* (Cantors.)

Alleluia. (Chorus.)[4]

---

[1] The whole piece is a responsory, or *responsorium*; but it is convenient to use this term, or the word *responsum*, also to designate the introductory element. For the modern arrangement see *Graduale*, p. xv.

[2] See Wagner, pp. 92–3.

[3] See Wagner, p. 100; Fortescue, *Mass*, p. 269.

[4] In the modern Mass of Easter the *Alleluia* is not repeated after the verse. See *Graduale*, p. 204.

For the purposes of the present treatise particularly significant is the fact that for the final *a* of the *Alleluia* was provided a prolonged and elaborate melody sung to the sound of *a*. This particular melody, often termed *melisma* or *jubilus*, was sung twice, by the whole chorus—at the end of the second *Alleluia*, immediately before the verse, and at the end of the final *Alleluia*. This *melisma* will be considered further in a later part of this treatise.[1]

On days of mourning and penitence the place of the *Alleluia* is taken by the tract (*tractus*), which may have derived its name from the fact that it was originally sung straight through without interruption (*tractim*).[2] Although the tract has no place in the liturgy of Easter, I pause to describe it as a part of our theoretical norm of the Mass. It usually consists of a series of psalm-verses, as in the following example from Monday of Holy Week:

> Versus: *Domine, non secundum peccata nostra quæ fecimus nos, neque secundum iniquitates nostras retribuas nobis.*
>
> Versus: *Domine, ne memineris iniquitatum nostrarum antiquarum, cito anticipent nos misericordiæ tuæ, quia pauperes facti sumus nimis.*
>
> Versus: *Adjuva nos, Deus salutaris noster, et propter gloriam nominis tui, Domine, libera nos; et propitius esto peccatis nostris, propter nomen tuum.*

At the present time the verses of the tract are sung in alternation between the cantors and the chorus, or between the two semichoruses.[3] In the Middle Ages the verses were sung through without interruption by a single cantor.[4]

8. Sequence (*Sequentia*).

Concerning the origin and varieties of sequences something will be said below.[5] Since from the ninth century to the fifteenth the number of these compositions ran into hundreds, or perhaps thousands, the Mass of any important feast would be likely to have its sequence. In the modern missal five fine examples are retained: for Easter, *Victimæ paschali*; for Pentecost, *Veni, sancte Spiritus*; for Corpus Christi, *Lauda Sion*; for the two feasts of the Seven Sorrows of the Blessed Virgin Mary, *Stabat Mater*; and for the Mass of the Dead, *Dies iræ*. The text of the sequence for Easter Day is as follows:

[1] See below, p. 182. On the repetition of the *melisma* see Fortescue, *Mass*, p. 269. This particular matter seems to be slighted by Wagner, pp. 97–103, and by Cabrol and Leclercq, i, 1226–9.

[2] See Wagner, p. 103; Fortescue, *Mass*, p. 271.

[3] See *Graduale*, p. xv.

[4] See Wagner, p. 103.

[5] See pp. 182 sqq.

Victimæ paschali laudes immolent Christiani.
Agnus redemit oves; Christus innocens Patri reconciliavit peccatores.
Mors et vita duello conflixere mirando; dux vitæ mortuus, regnat vivus.
Dic nobis, Maria, quid vidisti in via?
Sepulchrum Christi viventis, et gloriam vidi resurgentis.
Angelicos testes, sudarium et vestes.
Surrexit Christus, spes mea; præcedet vos in Galilæam.
Scimus Christum surrexisse a mortuis vere; tu nobis, victor Rex,
miserere. Amen. Alleluia.

In our day, the sentences of the sequence are sung in alternation
between the cantors and the chorus, or between the two semi-
choruses.[1]

9. Gospel (*Evangelium*).

Before the deacon intones, or sings, the gospel, he must first
prepare himself. Hence at the conclusion of the sequence, he
kneels before the altar and says this prayer:

Munda cor meum, ac labia mea, omnipotens Deus, qui labia Isaiæ
Prophetæ calculo mundasti ignito; ita me tua grata miseratione dignare
mundare, ut sanctum Evangelium tuum digne valeam nuntiare. Per
Christum Dominum nostrum. Amen.

The deacon then takes up the gospel-book from the altar, and
kneeling before the celebrant receives his blessing according to
the following form:

Jube, domne, benedicere. (Deacon.)
Dominus sit in corde tuo, et in labiis tuis, ut digne et competenter
annunties Evangelium suum. In nomine Patris, et Filii, et Spiritus
Sancti. Amen. (Celebrant.)

Then carrying the gospel-book to the north side of the choir,
accompanied by the subdeacon, a thurifer, and torch-bearers,
the deacon begins the following forms:

Dominus vobiscum. (Deacon.)
Et cum spiritu tuo. (Chorus.)
Sequentia sancti Evangelii secundum Marcum. (Deacon, making
the sign of the cross at the place where the proper gospel
begins in the book, and crossing himself likewise.)

[1] See *Graduale*, p. xv. The content of
Victimæ paschali will be amply considered below, pp. 273 sqq. As may be seen there, the
medieval text differs somewhat from the
modern. During the Middle Ages different
forms, of sequences were sung in different
ways. Sometimes parallel phrases or sentences were sung by alternating semi-
choruses; sometimes the whole chorus sang
the sequence straight through. See Wagner,
p. 261.

Gloria tibi, Domine. (Chorus, while the deacon censes the gospel-book.)

The deacon now intones the following gospel for Easter (Mark xvi, 1–7):

> *In illo tempore: Maria Magdalene, et Maria Jacobi, et Salome emerunt aromata, ut venientes ungerent Jesum. Et valde mane una sabbatorum, veniunt ad monumentum, orto jam sole. Et dicebant ad invicem: Quis revolvet nobis lapidem ab ostio monumenti? Et respicientes viderunt revolutum lapidem. Erat quippe magnus valde. Et introeuntes in monumentum viderunt juvenem sedentem in dextris, coopertum stola candida, et obstupuerunt. Qui dixit illis: Nolite expavescere; Jesum quæritis Nazarenum, crucifixum; surrexit, non est hic; ecce locus ubi posuerunt eum. Sed ite, dicite discipulis ejus, et Petro, quia præcedit vos in Galilæam; ibi eum videbitis, sicut dixit vobis.*

At the conclusion of the reading the subdeacon carries the gospel-book to the celebrant, who kisses the appropriate page, saying,

> *Per Evangelica dicta deleantur nostra delicta.*

Then the celebrant is censed by the deacon.

10. Creed (*Credo*, or *Symbolum*).

According to a very ancient tradition the gospel is appropriately followed by a sermon in the vulgar tongue. But since the creed was often regarded as in some way an extension of the gospel, the sermon might be introduced after the creed.[1] The vernacular homily need not concern us further here.

After the gospel (or the homily), the celebrant intones the opening words of the creed (*Credo in unum Deum*), and the chorus continues it to the end, either singing it straight through, or singing the clauses in alternation between two semi-choruses.[2] The form of creed used in the modern Mass is the following:

> *Credo in unum Deum. Patrem omnipotentem, factorem cæli et terræ, visibilium omnium, et invisibilium. Et in unum Dominum Jesum Christum, Filium Dei unigenitum. Et ex Patre natum ante omnia sæcula. Deum de Deo, lumen de lumine. Deum verum de Deo vero. Genitum, non factum, consubstantialem Patri; per quem omnia facta sunt. Qui propter nos homines, et propter nostram salutem descendit de cælis. Et incarnatus est de Spiritu Sancto ex Maria virgine; et homo factus est. Crucifixus etiam pro nobis, sub Pontio Pilato passus, et sepultus est. Et resurrexit tertia die, secundum Scripturas. Et ascendit*

---

[1] See Fortescue, *Mass*, pp. 284–5.   [2] See *Graduale*, p. xv.

in cœlum; sedet ad dexteram Patris. Et iterum venturus est cum gloria judicare vivos et mortuos; cujus regni non erit finis. Et in Spiritum Sanctum, Dominum et vivificantem, qui ex Patre Filioque procedit. Qui cum Patre et Filio simul adoratur, et conglorificatur; qui locutus est per Prophetas. Et unam sanctam Catholicam et Apostolicam Ecclesiam. Confiteor unum baptisma in remissionem peccatorum. Et expecto resurrectionem mortuorum. Et vitam venturi sæculi. Amen.

The creed is a relatively late addition to the Mass, having been introduced about the eleventh century. That it is not an essential element appears from the fact that it is not sung on all days of the year.[1]

II. The Oblation

11. Offertory (*Offertorium*).

As has been remarked above, the part of the Mass preceding the offertory stands by itself as a kind of introductory instructional and devotional service. It was anciently called the Mass of the Catechumens (*Missa Catechumenorum*), and after it the candidates for baptism were dismissed from the church. The Mass of the Faithful (*Missa Fidelium*), which then followed, appears to have opened with certain prayers; and although these are now lost, the formula introducing them has been retained even to the present day.[2] Thus, when the creed has been finished, one hears the following:

Versus: *Dominus vobiscum.* (Celebrant.)
Responsio: *Et cum spiritu tuo.* (Chorus.)
Oremus. (Celebrant.)

In the absence of the prayer, or prayers, to which the word *Oremus* should lead, the Mass proceeds with the next liturgical piece at hand, the offertory, the text of which is the following (Ps. lxxv, 9–10):

Terra tremuit, et quievit, dum resurgeret in judicio Deus, alleluia.

The opening word of the offertory is sung by the cantors, and the remainder by the chorus.[3]

From early times until about the eleventh century there occurred at the offertory a procession, in which those who were later to partake at the communion brought to the altar offerings of bread and wine for the consecration to follow. From the eleventh and twelfth centuries we hear of other gifts of a more

[1] See Fortescue, *Mass*, pp. 285–90.   [3] See *Graduale*, pp. xvi, 205.
[2] See *ibid.*, pp. 293–6.

worldly nature, of which the offering collected in our time is a
survival. The musical piece sung during this procession was
virtually identical with the introit in form, consisting of an antiphon and a succession of psalm-verses, the antiphon being repeated after each verse, or along with the doxology at the end.[1]
The number of psalm-verses would vary with the number of the
persons making offerings, and the whole piece would be concluded when the actual offering was completed.[2] When the
custom arose of committing the preparation of the bread and
wine to the clergy before Mass, the procession at the offertory was
no longer required, and the choral piece was eventually shortened to the minimum. It now consists usually, as in the case
before us, of a single sentence, which may be regarded as merely
the antiphon formerly repeated after the verses of a psalm.[3]

12. Prayers at the Offering of Bread and Wine (*Orationes*).

The offering of the bread and wine is accomplished through
five prayers said by the celebrant. In offering the bread, or Host
(*Hostia*), upon the paten, he says:

> *Suscipe, sancte Pater, omnipotens æterne Deus, hanc immaculatam
> Hostiam, quam ego indignus famulus tuus offero tibi Deo meo vivo et
> vero, pro innumerabilibus peccatis et offensionibus et negligentiis meis,
> et pro omnibus circumstantibus, sed et pro omnibus fidelibus Christianis
> vivis atque defunctis, ut mihi et illis proficiat ad salutem in vitam
> æternam. Amen.*

After this prayer the celebrant lays the Host upon the corporal,
a white linen cloth spread upon the altar-table. Then the deacon
holds the chalice while pouring wine into it, and the subdeacon
adds water. This mingling of wine and water the celebrant
blesses in the following prayer:

> *Deus, qui humanæ substantiæ dignitatem mirabiliter condidisti, et
> mirabilius reformasti, da nobis per hujus aquæ et vini mysterium, ejus
> Divinitatis esse consortes, qui humanitatis nostræ fieri dignatus est
> particeps, Jesus Christus Filius tuus, Dominus noster: Qui tecum vivit
> et regnat in unitate Spiritus Sancti Deus, per omnia sæcula sæculorum.
> Amen.*

The celebrant takes the chalice and offers it, saying, along with
the deacon, this prayer:[4]

---

[1] See above, p. 21.

[2] For further discussion of ceremonials associated with the offertory see below, ii, 32 sqq.

[3] See Fortescue, *Mass*, pp. 296–304; Wagner, pp. 110–7.

[4] See Fortescue, *Ceremonies*, p. 117.

*Offerimus tibi, Domine, calicem salutaris, tuam deprecantes clemen-
tiam, ut in conspectu divinæ Majestatis tuæ, pro nostra et totius mundi
salute cum odore suavitatis ascendat. Amen.*

After placing the chalice upon the corporal the celebrant says
two further prayers, accompanying them by appropriate gestures. He bows slightly, lays his hands, joined, on the altar in
front of him, meanwhile saying silently,

*In spiritu humilitatis, et in animo contrito suscipiamur a te, Domine,
et sic fiat sacrificium nostrum in conspectu tuo hodie ut placeat tibi,
Domine Deus.*

Then the celebrant stands erect, extends and raises his hands,
looks up for a moment, and then lowers his eyes and joins his
hands before his breast, saying meanwhile the following:

*Veni, sanctificator, omnipotens æterne Deus, et benedic hoc sacri-
ficium tuo sancto nomini præparatum.*

These five prayers, though all medieval, entered the Mass at
different periods.[1]

13. Prayers at the General Censing (*Orationes*).

After the prayers of oblation follows a general censing, including, in succession, the bread and wine, the altar, the celebrant,
and all other persons in the choir. First the celebrant blesses the
incense, praying thus:

*Per intercessionem beati Michaëlis Archangeli stantis a dextris
altaris incensi, et omnium electorum suorum, incensum istud dignetur
Dominus benedicere, et in odorem suavitatis accipere. Per Christum
Dominum nostrum. Amen.*

Then the celebrant takes the thurible and censes the bread and
wine, saying,

*Incensum istud, a te benedictum, ascendat ad te, Domine, et
descendat super nos misericordia tua.*

In censing the altar he prays as follows:

*Dirigatur, Domine, oratio mea sicut incensum in conspectu tuo:
elevatio manuum mearum sacrificium vespertinum. Pone, Domine,
custodiam ori meo, et ostium circumstantiæ labiis meis, ut non declinet
cor meum in verba malitiæ, ad excusandas excusationes in peccatis.*

In returning the thurible to the deacon the celebrant says,

*Accendat in nobis Dominus ignem sui amoris, et flammam
æternæ caritatis. Amen.*

[1] See Fortescue, *Mass*, pp. 304–8.

After this last prayer the celebrant is censed, and then the others in the choir, in order, without special prayers.

14. Psalm xxv (Washing of hands).

When the celebrant has been censed by the deacon, he washes his hands, saying meanwhile Psalm xxv:

Lavabo inter innocentes manus meas, et circumdabo altare tuum, Domine.

Ut audiam vocem laudis, et enarrem universa mirabilia tua.

Domine, dilexi decorem domus tuæ, et locum habitationis gloriæ tuæ.

Ne perdas cum impiis, Deus, animam meam, et cum viris sanguinum vitam meam.

In quorum manibus iniquitates sunt; dextera eorum repleta est muneribus.

Ego autem in innocentia mea ingressus sum; redime me, et miserere mei.

Pes meus stetit in directo; in ecclesiis benedicam te, Domine.

Gloria Patri, et Filio, et Spiritui Sancto.

Sicut erat in principio, et nunc, et semper, et in sæcula sæculorum. Amen.

15. Prayer of Oblation (*Oratio*).

After the washing of hands, the celebrant sums up the act of oblation in this appeal:

Suscipe, sancta Trinitas, hanc oblationem, quam tibi offerimus ob memoriam passionis, resurrectionis, et ascensionis Jesu Christi, Domini nostri; et in honorem beatæ Mariæ semper virginis, et beati Joannis Baptistæ, et sanctorum Apostolorum Petri et Pauli, et istorum, et omnium Sanctorum, ut illis proficiat ad honorem, nobis autem ad salutem, et illi pro nobis intercedere dignentur in cœlis, quorum memoriam agimus in terris. Per eumdem Christum Dominum nostrum. Amen.

This prayer was used somewhat optionally during the Middle Ages, not being generally prescribed until the sixteenth century.[1]

16. Prayer for Acceptance (*Oratio*).

At the conclusion of the prayer *Suscipe, sancta Trinitas* the celebrant kisses the altar. Joining his hands, he turns to the right towards the chorus. Facing thus he stretches out his hands and joins them again, meanwhile beginning the following succession of utterances:

Orate, fratres, ut meum ac vestrum sacrificium acceptabile fiat apud Deum Patrem omnipotentem. (Celebrant.)

---

[1] See Fortescue, *Mass*, p. 311.

Suscipiat Dominus sacrificium de manibus tuis ad laudem et gloriam nominis sui, ad utilitatem quoque nostram, totiusque Ecclesiæ suæ sanctæ. (Deacon and subdeacon.)

Amen. (Celebrant.)

17. Secret (*Secreta*).

The secret is said by the celebrant as the final prayer of the oblation. The designation may arise from the fact that it is said in a low voice; and since it is not generally audible, it is not introduced by the word *Oremus*. The form of secret for Easter is the following:

Suscipe, quæsumus, Domine, preces populi tui cum oblationibus hostiarum, ut paschalibus initiata mysteriis, ad æternitatis nobis medelam, te operante, proficiant. Per Dominum nostrum Jesum Christum Filium tuum, qui tecum vivit et regnat in unitate Spiritus Sancti Deus, per omnia sæcula sæculorum.

The concluding words *per omnia sæcula sæculorum* are said aloud, as an indication to the chorus and others that the preface is about to begin. To this concluding phrase the chorus responds *Amen*.

It has long been permissible for the celebrant to say all the prayers of the oblation (nos. 12, 13, 14, 15, 16, and 17) while the offertory is being sung, the result being, for good or ill, two simultaneous recitals: one in a low voice by the celebrant at the altar, and another aloud by the chorus in the choir. The offertory must, of course, be finished before the preface may properly begin.

III. The Consecration

18. Preface (*Præfatio*).

With the preface begins the central part of the Mass, during which the bread and wine are consecrated. The preface itself is introduced by several versicles and responses, which begin immediately after the *Amen* at the end of the secret. The complete text of these utterances is as follows:

Dominus vobiscum. (Celebrant.)
Et cum spiritu tuo. (Chorus.)
Sursum corda. (Celebrant.)
Habemus ad Dominum. (Chorus.)
Gratias agamus Domino Deo nostro. (Celebrant.)
Dignum et justum est. (Chorus.)
Vere dignum et justum est, æquum et salutare. Te quidem, Domine, omni tempore, sed in hac potissimum die gloriosius prædicare, cum

Pascha nostrum immolatus est Christus. Ipse enim verus est Agnus qui abstulit peccata mundi. Qui mortem nostram moriendo destruxit, et vitam resurgendo reparavit. Et ideo cum Angelis et Archangelis, cum Thronis et Dominationibus, cumque omni militia cœlestis exercitus, hymnum gloriæ tuæ canimus, sine fine dicentes. (Celebrant.)

While intoning this last paragraph, the preface itself, the celebrant stands facing the altar, with his hands extended on either side.

19. Sanctus.

The last word of the preface (*dicentes*) leads directly to the *Sanctus*,[1] which is properly sung through by the chorus, without interruption, in the following form:

Sanctus, Sanctus, Sanctus, Dominus Deus Sabaoth.
Pleni sunt cœli et terra gloria tua.
Hosanna in excelsis.
Benedictus qui venit in nomine Domini.
Hosanna in excelsis.

According to the general modern practice, when the chorus begins the *Sanctus*, the celebrant himself recites it, and then, while the chorus is singing as far as the word *Benedictus*, he proceeds with the silent, or almost silent, recital of the prayers of the Canon. Before the word *Benedictus* the chorus pauses, and postpones singing the latter part of the *Sanctus* until the elevation has occurred, after the consecration.[2] This is obviously a distortion of the structure of the Mass.[3]

20. The Canon (*Canon Missæ*).

As applied to the fundamental part of the Mass, the word *Canon* may mean merely the fixed and standard form according to which the consecration must be effected. The Canon is essentially a succession of prayers of which the dominant note is thanksgiving, in accordance with the tradition established by Christ Himself.[4] Except for a few words at the very end, the Canon is recited by the celebrant inaudibly. For purposes of exposition the prayers are here arranged in three groups, with reference to the central act of the consecration.

a. Prayers preceding the Consecration (*Orationes*).

The first of the five prayers preceding the consecration, and

---

[1] The ringing of a bell at the *Sanctus* appears to be a modern practice. See Fortescue, *Mass*, p. 343.

[2] See 20 *b* below.

[3] See Fortescue, *Mass*, p. 323.

[4] See above, p. 16.

the first element of the Canon, is the following petition on behalf
of the Church:

*Te igitur, clementissime Pater, per Jesum Christum Filium tuum
Dominum nostrum supplices rogamus ac petimus, uti accepta habeas,
et benedicas, hæc dona, hæc munera, hæc sancta sacrificia illibata, in
primis quæ tibi offerimus pro Ecclesia tua sancta catholica, quam
pacificare, custodire, adunare, et regere digneris toto orbe terrarum,
una cum famulo tuo Papa nostro N. et Antistite nostro N.[1] et omnibus
orthodoxis, atque catholicæ et apostolicæ fidei cultoribus.*

As the celebrant says this prayer he faces the altar, and during
the recital he makes appropriate gestures, which need not be
enumerated here.[2] Then follows the commemoration of the
living (*Commemoratio pro vivis*):

*Memento, Domine, famulorum famularumque tuarum N. et N.,[3] et
omnium circumstantium, quorum tibi fides cognita est, et nota devotio,
pro quibus tibi offerimus, vel qui tibi offerunt hoc sacrificium laudis,
pro se, suisque omnibus, pro redemptione animarum suarum, pro spe
salutis et incolumitatis suæ; tibique reddunt vota sua æterno Deo, vivo
et vero.*

The next prayer, designated *Infra actionem*[4] in the missal, is an
intercession for union between the worshippers present and the
saints:

*Communicantes, et diem sacratissimum celebrantes, Resurrectionis
Domini nostri Jesu Christi secundum carnem; sed et memoriam
venerantes, in primis gloriosæ semper virginis Mariæ, genitricis ejusdem Dei et Domini nostri Jesu Christi; sed et beatorum Apostolorum,
ac Martyrum tuorum, Petri et Pauli, Andreæ, Jacobi, Joannis,
Thomæ, Jacobi, Philippi, Bartholomæi, Matthæi, Simonis et Thad-
dæi; Lini, Cleti, Clementis, Xysti, Cornelii, Cypriani, Laurentii,
Chrysogoni, Joannis et Pauli, Cosmæ et Damiani, et omnium Sanctorum tuorum, quorum meritis precibusque concedas, ut in omnibus
protectionis tuæ muniamur auxilio. Per eumdem Christum Dominum
nostrum. Amen.*

[1] For the first 'N.' is to be said the name
of the reigning Pope, and for the second, the
name of the 'Ordinary', or bishop of the
diocese.

[2] The essential ceremonial movements accompanying this prayer, and the remaining
prayers of the Canon, are conveniently indicated by Fortescue, *Ceremonies*, pp. 52–7.

[3] In the place of the form 'N. et N.' the
celebrant names as many persons as he

wishes.

[4] Since it varies in content slightly from
time to time, this prayer commonly occupies
a place in the missal after the preface for the
particular day. Hence the rubric *Infra
actionem* ('Within the Canon') to separate it
from the preface preceding it. I give here, of
course, the text proper to Easter. See Fortescue, *Mass*, pp. 330–1.

For our present purpose the next two prayers of intercession require no introductory comment:[1]

> *Hanc igitur oblationem servitutis nostræ, sed et cunctæ familiæ tuæ, quam tibi offerimus pro his quoque, quos regenerare dignatus es ex aqua et Spiritu Sancto, tribuens eis remissionem omnium peccatorum, quæsumus Domine, ut placatus accipias, diesque nostros in tua pace disponas, atque ab æterna damnatione nos eripi, et in electorum tuorum jubeas grege numerari. Per Christum Dominum nostrum. Amen.*
>
> *Quam oblationem tu, Deus, in omnibus, quæsumus, benedictam, adscriptam, ratam, rationabilem, acceptabilemque facere digneris, ut nobis Corpus et Sanguis fiat dilectissimi Filii tui Domini nostri Jesu Christi.*

It is obvious that this latter petition, asking that the bread and wine may become the body and blood of Christ, leads directly to the final act of consecration.

b. The Consecration.

The two passages spoken by the celebrant at the final consecration of the bread and wine are slightly modified versions of sentences used by Christ Himself in instituting the Eucharist at the Last Supper.[2] The first passage is as follows:

> *Qui pridie quam pateretur, accepit panem in sanctas ac venerabiles manus suas, et elevatis oculis in cœlum, ad te Deum Patrem suum omnipotentem, tibi gratias agens, benedixit, fregit, deditque discipulis suis, dicens: Accipite, et manducate ex hoc omnes.* HOC EST ENIM CORPUS MEUM.

While saying the opening words *Qui pridie quam paieretur*, the celebrant takes the Host up from the altar-table. At the words *elevatis oculis in cœlum* he looks upward, and then lowers his eyes again. The words of consecration, HOC EST ENIM CORPUS MEUM, he says 'secretly, distinctly, and attentively',[3] bending meanwhile over the altar. When these words have been said, he stands erect and then genuflects. Rising again, and still facing the altar, he holds the consecrated Host up before him to such a height that it may be seen by all, above his head. He places it upon the altar again, and once more genuflects. During this elevation a bell is rung. Rising from the second genuflection, the celebrant says the following relating to the wine:

> *Simili modo postquam cœnatum est, accipiens et hunc præclarum*

---

[1] The first of these prayers (*Hanc igitur*) is given in the special form proper to Easter.

[2] See above, p. 16.

[3] Rubric of the missal.

Calicem in sanctas ac venerabiles manus suas, item tibi gratias agens, benedixit, deditque discipulis suis dicens: Accipite et bibite ex eo omnes. HIC EST ENIM CALIX SANGUINIS MEI, NOVI ET ÆTERNI TESTA- MENTI, MYSTERIUM FIDEI, QUI PRO VOBIS ET PRO MULTIS EFFUN- DETUR IN REMISSIONEM PECCATORUM. *Hæc quotiescumque feceritis, in mei memoriam facietis.*

The words of consecration, printed in capitals here, are said 'attentively, continuously, and secretly', the chalice being held slightly raised above the altar. The celebrant then genuflects, and after rising, elevates the chalice to a height at which it can be seen by all, above his head. He places it upon the altar again, and once more genuflects. During this elevation a bell may be rung again. Thus are accomplished the consecration and eleva- tion of the bread and wine. The tradition of performing an act of elevation in connexion with the consecration is, no doubt, very ancient. Since the later Middle Ages, however, the conspicuous- ness of the elevation may have led to some exaggeration of its relative importance. The central and original liturgical act, it should be remembered, is not the elevation but the consecra- tion.[1]

c. Prayers following the Consecration (*Orationes*).

After the consecration has been completed, the celebrant recites, in general silently, some six prayers, the ceremonial accompaniments of which need not be noticed here.[2] It will be observed that the third of these prayers is pre-eminent in beauty and sublimity.

Unde et memores, Domine, nos servi tui, sed et plebs tua sancta, ejusdem Christi Filii tui Domini nostri tam beatæ passionis, necnon et ab inferis resurrectionis, sed et in cœlos gloriosæ ascensionis, offerimus præclaræ Majestati tuæ de tuis donis ac datis, Hostiam puram, hostiam sanctam, hostiam immaculatam, Panem sanctum vitæ æternæ, et Calicem salutis perpetuæ.

Supra quæ propitio ac sereno vultu respicere digneris, et accepta habere, sicuti accepta habere dignatus es munera pueri tui justi Abel, et sacrificium Patriarchæ nostri Abrahæ, et quod tibi obtulit summus sacerdos tuus Melchisedech, sanctum sacrificium, immaculatam hostiam.

Supplices te rogamus, omnipotens Deus, jube hæc perferri per manus sancti Angeli tui in sublime altare tuum, in conspectu divinæ Majestatis tuæ, ut quotquot ex hac altaris participatione, sacrosanctum Filii tui

[1] See Fortescue, *Mass*, pp. 337–45; Bishop, p. 9.
[2] For ceremonial details see Fortescue, *Ceremonies*, pp. 56–7.

Corpus et Sanguinem sumpserimus, omni benedictione cœlesti et gratia repleamur. Per eumdem Christum Dominum nostrum. Amen.

Memento etiam, Domine, famulorum famularumque tuarum N. et N. qui nos præcesserunt cum signo fidei, et dormiunt in somno pacis. Ipsis, Domine, et omnibus in Christo quiescentibus, locum refrigerii, lucis, et pacis, ut indulgeas, deprecamur. Per eumdem Christum Dominum nostrum. Amen.[1]

Nobis quoque peccatoribus famulis tuis, de multitudine miserationum tuarum sperantibus, partem aliquam et societatem donare digneris cum tuis sanctis Apostolis et Martyribus: cum Joanne, Stephano, Matthia, Barnaba, Ignatio, Alexandro, Marcellino, Petro, Felicitate, Perpetua, Agatha, Lucia, Agnete, Cæcilia, Anastasia, et omnibus Sanctis tuis; intra quorum nos consortium, non æstimator meriti, sed veniæ, quæsumus, largitor admitte. Per Christum Dominum nostrum.

Per quem hæc omnia, Domine, semper bona creas, sanctificas, vivificas, benedicis, et præstas nobis. Per ipsum, et cum ipso, et in ipso est tibi Deo Patri omnipotenti, in unitate Spiritus Sancti, omnis honor et gloria. Per omnia sæcula sæculorum.

The last four words of the last prayer the celebrant intones aloud, and the chorus responds *Amen*. Thus ends the Canon.

IV. The Communion

21. Pater Noster.

Immediately after the final *Amen* of the Canon, the celebrant sings the *Pater Noster* with its brief introductory formula, and the chorus responds, as is shown in the following:

Oremus. Præceptis salutaribus moniti, et divina institutione formati, audemus dicere: Pater noster, qui es in cælis: Sanctificetur nomen tuum. Adveniat regnum tuum. Fiat voluntas tua, sicut in cælo, et in terra. Panem nostrum quotidianum da nobis hodie. Et dimitte nobis debita nostra, sicut et nos dimittimus debitoribus nostris. Et ne nos inducas in tentationem. (Celebrant.)

Sed libera nos a malo. (Chorus.)

Amen. (Celebrant, *secrete.*)

22. Prayers at the Fraction and the Commingling (*Orationes*).

Since at the Last Supper Christ took bread and broke it, the Mass has always included a similar act before the distribution at the communion. The prayer during the reciting of which the

---

[1] In the missal this prayer is headed by the rubric *Commemoratio pro Defunctis*. The formula 'N. et N.' may be omitted. See Fortescue, *Ceremonies*, p. 56.

celebrant breaks the Host is a kind of expansion of the *Pater Noster,* as follows:[1]

Libera nos, quæsumus, Domine, ab omnibus malis, præteritis, præsentibus et futuris; et intercedente beata et gloriosa semper virgine Dei genitrice Maria, cum beatis Apostolis tuis Petro et Paulo, atque Andrea, et omnibus Sanctis, da propitius pacem in diebus nostris, ut ope misericordiæ tuæ adjuti, et a peccato simus semper liberi, et ab omni perturbatione securi. Per eumdem Dominum nostrum Jesum Christum Filium tuum. Qui tecum vivit et regnat in unitate Spiritus Sancti Deus. Per omnia sæcula sæculorum.

The last four words the celebrant intones aloud, and the chorus responds *Amen.* The immediate sequel to the fraction is the commingling of the consecrated elements, brought about by the celebrant's letting a fragment of the Host fall into the chalice. Just before this act, is intoned this formula:

Pax Domini sit semper vobiscum. (Celebrant.)
Et cum spiritu tuo. (Chorus.)

During the act of commingling the celebrant recites this prayer:

Hæc commixtio et consecratio Corporis et Sanguinis Domini nostri Jesu Christi fiat accipientibus nobis in vitam æternam. Amen.

23. Agnus Dei.

The prayer *Hæc commixtio* is followed at once by the *Agnus Dei,* sung straight through by the chorus in the following triple repetition:[2]

Agnus Dei, qui tollis peccata mundi, miserere nobis.
Agnus Dei, qui tollis peccata mundi, miserere nobis.
Agnus Dei, qui tollis peccata mundi, dona nobis pacem.

Meanwhile the celebrant says these sentences silently.

24. Kiss of Peace (*Pax*).

At the conclusion of the *Agnus Dei* the celebrant says the following prayer:

Domine Jesu Christe, qui dixisti apostolis tuis: Pacem relinquo vobis, pacem meam do vobis, ne respicias peccata mea, sed fidem Ecclesiæ tuæ; eamque secundum voluntatem tuam pacificare et coadunare digneris. Qui vivis et regnas Deus, per omnia sæcula sæculorum. Amen.

[1] This prayer is called the embolism. For the ceremonial details of the fraction see Fortescue, *Ceremonies,* pp. 57–8. The Host is broken into three parts of unequal size. The smallest fragment is used in the commingling immediately to follow here; the other two parts are consumed by the celebrant later, at his communion. (See no. 25 below.)

[2] See *Graduale,* p. xvi.

Then he kisses the altar, and turning to the deacon at his right, gives him the Kiss of Peace (*Pax*), using this formula:

Pax tecum. (Celebrant.)
Et cum spiritu tuo. (Deacon.)

In the same way the deacon gives the *Pax* to the subdeacon, and the latter conveys it to the chorus.[1]

25. Prayers at the Communion of the Celebrant (*Orationes*).

While the *Pax* is being transmitted throughout the chorus, the celebrant proceeds with the following prayers, in preparation for his own communion:

Domine Jesu Christe, Fili Dei vivi, qui ex voluntate Patris, co-operante Spiritu Sancto, per mortem tuam mundum vivificasti, libera me per hoc sacrosanctum Corpus et Sanguinem tuum, ab omnibus iniquitatibus meis, et universis malis, et fac me tuis semper inhærere mandatis, et a te numquam separari permittas. Qui cum eodem Deo Patre et Spiritu Sancto vivis et regnas Deus in sæcula sæculorum. Amen.

Perceptio Corporis tui, Domine Jesu Christe, quod ego indignus sumere præsumo, non mihi proveniat in judicium et condemnationem, sed pro tua pietate prosit mihi ad tutamentum mentis et corporis, et ad medelam percipiendam. Qui vivis et regnas cum Deo Patre in unitate Spiritus Sancti Deus, per omnia sæcula sæculorum. Amen.

Panem cælestem accipiam, et nomen Domini invocabo.

Domine, non sum dignus ut intres sub tectum meum; sed tantum dic verbo, et sanabitur anima mea.

Corpus Domini nostri Jesu Christi custodiat animam meam in vitam æternam. Amen.

At the conclusion of this last petition the celebrant consumes the Host: that is to say, the two parts of it which remain after the previous commingling of the consecrated bread and wine.[2]

In preparation for the completion of his act of communion the celebrant says the two following prayers:

Quid retribuam Domino pro omnibus quæ retribuit mihi? Calicem salutaris accipiam, et nomen Domini invocabo. Laudans invocabo Dominum, et ab inimicis meis salvus ero.

Sanguis Domini nostri Jesu Christi custodiat animam meam in vitam æternam. Amen.

The celebrant now drinks from the chalice the Eucharist under

---

[1] For the details of the ceremonial see Fortescue, *Ceremonies*, pp. 27, 111, 119, 125.
[2] See no. 22 above. The ceremonial for the celebrant's communion is described by Fortescue, *Ceremonies*, pp. 58–60.

the appearance of wine, including the particle of the Host in it.[1]

26. Ablution (*Ablutio*).

After the completion of his communion the celebrant proceeds to the ablution. While the subdeacon pours wine into the chalice, the celebrant says the following:

Quod ore sumpsimus, Domine, pura mente capiamus; et de munere temporali fiat nobis remedium sempiternum.

He now drinks what is in the chalice. Then he holds the thumbs and forefingers of both hands over the chalice, and the subdeacon pours wine and water over the celebrant's fingers into the chalice, the celebrant meanwhile saying the following:

Corpus tuum, Domine, quod sumpsi, et Sanguis quem potavi adhæreat visceribus meis; et præsta ut in me non remaneat scelerum macula, quem pura et sancta refecerunt Sacramenta. Qui vivis et regnas in sæcula sæculorum. Amen.

Once more he drinks what is in the chalice.[2]

27. Communion (*Communio*).

After the communion of the celebrant, including the ablution, has been completed, the chorus sings the following piece, called the *communio*:

Pascha nostrum immolatus est Christus, alleluia; itaque epulemur in azymis sinceritatis et veritatis, alleluia, alleluia, alleluia.

Like the introit and the offertory, the *communio* was originally a chant of considerable length, consisting of a succession of psalm-verses with an antiphon. This liturgical piece was designed to occupy the period of time during which the members of the chorus and the congregation were partaking of the communion. The manner of singing such a composition has been explained above.[3] At a relatively early period in the Middle Ages, the *communio* was gradually shortened, as the number of communicants at the solemn Mass decreased.[4] The result is that now only the antiphon, without psalm-verses, remains.

28. Postcommunion (*Postcommunio*).

After the antiphon just considered, the celebrant says aloud

[1] See no. 22 above.
[2] For details of the ceremonial of the ablution see Fortescue, *Ceremonies*, pp. 61–2, 112.
[3] See p. 21.
[4] When Holy Communion is distributed at solemn Mass in our day, the distribution occurs after the communion of the celebrant and before the ablution. In regard to the ceremonial see Fortescue, *Ceremonies*, pp. 130–2.

the following collective prayer called the *postcommunio*, with the appropriate introductory formula:

Dominus vobiscum. (Celebrant.)
Et cum spiritu tuo. (Chorus.)
Oremus. Spiritum nobis, Domine, tuæ caritatis infunde, ut quos Sacramentis paschalibus satiasti, tua facias pietate concordes. Per Dominum nostrum Jesum Christum, Filium tuum, qui tecum vivit et regnat in unitate ejusdem Spiritus Sancti Deus per omnia sæcula sæculorum. (Celebrant.)
Amen. (Chorus.)

V. The Dismissal

29. Ite, missa est.

·The postcommunion is immediately followed by this formula:

Dominus vobiscum. (Celebrant.)
Et cum spiritu tuo. (Chorus.)

Then the deacon sings the words *Ite, missa est, alleluia, alleluia,* to which the chorus responds *Deo gratias, alleluia, alleluia.*[1] The deacon's utterance means, 'Go, it is the dismissal', or 'Go, there is dismissal', and the noun *missa* used here has given its name to the whole Eucharistic observance. The finality of the deacon's announcement indicates that the Mass ends at this point, and that what follows in the modern missal is a later addition.[2]

At the close of a schematic survey of the form of the Roman Mass one may appropriately emphasize again the fact that the completed structure now before us is the result of a somewhat complicated fusion and a long accretion. The central sacrificial act was present from the beginning, and the chief prayers and chants were fixed during the early Christian centuries; but later, from non-Roman sources, were adopted fresh forms of prayer, and, more conspicuously, several striking elements of ceremonial. 'We do not realize at once', observes Bishop, 'how much of novel and imposing ceremonial is involved in the addition, in the twelfth and thirteenth centuries, of the single act of the elevation of the Host and Chalice, with its accompanying lights and

[1] On days of sorrow or penance, instead of *Ite, missa est* is used *Benedicamus Domino* with the usual response *Deo gratias*. On these closing formulæ see Cabrol and Leclercq, ii, 659–60.

[2] See Fortescue, *Mass*, pp. 392–5; Bishop, p. 12. In the modern missal the dismissal is followed by the *Placeat* prayer, a benediction, and the reading of a passage from the Gospels.

torches, censing, bell-ringings, and genuflections.'[1] We are justified in concluding, therefore, that the Roman Mass, both in its
text and in its ceremonial, arose through a blending of the sober
directness of Rome itself with the sensuousness and imaginative
splendour of other customs of Eucharistic worship.

[1] Bishop, p. 9.

CHAPTER II

THE CANONICAL OFFICE

TO the sacred origin, sacrificial intention, and essential stability of the Roman Mass the devotional observances of the Canonical Office, or *Cursus*, present a significant contrast. Its eight daily services, or *horæ*, include no indispensable religious act, follow no explicit pattern enjoined by Christ Himself, arose very gradually during a period of several centuries, and differed widely from one community to another.[1]

The beginnings are to be found in the 'vigil', or service of preparation, which the early Christians observed during the night before Easter Sunday, and which was eventually attached to the eve of each Sunday, of each feast of a martyr, and of the fast-days, Wednesday and Friday.[2] The vigil lasted throughout the night, and consisted of three successive services: one in the evening, one in the middle of the night, at cock-crow, and one in the early morning. Each of these observances comprised the singing of psalms, the reading of passages from the Bible, the saying of prayers, and the delivering of homilies. In form and content they were, like the introductory part of the Mass, modelled on the ordinary assemblies of the Jewish Synagogue.[3] The three successive parts of the vigil may be regarded as the first forms, respectively, of Vespers (*Vesperæ*), Matins (*Matutinum*), and Lauds (*Laudes*). The original placing of Matins in the middle of the night is reflected in the fact that the three main divisions of this service have always been called *nocturni*.[4]

To the three separate services of the vigil the new conditions of the age of Constantine brought substantial additions. Churches were built freely, and worship could be conducted openly and daily. Since the faithful could not be expected to attend both vigil and Mass every day, there arose groups of ascetics who dedicated themselves to a life of chastity and continual prayer. Devoted worshippers such as these could not only conduct adequately the three night offices of Vespers, Matins, and Lauds, but could also undertake observances by day. Thus, during the

---

[1] For general bibliography relating to the Canonical Office see Notes, p. 546.

[2] For convenient accounts of the origin and development of the *horæ* see especially Cabrol, *Prayer*, pp. 137 sqq.; Batiffol, chap. i; Wagner, pp. 126 sqq.

[3] See Cabrol, *Origines*, p. 141, and above, p. 16.

[4] See below, pp. 51 sqq.

fourth century, arose at the third, sixth, and ninth hours of the day the offices of Terce (*Tertia*), Sext (*Sexta*), and None (*Nona*). The night services continued to be attended freely by the laity, but the observances during the day-time were primarily for the professional clergy. As the influence of the ascetic and monastic groups advanced, and as they devoted themselves ever more zealously to organized worship, there arose—entirely under monastic auspices—two additional services: one in the early morning, eventually called Prime (*Prima*); and one at bed-time, called Compline (*Completorium*, 'completion').[1]

Such, then, is the genesis of the eight daily devotional services known collectively as the Canonical Office, *Cursus*, or *Horæ*. In origin the series was in large measure monastic, and in practice it necessarily remained so, for only the clergy in the regular life could hope to maintain so ample a plan of worship. Counting the Mass, the separate services of the day numbered nine, in the following order: Matins, Lauds, Prime, Terce, Mass, Sext, None, Vespers, and Compline.

From the circumstances of its development, as well as from the nature of its content, the Canonical Office inevitably showed marked diversities from one community to another. Having no central sacramental purpose, and being largely the devotional exercise of relatively small, isolated groups, or of rival monastic orders, the several *horæ* often developed in detail according to local preference. Hence the monastic form differed from the secular, and from time to time each of these forms, within itself, developed local peculiarities. Of these divergences a substantial proportion have persisted to the present day, along with differences of more recent development.

Under these conditions one may well be in doubt as to the appropriate model to adopt for our present exposition. In the year 900, for example, there was no form of Canonical Office, which, in all its details, could be regarded as obligatory for all churches, monastic and secular, in Western Europe. If the necessary liturgical facts were available, one would be glad to describe the *Cursus* followed in some community in which church plays arose, such as Fleury or Winchester. In the absence of the required details of text and ceremonial, however, we may resort to the procedure which we adopted for the Mass, and construct our norm from the rubrics and practice of the Church of

---

[1] See especially Batiffol, pp. 27–8.

Rome to-day. This norm will serve as well as any other for illustrating the general form and content of the Canonical Office in the Middle Ages, and the medieval departures from it in detail can be considered at appropriate places in the course of the general exposition.

As a basis for the description that follows I adopt the *Cursus* for Christmas Day as it might be sung in any parish or cathedral church which provides an adequate liturgical chorus of the sort specified in the preceding chapter.[1] In a cathedral, the presence of a bishop would affect the ceremonial only slightly; and for our present purpose we may, if we wish, assume that the bishop is absent altogether.[2] Aside from the chorus—from which four cantors are singled out for special duties—the most important officiating persons are the hebdomadary (*hebdomadarius*),[3] who presides over the services of the week, and takes the initiative at many points, and the reader (*lector*), who reads the lessons (*lectiones*).[4] A somewhat larger proportion of the *Cursus* than of the Mass is 'proper', or variable from day to day. Since the Canonical Office includes no indispensable sacramental element which cannot be altered, almost any part of the *horæ* is subject to variation.

As in the case of the Mass, the extent to which the different parts of the text of the Canonical Office are distributed into separate volumes is governed by the convenience of the officiants who use them. For the Middle Ages the following might be considered a normal list:[5]

(1) A psalter (*psalterium*), providing the words and music for the chorus in singing the psalms.

(2) A lectionary (*lectionarium*), containing the homilies and Biblical passages read by the lector.

(3) A *liber responsalis*, or *responsoriale*, containing the respon-

---

[1] See above, p. 18. For my description of the Canonical Office I abandon Easter because Matins on that day takes a form which is much briefer than the norm for a great feast (see below, p. 64), and because Vespers of Easter also departs widely from the norm (see below, p. 71).

[2] If present, the bishop would, for example, assume certain of the functions assigned to the hebdomadary in the exposition below.

[3] This officiating person, in any particular service, may be called also the celebrant. See Fortescue, *Ceremonies*, pp. 236–7.

[4] For the sake of simplicity I assume that the cleric serving as hebdomadary retains his usual stall in the rows of the chorus, and that the one serving as lector occupies his usual stall, except when he is engaged in reading the lessons, or in acts immediately connected therewith. On a great feast, several separate lectors may be assigned to the reading of the separate lessons.

[5] The liturgical terminology used here will be elucidated below. In regard to the service-books for the Canonical Office see Wordsworth and Littlehales, pp. 69 sqq.

sories, invitatories, versicles and responses, and antiphons sung by the chorus.

(4) A *collectarium*, containing the prayers (*orationes*), or collects (*collectæ*), and possibly the Biblical passages called chapters, or *capitula*.[1]

(5) A hymnal (*hymnarium*), containing the hymns.[2]

(6) A martyrology (*martyrologium*), comprising the lives of the saints, for reading at the office of Prime.[3]

The volumes enumerated are, of course, capable of being combined in various ways, or of being further subdivided. Thus the hymnal might be united with the psalter, to form one volume; and the lectionary might be divided into two volumes, one containing Biblical passages, and the other, homilies. As a guide to the use of all these books in the ceremonial of the choir, every church would need at least one copy of the ordinary, or book of rubrics.[4] In modern times the complete liturgical text, without music, is codified in a single volume, or set of volumes, called the breviary (*breviarium*).[5]

With these preliminary observations in mind we are ready to survey the actual structure and text of the eight separate services of the Canonical Office.[6]

MATINS (*Matutinum*)

The general structure of Matins will be apparent from the following outline:[7]

I. INTRODUCTION

1. Pater Noster. Ave Maria. Credo.
2. Verses and Responses (*Versus et Responsiones*).
3. Gloria Patri. Alleluia.
4. Invitatory (*Invitatorium*. Proper). Psalm xciv (*Psalmus xciv*).
5. Hymn (*Hymnus*. Proper).

---

[1] See, for example, the outline of Lauds below, p. 64.

[2] Hymns were freely introduced into the Canonical Office relatively late in the Middle Ages.

[3] See below, p. 69.

[4] See above, p. 20.

[5] Concerning the structure of the breviary one may consult the manuals of Lietzmann and Thalhofer, mentioned in the general list of books below.

[6] For our present purpose we may ignore the fact that nearly all feasts begin liturgically with Vespers of the preceding day. Thus Vespers of December 24th is 'First Vespers' of Christmas, and Vespers of December 25th is 'Second Vespers'. We may here assume a liturgical day of eight separate *horæ*, beginning with Matins and ending with Compline.

[7] In order to familiarize the reader with liturgical terminology I have inserted in the subsequent outlines a number of the Latin terms; and I have indicated most of the parts whose texts are variable, or 'proper'.

II. NOCTURNS (*Nocturni*)

A. First Nocturn (*Primus Nocturnus*).

1. Antiphon. Psalm (*Antiphona. Psalmus.* Proper).
2. Antiphon. Psalm. (Proper.)
3. Antiphon. Psalm. Verse. Response. (Proper.)
4. Pater Noster.
5. Absolution. Response (*Absolutio. Responsio.* Proper).
6. Verse. Benediction. Response (*Versus. Benedictio. Responsio*).
7. First Lesson (*Lectio i.* Proper). Verse. Response.
8. Responsory (*Responsorium.* Proper).
9. Verse. Benediction. Response.
10. Second Lesson (*Lectio ii.* Proper). Verse. Response.
11. Responsory. (Proper.)
12. Verse. Benediction. Response.
13. Third Lesson (*Lectio iii.* Proper). Verse. Response.
14. Responsory. (Proper.)

B. Second Nocturn (*Secundus Nocturnus*).

1. Antiphon. Psalm. (Proper.)
2. Antiphon. Psalm. (Proper.)
3. Antiphon. Psalm. Verse. Response. (Proper.)
4. Pater Noster.
5. Absolution. Response.
6. Verse. Benediction. Response.
7. Fourth Lesson (*Lectio iv.* Proper). Verse. Response.
8. Responsory. (Proper.)
9. Verse. Benediction. Response.
10. Fifth Lesson (*Lectio v.* Proper). Verse. Response.
11. Responsory. (Proper.)
12. Verse. Benediction. Response.
13. Sixth Lesson (*Lectio vi.* Proper). Verse. Response.
14. Responsory. (Proper.)

C. Third Nocturn (*Tertius Nocturnus*).

1. Antiphon. Psalm. (Proper.)
2. Antiphon. Psalm. (Proper.)
3. Antiphon. Psalm. Verse. Response. (Proper.)
4. Pater Noster.
5. Absolution. Response.

6. Verse. Benediction. Response.
7. Seventh Lesson (*Lectio vii.* Proper). Verse. Response.
8. Responsory. (Proper.)
9. Verse. Benediction. Response.
10. Eighth Lesson (*Lectio viii.* Proper). Verse. Response.
11. Responsory. (Proper.)
12. Verse. Benediction. Response.
13. Ninth Lesson (*Lectio ix.* Proper). Verse. Response.

III. TE DEUM LAUDAMUS

Under the guidance of this comprehensive outline we are
prepared for examining the content of each part of Matins, and
for observing the manner in which it is performed.[1]

I. INTRODUCTION[2]

1. Pater Noster. Ave Maria. Credo.
These three liturgical texts are recited silently by all persons
in the choir, as follows:

*Pater noster, qui es in cœlis, sanctificetur nomen tuum. Adveniat
regnum tuum. Fiat voluntas tua, sicut in cœlo, et in terra. Panem
nostrum quotidianum da nobis hodie. Et dimitte nobis debita nostra,
sicut et nos dimittimus debitoribus nostris. Et ne nos inducas in tentationem; sed libera nos a malo. Amen.*

*Ave Maria, gratia plena; Dominus tecum; benedicta tu in mulieri-
bus, et benedictus fructus ventris tui Jesus. Sancta Maria, Mater Dei,
ora pro nobis peccatoribus, nunc et in hora mortis nostræ. Amen.*

*Credo in Deum, Patrem omnipotentem, Creatorem cœli et terræ. Et
in Jesum Christum, Filium ejus unicum, Dominum nostrum, qui con-
ceptus est de Spiritu Sancto, natus ex Maria Virgine, passus sub Pontio
Pilato, crucifixus, mortuus, et sepultus; descendit ad inferos; tertia die
resurrexit a mortuis; ascendit ad cœlos, sedet ad dexteram Dei Patris
omnipotentis; inde venturus est judicare vivos et mortuos. Credo in
Spiritum Sanctum, sanctam Ecclesiam catholicam, Sanctorum communionem, remissionem peccatorum, carnis resurrectionem, vitam
æternam. Amen.*

---

[1] For bibliography see Notes, p. 546. The
more important details of ceremonial are mentioned by Fortescue, *Ceremonies*, pp. 236 sq.,
and by Martinucci, pt. i, vol. ii, 24–30. The
assignment of parts to the several officiants
is indicated in *Directorium Chori*, pp. iv–v.

[2] Here, and elsewhere, I omit from consideration the preparatory prayers that may
be said privately, and hence are not strictly
liturgical.

2. Versicles and Responses (*Versus et Responsiones*).
These forms are the following:[1]

Versus: *Domine, labia mea aperies.* (Hebdomadary.)
Responsio: *Et os meum annuntiabit laudem tuam.* (Chorus.)
Versus: *Deus, in adjutorium meum intende.* (Hebdomadary.)
Responsio: *Domine, ad adjuvandum me festina.* (Chorus.)

3. Gloria Patri. Alleluia.
The full form is as follows:

Gloria Patri, et Filio, et Spiritui Sancto. Sicut erat in principio, et nunc, et semper, et in sæcula sæculorum. Amen.
Alleluia.

The doxology is sung by the chorus as a whole, or is divided between two semi-choruses, beginning with the words *Sicut erat.* The single word *Alleluia* is sung by the whole chorus.

4. Invitatory (*Invitatorium*). Psalm xciv (*Psalmus xciv*).
The invitatory verse is *Christus natus est nobis, venite adoremus.* This is sung in conjunction with the verses of Psalm xciv in the following special manner:

Christus natus est nobis, venite adoremus. (Cantors.)
Christus natus est nobis, venite adoremus. (Chorus.)
Venite, exsultemus Domino, jubilemus Deo salutari nostro; præoccupemus faciem ejus in confessione, et in psalmis jubilemus ei. (Cantors.)
Christus natus est nobis, venite adoremus. (Chorus.)
Quoniam Deus magnus Dominus, et Rex magnus super omnes deos: quoniam non repellet Dominus plebem suam, quia in manu ejus sunt omnes fines terræ, et altitudines montium ipse conspicit. (Cantors.)
Venite adoremus. (Chorus.)
Quoniam ipsius est mare, et ipse fecit illud, et aridam fundaverunt manus ejus: venite, adoremus, et procidamus ante Deum: ploremus coram Domino, qui fecit nos, quia ipse est Dominus Deus noster; nos autem populus ejus, et oves pascuæ ejus. (Cantors.)
Christus natus est nobis, venite adoremus. (Chorus.)
Hodie si vocem ejus audieritis, nolite obdurare corda vestra, sicut in exacerbatione secundum diem tentationis in deserto: ubi tentaverunt me patres vestri, probaverunt et viderunt opera mea. (Cantors.)
Venite adoremus. (Chorus.)
Quadraginta annis proximus fui generationi huic, et dixi: Semper hi

---

[1] As to the officiants see *Directorium Chori*, p. iv.

*errant corde: ipsi vero non cognoverunt vias meas, quibus juravi in ira
mea, si introibunt in requiem meam.* (Cantors.)

Christus natus est nobis, venite adoremus. (Chorus.)

*Gloria Patri, et Filio, et Spiritui Sancto: Sicut erat in principio, et
nunc, et semper, et in sæcula sæculorum. Amen.* (Cantors.)

Venite adoremus. (Chorus.)

Christus natus est nobis, venite adoremus. (Cantors and chorus.)

It is to be observed that the invitatory verse is sung twice at the
beginning, and that in later repetitions sometimes the whole
verse is sung, and sometimes only the latter part of it.

5. Hymn (*Hymnus*).

The hymn is *Jesu, redemptor omnium,* in seven stanzas, of which
the following is the first:

> *Jesu, redemptor omnium,*
> *quem lucis ante originem*
> *parem paternæ gloriæ*
> *pater supremus edidit.*[1]

In rendering the hymn two semi-choruses sing alternate
stanzas.[2]

II. NOCTURNS (*Nocturni*)

From a glance at the outline above one observes that the
essential part of Matins is contained in three divisions, virtually
identical in form, called Nocturns. Of each Nocturn the chief
content is three psalms,[3] with their respective antiphons, and
three lessons, or readings, with their respective responsories.

A. First Nocturn (*Primus Nocturnus*)

1. Antiphon. Psalm (*Antiphona. Psalmus*).

The first antiphon is *Dominus dixit ad me: Filius meus es tu, ego
hodie genui te,* and it accompanies Psalm ii (*Quare fremuerunt*). The
antiphon is first sung by the whole chorus, and then the psalm is
sung by semi-choruses which take alternating verses. After the
last verse of the psalm, is sung the doxology *Gloria Patri,* divided
between semi-choruses; and finally the antiphon is repeated by
the chorus as a whole.[4] This arrangement is shown in the following abbreviated text:

Antiphon: *Dominus dixit ad me: Filius meus es tu, ego hodie genui
te.* (Chorus.)

---

[1] See Chevalier, *R. H.,* no. 9632.
[2] See Martinucci, pt. i, vol. ii, 26.
[3] A *liturgical* psalm may contain only part

of a Biblical psalm, or it may combine two or
more *Biblical* psalms.
[4] See Martinucci, pt. i, vol. ii, 26–7.

Ps. ii, 1. *Quare fremuerunt gentes, et populi meditati sunt inania?* (First semi-chorus.)

2. *Astiterunt reges terræ, et principes convenerunt in unum adversus Dominum, et adversus Christum ejus.* (Second semi-chorus.)

. . . . .

12. *Apprehendite disciplinam, nequando irascatur Dominus, et pereatis de via justa.* (Second semi-chorus.)

13. *Cum exarserit in brevi ira ejus, beati omnes qui confidunt in eo.* (First semi-chorus.)
    Gloria Patri, et Filio, et Spiritui Sancto. (Second semi-chorus.)
    Sicut erat in principio, et nunc, et semper, et in sæcula sæculorum. Amen. (First semi-chorus.)

Antiphon: *Dominus dixit ad me: Filius meus es tu, ego hodie genui te.* (Chorus.)

It should be remembered, however, that in many communities during the Middle Ages the antiphonal arrangement was very different from what I have just described. It is supposed that at an early period the antiphon was repeated after every verse or two of the psalm, and sometimes several antiphons may have been used, in various ways, in the singing of a single psalm.[1] Although such practices may have achieved certain desirable effects, they must have impeded the natural movement of the psalm itself, and have added greatly to the length of the service.

2. Antiphon. Psalm.

The second antiphon is *Tamquam sponsus Dominus procedens de thalamo suo*, accompanying Psalm xviii (*Cæli enarrant*). The singing of these follows the form shown above for the first antiphon and psalm.

3. Antiphon. Psalm. Verse. Response.

The third antiphon is *Diffusa est gratia in labiis tuis, propterea benedixit te Deus in æternum*, accompanying Psalm xliv (*Eructavit cor meum*). The singing of these follows the form shown above for the first antiphon and psalm. Then are sung this verse and response:

Tamquam sponsus. (Cantors.)
Dominus procedens de thalamo suo. (Chorus.)

4. Pater Noster.

This prayer is recited silently by all persons in the choir,

---

[1] See Wagner, pp. 144–55.

except for the closing words, which are spoken aloud as follows:[1]

Et ne nos inducas in tentationem. (Hebdomadary.)
Sed libera nos a malo. (Chorus.)

5. Absolution. Response (*Absolutio. Responsio*).

Immediately after the *Pater Noster* the hebdomadary recites the following prayer:

Exaudi, Domine Jesu Christe, preces servorum tuorum, et miserere nobis: Qui cum Patre et Spiritu Sancto vivis et regnas in sæcula sæculorum.

The chorus responds *Amen.*[2]

6. Verse. Benediction. Response (*Versus. Benedictio. Responsio*).

The lector now asks for the blessing of the presiding person, and receives it, according to the following forms:[3]

Versus: *Jube, domne, benedicere.* (Lector.)
Benedictio: *Benedictione perpetua benedicat nos Pater æternus.* (Hebdomadary.)
Responsio: *Amen.* (Chorus.)

7. First Lesson (*Lectio i*). Verse. Response.

The lector reads the following first lesson:

Primo tempore alleviata est terra Zabulon, et terra Nephthali; et novissimo aggravata est via maris trans Jordanem Galilææ gentium. Populus, qui ambulabat in tenebris, vidit lucem magnam; habitantibus in regione umbræ mortis, lux orta est eis. Multiplicasti gentem, et non magnificasti lætitiam. Lætabuntur coram te, sicut qui lætantur in messe, sicut exsultant victores capta præda, quando dividunt spolia. Jugum enim oneris ejus, et virgam humeri ejus, et sceptrum exactoris ejus superasti sicut in die Madian. Quia omnis violenta prædatio cum tumultu, et vestimentum mistum sanguine, erit in combustionem, et cibus ignis. Parvulus enim natus est nobis, et filius datus est nobis, et factus est principatus super humerum ejus: et vocabitur nomen ejus, Admirabilis, Consiliarius, Deus, Fortis, Pater futuri sæculi, Princeps pacis.

The reading is brought to a conclusion by the following verse and response:

Tu autem, Domine, miserere nobis. (Lector.)
Deo gratias. (Chorus.)

---

[1] The full text may be seen above, at the beginning of Matins, p. 49.
[2] See Martinucci, pt. i, vol. ii, 28.
[3] See *ibid.*

8. Responsory (*Responsorium*).

The first lesson is followed by the singing of a responsory, of which the text is the following:

> *Hodie nobis cœlorum Rex de Virgine nasci dignatus est, ut hominem perditum ad cœlestia regna revocaret. Gaudet exercitus Angelorum, quia salus æterna humano generi apparuit.* Versus: *Gloria in excelsis Deo, et in terra pax hominibus bonæ voluntatis. Gaudet. Gloria Patri. Hodie nobis.*

In the actual singing, the several parts of the responsory are distributed as follows:[1]

1. *Hodie nobis cœlorum Rex de Virgine nasci dignatus est, ut hominem perditum ad cœlestia regna revocaret. Gaudet exercitus Angelorum, quia salus æterna humano generi apparuit.* (Cantors and chorus.)[2]

2. *Gloria in excelsis Deo, et in terra pax hominibus bonæ voluntatis.* (Cantors.)

3. *Gaudet exercitus Angelorum, quia salus æterna humano generi apparuit.* (Chorus.)

4. *Gloria Patri, et Filio, et Spiritui Sancto.* (Cantors.)

5. *Hodie nobis cœlorum Rex de Virgine nasci dignatus est, ut hominem perditum ad cœlestia regna revocaret. Gaudet exercitus Angelorum, quia salus æterna humano generi apparuit.* (Chorus.)

This arrangement may be considered normal in modern practice. It should be remarked, however, that the several responsories of festal Matins are not usually sung in precisely the same manner.[3] Thus on Christmas Day the second, fourth, fifth, and seventh responsories have no *Gloria Patri*, and hence lack the last two of the five divisions into which the responsory is divided in the norm displayed above. In the earlier Middle Ages, the singing of the responsory was more protracted than in any arrangement used to-day. During the Carolingian period, for example, the text before us might have been distributed among the singers as follows:[4]

---

[1] The part of the responsory preceding the *versus* may be conveniently referred to as the *responsum*. The single word (*Gaudet*) standing immediately after the *versus* indicates the point within the *responsum* at which the repetition of part of the *responsum* is to begin.

[2] The opening word is sung by the cantors, after which the chorus assumes the singing of the rest of the passage.

[3] For convenience of reference it is customary to speak of the psalms, lessons, and responsories as if they were numbered continuously throughout the three nocturns. Thus the last responsory of the second nocturn is referred to as the sixth, and the third lesson of the third nocturn, as the ninth. See below, p. 62.

[4] See Wagner, pp. 137–8.

Hodie nobis cœlorum Rex de Virgine nasci dignatus est, ut hominem perditum ad cœlestia regna revocaret. Gaudet exercitus Angelorum, quia salus æterna humano generi apparuit. (Cantor.)

Hodie nobis cœlorum Rex de Virgine nasci dignatus est, ut hominem perditum ad cœlestia regna revocaret. Gaudet exercitus Angelorum, quia salus æterna humano generi apparuit. (Chorus.)

Gloria in excelsis Deo, et in terra pax hominibus bonæ voluntatis. (Cantor.)

Hodie nobis cœlorum Rex de Virgine nasci dignatus est, ut hominem perditum ad cœlestia regna revocaret. Gaudet exercitus Angelorum, quia salus æterna humano generi apparuit. (Chorus.)

Gloria Patri, et Filio, et Spiritui Sancto. (Cantor.)

Gaudet exercitus Angelorum, quia salus æterna humano generi apparuit. (Chorus.)

Hodie nobis cœlorum Rex de Virgine nasci dignatus est, ut hominem perditum ad cœlestia regna revocaret. Gaudet exercitus Angelorum, quia salus æterna humano generi apparuit. (Cantor.)

Hodie nobis cœlorum Rex de Virgine nasci dignatus est, ut hominem perditum ad cœlestia regna revocaret. Gaudet exercitus Angelorum, quia salus æterna humano generi apparuit. (Chorus.)

Let it be remembered, however, that in this matter, as in many others connected with the Canonical Office, practice has always varied considerably from time to time, and from place to place.[1]

9. Verse. Benediction. Response.

At the conclusion of the first responsory the reading of the second lesson is prepared for by the blessing of the lector in the following form:

Versus: *Jube, domne, benedicere.* (Lector.)

Benedictio: *Unigenitus Dei Filius nos benedicere et adjuvare dignetur.* (Hebdomadary.)

Responsio: *Amen.* (Chorus.)

10. Second Lesson (*Lectio ii*). Verse. Response.

The lector reads the following second lesson:

Consolamini, consolamini, popule meus, dicit Deus vester. Loquimini ad cor Jerusalem, et advocate eam: quoniam completa est malitia ejus, dimissa est iniquitas illius, suscepit de manu Domini duplicia pro

---

[1] The modern singing of the responsories in Matins appears not to be specifically and adequately explained in the authorized service-books and manuals, or in the *Decreta Authentica Congregationis Sacrorum Rituum,* 7 vols., Rome, 1898–1927. My exposition of modern practice is based chiefly upon actual performance in certain European churches distinguished for their liturgical traditions.

omnibus peccatis suis. Vox clamantis in deserto: Parate viam Domini, rectas facite in solitudine semitas Dei nostri. Omnis vallis exaltabitur, et omnis mons et collis humiliabitur; et erunt prava in directa, et aspera in vias planas. Et revelabitur gloria Domini; et videbit omnis caro pariter quod os Domini locutum est. Vox dicentis: Clama. Et dixi: Quid clamabo? Omnis caro fœnum, et omnis gloria ejus quasi flos agri. Exsiccatum est fœnum, et cecidit flos, quia spiritus Domini sufflavit in eo. Vere fœnum est populus; exsiccatum est fœnum, et cecidit flos. Verbum autem Domini nostri manet in æternum.

This reading is brought to a conclusion by the following verse and response:

Tu autem, Domine, miserere nobis. (Lector.)
Deo gratias. (Chorus.)

11. Responsory.

The responsory associated with the second lesson is the following:

Hodie nobis de cœlo pax vera descendit: Hodie per totum mundum melliflui facti sunt cœli. Versus: *Hodie illuxit nobis dies redemptionis novæ, reparationis antiquæ, felicitatis æternæ. Hodie.*

The manner in which this text is sung is indicated above (II. *A*. 8).

12. Verse. Benediction. Response.

At the conclusion of the second responsory the reading of the third lesson is prepared for by the blessing of the lector in the following form:

Versus: *Jube, domne, benedicere.* (Lector.)
Benedictio: *Spiritus Sancti gratia illuminet sensus et corda nostra.*
              (Hebdomadary.)
Responsio: *Amen.* (Chorus.)

13. Third Lesson (*Lectio iii*). Verse. Response.

The lector reads the following third lesson:

Consurge, consurge, induere fortitudine tua Sion, induere vestimentis gloriæ tuæ Jerusalem civitas sancti: quia non adjiciet ultra ut pertranseat per te incircumcisus et immundus. Excutere de pulvere, consurge, sede Jerusalem; solve vincula colli tui, captiva filia Sion. Quia hæc dicit Dominus: Gratis venumdati estis, et sine argento redimemini. Quia hæc dicit Dominus Deus: In Ægyptum descendit populus meus in principio, ut colonus esset ibi; et Assur absque ulla causa calumniatus est eum. Et nunc quid mihi est hic, dicit Dominus, quoniam ablatus est populus meus gratis? Dominatores ejus inique agunt, dicit Dominus; et jugiter tota die nomen meum blasphematur. Propter hoc sciet populus meus nomen meum in die illa, quia ego ipse, qui loquebar, ecce adsum.

The reading is brought to a conclusion by the following verse and response:

> *Tu autem, Domine, miserere nobis.* (Lector.)
> *Deo gratias.* (Chorus.)

14. Responsory.

The responsory associated with the third lesson is the following:

> *Quem vidistis, pastores? Dicite, annuntiate nobis in terris quis apparuit? Natum vidimus, et choros Angelorum collaudantes Dominum.* Versus: *Dicite, quidnam vidistis? et annuntiate Christi nativitatem. Natum. Gloria Patri. Natum.*

The general arrangement according to which this text is sung is the one applied above to the first responsory, with this exception: the fifth division of that arrangement contains, in the case before us, only the *second half* of the *responsum*, beginning with the word *Natum*.

B. Second Nocturn (*Secundus Nocturnus*)

As appears from the schematic outline above, the second Nocturn resembles the first in virtually every detail of *form*. For the antiphons, psalms, lessons, and responsories, however, the second Nocturn has its own proper *texts*. These may be given here, or merely referred to, without comment.

1. Antiphon. Psalm.

> Antiphona: *Suscepimus Deus misericordiam tuam in medio templi tui.*
> Ps. xlvii (*Magnus Dominus*).

2. Antiphon. Psalm.

> Antiphona: *Orietur in diebus Domini abundantia pacis, et dominabitur.*
> Ps. lxxi (*Deus judicium tuum*).

3. Antiphon. Psalm. Verse. Response.

> Antiphona: *Veritas de terra orta est, et justitia de cœlo prospexit.*
> Ps. lxxxiv (*Benedixisti, Domine*).
> Versus: *Speciosus forma præ filiis hominum.* (Cantors.)
> Responsio: *Diffusa est gratia in labiis tuis.* (Chorus.)

4. Pater Noster.

The details are given above (II. *A.* 4).

5. Absolution. Response.

> Absolutio: *Ipsius pietas et misericordia nos adjuvet; qui cum Patre*
> *et Spiritu Sancto vivit et regnat in sæcula sæculorum.*
> (Hebdomadary.)
> Responsio: *Amen.* (Chorus.)

6. Verse. Benediction. Response.

> Versus: *Jube, domne, benedicere.* (Lector.)
> Benedictio: *Deus Pater omnipotens sit nobis propitius et clemens.*
> (Hebdomadary.)
> Responsio: *Amen.* (Chorus.)

7. Fourth Lesson (*Lectio iv*). Verse. Response.

> *Sermo Sancti Leonis Papæ.*

Salvator noster, dilectissimi, hodie natus est; gaudeamus. Neque
enim fas est locum esse tristitiæ, ubi natalis est vitæ: quæ, consumpto
mortalitatis timore, nobis ingerit de promissa æternitate lætitiam.
Nemo ab hujus alacritatis participatione secernitur. Una cunctis
lætitiæ communis est ratio, quia Dominus noster peccati mortisque
destructor, sicut nullum a reatu liberum reperit, ita liberandis omnibus
venit. Exsultet sanctus, quia propinquat ad palmam; gaudeat pec-
cator, quia invitatur ad veniam; animetur Gentilis, quia vocatur ad
vitam. Dei namque Filius secundum plenitudinem temporis, quam
divini consilii inscrutabilis altitudo disposuit, reconciliandam auctori
suo naturam generis assumpsit humani, ut inventor mortis diabolus, per
ipsam, quam vicerat, vinceretur. (Lector.)

> Versus: *Tu autem, Domine, miserere nobis.* (Lector.)
> Responsio: *Deo gratias.* (Chorus.)

8. Responsory.

O magnum mysterium, et admirabile sacramentum, ut animalia
viderent Dominum natum, jacentem in præsepio. Beata Virgo, cujus
viscera meruerunt portare Dominum Christum. Versus: *Ave Maria,*
gratia plena; Dominus tecum. Beata. (Cantors and chorus.)

9. Verse. Benediction. Response.

> Versus: *Jube, domne, benedicere.* (Lector.)
> Benedictio: *Christus perpetuæ det nobis gaudia vitæ.* (Heb-
> domadary.)
> Responsio: *Amen.* (Chorus.)

10. Fifth Lesson (*Lectio v*). Verse. Response.

In quo conflictu pro nobis inito, magno et mirabili æquitatis jure certatum est, dum omnipotens Dominus cum sævissimo hoste non in sua majestate, sed in nostra congreditur humilitate, objiciens ei eamdem formam, eamdemque naturam, mortalitatis quidem nostræ participem, sed peccati totius expertem. Alienum quippe ab hac nativitate est, quod de omnibus legitur: Nemo mundus a sorde, nec infans, cujus est unius diei vita super terram. Nihil ergo in istam singularem nativitatem de carnis concupiscentia transivit, nihil de peccati lege manavit. Virgo regia Davidicæ stirpis eligitur, quæ sacro gravidanda fœtu, divinam humanamque prolem prius conciperet mente, quam corpore. Et ne superni ignara consilii ad inusitatos paveret affatus: quod in ea operandum erat a Spiritu Sancto, colloquio discit angelico, nec damnum credit pudoris, Dei Genitrix mox futura. (Lector.)

Versus: *Tu autem, Domine, miserere nobis.* (Lector.)

Responsio: *Deo gratias.* (Chorus.)

11. Responsory.

Beata Dei Genitrix Maria, cujus viscera intacta permanent, hodie genuit Salvatorem sæculi. Versus: *Beata quæ credidit, quoniam perfecta sunt omnia quæ dicta sunt ei a Domino. Hodie.* (Cantors and chorus.)

12. Verse. Benediction. Response.

Versus: *Jube, domne, benedicere.* (Lector.)

Benedictio: *Ignem sui amoris accendat Deus in cordibus nostris.* (Hebdomadary.)

Responsio: *Amen.* (Chorus.)

13. Sixth Lesson (*Lectio vi*). Verse. Response.

Agamus ergo, dilectissimi, gratias Deo Patri, per Filium ejus in Spiritu Sancto, qui propter multam caritatem suam, qua dilexit nos, misertus est nostri; et cum essemus mortui peccatis, convivificavit nos Christo, ut essemus in ipso nova creatura novumque figmentum. Deponamus ergo veterem hominem cum actibus suis; et adepti participationem generationis Christi, carnis renuntiemus operibus. Agnosce, O Christiane, dignitatem tuam; et divinæ consors factus naturæ, noli in veterem vilitatem degeneri conversatione redire. Memento cujus capitis, et cujus corporis sis membrum. Reminiscere, quia erutus de potestate tenebrarum, translatus es in Dei lumen et regnum. (Lector.)

Versus: *Tu autem, Domine, miserere nobis.* (Lector.)

Responsio: *Deo gratias.* (Chorus.)

14. Responsory.

Sancta et immaculata virginitas, quibus te laudibus efferam, nescio:
Quia quem cæli capere non poterant, tuo gremio contulisti. Versus:
Benedicta tu in mulieribus, et benedictus fructus ventris tui. Quia.
Gloria Patri. Quia. (Cantors and chorus.)

C. Third Nocturn (*Tertius Nocturnus*)

1. Antiphon. Psalm.

   Antiphona: *Ipse invocabit me, alleluia; Pater meus es tu, alleluia.*
   Ps. lxxxviii (*Misericordias Domini*).

2. Antiphon. Psalm.

   Antiphona: *Lætentur cæli, et exsultet terra ante faciem Domini,*
       quoniam venit.
   Ps. xcv (*Cantate Domino*).

3. Antiphon. Psalm. Verse. Response.

   Antiphona: *Notum fecit Dominus, alleluia, salutare suum, alleluia.*
   Ps. xcvii (*Cantate Domino*).
   Versus: *Ipse invocabit me, alleluia.* (Cantors.)
   Responsio: *Pater meus es tu, alleluia.* (Chorus.)

4. Pater Noster.
The details are given above (II. *A*. 4).

5. Absolution. Response.

   Absolutio: *A vinculis peccatorum nostrorum absolvat nos omnipotens*
       et misericors Dominus. (Hebdomadary.)
   Responsio: *Amen.* (Chorus.)

6. Verse. Benediction. Response.

   Versus: *Jube, domne, benedicere.* (Lector.)
   Benedictio: *Evangelica lectio sit nobis salus et protectio.* (Heb-
       domadary.)
   Responsio: *Amen.* (Chorus.)

7. Seventh Lesson (*Lectio vii*). Verse. Response.[1]

   Lectio sancti Evangelii secundum Lucam.

In illo tempore: Exiit edictum a Cæsare Augusto, ut describeretur
universus orbis. Et reliqua. (Lector.)

[1] When Matins has nine lessons, the seventh usually includes the liturgical gospel of the day—that is, the passage from the Gospels read in the Mass on that day. Then the remainder of the seventh lesson, and the eighth and ninth lessons, are usually devoted to a homily upon the liturgical gospel. Christmas happens to have three liturgical gospels, for its exceptional three Masses (see above, p. 18); hence each of the last three lessons of Matins includes at least part of one of these three gospels. Easter, as we shall see (below, p. 64), has only one nocturn, of three lessons; hence the first of these includes the gospel. During the reading of the gospel the chorus stands. See Fortescue, *Ceremonies*, p. 237.

Homilia Sancti Gregorii Papæ.

Quia, largiente Domino, Missarum solemnia ter hodie celebraturi sumus, loqui diu de Evangelica lectione non possumus: sed nos aliquid vel breviter dicere Redemptoris nostri nativitas ipsa compellit. Quid est enim quod nascituro Domino mundus describitur, nisi hoc, quod aperte monstratur, quia ille apparebat in carne, qui electos suos adscriberet in æternitate? Quo contra de reprobis per Prophetam dicitur: Deleantur de libro viventium, et cum justis non scribantur. Qui bene etiam in Bethlehem nascitur. Bethlehem quippe Domus panis interpretatur. Ipse namque est, qui ait: Ego sum panis vivus, qui de cælo descendi. Locus ergo, in quo Dominus nascitur, domus panis antea vocatus est: quia futurum profecto erat, ut ille ibi per materiam carnis appareret, qui electorum mentes interna satietate reficeret. Qui non in parentum domo, sed in via nascitur, ut profecto ostenderet quia per humanitatem suam, quam assumpserat, quasi in alieno nascebatur. (Lector.)

Versus: *Tu autem, Domine, miserere nobis.* (Lector.)

Responsio: *Deo gratias.* (Chorus.)

8. Responsory.

Beata viscera Mariæ Virginis, quæ portaverunt æterni Patris Filium; et beata ubera, quæ lactaverunt Christum Dominum; Qui hodie pro salute mundi de Virgine nasci dignatus est. Versus: *Dies sanctificatus illuxit nobis; venite, gentes, et adorate Dominum. Qui.* (Cantors and chorus.)

9. Verse. Benediction. Response.

Versus: *Jube, domne, benedicere.* (Lector.)

Benedictio: *Per evangelica dicta deleantur nostra delicta.* (Hebdomadary.)

Responsio: *Amen.* (Chorus.)

10. Eighth Lesson (*Lectio viii*). Verse. Response.

Lectio sancti Evangelii secundum Lucam.

In illo tempore: Pastores loquebantur ad invicem: Transeamus usque Bethlehem, et videamus hoc verbum quod factum est, quod Dominus ostendit nobis. Et reliqua. (Lector.)

Homilia Sancti Ambrosii Episcopi.

Videte Ecclesiæ surgentis exordium, Christus nascitur, et pastores vigilare cæperunt: qui gentium greges, pecudum modo ante viventes, in caulam Domini congregarent, ne quos spiritualium bestiarum per offusas noctium tenebras paterentur incursus. Et bene pastores vigilant quos bonus pastor informat. Grex igitur populus, nox sæculum, pastores sunt sacerdotes. Aut fortasse etiam ille sit pastor cui dicitur: Esto vigilans, et confirma. Quia non solum Episcopos ad tuendum gregem Dominus ordinavit, sed etiam Angelos destinavit. (Lector.)

Versus: *Tu autem, Domine, miserere nobis.* (Lector.)

Responsio: *Deo gratias.* (Chorus.)

11. Responsory.

Verbum caro factum est, et habitavit in nobis: Et vidimus gloriam ejus, gloriam quasi Unigeniti a Patre, plenum gratiæ et veritatis. Versus: *Omnia per ipsum facta sunt, et sine ipso factum est nihil. Et. Gloria Patri. Et.*

12. Verse. Benediction. Response.

Versus: *Jube, domne, benedicere.* (Lector.)

Benedictio: *Verba sancti Evangelii doceat nos Christus Filius Dei.* (Hebdomadary.)

Responsio: *Amen.* (Chorus.)

13. Ninth Lesson (*Lectio ix.* Proper). Verse. Response.

Lectio sancti Evangelii secundum Joannem.

In principio erat Verbum, et Verbum erat apud Deum, et Deus erat Verbum. Et reliqua. (Lector.)

Homilia Sancti Augustini Episcopi.

Ne vile aliquid putares, quale consuevisti cogitare, cum verba humana soleres audire, audi quid cogites. Deus erat Verbum. Exeat nunc nescio quis infidelis Arianus, et dicat quia Verbum Dei factum est. Quomodo potest fieri ut verbum Dei factum sit, quando Deus per Verbum fecit omnia? Si et Verbum Dei ipsum factum est, per quod aliud verbum factum est? Si hoc dicis, quia hoc est verbum Verbi, per quod factum est illud: ipsum dico ego unicum Filium Dei. Si autem non dicis verbum Verbi, concede non factum, per quod facta sunt omnia. Non enim per seipsum fieri potuit, per quod facta sunt omnia. Crede ergo Evangelistæ. (Lector.)

Versus: *Tu autem, Domine, miserere nobis.* (Lector.)

Responsio: *Deo gratias.* (Chorus.)

Viewing the three Nocturns together one should observe that the lessons are numbered continuously throughout Matins, the second lesson of the third Nocturn, for example, being called the eighth lesson, and the responsory after it being referred to as the eighth responsory. One may bear in mind also the probability that on an important feast-day the reading of all the lessons will not be assigned to a single lector. Although communities will inevitably differ somewhat in their customs, it would be normal to appoint a separate lector for each of the lessons, the last being assigned to the hebdomadary or some other dignitary.[1]

III. Te Deum laudamus

At the conclusion of the ninth lesson—or, during the Middle Ages, after the ninth responsory,[2]—the hebdomadary, or some other dignitary, begins the singing of the *Te Deum*, and the chorus, standing, takes up the chant and carries it through.[3] During the Middle Ages it was sung by semi-choruses, which took the alternating verses or phrases.[4] Since this rhythmical hymn is mentioned frequently in connexion with the plays of the Church, the following complete text is offered here:

Te Deum laudamus; te Dominum confitemur.
Te æternum Patrem omnis terra veneratur.
Tibi omnes Angeli: tibi cæli, et universæ Potestates,
Tibi Cherubim et Seraphim, incessabili voce proclamant:
Sanctus, Sanctus, Sanctus, Dominus Deus Sabaoth.
Pleni sunt cæli et terra majestatis gloriæ tuæ.
Te gloriosus Apostolorum chorus,
Te Prophetarum laudabilis numerus,
Te Martyrum candidatus laudat exercitus.
Te per orbem terrarum sancta confitetur Ecclesia.
Patrem immensæ majestatis.
Venerandum tuum verum et unicum Filium.
Sanctum quoque Paraclitum Spiritum.
Tu Rex gloriæ Christe.
Tu Patris sempiternus es Filius.
Tu ad liberandum suscepturus hominem, non horruisti Virginis uterum.
Tu, devicto mortis aculeo, aperuisti credentibus regna cælorum.
Tu ad dexteram Dei sedes, in gloria Patris.
Judex crederis esse venturus.
Te ergo quæsumus, tuis famulis subveni: quos pretioso sanguine redemisti.
Æterna fac cum Sanctis tuis in gloria numerari.
Salvum fac populum tuum, Domine, et benedic hereditati tuæ.
Et rege eos, et extolle illos usque in æternum.

---

[1] See Martinucci, pt. i, vol. ii, 30; Fortescue, *Ceremonies*, p. 237.
[2] The practice of dropping the last responsory of Matins is modern.
[3] See Martinucci, pt. i, vol. ii, 30.
[4] See Wagner, p. 172.

Per singulos dies benedicimus te.

Et laudamus nomen tuum in sæculum, et in sæculum sæculi.

Dignare, Domine, die isto, sine peccato nos custodire.

Miserere nostri, Domine, miserere nostri.

Fiat misericordia tua, Domine, super nos, quemadmodum speravimus in te.

In te, Domine, speravi, non confundar in æternum.

For our general purposes here, we may regard Matins as ending with the *Te Deum*.[1] As we shall be reminded later, the singing of this hymn was often accompanied by the censing of the altar, or by other special ceremonials.[2]

The form of Matins now before us may be regarded as typical for the great feasts of the year, such as Epiphany, Palm Sunday, or Ascension. One should observe, however, that Matins of Easter—with which we shall have much to do—is exceptional in that it omits the second and third Nocturns altogether. Thus the office is brought to a close by the singing of the *Te Deum* immediately after the verse and response at the end of the third lesson. The medieval form of Easter Matins differed from this only in retaining the third responsory before the *Te Deum*.[3]

LAUDS (*Laudes*)

After Matins the next service of the Canonical Office is Lauds, which may be outlined as follows:

1. Pater Noster. Ave Maria.[4]
2. Verse (*Versus*). Response (*Responsio*).
3. Gloria Patri. Alleluia.
4. Antiphon. Psalm. (*Antiphona. Psalmus*. Proper.)
5. Antiphon. Psalm. (Proper.)
6. Antiphon. Psalm. (Proper.)
7. Antiphon. Psalm. (Proper.)
8. Antiphon. Psalm. (Proper.)
9. Chapter. Response. (*Capitulum. Responsio*. Proper.)
10. Hymn (*Hymnus*. Proper). Verse. Response. (Proper.)
11. Antiphon. (Proper.) Canticle (*Canticum: Benedictus*).

[1] For exceptional practices at the close of Christmas Matins see Notes, p. 547.

[2] See below, pp. 233 sqq.

[3] For further information concerning Easter Matins see Notes, p. 547.

[4] On the frequent occasions when Lauds follows Matins immediately, and is virtually a continuation of that office, no. 1 may be omitted. In the manuscripts Lauds is often called *Matutinæ Laudes*, or *Matutinæ*, and such expressions sometimes lead to a confusion with *Matutinum*, the designation for Matins. See, for example, below, p. 572.

12. Verse. Response. Prayer (*Oratio.* Proper). Response.
13. Verses and Responses.
14. Pater Noster. Verse. Response.
15. Antiphon B.M.V. (*Antiphona Beatæ Mariæ Virginis.*)
16. Verse. Response. Prayer. Response.
17. Verse. Response.

Since the comments already made upon the several divisions of Matins apply to considerable parts of Lauds, I allow myself, in the pages that follow, to reduce the exposition through frequent references to what has been said above.[1]

1. Pater Noster. Ave Maria.

The texts of the *Pater Noster* and *Ave Maria* may be seen above.[2] They are said *secreto* by all persons in the choir.

2. Verse (*Versus*). Response (*Responsio*).

The following are the forms:

> Versus: *Deus in adjutorium meum intende.* (Hebdomadary.)
> Responsio: *Domine, ad adjuvandum me festina.* (Chorus.)

3. Gloria Patri. Alleluia.

The text of this part, with comment, may be seen above.[3]

4. Antiphon. Psalm. (*Antiphona. Psalmus*).
5. Antiphon. Psalm.
6. Antiphon. Psalm.
7. Antiphon. Psalm.
8. Antiphon. Psalm.

Each of the five psalms, with its antiphon, is sung after the manner already explained.[4] The proper texts for Christmas are the following:

> Antiphona: *Quem vidistis, pastores? Dicite, annuntiate nobis in terris quis apparuit? Natum vidimus, et choros angelorum collaudantes Dominum, alleluia, alleluia.*
> Ps. xcii (*Dominus regnavit*).
> Antiphona: *Genuit puerpera Regem, cui nomen æternum, et gaudia matris habens cum virginitatis honore; nec primam similem visa est, nec habere sequentem, alleluia.*
> Ps. xcix (*Jubilate Deo*).
> Antiphona: *Angelus ad pastores ait: Annuntio vobis gaudium*

---

[1] For the ceremonial during Lauds see Fortescue, *Ceremonies*, pp. 199–208, 237. The assignment of officiants to the several parts is indicated in *Directorium Chori*, pp. v–vii.

[2] See p. 49.
[3] See p. 50.
[4] See pp. 51–2.

magnum, quia natus est vobis hodie Salvator mundi, alleluia.

Ps. lxii (*Deus, Deus meus*).

Antiphona: *Facta est cum Angelo multitudo cœlestis exercitus laudantium Deum, et dicentium: Gloria in excelsis Deo, et in terra pax hominibus bonœ voluntatis, alleluia.*

Canticum trium Puerorum. Daniel iii (*Benedicite*).

Antiphona: *Parvulus filius hodie natus est nobis; et vocabitur Deus, Fortis, alleluia, alleluia.*

Ps. cxlviii (*Laudate Dominum de cœlis*).

9. Chapter. Response. (*Capitulum. Responsio*).

After the singing of the antiphon at the end of the fifth psalm, are said the following chapter and response:

Multifariam, multisque modis, olim Deus loquens patribus in Prophetis; novissime diebus istis locutus est nobis in Filio, quem constituit hæredem universorum, per quem fecit et sæcula. (Hebdomadary.)

Responsio: *Deo gratias.* (Chorus.)

10. Hymn (*Hymnus*). Verse. Response.

The hymn, *A solis ortus cardine*,[1] is sung in a manner already explained.[2] Then follow this verse and response:

Notum fecit Dominus, alleluia. (Cantors.)
Salutare suum, alleluia. (Chorus.)

11. Antiphon. Canticle (*Canticum: Benedictus*).

The *Canticum Zachariæ* (Luke i, 68–79) and its antiphon are sung after the manner of the psalms and their antiphons in Matins.[3] The antiphon is the following:

Gloria in excelsis Deo, et in terra pax hominibus bonæ voluntatis, alleluia, alleluia.

During the singing of the canticle the hebdomadary censes the altar.[4]

12. Verse. Response. Prayer (*Oratio*). Response.

The distribution of parts within this liturgical group is as follows:

Versus: *Dominus vobiscum.* (Hebdomadary.)

Responsio: *Et cum spiritu tuo.* (Chorus.)

---

[1] Chevalier, *R. H.*, no. 26.
[2] See above, p. 51.
[3] See above, pp. 51–2.
[4] See Fortescue, *Ceremonies*, p. 237.

Oremus: Concede, quæsumus, omnipotens Deus, ut nos Unigeniti tui nova per carnem Nativitas liberet, quos sub peccati jugo vetusta servitus tenet. Per eumdem Dominum nostrum Jesum Christum, Filium tuum, qui tecum vivit et regnat in unitate Spiritus Sancti Deus, per omnia sæculorum. (Hebdomadary.)

Responsio: *Amen.* (Chorus.)

13. Verses and Responses.

After the *Amen* of the preceding prayer follow these forms:

Versus: *Dominus vobiscum.* (Hebdomadary.)
Responsio: *Et cum spiritu tuo.* (Chorus.)
Versus: *Benedicamus Domino.* (Hebdomadary.)
Responsio: *Deo gratias.* (Chorus.)[1]
Versus: *Fidelium animæ per misericordiam Dei requiescant in pace.* (Hebdomadary.)
Responsio: *Amen.* (Chorus.)

14. Pater Noster. Verse. Response.

The *Pater Noster* is said *secreto* by all persons in the choir. Then follow the verse and response:

Dominus det nobis suam pacem. (Hebdomadary.)
Et vitam æternam. Amen. (Chorus.)

15. Antiphon B.M.V. (*Antiphona Beatæ Mariæ Virginis*).

The hebdomadary begins, and the chorus continues and sings throughout, the following antiphon of the Blessed Virgin Mary:[2]

*Alma Redemptoris Mater, quæ pervia cœli
Porta manes, et stella maris, succurre cadenti,
Surgere qui curat, populo; tu quæ genuisti,
Natura mirante, tuum sanctum Genitorem,
Virgo prius ac posterius Gabrielis ab ore
Sumens illud Ave, peccatorum miserere.*

16. Verse. Response. Prayer. Response.

The texts within this liturgical group are distributed as follows:

Versus: *Post partum, Virgo inviolata permansisti.* (Hebdomadary.)
Responsio: *Dei Genitrix, intercede pro nobis.* (Chorus.)
Oremus: Deus, qui salutis æternæ, beatæ Mariæ virginitate fœcunda,

---

[1] The verse *Benedicamus Domino* and the response *Deo gratias*, now placed a considerable distance from the end of the service, were once a normal formula for bringing any religious office to a close, and were found at the conclusion of all the *horæ*, even of Matins.

See Thalhofer, ii, 571, 587; Cabrol and Leclercq, ii, 659–60; Gautier, *Tropes*, p. 171. For the use of this formula at the end of the Mass see above, p. 42.

[2] The term *antiphona* is used here in a somewhat unusual sense.

humano generi præmia præstitisti, tribue, quæsumus, ut ipsam pro nobis intercedere sentiamus, per quam meruimus auctorem vitæ suscipere, Dominum nostrum Jesum Christum, Filium tuum. (Hebdomadary.)

Responsio: *Amen.* (Chorus.)

17. Verse. Response.

The office closes with the following:

Versus: *Divinum auxilium maneat semper nobiscum.* (Hebdomadary.)

Responsio: *Amen.* (Chorus.)[1]

The remaining six *horæ* need not be reviewed in complete detail, since in their normal forms they have no significant relation to the plays of the Church. With Prime, Terce, Sext, None, and Compline the subsequent parts of this treatise are not concerned; and Vespers will appear only in a form so exceptional that a detailed exposition of the usual structure of this office would not aid us in interpreting the relevant dramatic pieces.[2] In general content, however, these six services resemble the *horæ* already explained. Psalms and their antiphons, for example, are sung in the same manner throughout the Canonical Office.[3] In order that our survey may be theoretically complete, however, I offer summary outlines of the remaining services, with a few observations upon their peculiarities.

PRIME (*Prima*)

The Office of Prime, it will be remembered, is purely monastic in origin.[4] It contains the following parts:

1. Pater Noster. Ave Maria. Credo.
2. Verse. Response.
3. Gloria Patri. Alleluia.
4. Hymn.
5. Antiphon. Psalm.
6. Chapter. Response.
7. Short Responsory (*Responsorium breve*). Verse. Response.
8. Verse. Response. Prayer. Response.
9. Verses and Responses. Martyrology (*Martyrologium*). Verse. Response.

---

[1] I omit here, and at the end of other *horæ*, certain additional forms which may be said privately, but which are not an essential part of the Canonical Office as sung in choir.

[2] See below, pp. 456 sqq.

[3] As has been said above (p. 51), a *liturgical* psalm may combine two or more *Biblical* psalms.

[4] See above, p. 45.

10. Prayer. Response.
11. Verses and Responses. Gloria Patri.
12. Kyrie eleïson. Pater Noster. Verses and Responses.
13. Prayer. Response.
14. Verse. Benediction. Response.
15. Short Lesson (*Lectio brevis*). Verse. Response.
16. Verses and Responses. Benediction. Response.
17. Pater Noster.

Of the liturgical pieces in this office we need consider only the short responsory (7), the martyrology (9), and the short lesson (15), with its introductory forms (14).[1]

7. Short Responsory (*Responsorium breve*). Verse. Response.
The text of the short responsory is as follows:

Christe, Fili Dei vivi, miserere nobis. Versus: *Qui natus es de Maria Virgine.*

In the singing of this text, the parts are distributed thus:

Christe, Fili Dei vivi, miserere nobis. (Cantors.)
Christe, Fili Dei vivi, miserere nobis. (Chorus.)
Qui natus es de Maria Virgine. (Cantors.)
Miserere nobis. (Chorus.)
Gloria Patri, et Filio, et Spiritui Sancto. (Cantors.)
Christe, Fili Dei vivi, miserere nobis. (Chorus.)

Then are sung a special verse and response:

Exsurge, Christe, adjuva nos. (Cantors.)
Et libera nos propter nomen tuum. (Chorus.)

9. Verses and Responses. Martyrology (*Martyrologium*). Verse. Response.

The reading of the martyrology is introduced by the following forms:

Versus: *Dominus vobiscum.* (Hebdomadary.)
Responsio: *Et cum spiritu tuo.* (Chorus.)
Versus: *Benedicamus Domino.* (Hebdomadary.)
Responsio: *Deo gratias.* (Chorus.)

Then is read by a lector a passage from the martyrology, which need not be specified here. The reading is followed by this verse and response:

Pretiosa in conspectu Domini. (Hebdomadary.)
Mors Sanctorum ejus. (Chorus.)

---

[1] Prime is briefly considered by Martinucci, pt. i, vol. ii, 9. See also *Directorium Chori*, p. vii.

14. Verse. Benediction. Response.

The reading of the short lesson (*lectio brevis*) is introduced by the following verse, benediction, and response:

Jube, domne, benedicere. (Lector.)
Dies et actus nostros in sua pace disponat Dominus omnipotens.
   (Hebdomadary.)
Amen. (Chorus.)

15. Short Lesson (*Lectio brevis*). Verse. Response.
The text of the short lesson is this:

Ipsi peribunt, tu autem permanebis; et omnes sicut vestimentum veterascent; et velut amictum mutabis eos, et mutabuntur; tu autem idem ipse es, et anni tui non deficient. (Lector.)
Then follow this verse and response:
   Tu autem, Domine, miserere nobis. (Lector.)
   Deo gratias. (Chorus.)

The remaining parts of Prime are liturgical forms which have been explained in relation to Matins and Lauds, and their texts need not be given here.

TERCE (*Tertia*), SEXT (*Sexta*), NONE (*Nona*)

The next three *horæ*, Terce, Sext, and None, may be dismissed very briefly.[1] Since they are identical in form, the following outline will serve for all:

1. Pater Noster. Ave Maria.
2. Verse. Response.
3. Gloria Patri. Alleluia.
4. Hymn.
5. Antiphon. Psalm.
6. Chapter. Response.
7. Short Responsory. Verse. Response.
8. Verse. Response. Prayer. Response.
9. Verses and Responses.
10. Pater Noster.

These three services contain no liturgical forms which have not been explained above. As a group, along with Prime, they are often called the 'Little Hours' (*Horæ minores, Horæ parvæ*).

---

[1] See *Directorium Chori*, p. vii.

VESPERS (*Vesperæ*)

The structure of Vespers is shown in the following outline:

1. Pater Noster. Ave Maria.
2. Verse. Response.
3. Gloria Patri. Alleluia.
4. Antiphon. Psalm.
5. Antiphon. Psalm.
6. Antiphon. Psalm.
7. Antiphon. Psalm.
8. Antiphon. Psalm.
9. Chapter. Response.
10. Hymn. Verse. Response.
11. Antiphon. Canticle (*Canticum: Magnificat*).
12. Verse. Response. Prayer. Response.
13. Verses and Responses.
14. Pater Noster. Verse. Response.
15. Antiphon of the Blessed Virgin Mary.
16. Verse. Response. Prayer. Response.
17. Verse. Response.

The arrangement of Vespers is precisely that of Lauds; hence the observations already made upon the latter service may be applied here.[1] The canticle used in Vespers, parallel to the *Benedictus* of Lauds, is the *Magnificat* (Luke i, 46–55). As has already been remarked, the form of Vespers with which we shall have most to do in our subsequent study of dramatic performances is very different from that now before us, and will demand detailed consideration by itself.[2]

COMPLINE (*Completorium*)

Compline, the last of the *horæ*, takes the following form:

1. Verse. Benediction. Response.
2. Short Lesson (*Lectio brevis*). Verse. Response.
3. Verse. Response. Pater Noster.
4. Confession by the Hebdomadary (*Confessio*). Responses.
5. Confession by the Chorus (*Confessio*). Responses.
6. Absolution. Response.
7. Verses and Responses. Gloria Patri. Alleluia.
8. Antiphon. Psalm.
9. Hymn.
10. Chapter. Response.

[1] See above, pp. 64 sqq.   [2] See below, pp. 456 sqq.

11. Short Responsory. Verse. Response.

12. Antiphon. Canticle (*Canticum: Nunc dimittis*).

13. Verse. Response. Prayer. Response.

14. Verses and Responses. Benediction. Response.

15. Antiphon of the Blessed Virgin Mary.

16. Verse. Response. Prayer. Response.

17. Verse. Response.

18. Pater Noster. Ave Maria. Credo.

Since Compline was originally a monastic office designed for a special purpose—probably for use in the dormitory at bedtime—it differs markedly from the other *horæ*; hence several of its parts require a few words of explanation.[1]

1. Verse. Benediction. Response.

The office is unique in beginning with a lesson, the reading of which is prepared for by the following formula:

Jube, domne, benedicere. (Lector.)

Noctem quietam, et finem perfectum concedat nobis Dominus omnipotens. (Hebdomadary.)

Amen. (Chorus.)

2. Short Lesson (*Lectio brevis*). Verse. Response.

The lector reads the following:

Fratres: Sobrii estote, et vigilate quia adversarius vester diabolus tamquam leo rugiens circuit, quærens quem devoret, cui resistite fortes in fide.

Then are said a verse and response:

Tu autem, Domine, miserere nobis. (Lector.)

Deo gratias. (Chorus.)

3. Verse. Response. Pater Noster.

The *Pater Noster* is preceded by a verse and response:

Adjutorium nostrum in nomine Domini. (Hebdomadary.)

Qui fecit cælum et terram. (Chorus.)

Then the *Pater Noster* is recited *secreto* by all.

4. Confession by the Hebdomadary (*Confessio*). Responses.

The hebdomadary makes this confession:

Confiteor Deo omnipotenti, beatæ Mariæ semper Virgini, beato Michaëli Archangelo, beato Joanni Baptistæ, sanctis Apostolis Petro et Paulo, omnibus Sanctis, et vobis, fratres: quia peccavi nimis

---

[1] See Martinucci, pt. i, vol. i, 12–3; *Directorium Chori*, pp. 60–70; Fortescue, *Ceremonies*, pp. 234–6.

cogitatione, verbo et opere: mea culpa, mea culpa, mea maxima culpa. Ideo precor beatam Mariam semper Virginem, beatum Michaëlem Archangelum, beatum Joannem Baptistam, sanctos Apostolos Petrum et Paulum, omnes Sanctos, et vos fratres, orare pro me ad Dominum Deum nostrum.

To this are made the following responses:

Misereatur tui omnipotens Deus, et dimissis peccatis tuis, perducat te ad vitam æternam. (Chorus.)
Amen. (Hebdomadary.)

5. Confession by the Chorus (*Confessio*). Responses.

The same form of confession as that of the hebdomadary is made by the chorus—with appropriate changes of pronouns and the word of address—and the same responses are used.

6. Absolution. Response.

The absolution and response are as follows:

Indulgentiam, absolutionem, et remissionem peccatorum nostrorum tribuat nobis omnipotens et misericors Dominus. (Hebdomadary.)
Amen. (Chorus.)

7. Verses and Responses. Gloria Patri. Alleluia.

The recitals that immediately follow the absolution and response are these:

Versus: Converte nos, Deus, salutaris noster. (Hebdomadary.)
Responsio: Et averte iram tuam a nobis. (Chorus.)
Versus: Deus, in adjutorium meum intende. (Hebdomadary.)
Responsio: Domine, ad adjuvandum me festina. (Chorus.)
Gloria Patri, et Filio, et Spiritui Sancto. (Hebdomadary.)
Sicut erat in principio, et nunc, et semper, et in sæcula sæculorum,
*　　Amen. Alleluia.* (Chorus.)

Of the remaining parts of the office need be mentioned only two:

12. Antiphon. Canticle (*Canticum: Nunc dimittis*).

The canticle *Nunc dimittis* (Luke ii, 29–32) is sung, with its antiphon, after the manner of the *Benedictus* at Lauds and the *Magnificat* at Vespers.[1]

15. Antiphon of the Blessed Virgin Mary.

The text of the antiphon *Alma Redemptoris* is given, and the singing of it is explained, in the course of the exposition of Lauds above.[2]

---

[1] See above, pp. 66, 71.　　　　[2] See p. 67.

Now that the structure and content of the *horæ* have been surveyed, a word remains to be said as to the distribution of these services, and of the Mass, among the hours of the day. The *horárium* followed, in a general way, under the rule of St Benedict during the Middle Ages was the following:[1]

Matins	2–2.30 a.m.
Lauds	4.30–5 a.m.
Prime	6 a.m.
Terce	9 a.m.
MASS	
Sext	12 noon.
None	4 p.m.
Vespers	4.30 p.m.
Compline	6 p.m.

This arrangement allowed substantial intervals for rest, meditation, and physical work. Although custom varied somewhat over Western Europe, some such distribution as this must have been followed in many monasteries and cathedrals. In modern times Matins and Lauds are usually sung continuously in the early morning; and the other services of the day are combined in groups which differ from place to place. Whatever the arrangement for the *horæ*, the Mass belongs to the period before noon.

The exposition of the liturgical system undertaken in these two chapters has, I trust, set forth with fair lucidity the general nature of the Roman plan of daily worship. This description must be regarded, however, merely as an attempt to present a norm for general liturgical guidance. Of the numerous variations in detail that may occur from day to day, and from season to season, only the slightest hints have been given; and of the special ceremonies, processions, and acts of ritual that occur within the general framework no mention has, as yet, been made. Certain of these will be considered when they are found to bear directly upon the main literary object of this treatise.[2] At such times one might also introduce a few observations upon matters of aesthetic, which have been excluded from the somewhat

---

[1] See C. Butler, *Benedictine Monasticism*, London, 1919, p. 281. The hours mentioned are those at which the services began. In this scheme I ignore the fact that, by exception, Christmas has three Masses: one after Matins, a second after Prime, and a third after Terce. The *horarium* before us applies to an average day in Lent.

[2] See, for example, the next chapter.

stern demonstration just completed. It must be admitted, however, that the most conspicuous elements of beauty in the Roman liturgy are almost completely irrelevant to the history of the drama. The sublimity of the prayers of the Canon of the Mass, the exquisite cadences effected by the final repetitions of the antiphons in the ordinary psalmody of the day, the touching directness and tenderness of the petitions in the several *horæ*— rare achievements such as these have, unhappily, no direct bearing upon the invention of plays, and almost none upon their development. The plays of the Church owe to the liturgy their very existence, and they assimilated much of its piety, splendour, and common sense; but they were powerless to reflect its deeper beauty and its pervasive majesty.

DRAMATIC AND OTHER LITERARY ASPECTS
OF THE ROMAN LITURGY

CHAPTER III

THE DRAMATIC ELEMENT IN THE LITURGY

FROM the somewhat formal consideration of liturgical matters in the last two chapters we now turn to our essentially literary inquiry as to how, within this impressive plan of worship, plays came into being. In this undertaking the first step must be an examination of the dramatic elements inherent in the authorized liturgy itself, and in certain seasonal observances which arose within the general liturgical frame-work, and which received the sanction of tradition.[1]

I

It is obvious that no satisfying study of these phenomena can be made without the guidance of a candid and practical definition of the term *drama*. By some criterion we must be able to discriminate between what is merely *dramatic* or *theatrical*, because of its similarity to things familiar upon the stage, and what is authentically a *play*. No one can have failed to observe that in its external resemblances to stage-performances the Roman liturgy is abundantly dramatic. A large proportion of liturgical utterance, for example, takes the form of dialogue. This appears in all those recitals of the chief officiant in the Mass or Canonical Office to which the chorus or the ministers make responses. It is obvious also in the antiphonal singing of two semi-choruses, or in the responsive singing in which a single cantor, or isolated group of cantors, alternates with the whole chorus. These antiphonal and responsive pieces, moreover, often contain direct discourse in the form of question and answer, as does the responsory *Quem vidistis, pastores?* exhibited above;[2] and in some instances the force of the interrogation and reply may have been accurately recognized in the partition of the sentences between two choral groups.[3] Certainly this particular effect must have been felt sometimes in the antiphonal singing of the psalms, as, for example, when two semi-choruses delivered these two verses:[4]

[1] For bibliography see Notes, p. 548.
[2] See above, p. 57, and below, ii, 20.
[3] See, for example, the responsory *Interrogabat Magos*, below, ii, 43, 52. Bartholomaeis (pp. 114–9) partitions the sentences of such responsories with a dramatic precision for

which I can find no secure authority.
[4] Ps. xxiv, 3–4. Numerous conjectures as to the dramatic rendering of Biblical passages in the liturgy are offered by E. King, *Dramatic Art and Church Liturgy*, in *Dublin Review*, cxxv (1899), 43–55.

First semi-chorus: *Quis ascendet in montem Domini? aut quis stabit in loco sancto ejus?*

Second semi-chorus: *Innocens manibus et mundo corde, qui non accepit in vano animam suam, nec juravit in dolo proximo suo.*

Another aspect of the liturgy which brings to mind the circumstances of the theatre is the movements and postures of those who participate.[1] Not only do various groups and individuals exchange speeches among themselves, but frequently one participant or another also moves about the choir, and performs certain physical acts. This is conspicuously true of the Mass, during which the celebrant and his ministers are constantly passing to and fro on the steps and footpace before the altar, transferring vessels or books from one place to another, making gestures, and communicating with one another by signs.

Dramatic externalities of this kind, however, must not be mistaken for genuine drama itself, in which the essential element is not forms of speech and movement, but *impersonation*. A play, that is to say, is, above all else, a story presented in action, in which the speakers or actors impersonate the characters concerned.[2] Dialogue is not essential, for a monologue is drama when the speaker impersonates the one from whom the utterance is represented as proceeding.[3] Even spoken language may be dispensed with, for pantomime is a true, though limited, form of drama, provided a story is successfully conveyed, and provided the actors pretend to be the personages concerned in this story.

As to the nature of impersonation in itself there can scarcely be any substantial disagreement. It consists in physical imitation. In some external and recognizable manner the actor must pretend to be the person whose words he is speaking, and whose actions he is imitating. The performer must do more than merely *represent* the chosen personage; he must also *resemble* him, or at least show his intention of doing so. It follows, then, that the dialogue and physical movements of those who participate in the liturgy will be transformed from the *dramatic* into *drama* whenever these persons convey a story and pretend to be the

[1] Concerning an alleged theatrical tendency in such matters see Notes, p. 548.

[2] I am following the definition expounded by Manly, *Literary Forms*, pp. 584–5. A similar view is advanced by Valentin, p. 67; Brinkmann, pp. 110–1, 127. This general position is challenged by G. La Piana, in *Bollettino di Letteratura critico-religiosa*, i (1914–5), 220–3.

[3] Chambers (i, 81) appears to regard dialogue as essential.

characters in this story. This pretence may be made apparent through realistic details of costume and gesture, through a trifling and suggestive rearranging of liturgical vestment, or, conceivably, through the conventional forms of the vestments themselves.

II

In our inquiry as to whether the Roman liturgy itself has ever conformed to this conception of drama, we may, if we wish, begin with the most sacred of all the ceremonies of Christian worship, the Mass itself. Assertions, more or less explicit, that the Eucharistic service is actually a play have been made for centuries, and are frequently heard in our own day. 'The Mass itself, when sung with all its due accompaniment of solemn ritual', writes Canon Westlake, 'was at once the most elementary as well as the highest drama of all.'[1] 'Holy Mass is a liturgical drama', declares Dom Lefebvre.[2] Lintilhac holds that the central act of the sacred ceremony is 'truly mimetic', and that 'the Mass, grafted upon the primitive liturgy of the Last Supper, was already a true drama'.[3] Modern observations like these—of which there are many[4]—are anticipated in a long succession of utterances running back at least as far as the ninth century. In that period, for example, Amalarius of Metz, in the preface to his *De Ecclesiasticis Officiis*, wrote as follows:[5]

Sacramenta debent habere similitudinem aliquam earum rerum quarum sacramenta sunt. Quapropter, similis sit sacerdos Christo, sicut panis et liquor similia sunt corpori Christi. Sic est immolatio sacerdotis in altari quodammodo ut Christi immolatio in cruce.

This would seem to be a declaration that in its action and physical aspects the Mass in some way resembles actualities in the life of Christ. What the subsequent treatise really conveys, however, is a congeries of suggestions as to ways in which liturgical details may be regarded as *symbols* of biographical episodes. Thus, under Amalarius's treatment, the Mass falls, broadly, into three parts, which symbolize three successive periods of Christ's life.[6] The part extending from the introit through the gospel presents the events up to the entry into

---

[1] H. F. Westlake, *The Parish Gilds of Mediaeval England*, London, 1919, p. 127.

[2] *Daily Missal with Vespers for Sundays and Feasts*, ed. G. Lefebvre, Lophem and St Paul [1925], p. xxxi.

[3] Lintilhac, p. 10.

[4] See Notes, p. 548.

[5] Migne, *P. L.*, cv, 989.

[6] See Migne, *P. L.*, cv, 1108–26, 1126–50, 1151–6; Franz, *Messe*, pp. 353–8; Moreau, *Explications allégoriques*, pp. 125–7.

Jerusalem: Christ's coming upon earth (*i.e.* the introit), the various incidents before the Passion and His preaching (*i.e.* the liturgical gospel). The second division, from the offertory through the *Pater Noster*, represents the Passion and subsequent burial: Christ's receiving the praise and prayers of the multitude at His entry into Jerusalem (*i.e.* the celebrant's receiving the oblation), the multitude's acclaiming Him (*i.e.* the *Sanctus*), His agony in the garden and the fleeing of His disciples (*i.e.* from *Te igitur* to the Consecration), His death on the cross (*i.e.* *Unde et memores* through *Supplices te*), and the confession of the centurion (*i.e.* *Nobis quoque peccatoribus*). The remaining part of the Mass exhibits the Resurrection and the Ascension: the re-uniting of Christ's body and spirit (*i.e.* the mingling of bread and wine); the recognizing of Christ in the breaking of the bread at Emmaus (*i.e.* the *Agnus Dei* and the fraction of the Host); and Christ's blessing His disciples, and His ascension to heaven (*i.e.* the blessing of the congregation directly before the singing of *Ite, missa est*).[1]

According to the text of Amalarius as a whole, however, the occurrences in the Mass do not represent the biographical events in so simple and orderly a sequence as this. A single liturgical piece, for example, may be required to indicate events in two separate biographical periods. Thus the *Gloria in excelsis*, which falls within the part of the service representing events before the entry into Jerusalem, is said actually to symbolize the joyous reception of Christ and the saints into heaven after the Resurrection.[2] The officiants, moreover, do not consistently represent always the same persons. The deacon and subdeacon are understood to be sometimes the prophets, and sometimes the disciples; and the subdeacon may be regarded as the symbol of the disciples, of Joseph of Arimathea, or of the women at the foot of the cross.[3]

Whatever the obscurities and confusions of Amalarius's method of symbolizing, it so effectually advanced the conception of the Mass as in some sense a dramatic representation of the life of Christ that his famous imitator, Honorius of Autun, writing his *Gemma Animæ* about the year 1100, ventured to insert the following passage:[4]

[1] The parts of the Mass mentioned in this paragraph can be identified in the exposition in chapter i.

[2] See Migne, *P. L.*, cv, 1115.

[3] See Franz, *Messe*, pp. 355–6. For extended examples of the symbolizing of Amalarius see Hirn, pp. 75 sqq.

[4] Migne, *P. L.*, clxxii, 570. For the inter-

Sciendum quod hi qui tragœdias in theatris recitabant, actus pugnantium gestibus populo repræsentabant. Sic tragicus noster pugnam Christi populo Christiano in theatro Ecclesiæ gestibus suis repræsentat, eique victoriam redemptionis suæ inculcat. Itaque cum presbyter *Orate* dicit, Christum pro nobis in agonia positum exprimit, cum apostolos orare monuit. Per secretum silentium, significat Christum velut agnum sine voce ad victimam ductum. Per manuum expansionem, designat Christi in cruce extensionem. Per cantum præfationis, exprimit clamorem Christi in cruce pendentis. Decem namque psalmos, scilicet a *Deus meus respice* usque *In manus tuas commendo spiritum meum* cantavit, et sic exspiravit. Per Canonis secretum innuit Sabbati silentium. Per pacem, et communicationem designat pacem datam post Christi resurrectionem et gaudii communicationem. Confecto sacramento, pax et communio populo a sacerdote datur, quia accusatore nostro ab agonotheta nostro per duellum prostrato, pax a judice populo denuntiatur, ad convivium invitatur. Deinde ad propria redire cum gaudio per *Ite missa est* imperatur. Qui gratias Deo jubilat et gaudens domum remeat.

The opening sentences of this passage clearly proclaim that in the Mass the celebrant as genuinely impersonates Christ as the tragic actor does the persons represented in the profane theatre. In what follows, however, Honorius does not consistently sustain the principle of realistic impersonation. The celebrant's moments of silence, and his extending of his arms, might conceivably be interpreted as mimetic; but only in a symbolic way can the singing of the preface and the silent recital of prayers in the Canon represent respectively the cry of Christ from the cross and the silence of the Saturday during which He lay in the tomb.

In spite of its inevitable inconsistencies, however, the interpretation of the Mass as a miscellany of symbols representing dramatically the life of Christ was continued throughout the Middle Ages by a succession of writers, of whom the most prominent were Sicardus of Cremona (†1215), Pope Innocent III (†1216), Albertus Magnus (1206–80), and Durandus of Mende (*c.* 1237–96).[1] The impress of their tradition in our own time appears, for example, in one of the most highly recommended of

pretation put upon this passage by William Prynne in England in the seventeenth century see Notes, p. 549.

[1] For comprehensive summaries of the tendency toward symbolizing everything connected with the liturgy see Alt, pp. 328–41; Hirn, pp. 73–87; Sauer, pp. 1–53; Franz, *Messe*, pp. 351–457; Moreau, *Explications allégoriques*, pp. 123–43; Frere, *Ceremonial*, pp. 145–61. On Durandus's exposition of the Mass as symbolizing the life of Christ see Taylor, ii, 102–4.

liturgical manuals, which includes an outline of the Mass as a drama in four acts, with subsidiary scenes.[1]

It is not to be supposed, however, that this kind of symbolizing has met with unqualified approval. Within the Church itself, especially since the sixteenth century, a vigorous succession of liturgiologists have undertaken to limit the influence of symbolistic interpretation, and to provide historical, in place of fanciful, explanations. Claude de Vert, the most prominent writer of this school, entitled his treatise *Explication simple, littérale et historique des Cérémonies de l'Église*,[2] thus making clear that his aim was to account for liturgical ceremonial not as dramatic expression, but as a natural outcome of ancient usages, of the demands of physical convenience, and of a desire to accompany the sacred word by reverent acts. Although the details of this controversy have no place in our present inquiry, the literary historian must ally himself with the 'literalists' against the symbolists in so far as the former discredit the interpreting of the Mass as a drama. In the nature of the case, to be sure, the Eucharistic service inevitably recalls the Last Supper, and in certain ceremonial acts, such as the breaking of the bread, or the raising of his eyes to heaven, the celebrant may, in a sense, be said to imitate acts of Christ Himself. He does not, however, attempt impersonation, and hence he is not an actor in a play.

The impossibility of there being impersonation in the liturgy of the Eucharist arises from the fact that since the early Christian centuries this rite has been regarded as a true sacrifice.[3] The central act is designed not to represent or portray or merely commemorate the Crucifixion, but actually to repeat it. What takes place at the altar is not an aesthetic picture of a happening

---

[1] See Wapelhorst, pp. 450–2. This author observes, however, that the patristic writings from which his dramatic outline derives are not free from confusion, and that their symbolizing is not to be regarded as the official doctrine of the Church. The view that the symbolizing of the liturgy is a kind of drama ('symbolisch-liturgisches Drama', 'dramma liturgico') is taken by Alt, pp. 328–41, and La Piana, *loc. cit.*, pp. 220–2. In such symbolism Brinkmann (p. 112) feels a substantial impulse towards drama. Stengel (pp. 233–4), on the other hand, seems to regard drama as fundamentally alien to medieval worship.

[2] Four vols., Paris, 1706–13, the second edition, revised by the author. Concerning the view represented by de Vert see Moreau, *Explication réaliste*, pp. 400–19; Cabrol, *Origines*, pp. 41–3; Cabrol and Leclercq, i, 1328; Frere, *Ceremonial*, pp. 103–16.

[3] Church doctrine in this matter down to the Reformation is treated comprehensively by Stone, *Eucharist*, vol. i. Considerable modern discussion of the sacrificial element in the Mass is summarized by Maurice de la Taille in *The Ecclesiastical Review*, lxxi (1924), 1–22. See also Hirn, pp. 74 sqq. I cannot share the view of Chambers (ii, 4), that when the Mass 'was looked upon as an actual repetition of the initial sacrifice, the dramatic character was only intensified'.

in the past, but a genuine renewal of it. Just as Christ sacrificed Himself on the Cross, so in the Mass He is present invisibly, and sacrifices Himself again. The consecrated elements *are* Christ, and through the words and acts of the celebrant, Christ accomplishes His own immolation, being Himself, in reality, both the victim and the priest.[1] The celebrant remains merely the celebrant, and does not undertake to play the part of his Lord. He is only the instrument through which Christ acts.

The Mass, then, has never been a drama, nor did it ever directly give rise to drama.[2] The dramatic features of this service, along with those of the Canonical Office, and the symbolizing of virtually every sentence, gesture and physical accompaniment—these phenomena may have contributed suggestions as to the possibility of inventing drama, and may, indirectly have encouraged it; but the liturgy itself, in its ordinary observances, remained always merely worship.

III

Hitherto we have been concerned only with the Mass and Canonical Office in what we may call their normal and simple state. It has, to be sure, been intimated that the texts of these services change somewhat from day to day,[3] but insufficient attention has thus far been given to the significance of the liturgical calendar, and to the amplifications of the standard liturgical forms on certain days of the year. Since these seasonal modifications or enlargements often exhibit uncommonly striking dramatic features, they must, in our present inquiry, be given particular attention.

The first step in the formation of a liturgical calendar during the first Christian centuries was the setting aside of Sunday for a weekly Eucharistic service and commemoration of Christ's Passion, Death and Resurrection.[4] The annual Sunday nearest to the date of the Resurrection was observed with special elaborateness, and developed into the feast which we know as

---

[1] See Hirn, p. 74; Broussolle, pp. 141 sqq.; Hedley, p. 232. For confirmatory citations from Thomas Aquinas, Albertus Magnus and the Council of Trent see H. A. Koestlin, *Geschichte des christlichen Gottesdienstes*, Freiburg, 1887, pp. 101–3.

[2] Broussolle (p. 166) writes as follows: 'La sainte messe est une représentation de la Passion et de la mort de Jésus-Christ, non pas en paroles, comme dans les tragédies et dans les drames, mais en vérité et essentiellement.'

[3] See above, pp. 18, 47.

[4] In this summary I follow especially Cabrol, *Origines*, pp. 174 sqq.

Easter. This celebration entailed a period of preparation, which we know as Lent, and was followed by a season dominated by the feast of Pentecost.

The gradual enrichment of the liturgical calendar was accomplished most conspicuously through the creation, in or near Jerusalem, of annual observances which enabled the faithful to live over again the events of Christ's life which had actually occurred in precisely these holy places. In the so-called *Peregrinatio Etheriæ*, a noble lady, probably from Galicia, describes a large number of the anniversary services which she witnessed in Jerusalem towards the end of the fourth century.[1] From her we learn, for example, that on the eve of Epiphany the faithful betook themselves to Bethlehem, six miles from Jerusalem, and in the church at the grotto of the Holy Manger sang a night office. Before dawn the clergy and people returned to Jerusalem singing *Benedictus qui venit in nomine Domini*. On Palm Sunday, a week before Easter, was celebrated the entry into Jerusalem. The most striking part of this ceremony occurred in the latter part of the afternoon, when the clergy and people gathered at the church of the Ascension, or *Imbomon*, on the summit of the Mount of Olives. Here was read the Gospel narrative of the event commemorated, after which the bishop moved forth from the church preceded by the people singing hymns and antiphons containing the refrain *Benedictus qui venit in nomine Domini*. The children in the gathering, and even the infants in arms, carried branches of palm. Thus accompanied, the bishop descended from the Mount of Olives, entered the city, and conducted the evening office in the church of the Anastasis, which enclosed the Holy Sepulchre.[2]

On the Thursday evening preceding Easter was commemorated, on the Mount of Olives, the agony that Christ had suffered in that spot after the Last Supper. On Friday occurred the commemoration of the Crucifixion, with services in the

[1] For a fresh text of the relevant parts of the *Peregrinatio Etheriæ*, with an English translation and a discussion of date and authorship, see Duchesne, pp. 490–523, 541–71. For a detailed exposition of the *Peregrinatio* see F. Cabrol, *Les Églises de Jérusalem: la Discipline et la Liturgie au quatrième Siècle*, Paris, 1895; and for a briefer survey see Cabrol, *Origines*, pp. 176 sqq.

[2] For the passage in the *Peregrinatio Etheriæ* describing this observance see Duchesne, pp. 505–6. In narrating the bishop's descent from the Mount, Etheria writes as follows: *Et sic deducetur episcopus in eo typo quo tunc Dominus deductus est*. From this passage Cabrol (*Églises*, pp. 93–4) infers that the bishop impersonated Christ at least to the extent of riding an ass. From the context, however, it seems clear that the bishop went afoot, and that no ass was provided. See Franz, *Benediktionen*, i, 471.

chapel of the Cross, at the church of Golgotha, or *Martyrium*, and at the Holy Sepulchre. The most striking ceremony on this occasion was the adoring of the Cross, at the *Martyrium*, which Etheria describes as follows:[1]

Et sic ponitur cathedra episcopo in Golgotha post Crucem, quæ stat nunc; residet episcopus hic cathedra; ponitur ante eum mensa sublinteata; stant in giro mensa diacones; et affertur loculus argenteus deauratus in quo est lignum sanctum Crucis; aperitur et profertur; ponitur in mensa quam lignum crucis quam titulus. Cum ergo positum fuerit in mensa, episcopus sedens de manibus suis summitates de ligno sancto premet; diacones autem qui in giro stant custodient. Hoc autem propterea sic custoditur, quia consuetudo est ut unus et unus omnis populus veniens, tam fideles quam cathecumini, acclinant se ad mensam, osculentur sanctum lignum, et pertranseant. Et quoniam, nescio quando, dicitur quidam fixisse morsum et furasse sancto ligno, ideo nunc a diaconibus qui in giro stant, sic custoditur, ne quis veniens audeat denuo sic facere. Ac sic ergo omnis populus transit, unus et unus, toti acclinantes se, primum de fronte, sic de occulis tangentes Crucem et titulum, et sic osculantes Crucem pertranseunt; manum autem nemo mittit ad tangendum.

In this ceremony the bishop, attended by deacons, holds the relic of the true Cross firmly in his hands, while the clergy and people make obeisance before it. Each worshipper kneels, touches the relic with his forehead and eyes, kisses it, and passes on.

The Ascension and Pentecost were celebrated on a single day, the former in the church on the spot whence Christ had ascended, and the latter in the Cenacle, or Church of Sion, at the place where the Holy Spirit had descended upon the disciples.[2]

From observances such as these, then, arose the liturgical calendar in the East. At Jerusalem, by the fourth century, had been established a succession of commemorations extending through the life of Christ from the Nativity to the Ascension and the Descent of the Holy Spirit, and distributed throughout the year. Of these ceremonies the most vivid in their appeal were those of the Holy Week preceding Easter; but all the commemorations of the year had a single purpose: to aid the faithful to

[1] Duchesne, p. 510.
[2] I omit Easter from consideration because of the relatively brief and simple nature of its ceremonies at Jerusalem. See Duchesne, pp. 512-3.

live over again, in the holy places themselves, the major events in the life of Jesus.

Through pilgrims to Palestine, and through other agencies, the cycle of Christian festivals observed in Jerusalem was made known, and largely adopted, in the West.[1] As modified by special influences in Western Europe the calendar eventually took form in the following succession of liturgical seasons:[2]

Advent. This season begins with the Sunday falling within the period from November 27th to December 3rd, and continues to the eve of Christmas. Within this period are four Sundays, referred to serially by number as *Dominica prima Adventus, Dominica secunda Adventus,* and so on.[3]

Christmas. This is a period of fourteen days extending from December 25th (*Nativitas Domini*) to the feast of Epiphany (*Epiphania Domini*) on January 6th.[4] During this season are commemorated especially the birth of Christ, and his appearing to the world. During the first three or four centuries these events were celebrated on Epiphany, January 6th, as were also, during the Middle Ages, the visit of the Magi, the baptism of Jesus in Jordan, and his first miracle at Cana.

After Epiphany follows a variable period, of from twelve to forty-six days, which may be regarded as an epilogue to the Christmas season, or as a transition to the next organized season of *Septuagesima.*

Septuagesima. This is a period of two weeks and two days preceding Lent, a period beginning with Septuagesima Sunday (*Dominica in Septuagesima*), and including the two succeeding Sundays, known as *Dominica in Sexagesima* and *Dominica in Quinquagesima.* The date of Septuagesima Sunday varies in accordance with the variation of that of Easter, between January 18th and February 21st. The sixteen days of Septuagesima eventually

[1] See Cabrol, *Origines,* p. 187. The fidelity with which the liturgical arrangements at Rome followed those of Jerusalem seems to be shown by the grouping of the churches in the part of the city surrounding St. John Lateran. In this grouping appears an attempt to reproduce the relative positions of the holy places at Jerusalem. See Cabrol, *Origines,* p. 187.

[2] The liturgical seasons are effectively reviewed by Cabrol, *Prayer,* pp. 155 sqq., and, of course, in numberless manuals, such as those of K. A. H. Kellner, *Heortology,* London, 1908, and V. Staley, *The Liturgical Year,* London, 1907.

[3] Here and elsewhere I mention the liturgical names of certain days as an aid to the reader in his interpretation of liturgical and dramatic texts to be considered later.

[4] In a more general sense the Christmas season may be regarded as extending to the Feast of the Purification, Feb. 2nd. See Cabrol, *Prayer,* p. 160. Interpreted in this extended sense the Christmas season often overlaps the succeeding liturgical season of *Septuagesima,* which begins on variable dates between Jan. 18th and Feb. 21st.

borrowed from Lent the character of penance, mourning, and preparation for Easter.

Lent. This season begins on the Wednesday (*Feria quarta*), called Ash Wednesday (*Dies Cinerum*), of the seventh week preceding Easter, and ends on Easter Eve (*Sabbato Sancto*).[1] Of the six Sundays, the first four are called, merely by numbers, *Dominica prima in Quadragesima, Dominica secunda in Quadragesima,* and so on.[2] The fifth Sunday is named Passion Sunday (*Dominica Passionis*), and the week which it opens is called Passion Week (*Hebdomada Passionis*). The sixth and last Sunday, called Palm Sunday (*Dominica Palmarum,* or *Dominica in Palmis*), opens Holy Week (*Hebdomada Major*). Thursday (*Feria quinta*) of Holy Week is called Maundy Thursday, and *Cœna Domini*; Friday (*Feria sexta*) is called Good Friday, and *Parasceve*. The whole period of Lent is devoted to a penitential preparation for Easter. During Passion Week the liturgy traces the events in Jesus' life before the actual approach to the Passion. Holy Week follows the occurrences from the entry into Jerusalem, commemorated on Palm Sunday, through the Passion itself. On Maundy Thursday is commemorated the Last Supper and the institution of the Eucharist. Good Friday recalls the Crucifixion, particularly in the ceremony of the Adoration of the Cross.[3]

Easter. The Easter season extends over a period of fifty days from Easter Sunday (*Pascha* or *Dominica Resurrectionis*) to Pentecost (*Dominica Pentecostes*). As a movable feast, Easter may fall on any day between March 22nd and April 25th; and Pentecost, or Whitsunday, on any day between May 10th and June 13th. The Feast of the Ascension occurs ten days before Pentecost; that is, on Thursday of the sixth week after Easter Day. Since during the Easter season are celebrated the Resurrection, the Ascension, and the Descent of the Holy Spirit, this is the period of liturgical rejoicing. The continuity of this rejoicing, however, is broken by a period of three days immediately before Ascension Day. This Monday, Tuesday, and Wednesday, collectively called Rogations (*In Rogationibus*), are devoted to special supplications for forgiveness of sin and for protection to the fruits of the earth.

---

[1] In the ecclesiastical calendar, the seven days of the week are ordinarily designated as follows, beginning with Sunday: *Dominica, Feria secunda, Feria tertia, Feria quarta, Feria quinta, Feria sexta, Sabbato.*

[2] From the first word of the introit of the Mass on that day, the fourth Sunday of Lent is often called *Lætare* Sunday.

[3] This ceremony is fully considered below, pp. 102, 118 sqq.

The Period after Pentecost. The long period of several months
from Pentecost to Advent is governed by no single or dominating
notion. It is referred to simply as the period after Pentecost, and
the Sundays are numbered serially as *post Pentecosten* (*e.g.
Dominica secunda post Pentecosten*). During the later Middle Ages,
in many places, the first Sunday after Pentecost was called
Trinity Sunday (*Dominica Trinitatis*), and on the Thursday after
this fell the feast of *Corpus Christi*.

From what has now been said it appears that both in its
origin and in its completed development the liturgical year is
based upon successive moments in the life of Christ. Since the
avowed purpose of all the seasonal observances was to bring
effectually to mind occurrences in Christ's life, and since even
the normal liturgy of ordinary worship contained elements of a
dramatic nature, we must now inquire whether the splendid
special ceremonies designed as vivid annual commemorations of
religious events ever attained to true drama.[1] It happens that
within the authorized liturgy the most conspicuously dramatic
ceremonials have always been found, not at such supreme feasts
as Christmas and Easter, but during Holy Week; hence we inevitably centre our attention especially upon this latter liturgical
period.[2]

IV

Of all the ceremonials of Holy Week the most animated and
splendid in its pageantry is the procession of the palms on Palm
Sunday, celebrating the Entry into Jerusalem. Etheria's description of this observance at Jerusalem itself in the fourth
century has been outlined above.[3] By the seventh century the
Oriental custom had been brought to the West, and by the tenth
century had developed, in widely separated communities, a
variety of elaborated forms.[4] The preferred arrangement pro-

---

[1] For loose assertions that the liturgical
year is itself a drama, or a succession of
dramas, see Gautier, *Poésie*, p. 7; Du Méril,
p. 42. For more or less orderly surveys of
special liturgical ceremonies through the
year see Chambers, ii, 4–6, 65–7; Du Méril,
pp. 48–53; Clément, pp. 92–285; Boutillier,
pp. 444–98; Deschamps de Pas, pp. 103–86.
[2] In regard to the essentially non-Roman
sensuousness of some of the ceremonies of

Holy Week see Bishop, p. 12.
[3] See p. 86.
[4] Concerning Western practices see especially [A. de Santi] *La Domenica delle Palme
nella Storia liturgica*, in *La Civiltà cattolica*, no.
1339 (1906), 3–18; no. 1340 (1906), 159–77;
Stapper, *Feier*, pp. 78–80; Thalhofer, i, 611–
5. For the complete text of one Palm Sunday
procession see below, pp. 94 sqq.

vided that the procession set forth from a hill, or elevated place, outside the town, and proceed to the gate, where those in the procession and certain choir-boys stationed on the tower sang antiphonally the hymn *Gloria, laus et honor*.[1] The procession then passed through the gate into the town singing the antiphon *Ingrediente*. Meanwhile the faithful raised palm-branches aloft, and cast garments in the path of the *cortège*. In this form the ceremony clearly reflects the actual topographical situation of Jerusalem, the elevated spot outside the town representing the Mount of Olives.

Symbolism of a more or less imitative sort appears in the frequent practice of carrying venerated objects in the procession. Thus an anonymous treatise of the tenth century describes the use of the gospel-book in this way:[2]

Hodie præparatur quoddam portatorium honestissime, in quo intromittitur sanctum Evangelium, quod intelligitur Christus, et statuitur in ecclesia ante aram, unde clerus processurus est. Deinde adunantur palmæ et flores, atque diversa genera frondium, seu olivarum, super quæ dicitur hæc oratio a sacerdote: *Omnipotens sempiterne Deus, qui antequam Filium tuum Dominum nostrum pro nobis mortem perpeti sineres.* Sequitur benedictio palmarum sive frondium: *Omnipotens Deus Christe.* His finitis, dantur a custodibus palmæ, accipienteque populo ramos arborum, olivarum, sive florum, inchoatur antiphona *Pueri Hebræorum.* Deinde suscipiunt diaconi suprascriptum portatorium cum Evangelio, bajulantes cum ingenti exsultatione jugum Christi suave et onus ejus leve, præcedente aqua benedicta cum candelabris atque thymiamateriis cum aliis ornamentis. Insuper etiam laicorum schola cum vexillis atque fanonibus a longe præeunte. Exeunte enim clero seu populo ab ecclesia, inchoatur antiphona *Cum appropinquaret Dominus.* Qua finita, inchoat schola antiphonam *Cœperunt omnes.* Item *Cum audissent.* Item *Appropinquante.* Cum ingressi fuerint civitatem, vel cœnobium, dicitur responsorium *Ingrediente Domino.* Item *Collegerunt pontifices. Unus autem.* His finitis, ante atrium ecclesiæ loco competenti subsistit schola cum bajulis et reliquo ornatu, et clerus seu populus expectant in loco atrii, inchoantes antiphonam *Occurrerunt.* Respondet schola cum angelis et pueris. Hac finita, inchoantur a duobus cantoribus quidam versus *Israel es tu rex.* Respondet chorus, aspiciens seu inclinans se ad suprascriptum sanctum Evangelium, *Gloria, laus et honor tibi sit.* Eo ordine sequuntur alii versus. His finitis, incipit schola cum bajulis antiphonam *Pueri Hebræorum.* Et tunc prosternit omnis plebs hinc inde frondes seu

---

[1] See Chevalier, *R. H.*, no. 7282.
[2] Migne, *P. L.*, ci, 1201–2. See Santi, *Palme*, pp. 159–62; Martene, iii, 71.

flores decantantes antiphonam *Osanna filio David*, usque ad altare. Et sic intrant ad Missas.

In this ceremony the gospel-book, symbolizing Christ Himself, serves to indicate that it is He who is entering the city. This intention is made still clearer in the *Decreta* of Lanfranc, which provides that along with two texts of the Gospel shall be carried also the consecrated Host, or *Corpus Domini*. This was a common custom in England and France.[1] At Bayeux the clergy bore the Gospel and relics of saints; at Aquileia, the cross.[2]

The dramatic effect of the procession was notably increased when it included a bit of dialogue in the form of a question and answer. At Winchester, for example, when the procession reached the gate of the city, it divided into two groups: those accompanying the bier (*feretrum*) on which the Host was carried, and, a stone's throw away, those accompanying the bishop. Then between the two occurred the following exchange of sentences:[3]

> Tunc pueri uersi ad feretrum dicant:
> *Quis est iste?*
> Illi uero qui sunt cum feretro, quasi Discipuli Christi, pueris interrogantibus respondeant:
> *Hic est qui uenturus erat pro salute populi.*
> Item interrogent illos pueri:
> *Qualis est iste?*
> Discipuli respondeant:
> *Hic est salus nostra et redemptio Israhel.*

Another type of dialogue, used in many French churches at the door of the church, is described in the following passage:[4]

> Quibus finitis,[5] olim episcopus, sive ille qui officio præerat, portas percutiebat dicens:
> *Attollite portas, principes, vestras, et elevamini, portæ æternales, et introibit rex gloriæ.*
> Cum⟨Cui?⟩ existentes in ecclesia reponebant:
> *Quis est iste rex gloriæ?*

---

[1] See Santi, *Palme*, pp. 163–5; Martene, iii, 71–2. For the similar use of Rome, Sarum and Hereford see Bishop, pp. 276–94.

[2] See Santi, pp. 168–9.

[3] Oxford, Bibl. Bodl., MS Rawlinson C. 892, Grad. Wintoniense sæc. xii–xiii, fol. 47ʳ. The text of this uncommonly long processional ceremony, still unpublished, occupies

fol. 44ʳ–49ʳ.

[4] Martene, iii, 72. See also *id.*, iii, 75–6; Young, *Harrowing of Hell*, pp. 892–3; R. Triger, *La Procession des Rameaux au Mans*, in *Revue historique et archéologique du Maine*, xiv (1883), 151–216, 316–85—especially 346–7.

[5] The reference is to the Palm Sunday processional hymn *Gloria, laus et honor*.

Ad quos cum ille tertio dixisset *Attollite portas*, similemque illi dedissent responsionem; ipse tandem clamabat:

Dominus virtutum, ipse est rex gloriæ.

Tunc clausæ aperiebantur valvæ.

In neither of these instances is the dialogue accompanied by impersonation, even though at Winchester one group speak *quasi Discipuli Christi*. The missing element, however, is occasionally found at one point or another in the procession, as we may see in the liturgical usage of Salisbury. In this church it was arranged that the procession should halt at four stations.[1] The first of these was before the cross in the cemetery north of the choir. Here was read the Gospel *Cum appropinquasset*,[2] ending with the words *Benedictus qui venit in nomine Domini*. At the moment when the reading was concluded arrived two boys carrying a bier containing relics and a Host. What then occurred is described as follows:[3]

Finito evangelio, unus puer ad modum Prophetæ indutus, stans in aliquo eminenti loco, cantet lectionem propheticam modo quo sequitur:

Hierusalem, respice ad orientem, et vide; leva, Hierusalem, oculos, et vide potentiam regis.

Tres clerici de secunda forma exeuntes ex eadem processione, habitu non mutato, conversi ad populum, stantes ante magnam crucem ex parte occidentali, simul cantent hunc versum hoc modo:

En rex venit mansuetus tibi, Sion filia mystica, humilis sedens super animalia, quem venturum jam prædixit lectio prophetica.

Post singulos versus exsecutor officii incipiat antiphonam *Salve*, conversus ad reliquias, quam prosequatur chorus cum genuflexione osculando terram; ab ipso quoque exsecutore officii, primo cum choro genuflectendo, dicatur sic: *Salve, quem Jesum*. Chorus in prostratione deosculando terram prosequatur resurgendo:

Testatur plebs Hebræorum,
Obvia cum palmis tibi clamans verba salutis.

Item Propheta cantet hoc quod sequitur:

Ecce salvator venit solvere te a vinculis; levate capita vestra.

Iterum clerici stantes ante reliquias simul, loco nec habitu mutato, dicant hunc versum sequentem:

Hic est qui de Edom venit tinctis Bozra vestibus, in stola sua formosus, gradiens virtutibus, non in equis bellicosis nec in altis curribus.

---

[1] See Henderson, pp. 47–54.　　[2] See Matt. xxi, 1–9.　　[3] Henderson, pp. 50–1.

Item exsecutor officii, loco nec habitu mutato, incipiat antiphonam
Salve rex mundi. Chorus resurgendo prosequatur:

> *Rex regum, gloria cæli,*
> *Cui manet imperium, laus et decus hic et in ævum*

Iterum Propheta:

> *Ecce appropinquabit redemptio vestra.*

Postea evanescat.

For our present purpose the significance of this ceremony lies
not so much in its liturgical content as in the participation of a
boy costumed as a prophet. A similar impersonation, representing Caiphas, seems to have been included in the Palm Sunday
procession at Wells.[1]

The most striking of all the ceremonials associated with the
procession of Palm Sunday is the bringing into the church of a
figure representing Christ riding on an ass. The use of this
Palmesel flourished especially in Germany, and during the later
Middle Ages. There is evidence of this custom at Augsburg,
however, as early as the time of St Ulrich (†973).[2] Although the
ceremonial details differed greatly from place to place, this kind
of observance may be illustrated by the following description
from a service-book of the fourteenth century used in the collegiate church of canonesses and canons at Essen:[3]

Quo facto, dyaconus cum campanario portante unum pondus
palmarum benedictarum post eum vadat ad chorum domicellarum,
distribuendo eas inter domicellas a dignioribus et senioribus incipiendo
in una parte chori et deinde in alia. Interim conventus cantabit antiphonam *Pueri Hebreorum tollentes ramos,* et cetera.

De processione. Qua finita, canonici reliqui preter presbiterum et
ministros ibunt cum scolaribus, qui tunc ibi presentes erunt, in processione ad ecclesiam Sancte Gertrudis pro Ymagine Christi heri illuc
cum Asino adducta. Via. Exeuntes monasterium per portam funerum
et ecclesiam Sancti Johannis cantantes in via hanc antiphonam.

Antiphona:

Cum appropinquaret Dominus Jherosolimam, misit duos de discipulis suis
dicens: Ite in castellum, quod contra vos est, et invenietis pullum asine alligatum,
super quem nullus hominum sedit; solvite et adducite michi. Si quis vos interro-

---

[1] See C. Brown, *Caiphas as a Palm-Sunday
Prophet,* in *Anniversary Papers by Colleagues and
Pupils of George Lyman Kittredge,* Boston, 1913,
pp. 105–17; and Notes, p. 549.
[2] This matter is treated especially by E.
Wiepen, *Palmsonntagsprozession und Palmesel,*

Bonn, 1903; Franz, *Benediktionen,* i, 489–97;
Santi, *Palme,* pp. 165–8; Chambers, i, 333–4.
[3] I quote the text of Arens, pp. 42–7. The
Essen *ordinarium* of the fourteenth century is
described by Arens, pp. vii sqq.

II. *Palmesel* from Steinen, Switzerland, in the Schweizerisches Landesmuseum, Zürich

gaverit, dicite: Opus Domini est. Solventes adduxerunt ad Jhesum et imposuerunt super eum vestimenta, et sedit super eum; alii expandebant vestimenta sua in via, alii ramos de arboribus externebant et qui sequebantur clamabant: Osanna, benedictus qui venit in nomine Domini, benedictum regnum patris nostri David. Osanna in excelsis, miserere nostri, fili David.

Cum autem processio venerit ad ecclesiam Sancte Gertrudis, non intrabit in ecclesiam, sed ante januam returnabit, et populus educet Ymaginem et per eandem viam quam venerat processio de monasterio, in monasterium revertetur, scolaribus precedentibus, deinde canonicis ac plebano Sancte Gertrudis induto cappa et portante pleonarium, deinde candelis, deinde Ymagine in Asino, deinde populo. Cantus. Et in reditu ad monasterium cantabuntur due subsequentes antiphone.

Antiphona:

Cum audisset populus quia Jhesus venit Jherosulimam, acceperunt ramos palmarum et exierunt ei obviam et clamabant pueri, dicentes: Hic est qui venturus est in salutem populi. Hic est salus nostra, et redemptio Israhel. Quantus est iste quem Throni et Dominationes adorant? Noli timere, filia Syon: ecce rex tuus venit tibi, sedens super pullum asine, sicut scriptum est. Salve rex, fabricator mundi, qui venisti redimere nos.

Antiphona:

Ante sex dies solempnitatis Pasche, quia venit Dominus in civitatem Jherusalem, occurrerunt pueri, in manibus portantes ramos palmarum, et clamabant voce magna, dicentes: Osanna in excelsis. Benedictus qui venisti in multitudine misericordie. Osanna in excelsis.

Interim antequam processio, ut predicitur, absens ex monasterio fuerit, exibit conventus chorum per januam versus summum altare et cum presbitero et ministris descendent in processione per gradus versus altare Sancti Georgii usque ad medium monasterii ante candelabrum, quod est ante altare Sancte Crucis, expectantes ibidem adventum Ymaginis et processionis. Cumque Ymaginem in reditu contigit descendere gradum introitus monasterii, appendet sacerdos digitis suis crucem argenteam, et aderit campanarius ibidem cum aqua benedicta et thure. Cum autem advenerint, fiet talis statio: Ymago cum Asino ponetur in medio monasterii prope altare Sancti Petri ad unum passum, facie Ymaginis versa ad orientem. Conventus manebit ante candelabrum versus altare Sancte Marie Magdalene, canonici ad partem meridionalem in sedilibus consuetis, et scolares ante eos; et in medio inter Ymaginem et conventum, que se invicem respicient, erunt strata tria tapeta per transversum monasterii ab invicem parum jacentia. Deinde plebanus Sancte Gertrudis et subdyaconus, quilibet cum pleonario, accedent et statuent se apud collum Asini, unus ad dexteram et alius ad sinistram. Deinde accedent sex cantatrices de conventu, bine et bine ultra dicta tapeta statuentes se retro inter altare Sancti Petri et

Ymaginem. His ita ordinatis, conventus incipiet hymnum *Gloria, laus,* cantatrices singulos versus, conventus repetitionem, et cetera, secundum ordinarium suum.

Ymnus:

Gloria, laus et honor tibi sit, Rex Christe Redemptor,
  Cui puerile decus prompsit Osanna pium.
Israel es tu rex, Davidis et inclita proles;
  Nomine qui in Domini, rex benedicte, venis. Gloria.
Cetus in excelsis te laudat celicus omnis,
  Et mortalis homo, et cuncta creata simul. Cui.
Plebs Hebrea tibi cum palmis obviam venit
  Cum prece, voto, ymnis assumus ecce tibi. Gloria.
Hi tibi passuro solvebant munia laudis;
  Nos tibi regnanti pangimus ecce melos. Cui.
Hi placuere tibi, placeat devotio nostra,
  Rex pie, rex clemens, cui bona cuncta placent. Gloria.

Quo finito et dictis cantatricibus ad conventum et duobus cum pleonariis ad clericos reversis, clerici incipient et cantabunt hanc antiphonam.

Antiphona:

Pueri Hebreorum vestimenta prosternebant in via et clamabant, dicentes: Osanna filio David, benedictus qui venit in nomine Domini.

Interim quod predicta antiphona cantatur, octo scolares vel circiter genuflectent super dictis tapetis facie versa ad Ymaginem, scilicet ad occidentem. Deinde cantabit conventus antiphonam *Occurrunt,* et interim omnes canonici preterquam presbiter et ministri genuflectentes se similiter prosternent.

Antiphona:

Occurrunt turbe cum floribus et palmis redemptori Domino et victori triumphanti digne dant obsequia; filium Dei olim gentes predicant et in laudem Christi voces tonant per nubila Osanna.

Deinde clerici iterum antiphonam *Turba multa.* Interim conventus similiter adorabit.

Antiphona:

Turba multa, que convenerat ad diem festum, clamabat Domino: Benedictus qui venit in nomine Domini, Osanna in excelsis.

Et cum conventus surrexerit, cantrix incipiet antiphonam *Ave,* quam conventus complebit nullo genuflectente.

Antiphona:

Ave rex noster, fili David, redemptor mundi, quem prophete predicaverunt salvatorem domui Israhel esse venturum, te enim ad salutarem victimam Pater misit in mundum, quem expectabant omnes sancti ab origine mundi, et nunc: Osanna filio David, benedictus qui venit in nomine Domini. Osanna in excelsis.

Qua antiphona finita, clerici cantabunt antiphonam *Scriptum est* subsequentem. Interim presbiter cum ministris similiter prostrati adorabunt, presbiter in medio, ministri hinc et hinc.

Antiphona:

Scriptum est enim, percutiam pastorem, et dispergentur oves gregis; postquam autem surrexero, precedam vos in Galileam; ibi me videbitis, dicit Dominus.

Qua finita, conventus cantabit antiphonam sequentem.

Antiphona:

Gaude et letare Jherusalem. Ecce rex tuus venit, de quo prophete predixerunt, quem angeli adoraverunt, cui Cherubin et Seraphin: Sanctus, Sanctus, Sanctus, proclamant.

Presbiter dicit *Oremus.*

Collecta:

Adjuva nos, Deus salutaris noster, et ad beneficia recolenda, quibus nos restaurare dignatus es, tribue venire gaudentes. Per Christum.

Qua finita, clerici ascendunt ad chorum canonicorum coram summo altari cantando responsorium *Ingrediente*, quod sequitur. Clerici cantabunt:

Ingrediente Domino in sanctam civitatem, Hebreorum pueri resurrectionem vite pronunciantes cum ramis palmarum Osanna clamabant in excelsis.

Quo finito, conventus manens inferius ante gradus cantabunt responsorium sequens, Ymagine cum Asino ante sepulchrum Sancti Alfredi posita. Conventus:

Circumdederunt me viri mendaces, sine causa flagellis ceciderunt me; sed tu, Domine defensor, vindica me.

Quo finito, presbiter leget collectam *Omnipotens sempiterne Deus, qui humano generi*, et cetera.

It is to be observed that in spite of the presence of the *Palmesel*, the ceremonial is simple and seriously liturgical, and the choral pieces are the usual ones of Palm Sunday in all countries. The procession occurred after the blessing of the palms, the canons leaving the monastic church to fetch the *Palmesel* from the church of St Gertrude. When the image had been taken thence and drawn to the church of the monastery, it was met at the door by a priest with a silver cross and by a *campanarius* with holy water. The *Palmesel* was then stationed in the middle of the church, facing east, with carpets laid before it. In the presence of the image the canonesses and varying groups of clerics sang the hymn *Gloria, laus et honor*, and a succession of antiphons, during some of which they knelt or prostrated themselves.

Eventually the *Palmesel* was drawn to a position before the tomb of St Alfred, and the ceremony closed with the saying of a collect.

Although the *Palmesel* aroused particular hostility among Protestant reformers, it was persistently used in some parts of Germany down through the eighteenth and nineteenth centuries.[1] The images themselves, of which a considerable number are preserved, seem usually to have been of almost life-size, and to have been mounted on wheels.[2]

Far less brilliant than the procession of Palm Sunday, but similar to it in the nearness of its approach to true dramatic action, is the ceremony of the washing of the feet of certain poor persons on Holy Thursday. This commemorates Christ's washing of the apostles' feet at the Last Supper, and his command that his disciples should do likewise for one another.[3] The ceremony is called the *Mandatum*, and the day is called Maundy Thursday, from the first antiphon sung: *Mandatum novum do vobis: Ut diligatis invicem, sicut dilexi vos.*[4] The commemoration has consisted traditionally in an actual repetition of the act performed by Christ.[5] It occurs after Mass and after the denuding of the altars; hence some time during the afternoon. The officiating cleric comes to the place appointed, accompanied by his ministers. After the liturgical gospel of the day, recounting Christ's washing of the feet of the apostles, has been read, the officiant girds himself with a towel, and proceeds with the washing of the feet of selected poor persons. Meanwhile are sung antiphons and psalm-verses. Not infrequently this part of the ceremony was followed by a conventual meal, during which food was distributed in commemoration of the Last Supper.[6] All these features appear in the following description of the ceremony at Besançon:[7]

Post expletionem Missæ, descendat pontifex in sacrarium mandans presbyteris quos voluerit. Cum autem venerint canonici claustrum, sint

---

[1] See Wiepen, pp. 19–23, and the texts of Kirchmayer and Googe in Appendix C.

[2] For descriptions see Wiepen, pp. 39–44; Chambers, i, 334. For photographs see Max Picard, *Mittelalterliche Holzfiguren*, Erlenbach-Zurich, 1920, plate 29; G. Lanson, *Histoire illustrée de la Littérature française*, i, Paris [1923], 145. Three examples, of the fifteenth and sixteenth centuries, are preserved in the Landesmuseum in Zurich. In regard to three specimens at Basel see Chambers, i, 334. An admirable example of the sixteenth century, from South Germany, may be seen in the Victoria and Albert Museum in London. See also plate ii.

[3] See John xiii, 1–15.

[4] See John xiii, 34.

[5] For medieval descriptions of the ceremony see Martene, iii, 99–100, 110, 119, 121.

[6] See Stapper, *Feier*, pp. 82–3, 151–2; Cox, *Churchwardens' Accounts*, pp. 70–1; Tolhurst, ii, 335–6.

[7] Martene, iii, 110. Concerning the manuscript Martene writes (iii, 109): 'Ex MS. Pontificali annorum circiter 600.'

ibi parati 60 pauperes, ut abluantur eorum pedes; et detur unicuique denarius, et panis, et metrem vini; et postea seniores eant refectorium. Interim ut comederint, denudentur altaria, et præparetur aqua ad abluenda altaria sive vinum vel pigmentum. Cum autem surrexerint seniores a refectione, præcinget se episcopus vel ipsi sacerdotes quibus ipse jusserit, ut abluantur altaria; et interim cantant seniores communiter in choro responsorium *Circumdederunt me.* Tractus *Qui habitat in adjutorio.* Tractus *De necessitatibus meis.* Tractus *Domine non secundum.* Et dum ista fiant, præparetur capitulum cortinis palleis ceterisque ornamentis. Diaconus autem præparat se sicut in diebus festis, tam ipse quam ceteri processores cum candelabris et thuribulis, et veniens capitulum legat evangelium *Ante diem festum Paschæ,* usque *ut dilectio qua dilexisti me in ipsis sit, et ego in ipsis.* Interim dum legitur evangelium, præparentur luteus, et manutergia, et præcinctoria, et cetera vasa quæ necessaria sunt ad abluendos pedes. Finito evangelio, præcingat se diaconus vel decanus, et ipsi quibus ipse jusserit, et ipsemet pontifex, et incipiat cantor *Dominus Jesus. Mandatum novum.* Psalmus *Beati immaculati. Ante diem festum,* et cetera. *Postquam surrexit,* et cetera. Psalmus *Deus misereatur nostri.* Antiphona *Domine, tu mihi lavas,* et cetera. Antiphona *Domine, non tantum pedes.* Antiphona *Si ego Dominus.* Antiphona *Diligamus nos invicem.* Psalmus *Quam dilecta.* Antiphona *In diebus illis,* et cetera. Responsorium *Felix Maria.* Responsorium *Pectore sincero,* et cetera. Responsorium *O felix.* Antiphona *Ubi caritas,* et cetera. Antiphona *Christus descendit.* Completa lavatione pedum, defertur aqua ad abluendas manus et manutergia; et interim dum cœna fit, dicant pueri hymnum, et seniores repetant semper primum versum. Interim dum cantatur hymnus, deferantur panes azymi et nebulæ et oblatæ, et benedicantur ab episcopo vel decano hoc modo: *Benedic, Domine, hanc creaturam panis, sicut benedixisti quinque panes in deserto, ut ex ea gustantes accipiant tam corporis, quam animæ sanitatem. Per.* Tunc distribuat episcopus vel decanus singulis dicens *Accipite, et sumite in commemoratione Dominicæ Cœnæ.* Et sic cœnent cum sobrietate, bibentes etiam sobrie, et cantantes honeste. Hymnus *Tellus ac æthera jubilent,* et cetera. Post hæc dicatur ab episcopo vel decano hæc oratio: *Adesto, Domine, officio servitutis nostræ,* et cetera. Si episcopus adest, dicit diaconus *Humiliate vos ad benedictionem. Benedicat vos Dominus, qui per Unigeniti sui passionem,* et cetera.

Obviously such an observance is perfectly adapted for transformation into drama. If by the slightest touch the officiating cleric were to impersonate Christ, the instantaneous result would be a play. But of such a transformation the available records make no mention.[1]

---

[1] For further information concerning the *Mandatum* see Deschamps de Pas, pp. 163, 165–6; Le Verdier, i, pp. xxxviii sq.; Wordsworth, *Notes,* pp. 184–5; Clément, pp. 207–8; Frere, *Use of Sarum,* ii, 164; Feasey, *Ceremonial,* pp. 95–113; Thalhofer, i, 628–9;

In comparison with the ceremonies of Palm Sunday and of Holy Thursday, the other observances of Holy Week cannot be said to approach very closely to the borders of true drama. One or two of these I shall describe briefly, however, chiefly in order that possible misconceptions may be avoided. It has been erroneously inferred, for example, that the dramatic method was used in the singing of the Passions during the Middle Ages. From at least as early as the fifth century the liturgy of Holy Week has included the intoning at Mass of the four canonical accounts of Christ's last days upon earth—that of Matthew on Palm Sunday, of Mark on Tuesday, of Luke on Wednesday, and of John on Good Friday.[1] In modern times these passages— called *Passiones*—are sung in a manner which is sympathetically described by Cardinal Wiseman as follows:[2]

This is performed by three interlocutors, in the habit of deacons, who distribute among themselves the parts, as follows: The narrative is given by one in a strong, manly tenor voice; the words of our Saviour are chaunted in a deep solemn bass and whatever is spoken by any other person is given by the third in a high contralto. This at once produces a dramatic effect; each part has its particular cadence, of old, simple, but rich chaunt, suited to the character represented, and worthy of ancient tragedy. That of the narrator is clear, distinct, and slightly modulated; that in which ordinary interlocutors speak, sprightly and almost bordering upon colloquial familiarity; but that in which our Saviour's words are uttered, is slow, grave, and most solemn, beginning low, and ascending by full tones, then gently varied in rich though simple undulations, till it ends by a graceful and expressive cadence, modified with still greater effect in interrogating phrases.

The distribution of the sentences of the *Passio* among three persons, as described here, results in a kind of dialogue, interrupted by brief passages of narrative; and to many observers this modern ceremony must have seemed not only highly dramatic, but also readily transformable, through touches of impersonation, into an actual play. To our present study, however, such impressions are irrelevant, for the modern practice of distributing the parts to three separate persons was unknown during the Middle Ages, having been introduced only about the fifteenth

Thurston, pp. 304 sqq.; Bishop, p. 294. For Herrad of Landsberg's distinction between an impersonated play and a mere liturgical observance such as the *Mandatum* see below, ii, 413.

[1] Matt. xxvi, 1—xxvii, 61; Mark xiv, 1— xv, 46; Luke xxii, 1—xxiii, 53; John xviii, 1— xix, 42.

[2] Nicholas P. S., Cardinal Wiseman, *Four Lectures on the Offices and Ceremonies of Holy Week, as performed in the Papal Chapels*, Baltimore, 1854, pp. 67–8.

century. Before that time the *Passio* was sung by a *single* deacon, who indicated the narrative passages, and the transition from the words of one person to those of another, merely by changing the pitch and intensity of his voice and the speed of his recital.[1]

During the Middle Ages, then, the reading of the *Passiones*, though deeply affecting, was far less dramatic in form than has commonly been supposed by most modern commentators. If there was any suggestion of theatrical adaptation, it arose not from the employment of several reciters, but from a few imitative or symbolic acts performed by persons other than the single reader or singer. Thus during the singing of the *Passio* from St Luke, on Wednesday, at the words *Et velum templi scissum est medium*, a curtain that had been hung before, or about, the altar might be dropped or torn; or at the words *Obscuratus est sol*, a curtain might be let down from above. Likewise during the *Passio* from St John, on Good Friday, at the words *Partiti sunt vestimenta mea sibi*, the attendant clerics might tear, or remove, certain linen altar coverings. In the singing of any of the *Passiones*, at the point where Christ's death is announced there was a pause in the recital, or an extinguishing of lights, as well as a general kneeling of the congregation.[2] Such symbolic or reverential acts were, under the circumstances, deeply impressive; but they did not lead directly to the invention of plays.

This general observation must be made also concerning the three beautiful services called *Tenebræ*, consisting of Matins and Lauds of Thursday, Friday, and Saturday of Holy Week.[3] At each service, according to modern practice, is set up in the choir a triangular candle-stick, or hearse, with accommodation for fifteen candles. At the conclusion of each of the psalms—nine in Matins and five in Lauds—one candle is extinguished; and during the *Benedictus* of Lauds the lights on the altar are also put out.[4] Thus at the end of the service the only light remaining in the church is the single candle at the summit of the candlestick. Finally this last candle is hidden behind the altar.

The modern form of *Tenebræ* thus outlined represents well enough the general medieval practice. Although the number

[1] For the evidence see Notes, p. 550.

[2] For evidence concerning all these practices see Young, *Passion-Play*, pp. 332–3.

[3] In modern times each service of *Tenebræ* is performed on the evening preceding the day from which the liturgical text is taken.

Hence Matins and Lauds of Thursday, Friday, and Saturday are sung on the evenings of Wednesday, Thursday, and Friday.

[4] For the structure of Matins and Lauds see above, pp. 47 sqq.

of candles varied somewhat from place to place, the beautiful effect of the observance was the same everywhere. The gradual descent of darkness through the church lent itself easily to symbolism, and the 'theatrical' use of lights was, no doubt, very telling; but the observance offers nothing from which to develop a play.[1]

A more promising dramatic germ was present in the vivid commemoration of the Crucifixion on Good Friday, known as the Adoration of the Cross. This ceremony was cultivated first at Jerusalem, and the form which it assumed there in the fourth century has already been described.[2] The oriental observance was transported to the West at least as early as the eighth century, and became an established part of the Roman liturgy. Although the ceremonial was not uniform throughout the West, the fundamental element of obeisance before the cross remained the same as in the East, and during the Middle Ages this central act advanced no further toward drama. A more intimate consideration of this ceremony, and of the dramatic features that eventually accumulated on its periphery, will be considered in an appropriate place below.[3]

The several other vivid liturgical acts of Holy Week need not be described here. The blessing of the new fire and of the baptismal fonts on Holy Saturday has always been accompanied by striking symbolic movements and by beautiful recitals; but none of these ever approached closely to the borders of drama.[4]

V

Passing from the ceremonies of the organized seasons of the liturgical year, we must give at least a moment's attention to a special liturgical observance which occupies no fixed position in the calendar of the Church as a whole, and which, in the nature of the case, varies in date from one community to another. I refer to the Consecration of a Church.[5] From a very early period the dedication of any new church building to regular Christian worship was solemnized in an impressive manner. The pilgrim, Etheria, reports that in the fourth century the annual commemoration of the consecration of the principal churches in

---

[1] Concerning *Tenebræ* in general see Wordsworth, *Notes*, pp. 290–1; Clément, pp. 204–5; D'Ancona, i, 27; Martene, iii, 81–2; iv, 122–4; Chambers, ii, 6; Feasey, *Ceremonial*, pp. 84–94; Thalhofer, i, 620–1; Thurston, pp. 238–73.

[2] See above, p. 87.
[3] See pp. 118 sqq.
[4] See Thalhofer, i, 637 sqq.; Martene, iii, 144 sqq.; Thurston, pp. 405 sqq.; Bishop, pp. 296–7.
[5] For bibliography see Notes, p. 551.

Jerusalem was a ceremony of great splendour.[1] The liturgical forms which were gradually developed for the consecratory observance during later centuries may be grouped under three divisions: the consecration of the church building, the consecration of the altar, and the translation of relics to the altar. Of these three we are at present concerned only with the first, the essential purpose of which is the purifying of the edifice. In its unconsecrated state the building is to be regarded as impure and as the dwelling-place of Satan. The ceremony of cleansing the place and of expelling the devil is arranged for as follows in an *Ordo Dedicationis Ecclesiæ* used by the bishop of Metz in the ninth century:[2]

Incipit pontifex aquam aspargere consecratam a foris, sequendo feretro reliquiarum, cleroque canente antifonam *Asperges me, Domine,* cum psalmo L^{mo}, sed uno ex clericis in nova ecclesia clausis hostiis quasi latente. Nam pontifex circumit ecclesiam ab hostio in partem aquilonarem prima vice usque iterum ad idem hostium; et cum illic perventum fuerit, pulsat hostium tribus vicibus, dicendo:

Tollite portas, principes, vestras, et elevamini, portæ æternales, et introibit rex gloriæ.

Ille deintus respondens dicat:

Quis est iste rex gloriæ?

Iterum circumienda est ecclesia secunda vice sicut prius, cum eadem antiphona et eodem psalmo, usquedum perveniatur ad hostium, atque iterum pulsetur sicut prius eisdem verbis et idem respondente deintus latente. Tunc tertio iterum circumienda est eodem modo cum eodem cantu usque iterum ad hostium. Tunc dicenti pontifici et pulsanti respondendum est ei sicut prius:

Quis est iste rex gloriæ?

Pontifex respondeat:

Dominus virtutum, ipse est rex gloriæ.

Tunc aperientur hostia et canenda est antiphona *Ambulate, sancti Dei, ingredimini in domum Domini,* cum psalmo *Lætatus sum in his quæ dicta sunt mihi,* et cetera. Et ille qui prius fuerat intus quasi fugiens egrediatur ad illud hostium foras, iterum ingressurus per primum hostium vestitus vestimentis ecclesiasticis.

According to this *ordo* the bishop begins the purifying of the building by sprinkling the exterior of the walls. The procession

---

[1] See Duchesne, pp. 522–3; Cabrol, *Prayer,* p. 204.

[2] I use the text printed by Duchesne, pp. 487–8, from Bibl. Nat., MS lat. 9428. This passage is reprinted by Young, *Harrowing of Hell,* p. 894. See Chambers, ii, 4.

of clerics marches round the exterior of the church three times, halting each time at the west door, and performing there a special ceremonial. The bishop strikes the door thrice with his staff, saying *Tollite portas*, and receives the response *Quis est iste rex gloriæ?* from a cleric concealed within the church. After the third recital of this dialogue, the bishop declares himself in the words *Dominus virtutum, ipse est rex gloriæ*, the doors are flung open, and the procession enters the building. Meanwhile the cleric who has been concealed behind the closed doors slips out and, resuming his vestments, joins the procession as the bishop proceeds with sprinkling the interior of the church.

Obviously this dramatic representation of the expulsion of evil approaches very close to being a play. Although the text now before us gives no evidence upon the point, it is difficult to believe that this symbolic ceremonial did not sometimes include an element of impersonation, such as a mimetic use of voice on the part of the cleric who represented the devil within the building.

VI

Our survey of dramatic ceremonies must include, finally, at least a brief consideration of the astonishing clerical revels admitted into the liturgy of many medieval cathedrals, collegiate churches and monasteries during the period of a fortnight or more following Christmas Day. The significance of these activities in the history of the drama has, no doubt, been frequently exaggerated; nevertheless they cannot be altogether omitted from a treatise such as the present one.

These festivities of Christmas and the New Year include some four special celebrations on four separate days, presided over by different ranks of the clergy as follows: the deacons on St Stephen's Day (Dec. 26), the priests on the feast of St John (Dec. 27), the choir-boys on Innocents' Day (Dec. 28), and the subdeacons on the feast of the Circumcision (Jan. 1), on Epiphany (Jan. 6), or on the octave of Epiphany (Jan. 13). These four observances are frequently referred to collectively as the 'Feast of Fools'; but this term is more appropriately restricted to the last of them, and I shall so restrict it here.[1]

The Feast of Fools was known, in different communities, by a variety of names, such as *festum stultorum*, *fatuorum*, or *follorum*,

---

[1] For bibliography see Notes, p. 551.

festum subdiaconorum, and *festum baculi*. It seems to have arisen about the twelfth century, to have been observed especially in France, and to have occurred most commonly on the feast of the Circumcision (Jan. 1). The nature of the celebration was determined by the fact that the control of the services of the day, both the Mass and the *Cursus*, was given over to the subdeacons. At First Vespers[1] their representative received the *baculus* of the master of ceremonies, assumed his authority, and retained it throughout the feast. The effect of these arrangements was to give to the subdeacons an unwonted prominence and a notorious opportunity for 'misrule'. The liturgical results arising from such licence can scarcely be expected to appear completely in the pages of a service-book; but a thirteenth-century manuscript from Beauvais gives some impression of what occurred in the cathedral there.[2] The normal *form* of the Mass and Canonical Office is retained, but the *text* is extended by interpolations, or tropes.[3] The ceremonial included a drinking-bout, the bringing of an ass into the church at the singing of the Prose of the Ass,

> Orientis partibus
> adventavit asinus,[4]

and the ending of certain liturgical pieces with a bray. A 're-formed' version of this celebration used at the cathedral of Sens in the thirteenth century, although it calls itself *asinaria festa*, omits the coarser elements of revelry.[5] It appears to be entirely serious in its intention, and might be described as simply a 'troped', or embellished, liturgical office for the feast of the Circumcision. The Feast of Fools, then, can scarcely be said to occupy a very significant place in dramatic history. Its activities have to do with licensed misbehaviour rather than with theatrical representation.

A somewhat closer approach to the drama is made in one of the other celebrations of the Christmas season mentioned above: the revels of the choir-boys on Innocents' Day (Dec. 28),[6] which

---

[1] For the meaning of the term see above, p. 47.

[2] This manuscript (London, Brit. Mus., MS Egerton 2615) was rediscovered by Chambers, and the ceremonials which were probably connected with it are described by him, i, 284–8.

[3] For the meaning of the term 'trope' see below, chap. vi.

[4] For the text of the Prose of the Ass see

Notes, p. 551. The amount of medieval symbolizing associated with the ass is considerable. See Cabrol and Leclercq, i, 2041–68.

[5] The office from Sens is described by Chambers, i, 279–84. The text has since been thoroughly re-edited by H. Villetard, *Office de Pierre de Corbeil* (*Bibliothèque musico-logique*, iv), Paris, 1907.

[6] For bibliography see Notes, p. 552.

appear to have been known as early as the tenth century.[1] Just as in the Feast of Fools the subdeacons take control, so here the choir-boys assume the highest responsibilities, flout their elders, and introduce as much levity as the community will allow. In these activities they are led by a Boy Bishop, or *Episcopus Puerorum*, whom they elect well in advance of the feast, often on St Nicholas' Day (Dec. 6). The Boy Bishop flourished in every country of Western Europe, and especially in France and England. In the latter country he is amply recorded from the thirteenth century to the sixteenth, and seems to have appeared in religious houses and schools, as well as in cathedrals and collegiate churches. Since the extant examples from Italy appear not to be numerous, I illustrate the revels of Innocents' Day in general from the customs recorded in an unpublished service-book used in the thirteenth century in the cathedral of Padua:[2]

In Uigilia Innocentum. Ad Uesperum[3] ut supra. Ad *Magnificat* antiphona *Iste est discipulus*. Et tunc sacerdotes deponunt pluuialia. Et duo acoliti induunt se pluuialibus, et tunc conferunt cereos et libros scolaribus. Finita oratione Sancti Iohannis, unus de supradictis acolitis confert antiphonam Innocentum maiori acolito, et episcopus dic*it* versum et orationem Innocentum; et postea prosecuntur antiphonas, versus, et orationes Natiuitatis Domini et Sancti Stephani. Et ita cantatur Uesperum quando non est aliquis Episcopellus. Sed quando est Episcopellus, tunc, finita oratione Sancti Iohannis, exit Episcopellus de secrestia inferiori preparatus cum clericis et capellanis suis cum pluuialibus, cum cruce et turribulo et cereis precedentibus; et uadunt cum processione tali ad altare Sancti Danielis cantando responsorium | *Centum quadraginta*. Et tunc Episcopellus ascendit ad altare, precedentibus cereis, et thurificat illud, et acolitus, accepto turribulo, thurificat Episcopellum, et postea acolitos qui regunt chorum, deinde canonicos et alios clericos et scolares secundum ordinem superius annotatum. Finito responsorio, unus acolitorum incip*it* antiphonam ad *Magnificat*, scilicet *Istorum est enim regnum celorum*. Oratio *Deus cuius hodierna die*, et cetera; et prosecuntur antiphonas et orationes Natiuitatis et Sancti Stephani, ut dictum est supra, quas orationes dicit Episcopellus. Et postea tres acoliti uel alij clerici cantant et secundant *Benedicamus Domino*, et Episcopellus benedicit clerum et populum.

Hic uadit Episcopellus ad domum episcopi ut hic dicitur. In sero uadit Episcopellus cum canonicis indutus pluuiali et mitra, precedenti-

---

[1] See Chambers, i, 338.
[2] Padua, Bibl. Capit., MS S, Ordin. Patavinense sæc. xiii, fol. 50ᵛ–53ᵛ, described by Dondi Orologio, pp. 42–3, 53–7, and by

Bartholomaeis, pp. 208–9, and now printed, I think, for the first time. Concerning the MS see Notes, p. 552.   [3] Uesperum] The persistent spelling of the MS.

bus scolaribus cum cereis et turribulo, ad domum episcopi, et in introitu hostij dicitur antiphona *Sinite paruulos.* Et tunc datur incensum Episcopello et episcopo antiquo et canonicis et clericis et scolaribus et etiam laycis qui intersunt, et omnes sedent. Et tunc Episcopellus querit ab episcopo utrum bene amistrauit bona ecclesie, et multe alie trufe dicuntur ibi. Et demum | Episcopellus precipit apportari uinum, et omnes bibunt. Et recepta benedictione ab Episcopello, recedunt.

Ad Matutinum. Ad Matutinum Episcopellus incipit Matutinum. Si Episcopellus non est, tunc incipit sacerdos ebdomadarius sine pluuiali. Quatuor acoliti cum pluuialibus cantant vitatorium in medio chori, quia Episcopellus ponit sedem suam iuxta pergamum, et dum cantatur vitatorium, Episcopellus uadit et incensat altare, et omnes thurificantur ordine supradicto. Et tunc duo acoliti cum pluuialibus regunt chorum et conferunt antiphonas et primo episcopo, postea scolaribus incipiendo a minoribus, et ita prosecuntur propriam ystoriam, scilicet *Sub altare Dei,* cum vitatorio et antiphonis et psalmis de Martyribus. Et omnia dicit et facit Episcopellus que faceret et diceret episcopus. Sex lectiones leguntur de propria legenda, scilicet *Hodie, fratres karissimi, natalem illorum infantium.* Maior acolitus legit primam lectionem, et sic degradando acoliti legunt lectiones. Omeliam legit diaconus, scilicet *Angelus Domini apparuit,* et cetera. Episcopellus legit nonam lectionem. *Te Deum laudamus* non cantatur, sed, finita nona lectione, uadit Episcopellus | cum clero suo post altare maius cantando nonum responsorium, scilicet *Centum quadraginta*; et ibi cantantur Laudes cum propriis antiphonis, scilicet *Herodes iratus est,* et cetera. Et tali modo prosecuntur psalmos, scilicet quia ab uno latere incipiunt *Dominus regnauit*; ab alio latere dicunt secundum versum; illi qui remanent in choro ab uno latere dicunt tercium uersum; ab alio latere dicunt quartum uersum; et tali ordine prosecuntur omnes psalmos Laudum, et *Benedictus Dominus Deus Israel.* Capitulum *Vidi supra montem.* Versus *Hii sunt qui cum mulieribus,* et cetera. Ad *Benedictus* antiphona *A bimatu et infra.* Oratio *Deus cuius hodierna die.* Et prosecuntur antiphonas et orationes Natiuitatis Domini, Sancti Stephani, et Sancti Iohannis.

Finito Matutino, Episcopellus benedicit clerum et populum. Si uero non est Episcopellus, tunc cantantur Laudes Matutine in choro ecclesie et non post altare.

Ad Missam. Post Primam quidam sacerdos dicit Missam Episcopelli ad altare Sancte Crucis, et ibi a dextro latere altaris preparatus est Episcopellus cum pluuiali et mitra, et cum capellanis suis. Officium *Ex ore infantium.* Epistola *Vidi supra montem Syon.*

Quam dicit quidam indutus quadam uili | stricta, et tenet in manu quandam hastam ligneam, quam prohicit uersus populum. Et ibi sunt quidam armati, qui secuntur dictam hastam, et circuiunt ecclesiam querendo Infantem cum Matre sua, scilicet Christum cum Beata Uirgine

Maria. Et est quidam indutus ad modum mulieris que sedet supra Asinam, habens filium in sinu suo; et quidam, qui presentat Ioseph, duc*it* asinam fugientem per ecclesiam, ad significationem Uirginis fugientis cum puero in Egypto secundum quod angelus Domini in sompnis dixerat Ioseph.

Non dicitur *Gloria in excelsis Deo*, nec *Alleluia*; sed loco *Alleluia*[1] dicitur *Laus tibi, Christe*. Euangelium *Angelus Domini apparuit*, et cetera, quod dic*it* diaconus cum stola tantum. Post euangelium descendit Episcopellus preparatus pluuiali, mitra, et baculo, assistentibus ei capellanis et clericis suis, ad gradus ante altare Sancte Crucis, et ibi sedens suscipit oblationem a populo, que oblatio sua est. Accepta oblatione, quidam capellanus suus facit confessionem secundum quod sibi uidetur; et postea Episcopellus benedicit clerum et populum suis benedictionibus.

Finita Missa, incipitur alia Missa pro pueris plana uoce cum eisdem | offertorio, oratione, epistola, et euangelio ut in prima Missa. Finito euangelio, mulieres offerunt denarios et candelas pro pueris defunctis, et postea finitur Missa.

Ad Terciam, ad Sextam, et ad Nonam tres prime antiphone Laudum super psalmos. Capitulum ad Terciam *Vidi supra montem*. Capitulum ad Sextam *Et audiui uocem*. Capitulum ad Nonam *Et uocem quam audiui*. Responsoria de Martyribus, que dicit maior acolitus, et incipit antiphonas super psalmos.

Qualiter Episcopellus post prandium uisitat. Sciendum est quod ecclesias sibi subditas Episcopellus in die Innocentum dat prandium omnibus canonicis, clericis, et scolaribus cum eo prandere uolentibus supra domum magnam. Et post prandium ascendit equum cum pluuiali et cyrotecis et anulo et mitra. Capellani sui similiter cum pluuialibus ascendunt equos, et quidam de canonicis et scolaribus et familia sua. Et circuit ciuitatem signando uiros et mulieres, et uisitando monasteria sibi tributaria, scilicet monasterium Sancte Justine, Sancti Stephani, Sancte Sophie, Sancti Leonardi, et Sancti Petri; et ad quodlibet istorum monasteriorum descendit cum clericis et familia sua. Et tunc recipitur honorifice ab abbatibus | et prioribus et abbatissis et a monachis et monialibus cum pluuialibus, incenso, et aqua sancta, et tunc intrat ecclesiam et prosternit se ante altare in oratione, et postea benedicit omnes, et intrant claustrum. Et Episcopellus precipit apportari uinum, et omnes bibunt. Et si aliquid istorum monasteriorum denegat sibi consuetum tributum prestare, scilicet spallas et fugacias et alia consueta, tunc dictus Episcopellus interdicit dictum monasterium ita quod per huiusmodi interdictum tempore quo dominus episcopus cum clero et populo uadit sollempniter cum letaniis, tunc non intrat ecclesiam dicti monasterij denegantis Episcopello tributum prestare; et huiusmodi interdictum seruatur donec dictum monasterium satis-

---

[1] Alleluia] Alle (MS).

fecerit dicto Episcopello ad uoluntatem acolitorum canonice Paduane; et tunc relaxabitur interdictum.

Ad Uesperum omnia in Uigilia Sancti Thome martyris ut supra. Capitulum *Vidi supra montem.* Ad *Magnificat* antiphona *Innocentes pro Christo.* Oratio ut supra.[1] Oratio Sancti Thome *Deus pro cuius ecclesia,* et cetera. Postea prosecuntur antiphonas et orationes Natiuitatis Domini, Sancti Stephani, et Sancti Iohannis. Completorium ut supra.

In this church the Boy Bishop assumes his authority and presides at Vespers on St John's Day (Dec. 27). That evening the *espiscopellus,* in cope and mitre, and preceded by boys carrying candles and thuribles, visits the house of the recognized bishop, who is interrogated as to his stewardship of the goods of the church, and is subjected to other forms of jesting (*multe alie trufe dicuntur ibi*). Then wine is brought, and all partake. During the *horæ* of the next morning there are no scandalous occurrences. The Boy Bishop presides at Matins, censes the altar, and reads the ninth lesson. After Prime, is celebrated a special Mass, during which the *episcopellus* assumes the place of a true bishop.[2] After the reading of the epistle, the reader throws a wooden spear towards the congregation. Then occurs a brief dramatization of the Flight into Egypt, in dumb show. Certain armed men circulate about in the church seeking Christ and his mother. Mary is impersonated by a cleric dressed as a woman holding a child in her arms and sitting on an ass. Another cleric, impersonating Joseph, leads the animal through the church.[3] After the gospel, the *episcopellus* receives a general offering from the congregation. At the conclusion of None he gives a dinner to all the canons, clerics, and choir-boys. At the conclusion of this ceremony he mounts a horse, and, accompanied by an appropriate retinue, visits all the monasteries tributary to the cathedral. At each house he demands wine for all, and either receives the customary contribution, or places the monastery under an interdict. For the close of the day no special activities are prescribed.

The general form and tone of this observance at Padua may be regarded as sufficiently typical for Western Europe. The impersonated scene of the Flight into Egypt appears to have

---

[1] For insertion here is written in the left margin the following passage: Ad *Magnificat* antiphona *Martyr Thoma, martyr Dei.*

[2] It should be observed that the *episcopellus*

himself does not celebrate Mass.

[3] For dramatic treatments of the Flight into Egypt see below, ii, 118, 189–90.

been a well-known feature of either the Feast of Fools or Innocents' Day in France.[1] In various places in England the Boy Bishop, as part of his assumption of mature responsibility, preached a sermon at Mass; and several examples of such discourses are still preserved.[2]

Although the Feast of Fools and the custom of the Boy Bishop contain occasional features which can be identified as drama, it is scarcely necessary to insist that in their fundamental conception they are allied to sheer revelry and hilarity rather than to the stage. The *episcopellus*, to be sure, does, in a sense, pretend to be the real bishop, and in some of his doings he may be said to imitate that dignified personage. It should be remembered, however, that the chief action in which he is engaged is not an *imitation* of the liturgy, or a dramatic representation of it, but the usual, authorized worship of the day. He is, therefore, not an *impersonation* of the true presiding bishop, but merely a ludicrous substitute.[3]

It is clear, then, that the dramatic phenomena reviewed in this chapter, cannot be regarded as effectual origins of the genuine drama of the Church. The Mass is excluded from the possibility of dramatization because of its fundamental meaning. It is not a representation of an action, but an actual re-creation of it. The *horæ* of the Canonical Office never gave promise of development into drama, since they were designed as devotional exercises, and exhibit no intention of representing actual events. Several of the special ceremonies of Holy Week, however, do show this intention, and might readily have been transformed into plays if this development had been desired. This transformation would have been especially feasible for the procession of Palm Sunday, the *Mandatum* of Holy Thursday, or the Adoration of the Cross on Good Friday. The first of these ceremonies, indeed, did occasionally include the impersonating of one of the subordinate personages. Likewise the observances presided over by the Boy Bishop sometimes included elements of genuine pantomime; but the chief occupations of that anniversary belong to the category of buffoonery rather than of dramatic representation. Certain ceremonial aspects of the Palm

[1] See Chambers, i, 287, 333.
[2] See especially Fletcher, pp. 16–9; Owst, p. 220; Meller, pp. 13–5.
[3] Creizenach (i, 91) rightly minimizes the effect of the Boy Bishop upon the drama; A. F. Leach (*Educational Charters and Documents, 598 to 1909*, Cambridge, 1911. p. xlvi) decidedly overestimates it.

Sunday procession, of the Adoration of the Cross, and of the ministrations of the Boy Bishop are, to be sure, reflected in plays to be considered later in this study;[1] but of the drama of the Church as a whole the liturgical observances now before us are not the essential beginnings.

[1] See below, pp. 503 sq., 519 sqq., and ii, 175.

CHAPTER IV

THE BURIAL OF CROSS AND HOST

IT has seemed convenient to reserve for separate consideration two special liturgical ceremonies which are not only in themselves more decisively dramatic than most of those reviewed in the preceding chapter, but which are also more directly and significantly related to the plays treated later in this study. These two special observances may be called the *Depositio* and the *Elevatio*, the former commemorating the burial of Christ, and the latter, the Resurrection. Although these commemorations are not invariably so elaborate as some that we have already considered, they are among the earliest in date, were very widely observed, and have persisted from at least the tenth century to the present time.[1]

I

The general nature of the *Depositio* and *Elevatio* may be seen in the following relatively simple versions of the fourteenth century from the monastery of St Blaise, in the Black Forest:[2]

⟨Depositio Hostiæ⟩[3]

Communicatis omnibus,[4] sonentur tabulæ omnes. Post hæc fiet oratio ante Vesperam. Interim sacerdos sumat Viaticum, eatque ad Sepulchrum cum incenso et candelis cantando responsorium:

> *Agnus Dei Christus ⟨immolatus est pro salute mundi; nam de parentis protoplasti fraude factor condolens, quando pomi noxialis morte morsu corruit; ipse lignum tunc notavit, damna ligni ut solveret. Versus: Christus factus est pro nobis obediens usque ad mortem, mortem autem crucis. Ipse lignum.⟩*

⟨Responsorium:⟩

> *Ecce quomodo moritur ⟨justus, et nemo percipit corde; et viri justi tolluntur, et nemo considerat; a facie iniquitatis oblatus est justus, et erit in pace memoria ejus. Versus: In pace factus est locus ejus, et in Sion habitatio ejus. Et erit.⟩*

cum versibus et repetitionibus; ponensque illud in Sepulchrum incenset, et claudens illud cantet responsorium:

> *Sepulto Domino, ⟨signatum est monumentum; volventes lapidem ad ostium monumenti; ponentes milites qui custodirent illud. Versus: Ne forte veniant*

---

[1] For bibliography see Notes, p. 552.

[2] I give the texts of Gerbert, *Monumenta*, part ii, 235, 236, previously reprinted by Young, *Dramatic Associations*, pp. 5-7. The *Depositio* is incompletely reprinted in *Decreta*, iv, 432.

[3] Gerbert, *Monumenta*, ii, 235.

[4] The reference is to the Communion of the Mass of the Presanctified on Good Friday. See below, p. 117.

discipuli ejus et furentur eum, et dicant plebi: Surrexit a mortuis. Po-
nentes.⟩[1]

cum versu et repetitione; ponaturque cereus ardens ante Sepulchrum.
Deinde legatur Vespera.

⟨ELEVATIO HOSTIÆ⟩[2]

Nocte sacratissima Resurrectionis Domini, cum tempus fuerit
pulsandi Matutinum, secretarius surgat, sumens laternam cum lumine
Domnum Abbatem excitabit, atque priorem, deinde alios de fratribus ad
compulsandas campanas, qui sibi placuerint. Surgens autem Domnus
Abbas ad ecclesiam eat, et induit se alba, stola et cappa, prior autem
alba, et cæteri fratres. Sumentesque duo thuribula cum incenso, præcedentibus candelabris, eant ad Sepulchrum cum responsorio:

> *Maria Magdalena ⟨et altera Maria ibant diluculo ad monumentum. Jesum*
> *quem quæritis, non est hic; surrexit sicut locutus est, præcedet vos in Galilæam;*
> *ibi eum videbitis, alleluia, alleluia. Versus: Cito euntes dicite discipulis ejus*
> *et Petro quia surrexit Dominus. Præcedet.*⟩[3]

cum versu. Et eant ad Sepulchrum, ac illud incensent exterius; deinde
levato tegimento, iterum incensent interius. Postea sumens Corpus
Domini super altare ponit cantans responsorium:

> *Surrexit pastor bonus ⟨qui animam suam posuit pro ovibus suis, et pro suo*
> *grege mori dignatus est, alleluia, alleluia, alleluia. Versus: Surrexit Dominus*
> *de sepulcro, qui pro nobis pependit in ligno. Et pro suo.*⟩[4]

cum versu. Interim levet Corpus Dominicum, incensisque candelis,
sonetur classis. Post ternas orationes incipiat Domnus Abbas xv Gradus.
Omnes qui in hac nocte aliquid cantare vel legere volunt, debent esse
revestiti albis præter puerum qui dicit versum. Infra xv Gradus
sonentur duo maxima signa in angulari; deinde duo maiora signa in
choro. Postea fiat compulsatio ab omnibus campanis. Tunc veniens
Domnus Abbas ante altare indutus cappa incipiat *Domine, labia mea
aperies.*[5]

It will be observed that the setting for these dramatic offices
is a receptacle called *sepulchrum*. In the absence of a description,
we can only infer, for the moment,[6] that this is some sort of chest
or enclosure, with a cover. The *Depositio* occurs on Good Friday,
between Mass and Vespers, and consists essentially in the burial

---

[1] This responsory, along with the two preceding, is from Matins of Holy Saturday. See Hartker, pp. 222–4; Migne, *P.L.*, lxxviii, 768.

[2] Gerbert, *Monumenta*, ii, 236.

[3] First responsory of Matins of Easter Monday. See Hartker, p. 232; Migne, *P.L.*, lxxviii, 771.

[4] The third responsory of Matins of Thursday after Easter. See Hartker, p. 237; Migne, *P.L.*, lxxviii, 773.

[5] The beginning of Matins. See above, p. 50.

[6] The *sepulchrum* is discussed at length in Appendix A. See also plates iii, viii, and ix.

in the sepulchre of a consecrated Host (*Viaticum, Corpus Domini*), in commemoration of the burial of Christ. The essence of the *Elevatio* is the taking up of the Host from the sepulchre, before Matins on Easter morning, in commemoration of the Resurrection. These observances are extra-liturgical, in that they are not essential and universally authorized elements of the Roman liturgy. The sentences sung during the ceremony, however, are not compositions invented for the occasion, but traditional pieces from the liturgy itself.

Although the *Depositio* and *Elevatio* must be regarded as extra-liturgical, they seem to be not so much an alien element in the Roman ceremonial as an extension of it. Various aspects of the dramatic ceremonies appear to have been suggested by the traditional observances of Holy Week. Such a suggestion may have been given, for example, by the ancient practice of reserving a Host from the Mass of Holy Thursday for the Mass of the Presanctified (*Missa Præsanctificatorum*) on Good Friday.[1] This reservation was necessary through the fact that from about the fifth century to the present time the Roman rite has not permitted the consecration of the sacred elements on Good Friday itself.[2] The result of this prohibition is the supplying of the Mass of Good Friday with a Host consecrated upon the previous day—a presanctified Host. Hence the term *Missa Præsanctificatorum*. The absence of the consecration of the Host from the Mass of Friday automatically eliminates a large part of the usual *Ordo Missæ*, including such central elements as the consecratory prayer of the Canon and the words of the Institution. This reduced form of Mass is, in fact, primarily a mere communion service, for which the Host is reserved from the day before.[3]

Our immediate interest in the Mass of the Presanctified, however, lies not so much in its liturgical content as in the implications of the reserving of the Host from Thursday to Friday. The laying away of the *Corpus Domini* from one day to another naturally attached to itself a special ceremonial, and was inevitably interpreted by a special symbolism. The development of such a ceremonial can be traced, for example, in the *Ordines*

---

[1] This reservation is considered at length by Raible, *Ueber Ursprung, Alter und Entwickelung der 'Missa Præsanctificatorum'*, in *Der Katholik* (Mainz), Dritte Folge, xxiii (1901), 143–56, 250–66, 363–74. See also Thalhofer, i, 624–5, 635–6.

[2] See Raible, *op. cit.*, pp. 152, 250, 261,

266. The reasons for this prohibition do not concern us here. See Raible, p. 144.

[3] The liturgical content of the *Missa Præsanctificatorum* is more precisely outlined below, p. 117. Concerning the Canon of the Mass see above, p. 34.

III. Easter Sepulchre, at Hawton, Nottinghamshire

Romani, which prescribed the papal use at Rome, and which had their influence in Western Europe generally. *Ordo I*, in passages that probably represent the traditions of the sixth century, provides that the reserved Host shall not be left upon the altar upon which it was consecrated on Thursday, but shall be kept over night in a place apart; *Ordo X*, treating ceremonials at least as old as the eleventh or twelfth century, describes a procession of some elaborateness to and from the place of reservation; and *Ordo XV*, of the fourteenth century, not only describes a procession, but also provides that the reserved Host be carried and kept in a chalice, and that this chalice, with its Host, be deposited in some sort of chest or tabernacle.[1] The use of France, as prescribed in the eleventh century for Rouen, by the archbishop, Jean d'Avranches, includes a procession, the sequestering of the reserved Host upon a special altar, and the placing of a light before it.[2]

Resemblances between the liturgical reservation from Holy Thursday to Good Friday and the extra-liturgical dramatic ceremonials are not difficult to discern. The chest, or tabernacle, in which the reserved Host is placed has a parallel in the *sepulchrum* of the *Depositio* and *Elevatio*; the placing of the Host upon a special altar points to the use of the altar itself as a *sepulchrum* in some versions of the dramatic ceremonials;[3] the light before the altar of the reservation is matched by lights used at the *sepulchrum*;[4] and the depositing of the reserved Host in a chalice is clearly a possible antecedent for a similar use of the chalice in certain versions of the dramatic observances.[5] Although the extant documents do not enable us to demonstrate that each of these ceremonials of the reservation of Holy Thursday antedates the earliest versions of the *Depositio* and *Elevatio*, in the tenth century,[6] the probability is that the authorized liturgical usages preceded the extra-liturgical ones. In any case, the traditional reservation of the Host, in some form, was available as an ancient model for the *Depositio* and *Elevatio*; and in some fashion, probably, it was so regarded.[7]

[1] For the relevant details concerning the *Ordines Romani* see Young, *Dramatic Associations*, pp. 11–3.

[2] See Migne, *P. L.*, cxlvii, 50; Young, *op. cit.*, pp. 12–3.

[3] For examples see below, pp. 240–1, 244, 288–9.

[4] See above, p. 113, and below, p. 165.

[5] See below, p. 155.

[6] See below, pp. 121–2, 132–3.

[7] Brooks (*Sepulchre*, pp. 32–3) and Brinkmann (pp. 124, 126) would minimize this influence. Brinkmann (pp. 124–5) holds that the Host became attached to the *Depositio* merely through the fact that after the Adoration of the Cross it was brought

This influence may have been supported, furthermore, by the medieval convention of symbolizing the receptacle for reserving the Eucharist—whether for the sick or for other purposes—as a tomb. Throughout the Middle Ages the symbolists interpreted the vessel or tabernacle enclosing the *Corpus Domini* as being a *sepulchrum*. Thus in early times the *capsa* for containing the Host was often designed in the form of a 'tower', the actual tomb of Christ in Jerusalem being conceived in this form; and in early Christian art the tabernacle quite regularly took the name *turris*.[1] Similarly the chalice and the altar itself were often symbolized as receptacles for burial;[2] hence the use of a chalice and of a special altar in the ceremonial of the Thursday reservation may have helped to establish this observance as a model for the *Depositio*.[3]

It may be remarked, in passing, that the influence of this sort of symbolizing is discernible in the misguided modern practice of revering the Place of Repose (*reposoir*) of the Host reserved from the Thursday Mass as if it were a sepulchre. At the end of the Middle Ages, with the general disappearance of the *Depositio* and *Elevatio*, or in places where these dramatic ceremonials had never been performed, there arose the custom, which still persists, of attaching to the *reposoir* the name and significance of *sepulchrum*. The Sacred Congregation of Rites has not failed to declare that the Place of Repose is not a *sepulchrum*, and that the modern use of this term in connexion with the ceremonial of Holy Thursday is inappropriate, in that the death of Christ is not commemorated until the next day; but the Congregation condones the incongruity, and justifies the Thursday 'sepulchre' by appealing to the symbolistic tradition mentioned above, according to which the chalice containing the reserved Host is the *novum sepulchrum*.[4] I scarcely need remark that, except through the ultimate symbolism by which it came into currency, the modern Thursday 'sepulchre' has no real connexion with the *sepulchrum* which serves as a setting for the dramatic ceremonials under discussion here.[5]

from the place of reservation for use in the Mass of the Presanctified. See below, p. 117.

[1] See Raible, *op. cit.*, p. 262; *Decreta*, iv, 419; Hirn, pp. 159–61; Young, *op. cit.*, p. 15.

[2] See Corblet, ii, 241, 295; *Decreta*, iv, 419–20.

[3] It should be remembered also that the Host to be used in the sepulchre was often consecrated along with the one which was to be reserved for the Mass of the Presanctified. See below, p. 123. Sometimes, however, the sepulchre was supplied with fragments from the Host used in this Mass. See below, for example, p. 155.

[4] See *Decreta*, iv, 419–21.

[5] For a more ample treatment of the dis-

II

For the sake of simplification, I have hitherto ignored the fact that in the performance of the *Depositio* and *Elevatio* the Host was not always the only object placed in the *sepulchrum*. In citing the Thursday-Friday reservation as a possible influence towards the formation of these dramatic offices I have offered no explanation of the fact that in a large proportion of the extant versions of them the burial included both a Host and a cross,[1] and that a considerable number of texts prescribe the burial of the cross alone.[2] In this use of the cross we readily discern a second fundamental influence upon the *Depositio* and *Elevatio*: namely, that of the liturgical Adoration of the Cross of Good Friday.[3]

The *Adoratio Crucis* is certainly one of the oldest of the liturgical observances of Holy Week, having been performed at Jerusalem at least as early as the fourth century, and having been introduced into the West in the seventh or eighth.[4] The position which the ceremony took in the Western liturgy of Good Friday will be more readily understood after a brief explanation of the structure of the Mass of the Presanctified into which the *Adoratio* was incorporated.[5]

This Mass is found not in the usual liturgical position, between Terce and Sext, but between None and Vespers. The office begins, somewhat abruptly, with the reading of two lessons, or *lectiones*, the first of which is followed by a tract and a prayer, and the second, by a tract alone.[6] Then after the Passion, from the Gospel of John,[7] and a series of special prayers (*Orationes solemnes*), occurs the *Adoratio Crucis*. The service closes with the bringing of the presanctified Host, and the communion. The office of Vespers normally follows immediately. These arrangements may be shown by the following outline, in which, for our subsequent convenience, I insert an indication of the three liturgical positions in any one of which the *Depositio* may be found:

tinction between the erroneous 'sepulchre' of Holy Thursday and the actual *sepulchrum* of the *Depositio* and *Elevatio* see Brooks, *op. cit.*, pp. 49–52; Young, *op. cit.*, p. 16.

[1] See below. pp. 143 sqq.
[2] See below, pp. 132 sqq.
[3] This general observation is made in *Decreta*, iv, 432, and by Chambers, ii, 17–8. The matter is treated in detail by Young,

op. cit., pp. 18–27, and by Brooks, *op. cit.*, pp. 31–2. See also Brinkmann, pp. 119–22.
[4] The Eastern observance is briefly described above, p. 87.
[5] The general nature of this Mass is briefly explained above, p. 114.
[6] Concerning the tract see above, p. 26.
[7] See above, p. 100.

Nona
Missa Præsanctificatorum
   Lectio i
      Tractus
      Oratio
   Lectio ii
      Tractus
   Passio
   Orationes Solemnes
   Adoratio Crucis
     ⟨Depositio⟩
   Communio Fidelium
     ⟨Depositio⟩
Vesperæ
     ⟨Depositio⟩

With the general structure of the Mass of Good Friday now before us, we may centre our attention upon the *Adoratio Crucis* as observed in Western Europe. An early text of this ceremonial is forthcoming from the famous *Regularis Concordia* of St Ethelwold:[1]

Quibus expletis per ordinem, statim preparetur Crux ante altare, interposito spatio inter ipsam et altare, sustentata hinc et inde a duobus diaconibus. Tunc cantent:

Popule meus, ⟨quid feci tibi?⟩

Respondentes autem duo subdiaconi stantes ante Crucem canant grece:
   Agios o Theos, Agyos y⟨s⟩chiros, Agios athanathos, eleïson ymas.
Itemque scola idipsum latine:

Sanctus Deus.

Deferatur tunc ab[2] ipsis diaconibus ante altare, et eos accolitus cum puluillo sequatur super quem sancta Crux ponatur. Antiphonaque finita quam scola respondit latine, canant ibidem sicut prius:

Quia eduxi[3] uos per desertum.

Item uero respondeant subdiaconi grece sicut prius *Agios*, ut supra.
Itemque scola latine ut prius *Sanctus Deus*.
Itemque diaconi leuantes Crucem canant sicut prius:

---

[1] London, Brit. Mus., MS Cotton Tiberius A. III. fol, 18ᵛ–19ᵛ. I print from the MS with a result differing in no essential way from the text of W. S. Logeman, in *Anglia*, xiii (1891), 418–21. For the bibliography of the MS see below, p. 582.
[2] ab] ad (MS).
[3] Quia eduxi] Qua edux (MS).

Quid ultra ⟨debui facere tibi, et non feci?⟩

Ite⟨m⟩ subdiaconi sicut prius *Agyos*, ut supra.

Itemque scola latine *Sanctus Deus*, ut supra

Post hec uertentes se ad clerum, nudata Cruce, dicant antiphonam:

Ecce lignum crucis.

Alia: *Crucem tuam adoramus.*

Alia: *Dum fabricator mundi.* |

    ⟨P⟩*ange lingua.*

Ilico ea nudata, ueniat abbas ante Crucem sanctam ac tribus uicibus se prosternat cum omnibus fratribus dexterioris chori, scilicet senioribus ac iunioribus, et cum magno cordis suspirio vii^m poenitentie psalmos cum orationibus sancte Cruci competentibus decantando[1] peroret. In prima quidem oratione tres psalmos primos cum oracione:

Domine Ihesu Christe, adoro te in cruce ascendentem. Deprecor te ut ipsa crux liberet me de diabolo percutiente.

Domine Ihesu Christe, adoro te ut ipsa uulneratum. Deprecor te ut ipsa uulnera remedium sint anime mee.

Domine Ihesu Christe, adoro te descendentem ad inferos, liberantem captiuos. Deprecor te ut non ibi me dimittas introire.

Domine Ihesu Christe, adoro te resurgentem ab inferis, ascendentem ad celos. Deprecor te miserere mei.

Domine Ihesu Christe, adoro te uenturum iudicaturum. Deprecor te ut in tuo aduentu non intres in iudicio cum me peccante, sed deprecor te ut ante dimittas quam iudices, qui uiuis et regnas.

In secunda duos medios cum sequente[2] oratione:

Domine Ihesu Christe, gloriosissime conditor mundi, qui cum sis splendor glorie coeternus Patri Sanctoque Spiritui ideo dignatus es carnem ex inmaculata uirgine sumere et gloriosas palmas tuas in crucis patibulo permisisti configere, ut claustra dissipares inferni et humanum genus liberares de morte, respice et miserere michi misero obpresso facinorum pondere multarumque nequitiarum labe polluto no⟨n⟩ me digneris derelinquere, piissime Pater, sed indulge quod impie gessi. Exaudi me prostratum coram adoranda gloriosissima cruce tua, ut merear | tibi mundus adsistere et placere conspectui tuo. Qui cum[3] Patre.

⟨I⟩n tertia ultimos duos cum oratione:

Deus omnipotens, Ihesu Christe, qui tuas manus mundas propter nos in cruce posuisti, et de tuo sancto sanguine nos redemisti, mitte in me sensum et intelli-gentiam[4] quomodo habeam ueram penitentiam et habeam bonam perseuerantiam omnibus diebus uite mee, Amen.

---

[1] competentibus decantando] compeni-tentibus decantato (MS).

[2] medios cum sequente] medioximus

sequentem (MS).

[3] cum] con (MS).

[4] intelligentiam] intellegentiam (MS).

Et eam humiliter deosculans surgat. Dehinc sinisterioris chori[1] omnes fratres eadem mente deuota peragant. Nam salutata ab abbate uel omnibus Cruce, redeat ipse abbas ad sedem suam usque dum omnis clerus ac populus hoc idem faciat.[2]

According to this *ordo* the Adoration opens with the *Improperia*, or 'Reproaches'. Two deacons supporting the cross before the altar begin the utterances of Christ (*Popule meus*), to each of which two subdeacons respond in Greek, and the chorus, in Latin. After the first of these responses the cross is laid upon a cushion. After the singing of the *Improperia*, the cross is uncovered, and three antiphons and the hymn *Pange lingua* are sung. Then the abbot, along with half the chorus, prostrates himself before the cross and sings the seven penitential psalms, with appropriate prayers. The ceremony closes with the kissing of the cross.

In its general content the *Adoratio* of St Ethelwold's *Concordia* is sufficiently representative; it conforms, indeed, to the authorized use of Rome itself as prescribed in the *Ordines Romani*. One striking feature of the papal ceremonial, however, seems to deserve our special notice in view of its conspicuousness and its possible influence, direct or indirect, upon our special dramatic ceremonials. I refer to the papal procession before and after the Mass of Good Friday. The papal station on that day was the church of the Holy Cross. Before proceeding from the Lateran Palace to this church, the Pope entered the chapel of St Lawrence (*Sancta Sanctorum*), adjoining the palace, took a cross from a chest under the altar, and proceeded with it to the church of the Lateran. Thence the procession, bearing the cross from the *Sancta Sanctorum*, together with a reserved Host from the church of the Lateran, moved through the city to the church of the Holy Cross. The cross served for the *Adoratio*, and the Host, for the communion of the Mass. After Mass and Vespers, the Pope carried the cross in procession back from the church of the Holy Cross to the *Sancta Sanctorum* and deposited it in its chest under the altar. These processions occurred from the eighth century onwards throughout the Middle Ages.[3]

In view of the facts now before us the relation between the *Adoratio* and the *Depositio* may be inferred with some confidence.

---

[1] chori] choris (MS).

[2] Followed immediately by the *Depositio* printed below, p. 133.

[3] For a detailed exposition of these matters see Young, *op. cit.*, pp. 22–6.

Since the *Adoratio* itself is a vivid commemoration of the Crucifixion, nothing could be more natural than that a vivid commemoration of the Burial should be invented as a sequel. Any
taking down of the cross after the ceremony of the *Adoratio* must
inevitably bring to mind the burial of the crucified Christ Himself.[1] Such an act as the carrying back of the cross from the
Adoratio in the church of the Holy Cross to the chest under the
altar of the *Sancta Sanctorum* may at times have been a conscious
ceremonial of burial.[2] Viewed in the light of the widespread
symbolizing of the altar as a tomb, spoken of above, a procession
of this sort clearly suggests the carrying of Christ to His grave,
which is precisely the intention of the *Depositio*. The fact that
the *Depositio* did not thrive at Rome itself does not preclude the
possibility that traditional and widely-known Roman ceremonials
of Good Friday had an influence upon the invention of the *Depositio* elsewhere.[3]

It is to be observed, however, that none of the observances
connected with the Adoration contributes anything toward the
forming of the *Elevatio*. For this a model may have been found
in the taking up of the presanctified Host from the place of
reservation for the Mass of Good Friday. More probably no
such specific inspiration was required; for, once the object,
whether Host or Cross, was 'buried', it must eventually be
'raised'. Given the *Depositio* of Good Friday, an *Elevatio* at some
time before dawn on Easter Day became inevitable.[4]

How early the *Depositio* and *Elevatio* arose as distinct additions
to the authorized ceremonial we cannot tell with precision. It
has been asserted that the *Depositio* is as old as the seventh
century;[5] but for so early a date there is no proof. One infers
that the *Depositio Hostiæ* was customary at Augsburg about the
middle of the tenth century, for it appears to be mentioned in
a life of St Ulrich, bishop of that diocese, which was probably
written within some twenty years from the date of his death.[6]

[1] For evidence that the cross used in the
Depositio was the same as that used in the
preceding *Adoratio* see below, p. 595.

[2] Santi (*Pasqua*, p. 12) seems to regard this
as an example of the *Depositio*, or, at least, as a
definite symbolic representation of Christ's
burial in a *sepulchrum*.

[3] Brooks (*Sepulchre*, p. 32) and Brinkmann
(pp. 121, 123, 127) seem to regard this
Roman influence as possible, but unnecessary. I do not insist upon it.

[4] Certain papal ceremonies on Easter
morning which may possibly be reflected in
the *Elevatio* are discussed by Young, *op. cit.*,
pp. 27–9. Brinkmann (pp. 122–3) appears
to regard these as of some significance.

[5] J. N. Dalton, *The Collegiate Church of
Ottery St Mary*, Cambridge, 1917, pp. 252–3.

[6] See Notes, p. 553.

Also of the tenth century are the *Depositio Crucis* and *Elevatio Crucis* found in the *Regularis Concordia*, a monastic consuetudinary drawn up, probably between 965 and 975, by St Ethelwold and others.[1] From the period before the tenth century no evidence of such dramatic ceremonials is forthcoming. Whether the object 'buried' in the original form of the *Depositio* was the Host or the Cross we do not know. Since the most obvious inspiration of the ceremony was the Adoration of the Cross, and since eventually the cross was the object most frequently used, one is tempted to infer that it was present at the beginning. But of this we cannot be certain.[2]

III

From questions of origin we now pass to a consideration of the extant texts of the *Depositio* and *Elevatio* themselves. These may be conveniently divided into three groups. In the first I place the versions in which the object 'buried' is the Host, in the second group this central object is the cross, and in the versions of the third are found both the Host and the cross. Certain examples of the *Elevatio* which present the special theme of the Harrowing of Hell will be treated separately.[3] In arranging the texts within each group I shall proceed, in general, from the simple to the more highly elaborated. Hence I am guided not so much by the chronology of the recorded texts, or by geographical contiguity, as by amplitude of speech and action. One scarcely need remark that the simpler, and often earlier, versions are sometimes preserved in records later than those containing more elaborate examples. I do not pretend, however, that the order followed here demonstrates the authentic historical development. For such a demonstration the known facts are, I think, insufficient. The following survey, then, attempts not so much to establish an historical sequence as to offer an orderly description. At all times I shall consider the *Depositio* and *Elevatio* as mutually related, and, as far as possible, shall allow the two ceremonies to elucidate each other. Unhappily, however, a good many of the manuscripts lack one or the other—a defect which does not in itself, of course, prove the absence of the missing ceremony from the use of the church concerned.

Beginning, then, with ceremonies in which only the Host is

---

[1] See below, pp. 132–4, 582.
[2] Brinkmann (pp. 126, 127) infers that the *Depositio Crucis* antedated the *Depositio*

Hostiæ, and arose early in the tenth century.
[3] See chap. v.

used, we may observe first the following very simple version of the *Depositio* from Constance:[1]

Post communionem legantur Vesperæ sub silentio. His omnibus peractis, procedunt cum Corpore Domini ad locum ubi debet recondi, nihil cantantes; sed dum venitur ad locum, cantor imponit antiphonam:

In pace in idipsum dormiam et requiescam.[2]

Alia antiphona:

Caro mea requiescet in spe.[2]

In reditum ad chorum canitur responsorium:

Sepulto Domino, signatum est monumentum; voluentes lapidem ad ostium monumenti; ponentes milites qui custodirent eum. Versus: *Ne forte veniant discipuli eius et furentur eum, et dicant plebi: Surrexit a mortuis. Ponentes milites.*

From this text we learn only that the Host was carried silently to the place of burial, and, during the singing of two antiphons, was laid away. The processional for the return to the choir is the responsory *Sepulto Domino.*

A more generous description of the ceremonies at the sepulchre is found in a service-book of the year 1580 from the diocese of Gran, in Hungary. Provision is made, in the first place, for the reservation on Holy Thursday of two Hosts for Good Friday— one for the Mass of the Presanctified, and one for burial in the *sepulchrum*:[3]

Et pro die crastina consecrantur Hostiæ duæ: altera quam sumpturus est episcopus vel sacerdos officium peracturus, altera quæ reponetur in Sepulchrum.

After Vespers on Good Friday the *Depositio* was performed as follows:[4]

Demum pontifex[5] vel sacerdos officians, exuta casula, portans in manibus alteram Hostiam consecratam quæ pro sepultura heri fuit reseruata,

[1] *Agenda seu Obsequiale . . . Ecclesiæ et Episcopatus Constantiensis,* 1570, fol. xcivᵛ– xcviʳ, previously reprinted by Young, *op. cit.,* pp. 31–2. Virtually the same text is found in *Benedictionale ecclesiæ . . . Constantiensis,* Constance, 1597, pp. 117–20. Concerning the special form of *Elevatio* in these books see below, p. 301. See also the simple versions of *Depositio* and *Elevatio* from St Quentin MS 86, printed below, p. 684. For the *sepulchrum* at Constance see plate viii.

[2] Antiphons of Matins of Holy Saturday. See Hartker, p. 222; Migne, *P.L.,* lxxviii, 767, 768.

[3] *Ordinarium Officii Divini secundum consuetudinem Metropolitanæ Ecclesiæ Strigoniensis,* Tirnova, 1580, sig. H 7 recto. The passages from this book given here have been previously reprinted by Young, *op. cit.,* pp. 32–3. Concerning the use of the *Depositio* and *Elevatio* in Hungary see Dankó, *Feier,* pp. 175 sqq. Concerning the *Visitatio Sepulchri* from the *Ordinarium* of 1580 see below, p. 306. For texts which may be associated with those now before us see Notes, p. 553.

[4] *Ordinarium,* 1580, sig. I 4 recto.

[5] pontifex] pontefex (Print).

in patena supra calicem collocatam, palla et linteolo tectam, descendit
cum ministris versus Sepulchrum, præcedentibus ceroferariis et turribulo,
quod semel circumit. Deinde reponit in illud eandem Hostiam una cum
calice, claudit, obsignat, et per circuitum incensat, choro cantante
responsoria:

> Hierusalem, luge, ⟨et exue te vestibus jucunditatis; induere cinere cum cilicio,
> quia in te est occisus Salvator Israel. Versus: Montes Gelboe, nec ros, nec
> pluvia super vos descendat. Quia.⟩;[1]

et:
> Sepulto Domino.

Quibus completis, cantat versus Adoramus te, Christe, et cetera; Omnis
terra, et cetera; et orationem Deus, qui pro nobis. Completorium hora
consueta legitur ut heri.

The ceremonial is here described in some detail. In the procession to the sepulchrum the bishop carries the Host upon a paten
placed over the mouth of a chalice, the whole being covered
with cloths. Eventually the Host, paten, and chalice are placed
in the sepulchrum, which is closed, sealed, and censed during the
singing of the responsories Jerusalem, luge and Sepulto Domino.
The office closes with versicles and a prayer.

The related Elevatio is provided for in the following rubric:[2]

> In Festo Gloriosissimæ Resurrectionis Domini Nostri Iesu Christi.
> Priusquam pulsetur ad Matutinum, clausis ianuis templi, succustos[3]
> aperit Sepulchrum, et apertum relinquit. Corpus Domini, quod in
> Sepulchro positum fuit, reponit in monstrantiam, quam in mensa indu-
> mento altaris decenter vestita ante ostium Sepulchri supra corporale
> collocat, cum duabus candelis in candelabris ardentibus. Sicut enim
> certum est Christum, antequam Mulieres et Discipuli ad Sepulchrum
> venirent, resurrexisse, ita conuenit hanc cæremoniam peragi priusquam
> populus in templum conueniat.

One or two of the details in the rubric deserve particular notice.
Not only are we told that this office is performed by the sacristan
in secret before Matins; we are also given the reason for the
secrecy. It appears that since Christ rose before the arrival of
the Marys and the disciples at the tomb, the commemoration
of the Resurrection should be made before the entrance of the
people into the church.[4] It should be observed further that

---

[1] Responsory of Matins of Holy Saturday.
See Hartker, p. 222; Migne, P.L., lxxviii,
768.
[2] Ordinarium, 1580, sig. I 8 recto.
[3] succustos] succostos (Print).
[4] Concerning other reasons given for
excluding the congregation until after the
Elevatio see Notes, p. 553.

after being taken up, the Host is placed in a monstrance[1] and put upon the altar, before the *sepulchrum*. This arrangement suggests that in this case the sepulchre is the tabernacle behind the altar-table.

A somewhat different location of the sepulchre is indicated in the following rubric of the year 1417 from the cathedral of Parma:[2]

Finita dicta Missa, descendant Dominus Episcopus cum canonicis et toto clero ad cappellam Sanctæ Agathæ, et Corpus Christi quod est ibi reconditum cum ea processione modo et forma et solemnitate quibus portatum fuit, inde devote accipiatur, et reportetur, et in Paradiso post altare maius reverenter recondatur, ut in Sepulcro, ibi dimisso lumine copioso per totam noctem duraturo, clericis cantantibus responsorium *Sepulto Domino*, et cetera. Quo finito, dicuntur Vesperæ[3] ante ostium Paradisi[4] a Domino Episcopo et clericis suis genuflexis, submissis vocibus; et ipsis finitis, denudatur altare.

It appears that at Parma the ceremony of the *Depositio* occurred after Mass, and that the Host to be 'buried' had been reserved in a chapel of the cathedral, from which it was carried, in a procession of the bishop and clergy, to a structure called *Paradisus* situated behind the main altar. Here the Host was deposited, during the singing of the responsory *Sepulto Domino*. Vespers was then said before the door of the *Paradisus*, and lights were kept burning during the night.

The simple ceremonials that have been described thus far are impressively overshadowed by the elborate dramatic observances recorded in the famous *Liber Sacerdotalis* printed in 1523 under the editorship of Alberto Castellani.[5] This editor, it appears, compiled this book from the medieval liturgical customs of various localities other than Rome, and none of the several editions received complete papal sanction.[6] It is,

---

[1] The use of the monstrance appears to be a relatively late practice. See *Decreta*, iv, 433–9; Brooks, *Sepulchre*, pp. 44 sqq.

[2] Barbieri, pp. 140–1, previously reprinted by Young, *op. cit.*, pp. 43–4. The reservation of *two* Hosts on Holy Thursday is ordered thus (Barbieri, p. 134): *Et redit clerus ad episcopum qui Missam perficiat, reservatis duabus Hostiis consecratis, quæ, finita Missa, in sacrario reverenter includantur.* Concerning the related *Elevatio* see below, p. 300.

[3] Vesperæ] Vesperi (Print).

[4] The editor provides the following foot-note: 'Questo particolare non lascia dubbio che l'edificio, chiamato *Paradisus*, fosse chiuso; e così appunto esser dovea, in grazia del nome attribuitogli, da poi ch'esso tanto vale quanto *hortus conclusus* (v. Isid. *Orig.* xiv, iii, 1, 3).'

[5] *Liber Sacerdotalis nuperrime ex libris Sancte Romane Ecclesie et quarumdam aliarum ecclesiarum et ex antiquis codicibus . . . collectus*, Venice, 1523. For other dramatic ceremonials from this book see below, p. 622.

[6] See Notes, p. 554.

therefore, impossible to identify the community, or communities, for which the sepulchre ceremonies were designed. The *Depositio* is prescribed in the edition of 1523 as follows:[1]

DE PROCESSIONE IN FERIA VI IN PARASCEUE AD PONENDUM CORPUS DOMINI IN SEPULCHRO

Feria vi in Parasceue post officium Misse, vel etiam post prandium, ordinatur solennis sed lugubris processio. Paratur enim sacerdos omnibus paramentis et pluuiali desuper cum diacono et subdiacono cum dalmaticis nigri coloris. Parantur etiam quatuor sacerdotes, vel duo ad minus, induti camisiis nigris cum amictu et cingulo eiusdem coloris; si haberi possunt alios, in albis parantur etiam duo alii sacerdotes, vel unus tantum ubi pauci fuerint sacerdotes, cum amictu, alba, cingulo, manipulo, et stolla, et duo thuriferarii in albis. Preparetur etiam feretrum a quatuor portandum cum superiori coopertura in modum semicirculi, et cooperiatur aliquo panno nigro de serico, si haberi poterit, in quo Sacramentum deportetur. Parantur etiam luminaria: scilicet intortitia et cerei ad illuminandum Corpus Christi. Et congregato populo, sacerdos accipit reuerenter Sacramentum de altari et tenens illud in manibus versus ad populum, omnibus aliis genuflexis, ipse stans incipit responsorium *Plange*, ceteris prosequentibus:

> *Plange quasi virgo, plebs mea; vlulate, pastores, in cinere et cilicio; quia venit dies Domini magna et amara valde.* Duo clerici cantent versum:[2]
> *Accingite vos, sacerdotes, et plangite; ministri altaris, aspergite vos cinere. Quia.*[3]

Completo responsorio cum versu et replica, duo sacerdotes apparati cum stollis vt supra stantes ante Sacramentum versis vultibus ad populum cantent versum *Popule me⟨us⟩*, omnibus aliis preter eum qui facit officium genuflexis et versis vultibus ad Sacramentum:

> *Popule meus, quid feci tibi, aut in quo contristaui te? responde mihi. Quia eduxi te de terra Egypti, parasti crucem Saluatori tuo.*

Dicto versu predicto, chorus genuflexus vt supra cantet:

> *Sanctus Deus, sanctus fortis, sanctus et inmortalis, miserere nobis.*

Hoc dicto, sacerdos ponat Corpus Domini reuerenter in feretro quod portabunt quatuor sacerdotes predicti, vel duo vbi paucitas sacerdotum est, in albis parati, capitibus amicto coopertis, et incepto responsorio *Recessit pa⟨stor⟩*, procedit processio isto ordine: Primo acoliti cum cereis accensis et cruce; postea clerici, iunioribus precedentibus; vltimo duo sacerdotes parati qui cantauerunt *Popule meus*. Post ipsos sequitur feretrum cum Corpore Domini portatum a quatuor vel duobus, vt supra; et super Sacramentum baldachinum nigrum portetur ab aliqui-

---

[1] Castellani, fol. 263ʳ–269ᵛ.
[2] versum] Printed twice.
[3] Responsory of Matins of Holy Saturday.

See Hartker, p. 222; Migne, *P. L.*, lxxviii, 768.

bus personis magis dignis. Ex latere sint duo acoliti cum turribulis, qui continuo Sacramentum incensabunt circum; circa sint luminaria et intortitia. Post feretrum sequitur sacerdos cum pluuiali et dyaconus et subdiaconus; et vltimo seculares, maioribus precedentibus. Processione isto modo ordinata, procedunt cum deuotione quousque dicta fuerit replica post versum responsorii, quem versum dicent duo clerici, et idem seruetur in aliis responsoriis sequentibus. Responsorium:

> *Recessit pastor noster, fons aque viue, **ad** cuius transitum sol obscuratus est; nam et ille captus est qui captiuum tenebat primum hominem. Hodie portas mortis et seras pariter Saluator noster dirupit. Versus: Destruxit quidem claustra inferni et subuertit potentias dyaboli. Nam et.*[1]

Finita replica post versum, firmetur processio, et omnes flectant genua, exceptis illis qui portant feretrum et duobus sacerdotibus qui cantauerunt *Popule meus*, qui stantes versis vultibus[2] ad populum, omnibus aliis genuflexis ha⟨ben⟩tibus vultus suos ad feretrum conuersos, cantent versum *Quia eduxi*; et hoc quidem seruetur in omnibus sequentibus stationibus. Versus:

> *Quia eduxi te per desertum quadraginta annis et manna cibaui te, et introduxi in terram satis optimam, parasti crucem Saluatori tuo.*

Chorus: *Sanctus Deus*, vt supra. Quo dicto, surgant omnes et incipiatur responsorium *Ecce uidimus*, et procedatur ad secundam stationem cantando responsorium totum vsque in finem cum versu et replica. Responsorium:

> *Ecce vidimus eum non habentem speciem neque decorem; aspectus eius in eo non est; hic peccata nostra portauit, et pro nobis dolens; ipse autem vulneratus est propter iniquitates nostras, cuius liuore sanati sumus. Versus: Vere languores nostros ipse tulit, et dolores nostros ipse portauit. Cuius.*[3]

Omnibus genuflexis, duo sacerdotes stantes vt prius[4] dicant versum:

> *Quid vltra debui facere tibi, et non feci? Ego quidem plantaui te vineam meam speciosissimam; et tu facta es mihi nimis amara; aceto namque sitim meam potasti, et lancea perforasti latus Saluatori tuo.*

Chorus: *Sanctus Deus*. Totum dicitur vt supra. Surgentibus omnibus, incipiatur responsorium *Hierusalem*, et procedatur ad tertiam stationem vt supra. Responsorium:

> *Hierusalem, luge, et exue te vestibus iocunditatis; induere cinere et cilicio, quia in te occisus Saluator Israel. Versus: Deduc quasi torrentem lachrymas per diem, et nocte non taceat pupilla oculi tui. Quia in.*[5]

---

[1] Responsory of Matins of Holy Saturday. See Hartker, p. 223; Migne, *P.L.*, lxxviii, 768.
[2] vultibus] vulbentibus (Print).
[3] Responsory of Matins of Holy Thursday. See Hartker, p. 178.

[4] prius] primus (Print).
[5] Responsory of Matins of Holy Saturday. See Hartker, p. 222; Migne, *P.L.*, lxxviii, 768.

Omnibus vt prius genuflexis, duo sacerdotes stantes dicant versum:

Ego propter te flagellaui Egyptum cum omnibus primogenitis suis; et tu me flagellatum ad crucifigendum cum latronibus tradidisti.

Chorus: *Sanctus Deus*, vt supra. Quo dicto, omnes surgant, et incipiatur responsorium *Calligauerunt*, et procedat processio ad quartam stationem que fiat circa ingressum ecclesie redeundo ante Sepulchrum. Responsorium:

Calligauerunt oculi mei a fletu meo, quia elongatus est a me qui consolabatur me. Videte, omnes populi, si est dolor similis sicut dolor meus. Versus: *O vos omnes qui transitis per viam, attendite et videte. Si est.*[1]

Omnibus vt prius genuflexis, duo sacerdotes predicti stantes cantent versum vt supra:

Ego dedi tibi sceptrum regale, et tu meo capiti coronam spineam; ego te exaltaui magna virtute, et tu me suspendisti in patibulo crucis.

Finito versu, chorus cantet *Sanctus*, totum vt supra, *Sanctus Deus*. Dicto *Miserere nobis*, sacerdos cum reuerentia accipiat Corpus Domini de feretro et illud in manibus eleuatum teneat conuersus ad populum et versis renibus ad Sepulchrum. Tunc duo clerici genuflexi cantent versum *Cum autem venissent*, et reliquos infra notatos:

Versus: *Cum autem venissent ad locum ubi crucifigendus erat filius meus, statuerunt eum in medio omnis populi, et vestibus expoliatis, nudum dimiserunt corpus sanctissimum.*

Versus: *O dulcissime filie Syon, o dulcissime, videte dolorem meum. Inspicite nudum in medio omnis populi filium meum dulcissimum; vulneratus est in medio eorum.*

1 Versus: *Cum vero venissent ad locum vbi sepeliendus erat filius meus, statuerunt eum in medio mulierum; et syndone inuoluentes sepultum dimiserunt corpus sanctissimum.*

2 Versus: *O vos omnes qui transitis per viam, venite et videte si est dolor sicut meus; desolata sum nimis; non est qui consoletur me; salus mea infirmata est; vita occiditur et a me tollitur.*

3 Versus: *O nimis triste spectaculum, o crudele supplitium impensum filio, o felix rex tam indecenti morte coronatus, pontifices iniquitatis tantum ne in vestrum exardescitis Deum?*

4 Versus: *Attendite vos, o populi et vniuerse plebes, dolorem maximum: morte turpissima mactauerunt filium meum. Vos optime sorores, flete vna mecum; de filio conqueramur.*

5 Versus: *Cum vero deposuissent corpus Iesu de cruce, statuerunt illud in gremio matris sue, in medio mulierum amarissime flentium, mestissima matre filium nimis deplorante.*

Cantatis predictis versibus vel eorum parte, sacerdos eleuatis manibus

[1] Responsory of Matins of Good Friday. See Hartker, p. 219; Migne, *P.L.*, lxxviii, 767.

cum Corpore Christi in modum crucis benedicat populum et cum reuerentia illud ponat in Sepulchro, et ipsum claudat et sigillo suo signet. Responsorium:

> *Sepulto Domino, signatum est monumentum; voluentes lapidem ad hostium monumenti; ponentes milites qui custodirent illum.* ⟨Versus:⟩ *Ne forte veniant discipuli eius et furentur eum, et dicant plebi: Surrexit a mortuis.*

Finito responsorio predicto, duo clerici dicant versum:

> *In pace factus est locus eius.*

Responsio:

> *Et in Syon habitatio eius.*

Et sacerdos, sine *Dominus vobiscum* vel *Oremus*, dicat absolute orationem:

> *Respice, quesumus, Domine, super hanc familiam tuam pro qua Dominus noster Iesus Christus non dubitauit manibus tradi nocentium, et crucis subire tormentum.*

Et non dicat *Qui tecum*, nec respondeatur *Amen*. Et sic terminetur processio.

Si processio debet fieri prolixior et in ea plures mansiones seu stationes fieri oporteat, finito responsorio *Caligauerunt* cum versu et aliis que sequuntur, repetatur aliquod responsorium de predictis cum suo versu et aliis que sequuntur, ita quod responsorium *Sepulto* vltimo loco reseruetur quando Corpus Domini ponitur in Sepulchro.

Supra posita processio more Veneto fit infrascripto ordine. Paratis omnibus vt supra in precedenti processione, notatum est loco responsorii *Plange*, incipitur a duobus clericis genuflexis antiphona *Venite et ploremus*, in cantu vt inferius notatum est. Postmodum totus chorus surgens dicat versum *Popule*, vt supra. Quo finito, illi duo clerici qui cantauerunt *Venite et plo⟨remus⟩*, cantant versum *Quia edu⟨xi⟩*, et chorus repetit versum *Popule*. Item duo clerici dicant versum *Ego propter te fla⟨gellaui⟩*, et chorus repetit versum *Popule*. Et sic alternatim dicantur *Improperia* pro-vt supra signatum est in Adoratione Crucis, fo. 258. Vel ipsa *Improperia* cantantur in sexto tono psalmorum. Et cum in dicta processione fieri debet aliqua statio seu mansio, omnes genuflectant et illi duo cantent antiphonam *Venite et*, vt supra. Qua dicta, surgant omnes et sequantur processionem cantando versum *Popule*, et *Improperia*, vt supra. Cum autem peruenerint ad Sepulchrum, faciant omnia vt supra in precedenti processione.

> *Venite et ploremus ante Dominum, qui passus est pro nobis dicens.*[1]

According to this *ordo* the *Depositio* is performed either after the Mass of the Presanctified or later, after dinner. The procession is made especially impressive through the use of a bier

---

[1] The last word is written twice, with varying musical notation, and is followed immediately by a rubric beginning *Sabbato Sancto*.

(*feretrum*) and a canopy (*baldachinum*). The ceremonial begins with the priest's taking the Host reverently from the altar at the singing of the responsory *Plange quasi virgo*. At the conclusion of this, two priests begin the *Improperia* (*Popule meus*),[1] to which the chorus responds (*Sanctus Deus*). The priest places the Host on the bier, over which a canopy is held, and beside which are carried thuribles and lights. The procession to the *sepulchrum* is made in four stages, each stage having its processional responsory. At each station the two priests already mentioned sing a verse of the *Improperia*, to which the chorus makes a response. The fourth station occurs before the sepulchre where, after a final verse of the *Improperia*, followed by the *Miserere*, the priest takes the Host from the bier and holds it aloft before the congregation while two clerics kneeling sing a series of *versus*. The priest now blesses the congregation with the Host and reverently places it in the *sepulchrum*. During the singing of the responsory *Sepulto Domino* he closes the sepulchre and seals it. The office closes with a versicle, a response, and a prayer.

More significant than the splendour of this procession is the use of the *Improperia*, borrowed directly from the traditional *Adoratio Crucis* of the Mass of the Presanctified. The presence of this liturgical element seems to be definite proof of the influence of the *Adoratio* upon the *Depositio*. It will be observed, however, that with all its careful construction and ceremonial elaboration, this dramatic office contains no impersonation, and hence stops short of true drama.

With the sepulchre ceremonies in which the Host is the centre of interest we must include the brief observance prescribed in a breviary of the eleventh century from St Gall:[2]

Sublato igitur Corpore Domini de Monumento, incip*iat* cantor responsorium:

> *Angelus Domini descendit* ⟨*de cœlo, et accedens revolvit lapidem, et super eum sedit, et dixit mulieribus: Nolite timere; scio enim quia crucifixum quæritis; jam surrexit, venite et videte locum ubi positus erat Dominus, alleluia.* Versus: *Angelus Domini locutus est mulieribus dicens: Quem quæritis, an Jesum quæritis? Jam surrexit*⟩.[3]

---

[1] See above, pp. 118 sqq.

[2] St Gall, Stiftsbibl., MS 387, Brev. Sangallense sæc. xi, p. 55, previously printed by Young, *Harrowing*, pp. 897–8, and Young, *Dramatic Associations*, p. 30. In the MS the text is immediately preceded by the usual third responsory *Dum transisset*. The MS contains no *Depositio* or *Visitatio Sepulchri*, but has a procession before Mass in which the *Quem quæritis* dialogue is embodied. See below, p. 227. For related texts see Notes, p. 554.

[3] See Hartker, pp. 228–9; Migne, *P. L.*, lxxviii, 769.

Intrantibus aùtem in chorum incip*iat* cantor antiphonam:

Surrexit Christus et illuxit populo suo, quem redemit sanguine suo, alleluia.

Versus:

> *Haec est alma dies in qua spoliatur auernus;*
> *Resurrexit homo Deus, exultate redempti.*
> *Te Deum lavdamvs.*[1]

This brief text provides for the raising of the *Corpus Domini* from the sepulchre at the *end* of Matins. In carrying the Host to the choir the procession sings the responsory *Angelus Domini* and the antiphon *Surrexit Christus*. The two hexameters which follow may be regarded as an embellishment, or 'trope', of the *Te Deum*;[2] and they contain a suggestion of the Harrowing of Hell, a theme which, as we shall see, forms a prominent part of many versions of the *Elevatio*.[3]

Among the exceptional features of the particular ceremony now before us the most puzzling is its position in the liturgy—at the *end* of Matins—since, as we shall see, this is the place commonly occupied by a dramatic performance, the *Visitatio Sepulchri*, representing not the Resurrection, but the visit of the Marys to the empty tomb.[4] The fact that the symbolists interpreted the *Te Deum* of Easter Matins as marking the moment of the Resurrection might be supposed to justify the presence of the *Elevatio* just before this liturgical piece.[5] Nevertheless this position was usually dedicated not to the *Elevatio* but to the *Visitatio Sepulchri*, and the appearing of the former at the end of Matins here seems to have resulted merely from the fact that at St Gall the *Visitatio* did not thrive.[6] It is partly to its liturgical position that one must attribute certain textual incongruities in the present ceremony. The responsory *Angelus Domini*, for example, recounting the address of the angel to the Marys, is inappropriate as a processional accompaniment to the taking up of the Host, as is also the responsory *Dum transisset* sung immediately before the action occurs.[7]

Although the few examples of the *Depositio* and *Elevatio* just reviewed are not the only versions in which the Host alone is

---

[1] Followed immediately by the rubric *In Matutinis Laudibus.*

[2] See below, p. 191.

[3] See below, chap. v.

[4] See below, chap. viii.

[5] Concerning this symbolizing of the *Te Deum* see below, p. 231.

[6] See below, p. 563. Brooks (*Sepulchre,*

p. 41) and Brinkmann (pp. 133, 134, 138–9) agree in the opinion that the placing of the *Elevatio* at the *end* of Matins is merely exceptional, and in no way reflects the original arrangement.

[7] Concerning the content of *Dum transisset* see below, p. 232.

employed,[1] it is a noteworthy fact that during the long period
before the sixteenth century this use of the Host is relatively
rare. The simple reason is that, for the burial ceremony of the
Depositio, the Host is essentially inappropriate, as the following
words from a thirteenth-century text clearly show:[2]

> Contra omnem rationem est, quod in quibusdam ecclesiis Eucharistia
> in huiusmodi archa Sepulchrum representante poni consuevit et claudi.
> Ibi enim Eucharistia, que est uerum et uiuum Corpus Christi, ipsum
> Christi Corpus mortuum representat, quod est indecens penitus et
> absurdum.

As the living Body of Christ, then, the Host could not fittingly
be used to represent the dead, or be enclosed within a *sepulchrum*.
Sometimes, however, it could have an appropriate part in the
ceremonial of the *Elevatio*. When the object buried was a cross,
the raising of it could be very effectively accompanied by the
exhibiting of the Host. Hence we shall observe presently that
in a number of churches the Host was altogether absent from
the *Depositio*, but was brought forward—not from within the
sepulchrum, but from a more fitting place—for use in the procession
at the *Elevatio*.[3] During the later Middle Ages the prominence
given to the Eucharist in this ceremony was sometimes, no doubt,
a reflection from the splendour of the procession of Corpus
Christi Day.[4]

IV

When we pass to a consideration of the use of the cross in
these ceremonies we find not only a much larger number of
extant texts, but also, in some instances, a more intimate relationship between the dramatic office and the authorized liturgy.
Since, as we have already observed, the commemoration of the
Crucifixion in the Adoration of the Cross may very naturally
and appropriately be followed by a lowering and burying of the
object adored, we may expect to find that a certain number of
versions of the *Depositio Crucis* attach themselves to the *Adoratio*
so directly as to form with it a continuous ceremony. This is
true, for example, of the earliest extant text of the *Depositio*,
contained in the *Regularis Concordia* drawn up in the tenth cen-

---

[1] See chap. v *passim*, and below, pp.
300 sqq.

[2] Zurich, Zentralbibl., MS C. 8 b, Ordin.
Turicense anni 1260, fol. 52[r]. The *Depositio*
containing this passage was published by
Brooks, *Sepulchre*, p. 109, and is re-edited

below, p. 154.

[3] See Brooks, *Sepulchre*, p. 40; Brooks,
Sepulchrum Christi, pp. 156-7; below, pp. 141,
304, 305.

[4] See Brooks, *Sepulchre*, pp. 44-6.

tury by St Ethelwold, for the Benedictine monasteries of England. The *Adoratio Crucis* in this monastic rule, printed in full above,[1] is immediately continued by the following form of *Depositio*:[2]

Nam quia ea die depositionem Corporis Saluatoris nostri celebramus, usum quorundam religiosorum imitabilem ad fidem indocti uulgi ac neofitorum corroborandam equiparando sequi, si ita cui uisum fuerit uel sibi taliter placuerit hoc modo decreuimus. Sit autem in una parte altaris, qua uacuum fuerit, quedam assimilatio Sepulchri, uelamenque quoddam in gyro tensum quod, dum Sancta Crux adorata fuerit, deponatur hoc ordine. Ueniant diaconi qui prius portauerunt eam, et inuoluant eam sindone in loco ubi adorata est. Tunc reportent eam canentes antiphonas *In pace in idipsum; Habitabit;* item *Caro mea requiescet in spe,* donec ueniant ad locum monumenti;[3] depositaque Cruce, ac si Domini Nostri Ihesu Christi Corpore sepulto, dicant antiphonam:

> *Sepulto Domino, signatum est monumentum; ponentes milites qui custodirent eum.*[4]

In eodem loco Sancta Crux cum omni reuerentia custodiatur usque Dominice[5] noctem Resurrectionis. Nocte uero ordinentur duo fratres aut tres aut plures, si tanta fuerint congregatio, qui ibidem | psalmos decantando excubias fideles exerceant.

This text of the *Depositio* not only shows a direct attachment of this office to the *Adoratio,* but it also explains the didactic purpose of the dramatic ceremonial. The *Depositio,* it appears, is designed for enforcing the intention of the *Adoratio,* and for strengthening the faith of the unlearned and of the neophytes. In a vacant part of the altar is prepared a likeness of the sepulchre, with a veil stretched upon a ring. The deacons who have carried the cross for the *Adoratio* wrap it in a cloth in the place of the adoration, and carry it to the *sepulchrum* singing antiphons. They then deposit it in the sepulchre as if it were the buried body of Christ, meanwhile singing the antiphon *Sepulto Domino.* Here the cross is guarded until the night of the Resurrection. Two, three, or more brothers are appointed to keep faithful watch by night, singing psalms.

---

[1] See pp. 118 sqq.

[2] London, Brit. Mus., MS Cotton Tiberius A. III, Regularis Concordia saec. xi, fol. 19ᵛ–20ʳ, published by W. S. Logeman, in *Anglia,* xiii (1891), 421–2. The *Depositio* and *Elevatio* from the *Regularis Concordia* are discussed by Brinkmann, pp. 114–9. Concerning the MSS, previous editions, and historical relationships of the *Regularis Concordia,* see below, p. 582.

[3] monumenti] monumento (MS).

[4] Antiphon of Lauds of Holy Saturday. See Hartker, p. 225.

[5] Dominice] dominica (MS).

Our knowledge of the related *Elevatio* is confined to the following sentence:[1]

Eiusdem tempore noctis antequam Matutinorum signa moueantur, sumant editui Crucem et ponant in loco sibi congruo.

In this brief rubric the sacristans of the church are charged with taking the cross from the *sepulchrum* and putting it in an appropriate place—this to be done before Matins on Easter morning.

Before leaving these ceremonies taken from the *Regularis Concordia*, I bring forward for particular notice the following simple sentence in the *Depositio: Veniant diaconi qui prius portaverunt eam, et involvant eam sindone.* The use of a cloth, or cloths, as a wrapping for the cross is an important step towards realism, which not only added notably to the impressiveness of the *Depositio*, but which eventually contributed also striking theatrical effects to many versions of the *Visitatio Sepulchri* to be considered later.[2]

As to the preparation of Christ's body for burial the first three Gospels tell us merely that it was wrapped in a clean linen cloth.[3] In the Gospel of John we are told that the body was buried with linen cloths and spices according to the usual Jewish custom; and that when Peter and John visited the tomb after the Resurrection, they found not only linen cloths, but also, in a place apart, the sudary (*sudarium*) which had been placed over the head of Christ.[4] The burial custom of the Jews was to wrap a body in a shroud, and then to bind the shroud to the body by winding long strips of cloth about it. The *sudarium* might be identified as the shroud covering the whole body,[5] or as a separate covering for the head.[6] Whatever the number of separate cloths actually used in the burial of Christ, plastic art seems usually to have followed the Gospel of John in representing the tomb on Easter morning as containing two separated objects: the *sudarium* and the *linteamina*.[7] The dramatic ceremonies at the sepulchre, as we shall see, followed the Gospel traditions with considerable freedom, using sometimes a single cloth, called *sindo* or *linteum*, as in the *Depositio* from the *Regularis Concordia*, sometimes a cloth

---

[1] MS Cotton Tiberius A. III, fol. 21ʳ. With this rubric concerning the *Elevatio* may be associated a text from Paris, Bibl. Nat., MS lat. 2402, printed in Notes, p. 555.

[2] See chaps. ix–xiii *passim*.

[3] Et accepto corpore, Joseph involvit illud in sindone munda (Matt. xxvii, 59). Cf. Mark xv, 46; Luke xxiii, 53.

[4] See John xix, 39–40; xx, 6–7.

[5] See H. Thurston, *The Holy Shroud*, in *Catholic Encyclopedia*, xiii, 762–3.

[6] U. Chevalier, *Étude critique sur l'Origine du Saint Suaire de Lirey-Chambery-Turin*, Paris, 1900, p. 9, note 2; C. Rohault de Fleury, *Mémoire sur les Instruments de la Passion*, Paris, 1870, p. 34.

[7] See Brooks, *Sepulchre*, figures 10, 11, 13, 14, and 15.

called *sudarium*, sometimes several pieces called *linteamina*, and
again both a *sudarium* and *linteamina*. These dramatic usages may
have been in part responsible for the production of painted
sudaria which have sometimes been mistaken for authentic relics
of the Passion.[1]

Returning to the texts of the dramatic ceremonies, we observe
that the close relationship between the *Depositio* and the Adoration of the Cross is shown particularly well in the following from
a thirteenth-century gradual of the cathedral of Rouen:[2]

Quando Crux adorata fuerit a clero et populo, eleuet eam sacerdos
alte, et incipiat cantor hanc antiphonam:

> *Super omnia ligna cedrorum, tu sola excelsior, in qua uita mundi pependit, in
> qua Christus triumphauit, et mors mortem superauit in eternum.*

Quo uiso, clerus et populus genuflectant, et chorus finiat antiphonam.
Qua cantata, Crux paruula in commemoratione sanguinis et aque de-
flentis de latere Redemptoris aqua et uino lauetur, de quo commemora-
tionem sacram clerus bibat et populus, et ad opus infirmorum reseruetur.
Quo facto, sacerdotes et clerici accipiant Crucifixum et portent ad
Sepulchrum preparatum cantantes hoc responsorium:

> *Sicut ouis ad occisionem ductus est, et dum male tracta|retur, non aperuit os
> suum, traditus est ad mortem ut uiuificaret populum suum.* Versus: *In pace
> factus est locus eius, et in Syon habitatio eius.* Responsorium: *Vt uiuificaret.*[3]

Et tunc ponatur in Sepulcro, pedibus uersis ad orientem, et cooperiatur
pallio, et incensando illum dicat archiepiscopus uel sacerdos hanc antiphonam:

> *In pace in idipsum dormiam et requiescam.*

Qua cantata, claudat hostium Sepulchri. Responsorium:

> *Sepulto Domino, signatum est monumentum; uoluentes lapidem ad hostium
> monumenti; ponentes milites qui custodirent illud.* Versus: *Ne forte ueniant
> discipuli eius et furentur eum, et dicant plebi: Surrexit a mortuis.* Responso-
> rium: *Voluentes.*

His expletis, ministri Crucis casulis induti afferant ad altare cum uino
non consecrato reseruatum Corpus Domini.

---

[1] See Thurston, *op. cit.*, p. 763. The matter
of mistaken authenticity, and of the burial
cloths generally is treated with especial fullness and incisiveness by Chevalier, *op. cit.*

[2] Paris, Bibl. Nat., MS lat. 904, Grad.
Rothomagense sæc. xiii, fol. 92ᵛ–93ʳ, previously printed by Young, *Dramatic Associations*, pp. 74–5. A photographic reproduction
of this MS occupies the second volume of *Le*

Graduel de l'Église cathédrale de Rouen, edited
by H. Loriquet, J. Pothier, and A. Collette,
Rouen, 1907. The MS provides music. For
bibliography of relevant Rouen MSS see
Young, *Rouen*, pp. 224–7.

[3] Responsory of Matins of Holy Saturday.
See Hartker, p. 222; Migne, *P.L.*, lxxviii,
768.

The *Adoratio Crucis*, it will be observed, ends with the exceptionally suggestive ceremonial of the washing of the cross with wine and water.[1] Then follows immediately the *Depositio* proper. After being carried to the place of burial during the singing of the responsory *Sicut ovis*, the cross is laid in the sepulchre, covered with a winding sheet, and censed. After the closing of the door of the *sepulchrum* is sung the responsory *Sepulto Domino*. Then occurs immediately the communion of the Mass of the Presanctified.

The extant service-books of Rouen contain no text of the *Elevatio*. It is briefly described, however, in the *Liber de Officiis* of Jean d'Avranches, archbishop of Rouen in the eleventh century, and must have been in use there during later centuries.[2] It is, indeed, not easily conceivable that a church which performed the *Depositio* and *Visitatio Sepulchri* should omit the intermediate office.[3]

Concerning the sepulchre offices in the Abbey Church of Durham we have unusual sources of information. In a missal of the fourteenth century the *Depositio* is prescribed as follows:[4]

Et sciendum quod dum Crux portatur et reportatur per me|dium chori, adorari debet ab omnibus flexis genibus. Cum uero peruenerint ad gradus pauimenti, procedant duo fratres cum candelabris, et tertius cum thuribulo, precedentes Crucis portatores et episcopum uel priorem, qui, cum portatoribus Crucis, Crucem in Sepulcro collocaturus est. Finita antiphona *Super omnia*, incipiat cantor responsorium:

> *Tenebre ⟨factæ sunt dum crucifixissent Jesum Judæi, et circa horam nonam exclamavit Jesus voce magna: Deus, Deus, ut quid me dereliquisti? Tunc unus ex militibus lancea latus ejus perforavit, et inclinato capite emisit spiritum. Versus: Et velum templi scissum est a summo usque deorsum, et omnis terra tremuit. Tunc unus.⟩.*[5]

Quo decantato, collocetur Crux in Sepulcro, incensato loco ante posicionem et post. Dum hec aguntur incipiat cantor has antiphonas:[6]

> *Proprio filio suo non pepercit Deus, ⟨sed⟩ pro nobis omnibus tradidit illum.*

Antiphona:

> *Caro mea requiescet in spe.*

---

[1] Cf. the *Depositio* from Barking below, p. 164. See Feasey, *Ceremonial*, p. 130.

[2] See Notes, p. 555.

[3] For the *Visitatio Sepulchri* from Rouen see below, p. 370.

[4] London, Brit. Mus., MS Harl. 5289, Miss. Dunelmense sæc. xiv, fol. 177^r–177^v, previously edited by Young, *Dramatic Associations*, pp. 77–8. The MS contains no *Elevatio*

or *Visitatio*. Concerning a *Depositio* which may be associated with that now before us see Notes, p. 555.

[5] Responsory of Matins of Good Friday. See Hartker, p. 218; Migne, *P.L.*, lxxviii, 766–7.

[6] For the six antiphons of Holy Week which follow see Hartker, pp. 181, 219, 222, 225.

Antiphona:

Dominus tanquam ouis ad uictimam ductus est et non aperuit os suum.

Antiphona:

Oblatus est quia ipse uoluit, et peccata nostra ipse portabit.

Antiphona:

In pace in idipsum dormiam et requiescam.

Deinde duo uertentes uultum ad conuentum canant hanc antiphonam:

Ioseph ab Arimathia petiit corpus Ihesu et sepelliuit eum in sepulcro suo.

Eaque percantata, descendat in reuestiarium qui officium celebrat.[1]

At the conclusion of the *Adoratio*, in this case, is sung the responsory *Tenebræ*, after which the cross is put into the sepulchre, and the place is censed. During the laying down of the cross are sung a series of five antiphons. Then two clerics, turning toward the *conventus*, close the office with the singing of the antiphon *Joseph ab Arimathia*.

For the end of the Middle Ages our knowledge of the dramatic ceremonies at Durham is greatly enlarged through an anonymous record compiled in the year 1593.[2] Of the Adoration of the Cross and its sequel this printed book gives us the following description:[3]

Within the Abbye Church of Durham, uppon Good Friday theire was maruelous solemne seruice, in the which seruice time, after the Passion was sung, two of the eldest monkes did take a goodly large Crucifix, all of gold, of the picture of our Sauiour Christ nailed uppon the crosse, lyinge uppon a ueluett cushion, hauinge St Cuthbert's armes uppon it all imbroydered with gold, bringinge that betwixt them uppon the said cushion to the lowest greeces in the quire, and there betwixt them did hold the said picture of our Sauiour, sittinge of euery side, on ther knees, of that, and then one of the said monkes did rise and went a prettye way from it, sittinge downe uppon his knees, with his shooes put of, uerye reuerently did creepe away uppon his knees unto the said Crosse, and most reuerently did kisse it. And after him the other monke did so likewise, and then they did sitt them downe on euery side of the

---

[1] The Mass of the Presanctified follows.

[2] *Rites of Durham, being a Description or Brief Declaration of all the Ancient Monuments, Rites, and Customs belonging or being within the Monastical Church of Durham before the Suppression. Written 1593*, edited by J. T. Fowler, from seven manuscripts, in *Publications of the Surtees Society*, cvii (1903).

[3] *Surtees Society*, cvii, 11–2. I have modernized somewhat the punctuation and capitalization. The passages that I quote have been reprinted from the less comprehensive edition of J. Raine (*Surtees Society*, xv) by Chambers, ii, 310–1, and Adams, pp. 4–5. See also Feasey, *Ceremonial*, pp. 135–6, 170–1; Rock, iv, 288–90.

said Crosse, and holdinge it betwixt them, and after that the prior came forth of his stall, and did sitt him downe of his knees, with his shooes of, and in like sort did creepe also unto the said Crosse, and all the monkes after him, one after an nother in the same order, and in the meane time all the whole quire singinge an himne. The seruice beinge ended, the two monkes did carrye it to the Sepulchre with great reuerence, which Sepulchre was sett upp in the morninge, on the north side of the quire, nigh to the high altar, before the seruice time; and there did lay it within the said Sepulchre with great deuotion, with another picture of our Sauiour Christ, in whose breast they did enclose, with great reuerence, the most holy and blessed Sacrament of the altar, senceinge and prayinge vnto it uppon theire knees a great space, settinge two tapers lighted before it, which tapers did burne unto Easter day in the morninge, that it was taken forth.

The *Elevatio* is described thus:[1]

There was in the Abbye Church of Duresme uerye solemne seruice uppon Easter Day, betweene 3 and 4 of the clocke in the morninge, in honour of the Resurrection, where 2 of the oldest monkes of the quire came to the Sepulchre, beinge sett vpp upon Good Friday, after the Passion, all couered with redd ueluett and embrodered with gold, and then did sence it, either monke with a paire of siluer sencors sittinge on theire knees before the Sepulchre. Then they both risinge came to the Sepulchre, out of the which, with great reverence, they tooke a maruelous beautifull Image of our Sauiour, representinge the Resurrection, with a crosse in his hand, in the breast wherof was enclosed in bright christall the Holy Sacrament of the altar, throughe the which christall the Blessed Host was conspicuous to the behoulders. Then, after the eleuation of the said picture, carryed by the said 2 monkes uppon a faire ueluett cushion, all embrodered, singinge the anthem of *Christus resurgens*, they brought ⟨it⟩ to the high altar, settinge that on the midst therof, whereon it stood, the two monkes kneelinge on theire knets before the altar, and senceing it all the time that the rest of the whole quire was in singinge the foresaid anthem of *Christus resurgens*. The which anthem beinge ended, the 2 Monkes tooke up the cushines and the picture from the altar, supportinge it betwixt them, proceedinge, in procession, from the high altar to the south quire dore, where there was 4 antient gentlemen, belonginge to the prior, appointed to attend their comminge, holdinge upp a most rich cannopye of purple ueluett, tached round about with redd silke and gold fringe; and at euerye corner did stand one of theise ancient gentlemen, to beare it ouer the said Image, with the Holy Sacrament, carried by two monkes round about the church, the whole quire waitinge uppon it with goodly torches and great store of other

---

[1] *Surtees Society*, cvii, 12–3.

lights, all singinge, reioyceinge, and praising God most deuoutly, till they came to the high altar againe, wheron they did place the said Image there to remaine untill the Assencion day.

For our present purpose the chief interest of these charming descriptions lies in the details concerning the objects buried in the sepulchre, as to which we are given the following additional information:[1]

⟨Over a certain altar in the 'south alley of the lantern'⟩ was a merveylous lyvelye and bewtifull Immage of the picture of our Ladie, socalled the Lady of Boultone, whiche picture was maide to open with gymmers from her breaste downdward. And within the said Immage was wrowghte and pictured the Immage of our Saviour, merveylouse fynlie gilted, houldinge vppe his handes, and holding betwixt his handes a fair and large Crucifix of Christ, all of gold, the whiche Crucifix was to be taiken fourthe euery Good Fridaie, and euery man did crepe vnto it that was in that churche as that daye. And ther after yt was houng vpe againe within the said Immage.

From what is now before us it appears that for use in the *Depositio* and *Elevatio* the Abbey at Durham possessed a remarkable image 'of our Saviour Christ', in the breast of which was a cavity large enough for receiving the Host enclosed in transparent crystal. Held in the uplifted hands of this figure, but detachable from it, was a crucifix, or 'picture of our Saviour Christ nailed upon the crosse'. Guided by certain Continental usages, to be mentioned below, we may call the former object the *Imago Resurrectionis*, and the latter, the *Imago Crucifixi*.[2] Although the language of the tract is none too clear, I infer that in the dramatic ceremonies of the *sepulchrum* the two effigies are buried and raised together, the *Imago Crucifixi* being held in the uplifted hands of the *Imago Resurrectionis*. It will be observed that as it lies in the sepulchre the *Imago Resurrectionis* contains in its cavity 'the most holy and blessed Sacrament of the Altar', in defiance of the doctrine that the consecrated Host has no proper place in a tomb.[3] A figure of this general kind lying in the *sepulchrum*, along with the Host, is unsympathetically described in *The Popish Kingdome* of Barnabe Googe, translated in the year 1570 from the *Regnum Papisticum* (1553) of the German anti-Catholic poet, Thomas Kirchmayer (Naogeorgus):[4]

---

[1] *Id.*, p. 30.
[2] See, for example, below, pp. 157 sqq.
[3] See above, p. 132.

[4] *The Popish Kingdome, or reigne of Antichrist, written in Latine verse by Thomas Naogeorgus, and englyshed by Barnabe Googe,*

An other Image doe they get, like one but newly deade,
With legges stretcht out at length, and handes vpon his body spreade.
And him with pompe and sacred song they beare vnto his graue,
His bodie all being wrapt in lawne, and silkes and sarcenet braue.
The boyes before with clappers go, and filthie noyses make;
The Sexten beares the light, the people hereof knowledge take;
And downe they kneele, or kisse the grounde, their handes helde vp
  abrod,
And knocking on their breastes they make this woodden blocke a God.
And least in graue he shoulde remaine without some companie,
The singing bread is layde with him, for more idolatrie.

In order to avoid burying the *Imago Resurrectionis* and its Host,
some churches separated this effigy completely from the *Imago
Crucifixi* in the ceremonies at the sepulchre. Thus in the performance of the *Depositio* at Prüfening, as we shall see, only the
latter was used, the *Imago Resurrectionis* being brought forth only
for the *Elevatio*.[1]

Proceeding with our survey of the dramatic observances we
may consider one or two versions of the *Depositio* in which the
cross is the centre of attention, but which are not direct con-
tinuations of the *Adoratio*. Such is the following example from
Moosburg, with its accompanying *Elevatio:*[2]

⟨DEPOSITIO CRUCIS⟩[3]

Expleta communione, Corpus Christi quod superfuerit diligenter et
reuerenter in corporali involuto et super altari mobili posito portatur
ad locum in quo Crucifixus est adoratus, et ibi Sepulchrum pro sepultura Crucifixi debet esse positum et circumductis pannis decenter preparatum. Et Corpus Christi cum altari mobili primo super Sepulchrum
ponitur, et clericis deuote circumstantibus incipiatur Vespera subpressa
voce, *Confitebor tibi* cum reliquis psalmis ferialibus et *Magnificat.* Hec
omnia continuatim sine *Gloria Patri.* Sequitur, flexis genibus, *Miserere
mei* et *Pater Noster* et versus *Proprio filio suo non pepercit.* Deinde recipiatur
Crucifixus, et voce lenta et lugubri cantetur responsorium *Ecce quomodo
moritur.* Versus *In pace in idipsum.* Finito responsorio, collocetur Crucifixus in Sepulchrum, et lintheaminibus et sudario cooperiatur. Deinde
lapis, videlicet altare mobile, sub capite sev sub dextero latere ponatur
cum alio sanctuario, et signetur sepulchrum aliqua clausura, et cantetur

---

London, 1570, fol. 51[v]. For the setting of
this description, and of the original passage
in the *Regnum Papisticum*, see Appendix C,
below, ii, 528, 534.

[1] For the text from Prüfening see below,
p. 157. See also Notes, p. 555.

[2] Munich, Staatsbibl., MS lat. 9469, Brev.

Mosburgense sæc. xv–xvi, fol. 56[v], 58[v]–59[r],
previously edited by Brooks, *Sepulchre*, p. 104.
With the texts before us may be associated
several others printed or mentioned in Notes,
p. 556.

[3] Munich MS lat. 9469, fol. 56[v].

remisse responsorium *Sepulto Domino*. Versus *Ne forte veniant*. Responsorium *Recessit pastor*. Versus *Ante cuius conspectum*. Aspergatur et thurificetur. Sequitur versus *In pace factus est locus*, et sic est finis. Corpus Christi deinde reuerenter ad altare publicum deportatur, et ibi diligenter reseruatur et pro communicantibus distribuitur.[1]

⟨ELEVATIO CRUCIS⟩[2]

In ipsa sancta nocte ante pulsacionem clam surgitur, sintque parata thuribula cum thure et mirra et thymiamathe et aspersorio. Et excludantur layci, si commode fieri potest, nam nobiscum viri et mulieres in ecclesia sacras vigilias obseruant; et ueniente tempore Matutinarum, clerici eos sine scandalo repellere nequeunt propter antiquam consvetudinem vigilandi, de qua dicit Ieronimus, vt dicit auctor Racionalis: Reor, inquit, tradicionem apostolicam permansisse vt die vigiliarum Pasche ante noctis medium dimittere non liceat populos expectantes Christi aduentum, vt resurgenti Saluatori occurrant et postquam tempus illud transierit securitate presumpta festum cunctos agere diem; hec Ieronimus.

Deinde decanus et seniores humiliter | progrediantur ante altare Sancte Crucis et dicant sibi mutuo *Confiteor* et *Misereatur*. Deinde cum summa reuerencia insimul accedant ad Sepulchrum et dicant psalmos: *Domine, quid multiplicati*; psalmus *Miserere mei, Deus, miserere mei, quoniam in te confidit*; psalmus *Domine probasti me*. *Ky⟨rie eleïson⟩, Ch⟨riste eleïson⟩, Ky⟨rie eleïson⟩. Pater Noster. Et ne nos.* Versus *Exurge, Domine, adiuua*; versus *Domine Deus virtutum*; versus *Domine, exaudi orationem*. *Dominus vobiscum. Oremus: Da nobis, Domine, auxilium*. Et thurificent et aspergant Ymaginem Crucifixi, sublatamque de Sepulchro secum portent ante aram Sancti Iohannis cantando humili voce responsorium *Dum transisset sabbatum*, cum versu *Et ualde*.[3] Sacerdos subiungat versum *Surrexit Dominus vere et apparuit*. Oratio *Deus qui hodierna die per unigenitum tuum*. Qua finita, stantes ante altare se invicem mutua caritate deosculantes, vel ad minus Crucifixum, dicant *Surrexit Dominus*. Alij respondeant *Gaudeamus omnes*. Deinde statim sollempniter pulsetur.[4]

It is obvious that at Moosburg the *Depositio* is made vivid through the use of several realistic accompaniments. After Mass the vessel containing the part of the Eucharist which remains is placed upon a portable stone altar, and both objects are laid upon a sepulchre prepared at the place where the Adoration occurred; and here Vespers is said quietly. When the crucifix is put into the sepulchre, it is covered not merely by linen cloths

---

[1] Followed by the rubric *Completorium*.
[2] Munich MS lat. 9469, fol. 58ᵛ–59ʳ.
[3] For the full text of this responsory, commonly used as the last of Easter Matins, see below, p. 232.
[4] Followed by the rubric *Ad Matutinum*.

(*lintheamina*), but also by a *sudarium*, in accordance with the tradition established by the Gospel of John.[1] In the closing of the sepulchre the altar stone, or *lapis*, is used in some manner, after the Eucharist has been carried to a separate place for other purposes. Some versions of the *Depositio* provide explicitly that the *lapis* shall serve as the covering and closure for the sepulchre;[2] and in any of these arrangements it supplies an acceptable bit of realism and prepares for the interrogation *Quis revolvet nobis lapidem ab ostio monumenti?* or *Quis revolvet nobis ab ostio lapidem quem tegere sanctum cernimus sepulchrum?* with which numerous versions of the *Visitatio Sepulchri* open.[3]

In the description of the *Elevatio* is given a naïve explanation of the difficulty of excluding laymen from this popular observance.[4] Noticeable also is the use of the responsory *Dum transisset*. This liturgical piece, recounting the visit of the Marys to the empty tomb, is obviously inappropriate to a ceremony symbolizing the act of the Resurrection itself.[5]

Especially careful provision for the dramatic use of the gravecloth is made in the following versions from Treves:[6]

⟨DEPOSITIO CRUCIS⟩[7]

Hiis peractis, exuat sacerdos casulam et induatur cappa purpurea, et ad requirendam Crucem descendatur hoc ordine. Precedat alicus indutus cappa cum aqua benedicta; sequantur duo acoliti in tunicis cum cereis, in medio eorum acolitus in cappa cum thuribulo; post hos subdiaconus in subtili cum textu; duo alici induti tunicis a dextris et a sinistris eius cum crucibus sollempnibus; sequatur dyaconus in dalmatica; deinde sacerdos in cappa prout dictum est. Procedant sic ordinati ad Sanctam Agnetem. Ibi inueniri debet Crux ante altare uelata, quam teneant a dextris et a sinistris duo subdiaconi induti casulis rubeis. Accedat sacerdos, et leuato uelamine aspergat Crucem aqua benedicta. Post aspersionem reponatur uelamen super Crucem, et incipiat cantor responsorium *Iherusalem luge*; deinde uersum *Plange quasi uirgo*; que cantentur uocibus submissis cum versibus et repetitionibus, et procedat omnis processio suo ordine. Subdiaconi vero portantes

---

[1] See above, p. 134.
[2] See, for example, the *Depositio* from Andechs (Munich MS lat. 24882) printed below, p. 556. See also the text from Berlin MS 4°. 113 below, p. 152.
[3] See below, pp. 259 sqq. For the *Visitatio Sepulchri* from Moosburg itself see below, p. 361.
[4] See above, p. 124.

[5] See above, p. 131.
[6] London, Brit. Mus., MS Harl. 2958, Ordin. Trevirense sæc. xiii, fol. 36ʳ–36ᵛ, 37ʳ, previously edited by Young, *op. cit.*, pp. 83–4. For the *Visitatio Sepulchri* from this MS see below, p. 280. With the texts before us may be associated several mentioned or printed in Notes, p. 558.
[7] MS Harl. 2958, fol. 36ʳ–36ᵛ.

Crucem uelatam immediate sequantur sacerdotem. Cum peruenerint in criptam ante Sepulcrum, sacerdos aspergat Sepulcrum aqua benedicta et thurificet. Deinde Crux ponatur in Sepulcrum et ueletur panno albo, et incipiat cantor responsorium *Ecce quomodo moritur iustus*, uoce submissa cum versu et repetitione. Post modum claudatur Sepulcrum, et incipiat cantor responsorium *Sepulto Domino*, cum versu et rep⟨et⟩itione. Sacerdo⟨s⟩ uero dicat versiculum *In pace factus est locus eius*. Et | respondeatur *Et in Syon habitatio eius*. Quibus peractis, egrediatur processio.[1]

⟨ELEVATIO CRUCIS⟩[2]

In die sancto Pasce mane ante pulsationem Matutini, reuertatur processio ad Sepulcrum sicut processit ad sepeliendum. Et sacerdos, flexis genibus, dicat orationes, et aspergat aqua benedicta Crucem, et thurificabit; et, ablato velamine, dicat versum *Surrexit Dominus uere*, leuando Crucem. Et cantor immediate incipiat antiphonam *Christus resurgens*, et versum *Dicant nunc*, cum repetitione. Deinde egrediatur processio, relicto sudario in monumento, et pulsetur ad Matutinum.

The text of the *Depositio* reveals two somewhat unusual conditions: the performing of the office after Vespers, and the locating of the sepulchre in the crypt. In the *Elevatio* especial interest attaches to the rubric prescribing that the *sudarium* covering the cross shall be left behind when the latter is removed from the sepulchre. Thus the sudary is in place for use in the subsequent *Visitatio Sepulchri*.[3]

V

Among the burial ceremonies which seem to centre essentially in the cross we have already considered versions in which the Host appears at least in a subsidiary way.[4] To these we may now add one or two examples in which the two objects are equally prominent, and are unmistakably enclosed within the sepulchre together. This is the arrangement, for example, in the following offices from Aquileia:[5]

[1] Followed by the rubric *Sabbato Sancto ad Matutinum*.

[2] MS Harl. 2958, fol. 37ʳ. For the liturgical pieces employed see Hartker, pp. 203, 241.

[3] See below, p. 281.

[4] See above, pp. 138, 140.

[5] The *Depositio* is from *Agenda Dioecesis Sanctæ Ecclesiæ Aquilegiensis*, Venice, 1575, pp. 120–3, previously reprinted by Young, *op. cit.*, pp. 93–4. The *Elevatio*, from an undated print, is given by Rubeis, p. 339, from whom I reprint here. For a version of the *Visitatio Sepulchri* from Aquileia see below, p. 321. With the texts before us may be associated others mentioned or printed in Notes, p. 560.

⟨Depositio Crucis et Hostiæ⟩[1]

Oratione[2] vero expleta, et Sepulchro preparato et decenter ornato, assint inpromptu tria thuribula cum incenso thuris, mirrhe, et thimiamatis, et quatuor candele ardentes; et ministri cum sacerdotibus portent Imaginem Crucifixi versus Sepulchrum, et officians sequatur portans Sacramentum Eucharistie in sanctuario repositum. Chorus vero in tali processione lugubri voce cantet responsorium cum suo versu:

Ecce quomodo moritur iustus, et nemo percipit corde; et viri iusti tolluntur, et nemo considerat; a facie iniquitatis oblatus est iustus, et erit in pace memoria eius. ⟨Versus:⟩ *In pace factus est locus eius, et in Syon habitatio eius. Et erit in pace.*

Quo finito et dum ad Sepulchrum ventum sit, officians locet Sacramentum in sanctuario reposito ad locum in Sepulchro ad hoc paratum. Deinde ministri et sacerdotes Imaginem Crucifixi collocent in Sepulchro, et cooperiant lintheaminibus et sudario, et supponant lapidem. Chorus cantet responsorium cum suo versu:

Recessit pastor noster, fons aque viue, ad cuius transitum sol obscuratus est; nam et ille captus est qui captiuum tenebat primum hominem. Hodie portas mortis et seras pariter Saluator noster destruxit. Versus: *Ante cuius conspectum mors fugit, ad cuius vocem mortui resurgunt; videntes autem eum porte mortis confracte sunt. Hodie portas.*

Officians vero thurificet Imaginem Crucifixi sic in Sepulchrum positam, et aspergat aqua benedicta. Et postea clauditur Sepulchrum, et clauso apponunt sigilla officiantes et laici presidentes, et chorus cantet responsorium sequentem cum suo versu:

Sepulto Domino, signatum est monumentum; voluentes lapidem ad hostium monumenti; ponentes milites qui custodirent illud. ⟨Versus:⟩ *Ne forte veniant discipuli eius et furentur eum, et dicant plebi: Surrexit a mortuis. Ponentes.*

Quo finito, officians dicat versiculum:

In pace factus est locus eius.

Et respondent ministri et sacerdotes:

Et habitatio eius in Syon.

Tandem circa Sepulchrum dicantur Vespere secundum rubricam breuiarii. Et sub *Magnificat* officians et ministri cum tribus thuribulis Sepulchrum thurificent, et sacerdos aqua benedicta aspergat. Finitis autem Vesperis, scholares secundum morem patrie incipiunt legere psalterium.

---

[1] *Agenda*, Venice, 1575, pp. 120–3.
[2] This is the closing prayer of the Mass of the Presanctified.

⟨ELEVATIO CRUCIS ET HOSTIÆ⟩[1]

Ad Matutinum clam surgitur. Et sint parata tria thuribula cum thure, myrrha, et thimiamate. Et officians, præsentibus sacerdotibus et laico, qui nuper sigillum apposuerat, Sepulchrum accedat, et aperiat cum reverentia. Et officians dicat cum sacerdotibus psalmos sequentes:

Domine, quid multiplicati sunt.
Domine, probasti me.
Miserere mei, Deus, miserere mei.

Quibus finitis, officians thurificet Imaginem Crucifixi; et sacerdotes reverenter de Sepulcro eam tollant, relictis linteaminibus et sudario in Sepulcro, et ad chorum super altare portent. Officians vero Sacramentum Eucharistiæ in Sepulcro collocatum, præcedente lumine, in locum suum ferat. Et cantent portantes Imaginem:

Surrexit pastor bonus, qui posuit animam suam.

Quo finito, officians stet cum sacerdotibus in choro, et dicat versum:

Surrexit Dominus vere. Responsio *Et apparuit Simoni.*

Oratio: *Oremus: Omnipotens sempiterne Deus, qui hac sacratissima nocte.* Alia: *In memoriam et laudem gloriosæ Resurrectionis tuæ.* Alia: *Cæli et terræ conditor, quo moriente, illuminata sunt tartara.* Alia: *Adesto, pie Pater, invocationibus nostris.* Alia: *Domine Jesu Christe, propter hoc gaudium.* Deinde, pulsatis campanis, incipiatur Officium Matutinale.

At Aquileia the *Depositio* occurs immediately after Mass. In the procession the ministers of the Mass carry the *Imago Crucifixi*, and the celebrant, the Host. Each object is deposited in a part of the sepulchre especially prepared for it.[2] After laying down the crucifix, the ministers cover it with linen cloths and a sudary, and put the stone in its place. The crucifix is then censed and sprinkled, and the sepulchre is sealed. In the *Elevatio* the most informing detail is the leaving in the sepulchre of the *lintheamina* and *sudarium*, for dramatic use in the *Visitatio* to follow.[3]

For another example of the close association of the cross and Host we may cite the use of Sarum, as representing a widely influential practice in England. The following are representative texts:[4]

[1] Rubeis, p. 339.

[2] The *sanctuarium* in which the Host is deposited is, no doubt, a box or cavity. For the *sepulchrum* at Aquileia see plate ix, and below, ii, 509.

[3] For the text of the *Visitatio* see below, p. 321.

[4] Henderson, pp. 72-3, 91-2. For a fuller display of Sarum texts bearing upon the ceremonies at the sepulchre see Frere, *Sarum*, i, 6, 115, 153-4, 219-20; ii, 166, drawn upon by Chambers, ii, 312-5. For the *Depositio* see also *Graduale Sarisburiense*, ed. W. H. Frere, London, 1894, plate 104; *The Sarum Missal*, ed. J. W. Legg, Oxford, 1916, p. 115. For the *Elevatio* see also *Antiphonale Sarisburiense* (*Plainsong and Mediæval Music Society*), London, 1901-25, plate 235. See also

⟨DEPOSITIO CRUCIS ET HOSTIÆ⟩[1]

Finitis Vesperis, exuat sacerdos casulam, et sumens secum unum de prælatis in superpelliceis, discalceati reponant Crucem cum Corpore Dominico in Sepulcrum, incipiens ipse solus hoc responsorium: *Æstimatus sum*, genuflectendo cum socio suo; quo incepto statim surgat. Similiter fiat in responsorio *Sepulto Domino*. Chorus totum responsorium prosequatur cum suo versu, genuflectendo per totum tempus usque ad finem servitii. Responsoria ut sic:

Æstimatus sum, chorus prosequatur, *cum descendentibus in lacum; factus sum sicut homo sine adjutorio, inter mortuos liber.* Versus: *Posuerunt me in lacu inferiori, in tenebrosis et in umbra mortis. Factus.*[2]

Dum prædictum responsorium canitur cum suo versu, prædicti duo sacerdotes thurificent Sepulcrum, quo facto et clauso ostio, incipiet idem sacerdos responsorium:

Sepulto Domino, signatum est monumentum; volventes lapidem ad ostium monumenti; ponentes milites qui custodirent illud. Versus: *Ne forte veniant discipuli ejus et furentur eum, et dicant plebi: Surrexit a mortuis. Ponentes.*

Item prædicti duo sacerdotes dicant istas tres antiphonas sequentes genuflectendo continue. Antiphona:

In pace, chorus prosequatur, *in idipsum dormiam et requiescam.*
Iterum sacerdotes:

In pace factus est, chorus prosequatur, *locus ejus, et in Sion habitatio ejus.*
Sacerdotes:

Caro mea, chorus prosequatur, *requiescet in spe.*

⟨ELEVATIO CRUCIS ET HOSTIÆ⟩[3]

Ante Matutinas et ante campanarum pulsationem conveniant clerici ad ecclesiam et accendantur omnia lumina per ecclesiam. Duo excellentiores cum ceroferariis et thuribulariis et clero circumstante ad Sepulcrum accedant, et incensato prius Sepulchro cum magna veneratione statim post thurificationem, videlicet genuflectendo, Corpus Domini privatim super altare deponant. Iterum accipiant Crucem de Sepulchro, et incipiat excellentior persona *Christus resurgens*, cum qua eat processio per ostium presbyterii australe incedendo per medium chori, et regrediens cum prædicta Cruce de Sepulchro assumpta inter duos sacerdotes prædictos super eorum brachia venerabiliter portata cum thuribulariis et ceroferariis præcedentibus per ostium presbyterii boreale, exeundo ad unum altare ex parte boreali ecclesiæ, choro

Bishop, p. 295. Concerning texts to be associated with those before us see Notes, p. 561
[1] Henderson, pp. 72–3.
[2] For a responsory of Holy Saturday of similar beginning see Hartker, p. 224; Migne, *P. L.*, lxxviii, 768.
[3] Henderson, pp. 91–2.

sequente habitu non mutato, excellentioribus præcedentibus, Corpore vero Domini super altare in pyxide dimisso in subthesaurarii custodia, qui illud in prædicta pyxide in tabernaculo dependat, ut patet in ista statione præcedente. Et tunc pulsentur omnes campanæ in classicum, et cantetur antiphona:

> *Christus resurgens ex mortuis, jam non moritur; mors illi ultra non domina-*
> *bitur, quod enim vivit, vivit Deo, alleluia, alleluia.* Versus: *Dicant nunc*
> *Judæi quomodo milites custodientes sepulchrum perdiderunt regem ad lapidis*
> *positionem. Quare non servabant petram justitiæ? Aut sepultum reddant, aut*
> *resurgentem adorent, nobiscum dicentes.*

Chorus respondeat hoc modo quo sequitur: *Alleluia, alleluia.*

The ceremonial of the *Depositio* is here very simple, consisting merely in the laying down of the cross and Host together, and the censing and closing of the sepulchre. The notable feature of the *Elevatio* is the careful separation of the Host and the cross in the ceremonial. The Host is removed from the sepulchre first, and taken *privatim* to the altar; then follows an elaborate procession for the carrying forth of the cross.

Because of their exceptional details we must consider, finally, the following versions from Hungary:[1]

⟨DEPOSITIO CRUCIS ET HOSTIÆ⟩[2]

Interim subcustos exportat monstrantiam cum Sacramento pro sepultura ad altare magnum. His peractis, descendat chorus processionaliter ad locum vbi sepultura ordinata[3] est, episcopo ipsos cum Sacramento sequente, precedentibus quattuor precedentibus seu iuuenibus cum bacculis auratis cum candelis accensis. Et Dominus Episcopus recondat Crucem cum Sacramento reuerenter, thurificando et aspergendo ac sigillando Sepulchrum. Interim chorus cantet responsoria: *Hierusalem luge. Ecce vidimus. Plange quasi virgo. Recessit pastor bonus.* Recondito Sacramento, chorus cantet responsorium *Sepulto Domino.* Et postea Dominus Episcopus dicat versum et orationem ut in missali. Tandem facta reuerentia, recedat.[4]

⟨ELEVATIO CRUCIS ET HOSTIÆ⟩[5]

Item in Matutino post vltimam omeliam, dum chorales incipiunt ad responsorium *Dum transisset*, debent procedere usque ad Sepulchrum; et ibidem chorales versiculum cum *Gloria Patri* sollemnisabunt. Ibique

---

[1] I reprint the texts of Dankó, *Hymnarium*, pp. 535–6, 537–8, from 'Ordinarius Scepusiensis sive Strigoniensis sæculi decimi quinti e codice manuscripto Bibliothecæ R. Universitatis Budapestinensis'. These texts have been reprinted also by Young, *Dramatic Associations*, pp. 122–3. The *Depositio* is immediately preceded by Vespers.

[2] Dankó, *Hymnarium*, pp. 535–6.

[3] sepultura ordinata] sepulturum ordinatam (Dankó).

[4] Followed immediately by the rubric *In Completorio.*

[5] Dankó, *Hymnarium*, pp. 537–8.

ministri stantes candelis accensis, thure et thuribulo ibi existentibus, et interim vnus leuabit Sepulchrum et Hostiam, et Dominus Pontifex siue plebanus precedentes sollemniter thurificabit. Dein Corpus cum parua Cruce excipiet, quod impositum fuit feria sexta majoris ebdomade. Et excipit cum versiculo isto: *Surrexit Dominus de sepulchro, alleluia, qui pro nobis*. Et interea circa altare Beate Virginis calicem cum corporalibus preparant. Tunc Dominus Pontifex seu plebanus accedens Corpus Christi super patenam tenens in manu honorifice et ad maximam reuerenciam vertat se tribus vicibus ad populum cum Corpore Christi cantando *Pax vobis*, cum suo *Alleluia*. Chorus respondet *Nolite timere, alleluia*. Deinde processio canendo redibit ad chorum sollemnisando *Te Deum*.

In contrast to the prominence given, in certain of the preceding versions, to the cross, one notes here the conspicuous use of the Host. From the rubrics of the *Depositio* it appears that the Sacrament is carried to the sepulchre in a monstrance. In the ceremony of the *Elevatio*, after it has been taken out of the sepulchre, the Host is used in a triple blessing of the congregation. The *sepulchrum* itself seems to be a portable chest of some sort, placed, for the present purpose, at the main altar. Most noteworthy of all is the unusual liturgical position of the *Elevatio:* before the *Te Deum* at the end of Easter Matins. The general impropriety of this arrangement has already been mentioned.[1]

The versions of the ceremonies at the sepulchre reviewed thus far give the impression of having promised more in a dramatic way than they actually succeeded in accomplishing. As a whole the arrangements for stage-setting are ample. In one community or another were used a carefully arranged enclosure for the *sepulchrum*, an effigy for burial, grave-cloths for winding it, and a stone for closing the tomb. The utterances, however, remain merely the familiar liturgical forms of the season, accompanied by no more attempt in the way of dialogue than is usual in normal daily worship, and, above all, spoken with no effort toward impersonation on the part of the performers. From what we have seen, therefore, we should infer that the *Depositio* and *Elevatio* were merely striking examples of symbolism. As liturgical exercises they are uncommonly tender or vivid or splendid; but they lack the essential of true drama.[2] The removal of this deficiency appears to have been attempted in some of the examples brought forward in the next chapter.

[1] See above, p. 131.
[2] Concerning impersonation as the essential element of drama see above, p. 80.

CHAPTER V

THE HARROWING OF HELL

IN the ceremonies surveyed in the preceding chapter we have encountered scarcely a hint of a theme which in many communities assumed a conspicuous place in the dramatic observances at the sepulchre, and which was eventually to be treated with impressive amplitude in the vernacular drama of Western Europe. I refer to the traditional narrative of the Harrowing of Hell.[1]

I

The chief inspiration for a literary treatment of this theme is, directly or indirectly, the Gospel of Nicodemus. In its complete form this apocryphal narrative is composed of two parts, the *Acta Pilati* and the *Descensus Christi ad Inferos*, which were probably written at different times, and in complete independence of each other. It is with the older of these, the *Descensus*, assigned to the second or third century, that we are concerned here.[2]

The *Descensus* contains a lively and dramatic account of Christ's descent into Hades in the interval between the Crucifixion and the Resurrection, of his breaking down the gates, of his binding Satan, and of his releasing the souls of the patriarchs from their long imprisonment. The most vivacious part of the narrative, and the part which is most directly related to the drama, is found in the following passage of the Latin version:[3]

Et cum hæc ad invicem loquerentur Satan princeps et inferus, subito facta est vox ut tonitruum et spiritualis clamor: *Tollite portas, principes, vestras, et elevamini, portæ æternales,*[4] *et introibit rex gloriæ.* Hæc audiens inferus dixit ad Satan principem: Recede a me et exi de meis sedibus foras; si potens es præliator, pugna adversum regem gloriæ. . . . Hæc autem audiens omnis multitudo sanctorum cum voce increpationis dixerunt ad inferum: Aperi portas tuas ut intret rex gloriæ. . . . Hæc autem audientes omnes sancti ab Esaia dixerunt ad inferum: Aperi portas tuas: nunc victus, infirmus et impotens eris. Et facta est vox magna ut tonitruum dicens: *Tollite portas, principes, vestras, et elevamini,*

---

[1] In certain of the texts examined above this theme is touched upon fleetingly, as, for example, in the verses *Hæc est alma dies* and in the responsory *Recessit pastor noster.* See pp. 131, 144. For bibliography see Notes, p. 561.

[2] See A. Harnack, *Geschichte der altchristlichen Litteratur,* i, Leipzig, 1893, pp. 21–4; E. von Dobschütz, *Gospel of Nicodemus,* in

Hastings, *Bible,* iii, 544–7. For the text see Tischendorf, *Evangelia,* pp. 389 sqq.

[3] Tischendorf, *Evangelia,* pp. 397–400. I have italicized the sentences with which we are chiefly concerned here.

[4] As Tischendorf suggests (p. 397), *æternales* and *infernales* appear to have exchanged places occasionally in the MS.

portæ infernales,[1] *et introibit rex gloriæ.* Videns inferus quia duabus vicibus hæc clamaverunt, quasi ignorans dicit: *Quis est rex gloriæ?* Respondens David ad inferum ait: Ista verba clamoris cognosco, quoniam ego eadem per spiritum eius vaticinatus sum. Et nunc quæ supra dixi dico tibi: *Dominus fortis et potens, dominus potens in prælio, ipse est rex gloriæ.* Et ipse dominus de cælo in terris prospexit ut audiret gemitus compeditorum et ut solveret filios interemptorum. Et nunc, spurcissime et fœtidissime infere, aperi portas tuas ut intret rex gloriæ. Hæc dicente David ad inferum supervenit in forma hominis dominus maiestatis, et æternas tenebras illustravit et indissolubilia vincula disrupit: et invictæ virtutis auxilium visitavit nos sedentes in profundis tenebris delictorum et in umbra mortis peccatorum. . . . Tunc rex gloriæ maiestate sua conculcans mortem et comprehendens Satan principem tradidit inferi potestati, et attraxit Adam ad suam claritatem.

It would be convenient to infer that for their representations of the Harrowing of Hell the dramatic writers of the Middle Ages used this passage directly, arranging it as a dialogue, and adopting its suggestions as to impersonation. Before drawing this inference, however, we are bound to consider certain resemblances between the narrative of the *Descensus* and passages both in the Vulgate and in the liturgy itself. The following, for example, are the last four verses of the twenty-fourth Psalm:

Attollite portas, principes, vestras, et elevamini, portæ æternales, et introibit rex gloriæ.

Quis est iste rex gloriæ? Dominus fortis et potens, Dominus potens in prælio.

Attollite portas, principes, vestras, et elevamini, portæ æternales, et introibit rex gloriæ.

Quis est iste rex gloriæ? Dominus virtutum, ipse est rex gloriæ.

These verses constitute a triumphal procession of some sort, quite separate in origin from the rest of the psalm, and representing in some way the source of the parallel passages in the *Descensus*.[2] The dramatic effect of this passage cannot have escaped those who sang the psalm antiphonally in the Canonical Office;[3] and this effect is reinforced by the use of at least one of these sentences in other liturgical pieces, such as the following gradual of one of the Masses in Advent:[4]

[1] As Tischendorf suggests (p. 397), *æternales* and *infernales* appear to have exchanged places occasionally in the MS.

[2] See B. Duhm, *Die Psalmen*, Tübingen, 1922, pp. 102–3; G. H. A. von Ewald, *Commentary on the Psalms*, i, London, 1880, pp. 79–82. In our present study the relation of the verses of the psalm to the parallels in the *Evangelium Nicodemi* is of no great importance. The psalm-verses are, of course, the earlier.

[3] On the singing of psalms see above, p. 51.

[4] Migne, *P. L.*, lxxviii, 643. For other

Tollite portas, principes, vestras, et elevamini, portæ æternales, et introibit rex gloriæ. Versus: Quis ascendet in montem Domini, aut quis stabit in loco sancto ejus? Innocens manibus, et mundo corde.

Most impressive of all are the uses of the formula *Tollite portas* at the city gates or at the church door in the processions of Palm Sunday and of the ceremony for dedicating a church-building, which have been described in an earlier chapter.[1] The latter of these ceremonies, as we have observed, includes a personage hidden within the church to represent, or symbolize, Satan, whose eventual expulsion from the building directly reflects the story of the Harrowing of Hell as narrated in the *Descensus*. The other interrelations which may have existed among the Gospel of Nicodemus, the psalter, the choral passages of the regular liturgy, and the special dramatic processions, it would probably be idle to attempt to calculate. Of the bearing of all these forms upon the dramatic ceremonies of the sepulchre we may judge as we proceed.

Before examining the versions of *Depositio* and *Elevatio*, however, we must pause over one more liturgical piece of some importance in the development that we are considering. This is the following famous antiphon: [2]

Cum rex gloriæ Christus infernum debellaturus intraret, et chorus angelicus ante faciem ejus portas principum tolli præciperet, sanctorum populus, qui tenebatur in morte captivus, voce lacrimabili clamaverat: Advenisti desiderabilis, quem expectabamus in tenebris, ut educeres hac nocte vinculatos de claustris. Te nostra vocabant suspiria; te larga requirebant tormenta; tu factus es spes desperatis, magna consolatio in tormentis.

This *Canticum triumphale*, as it has been appropriately named, was frequently used in the processions of Easter.[3] It obviously reflects the story in the *Descensus*, but it may have been composed under the influence of a sermon on this theme often assigned to St Augustine.[4] For our present purpose it may be regarded as an independent liturgical composition, available for

liturgical uses of the hortatory *Tollite portas* see Hartker, pp. 15–6, 327: Wagner, p. 113. For evidences of the *Descensus* theme in the liturgy see Cabrol and Leclercq, iv, 682–93; Kretzmann, pp. 120–1; Schmidt, p. 23; Young, *Harrowing of Hell*, pp. 892–5.

[1] See above, pp. 92, 103.
[2] Chevalier, *R. H.*, no. 4103, printed by Daniel, *Thesaurus*, ii, 315.

[3] See Cabrol and Leclercq, iv, 690; Marbach, pp. 540–1; Grünewald, pp. 67–8; Wilmart, pp. 38, 104–5.
[4] See Cabrol and Leclercq, iv, 690–1; Marbach, p. 541; Kretzmann, p. 126. The sermon, often referred to as 'Sermo clx. De Pascha II. Alias de Tempore 137', may be seen in Migne, *P. L.*, xxxix, 2059–61.

any festal ceremony, and destined for conspicuous use in the *Elevatio*.

It is to this ceremony of the Resurrection, rather than to the *Depositio*, that the theme of the Harrowing of Hell naturally attaches itself; hence the primary purpose of the pages that follow is to describe a particular development within the *Elevatio*.[1] In this survey, however, I shall include with each version of the *Elevatio* the related *Depositio*, if it is extant. In grouping the texts I shall not be essentially guided, as in the preceding chapter, by the nature of the object, or objects, used in the burial ceremony.

II

MAGDEBURG

The simplest treatment of the theme of the *Descensus* is the mere insertion in the *Elevatio* of the antiphon *Cum rex gloriæ*. This use may be seen in the dramatic ceremonies used in the fifteenth century in the cathedral of Magdeburg:[2]

⟨DEPOSITIO CRUCIS⟩[3]

Quando hora nona reddidit, parabunt eciam ymaginarium Sepulcrum Domini ante altare Sancti Laurencii, vbi eciam subcustos tempore suo habebit duos lapides ad sepulturam Crucis necessarios, et duo mundissima linthea alba, quorum vnum Cruci substernetur et alio cooperietur, quia Ioseph corpus Domini inuoluit in syndone munda. . . . | Completo officio[4] et preparamentis depositis, archiepiscopus et seniores domini tollent Crucem et deuotissime ferent ad preparatum locum ymaginarii Sepulcri. Et precedent eos duo thuribularii et predicti duo pueri canonici in albis cum candelis ardentibus. Et portando Crucem cantabitur submisse responsorium:

Ecce quomodo moritur,

et responsorium:

Sicut ouis,

cum suis versibus et repeticionibus. Et substernetur Cruci ab episcopo mundissimum lintheum, et alio lintheo mundissimo operietur, quia, vt supra dictum est, Ioseph inuoluit corpus Domini syndone munda. Et

---

Schmidt (pp. 23–4) examines the resemblances between the antiphon and the sermon in some detail.

[1] We need not concern ourselves with the theological dispute (see Meyer, pp. 62, 99–100) as to whether Christ invaded Hell as a spirit (*i.e.* before the Resurrection) or in the flesh (*i.e.* after the Resurrection). The playwrights, consciously or unconsciously, treated the matter with great freedom.

[2] Berlin, Staatsbibl., MS theol. lat. 4º. 113, Ordin. Magdeburgense sæc. xv, fol. 82ᵛ, 84ᵛ, 88ʳ–88ᵛ, published by Brooks, *Sepulchre*, p. 103. For the related *Visitatio Sepulchri* see below, p. 630. Concerning associated texts see Notes, p. 561.

[3] Berlin MS 4º. 113, fol. 82ᵛ, 84ᵛ.

[4] The reference is to Vespers.

sic cum deuotione et reuerencia locabitur in Sepulcro. Ponentur eciam ab archiepiscopo duo lapides, vnus ad caput Crucis et alius ad pedes. Deinde, Cruce thurificata ab episcopo, cantatur responsorium:

Sepulto Domino,

cum versu et repeticione. Et tunc dicet episcopus versum:

In pace factus est locus eius,

respondente conuentu:

Et in Syon ha⟨bitatio⟩ eius.

Et tunc ceroferarii et thuribularii ad sacrarium reuertentur.

⟨ELEVATIO CRUCIS⟩ [1]

In sancta nocte Pasce ante pulsationem Matutinarum veniet archiepiscopus et domini canonici ad monasterium et alii qui voluerint, et precedent eos ad ymaginarium Sepulcrum duo domini cum thuribulis, et deinde duo cum cereis quos accipient in sanctuario, inter cereos septem proximos extremis. Et archiepiscopus Crucem discooperiens thurificabit. Et tunc archiepiscopus et maiores domini cum multa | veneratione eleuantes Crucem cantabunt omnes submisse, archiepiscopo inchoante,

Cum rex glorie.

Tunc prepulsabuntur Matutine. Et sic cantantes reuerenter portabunt Crucem retro summum altare et sistent eam ante sedem episcopalem, ponentes hinc et inde duo candelabra cum candelis. Ibi salutabunt eam qui volunt.

The most noteworthy aspect of the *Depositio* here is the use of two linen cloths and two stones. One cloth is placed under, and one over, the buried cross, in imitation of the act of Joseph of Arimathea. The use of two stones, one at the head and the other at the foot of the cross, we now encounter for the first time.[2] The ceremonial of the *Elevatio* is extremely simple, the cross being merely uncovered and censed, and then carried to the main altar while the chorus sings *Cum rex gloriæ* as a processional. Since this antiphon is the only utterance, the ceremony would seem to be dominated by the theme of the Harrowing of Hell; but of this situation there is no recognition in the accompanying action.

The opening of the way towards dramatic action is suggested in a version of the *Elevatio* from Zurich: [3]

[1] Berlin MS 4º. 113, fol. 88ʳ–88ᵛ.

[2] Concerning the use of cloths and a stone see above, pp. 134, 142.

[3] Zurich, Zentralbibl., MS C. 8 b, Brev. chori Turicensis anni 1260, fol. 51ᵛ–52ʳ, 54ᵛ–55ʳ, previously edited by Brooks, *Sepulchre*, p. 109. The passages enclosed within square brackets are written in the MS by a somewhat later hand, over erasures, between the lines, or in the margins. The *Depositio* is

⟨Depositio Crucis⟩ [1]

Tam ipse [sacerdos] ferens aliquam Crucem uelatam quam omnes canoni|ci, habentes in manibus candelas accensas cum diuersis turibulis, per hostium altaris Sancte Marie ad altare Martyrum procedentes, remisse cantant responsorium:

Recessit pastor [*noster*]. Versus: *Ante cuius conspectum* [*hodie portas mortis*].

Psalmus: *Miserere mei, Deus*, vel psalmus: *Notus in Iudea*.

[Interdum tamen ambo psalmi leguntur.]

Versus: *In pace factus est locus eius.*

Postea dicit sacerdos orationem:

Omnipotens sempiterne Deus, [*fac nos ita Dominice Passionis sacramenta peragere vt indulgentiam percipere mereamur. Per Christum Dominum nostrum*].

Sed interim dum legitur [predictus psalmus] *Miserere mei, Deus,* [uel psalmus *Notus in Iudea Deus*], sacerdotes predictam paruam Crucem ponunt et signando claudunt in archam que intra testudinem retro altare Martyrum, candido uelo circumpendente, posita Sepulchrum Dominicum representat. Nam contra omnem rationem est quod in quibusdam ecclesiis Eucharistia in huiusmodi archa sepulchrum representante poni consueuit et claudi. Ibi enim Eucharistia, que est uerum et uiuum Corpus Christi, ipsum Christi corpus mortuum representat, quod est indecens penitus et absurdum. In reditu uoce remissa cantatur responsorium:

Sepulto Domino. Versus: *Ne forte ueniant* [*ponentes milites*].

Et candelis edituo restitutis, a binis et binis Vespere dicuntur.

⟨Elevatio Crucis⟩ [2]

In Sancta Nocte Pasche ad Visitationem Sepulchri.

Ante pulsationem Matutini canonici per seruos editui latenter conuocati, cum turibulis et candelis accensis [solummodo superpelliciati], procedentes per hostium altaris Sancte Marie cantant remisse:

Cum rex glorie.

Sed ad Sepulchrum legitur psalmus *Domine, probasti me*, per totum. Sequitur *Kyrieleyson. Pater noster.* Versus *In resurrectione tua, Christe.* Oratio *Deus, qui hodierna die per unigenitum tuum.* Et dum hec [fiunt] a canonicis, sacerdos cum suis ministris in|trat testudinem et locum Sepulchri, et inde tollit linteum, et facit alia que representant Resurrectionem. In redeundo per hostium cancellorum canitur, uoce remissa, *Terra tremuit.* Et edituo candele resti[tu]untur.

---

preceded by the communion of the Mass of the Presanctified. For the related *Visitatio Sepulchri* see below, p. 314.

[1] Zurich MS C. 8b, fol. 51ᵛ–52ʳ.
[2] Zurich MS C. 8b, fol. 54ᵛ–55ʳ.

Et nota [quod concanonicus noster, Heinricus Sluzzelli emerit predium in Niderun Glatta, soluens annuatim ii quatrinos, sic instituens de consensu prepositi et capellani ut thesaurarius ecclesie Turicensis qui] pro tempore fuerit, candelas que habentur a canonicis et clericis in Parasceue ad representandum dominicam sepulturam et quas habent in sancta nocte ad uisitationem Sepulchri ex officio suo tenetur dare distribuere et postmodum a singulis redditas fideliter conseruare.

Visitatione Sepulchri finita, more sollempni pulsatur Matutinum.

Particularly arresting in the *Depositio* from Zurich is the passage, already referred to, in which we are given the reason for excluding the Host from the burial ceremony: the inappropriateness of using the *verum et vivum corpus Christi* to represent the *Christi corpus mortuum*.[1] In the *Elevatio* the antiphon *Cum rex gloriæ* is employed merely as the processional for the approach to the sepulchre. More important is the rubric *Et facit ⟨sacerdos⟩ alia quæ representant Resurrectionem.* This seems to give to the officiating priest a certain latitude in introducing bits of ceremonial; and it indicates that what is prescribed in the rubrics of the sepulchre ceremonies is only part of the dramatic movement which actually occurred.

Although the *Elevatio* from Eichstätt shows no advance towards a fuller representation of the Harrowing of Hell, it contains other novelties which must be noticed here. The form which the two sepulchre offices took in this diocese may be represented by the following:[2]

⟨DEPOSITIO CRUCIS ET HOSTIÆ⟩ [3]

Demum sacerdos cum particulis minoribus retentis et calice vacuo ac Cruce quam prius subdiaconi gestabant, procedat ad Sepulchrum et hec in Sepulchro honorifice recondat, choro submissa voce canente responsorium:

> *Recessit pastor noster,*

et responsorium:

> *Ecce quomodo moritur iustus.*

Et ibidem Vespere sub silentio.

---

[1] See above, p. 132.

[2] The text of the *Depositio* is from *Missale secundum Chorum et Ritum Eiistetensis Ecclesie,* Nuremberg, 1517, fol. lxxxvʳ. This volume contains no *Elevatio* or *Visitatio Sepulchri.* The text of the *Elevatio* is from Munich, Staatsbibl., MS lat. 3918, Ordin. Eystettense sæc. xiv, fol. 75ʳ–75ᵛ. This MS contains no *Depositio.* Both texts have been printed, with further bibliography, by Young, *Dramatic Associations,* pp. 104–6. For the related *Visitatio Sepulchri* see below, p. 283. In regard to associated versions of the *Depositio* and *Elevatio* see Notes, p. 562.

[3] *Missale,* Nuremberg, 1517, fol. lxxxvʳ. The *Depositio* is preceded by the communion of the Mass of the Presanctified.

⟨ELEVATIO CRUCIS ET HOSTIÆ⟩ [1]

Incipit ordo in festo sancte Pasce. Item ante Matutinum itur ad Sepulchrum et canuntur antiphone subscripte. Et tres domini simul cantent preuiam antiphonam: [2]

Ad monumentum venimus gementes, angelum Domini sedentem vidimus et dicentem quia surrexit Ihesus.

Primus eorum canit antiphonam sequentem:

Surrexit Dominus de sepulchro, qui pro nobis pependit in ligno, alleluia.

Secundus eorum canit antiphonam:

Surrexit Christus et illuxit populo suo, quem redemit sangwine suo, alleluia.

Tercius canit antiphonam:

Venit Maria nuncians discipulis; Quia vidi Dominum, alleluia.

Deinde legantur orationes que in Parasceve [3] legebantur ante Crucem flexis genibus, scilicet:

Domine Ihesu Christe, gloriosissime conditor,

et cetera, ut supra patescunt.[4] Finitis autem orationibus, portatur Corpus Christi ad chorum sew ad locum suum deputatum, et canitur antiphona subscripta: |

Cum rex glorie Christus infernum debellaturus intraret, et chorus angelicus ante faciem eius portas [5] principum tolli preciperet, sanctorum populus qui tenebatur in morte captiuus voce lacrimabili clamauerat: Advenisti desiderabilis, quem exspectabamus in tenebris, ut educeres hac nocte vinculatos de claustris. Te nostra vocabant suspiria, te larga requirebant lamenta; tu factus es spes desperatis, magna consolacio in tormentis.[6]

It appears that the Eucharist used in the *Depositio* before us is not a separate Host consecrated for this special purpose, but certain particles retained from the preceding Mass of the Presanctified. The rubrics seem to indicate that the cross is buried also, although this second object is not mentioned in the *Elevatio*.[7] The significance of this latter ceremony lies not so much in the use of the antiphon *Cum rex gloriæ*, which is still a mere processional, as in the approach to a dramatic treatment of the visit of the three Marys to the empty tomb. At the opening of the *Elevatio*, three clerics together sing *Ad monumentum venimus*, and then each in turn sings a separate antiphon. In all these utterances it is assumed that the Resurrection has already

---

[1] Munich MS lat. 3918, fol. 75ʳ–75ᵛ.

[2] antiphonam] antiphanam (MS). Same spelling in the succeeding two rubrics.

[3] Parasceve] parascave (MS).

[4] patescunt] Reading uncertain (MS).

[5] portas] portans (MS).

[6] Followed by the rubric *Deinde Matutinum peragitur more suo.*

[7] Brooks (*Sepulchre*, pp. 35–6) expresses doubt as to there having been two objects in the sepulchre.

occurred, and one of them is taken directly from the Gospel narrative concerning the Marys.[1] It scarcely need be said that the introduction of this theme while the *Corpus Christi* still lies in the sepulchre results in a patent incongruity. Of this particular ineptitude we shall see other examples below.[2]

We may bring forward, finally, one more example of the *Elevatio* in which the story of the *Descensus* is represented merely by the processional use of the antiphon *Cum rex gloriæ*. This office, from the monastery of Prüfening, demands consideration because it, and the related *Depositio*, contain unusual evidences of dramatic realism. The texts of the two ceremonies are as follows:[3]

⟨Depositio Crucis et Hostiæ⟩[4]

Deinde Dominus Abbas et qui Crucem cum eo portat imponunt responsorium *Vadis propiciator*, cum quo cantu fit processio de choro ad monasterium, et precedit primo conuentus, deinde ministri, videlicet diaconus et subdiaconus, post hos duo iuuenes cum candelis, vltimo portitores Crucis; et fit stacio ante altare Sancte Crucis quod antea a custode loco Dominici Sepulchri lintheo magno specialiter ad hoc apto velatum existit.[5] . . . Quibus omnibus rite expeditis, singulis rursum genua flectentibus, cantor imponit antiphonam *Super omnia ligna cedrorum*, tractim a choro canendam; qua inchoata, Dominus Abbas et qui cum eo Crucem tenuit Ymaginem Crucifixi coram populo de Cruce deponunt, quam Dominus Abbas intra velum ante altare Sancte Crucis protensum in eodem altari vice Dominici Sepulchri preparato ponit et pannis ac lintheis ibidem positis reuerenter operit. Crucem vero in qua dicta Ymago pependit custos per ministrum suum ad locum debitum deportari facit. Ipse vero mox chorum ingrediens scrineum reliquiarum retro altare in quo Corpus Dominicum reconditum est aperit, aspersoriumque cum turribulo ut ibidem habeantur et reliqua necessaria pro communione sancta rite disponit.[6] . . .

De Corpore Dominico in sarcofago in altari Sancte Crucis loco

---

[1] For the 'antiphon' *Venit Maria* see John xx, 18. Concerning the opening utterance *Ad monumentum* see below, pp. 258, 268. For the antiphons *Surrexit Dominus* and *Surrexit Christus* see Hartker, pp. 240, 241; Migne, *P. L.*, lxxviii, 775, 776.

[2] See pp. 301 sqq.

[3] Munich, Staatsbibl., MS lat. 12018, Ordin. Pruveningense sæc. xv–xvi, fol. 64v, 65v, 66v–67v, 73v–74v, previously edited by Brooks, *Sepulchre*, pp. 105–7. The MS contains no *Visitatio Sepulchri*. For texts that may be associated with those before us see Notes, p. 562.

[4] Munich MS lat. 12018, fol. 64v, 65v, 66v–67v. The text as printed here is immediately preceded by the *Improperia* of the Adoration of the Cross.

[5] The passage omitted here (fol. 64v–65v) concerns the continuation of the Adoration of the Cross. My text (fol. 65v) then brings this ceremony to its conclusion.

[6] The passage omitted here (fol. 65v–66v) concerns the communion of the Mass of the Presanctified.

Dominici Sepulchri preparato recondendo. Expeditis | omnibus supradictis, postquam Dominus Abbas, reposito iam retro altare Sacramento, redierit ad altare, sumit[1] capsulam alteram in quam prius particulam vnam Eucharistie reposuit, et defert eam sub casula ad altare Sancte Crucis, vice Dominici Sepulchri preparatum. Et precedit eum totus conuentus processionaliter de choro egredientes et ante Sepulchrum in vtroque choro stacionem facturi. Et post conuentum secuntur duo ceroferarii et altaris ministri eo ordine quo supra in deportacione Sacramenti precesserant, post hos Dominus Abbas cum Sacramento, deinde capellanus. Custos autem prouideat ut illico quinque lampades circa Sepulchrum locentur, moxque incendantur vsque ante Nocturnos in sancta nocte Dominice Resurreccionis iugiter arsure, que tamen cum ceteris luminibus hac proxima nocte ad Matutinum extinguuntur; post hoc autem vice uersa incenduntur. In ipso autem egressu processionis de choro cantor imponit responsorium *Ecce quomodo moritur iustus.* Quo cantato in ipsa stacione, sequitur responsorium *Recessit pastor noster;* deinde antiphona *Ioseph ab Arimathia;* post hoc, responsorium *Sepulto Domino.* Dictorum vero responsoriorum versus cantare debent cantores ante Sepulchrum. Insuper est notandum quod ceroferarii Sepulchrum non ingrediuntur sed, candelabris ante Sepulchrum in vtroque choro in terra locatis, stabunt ad loca sua; nec extinguuntur ille candele vsque ad finem Vesperarum. Dominus Abbas vero et ministri nec non capellanus huius Sepulchrum, idest intra velum ante altare Sancte Crucis circumtensum, ingrediuntur. Est autem in ipso altari prius per custodem sarcophagum quoddam reliquiarum positum in quod mox ut Dominus Abbas ingreditur reponit capsam cum Corpore Dominico, statimque cum ministris et capellano legit responsorium *Ecce quomodo;* responsorium *Recessit pastor;* antiphonam *Joseph ab Arimathia.* Deinde claudit Dominus Abbas sarcofagum. Quo clauso et lintheis quibus et Ymago Crucifixi operta est cooperto, subiungunt responsorium *Sepulto Domino.* Versus autem predictorum responsoriorum pronuncientur a capellano. Deinde subiungit Dominus Abbas versiculum *Tu autem, Domine, miserere mei.* Respondent ministri *Et resuscita me et retribuam eis.* Dominus Abbas dicit *Dominus vobiscum. Oremus: Omnipotens sempiterne Deus, qui Christi filii tui beatam passionem.* Et concludit hanc collectam cum particula *Per eundem Christum Dominum nostrum.* Respondent ministri *Amen.* Deinde tam Dominus Abbas quam ministri flexis genibus dicentes *Pater Noster,* denuoque surgentes similiter orent versus in Sepulchro secundum rubricam infra scriptam. Quibus dictis, Dominus Abbas aqua benedicta aspergit et deinde | thurificat tam sarcofagum Sacramenti quam Ymaginem Crucifixi. Quo facto, Dominus Abbas et ministri et capellanus non expectantes conuentum mox ad chorum vel ad sacristiam vadunt et vestibus sacris se exuunt.

---

[1] sumit] summit (MS).

⟨Elevatio Hostiæ et Imaginis Resurrectionis⟩ [1]

⟨F⟩estum Resurreccionis Domini nostri Ihesu Christi in summis et in septem luminibus solemnissimo et deuotissimo ritu agitur. Igitur in sancta nocte, instante iam hora vndecima aut paulo antea, custos Ymaginem Dominice Resurreccionis ponit in Sepulchro Domini, id est in altari Sancte Crucis. Deinde disponit pontificalia pro Domino Abbate, et tam pro eo quam pro capellano et duobus ceroferariis superpellicia et cappas in altari Apostolorum locat. Moxque in dormitorio fit excitacio fratrum cum campanella. Pulsus vero in ecclesia non fit, sed differtur vsque post processionem infrascriptam. Conueniunt itaque Dominus Abbas et fratres in ecclesiam ante altare Apostolorum, vbi Dominus Abbas pontificalibus, humerali, superpellicio, stola et cappa induitur. Capellanus quoque et duo ceroferarii iuuenes similiter superpelliciis et cappis induuntur. Moxque ad Sepulchrum Domini omnes procedunt et hoc ordine: primo precedunt duo conuersi vel iuuenes deferentes duo candelabra cum candelis accensis, sicut in solemnibus processionibus processioni post vexilla solent preferri. Deinde conuentus per ordinem bini et bini; post hoc duo iuuenes ceroferarii, superpelliciis et cappis induti, cum candelis | accensis et cimbalis postea ante Sacramentum pulsandis. Hos sequitur Dominus Abbas et capellanus. Cumque ante Sepulchrum, id est ante altare Sancte Crucis extra velum, singuli ordinate circumsteterint, Domino Abbate incipiente submissa voce, dicunt per choros hos psalmos: *Miserere mei, Deus, miserere mei, quoniam in te confidit; Domine probasti*; continuando sub vno *Gloria Patri*. Deinde Dominus Abbas vicissim cum conuentu dicit *Confiteor Deo Patri*, et cetera, more consueto. Post hoc ingreditur Dominus Abbas cum capellano intra velum ad altare Sancte Crucis, et primo aspergit aqua benedicta et thurificat sarchofagum Sacramenti, deinde Ymaginem Crucifixi, lintheis ab inde depositis post thurificacionem. Moxque ipse Dominus Abbas leni et mediocri voce incipit antiphonam *Alleluia, exurge, gloria mea*, quam chorus complet addendo sub nota consueta versum *Christe salus rerum*; versum *Pollicitam sed redde fidem*; versum *Redde tuam faciem*. Interim Dominus Abbas cum debita reuerencia capsam Sacramenti de sarcophago reliquiarum tollit. Et capellanus Ymaginem Resurreccionis accipit, altera Ymagine Crucifixi in altari relicta. Moxque finitis versibus predictis, cantor imponit *Surrexit pastor bonus*, cum quo cantu processionaliter redeunt ad altare Apostolorum, conuentu precedente ordine quo prius; secunturque conuentum ceroferarii cum candelis accensis et sonantibus cimbalis; deinde Dominus Abbas deferens Sacramentum; postea capellanus cum Ymagine Resurreccionis. Cumque ante altare Apostolorum steterit conuentus per choros singuli in ordine suo in ipso accessu Domini Abbatis cum Sacramento, omnes veniam super genua petunt, donec Dominus Abbas, versa ad conuentum

---

[1] Munich MS lat. 12018, fol. 73ᵛ–74ᵛ.

facie, cum capsa Sacramenti pro benediccione signum crucis faciat et sic eciam deinceps et in choro similiter fiat. Finito autem predicto cantu et addito in fine *Alleluia,* mox sine intermissione imponit cantor antiphonam:

Cum rex glorie,

quam cantando fit processio per ambitum, itemque reditur ad altare Apostolorum ordine suprascripto. Finita autem antiphona predicta, imponit cantor *Surgens Ihesus Dominus noster,*[1] addito in fine *Alleluia.* Deinde subiungit Dominus Abbas versiculum *In resurreccione tua, Christe, alleluia. Dominus vobiscum. Oremus: Deus, qui ad eternam vitam in Christi resurreccione nos reparas, ita concludendo Ihesus Christus, Filius tuus, Dominus noster.* Respondet conuentus *Amen.* Moxque processionaliter intrando ad chorum ordine quo supra, cantore imponente, cantantur hii versus: *O vere digna hostia; Gloria tibi, Domine, qui surrexisti a mortuis.*[2] Et relinquitur Ymago Dominice Resurreccionis in altari Apostolorum. Capsam vero Dominici Sacramenti Dominus Abbas, pre|cedentibus eum cero-'ferariis cum cimbalis, defert ad chorum, factoque ante summum altare versus conuentum pro benedictione signo crucis, retro altare vadit et ipsum Sacramentum in scrinio reliquiarum super altari viatico, vbi et in Cena Domini et in Parasceue Sacramentum reconditum erat, honorifice reponit, locumque ipsum mox aqua benedicta aspergit et thurificat, custosque cum diligencia claudit. Rediensque Dominus Abbas ante summum altare, pontificalibus aliisque ornamentis exuitur, similiter et capellanus et ceroferarii superpelliciis et cappis exuuntur. Post hoc inmediate fit pulsus cum omnibus campanis, deinde bine et bine campane pulsantur, itemque omnes simul compulsantur, sicut in maximis festis fieri solet. Sub hoc autem pulsu tolluntur de altari Sancte Crucis per custodem linthea quibus sarchofagum et Ymago Crucifixi obuoluta erant, similiter et velum maius ante idem altare circumtensum deponitur. Ipsaque Ymago Crucifixi et sarchofagum reliquiarum ad locum suum deportantur. Lampades eciam que circa Sepulchrum ardebant extincte inde deponuntur. Candela vna in altari Apostolorum ante Ymaginem Resurreccionis accenditur, et vsque post Matutinas Laudes donec ipsa Ymago per custodem ad summum altare portetur, ardere permittitur.[3]

For the sepulchre at Prüfening is used the altar of the Holy Cross, upon which, or before which, is placed a box surrounded by curtains. The *Depositio* may be said to consist of two separate ceremonies. The first, immediately after the Adoration of the

---

[1] For a responsory of Easter Monday beginning thus see Hartker, p. 232.

[2] These verses are from the hymn *Ad cœnam agni,* for the full text of which see Notes, p. 562.

[3] What follows concerns the singing of Matins.

Cross, includes a special touch of realism in that, when the crucifix is brought to the sepulchre, the *Corpus*, or *Imago Crucifixi*, is detached from the cross before the eyes of the congregation, laid in the tomb, and covered with cloths. Meanwhile the bare cross itself is carried aside. In the second ceremony, after the Mass, a particle of the Eucharist remaining from the preceding communion is put into a box in the sepulchre, beside the *Imago Crucifixi*, and both the *Imago* and the box are wrapped in cloths.

For use in the *Elevatio* is placed in the sepulchre, before the participants arrive, a third object, the *Imago Resurrectionis*. This is presumably an image of Christ bearing in his hand some emblem of the Resurrection, such as a cross with a banner attached to it.[1] In the course of the ceremony the Eucharist and *Imago Resurrectionis* are taken up from the sepulchre and carried together to the altar of the Apostles, where the *Imago* is left, the Eucharist being taken eventually to a chest behind another altar. Meanwhile the *Imago Crucifixi*, which had been buried on Good Friday, is completely ignored, being left for the sacristan to remove privately, along with the sepulchre cloths and curtains, before the opening of Matins. The effort towards realism here consists essentially in the substitution of the *Imago Resurrectionis* for the *Imago Crucifixi*. The latter is the only object suitable for burial on Good Friday, whereas for issuing from the tomb on Easter morning, only the former object is appropriate.

III

Although the liturgical offices reviewed thus far are noteworthy for their apt and realistic symbolism, this ceremonial elaboration has not served to develop within the *Elevatio* the theme of the Harrowing of Hell latent in the antiphon *Cum rex gloriæ*. The fact is that the more vivid representation of the *Descensus ad inferos* arose not through action attached to this antiphon, but through the use of the dialogue *Tollite portas*, the origins of which have already been considered.[2] In surveying the dramatic adaptations of this dialogue, then, we begin with a brief form of *Elevatio* such as that found at Mainz:[3]

---

[1] Concerning the *Imago Resurrectionis* and *Imago Crucifixi* see above, p. 139.

[2] See above, pp. 149 sqq.

[3] Rome, Bibl. Vatic., MS Palat. lat. 448, Rituale-Agendum Moguntinum sæc. xv, fol. 51r–51v, 63r–63v, previously edited by Young, *Harrowing of Hell*, pp. 914–5. The MS contains no *Visitatio Sepulchri*.

MAINZ

⟨Depositio Crucis⟩ [1]

Completa communione, statim dicantur Vespere sub silentio sicut here. Post Vesperas sacerdos Corpus Domini in mundissima theca diligenter reconditum portetur ad locum ad hoc preparatum, et in eo quasi sepeliendo ponatur cum hoc responsorio:

> *Ecce quomodo moritur iustus, et nemo percipit corde; uiri iusti tolluntur, et nemo considerat; a facie iniquitatis sublatus est iustus, et erit in pace | memoriam eius.* Versus: *In pace factus est locus eius, et in Syon habitacio eius.*

In recessu cantatur hoc responsorium:

> *Sepulto Domino, signatum est monumentum; uoluentes lapidem ad[2] hostium monumenti; ponentes milites qui custodirent illud.* Versus: *Ne forte ueniant discipuli eius et furentur eum, et dicant plebi: Surrexit a mortuis. Ponentes.*

Ac ita usque in diem tercium lumina iii ibi iugiter ardencia cum magna cautela seruetur.

⟨Elevatio Crucis⟩ [3]

Hic nota quod in sacra nocte Paschali prope diem Matutine pulsentur. Et campanarius cum ipso sacerdote, ambo portantes incensum cruce et candela precedente[4] eos, uisitant locum ubi Crux Domini deposita est, et ipse sacerdos osculat stigmata Crucis et thurificet et aspergatur aqua | benedicta. Et sacerdos tollens Crucem procedens ad ostium templi quod aptum est ad hoc cantans submissa uoce antiphonam:

> *Tollite portas, principes, uestras, et eleuamini porte eternales.*

Et trudens ter ad ostium et cantat ter antiphonam suprascripta⟨m⟩. Hoc facto, sacerdos cantat sub silencio antiphonam hanc:

> *Cum rex glorie.*

Finita antiphona, sacerdos deponat Crucem clam in armarium uel ad locum sibi tunc deputatum; et tunc pulsantur Matutine.

Confining our attention to the *Elevatio*,[5] we observe that after the priest has kissed the *stigmata* of the body on the cross, he carries the crucifix forth and with it strikes the door of the church thrice, each time singing the antiphon *Tollite portas*. Then, after singing *Cum rex gloriæ* in a low voice, he puts the crucifix away in a cupboard. Although the realistic intention of this ceremonial is obvious, the dramatic possibilities are not carried very far. Apparently the door is not opened in response to the words *Tollite portas*, and certainly no dialogue is spoken.

---

[1] Rome MS Palat. lat. 448, fol. 51r–51v.
[2] ad] ab (MS).
[3] Rome MS Palat. lat. 448, fol. 63r–63v.
[4] precedente] procedente (MS).
[5] The *Depositio* mentions only the *Corpus*

Domini as being buried, and the *Elevatio*, only the crucifix. Brooks (*Sepulchre*, p. 36) suggests that '*Corpus Domini* would seem not to have its usual meaning here but to be equivalent to *Crux Domini*'.

A slight advance in these matters appears in the fifteenth-century practice of the monastery of St Gall, from which we have the following:[1]

⟨DEPOSITIO CRUCIS⟩[2]

Antiphona finita, omnes ascendunt circa altare et Dominus Abbas exuens casulam, stantes ante Crucem ad dextrum[3] cornu altaris cantantes responsorium:

Ecce quomodo, submissa voce. Versus: *In pace factus*. Repeticio: *Et erit*.

Post accipentes Crucem Dominus Abbas et seniores portantes ad Sepulchrum cantantes responsorium:

Sicut ouis. Versus: *In pace.* Repeticio: *Traditus.*

Interim ponent Crucem in Sepulcro et claudunt eum, ponentes ante Sepulchrum quatuor lumina iugiter ardentia, cantantes responsorium:

Sepulto Domino. Versus: *Ne forte.* Repeticio: *Ponentes mi⟨lites⟩.*

Deinde Dominus Abbas dicat versum *In pace factus est locus eius*; collecta *Respice, Domine*; et aspergens Sepulcrum aqua benedicta, et thurificetur cum incensu, et misse sunt.

⟨ELEVATIO CRUCIS⟩[4]

Ordo ad leuandum Crucem Sanctam in Sacratissima Nocte Pascali.

Parum ante Matutinas Dominus Abbas, prepositus decanus, custos, et seniores ad hoc deputati surgant diluculo, et induunt se albis et cappis, pergentes cum summa reuerencia, cum ministris portantes aquam benedictam cum incensu, et cum silencio, ad Sepulcrum. Et Dominus Abbas cum summo honore totaque deuotione flexis genibus deponat sudarium et linteamina cum quibus Sancta Crux est inuoluta, et aspergens aqua benedicta, et thurificetur cum incensu, et cantent submissa voce:

Christe, salus rerum. Versus: *Pollicitam*, vsque *Surge, sepulte meus.*

Et eleuantes Crucem de[5] Sepulchro cantent hos versus: *Solue cathenatus.* Versus: *Redde tuam faciem.* Quibus finitis, cantatur antiphona:

Cum rex glorie,

submissa voce, portantes Crucem ante chorum in monasterio. Antiphona finita, cantant antiphonam:

Attollite portas, prin⟨cipes⟩,

[1] St Gall, Stiftsbibl., MS 448, Ordin. San-gallense sæc. xv, pp. 102, 105, previously edited by Young, *Some Texts*, pp. 319–21, and by Young, *Dramatic Associations*, pp. 90–1. For the related *Visitatio Sepulchri* see below, p. 667. For further observations on the MS see Notes, p. 563.

[2] St Gall MS 448, p. 102. The antiphon mentioned at the beginning of the text is that of the *Magnificat* at Vespers.
[3] dextrum] dextram (MS).
[4] St Gall MS 448, p. 105.
[5] de] Written above *in* (MS).

tribus vicibus, pulsantes contra ianuam cum pede Crucis in signum redempcionis animarum ex limbo. Ad istum pulsum ianua aperitur. Postea ponatur Crux ante altare Beate Virginis, panno supposito ac lumine accenso, vt a populis adoretur. Deinde Dominus Abbas dica⟨t⟩ versum *In resurrectione tua, Christe.* Collecta *Presta, quesumus, omnipotens Deus.* Hys finitis, adorent Crucem osculando ac rigando lacrimis vulnera eius. Et tunc fiat compulsacio omnium campanarum, pulsantque tribus vicibus in signum Resurrectionis. Post hoc pulsantur Matutine.

In this version of the *Elevatio*, the processional *Cum rex gloriæ* accompanies the carrying of the cross to the door of the choir. Here the antiphon *Attollite portas* is sung thrice, and the door is struck three times with the shaft of the cross, *in signum redemptionis animarum ex limbo.* At the third striking, the door is opened, and the cross is placed before the altar of the Blessed Virgin for adoration by all present.

A far more impressive effort in the way of dramatic realism is to be observed in the following ceremonies from the monastery of Barking, near London: [1]

BARKING

⟨DEPOSITIO CRUCIS⟩ [2]

Cum autem Sancta Crux fuerit adorata, sacerdotes de loco predicto Crucem eleuantes incipiant antiphonam:

Super omnia ligna,

et choro illo subsequente totam concinant, cantrice incipiente. Deferant Crucem ad magnum altare, ibique in specie Ioseph et Nichodemi, de ligno deponentes Ymaginem, uulnera Crucifixi uino abluant et aqua. Dum autem hec fiunt, concinat conuentus responsorium:

Ecce quomodo moritur iustus,

sacerdote incipiente et cantrice respondente et conuentu succinente. Post uulnerum ablucionem cum candelabris et turribulo deferant illam ad Sepulcrum has [3] canentes antiphonas: *In pace in idipsum.* Antiphona *Habitabit.* Antiphona *Caro mea.* Cumque in predictum locum tapetum palleo auriculari quoque et lintheis nitidissimis decenter ornatum illam cum reuerencia locauerint, claudat sacerdos Sepulcrum et incipiat responsorium:

Sepulto Domino.

---

[1] Oxford, University College, MS 169, Ordin. Berkingense sæc. xv, pp. 108–9, 119–21, previously edited by Young, *Harrowing of Hell*, pp. 926–9; Young, *Dramatic Associations*, pp. 119–21; Tolhurst, i, 100, 107–8. For the related *Visitatio Sepulchri* see below, p. 381.

[2] Univ. Coll. MS 169, pp. 108–9.

[3] has] hac (MS).

Et tunc abbatissa offerat cereum, qui iugiter ardeat ante Sepulcrum, nec extinguatur donec Ymago in nocte Pasche post Matutinas de Sepulcro cum cereis et thure et processione resumpta, suo reponatur in loco. Hiis itaque gestis, redeat conuentus in chorum, | et sacerdos in uestiarium.

⟨ELEVATIO HOSTIÆ⟩ [1]

Nota quod secundum antiquam consuetudinem ecclesiasticam Resur-⟨r⟩exio Dominica celebrata fuit ante Matutinas, et ante aliquam campane pulsacionem in die Pasche. Et quoniam populorum concursus temporibus illis videbatur deuocione frigessere, et torpor humanus maxime accrescens, venerabilis Domina [2] Katerina de Suttone, tunc pastoralis cure gerens vicem, desiderans dictum torporem penitus exstirpare et fidelium deuocionem ad tam celeb⟨r⟩em celebracionem magis excitare, vnanimi consororum consensu instituit ut statim post iii responsorium Matutinarum die Pasche fieret Dominice Resur⟨r⟩exionis celebracio, et hoc modo statuetur processio.

In primis eat Domina Abbatissa cum toto conuentu et quibusdam sacerdotibus et clericis capis indutis, quolibet sacerdote et clerico palmam et candelam extinctam manu deferente [3]; intrent capellam Sancte Marie Magdalene, figurantes animas sanctorum Patrum ante | aduentum Christi ad inferos descendentes, et claudant sibi ostium dicte capelle. Deinde superueniens sacerdos ebdomadarius ad dictam capellam appropians alba indutus et capa, cum duobus diaconis, vno Crucem deferente cum uexillo dominico desuper pendente, altero [4] cum turribulo manu sua baiulante, et aliis sacerdotibus et clericis cum duobus pueris cereos deferentibus, ad ostium dicte capelle incipiens ter hanc antiphonam:

Tollite portas.

Qui quidem sacerdos representabit personam Christi ad inferos descensuram et portas inferni dirupturam, et predicta antiphona vnaquaque uice in altiori uoce incipiatur, quam clerici tociens eandem repetant, et ad quamquam incepcionem pulset cum Cruce ad predictum ostium, figurans dirupcionem portarum inferni; et tercia pulsacione ostium aperiat. Deinde ingrediatur ille cum ministris suis. Interim incipiat quidam sacerdos in capella existens [5] antiphonam:

A porta inferi,

quam subinferat cantrix cum toto conventu:

Erue, Domine,

---

[1] Univ. Coll. MS 169, pp. 119–21. The text is immediately preceded by the third responsory *Dum transisset*, concerning which see below, pp. 232–3.

[2] Domina] Written twice (MS).
[3] deferente] deferentem (MS).
[4] altero] albo (MS).
[5] existens] existente (MS).

et cetera.[1] Deinde extrahet sacerdos ebdomadarius omnes essentes in capella predicta, et interim incipiat sacerdos antiphonam:

Domine, abstraxisti,

et cantrix subsequatur:

Ab inferis.[2]

Tunc omnes exeant de capella, id est, de limbo Patrum, et cantent sacerdotes et clerici antiphonam:

Cum rex glorie,

processionaliter per medium chori ad Sepulcrum portantes singuli palmam et candelam, designantes victoriam de hoste recuperatam, subsequentibus Domina Abbatissa, priorissa, et toto conuentu sicut sunt priores.

Et cum ad Sepulcrum peruenerint, sacerdos | ebdomadarius Sepulcrum thurificet et intret Sepulcrum incipiendo versum *Consurgit.*[3] Deinde subsequatur cantrix *Christus tumulo.*[4] Versus *Quesumus, auctor.* Versus *Gloria tibi, Domine.* Et interim asportabit Corpus Dominicum de Sepulcro incipiendo antiphonam *Christus resurgens,* coram altari, verso uultu ad populum, tenendo Corpus Dominicum in manibus suis inclusum cristallo. Deinde subiungat cantrix *Ex mortuis.* Et cum dicta antiphona faciant processionem ad altare Sancte Trinitatis cum solenni apparatu, videlicet cum turribulis et cereis. Conuentus sequatur cantando predictam antiphonam cum versu *Dicant nunc,*[5] et uersiculo[6] *Dicite in nacionibus.* Oratio *Deus qui pro nobis Filium tuum.* Et hec processio figuratur per hoc quomodo Christus procedit post Resur⟨r⟩exionem in Galileam, sequentibus discipulis.[7]

The *Depositio* of Barking may be regarded as a direct continuation of the Adoration of the Cross. Especially striking, in the way of realism, is the detaching of the *Corpus* from the cross, and the washing of the wounds painted upon the figure (*vulnera Crucifixi*).[8] By the rubric *in specie Joseph et Nichodemi* one is strongly tempted to infer impersonation; but this temptation, probably, must be resisted.

From the generous rubrics of the *Elevatio,* we learn that the present form of this office is due to the reform of Katherine of Sutton, abbess of Barking from 1363 to 1376.[9] Although she recognizes the tradition of placing the *Elevatio before* Easter

---

[1] The antiphon is *A porta inferi erue, Domine, animam meam.* See Hartker, p. 225.

[2] The antiphon is *Domine, abstraxisti ab inferis animam meam.* See Hartker, p. 223.

[3] This verse and the two that follow are from the hymn *Ad cœnam agni,* printed below, p. 562.

[4] tumulo] timulo (MS).

[5] In regard to this antiphon see below, p. 587.

[6] uersiculo] uersiculus (MS).

[7] Immediately followed by the *Visitatio Sepulchri,* printed below, pp. 381 sqq.

[8] See above, p. 136.

[9] W. Dugdale, *Monasticon Anglicanum,* i, London, 1849, p. 437.

Matins, she undertakes to establish at Barking a special form of this dramatic ceremony for observance *at the close of* Matins, immediately before the usual *Visitatio Sepulchri*.[1]

The *Elevatio* from Barking appears to fall into two parts: an introduction representing the *Descensus*, and the actual raising of the Host from the *sepulchrum*. The representation of the *Descensus* occurs at the chapel of St Mary Magdalen. Behind the closed doors of this room are imprisoned all the members of the convent, representing the souls of the patriarchs confined in Hell and awaiting the coming of Christ. After the priest outside has uttered *Tollite portas* three times, the door of the chapel is flung open, and all the imprisoned spirits, carrying palms of victory, are allowed to depart in procession towards the sepulchre during the singing of several antiphons, the last of which is *Cum rex gloriæ*. The subsequent raising of the Host from the sepulchre includes one or two unusual features. During the ceremony, for example, are sung three stanzas from the hymn *Ad cœnam agni*. Particularly noteworthy also is the displaying of the Host placed in a monstrance.[2] The concluding procession from the main altar to the altar of the Holy Trinity is interpreted for us symbolically as representing the journey of Christ into Galilee.

It is impossible, perhaps, to determine with certainty whether or not the ceremonies before us included an element of impersonation and thus became true drama. Particularly suggestive is such a rubric as this: *Sacerdos repræsentabit personam Christi ad inferos descensuram*. From such a sentence one would like to infer that in some gesture or detail of vestment the priest actually undertook to resemble physically the Person in whose name he spoke; but such an inference would be insecure. Of this much, however, we may be sure: the Lady Abbess of Barking succeeded in her desire to arrange a dramatic observance such as should 'dispel completely the sluggish indifference of the faithful'.

Even so animated a version of the *Elevatio* as that from Barking, however, fails to avail itself of the most obviously dramatic

---

[1] As to the liturgical position of the *Visitatio Sepulchri* see below, pp. 231 sqq.

[2] In regard to the prominence given to the Host in ceremonies of the later Middle Ages see above, p. 125. As Brooks observes (*Sepulchre*, p. 36), there is some doubt as to what objects were actually 'buried' at Barking. The *Depositio* mentions only the *Imago Crucifixi*, which seems to mean here the *corpus* detached from the crucifix—which *corpus* may have contained a cavity for receiving the Host enclosed in crystal. The *Elevatio* mentions only the *Corpus Dominicum*, which might mean the *corpus* from the crucifix; but since it is enclosed in crystal, it is probably the Host.

feature of the narrative of the *Descensus*: namely, the dialogue. For an example of at least a tentative use of this element, then, we may turn to the ceremonies of the church of St John the Evangelist, in Dublin, from which we have the following three texts: [1]

⟨DEPOSITIO CRUCIS ET HOSTIÆ⟩ [2]

Finitis Vesperis, exuat sacerdos casulam, et assumens unum de prelatis in superpelliciis discalciari, reponant Crucem pariter cum Corpore Dominico in Sepulcro, incipiens ipse solus hoc responsorium *Estimatus sum*, genuflectendo cum socio suo, quo incepto, statim surgat. Similiter fiat in responsorio *Sepulto Domino*. Chorus totum responsorium prosequatur cum suo versu genuflectendo per totum tempus usque ad finem seruicii responsorii. |

Estimatus sum. Chorus prosequatur responsorium *Cum descendentibus in lacum, factus sum sicut homo sine adiutorio, inter mortuos liber.* Versus: *Posuerunt me in lacu inferiori in tenebrosis et in umbra mortis. Factus.*

Dum predictum responsorium cum suo versu canitur, predicti duo sacerdotes thurificent Sepulcrum, quo facto et clauso ostio, incipiat idem sacerdos hoc sequens responsorium:

Sepulto Domino. Chorus respondeat *Signatum est monumentum; uoluentes lapidem ad ostium mo|numenti: ponentes milites qui custodirent illud.* Versus: *Ne forte ueniant discipuli eius et furentur eum et dicant plebi: Surrexit a mortuis. Ponentes.*

Sacerdos antiphonam:

In pace. Chorus prosequatur *In idipsum dormiam et requiescam.*

Sacerdos antiphonam:

In pace factus est. Chorus prosequatur *Locus eius, et in Syon habitacio eius.*

Sacerdos antiphonam:

Caro mea. Chorus prosequatur *Requiescet in spe.*

Ad istas tres antiphonas genuflectentur predicti duo sacerdotes continue. Hiis finitis, ordine | non seruato reinduat sacerdos casulam et eodem modo quo accessit in principio seruicii cum diacono et subdiacono et ceteris ministris abs⟨c⟩edat, dictis prius orationibus ad placitum secrete ab omnibus cum genuflectione, omnibus aliis ad libitum recedentibus. Exinde continue ardebit unus cereus ad minus ante Sepulcrum usque ad processionem que fit in Resurreccione Dominica in die Pasche, ita

---

[1] Oxford, Bibl. Bodl., MS Rawlinson Liturg. d. iv, Process. Sancti Johannis Evangelistæ Dublinensis sæc. xiv, fol. 68v–70r, 85v–86v, 127v–130r, previously edited by Young, *Harrowing of Hell*, pp. 916–20. The MS provides music. For the related *Visitatio Sepulchri* see below, p. 347. Concerning the MS, and concerning associated versions, see Notes, p. 563.

[2] Oxford MS Rawlinson Liturg. d. iv, fol. 68v–70r.

tantum quod dum psalmus *Benedictus* canitur et cetera que secuntur in sequenti nocte, extinguatur. Similiter et extinguatur in vigilia Pasce dum benedicitur Nouus Ignis usque accendatur Cereus Paschalis.[1]

⟨ELEVATIO CRUCIS ET HOSTIÆ⟩[2]

In die Pasce ante Matutinas et ante campanarum pulsacionem conueniant clerici ad ecclesiam, et accendantur omnia luminaria per totam ecclesiam. Duo excellenciores presbyteri in superpelliciis cum ceroferariis[3] et thuribulariis et clero circumstante ad Sepulcrum accedant, et, incensato prius Sepulcro cum magna ueneracione, statim post thurificacionem, videlicet genuflectendo, Corpus Dominicum priuatim super altare deponant, interim accipientes Crucem de Sepulcro, incipiat excellencior primam antiphonam:

Christus resurgens.

Cum qua eat processio per ostium presbyterii australe et per medium chori regrediens cum predicta Cruce de Sepulcro assumpta inter duos sacerdotes predictos, super eorum brachia uenerabiliter par|ata, cum thuribulariis et ceroferariis precedentibus ad vnum altare ex parte boriale, choro sequente habitu non mutato, excellencioribus precedentibus; Corpore uero Dominico super altare in pixide dimisso sub thesaurarii custodia, qui illud statim in predicta pixide in tabernacula dependeat. Et tunc pulsentur omnes campane in classicum. Antiphona:

Christus resurgens ex mortuis iam non moritur; mors illi ultra non dominabitur, quod enim viuit, viuit Deo, alleluya, alleluya.

Versus:

Dicant nunc Iudei quomodo milites custodientes sepulcrum perdiderunt regem ad lapidis positionem.[4] *Quare non seruabant petram iusticie? | Aut sepultum reddant aut resurgentem adorent,*[5] *nobiscum dicentes.* Chorus dicat sic: *Alleluya, alleluya.*

Finita antiphona cum suis versibus a toto choro, dicat excellencior persona in ipsa stacione ante altare versiculum:

Surrexit Dominus de sepulcro.

Responsio:

Qui pro nobis ⟨pependit in ligno, alleluia, alleluia⟩.

Oremus.

Oratio:

Deus qui pro nobis Filium tuum crucis patibulum subire uoluisti, ut inimici a nobis expelleres potestatem, concede nobis, famulis tuis, ut in resurreccionis eius gaudiis semper uiuamus. Per eundem Christum.

---

[1] Followed by the rubric *Sabbato in uigilia Pasce.*

[2] Oxford MS Rawlinson Liturg. d. iv, fol. 85v–86v.

[3] ceroferariis] ceroferarius (MS).

[4] positionem] posissionem (MS).

[5] adorent] adorant (MS).

Nec precedat nec subsequatur *Dominus uobiscum*. Finita oratione, omnes cum gaudio genuflectant ibidem, et ipsam Crucem adorent, inprimis digniores persone. Et secrete sine processione chorum intrent. Hiis itaque gestis, discooperiantur cruces per ecclesiam et omnes ymagines; et interim pulsentur campane ad Matutinas more solito.

⟨ELEVATIO CRUCIS ET HOSTIÆ⟩ [1]

In die Pasche ante Matutinas, et ante campanarum pulsacionem, conueniant clerici ad ecclesiam, extinctis prius omnibus ecclesie | luminaribus, exceptis luminaribus infra Sepulcrum et magno Cereo Paschale, singuli quoque clerici et alii cereos extinctos in manibus deferentes. Incipiat cantor hanc antiphonam *Cum rex glorie*, et percantetur a choro:

> *Cvm rex glorie Christus infernum debellaturus intrasset, et chorus angelicus portas principum tolli preceperat, sanctorum anime que tenebantur in morte captiue, uoce lacrimabili clamauerunt: Aduenisti desiderabilis, quem expectabamus in tenebris, ut educeres hac nocte uinculatos de claustris. Te nostra uocabant | suspiria; te larga requirebant lamenta; tu factus es spes desolatis, magna consolacio in tormentis.*

Et interim duo excellenciores sacerdotes in superpelliciis cum thuribulariis ad Sepulcrum accedant, et, finita antiphona, excellencior persona incipiat antiphonam humili uoce sic:

> *Eleuamini, porte eternales, et introibit rex glorie!*

Chorus prosequatur versum:

> *Quis est iste rex glorie? Dominus uirtutum, ipse est rex glorie.*

Item idem sacerdos parum alcius incipiat antiphonam:

> *Eleuamini, ⟨portæ æternales, et introibit rex gloriæ!⟩*

Chorus prosequatur versum:

> *Quis est iste rex glorie? Dominus fortis et potens, Dominus potens in prelio.*

Item idem sacerdos tercio alcius incipiat antiphonam: |

> *Eleuamini, ⟨portæ æternales, et introibit rex gloriæ!⟩*

Chorus prosequatur versum:

> *Quis est iste rex glorie? Dominus uirtutum, ipse est rex glorie.*

Tunc, incensato Sepulcro et aperto ostio predicti, sacerdotes cereos suos de lumine infra Sepulcrum acce⟨n⟩dant, ex quibus ceteri cerei per ecclesiam illuminentur. Deinde predicti sacerdotes eleuantes Crucem de Sepulcro, et Corpore Dominico super altare prius deposito, excellencior sacerdos incipiet antiphonam:

> *Domine, abstraxisti ab inferis animam meam.* [2]

---

[1] Oxford MS Rawlinson Liturg. d. iv, fol. 127ᵛ–130ʳ.
[2] For this antiphon see Hartker, p. 223.

Chorus prosequatur psalmum:

Exaltabo te, Domine, quoniam suscepisti me, nec delectasti inimicos meos super me.[1]

Et post unumquemque versum repetatur a choro antiphona *Domine, abstraxisti,* ut supra, et sic fiat repeticio quousque Sancta Crux a predictis sacerdotibus honorifice super altare apponatur.[2] Quibus factis, predicti sacerdotes alta uoce incipiant ante altare hunc versum:

Consurgens Christus tumulo.[3]

Chorus prosequatur:

Victor redit de baratro,
tyrannum trudens uinculo,
et reserans | paradisum. ,

Deinde predicti sacerdotes dicant versum:

Quesumus, auctor omnium.

Chorus prosequatur:

In hoc paschali gaudio,
ab omni mortis impetu
tuum defende populum.

Item predicti sacerdotes:

Gloria tibi, Domine.

Hic omnes genuflectant, et pulsentur omnes campane, et chorus prosequatur:

Qui surrexisti a mortuis,
cum Patre et Sancto Spiritu
in sempiterna secula.

Hiis finitis, incipient predicti sacerdotes antiphonam *Christus resurgens.* Chorus prosequatur *Ex mortuis.* Cum qua antiphona eat processio per medium chori cum predicta Cruce de Sepulcro assumpta inter predictos duos sacerdotes, super eorum brachia uenerabiliter peracta, cum thuribulariis et ceroferariis precede⟨n⟩tibus ad aliquod altare extra chorum, choro sequente habitu non mutato, excellencioribus precedentibus, Corpore uero Dominico super altare in pixide dimisso. Quod quidem interim sacrista in tabernacula honorabiliter reponat.[4] Finita antiphona cum suo versu a toto choro, *dicat* principalis sacerdos in ipsa stacione conuersus ad altare hunc versiculum: *Surrexit Dominus de sepulcro.* Oratio *Deus, qui pro nobis Filium.* Finita oratione, omnes genuflectant ibidem, et ipsam Crucem adorent, | inprimis digniores persone. Et secrete sine processione in chorum redeant. Hiis itaque gestis, discooperiantur

[1] Ps. xxx, 1.
[2] apponatur] apponant (MS).
[3] tumulo] timulo (MS). This line and the eleven which follow are from the hymn *Ad cœnam agni,* for the full text of which see below, p. 562.
[4] reponat] reponant (MS).

cruces et ymagines per ecclesiam; et interim pulsentur campane more solito ad Matutinas.

Since the *Depositio* and first *Elevatio* from Dublin are of no special interest for our present purpose, we may confine our attention to the second version of the *Elevatio*. This opens with a procession to the sepulchre, during the singing of *Cum rex gloriæ*. At the door of the sepulchre the senior priest speaks the challenge *Elevamini, portæ æternales*, to which the chorus responds *Quis est iste rex gloriæ?* This exchange of utterances occurs three times, the priest raising the pitch of his voice at each repetition. The subsequent taking up from the sepulchre of the cross and Host is accompanied by the singing of several liturgical pieces, among them three stanzas of the hymn *Ad cœnam agni*.

The treatment of the theme of the *Descensus* here can scarcely be considered highly successful. Inept, for example, is the arrangement whereby, after saying *Quis est iste rex gloriæ?* the chorus, in the same breath, answers its own question. Still less acceptable is the reciting of the dialogue at the door of the sepulchre, a place to which the intention of the passage is quite alien.

For anything that can be called an adequate use of the dialogue under consideration we must resort, apparently, to the printed books which probably record, in general, the elaborated usages of the end of the Middle Ages. Convenient for our purpose is a service-book of Bamberg of the year 1587, in which we find the following texts of the *Depositio* and *Elevatio*: [1]

⟨Depositio Crucis et Hostiæ⟩ [2]

Postea redeat ad altare, et accipiat Hostiam magnam consecratam, una cum parva Cruce, ibi relictam, eamque ad Sepulchrum portet, iterum præcedente lumine, et sonante tabula. Sacerdotem immediate sequatur chorus cantans lugubri voce responsorium:

Ecce quomodo moritur iustus, et nemo percipit corde; viri iusti tolluntur, et nemo considerat; a facie iniquitatis sublatus est iustus, et erit in pace memoria eius. Versus: *In pace factus est locus eius, et in Syon habitatio eius. Et erit,* et cætera.

[1] *Agenda Bambergensia . . .*, Ingolstadt,1587, part ii, pp. 522-7, 585-97. The *Elevatio* is reprinted by Lange, in *Z.f.d. A.*, xxix (1885), 247-50, and the *Depositio* and *Elevatio*, by Young, *Dramatic Associations*, pp. 114-8. For the *Visitatio Sepulchri* see below, p. 323. With the texts before us may be associated the Augsburg and Würzburg versions referred to by Young, *op. cit.*, p. 114. On the Augsburg versions see Hoeynck, pp. 215-6, 219-20; Brooks, *Sepulchre*, p. 43.

[2] *Agenda Bambergensia*, Ingolstadt, 1587, pp. 552-7. The text as printed here is immediately preceded by rubrics concerning the communion of the Mass of the Presanctified.

Cum ad Sepulchrum pervenerit sacerdos, Corpus Christi una cum Sancta Cruce reverenter deponat in Sepulchrum, factaque thurificatione, ac lustralis aquæ aspersione, claudat, et sera diligenter muniat Sepulchrum, ne Christi Corpus, per impios aut hæreticos vel Iudæos inde auferri, vel alia queuis contaminatio fieri queat. Deinde sequens cantetur responsorium:

> *Sepulto Domino, signatum est monumentum; voluentes lapidem ad ostium monumenti; ponentes milites qui custodirent illud.* Versus: *Ne forte veniant discipuli eius et furentur eum, et dicant plebi: Surrexit a mortuis. Ponentes,* et cætera.

Postea sacerdos cum ministris, vel choro, flexis genibus, legat clara voce Vesperas, secundum ritum in breviario descriptum. Curent postremo parochi ut in honorem venerabilis Sacramenti sint et maneant continue ad Sepulchrum cerei ardentes; et psalterium quoque per pueros vel alios lugubri lentaque voce legatur usque ad horam Resurrectionis. Sub divinis tamen lectio psalmorum debet omitti.

⟨ELEVATIO CRUCIS ET HOSTIÆ⟩ [1]

Ordo Celebrandi Commemorationem Dominicæ Resurrectionis in Sancta Nocte.

Et hæc quoque Dominicæ Resurrectionis commemoratio celebrioribus servit ecclesiis. Unde aliarum ecclesiarum, utpote minorum et ruralium, rectores et parochi, ex ordine hic descripto aliquid saltem desumere possunt, quod pro loci et personarum illic convenientium qualitate commodum fore iudicaverint.

Ubi igitur Corpus Domini in die Parasceves Sepulchro impositum, inde elevandum est, sequens servetur modus. Circa horam noctis huius sacræ undecimam populus Christianus ad Sepulchrum Domini conveniat, sacerdos vero superpelliceo, stola et pluuiali, seu cappa, ut vocant, chorali indutus, e sacrario prodeat, versusque Sepulchrum lento gradu pergat, præcedentibus ipsum duobus ceroferariis, unoque et altero clerico similiter superpelliceato sequente. Ad Sepulchrum ubi pervenerint, in genua procumbant, sicque coram venerabili Sacramento sequentes duos psalmos, flexis genibus, deuote recitent:

> Psalmus iii. *Domine, quid multiplicati* [2] *... super populum tuum benedictio tua. Gloria Patri et Filio et Spiritui Sancto. Sicut erat in principio,* et cætera.
> Psalmus cxxxviii. *Domine, probasti* [2] *... et deduc me in via æterna. Gloria Patri et Filio et Spiritui Sancto. Sicut erat in principio, et nunc et semper, et in secula seculorum, Amen.*
> *Kyrie eleison. Christe eleison. Kyrie eleison.*

---

[1] *Agenda Bambergensia*, Ingolstadt, 1587, pp. 585–97.
[2] In the *Agenda* the two psalms are given in full, Ps. iii extending from p. 586 to p. 587, and Ps. cxxxviii (cxxxix), from p. 587 to p. 590.

Pater noster, et cætera. *Et ne nos inducas in tentationem. Sed libera,* et cætera.

Versus: *In resurrectione tua, Christe, alleluia.*

Responsio: *Cœlum et terra lætentur, alleluia.*

Oremus.

Gregem tuum, Pastor bone, placatus intende, et oves, quas pretioso sanguine redemisti, diabolica non sinas incursione lacerari. Qui cum Deo Patre in unitate Spiritus Sancti vivis ac regnas Deus, per omnia secula seculorum.

Responsio: *Amen.*

His dictis, aperiatur Sepulchrum, fiatque thurificatio et aquæ benedictæ aspersio super venerabile Sacramentum, et parvam Crucifixi Imaginem, quæ utraque deinde sacerdos reverenter in manus capiat, versusque ad populum sequentem antiphonam tribus vicibus, voce semper altius elevata, incipiat, ac reliquum chorus prosequatur:

Surrexit Dominus de sepulchro.

Chorus:

Qui pro nobis pependit in ligno, alleluia.

Postea instituatur processio, vel per cœmiterium, vel (si tutum non videbitur) per templi ambitum, hoc modo: Primo præcedant duo ceroferarii prædicti, quos immediate sequantur duo sacerdotes, vel clerici, portantes eam Crucifixi Imaginem magnam, quam casula coopertam, in die Parasceves gestaverunt duo sacerdotes. Deinde subsequatur sacerdos cum venerabili Sacramento et Sancta Cruce, quæ utraque paulo ante ex Sepulchro levavit; chorus vero cantet antiphonam:

Cum rex gloriæ Christus infernum debellaturus intraret, et chorus angelicus ante faciem eius portas principum tolli præciperet, sanctorum populus, qui tenebatur in morte captivus, voce lacrymabili clamaverat: Advenisti desiderabilis, quem expectabamus in tenebris, ut educeres hac nocte vinculatos de claustris. Te nostra vocabant suspiria, te larga requirebant lamenta, tu factus es spes desperatis, magna consolatio in tormentis, alleluia.

Ubi ad primam vel proximam templi ianuam ventum fuerit, duo sacerdotes prædicti cum stipite Crucifixi tribus vicibus fortiter percutiant ianuam, huncque in modum inter percutiendum cantent:

Tollite portas, principes, vestras, et elevamini, portæ æternales.

Chorus quod sequitur canit:

Et introibit Rex gloriæ.

Sit deinde aliquis in templo (si tamen extra templum processio fit; si vero in templo instituatur processio, sit is extra templum) qui Diaboli personam simulans, ferro, malleo, aut cathena, fortiter quoque impingat in ianuam eandem, dicatque vel clamet alta voce:

Quis est iste Rex gloriæ?

Mox chorus, vel eo deficiente, sacerdos subiungat:

Dominus fortis et potens, Dominus potens in prælio.

Post hæc chorus in incœpta, et paulo ante interrupta antiphona *Cum Rex gloriæ,* et cætera, canere pergat, totaque processio, ordine prædicto, versus secundam templi ianuam progrediatur, apud quam omnia fiant uti apud primam. Et notandum quod hæc utraque ianua manere debet clausa. Quando vero ad ultimam ianuam venerint, factis ibidem quoque iis quæ circa primam indicauimus, aperiri debet illa. Per quod designatur, vel circumstanti populo ad oculum repræsentatur, quomodo Christus Dominus post Passionem suo ad inferos descensu, eum inferni locum qui Patrum Lymbus dicitur aperuerit, vel quod alibi dicitur, portas æreas vel vectes ferreos confregerit, suosque captivos inde liberaverit. Deinde continuetur antiphona *Cum Rex gloriæ,* et cætera, usque ad finem, pergatque processio ad chorum templi. Sacerdos vero gradus altaris ascendat, ibique versus populum consistens, ac Christi Corpus adhuc in manibus tenens, cantet tribus vicibus, voce semper altius elevata, *O vere digna hostia,* et caetera, choro versum illum prosequente.

O vere digna Hostia.[1]

Chorus: *Per quam fracta sunt tartara,*
redempta plebs captivata,
redit ad vitæ præmia.

Addatur deinceps eiusdem hymni ultimus versus, sacerdote incipiente:

Gloria tibi, Domine.

Chorus: *Qui surrexisti a mortuis,*
cum Patre et Sancto Spiritu,
in sempiterna secula, Amen.

Sub hoc ultimo versu, sacerdos, facto signo crucis super populum cum venerabili Sacramento, portet illud ad suum locum in quo conseruari solet; chorus vero incipiat:

Victimæ paschali laudes,

et cætera. Et post quemlibet versum, inserat unum tantum paschalem Germanicum, quem populus quoque celebriter decantet; sitque primus:

Christ ist erstanden,

et cætera. Hos cantus invenies in fine huius libri. Post hæc incipiantur Matutinæ.

The *Depositio* at Bamberg, performed after Mass, includes in the burial both Host and cross, and is notable especially for the precaution taken against the possible desecration of the Host by Jews, heretics, or others. This is one of many indications that, during the late Middle Ages and the period of the Reformation,

---

[1] This line and the seven which follow are from the hymn *Ad cœnam agni,* for the full text of which see below, p. 562.

the security of the Eucharist used in the ceremonies at the sepulchre was a matter of some anxiety.[1]

The *Elevatio* is of unusual fullness and importance. Before the beginning of the observance the lay congregation is allowed to gather at the sepulchre, there to be joined by a procession of the clergy from the sacristy. After the reciting of two psalms and of several familiar liturgical forms, the sepulchre is opened, and the Host and cross are censed, sprinkled, and elevated into general view. Then both objects are carried through the cemetery outside the church, the chorus singing the antiphon *Cum rex gloriæ*. When the procession reaches the first portal of the church, two priests, carrying an especially large crucifix, strike the door with the shaft three times, singing *Tollite portas*. A person within the building, representing Satan, responds with the words *Quis est iste rex gloriæ?* The chorus outside replies *Dominus fortis*. Since the door remains closed, the procession passes on and conducts the dialogue at a second portal, and then at a third. When this door yields, the procession enters the church and advances to the choir. Here the officiating priest raises the Host aloft and blesses the congregation, singing three times the verse *O vere digna Hostia*. After the Eucharist has been put away in its appropriate place, the chorus sings the sequence *Victimæ paschali*, the congregation responding to the several sentences with vernacular songs such as *Christ ist erstanden*.[2]

In this observance the theme of the Harrowing of Hell approaches genuine dramatization more nearly than in any of the versions of the *Elevatio* considered hitherto. In the diocese of Bamberg it is no longer treated in a merely incidental way, but is used to form the central and most conspicuous action of the ceremony. Although most of the text and ceremonial is still purely liturgical, Satan, at least, is carefully impersonated, and the intention of conveying a story in action is expressed in such words as the following:

Per quod designatur, vel circumstanti populo ad oculum repræsentatur, quomodo Christus Dominus post Passionem suo ad inferos descensu, eum inferni locum qui Patrum Lymbus dicitur aperuerit, vel quod alibi dicitur, portas æreas vel vectes ferreos confregerit, suosque captivos inde liberaverit.

[1] See Brooks, *Sepulchre*, pp. 40–1. In regard to the Bamberg custom of reserving and adoring the special Host consecrated on Thursday for the ceremonies at the sepulchre see Notes, p. 564.

[2] Concerning *Victimæ paschali* and *Christ ist erstanden* see below, pp. 273, 323.

It is obvious that the cleric who wrote this sentence had a feeling for the stage, and was ready to abandon symbolism in favour of drama.

In view of the opening of the way towards impersonation in the *Elevatio* from Bamberg, one is at a loss to account for the general absence of this essential dramatic element from the ceremonies at the sepulchre during the Middle Ages. One would have surmised that the clerics who ventured to introduce into the *Elevatio* the vivacious action and dialogue of the scene in Hell need not have waited until the approach of modern times before venturing upon something realistic, or at least suggestive, in the way of costume and personal mannerism. Surely the abbess of Barking, Lady Katherine of Sutton, was not lacking in militancy and independence; and yet the spirited performance which she arranged at the door of the chapel of St Mary Magdalen seems to stop short of true drama. The fact appears to be that from the very outset the *Depositio* and *Elevatio* were committed to a close dependence upon the text and mood of the authorized liturgy of Holy Week. Since they were not part of the authorized worship of Rome they were, to be sure, extra-liturgical; but in their utterances they followed accepted Roman forms, and in their temper they were generally governed by Roman sobriety and simplicity. Particularly noteworthy in these ceremonies is the subdued tone which usually pervades the *Elevatio*. This celebration of the happiest event in Christian history might have been expected to cast off the mourning which necessarily surrounds the *Depositio*, and to have shared in the public enthusiasm of Easter. In reality, as we have seen, the *Elevatio* was often performed almost privately, in a subdued voice, and behind closed doors. The performance was usually given not for rejoicing throngs of laymen, but rather for small groups of penitent clerics. Reticence such as this does not make for effectual drama.

CHAPTER VI

LITERARY EMBELLISHMENTS OF THE
LITURGY : TROPES

IT is now apparent that the plays of the Church did not arise directly or primarily from the ceremonies regularly used in Christian worship. Although these observances were often highly theatrical, and were sometimes of a sort readily capable of transformation into drama, they do not lead us into the main current of dramatic development. The effectual beginnings of medieval religious drama are to be found not in the elaboration of elements present in the traditional forms of worship, but in certain deliberate, and perhaps unsanctioned, literary additions to the authorized liturgical text. Although, as we shall see, the variety of these literary embellishments is very large, the whole body of them may be conveniently called *tropes*.[1]

I

In its broadest sense a trope may be defined as a verbal amplification of a passage in the authorized liturgy, in the form of an introduction, an interpolation, or a conclusion, or in the form of any combination of these. A simple example may be drawn from among the tropes of the concluding formula of the Mass. The end of this service, as we have seen, is normally announced by the deacon in the words, *Ite, missa est*, to which the chorus responds, *Deo gratias*.[2] Into these two brief and adequate utterances a zealous monk of St Gall interpolated some sixteen words of his own, in the form of the following trope:[3]

Ite *nunc in pace, spiritus sanctus super vos sit, iam* missa est.
Deo *semper laudes agite, in corde gloriam et* gratias.

Although this meagre example illustrates inadequately the form and scope of tropes as a whole, it discloses sufficiently well the central intention of all these liturgical embellishments. Their purpose is to adorn the liturgical text, to enforce its meaning, and to enlarge its emotional appeal. The trope often undertakes

[1] For observations on the term *trope*, and for bibliography, see Notes, p. 565.

[2] See above, p. 42.

[3] *A. H.*, xlvii, 412. In the present chapter, in a quotation containing both liturgical words and words constituting a trope, the words of the trope are printed in Italics, the authorized liturgical part and its accompanying rubrics appearing in Roman.

to become an inseparable part of the whole piece,
has no meaning apart from the passage which :
Sometimes, however, the embellishment is so lengthy
the authorized text to which it is attached, and in ma
it severs the attachment decisively, and stands for
contained and apparently independent composition. Tropes of
this last sort are usually given special names, the largest group
of them being called *sequences*, or *proses*. Of these various types
ample illustrations will be given below.

The very beginnings of the practice of embellishing the
accepted liturgical text are, it must be confessed, hidden in
obscurity. Since during the early Middle Ages liturgical usage
was by no means so firmly established as in modern times,
unauthorized embellishments may have been occasionally introduced at a very early period. Intrusions into the liturgy, of one
sort or another, are mentioned in church councils and papal
decrees from the fourth century onwards.[1] The particular form
of literary activity with which we are immediately concerned,
however, came into prominence in the empire of the Carolingians during the ninth century, and seems to have been one
manifestation of the general intellectual and creative movement
conveniently called the Carolingian Renaissance.[2]

Few undertakings in the realm of art and letters have been
more grandiose in conception or more potent in effect than
Charlemagne's project for reviving the glory of antiquity within
his own Christian domain. His primary purpose, no doubt, was
the reviving of the inner life of the Church, for it was sufficiently
apparent that his royal predecessors had left this institution upon
a low spiritual and intellectual level. For this undertaking the
first requisite was an adequately educated clergy, and a substantial body of cultivated laymen. By way of providing the
necessary intellectual leadership, the king summoned from the
more advanced educational centres of Europe a group of celebrated teachers and writers, among whom the most distinguished
was Alcuin (735–804), the most learned man of his day, and
eventually the pre-eminent organizer of learning upon the Continent. It was such men who developed the court school from
a mere royal seminary into an academy of national importance.
Here, under the influence of the sovereign, the ablest scholars

[1] See Muller, pp. 545–50.
[2] For bibliography bearing upon the Carolingian Renaissance see Notes, p. 566.

of Europe associated themselves not only with the royal family and the aristocracy, but with the humblest of learners as well. From this centre issued the means for advancing education throughout Charlemagne's dominions. At monasteries and cathedrals, schools and libraries were developed. The service-books of the Church were corrected, and the Latin text of the Bible was re-edited and expounded. The poetry of early Christian and pagan poets was reverently studied, and matters of ethical, theological, and historical interest were expressed in verse. The creative impulse manifested in education and letters appeared abundantly also in the arts generally. On all sides arose churches, the interiors of which were beautified by mosaics and mural paintings, and the vaultings of which resounded with perfected liturgical singing. The sacristies and treasuries of cathedrals and monasteries were enriched with fine examples of goldsmithing and ivory-carving. Manuscripts were beautified through the adoption of a clearer and more elegant hand-writing, through miniature painting, and through elaboration of binding.

This intellectual and artistic revival fostered by Charlemagne continued throughout the century following him, and with it, in some fashion, must be associated the rise of those extra-liturgical compositions which we call tropes.[1] The relation of trope-writing to the other activities of this renaissance, however, is not entirely clear, for one of Charlemagne's specific under-takings would seem to have been directly hostile to the particular kind of writing which we are now considering. The Church service-books current in his kingdom when he took the throne in 769 were in a state which has been pungently characterized as liturgical anarchy,[2] and nothing is more truly illustrative of the king's reforming spirit than the zeal with which he brought into effect a genuine renovation of liturgical texts, in accordance with the use of Rome. He required that service-books be care-fully collated from pure Roman models, and strengthened his purpose by founding the first great school of liturgical study, in which such scholars as Alcuin, Amalarius, and Rabanus Maurus became prominent figures.[3] The work of such men unquestion-ably made for a firm contact with Roman tradition, and for the

[1] See Meyer, p. 173.
[2] See Bishop, p. 15.
[3] In regard to Charlemagne's projects in liturgiology see especially Cabrol and Le-clercq, iii, 807–25; Van Doren, pp. 39–69.

exclusion of precisely such liturgical excrescences as we are now considering.[1]

How, then, are we to account for the presence of tropes in the very liturgical books which the Carolingians are presumed to have been purifying? To this question the available facts provide no single lucid answer. It has sometimes been asserted that the Roman hierarchy itself never consistently opposed the invention, for liturgical uses, of new melodies and of new words to accompany them;[2] and there is a tradition that one ninth-century pope actually encouraged the writing of tropes,[3] and that one noted producer of them exchanged compositions of this sort with Charles the Fat (882–7).[4] This explanation implies that what Rome required, and the Carolingians enforced, was uniformity in the more essential parts of the liturgy, such as the prayers and the lessons, the musical pieces being left open to modification.[5] Thus the introits, offertories or responsories might be decorated, provided the Canon, the gospels, and the homilies were kept intact. Another explanation is that, although Charlemagne may have been intent originally upon liturgical uniformity, his reforming energy was spent not upon purity of content but upon correctness of Latinity. A trope, therefore, could attain liturgical legitimacy through appropriateness of form.[6] Less precise—though not necessarily less adequate—is the explanation that the monarchs who succeeded to Charlemagne's throne relaxed their ecclesiastical supervision, and carelessly admitted liturgical irregularities;[7] or that of the two opposing impulses encouraged by Charlemagne—the one for liturgical purism and the other for artistic creation—the latter merely triumphed over the former.[8]

---

[1] Meyer (p. 35) presents this conflict clearly. A. Kleinclausz (E. Lavisse, *Histoire de France*, ii, part i, Paris, 1903, p. 342) appears to credit Charlemagne with the deliberate elimination of tropes from the service-books.

[2] See Bäumer, i, 418–9; Muller, pp. 544–50.

[3] See Muller, p. 544.

[4] See Wagner, p. 277; Schubiger, *Sängerschule*, pp. 29, 59. Concerning the metrical compositions said to have been contributed by Charles the Bald (843–77) to the Gallican liturgy see J. B. Mullinger, *The Schools of Charles the Great*, London, 1877, p. 160.

[5] See A. Hauck, *Kirchengeschichte Deutsch-*

lands, ii, Leipzig, 1890, pp. 608–9; F. Cabrol, *Origines*, p. 92. G. Paris (*Journal des Savants*, 1892, p. 684) somewhat vaguely suggests that the Carolingian renovation of the liturgy included the insertion of extra-liturgical compositions.

[6] See Muller, pp. 533–74.

[7] See Hauck, *op. cit.*, ii, 555–610; A. Molinier, *Les Sources de l'Histoire de France*, i, Paris, 1901, pp. 183–4; Van Doren, pp. 43–5; Meyer, p. 35.

[8] This view seems to be implied, though it is not explicitly stated, by J. A. Ketterer, *Karl der Grosse und die Kirche*, Munich and Leipzig, 1898, pp. 232–50.

Among these opinions, or speculations, as to why literary adornments were allowed to invade the authorized liturgy we are, fortunately, not required to choose. We may accept the unquestioned fact that during the Carolingian period, and under the general circumstances of a literary renaissance, tropes took a striking place in public worship in certain communities of France and neighbouring countries; and we may proceed to examine the results of this special phenomenon.

II

We may begin, then, with the group of extra-liturgical compositions which have often been regarded as the earliest writings of this sort, and which are, in any case, the most prolific. For reasons that will appear presently, this group of tropes are called *sequences*, or *proses*. The origin and nature of the sequence will be more readily understood if we revert to the liturgical piece to which it was originally attached: the *Alleluia* and its verse, sung during the introductory part of the Mass. In the third Mass of Christmas Day, for example, this piece was rendered in the following general form:[1]

> Alleluia. (Cantors.)
> Alleluia. (Chorus.)
> Versus: Dies sanctificatus illuxit nobis; venite,
> gentes, et adorate Dominum, quia hodie
> descendit lux magna super terram. (Cantors.)
> Alleluia. (Chorus.)

Although the manner of singing the *Alleluia* and its verse was probably not precisely uniform throughout the part of Western Europe dominated by Roman usage, the arrangement described here may be assumed to represent the norm for a great feast-day in any organized ecclesiastical community. From a very remote period it was customary to sing the final *a* of the second and the third *Alleluia* to an uncommonly long and elaborate melody, appropriately called by a variety of names such as *melisma, neuma, sequela, jubilus,* and *jubilatio*.[2] To these unusual vocalizations the symbolists of the Church, from the tenth century onwards, did not fail to draw attention, interpreting them, for

[1] See Wagner, p. 100; Fortescue, *Mass*, p. 269; and above, pp. 18, 25. For an early text of this *Alleluia* and its verse see the tenth-century gradual of St Gall published in *Paléographie musicale*, i—St Gall MS 339, p. 44. For bibliography concerning the origin and development of sequences see Notes, p. 566.

[2] For additional names see Gautier, *Tropes*, p. 14. In regard to early examples see Wagner, pp. 43–6; Cabrol and Leclercq, vii, 2770–2.

IV. *Sequentiæ* from the Winchester Troper, in Oxford,
Bodleian Library, MS Bodl. 775, fol. 122^r

example, as representations of man's incompetence for praising God adequately, or of human longing for the heavenly life[1]. The length of the melody was such that, for convenience, it was divided by pauses into shorter musical phrases, each of which was called a *sequentia*, or *clausula*, the whole succession of sub-divisions being called, collectively, *sequentiæ*.[2] Probably each of these phrases, except an occasional very short one, was sung twice, by separate groups of singers, or semi-choruses. As an aid towards remembering the melodies, or for some other pur-pose, the practice arose of providing words for some of the phrases, and eventually for the whole succession of them. The resulting combination of words and music was appropriately described either as *sequentiæ cum prosa* or as *prosa ad sequentias*. In France, during the Middle Ages, such a composition was usually called *prosa*, or *prose*, and in Germany, *sequentia*, or *sequenz*. In modern English the accepted term is *sequence*.

The earliest extant sequences are associated with the name of Notker Balbulus (c. 840–912), the vivacious and accomplished monk of St Gall, and it has been customary to credit him with the invention of this sort of composition. The evidence upon which this attribution rests is the following passage from a letter addressed to Liutward, bishop of Vercelli, which Notker pre-fixed to his own *Liber Sequentiarum*:[3]

Cum adhuc juvenculus essem, et melodiæ longissimæ, sæpius memoriæ commendatæ, instabile corculum aufugerent, cœpi tacitus mecum vol-vere quonam modo eas potuerim colligare. Interim vero contigit ut presbyter quidam de Gimedia, nuper a Nordmannis vastata, veniret ad nos, antiphonarium suum secum deferens, in quo aliqui versus ad sequentias erant modulati, sed jam tunc nimium vitiati. Quorum, ut visu delectatus, ita sum gustu amaricatus. Ad imitationem tamen eorum cœpi scribere *Laudes Deo concinat orbis universus, qui gratis est liberatus*, et infra, *Coluber Adæ malesuasor*. Quos cum magistro meo Ysoni obtulissem, ille, studio meo congratulatus imperitiæque compassus, quæ placuerunt laudavit; quæ autem minus, emendare curavit, dicens, 'Singuli motus cantilenæ singulas syllabas debent habere'. Quod audiens, ea quidem quæ in *ia* veniebant, ad liquidum correxi. Quæ vero in *le* vel *lu* quasi impossibilia vel attemperare neglexi, cum et illud postea visu facillimum deprehenderim, ut testes sunt *Dominus in Sina*,

[1] See Gautier, *op. cit.*, pp. 13–4; Wagner, pp. 99–100.
[2] For examples of *sequentiæ* see plate iv.
[3] I quote the corrected text of Gautier, *Tropes*, pp. 20–1, which differs in no essential way from that in Migne, *P. L.*, cxxxi, 1003–4.

Other more or less critical texts are given by Werner, pp. 97–8, and by E. Dümmler, in *Mittheilungen der antiquarischen Gesellschaft in Zürich*, xii (1858–60), 224. For further bib-liography see Notes, p. 566.

et *Mater*. Hocque modo instructus, secunda mox voce dictavi *Psallat Ecclesia, mater inlibata*. Quos versiculos, cum magistro meo Marcello præsentarem, ille, gaudio repletus, in rotulos eos congessit et pueris cantandos aliis alios insinuavit.

From this passage it appears that soon after the destruction of the monastery of Jumièges by the Northmen, in 851,[1] a monk from that community visited St Gall, bringing with him his choir-book. Notker observed that in this volume, under the long melodies at the *Alleluia*, were written words—*versus ad sequentias*. Having found difficulty in remembering the wordless melodies themselves, he was highly pleased over the new mnemonic resource. Since, however, the verses in the book of the visiting monk were offensive to his taste, he composed certain texts of his own—a single syllable for each musical note—and perfected them under the guidance of his master, Yso. Eventually, we may be sure, he not only composed the words for a considerable number of sequences, but also revised the original melodies.[2]

From Notker's own letter, then, it is clear that he was not the first to write words as an accompaniment to the final melodies of the *Alleluia*.[3] Although the extra-liturgical verses in the volume from Jumièges may have been far from distinguished in their literary form, they anticipated Notker's efforts, and they represented a kind of composition which may have been cultivated in France for a considerable time before the year 851.[4] It can scarcely be denied, in any case, that the oldest extant sequences from France exhibit a less highly developed, and hence probably an earlier, form than that of the Notkerian compositions, and that these latter also bear some evidences of French influence.[5] We may be reasonably certain, therefore, that the original home of sequences is not St Gall, but, in all probability, some French monastic community such as Limoges, Luxeuil, Moissac, or St-Benoît-sur-Loire.[6] Notker's real service

---

[1] On the date see Van Doren, p. 81; Moser, i, 90.

[2] See Werner, pp. 102–3. It has usually been assumed that the series of wordless melodies following the final *a*'s of the *Alleluias* in certain early MSS are the original *jubili* which existed before words were supplied. See Wagner, pp. 252–3; Adams, opposite p. 3. Blume (*A. H.*, liii, pp. xxi–xxii) believes that all extant examples of *jubili* were written for words.

[3] See Gautier, *Tropes*, p. 29.

[4] Blume (*A. H.*, liii, p. xix) infers that

sequences may have originated in the eighth century, and Raby (p. 213) accepts this inference.

[5] See Blume, in *A. H.*, liii, pp. xiv sqq.

[6] See Blume, in *Catholic Encyclopedia*, xii, 486; Raby, p. 213. Moser (i, 91) hesitates to follow Blume in assigning the priority to France, and infers that, at the beginning of the tenth century, the writing of sequences was 'in the air' in other countries. Clark (pp. 180 sqq.) regards the developments in France and at St Gall as parallel.

seems to have lain not in creating a new literary *genre*, but in giving prominence to an improved form of sequence, in establishing its vogue in Germany, and in bringing to his own monastery a renown which, in respect to this sort of writing, historians have, perhaps, somewhat exaggerated.[1]

Although in their beginnings the sequences were closely attached to the *Alleluia* of the Mass, and although some of the extant examples seem to disclose this original attachment through beginning with the word *Alleluia*,[2] the great majority stand forth as independent compositions. When sung in the Mass, the sequence occupied its historical position between the *Alleluia* and the gospel; but pieces composed for use in the Mass were sometimes sung also in other parts of the liturgy.[3] The number and variety of the sequences written throughout the Middle Ages was very large. Notker himself is often credited with some fifty or more, and his anonymous imitators and successors all over Western Europe produced many hundreds.[4]

Within this large body of extant sequences it is relatively easy to distinguish three different types, which may be regarded as representing three stages of literary development.[5] The earliest examples, composed largely before the end of the tenth century, consist essentially of a succession of pairs of sentences, or strophes, the two strophes of a pair containing an equal number of syllables, but the pairs themselves varying in length. Syllables are counted, but the quantities of vowels are disregarded. This symmetrical structure is introduced or concluded, or both introduced and concluded, by a single additional sentence or phrase, or by the word *Alleluia*. These additional sentences, like the strophes, usually end in *a*. This type may be illustrated by the following:[6]

1. Eia, recolamus laudibus piis digna

2a. Huius diei carmina,	2b. Noctis interit nebula,
in qua nobis lux	pereunt nostri
oritur gratissima;	criminis umbracula.

---

[1] The pre-eminence of St Gall is upheld, for example, by Meyer, p. 35. The corrective is supplied by Van Doren, pp. 93, 147–53; Clark, pp. 179, 188.

[2] See, for example, *A. H.*, liii, 11–4, 31, 33, 35.

[3] For the use of the sequence *Victimæ paschali* in Vespers see below, p. 482.

[4] The estimates of the number of sequences written by Notker have varied between fourteen and seventy-eight. See Van Doren, p. 84. Quantities of sequences have been published, or re-published, in *A. H.*, vii–x, xxxiv, xxxvii, xxxix, xl, xlii, xliv, liii, liv.

[5] See Blume, in *Catholic Encyclopedia*, xii, 484–6.

[6] *A. H.*, liii, 23–4.

3a. Hodie sæculo
    maris stella
    est enixa
    novæ salutis gaudia;

3b. Quem tremunt barathra,
    mors cruenta,
    pavet ipsa,
    a quo peribit mortua.

4a. Gemit capta pestis antiqua,
    coluber lividus perdit spolia;

4b. Homo lapsus, ovis abducta
    revocatur ad æterna gaudia.

5a. Gaudent in hac die agmina
    angelorum cælestia,

5b. Quia erat drachma decima
    perdita et est inventa.

6a. O culpa nimium beata,
    qua redempta est natura!

6b. Deus, qui creavit omnia,
    nascitur ex femina.

7a. Mirabilis natura,
    mirifice induta,
    assumens, quod non erat,
    manens, quod erat,

7b. Induitur natura
    divinitas humana.
    Quis audivit talia,
    dic, rogo, facta?

8a. Quærere venerat
    pastor pius, quod perierat;

8b. Induit galeam,
    certat ut miles armatura.

9a. Prostratus in sua
    propria
    ruit hostis spicula;
    auferuntur tela,

9b. In quibus fidebat;
    divisa
    sunt illius spolia
    capta præda sua.

10a. Christi pugna fortissima
     salus nostra est vera;

10b. Qui nos suam ad patriam
     duxit post victoriam,

11. In qua sibi laus est æterna.

It cannot be said that all sequences of the first period conform exactly to this form in all respects. In *Psallat Ecclesia, mater illibata*, mentioned in Notker's letter to Liutward, for example, fewer than half of the strophes end in *a*, or contain this vowel in the final syllable.[1] The text before us, however, may be regarded as representative of the usual Notkerian structure.

The second, or transitional, period covers the eleventh century, during which the new sequences show a tendency towards rhyme and regularity of rhythm. Of this type *Victimæ paschali*, still retained in the Mass of Easter, is a perfect example. This poem, already displayed above, will claim our closer attention in a later chapter.[2] The transitional style of sequence may be illustrated here by the following from the eleventh century, composed in honour of St Nicholas:[3]

1a. Congaudentes exultemus
    vocali concordia.

1b. Ad beati Nicholai
    festiva sollemnia,

[1] For the text see *A. H.*, liii, 398.
[2] See above, p. 27, and below, chap. x.
[3] *A. H.*, liv, 95–6, quoted also by Raby,
pp. 345–6. In regard to the legends referred
to in this sequence considerable information
is given below, chap. xxvi.

2a. Qui in cunis adhuc iacens
    servando ieiunia,

2b. Ad papillas cœpit summa
    promereri gaudia.

3a. Adulescens amplexatur
    literarum studia,

3b. Alienus et immunis
    ab omni lascivia.

4a. Felix confessor,
    cuius fuit dignitatis
    vox de cælo nuntia,

4b. Per quam provectus
    præsulatus sublimatur
    ad summa fastigia.

5a. Erat in eius animo
    pietas eximia,
    et oppressis impendebat
    multa beneficia:

5b. Auro per eum virginum
    tollitur infamia,
    atque patris earundem
    levatur inopia;

6a. Quidam nautæ navigantes
    et contra fluctuum
    sævitiam luctantes
    navi pæne dissoluta,

6b. Iam de vita desperantes
    in tanto positi
    periculo clamantes
    voce dicunt omnes una:

7a. 'O beate Nicolae,
    nos ad portum maris trahe
    de mortis angustia;

7b. Trahe nos ad portum maris,
    tu qui tot auxiliaris
    pietatis gratia.'

8a. Dum clamarent nec incassum,
    ecce, quidam dicens: 'Assum
    ad vestra præsidia.'

8b. Statim aura datur grata,
    et tempestas fit sedata,
    quieverunt maria.

9a. Ex ipsius tumba manat
    unctionis copia,

9b. Quæ infirmos omnes sanat
    per eius suffragia.

10a. Nos qui sumus in hoc mundo
    vitiorum in profundo
    iam passi naufragia,

10b. Gloriose Nicolae,
    ad salutis portum trahe,
    ubi pax et gloria;

11a. Illam nobis unctionem
    impetres ad Dominum
    prece pia,

11b. Qui sanavit læsionem
    multorum peccaminum
    in Maria.

12a. Huius festum celebrantes
    gaudeant per sæcula,

12b. Et coronet eos Christus
    post vitæ curricula.

In this piece rhyme and rhythm are used with notable skill, and with not a little beauty of effect.

The third type of sequence, composed from about the year 1100 onwards, attains regularity of metre, purity of rhyme, and uniformity in the arrangement of stanzas. Such is the poem *Lauda, Sion,* written by Thomas Aquinas in 1263 for the Mass of Corpus Christi Day, and still retained there. Among the sequences of this third period are found some of the most beautiful poems of the Middle Ages, including those of Adam of St Victor († 1192), the *Dies iræ* of Thomas of Celano (fl. 1220–49), and the *Stabat mater*.[1]

---

[1] Concerning the sequences of the more advanced type see especially Wagner, pp. 266–74. The sequences retained in the modern missal are mentioned above, p. 26.

III

Because of the special circumstances of their origin at the *Alleluia* of the Mass, and because of their independence of the liturgy as self-contained compositions, it has been convenient to consider sequences in a group by themselves. We have now to extend our survey to the numerous other literary excrescences found in other parts of the liturgy, both of the Mass and of the Canonical Office.[1] It is to these more varied pieces that writers have often applied the term *tropes* in the more restricted sense; and the use of a separate collective term for these miscellaneous compositions may often be useful, for, as a whole, they differ from the developed sequences in form and in the intimacy of their attachment to the authorized liturgy. Whereas sequences are usually independent poems, freely detachable from the true liturgy, tropes commonly maintain the original attachment. Most tropes may be viewed as commentaries, more or less poetical, upon the genuine liturgical text, and as meaningless, or ineffectual, without its support.

The precise origin of tropes is even more obscure than that of sequences.[2] Probably the process in the two cases was similar, and, in a general way, contemporaneous. We may assume that just as, from very early times, elaborate melodies were sung to the final *a* of the *Alleluia*, so similar melodies were provided for, let us say, the final *a* of *Gloria* in the *Gloria in excelsis*, and for the *e* in *Kyrie*, and that for these latter melodies were eventually supplied extra-liturgical words. A development of this sort would seem to explain, for example, a trope such as the following:[3]

I

a. Kyrie, *fons bonitatis,*
　pater ingenite,
　a quo bona cuncta
　procedunt,
　eleïson.

b. Kyrie, *qui pati natum*
　mundi pro crimine,
　ipsum ut salvaret,
　misisti,
　eleïson.

c. Kyrie, *qui septiformis*
　dans dona pneumatis,
　a quo cælum, terra
　replentur,
　eleïson.

---

[1] For bibliography see Notes, p. 566.
[2] I follow especially C. Blume's treatment of the matter in *A. H.*, xlvii, 17–9, and in

Catholic Encyclopedia, xv, 65–6.
[3] *A. H.*, xlvii, 53–4. For the normal form of *Kyrie eleïson* see above, p. 23.

2

a. Christe, *unice*   b. Christe, *hagie,*
   Dei patris genite,   *cæli compos regiæ*
   quem de virgine   *melos gloriæ*
   nasciturum   *cui semper*
   mundo mirifice   *astans pro munere*
   sancti prædixerunt prophetæ,   *angelorum decantat apex,*
   eleïson.   eleïson.

      c. Christe, *cælitus*
        assis nostris precibus,
        pronis mentibus
        quem in terris
        devote colimus;
        ad te, pie Iesu, clamamus:
        eleïson.

3

a. Kyrie, *spiritus alme,*   b. Kyrie, *qui baptizato*
   cohærens patri natoque,   *in Iordanis unda Christo*
   unius usiæ   *effulgens specie*
   consistendo,   *columbina*
   flans ab utroque,   *apparuisti*
   eleïson.   eleïson.

      c. Kyrie, *ignis divine,*
        pectora nostra succende,
        ut digni pariter
        proclamare
        possimus semper,
        eleïson.

One may reasonably infer, then, that more or less elaborate melodies might have arisen at this or that vowel in almost any choral part of the liturgy, and that any of these tunes might be provided with words. In many cases also a composer of words might, presumably, have invented or modified the music to fit his verbal text. Through some such process, then, were produced tropes of virtually all the musical parts of the Mass: introit, *Kyrie eleïson, Gloria in excelsis*, gradual, offertory, *Sanctus, Agnus Dei*, communio, and *Ite, missa est*. In the course of this general development extra-liturgical words were attached, more or less intimately, also to the epistle and the gospel.[1]

The most celebrated writer of tropes was Notker's friend,

---

[1] The standard collection of all forms of tropes of the Mass is that of C. Blume and H. M. Bannister, in *A. H.*, xlvii and xlix. For a liberal selection of texts see Gautier, *Tropes*, pp. 147 sqq. For a troped, or 'farced', epistle see below, ii, 461.

Tutilo, of whose life we know only that it was spent at St Gall and that it ended soon after 912.[1] Just as Notker has often been credited with the invention of sequences, so his fellow monk is often spoken of as the first writer of tropes.[2] Although this assignment of priority is doubtful,[3] we can assert with confidence that in his particular *genre* no early writer achieved greater acclaim.

Like the sequences, the tropes distributed throughout the Mass show a gradual transformation from prose into verse.[4] Tutilo and his immediate imitators used prose, and the great majority of tropes take this form. Into the midst of the prose, however, crept an occasional hexameter, and after about the middle of the eleventh century arose a considerable body of rhymed compositions in regular trochaic and iambic metres. These stages of development may be illustrated by the following three tropes of the *Agnus Dei*:

(1) Agnus Dei, qui tollis peccata mundi, *qui sedes ad dexteram Patris, solus inuisibilis rex*, miserere nobis.
Agnus Dei, qui tollis peccata mundi, *rex regum, gaudium angelorum, Deus*, miserere nobis.
Agnus Dei, qui tollis peccata mundi, *lux indeficiens, pax perpetua, omniumque redemptio sancta*, miserere nobis.[5]

(2) Agnus Dei, *Patris Filius æterni*, qui tollis peccata mundi, *auxilium quærentibus* miserere nobis.
Agnus Dei, *custos et pastor ovium*, qui tollis peccata mundi, *nostra te confidentibus* miserere nobis.
Agnus Dei, *defensor noster, adveni*, qui tollis peccata mundi, *tuam in te sperantibus* dona nobis pacem.[6]

(3)
Agnus Dei, qui tollis peccata mundi,	Agnus Dei, qui tollis peccata mundi,
causa rerum,	*cuius tactus*
lumen verum,	*regit actus,*
dulcis potus	*voluisse*
mundis notus,	*cui fecisse,*
sanans febres animæ,	*magistrorum optime,*
miserere nobis.	miserere nobis.

---

[1] See Gautier, *Tropes*, pp. 35–8; Wagner, pp. 274–5.
[2] See Gautier, *Tropes*, pp. 37–8.
[3] Blume (*Catholic Encyclopedia*, xv, 66) asserts that tropes, in some form, arose as early as the eighth century.
[4] See Gautier, *Tropes*, pp. 147–65; Wag-

ner, pp. 278–86.
[5] St Gall, Stiftsbibl., MS 484, Trop. Sangallense sæc. x, pp. 243–4. My text differs in a few details from that of Gautier, *Tropes*, p. 164. For the normal form of the *Agnus Dei* see above, p. 39.
[6] *A. H.*, xlvii, 387:

Agnus Dei, qui tollis peccata mundi,
  fovens cura
  sed secura,
    unge mentes
    te petentes,
    fructus spei maximæ,
      dona nobis pacem.[1]

In the first of these examples the embellishment is in plain prose. The amplifications of the liturgical text in the second case approach rhythmical regularity. In the third trope the rhyme and orderly trochaic movement are obvious.

The lavish effort expended upon embellishing the liturgy of the Mass was not applied in like measure, during the tenth and eleventh centuries, to the Canonical Office.[2] This apparent neglect is probably to be explained by the melodic simplicity of the music used in the *horæ*. In these services there were relatively few lengthy vocalizations, or wordless *jubili*, to which literary inventions might be fitted.[3] A few sequences, written primarily for use in the Mass, are sometimes found also in Lauds or Vespers.[4] Most of the extant tropes written specifically for the Canonical Office are associated with the responsories of Matins, and show the sophistications of rhyme and metre characteristic of the later Middle Ages. In the manuscripts these particular compositions are often given the special names *verbeta*, *prosula*, or *prosella*.[5] Tropes more or less similar to these in character were attached also to the formula *Deus in adjutorium*, the invitatory, the *lectiones* of Matins, the *Te Deum*, the *Magnificat*, the *Benedicamus*, and the antiphon of the Blessed Virgin Mary. Of several of these types of tropes examples will be found below.[6]

With such embellishments of the liturgy of the Canonical Office should be associated the ambitious literary productions known as rhymed offices, or *historiæ*.[7] These elaborate composi-

---

[1] *A. H.*, xlvii, 399.

[2] For tropes of the Canonical Office see Gautier, *Tropes*, pp. 165–73; Wagner, pp. 286–90; C. Blume, *Zur Poesie des kirchlichen Stundengebetes im Mittelalter*, in *Stimmen aus Maria-Laach*, lv (1898), 132–45; Villetard, *Corbeil*, pp. 87, 89–90, *et pass.*; Hoeynck, pp. 379–82. No comprehensive study of these particular tropes has yet been published, but it is expected that in *A. H.* a volume will be devoted to them. See *A. H.*, xlvii, 17. The general structure and content of the Canonical Office are explained above, chap. ii.

[3] See Wagner, p. 286.

[4] See, for example, below, p. 482.

[5] For examples of tropes of responsories see pp. 234, 574.

[6] See, for example, i, 567; ii, 18–9.

[7] For bibliography and an example see Young, *Miracle Play*, pp. 257–64. The subject is treated by Wagner, pp. 133, 294–312; Bäumer, ii, 73–86. Examples are found in *A. H.*, v, xiii, xvii, xviii, xxiv, xxv, xxvi, xxviii, xxix, and xlva.

tions may be described as attempts to versify all the choral pieces of the *Cursus* except the psalms themselves. From the tenth century onwards, *historiæ* of this sort were composed in very large numbers, especially for honouring particular saints or patrons. Naturally enough the various examples differ among themselves as to the completeness with which the process of versification is carried through the series of antiphons and responsories. Sometimes only parts of a few responsories appear as verse, whereas again every musical piece is transformed into rhymed metre, and the whole liturgical framework becomes a poem. Such rhymed offices can hardly be regarded as tropes in the sense assumed hitherto, for they are not so much *additions* to the established liturgical text as *substitutions* for it. Many of them, no doubt, are merely parochial inventions designed for honouring local saints, rather than for wide currency. Nevertheless they must be reckoned along with tropes in general as part of a pervasive literary effort which piously sought beauty and encouraged devotion, but which, in all countries of Western Europe, was a menace to the dignity and force of Roman worship.

IV

The literary content of tropes and the qualities of their style are determined by the general purposes for which they were composed.[1] Since they undertook to strengthen the emotions and elucidate the meanings inherent in the liturgy to which they were attached, they are primarily expositions of doctrine, and expressions of the varying moods of the liturgical year. In them one feels the freshness of Christmas, the austerity of Lent, the rejoicing of Easter, and the repose of the summer season of Pentecost. They do not, however, often penetrate into the liturgy of Holy Week; they almost never undertake to express the overwhelming grief aroused by the Passion. The characteristic note of the tropes is joy, expressed in impulsive sentences such as these:[2]

> Nubium cursus, ventorum volatus, fulgurum coruscatio, et tonitruum sonitus dulce consonent simul, Alleluia!

> Fluctus et undæ, imber et procellæ, tempestas et serenitas, cauma, gelu, nix, pruinæ, saltus, nemora pangant, Alleluia!

[1] By *tropes* I mean here all forms of liturgical embellishment, including sequences. The most comprehensive study of the content and style of tropes is that of L. Gautier, *La Poésie religieuse dans les Cloîtres des IXe–XIe siècles*, Paris, 1887.

[2] *A. H.*, liii, 60.

Hundreds of passages conclude with the joyous exclamation *Eia!*[1] The effort to expound doctrine may be illustrated by the following passage from a sequence on the Trinity:[2]

1. Vox clarescat, mens purgetur,
   homo totus emundetur,
   dulci voci conformetur
   pura conscientia;

2. Patri, proli iubilemus,
   sacrum neuma prædicemus,
   unam laudem tribus demus,
   quos unit essentia.

3. Pater creans increatus,
   nascens ab æterno natus,
   amor ab his derivatus
   sunt una substantia.

4. Tres personæ trinitatis
   unum esse deitatis,
   sunt eiusdem maiestatis
   et idem per omnia.

The doctrine of the Redemption is elucidated in a trope of the *Kyrie eleïson* thus:[3]

    a. Kyrie,
      magnæ Deus potentiæ,
      liberator hominis,
      transgressoris mandati,
      eleïson.

b. Kyrie *mirifice,*
  qui natum de virgine
  misisti redimere,
  nos pie eleïson.

c. Kyrie *magnifice,*
  qui carnem pro ovibus
  perditis assumpsisti
  humanam, eleïson.

For particularly sincere and adequate expression one may turn to phrases like these applied to the Holy Spirit:[4]

1. Te docente, nil obscurum,
   te præsente, nil impurum;
   sub tua præsentia

2. Gloriatur mens iucunda,
   per te læta, per te munda
   gaudet conscientia.

3. O iuvamen oppressorum,
   O solamen miserorum,
   pauperum refugium.

Or one may cite such earnest expressions as the following concerning the Eucharist:[5]

Cordium via, vita, veritas, cibus mentium, in quo sistit summa suavitas.

Cenæ supernæ redundans bonitas, panem mittens de cælo verum.

Beyond question, then, the writers of tropes often uttered significant thought and feeling in adequate language; their expression

---

[1] For examples see below, pp. 208, 209.
[2] *A. H.*, liv, 254.
[3] *A. H.*, xlvii, 158–9.
[4] *A. H.*, liv, 241–2. I have re-numbered the strophes.
[5] *A. H.*, xlvi i, 134.

is sometimes touching, and occasionally distinguished. As a whole, however, tropes bear the stamp of literary mediocrity. This failure in style arises, probably, not only from a lack of literary endowment in the writers, but also from the limitations imposed upon them by the circumstances. For a century or two these compositions were produced, in large measure, either as texts for pre-existing melodies, or in conformity with established conventions as to number of syllables and as to assonance. Under these conditions the temptation towards artificiality must have been strong. The result, in any case, was often commonplace or insincere. Affectation is seen, for example, in the excessive use of diminutives, of superlatives, and of words newly formed with suffixes such as *-fluus*.[1] Still more disheartening are the punning and verbal frivolities seen in such passages as the following:[2]

1a. Dum immundum et egenum   1b. Christus spinam hanc sacravit
    et immundis mundum plenum   et spineti spinas lavit
      mundavit a crimine,   suo sacro sanguine.

      Sis nobis vena veniæ.
      Sub securi stat securus.
      Dum torretur, non terretur.
      O quam beata curia,
      Quæ curæ prorsus nescia.

Although, in fairness, one must grant that ingenuities of this sort do not appear in all tropes, they are nevertheless so frequent as to indicate the literary level of these writings as a whole. In their simplest and least spirited form the tropes are mere prosaic amplifications of sentences in the liturgy. At their worst they transform the majestic common sense of Catholic worship into something lengthy, turgid, or fantastic; at their best they are genuine, and sometimes poetical, expressions of devotion and joy.

    Of the pleasure which these liturgical pieces gave to medieval worshippers we have such evidences as the following lines of Gautier de Coincy:[3]

      Chantons, chantons, clercs et clergesses,
      Les samedis les bèles messes
      De la Dame de paradis.

[1] See Gautier, *Poésie*, pp. 34–40; *A. H.*, xlvii, 170; xlix, 27, 83, 88, 135, 297; liii, 35, 63, 256; liv, 157, 357.

[2] *A. H.*, liv, 209; xlix, 336; R. C. Trench, *Sacred Latin Poetry*, London and Cambridge, 1864, pp. 56–7.

[3] *Les Miracles de la Sainte Vierge traduits et mis en vers par Gautier de Coincy*, ed. A. E. Poquet, Paris, 1857, p. 678. See Lintilhac, p. 23.

Chantons, chantons les samedis
Les déliteuses kyrièles,
Les séquences plaisans et bèles
A haute voiz et à haut tons.

The success of these extra-liturgical writings, moreover, appears not merely in the Latin versions written for use in churches, but also in the immense body of secular pieces which they inspired in the several vernaculars. The music and the words of tropes had a most pervasive influence upon European lyrical poetry in general. Many a *cantio*, cantata or motet of the most mundane character had its ultimate origin in pieces devised as embellishments of the liturgy of the Church.[1]

V

Our more immediate interest in tropes, however, lies not so much in their stylistic detail as in the dramatic form which a certain number of them display. Of this feature a striking example appears in the following piece composed by Tutilo himself:[2]

> *Hodie cantandus est nobis puer, quem gignebat ineffabiliter ante tempora Pater, et eundem sub tempore generauit inclyta mater.*
>
> Interrogatio: *Quis est iste puer quem tam magnis preconiis dignis uociferatis? Dicite nobis, ut collaudatores esse possimus.*
>
> Responsio: *Hic enim est quem presagus et electus symmista Dei ad terras uenturum preuidens longe ante prenotauit, sicque predixit:* Pver natvs est.[3]

This famous dialogue, composed as an introduction to the introit of the third Mass of Christmas, shows ample dramatic promise, and has sometimes been proclaimed the germ of medieval drama; but, as we shall see, it never became a play.[4] A similar dramatic ineffectualness attended several tropes containing dialogue, such as the following embellishment of the *Kyrie eleïson*:[5]

---

[1] See Meyer, pp. 166–84; J. Beck, *La Musique des Troubadours*, Paris [1910], pp. 23–4; Lintilhac, p. 23; Clark, p. 192; C. Blume, in *Festschrift Georg von Hertling*, Kempten and Munich, 1913, i, 128.

[2] Vienna, MS lat. 1845, Trop. Bambergense sæc. xi, fol. 58ᵛ. Possibly this particular text is now first printed. For numerous other texts see *A. H.*, xlix, 7–8; Young, *Offi-*

cium Pastorum, pp. 362–8. See also Gautier, *Tropes*, pp. 43, 61–4, 139, 209, 218; Schubiger, *Sängerschule*, p. 60; Meyer, p. 34; Frere, *Winchester Troper*, pp. 4–5; Chambers, ii, 8–9; Bartholomaeis, p. 126.

[3] The last three words are the *incipit* of the introit of the third Mass of Christmas.

[4] See below, ii, 23–4.

[5] *A. H.*, xlvii, 186–7, from a MS of the

1

a. Ad monumentum Domini
   plorabant mulieres;

b. Maria vidit angelum
   amictum cum splendore;

c. Cum lacrimis interrogat
   de Christo salvatore:

2

a. 'Ubi est meus Dominus
   et filius excelsi,

b. Quem Iudas tradit osculo,
   ut agnum crucifixit?

c. Iam lapis revolutus est
   ab ore monumenti.'

3

a. Sedit desuper angelus,
   mulieribus dixit:

b. 'Ille, quem quæris, mulier,
   surrexit, sicut dixit;

c. In Galilæam pergite;
   ibi eum videbitis.'

Dialogue is embedded also in a trope of the introit (*Nunc scio vere*) for the feast of St Peter (Aug. 1st):[1]

> *Petro ad ostium pulsanti occurrit puella illum interrogans ocius: 'Quis es, domine, pulsansque iamiam fortiter ianuam nostram?'*
>
> *'Assum Petrus,' ille respondens; 'dudum missus Christi in carcerem pro confessione: aperi, Roda!'*
>
> *At illa, illius vocem cognoscens, præ gaudio quæ fleverat, valvas non reclusit, fratribus enuntiavit.*
>
> *Alleluia, Alleluia. Viso Petro, omnes mergebant præ gaudioque fleverant; voce magna et Petrus inquit*: Nunc scio vere.

Dramatic possibilities are still more apparent in a trope of the introit (*Viri Galilæi*) of Ascension Day:[2]

> *Quem creditis super astra ascendisse, o Christicolæ?*
> *Iesum qui surrexit de sepulcro, o cælicolæ.*
> *Iam ascendit, ut prædixit: Ascendo ad patrem meum et patrem vestrum, Deum meum et Deum vestrum, alleluia.*
> *Regna, terræ, gentes, linguæ, decantate Domino.*
> *Quem adorant cæli cives in paterno solio. Eia!* Viri Galilæi.

---

twelfth century. Before each of the nine divisions of the trope were sung the words *Kyrie* (or *Christe*) *eleïson*.

[1] *A. H.*, xlix, 10, from a MS of the eleventh century. See Gautier, *Tropes*, p. 219; Bartholomaeis, p. 130.

[2] *A. H.*, xlix, 10. For other texts see Lange, p. 20; Frere, *Winchester Troper*, p. 110; Gautier, *Tropes*, p. 219; Young, *Some Texts*, p. 309. See also Chambers, ii, 11; Bartholomaeis, p. 148; Chevalier, *R. H.*, no. 16275; Blume, *Repertorium*, p. 268.

The manner in which such a trope might be sung is seen in a text, of uncertain date, from Vienne:[1]

Viennæ vero in Gallia diaconus et subdiaconus una cum archiepiscopo mitrati incedebant; et in reditu omnibus in navi stantibus, duo canonici ad cantores accedebant, quibus isti dicebant:

Quem creditis?[2]

Respondentibus illis:

Jesum qui resurrexit,

cantores reponebant:

Jam ascendit, sicut dixit.

Tum canonicis subjungentibus *Alleluia,* omnes chorum intrabant, Missamque solemniter decantabant.

We have also a similar trope for the introit (*De ventre*) of the feast of the Nativity of St John the Baptist (June 24th):[3]

Qvem creditis natum in orbe, o Deicole?
Iohannem precursorem ortum de sterili, angelo nunciante, o celicole.
Iam natus est,| ut dixit Saluator: Mitto angelum meum ante me qui preparet uiam meam.
Eia! Psallite, omnes cristicole: De ventre.

All of these tropes, with their bits of dialogue, show dramatic promise.[4] Through the use of impersonation any one of them might have become a diminutive play. This development, however, seems never to have occurred. Although we have only slight information as to the manner in which such pieces were sung, we may safely assume that those who uttered the dialogues never undertook to act them out.[5] The use of impersonation, indeed, seems to have been reserved especially for one particular trope which has not yet been mentioned, and which, because of its dramatic importance, must be considered by itself in the next chapter.

[1] Martene, iii, 193.
[2] creditis] quæritis (Martene).
[3] Vich, Museo, MS 111, Trop. Ripollense sæc. xii, fol. 19v–20r, previously printed by Young, *Some Texts,* p. 309.

[4] Concerning other dramatic tropes see Notes, p. 566.
[5] I have found no evidence in support of Gayley's statement (*Forefathers,* p. 31) that the Ascension trope developed into a play.

PLAYS ASSOCIATED WITH
THE RESURRECTION AND THE PASSION

CHAPTER VII

DRAMATIC TROPES OF THE MASS OF EASTER

AFTER our brief glance at several slight inventions of a dramatic sort in the preceding chapter, we are now to linger somewhat more attentively over a trope which, in its original form, is no more impressive or dramatically promising than the others, and which, indeed, probably served as a model for at least two of them.[1] Its pre-eminence is due, then, not to the boldness of its conception, but to the fact that out of it happened to be developed the earliest recorded play of the medieval Church.[2]

I

This prose trope is commonly attached to the introit of the Mass of Easter, and the simplest version of it runs as follows in a manuscript of the tenth century from the monastery of St Gall:[3]

ITEM DE RESVRRECTIONE DOMINI

Interrogatio:

Quem quęritis in sepulchro, Christicolę?

Responsio:

Iesum Nazarenum crucifixum, o caelicolae.

Non est hic, surrexit sicut predixerat; ite, nuntiate quia surrexit de sepulchro.

Resurrexi.

The trope, it will be seen, serves merely as an introduction to the introit, the complete text of which is as follows:[4]

Resurrexi, et adhuc tecum sum, alleluia; posuisti super me manum tuam, alleluia; mirabilis facta est scientia tua, alleluia, alleluia. Psalmus: Domine, probasti me, et cognovisti me; tu cognovisti sessionem meam, et resurrectionem meam.

[1] On the dependence of the Ascension trope *Quem creditis (cernitis)* and of the Christmas *Quem quæritis in præsepe* see Chambers, ii, 10–1.

[2] This trope is studied by Young, *The Origin of the Easter Play*, in *P.M.L.A.*, xxix (1914), 1–58. Some twelve examples of it are published, or referred to, by Blume, in *A.H.*, xlix, 9–10. See also Chambers, ii, 9–10; Gautier, *Tropes*, pp. 219–21; and Notes, p. 568.

[3] St Gall, Stiftsbibl., MS 484, Trop. Sangallense sæc. x, p. 111, previously printed, for example, by Gautier, *Tropes*, p. 220; Bartholomaeis, p. 128; Chambers, ii, 9; Young,

op. cit., p. 2; Adams, p. 3. For facsimiles see plate v, and Gautier, p. 216. The first word *Item* indicates that this is one of a series of tropes of the introit. The word *Resurrexi*, at the end, is the first word of the introit. For further bibliography see Notes, p. 568. In the examples of tropes given in the present chapter, the spoken text of the tropes is printed in Italics, the rubrics and the authorized liturgical text, in Roman type. In the MSS virtually all tropes have music.

[4] In regard to the singing of the introit see above, p. 21.

Clearly the literary embellishment in no way enters or disturbs the liturgical text. That it constitutes a dialogue appears both from the content and from the rubrics. The subject is the visit of the Marys to Christ's empty sepulchre, the first sentence containing the question asked by the angel, or angels,[1] stationed there, the second containing the reply of the Marys, and the third, *Non est hic*, the angelic announcement of the Resurrection. The omission of a rubric before the third sentence might suggest that the second and third utterances were delivered by the same persons. From other versions of the trope to be seen below, however, we infer that this undramatic form of rendition was avoided, and that the third sentence was spoken by the persons who spoke the first. In the text before us we have no indication as to how the parts were distributed: whether between two semi-choruses, or between a cantor and the whole chorus, or between two cantors, or groups of cantors.

In seeking the source of this addition to the liturgy we turn most naturally to the Gospel narratives of the Resurrection in the Vulgate, the relevant parts of which are as follows:[2]

Matthew xxviii.	Mark xvi.	Luke xxiv.
5. Respondens autem angelus, dixit mulieribus: Nolite timere vos; scio enim quod Jesum, qui crucifixus est, quæritis.	5. Et introeuntes in monumentum, viderunt juvenem sedentem in dextris coopertum stola candida, et obstupuerunt.	4. Et factum est, dum mente consternatæ essent de isto, ecce duo viri steterunt secus illas in veste fulgenti.
6. Non est hic; surrexit enim, sicut dixit. Venite et videte locum ubi positus erat Dominus.	6. Qui dicit illis: Nolite expavescere; Jesum quæritis Nazarenum, crucifixum; surrexit, non est hic; ecce locus ubi posuerunt eum.	5. Cum timerent autem, et declinarent vultum in terram, dixerunt ad illas: Quid quæritis viventem cum mortuis?
7. Et cito euntes, dicite discipulis ejus quia surrexit; et ecce præcedit vos in Galilæam; ibi eum videbitis; ecce prædixi vobis.	7. Sed ite, dicite discipulis ejus, et Petro, quia præcedit vos in Galilæam; ibi eum videbitis, sicut dixit vobis.	6. Non est hic, sed surrexit; recordamini qualiter locutus est vobis, cum adhuc in Galilæa esset.
10. Tunc ait illis Jesus: Nolite timere; ite, nunciate fratribus meis ut eant in Galilæam; ibi me videbunt.		

---

[1] The question of the number of angels at the tomb will be discussed below, p. 217. When the number is not indicated in the text under discussion, I shall often make my references in the singular.

[2] For discussions of the relation of *Quem quæritis* to the Vulgate see, for example, Young, *op. cit.*, pp. 6–8; Lintilhac, i, 25–6.

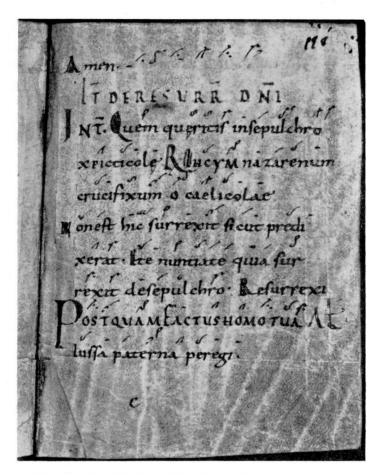

v. The Simplest Version of the Easter Dramatic Trope *Quem quæritis*, in St Gall, Stiftsbibliothek, MS 484, p. 111

It appears, in the first place, that none of the Gospels recounts the visit of the Marys in the form of a dialogue. In only one account, that of St Luke, is there an angelic interrogation, and this is far from identical with that in the trope. It is clear, moreover, that in none of the accounts do the Marys explicitly reply to the angelic address. Certainly, then, although the Vulgate provides the content and some of the words of the trope, it does not provide the dialogue form.[1] It might be suggested that the influence of St Luke's version is to be seen in the plural form *caelicolae* of the trope, since only in the third Gospel are two angels mentioned. The plural form, however, is almost certainly due to the rhyme with the inevitable plural *Christicole*.[2]

As another possible source we may turn to the liturgy itself, which the trope-writer was engaged in embellishing. During the Easter season he shared in the singing of such suggestive antiphons as the following:[3]

Antiphona: Jesum, quem quæritis, non est hic, sed surrexit; recordamini qualiter locutus est vobis dum adhuc in Galilæa esset, alleluia.

Antiphona: Nolite expavescere, Jesum Nazarenum quæritis crucifixum; non est hic, surrexit, alleluia.

Antiphona: Jesum qui crucifixus est quæritis, alleluia; non est hic, surrexit enim sicut dixit vobis, alleluia.

Likewise familiar were the following two well-known responsories:[4]

Angelus Domini descendit de cœlo, et accedens revolvit lapidem; et super eum sedit, et dixit mulieribus: Nolite timere; scio enim quia crucifixum quæritis. Jam surrexit. Venite et videte locum ubi positus erat Dominus, alleluia. Versus: Angelus Domini locutus est mulieribus dicens: Quem quæritis, an Jesum quæritis? Jam.

Angelus Domini locutus est mulieribus dicens: Quem quæritis, an Jesum quæritis? Jam surrexit, venite et videte, alleluia, alleluia. Versus: Ecce præcedet vos in Galilæam; ibi eum videbitis, sicut dixit vobis. Jam.

In view of the varied and somewhat elaborate methods employed in the singing of responsories during the Middle Ages, it might be surmised that in the rendering of the two texts before us the parts were so distributed among groups of the chorus as

---

[1] Lintilhac (i, 25–6) is clear on this point. Schiffmann (*Drama*, p. 9) regards the Gospel as already in dialogue form.

[2] See Gaston Paris, in *Journal des Savants*, 1892, p. 684.

[3] See Hartker, p. 230; Migne, *P. L.*, lxxviii, 769, 774. Here may be quoted also

the offertory of the Mass for Easter Monday (Migne, *P. L.*, lxxviii, 678): *Angelus Domini descendit de cœlo, et dixit mulieribus: Quem quæritis surrexit, sicut dixit, alleluia.*

[4] See Hartker, pp. 228–9; Migne, *P. L.*, lxxviii, 769–70.

to separate the interrogations from the enclosing narrative, and thus point the way more decisively towards dialogue.[1] As a matter of fact, however, we have no evidence that such an arrangement of parts was ever made; and, most significantly of all, these responsories, along with the antiphons cited, fail to provide an utterance for the Marys.

In another part of the liturgy, however, in an irrelevant context, are found certain brief passages that may have served the writer of *Quem quæritis* as a formal nucleus. During Mass on Good Friday he was accustomed to stand for an hour while the deacon sang the Passion according to St John. In the course of this impressive ceremony he heard the following:

(1) Quem quæritis?
Responderunt ei:
Jesum Nazarenum.[2]

(2) Quem quæritis?
Illi autem dixerunt:
Jesum Nazarenum.[3]

Since in the chanting of each of these passages each of the three utterances was marked by a change of pitch and tempo on the part of the deacon, the force of the question and answer could not escape a listener.[4] It will be remembered, however, that the three utterances are those of Christ, the narrator, and the Jews, respectively, and that they have no association with the visit of the Marys to the Tomb.

It appears, therefore, that whether or not any of these Biblical or liturgical passages served the author of *Quem quæritis* as a point of departure, none of them approaches the effectual dramatic form of the trope itself. *Quem quæritis in sepulchro* must be regarded as an original composition, in which we can discern a fusion of passages from the Vulgate and, possibly, from the liturgy.[5]

The author of this trope cannot be identified with any certainty. The oldest extant text, as we shall see, is found in a manuscript written at the monastery of St Martial at Limoges within the period 923–34.[6] This text, however, does not show

---

[1] Concerning the singing of the responsories see above, p. 54, and Young, *op. cit.*, pp. 8–11.

[2] John xviii, 4–5.

[3] *Id.*, xviii, 7.

[4] Concerning the medieval manner of singing the Passions during Holy Week see above, p. 100. Bartholomaeis (p. 127) appears

to accept the singing of the Passion as an influence upon the author of *Quem quæritis*.

[5] The general consensus of opinion upon this point is recorded by Young, *op. cit.*, p. 12, note 21. See also Brinkmann, p. 110.

[6] The MS (Paris, Bibl. Nat., MS lat. 1240), and the text from it, are dealt with below, p. 210. As to the date see the facts advanced

the trope in its simplest state. The *simplest* form, and, as we may rather confidently say, the *original* one, is that printed above from a manuscript of St Gall. Although this manuscript cannot be assigned to a date earlier than the middle of the tenth century,[1] the version of *Quem quæritis* preserved in it may be supposed to have originated at a date earlier than the period 923–34, from which we have a text of an elaborated version.[2] If, then, the original version of our trope seems to be located at St Gall, and if it arose at a date somewhat anterior to 923–34, one is tempted to mention as the probable author, the famous Tutilo, who was actively engaged in this sort of composition during the early years of the tenth century, and was still living in 912.[3] In support of this tentative attribution may be mentioned the fact that the St Gall manuscript, no. 484, which preserves the earliest text of the simplest version of *Quem quæritis in sepulchro*, contains also two tropes which have been decisively assigned to Tutilo,[4] and that one of these, *Hodie cantandus est*, is strikingly dramatic in form.[5]

II

Proceeding, then, to our survey of the career of *Quem quæritis* as a trope of the introit of Easter, we may observe first a trifling peculiarity in a version of the twelfth century from Vercelli:[6]

IN PASCHA INTROITUM

Quem queritis in sepulchro, o Christicole?
Versus: *Hiesum Nazarenum crucifixum.*
Versus: *Non est hic, surrexit sicut predixerat;[7] ite, nunciate quia surrexit.[8]*
Antiphona: Resurrexi.

The shortening of the second sentence here removes the usual rhyme *Christicolæ: cælicolæ*. This variation may have arisen through scribal error, although it appears in two other manuscripts.[9]

by H. M. Bannister, in *Journal of Theological Studies*, ii (1901), 420 sqq.
[1] See Bannister, *op. cit.*, p. 421.
[2] This reasoning seems to accord with the general view of Blume, in *A.H.*, xlix, 10.
[3] See Gautier, *Tropes*, pp. 35–6, and above, p. 190. Wilmotte (p. 15) regards Tutilo as the author, and to Brinkmann (p. 110) this assignment seems reasonable. See also Flood, pp. 546–7.
[4] See Gautier, *Tropes*, p. 34.

[5] Concerning *Hodie cantandus est* see above, p. 195.
[6] Vercelli, Bibl. Capit., MS 161, Grad.-Trop. Vercellense sæc. xii, fol. 121ʳ, previously edited by Young, *op. cit.*, p. 14, along with similar texts from Vercelli MSS 146 and 162.
[7] predixerat] prediscerat (MS).
[8] surrexit] susrexit (MS).
[9] MSS 146 and 162, treated by Young, *op. cit.*, p. 14.

Of the trope in the simple form of three sentences we have only the versions of St Gall and Vercelli. It is usually found with additional utterances at the beginning or the end, or at both beginning and end. In considering first the additions inserted at the close, we shall be interested especially in any efforts made towards improving the transition between the trope and the introit, for at this point lurks an incongruity in sense. The dialogue between the Marys and the angel, it will be observed, does not combine happily with the opening words of the introit: *Resurrexi, et adhuc tecum sum.* This sentence, taken from the Psalms,[1] is, in its present position, obviously intended as an utterance of the risen Christ, and in a text to be examined presently it is definitely referred to as being *verba Christi.*[2] Since, therefore, the outcome of the preceding dialogue is the assurance that Christ is *not* at the tomb (*Non est hic*), the *Resurrexi* of the introit, implying his presence, conveys an impression of abruptness or inconsistency. We may surmise, then, that some of the writers of tropes who, from time to time, enlarged the original form of *Quem quæritis* were conscious of this ineptitude, and undertook to remove it through providing a suitable transition between the trope and introit itself. Possibly an effort in this direction is discernible in a version of the eleventh or twelfth century from Ravenna:[3]

DOM*inicum* DIEM S*anctu*M PASCHE TROPH*i*[4]

Quem queritis in sepulchro, Cristicole?
Hiesum Nazarenum crucifixum, o celicole.
Non est hic, surrexit enim sicut predixerat; ite, nunciate quia surrexit dicentes:
Alleluia, resurrexit Dominus, hodie resur⟨r⟩exit leo fortis, Christus, filius Dei. Deo gracias, dicite eia, alleluia!
Resurrexi.[5]

In the absence of rubrics, it is quite impossible to determine how the added sentences here were distributed among the speakers. From other versions we may infer that they are felt as constituting a second speech for the *Christicolæ*, addressed to the chorus.[6] As a transition between the trope and the introit

[1] Ps. cxxxix, 18.
[2] See below, pp. 208, 209.
[3] Modena, Bibl. Capit., MS O.1.7, Trop. Ravennatense sæc. xi–xii, fol. 102ʳ–102ᵛ, previously edited by Young, *op. cit.*, p. 20. For similar texts see Notes, p. 568.

[4] I resist the temptation to emend the baffling introductory rubric of this text, and of others below.
[5] The word *Resurrexi* (MS *Resurrexit*) is followed by the rubric *Aliter.*
[6] For a parallel to this use of *dicentes* by one

the addition is not entirely negligible, for it serves, at least, to increase the separation between the words *Non est hic* and *Resurrexi, et adhuc tecum sum,* and softens the incongruity between the two passages. The exclamation *eia,* which has been noted as a special characteristic of tropes, will appear frequently in those of Easter.[1]

A somewhat similar enlargement of the trope appears in a version from the monastery of Bobbio:[2]

INCIPIUNT TROPHI IN DIE SANCTO[3] PASCE ANTE INTROITUM

Quem queritis in sepulchro, Christicole?
Hiesum Nazarenum crucifixum, o celicole.
Non est hic, surrexit sicut locutus est; ite, nuntiate quia surrexit, dicentes:
Alleluia, alleluia, resurrexit Dominus.

Item Trophi:

Pascha nostrum Christus est, immolatus agnus est, etenim pascha nostrum immolatus est Christus.
Hodie exultent iusti; resurrexit leo fortis; Deo gratias, dicite eia!

Item introitum: Resurrexi.

I assume that what follows the rubric *Item Trophi* is intended as a continuation of what precedes, and is meant primarily as an expression of liturgical rejoicing.

A far more definite effort towards transition is seen in a Benedictine version of the tenth or eleventh century from a monastery in the Abruzzi:[4]

DIEM DOMINICUM SANCTUM PASCHE
STATIO AD SANCTAM MARIA⟨M⟩ MAIORE⟨M⟩

INTROITUM

Quem queritis in sepulchro, Christicole?
Ihesum Nazarenum crucifixum, celicole.
Non hic est, surrexit sicut predixerat; ite, nuntiate quia surrexit.
Alleluia, resurrexit Dominus, hodie resurrexit leo fortis.

speaker for introducing the utterance of another speaker see the preface of the Mass above, p. 34.

[1] See above, p. 193.
[2] Turin, Bibl. Reale, MS G.V. 20, Grad.-Trop. Bobbiense sæc. xi, fol. 97ʳ, previously edited by Young, *op. cit.,* p. 31. Another text of the same version, from Turin MS F.IV.18, Trop. Bobbiense sæc. xii, fol. 85ᵛ, is printed *ibid.*
[3] Sancto] sc̄m (MS).

[4] Rome, Bibl. Vatic., MS lat. 4770, Miss. Benedictinum Sancti Petri in Aprutio sæc. x–xi, fol. 117ʳ. Bibliography bearing upon the MS, along with facsimiles showing the text before us, is given by E. Carusi and V. De Bartholomaeis, *Monumenti paleografici degli Abruzzi,* i, fasc. i, Rome, 1924, plates 12 and 13. For previous printings of the present text see Young, *op. cit.,* p. 30; Bartholomaeis, pp. 517–8; Stapper, *Münster,* p. 21.

⟨D⟩eo gratias, Deo gratias, Deo gratias; dicite omnes alleluia!
Eia, pleps deuota, Deo nunc corde sereno cum Christo Deo celebremus
Pascham canentes:
Resurrexit sicut dixit Dominus; in Galilea apparuit discipulis. Resurrexi[1]
et adhuc tecum sum. Ve tibi, Iuda, qui tradidisti Dominum, et cum Iudeis accepisti pretium.⟨Posuisti super me manum tuam, alleluia.⟩ Mulieribus que[2]
ad sepulchrum uenera⟨n⟩t angelus dixit quia surrexit Dominus. Mirabilis ⟨facta
est scientia tua, alleluia, alleluia⟩. Cito euntes, dicite, discipuli,[3] alleluia,
alleluia. Resurrexi.[4] Lux mundi, Dominus resurrexit hodie. Posui⟨sti⟩.[5]
Manus tua,[6] Domine, saluauit mundum hodie. Mirabilis. Scientia Dei mirabile facta est hodie, alleluia, alleluia. Resurrexi[7] et adhuc tecum sum,
alleluia. ⟨Ch⟩ristus hodie resurrexit a mortuis, et Patrem glorificans ait.
Posuisti super me manum tuam, alleluia. Quoniam mors mea facta est
mundi uita. Mirabilis facta est s⟨c⟩ientia tua. Quem celum ⟨et⟩ terra simul
collaudant dicentes alleluia, alleluia! Psalmus: Domine probasti.[8]

The sentence in this version beginning Eia, plebs devota is clearly
designed to introduce the introit and its further trope Resurrexit
sicut dixit. It aptly refers to the introit as being an utterance of
Christ, and invites the chorus to join in singing it. Admonition
of this sort leads, obviously, in the direction of liturgical, rather
than dramatic, expression.

The liturgical element is still more prominent in a trope of
the eleventh or twelfth century used, probably, at Vercelli:[9]

Quem queritis in sepulchro, Christicole?
Hiesum Nazarenum crucifixum, o celicole.
Non est hic, surrexit sicut predixerat; ite, nunciate quia surrexit, dicentes:
Alleluia, resurrexit Dominus, eia!
Karrissimi, uerba canite Christi.[10]
Psallite, fratres, hora est; surrexit Dominus, eia et eia!
Resurrexi.

Here the last two sentences are mere liturgical exhortations
designed for introducing the introit. Although such utterances
contribute nothing towards extending the preceding dialogue,
they provide a link between it and the liturgical text that follows.
This linking is still more intimate in a version of the eleventh
century from Monza:[11]

[1] discipulis. Resurrexi] dissipulis. Resurrexit (MS).
[2] Mulieribus que] Mulieres qui (MS).
[3] discipuli] dissipuli (MS).
[4] Resurrexi] Resurrexit (MS).
[5] Posui⟨sti⟩] Possui (MS).
[6] tua] tue (MS).
[7] Resurrexi] Resurrexit (MS).

[8] A trope of the Kyrie follows immediately.
[9] Vercelli, Bibl. Capit., MS 56, Miss.
Vercellense (?) sæc. xi-xii, fol. 87ᵛ, previously edited by Young, op. cit., p. 27.
[10] Christi] Xpiste (MS).
[11] Monza, Bibl. Capit., MS C. 13/76,
Grad.-Trop. Modœtinum sæc. xi, fol. 98ᵛ-99ʳ,
printed by Young, op. cit., p. 29. The last

TROPHus

Versus: *Quem queritis in sepulchro, Christicole?*
Versus: *Hiesum Nazarenum crucifixum, o celicole.*
Versus: *Non est hic, surrexit sicut predixerat; ite, nuntiate quia surrexit,*
dicentes:
    Alleluia, resurrexi⟨t⟩ hodie; hodie resurrexit leo fortis, Christus, filius
Dei; | Deo gratias, dicite eia!
    Resurrexi ⟨et adhuc tecum sum, alleluia; posuisti super me
manum tuam, alleluia; mirabilis facta est scientia tua, alleluia,
alleluia⟩.
    Eia, karissimi, uerba canite Christi.
Psalmus: Domine, probasti me, ⟨et cognovisti me; tu cognovisti
sessionem meam, et resurrectionem meam.
    Gloria Patri, et Filio, et Spiritui Sancto. Sicut erat in principio,
et nunc, et semper, et in sæcula sæculorum, Amen.⟩
    Psallite, fratres, ⟨h⟩ora est; surrexit Dominus, eia et eia!
Resurrexi.

In this instance the exhortations *Eia, karissimi* and *Psallite, fratres*
are enclosed within the sentences of the introit itself.

Another form of transition appears in a composition of the
eleventh century from Limoges: [1]

TROPOS IN RESURRECTIONE

Quem queritis in sepulchro, o Christicole?
Iesum Nazarenum crucifixum, o celicole.
Non est hic, surrexit sicut predixerat; ite, | nunciate quia surrexit.
Alleluia, ad sepulcrum residens angelus nunciat resurrexisse Christum.
En ecce completum est illud quod olim ipse per prophetam dixerat ad Patrem,
taliter inquiens:
    Resur⟨rexi⟩.

The sentence *Alleluia, ad sepulchrum* may be regarded as an undramatic narrative addition, as some critics have remarked,[2] or
it may be conceived of as an announcement of the Resurrection,
sufficiently appropriate for utterance by the *Christicolæ*. The
last sentence of the trope leads carefully up to the introit,
specifically recognizing its source in the Old Testament (*per
prophetam*), and marking it as an utterance of Christ Himself.

word *Resurrexi* indicates a repetition of the
antiphon of the introit. A similar text is to be
found in the same library, MS 77, Grad.
Modœtinum sæc. xii, fol. 81ʳ.
  [1] Paris, Bibl. Nat., MS lat. 1119, Trop. S.
Augustini Lemovicensis sæc. xi, fol. 21ʳ–21ᵛ,
previously edited by Young, *op. cit.*, p. 24.

This text is dealt with somewhat imperfectly
by Lange, *Osterfeiern*, no. 9, p. 22. Concerning similar texts from other MSS see Notes,
p. 569.
  [2] See Chambers, ii, 10; Gautier, *Tropes*,
p. 220.

III

As we approach those versions of *Quem quæritis* in which the simplest form is expanded by prefatory sentences, our attention is drawn first to a text from the monastery of St Martial, at Limoges, which antedates, by at least a few years, all other extant examples of this trope:[1]

TROPHI[2] IN ⟨DIE⟩ PASCHE

Psallite regi magno, deuicto mortis imperio!
Quem queritis in sepulchro, o Christicolę?

Responsio:

Ihesum Nazarenum crucifixum, o celicole.

Responsio:

Non est hic, surrexit sicut ipse dixit; ite, nunciate quia surrexit.
Alleluia, resurrexit Dominus, hodie resurrexit leo fortis, Cristus, filius Dei;
Deo gratias, dicite eia!

⟨Resurrexi, et adhuc tecum sum, alleluia.⟩ *Dormiui, Pater, et surgam diluculo, et somnus meus dulcis est michi.* Po⟨suisti super me manum tuam, alleluia⟩. *Ita, Pater, sic placuit ante te, ut moriendo mortis mors fuissem, morsus inferni, et mundo uita.* Mirabilis ⟨facta est scientia tua, alleluia, alleluia⟩. *Qui abscondisti hec sapientibus, et reuelasti paruulis, alleluia.*

The introductory sentence here might possibly be regarded as a sufficiently appropriate dramatic utterance for the angel who is conceived of as uttering the interrogation that follows; but the words *Psallite regi* suggest rather a purely liturgical exhortation, similar to the *Psallite, fratres* which we have already observed at the close of another version of the trope.

Another form of liturgical summons introduces a version of the eleventh century from Mantua:[3]

In die sancto[4] Pa⟨s⟩che ad Missam sint omnes ordinati in choro, et incipiat cantor ita dicens:

Hora est, psallite; [5] *iubet domnus canere; eia dicite!*

Respondet scola:[6]

Quem queritis in sepulchro, o Cristicole?

---

[1] Paris, Bibl. Nat., MS lat. 1240, Trop. Sancti Martialis Lemovicensis sæc. x, fol. 30ᵛ, printed by Young, *op. cit.*, p. 22, where earlier printings are mentioned. Concerning the date see above, p. 204. The text as printed here is followed immediately by the rubric *Item,* introducing another trope. See plate vi.

[2] Trophi] Tropum (? MS).

[3] Verona, Bibl. Capit., MS 107, Trop. Mantuanum sæc. xi, fol. 11ʳ, previously edited by Young, *op. cit.*, p. 19. Concerning other texts of this trope see Notes, p. 570.

[4] sancto] sēm (MS).

[5] psallite] spallite (MS).

[6] The use of the word *schola* as a designation for any liturgical chorus arose from the

VI. The Earliest Text of the Easter Dramatic Trope *Quem quæritis*, in Paris, Bibliothèque Nationale, MS lat. 1240, fol. 30ᵛ

Respondet cantor:

Hiesum Nazarenum crucifixum, o celicole.

Respondet scola:

Non est hic, surrexit sicut predixerat; ite, nunciate quia surrexit, dicentes:
Resurrexi.

The sentence beginning *Hora est,* which is, obviously, no part of the dialogue, may arise from a passage in the Epistle to the Romans: *Hora est iam nos de somno surgere.*[1] It is found apart from *Quem quæritis* in the following Easter trope of the twelfth century:[2]

⟨*H*⟩*ora est, psallite; iubet domnus canere; eia dicite.*
Christus, devicta morte, resonat voce preclara, Patri dicens:
Resurrexi et adhuc tecum sum.

Particularly welcome in the text from Mantua are the rubrics. Although regrettably brief, they assure us that the sentences are delivered responsively, between a single cantor and the whole chorus (*schola*). This arrangement recognizes the fact that the trope is in dialogue form; but it does not attempt precise dramatic appropriateness.

The presence of both the hortatory introduction and familiar transitional sentences before the introit is seen in a tenth-century form from Limoges:[3]

In die sancto Pasche Stacio ad Sanctum Petrum

Item Tropos in Die

Hora est, psallite; iubet[4] *dompnus canere; eia, eia dicite!*
Quem queritis in sepulcro, o Christicole?

Respondent:
Iesum Nazarenum crucifixum, o celicole.
Respondent:
Non est hic,[5] *surrexit sicut predixerat; ite, nunciate quia surrexit.*
Respondent:
Alleluia, ad sepulcrum residens angelus nunciat resurrexisse Christum.

---

term *schola cantorum,* which was applied to a school of liturgical singing, or, more particularly, to the pre-eminent *schola cantorum* established at Rome by Gregory the Great. See Wagner, pp. 214–9; Bäumer, i, 300–5; Braun, *Handlexikon,* p. 311.

[1] Rom. xiii, 11.

[2] I give the text of Bartholomaeis (p. 141),

published from an Italian missal of the twelfth century (MS Vat. lat. 10646).

[3] Paris, Bibl. Nat., MS lat. 1118, Trop. Sancti Martialis Lemovicensis sæc. x (988–96), fol. 40ᵛ, previously edited by Young, *op. cit.,* p. 26.

[4] iubet] iuba (MS).

[5] hic] ihc (MS).

En ecce completum est illud quod olim ipse per prophetam dixerat, ad Patrem taliter inquiens:

Resurrexi.[1]

Of this same type is the following from Apt, in France:[2]

IN PASCHA

Hora est, psallite; iube⟨t⟩ dominus canere; eia dicite!
Quem queritis in sepulchro, Chri⟨s⟩ticole?
Ihesum Nazarenum crucifixum, o celicole.
Non est hic, surrexit sicut predixerat; ite, nunciate quia surrexit dicentes:
Alleluia, resurrexit Dominus, hodie resurrexit | leo fortis, Christus, filius Dei; Deo gracias, dicite eia!
En ecce completum est illud quod olim ipse per prophetam dixerat, ad Patrem taliter inquiens:[3]

Antiphona: Resurrexi.[4]

In these two versions the original three sentences of the simplest form of the trope lose their salience in the midst of utterances which enhance the liturgical vivacity of the composition rather than its dramatic promise.

A genuine addition to the dialogue appears, finally, in a somewhat incomplete version of the eleventh century from Limoges:[5]

⟨H⟩OC EST DE MULIERIBUS

Vbi est Christus, meus Dominus et filius excelsus? Eamus uidere sepulcrum.
Quem queritis in sepulcro, o Christicole?
⟨Jesum Nazarenum crucifixum, o cœlicolæ.⟩[6]
Non est hic, surrexit sicut predixerat; ite, nuntiate discipulis eius quia precedet uos in Galileam.
Vere surrexit Dominus de sepulcro cum gloria, alleluia.

A complete text containing the same novelty is forthcoming from the monastery of Ripoll, in Spain:[7]

---

[1] Resurrexi] Resurrexit (MS). Followed immediately by the rubric *Item alius.*

[2] Apt, Bibl. Capit., MS 4, Trop. Aptense sæc. x–xi, fol. 33ᵛ–34ʳ, incompletely edited by Young, *op. cit.*, p. 23.

[3] En ecce . . . inquiens] Written in another hand, of the eleventh century, in the upper margin of fol. 34ʳ.

[4] Resurrexi] Resurrexit (MS).

[5] Paris, Bibl. Nat., MS lat. 1139, Trop. Sancti Martialis Lemovicensis sæc. xi–xii, fol. 53ʳ, printed by Young, *op. cit.*, p. 34. For a list of earlier printings see Lange, p. 4. Lange's own text (p. 22) is incomplete. Con-cerning the MS see below, ii, 456. In the MS the text is preceded by irrelevant *versus*, and followed by the rubric *Sponsus*, introducing the famous play of that name (see below, ii, 362). For a somewhat similar text see Notes, p. 570.

[6] This sentence is supplied also in the text printed by Morf, p. 391.

[7] Vich, Museo, MS 32, Trop. Ripollense sæc. xii–xiii, fol. 48ᵛ. The same text is found *ibid.*, MS 124, fol. Bᵛ–Cʳ, under the rubric *Tropus in die sancto Pasche.* Both texts have been edited by Young, *op. cit.*, pp. 33–4, the first of the MSS being numbered 31 there.

IN DIE SANCTO PASCHE TROPUS

⟨*H*⟩*ora est, psallite; iubet domnus canere; eia dicite!*
Vbi est Christus, meus Dominus et filius excelsi? Eamus uidere sepulcrum.
Quem queritis in sepulcro, Christicole?
Ihesum Nazarenum crucifixum, o celicole.
Non est hic, surrexit sicut predixerat; ite, nunciate quia surrexit, dicentes:
Alleluia, ad sepulcrum residens angelus nunciat resurrexisse Christum.

En ecce completum est illud quod olim ipse per prophetam dixerat, ad Patrem taliter inquiens:
Resurrexi.

The additional passage *Ubi est Christus*, in these two texts, is an appropriate utterance for one of the *Christicolæ*, and, as we shall see, was assigned to one of the Marys in the eventual dramatization of this form of the trope.[1] It has been suggested that the words *Eamus videre sepulchrum* indicate the actual presence of some sort of sepulchre as *mise en scène* for the dialogue;[2] but of this there is no certainty.

The versions of *Quem quæritis in sepulchro* reviewed above illustrate sufficiently the textual expansion of this trope while it remained attached to the introit of the Mass of Easter.[3] Noteworthy is the fact that the sequence of sentences as found in the simplest form of the composition is not disturbed. We must infer, therefore, that the various expanded versions were not original and independent creations in separate localities, but were all developments from a single form contrived by a single author.[4] The additions are, in general, not sentences borrowed from the authorized liturgy, but free inventions like the original trope itself.[5] A few of the increments may be regarded as additions to the dialogue; but, as a whole, they express liturgical rejoicing rather than a sense for drama.

IV

For estimating the dramatic significance of these tropes, however, our most serious limitation hitherto has been the almost

[1] See below, p. 271. I do not understand why Chambers (ii, 29) thinks this utterance appropriate only to the Blessed Virgin Mary, who was not one of the women visiting the empty sepulchre. For a trope of the *Kyrie* containing the sentence under consideration see above, p. 196. In this instance *Ubi est Christus* is clearly understood to be the utterance of one of the three *mulieres* who visit the empty tomb.

[2] See Gautier, *Tropes*, p. 221.
[3] Such a version as that from Paris MS lat. 1139, to be sure, may not be a genuine introit trope; but probably it is.
[4] This is the view, for example, of Milchsack (p. 32), Davidson (pp. 31-2), and Brinkmann (p. 110). For the contrary opinion see R. Bechstein, in *Literaturblatt für germanische und romanische Philologie*, 1881, col. 201-2. [5] See Young, *op. cit.*, p. 58.

total absence of information as to the circumstances in which they were sung. As to physical surroundings, or *mise en scène*, the meagre rubrics have been silent. It is possible that one or another of the versions examined above was sung before some sort of representation of a sepulchre, with an appropriate distribution of parts among the participants, and amid a suggestive ceremonial; but of such effects we have, as yet, heard nothing explicit. We are now ready, therefore, to consider a few versions of *Quem quæritis* which offer nothing new in their content, but which bear at least the beginnings of evidence as to the arrangements for singing them. Informing details are found, for example, in the following text of the eleventh century from Monte Cassino:[1]

Finita Tertia, uadat unus sacerdos ante altare, alba ueste indutus, et uersus ad chorum dicat alta uoce:

Quem queritis?

Et duo alii clerici stantes in medio chori respondeant:

Iesum Nazarenum.

Et sacerdos:

Non est hic, surrexit.

Illi uero conuersi ad chorum dicant:

Alleluia, resurrexit Dominus.

Post hec incip*iatur* tropos. Seq*uatur* introitus: Resurrexi.

The arrangement here is that a single priest, standing before the altar, addresses the angel's question to two clerics standing in the middle of the choir. The two clerics deliver the reply of the Marys, and after receiving the angelic assurance, address to the chorus their *Alleluia, resurrexit*. In the assignment of parts we may discern an attempted approach to dramatic appropriateness—one person speaking for the angel, and two persons for the Marys.[2] The stationing of the personages *ante altare* points to the possibility that the altar itself may be used consciously as a dramatic setting.

This possibility is suggested still more directly by another version from Monte Cassino:[3]

---

[1] Monte Cassino, MS 127, Miss.–Monasticum sæc. xi, fol. 105ᵛ, previously printed by Young, *op. cit.*, pp. 35–6, and by A. de la Fage, *Essais de Diphthérographie musicale*, Paris, 1862, p. 473. The text before us is preceded by a heading which seems to read, Dom*inicum* S*anctum* Pa*s*cha. A somewhat similar text is calendared in *Bibliotheca Casinensis*, iv, Monte Cassino, 1880, p. 124. See Chambers, ii, 12; Young, *op. cit.*, p. 36.

[2] See below, p. 217.

[3] Martene, iv, 147–8, from an unidentified manuscript older than the year 1105. The text has been previously reprinted by Lange,

Processione finita, vadat sacerdos post altare, et versus ad chorum dicat alta voce:

Quem quæritis?

Et duo alii clerici stantes in medio chori respondeant:

Jesum Nazarenum.

Et sacerdos:

Non est hic.

Illi vero conversi ad chorum dicant:

Alleluja.

Post hæc alii quatuor cantent tropos, et agatur Missa ordine suo.

In this case the priest who speaks the words of the angel stands *behind* the altar, addressing two clerics who stand on the other side of it; hence the dialogue is carried on *across* the altar in such a way as to include it unmistakably in the setting. Similar conditions are found in several other versions—for example, in this one of the twelfth century from Benevento:[1]

Indutus presbyter sacris uestibus stet post altare, et dic*at* alta uoce:
Quem queritis in sepulcro, Christicole?

Respondeat diaconus:

Hiesum Nazarenum, o celicole.

R*espondeat* presbyter:

Non est hic, surrexit sicut predixerat; ite, nunciate quia surrexit.

Tunc pergit diaconus canendo hec usque in choro:

Alleluia, resurrexit Dominus.

Item versus de introitu:

Hodie exultent iusti, resurrexi⟨t⟩ leo fortis; Deo gracias dicite omnes.
Resurrexi.[2]

The words of the angel, it will be observed, are here said by a single priest, and those of the Marys, by a single deacon.

In a text of the eleventh century from Novalesa is seen a slightly different distribution of parts:[3]

In die sancto Pasce, cum omnes simul convenerint in ecclesiam ad

no. 23, p. 23; Chambers, ii, 12; Young, *op. cit.*, p. 42; Bartholomaeis, p. 517. Here may be mentioned a confused text of the thirteenth century from St Denis, printed by Martene, iv, 147, and reprinted by Lange, no. 1, p. 21 (incompletely), and by Chambers, ii, 12.

[1] Benevento, Bibl. Capit., MS 27, Trop. Beneventanum sæc. xii, fol. 47ᵛ, previously edited by Young, *op. cit.*, pp. 37-8. The text

before us is preceded by the rubric, Domi*nicum* S*anctum* Pascha, S*tatio* ad S*anctam*Maria⟨m⟩. For similar tropes from the Beneventan MSS 25, 26, 28 and 29, see Young, pp. 37-9.

[2] The trope continues within the introit. See Young, pp. 37-8.

[3] Oxford, Bibl. Bodl., MS Douce 222, Trop. Novaliciense sæc. xi, fol. 18ᵣ-19ᵣ, previously edited by Young, *op. cit.*, p. 40;

Missam celebrandam, stent parati duo diaconi induti dalmaticis retro altare dicentes:|

Quem queritis in sepulchro, Christicole?

Respondeant duo cantores stantes in choro:

Iesum Nazarenum crucifixum, o celicole.

Item diaconi:

Non est hic, surrexit sicut predixerat; ite, nunciate quia resurrexit, dicentes.

Tunc cantor dicat excelsa uoce:

Alleluia, resurrexit Dominus.

Tunc psallat scola:

Resurrexi, ⟨et adhuc tecum sum, alleluia.⟩ *Qui dicit Patri prophetica uoce.*| Posuisti ⟨super me manum tuam, alleluia; mirabilis facta est scientia tua, alleluia, alleluia⟩. *Mirabile laudat filius Patrem.* Psalmus: Domine, probasti me, ⟨et cognovisti me; tu cognovisti sessionem meam et resurrectionem meam.⟩ *Eia, karissimi, uerba canite Christi.* Resurrexi, ⟨et adhuc tecum sum, alleluia.⟩ *Victor ut ad celos, calcata morte, redire.* Posuisti ⟨super me manum tuam, alleluia⟩. *Quo genus humanum, pulsis erroribus, altum scanderet ad celum.* Mirabilis ⟨facta est scientia tua, alleluia, alleluia⟩. *Nunc omnes cum ingenti gaudio celsa uoce gloriam Christo canite.* Gloria ⟨Patri, et Filio, et Spiritui Sancto; sicut erat in principio, et nunc et semper, et in sæcula⟩ seculorum, Amen.[1]

Here the words of the angel are said by two deacons standing behind the altar, and those of the Marys by two cantors standing on the other side of it.

A less definite indication of the number of the speakers is given us, finally, in a version of the end of the eleventh century, or the beginning of the twelfth, from Piacenza:[2]

IN DIE SANCTO [3] PASCE TROPI

Finita Tercia, cantor cum aliis uadat retro altare; excelsa uoce incipiat:

Quem queritis[4] in sepulcro, Christicole?

Qui ante altare fuerint respondeant:

Hiesum Nazarenum crucifixum, o celicole.

Illi uero ⟨qui⟩ retro fuerint dicent:

Non est hic, surrexit sicut predixerat; ite, nunciate quia surrexit, dicentes.

Brooks, *New Texts*, pp. 463–4; Young, *Officium Pastorum*, p. 309.

[1] Here follows another trope beginning *Christus surrexit a mortuis.*

[2] Piacenza, Bibl. Capit., MS 65, Grad.-Trop. Placentinum sæc. xi–xii, fol. 235ᵛ,

printed by Young, *Easter Play*, p. 41. Somewhat similar rubrics are found in Pistoia, Bibl. Capit., MS 70, Trop. Pistoriense sæc. xi–xii, fol. 32ʳ.

[3] Sancto] scm (MS).

[4] Quem queritis] Written twice (MS).

Qui ante *respondeant:*

> Alleluia, alleluia, resurrexit Dominus.

Illi qui retro dicant:

> Eia, carissimi, uerba canite Christi.

His finitis, qui retro fuerint, ante altare ueniant et cum aliis simul cantant: Resurrexi.[1]

According to the custom of this church some three or more cantors gather behind the altar to sing the words of the angel, and an undetermined number respond for the Marys. At the end of the dialogue, the cantors behind the altar come forward to join those in front for the singing of the introit.

In view of the fact that several of the versions now before us assign the sentences of the dialogue to definite persons, or groups, it is time to inquire what the appropriate number of participants really is. According to St Matthew two Marys visited the tomb, and encountered one angel stationed outside it.[2] In St Mark's account there are three Marys, and one angel seated within the tomb.[3] St Luke does not mention the number of the women, but speaks of two angels within.[4] In recounting the visit of Mary Magdalen to the Sepulchre, St John mentions two angels.[5] Omitting from consideration the visit of Mary Magdalen, which obviously is not the subject of the trope, we observe that the Gospels may be said to sanction any arrangement employing either two or three Marys, and either one or two angels. As to the number of the angels, the authorized liturgy shows no consistent usage, but an apparent preference for the one angel stationed outside, in accordance with the account of St Matthew. Hartker's *Liber responsalis*, of the tenth century, illustrates its Easter section by a notable picture showing one angel, outside the sepulchre, in conversation with three women;[6] and in adapting the Gospel passage *vidit duos angelos in albis sedentes*[7] to liturgical use, the same authority alters it to read *vidit angelum in albis sedentem.*[8] The version of *Quem quæritis* in the same manuscript, however, has the usual plural *cælicolæ.*[9] Since the text of the trope itself usually refers to both the Marys and

---

[1] For the continuation of the trope within the introit see Young, *op. cit.*, pp. 41–2.

[2] See Matt. xxviii, 1, 2, 5–7.

[3] See Mark xvi, 1, 5.

[4] See Luke xxiii, 56; xxiv, 1, 4, 23.

[5] See John xx, 11–21.

[6] See Hartker, p. 227 (St Gall MS 391,

p. 33), reproduced as frontispiece, plate i.

[7] John xx, 12.

[8] Hartker, p. 237. For a general discussion of the number of the angels see Meyer, pp. 82–5.

[9] See Hartker, p. 231.

the angels in the plural, it would seem that dramatic appropriateness must require at least two speakers for each part in the dialogue. To this condition only the versions from Novalesa and Piacenza can be said to conform. But the varying evidences of the Gospels and the liturgy obviously encourage other arrangements, inconsistent with the content of the trope itself, such as that shown by the version from Monte Cassino, with one speaker for the part of the angel, and two for the part of the Marys.

From these observations upon the distribution of parts in the few tropes before us it should not be inferred that I am contending for a conscious attempt at complete dramatic fitness on the part of the writers. The various arrangements in these texts may have resulted merely from the accidents of local circumstance. Above all, it should be observed that we have as yet encountered no evidence whatever of dramatic impersonation. So far as we can tell from the rubrics, the participating clerics are vested, and conduct themselves, in the usual liturgical manner.[1]

Considerably more significant than the tentative distribution of parts, in the group of texts before us, is the delivering of the dialogue across the altar, for this practice at once raises the question as to whether this particular locale was adopted merely by chance, or was deliberately chosen for its dramatic appropriateness. That the latter is the case seems to be established by the fact that both through its physical history and through its symbolical implications the altar has always been regarded as a sepulchre, and often, more specifically, as the sepulchre of Christ.[2]

During the years immediately following the Crucifixion, the altars used in renewal of the Last Supper were probably mere tables of wood (*mensæ*) in the houses of the faithful.[3] Later, during a century or two of persecution, the observance often occurred in special and remote localities, such as the catacombs about Rome, and similar places of burial. In such cemeteries the altar was inevitably placed, in some manner, over the body of a martyr or saint. It may have been constructed in a grave-chapel above ground,[4] or it may have been the very cover of

[1] For an *ordo* of the fourteenth century concerning the stationing of two cardinal deacons behind the altar, 'ad similitudinem seu repræsentationem angelorum monumentum custodientium,' in the Papal Mass at Rome, see Migne, *P.L.*, lxxviii, 1331.
[2] See Braun, *Altar*, i, 608–61, 753; Young *op. cit.*, pp. 43 sqq.; above, p. 115.
[3] See Rohault de Fleury, *Messe*, i, 103 237.
[4] See Hirn, pp. 14–8.

a sarcophagus, in a chamber under ground.[1] Whatever its particular form, the Christian altar very early became closely associated with the tomb of a martyr or saint. As one writer has remarked, 'The "arca", *i.e.* the chest which contained the martyr's bones, became an "ara", *i.e.* a table bearing the flesh and blood of the divine man.'[2] It was natural, then, that with the erection of altars in churches, after the Peace of the Church, the identification of tomb and altar should have been piously maintained, and that the church altar should have been built, normally, over the tomb of a saint, or, to reverse the relation, that the relics of a saint (*Sancta Sancti*) should have been buried under the altar.[3] Thus it happens that to this day, under the main altar of many a church edifice, may be found the tomb of a saint, the saint's place of rest being variously called *Confessio*, *Martyrium*, or *Testimonium*.

As the number of churches increased throughout the Christian world, however, it became impossible to provide for each altar the entire remains of a saint, and a subdividing of relics became necessary. Instead of resting over the entire body of a sanctified person, the altar could now be associated with only a small particle, or small particles. These relics were sometimes placed in an appropriate reliquary under the altar, or, as was more common, in an excavation in the top of the stone altar-table, the cavity being regularly called *sepulchrum*. In the *sepulchrum* was placed a closed box (*capsa*)—usually a small envelope of lead—containing the relics, and the *sepulchrum* cavity was closed with a stone seal (*sigillum*).[4]

For the medieval worshipper the transition was easy from the use of the altar as the tomb of a saint to the notion of the altar as the sepulchre of Christ. It appears, indeed, that in the *sepulchrum* of the altar the relics of the saint were sometimes actually replaced by 'fragments of the Saviour's body', that is, by pieces of a consecrated wafer.[5] In such a case the altar became in an actual sense the grave of Christ.

Whether or not the altar was often recognized as *Sepulchrum Christi* through such material means, we have sufficient evidence that it was so accepted symbolically.[6] In the *Theoria* of

[1] See Rohault de Fleury, *Messe*, i, 103–9, 237.

[2] Hirn, p. 23.

[3] See *id.*, p. 26.

[4] See Thalhofer, i, 431; Hirn, p. 26 Otte,

i, 131, 134.

[5] See Hirn, p. 68.

[6] See Rohault de Fleury, *Messe*, i, 107–9, 239.

Germanus I, Patriarch of Constantinople († 733), for example, we read:[1]

> Altare est Propitiatorium in quo offerebatur pro peccato, iuxta sanctum monumentum Christi, in quo altari victimam se Christus obtulit Deo et Patri, per oblationem corporis sui. . . . Altare est et dicitur præsepe, et sepulchrum Domini.

A similar interpretation is given by Amalarius of Metz, in the ninth century, in his *De Ecclesiasticis Officiis*:[2]

> Per particulam oblatæ immissæ in calicem ostenditur Christi corpus, quod jam resurrexit a mortuis; per comestam a sacerdote vel a populo, ambulans adhuc super terram, per relictam in altari, jacens in sepulcris.

Again, in his *Ecloga de Officio Missæ* Amalarius writes the following verse:[3]

> Ecce habes hic tumulum Christi quam conspicis aram.

Further testimony as to the symbolism of the altar, and as to the fitness of the arrangement seen in the dramatic texts under consideration, is found in the famous *Rationale* of Durandus, Bishop of Mende († 1296):[4]

> Nec est omittendum, quod in quibusdam ecclesijs in his septem diebus duo cum albis superpellicijs incipiunt responsorium *Hec dies*; et in alijs, quosdam tropos post altare,—quod representat sepulcrum pro eo quod corpus Iesu in eo sacramentaliter collocatur et consecratur—gerentes typum duorum angelorum qui stantes in sepulcro Christum resurrexisse retulerunt.

Durandus's description of *tropos post altare* seems to apply precisely to versions of *Quem quæritis in sepulchro* sung in the manner customary at Monte Cassino, Benevento, Novalesa, and Piacenza, and to give substantial support to our inference that the altar was adopted deliberately as the appropriate setting for this dialogue. Further confirmation will appear in numerous versions of the Easter play exhibited in subsequent chapters.

V

The accompaniment of an appropriate setting, however, does not in itself give assurance that the process of dramatization is complete. The final dramatic result, as we have seen, is achieved only when those who speak actually attempt to impersonate, in some manner, the characters whom they represent. This essential requirement is met by none of the versions of *Quem quæritis*

---

[1] *Maxima Bibliotheca Veterum Patrum*, xiii, Lyons, 1677, p. 51.
[2] Migne, *P.L.*, cv, 1154–5.
[3] *Id.*, col. 1326.
[4] Durandus, fol. ccxiiii[r].

reviewed above, nor by any other known trope of the introit, unless it be the following one of the fifteenth century from Brescia:[1]

In die Pasce cantoria accipiant duas dominas et ponant post altare maius in loco Angelorum, et cantent istam tropham, scilicet:

Quem queritis?

Et cantoria accipiant tres dominas que habeant singula vassa argentea[2] in manibus, et canere debeant in medio choro ad modum[3] tres Marie et respondeant Angelis, scilicet:

Ihesum Nazarenum.

Respondeant Angeli:

Non est hic, sur⟨r⟩exit.

Tres Marie et cante⟨n⟩t adhuc tropha⟨m⟩, scilicet:

Alleluia, resurrexit.

Et hoc facto, ebdomodaria epistole[4] teneat sepulcrum eboris in manibus in medio choro donec expleat epistolam, et incipiat officium[5] Misse:

Resur⟨r⟩exi, et adhuc tecum sum.

Et tres Marie respondeant istam tropham:

Qui dicit Patri propheti⟨c⟩a uoce.

Et chorus respondeat, scilicet:

Posuisti super me manum tuam.

Tres Marie respondeant:

Mirabilem laudat filius Patrem.

Chorus respondeat:

Mirabillis facta est scientia tua.

Et tres Marie vadant deorsum tunc ad altare maius ad offerendum tria vasa argentea, et chorus dicat versum:

Domine, probasti me.

Et chorus incipiat officium:

Resurrexi.[6]

Et alius chorus dicat:

Gloria Patri.

Et hoc dicto, ueniant tres[7] Marie. Respondeant superius in medio choro et dicant istam tropham, scilicet:

Hodie resurrexit.

[1] Brescia, Bibl. Civica Queriniana, MS H.vi.11, Ordin. Ecclesiæ Sanctæ Juliæ anni 1438, fol. 30ʳ, previously edited by Young, *op. cit.*, pp. 47–8. The MS provides no music.
[2] argentea] arientea (MS).
[3] modum] modom (MS).

[4] epistole] epistola (MS).
[5] officium] offitium (MS). *Officium* is the usual word for introit in France, and is thus used also in other countries.
[6] officium: Resurrexi] offitium Resurexit (MS).
[7] tres] et hoc dicto tres (MS).

Et hiis finitis, tres Marie reuertant ad loca sua; et ebdomodaria incipiat adhuc officium Misse:

Resurrexi.[1]

Et chorus expleat, et cantoria incipiat prosam, scilicet:

Domine redemptor.

Et ebdomodaria incipiat: Kyrie.

From the extraordinary Latinity of this text we can, perhaps, extract the essentials of the dramatic performance. Since the three nuns in the middle of the choir carry silver vessels and avowedly impersonate the three Marys, we may assume that the two behind the altar impersonate the angels. The dialogue is delivered across the altar in a manner with which we are already acquainted. The handling of the *sepulchrum eboris* by the *hebdomadaria* is not clearly explained. This personage appears to have some association with the epistle, the reading of which at the introit cannot, of course, be contemplated. I can only surmise that a small representation of the sepulchre, in ivory, had been placed upon the altar as part of the general *mise en scène*, and that, at the conclusion of the dramatic dialogue, the one who was eventually to read the epistle took the ivory sepulchre from the altar and held it until after the epistle was finished. It is interesting to observe that after they have completed their dramatic action, the three Marys take part in the singing of the internal troping of the introit, the chorus delivering the liturgical text, and the Marys, the trope.

If I interpret this text correctly, it is the only one yet published which presents a completely dramatized form of the trope *Quem quæritis* in its direct attachment to the introit of Easter. Such a result is a natural outcome of the earlier developments of this dialogue which have been surveyed in the preceding pages. The uniqueness and late date of the version from Brescia, however, seem to indicate that during the Middle Ages as a whole an Easter play at the introit was unknown. It is possible that the dramatic arrangement before us arises merely through imitation of the plays which, as we shall see, had been common for centuries at the end of Easter Matins.[2]

---

[1] officium Misse: Resurrexi] offitium Misse Resurexit (MS).

[2] See Brinkmann, p. 111; and below, chaps. ix–xiv.

CHAPTER VIII

THE EASTER INTROIT TROPE IN TRANSITION

FOR the fact that the dialogue *Quem quæritis in sepulchro* achieved so meagre a dramatic development at the introit of the Mass of Easter there appears to be no adequate explanation. One is at liberty to conjecture that the incongruity in content between the trope and the introit, already commented upon, was a deterrent;[1] or that a more ample dramatic ceremony would have been censured as displacing or overshadowing the authorized liturgical observances at the beginning of Mass.[2] In the absence of genuine information, however, our best course is to resist speculation, and to confine our attention to the actual evidences showing that, in seeking dramatic freedom, the trope gradually detached itself from the introit and the Mass altogether.

I

The beginnings of this process of detachment may, perhaps, be discerned in one or two of the texts considered in the preceding chapter. In the version from Bobbio, for example, *Quem quæritis* is separated from the introit by substantial sentences of no dramatic significance,[3] and in one of the texts from Monte Cassino, the dialogue is followed by a rubric—*Post hec incipiatur tropos. Sequitur introitus*—which seems to indicate that at this place a separate trope intervenes.[4] A similar indication is given in the following text of the early eleventh century from Ivrea, in Italy:[5]

VERSUS AD SEPULCHRUM

Quem queritis in sepulchro, o Christicole?
Versus: *Hiesum Nazarenum crucifixum, o celicole.*
Versus: *Non est hic, surrexit sicut predixerat; ite, nuntiate quia surrexit dicentes.*

Tropus

Alleluia, resurrexit Dominus, eia!
Versus: *Karissimi, uerba canite Christi.*
Versus: *Psallite, fratres, hora est; resurrexit Dominus, eia et eia!*

[1] See above, p. 206.
[2] See Clark, p. 206. Concerning the normal ceremonial at the introit see above, pp. 21 sqq.
[3] See above, p. 207.
[4] See the text from Monte Cassino MS 127, above, p. 214.
[5] Ivrea, Bibl. Capit., MS 60, Trop. Eporediense sæc. xi (1001–11), fol. 69ᵛ, previously edited by Young, *Easter Play*, p. 28. For a text which may be appropriately associated with this one see Notes, p. 570.

Tro*pus*

Christus, deuicta morte, persona uoce preclara Patri dicens: Resurrexi.

Versus: *Cum seuiens Iudeorum me circumdare⟨t⟩ turba.* Posuisti.

Versus: *Cuncta quia oculi⟨s⟩ maiestatis tue sunt aperta.* Mirabilis.[1]

The opening rubric here may indicate that the dialogue was
sung at some sort of structural *sepulchrum*, or it may mean
merely that the sentences following are concerned with events
which occurred *ad sepulchrum*. Our immediate interest, in any
case, is in the repeated rubric *Tropus* after the dialogue, which
points to a separation between the *Versus ad Sepulchrum* and the
introit. The question arises also as to whether in the textually
similar version from Vercelli, printed in the preceding chapter,
the same separation was intended.[2]

A related consideration arises from the following composition,
of uncertain date, once in use in the church of St Martin, at
Tours:[3]

Processionem sequebatur Missa, quæ antequam incipiatur, inquit
Turonense S. Martini ordinarium, veniat ordo Missæ revestitus in
chorum, et sit cantor cum succentoribus ante januam chori, duobus
pueris albis in dalmaticis existentibus. Duo vero vicarii levitæ revestiti
in dalmaticis albis stantes ante Sepulchrum beatissimi Martini, versis
vultibus ad cantorem, incipiant:

> *Quem quæritis?*

Et duo pueri stantes ante cantorem respondent:

> *Jesum Nazarenum.*

Levitæ:

> *Non est hic.*

Pueri:

> *Alleluja, resurrexit Dominus.*

Tunc unus puer solus dicat ter:

> *Accendite,*

exaltando vocem. Et alter puer respondet totidem vicibus:

> *Psallite, fratres.*

Sequitur solus puer una vice:

> *Accendite.*

Alter puer respondet:

> *Psallite, fratres.*

---

[1] Here follow the complete introit of
Easter, and further tropes.

[2] See above, p. 208.

[3] Martene, iii, 173, previously reprinted,
incompletely, by Lange, no. 25, p. 24.

Puer:

Accendite.

Alter puer respondet:

Psallite, fratres.

Deinde puer:

Accendite.

Alter puer:

Psallite, fratres.

Et his peractis, simul pueri, versis vultibus ad cantorem, dicant:

Hora est; cantate Deo, eja!

se inclinando. Quo dicto, incipit cantor officium Missæ.

The presence of the summonses *Psallite, fratres* and *Hora est* relates this introit trope, obviously, to several texts brought forward in the preceding chapter.[1] The significance of the version before us lies partly in the delivering of the *Quem quæritis* dialogue at the tomb of St Martin, but more especially in the prominence given to the repeated liturgical exhortations which follow the dialogue and lead up to the singing of the introit. This feature tends towards the minimizing of the Easter dialogue in favour of the Easter liturgy, and points once more towards the eventual severing of relations between the dramatic trope and the authorized text of the Mass.

II

The removal of *Quem quæritis* from the introit becomes relatively complete when the dialogue is employed in the procession which, on days of liturgical importance, followed Terce and preceded the Mass as an independent liturgical ceremony.[2] The simplest use of the trope in this way is seen in the following, of the eleventh century, from Heidenheim:[3]

IN PROCESSIONE DOMINI

Hora est, psallite; iubet domnus canere; eia dicite!

Interrogatio:

Quem que|ritis in sepulchro, o Christicole?

Responsio:

Ihesum Nazarenum crucifixum, o celicole.

Non est hic, surrexit sicut predixerat; ite, nuntiate quia surrexit, dicentes:

[1] See above, pp. 210 sqq.

[2] Concerning such processions see Gautier, *Tropes*, pp. 195–204.

[3] Oxford, Bibl. Bodl., MS Selden supra 27, Trop. Heidenhemense sæc. xi, fol. 69ᵛ–70ʳ, previously edited by Young, *op. cit.*, p. 50.

Surrexit enim ⟨sicut dixit Dominus; ecce præcedet vos in Galilæam, alleluia; ibi eum videbitis, alleluia, alleluia, alleluia⟩.[1]

In this instance the trope itself, in a general form already familiar,[2] appears to constitute the whole of the procession. This situation is so unusual that one may surmise the loss of part of the text. The more normal form of procession, in any case, includes, along with the *Quem quæritis* dialogue, a substantial amount of liturgical text. Such, for example, is the following processional piece from Monza:[3]

IN PROCESSIONE

Sedit angelus ad sepulchrum Domini stola claritatis coopertus; uidentes eum mulieres nimio terrore perterrite astiterunt a longe. Tunc locutus est angelus et dixit eis: Nolite metuere; dico uobis quia illum quem queritis mortuum iam uiuit, et uita hominum cum | eo surrexit, alleluia.

Quem queritis in sepulchro, Christicole?

Iesum Nazarenum crucifixum, o celicole.

Non est hic, surrexit sicut locutus est; ite, nuntiate quia surrexit, dicentes: Alleluia, resurrexit Dominus.

Nolite.[4]

The essential observation to be made upon this text is that the liturgical piece *Sedit angelus* with which *Quem quæritis* is combined, anticipates the theme of the latter and weakens its dramatic effect.[5] This result, at least, is avoided in the following more ambitious version from St Gall:[6]

IN DOMINICO DIE SANCTI PASCAE
IN PROCESSIONE AD SEPULCRUM

Quem queritis in sepulcro, o Christicole?

Iesum[7] *Nazarenum crucifixum, o caelicole.*

Non[7] *est hic, surrexit sicut predixerat; ite, nuntiate quia surrexit de sepulcro.*

---

[1] *Surrexit enim* is an authorized liturgical antiphon of Easter. See Hartker, p. 231; Migne, *P. L.*, lxxviii, 776. The procession printed here is followed immediately in the MS by the rubric *In die Sancto Pasche*, introducing a series of introit tropes.

[2] See, for example, the version from Mantua, printed above, p. 210.

[3] Monza, Bibl. Capit., MS K.11, Grad.-Trop. Modœtinum sæc. xii, fol. 60ʳ–60ᵛ, previously edited by Young, *op. cit.*, pp. 54–5.

[4] *Nolite* indicates that the latter part (*Nolite . . . surrexit, alleluia*) of *Sedit angelus* is repeated here. In the manuscript the text here printed is followed immediately by the

rubric *Trophus ad introitum Misse.*

[5] Concerning *Sedit angelus* see Gautier, p. 203. For the complete processional antiphon from which it is taken see Hartker, pp. 231–2.

[6] St Gall, Stiftsbibl., MS 376, Trop. Sangallense sæc. xi, pp. 196–7, previously edited by Young, *op. cit.*, pp. 53–4. The processional text is entirely detached from that of the introit, which begins on p. 199 of the manuscript, after an illumination occupying all of p. 198.

[7] The words *Iesum* and *Non* are preceded by blank spaces, obviously left for rubrics.

Surrexit enim sicut dixit Dominus; ecce precedet uos in Galileam; ibi eum uidebitis, alleluia, alleluia.[1]

Sedit angelus ad sepulcrum Domini stola claritatis coopertus; uidentes eum mulieres nimio terrore perterrite substiterunt a longe. Tunc locutus est angelus et dixit eis: Nolite metuere, dico uobis quia illum quem queritis mortuum iam uiuit, et uita hominum cum eo surrexit, alleluia.

Recordamini quomodo predixit quia oportet filium hominis crucifigi, et tercia die a morte suscitari.

Crucifixum Dominum laudate, et sepultum propter nos glorificate, resurgentemque a morte adorate, alleluia.

Since the opening rubric of this text directs that the chorus which sings the procession shall visit the *sepulchrum*, we may infer that *Quem quæritis* was sung there as a dialogue, though without impersonation.[2] The succeeding antiphons are related to the trope in content, but are used here as mere processional utterances.

Additional liturgical pieces appear in another processional text of the eleventh century from St Gall:[3]

AD PROCESSIONEM

Antiphona: *In die resurrectionis meae, dixit*[4] *Dominus, alleluia: Congregabo gentes, et colligam regna, et effundam super uos aquam mundam, alleluia.*

Antiphona: *Vidi aquam egredientem de templo a latere dextro, alleluia, et omnes ad quos peruenit aqua ista salui facti sunt, et dicent alleluia, alleluia.*

Interrogatio: *Quem queritis in sepulchro, Christicolae?*

Responsionis versus: *Iesum Nazarenum crucifixum, o celicolae.*

Item: *Non est hic, surrexit sicut predixerat; ite, nuntiate quia surrexit de sepulchro.*

Antiphona: *Surrexit enim sicut dixit Dominus; ecce precedet uos in Galileam; ibi eum uidebitis, alleluia, alleluia.*

Antiphona: *Sedit angelus ad sepulchrum Domini stola claritatis coopertus; uidentes eum mulieres nimio terrore perterrite substiterunt a longe. Tunc locutus est angelus et dixit eis.*

Versus: *Recordamini quomodo predixit quia oportet filium hominis crucifigi, et tercia die a morte suscitari. Nolite metuere; dico uobis quia illum quem quaeritis mortuum iam uiuit, et uita hominum cum eo surrexit, alleluia.*

---

[1] *Surrexit . . . alleluia,* unlike the rest of the text, has no musical notation.

[2] For other evidence as to the existence of a *sepulchrum* at St Gall as early as the eleventh century, see above, p. 130.

[3] St Gall, Stiftsbibl., MS 387, Brev. Sangallense sæc. xi, pp. 57–8, now completely pub-

lished, I think, for the first time. Lange (no. 4, p. 22) extracts the *Quem quæritis* dialogue, without indicating its associations. In regard to other versions generally similar to that before us see Notes, p. 571.

[4] dixit] dicit (MS).

Antiphona: *Et recordate sunt uerborum eius, et regresse a monumento nuntiaue-runt haec omnia illis undecim et ceteris omnibus, alleluia.*

Versus: *Crucifixum Dominum laudate, et sepultum propter nos glorificate, resurgentemque a morte adorate, alleluia.*[1]

In this version the dialogue in which we are interested is plainly surrounded and overshadowed by liturgical pieces, the first two of which are scarcely related to it in content. We may infer that at one station in the procession—perhaps at a sepulchre— *Quem quæritis* was sung as a recognizable dialogue.

III

The interpretation of the preceding processional texts has been especially difficult and hesitating because of the absence of rubrics. We are fortunate, therefore, in possessing one or two examples in which this deficiency is generously met, as, for instance, in the following text of the thirteenth century from Monza:[2]

Cantata Tertia, uadimus ad Sanctum Michaëlem cum duobus testa-uangeliis,[3] que testa portant duo diacones in cappis et cum quatuor cirostris non accensis, cruce aurea precedente et sceptro deferente ante archipresbiterum. Et ibi reuestitur archipresbiter uel sacerdos ebdoma-darius cum planeta, et alii cum pluuialibus, exceptis duobus diaconibus et duobus subdiaconibus qui sunt reuestiti cum dalmaticis. Et postea redimus cum processione, cereis accensis, canendo antiphonam de Laudibus *Angelus Domini,* et cetera, et *Stetit angelus.* Et cum intramus ecclesiam,[4] dicitur *Pro eo quod non credidisti uerbis meis.*[5] Et cum sumus in ecclesia, stamus et dicitur antiphona:

> *Et ualde mane ⟨una sabbatorum veniunt ad monumentum, orto jam sole, alleluia⟩,*[6]

archipresbitero sedente super foldestorio. Et hoc dicitur ter, et chorus semper similiter respondet.[7] Et cum intramus chorum, custos, leuata cruce aurea cum candelis accensis desuper, ponit ignem in corona lampa-darum circumdata et tota cooperta bombice, quod dicitur farum. Et postea intramus chorum, et iuxta altare ponitur faldestodium cooperto

---

[1] Followed immediately by the rubric *Ad Tertiam.*

[2] Printed by A. F. Frisi, *Memorie storiche di Monza e sua Corte,* iii, Milan, 1794, pp. 195–7, from MS B.43, said to be preserved in the Chapter Library of the Metropolitan Church at Milan. This manuscript, an *ordinarium* of the thirteenth century from Monza, I have not seen. Although this procession differs in details from that printed above from Monza MS K.11, the two are closely related. See above, p. 226.

[3] *Testavangelium* is the gospel-book. See Du Cange, *sub voc.*

[4] The basilica of St John the Baptist.

[5] Antiphon in honour of St John the Baptist. See Hartker, p. 273.

[6] For this antiphon see Hartker, p. 229.

[7] respondet] respondit (Frisi).

pallio. Et duo clerici cum pluuialibus reuestiti euntes et exeuntes per hostium Regine, quod est iuxta lectos custodum, uenientes per corpus ecclesie intrant chorum et stant ante altare; et duo alii clerici cum pluuialibus reuestiti stantes iuxta dictum faldestodium, quod est in loco Sepulchri, et cantant:

> Quem queritis in sepulchro, Christicole?

Et qui sunt ante altare respondent:

> Ihesum Nazarenum, o celicole.

Et alii respondent:

> Non est hic, sed surrexit sicut predixerat; ite,

et cetera, ut in antiphonario continetur. Postea incipitur Missa tali modo. Dicitur tropha. Postea dicitur *Resurrexi et adhuc*, et cetera.[1]

This ceremony occupies the appropriate position immediately after Terce and before the Mass. After certain preliminary ceremonials, the procession enters the basilica, and advances towards the choir during the triple repetition of the antiphon *Et valde mane*. As the singers and clergy enter the choir, a crown of lights, of candles and cotton, is set ablaze over a gilded cross. The dramatic dialogue now takes place before the altar. Near the altar is a faldstool covered with a drapery, to represent the sepulchre. Standing beside this two clerics vested in copes represent the angels, and two other clerics similarly vested, standing before the altar, sing the part of the Marys. With the familiar dialogue the procession is concluded, and after a separate trope of the introit, the Mass begins. Such a ceremonial almost achieves genuine drama. The improved setting is sufficiently adequate, but impersonation, it appears, is not attempted.

Of a similar nature is a processional ceremony, of uncertain date, from Vienne:[2]

Ad majorem Missam debent esse sex suburbani, diaconi septem, subdiaconi totidem, et septem ceroferarii clericuli in albis. Septimus habeat albam paratam cum amictu parato. Archiepiscopus adornetur in vestiario ornamentis pontificalibus; suburbani, diaconi, et subdiaconi, et ceroferarii induantur, et clerici de majori choro in cappis sericis.

Fiat processio ad Sepulcrum sic. Primo pergant ceroferarii; postea

---

[1] Here follows the rubric *In Uesperis.*
[2] Martene, iii, 180. See U. Chevalier, *Étude historique sur la Constitution de l'Église métropolitaine et primatiale de Vienne*, i, Vienne, 1922, pp. 200–1; Moléon, p. 28. From the text before us Lange (no. 32, pp. 26–7) prints a mere excerpt.

archidiaconus de turre portans crucem auream; deinde chorus gradatim et cantores; postea sex subdiaconi, postremo subdiaconus major deferens textum aureum; deinde diaconi sex et archiepiscopus, quem sequuntur suburbani. Duo vero majores decani stent a latere archiepiscopi ad serviendum ei, et sedeat archiepiscopus in faldistorio ante Sepulcrum. Cantores de retro, verso dorso ad Sepulcrum, decanus, et capiscolus, sumpta ab archiepiscopo benedictione, assumant socios ex utraque parte, quos voluerint, et pergant per medium chorum retro majus altare, et ibi incipiant alte voce antiphonam *O mors*, cum versu.[1] Et repetita antiphona, redeant ad processionem. Deinde ceroferarii dicant alta voce antiphonam *Ite, nunciate*.[2] Qua finita, duo canonici de mandato capiscoli accedant ad Sepulcrum ante cantores stantes. Cantores incipiant:

Quem quæritis?

Duo canonici:

Jesum Nazarenum.

Cantores respondent:

Non est hic.

Et canonici dicant:

Alleluia.

Chorus decantet:

Resurrexit Dominus.

Et sic intrent omnes in chorum, archiepiscopo et aliis cum eo indutis in navi stantibus, donec incipiatur *Gloria*. Introitus a cantoribus.

After the elaborate ceremonial with which this procession begins, the Easter dialogue is sung in the presence of the archbishop at a *sepulchrum* located, probably, behind the altar. The number of the singers who deliver the words of the angels is not mentioned; the Marys are represented by two canons. At the conclusion of the dialogue, the procession enters the choir and proceeds with the Mass.

The generous rubrics of the versions from Monza and Vienne are valuable not only in elucidating the processional uses of the Easter dialogue in those two communities, but also in suggesting the probability that a similar vivid ceremonial accompanied less informing texts, such as those from Heidenheim and St Gall, presented earlier in this chapter. In spite of their elaborateness, however, none of these processions appears to have included genuine impersonation.

---

[1] See Hartker, p. 224.   [2] See *id.*, p. 241.

IV

From our survey of the uses of *Quem quæritis* both as a preface to the introit, and as a part of the independent liturgical procession which preceded the introit, we may confidently assert that in its association with the Mass this trope did not attain true dramatization or free textual development. The single version which shows impersonation, that from Brescia, seems to be an isolated example from the close of the Middle Ages, and to show no palpable advance in dramatic content beyond that of the original trope in its tenth-century form.[1] The dramatic potentialities of *Quem quæritis* were realized, then, only when it was withdrawn from the Mass altogether, and was given a lodging-place in the Canonical Office. In this new position it achieved a generous amount of literary freedom, and developed into an authentic Easter play. To this we may refer henceforth as the *Visitatio Sepulchri*.[2]

The general location of this dramatic piece among the *horæ* would seem to have been predetermined by its content. A dialogue of the Marys and the angel at the tomb in the early morning could be appropriately placed only at Matins; and there is no indication that any other anchorage was ever seriously considered.[3] Nor does there appear to have been much doubt as to the precise position which the play should take within the structure of Matins. In rare instances the performance occurred before the beginning of the office;[4] but normally it is found at the close, between the last responsory and the *Te Deum*.[5] This location may have been chosen primarily for mere convenience, the position before the office being usually occupied by the *Elevatio*, and the end being the most acceptable place remaining.[6] Probably, however, the choice was made for special reasons of liturgical appropriateness.

Of these reasons the least weighty, perhaps, is that given by the medieval symbolists, who declare that the play belongs at the end of Matins because the *Te Deum* here marks liturgically the moment at which Our Lord rose.[7] This symbolical explana-

---

[1] See above, p. 221.

[2] In regard to this designation see below, p. 576.

[3] For relatively unimportant evidences as to exceptions see Notes, p. 571.

[4] See below, pp. 298 sqq., 658.

[5] For the structure of Easter Matins see above, p. 64.

[6] As to the position of the *Elevatio* see above, p. 114.

[7] Durandus of Mende expresses the notion thus: Hic ⟨i.e. the position immediately before the *Te Deum*⟩ est proprior locus, eo quod *Te Deum laudamus* exprimit horam qua

tion is scarcely adequate, for the coming of the Marys, represented in the *Visitatio Sepulchri*, occurred historically not at the precise moment of the Resurrection, but at a later time. The hour at which the Marys are reported to have made their visit, indeed, suggests another and more valid reason for performing the play at the end of Matins. They set out, the Gospels tell us, very early in the morning, at the beginning of dawn.[1] Now in early liturgical tradition, from the time of Charlemagne onward, the beginning of the day was marked precisely by the transition from Matins to Lauds. Sometimes, to be sure, Matins may have been completed well before dawn, with the result of allowing the clergy an interval of repose before the beginning of Lauds. So strict was the tradition of ending Matins at dawn, however, that if this office was still unfinished at that time, it was abruptly discontinued, in order that Lauds might begin at the appropriate moment.[2] Thus the *Te Deum*, which stood at the end of Matins and immediately before Lauds, came to be regarded as marking the division between night and day.[3] Since, then, the *Visitatio Sepulchri* represents an event which occurred at dawn on Easter morning, one could suggest no more appropriate liturgical position for the performance than that to which it was normally assigned.

The appropriateness of this arrangement becomes still more apparent when one considers the content of the authorized liturgical piece which immediately precedes and, as it were, introduces the dramatic performance.[4] This third, and last, responsory of Easter Matins is found in the following four forms:

(1) Dum transisset sabbatum, Maria Magdalena et Maria Jacobi et Salome emerunt aromata, ut venientes ungerent Jesum, alleluia, alleluia. Versus: Et valde mane una sabbatorum veniunt ad monumentum, orto iam sole.[5]

(2) Et valde mane una sabbatorum veniunt ad monumentum, orto

Dominus resurrexit. For further evidences see Notes, p. 573.

[1] Vespere autem sabbati, quæ lucescit in prima sabbati (Matt. xxviii, 1); valde mane (Luke xxiv, 1); valde diluculo (Luke xxiv, 1).
[2] See Batiffol, p. 83. A rubric in a monastic ordinary of about the year 1100 (Munich, Staatsbibl., MS lat. 14765, fol. 92ᵛ, printed below, p. 557) prescribes that the moment for beginning Matins be so chosen that the last lesson shall be begun at the first appearance

of dawn. See also the singing of a stanza from the hymn *Aurora diem nuntiat* in a version of the *Visitatio* from Regensburg, printed below, p. 296.
[3] See H. Bone, *Das Te Deum*, Frankfurt, 1880, pp. 107–8.
[4] This matter has been considered by Brinkmann, p. 113.
[5] See Hartker, p. 229; Migne, *P. L.*, lxxviii, 770.

iam sole, alleluia, alleluia. Versus: Et respicientes viderunt revolutum lapidem, erat quippe magnus valde.[1]

(3) Et valde mane una sabbatorum veniunt ad monumentum, orto iam sole, alleluia. Versus: Mulieres emerunt aromata; summo diluculo veniunt ad monumentum.[2]

(4) Et valde mane una sabbatorum veniunt ad monumentum, orto iam sole, alleluia. Versus: Maria Magdalena et Maria Jacobi et Salome venerunt diluculo ad monumentum.[3]

It will be observed that these four versions—of which the first is very much the most common[4]—all recount the same narrative: the journey of the Marys to the tomb at dawn on the first Easter morning. Since in sacred history this action immediately precedes the occurrence at the sepulchre which is the nucleus of the *Visitatio Sepulchri*, the transition from the liturgy to the play leaves nothing to be desired. That the clerics who conducted performances of the *Visitatio* were conscious of the appropriateness of this arrangement is shown by the fact that in numerous versions of the play the responsory is made to serve explicitly as a processional for the entrance of the Marys.[5]

Although the reasons already advanced seem to account sufficiently for the placing of the Easter play at the close of Matins, additional explanations can be offered. One of these is the traditional use of incense here. From the fact that in many versions of the *Visitatio* the Marys carry thuribles instead of, or in addition to, the spices mentioned in the Gospels,[6] it has been inferred that the play grew out of the custom of censing the sepulchre at this place in the liturgy.[7] Certainly the use of incense at the singing of the *Te Deum* in Matins was very general during the Middle Ages. The object most often censed at Easter, to be sure, seems to have been the altar;[8] but the altar, as we have seen, was quite generally felt to be *sepulchrum Christi*.[9] Certainly the plays themselves exhibit numerous details of impersonation and stage-action which can be conveniently accounted for through their derivation from the

---

[1] See Young, *Some Texts*, p. 298, from Paris, Bibl. Nat., MS lat. 1293, fol. 113ʳ.

[2] See Paris, Bibl. Nat., Nouvelles Acquisitions, MS latin 840, fol. 44ʳ.

[3] Paris, Bibl. Nat., MS lat. 750, fol. 4ᵛ.

[4] Chambers (ii, 25, note 4) seems to assume that this first form is the only one.

[5] See below, for example, pp. 288–9.

[6] Maria Magdalene et Maria Jacobi et Salome emerunt aromata, ut venientes ungerent Jesum (Mark xvi, 1); venerunt ad monumentum portantes, quæ paraverant, aromata (Luke xxiv, 1).

[7] See Chambers, ii, 25.

[8] See Atchley, pp. 149, 377, 387, 390; Frere, *Sarum*, i, 32, 155. In regard to special censings of the sepulchre at Soissons see Notes, p. 573.

[9] See above, pp. 218 sqq.

liturgical use of incense. In several versions—and among them some of the earliest—the Marys carry only thuribles.[1] Again, they carry both vessels and thuribles;[2] and sometimes the women carrying vessels or boxes are preceded in the procession to the sepulchre by clerics bearing thuribles.[3] Particularly noteworthy is the action in the *Visitatio* at Rouen, in which the Marys bear vessels to the tomb, but at the close of which the archbishop or a priest, in beginning the *Te Deum*, censes the altar with a thurible.[4] It can, of course, be urged that the thuribles used by the Marys, like their pyxes and other vessels, were suggested merely by the *aromata* of the Gospel narratives;[5] and certainly it must be admitted that the censer and incense-boat would represent the Scriptural spices quite aptly enough. The probability is, however, that the thuribles and incense in many versions of the *Visitatio* are there through imitation of a purely liturgical act, and that the play is, in part, an amplification of this ceremony.

The use of incense in the *Visitatio* suggests that we consider, finally, another liturgical act performed at the end of Easter Matins which includes a censing and which bears otherwise upon the matter before us. From a very early period it was customary to read, or intone, at the end of Matins the passage from the Gospels proper to the day.[6] Since texts for this ceremony on Easter Day are not conveniently accessible, I offer here an example which shows, after the last responsory, not only the liturgical gospel, but a highly developed trope, or *prosa*, as well:[7]

Responsorium: *Dum transisset sabbatum, Maria Magdalene et Maria Iacobi et Salome emerunt aromata, vt uenientes ungerent Ihesum, alleluia, alleluia.* Versus: *Et ualde mane una sabbatorum ueniunt ad monumentum, orto iam sole. Vt uenientes. Gloria.* | Responsorium: *Dum transisset.*

PROSA

1. *Mane prima sabbati*[8]
   surgens Dei filius,
   nostra spes et gloria,

2. *Victo rege sceleris,*
   rediit ab inferis
   cum summa uictoria.

---

[1] See below, for example, pp. 249, 260.
[2] See below, for example, pp. 258, 264.
[3] See below, for example, p. 290.
[4] See below, p. 371.
[5] This appears to be the opinion of Atchley, p. 300.
[6] See Bäumer, i, 397; A. Gastoué, *Les Vigiles nocturnes*, Paris, 1908, p. 57.

[7] Paris, Bibl. Nat., MS lat. 1041, Brev. Benedictinum sæc. xiv, fol. 140^r–140^v. The trope *Mane prima sabbati* (Chevalier, *R.H.* no. 11064) is printed by Daniel, *Thesaurus* ii, 255–6. For other examples see below, pp. 277, 287.
[8] sabbati] After this word a cursive hand of the fifteenth century or later has written

3. Cuius resurrectio,
omni plena gaudio,
consolatur omnia.

4. Resurgentis[1] itaque
Maria Magdalene
facta est prenuntia,

5. Ferens Christi fratribus,
eius morte tristibus,
expectata gaudia.

6. O beati oculi,
quibus regem seculi,
morte iam deposita,
prima est intuita.

7. Hec est illa femina
cuius cuncta crimina
ad Christi uestigia
eius lauit gratia.

8. Que dum plorat ·
et mens orat
sancto clamat
quod cor amat
Ihesum super omnia.

9. Non ignorat
quem adorat,
quid precetur
se deletur,
quod mens timet conscia.

10. O Maria,
Mater pia,
Stella maris
appellaris
operum per merita.

11. Matri Christi
coequata
dum fuisti
sic uocata
sed honore subdita.

12. Illa mundi imperatrix,
ista beata peccatrix,
leticie primordia
fuderunt in ecclesia.

13. Illa enim fuit porta
per quam fuit lux exorta.
Hec resurgentis nuntia
mundum replet leticia.

14. O Maria Magdalena,
audi uota laude plena
apud Christum chorum istum
nostra mens concilia.

15. Vt fons summe pietatis
qui te lauit a peccatis
seruos suos a⟨t⟩que tuos
mundet data uenia.

16. Hoc det eius gratia
qui regnat per omnia.
Alleluia.

SECUNDUM MARCUM

In illo tempore, Maria Magdalene et Maria Iacobi et Salome emerunt aromata, ut uenientes ungerent Ihesum. Et ualde mane una sabbatorum ueniunt ad monumentum, orto iam sole. Et dicebant ad inuicem: Quis reuoluet nobis lapidem ab hostio monumenti? Et respicientes uiderunt reuolutum lapidem. Erat quippe magnus ualde. Et introeuntes in monumentum uiderunt iuuenem sedentem in

Require folio 4° ante cum alia prosa Victime. The remainder of the prose, through stanza 16, is taken, therefore, from fol. 138[r], where it is written in a hand of the fourteenth century. The numerals attached to the stanzas are supplied by the editor. With the heading *Secundum Marcum* is resumed the text found on fol. 140[v].

[1] Resurgentis] resurgens (MS).

dextris coopertum stola candida, et obstupuerunt. Qui dicit illis: Nolite expauescere;
Ihesum queritis Nazarenum crucifixum; surrexit, non est hic. Ecce locus ubi
posuerunt eum. Sed ite, dicite discipulis eius, et Petro, quia precedit uos in Galyleam;
ibi eum uidebitis sicut dixi⟨t⟩ uobis.[1]

Here the narrative recounting the visit of the Marys to the
empty tomb occupies the position usually assigned to the
dramatic performance.[2] Since the reading of the gospel was
undoubtedly accompanied by censing,[3] we are to visualize a
conspicuous liturgical ceremony, the festal nature of which is,
in the present instance, emphasized by the use of a somewhat
ambitious trope. One is tempted to surmise, therefore, that the
ceremonious reading of the Easter narrative may have had some
influence in attracting to this liturgical position the presentation
of the same story in dramatic form.[4]

It is now obvious that for placing the *Visitatio Sepulchri* after
the last responsory of Easter Matins there were ample reasons.
Without attempting to estimate the relative force of each of
these, we may simply accept the assured fact, that the play took
its preferred position under highly appropriate circumstances.
It should be remembered, moreover, that the *Visitatio* was only
one of a large number of extra-liturgical compositions which
arose in precisely this part of the *Cursus*. The tropes which
invaded the Canonical Office during the later Middle Ages
seem to have attached themselves most often to the responsories,
and the last responsory of Easter Matins appears to have been
particularly hospitable to such embellishments. To the one
example just given, many others might be added.[5] In taking its
new position, therefore, the trope *Quem quæritis in sepulchro* was
merely sharing in a general literary tendency.

V

Among the most important results of the transfer of the
dramatic trope from the Mass to Matins was its more direct
association with the *Depositio* of Good Friday and the *Elevatio*
performed during the earlier hours of Easter.[6] After these two
ceremonies the *Visitatio Sepulchri* followed as a natural third in
a series of dramatic observances at the *sepulchrum*, and it was

---

[1] Followed immediately in the manuscript
by the rubric *In Laudibus.*

[2] Possibly, however, it was intended that
the *Te Deum* be sung just before the reading
of the gospel. See below, p. 676.

[3] See Atchley, p. 149.

[4] To this observation, however, I attach
no great force.

[5] See Notes, p. 574.

[6] See above, chaps. iv and v.

partly under the influence of these new associations, no doubt, that the dialogue *Quem quæritis* acquired the additional dramatic features which transformed it into a successful and expanding play.[1] The *Depositio* and *Elevatio*, to be sure, were mutually dependent and complete, and required no sequel; and a number of churches—particularly, during the later Middle Ages, the more prominent ones in England—seem to have provided none.[2] Some English communities, however,[3] and a far larger number on the Continent, adopted the *Visitatio* as the appropriate conclusion for the two dramatic offices which preceded.

That the *Depositio* and *Elevatio* were the earlier development, and that the *Visitatio* attached itself to the *sepulchrum* somewhat later, can hardly be doubted.[4] In support of this view may be cited, in the first place, the difference between the *Depositio* and *Elevatio* on the one hand, and the *Visitatio* on the other, in content and tone. Whereas the first two ceremonies are completely liturgical in content, and are devoid of original writing and of dialogue, the last is essentially a free composition. Although, as we shall see, the developed versions of the *Visitatio* include numerous liturgical pieces, the invariable central element of this play is an independent literary production: the dialogued trope *Quem quæritis in sepulchro*. We may, then, fairly assume that if the *Visitatio* had preceded the other two dramatic ceremonies in its attachment to the sepulchre, these latter would have reflected somewhat of the dialogue and freer composition of the *Visitatio*. That the *Visitatio* should not have conformed to the liturgical rigour of the other two ceremonies appears to have been due, in part at least, to the fact that it brought to the *sepulchrum* an independent literary dialogue ready for dramatic use.

Another consideration leads to the same conclusion as to the priority of the *Depositio* and *Elevatio*. From our study of these two offices it is manifest that, however dramatic their ceremonial, they never in themselves developed true drama. Although the symbolical acts are often highly imitative, the agents in the

---

[1] See Clark, p. 205.

[2] See Chambers, ii, 25, and the treatment of the *Depositio* and *Elevatio* from Durham and Sarum above, chap. iv.

[3] See the examples of the *Visitatio* from the *Regularis Concordia* of St Ethelwold, from Dublin, and from Barking below, pp. 249, 347, 381.

[4] This matter is discussed by Young, *Dramatic Associations*, pp. 127–30; Brooks, *Sepulchre*, pp. 47–9. The inference of Chasles (p. 69) that some form of *Visitatio* existed as early as the year 830 appears to have arisen from a misinterpretation of the symbolism of Amalarius.

action did not attempt to impersonate the characters in the story behind this action.[1] In the *Visitatio*, on the other hand, impersonation became customary as early as the latter half of the tenth century. It is safe to infer, then, that if the *Visitatio*, with its characteristic of impersonation, had developed at the sepulchre before the advent of the *Depositio* and *Elevatio*, these would have shown the influence of the other dramatic office in this most important respect. The consistent absence of this element from the *Depositio* and *Elevatio* seems to indicate that they attained their relatively rigid liturgical character before they became associated with the *Visitatio*.[2]

[1] An apparent exception is the impersonation of Satan in the Bamberg *Elevatio* of 1587. See above, p. 176. This text may represent a relatively modern custom. Moreover, the representation of the harrowing of Hell, in which the impersonation occurs, is not, in general, a central element in the *Elevatio*.

[2] This general view is accepted by Brooks, *Sepulchre*, p. 47. For a further observation upon the fundamental distinction between the *Visitatio* and the other two offices see Notes, p. 575.

CHAPTER IX

THE VISIT TO THE SEPULCHRE
FIRST STAGE

THE pleasure which medieval worshippers found in the
Easter play, or *Visitatio Sepulchri*, is plainly shown by the
astonishing number of examples still preserved in manuscripts
and early printed books of all countries of Western Europe.[1] In
the pages to follow will be printed, or mentioned, more than
four hundred texts. Since a considerable number of such
dramatic pieces are very brief and inconspicuous, probably some
of the shorter ones already in print have escaped my notice;
and beyond doubt some lie hidden in liturgical manuscripts
still unexamined, particularly in the less orderly libraries and
chapter-houses of Southern and South-eastern Europe. It
seems improbable, however, that the eventual publication of
additional examples will substantially extend the boundaries
of the subject, for the uniformity among large groups of texts
now available, and the conventional limitations under which
the writers seem to have worked, point to the likelihood that
we shall discover few, if any, new types of importance. This
inference is confirmed, at any rate, by the relatively slight
disclosures arising from a score or more of hitherto unpublished
versions offered in appropriate places below.

In surveying the numerous texts of the *Visitatio Sepulchri* it is
convenient to recognize three marked stages in the growth of
the play: one in which the dialogue is conducted by the Marys
and the angel, a second in which are added the apostles, Peter
and John, and a third which provides a role for the risen Christ.[2]
In the present chapter I consider the first of these stages. The
texts are arranged, in general, in accordance with the increasing
elaboration of their content. The chief interest of a good many
versions, however, arises not so much from the dramatic utterances themselves as from the accompanying rubrics. The
speeches, as we shall see, are in large measure formalized, and
lack variety, whereas the stage-directions frequently disclose
fresh details as to the manner in which the words are spoken,

[1] For bibliography, and observations upon
the term *Visitatio Sepulchri*, see Notes, p. 576.
[2] This classification was first applied comprehensively by C. Lange, *Die lateinischen Osterfeiern*, Munich, 1887. See also, for example,
Chambers, ii, 12–33; Lintilhac, i, 27–31.

as to the physical setting, and, most important of all, as to the impersonating of the characters. Although the absence of rubrics does not necessarily imply the absence of stage-setting and impersonation from the actual performance, the presence of explicit descriptions of the acting is sometimes a particularly welcome contribution of an otherwise commonplace text. In exhibiting representative examples of the several types, therefore, I have usually given most prominence to the texts containing the fullest rubrics.[1] The sequence of versions within a particular group, moreover, although it commonly proceeds from the simplest to the most elaborate, does not pretend to demonstrate a strict historical evolution, or to elucidate the complexities of geographical relationships. The general arrangement probably represents fairly enough the broad development of the several types, and it does not entirely ignore textual interrelations and regional groupings; but it makes no claim to final precision in these respects—a precision for which our present knowledge, as a matter of fact, is inadequate. I undertake, then, not so much an exact demonstration of historical sequence as an orderly description of experiments and achievements.[2]

<h1 style="text-align:center">I</h1>

In approaching the numerous versions of the *Visitatio Sepulchri* which are restricted in scope to a dialogue between the Marys and the angel, one would be glad to begin with an example consisting merely of the trope *Quem quæritis* in its simplest form, of three sentences;[3] but of such a version we have no unequivocal text.[4] We must, then, proceed to versions of the play in which the simple dialogue is extended by the addition of a familiar liturgical piece, as, for example, in the following from Tours:[5]

Post hæc[6] duo pueri in albis, unus ad dextram altaris, alius ad sinistram cantant:

Quem quæritis ⟨in sepulchro, o Christicolæ⟩?

---

[1] Lange's indifference to the dramatic significance of the rubrics is justly censured, for example, by Creizenach (i, 46) and Wilmotte (pp. 30–1).

[2] As I have remarked in the Preface, this observation applies to the present treatise as a whole.

[3] This form, as found in St. Gall MS 484, is printed above, p. 201.

[4] For a doubtful example see Notes, p. 576.

[5] Martene, iii, 179–80, previously reprinted by Lange, no. 24, p. 24, and by Adams, p. 6. Martene (i, p. xxiii) speaks of the MS as 'ante 300 annos exaratum.' For texts of the *Visitatio* which may be associated with the example before us see Notes, p. 577.

[6] The reference is to the preceding third responsory of Easter Matins—probably *Dum transisset*. See above, p. 232.

Tres capellani cum dalmaticis albis, coopertis capitibus, ante altare respondent:

> *Jesum Nazarenum ⟨crucifixum, o cœlicolæ⟩.*

Item pueri:

> *Non est hic, ⟨surrexit sicut prædixerat; ite, nuntiate quia surrexit de sepulchro.⟩*

Deinde illi tres accedentes ad altare, et intro aspicientes, versi ad chorum dicunt alta voce:

> *Alleluia, surrexit Dominus ⟨de sepulchro, qui pro nobis pependit in ligno, alleluia⟩.*[1]

Post hæc cantor incipit *Te Deum.*

In this play the sepulchre is supplied by the altar, according to the tradition already explained above.[2] The words *intro aspicientes* probably indicate either that the Marys look through the grill, which was not uncommon under altar-tables, or that they inspect the actual *sepulchrum* inserted in the altar-table itself. The representing of the angels by two persons, and of the Marys by three, conforms sufficiently well to the narrative of the Gospels, and to the form of the responsory which usually precedes.[3] The covered heads of the three *capellani* seem to show clearly that impersonation is intended.

Additional dramatic details are disclosed in the following example, of the eleventh or twelfth century, from an unidentified monastery:[4]

Post tercium responsorium ueniant duo sacerdotes in albis cappis retro altare, qui Angeli sedentis ad Sepulcrum Domini uicem debent gerere; et ueniant duo diaconi in dalmaticis portantes incensum in duobus turibulis, amictis capitibus in significatione Mulierum Dominum querentium cum aromatibus ad Sepulcrum. Sic alloquantur:

> *Quem queritis in sepulcro, o Christicole?*

Responsio diaconorum, uice Mulierum, humili uoce:

> *Ihesum ⟨Nazarenum⟩ crucifixum, o celicole.*

Iterato presbiteri, uice Angeli, uoce exultanti:

> *Non est hic, surrexit sicut predixerat; ite, nunciate[5] quia surrexit a morte.*

---

[1] For this antiphon see Hartker, p. 241; Migne, *P. L.,* lxxviii, 771, 776.

[2] Concerning the association of the notion of the sepulchre with the altar see above, p. 218.

[3] See above, pp. 217, 232.

[4] Found on a sheet, from a monastic *ordinarium* of the eleventh or twelfth century, attached to the front cover of MS 1056 in the Stiftsbibliothek, Melk, and now printed, I think, for the first time. For associated texts see Notes, p. 577.

[5] nunciate] nunciante (MS).

Interim diaconi discooperiant altare. Nunciantes autem conuertuntur ad fratres uoce clara cantantes antiphonam:

Surrexit Dominus de sepulcro, ⟨qui pro nobis pependit in ligno, alleluia.⟩

Qua finita, cantet chorus *Te Deum laudamus.*

This version arranges for the impersonation of the two Marys in careful detail, specifying the covering of the head, the carrying of thuribles and incense, and the uncovering of the altar-sepulchre by way of demonstrating the fact of the Resurrection. The rubric concerning the number of angels is somewhat puzzling; for, although *two* priests sing the part, they seem to be thought of as representing only *one* angel. In the rubric the writer appears to be adhering somewhat desperately to the narrative of Matthew, with its two Marys and one angel; but in the spoken text the angels are addressed in the plural.[1] From the variations among the several Gospel narratives inevitably arise similar variations, and, as we shall see, frequent incongruities, in the dramatic texts. The Marys announce the Resurrection to the chorus merely by singing the antiphon *Surrexit Dominus.* In another play, similar to the one before us, this announcement is accompanied by the displaying of a crucifix from which the *corpus* has been removed.[2] The members of the chorus who are thus addressed must be regarded, in a general way, as representing the disciples, and one would like to infer that this representation was often made specific by some realistic or symbolic detail. Unfortunately, however, except for Peter and John, whose role will be considered below,[3] this dramatic step seems to have been taken very rarely.[4]

The simple type of play now before us occasionally shows textual variations which, though of minor importance, cannot be entirely ignored. An example may be seen in the following version of the twelfth century from Utrecht:[5]

AD SEPULCRUM

Versus:[6]

Quem queritis in sepulchro, o Christicole?

[1] See above, p. 217.

[2] See the version from Verdun below, p. 578.

[3] See chaps. xi and xii.

[4] See below, pp. 383, 384, 398, 401.

[5] Utrecht, Bibl. de Rijksuniversiteit, MS 407 (*olim* Script. Eccles. 316), Lib. resp. Ultrajectensis sæc. xii, fol. 116ᵛ (A), previously edited by Lange, no. 19, p. 23. The text as printed here is immediately preceded by the responsory *Dum transisset.* I give the variant from the text found *ibid.*, MS 406 (*olim* Script. Eccles. 318), Lib. resp. Ultrajectensis sæc. xii, fol. 97ᵛ (B), previously edited by Milchsack, p. 65, and Van Mierlo, p. 36, and mentioned by Lange, no. 20, p. 23. For associated versions see Notes, p. 578.

[6] Versus] Angel*us* (B).

Mulieres:

Ihesum Nazarenum crucifixum, o celicole.

Angelus:

Non est hic, surrexit sicut predixerat; ite, nunciate quia surrexit, dicentes:

Antiphona:

Surrexit Dominus de sepulchro, ⟨qui pro nobis pependit in ligno, alleluia.⟩
⟨T⟩e Deum laudamus.

The transitional word *dicentes*, which we have already observed among the introit tropes,[1] can hardly be considered fortunate dramatically, since it has the effect of reducing the spontaneity of the next speaker, and, indeed, raises a doubt, in the present instance, as to who the next speaker is. The absence of a rubric before the antiphon *Surrexit* would suggest that it is to be spoken by the angel; but the rubrics in other versions assign it specifically to the Marys.[2]

Another slight variation appears in the following example of the fifteenth century from Fulda:[3]

AD SEPULCRUM

Quem queritis in sepulcro, o Christicole?

Versus: *Ihesum Nazarenum crucifixum, o celicole.*

Versus: *Non est hic, surrexit sicut predixerat; ite, nunciate | quia surrexit de sepulchro.*

⟨Versus:⟩ *Surrexit Dominus de sepulchro, qui pro nobis pependit in ligno, alleluia.*

Chorus: *Deo gratias, alleluia, alleluia, alleluia.*

Te Deum laudamus.

The addition here of the response *Deo gratias*—familiar in the authorized liturgy and in the introit tropes—has at least the effect of drawing the chorus into the dialogue.[4]

A fresh liturgical antiphon is present in a version of the *Visitatio*, of the eleventh century, from Minden:[5]

IN DIE SANCTO PASCHE PRIMO MANE AD UISITANDUM SEPULCHRUM DOMINI

Interrogatio:

Quem quaeritis in sepulchro, o[6] *Christicolae?*

---

[1] See above, pp. 206 sq.

[2] See, for example, below, p. 244. On the use of *dicentes* at the *Sanctus* in Mass see above, p. 34.

[3] Rome, Bibl. Vatic., MS Palatino 525, Brev. Fuldense saec. xv, fol. 208ᵛ–209ʳ, previously edited by Young, *Some Texts*, p. 318. In the MS the text is preceded by the third responsory *Dum transisset.*

[4] See above, for example, pp. 42, 210.

[5] Berlin, Staatsbibl., MS theol. lat. 4°.15, Grad. Mindense saec. xi, fol. 120ʳ (A), referred to by Lange, no. 7, p. 22. The text is provided with musical notation. I give the variant from the text found *ibid.*, MS theol. lat. 4°. 11, Grad. Mindense saec. xi, fol. 45ᵛ–46ʳ (B), now first published. For a similar text see Notes, p. 579. [6] o] Omitted (B).

Responsio:

> *Ihesum Nazarenum crucifixum, o celicole*

⟨Versus:⟩

> *Non est hic, surrexit sicut praedixerat; ite, nuntiate quia surrexit de sepulchro.*

Antiphona:

> *Surrexit enim sicut dixit Dominus, et praecedet uos in Galileam, alleluia; ibi eum uidebitis, alleluia, alleluia, alleluia.*[1]

The antiphon *Surrexit enim,*[2] not found among the introit tropes, is a form of announcement particularly appropriate to those who may be regarded as representing, though not impersonating, the disciples. Although the position of the performance in the liturgy is not indicated, the words *primo mane* point to Matins.

In the following text of the fourteenth century from Clermont-Ferrand one finds an increased definiteness in the rubrics, and a fresh concluding speech for the Marys:[3]

Quo finito,[4] duo pueri iuxta altare ornati sicut Angeli excelsa uoce cantent versum:

> *Quem queritis in sepulcro, o Christicole?*

Deinde tres ante altare induti[5] capis, cum candelabris, tenentes tria turribula, humili uoce respondeant versum:[6]

> *Ihesum Nazarenum crucifixum, o celicole.*

Item duo pueri versum:

> *Non est hic, surrexit sicut predixerat; ite, nunciate quia surrexit dicentes:*

Tunc tres presbyteri uertant se ad chorum et cante⟨n⟩t tribus uicibus:

> *Alleluia, resurrexit Dominus.*

Deinde cantent similiter hunc versum:

> *Hodie resurrexit leo fortis, Christus, filius Dei.*

Psalmus: *Te Deum.*

In this instance the intention of impersonation is made uncommonly clear by such words as *ornati sicut Angeli,* applied to the two *pueri.* Once again the altar appears to serve as the sepulchre. The last utterance of the Marys, *Alleluia, resurrexit,* which we have already observed among the introit tropes, is made

---

[1] Followed by the rubric: Ad Processionem *Salue festa dies.* Of the concluding antiphon B has only the first two words *Surrexit enim.*

[2] See Hartker, p. 231; Migne, *P. L.,* lxxviii, 776.

[3] Paris, Bibl. Nat., MS lat. 1274, Brev. Claromontense sæc. xiv. fol. 128ᵛ, previously

edited by Lange, no. 33, pp. 26–7, but with an erroneous reference to MS lat. 1272.

[4] The reference is to the responsory *Dum transisset.*

[5] induti] indutis (MS).

[6] versum] versus (MS).

particularly effective through the triple repetition of the opening words.

Closely related to the version of Clermont-Ferrand in content is the following from Senlis:[1]

Finita repetitione,[2] illi qui tenebunt chorum ibunt ante altare. Et duo presbyteri, vnus ad dextram altaris et alius ad sinistram, albis non paratis induti, cantabunt versum sequentem:[3]

Qvem queritis in sepulchro, o Christicole?

Custodes chori respondebunt:[4]

Ihesum Nazarenum crucifixum, o celicole.

Tunc presbyteri eleuantes palam altaris dicent:[5]

Non est hic, surrexit sicut predixerat; ite, nunciate quia surrexit.

Et custodes chori reuertentes se ad chorum dicent versum:

Alleluya, resurrexit Dominus, hodie resurrexit leo fortis, Christus, filius Dei.

Chorus:

Deo gracias dicite, eya!

Quo dicto, incipietur[6] *Te Deum.* Et ibunt omnes osculari[7] Sepulchrum.

The use of the altar as the sepulchre is here enlivened by a touch of realistic action; for when they sing the words *Non est hic*, the angels raise the altar-cloth, by way of demonstrating the fact of the Resurrection. Once more, also, the chorus utters the concluding *Deo gratias*.

In this division of our survey we must include, finally, two versions which convey no information as to *mise en scène* or personnel, but which contain fresh textual details. The first is of the eleventh century, from Arras:[8]

Quem queritis in sepulchro, o Christicole?

Respondent duo:

Ihesum Nazarenum querimus crucifixum, o caelicole.

Non est hic, surrexit sicut predixerat; ite, nunciate quia surrexit a morte.

Alleluia, resurrexit Dominus.

Eia, karissimi, uerbis canite cuncti.

Te Deum laudamus.

[1] Paris, Bibl. Nat., MS lat. 1268, Brev. Silvanectense sæc. xiv, fol. 300ʳ (A), previously edited by Lange, no. 35, pp. 27–8. I give the variants from Paris, Bibl. Sainte-Geneviève, MS 2636 (B.Bl. 4°. 22), Brev. Silvanectense sæc. xv, fol. 187ʳ (B), mentioned by Lange, no. 37, p. 28, and now first published. For associated texts see Notes, p. 579.

[2] The reference is to the singing of the responsory *Et valde mane.* See above, p. 233.

[3] sequentem] sequentem versum (B).

[4] respondebunt] respondebunt versum (B).

[5] dicent] dicent versum (B).

[6] incipietur] dicitur (B).

[7] osculari] Omitted (B).

[8] Cambrai, Bibl. de la Ville, MS 75, Grad.-Trop. Sancti Vedasti Atrebatensis sæc. xi, fol. 11ᵛ, now published, I think, for the first time. The text as printed here is preceded in the MS by irrelevant antiphons for the last three days of Holy Week, and is followed by the rubric *In die ad Missam.*

The hortatory sentence at the end of this version, *Eia, karissimi,* which appears to serve as a transitional introduction to the *Te Deum,* may be an adaptation of a similar formula which we have found in certain of the introit tropes and processionals.[1]

The last text requiring notice here is the following, of the twelfth century, from St Gall:[2]

IN UISITATIONE SEPULCHRI VERSUS

Quem queritis in sepulchro, Christicole?
Ihesum Nazarenum crucifixum, o celicole.
Non est hic, surrexit sicut predixerat; ite, nunciate quia surrexit de sepulchro.

Antiphona:

Surrexit enim sicut dixit | *⟨Dominus; ecce præcedet vos in Galilæam; ibi eum videbitis, alleluia, alleluia⟩.*[3]

Antiphona:

Christus resurgens ⟨ex mortuis, jam non moritur; mors illi ultra non domi-nabitur, quod enim vivit, vivit Deo, alleluia, alleluia⟩.[4]

The addition in this instance is a traditional liturgical piece *Christus resurgens,* which serves well as a conclusion of the dramatic performance, and which will appear frequently in other types of the Easter play.

II

In the versions of the *Visitatio Sepulchri* surveyed thus far, the slight enlargements of the original form of the trope *Quem quæritis* have consisted merely in sentences which the Marys could use for announcing the Resurrection to the chorus, at the end of the performance, and in a few expressions with which the chorus might respond. Since the chorus shows no sign of impersonation, these announcements and responses may be regarded as liturgical, rather than dramatic, additions. A more decisive enlargement of the essential action of the little play arises with the adoption of the antiphon *Venite et videte locum ubi positus erat Dominus.*[5] This utterance of the angels supplies a motivation for the act of raising the altar-cloth, or of peering within the sepulchre, on the part of the Marys. In disposing

---

[1] See above, pp. 209, 217, 223.

[2] St Gall, Stiftsbibl., MS 360, Versus Sangallenses sæc. xii, pp. 31–2, mentioned by Gautier, *Tropes,* p. 221, and by Brooks, *Neue Osterfeiern,* p. 298, and now first printed. In the MS this text has music, is preceded by irrelevant verses, and is followed by the rubric *Ad Vesperas per totam ebdomadam Pasce.*

[3] See Hartker, p. 231.

[4] See Hartker, p. 203.

[5] See Hartker, p. 226; Migne, *P. L.,* lxxviii, 769, 771. The antiphon is taken from Matt. xxviii, 6.

of this speech within the fabric of the performance, however, the writers seem not to have been very adroit. According both to the Gospel narrative (Matt. xxviii, 5–7) and to common sense this exhortation ought to be uttered between the two parts of the angels' second speech, after they have announced the Resurrection, but before they have sent the Marys on their way by the words *Ite, nuntiate.* This arrangement, however, is found very seldom.[1] In the great majority of the plays the words *Venite et videte* are spoken after the Marys have left, or turned away from, the sepulchre in order to make their announcement to the chorus and congregation. This inept arrangement arises apparently from a reverent unwillingness to disturb the original simple structure of the trope *Quem quæritis*—and from a lack of dramatic resourcefulness.

In examining the shorter versions of the *Visitatio* which contain the speech *Venite et videte* we may begin conveniently with several examples in which the other utterances are already familiar, as, for instance, in this text of the fourteenth century from Speyer:[2]

Finita repeticione post *Gloria Patri,* incipi*tu*r responsorium[3] ab inicio, quod cantans chorus cum processione descend*it* in medium monasterium. Interea duo diaconi induti dalmaticis ueniunt ad Sepulchrum, et unus sedet ad caput et alius ad pedes. Post hec ueniunt tres sacerdotes induti cappis albis, cum tribus thuribulis, iuxta Sepulchrum stantes. H*ec* uidentes dyaconi cantant:

> *Quem queritis ⟨in sepulchro, o Christicolæ⟩?*

Presbyteri:

> *Ihesum Nazarenum ⟨crucifixum, o cœlicolæ⟩.*

Diaconi:

> *Non est hic, ⟨surrexit sicut prædixerat; ite, nuntiate quia surrexit.⟩*

Antiphona:

> *Venite ⟨et videte locum ubi positus erat Dominus, alleluia⟩.*

Psalmus: *Te Deum laudamus.* Cum quibus et laici incipiunt suam laudem alta uoce.

The new antiphon appears here as a mere additional utterance of the deacons who take the role of the angels. Unfortunately the generous rubrics with which the play opens do not continue

---

[1] For exceptional instances see below, for example, pp. 251, 270, 349, 379.

[2] Vienna, Nationalbibl., MS lat. 1882, Directorium Spirense sæc. xiv, fol. 41ᵛ, pre-viously edited by Lange, no. 47, pp. 33–4. For associated texts see Notes, p. 581.

[3] The responsory is *Dum transisset.*

with information as to the action accompanying the *Venite*. At the conclusion of the *Te Deum* the lay congregation sing a *laus*—presumably the vernacular *Christ ist erstanden*—which we shall encounter frequently in the longer Easter plays.[1]

A far more adequate arrangement appears in the following composition of the twelfth century from the abbey of Remiremont:[2]

⟨I⟩N UISITATIONE SEPULCHRI INFRA MAT⟨UT⟩INAS

Duo presbyteri ueniant cum thuribulis ad Sepulchrum, quibus duo diacones induti albis et stolis dicant:

Quem queritis in sepulchro, Christicole?

Presbyteri resp*ondeant:*

Ihesum Nazarenum crucifixum, o celicole.

Diacones dicunt:

Non est hic, surrexit sicut predixerat; ite, nuntiate quia surrexit a morte.
Venite et uidete locum ubi positus erat Dominus, alleluia, alleluia.

Tunc presbyteri, accepto sudario, reuertentes cantent clam| antiphonam:

Surrexit Christus et illuxit populo suo, quem redemit sanguine suo, alleluia.[3]

Alia antiphona:

Surrexit enim sicut dixit Dominus, et precedet uos in Galileam, alleluia; ibi eum uidebitis, alleluia, alleluia, alleluia.

Post hec manifeste et alta uoce antiphona:

Surrexit Dominus de sepulchro, qui pro nobis pependit in ligno, alleluia, alleluia, alleluia.

Finita antiphona, incipiat abbas *Te Deum laudamus.*

From the brief rubrics before us, and from the *Depositio* used in this same church,[4] we can infer a considerable part of the dramatic action in the *Visitatio*. When the Host and cross were buried on Good Friday, they were covered by a *sudarium*; and we may assume that in the ceremony of the *Elevatio*,[5] before Matins, the sudary was left in the sepulchre, as in similar ceremonies elsewhere.[6] In the *Visitatio* before us, then, at the words *Venite et videte*, the two Marys inspect, and perhaps enter, the sepulchre,

---

[1] See below, pp. 322 sqq.

[2] Paris, Bibl. Nat., MS lat. 9486, Ordin. Romaricense sæc. xii, fol. 60ʳ–60ᵛ, previously edited by Brooks, *New Texts*, p. 466, and by Young, *Passion-Play*, p. 351. For the related *Depositio* see below, p. 560. With the text before us may be associated that published by Dankó (*Feier*, p. 176), from Budapest, Nationalmuseum, MS Quart. Hung. 387,

Sacramentarium Bolduense sæc. xii.

[3] For this antiphon see Hartker, p. 240; Migne, *P. L.*, lxxviii, 775, 776.

[4] See below, p. 560.

[5] The MS omits the text of the *Elevatio*. Concerning the use of the *sudarium* see above, p. 134.

[6] See above, for example, pp. 143, 145.

take up the *sudarium*, and, no doubt, display it when they sing one or another of the antiphons that follow.

The taking up and displaying of the sudary, or *linteamina*, are described with considerably more detail in the most familiar and famed of all versions of the *Visitatio*: namely, that included in the *Regularis Concordia* of St Ethelwold, prepared at Winchester within the period 965–75, for the use of the Benedictine monasteries of England:[1]

Dum tertia recitatur lectio, quatuor fratres induant se, quorum unus alba[2] indutus acsi ad aliud agendum ingrediatur, atque latenter Sepulchri locum adeat, ibique manu tenens palmam, quietus sedeat. Dumque tertium percelebratur responsorium, residui tres succedant, omnes quidem cappis induti, turribula cum incensu manibus gestantes ac pedetemptim ad similitudinem querentium quid, ueniant ante locum Sepulchri. Aguntur enim hęc ad imitationem Angeli sedentis in monumento, atque Mulierum cum aromatibus uenientium, ut ungerent corpus Ihesu. Cum ergo ille residens tres uelut erraneos, ac aliquid querentes, uiderit sibi adproximare, incipiat mediocri uoce dulcisone | cantare:

   Quem queritis ⟨in sepulchro, o Christicolæ⟩?

Quo decantato fine tenus, respondeant hi tres uno ore:

   Ihesum Nazarenum ⟨crucifixum, o cælicola⟩.

Quibus ille:

   Non est hic, surrexit sicut predixerat; ite, nuntiate quia surrexit a mortuis.

Cuius iussionis[3] uoce uertant se illi tres ad chorum dicentes:

   Alleluia, resurrexit Dominus, ⟨hodie resurrexit leo fortis, Christus, filius Dei.⟩

Dicto hoc, rursus ille residens uelut reuocans illos dicat antiphonam:

   Venite et uidete locum ⟨ubi positus erat Dominus, alleluia⟩.

Hęc uero dicens surgat, et erigat uelum, ostendatque eis locum Cruce nudatum, sed tantum linteamina posita, quibus Crux inuoluta erat. Quo uiso, deponant turribula, quę gestauerant in eodem Sepulchro, sumantque linteum et extendant contra clerum, ac ueluti ostendentes, quod surrexerit Dominus et iam non sit illo inuolutus, hanc canant antiphonam:

   Surrexit Dominus de sepulchro, ⟨qui pro nobis pependit in ligno, alleluia⟩.

---

[1] London, Brit. Mus., MS Cotton Tiberius A. III, Regularis Concordia sæc. xi, fol. 21ʳ– 1ᵛ, previously edited by W. S. Logeman in *Anglia*, xiii (1891), 426–8, and reprinted therefrom by Manly, i, pp. xix–xx; Chambers, ɪ, 309, and Adams, pp. 9-10. See plate vii. A less correct version of the *Visitatio Sepulchri* found in the *Regularis Concordia* in Brit. Mus., MS Cotton Faustina B. III, sæc. xi, fol. 188ᵛ–

189ᵛ, of which I give the text in Notes, p. 581, along with information concerning historical relationships and other MSS and editions. Neither text of the *Visitatio* has music in the MS. The text in MS Tiberius A. III is accompanied by Old English glosses.

[2] alba] abba (MS).

[3] iussionis] iussimus (MS).

Superponantque linteum altari. Finita antiphona, prior congauden
pro triumpho regis nostri, quod deuicta morte surrexit, incipiat hymnun
Te Deum laudamus. Quo incepto, una pulsantur omnia signa.

From the *Depositio* and *Elevatio* associated with this play w
have already learned that the sepulchre for the performance i
arranged in a vacant part of the altar, and is provided with a
curtain stretched upon a ring.[1] We may assume that by th
drawing of this curtain the sepulchre is opened or closed. Th
impersonation of the Marys and the angel is described witl
touching explicitness. The angel, wearing an alb and carryin
a palm, is to go to the sepulchre without attracting attention
and is to sit there quietly. The Marys, vested in copes an
carrying thuribles, are to walk slowly, after the manner c
persons who are looking for something.[2] Somewhat less satisf
ing than the rubrics concerning costume and gesture is th
arrangement of the speeches. The angel's words *Venite et vide*
are decisively separated from his declaration *Non est hic.* Afte
the Marys have been dismissed by the command *Ite, nuntiate*
they appropriately turn away and announce the Resurrectio
to the chorus. Then the angel must summon them back an
convince them that Christ has risen by drawing the curtain, an
calling attention to the absence of the cross, and to the *linteamin*
in which it was wrapped. The Marys now lay down thei
thuribles, take up the grave-cloths, and exhibiting them to th
chorus, once more declare the Resurrection. The prior bring
the play to a joyful conclusion by beginning the *Te Deum,* thu
signalling the sounding of all the bells.

From a text so sound and authoritative as that from th
Regularis Concordia one passes somewhat reluctantly to a versio
of the play which, though it probably represents medieva
custom, is known to us only through unauthenticated texts c
the seventeenth and eighteenth centuries. Our special interes
in the *Visitatio* from Angers arises from the fact that it is one c
the rare examples in which the speech *Venite et videte* occupie
the natural place assigned to it in the Biblical narrativ
Eveillon describes the play as follows:[3]

[1] See above, p. 133.
[2] Cf. the use of the antiphon *Ardens est* in the *Visitatio* from Xanten below, p. 269.
[3] [J. Eveillon,] *De Processionibus Ecclesiasticis Liber,* Paris, 1655, pp. 177–9. With variations only in unimportant details the *Visitatio*
is described also by Macri, ii, 175, ar Moléon, p. 98. The description of the latte in the edition of 1757, is reprinted by Lang no. 59, p. 39. Concerning plays which r semble the present one in the position *Venite et videte* see above, p. 247.

fribus cantuas officio prebeatur. Completorium sonoriter cele
bretur more canonicorum.

Iidem sco pasche separim canonice hore amonadius ineccelesia dei
more canonicorum. propter auctoritate beati GREGORII pape
sedis aplice quam ipse antiphonario dictautur. celebrende sunt. Cuisde
tempore nocas antequam matutinorum signa moueantur. sumant
edicui crucem. & ponant inloco sibi congruo. Inprimis adnoceuma
abbate seu quolibet sacerdote dum nituir lausdi. inaeecta dicar.

Dnie labia mea aperies. semel tantum. postea. Ds inadiutorium
meam intende. cum gla. Psalmo autem dnie quid multiplicati
sunt dimisso. cantor incipiat muitatorium. Tunc tres anaph
cum tribus psalmis. Quibus finitas uersus conuenions dicautur.
Deinde tot lectionis cum responsonis adhoc nre pertinentibus.
Dum tertia recitatur lectio iiii. frs induant se quorum unus
abba indutus. ac si adaliud agendum ingrediatur. acq; latenter
sepulchri locum adeat. ibiq; manu tenens palmam quietus
sedeat. Dumq; tertium percelebitur responsorium. residui
tres succedant. Omis quidem cappis induta. turibula cumincensu
manibus gestantes. acpede tentum. dsimilitudinem queren
tium. quid iuenant. ante locum sepulcon. Aquuntur enim
hec adimirationem angeli sederas inmonumento. Acq; mu
erum cum aromatibus uenientium ite unguere corpus ihu
Cum ergo ille residens. tres uelut errineos ab aliquid querentes
uident sibi adproximare. incipiat mediocri uoce dulcisone

In ecclesia Andegauensi celebratur hoc mysterium, finito tertio responsorio Matutini, hoc modo. Paratur altare maius vice Monumenti Christi, velis supra et ab anteriori parte obtentis, quasi tabernaculum extemporaneum. Adhærent altari duo maiores capellani, superpellicio et cappa candida induti, alter ad cornu dextrum, alter ad sinistrum, qui repræsentent Angelos ad Monumentum sedentes. Tum procedunt a secretario duo corbicularii,[1] alba et dalmatica candida ornati, capite amictu circumtecto, sed amictui superinducta mitella purpurea, Mulieres ad Monumentum venientes exhibituri, præcedentibus duobus pueris symphoniacis cum thuribulis. Hos,[2] ubi in aditu altaris constiterint, illi canentes interrogant:

Quem quæritis in sepulcro, ⟨o Christicolæ?⟩

Respondent hi, similiter canentes:

Iesum Nazarenum crucifixum, ⟨o cælicolæ.⟩

Tum illi:

Non est hic, surrexit sicut prædixerat.
Venite et videte locum ubi positus erat Dominus.

Hoc audito, corbicularii introeunt in Monumentum et illud venerantur, osculantes altare in medio quasi Dominum suum, cuius desiderio venerant, præ suauitate amoris basiantes; atque interea duo pueri altare terno ductu incensant. Tunc capellani:

Ite, nuntiate discipulis eius quia surrexit.

Ad hanc vocem corbicularii pergunt in chorum, præcedentibus duobus pueris, cantantes elata voce:

Alleluia, resurrexit Dominus, hodie resurrexit leo fortis, Christus, filius Dei.

Quibus una voce respondet omnis chorus:

Deo gratias, dicite eia.

Interea vero duo illi corbicularii accedentes ad episcopum, facta reuerentia, eum osculo salutant submissa voce quasi in aurem dicentes:

Resurrexit Dominus, alleluia.

Quibus respondet episcopus osculum reddens:

Deo gratias, alleluia.

Et statim præ lætitia in iubilum erumpens, intonat hymnum *Te Deum laudamus*, duobus pueris interea thus ei adolentibus. Deinde ambo corbicularii simul procedentes cantori suo loco stanti eumdem nuntium perferunt, osculumque libant; atque inde discedentes, alter ad dextram, alter ad sinistram partem chori, aliis dignitatibus et canonicis cæterisque in choro versantibus per ordinem, eadem verba insinuant, addito osculo, et pueris ad singulos incensum mittentibus. Respondent vero etiam singuli, osculum osculo reddentes, *Deo gratias, alleluia.*

---

[1] *Corbicularius* appears to be a term peculiar to Angers, and denotes a cleric vested in a certain sort of surplice. See Du Cange, *sub voc.*
[2] Hos] Hi (Print).

For the sepulchre at Angers is used the main altar, in front of which a certain space is enclosed by curtains. Impersonation of the two Marys and two angels is accomplished, as usual, through the adaptation of vestments. When the angels say *Venite et videte*, the Marys enter the enclosure, and kiss the altar, while their acolytes cense it. Then at the command *Ite, nuntiate* the Marys proceed into the choir and announce the Resurrection, first to the chorus and then to the bishop. The ceremony closes with the *Te Deum*, a general censing, and the giving of the Pax.

The liturgical pieces which we have thus far found associated with the speech *Venite et videte* in the latter part of the play are merely antiphons with which we have already become familiar in earlier parts of this study, and which provide no specific motivation or description of dramatic action.[1] What the writers appear to have felt the need of was a second form of dismissal which the angels could address to the Marys after having summoned them back again to the sepulchre. For this purpose, therefore, they adopted the antiphon *Cito euntes, dicite discipulis quia surrexit Dominus, alleluia*,[2] as, for example, in the following text from the monastery of St Maximin, near Treves:[3]

Vltimum responsorium post *Gloria Patri* repetitur a capite. Quo finito, antequam *Te Deum laudamus* incipiatur, duo dyaconi in albis stent apud Sepulchrum, et duo presbiteri in albis et cappis veniant ad eos. Tunc dyaconi cantent mediocriter:

> *Quem queritis, in sepulchro, o Christicole?*

Sacerdotes:

> *Ihesum Nazarenum ⟨crucifixum⟩, o celicole.*

Dyaconi: ·

> *Non est hic, surrexit sicut predixerat.*

Item dyaconi:

> *Venite et videte locum ⟨ubi positus erat Dominus, alleluia, alleluia⟩.*

Item dyaconi:

> *Cito euntes, ⟨dicite discipulis quia surrexit Dominus, alleluia.⟩*

Post hec sacerdotes accipiant sudarium de Sepulchro, et vadant supra gradus presbiterij, et extendentes sudarium cantent alta voce:

---

[1] For the use of a less familiar antiphon see Notes, p. 583.

[2] See Migne, *P. L.*, lxxviii, 769, 770; Hartker, p. 226.

[3] Treves, Stadtbibl., MS 1635, Ordin. monasterii Sancti Maximini sæc. xv, fol. 79ᵛ, previously edited by Brooks, *New Texts*, pp. 469–70. For associated texts see Notes, p. 583.

Surrexit Dominus de sepulchro, qui pro nobis pependit in ligno, alleluia, alleluia, alleluia.

Sequitur *Te Deum laudamus.*

As a form of dismissal, the antiphon *Cito euntes* is particularly appropriate here, in that it motivates the succeeding announcement of the Marys to the chorus or congregation, who may be regarded, in a general way, as representing the disciples. Fortunate also is the apparent shortening of the second speech of the *dyaconi*; for the omission of the usual *ite, nuntiate* restores perfectly the natural sequence of the narrative of St Matthew: *Non est hic, surrexit enim sicut dixit; venite et videte locum ubi positus erat Dominus. Et cito euntes, dicite discipulis ejus quia surrexit.*[1]

The use of the new antiphon under somewhat altered surroundings may be seen in the following play from Raitenbuch:[2]

Et cantor incipit responsorium a capite. Deinde de choro exeunt cum reuerencia portantes in manibus candelas ardentes, sub typo Mulierum, tres superiores induti bonis cappis. Vadunt ad Sepulchrum, et ibi sedent duo dyaconi induti dalmaticis sub vice Angelorum, qui dicunt eis:

Quem queritis, o tremule mulieres, in hoc tumulo plorantes?

Respondent presbyteri:

Ihesum Nazarenum crucifixum querimus.

Angeli:

Non est hic quem queritis, sed cito euntes nunctiate discipulis eius et Petro quia surrexit Ihesus.

Angeli:

Venite et videte locu⟨m⟩ ubi positus erat Dominus, alleluia.[3]

Angeli:

Cito euntes, dicite discipulis quia surrexit Dominus, alleluia, alleluia.

Tunc sacerdotes intrantes Sepulchrum lintheamina inde tollunt, et portantes ante se cantant et ostendunt omnibus, et dicunt antiphonam:

Surrexit Dominus de sepulchro, qui pro nobis pependit in ligno, alleluia.

Deinde cantor incipit *Te Deum lau⟨damus⟩.*

Of this version the most arresting feature is the elaborated form of the dialogue *Quem quæritis.* Just as the original trope is a free adaptation of passages in the Gospels,[4] so the dialogue before us is an independent revision of the trope itself. One observes,

---

[1] Matt. xxviii, 6–7.
[2] Munich, Staatsbibl., MS lat. 12301, Ordin. Raitenbuchense anni 1431, fol. 90ᵛ, described by Brooks, *Neue Osterfeiern*, p. 299, and now printed, I think, for the first time. The text is preceded by a rubric concerning

the third responsory *Dum transisset.* For a similar version of the *Visitatio* see Notes, p. 586.
[3] alleluia] After this word is an unintelligible entry which appears to be *namazaize.*
[4] See above, pp. 202–3.

however, that in the second speech of the angels the reviser is obviously influenced by the following sentences of the Vulgate: *Et cito euntes, dicite discipulis ejus quia surrexit;*[1] *Sed ite, dicite discipulis ejus, et Petro, quia præcedit vos in Galilæam.*[2] The words *cito euntes* in this speech are, in the play before us, somewhat awkwardly repeated at the beginning of the final dismissal uttered by the *angeli.* Of this ineptitude we shall see other examples. A noticeable aspect of the new form of dialogue is the removal of the word *Christicolæ,* and of the more or less inevitable rhyming word *cælicolæ.* It is obvious that this traditional rhyme may have caused embarrassment when a church wished to represent a single angel, according to the narratives of Matthew and Mark. Hence one critic has suggested that the revision was inspired by a desire for a form which could be used without regard to the number of actors.[3] We shall find, in any case, that the new arrangement is confined almost exclusively to Germany, or to places known to be rather specifically under German influence.[4]

In the two plays just examined the Marys proclaim the Resurrection to the congregation only once. To the angels' first command, in other words, they do not accede. For an example of a double proclamation, then, we turn to the following from the venerable tenth-century troper of Winchester:[5]

Angelica de Christi[6] Resurrectione:
> *Quem queritis in sepulchro, Christicolae?*

Sanctarum Mulierum responsio:
> *Ihesum Nazarenum crucifixum, o cęlicola.* |

Angelice uocis consolatio:[7]
> *Non est hic, surrexit sicut predixerat; ite, nuntiate quia surrexit, dicentes:*

Sanctarum Mulierum ad omnem clerum modulatio:
> *Alleluia, resurrexit Dominus, hodie ⟨resurrexit⟩ leo fortis, Christus, filius Dei. Deo gratias, dicite eia!*

Dicat Angelus:
> *Venite et uidete locum ubi positus erat Dominus, alleluia, alleluia.*

Iterum dicat Angelus:
> *Cito euntes, dicite discipulis quia surrexit Dominus, alleluia, alleluia.*

---

[1] Matt. xxviii, 7.
[2] Mark xvi, 7.
[3] See Meyer, p. 84, note 1.
[4] See Meyer, p. 119.
[5] Oxford, Bibl. Bodl., MS 775, Trop. Wintoniense sæc. x (978–80), fol. 17ʳ–17ᵛ,

published by Frere, *Winchester Troper,* p. 17; Manly, i, p. xxi; Chambers, ii, 13. Manly's text is reprinted by Beeson, pp. 201–2. For a text from another MS see Notes, p. 586.
[6] Christi] X̄P̄E (MS).
[7] uocis consolatio] uoces consolatus (MS).

Mulieres[1] una uoce canant iubilantes:

Surrexit Dominus de sepulchro, qui pro nobis pependit in ligno, alleluia.[2]

Although the rubrics in this text are tantalizingly laconic, we may reasonably assume that it represents a normal form of *Visitatio* designed for performance, with impersonation, at Easter Matins.[3] One observes that the word *cælicolæ* of the original trope has here been appropriately changed to the singular *cælicola*, in recognition of the fact that only one angel is present.

In their proclamation of the Resurrection the Marys do not always confine their utterances to the mild and simple antiphons which we have been examining. They occasionally allow themselves a somewhat militant outburst against the Jews, beginning with the words *Dicant nunc Judæi*.[4] This usage is fully illustrated by the liturgy of Strassburg in texts ranging in date from the thirteenth to the sixteenth century. For the sake of its superior rubrics we may avail ourselves here of the following from a service-book printed in 1590:[5]

Lecta autem tertia lectione, duo eliguntur qui vadunt ad Sepulchrum, induti cappis albis vel superpelliciis, et sedeant unus ad caput, alter ad pedes, expectantes visitatores eiusdem Sepulchri. Finito autem tertio responsorio, tres sacerdotes, quibus hoc cantor iniunxerit, cappis induti, singuli thuribulum cum incenso plurimo portantes, ad Sepulchrum procedant. Quos Caelicolae duo, scilicet stantes in Sepulchro, interrogant. Versus:

Quem queritis in sepulchro, o Christicole?

Respondent Christicolae, tres scilicet sacerdotes:

Iesum Nazarenum crucifixum, o caelicolae.

Item Caelicolae. Versus:

Non est hic, surrexit sicut praedixerat; ite, nunciate quia surrexit de sepulchro.

Deinde Caelicolae leuantes velamen Sepulchro superpositum dant eis sudarium cantando hanc antiphonam:

Venite et videte locum ubi positus erat Dominus, alleluia, alleluia.

Accepto sudario, redeant in chorum. Et tres in choro cantent voce sonora hanc antiphonam:

Dicant nunc Iudei quomodo milites custodientes sepulchrum perdiderunt regem

---

[1] Mulieres] Mulieri (MS).

[2] Followed by the rubric *Sabbato Sancto primum Benedictio Cerei.*

[3] For observations on the liturgical position of this piece see Notes, p. 587.

[4] For remarks on this liturgical piece see Notes, p. 587.

[5] *Agenda Ecclesiae Argentinensis*, Cologne, 1590, pp. 252–5, mentioned by Lange, no. 75, p. 50, and reprinted by Young, *Harrowing of Hell*, pp. 913–4. Concerning the related *Depositio* and *Elevatio* see below, p. 562; and concerning other texts of the *Visitatio* see Notes, p. 587.

ad lapidis positionem. Quare non seruant petram iustitiae? Aut sepultum reddant, aut resurgentem adorent, nobiscum dicentes alleluia, alleluia.

Venientibus autem super chorum, vultibus versis ad clerum, et stantes in supremo gradu ante maius altare, expanso inter se sudario, canentes Christicolae antiphonam:

> *Surrexit Dominus de sepulchro, qui pro nobis pependit in ligno, alleluia.*

Chorus cantet antiphonam:

> *Surrexit Christus, et illuxit populo suo, quem redemit sanguine suo, alleluia.*

Christicolae cantent antiphonam:

> *Surrexit enim sicut dixit Dominus, et praecedet vos in Galilaeam, alleluia; ibi eum videbitis, alleluia, alleluia, alleluia.*

Deinde cantor prosequatur *Te Deum laudamus.* Haec praescripta Visitatio Sepulchri observetur secundum consuetudinem cuiuslibet ecclesiae.

The absence here of a speech dismissing the Marys after they have received the sudary gives the impression of a certain abruptness. The *mise en scène*, however, is uncommonly adequate, the sepulchre being a curtained structure large enough to enter. Particularly effective in the action is the displaying of the large sudary by the Marys from the top altar-step, and their subsequent antiphonal dialogue with the chorus.

The appropriate form of dismissal, after the antiphon *Dicant nunc Judæi*, is found in a text from the monastery of St Emmeram:[1]

AD SEPULCHRUM

> *Qvem queritis in sepulchro, o Christicole?*

Antiphona: *Ihesum Nazarenum crucifixum, o celicole.*

Antiphona: *Non est hic, surrexit sicut[2] predixerat; ite, nunciate quia surrexit de sepulchro.*

Antiphona: *Venite et uidete ⟨locum ubi positus erat Dominus, alleluia, alleluia⟩.*

Antiphona: *Dicant nunc Iudei quomodo milites custodientes sepulchrum perdiderunt regem ad lapidis positionem. Quare non seruabant petram iusticie? Aut sepultum reddant, aut resurgentem adorent, nobiscum dicentes alleluia.*

Angeli antiphona: *Cito euntes dicite discipulis ⟨quia surrexit Dominus, alleluia⟩.*

Antiphona: *Surrexit enim sicut dixit ⟨Dominus; et præcedet vos in Galilæam, alleluia; ibi eum videbitis, alleluia, alleluia, alleluia⟩.*

> *Te Deum laudamus.*

In the absence of adequate rubrics we may assume that it is the Marys who sing the antiphon *Dicant nunc Judæi*, before they depart from the sepulchre.

---

[1] Munich, Staatsbibl., MS lat. 14741, Brev. Sancti Emmerami sæc. xiv, fol. 207ʳ, previously edited by Lange, no. 79, p. 53.

For associated texts see Notes, p. 588.
[2] sicut] Written twice (MS).

A fresh utterance and an unusual bit of stage-action are assigned to the Marys in the following *Visitatio* from Fritzlar:[1]

Quo finito, duo scolares sedentes in Sepulchro cantent:
Quem queritis, o ⟨tremulæ mulieres, in hoc tumulo plorantes⟩?
Tunc tres scolares induti cappis sericis uel uestibus muliebribus uenientes apud[2] Sepulchrum cum thuribulis et candelis accensis respondeant cantantes:
Ihesum Nazarenum ⟨crucifixum quærimus⟩,
fungentes officio Mariarum. Iterum | scolares in Sepulchro cantent:
Non est hic ⟨quem quæritis, sed cito euntes nuntiate discipulis ejus et Petro, quia surrexit Jesus.⟩
Et statim surgentes in Sepulchrum, exeuntes Sepulchrum discooperiant in parte illa ubi exeunt, et habentes cooperimentum Sepulchri in manibus cantent:
Venite et uidete locum ⟨ubi positus erat Dominus, alleluia, alleluia⟩.
Tunc tres Marie abeuntes et crucifixum accedentes paulatim cantent:
Ad sepulchrum uenimus gementes; ⟨angelos Domini sedentes vidimus et dicentes quia surrexit Jesus.⟩
Quo finito, statim stantes contra chorum et eleuato crucifixo in altum cantent:
Surrexit Dominus de sepulchro, ⟨qui pro nobis pependit in ligno, alleluia.⟩
Postea cantor incipiat *Te Deum laudamus.*

The passage *Ad sepulchrum venimus* is not among the traditional liturgical pieces in the service-books, and appears to have been composed specifically for use in the *Visitatio*, in the more extended versions of which we shall find it frequently.[3] In the play before us it is used by the Marys for a processional as they proceed to the place where the cross is stationed. Their raising of the cross when they proclaim the Resurrection is exceptionally effective.

A variant of the passage *Ad sepulchrum venimus*, and a quite different disposition of the action, are seen in a play of the fourteenth century from Würzburg:[4]

Infra tercium responsorium duo canonici dyaconi, induti dalmaticis albis, precedentibus eis duobus pueris cum candelis, per hostium chori

---

[1] Cassel, Landesbibl., MS Theol. 2°. 99, Directorium Chori Fredeslariense sæc. xv, fol. 88ᵛ–89ʳ, previously edited by Brooks, *Sepulchre*, p. 100. The text is preceded by the third responsory *Dum transisset.* Concerning the related *Depositio* see below, p. 561; and concerning associated texts of the *Visitatio* see Notes, p. 588.

[2] apud] apłi (MS).
[3] In regard to this piece, and its variants, see Lange, pp. 31, 54–6, 167; Meyer, p. 78.
[4] Würzburg, Universitätsbibl., MS Theol. 2°. 127a, Brev. Wirceburgense sæc. xiv, fol. 68ᵛ–69ʳ, previously edited by Lange, no. 80, pp. 53–4. The text is preceded by the third responsory *Dum transisset.*

iuxta altare Sancti Petri descendunt in criptam, et quasi Angeli supra Sepulcrum sedentes, et visitationem Sepulcri per tres Marias exspectantes. Deinde dominus decanus cum duobus sacerdotibus canonicis, cappis albis induti, quasi tres Marie, cum tribus thuribulis et tribus pixidis, precedentibus eis duobus pueris | cum candelis, per hostium iuxta altare Sancti Martini descendunt in criptam ad visitandum Sepulcrum. Cum autem Sepulcrum[1] venerint, duo dyaconi quasi Angeli in Sepulcro sedentes cantent hos versus:

> *Quem queritis, o tremule mulieres, ⟨in hoc tumulo plorantes?⟩*

Marie respondent:

> *Ihesum Nazarenum crvcifixum querimus.*

Angeli cantent:

> *Non est hic, surrexit.*

Deinde Angeli sumentes lintheum in manibus suis extendant et cantent antiphonam:

> *Venite et videte locum ⟨ubi positus erat Dominus, alleluia, alleluia⟩.*

Interea tres scolares iuxta summum altare in latere dextro stantes, finito tertio responsorio, cantent hos versus:

> *Ad tumulum venere gementes,*

choro reliquam notam repetente. Interim tres Marie cum lintheo de cripta[2] venientes, stantes ante altare Sancti Martini, et finitis versibus, incipiunt antiphonam:

> *Dicant nunc Iudei,*

choro prosequente. Deinde Marie chorum ascendentes et super gradus iuxta tumbam episcopi stantes, lintheum dominis et populo ostendant cum antiphona:[3]

> *Surrexit Dominus de sepulcro, ⟨qui pro nobis pependit in ligno, alleluia⟩,*

simul cantando. Qua finita, rectores chori simul incipiant *Te Deum laudamus.*

According to the arrangement before us, the dialogue of the angels and Marys occurs at a sepulchre in the crypt during the singing of the third responsory in the choir above. At the simultaneous conclusion of the dialogue and the responsory, three singers at the main altar herald the ascent of the Marys to the upper church by singing the narrative passage *Ad tumulum venere gementes.*[4] After beginning the antiphon *Dicant nunc Judæi,* the Marys re-enter the choir and, exhibiting the grave-cloth to the congregation, conclude the performance.

---

[1] Sepulcrum] sepulcū (MS).
[2] cripta] criptam (MS).
[3] antiphona] antiphonam (MS).
[4] Concerning this passage see below, p. 585.

III

Having considered somewhat amply the textual variations and additions used by way of enlarging the latter part of the *Visitatio*, we have now to examine certain passages which were adopted by way of preface. Of these the most relevant and persistent is the Easter antiphon *Et dicebant ad invicem: Quis revolvet nobis lapidem ab ostio monumenti?*[1] The dramatic use of this passage for introducing the *Quem quæritis* dialogue was prompted not only by its position in the Gospel narrative of the approach of the Marys to the tomb, but also by certain anticipations found in the *Depositio* and *Elevatio*. It is clear that a considerable number of these latter ceremonies included the use of some sort of stone, or *lapis*, for closing the *sepulchrum* at the conclusion of the burial on Good Friday, and hence for removal from the *ostium sepulchri* early on Easter morning.[2] In some communities the object used to represent the *lapis* seems to have been a portable stone altar.[3] Although we have, of course, no evidence showing that every church which used *Quis revolvet* in its *Visitatio* provided an anticipatory *lapis* in a preceding *Depositio* and *Elevatio*, we may infer that this arrangement prevailed rather widely.

An early use of the new antiphon may be seen in the following simple text of the tenth or eleventh century from Reichenau:[4]

AD VISITANDVM SEPVL*chrum*

Presbyteri vice Mvliervm:

Et dicebant ad invicem: Quis reuoluit nobis lapidem ab hostio monumenti? Alleluia, alleluia!

Interrog*ant* Angel*i*:

Quem queritis in sepulchro, Christicole?

R*esponsio*:

Ihesum Nazarenum crucifixum, o caelicolae.|

Econtra:

Non est hic, surrexit sicut predixerat; ite, nunciate quia surrexit de sepulchro.

---

[1] See Hartker, p. 230; Migne, *P.L.*, lxxviii, 770. The antiphon is derived from Mark xvi, 3.
[2] For an example see above, p. 142.
[3] See above, for example, pp. 140–2.
[4] Bamberg, Staatsbibl., MS lit. 5 (Ed.

V. 9), Trop. Augiense sæc. x–xi, fol. 45^r–45^v, previously edited by Lange, no. 39, p. 29. In the MS the present text has neums, and is preceded by liturgical pieces from the Adoration of the Cross, of Good Friday.

Presbyteri:

Svrrexit enim ⟨sicut dixit Dominus, et præcedet vos in Galilæam, alleluia; ibi eum videbitis, alleluia, alleluia, alleluia⟩.

Te Deum lavdamvs.

The new preface here provides an obviously appropriate utterance for the Marys as they approach the tomb. The retention in their speech of the narrative words *Et dicebant ad invicem*, however, is a naïve dramatic blemish which the ecclesiastical playwrights did not fail to recognize, for it is not found often.[1] The offending passage is absent, for example, from the following form of the play used in the monastery of St Blaise:[2]

Tertium vero responsorium cantent tres cantores in cappis, quorum duo incensent altare, ut supra scriptum est. Responsorium *Dum transisset*, quod post *Gloria Patri* reincipiendum est. Interim duo sacerdotes se cappis induunt summentes duo thuribula, et humeraria in capita ponent, intrantes chorum, paulatim euntes versus Sepulchrum, voce mediocri cantantes:

Quis revolvet nobis lapidem ⟨ab ostio monumenti⟩?

Quos Diaconus, qui debet esse retro Sepulchrum, interroget psallendo:

Quem quæritis ⟨in sepulchro, o Christicolæ⟩?

Deinde illi:

Iesum Nazarenum ⟨crucifixum, o cœlicola⟩.

Quibus Diaconus respondet:

Non est hic, ⟨surrexit sicut prædixerat; ite, nuntiate quia surrexit de sepulchro.⟩

Mox incensent Sepulchrum, et dicente diacono *Ite, nuntiate*, vertent se ad chorum, remanentes super gradum, et cantent:

Surrexit Dominus de sepulchro,

usque in finem. Finita antiphona, domnus abbas incipiat *Te Deum laudamus* in medio ante altare. Moxque campanæ sonentur in angularibus.

This version follows the tradition of St Matthew, with its one angel and two Marys.[3] The details of impersonation and the censing of the sepulchre are in the established manner of liturgical drama. Although the sudary is not mentioned here, or in the related *Depositio* and *Elevatio*,[4] it may well have been used in connexion with the words *Surrexit Dominus*.[5]

---

[1] For another example see below, p. 629.

[2] The text is published by Gerbert, *Monumenta*, ii, 237, 'Ex ordine operis Dei San-Blas. Msc. sæc. XIV,' and reprinted by Lange, no 44, pp. 30–1, and by Young, *Dramatic Associations*, p. 7. For earlier reprints see Lange, p. 6; for the related *Depositio* and *Elevatio* see above, pp. 112 sqq.; and for associated texts of the *Visitatio* see Notes, p. 589.

[3] See above, p. 217.

[4] See above, pp. 112 sqq.

[5] See the *Visitatio* from Andenne below, p. 589.

A similar *Visitatio*, with important rubrical details, is the following from Metz:[1]

Ordo ad Visitandum Sepulchrum

Interim dum ultimum responsorium est reinceptum post *Gloria*, duo diaconi egressi a choro, induti dalmaticis albis, ferentes in manibus thuribula, tenentes etiam palmas in manibus ita quod in una manu, scilicet dextra thuribulum teneant, in reliqua vero palmam, debent paulatim procedere versus altare et cantare bis:[2]

Quis revolvet nobis lapidem ab ostio monumenti?

Duo autem sacerdotes induti casulis stent retro altare et cantent:

Quem quaeritis in sepulchro, o Christicole?

Duo vero diaconi stantes juxta cornua ipsius altaris interim debent thurificare anteriorem partem altaris, et cantare quasi respondendo:

Jesum Nazarenum querimus crucifixum, o celicole.

Tunc duo sacerdotes respondeant:

Non est hic, surrexit sicut predixerat; ite, nuntiate quia surrexit a morte.

Et interim discooperiant capsam argenteam quæ est super altare sublevando levamen cum duobus baculis. Diaconi vero vertant se ad chorum, et eant super gradus, et ibi cantent alta voce:

Surrexit Dominus de sepulchro, ⟨qui pro nobis pependit in ligno, alleluia.⟩

Et statim episcopus vel alia persona incipiat ad præceptum cantoris *Te Deum laudamus*, diaconis ipsis recedentibus.

Each of the deacons who impersonate the Marys in this play holds a thurible in his right hand and a palm in his left. The angels stand behind the altar, which serves as the sepulchre. In announcing the Resurrection to the Marys the angels, by using two rods, raise a cloth from the altar-table and disclose a silver *capsa*, or box. This *capsa* is probably the enclosure of the relics regularly placed in an excavation in the top of the altar-stone, and actually called *sepulchrum*.[3] The appropriateness of this stage-action is obvious.

In a relatively small number of versions of the play, all of them of French origin, the opening interrogation *Quis revolvet?* is preceded by the exclamation *O Deus!* Among these versions is one which, in at least a single respect, might fairly be con-

---

[1] Paris, Bibl. Nat., MS lat. 990, Liber de Ordinatione et Officiis totius anni in ecclesia Metensi, fol. 52ʳ. This is a seventeenth-century copy of an original of unknown date. The *Visitatio* has been previously edited by Brooks, *New Texts*, pp. 464–5. Concerning associated texts see Notes, p. 590.

[2] bis] Brooks conjectures that this is a scribe's mistake for *Deus*, with which the succeeding speech may have begun.

[3] See above, p. 219.

sidered the most noteworthy Easter play in the world, for it was performed not in an improvised Western *mise en scène*, but at the original Holy Sepulchre in Jerusalem itself. Of this sacred ceremony the oldest extant text is the following, of the year 1160:[1]

Quod[2] dum cantatur, sint parati tres clerici juuenes in modum Mulierum retro altare, iuxta consuetudinem antiquorum. Quod non facimus modo propter astancium peregrinorum multitudinem. Interim finito scilicet responsorio, procedunt inde, preeuntibus[3] candelabris et turibulis, deferentes in manibus unusquisque uas aureum uel argenteum intus habens aliquod unguentum, cantando ter antiphonam:

O Deus! Quis reuoluet ⟨nobis lapidem ab ostio monumenti⟩?

Cumque ad portam Sepulchri Gloriosi appropinquauerint, duo alij clerici ante portam uel iuxta predicti Sepulcri tenentes cereos in manibus, habentes amictus super capita, respondentes cantabunt:

Quem queritis ⟨in sepulchro, o Christicolæ⟩?

Respondebunt Mulieres:

Ihesum Nazarenum ⟨crucifixum, o cælicolæ⟩.

Respondebunt tunc illi duo:

Non est hic, surrexit ⟨sicut predixerat; ite, nuntiate quia surrexit⟩.

Illis[4] canentibus, ingredientur Sepulchrum Mulieres, ibique facta breui oratione regredientur, atque in medio choro stantes alta uoce cantando nunciabunt:

Alleluia, resurrexit Dominus, ⟨hodie resurrexit leo fortis, Christus, filius Dei.⟩

Quo finito, patriar|cha incip*iat Te Deum laudamus.*

This play is of a general type with which we are now familiar, and the speeches themselves require no elucidation. By way of impersonation the angels have amices over their heads and carry candles; and each of the Marys carries a gold or silver vessel containing ointment. Our peculiar interest in this version of the *Visitatio* arises, then, not from its content but from the circumstances under which it was performed. It is a French liturgical observance brought to Jerusalem by the Crusaders and adapted to the sanctity of the Holy Places. Some time between the date of their arrival (1099–1100) and the year 1160, however, the performance was discontinued, because of the throngs of pilgrims who came to see it. We must be grateful

---

[1] Rome, Bibl. Vatic., MS Barberini lat. 659, Ordin. ad usum Hierosolymitanum anni 1160, fol. 75ᵛ–76ʳ, published by Young, *Home of the Easter Play*, p. 76. The MS contains no *Depositio* or *Elevatio*. For another text of this *Visitatio*, with bibliography, see Notes, p. 591.

[2] Referring to the third responsory *Dur transisset.*

[3] preeuntibus] pereuntibus (MS).

[4] Illis] ille (MS).

for the vivifying phrase *propter astancium peregrinorum multitudinem*, which enables us to visualize the jostling crowds of worshippers who had streamed into the none too ample church of the Anastasis and had turbulently surrounded the rock of the Holy Sepulchre in their desire to see a dramatization of a Christian mystery.[1]

For the use of the introductory *Quis revolvet* in more extended forms of the *Visitatio* we proceed to such a text as the following from an unidentified monastery in Germany:[2]

Cum autem tercium responsorium post *Gloria Patri* ab initio repetitur, duo conuersi cum candelabris, et post eos domnus abbas, et duo pueri[3] cappis induti cum singulis thuribulis, incenso imposito, precedant; quos subsequantur tres cantores, deinde pueri, et post eos totus conuentus; atque hoc ordine procedant ad uisitandum | Sepulchrum. Quo dum peruenerint, omnibus ordinate stantibus, hi tres cum thuribulis stent procul a Sepulchro expectantes donec finiatur responsorivm, conuersis utroque latere astantibus. Finito responsorio, incipiant hi tres submissa uoce:

> Quis reuoluet nobis lapidem ⟨ab ostio monumenti⟩?

Et conuersis cum candelabris preeuntibus sic decantando eant usque ad hostium Sepulchri. Duo autem diaconi cum alba et stola dalmaticis induti intrinsecus sedentes, qui et propter hoc ipsum infra terciam lectionem illuc intrauerant, interrogent eos canendo hunc versum:

> Quem queritis in sepulchro, o Christicole?

Et illi respondeant:

> Ihesum Nazarenum crucifixum, o celicole.

Et diaconi econtra:

> Non est hic, surrexit sicut predixerat; ite, nunciate quia surrexit.

Statimque adiungentes cum dicunt:

> Venite ei uidete locum ubi positus erat Dominvs, alleluia, alleluia,

intrent illi cum thuribulis et incensent Sepulchrum, sublatoque lintheo uel sudario, quod inuenerint, tam ipsi quam et diaconi egrediantur, et ante altare sese ad conuentum uel ad populum conuertentes inter manus extendant sudarium ante se, et diaconibus ex utroque latere astantibus canant hi quinque hanc antiphonam:

> Sur⟨r⟩exit Dominus de sepulchro, ⟨qui pro nobis pependit in ligno, alleluia⟩.

Moxque stent tres cantores in medio; incipiant *Te Deum laudamvs*. | Et conuentus regrediatur in chorum.

---

[1] Concerning the Anastasis and the Holy Sepulchre see Appendix A.

[2] Munich, Staatsbibl., MS lat. 14765, Consuetudines Sigiberti Abbatis saec. xi–xii, fol. 93ʳ–94ʳ, published by B. Albers, in *Revue bénédictine*, xx (1903), 427–8, and by Albers, *Consuetudines*, ii, 104–6; v, 39. For bibliography and associated texts see Notes, pp. 557, 592.

[3] duo pueri] duos pueros (MS).

Noticeable here is the size of the sepulchre, which can accommodate at least five persons. The two angels seat themselves within it at the reading of the third lesson. In response to the *Venite et videte*, the three Marys also enter it, cense it, and take up the grave-cloth. Then all five persons come forth, exhibit the sudary to the convent, and sing in unison the antiphon *Surrexit Dominus*.

A certain expansion of dialogue and variation in costume are observable in the following play of the fourteenth century from the monastery of Fécamp:[1]

Post tercium responsorium tres fratres in specie Mulierum, quorum unus in capa rubea portet thuribulum inter duos alios, et ceteri duo ex utroque latere eius in dalmaticis candidis portent uasa in modum pissidarum, stantesque iuxta candelabrum cantent humiliter, ita conquerentes:

O Deus! Quis reuoluet nobis lapidem ab ostio monumenti?

Hinc procedant lente usque ad ostium iuxta altare, et unus frater in albis in specie Angeli stans iuxta Sepulchrum respondeat:

Quem queritis in sepulchro, o Christicole?

Mulieres ad Angelum:

Ihesum Nazarenum crucifixum, o celicola.

Angelus:

Non | est hic, surrexit sicut predixerat; ite, nunciate quia surrexit dicentes:

Mulieres:

Alleluia, resurrexit Dominus.

Angelus:

Alleluia, resurrexit Dominus.

Mulieres ad populum:

Alleluia, surrexit Dominus.

Angelus ad Mulieres:

Venite et uidete locum ubi positus erat Dominus, alleluia, alleluia.

Mulieres ad populum:

Surrexit Dominus de sepulchro, qui pro nobis pependit in ligno, alleluia, alleluia, alleluia.

Incipiat abbas et cantor, deinde chorus percantet ymnum *Te Deum lau|damus.*

In this performance an effort towards differentiation appears in the costuming of the Marys, one of them, presumably Mary

---

[1] Rouen, Bibl. de la Ville, MS 253 (*olim* A. 538), Ordin. Fiscannense sæc. xiv, fol. 54ʳ-55ʳ, previously edited by Lange, no. 57, pp. 36-7; Young, *Harrowing of Hell*, pp. 903-4. Concerning the related *Depositio* and *Elevatio* see below, p. 555.

Magdalen, wearing a red cope and carrying a thurible, whereas the others are vested in white dalmatics and carry vessels resembling pyxes. After the triple repetition of the words *Alleluia, resurrexit Dominus* at the dismissal *Ite, nuntiate*, the subsequent return of the Marys to the sepulchre seems almost like a separate scene. Noticeable also is the appropriate use of the singular form *celicola*.

Although the speeches in the following version from Toul resemble those in the play just examined, the details of *mise en scène* deserve separate consideration:[1]

In tercio responsorio, | dum dicti tres cantores cantant versum, pueri quatuor eant ad maius altare et sumant ibi duas cruces et duo candelabra cum cereis, redeantque in chorum cum thuribulario, et stent ad gradum chori expectantes ibi reiterationem responsorii post *Gloria Patri* faciendam. Finita uero reiteratione post *Gloria Patri*, reincipitur idem responsorium a cantoribus, et chorus prosequitur, uaduntque omnes cantando cum processione ante altare Sancte Crucis, precedentibus crucibus, thuribulario et ceroferariis. Tres uero cantores, qui et Marie dicuntur, uadant ad altare Sancti Apri et accipiant vascula ibi posita. Finitoque responsorio, eant ad Sepulchrum, capitibus uelatis amictibus suis, et cantent:

> *O Deus! Quis ⟨revolvet nobis lapidem ab ostio monumenti⟩?*

Puer uero, qui Angelum representat, stans in Sepulchro, palmam manu tenens, et in capite fanulum largum habens, respondeat:

> *Quem queritis ⟨in sepulchro, o Christicolæ⟩?*

Marie:

> *Ihesum Nazarenum ⟨crucifixum, o cælicola⟩.*

Angelus:

> *Non est hic, ⟨surrexit sicut prædixerat; ite, nuntiate quia surrexit.⟩*

Marie:

> *Alleluia, resurrexit Dominus, ⟨hodie resurrexit leo fortis, Christus, filius Dei.⟩*

Iterum respondeant Marie:

> *Alleluia, resurrexit Dominus, ⟨hodie resurrexit leo fortis, Christus, filius Dei.⟩*

Angelus:

> *Venite et uidete ⟨locum ubi positus erat Dominus, alleluia, alleluia⟩.*

Finita hac antiphona, exeat Angelus de Sepulchro per hostium ante. Marie uero intrent per hostium retro et offerant uascula sua, osculando

---

[1] Paris, Bibl. Nat., MS lat. 975, Ordin. Tullense sæc. xiii, fol. 29ᵛ–30ʳ, previously edited, in somewhat shortened form, by Lange, no. 60, pp. 39–40. In the MS the text is preceded by the responsory *Dum transisset*. For a version from the same community, from an unidentified MS, see Martene, iv, 146, mentioned by Lange, no. 61, p. 39. For associated versions see Notes, p. 594.

altare. Postea exeant de Sepulchro per hostium, per quod Angelus exiuit, capitibus denudatis, et stantes ante crucifixum, conuerse ad populum, incipiant hanc antiphonam:

Surrexit,

et chorus prosequatur *Dominus de sepulchro,* et residuum antiphonae. Interim duo socii cantoris ad loca sua reuertantur, et cum aliis stent fratribus, solo cantore in medio remanente. Finita uero predicta antiphona, incipiatur a cantore:

Angelus Domini,[1]

et chorus prosequatur. Et cantetur similiter:

Respondens autem ⟨angelus dixit mulieribus: Nolite timere, scio enim quod Jesum queritis⟩;[2]

et in fine dicitur *Alleluia.* Interim dum hec cantantur, portetur ab abbate incensum in Sepulchrum, duobus ceroferariis ipsum precedentibus. Finito autem *Alleluia* predicto, incipiatur ab ipso abbate, cantore sibi innuente, *Te Deum laudamus.* Quo cantato usque post *Sanctus,* reuertantur omnes in chorum, residuum predicti ymni cantando.

The aspect of this text which one needs especially to observe is not the admirable provision for impersonation, or the unusual liturgical censing of the sepulchre by the abbot at the end, but rather the following innocent rubric: *Tres uero cantores, qui et Marie dicuntur, uadant ad altare Sancti Apri et accipiant vascula ibi posita.* This special detour of the Marys to a side-altar for the purpose of receiving their vessels may, perhaps, be considered an embryonic form of their scene with the spice-merchant, or *unguentarius,* as we find it in more highly developed versions of the Easter play.[3]

A new form of the introductory speech of the Marys meets us for the first time in the following play from the monastery of Zwiefalten:[4]

Tercio responsorio denuo percantato, tres presbyteri siue diaconi, albis cappis induti, capita humeralibus obuoluta habentes et thuribula cum incenso in manibus tenentes, progrediuntur ad altare ubi paratum est Sepulcrum Domini cantantes multum suppressa uoce:

Quis reuoluet nobis ab hostio lapidem quem tegere sanctum cernimus sepulcrum?

Qua finita, subsistunt | non longe ab illis duobus fratribvs qui induti dal-

---

[1] For several liturgical pieces beginning thus see Migne, *P. L.,* lxxviii, 678, 769; Hartker, pp. 204, 228, 229.

[2] See Hartker, p. 230.

[3] See below, pp. 401 sqq.

[4] Stuttgart, Landesbibl., MS 4°. 36, Lib. resp. Zwifaltensis sæc. xii, fol. 122ᵛ–123ᵛ, now printed, I think, for the first time. The MS provides music. For associated texts see Notes, p. 596.

maticis, uelatis similiter capitibus, sedent infra Sepulcrum, quique
statim subinferunt hanc:

> *Quem queritis in sepulchro, o Christicole?*

Econtra isti qui uicem Mulierum agunt respondent:

> *Iesum Nazarenum crucifixum, o celicole.*

Item illi qui uicem Angelorum agunt:

> *Non est hic, surrexit sicut predixerat; ite, nunciate quia surrexit de sepulchro.*

Mox isti intrant Sepulcrum, et illis interim canentibus:

> *Venite et uidete locum ⟨ubi positus erat Dominus, alleluia⟩,*

thurificant locum ubi positvs erat Crucifixus; nam antequam pulsaretur
ad Nocturnos, sublatvs est inde cum Corpore Domini a custodibvs
ecclesie.[1] Sicque tollentes linteum quo erat | coopertvs, portant illud inter
se expansum, dextra leuaque gestantes thuribula, et cantantes mediocri
uoce antiphonam ambrosianam:

> *Dicant nunc Iudei quomodo milites custodientes sepulcrum perdiderunt regem*
> *ad lapidis positionem.[2] Quare non seruabant petram iusticie? Aut sepultum*
> *reddant, aut resurgentem adorent, nobiscum dicentes alleluia, alleluia.*

Regrediuntur eadem uia qua uenerunt, et finita antiphona ante introitum chori, intrant et super gradum sanctuarii consistentes, uersa facie
in chorvm, linteo adhuc expanso, excelsa uoce intonant antiphonam:

> *Surrexit enim sicut dixit Dominus.*

Quo facto inponitur *Te Deum laudamvs.*

The enlarged form of the antiphon *Quis revolvet*, seen here, will
appear in numerous other versions of the *Visitatio* from German
territory to be considered below. One is surprised that, in the
present instance, it is followed by the unrevised form of the
Quem quæritis dialogue.[3] Noticeable also in the play before us
is the special prominence given to the *sudarium*, which is exhibited first at the sepulchre outside the choir, with the accompaniment of *Dicant nunc Judæi*, and later from the steps before
the main altar, at the singing of the antiphon *Surrexit*.

A more definite advance in dramatic appropriateness appears
in a detail in the following *Visitatio* from the cathedral of
Cividale:[4]

---

[1] This refers, of course, to the *Elevatio Crucis* before Matins.

[2] lapidis positionem] lapidem posicionis (MS).

[3] See above, p. 253.

[4] Coussemaker, pp. 307–10, published this text from MS T. VII, of the fourteenth century, in the archives of the cathedral of Cividale, and his text is reprinted by Lange,

no. 85, pp. 58–9. The MSS of the cathedral are now in the Reale Museo Archeologico at Cividale, but the MS under consideration cannot be found among them. A search was made for me through the generosity of Signore Giuseppe Vale, Librarian of the Archbishop's Library at Udine. I reprint, therefore, the text of Coussemaker. For an associated text see Notes, p. 597.

In Resurrectione Domini N.J.C. Ad Matutinum

Finito tertio responsorio, tres Marie de sacrario veniant aptate et cum thuribulis et incenso; et vadant ad Sepulchrum canendo submissa voce hos versus:

> *Quis revolvet nobis ab ostio lapidem quem tegere sanctum cernimus sepulchrum?*

Angelus sedens in dextera Sepulchri respondeat cantando hunc versum:

> *Quem queritis, o tremule mulieres, in hoc tumulo plorantes?*

Marie:

> *Jhesum Nazarenum crucifixum querimus.*

Respondet Angelus:

> *Non est hic quem queritis; sed cito euntes nuntiate discipulis ejus et Petro quia surrexit Jhesus.*

Finito versu, Angelus levat cortinam, et cantat hanc antiphonam:

> *Venite et videte locum ubi positus erat Dominus, alleluia, alleluia.*

Deinde Marie intrant ad Sepulchrum et tollunt lintheamina; et intrant chorum cantando hos versus, usque in medium chori:

> *Ad monumentum venimus gementes; angelum Domini sedentem vidimus et dicentem quia surrexit Jhesus.*

Finito isto versu, vertunt se Marie versus chorum; et extendunt lintheamina et cantant alta voce hoc carmen:

> *Cernitis, o socii, ecce lintheamina et sudarium, et corpus non est in sepulchro inventum.*

Hoc peracto, incipiunt chorarii alta voce antiphonam:

> *Surrexit Dominus de sepulchro, qui pro nobis ⟨pependit in ligno, alleluia⟩.*

Finita ea antiphona, statim inchoetur *Te Deum laudamus.*

As an utterance for the Marys when they exhibit the grave-cloths nothing could be more suitable than the speech beginning *Cernitis, o socii, ecce lintheamina et sudarium*, which we now observe for the first time. This sentence, unknown to the authorized liturgy, was probably composed specifically for use in the *Visitatio*, and it will be found below in numerous examples.[1] Likewise peculiar to the Easter play is the preceding speech of the Marys, *Ad monumentum venimus*, of which we have seen a variant form above.[2] Noteworthy also in the text before us are the revised versions of *Quis revolvet* and of the *Quem quæritis* dialogue.

---

[1] See Lange, p. 167.　　　　[2] See above, p. 258.

IV

In a group by themselves belong a few relatively simple versions of the *Visitatio* in which the introductory *Quis revolvet* is preceded, or replaced, by other utterances. An example is the following from Xanten:[1]

⟨Mulieres:⟩[2]

>*Ardens est cor meum; desidero uidere Dominum meum; quero et non invenio vbi posuerunt eum, alleluia.*
>
>*Quis reuoluet nobis lapidem ab hostio monumenti, alleluia, alleluia?*

Angeli:

>*Quem queritis in sepulcro, o Christicole?*

Mulieres:

>*Ihesum Nazarenum crucifixum, o celicole.*

Angeli:

>*Non est hic, surrexit sicut predixerat; ite, nunciate quia surrexit.*

Mulieres:

>*Alleluia, resurrexit Dominus, ⟨hodie resurrexit leo fortis, Christus, filius Dei.⟩ Te Deum laudamus.*

The antiphon *Ardens est* will be recognized as a particularly appropriate utterance for the Marys on their way to the tomb, since it expresses precisely the mood of persons 'erranei, ac aliquid querentes'.[3]

A more ambitious, and still more acceptable, prelude appears in a form of the play found in a Norman service-book adapted to the use of Sicily:[4]

In Die Resurrectio⟨n⟩is Domini Versus Mulierum

Prima:

>*Hev! misere, cur contigit*
>*uidere mortem Saluatoris?*

---

[1] Paris, Bibl. Nat., MS lat. 1307, Brev. Xantense sæc. xv, fol. 92ᵛ, first published by Lange, no. 42, pp. 29–30. For associated texts see Notes, p. 598.

[2] The incomplete text of this version of the *Visitatio* in Paris, Bibl. Nat., MS lat. 1308, fol. 101ʳ (see below, p. 598), has here the rubric *Due Marie*. For the Easter antiphon *Ardens est* see Migne, *P.L.*, lxxviii, 773; Hartker, p. 237. The text printed above is immediately preceded by the third responsory *Dum transisset.*

[3] See the *Visitatio* from the *Regularis Concordia* above, p. 249.

[4] Madrid, Bibl. Nac., MS C. 132, Grad. ad usum ecclesiæ Siculorum sæc. xii, fol. 102ᵛ–103ʳ, now first printed. In the MS the text has music, and is preceded, at the bottom of fol. 102ʳ, by choral pieces for First Vespers of Easter. Concerning the MS see A. Legris, *La Liturgie rouennaise en Italie*, in *Revue des Questions historiques*, Nouvelle Série, xlix (1913), 450–60; and below, p. 476.

Secunda:

> *Heu! redemptio Israhel,*
> *ut quid taliter agere uoluit.*

Tertia:

> *Heu! consolatio nostra,*
> *ut quid mortem sustinuit.*

Insimul omnes:

> *O Deus! Quis reuoluet nobis ⟨lapidem ab ostio monumenti⟩?*

Versus Marie mul*ieris:*

> *Qvis reuoluet nobis lapidem ab hostio monumenti?*
> *Ecce lapis reuolutus, et iuuenis stola candida coopertus!*

Angelus:

> *Nolite timere uos; dicite quem queritis ad sepulcrum, Christicole?*

Mvlieres:

> *Hiesum Nazarenum crucifixum querimus, o celicole.*

Angelus:

> *Non est hic, surrexit sicut predixerat.*
> *Uenite et uidete locum ubi positus erat Dominus.*
> *Ecce locus ubi posuerunt eum.*
> *Ite, dicite discipulis eius quia surrexit de sepulchro; et ecce precedet uos in*
> *Galileam; ibi eum | uidebitis, sicut dixit uobis.*

Mulieres:

> *Eamus nuntiare mirum quod uidimus, et gaudium quod accepimus.*
> *Surrexit uere sicut dixit Dominus; precedet uos in Galileam, alleluia; ib*
> *eum uidebitis, alleluia, alleluia, alleluia.*

Chorvs:

> *Deo gratias, alleluia, alleluia, alleluia.*

Episcopus: *Te Deum laudamus.*[1]

This composition shows a dramatic adroitness and a literary skill not exhibited by any of the plays examined hitherto. The touching introductory lament of the three Marys, which we shall see later in other versions, is here completely appropriate. Especially noteworthy also is the surprise expressed in the exclamation of one of the Marys when she observes the open door of the sepulchre (*Ecce lapis reuolutus!*) and the angel clad in white. The speeches of the angel are agreeably lengthened by a successful use of passages from the Gospels,[2] and the invitation *Venite et videte* is disposed of aptly. The last speech of the Marys

---

[1] Followed by the rubric *In Die sčm Pasche*, and the introit of the Mass.
[2] See especially Matt. xxviii, 5–7.

successfully conveys first their desire to report to the disciples, and then their actual announcement of the Resurrection.

Our survey of the simpler types of *Visitatio* concludes with an example containing an introductory sentence not easily found elsewhere, except in a few texts of the trope of the Easter introit.[1] This rare version is the following from a service-book formerly possessed by the monastery of St Martial, at Limoges:[2]

PROSA

> *Ubi est Christus, meus Dominus, et filius excelsus?*
> *Eamus videre sepulcrum.*
> Versus: *Quem queritis in sepulcro, o Christicole?*
> Versus: *Ihesum Nazarenum crucifixum, o celicole.*
> Versus: *Non est hic, surrexit sicut predixerat; ite, nunciate discipulis eius quia precedet uos in Galileam, alleluia.*
> Versus: *Alleluia, alleluia!*
> Versus: *Vere surrexit Dominus de sepulcro cum gloria, alleluia, alleluia.*

Since this composition has as a heading only the word *Prosa*, and lacks dramatic rubrics, one would naturally infer that it was intended merely as a liturgical embellishment of the preceding responsory, and was not performed as a play; and this inference may be correct for the text before us. That this particular version of the dialogue *Quem quæritis* was sometimes delivered with impersonation, however, is established by the following text from Poitiers:[3]

> Finitis Matutinis, accedunt ad Sepulchrum portantes luminaria. Tunc incipit Maria:
>> *Ubi est Christus meus?*
> Respondet Angelus:
>> *Non est hic.*
> Tunc Maria aperit os Sepulchri, et dicit publica voce:
>> *Surrexit Christus.*
> Et omnes respondent:
>> *Deo gratias.*

Although this passage is obviously incomplete and imperfect, it certainly describes a liturgical play. As to the speaker of the

[1] See above, p. 212.

[2] Paris, Bibl. Nat., MS lat. 784, Lib. resp. Sancti Martialis Lemovicensis (?) sæc. xiii–xiv, fol. 106ᵛ, now first printed. The text before us has music, and is preceded in the MS by the responsory *Dum transisset*, without

further introduction, and is followed by the rubric *In Laudibus*.

[3] Martene, iii, 173, from a 'vetustissimum Rituale' from Poitiers. See Chambers, ii, 29. Martene's text does not show what follows in the MS.

opening sentence we learn only that she is one of the Marys. One critic has expressed the opinion that this speech could be appropriately uttered only by the Virgin Mary, who never appears in other versions of the *Visitatio*.[1] Neither from the text nor from the general circumstances, however, is it clear that the speaker might not be any one of the usual three Marys.

V

The forms of the *Visitatio Sepulchri* surveyed thus far exhibit, within the restricted scope of their action, a considerable variety of content.[2] Most of the utterances added to the original dialogue of *Quem quæritis*, to be sure, are passages from the authorized liturgy, adopted into the play with very little effort towards readjustment. Of this casual procedure a conspicuous example is the use of the antiphon *Venite et videte*. A few of the enlargements, however, are employed far more successfully. The traditional antiphon *Quis revolvet*, for example, serves admirably as an introductory speech for the Marys, and the original sentences *Cernitis, o socii* and *Ad monumentum venimus* are entirely adequate in the positions for which they were invented. The play from Sicily, with its verses of lament, and free use of the Biblical narrative, is a genuine literary achievement.

From the dates of the manuscripts we must infer that plays of the simple sort now under review were in use for more than five hundred years. Although during the later Middle Ages arose far more ambitious forms of the *Visitatio Sepulchri*, many churches adopted or retained the elementary type. The earliest of these plays can be assigned to the second half of the tenth century, and texts of them are still found in manuscripts of the fifteenth century and in numerous printed books of the sixteenth.[3]

[1] See Chambers, ii, 29.

[2] For a few special texts, not otherwise treated in this chapter, see Notes, p. 599.

[3] From the fact that, in some ninth-century iconographic representations, the Marys carry thuribles rather than the Scriptural ointment-boxes, Weber (*Kunst*, p. 32) infers that the influence of the *Visitatio* is to be discerned at that date. For vaguer reasons, Mme Chasles (p. 69) also holds that the *Visitatio* was known in the ninth century. The evidences advanced for proving the existence of a genuine Easter play before the tenth century are, I think, inadequate.

CHAPTER X

THE VISIT TO THE SEPULCHRE

FIRST STAGE (*continued*)

TO the minor enlargements of the *Visitatio Sepulchri* surveyed in the preceding chapter is now to be added a new dramatic element of considerably greater scope and importance. This is the Easter sequence *Victimæ paschali*, composed in the eleventh century, probably by Wipo, priest and chaplain to the emperors Conrad II and Henry III.[1]

I

Of this famous composition we have already seen the somewhat abbreviated form in which it appears in the modern Mass of Easter.[2] The complete version current during the Middle Ages is as follows:[3]

1. Victimæ paschali laudes
   immolent Christiani.

2. Agnus redemit oves,
   Christus innocens Patri
   reconciliavit
   peccatores.

3. Mors et vita duello
   conflixere mirando;
   dux vitæ mortuus,
   regnat vivus.

4. Dic nobis, Maria,
   quid vidisti in via?
   'Sepulchrum Christi viventis,
   et gloriam vidi resurgentis;

5. Angelicos testes,
   sudarium et vestes.
   Surrexit Christus, spes mea;
   præcedet suos in Galilæa.'

6. Credendum est magis soli
   Mariæ veraci
   quam Judæorum
   turbæ fallaci.

7. Scimus Christum surrexisse
   ex mortuis vere;
   tu nobis, victor
   rex, miserere.

In the general development of sequences, outlined in an earlier chapter, this piece occupies a position midway between the earlier prose productions of Notker and the completely rhymed pieces of a later period.[4] Its first three divisions are in prose, the next two are rhymed with some care, and the last two show at least a tendency in the same direction. In interpreting

[1] For bibliography bearing on *Victimæ paschali* see Notes, p. 605.
[2] See above, p. 27.
[3] I give the text from *A.H.*, liv, 12–3.
[4] See above, p. 186.

its content, we are to regard the first three stanzas as a lyrical utterance of Christ's followers, inciting all Christians to rejoice in His victory. The next three stanzas constitute a dialogue between the Christian disciples and Mary Magdalen, and the last may be regarded as an extension of this dialogue, or as an independent lyrical conclusion.[1]

The trenchant language, the palpable emotion, and, above all, the element of dialogue in this composition led inevitably to its being used in the drama of the Church. We have already found it serving a dramatic purpose in the *Elevatio* before Easter Matins,[2] and there is the following isolated record of a dramatic use of it in the Mass, at Vienne:[3]

Tunc intrantes in vestiarium, sacerdos planeta alba, diaconus dalmatica alba, subdiaconus tunica talari alba, et thuriferarius induantur, et sic præeuntibus ceroferariis indutis etiam albis, procedant ad Sepulcrum, ubi Missa matutinalis celebretur.[4] Et caput scholæ ex officio suo, quæ in aliis Missis cantores incipere solent, ipse solus incipiat alta voce; et in aliis Missis matutinalibus per hebdomadam magister scholæ omnia ipse solus incipere debet, sicut et caput scholæ. Prosa *Victimæ paschali.* Finito versu *Dic*[5] *nobis, Maria,* clericulus stans in Sepulcro cum amictu parato et stola dicat versum:

Angelicos testes.[6]

Chorus respondeat:

Dic nobis, Maria, ⟨quid vidisti in via?⟩

Clericulus dicat:

Angelicos testes, ⟨sudarium et vestes.⟩

Clericus dicat:

Surrexit Christus, ⟨spes mea; præcedet suos in Galilæa.⟩

Chorus:

Credendum est magis,
usque ad finem.[7]

[1] Slightly varying interpretations are given by Du Méril, pp. 43-4; Clichtoveus, fol. 162ʳ; Grieshaber, p. 12; N. Gihr, *Die Sequenzen des römischen Messbuches,* Freiburg, 1887, p. 131.   [2] See above, p. 175.

[3] Martene, iii, 180. The ceremony described here is preceded by Lauds. At a later time in the day, according to the use of Vienne, follows a processional use of the trope *Quem quæritis,* treated in an earlier chapter. See above, pp. 229-30.

[4] Monasteries, and other communities,

often celebrated two solemn Masses in one day. The first—called *Missa matutinalis, Missa capitalis,* or *Missa parva*—was usually conducted not at the high altar, but at another special altar in the choir or apse. See Tolhurst, ii, 367.

[5] Dic] Dicat (Martene).

[6] Presumably the passage really intended here is *Sepulchrum Christi viventis, et gloriam vidi resurgentis.*

[7] Followed by the words *Evangelium dicat diaconus.*

This passage describes the rendering of the sequence in an early morning Mass performed at the *sepulchrum*. The part beginning with *Dic nobis* is recited between the chorus and a choir-boy standing within the sepulchre. Impersonation seems not to be intended. Although this ceremony is strikingly dramatic, neither the text before us nor any other evidence lends support to the inference sometimes drawn, that this sequence is the common origin of all forms of the *Visitatio Sepulchri*.[1] From what we have observed above, it is clear that the play was well established during the century preceding that in which *Victimæ paschali* was written.[2] In the development of the play, therefore, the sequence was an amplifying, rather than an originating, element.

II

In surveying the variety of ways in which this amplification was attempted, one observes that a large number of the plays accepted the text of *Victimæ paschali* in its entirety, both the lyrical introductory sentences, and the latter part in dialogue. There are apparent indications, indeed, that its potentialities in the way of dialogue were sometimes ignored, as in the following version of the fifteenth century from the use of Paris:[3]

Finito responsorio, statim debet fieri representacio Sepulcri. Et Angeli ad Mulieres:

    Alleluia! Quem queritis in sepulchro, o Christicole?

⟨Mulieres:⟩

    Ihesum Nazarenum crucifixum, o celicole.

Versus:

    Non est hic, surrexit sicut predixerat.

Versus:

    Ite, nunciate quia surrexit.

Tunc uertant se Mulieres ad chorum, et cantent hymnum:[4]

    Victime paschali laudes immolant Christiani.
    Agnus redemit oues, Christus innocens Patri reconciliauit peccatores.
    Mors et vita duello conflixere mirando; dux vite mortuus, regnat viuus.
    Dic nobis, Maria, quid vidisti[5] in via?

---

[1] Concerning this inference see Notes, p. 605.

[2] See above, p. 249.

[3] Paris, Bibl. de l'Arsenal, MS 133, Brev. Parisiense sæc. xv, fol. 226ʳ, mentioned by Brooks, *New Texts*, p. 475, and now printed, I think, for the first time. In the MS the text is preceded by the responsory *Et valde mane*, concerning which see above, p. 232.

[4] hymnum] hy*mnus* (MS).

[5] vidisti] vidistis (MS).

Sepulchrum Christi viuentis, et gloriam vidi resurgentis.
Angelicos testes, sudarium et vestes.
Surrexit Christus, spes nostra; precedet suos in Galileam.
Credendum est magis soli Marie veraci quam Iudeorum turbe fallaci.
Scimus Christum surrexisse a mortuis vere; tu nobis, uictor rex, miserere.
Psalmus: *Te Deum.*

From this text as it stands one is forced to infer that, after the usual brief dialogue of Marys and angels, the former are to sing the entire sequence through in unison, without pause and without the participation of others. It is difficult to believe, however, that this represents accepted practice. The other texts from the same diocese, in any case, show that this procedure was not the normal one. The usual custom of Paris is adequately represented by the following *Visitatio* of the fourteenth century:[1]

Post tercium responsorium ueniant tres Marie[2] ad Sepulcrum. Duo Angeli cantent:

Quem queritis in sepulchro, o Christicole?

Tres Mulieres respondent:

Ihesum Nazarenum crucifixum, o celicole.

Tunc Angeli discooperiunt Sepulcrum et dicent:

Non est hic, surrexit sicut predixerat; ite, nunciate quia surrexit.

Tunc uertunt se Mulieres[3] ad chorum et cantat prima Mulier:

Victime paschali laudes immolant Christiani.

Secunda Mulier:

Agnus redemit oues, Christus innocens Patri[4] reconciliauit peccatores.

Tercia Mulier:

Mors et uita duello conflixere mirando; dux uite mortuus, regnat uiuus.

Cantor indutus capa serica cantat ad Mulieres:

Dic nobis, Maria, quid uidisti in uia?

Prima Mulier *respondet* sola:

Sepulcrum Christi uiuentis, et gloriam uidi resurgentis.

Secunda Mulier:

Angelicos testes, sudarium et uestes.

Tertia Mulier:

Sur|rexit Christus, spes nostra; precedit suos in Galileam.

---

[1] Paris, Bibl. Nat., MS lat. 1264, Brev. Parisiense sæc. xiv, fol. 101^v–102^r, previously edited by Lange, no. 88, pp. 60–2. The responsory preceding the text is *Et valde mane.*   In regard to other texts of the same version see Notes, p. 605.   [2] Marie] Maries (MS).   [3] Mulieres] muleres (MS).   [4] Patri] patris (MS).

Cantor ad chorum:

Credendum est magis soli Marie ueraci quam Iudeorum turbe fallaci.

Chorus:

Scimus Christum surrexisse a mortuis uere; tu nobis, uictor rex, miserere.

Psalmus: *Te Deum.*

Here the dramatic possibilities of the sequence are recognized with considerable fullness, and it is made to serve admirably as a means whereby the Marys report the Resurrection to the chorus. Each of the women sings one of the first three sentences; and then, in response to the interrogation of the cantor, each replies with a separate utterance.[1] The play concludes with the singing of the last two sentences by the cantor and chorus respectively. This arrangement results in a certain lack of dramatic fitness in that the cantor's question to a single *Maria* is responded to by three separate persons. In reviewing the numerous situations of this sort, one wonders at the apparent unwillingness of the performers to alter the text of the sequence —from a singular to the plural—in accordance with the dramatic circumstances. Noticeable also is the merging of drama and liturgy in the circumstance that the cantor is merely a member of the usual liturgical chorus, whereas the Marys with whom he speaks are, no doubt, impersonated figures in a play. The presence of liturgical personages in the midst of genuine drama is, as we have already seen, a natural and common characteristic of the plays of the Church.

Still another Paris text, used in Sainte-Chapelle, deserves attention for the sake both of its rubrics and of its speeches:[2]

Finito autem ultimo responsorio, debent uenire tres Marie, vna post aliam, ad Sepulchrum, indute albis non paratis, et habentes amictus desuper capita sua, cantantes simul submissa uoce:

Mane prima ⟨sabbati⟩.[3]

Quando autem ueniunt ante Sepulchrum, debent se ordinate ponere coram eo. Et tunc duo Angeli stantes vnus a dextris et alius a sinistris dicant ad Mulieres:

Quem queritis ⟨in sepulchro, o Christicolæ⟩?

---

[1] In the Paris *Visitatio* the three Marys sometimes sing these three sentences in unison. See the text from London, Brit. Mus., Add. MS 37399, printed in Notes, p. 610.

[2] Paris, Bibl. Nat., MS lat. 1435, Ordin. ad usum Capellæ Regis sæc. xiv, fol. 17ᵛ–18ʳ, previously edited by Brooks, *New Texts*,

pp. 473–4. The *incipits* have musical notation. For another version used in Sainte-Chapelle, see the Arsenal (Paris) MS 114, treated below, p. 286.

[3] For the full text of this sequence, and for observations on other uses of it, see above, p. 234.

Mulieres ad eos:

Ihesum Nazarenum ⟨crucifixum, o cœlicolæ⟩.

Angeli ad eas:

Non est hic, ⟨surrexit sicut prædixerat; ite, nuntiate quia surrexit.⟩

Tunc Mulieres eant ad Sepulchrum, una post aliam, palpando Sepulchrum. Tunc secunda Maria accipit sudarium quod abscondit penes se. Postea uertant se ad chorum, et dicat prima:

Victime paschali ⟨laudes immolent Christiani⟩.

Secunda:

Agnus | redemit ⟨oves, Christus innocens Patri reconciliavit peccatores⟩.

Tercia:

Mors et uita duello ⟨conflixere mirando; dux vitæ mortuus, regnat vivus⟩.

Tunc unus de choralibus stans coram eis dicat:

Dic nobis, ⟨Maria, quid vidisti in via?⟩

Prima Mulier sola versum.

Sepulchrum Christi ⟨viventis, et gloriam vidi resurgentis⟩,

ostendendo illud cum digito. Secunda Mulier sola dicat versum:

Angelicos testes, ⟨sudarium et vestes,⟩

ostendendo digito; dicendo autem *sudarium* ostendat manifeste sudarium quod prius absconderat, et teneat illud in manu sua. Tercia Mulier sola dicat versum:

Surrexit Christus, spes nostra; ⟨præcedet suos in Galilæa.⟩

Tunc unus de choralibus solus dicat versum:

Credendum est magis ⟨soli Mariæ veraci quam Judæorum turbæ fallaci⟩.

Postea totus chorus dicat versum:

Scimus Christum ⟨surrexisse a mortuis vere; tu nobis, victor rex, miserere⟩.

Et tunc recedant Mulieres cum duobus cereis. Hiis finitis, incipiat sacerdos *Te Deum.*

Although the sequence *Mane prima sabbati*, sung by the Marys on their way to the sepulchre, is appropriate to Easter, it is hardly a fitting utterance for persons who have not yet been informed of the Resurrection. The nature of the incongruity may be inferred from the opening lines:

> Mane prima sabbati
> surgens Dei filius,
> > nostra spes et gloria,
> Victo rege sceleris,
> rediit ab inferis
> > cum summa victoria.

The inapplicability of the poem to the three Marys is emphasized further by the fact that it celebrates especially Mary Magdalen, as being the *beata peccatrix* and first herald of the Resurrection. The singing of *Victimæ paschali* in this play is noteworthy for the dramatic gestures that accompany it. At the words *Sepulchrum Christi*, the first Mary points to the sepulchre; and in the succeeding speech, the second Mary, in saying *Angelicos testes*, points to the angels, and at the word *sudarium*, displays the grave-cloth which she has previously taken from the sepulchre and hidden under her garment. It was, of course, to be expected that the mention of the *sudarium* in the sequence should bring this object into increasing prominence in the dramatic performances.[1]

Additions to both the text and the action appear in a play of the thirteenth century from Châlons-sur-Marne:[2]

Dum cantatur tercium responsorium, duo pueri induti albis uestibus sedentes iuxta altare, unus a dextris et alius a sinistris, quasi duo Angeli ad Sepulchrum Domini, operto eorum uultu de amictibus, tres diaconos dalmaticis albis indutos, tenentes thuribula et palmas in manibus, exeuntes de sacrario cum cruce et duobus cereis atque torca per partem dexteram uenientes ad introitum chori sub crucifixo et per partem chori dexteram uenientes, et ante altare astantes, tamquam Mulieres ad Sepulchrum Domini uenientes, cantando interrogant:

Quem queritis in sepulchro, ⟨o Christicolæ?⟩

Quibus diaconi, tamquam Mulieres, respondent:

Ihesum Nazarenum ⟨crucifixum, o cælicolæ⟩.

Pueri uero discooperientes altare de panno albo, tamquam de sudario, respondent:

Non est hic, ⟨surrexit sicut prædixerat; ite, nuntiate quia surrexit.⟩

Et diaconi uertentes se ad chorum cantant:

Alleluia, resurrexit Dominus, ⟨hodie resurrexit leo fortis, Christus, filius Dei.⟩

Et eis lento passu uenientibus uersus chorum, prima Maria cantat uersum:

Victime ⟨paschali laudes immolent Christiani⟩.

Secunda:

Agnus redemit ⟨oves, Christus innocens Patri reconciliavit peccatores⟩.

Tercia:

Mors et uita ⟨duello conflixere mirando; dux vitæ mortuus, regnat vivus⟩.

---

[1] See Meyer, pp. 49–50. Concerning the use of the *sudarium* in the *Depositio* and *Elevatio* see above, pp. 134 sqq.

[2] Paris, Bibl. Nat., MS lat. 10579, Ordin.

Catalaunense sæc. xiii, fol. lxxvi[v]–lxxvii[r], previously edited, with substantial omissions, by Lange, no. 97, pp. 62–3. For a similar version see Notes, p. 610.

Tunc succentor ueniens | eis obuiam ad primum gradum presbyteri interrogat primam Mariam cantans:

Dic nobis, Maria, ⟨quid vidisti in via?⟩

Cui illa respondet cantando:

Sepulchrum ⟨Christi viventis, et gloriam vidi resurgentis⟩.

Secunda:

Angelicos testes, ⟨sudarium et vestes.⟩

Tercia:

Surrexit Christus, spes mea; ⟨præcedet suos in Galilæa.⟩

Tunc succentor[1] choro annuntiat Resurrectionem Domini cantans:

Credendum est magis soli Marie,

eam digito demonstrans; cantat:

Ueraci,[2] quam Iudeorum turbe fallaci.

Tunc omnes de choro generaliter cantant versum:

Scimus Christum surrexisse ⟨a mortuis vere; tu nobis, victor rex, miserere⟩.

Interim Mulieres per uiam qua uenerunt in sacrarium reuertuntur. Finito dicto versu, episcopus uel cantor incipit *Te Deum laudamus.*

The spoken text is here enlarged by the familiar *Resurrexit Dominus*, used by the Marys as a kind of preliminary announcement before singing the sequence. The rubrics concerning the action indicate that the altar-sepulchre is guarded by two angels in white, who, at the words *Non est hic*, lift up from the altar-table a white cloth representing the sudary. When the cantor 'announces the Resurrection of the Lord' in the words *Credendum est magis soli Mariæ*, he points to one of the Marys—presumably to her who has sung *Surrexit Christus*. By his words and action he inevitably emphasizes the fact that the text of the sequence is not perfectly adapted for recital by *three* Marys.

Further enlargements of the dialogue are seen in the following version of the thirteenth century from Treves:[3]

Finito responsorio et versu cum *Gloria Patri*, reincipiat cantor idem responsorium *Dum transisset*, et egrediatur processio candelis accensis, et stationem in medio ecclesie ⟨faciat⟩. Ante egressum processionis in superiori parte chori tres domini egrediantur cum candelis suis et assumptis cappis purpureis; dentur eis tria thuribula cum incensu et vadant visitare Sepulcrum. Cum autem peruenerint ad Sepulcrum

---

[1] succentor] Corrected from *Christus* (MS).
[2] Ueraci] uelaci (MS).
[3] London, Brit. Mus., MS Harl. 2958, Ordin. Trevirense sæc. xiii, fol. 37[v], previously edited, with substantial missions, by

Lange, no. 105, pp. 71–4. For the related *Depositio* and *Elevatio* see above, p. 142. For other texts of the *Visitatio* from Treves see Notes, p. 611.

inuenire debent duos sacerdotes indutos dalmaticis in Sepulcro, vnum ad caput et alium ad pedes, qui dicant venientibus:

Quem queritis in sepulcro, o Christicole?

Respondere debent:

Ihesum Nazarenum crucifixum, o celicole.

Deinde dicere debent intus sedentes:

Non est hic, surrexit sicut predixerat: ite, nunciate quia surrexit.
Venite et videte locum vbi positus erat Dominus, alleluia, alleluia.

Deinde accedant dicti tres, et sudarium recipiant. In Sepulcro vero sedentes dicant:

Cito euntes, dicite discipulis eius quia surrexit Dominus, alleluia.

Recedant statim illi tres ad gradus cripte. Ibi manentes cantent primos tres versus de sequentia *Victime paschali* insimul. Quibus versibus sic cantatis, chorus cantet:

Dic nobis, Maria, quid vidisti in via?

Et tunc procedant dicti tres vsque ad tumbam Theoderici archiepiscopi; ibi respondeat iterum vnus ex tribus:

Sepulcrum Christi viuentis, et gloriam vidi resurgentis.

Secundus:

Angelicos testes, sudarium et vestes.

Cum dicitur hoc verbum *sudarium*, eleuent omnes tres sudarium. Tercius:

Surrexit Christus, spes mea; ⟨ præcedet suos in Galilæa.⟩

Chorus:

Credendum est magis,

et finiat sequenciam. Redeundo in chorum cantor incipiat antiphonam:

Et recordate sunt verborum eius, ⟨et regressæ a monumento nuntiaverunt hæc omnia illis undecim et ceteris omnibus, alleluia.⟩[1]

Et cum in chorum peruenerint, finita antiphona, incipiat maior *Te Deum laudamus*, quod totum cantatur candelis accensis.

In their preparation for descending to the sepulchre—which here appears to be in the crypt—the Marys are handed three thuribles with incense. As has been said above, this simple action may, perhaps, be regarded as a first step towards a scene of which the *unguentarius* is to be the centre.[2] After receiving the sudary, at the close of the usual dialogue, the Marys are dismissed by the words *Cito euntes*. Proceeding to the steps leading up from the crypt, the Marys pause there to sing in unison the first part of the sequence. When challenged by the words *Dic nobis*, they ascend to the tomb of Theodoric, and there

---

[1] For this antiphon see Hartker, p. 232. [2] See above, p. 266, and below, p. 401.

each in turn delivers her part of the reply. At the word *sudarium*, all three raise aloft the grave-cloth. As they pass into the choir, the cantor sings *Et recordatæ*. Since this antiphon narrates the departure of the Marys from the tomb on their errand of reporting their experiences to the disciples, its use here seems to indicate that the latter are understood as being represented, in a general way, by the chorus.

That the textual development in the versions just examined was not always accompanied by appropriate impersonation is shown by the following *ordo* from the diocese of Würzburg:[1]

Finito tercio responsorio, sacerdos accipiat candelas et thuribulum cum odore incensi et visitet Sepulchrum, repetendo responsorium *Dum transisset;* et dum venit ad monumentum, incipiat antiphonam:

> *Quis reuoluet nobis ⟨ab ostio lapidem quem tegere sanctum cernimus sepulchrum⟩?*

Respondet scolaris:

> *Quem queritis, ⟨o tremulæ mulieres, in hoc tumulo plorantes?⟩*

Sacerdos respon*det*:

> *Ihesum Nazarenum ⟨crucifixum quærimus⟩.*

Scolaris respon*det*:

> *Non est hic quem queritis; ⟨sed cito euntes nuntiate discipulis ejus et Petro quia surrexit Jesus.⟩*

Et monstret pannum, quo Crux tegebatur, cantans antiphonam:

> *Venite et uidete ⟨locum ubi positus erat Dominus, alleluia, alleluia⟩.*

Sacerdos accipiat lintheolum cantans solus:

> *Victime pascali ⟨laudes immolent Christiani.*
> *Agnus redemit oves, Christus innocens Patri reconciliavit peccatores.*
> *Mors et vita duello conflixere mirando; dux vitæ mortuus, regnat vivus⟩.*

Respon*detur* in choro:

> *Dic nobis, Maria, ⟨quid vidisti in via?⟩*

Sacerdos iterum:

> *Sepulcrum Christi viuentis.*

Respondent per totum. Tunc sacerdos, stans in hostio chori, monstrans populo lintheolum, et incipiant omnes cum eo:

> *Surrexit Dominus de sepulchro, ⟨qui pro nobis pependit in ligno, alleluia.⟩*

Et tunc populus incipit ymnum suum *Te Deum laudamus.*

The arresting aspect of this version of the *Visitatio* is the representing of the Marys by a *single* priest. This results, of course, in

[1] *Directorium Herbipolense*, Speyer, 1477, fol. 39ᵛ, previously reprinted by Lange, no. 101, p. 67. Concerning the *Depositio* and *Elevatio* of Würzburg see above, p. 172. With the text before us may be associated a *Visitatio* reprinted in Notes, p. 612.

several inconsistencies, but for the dialogue beginning *Dic nobis, Maria* it is appropriate. Although the grave-cloth is amply used in the action, there is no sign of impersonation. Beyond question the simplicity of the arrangement here arises from the intention of adapting the performance to the restricted resources of small churches in the diocese.

As an example of the form of *Visitatio* used at Eichstätt, which requires attention at this point, we may select the following text of the fourteenth century:[1]

Finito tercio responsorio, reincipitur, et cum eodem itur ad mona-sterium, et canitur ipsum responsorium totaliter. Quo finito, precentores[2] cum cantore cantent ante Sepulchrum antiphonam istam:

Quis reuoluet nobis ab hostio lapidem quem tegere[3] sanctum cernimus sepul-chrum?

Duo scolares in Sepulchro respondeant; vnus eorum canit antiphonam:|

Qvem queritis, o tremule mulieres, in hoc tumulo gementes?

Precentores respondeant:

Ihesum Nazarenum[4] crucifixum querimus.

Secundus scolaris canit:

Non est hic quem queritis, sed cito euntes, nuncciate discipulis eius et Petro quia surrexit Ihesus.

Deinde scolares exeant de Sepulchro cum lintheo, quod ostendant pre-centoribus, et cantent hanc antiphonam:

Venite et videte locum vbi positus erat Dominus, alleluia, alleluia.

Post hoc precentores reuertuntur ad monasterium, et cantent anti-phonam sequentem:

Ad monumentum[5] venimus gementes, angelum Domini sedentem vidimus et dicentem quia surrexit Ihesus, alleluia.

Finita autem hac antiphona, chorus incipit hanc sequenciam:

Victime pascali laudes ymolent Cristiani.
Agnus redemit oues, Cristus innocens Patri reconciliauit peccatores.|
Mors et vita duello conflixere mirando; dux vite mortuus, regnat viuus.
Dic nobis, Maria, quid vidisti in via?

Vnus precentorum respondet:

Sepulchrum Christi viuentis, et gloriam vidi resurgentis.

---

[1] Munich, Staatsbibl., MS lat. 3918, Ordin. Eystettense sæc. xiv, fol. 75ᵛ–76ᵛ, described by Brooks, *Neue Osterfeiern*, pp. 302–3, and now printed for the first time. For the related *Depositio* and *Elevatio* see above, p. 155. Con-cerning associated texts of the *Visitatio* see

Notes, p. 612.
[2] precentores] pretentores (MS).
[3] tegere] tergere (MS).
[4] Nazarenum] nasarenum (MS).
[5] Ad monumentum] De monumento (MS).

Iterum chorus cantat:
> *Dic nobis, Maria, quid vidisti in via?*

Aliter[1] precentor respondet:
> *Angelicos testes, sudarium et vestes.*

Chorus tercio repetit:
> *Dic nobis, Maria, quid vidisti in via?*

Cantor respondet:
> *Surrexit Christus, spes mea; precedet suos in Gallileam.*

Deinde tunc finitur sequencia per chorum totaliter:
> *Credendum est magis soli Marie veraci quam Iudeorum turbe fallaci.*
> *Scimus Cristum surrexisse ex mortuis vere; tu nobis, victor rex, miserere.*

Finita sequencia, canitur *Te Deum laudamus.*

One's chief interest in this version arises not from matters of *mise en scène*, but from the unusual assignment of the speeches. Of the two *scolares* who represent the angels, one sings *Quem quæritis*, the other, *Non est hic*, and both together, the antiphon *Venite et videte*. The singing of *Non est hic* by a single person brings the action into conformity with the singular *angelum* in a later speech of the Marys, *Ad monumentum venimus*. More important is the assignment of the parts of *Victimæ paschali*. The first division of the sequence is sung by the chorus, which also sings *Dic nobis* three times, addressing it to each of the three Marys in turn, and receiving a reply from each. In so far as the chorus is regarded as representing the disciples, it may appropriately sing the first division of the sequence, for the announcement of the Resurrection has previously been made by the Marys. The repetition of *Dic nobis, Maria* to each of the Marys as an individual removes the incongruity which arises when the singular *Maria* is addressed to the three Marys as a group. The absence from this text of rubrics specifying impersonation is disappointing.

Striking additions both to the spoken text and to the *mise en scène* appear in the following version from Narbonne:[2]

Post ultimum responsorium sequitur prosellus:
> *Almum te ⟨proclamat cetus ecce*
> *Nunc noster vnicus assidue*
> *Christe, proles Dei, Domine,*
> *Poculum qui bibisti letale,*

---

[1] Aliter] *Alter* may have been intended.
[2] Martene, iii, 172–3, prints this text from a Narbonne ordinary 'ante annos 300 exaratum'. It is reprinted by Lange, no. 99, pp. 64–6, with references (p. 9) to earlier reprintings.

Atque de morte voluisti surgere,
Ideoque canamus, Alleluia⟩.[1]

Quo finito, sint parati clerici cum cappis albis et amictibus in capitibus eorum, portantes quilibet eorum in manibus ampullam argenti, et ille qui fungitur officio Magdalenæ vadat in medio. Et introitu chori incipiant cantando insimul primum versum:

Omnipotens pater altissime,
⟨angelorum rector mitissime,
quid faciunt istæ miserrimæ?⟩

Et in fine ipsorum versuum flexis genibus[2] dicant:

Heu, quantus est dolor noster!

Deinde procedant ad pulpitum, et coram eo dicant versum:

Amisimus enim solatium,
⟨Jesum Christum, Mariæ filium;
ipse erat nobis consilium.
Heu, quantus est dolor noster!⟩

Postea accedant ante altare, et ibi dicant alium versum:

Sed eamus unguentum emere,
⟨ut hoc corpus possimus ungere,
quod numquam vermes possint commedere.
Heu, quantus est dolor noster!⟩

Quibus dictis, sint duo pueri super altare, induti albis et amictibus cum stolis violatis et sindone rubea in facies eorum et alis in humeris, qui dicant:

Quem quæritis in sepulcro, ⟨o Christicolæ?⟩

Quo dicto, omnes Mariæ insimul respondeant:

Jesum Nazarenum ⟨crucifixum, o cælicolæ⟩.

Deinde pueri dicant:

Non est hic, ⟨surrexit sicut prædixerat; ite, nuntiate quia surrexit.⟩

Levent cum filo pannum, qui est super libros argenti super altare in figura Sepulcri, et facta responsione a pueris, omnes Mariæ insimul vertant se versus chorum, et Magdalena cantet sola versum:

Victimæ paschali laudes ⟨immolent Christiani⟩.

Deinde Jacobi:

Agnus redemit oves, ⟨Christus innocens Patri reconciliavit peccatores.⟩

Postea Salome:

Mors et vita duello ⟨conflixere mirando; dux vitæ mortuus, regnat vivus⟩.

Hoc dicto, duo canonici, tamquam Apostoli, sint parati retro pulpitum, et dicant omnes insimul versum:

Dic nobis, Maria, ⟨quid vidisti in via?⟩

---

[1] This trope of the responsory *Dum transisset* is found in *Breviarium secundum consuetudinem Elnensis Ecclesie*, Heidelberg, 1500, fol. 100[r], mentioned by Chevalier, *R.H.*, no. 923.

[2] genibus] gentibus (Martene).

Deinde Magdalena sola respondeat:

> *Sepulcrum Christi viventis, ⟨et gloriam vidi resurgentis.*
> *Angelicos testes, sudarium et vestes.⟩*   .

Et quando dicitur *Angelicos testes*, vertat se ad altare sola, ac demonstret cum digito Angelos prædictos, stantes super altare, pronunciando versum supradictum; monstratis Angelis, vertat se ad chorum et dicat:

> *Surrexit Christus, spes mea; ⟨præcedet vos in Galilæa.⟩*

Finito versu, chorus dicat:

> *Credendum ⟨est⟩ magis soli ⟨Mariæ veraci quam Judæorum turbæ fallaci⟩;*

ac etiam:

> *Scimus Christum surrexisse ⟨a mortuis vere; tu nobis, victor rex, miserere⟩.*

His omnibus finitis, regentes chorum incipiant *Te Deum laudamus*. Interim prædictæ Mariæ et pueri intrent vestiarium ad deponenda vestimenta.

The none too intelligible trope *Almum te* is to be regarded here as an embellishment of the last responsory rather than as an introduction to the *Visitatio*. The play itself begins with three touching stanzas of lament sung by the Marys with admirable appropriateness as they approach the sepulchre. The third stanza proposes the buying of ointment, and thus points, once more, towards a scene with the *unguentarius*.[1] These four-line stanzas, composed of three lines of ten syllables and a refrain, will be seen again in more highly developed forms of the play.[2] The Narbonne text provides some notable details of staging. Each Mary carries a silver vessel, and the angels wear wings. Silver-bound books are arranged on the altar to form a temporary sepulchre, and over this is a cloth, which the angels lift when they sing *Non est hic*. The dialogued part of *Victimæ paschali* is delivered in an uncommonly effectual manner between two canons representing apostles (*tamquam Apostoli*) and Mary Magdalen alone. The suppression of the other two Marys here lends aptness to the singular number in *Dic nobis, Maria*. The reciting of these last words by two *apostoli* is at least a step towards a separate scene centring in Peter and John.[3]

For the sake of at least one special dramatic feature, we must notice here a second text of the *Visitatio* used in Sainte-Chapelle, in Paris:[4]

Finito responsorio, chorales et adiutores debent reincipere *Et valde*; et

---

[1] See above, p. 281, and below, pp. 401 sqq.
[2] See below, for example, pp. 439, 677.
[3] See chaps. xi and xii below.
[4] Paris, Bibl. de l'Arsenal, MS 114, Ordo

divini officii secundum usum Sacræ Cappellæ sæc. xv, fol. 73ᵛ–74ʳ, previously edited by Brooks, *New Texts*, pp. 471–3. The text is preceded by the responsory *Et valde mane*.

finito responsorio, tres Marie, albis amictis non paratis, dalmaticis aut tunicis albis ornate, vultus siue facies semitecte, voce submissa et humili, subtus organa existentes debent subsequiter et vna[1] post aliam per ordinem accedere ad chorum cappelle cantando, videlicet prima *Mane prima sabbati,*[2] et secunda secundum versum, et tercia tercium, semper et pedetentim[3] transeundo; et dum fuerint ad hostium chori, cantabunt insimul et vna voce simplici antiphonam:

O Deus! Quis reuoluet ⟨nobis lapidem ab ostio monumenti⟩?

Qua cantata, duo Angeli existentes et custodientes Sepulchrum, vnus ad caput et alius ad pedes, inuitant ipsas Marias cantando antiphonam:

Venite, venite, et nolite timere vos.

Et hoc cantato, predicte Marie accedunt ad Angelos et, dum ibi fuerint, prefati Angeli cantant insimul:

Quem queritis in sepulchro, o Christicole?

Marie respondent Angelis:

Ihesum Nazarenum crucifixum, o celicole.

Angeli ad eas:

Non est hic, surrexit sicut predixit; ite, nunciate quia surrexit.

Quo finito, statim predicte Marie, vna post aliam, eant ad Sepulchrum ipsum palpando, et dum ibi fuerit, secunda Maria accipiat sudarium et abscondat penes se. | Postea vertant se omnes ad chorum, et dicat prima Maria sola:

Victime paschali ⟨laudes immolent Christiani⟩.

Secunda:

Agnus redemit ⟨oves, Christus innocens Patri reconciliavit peccatores⟩.

Tertia:

Mors et vita ⟨duello conflixere mirando; dux vitæ mortuus, regnat vivus⟩.

Cantor dicat eas respiciendo:

Dic nobis, Maria, ⟨quid vidisti in via?⟩

Respondeat prima Maria sola:

Sepulchrum Christi viuentis,

et ostendat illud cum digito. Et secunda Maria sola dicat statim post primam versiculum *Angelicos testes,* eos ostendendo, *sudarium et vestes,* ostendendo manifeste sudarium quod penes se absconderet et illud teneat in manu sua. Tercia Mulier dicat sola versum:

Surrexit Christus, spes nostra,

vsque in finem. Alius choralis versum:

Credendum est magis soli,

---

[1] vna] vnam (MS.).
[2] For the text of *Mane prima sabbati* see above, p. 234.
[3] pedetentim] pedetantim (MS).

et cetera, vsque in finem. Postea totus chorus dicat versum:

    Scimus Christum surrexisse,

vsque in finem. Quibus gestis, surgant Milites, si ibidem fuerint, et faciant quod eis bonum viderint faciendum; et dum factum suum compleuerint, pueri dicant:

    Adest dies,

et cetera.[1] Et istis completis, episcopus vel thezaurarius incipiat alta voce *Te Deum.*

In most respects this play closely resembles the other one from Sainte-Chapelle considered earlier in this chapter.[2] The two open with the sequence *Mane prima*, and provide the same stage-action for the Marys. The present version stands by itself in containing the speeches *O Deus, quis revolvet* and *Venite, venite.* Its special distinction, however, arises from the rubric *Surgant Milites, si ibidem fuerint, et faciant quod eis bonum viderint faciendum.* This optional provision for a dumb-show by Roman soldiers prepares us for a more liberal use of these personages in some of the elaborated Easter plays to be considered in later chapters.[3]

III

From what we have now seen, we may fairly conclude that the adoption of the *Victimæ paschali* into the *Visitatio* was highly successful. The introductory lyrical part of the sequence has served well as an announcement of the Resurrection to the chorus, or to the apostles, and the part in dialogue, although it has given rise to some dramatic incongruities, has effectually enlarged the role of the Marys. In many versions of the play, a certain discrimination is shown in the elimination of the introductory part, as being unnecessary to the action, and in a more attentive developing of the dramatic passage beginning *Dic nobis, Maria.* This disposal of the text is seen, for example, in a version from Le Mans:[4]

Lectis autem lectionibus, dum tertium responsorium cantabitur, veniant duo pueri induti albis et operti capita, et sedeant iuxta altare,

---

[1] From the large number of hymns or sequences beginning *Adest dies* (Chevalier, *R.H.*, nos. 335–96), it is impossible to identify the one used here. It may be the Ascension hymn *Adest dies sanctus Dei, claro resplendens lumine* (no. 392).　　　[2] See above, p. 277.

[3] See below, pp. 408 sqq., 421 sqq.

[4] Le Mans, Bibl. de la Ville, MS 165 (*olim* 1175), Ordin. Cenomanense sæc. xv,

fol. 20ᵛ, previously edited by P. Piolin, in *Revue historique et archéologique du Maine*, xxix (1891), 210–1, and in his *Le Théâtre chrétien dans le Maine*, Mamers, 1892, p. 19. Lange's reprint, no. 224, pp. 66–7, is incomplete. My text has been collated with the MS through the courtesy of M. Julien L'Hermitte, Conservateur de la Bibliothèque du Mans. For associated versions see Notes, p. 613.

unus a dextris et alius a sinistris. Interim tres iuvenes clerici, induti dalmaticis albis, opertis capitibus candidis amictibus, faciant processionem eundo ante omnia altaria et visitando ea, precedentibus duobus clericis in cappis sericis portantibus duas torchias, et exeant silendo vel dicendo submissa voce, *Surrexit, non est hic,* osculando quodlibet altare. Finito vero tertio responsorio, veniant illi tres clerici ante magnum altare, quibus semel altare circumeuntibus, duo predicti pueri qui iuxta altare sederint dicant submissa voce:

Quem queritis in sepulcro, o Christicole?

Quibus tres predicti clerici humili voce respondeant:

Ihesum Nazarenum crucifixum, o celicole.

Item duo pueri nichilominus respondeant:

Non est hic, surrexit sicut predixit; ite, nunciate quia surrexit.

Tunc tres clerici accedentes ad altare cum reverentia sublevent pallium cum quo Sepulcrum fuerit coopertum, et sic osculato altari, recedentes veniant ante chorum, et verso dorso ad altare, versus chorum vultu cantent alta voce:

Alleluia, resurrexit Dominus, hodie resurrexit leo fortis, Christus, filius Dei.

Duo succentores in medio chori et Marie in introitu dicant alta voce:

Dic nobis, Maria, quid vidisti in via?

Una illarum respondet:

Sepulcrum Christi viventis, et gloriam vidi resurgentis.

Secunda dicat:

Angelicos testes, ⟨sudarium et vestes.⟩

Tertia dicat: ·

Surrexit Christus, spes nostra,

et cetera. Tunc succentores dicant:

Credendum est magis soli Marie,

et cetera. Et tunc chorus alta voce dicat:

Scimus Christum surrexisse,

et cetera. Et sic incipiat episcopus *Te Deum.* Predicti vero tres clerici veniant in chorum et dent pacis osculum omnibus, incipientes a senioribus ac dicentes unicuique *Resurrexit Dominus,* quibus singuli respondeant *Deo gratias.*

One of the most arresting features of this play is the procession of the Marys to the sepulchre, at the main altar, during which they visit the several subsidiary altars of the church, kissing one or another of them, and meanwhile saying nothing, or, in a low voice, *Surrexit, non est hic.* This elaborated procession is appropriately accompanied by the singing of the third responsory, which recounts the journey of the Marys to the tomb.[1] The

---

[1] See above, p. 233.

words *Surrexit, non est hic*, however, are spoken somewhat in-congruously by persons who have not yet been informed of the Resurrection. The manner in which the dialogue beginning with *Dic nobis* is recited is no more noteworthy than in several versions already surveyed. The two cantors who address the Marys here are, presumably, to be regarded as *apostoli*, as in the play from Narbonne.[1]

The familiar introductory sentence *Quis revolvet*, along with uncommonly informative rubrics, is found in the following play performed in the church of St John the Evangelist, at Besançon:[2]

In die sancto Pasche ad Matutinas fit sicut est consuetum. Primum re-sponsorium debent dicere pueri, secundum responsorium duo canonici in medio chori sine capis nigris, et tercium responsorium tres familia-res ante maius altare. Quando tercia lectio dicitur, debent esse parati tres canonici seu tres famuliares in capella Sancti Eugendi ad faciendum Marias, et in hunc modum ornari. Primo | debent habere capitagia super capita ita quod cooperiant frontes, et dalmaticas albas, et in manibus portantes fialas aureas uel argenteas. Et ita procedunt de capella Sancti Eugendi post tertium responsorium, precedente cantore cum capa et baculo, precedentibus cereis et turibulo cum quatuor torchiis, euntes usque ad altare Sancte Crucis, et ibi uertant versus maius altare can-tando insimul:

> *Quis revolvet ⟨nobis lapidem ab ostio monumenti⟩?*

Et in medio ecclesie et ad introitum chori incipiunt ultimam uicem. Interim sint parati duo pueri a[3] dextris et a sinistris altaris inducti admictis albis paratis, et super humeros alas habentes et stolas rubeas super humeros circumdantes alas in modum quo ponunt diaconi, respondentes Mulieribus sic:

> *Quem queritis ⟨in sepulchro, o Christicolæ⟩?*

cantando. Et Mulieres:

> *Jhesum Nazarenum ⟨crucifixum, o cælicolæ⟩.*

Et Angeli:

> *Non est hic, surrexit ⟨sicut prædixerat; ite, nuntiate quia surrexit⟩.*

Et discooperiunt altare Angeli linteaminibus quibus erat altare uelatum. Et Mulieres statim cantant:

> *Alleluia, surrexit Dominus, hodie ⟨resurrexit leo fortis, Christus, filius Dei⟩,*

usque ad maius altare, et super altare offerunt fialas suas genu flexo. Post

---

[1] See above, p. 286.

[2] Besançon, Bibl. de la Ville, MS 99, Liber ceremoniarum ecclesiæ Bisuntinæ Sancti Johannis Evangelistæ sæc. xiv, fol. 29^v–30^r, previously edited by Brooks, *Sepulchre*, p. 95. For a similar version from another Besançon MS see Notes, p. 614.

[3] a] ad (MS).

veniunt super gradus quelibet in loco suo; tunc uenit cantor ad eas et dicit ad primam Mariam cantando:

Dic nobis, Maria, quid uidisti in uia?

Respondet prima:

Sepulchrum Christi ⟨viventis, et gloriam vidi resurgentis⟩.

Et altera que portat sudarium loco suo dicit:

Angelicos testes, sudarium et uestes.

Et tercia Maria dicit:

Surrexit Christus, spes nostra; ⟨præcedet suos in Galilæa.⟩

Et cantor respiciendo chorum cantat:

Credendum est magis,

totum. Et chorus alta uoce:

Scimus Christum,

totum. Et statim incipitur *Te Deum* ab illo qui regit chorum, et Marie redeunt in capella ut supra. Et chorus deponit capas nigras usquequo cantatum fuerit *Te Deum.*

In this instance the three Marys are impersonated with especial care, and they advance to the sepulchre, at the main altar, in a somewhat formal procession, preceded by a cantor carrying a staff, and by attendants carrying lights and a thurible. The costumes of the two angels include amices, red stoles, and wings. The action is unusual only in that in singing *Alleluia, surrexit Dominus* the Marys kneel and deposit their vessels of gold or silver upon the altar of the sepulchre.

In the following form of *Visitatio*, from Troyes, we encounter a somewhat striking literary embellishment:[1]

Post hoc responsorium[2] tres Marie introducantur querentes sepultum, quas precedant pueri tenentes candelas accensas superpositas uirgis exornatis,[3] albis tunicis, cantantes ⟨*H*⟩*ortum predestinatio,*[4] donec ueniant in medio choro, paruum persubsistentes et cantantes:

O Deus! ⟨Quis revolvet nobis lapidem ab ostio monumenti?⟩

Et procedentes stent ante altare inter duas tumbas. Tunc duo sacerdotes in signum Angelorum a dextris et a sinistris stantes iuxta magnum altare dicant:

Quem queritis,

---

[1] Troyes, Bibl. de la Ville, MS 1150, Ordin. Trecense sæc. xiv, fol. 172^r–172^v, previously edited by Brooks, *Sepulchre*, p. 108. The MS contains no *Depositio* or *Elevatio*. For versions of the *Visitatio* which may be associated with the text before us see

Notes, p. 615.
[2] The responsory is *Et valde mane.*
[3] exornatis] Virtually illegible, and highly doubtful.
[4] For the complete text of this poem see below, pp. 615, 616.

et cetera. Marie respondeant:

Ihesum Nazarenum,

et cetera. Angeli:

Non est hic, surrexit,

et cetera. Quod dum cantant, amoueant albos pannos superpositos magno altari. Tunc Marie uertentes se ad chorum dicant:

Alleluia, resurrexit Dominus,

et cetera. Quo percantato, duo alii presbyteri in signum Apostolorum stantes in choro, unus a dextris et alter a sinistris, dicant:

Dic nobis, Maria,

et cetera. Una illarum respondeat:

Sepulchrum Christi,

et cetera. Et hec se uertens ad altare digito monstret dicens:

Angelicos testes, ⟨sudarium et vestes.⟩

Et ipsa, uerso uultu ad populum, dicat ut sequitur:

Surrexit Christus,

et cetera. Tunc illi duo presbyteri | memorati dicant:

Credendum est,

et cetera. Chorus:

Scimus Christum,

et cetera. Chorarius: *Te Deum laudamus.*

The procession of the three Marys to the sepulchre is accompanied here by the singing of the poem *Hortum prædestinatio.*[1] This fanciful, not to say fantastic, composition, although appropriate to the theme of Easter, is hardly fitting as a processional for the Marys at a point in the action at which it is assumed that they have not been informed of the Resurrection itself.[2] It may therefore be regarded as a festal, rather than a dramatic, enlargement of the play. In the action that follows, one need note only that, once again, the two priests who sing *Dic nobis,* although probably not costumed for impersonation, are understood to represent apostles.[3]

Another introductory poem, more successfully adapted to

---

[1] I am uncertain as to whether the poem is sung by the Marys or by others.

[2] At Sens, *Hortum prædestinatio* was regarded as merely a trope of the preceding responsory. See below, p. 616, and Chevalier, *R.H.*, no. 8045.

[3] See the versions from Narbonne and Le Mans above, pp. 286, 290.

the dramatic situation, is seen in the following from an unidentified French monastery:[1]

PROSA[2]

O quam magno dies ista   celebranda gaudio!
Quam ingenti, quam deuoto   recolenda studio!
In qua Christus iam misertus   hominis exitio,
Morte ui⟨c⟩ta, debellato   demonis imperio,
De tormentis traxit suos   in uirtutis brachio.

Hac in die resurrexit   potestate deica.
Angelus stat ad sepulchrum;   fugit plebs Iudaica.
Mulieres uisione   pauentes angelica
Secum uasa cum unguentis   ferunt aromatica;
Quibus angeli letantes   uoce dicunt publica.

Eis ante altare peruenientibus, duo pueri stantes iuxta altare, unus a
dexteris, alius a sinistris, albis induti, rubicundis amictis capitibus et
uultibus coopertis,[3] cantando dicant versum:

Quem queritis in sepulcro, o Christicole?

Tunc respondeant diachoni, et cantando dicant versum:

Ihesum Nazarenum crucifixum, o celicole.

Et respondeant pueri versum:

Non est hic, surrexit sicut predixerat; ite, nuntiate quia surrexit.

Et discooperiant altare pallio quo opertum est. Tunc unus ex custodibus
ecclesie tollat pallium desuper altare. Quo aperto, conuerta⟨n⟩t uultus
diaconi uersus chorum, et cantor siue succentor dicat cantando:

Dic nobis, Maria, quid uidisti[4] in uia?

Tunc medius eorum respondeat solus:

Sepulchrum Christi uiuentis, et gloriam uidi resurgentis.
Angelicos testes, sudarium et uestes.
Surrexit Christus, spes mea; | precedet suos in Galileam.

Quo finito, dicant tres diaconi simul:

Alleluia, resurrexit Dominus, ⟨hodie resurrexit leo fortis, Christus, filius Dei.⟩
Te Deum laudamus.

We may assume that the lyrical *prosa* before us is sung while the
three Marys advance to the tomb. Although, like *Hortum
prædestinatio*, it prematurely mentions the Resurrection, it is, in

---

[1] Paris, Bibl. Nat., MS lat. 1255, Brev.
monasticum Gallicanum sæc. xiii, fol. 151ᵛ–
152ʳ, now printed, I think, for the first time.
The speeches are provided with music. For
a play with similar speeches, but meagre
rubrics, see Notes, p. 616.

[2] Immediately preceded by the responsory
Dum transisset. For a prose similar to *O quam
magno dies* see Chevalier, *R.H.*, no. 13526.

[3] coopertis] cohopertis (MS).

[4] uidisti] uidistis (MS).

its last lines, skilfully fitted to the action that immediately follows. One observes with satisfaction that later in the play the sentences of response after *Dic nobis* are spoken appropriately by a *single* Mary, who is, no doubt, understood to be Mary Magdalen. This understanding is made explicit in the following *Visitatio* of the thirteenth century from the cathedral of Padua:[1]

Finitis lectionibus, chorus clericorum descendit cum cereis, cantando tercium responsorium *Dum transisset sabbatum*, in corpore ecclesie; et ibi extenditur ita quod episcopus stat iuxta monumentum quod est in corpore ecclesie. Et finito responsorio, magister scolarum uel cantor descendit ab altare Sancte Crvcis et duc*it* tres scolares ad modum Mulierum indutos, qui significant tres Marias ad Sepulcrum Christi cum unguentis et aromatibus uenientes. Que tres Marie deferunt uguenta et turribulum, et incipiunt canere plana uoce, ita tantum quod audiri possint, *Nos mulieres*,[2] et cetera. Et transeunt ita canendo per chorum clericorum, quousque ueniunt ante altare Sancti Danielis. Et duo scolares ad modum Angelorum, cum alis et liliis in manibus preparati, stant superius iuxta Sepulcrum Christi; qui uidentes dictas Mulieres Sepulcrum Christi querentes, dicunt eis concinendo:

> *Quem queritis in sepulcro,* | *Christicole?*

Respondent Mulieres:

> *Iesum[3] Nazarenum crucifixum, o celicole.*

Respondent Angeli:

> *Non est hic, surrexit sicut predixerat,*

et cetera. Et tunc dicte Marie ascendunt per scalas uersus meridiem ad Sepulcrum Christi. Angeli uero per scalas uersus aquilonem descendunt. Et dicte Marie diligenter leuantes pallium, huc et illuc in Sepulcro conspicientes, et non inuento corpore Christi, accipiunt pallium in testimonium Resurrectionis Christi, et descendunt cum dicto pallio per scalas per quas Angeli descenderunt, et ueniunt usque ad introitum Sancti Danielis, iuxta cancellos; et leuantes pallium, cantant hanc antiphonam:

> *Surrexit Dominus de sepulcro, qui pro nobis pependit in ligno, alleluia.*

Et ueniunt uersus episcopum et chorum clericorum. Et tunc magister scolarum et cantor locuntur ad Mariam Magdalenam, et concinendo dic*unt*:

> *Dic nobis, Maria, quid uidisti in uia?*

Que respondet:

> *Sepulcrum Christi uiuentis, et gloriam uidi resurgentis.*

---

[1] Padua, Bibl. Capit., MS S, Ordin. Patavinense sæc. xiii, fol. 98^r–99^r, summarized by Dondi Orologio, pp. 50–2, and previously edited by Bartholomaeis, pp. 520–1. Concerning the MS see below, p. 552. For texts of the *Depositio* and *Elevatio*, and for associated versions of the *Visitatio*, see Notes, p. 617.

[2] *Nos mulieres* I have not identified.

[3] Iesum] Qiesum (MS).

Item dicta Maria ostendendo eis Angelos et pallium dic*it*:

> *Angelicos testes, sudarium et uestes.*

Item dic*it* concinendo:

> *Surrexit Christus, spes mea; precedet uos in Galileam.*

Et tunc chorus clericorum concinendo respondet:

> *Credendum est magis soli Marie ueraci,*

et cetera. Et perficit chorus sequentiam. Et interim Maria Magda|lena confert pacem episcopo et canonicis et omnibus pacem uolentibus. Et finita sequentia, duo clerici ad altare Sancti Danielis cantant hanc anti-phonam:

> *Dicant nunc Iudei* ⟨*quomodo milites custodientes sepulchrum perdiderunt regem ad lapidis positionem. Quare non seruabant petram justiciæ? Aut sepul-tum reddant, aut resurgentem adorent, nobiscum dicentes alleluia, alleluia*⟩.

Qua finita, episcopus ex collatione magistri scolarum incipit *Te Deum laudamus*. Et tunc omnes clerici ascendunt chorum concinendo *Te Deum laudamus*.

In this church the sepulchre is arranged before the altar of St Daniel,[1] where are stationed the two angels with wings on their shoulders and lilies in their hands. On their way to this place the three Marys, fully impersonated, sing a processional *Nos mulieres*. One of the women is distinguished from the others as representing Mary Magdalen, and it is she alone who responds to the inquiry *Dic nobis*, and who, at the appropriate words, points to the angels and displays the *sudarium* brought from the sepulchre. At the end of the play she also gives the kiss of peace to the bishop.

Literary elements which we have not encountered hitherto appear in a play performed in the fifteenth century in the monas-tery of St Emmeram, at Regensburg, as follows:[2]

Dum idem responsorium cantatur, Dominus Abbas et vniuersaliter | omnes in conuentu, acceptis candelis a custode et accensis.[3] Dum finitum est responsorium cum versu et *Gloria Patri*, incipit cantor iterum idem responsorium *Dum transisset sabbatum*, et sic processionaliter veniunt ad monasterium[4] ante altare Sancte Crucis. Medio tempore introducit

---

[1] See the *Depositio* printed below, p. 617.

[2] Munich, Staatsbibl., MS lat. 14183, Ordin. Sancti Emmerammi Ratisponensis sæc. xv, fol. 50^v–51^r (A), printed by Brooks, *Neue Osterfeiern*, pp. 300–02. On p. 302 Brooks mentions similar texts to be found in MSS lat. 14428 and 14073 in the same library. The text in the latter manuscript is seriously mutilated; the variants in the text in MS lat.

14428, Ordin. Sancti Emmerammi Ratisponensis sæc. xv, fol. 57^r–57^v (B), are appended to the text printed here.

[3] The first sentence is incomplete in both MSS.

[4] *Monasterium* is used here to indicate the church building, particularly the nave or the part outside the choir.

cantor tres pueros ad chorum indutos vestibus puellaribus, tanquam tres Marias; et circa ianuam per quam itur de choro ad monasterium prima Maria cantat primum versum:

> *Aurora diem nuncciat,*
> *⟨et terram ros inebriat;*
> *nos verus sol justitiæ*
> *rore perfundat gratiæ.⟩*[1]

Secunda Maria versum:

> *Propere eamus.*[2]

Tercia Maria versum:

> *Sed o pie Deus.*

Tunc omnes tres intrant ante Sepulchrum, et simul cantant versum:

> *O quam dolenda passio.*

Tunc Angeli cantant versum:

> *Nolite metuere.*

Item Marie versum:

> *Quis reuoluet ⟨nobis lapidem ab ostio monumenti⟩?*

Et Angeli respondent versum:

> *Quem queritis, ⟨o tremulæ mulieres, in hoc tumulo plorantes?⟩*

Respondent Marie versum:

> *Ihesum Nazarenum ⟨crucifixum querimus⟩.*

Item Angeli:

> *Non est hic ⟨quem quæritis, sed cito euntes nuntiate discipulis ejus et Petro quia surrexit Jesus⟩.*
> *Venite et videte ⟨locum ubi positus erat Dominus, alleluia, alleluia⟩.*

Tunc Marie simul veniunt et stant ante altare Sancte Crucis contra conuentum, et simul cantant versum:

> *Resurrexit victor ab inferis,*
> *⟨pastor ovem reportans humeris.⟩*

Conuentus respondet:

> *Alleluia.*

Item Marie versum:

> *Reformator ⟨ruina veteris*
> *causam egit humani generis⟩.*

Conuentus:

> *Alleluia.*

---

[1] For the text of this hymn see Notes, p. 618.
[2] This speech and the succeeding two speeches are not parts of the version of the hymn *Aurora diem nuntiat* which I cite.

¹Item Marie versum:

Vespertina ⟨migravit hostia
matutina suscepta gloria⟩.

Conuentus:

*Alleluia.*¹

Tunc omnes tres incipiunt versum:

Dicant nunc Iudei.

Chorus, et cetera.² Postea Dominus Abbas et duo seniores cantant versum:

Dic nobis, Maria, ⟨quid vidisti in via?⟩

Respondent Marie:

Sepulchrum ⟨Christi viventis, et gloriam vidi resurgentis⟩.

Iterum Dominus Abbas et seniores versum:

Dic nobis, Maria, ⟨quid vidisti in via?⟩

Respondent Marie:

Angelicos testes, ⟨sudarium et vestes.⟩

Tercio Dominus Abbas et seniores versum:

Dic nobis, Maria, ⟨quid vidisti in via?⟩

Et Marie versum:

Surrexit Christus, spes mea; ⟨præcedet suos in Galilæa.⟩

Conuentus versum:

Credendum est magis,

usque ad finem sequencie. Tunc populus incipit leta voce *Crist*³ *ist erstanden.* Post hoc cantatur in organo *Alleluia, surrexit pastor.*⁴ Et conuentus intrat chorum, et restitutis candelis ac finito cantu in organo, Dominus Abbas incipit *Te Deum laudamus.* Quo finito, pulsantur due magne campane post Matutinum, et Dominus Abbas incipit Laudes.

On their way to the sepulchre, according to this text, the three Marys sing several unusual processional pieces, the first Mary beginning with a stanza of the hymn *Aurora diem nuntiat* particularly appropriate for a representation of a journey at dawn. The next three utterances appear to comprise a lament. For their eventual proclamation of the Resurrection to the members of the convent the Marys use parts of a composition in tensyllable couplets, *Resurrexit victor ab inferis,* the full form of which may be seen below.⁵ After each couplet sung by the Marys in unison, the chorus responds *Alleluia.* The remainder of the

---

¹⁻¹ Omitted from B.
² For the complete antiphon see above, p. 295.   ³ Crist] Crist der (B).

⁴ For this Easter responsory see Migne, *P. L.,* lxxviii, 773; Hartker, p. 237.
⁵ See Notes, p. 619.

play is noteworthy only for the presence, at the end, of the vernacular song *Christ ist erstanden*, sung by the congregation. This chant we shall find in numerous other plays from Germany.[1]

IV

At the end of our survey of the *Visitatio Sepulchri* in the first stage of its development, I bring together certain versions which, because of one peculiarity or another, stand apart from the normal varieties of the play considered hitherto. A few relatively simple forms, for example, are found not in the usual position of the *Visitatio*, at the *end* of Matins, but immediately before the beginning of this office. This practice is illustrated by the following fourteenth-century version from Udine:[2]

In die Resurrectionis surgimus mane ad Matutinum. Omnia signa simul mouentur sicut classicum mortuorum; sed in fine non remaneant simul, sed sicut in aliis festis. Classico uno *tantum* finito, sit paratus clerus et populus in ecclesia ad processionem albam faciendam cum superpelliciis albis, tenentes singulis candelam in manibus accensam. Et procedant ordinatam processionem facientes,[3] cruce, ceroferariis, et turribulo precedentibus, nil dicendo. Et cum ordinata fuerit processio in ecclesia, sint duo pueri in loco aliquo alto absconsi intra ecclesiam; et cantent hunc uersum alta uoce:

> *Quem queritis in sepulcro, o Christicole?*

Et chorus respondet:

> *Ihesum Nazarenum crucifixum, o celicole.*

Iterum pueri dicant hunc uersum:

> *Non est hic, surrexit sicut predixerat; ite, nunciate quia surrexit.*

Deinde episcopus autem uel sacerdos incipit antiphonam:

> *Christus resurgens ⟨ex mortuis, iam non moritur; mors illi ultra non dominabitur, quod enim vivit, vivit Deo, alleluia, alleluia⟩.*

Qua finita, cantores dicant antiphonam:

> *Dicant nunc ⟨Judæi quomodo milites custodientes sepulchrum perdiderunt regem ad lapidis positionem. Quare non servabant petram justitiæ? Aut sepultum reddant, aut resurgentem adorent, nobiscum dicentes alleluia, alleluia⟩.*

Quo finito, pueri dicant versum *In resurrectione tua, Christe*. Et Dominus Episcopus uel sacerdos dicat orationem *Presta, quesumus, omnipotens Deus, ut intercedente*. Qua finita, intrent chorum; et dum sunt in choro ordinati,

---

[1] See below, pp. 322 sqq.
[2] Paris, Bibl. Nat., MS lat. 1234, Ordin. Utinense sæc. xiv, fol. 10ᵛ, now printed, I

think, for the first time.
[3] facientes] facientem (MS).

Dominus Episcopus uel sacerdos incipit *Domine, labia mea*; postea *Deus in adiutorium*, et cetera; et cantores incipiunt invitatorium.[1]

This is a description of a procession of the clergy and others in the course of which the dialogue *Quem quæritis* is sung between two choir-boys hidden aloft in the church, as representing angels, and the whole chorus, speaking for the Marys. Since there is no sepulchre for *mise en scène*, and no impersonation, the ceremony must be regarded as a liturgical observance rather than as a play.

More genuinely dramatic is the following simple type of performance, from an unidentified monastery:[2]

Dum autem primum pulsentur in ipsa nocte omnia signa, statim post tres oraciones preparent se duo presbyteri ac duo diaconi, ambo prioris et ipsius ebdomade. Ad vltimum vero signum abbas cum omni congregacione veniat vbi Crux secundum ritum sepulta iacuerat expectantes Resurrectionem Domini. Tunc predicti duo presbyteri planetis induti, cum timiamate incenso stantes in medio, predictis diaconibus ad Sepulcrum in dalmaticis sedentibus, ad presbyteros iubilantes versum:

Quem queritis ⟨in sepulchro, o Christicolæ⟩?

illis respondentibus versum:

Ihesum Nazarenum ⟨crucifixum, o cœlicolæ⟩.

Tunc iterum diaconi respondent versum:

Non est hic, ⟨surrexit sicut praedixerat; ite, nuntiate quia surrexit⟩

tenentes ad invicem, que superiacuerat, facitergulam albam; tunc vero presbyteri antiphonam alte vociferantes:

Surrexit Dominus de sepulcro, ⟨qui pro nobis pependit in ligno, alleluia⟩

omnibus signis pulsatis, et abbate tandem *Te Deum laudamus* iubilante, et in chorum cum fratribus procedente; ac sic Matutinum incipit.

The action in this instance centres in a sepulchre, in which, no doubt on Good Friday, a cross was buried,[3] and the rubrics disclose at least a mild effort towards impersonation. At the words *Non est hic* the two deacons who represent the Marys display a white cloth as a *sudarium*. Although this performance clearly occurs before Matins, it resembles the usual *Visitatio* in closing with the *Te Deum*. It would seem, therefore, that, for some reason, a normal version of the play had been transposed, along with the *Te Deum*, from the end of Matins to the beginning.

---

[1] The MS proceeds with the *ordo* for Matins.

[2] Treves, Stadtbibl., MS 1238, Consuetudines monasticæ sæc. xv, fol. 202ᵛ, pre-viously edited by Albers, *Consuetudines*, v, 39–41.

[3] The MS contains no *Depositio* or *Elevatio*.

A more elaborate ceremonial is described in the following text from the cathedral of Parma:[1]

Hora quasi nona noctis pulsetur Baionus[2] solemniter cum aliis, ornetur altare solemnius quam ornari possit, et omnia luminaria ecclesiæ ut in Nativitate accendantur. Ante inchoationem Matutini duo guarda-chorii et duo cantores cum pivialibus Sepulchrum Domini reverenter intrant cum thuribulis et incenso, cereis ante Sepulcri ostium duobus positis. Et incensantes Sepulcrum[3] quærunt de Corpore Christi [quod ante hunc actum sacrista pervigil inde abstulisse debuit, et in sacrario deputato reverenter recondidisse],[4] et palpant linteamina munda, qui-bus id erat involutum. Quod non invenientes, revertuntur ad ostium Sepulcri, foris tamen non euntes, sed versus altare maius, iuxta quod sint aliqui clerici dicentes:

Quem quæritis?

Qui clerici respondentes dicant:

Iesum Nazarenum.

Quibus primi respondeant:

Non est hic, surrexit sicut dixit,

et cetera. Postea egrediuntur Sepulcrum isti quatuor, præviis dictis cereis, et dicunt versus populum antiphonam:

Surrexit Christus, iam non moritur.

Qua finita, maior illorum quatuor ad episcopum accedit sine lumine, et ei dicit plane *Surrexit Dominus*, et osculatur eum. Et episcopus dicit *Deo gratias*. Qui episcopus alta voce deinde dicit *Te Deum laudamus*, et incen-sat altare, dictis dupleriis ardentibus; et, dum dicitur *Te Deum laudamus*, ille qui nuntiavit Domino Episcopo Christum resurrexisse similiter nun-tiet Dominis Canonicis. Finito *Te Deum laudamus*, incipit Dominus Episcopus *Domine, labia mea aperies*.

From the ceremony of the *Depositio* at Parma, described in an earlier chapter,[5] we learn that the sepulchre is an enclosure of considerable size, behind the main altar; and in the rubrics before us we are told that at a very early hour on Easter morning it is opened, and that the Host buried on Good Friday is secretly removed. At the opening of the *Visitatio*, at the ninth hour, four choristers, with thuribles and lights, enter the sepulchre, touch the grave-cloths, and, not finding the Host, return to the door.

---

[1] Edited from unidentified sources by Barbieri, pp. 147–9, and from him reprinted by D'Ancona, i, 30–1; Lange, no. 38, p. 28; Young, *Dramatic Associations*, pp. 44–5; Bartholomaeis, p. 519. I give the text of Barbieri.

[2] The name of a large bell.
[3] sepulcrum] sepulcro (Barbieri).
[4] I assume that this passage, though printed within square brackets, is in the MS.
[5] See above, p. 125.

At this moment certain clerics standing beside the altar, near by, begin the usual dialogue with the question *Quem quæritis?* At the words *Non est hic*, the four choristers, preceded by lights, emerge from the sepulchre, say *Surrexit Christus*, and give the kiss of peace to the bishop. After the *Te Deum*, Matins begins. The act of entering and searching the sepulchre by the four choristers before the beginning of the dialogue appears to be unique. The inappropriate representing of the Marys by four persons, and the absence of impersonation, seem to indicate that this ceremony, like that from Udine, is merely a liturgical observance.

The number of instances in which the dialogue *Quem quæritis* is placed before the beginning of Matins is relatively small; and the three texts just reviewed are the only ones known to me in this liturgical position which represent the story of the visit of the Marys in what we may call an uncontaminated state. Since the position immediately before Matins is normally occupied by the *Elevatio*, however, the bringing of *Quem quæritis* to this place inevitably resulted, now and then, in the combining of two dramatic ceremonies treating themes which are historically separated in time. The *Elevatio* undertakes to represent symbolically the actual occurrence of the Resurrection, whereas the *Visitatio* presents through dialogue, and more or less impersonation, a later and separate event. In the combining of the two, therefore, we may be prepared to observe a certain amount of incongruity,[1] of the sort illustrated mildly by the following text from the cathedral of Constance:[2]

Ad Matutinum ante compulsationem fit processio ad tollendum venerabile Sacramentum in Sepulchro positum,[3] cum luminibus, thuribulo, et aqua benedicta. Primo cantet Angelus:

> *Quem quæritis in sepulchro, o Christicolæ?*

Cantent Mariæ:

> *Iesum Nazarenum crucifixum, o cælicolæ.*

Alius Angelus:

> *Non est hic, surrexit sicut prædixerat.*

---

[1] A forecast of this situation is made above, p. 157. See also Brooks, *Sepulchre*, pp. 43–4.

[2] *Benedictionale Ecclesiae et Diocoesis Constantiensis*, Constance, 1597, pp. 183–7 (A), referred to by Lange, no. 71, p. 47, and previously reprinted by Schubiger, *Spicilegien*, pp. 75–6, and therefrom by Lange, *Programm*, p. 10. The speeches are provided with music.

I give the variants from *Obsequiale . . . Ecclesiæ et Episcopatus Constantiensis*, Ingolstadt, 1560, fol. xcix⟨r⟩–c⟨v⟩ (B), mentioned by Lange, no. 69, p. 47. For the *sepulchrum* at Constance see plate viii.

[3] tollendum . . . positum] sanctum sepulchrum (B).

Tertius Angelus:

Ite, nunciate quia surrexit de sepulchro.

Angeli simul cantent:

Venite et videte locum ubi positus erat Dominus, alleluia, alleluia.

Chorus:

Et recordatæ sunt verborum eius, et regressæ sunt a monumento; nunciauerunt hæc omnia illis undecim et cæteris omnibus, alleluia.

In choro imponit sacerdos antiphonam sequentem[1] ter, et per cantores impletur:

Surrexit Dominus de sepulcro, qui pro nobis pependit in ligno, alleluia.

Sequitur *Te Deum laudamus*.[2]

The relation of the *Elevatio* and *Visitatio* here is not entirely clear. From the text as it stands we must infer that the dialogue *Quem quæritis* follows immediately after the *Elevatio*, but without organic relation to it. The *Visitatio* is unusual in that *three* angels participate, each with a separate speech, and in that the Marys take no part in the announcement of the Resurrection in the latter part of the performance.

A more intimate relationship between *Elevatio* and *Visitatio* appears in the following dramatic ceremony from the cathedral of Laon:[3]

In Pascha ad Matutinas due campane insimul pulsantur; sex cerei iuxta magnum cereum ante altare ponuntur.[4] Dum campane pulsantur, processio ante altare in hunc modum ordinata uadit ad Sepulchrum. Precedunt clericuli[5] cum cereis, duo cum thuribulis,[6] duo diaconi, alij duo cantaturi *Dicant nunc*, cantor et succentor. Omnes isti albis capis induti; alij sequuntur in ordine, unusquisque cereum accensum deferens. Predicti uero diaconi ad ostium Sepulchri uenientes incipiunt:

Ardens est ⟨cor meum, desidero videre Dominum meum; quæro et non invenio ubi posuerunt eum⟩.[7]

Clericulus in Sepulchro:

Quem queritis ⟨in sepulchro, o Christicolæ⟩?

---

[1] sequentem] Omitted (B).

[2] Followed by the rubric *Ordo Benedicendi Agnum Paschalem*.

[3] Laon, Bibl. de la Ville, MS 215, Ordin. Laudunense sæc. xiii, fol. 129ʳ–129ᵛ, previously edited by Chevalier, *Laon*, pp. 118–9. This *ordinarium* was compiled in the twelfth century (see Chevalier, p. xviii), and the manuscript under consideration was written early in the thirteenth century. In the margins and between the lines a hand of the middle of the thirteenth century has entered substantial modifications, all of which are entered in my foot-notes. I denote the original hand and the later one by M¹ and M² respectively. For further bibliography see Notes, p. 620.

[4] due campane . . . ponuntur] Marked *vacat* (M²).

[5] clericuli] duo clericuli (M²).

[6] duo cum thuribulis] Crossed out (M²).

[7] For this antiphon see Hartker, p. 237.

VIII. Easter Sepulchre in the Cathedral of Constance

Diaconi:

Ihesum Nazarenum ⟨crucifixum, o cœlicola⟩.

Clericulus: •

Non est hic, ⟨surrexit sicut prædixerat; ite, nuntiate quia surrexit, dicentes.⟩

Quo finito,[1] sacerdos alba casula uestitus portans calicem cum Corpore Christi egrediens de Sepulchro repperit ante ostium quatuor clericulos[2] pallium super baculos tollentes, et illo protectus incedit ante processionem,[3] precedentibus clericulis[4] cum cereis, astantibus[5] alijs | duobus iuxta ipsum cum thuribulis. Tunc diaconi predicti dicunt:

Surrexit Dominus uere, alleluia.

Post hec cantor et succentor incipiunt illam partem antiphone:[6]

Cum rex glorie Christus.

Aduenisti desiderabilis.

Et sic cantando procedunt omnes in medio ecclesie ante crucifixum. Post antiphona:

Christus resurgens.[7]

Duo canonici cum capis versum *Dicant nunc.* Post uersum processio cantando *Quod enim uiuit, uiuit Deo,* intrat chorum.[8] Sacerdos calicem super altare deponit. Interim campane insimul pulsantur. Episcopus stans in cathedra mitra et capa preparatus incipit *Domine, labia mea aperies.*

In this church the procession, before Matins, sets out from the main altar, and when it reaches the door of the sepulchre, two deacons in the procession sing the antiphon *Ardens est.*[9] A cleric

---

[1] Precedunt clericuli cum cereis . . . Quo finito] Marked *vacat* (M[2]). In place of this passage M[2] offers, in the margin, the following: Precedunt primo clericulus aquam benedictam deferens; hunc secuntur duo clericuli ferentes insignia; deinde duo alii clericuli ferentes duos cereos, duo alii clericuli capis sericis induti ferentes duas cruces aureas; hos secuntur clericuli; deinde cantor et succentor, capis sericis induti, portantes baculos deargentatos in manibus; deinde duo diaconi similiter capis sericis induti, et quatuor canonici subdiaconi albis tunicis induti, pallium super baculos tollentes; hos secuntur omnes alii combinati, unusquisque cereum accensum deferens. Predicti vero dyaconi ad ostium sepulcri uenientes incipiunt *Ardens est.* Clericulus stans in sepulcro respondet *Quem queritis?* Dyaconi *Ihesum Nazarenum.* Clericulus *Non est hic.* Postea cantor et succentor incipiunt *Surrexit Dominus vere, alleluia;* deinde prosam *Victime paschali laudes;* et sic cantando procedunt ante crucifixum in medio ecclesie.

[2] clericulos] subdiaconos albis tunicis indutos (M[2]).

[3] ante processionem] in fine processionis (M[2]).

[4] clericulis] duobus clericulis (M[2]).

[5] astantibus] et (M[2]).

[6] antiphone] Corrected from *antiphonam* (M[1]). For the text of the antiphon see above, p. 151.

[7] For the full text of this antiphon see above, p. 169.

[8] Tunc diaconi predicti . . . intrat chorum] Marked *vacat* (M[2]). In place of this passage M[2] offers the following, written in the margin of the preceding page: Dum autem processio peruenerit in medio ecclesie, cantor et succentor incipiunt responsorium *Christus resurgens;* duo dyaconi predicti cantant versum *Dicant nunc.* Quo cantato processio intrat chorum cantando *Quod enim uiuit.*

[9] In this exposition I follow the unrevised text, which, as a matter of fact, does not differ essentially from the revised form.

within the sepulchre now begins the dialogue *Quem quæritis,* ending with the usual announcement of the Resurrection (*Non est hic*). Then a priest issues from the sepulchre bearing a chalice containing the Host, which is carried in procession to a place before the crucifix, appropriate persons meanwhile singing *Surrexit Dominus* and *Cum rex gloriæ.* At the crucifix are sung *Christus resurgens* and *Dicant nunc Judæi,* after which the priest places the chalice upon the main altar. As we know from other sources, the Host was placed in the sepulchre not during the course of a *Depositio* on Good Friday, but at an earlier hour on Easter morning, merely in order that it might be carried forth in a representation of the Resurrection.[1] This arrangement, however, results in an incongruity, for the carrying forth of the Host occurs *after* the Resurrection has been announced, and *after* the tomb has been declared empty. This defect is rendered somewhat less conspicuous, perhaps, by the absence of impersonation; for the ceremony before us, it appears, is not a play, but a liturgical celebration.[2]

By exception, the combination of *Elevatio* and *Visitatio* is found, at least once, *after* Matins. We have already observed that the *Elevatio* itself occasionally occupied this position;[3] hence we are in some measure prepared for a dramatic text such as the following, from Soissons:[4]

Quo finito, cum *Gloria,* iterum incipiant ipsum cantor et succentor responsorium *Dum transisset.* Tunc eat processio ad Sepulchrum sic. Pueri primum ferentes tintinabula, alij cum uexillis; dein candelabra, thuribula, cruces quatuor. Subdiaconus in albis hos sequatur. Duo presbyteri cum capis de pallio, ceteri quoque in ordine suo. Ad ultimum episcopus cum baculo pastorali et mitra et capa de pallio, cum ipso uero capellanus. Et cum peruentum fuerit ad Sepulchrum, inueniantur ibi preparati duo diacones albis simplicibus, capitibus amictis coopertis, niueis dalmaticis superindutj. Hij in similitudinem Angelorum ad fenestram stantes Sepulchri, unus ad dexteram, alius ad sinistram, uoce humil⟨l⟩ima et capitibus inclinatis uersisque ad Sepulchrum:

Quem queritis in sepulchro, o Christicole?

[1] See Notes, p. 620. The service-books of Laon contain no *Depositio.*
[2] Concerning other more or less similar liturgical ceremonies see Notes, p. 621.
[3] See above, p. 131.
[4] *Rituale seu Mandatum insignis ecclesiæ Suessionensis,* Soissons, 1856, pp. 109–10, previously reprinted by Young, *Dramatic Associations,* pp. 47–8. The MS. of the late twelfth or early thirteenth century, is described in the *Rituale,* pp. vii–x. Martene (iii, 178) publishes a similar version from a MS of the thirteenth century, and his text is partly reprinted by Lange, no. 30, p. 26.

Duo presbyteri predicti cum capis de pallio in loco Mariarum:

 Jhesum Nazarenum crucifixum, o celicole.

Duo diaconi Angeli:

 Non est hic, surrexit sicut predixerat; ite, nuntiate quia surrexit.

Presbyteri, qui et Marie dicuntur, uoce altiori respondeant:

 Alleluya, resurrexit Dominus, hodie resurrexit leo fortis, Christus, filius Dei.
 Deo gracias, dicite eya.

Tunc capellanus de Sepulchro ab intus in superpellicio stans porrigat
diaconis uasculum cum Corpore Dominico, et statim pulsentur tintin-
nabula et omnia signa ecclesie. Cantor autem incipiat:

 Christus resurgens ⟨*ex mortuis, iam non moritur; mors illi ultra non*
 dominabitur, quod enim vivit, vivit Deo, alleluia, alleluia⟩.

Tunc extendat uelum quoddam super Corpus Dominicum a subdia-
conis quatuor; cerei quoque cum uexillis, thuribulis, et crucibus precedant. Presbyteri nempe predicti, acceptis thuribus, conducant illud
semper incensantes, unus a dexteris et alius a sinistris, stella predicta
semper duce.[1] Quo deportato a diaconis honorifice et super altare
oblato, ferra circa altare claudatur; finitaque antiphona superiori,
Christus resurgens, episcopus in sede sua stans iussu cantoris incipiat *Te
Deum laudamus*. Qui dum cantatur a choro, duo maiora signa tantum-
modo pulsentur. Interea vexille, cruces, cerei, thuribula cum tintin-
nabulis sonantibus ante altare morentur. Finito *Te Deum*, iterum omnia
signa pulsentur. Incensum quoque illud quod a presbyteris Dominico
Corpori offertur, ab ipsis episcopo, cantori et succentori, et omnibus
presbyteris in choro defertur. Dein a clericulis ceteris deportetur.

The preparations for this ceremony are described earlier in the
same service-book.[2] It appears that at Soissons, as at Laon, the
Host was not buried in the sepulchre on Good Friday, but was
reserved in the sacristy from Holy Thursday until immediately
before Matins on Easter morning. At this time it was brought
forth and placed upon the altar of the sepulchre, in readiness
for the ceremony now before us. This begins with a procession
to the sepulchre, where the usual dialogue is spoken between
two deacons and two priests representing respectively the angels
and the Marys. After the announcement of the Resurrection,
the Host is brought forth from the altar in the sepulchre and
carried in procession to the main altar during the singing of
Christus resurgens. In so far as this last part of the ceremony
represents the Resurrection itself, it follows very inappropriately
the *Non est hic* of the dialogue between the angels and the Marys.

---

[1] In regard to the *stella* see the description of preparations for this ceremony given

below, p. 625.

[2] These passages are given in Notes, p. 624.

The last exceptional version of the *Visitatio* requiring consideration here is the following from the use of Gran, in Hungary:[1]

Ad Matutinum inuitatorium et alia omnia ut in libro. Dum autem lectiones cantantur, induuntur in sacrario diaconus et subdiaconus, pro hoc festo in tabula notati, vestibus albis, suo ordini conuenientibus. Disponuntur duo ad ferendum thus et turribulum; item duo alii ad portanda vexilla. Et finita ultima lectione, dum in organo incipitur responsorium *Dum transisset sabbatum*, descendit officians cum prædictis et aliis ministris processionaliter ad Sepulchrum, et illud semel circumit, statque ante mensam in qua est monstrantia posita. Ubi finito responsorio, incensat primum; deinde sumit in manus monstrantiam, incipitque et chorus prosequitur introitum *Resurrexi*, sine versu. Qui dum a choro cantatur, portat et ponit Sacramentum ad altare Sanctæ Crucis. Et postquam introitus fuerit finitus, duo pueri veniunt ad ostium Sepulchri, quorum unus cantat:

Quem quæris, mulier, alleluia?

Alter vero respondet:

Iesum Nazarenum, alleluia.

Rursus primus:

Surrexit, non est hic, alleluia; ecce locus ubi posuerunt eum, alleluia.

Deinde accipiens in manus monstrantiam, officians ibidem apud altare Sanctæ Crucis, vertit se ad populum, incipitque antiphonam:

Pax vobis, ego sum, alleluia,

quam chorus prosequitur. Et hoc fit ter, voce semper altius eleuata. Quibus peractis, cantatur *Te Deum laudamus*, ac reuertitur processio ad chorum, et monstrantia collocatur in altari maiori super corporale, et ibi stat usque ad finem Laudum.[2]

This ceremony begins, after the third responsory of Matins, with the singing of the Easter introit *Resurrexi et adhuc tecum sum*,[3] during which the officiating cleric carries the Host from the altar of the sepulchre—where it had been placed in the earlier *Elevatio*[4]—to the altar of the Holy Cross. This ceremonial act, for which the introit is an appropriate accompaniment, clears the sepulchre for the subsequent dialogue between the two choir-boys. Although impersonation is not attempted, the singular form of address (*Quem quæris, mulier?*) is used with dramatic appropriateness.

---

[1] *Ordinarium Officii Divini secundum consuetudinem Metropolitanæ Ecclesiæ Strigoniensis*, Tirnovo, 1580, sig. I 8 recto—K 1 recto, previously reprinted by Lange, in *Z. f. d. A.*, xli (1897), 81–2, and by Young, *Dramatic Associations*, pp. 34–5. See also J. Dankó, *Feier*, pp. 183–7. For the related *Depositio* and *Elevatio* see above, p. 123. In regard to a few remaining texts of an exceptional nature see Notes, p. 625.

[2] Followed immediately by the rubric *Ad Laudes*.

[3] See above, p. 21.

[4] See above, p. 124.

CHAPTER XI

THE VISIT TO THE SEPULCHRE
SECOND STAGE

THE forms of the *Visitatio Sepulchri* reviewed so far have disclosed no dramatic personages except those implied in the original dialogue from which the play arose: the Marys and the angels. To these one might add, perhaps, the liturgical chorus, or the congregation, the members of which do not participate through impersonation, but may be regarded as representing the disciples to whom the Marys announce the Resurrection. The significant enlargement of the play to be considered in the present chapter is a scene in which the central figures are Peter and John. It is possible, of course, that the presence of these two apostles is implied in a few of the plays already examined, for the number of the clerics who address the words *Dic nobis* to the Marys is sometimes prescribed as *two*,[1] and Peter is named in the sentence *Cito euntes, nuntiate discipulis ejus et Petro quia surrexit Jesus*, occasionally spoken by the angels.[2] Hitherto, however, we have not found the presence of Peter and John upon the stage indicated explicitly.

The ultimate source of the new scene is the following passage in the Vulgate:[3]

1. Una autem sabbati, Maria Magdalene venit mane, cum adhuc tenebræ essent, ad monumentum, et vidit lapidem sublatum a monumento.

2. Cucurrit ergo, et venit ad Simonem Petrum, et ad alium discipulum, quem amabat Jesus, et dicit illis: Tulerunt Dominum de monumento, et nescimus ubi posuerunt eum.

3. Exiit ergo Petrus, et ille alius discipulus, et venerunt ad monumentum.

4. Currebant autem duo simul, et ille alius discipulus præcucurrit citius Petro, et venit primus ad monumentum.

5. Et cum se inclinasset, vidit posita linteamina, non tamen introivit.

6. Venit ergo Simon Petrus sequens eum, et introivit in monumentum, et vidit linteamina posita.

7. Et sudarium, quod fuerat super caput ejus, non cum linteaminibus positum, sed separatim involutum in unum locum.

[1] See, for example, the plays from Narbonne and Le Mans above, pp. 286, 290.
[2] See, for example, the play from Eichstätt above, p. 283. Probably this sentence is used in some other texts in which the speeches of the angels are not given in full.
[3] John xx, 1–10.

8. Tunc ergo introivit et ille discipulus, qui venerat primus ad monumentum, et vidit, et credidit.

9. Nondum enim sciebant Scripturam, quia oportebat eum a mortuis resurgere.

10. Abierunt ergo iterum discipuli ad semetipsos.

Here it is recorded that after seeing the open tomb, Mary Magdalen hastened to inform Peter and John. These two apostles responded by running to the place, John reaching it first, but delaying his entry into the sepulchre until Peter should arrive and precede him. Within the tomb they saw the sudary and linen cloths, but did not remove them.

I

A very simple, and somewhat halting, dramatic use of this narrative is seen in the following, from Zurich:[1]

Et responsorium illud[2] reincipitur, infra quod transitur ad Monumentum Domini, ubi cantabunt duo sacerdotes versum:

> *Quis reuoluet nobis lapidem ab hostio quem tegere sanctum cernimus sepulchrum?*

Quibus *respondet* plebanus in persona Angelorum versum:

> *Quem queritis, o tremule mulieres, in hoc tumulo plorantes?*

Et alii in persona Mulierum:

> *Ihesum Nazarenum crucifixum querimus.*

Quibus ille:

> *Non est hic quem queritis; sed cito[3] euntes dicite discipulis eius et Petro quia surrexit Ihesus.*

Et illi:

> *Ad monumentum venimus gementes, angelum Domini sedentem vidimus et dicentem quia surrexit Ihesus.*

Deinde chorus:

> *Currebant duo simul, et ille alius discipulus precucurrit citius Petro, et venit prior ad monumentum, alleluia.*

Deinde plebanus, accepta sindone, coram tota plebe in sublime expandit, atque clara uoce dicet antiphonam:

> *Cernitis, o socij, ecce lintheamina et sudarium, et corpus in sepulchro non est inuentum.*

---

[1] Einsiedeln, Stiftsbibl., MS 81, Brev. Turicense anni 1462, fol. 141ᵛ, previously edited by Lange, no. 126, pp. 87–8. Precisely the same form of *Visitatio*, in mutilated condition and devoid of rubrics, is found in Munich, Staatsbibl., Cod. lat. 6423, Lib. resp. Frisingensis sæc. xiv, fol. 1ᵛ, published by Lange, no. 125, pp. 87–8. In the latter MS the text has music.

[2] The responsory is *Dum transisset.*

[3] cito] citto (MS).

Statim post hoc cantor incipiet *Te Deum laudamus*, concrepantibus signis campanarum.

In this version the new theme is so imperfectly developed that Peter and John themselves seem not to appear. It is possible that while the chorus sings the narrative of their race to the tomb, they may cross the stage; but they have no speaking part. The two new utterances found in this text, however, are standard for virtually all the plays in which Peter and John are included. The antiphon *Currebant duo* is an ancient liturgical piece[1] which, as describing an event in the third person, is appropriately assigned to the chorus. The speech *Cernitis, o socii* appears to have been invented for the special purposes of the *Visitatio*, and we have already observed its use by the Marys at the moment of their displaying the *sudarium*.[2] In the text before us it is somewhat inappropriately delivered by the *plebanus*, or priest, who takes the part of the angels. In the versions to follow it is Peter and John who usually assume the duty of displaying the grave-cloths, and of reciting the words *Cernitis, o socii*.[3] The representing of the angels by a single person has at least the virtue of conforming to the singular number, *angelum*, in the report (*Ad monumentum*) of those who represent the Marys. Although impersonation is not indicated specifically, it may safely be inferred.

The actual presence of the two disciples is vouched for in the following monastic text from South Germany:[4]

Post *Gloria* huius[5] *Patri* incipiat cantor responsorium a capite, et exeant de choro cum magna reverencia portantes candelas in manibus ardentes. Illis ergo ordinatim stantibus, tres presbiteri maioris persone induti[6] bonis cappis, cum turribulis fumigantibus, sub typo sanctarum Mulierum uadunt ad Sepulchrum. Ibi sedent duo diaconi dalmaticis uestiti, sub uice Angelorum. Presbiteri vero loco Mulierum dicant hunc versum:

> *Qvis reuoluit[7] nobis ab hostio lapidem quem tegere sacrum cernimus sepulchrum?*

Angeli r*espondeant:*

> *Qvem queritis, o tremule mulieres, in hoc tumulo plorantes?*

---

[1] See Hartker, p. 238.
[2] See above, for example, p. 268.
[3] In regard to this speech and its uses see Lange, pp. 79–80.
[4] Oxford, Bibl. Bodl., MS Misc. Liturg. 202, Brev. Dominicanum sæc. xiii, fol. 72ᵛ–73ʳ, previously edited by Lange, no. 108, pp. 81–2.

The text has musical notation. Concerning the related *Elevatio* see below, p. 558.
[5] This refers to the third responsory *Dum transisset*.
[6] induti] unditi (MS).
[7] Qvis reuoluit] Written twice, the first time without melody.

Mvlieres:

> *Iesum querimus Nazarenum crucifixum.*

Angeli:

> *Non est hic quem queritis, sed cito euntes nunciate discipulis eius et Petro quia surrexit Iesus.*

Antiphona:

> *Venite et uidete locum ubi positus erat Dominus, alleluia, alleluia.*

Tunc Petrus et Johannes currebant ad Sepulcrum:

> *Cvrrebant duo simul, et ille alius discipulus precucurrit cicius Petro, et uenit prior ad monumentum, alleluia.*

Tunc sacerdotes intrantes locum sepulture, linteamina inde accipiunt et portent ante se usque ad medium monasterium, illudque omnibus ostendentes | dicant hanc antiphonam:

> *Surrexit Dominus de sepulchro, qui pro nobis pependit in ligno, alleluia.*

Tunc cantor alte incipiat *Te Deum laudamus*, et populus *Kyrie*, campanis clare sonantibus.

The lack of dramatic finish in this play appears especially in the abruptness with which Peter and John make their appearance upon the stage—immediately after the scene between the Marys and the angel, and without receiving from the Marys any announcement of the Resurrection. Whether they enter the sepulchre, or speak, we cannot tell. It is possible that they are the *sacerdotes* who exhibit the grave-cloths, and sing *Surrexit Dominus*. In any case, their characteristic utterance *Cernitis, o socii* is not included in this version. It seems likely that those who enter the tomb and sing *Surrexit* are the three priests (*presbyteri*) who impersonate the Marys. This probability is, perhaps, strengthened by details disclosed in a version of the twelfth century from Augsburg:[1]

> Post *Gloria Patri* repetitur responsorium[2] ab initio, et uadunt cum processione ad locum sepulture, vbi reposita fuit Crux et Corpus Domini in imaginario Sepulcro, et alternatim circumstent illud. Interea duo dyaconi, dalmaticis induti, vnus ad caput, alter ad pedes, in ipso Sepulcro collocentur. Et silentio facto, procedant duo sacerdotes casulis induti, et cantent ex personis Mvlierum:
>
> > *Quis reuoluet nobis ⟨ab ostio lapidem quem tegere sanctum cernimus sepulchrum⟩?*

---

[1] Munich, Staatsbibl., MS lat. 226, Ordin. Augustense sæc. xii, fol. 10ᵛ–11ʳ, previously edited by Lange, no. 110, pp. 82–3.   For the related *Elevatio* see below, p. 560.   [2] *Dum transisset.*

Et dyaconi deintus respondent ex persona Angelorum:

Quem queritis, o tremule ⟨mulieres, in hoc tumulo plorantes⟩?

Et iterum illi:

Ihesum Nazarenum crucifixum ⟨querimus⟩.

Et dyaconi:

Non est hic ⟨quem quæritis, sed cito euntes nuntiate discipulis ejus et Petro quia surrexit Jesus⟩.

Tunc presbyteri predicti cum silentio introeant, et thurificato loco, tollant linteum quo Crux fuerat cooperta, et exeuntes foras cantent:

Ad monumentum venimus ⟨gementes, angelum Domini sedentem vidimus et dicentem quia surrexit Jesus⟩.

Et post interuallum, stantes in medio, linteum in publicum ostendentes cantent:

Cernitis, o socii, ⟨ecce lintheamina et sudarium, et corpus non est in supulchro inventum.⟩

Tunc duo ad hoc parati, ex persona Discipulorum Petri et Johannis; et currendo ad Monumentum vnus precedat, quo non intrante, posterior introeat, choro cantante antiphonam:

Currebant duo simul, ⟨et ille alius discipulus præcucurrit citius Petro, et venit prior ad monumentum, alleluia.⟩

Interim sacerdotes predicti, Crvce nvdata | aspersa et thurificata, pro-nuntient omnibus Resurrectionem, cantando antiphonam:

Surrexit Dominus de sepulchro, ⟨qui pro nobis pependit in ligno, alleluia.⟩

Chorus autem, audita Resurrectione, prorumpens in gaudium, alta voce communiter imponat *Te Deum laudamus.*[1] Populus more suo concinat, et Crux in altum trahatur.

In this instance it is clearly the Marys who cense the sepulchre, take up the linen cloth, and sing *Cernitis, o socii.* After this, during the singing of *Currebant duo,* Peter and John race to the sepulchre, still without a speaking part. In Augsburg versions of a later date, however, the role of the apostles is developed more adequately, as we see from the following printed text of the year 1495:[2]

Processio[3] in Die Sancto Pasce mane ad visitandum Sepulcrum

Primo Mulieres cantent versum:

Quis reuoluet nobis ab ostio lapidem quem tegere sanctum cernimus sepulcrum?

---

[1] Here occurs the following marginal entry: Per *Te Deum laudamus,* quod alte cantatur, hora Resurrectionis signatur. See above, p. 231.

[2] ⟨*Breviarium Augustense,*⟩ Augsburg, 1495, fol. 253ʳ, now reprinted, so far as I know, for the first time, from a copy in the British Museum (I.A. 6762). This copy lacks the title-page. In regard to the *Depositio* and *Elevatio* from Augsburg service-books see above, p. 172. For associated versions of the *Visitatio* see Notes, p. 626.

[3] The responsory *Dum transisset* precedes.

Angeli cantent versum:

> *Quem queritis, o tremule mulieres, in hoc tumulo plorantes?*

Mulieres cantent versum:

> *Ihesum crucifixum Nazarenum querimus.*

Angeli cantent versum:

> *Non est hic quem queritis, sed cito euntes nunciate discipulis eius et Petro quia surrexit Ihesus.*

Mulieres cantent versum:

> *Ad monumentum venimus gementes, angelum Domini sedentem vidimus et dicentem quia surrexit Ihesus.*

Cantores cantent antiphonam:

> *Currebant duo simul, et ille alius discipulus precucurrit citius Petro, et venit prior ad monumentum, alleluia.*

Apostoli cantent versum:

> *Cernitis, o socii, ecce lintheamina et sudarium, et corpus non est in sepulchro inuentum.*

Cantores cantent antiphonam tribus vicibus eam incipiendo:

> *Surrexit Dominus de sepulchro, qui pro nobis pependit in ligno, alleluia,* ter incipiendo *Surrexit.*

> *Te Deum laudamus.*

Here at last Peter and John are allowed full participation in the normal sequence of the action. In dismissing the Marys the angels mention Peter, the Marys report their experience at the tomb, the chorus sings the narrative antiphon *Currebant duo* to accompany the action of the apostles, and the latter sing *Cernitis, o socii*, displaying, no doubt, the grave-cloth. One notes, in passing, the mild incongruity between the Marys' mention of a *single* angel and the actual presence of *two* angels. This naïve oversight is by no means unusual.

A slight extension of the dialogue, along with more ample rubrics, appears in the following play from an unidentified German monastery:[1]

> Duodecimo[2] responsorio imposito, tres presbyteri siue diaconi albi induuntur et cappis, capita uelata humeralibus habentes. Responsorio tercia uice finito, Sepulchrum hoc[3] ordine uisitantes, singuli singula cun

---

[1] Oxford, Bibl. Bodl., MS Misc. Liturg. 325, Ordin. Benedictinum sæc. xiii, fol. 82ʳ–82ᵛ, previously edited by Young, *Some Texts*, p. 312. The speeches have musical notation. In regard to the related *Depositio* and *Elevatio* see below, p. 556. With this *Visitatio* may be associated the texts treated in Notes, p. 628.

[2] This is one of the few examples of the *Visitatio* found in the monastic type of Easter Matins, with three Nocturns and twelve lessons. See below, p. 547. The twelfth responsory is *Dum transisset.*

[3] hoc] hunc (MS).

incenso turribula in manibus tenentes, pedetemptim procedunt ad Sepulchrum cantantes submissa uoce antiphonam:

> *Quis reuoluet nobis ab hostio lapidem quem tegere sacrum cernimus sepulchrum?*

Qva finita, duo diaconi | induti dalmaticis uelatis similiter capitibus sedent infra Sepulchrum; quique statim quasi uice Angelorum illos ad imitationem Mulierum uenientes ita compellant. Angelus deintus *respondet:*

> *Quem queritis, o tremule mulieres, in hoc tumulo gementes?*

Econtra isti versum:

> *Iesum Nazarenum crucifixum querimvs.*

Item illi versum:

> *Non est hic quem queritis, sed cito euntes nunciate discipulis eius et Petro quia surrexit Ihesus.*

Tunc isti intrant Sepulchrum, illis interim canentibus antiphonam:

> *Venite et uidete locum ubi positus erat Dominus, alleluia, alleluia.*

Thurificant locum ubi Crux posita erat, et tollentes linteum reportant illut inter se expansum; simul etiam gestantes turibula, et cantantes mediocri uoce, reuerse *sunt* a Monumento; cantant versum:

> *Ad monumentum uenimus gementes, angelum Domini sedentem uidimus et dicentem quia surrexit Iesus.*

Tunc armarius impon*at* antiphonam:[1]

> *Currebant duo simul,* ⟨*et ille alius discipulus præcucurrit citius Petro, et venit prior ad monumentum, alleluia.*⟩

Duo seniores tollentes linteamina:

> *Cernitis, o socii, ecce linteamina et sudarium, et corpus non est in sepulchro inuentum.*

Chorus cantat antiphonam:

> *Surrexit enim sicut dixit Dominus;* ⟨*et præcedet vos in Galilæam, alleluia; ibi eum videbitis, alleluia, alleluia, alleluia.*⟩

Qua ab eis percantata, imponitur *Te Deum laudamus.*

Passing over the informing details of costume here, one observes that, if the scribe is accurate, a single angel sings *Quem quæritis*, whereas the two together sing *Non est hic*. The grave-cloths appear to be displayed twice: first by the Marys, and later by the two *seniores* representing Peter and John.

II

Although it has no direct bearing upon the scene in which the apostles appear, one must notice that the greater part of

---

[1] antiphonam] Written twice (MS).

the plays of the stage that we are now considering open with the so-called antiphon *Maria Magdalena et alia Maria ferebant diluculo aromata, Dominum quærentes in monumento*. This sentence, composed in accordance with the narrative of St Matthew (xxviii, 1), and similar to several traditional liturgical pieces,[1] is usually sung by the chorus as the Marys enter at the beginning of the play. As a choral introduction to the scene between the Marys and the angels it is altogether appropriate, provided the number of the Marys in the play is two, as, for example, in a play of the thirteenth century from Zurich:[2]

Responsorium *Dum transisset* reincipitur, et interim canonicus representaturus Angelum, candidissima dalmatica indutus, per hostium altaris Sancte Marie in choro transiens, ponit se super sedem ad dextrum latus [inferioris] altaris sanctorum Martyrum, capite uelato per humerale. Sed clerus in cantando responsorium *Dum transisset* cum turibulo et cruce processionaliter descendit per hostium cancellorum stans inter et ante altaria Karoli et Marie Magdalene. Et finito responsorio *Dum transisset*,[3] subiungetur responsorium *Maria Magdalena* [vel pocius hec breuis antiphona *Maria Magdalena et alia Maria ferebant diluculo aromata*], et duo de canonicis cappati et ferentes thuribula cum incenso, representaturi Mulieres Marias Sepulchrum Domini uisitantes, progrediuntur ad altare Martyrum et stantes quasi in opposito Angeli deuote cantant:

Quis reuoluet ⟨ab ostio lapidem quem tegere sanctum cernimus sepulchrum⟩?

Angelus:|

Quem queritis, ⟨o tremulæ mulieres, in hoc tumulo gementes?⟩

Mulieres:

Ihesum Nazarenum ⟨crucifixum quærimus⟩.

Angelus:

Non est hic ⟨quem quæritis, sed cito euntes nuntiate discipulis ejus et Petro quia surrexit Jesus⟩.

Mulieres redeuntes [versus] locum stationis clericorum cantant:

Ad monumentum ⟨venimus gementes, angelum Domini sedentem vidimus et dicentem quia surrexit Jesus⟩.

Quo finito, clerus cantat aliquantulum remisse antiphonam:

Currebant duo simul, ⟨et ille alius discipulus præcucurrit citius Petro, et venit prior ad monumentum, alleluia.⟩

---

[1] See below, pp. 600–1.
[2] Zurich, Zentralbibl., MS C. 8b, Brev. Turicense anni 1260, fol. 55ᵛ–56ʳ, incompletely edited by Gerbert, *Vetus Liturgia*, p. 864 (later reprints of which are listed by Lange, no. 136, p. 12), and republished from the MS by Brooks, *Sepulchre*, p. 110. In the present edition the marginal and interlinear

additions, by a somewhat later hand, are enclosed in *square* brackets. Additions of the present editor are, as usual, enclosed in *pointed* brackets. For the related *Depositio* and *Elevatio* see above, pp. 154 sq. Concerning associated versions of the *Visitatio* see Notes, p. 630.
[3] transisset] transsisset (MS).

Et interim duo antiquiores et honorabiliores canonici casulati representaturi Petrum et Iohannem quasi festinanter uadunt ad [inferius] altare Martyrum, sed iunior citius seniore. Et ibi duobus candidissimis linthe[ol]is [ab ipso canonico Angelum representante] receptis, ipsa lintheola publice reportantes ad clerum et ostendentes cantant:

> *Cernitis, o socij, ⟨ecce lintheamina et sudarium, et corpus non est in sepulchro inventum.⟩*

Et statim chorus alta uoce subiungens *Te Deum laudamus* in chorum reuertitur,[1] predictis lintheolis super brachiola crucis quam scolaris prefert positis modo debito et consueto. [Hec eadem linteola, quasi formam stolarem habentia, in precessionibus pascalis temporis super brachiola crucis bacularis deferuntur, alias super brachia maioris crvcis que retro publicum altare inter archas sanctorum Martyrum stat. Eadem posita remanebunt tempore pernotato.]

Although the antiphon *Maria Magdalena* is a fitting introduction for the action that follows here, it emphasizes somewhat the incongruity between the *two* Marys of the play and the *three* Marys mentioned in the responsory *Dum transisset* which immediately precedes.[2] Peter and John are impersonated by two of the elder canons, who not only race to the sepulchre, but also assume, very appropriately, the exhibiting of the grave-cloths.

A slight addition to the dialogue appears in a text from Halberstadt:[3]

> Responsorium repetitur, et cum responsorio in ecclesia Halberstadense itur cum processione ad monasterium,[4] vbi cantantur sequentes antiphone:
> *Maria Magdalena et alia Maria ferebant diluculo aromata, Dominum querentes in monumento.*
> Due Marie eundo ad Sepulchrum cantant:
> *Quis reuoluet nobis ab ostio lapidem quem tegere sanctum cernimus sepulchrum?*
> Duo Angeli sedentes in Sepulchro:
> *Quem queritis, o tremule mulieres, in hoc tumulo plorantes?*
> Mulieres:
> *Jesum Nazarenum crucifixum querimus.*
> Angeli:
> *Non est hic quem queritis, sed cito euntes nunciate discipulis eius et Petro quia surrexit Iesus.*

[1] reuertitur] Corrected from *reuertuntur* (MS).
[2] See above, pp. 232–3.
[3] *Breviarium . . . ecclesiæ Halberstadensis*, Nuremberg, 1515, fol. 39ʳ, previously edited by Lange, no. 139, pp. 91–2. The text is preceded by the responsory *Dum transisset*. For similar versions see Notes, p. 635.
[4] *Monasterium*, as often, appears to mean 'church,' or 'nave'.

Angeli:

> *Venite et videte locum vbi positus erat Dominus, alleluia, alleluia.*

Mulieres:

> *Ad monumentum venimus gementes, angelum Domini sedentem vidimus et dicentem quia surrexit Iesus.*

Cantores incipiant:

> *Currebant duo simul, et ille alius discipulus precucurrit citius Petro, et venit prior ad monumentum, alleluia.*

Duo presbyteri ferentes linteamina in Sepulchro inuenta cantant:

> *Cernitis, o socii, ecce linteamina et sudarium, et corpus Iesu non est in sepulchro inuentum.*

In ambone cantatur antiphona:

> *Surrexit Dominus de sepulchro, qui pro nobis pependit in ligno, alleluia.*

Qua finita, dicitur *Te Deum.*

In this play the angels add the invitation *Venite et videte,* and for the more effectual displaying of the grave-cloths the priests who represent Peter and John mount a pulpit and sing *Surrexit Dominus.*[1] The text seems to include a double incongruity in the number of personages cited. As the performers enter is sung the responsory *Dum transisset,* mentioning *three* women, and this is followed immediately by the antiphon *Maria Magdalena* mentioning *two.* The number of angels is two, but in their speech *Ad monumentum venimus,* the Marys speak of only one. This latter ineptitude is avoided in a play of the fifteenth century from the cathedral of Cracow:[2]

Chorus eundo ad monumentum cantet responsorium *Dum transisset.* Dum Mulieres procedunt ad Sepulchrum, chorus cantet hanc antiphonam:

> *Maria Magdalena et alia Maria ferebant diluculo aromata, Dominum querentes in monumento.*

Ante Sepulchrum Mulieres cantent hanc antyphonam:

> *Quis reuoluet nobis ab ostio lapidem quem tegere sanctum cernimus sepulchrum?*

Angelus in Sepulchro:|

> *Quem queritis, o tremule mulieres, in hoc tumulo plorantes?*

---

[1] It is, of course, possible that *Surrexit Dominus* is sung, not by Peter and John, but by cantors.

[2] Cracow, Bibl. Capit., MS 85, Lib. resp. Cracoviensis anni 1471, fol. 116ᵛ–117ʳ, published by Windakiewicz, p. 352, along with a photographic facsimile of fol. 117ʳ. I have no knowledge of the MS beyond what Windakiewicz provides. The speeches are accompanied by music. Concerning another text of the same version see Notes, p. 636.

Item Mulieres:

Ihesum Nazarenum crucifixum querimus.

Item Angelus:

Non est hic quem queritis, sed cito euntes nunciate discipulis eius et Petro quia surrexit Ihesus.

Item Angelus:

Venite et uidete locum ubi positus erat Dominus, alleluia, alleluia.

Deinde Mulieres reuertantur ad chorum et cantent:

Ad monumentum uenimus gementes, angelum Domini sedentem uidimus et dicentem quia surrexit Ihesus.

Post hec duo currant ad Monumentum, choro canente antiphonam:

Currebant duo simul, ⟨et ille alius discipulus præcucurrit citius Petro, et venit prior ad monumentum, alleluia.⟩

Hanc antiphonam require in sabbato. Deinde sudario accepto, reuertantur ad chorum, et ostendendo sudarium cantent hanc antiphonam:

Cernitis, o socij, ecce lintheamina et sudarium, et corpus non est in sepulchro inuentum.

Deinde chorus cantet antiphonam:

Surrexit Dominus de sepulchro, ⟨qui pro nobis pependit in ligno, alleluia.⟩

Deinde cantatores alta uoce incipiant *Te Deum laudamus.*

In this case the one angel of the dialogue is correctly referred to in the singular in the speech *Ad monumentum venimus.* The scene of the apostles is conducted in the manner which we may now regard as normal.

Slightly more extended than the texts reviewed hitherto is the following from Klosterneuburg:[1]

Sicque,[2] ut mos[3] habet, Sepulchrum uisitatur; ibique clero in duos ordines diuiso, ut fieri solet in choro, cantores imponant antiphonam:[4]

Maria Magdalena et alia Maria ferebant diluculo aromata, Dominum querentes in monumento.

Tunc tres presbyteri ad hoc officium dispositi portantes thuribula et incensum, et in eundo ad Sepulchrum in persona Mulierum ad inuicem cantent hanc antiphonam:|

Quis reuoluet nobis ab ostio lapidem quem tegere sanctum cernimus sepulchrum?

---

[1] Klosterneuburg, Stiftsbibl., MS 1021, Rituale Claustroneoburgense sæc. xiv, fol. 60ᵛ–61ᵛ (A), previously edited by Pfeiffer, pp. 17–9, along with the version found *ibid.*, MS 629, Rituale Claustroneoburgense sæc.

xv, fol. 103ᵛ–105ʳ (B), from which I give the variants. The latter MS provides music.

[2] The responsory *Dum transisset* precedes.

[3] mos] mor (A).

[4] antiphonam] hanc antiphonam (B).

Et dyaconus, in[1] persona Angeli, humili ⟨voce⟩ respondeat:

> *Quem queritis, o tremule mulieres, in hoc tumulo gementes?*

Item presbyteri respondeant:[2]

> *Ihesum Nazarenum crucifixum querimus.*

Et Angelus respondeat:

> *Non est hic, quem queritis, sed cito euntes nunciate discipulis eius et Petro quia surrexit Ihesus.*

Item subiungat antiphonam:

> *Venite et uidete locum ubi positus erat Dominus, alleluia, alleluia.*

Et ab⟨s⟩cedente Angelo, presbyteri ad clerum se uertentes cantent:

> *Ad monumentum uenimus gementes, angelum Domini sedentem uidimus et dicentem quia surrexit Ihesus.*

Et illis abeuntibus, chorus cant*et* antiphonam:

> *Currebant duo simul, et ille alius discipulus pre⟨cu⟩currit cicius Petro, et uenit prior ad monumentum, alleluia.*

Interim dum canitur hec antiphona, duo presbyteri sub persona Johannis et Petri ad Sepulchrum uenientes tollunt sudarium, et ad clerum populumque conuersi proced*unt* sic cantantes[3] antiphonam:

> *Cernitis, o socii, ecce lintheamina et sudarium, et corpus non est in sepulchro in|uentum.*

Tunc clerus succinat omnis antiphonam:

> *Surrexit enim sicut dixit Dominus; precedet uos in Galyleam, alleluia; ibi eum uidebitis, alleluia, alleluia, alleluia.*

Cantores[4] versum:

> *Dicant nunc Iudei quomodo milites custodientes sepulchrum perdiderunt regem ad lapidis posicionem. Quare non seruabant petram iusticie? Aut sepultum reddant, aut resurgentem adorent, nobiscum dicentes.*

Sequitur[5] *Te Deum laudamus.*[6]

A fresh incongruity arises here from the fact that, in defiance of the antiphon *Maria Magdalena*, the number of Marys in the action is *three*. One notes with interest the provision that after the dialogue between the Marys and the angel, all four performers withdraw from the playing-space. This arrangement appears to recognize the supposed fact that, according to the narrative of St John, neither Marys nor angels were present

---

[1] in] sollempni ac alba ueste uestitus intra sepulchrum residens in (B).

[2] respondeant] in persona mulierum aromata ferencium respondeant (B).

[3] procedunt sic cantantes] protendunt sic decantantes (B).

[4] Cantores] •: deinde cantores (B).

[5] Sequitur] Hec finita imponatur (B).

[6] Followed immediately by the rubric *Benediccio Agni in Pascha.*

when the two apostles visited the tomb.¹ The choral *Dicant nunc Judæi* provides a vigorous, but none too graceful, ending for the play.

At this point in our survey belongs a somewhat exceptional version of the thirteenth century from Harlem:²

Ordo ad uisitandum Sepulchrum

Mulieres:

> *Maria Magdalena et alia Maria ferebant diluculo aromata, Dominum querentes in monumento.*

Mulieres:

> *Quis reuoluet nobis ab hostio lapidem quem tegere sanctum cernimus sepulchrum?*

Angeli:

> *Quem queritis, o tremule mulieres, in hoc tumulo plorantes?*

Mulieres:

> *Ihesum Nazarenum crucifixum querimus.*

Angeli:

> *Non est hic quem queritis, sed cito euntes nunciate discipulis eius et Petro quia surrexit Ihesus.*

Chorus:

> *Cito euntes, ⟨dicite discipulis quia surrexit Dominus, alleluia.⟩*

Mulieres, presbyteri remouendo se parum a Sepulchro cantent:³

> *Ad monumentum uenimus gementes, angelum Domini sedentem uidimus et dicentem quia surrexit Ihesus.*

Chorus; iterum redeant cantores:⁴

> *Currebant duo simul, et ille alius discipulus precucurrit citius Petro, et uenit prior ad monumentum, alleluia.*

Tunc accipiatur sudarium in Sepulcro, et eleuetur coram populo.

Cantores:

> *Cernitis, o socii, ecce lyntheamina et sudarium, et corpus non est in sepulchro inuentum.*

---

¹ From the Vulgate one infers that Mary Magdalen may have been at the tomb during at least part of the time when Peter and John were there, for immediately after the mention of their departure the text proceeds (xx, 11), *Maria autem stabat ad monumentum foris.*

² Harlem, Episcopal Museum, MS 258, Brev. Harlemense sæc. xiii, fol. 44ᵛ, previously edited by Lange, no. 142, pp. 93–5; Van Mierlo, pp. 51–2. The speeches are provided with music. In regard to the related *Elevatio* see below, p. 561. It is fair to say that

since the rubrics of the *Visitatio* are partly in the margins of the MS, the interpretation of some details in the play is uncertain.

³ presbyteri . . . cantent] Written apart from the preceding word *Mulieres*, in a different hand; hence intended, possibly, as a substitute for *Mulieres*.

⁴ iterum . . . cantores] Written apart from the preceding word *Chorus*, in a different hand; hence intended, possibly, as a substitute for *Chorus*.

Mulieres:

Surrexit Dominus de sepulchro, ⟨qui pro nobis pependit in ligno, alleluia.⟩

Tunc descendant ad crucem cantando antiphonam:

In Galilea Ihesum uidebitis, sicut dixit uobis, alleluia.[1]

Tunc erigat crucem presbyter cantando alte:

Christus Dominus resurrexit.

Responsio:

Deo gratias.

Iterum eleuat eam cantando altius:

Christus Dominus resurrexit.

Responsio:

Deo gratias.

Tercio erigat eam cantando altissime:

Christus Dominus resurrexit.

Responsio:

Deo gratias.

Hoc facto, portetur ad chorum cantando *Te Deum laudamus.*

The processional antiphon *Maria Magdalena* is here sung, inappropriately, by the *mulieres* themselves; and the command *Cito euntes*, after having been sung by the angels in the speech beginning *Non est hic*, appears to be repeated by the chorus. Especially noteworthy is the procession at the end of the play, with the antiphon *In Galilæa*, and the triple elevation of the cross.

III

A conspicuous feature of a considerable number of the plays of the general type now before us is the congregational singing at the conclusion.[2] Since, however, this participation of the populace is obviously not an enlargement of the action of the play, but only an added element of liturgical rejoicing, it need not be treated extensively here.[3] The plays which exhibit this practice, indeed, are of interest to us chiefly for other reasons.

A very simple example of the custom of congregational singing is found in a service-book from Aquileia:[4]

---

[1] For this antiphon of Easter Lauds see Hartker, p. 230.

[2] Singing of this sort is indicated also in simpler versions of the *Visitatio.* See, for example, above p. 297.

[3] For examples in plays treated earlier in this chapter see above, pp. 310, 311.

[4] *Agenda Dyocesis Aquilegiensis*, Venice, 1495, fol. 126ᵛ–128ᵛ (A), previously reprinted by Lange, no. 166, pp. 105–6. I give the variants from *Agenda Dioecesis Sanctæ Ecclesiæ Aquilegiensis*, Venice, 1575, pp. 115–7 (B). The same version is found in a *Processionale* of the year 1575 from Aquileia, men-

IX. Easter Sepulchre in the Cathedral of Aquileia

Finito autem tercio responsorio, vbi est consuetudo loci, omnis clerus portans cereos accensos procedit ad visitandum Sepulchrum. Dyaconus vero acturus officium Angeli precedat et sedeat in dextera parte Sepulchri, coopertus stola candida, et chorus cantet antiphonam:

Maria Magdalena et alia Maria ferebant diluculo aromata, Dominum querentes in monumento.

Tres presbyteri induti cappis cum totidem thuribulis, figuram Mulierum tenentes, procedunt versus Sepulchrum, et stantes cantent:

Quis reuoluet nobis ab ostio lapidem quem tegere sanctum cernimus sepulchrum?

Angelus respondet:

Quem queritis, o tremule mulieres, in hoc tumulo plorantes?

Mulieres respondent:

Iesum Nazarenum crucifixum querimus.

Angelus respondet:

Non est hic quem queritis, sed cito euntes renunciate discipulis eius et Petro quia surrexit Iesus.

Et cum ceperit cantare Angelus *Sed cito euntes*, Mulieres thurificent Sepulchrum, et festinanter redeant, et versus chorum stantes cantent:

Ad monumentum venimus gementes, angelum Domini sedentem vidimus et dicentem quia surrexit Iesus.

Tunc chorus imponit[1] antiphonam:

Currebant duo simul, et ille alius discipulus[2] precucur⟨r⟩it cicius Petro, et venit prior ad monumentum, alleluia.

Et cantores, quasi Petrus et Ioannes, currant, precurratque Ioannes, sequente Petro, et ita veniant ad Monumentum, et auferant lintheamina et sudarium quibus Ymago Domini erat inuoluta, et vertentes se ad chorum ostendendo ea et[3] cantent:

Cernitis, o socij, ecce lintheamina et sudarium, et corpus non est in sepulchro inuentum.

Chorus cantet antiphonam:

Surrexit enim sicut dixit Dominus; precedet vos in Galileam, alleluia; ibi eum videbitis, alleluia, alleluia, alleluia.

Interim clerus redit ad chorum, et populus cantet *Christus surrexit*. Et sequitur *Te Deum laudamus.*

The share of the congregation in this instance is the singing of *Christus surrexit* at the very end of the play, immediately before

tioned by Lange, no. 167, p. 107, and reprinted by Vale, col. 199–200. A similar text from Aquileia, from a 'Rituale impressum', is reprinted by Rubeis, pp. 340–1, and reprinted from him by Bartholomaeis, p. 522. For the *sepulchrum* at Aquileia see plate ix, and below, ii, 509.

[1] imponit] incipit (B).
[2] discipulus] discipulis (A).
[3] et] Omitted (B).

the *Te Deum*. However sceptical we may be as to the proficiency of the medieval populace in Latin, we must accept the plain evidence before us that on this occasion they are assigned a song written in the language of the Church itself. This occurrence, however, is unusual, for in most of the recorded instances the words sung are in the vernacular; and since the texts of the plays are from German communities, the song is in that language, and is, almost invariably, some part of the well-known composition beginning *Christ ist erstanden*. These words appear, for example, in a simple and normal form of the play from Freising:[1]

Responsorium[2] iteretur, et fit interea processio ad Sepulchrum; et ibi representatur planctus Mulierum Sepulchrum visitantium, Angelorum quoque apparitio Christi Resurrectionem nunciantium, cum antiphonis sequentibus. Antiphona:

> *Quis reuoluet nobis ab ostio lapidem quem tegere sanctum cernimus sepulchrum?*

Angeli:

> *Quem queritis, o tremule mulieres, in hoc tumulo plorantes?*

Mulieres:

> *Jesum Nazarenum crucifixum querimus.*

Angeli:

> *Non est hic quem queritis, sed cito euntes nunciate discipulis eius et Petro quia surrexit Iesus.*

Mulieres:

> *Ad monumentum uenimus gementes, angelum Domini sedentem uidimus et dicentem quia surrexit Iesus.*

Chorus:

> *Currebant duo simul, et ille alius discipulus precucurrit citius Petro, et venit prior ad monumentum, alleluia.*

Apostoli:

> *Cernitis, o socii, ecce lintheamina et sudarium, et corpus non est in sepulchro inuentum.*

---

[1] *Breviarium Frisingense*, Venice, 1516, fol. 197ᵛ–198ʳ, previously reprinted by Lange, no. 160, pp. 102–3. Precisely the same version, without verbal variants, is found in a Freising *Scamnalia* of 1520, mentioned by Lange, no. 161, p. 103; and similar versions in Freising breviaries of 1482 and 1491,which I have not seen, are mentioned by Brooks, *Neue Osterfeiern*, p. 307. In regard to the related *Depositio* and *Elevatio* see below, p. 558.

[2] *Dum transisset.*

Chorus:

Surrexit enim sicut dixit Dominus; et precedet vos in Galileam; ibi eum videbitis, alleluia, alleluia, alleluia.

Populus: *Crist ist erstanden.* Chorus: *Te Deum laudamus.*

The share taken by the congregation in this version, as in most of the others reviewed below, is sufficiently obvious. At the end of the action the people simply proclaim the Resurrection in their own language. Perhaps they often sing only the three words *Christ ist erstanden,* and thus merely translate the *Christus surrexit* of such a play as that from Aquileia considered above; possibly they sing a few lines more. Examples of such a continuation appear in other dramatic texts.[1] In general, however, the length of the vernacular utterance cannot be determined.[2]

In other respects the *Visitatio* from Freising requires no comment. In general content, indeed, the plays to which *Christ ist erstanden* is attached resemble the versions already reviewed. In the pages that immediately follow, therefore, I shall bring forward only a few texts in which the congregational part is in some way unusual, or which are noteworthy in mentioning other details of the performance. A printed version of the sixteenth century from Bamberg, for example, presents an uncommonly generous description of the arrangement of the stage:[3]

Ordo visitandi Sepulchrum Domini

Visvm est pro celebrioribus ecclesiis, aliunde petere, atque hunc in locum ponere modum quendam, quo Visitationis Sepvlchri Dominici commemoratio pie celebrari potest. Vbi notandum est quod in templo designari, atque tapete vel antipendio claudi, debet locus quidam ad repræsentandum Christi Sepvlchrvm conueniens, in quo inter cætera stratum iaceat linteum, seu sudarium album et subtile, designans syndonem quo[4] Christi corpus mortuum inuolutum fuit, quod relicta iam ibi syndone, rediuiuum ex Sepulchro surrexit.

Peractis igitur Matutinis, instituatur processio ad Sepulchrum, in qua cantetur responsorium de Resurrectione quod in Matutinis fuit vltimum, videlicet *Dum transisset sabbathum*, etc. Adsint deinde pueri, qui tres Marias Sepulchrum visitantes, item Angelos quoque, et Apostolos, tum voce, tum etiam habitu externo repræsentent. Primo igitur tres pueri a

---

[1] See, for example, below, p. 330.
[2] For further discussion of *Christ ist erstanden* see Notes, p. 636.
[3] *Agenda Bambergensia*, Ingolstadt, 1587, pp. 597–604. The speeches are provided with music. Lange (no. 141, pp. 93–5)

prints virtually this identical text as from a Bamberg *Agenda* of 1597. See also Lange, in *Z.f.d.A.*, xxix (1885), 250–1. For the related *Depositio* and *Elevatio* see above, p. 172.
[4] quo] cui (Print).

choro versus Sepulchrum prodeuntes, tres illas Mulierculas deuotas, atque ob lapidem ostio monumenti admotum anxias, designantes, querula voce cantent:

Quis reuoluet nobis ab ostio lapidem quem tegere sanctum cernimus sepulchrum?

Angeli in Sepulchro autem cantent sequenti modo:

Quem quæritis, o tremulæ mulieres, in hoc tumulo plorantes?

Respondeant Mulieres iterum in choro:

Iesum crucifixum Nazarenum quærimus.

Respondeant Angeli de Sepulchro, cantantes:

Non est hic quem quæritis, sed cito euntes nunciate discipulis eius et Petro quia surrexit Iesus.

Interim dum Angeli hoc cantant, Mulieres Sepulchro appropinquent; Angeli vero illud subito aperientes, atque Mulieribus monstrantes, alacri voce cantent:

Venite et videte locum vbi positus erat Dominus, alleluia, alleluia.

Tunc Mulieres penitius intueantur Sepulchrum, indeque recedentes cantent:

Ad monumentum venimus gementes, angelum Domini sedentem vidimus et dicentem quia surrexit Iesus.

Veniant denique in persona Ioannis et Petri Apostolorum duo alij celeri gressu, vnoque alterum præcurrente ad Sepulchrum, et postquam illud intuiti fuerint, cantent etiam querula voce:

Cernitis, o socij, ecce linteamina et sudarium, et corpus non est in sepulchro inuentum.

Postremo chorus ter cantat, et subinde altius, incipit hunc versum:

Surrexit Dominus de sepulchro, qui pro nobis pependit in ligno, alleluia.

Postremo potest chorus populo iterum præcinere cantilenas paschales Germanicas.[1]

The sepulchre is here described as a kind of room formed by curtains, with a piece of fine white linen lying within, for a shroud. During the procession to this place is sung the responsory *Dum transisset*, in which the mention of *three* Marys is appropriate to the circumstances. The absence of the narrative antiphon *Currebant duo* as an accompaniment of the race of Peter and John produces an effect of dramatic directness in the action. Particularly informing are the details concerning acting. All the roles are assigned to choir-boys, but unusual care is

---

[1] Followed by the rubric *Benedictiones escarum in die sancto Paschæ*. A note at the end of the book (p. 770) announces that the German vernacular pieces referred to *passim* will be printed in a separate volume.

taken that Marys, angels, and apostles shall have both costumes and voices appropriate to their parts, and shall make fitting gestures. The angel opens the sepulchre 'suddenly' (*subito*), the Marys inspect it 'searchingly' (*penitius*), the apostles represent their race with realistically 'rapid step' (*celeri gressu*), and both Marys and apostles, at the fitting moments, sing in a 'voice of complaint' (*querula voce*). The *cantilenæ pascales Germanicæ* at the conclusion of the play undoubtedly include *Christ ist erstanden*.

In the following text of the fifteenth century, of uncertain provenance, are additional details of some interest:[1]

Exacto responsorio[2] cum *Gloria Patri*, iterum repetitur, sicque, ut mos habet, Sepulchrum uisitatur. Ibique clero in duas partes diuiso, ut fieri solet in choro, imponat cantor antiphonam:

> *Maria Magdalena ⟨et alia Maria ferebant diluculo aromata, Dominum quærentes in monumento⟩.*

Tunc duo uel tres presbyteri, ad hoc officium dispositi, portantes thuribula et incensum, et in eundo ad Sepulchrum ad inuicem cantent:

> *Quis reuoluet nobis lapidem ab ostio monumenti?*

Et diaconus sollempni ueste uestitus et iuxta Sepulchrum residens, in persona Angeli respondeat:

> *Quem queritis, o tremule mulieres, in hoc tumulo gementes?*

Item presbyteri in persona Mulierum aromata ferentium respondent:

> *Ihesum Nazarenum crucifixum querimus.*

Angelus respondit:

> *Non est hic quem queritis, sed cito[3] euntes nunciate discipulis eius et Petro quia surrexit Ihesus.*

Et abscedente Angelo, presbyteri ad populum se uertentes cantent:

> *Ad monumentum uenimus gementes, angelum Domini sedentem uidimus et dicentem quia surrexit Ihesus.*

Et illis abeuntibus, imponitur antiphona:

> *Currebant duo simul, et ille alius discipulus precucurrit cicius Petro, et uenit prior ad monumentum, alleluia.*

Interim dum canitur hec antiphona, duo presbyteri sub persona Iohannis et Petri ad Sepulchrum uenientes tollunt sudarium, et ad clerum populumque uersi protendunt, sic decantantes:

> *Cernitis, o socii, ecce lintheamina et sudarium, et corpus Ihesv non est in sepulchro inuentum.*

---

[1] Vienna, Nationalbibl., MS lat. 1768, Brev. Vindobonense (?) sæc. xiii, fol. 190[r], previously edited by Milchsack, pp. 124–5; Lange, no. 165, pp. 104–5. Lange assigns the MS to the fifteenth century. For a similar version see Notes, p. 636.

[2] The third responsory *Dum transisset*.

[3] cito] scito (MS).

Tunc clerus succinit omnis antiphonam:

Surrexit enim sicut dixit Dominus, et precedet ⟨vos⟩ in Galyleam, alleluia.
Hac autem finita, imponitur ymnus *Te Deum laudamus.* Ac deinde, pre-
duce clero, concordet populus *Christ ist erstanden,* clero in chorum
redeunte.

The rubrics of this version inform us that after the singing of
the antiphon *Maria Magdalena,* with its specific mention of *two*
Marys, these personages may be actually impersonated by
either *two* or *three* actors. At the conclusion of the dialogue
between the Marys and the angel, it is provided that the latter
shall withdraw—a fortunate arrangement which we have
observed in at least one other text, and which we may infer for
a good many versions in which the rubrics are less communica-
tive.[1] The singing of *Christ ist erstanden* appears to be postponed
until after the completion of the *Te Deum,* and hence is not
directly connected with the play itself.

Certain precise details as to stage-action are added in a text
of the fifteenth century from the cathedral of Salzburg:[2]

Post *Gloria Patri* responsorium a principio repetatur, et omnis clerus
portans cereos accensos procedit ad visitandum Sepulchrum. Dyaconus
vero qui legerat evvangelium, acturus officium Angeli, precedat, sedeatque in dextera parte coopertus stola candida. At vbi chorus cantare
inceperit antiphonam *Maria Magdalena,* tres presbyteri induti cappis
cum totidem thuribulis, figuram Mulierum tenentes, et incenso, procedunt versus Sepulchrum, et stantes cantant:

*Quis reuoluet ⟨nobis ab ostio lapidem quem tegere sanctum cernimus sepul-
chrum⟩?*

Angelus respondit:

Quem queritis, ⟨o tremulæ mulieres, in hoc tumulo gementes?⟩

Mulieres:

Ihesum Nazarenum ⟨crucifixum quærimus⟩.

Angelus respondit:

*Non est hic ⟨quem quæritis, sed cito euntes nuntiate discipulis ejus et Petro
quia surrexit Jesus⟩.*

Et cum ceperit cantare Angelus *Sed cito euntes,* Mulieres thurificent Sepul-
chrum, et festinanter redeant, et versus chorum stantes can|tant:

*Ad monumentum venimus ⟨gementes, angelum Domini sedentem vidimus et
dicentem quia surrexit Jesus⟩.*

---

[1] See the play from Klosterneuburg MS 1021, above, p. 318.

[2] Munich, Staatsbibl., MS lat. 24900, Brev. Salisburgense saec. xv, fol. 69ʳ–69ᵛ,

mentioned by Lange, no. 153, p. 102, and now first printed. The text is preceded by the responsory *Dum transisset.* For associated versions see Notes, p. 637.

Tunc chorus inponat antiphonam:

> *Currebant duo simul,* ⟨*et ille alius discipulus præcucurrit citius Petro, et venit prior ad monumentum, alleluia.*⟩

Et cantores quasi Petrus et Iohannes currant, precurratque Iohannes, sequente Petro, et ita veniunt ad Monumentum. Et auferant lintheamina et sudarium quibus Ymago Domini erat inuoluta, et vertentes se ad chorum ostendendo ea, et cantent:

> *Cernitis, o socii,* ⟨*ecce lintheamina et sudarium, et corpus non est in sepulchro inventum.*⟩

Chorus:

> *Surrexit enim* ⟨*sicut dixit Dominus, et præcedet vos in Galilæam, alleluia; ibi eum videbitis, alleluia, alleluia, alleluia*⟩.

Populus: *Crist ist erstanden.*[1] Et ita clerus redeat ad chorum cantando antiphonam *Surrexit enim*; sed si non suffecerit,[2] repetatur. Tunc pontifex siue prepositus incipiat *Te Deum laudamus.*

Perhaps the most noteworthy aspect of this text is the rubric prescribing that Peter and John shall display both the *sudarium* and the *lintheamina.* The Biblical narrative, as we have seen, mentions both of these objects, but does not say that the disciples took them up and displayed them. From the final rubrics it would appear that the performance concludes in a highly festal manner, with the singing of *Christ ist erstanden* by the congregation in the nave of the church, and of the antiphon *Surrexit* by the clergy as they withdraw in procession into the choir.

To the general arrangement of speeches in the type of play now before us a naïve addition is made in the version from Chiemsee:[3]

Post *Gloria Patri* repetatur responsorium a principio. Et interim clerus portans cereos accensos procedit ad uisitandum Sepulchrum. Dyaconus uero qui legebat euangelium, acturus officium Angeli, precedat, sedeatque in dextera parte Sepulchri coopertus stola candida. Et chorus cantare incipiat:

> *Maria Magdalena et | alia Maria ferebant diluculo aromata, Dominum querentes in monumento.*

---

[1] erstanden] derstanden (MS).
[2] suffecerit] suffecerat (MS).
[3] Munich, Staatsbibl., MS lat. 5349, Brev. Chiemense sæc. xv, fol. 199ʳ–199ᵛ, previously edited by Lange, no. 162, pp. 102–3. The text is preceded by the third responsory *Dum* transisset. Concerning the related *Depositio* and *Elevatio* see below, p. 558. A similar *Visitatio* from a printed Chiemsee breviary of 1515 is mentioned by Brooks, *Neue Osterfeiern*, p. 307.

Et figuram Mulierum tenentes procedant versus Sepulchrum, et stantes cantant:

Quis reuoluet nobis ab hostio lapidem quem tegere sanctum cernimus sepulchrum?

Angelus respondit:

Quem queritis, o tremule mulieres, in hoc tumulo plorantes?

Iterum Mulieres:

Ihesum Nazarenum crucifixum querimus.

Angelus:

Non est hic quem queritis, sed cito euntes nunciate discipulis eius et Petro quia surrexit Ihesus.

Item:

Venite et videte locum vbi positus erat Dominus, alleluia, alleluia.

Et cum hec ceperit cantare Angelus *Sed cito euntes,* ut supra, Mulieres thurificent Sepulchrum, et festinanter redeant, et versus chorum stantes cantant Mulieres:

Ad monumentum venimus gementes, angelum Domini sedentem vidimus et dicentem quia surrexit Ihesus, alleluia.

Tunc chorus imponat antiphonam:

Currebant duo simul, et ille alius discipulus precucurrit cicius Petro, et venit prior ad monumentum, alleluia.

Et duo, quasi Petrus et Iohannes currant, precurratque Iohannes Petro, et ita veniunt ad Monumentum; et auferant lintheamina et sudarium quibus inuoluta erat Ymago, et vertentes se ad populum ostendendo ⟨ea⟩ cantent:

Cernitis, o socij, ecce lintheamina et sudarium, et corpus non est in sepulchro inuentum.

Chorus respondet:

Surrexit enim sicut dixit Dominus; precedet vos in Galileam, alleluia; ibi eum videbitis, alleluia, alleluia.

Et populus cum hoc incipiat cantare *Crist ist erstanden von der.* Et ita redeant ad chorum, et presbyter incipiat *Te Deum laudamus.*

If we follow confidently the careful rubrics before us, we must infer that when the angel sings *Cito euntes nunciate,* the Marys cense the sepulchre and promptly hasten away to report the Resurrection to the chorus, without waiting to hear the angel's subsequent invitation *Venite et videte.* It is possible that this invitation is sung during the censing, before the Marys depart; but in any case it is clear that after the dismissal which precedes, the words *Venite et videte* are noticeably intrusive.[1]

[1] See above, p. 247.

A more considerate disposal of the speech *Venite et videte*, and the inclusion of the antiphon *Dicant nunc Judæi*, are to be seen in a play of the fourteenth century from the monastery of Klosterneuburg:[1]

Exacto tercio responsorio cum *Gloria Patri*, iterum repetitur responsorium *Dum transisset*, sicque ut mos habet, Sepulchrum visitatur. Ibique clero in duos ordines diuiso, vt fieri solet in choro, cantores imponant antiphonam:

> *Maria Magdalena ⟨et alia Maria ferebant diluculo aromata, Dominum quærentes in monumento⟩.*

Tunc tres presbyteri ad hoc officium dispositi, portantes thuribula et incensum, et in eundo ad Sepulchrum ad inuicem cantent antiphonam:

> *Quis reuoluet ⟨ab ostio lapidem quem tegere sanctum cernimus sepulchrum⟩?*

Et dyaconus sollempni ac alba veste vestitus, intra Sepulchrum residens in[2] persona Angeli, humili | respondeat:

> *Quem queritis, o tremule ⟨mulieres, in hoc tumulo gementes⟩?*

Iterum presbyteri in[2] persona Mulierum aromata ferentium respondeant:

> *Ihesum Nazarenum ⟨crucifixum quærimus⟩.*

Et Angelus respondeat:

> *Non est hic ⟨quem quæritis, sed cito euntes nuntiate discipulis ejus et Petro quia surrexit Jesus⟩.*

Item antiphonam subiungat:

> *Venite et uidete ⟨locum ubi positus erat Dominus, alleluia, alleluia⟩.*

Et abscedente Angelo, presbyteri ad clerum se vertentes cantent:

> *Ad monumentum venimus gementes, ⟨angelum Domini sedentem vidimus et dicentem quia surrexit Jesus.⟩*

Et illis abeuntibus, chorus cantet antiphonam:

> *Currebant duo simul, ⟨et ille alius discipulus præcucurrit citius Petro, et venit prior ad monumentum, alleluia.⟩*

Interim, dum canitur hec antiphona, duo presbyteri sub persona Iohannis et Petri ad Sepulchrum venientes tollunt sudarium, et ad clerum populumque conuersi protendunt sic decantantes antiphonam:

> *Cernitis, o socij, ⟨ecce lintheamina et sudarium, et corpus non est in sepulchro inventum.⟩*

Tunc clerus succinat omnis antiphonam:

> *Surrexit enim sicut dixit Dominus, ⟨et præcedet vos in Galilæam, alleluia; ibi eum videbitis, alleluia, alleluia, alleluia.⟩*

---

[1] Klosterneuburg, Stiftsbibl., MS 1213, Ordin. Claustroneoburgense anni 1325, fol. 83^r–83^v (A), previously edited by Pfeiffer, pp. 17–9. I give the variants from the text found *ibid.*, MS 635, Ordin. Claustro-neoburgense sæc. xv, fol. 57^v–58^r (B), previously edited by Pfeiffer, *ibid.* For associated texts see Notes, p. 639.

[2] in] im (A).

Ac deinde cantores antiphonam:

> Dicant nunc Iudei ⟨quomodo milites custodientes sepulchrum perdiderunt regem ad lapidis positionem. Quare non servabant petram justitiæ? Aut sepultum reddant, aut resurgentem adorent, nobiscum dicentes alleluia⟩.

Hac finita, imponatur *Te Deum laudamus*. Et clero ad chorum redeunte, populus succinat:

> Christ der[1] ist erstanden von der marter alle.
> Des svll wir alle fro[2] sein, Christ sol vnser[3] trost sein.
> Kyrieleyson.[4]

According to the arrangement here the Marys delay their departure from the sepulchre until the angel has said *Venite et videte* and has withdrawn. The militant antiphon *Dicant nunc Judæi* is among the liturgical utterances at the close of the performance rather than part of the dramatic action. The finale is *Christ ist erstanden*, seen here for the first time in the full form which we may assume to be the one usually employed in connexion with the plays.[5]

An exceptional bit of ceremonial appears in a form of *Visitatio* found in a sixteenth-century service-book from Meissen:[6]

> Tertio responsorio *Dum transisset* cum versu, *Gloria Patri* et repetitione cantato,[7] reincipitur responsorium. Et domini cappis festiualibus induti, candelas ardentes singuli in manibus portantes, processionaliter procedant ad monasterium per choros alternatim stantes. Responsorio finito, prouisores ante tumbam Bennonis incipiant antiphonam:
>
> > Maria Magdalena ⟨et alia Maria ferebant diluculo aromata, Dominum quærentes in monumento⟩.

Qua finita, due Marie casulis rubeis indute stantes ante Sepulchrum cantent antiphonam:

> Quis reuoluet ⟨nobis ab ostio lapidem quem tegere sanctum cernimus sepulchrum⟩?

Angeli in Sepulchro, dalmaticis albis induti, respondeant cantantes:

> Quem queritis, ⟨o tremulæ mulieres, in hoc tumulo plorantes?⟩

Item Marie:

> Jesum Nazarenum ⟨crucifixum quærimus⟩.

---

[1] der] Omitted (B).
[2] svll...fro] schulle...vro (B).
[3] vnser] Written twice (B).
[4] Followed by the rubric *Mox instant Laudes*. The lines in German and the concluding *Kyrieleyson* have musical notation in A.

[5] See below, p. 636.
[6] *Breviarius ... insignis et ingenue Misnensis ecclesie*, Meissen, 1520, sig. F4 verso—F5 recto, reprinted by Lange, in *Z.f.d.A.*, xli (1897), 82–3. Concerning the related *Depositio* and *Elevatio* see below, p. 562.
[7] cantato] cantatis (Print).

Item Angeli:

Non est hic ⟨quem quæritis, sed cito euntes nuntiate discipulis ejus et Petro quia surrexit Jesus⟩.

Post hec Angeli Sepulchrum aperientes cantent:

Venite et videte ⟨locum ubi positus erat Dominus, alleluia, alleluia⟩.

Marie, inspecto Sepulchro, redeant, et stantes ante altare crucis, versis vultibus ad orientem, cantent:

Ad monumentum venimus ⟨gementes, angelos Domini sedentes vidimus et dicentes quia surrexit Jesus⟩.

Tunc chorus:

Currebant duo simul, ⟨et ille alius discipulus præcucurrit citius Petro, et venit prior ad monumentum, alleluia.⟩

Interea Petrus et Ioannes dalmaticis rubeis vestiti, Petro claudicante, cursorie vadant ad Sepulchrum. Et accepto sudario, revertantur; stantes ante altare crucis, faciebus versis ad occidentem, cantent:

Cernitis, o socii, ⟨ecce lintheamina et sudarium, et corpus non est in sepulchro inventum.⟩

Postea duo sacerdotes vicarii seniores casulis induti stantes intra hostium Domini Decani ostendentes Ymaginem Resurrectionis cantent:

Surrexit Dominus de sepulchro;

et chorus:

Qui pro nobis pependit in ligno, alleluia.

Idem duo sacerdotes predicti: *Surrexit Dominus;* et chorus: *Qui pro nobis.* Tertio iidem sacerdotes incipient *Crist ist enstanden,* et chorus prosequitur. Postea, sine interuallo, *Te Deum laudamus.*

A touch of colour is given to this performance by the red vestments of the Marys and the apostles; and realism appears in the limping gait prescribed for Peter. The action closes strikingly by the displaying of the *Imago Resurrectionis*, placed upon the main altar during the earlier ceremony of the *Elevatio.*[1]

A version of the fifteenth century from Indersdorf contains utterances not found among the related plays that we have been examining:[2]

Tercium responsorium post *Gloria Patri* reincipitur, et tunc fit Visitacio Sepulchri taliter. Conuentu manente in choro, tres persone, | precedentibus duabus accensis candelis, cantent ad Sepulchrum simul versum:

Ihesu, nostra redempcio,
⟨amor et desiderium,

---

[1] Concerning the *Imago Resurrectionis* see above, p. 139.

[2] Munich, Staatsbibl., MS lat. 7691, Brev. Indersdorfense sæc. xv, pp. 120–1, previously edited by Lange, no. 168, pp. 107–8; Young, *Harrowing of Hell*, pp. 905–6. For the related *Depositio* and *Elevatio* see below, p. 559.

deus creator omnium,
homo in fine temporum,

Quæ te vicit clementia,
ut ferres nostra crimina,
crudelem mortem patiens
ut nos a morte tolleres?⟩[1]

Et statim subiungant circueundo Sepulchrum versum:

Sed eamus ⟨*unguentum emere,*
ut hoc corpus possimus ungere,
quod numquam vermes possint commedere.
Heu, quantus est noster dolor⟩*!*

Et statim post versum:

Quis reuoluet nobis ⟨*ab ostio lapidem quem tegere sanctum cernimus*
sepulchrum⟩*?*

Tunc Angeli sedentes cum Sepulchro cantent versum:

Quem queritis, ⟨*o tremulæ mulieres, in hoc tumulo plorantes?*⟩

Iste tres persone respondent versum:

Ihesum Nazarenum ⟨*crucifixum quærimus*⟩*.*

Angeli:

Non est hic ⟨*quem quæritis, sed cito euntes nuntiate discipulis ejus et Petro*
quia surrexit Jesus⟩*.*

Et sic statim surgentes de loco ostendant Sepulchrum esse vacuum
cantantes versum:

Venite et videte ⟨*locum ubi positus erat Dominus, alleluia, alleluia*⟩,

ostendentes humerale. Postea subiungant circueundo Sepulchrum tres
persone versum:

Hew, hew!

Et iterum versum:

Ad monumentum uenimus ⟨*gementes, angelos Domini sedentes vidimus et*
dicentes quia surrexit Jesus⟩*.*

Et sic recedent. Deinde chorus cantet antiphonam:

Currebant duo simul, ⟨*et ille alius discipulus præcucurrit citius Petro, et venit*
prior ad monumentum, alleluia.⟩

Et duo venientes ad Sepulchrum cantent versum:

Cernitis, o socij, ⟨*ecce lintheamina et sudarium, et corpus non est in sepulchro*
inventum,⟩

tenentes in manibus sudarium positum in Sepulchro. Et statim subiungit chorus antiphonam:

---

[1] Concerning this hymn see Chevalier, *R.H.*, no. 9582. For the complete text from *A.H.*,
li, 95–6, see Notes, p. 641.

Surrexit enim sicut dixit ⟨Dominus; et præcedet vos in Galilæam, alleluia; ibi eum videbitis, alleluia, alleluia, alleluia⟩.

Qua finita, incipiant hij duo *Crist ist erstanden.* Et omnia signa pulsentur eciam circa altaria. Et post prelatus incipiat canticum *Te Deum laudamus.*

The one or more stanzas of the hymn *Jesu, nostra redemptio,* sung by the Marys at the sepulchre, provide a very appropriate lament. If I have rightly identified the succeeding verses, beginning *Sed eamus,*[1] we have here one more precursor of the scene in which the Marys visit the *unguentarius.*[2]

The present chapter may be appropriately concluded with a version of the *Visitatio* preserved in unusual fullness in a manuscript of the fourteenth century from the collegiate church of canonesses and canons at Essen:[3]

DE VISITATIONE SEPULCHRI

Finito autem tertio responsorio ante *Te Deum laudamus,* fit iterum statio communis per conventum, canonicos et scolares in medio monasterii ante candelabrum in sedilibus ibidem. Et nota, quod quotiescunque in hoc loco fit communis statio, ut hodie, conventus semper manebit ad partem aquilonarem, canonici vero et scolares ad australem. | In hac autem statione omnes canonici erunt induti cappis preter duos, qui erunt Angeli. Isti erunt induti dalmaticis albis super superpeliciis suis; ipsi etiam non ibunt cum aliis ad stationem nisi in fine, ut infra dicetur; sed statione se congregante, dicti Angeli ibunt ad Sepulchrum per chorum domicellarum et per tronulum et altum transitum, qui est versus aquilonem, et intrantes tentorium sedeant super Sepulchrum, scilicet archam supradictam, et habeant librum, in quo contineatur cantus, quem cantaturi erunt, si exterius nesciunt et lumen, ut videre possint, expectantes tres Marias ad Sepulchrum venturas, que Marie, scilicet tres canonice, per alium altum transitum, qui est versus meridiem, advenient. Interim autem quod ipse Marie ad Sepulchrum vadunt, conventus cantabit in statione antiphonam:

Conventus:
VISITATIO SEPULCHRI

Maria Magdalena et alia Maria ferebant diluculo aromata, Dominum querentes in monumento.

---

[1] This may be the *incipit* of the following quite different verses:
> Sed eamus et ad eius
> properemus tumulum;
> si dileximus viventem,
> diligamus mortuum.

See below, pp. 375, 378.

[2] See the version from Narbonne above, p. 286; and see below, p. 401.

[3] Essen, Münsterarchiv, MS sine sig.,

Ordin. Assindense sæc. xiv, pp. 80–3, previously edited by Arens, pp. 73–6, and reprinted from him by Brooks, *Sepulchre,* pp. 98–9. I am indebted to the Reverend Chaplain Kreidt, of the Münsterarchiv, for collating the present text with the MS. The MS is described by Arens, pp. vii sqq., and the *Visitatio* by him, pp. 163–5. In regard to the related *Depositio* and *Elevatio* see below, p. 562.

Et cum Marie omnes tres conveniant, stabunt apud Sepulchrum a longe, cantantes per iter hanc antiphonam—Marie:

Quis revolvet nobis ab hostio lapidem quem tegere sanctum cernimus sepulchrum?

Tunc Angeli in Sepulchro respondentes cantabunt hanc antiphonam—Angeli:

Quem queritis, o tremule mulieres, in hoc tumulo plorantes?

Tunc iterum Marie cantabunt hanc antiphonam—Marie:

Ihesum Nazarenum crucifixum querimus.|

Tunc Angeli iterum respondendo cantent—Angeli:

Non est hic quem queritis, sed cito cuntes nuntiate discipulis eius et Petro quia resurrexit Jhesus.

Tunc quelibet Mariarum singulariter accedet ad tentorium, respiciendo in tentorium una post aliam, et dicendo ad Angelos sic: *Ubi est Jhesus?* vel similia verba. Angeli respondebunt sic: *Surrexit, non est hic,* vel etiam similia verba. Quo facto, Marie ascendentes per iter ad organa cantabunt hanc antiphonam—Marie:

Ad monumentum venimus trementes, angelum Domini sedentem vidimus et dicentem quia surrexit Jhesus.

Tunc statim duo alii canonici de statione, unus senior et alius junior, loco duorum Apostolorum Petri et Johannis, ibunt velociter ad Sepulchrum per chorum domicellarum et altum transitum, per quem Angeli iverant; sed junior vadat citius seniore, et veniat prior ad monumentum Interim istis Apostolis sic euntibus, clerici in statione cantabunt antiphonam—clerici:

Currebant duo simul, et ille alius discipulus precucurrit citius Petro, et veni prior ad monumentum.

Cum autem senior advenit ad juniorem apud Sepulchrum, tunc ambo intrabunt in tento|rium, et senior intrabit prior, licet posterior advenerit Tunc Angeli tenentes et levantes aliquantulum pallam seu sudarium cantant hanc antiphonam—Angeli:

Cernitis, o socii, ecce linteamina et sudarium, et corpus non est inventum.

Tunc unus Apostolorum ascendet ad organa et versus ad stationem clamabit sic—Apostolus:

Christus Dominus surrexit.

Conventus respondebit *Deo gratias.* Sic clamabit tribus vicibus, primo in gravibus, secundo altius, et tertio bene alte, et conventus respondebit e toties in simili tono. Quo facto, populus cantat cantionem teutonicam de Resurrectione. Tunc hac cantione finita, cantrix incipiet *Te Deum laudamus,* et conventus complebit primum versum, clerici secundum, e sic de aliis usque ad finem vel, quod tamen hic prius non vidi, organa incipient et cantabunt primum versum, conventus secundum, clerici tertium, et sic de aliis.

Qualiter Apostoli et Angeli redibunt. Interim Apostoli cum Angelis redibunt per iter ad stationem euntes per alium transitum versus meridiem, per quem Marie advenerunt, Apostolis precedentibus et Angelis sequentibus. Marie vero redibunt econverso per alium transitum versus aquilonem, per quem Angeli et Apostoli advenerunt. Et cum Apostoli et Angeli ad stationem pervenerint, accedant in medium inter conventum et clericos, statuentes se linealiter, alter apud alterum, facie versa orientem ita quod Apostoli sint hinc et hinc in finibus et Angeli in medio; et sic inclinatione facta simul, ad orientem revertentur ad clericos ad loca sua.

The sepulchre in this church is a chest, or shrine (*archa*), placed in a tent in front of the altar of St Michael on a raised passage, or gallery, in the west end of the church. The two canons who represent the angels take their positions at the sepulchre after passing the length of the church along the raised gallery on the north side; and in case they cannot remember their melodies, they may have a book and a light. The three canonesses who take the parts of the Marys approach the place along the gallery on the south side. The usual dialogue is extended somewhat touchingly, for after being dismissed by the angels, the Marys, one after the other, peer within the tent, saying *Ubi est Jesus?* or similar words, and the angels reply with some such utterance as *Surrexit, non est hic.* The race of Peter and John, represented by two canons, is conducted in the traditional manner. It is the angels, however, who sing *Cernitis, o socii*, after which, one of the apostles mounts to the organ-loft and sings *Christus Dominus surrexit* three times. Then follow the vernacular song of the congregation and the *Te Deum* of the canonesses and clergy. Although the performance is elaborate, it is liturgical, rather than theatrical, in tone. The fact that the Marys are represented by women, and the angels and apostles by men, leads to no noteworthy realism in the impersonation.

CHAPTER XII

THE VISIT TO THE SEPULCHRE
SECOND STAGE (*continued*)

THE form of the *Visitatio Sepulchri* in which the scene of the apostles, Peter and John, is the characteristic element achieved its final elaboration through incorporating all, or part, of the dramatic sequence *Victimæ paschali*. The use of this liturgical poem even in the simpler types of the play, as we have seen, confronted the clerical playwrights with certain problems of dramatic adaptation which they solved with only a moderate degree of success.[1] In the sort of *Visitatio* now before us these difficulties recur in somewhat aggravated form. In the present chapter, then, our attention will be centred especially upon the efforts made towards utilizing *Victimæ paschali* to enlarge the scene of Peter and John both vividly and gracefully.

I

The arrangement requiring the minimum of effort on the part of the playwright is that in which the entire sequence is used merely as a conclusion to the performance, as in the following text, of uncertain provenance, preserved in a manuscript of the fifteenth century:[2]

Cum uisitatur Sepul⟨chrum⟩:

> *Maria Magdalena et alia Maria ferebant diluculo aromata, Dominum querentes in monumento.*

Mul*ieres*:|

> *Quis reuoluet nobis lapidem ab hostio quem tegere[3] sanctum cernimus sepulcrum?*

Angel*us*:

> *Quem queritis, o tremule mulieres, in hoc tumulo gementes?*

Mulieres:

> *Ihesum Nazarenum crucifixum querimus.*

Angelus:

> *Non est hic quem queritis, sed cito euntes nunciate discipulis eius et Petro quia surrexit Ihesus.*

---

[1] The sequence and its uses have been considered above, chap. x.

[2] Munich, Staatsbibl., MS lat. 23181, Brev. sæc. xv, fol. 265ʳ–265ᵛ, described by

Brooks, *Neue Osterfeiern*, p. 303, and now first printed. The text is immediately preceded in the MS by the responsory *Dum transisset*.

[3] tegere] tangere (MS).

Mulieres:

> Ad monumentum venimus gementes, angelum Domini sedentem uidimus et dicentem quia surrexit Ihesus.

Clerus antiphonam:

> Currebant duo simul, et ille alius discipulus pre⟨cu⟩currit cicius Petro, et uenit prior ad monumentum, alleluia.

Petrus et Iohannes:

> Cernitis, o socij, ecce linteamina et sudarium, et corpus non est inuentum in sepulchro.

Chorus:

> Surrexit enim sicut dixit Dominus; ecce precedet uos in Galileam, alleluia; ibi eum uidebitis, alleluia, alleluia, alleluia.

Sequencia Victime paschali.

Sequitur Te Deum laudamus. Secuntur Laudes.

In this version the meagreness of the rubrics is such that one hesitates to interpret the text with full strictness. We must infer, however, that the chorus sings the Victimæ paschali straight through, merely by way of giving the performance a festive conclusion. This arrangement is, in any case, unusual, for most versions of the Visitatio which place the sequence after the visit of Peter and John to the sepulchre, employ only the latter part of it, as was done, for example, in the fifteenth-century practice of Passau:[1]

> Responsorium iteratur; fiat processio in monasterium, omnes portantes cereos accensos. Angelus precedat sedeatque in dextra parte ad caput Sepulchri coopertus stola candida. Ordinata stacione et finito responsorio, cantores incipiant, choro prosequente:
>
> > Maria Magdalena et alia Maria ferebant diluculo aromata, Dominum querentes in monumento.
>
> Interim duo vel tres cum totidem thuribulis figuram Mulierum tenentes precedant ad Sepulchrum et stantes cantent:
>
> > Quis revolvet nobis ab hostio lapidem quem tegere sanctum cernimus sepulchrum?
>
> Angelus sedens in dextra parte Sepulchri respondeat:
>
> > Quem queritis, o tremule mulieres, in hoc tumulo plorantes?
>
> Mulieres:
>
> > Jhesum Nazarenum crucifixum querimus.

---

[1] Kremsmünster, Stiftsbibl., MS 274, Brev. Pataviense sæc. xv, fol. 306ᵛ, previously edited by Brooks, New Texts, pp. 484–5. The text is preceded by the responsory Dum transisset. For an associated text see Notes, p. 642.

Angelus:

> *Non est hic quem queritis, sed cito euntes nunciate discipulis eius et Petro quia surrexit Jhesus.*

Et cum Angelus ceperit cantare *Sed cito euntes,* Mulieres thurificent Sepulchrum, et festinanter redeant, et versus chorum stantes cantent antiphonam:

> *Ad monumentum venimus gementes, angelum Domini sedentem vidimus et dicentem quia surrexit Jhesus.*

Qua finita, chorus cantet:

> *Currebant duo simul, et ille alius discipulus precucurrit cicius Petro, et venit prior ad monumentum.*

Et duo quasi Petrus et Johannes currant, precurrat Johannes, sequente Petro, et venient ad Monumentum, et auferant lintheamina et sudarium quibus involuta erat Ymago Domini, et vertentes se ad chorum ostendendo ea cantent antiphonam:

> *Cernitis, o socii, ecce lintheamina et sudarium, et corpus non est in sepulchro inventum.*

Post hoc chorus cantet:

> *Dic nobis, Maria, quid vidisti in via?*

Et veniens unus loco Marie Magdalene cantet:

> *Sepulchrum Christi viventis, et gloriam vidi resurgentis.*

Versus:

> *Angelicos testes, sudarium et vestes.*

Versus:

> *Surrexit Christus, spes mea; precedet suos in Galilea.*

Chorus:

> *Credendum est magis soli Marie veraci quam Judeorum turbe fallaci.*

Versus:

> *Scimus Christum surrexisse ex mortuis vere; tu nobis, victor rex, miserere.*

Quo finito, cantores incipiant *Te Deum laudamus.*

Here the sequence furnishes a part of the dialogue of the play. After Peter and John have displayed the sudary and linen, and have declared the tomb empty, the choristers elicit from Mary Magdalen her testimony concerning the angelic message and the grave-cloths, and then declare their belief in the Resurrection. It may fairly be observed that the questioning of Mary Magdalen and her reply would be more natural, and more in accord with the sequence of events in the Gospel,[1] if placed *before* the scene of Peter and John, as is done in some of the plays

---

[1] See John xx, 1–8.

to be examined presently. But although her testimony as to the grave-cloths becomes somewhat anticlimactic after the two apostles have already exhibited them, there is nothing incongruous or illogical in her added confirmation.[1]

A slightly more animated use of the sequence is seen in the following example of the fifteenth century from St Florian:[2]

Responsorium[3] repetatur,[4] et fiat processio ad Sepulchrum. Postea cantetur antiphona:[5]

> *Maria Magdalena et altera Maria ferebant diluculo aromata, Dominum querentes in monumento.*

Postea veniant tres Marie et cantent:

> *Quis reuoluet nobis[6] ab hostio lapidem quem tegere[7] sanctum cernimus sepulchrum?*

Angelus:

> *Quem queritis, o tremule mulieres, in hoc tumulo gementes?*

Mulieres:

> *Ihesum Nazarenum crucifixum querimus.*

Angelus:

> *Non est hic quem queritis, sed cito euntes annunciate[8] discipulis eius et Petro quia surrexit Ihesus.*

Mulieres:

> *Ad monumentum venimus gementes, angelum Domini sedentem vidimus et dicentem[9] quia surrexit Ihesus.*

Chorus:[10]

> *Currebant duo simul, et ille alius discipulus precucurrit cicius Petro, et venit prior ad monumentum, alleluia.*

Petrus et Iohannes:[11]

> *Cernitis, o socij, ecce lintheamina et sudarium, et corpus non est in sepulchro inuentum.*

Post hoc[12] chorus cantet hunc versum:

> *Dic nobis, Maria, ⟨quid vidisti in via?⟩*

---

[1] Meyer (pp. 78–9) appears rather to hold the contrary view.

[2] St Florian, Stiftsbibl., MS XI.435.2°, Brev. Florianense sæc. xv, fol. 226ᵛ (A), previously edited by Lange, no. 186, pp. 116–8. I give the variants, except in details of spelling, from Vienna, Nationalbibl., MS lat. 1843, Brev. Pataviense sæc. xv, fol. 271ᵛ–272ʳ(B), mentioned by Lange, no. 187, p. 118.

[3] The third responsory *Dum transisset.*

[4] repetatur] repitetur (B).

[5] Postea . . . antiphona] et cantetur (B).

[6] reuoluet nobis] reuoluet (A); reuoluit nobis (B).

[7] quem tegere] tangere (B).

[8] annunciate] annunctiate (A); nuncciate (B).

[9] angelum . . . sedentem . . . dicentem] angelos . . . sedentes . . . dicentes (B).

[10] Chorus] Chorus cū (B).

[11] Iohannes] Iohannes *cantent* (B).

[12] Post hoc] Omitted (B).

Maria respondit:[1]

 Sepulchrum Christi ⟨viventis, et gloriam vidi resurgentis⟩.

Chorus item:[2]

 Dic nobis, Maria, ⟨quid vidisti in via?⟩

Maria:

 Angelicos testes, ⟨sudarium et vestes.⟩

Chorus:

 Dic nobis, ⟨Maria, quid vidisti in via?⟩

Maria respondet:[3]

 Surrexit Christus, ⟨spes mea; præcedet suos in Galilæa.⟩

Chorus:

 Credendum est magis ⟨soli Mariæ veraci quam Judæorum turbæ fallaci⟩.

Versus:

 Scimus Christum surrexisse ⟨ex mortuis vere; tu nobis, victor rex, miserere⟩.

Postea incipiatur *Te Deum laudamus.* Et populus cantet *Christ ist erstanden.*[4]

The repetition of the words *Dic nobis* now adds a touch of vivacity to the scene between the chorus and Mary Magdalen, but can scarcely be said to increase the effect of naturalness. The vernacular song *Christ ist erstanden,* here placed after the *Te Deum,* has appeared in numerous plays reviewed above, and it will be seen frequently again in the latter part of the present chapter.[5]

 Noteworthy additions both to the spoken text and to the ceremonial appear in the following play of the sixteenth century from the collegiate church at Halle:[6]

 Ad tertiam lectionem ministrabuntur omnibus personis ecclesie iterum candele accense, et post *Gloria Patri* tertij responsorij cantor et regentes incipient loco repetitionis responsorium a principio *Dum transisset.* Et tunc processio exibit ad Sepulchrum, quam precedent primo cammerarij et duo pueri portantes cereos, deinde alij duo portantes cruces cum vexillis. Hi stabunt circa baptisterium vel Sepulchrum hinc inde. Chorus vero stabit hoc modo, vt chorales sint ad occidentem; vicarij vero et domini ad orientem; et chori stabunt versi contra se inuicem. Tunc duo cantores post regentes in cappis suis, accipientes duo thuri-

---

[1] respondit] respondit hunc versum (B).
[2] item] Omitted (B).
[3] respondet] Omitted (B).
[4] Postea . . . erstanden] Omitted (B).
[5] See above, pp. 322 sqq.
[6] Bamberg, Staatsbibl., MS lit. 119 (Ed.

VI. 3), Brev. Hallense sæc. xvi, fol. 98ʳ–98ᵛ, previously edited by Brooks, *Osterfeiern,* pp. 56–7. Concerning the related *Depositio* and *Elevatio* see below, p. 562. A similar version of the *Visitatio* is printed in Notes, p. 643.

bula que utraque ibi parata subcustos habebit, representabunt Mulieres et visitabunt Sepulchrum. Interim precentor cum choro cantabit:

Maria Magdalena ⟨et alia Maria ferebant diluculo aromata, Dominum quærentes in monumento⟩.

Ad Sepulchrum sedebunt duo vicarij preparati, vnus ad dexteram, alius ad sinistram, qui representabunt duos Angelos; et Mulieres cantabunt non clamose:

Quis reuoluet nobis lapidem ⟨ab ostio monumenti, alleluia, alleluia⟩?

Tunc Angeli cantabunt interrogando:

Quem queritis, ⟨o tremulæ mulieres, in hoc tumulo plorantes?⟩

Respondebunt Mulieres:

Jesum Nazarenum ⟨crucifixum quærimus⟩.

Iterum Angeli:

Non est hic ⟨quem quæritis, sed cito euntes nuntiate discipulis ejus et Petro quia surrexit Jesus⟩.

Tunc Mulieres, thurificato Sepulchro, reuertentur et stantes inter Sepulchrum et altare Sancte Crucis cantabunt aperta voce:

Ad monumentum venimus ⟨gementes, angelos Domini sedentes vidimus et dicentes quia surrexit Jesus⟩.

Hoc cantato, parati erunt duo imponentes, qui representabunt Petrum et Joannem, et preuenit vnus citius alio, sicut Ioannis cucurrit citius Petro; nec tamen Joannes Sepulchrum introiuit nisi cum Petro. Interim chorus cantat:

Currebant duo simul, ⟨et ille alius discipulus præcucurrit citius Petro, et venit prior ad monumentum, alleluia.⟩

Illi venientes ad Sepulchrum accipient sudarium et cantabunt:

Cernitis, o socij, ⟨ecce lintheamina et sudarium, et corpus non est in sepulchro inventum.⟩

Quo cantato, dabunt preposito et decano, qui similiter erunt induti cappis, et cantori, sudarium in manibus. Tunc processio redibit ad chorum, et cantat chorus:

Dicant nunc Iudei ⟨quomodo milites custodientes sepulchrum perdiderunt regem ad lapidis positionem. Quare non servabant petram justitiæ? Aut sepultum reddant, aut resurgentem adorent, nobiscum dicentes, alleluia⟩.

Venientibus tribus prelatis ad summum altare, vultibus versis ad chorum, chorus incipit:

Dic nobis, Maria, quid vidisti in via?

Prepositus solus cantabit:

Sepulchrum Christi viuentis, et gloriam vidi resurgentis.|

Decanus:

Angelicos testes, sudarium et vestes.

Cantor:

Surrexit Christus, spes mea; precedet suos in Galileam.

Chorus: *Credendum est,* et *Scimus Christum,* et cetera. Interim prepositus solus thurificabit et osculabitur crucem ante altare, et cantant illi tres simul ter cum ostensione crucis:

Surrexit Dominus de sepulchro.

Chorus:

Qui pro nobis pependit in ligno, alleluia.

Deinde ligant crucem cum stola, et tradunt diuulgantibus Resurrectionem. Audita Christi Resurrectione, cantor et regentes prorumpunt in vocem et alte cantant in choro et organo *Te Deum laudamus.* Finito cantico isto, prepositus dicit versiculum *Surrexit Dominus de sepulchro.* Deinde Laudes.

According to this text, the *Visitatio* itself, including the scene of Peter and John, is performed at a sepulchre at some distance from the sanctuary. This part of the action is followed by a procession to the main altar, before which occurs a special ceremony. When the chorus sings *Dic nobis,* the replies are given by three separate clerics in turn. After the sequence has been concluded by the chorus, the chief cleric censes and kisses the cross, and elevates it three times, singing *Surrexit Dominus.* In this arrangement *Victimæ paschali* serves as the basis of a liturgical observance virtually separate from the play proper.

II

From the versions of the *Visitatio* in which the sequence tends to be used as a mere liturgical conclusion to the dramatic representation we pass to those which bring *Victimæ paschali* more intimately into the dramatic action by placing it *before* the scene of Peter and John. In this position, through its mention of the *sudarium et vestes,* it may be said to provide a fresh motivation for the subsequent action of the apostles. This very satisfactory order of events is somewhat imperfectly achieved in the practice of Halberstadt as shown in the following play of the fifteenth century:[1]

Post *Gloria Patri* rectores iterum incipiant *Dum transisset,* et processio intrabit monasterium. Finito responsorio, rectores incipiant antiphonam:

---

[1] Halberstadt, Bibl. des Domgymnasiums,   27ʳ–27ᵛ, previously edited by Lange, no. 145, MS 92, Ordin. Halberstadense sæc. xv, fol.   p. 98.

Maria Magdalena ⟨et alia Maria ferebant diluculo aromata, Dominum quærentes in monumento⟩.

Mulieres:

Quis reuoluet ⟨nobis ab ostio lapidem quem tegere sanctum cernimus sepulchrum⟩?

Angelus:

Quem queritis, ⟨o tremulæ mulieres, in hoc tumulo gementes?⟩|

Mulieres:

Ihesum Nazarenum ⟨crucifixum quærimus⟩

Angelus:

Non est hic ⟨quem quæritis, sed cito euntes nuntiate discipulis ejus et Petro quia surrexit Jesus⟩.

Mulieres:

Ad monumentum ⟨venimus gementes, angelum Domini sedentem vidimus et dicentem quia surrexit Jesus⟩.

Et postquam tercia Maria cantauit *Victimæ* vsque ad versum *Credendum est*, rectores incipiant *Credendum est*; et istis duobus versibus cantatis, rectores iterum incipiant:

Hec est illa Maria, que resurgentem.[1]

Quo cantato, duo domini sacerdotes ad hoc terminati ibunt ad Sepulcrum; tollentes inde sudarium, currunt ad altare Sancte Crucis. Regentes chorum[2] incipiant antiphonam:

Currebant duo ⟨simul, et ille alius discipulus præcucurrit citius Petro, et venit prior ad monumentum, alleluia⟩.

Quo cantato, illi duo tollant sudarium; cantent ad populum:

Cernitis, o socii,[3] ⟨ecce lintheamina et sudarium, et corpus non est in sepulchro inventum,⟩

ostendendo sudarium. Tunc domini tres cantent in ambone antiphonam:

Surrexit Dominus ⟨de sepulchro, qui pro nobis pependit in ligno⟩,

cum tribus *Alleluia* in fine, tenentes cereos et ostendentes crucem, que fuerat sepulta. Finita antiphona, rectores incipiant *Te Deum*.

If we are to credit the rubrics before us, the third Mary—whom we may assume to be Mary Magdalen—sings the entire sequence, except the last two sentences, which are sung by the leaders of the chorus. Then by way of emphasizing the message of Mary,

---

[1] The following trope of the *Alleluia*, referred to by Chevalier (*R.H.*, no. 7597), is found in Munich, Staatsbibl., MS lat. 14083, fol. 1ᵛ: *Haec est illa Maria cui dimissa sunt peccata multa, quia dilexit multum.* This, however, cannot be the piece sung in the play before us.

[2] chorum] *corum* (MS).

[3] socii] *soci* (MS).

these singers add a passage beginning *Hæc est illa Maria*. Having heard the Resurrection announced, two priests representing Peter and John, visit the sepulchre, presumably in the usual way. Finally three clerics with candles, standing at a pulpit, sing *Surrexit Dominus* and raise aloft a cross.

A more discriminating use of the sequence is seen in a version of the late fourteenth century from Prague:[1]

Hoc responsorium cantantes secedant in medium ecclesie, precedentibus candelis et vexillis. Canonici cappis vestiantur, et cereos in manibus baiulantes. Ibique responsorio cum versu et *Gloria Patri* debite finito, choro ad occidentem verso, procedentibus duobus ad Sepulchrum more muliebri ornatis et habentibus duo thuribula et duo cereos, incip*it* prelatus:

> *Maria Magdalena et alia Maria ferebant diluculo aromata, Dominum querentes in monumento,*

quam chorus finit. Tunc vice Mulieres stantes ante Sepulchrum cantent:|

> *Quis reuoluet nobis ab hostio lapidem quem tegere sanctum cernimus sepulchrum?*

Vice Angelus sedens ad Sepulchrum indutus albis, et stolam habens in capite, respondet:

> *Quem queritis, o tremule mulieres, in hoc tumulo plorantes?*

Vice Mulieres:

> *Iesum Nazarenum crucifixum querimus.*

Vice Angelus:

> *Non est hic quem queritis, sed cito euntes nunciate discipulis eius et Petro quia surrexit Ihesus.*

Tunc vice Mulieres reuerse ad chorum, versis vvltibus ad orientem cantant hanc antiphonam:

> *Ad monumentum venimus gementes, angelum Domini sedentem vidimus e dicentem quia surrexit Ihesus.*

Inde prelatus:

> *Dic nobis, Maria, ⟨quid vidisti in via?⟩*[2]

quod chorus finit. Vna Mulierum respondet:

> *Sepulchrum Christi vi⟨ventis, et gloriam vidi resurgentis⟩;*
> *Angelicos testes, ⟨sudarium et vestes;*
> *Surrexit Christus, spes mea; præcedet suos in Galilæa;⟩*

---

[1] Prague, Národni Museum, MS XV.A.10, Brev. Pragense sæc. xiv, fol. 192^r–192^v, now printed, I think, for the first time. The text is preceded by the responsory *Dum transisset*.

Most of the speeches have musical notation For associated versions see Notes, p. 643.

[2] For this speech and the three succeeding ones there is no music.

quod totum ipsa terminat. Chorus:

> *Credendum est magis ⟨soli Mariæ veraci quam Judæorum turbæ fallaci⟩.*
> *Scimus Christum ⟨surrexisse a mortuis vere; tu nobis, victor rex, miserere⟩.*

Deinde prelatus incipit antiphonam: .

> *Currebant ⟨duo simul, et ille alius discipulus præcucurrit citius Petro, et*
> *venit prior ad monumentum, alleluia⟩,*

quam chorus finit. Interim duo de fratribus portantes cereos et induti cappis vadunt ad Sepulchrum, et acceptis duobus lintheaminibus, reuersi ad chorum, stantes ad orientem, cantant antiphonam duo:

> *Cernitis, o socii, ecce lintheamina et sudarium, et corpus non est in sepulchro*
> *inuentum.*

Hoc finito, incipit prelatus antiphonam:

> *Surrexit Dominus de sepulcro, ⟨qui pro nobis pependit in ligno, alleluia,⟩*[1]

quam chorus finit. Interim deponuntur lintheamina in altare Sancte Crucis. Tunc prelatus portans cereum progreditur in medium chori, versoque vvltu ad orientem cum trina genuflexione cantet solus:[2]

> *Christus Dominus resurrexit.*

Chorus respondet:

> *Deo gracias, gaudeamus.*

Et sic ter dicatur et cum genuflexione. Post hec accedens prelatus deosculatur lintheamina, et dat pacem ad fratres et ad populum. Deinde incipit prelatus *Te Deum laudamus, Te Do⟨minum,⟩* quod cantantes redeunt ad chorum.

At the conclusion of the usual action at the sepulchre, in this play, the celebrant and chorus deliver the question *Dic nobis?* one of the Marys makes the threefold reply, and the chorus immediately completes the sequence. Moved by what they have heard, the two apostles proceed to the tomb, display the grave-cloths, and presently lay them upon the altar of the Holy Cross. Subsequently the celebrant kisses the linens, and then gives the kiss of peace to the clergy and the congregation. The care with which this text is composed appears not only in the fortunate position of the sequence, but also in the provision of *two* Marys, in accordance with the opening antiphon, *Maria Magdalena*, and of *one* angel, in conformity with the speech *Ad monumentum.*

A still more thoughtful adaptation of *Victimæ paschali* to the scene of the apostles is observable in a play of the fourteenth century from Moosburg:[3]

---

[1] For this antiphon there is no music.
[2] cantet solus] Corrected from *cantent* (MS).
[3] Munich, Staatsbibl., MS lat. 23068,

Brev. Mosburgense sæc. xiv, fol. 295ᵛ, described by Brooks, *Neue Osterfeiern*, p. 309, and now first printed. In the MS the text is preceded by the responsory *Dum transisset.*

AD UISITANDUM SEPULCHRUM

Primo Mulieres:

Quis reuoluet nobis lapidem ab hostio monumenti quem tegere sanctum cerni-mus[1] sepulchrum?

Angeli:

Quem queritis, o tremule mulieres, in hoc tumulo gementes?

Mulieres:

Ihesum Nazarenum crucifixum querimus.

Angeli:

Non est hic quem queritis, sed cito euntes nunciate discipulis eius et Petro quia surrexit Ihesus.

Venite et videte locum vbi positus erat Dominus, alleluia, alleluia.

Mulieres:

Ad monumentum venimus gementes, angelum Domini sedentem vidimus et dicentem quia surrexit Ihesus.

Apostoli:

Dic nobis, Maria, quid vidisti in via?

Mulier:[2]

Sepulchrum Christi viuentis, et gloriam vidi resurgentis.

Apostoli:

Dic ⟨nobis, Maria, quid vidisti in via⟩?

Mulier:

Angelicos teste⟨s⟩, sudarium et vestes.

Apostoli:

Dic nobis, ⟨Maria, quid vidisti in via?⟩

Mulieres:

Surrexit Christus, spes mea; precedet suos in Galileam.

Chorus:

Currebant duo simul, et ille alius discipulus precucurrit cicius Petro, et venit prior ad monumentum, alleluia.

Apostoli:

Cernitis, o socii, ecce lintheamina et sudarium, et corpus non est in sepulchro inventum.

Chorus:

Credendum est magis soli Marie veraci quam Iudeorum turbe fallaci.

Versus:

Scimus Christum surrexisse ex mortuis vere; tu nobis, victor rex, miserere.

Psalmus: *Te Deum lau⟨damus⟩.*

---

[1] tegere sanctum cernimus] tangere sanctum cernere (MS).

The scribe's wavering abbreviations sometimes leave one uncertain as to whether he intends the singular or plural of this word.

The sequence is here used with obvious freedom, and the result is a palpable dramatic advance. By assigning the question *Dic nobis?* to the apostles, and thus bringing Mary Magdalen into direct contact, not with the chorus, but with Peter and John themselves, some discerning writer has transmuted a liturgical passage into a true dramatic action. The succession of events now follows the natural order of the Gospel narrative: Mary Magdalen carries her report to the two apostles, they visit the tomb themselves, and then convey their announcement to the chorus, which may be regarded as representing the whole body of disciples. The closing sentences of the sequence are very appropriately sung by the chorus after Peter and John have confirmed the report of Mary Magdalen.

Of all the extant versions of the *Visitatio* which use the Easter sequence as part of the dialogue, the one which exhibits the most dramatic skill and literary finish is from the church of St John the Evangelist, in Dublin. This composition, moreover, is conspicuous among the plays of the present chapter as being the only one from outside German territory:[1]

Finito tertio responsorio cum suo versu et *Gloria Patri,* uenient tres persone in superpelliceis et in capis sericis, capitibus uelatis, quasi tres Marie querentes Ihesum,[2] singule portantes pixidem in manibus quasi aromatibus, quarum[3] prima ad ingressum chori uersus[4] Sepulcrum precedat.[5] Per se[6] quasi lamentando dicat:

> Heu! pius pastor occiditur,
> quem nulla culpa infecit.
> O mors lugenda!

Factoque modico interuallo, intret secunda Maria consimili[7] modo et dicat:

> Heu! nequam gens Iudaica,
> quam dira frendet uesania.
> Plebs execranda!

---

[1] I print the text from Oxford, Bibl. Bodl., MS Rawlinson Liturg. d.iv, Process. ad usum ecclesiæ Sancti Johannis Evangelistæ Dublinensis sæc. xiv, fol. 130ʳ–132ʳ (A), previously edited by Chambers, ii, 315–8; Young, *Harrowing of Hell,* pp. 920–4. The essential part of fol. 130ʳ is facsimiled by Chambers, ii, frontispiece. Chambers's text is reprinted by Adams, pp. 11–4. I give the variants, except in details of spelling, from Dublin, Archbishop Marsh's Library, MS Z.4.2.20 (*olim* V.3.2.10), Process. ad usum ecclesiæ Sancti Johannis Evangelistæ Dub-

linensis sæc. xiv, fol. 59ʳ–61ʳ (B), previously edited by Manly, *Specimens,* i, pp. xxii–xxvi; Chambers, ii, 315–8. Fol. 59ᵛ–61ʳ are facsimiled by Frere, *Winchester Troper,* plate 26ᵇ. Both MSS provide music. For the related *Depositio* and *Elevatio* see above, pp. 168 sqq.

[2] Ihesum] Christum (B).

[3] quarum] quasi (A).

[4] uersus] usque (B).

[5] precedat] procedat (B).

[6] se] In B supplied by a later hand in margin. [7] consimili] simili (B).

Deinde tertia Maria consimili modo dicat:[1]

> *Heu! uerus doctor obiit,*
> *qui uitam functis contulit.*
> *O res plangenda!*

Adhuc paululum procedendo prima Maria dicat:[2]

> *Heu! misere cur contigit*
> *uidere mortem Saluatoris?*

Deinde secunda Maria dicat:[3]|

> *Heu! consolacio nostra,*
> *ut quid mortem sustinuit!*

Tunc[4] tertia Maria:

> *Heu! redempcio nostra,*
> *ut quid taliter agere uoluit!*

Tunc se coniungant et procedant ad gradum chori ante altare simul[5] dicentes:

> *Iam iam, ecce,[6] iam properemus ad tumulum,*
> *unguentes dilecti[7] corpus sanctissimum.*

[8]Deinde procedant simul prope Sepulcrum, et prima Maria dicat per se:

> *Condumentis aromatum*
> *ungamus corpus sanctissimum,*
> *quo preciosa.*[8]

Tunc secunda Maria dicat per se:

> *Nardi uetet commixtio,*
> *ne putrescat in tumulo[9]*
> *caro beata.*

Deinde tertia Maria dicat per se:[10]

> *Sed nequimus hoc patrare   sine adiutorio.*
> *Quisnam saxum hoc reuoluet[11] | a monumenti ostio?*

Facto interuallo, Angelus iuxta Sepulcrum apparuit[12] eis, et dicat hoc modo:

> *Quem queritis ad sepulcrum, o Cristicole?*

Deinde respondeant tres Marie; simul dicant:[13]

> *Ihesum Nazarenum crucifixum, o celicola.*

---

[1] dicat] Omitted (B).
[2] dicat] dicat hoc modo (B).
[3] dicat] Omitted (B).
[4] Tunc] Deinde (B).
[5] simul] Omitted (B).
[6] ecce] esse (A.B).
[7] dilecti] delecti(A).
[8–8] Omitted, with the speech, but not the rubric, entered by a later hand at the top of the preceding page as follows: Condimentis aromatum vnguentes corpus sanctissimum quo preciosa (B).
[9] tumulo] timulo (A).
[10] dicat per se] Omitted (B).
[11] reuoluet] reuoluit (B).
[12] apparuit] appariat (B).
[13] dicant] Omitted (B).

Tunc Angelus dicet:[1]

Surrexit, non est hic, sicut dixit.
Uenite et uidete locum ubi positus fuerat.

Deinde predicte Marie Sepulcrum intrent, et[2] inclinantes se et pro-
spicientes undique intra[3] Sepulcrum alta uoce quasi gaudentes et admirantes et parum a Sepulcro recedentes simul dicant:[4]

Alleluya, resurrexit Dominus!
Alleluya, resurrexit Dominus hodie!
Resurrexit potens, fortis, Christus, Filius Dei!

Deinde Angelus ad eas:[5]

Et euntes dicite discipulis eius et Petro quia surrexit.|

In qua reuertant ad Angelum quasi mandatum suum ad implendum
parate, simul dicentes:[6]

Eya! pergamus propere
mandatum hoc perficere.

Interim ueniant ad ingressum chori due persone nude pedes, sub personis Apostolorum Iohannis et Petri, indute albis sine paruris cum tunicis, quarum Iohannes amictus tunica alba, palmam in manu gestans,
Petrus uero rubea tunica indutus, claues in manu ferens;[7] et predicte
Mulieres de Sepulcro reuertentes et quasi de choro simul exeuntes dicat
prima Maria per se[8] sequencia⟨m⟩:

Victime paschali laudes immolant Cristiani.
Agnus[9] redemit oues; Christus innocens Patri reconciliauit[10] peccatores.
Mors[11] et uita duello conflixere mirando; dux uite mortuus,[12] regnat uiuus.

Tunc obuiantes eis in medio chori predicti Discipuli interrogantes simul
dicant:

Dic nobis, Maria, quid uidisti in uia?

Tunc prima Maria respondet[13] quasi monstrando:

Sepul|crum Christi uiuentis, et gloriam uidi resurgentis.

Tunc secunda Maria respondet[14] similiter[15] monstrando:

Angelicos testes, sudarium et uestes.

Tunc[16] tertia Maria respondeat:

Surrexit Christus, spes nostra; precedet uos in Galileam.

Et sic precedant simul ad ostium chori. Interim[17] currant duo ad Monu-

---

[1] dicet] dicat sic (B).
[2] et] Omitted (B).
[3] intra] infra (A).
[4] simul dicant] dicant simul (B).
[5] eas] eas dicens (B).
[6] parate simul dicentes] parare simul
dicentes (A); parate dicentes simul (B).
[7] ferens] deferens (B).
[8] per se] Omitted (B).

[9] Agnus] Secunda Maria Agnus (B).
[10] reconciliauit] reconsiliauit (A.B).
[11] Mors] Tercia Maria Mors (B).
[12] mortuus] mortuis (A.B).
[13] respondet] respondeat (B).
[14] respondet] respondeat (B).
[15] similiter] quasi (B).
[16] Tunc] Omitted (B).
[17] Interim] et interim (B).

mentum; uerumptamen ille discipulus quem diligebat Ihesus uenit prior ad Monumentum, iuxta Euangelium: Currebant autem duo simul, et ille alius discipulus[1] precucurrit cicius Petro, et uenit prior ad monumentum; non tamen introiuit. Videntes Discipuli predicti[2] Sepulcrum uacuum, et uerbis Marie credente⟨s⟩ reuertant se ad chorum dicentes:[3]

Credendum est magis soli Marie ueraci quam Iudeorum turbe fallaci.

Tunc audita Christi Resurreccione, chorus presequatur alta uoce quasi gaudentes et exultantes sic dicentes:[4]

Scimus Christum surrexisse a mortuis uere; tu nobis, uictor rex, miserere.

Qua finita, executor officii incipiat *Te Deum laudamus*;[5] et sic recedant, scilicet Marie, Apostoli, et Angelus.[5]

The three veiled Marys, carrying pyxes for ointment boxes, open the play with a succession of touching laments in verse. As they draw near to the sepulchre they express their intention of anointing the body of Christ. The dialogue with the angel follows the usual course, except in that the angel's words *Venite et videte* are here appropriately uttered before the Marys are dismissed.[6] As the women leave the sepulchre, they meet Peter and John, to whom Mary Magdalen sings the lyrical first part of the sequence.[7] When the apostles ask the question *Dic nobis?* each of the Marys, in turn, makes a reply. The apostles now hasten to the sepulchre, and return bringing to the chorus their confirmation in the appropriate words *Credendum est*. Since they do not carry the grave-cloths, they necessarily omit the usual sentence *Cernitis, o socii*. The chorus closes the play by singing the last sentences of the sequence.

One observes that the entire text of *Victimæ paschali* is here employed with distinct dramatic success. The only incongruity is a slight one: the question *Dic nobis?* is responded to by each of the three Marys in turn, whereas the later declaration *Credendum est magis soli Mariæ* implies that only a single Mary has spoken. Aside from the sequence, the text is to a considerable extent original. We now see for the first time the stanzas of lament at the beginning of the play, and modified forms of one or two speeches at the sepulchre.[8] The costumes of the apostles are described in unique detail: their bare feet, the white tunic and palm of John, and the red tunic and keys of Peter.

[1] discipulus] discipulis (B).
[2] predicti] Omitted (B).
[3] dicentes] dicentes hoc modo (B).
[4] dicentes] dicant (B).
[5-5] Omitted (B).

[6] See above, p. 247.
[7] According to the text from Dublin MS Z.4.2.20, each of the three Marys sings a sentence.
[8] See below, p. 393.

III

Among the texts of the general type now under consideration a substantial number—all from the region of Germany—include not only the sequence *Victimæ paschali* but also the vernacular song of the congregation.[1] Since most of the dramatic features of such plays have already been exhibited in the preceding part of this chapter, our treatment of the succeeding examples need not be extensive.

A characteristic form of congregational participation is prescribed in an Augsburg service-book of the sixteenth century:[2]

ORDO SÉRVANDUS AD VISITANDUM SEPULCHRUM,

VT VOCANT, IN DIE SANCTO PASCHÆ

Peractis, vt dictum est, in choro Matutinis, et præcedentibus duobus ceroferarijs, cum solemnis processio ad Sepulchrum Domini tendit, cantatur iterum tertium et vltimum responsorium, et statio apud locum Sepulchri ab omnibus celebratur. Hic seruari solet cæremonia quædam in maioribus ecclesijs, vt piarum Mulierum, Angelorum, et Apostolorum qui circa Sepulchrum Domini versabantur, quædam fiat repræsentatio, eaque cæremonia et consuetudo, vbi fieri solet, retineatur. In persona Mulierum tunc a quibusdam hæc veteri ex more cantantur in choro:

> *Quis reuoluet nobis ab ostio lapidem quem tegere sanctum cernimus sepulchrum?*

Angeli vero in Sepulchro cantant sequenti modo:

> *Quem quæritis, o tremulæ mulieres, in hoc tumulo plorantes?*

Respondent Mulieres iterum in choro:

> *Iesum crucifixum Nazarenum quærimus.*

Rursus Angeli de Sepulchro cantant:

> *Non est hic quem quæritis, sed cito euntes nunciate discipulis eius et Petro quia surrexit Iesus.*

Iterum autem in persona Mulierum ex choro cantatur:

> *Ad monumentum venimus gementes, angelum Domini sedentem vidimus et dicentem quia surrexit Iesus.*

---

[1] One version in which *Christ ist erstanden* is sung after the *Te Deum* has been presented earlier in this chapter; see above, p. 340. Concerning this vernacular song see below, p. 636.

[2] *Ritus Ecclesiastici Augustensis Episcopatus*, Dillingen, 1580, pp. 593–8, previously reprinted by Milchsack, pp. 131–2; Lange, no. 170, pp. 108–10. In the copy in the British Museum, which I use, the page-numbers 595 and 596 are used twice. The speeches have music. Concerning the related *Depositio* and *Elevatio* see above, p. 172. For associated texts of the *Visitatio* see Notes, p. 645.

Chorus ita cantat:

> *Currebant duo simul, et ille alius discipulus præcucurrit citius Petro, et venit prior ad monumentum, alleluia.*

Sequitur cantus Apostolorum ante ingressum Sepulchri:

> *Cernitis, o socij, ecce lintheamina et sudarium, et corpus non est in sepulchro inuentum.*

Postremo chorus ter cantat, et subinde altius incipit hunc versum:

> *Surrexit Dominus de sepulchro, qui pro nobis pependit in ligno, alleluia.*

Sacerdos interim ad altare procedit, et thurificationem facit Venerabili Sacramento et Imagini Crucifixi, quæ in loco aliquo, vbi seruari alioquin solet, reponatur. Hinc cantat Chorus notam sequentiam:

> *Victimæ paschali,*

et cetera; et singulis eius versibus interponatur canticum Germanicum, quod etiam a populo celebriter decantatur:

> *Christ ist erstanden.*

Postremo a Choro decantatur *Te Deum laudamus.*

The noteworthy aspect of this play is the intertwining of *Victimæ paschali* and the vernacular song. After each verse of the sequence is sung a passage from *Christ ist erstanden.* This *mélange* is no part of the dramatic action itself, but merely a festive liturgical conclusion. Of some interest also is the censing of the Host and the *Imago Crucifixi* just before the singing of the Easter sequence.[1]

A less intrusive use of the German song and a more dramatic disposal of the sequence are shown in the following from the diocese of Passau:[2]

> Responsorium[3] repetatur, et fiat processio in monasterium, omnes portantes cereos accensos. Angelus[4] precedat sedeatque in dextera parte ad caput Sepulchri, coopertus stola candida. Ordinata statione et finito responsorio, cantores incipiant antiphonam, choro prosequente:
>
> > *Maria Magdalena et alia Maria ferebant diluculo aromata, Dominum querentes in monumento.*
>
> Interim duo vel tres cum totidem thuribulis, figuram Mulierum tenentes procedant ad Sepulchrum, et stantes cantant:
>
> > *Quis reuoluet nobis ab ostio lapidem quem tegere[5] sanctum cernimus[6] sepulchrum?*

---

[1] Concerning the use of the Host and *Imago Crucifixi* in dramatic ceremonies at the Easter sepulchre see above, pp. 113 sqq., 139.

[2] Melk, Stiftsbibliothek, MS 1671, Brev. Pataviense sæc. xv, fol. 510ᵛ–511ᵛ, previously edited by Lange, no. 183, pp. 114–6. For

associated versions of the *Visitatio* see Notes, p. 646.

[3] *Dum transisset.*

[4] Angelus] angelos (MS).

[5] tegere] tangere (MS).

[6] cernimus] cernitis (MS).

Angelus sedens in dextera parte Sepulchri respondeat:

Quem queritis, o tremule mulieres, in hoc tumulo | plorantes?

Mulieres:

Ihesum Nazarenum crucifixum querimus.

Angelus:

Non est hic quem queritis, sed cito euntes nuncciate discipulis eius et Petro quia surrexit Ihesus.

Et cum Angelus ceperit cantare *Sed cito euntes*, Mulieres thurificent Sepulchrum et festinanter redeant,[1] et versus chorum stantes cantant antiphonam:

Ad monumentum venimus gementes, angelum Domini sedentem vidimus et dicentem quia surrexit Ihesus.

Qua finita, chorus cantet:

Currebant duo simul, et ille alius discipulus precucurrit citius Petro, et uenit prior ad monumentum, alleluia.

Et duo quasi Petrus et Iohannes ⟨currant precurratque Iohannes⟩, sequente Petro, et veniant ad Monumentum et auferant lintheamina et sudarium, quibus involuta erat Ymago Domini, et vertentes se ad chorum ostendendo ea cantent antiphonam:

Cernitis, o socij, ecce lintheamina et sudarium, et corpus non est in sepulchro inventum.

Post hoc chorus cantet hunc versum:

Dic nobis, Maria, quid vidisti in via?

Tunc veniens vnus in medium loco Marie Magdalene cantet:

Sepulchrum Christi viuentis, et gloriam vidi resurgentis.

Versus:

Angelicos | testes, sudarium et vestes.

Versus:

Surrexit Christus, spes mea; precedet suos in Galilea.

Chorus:

Credendum est magis soli Marie veraci quam Iudeorum turbe fallaci.

Versus:

Scimus Christum surrexisse ex mortuis vere; tu nobis, victor rex, miserere.

Quo finito chorus incipiat *Te Deum laudamus*. Populus cantet *Christ ist erstanden*.

Since this version is, in most respects, identical with one considered earlier in this chapter,[2] it is necessary to remark here only that the singing of *Christ ist erstanden* after the *Te Deum*

---

[1] redeant] reddeant (MS).
[2] See the text from Kremsmünster MS 274 above, p. 337.

is really no part of the dramatic performance. This extreme detachment of the vernacular song from the action of the play is reduced somewhat in another version from the same diocese:[1]

VISITATIO SEPULCHRI

Fiat processio ad Sepulchrum. Omnes portant cereos accensos; et unus aptam vocem habens, acturus vocem Angeli, sedeat ad capud in dextra parte coopertus stola candida; et tres figuram Mulierum habentes cum tribus thuribulis cantent:

Maria Magdalena et altera Maria ferebant diluculo aromata, Dominum querentes in monumento.[2]

Angeli:

Quem queritis?[3]

Item Marie cantent:

Quis revolvet nobis ⟨ab ostio lapidem quem tegere sanctum cernimus sepul-chrum⟩?

Angeli:

Quem queritis, ⟨o tremulæ mulieres, in hoc tumulo plorantes?⟩

Marie cantent:

Jhesum Nazarenum ⟨crucifixum querimus⟩.

Angeli cantent:

Non est hic quem queritis, ⟨sed cito euntes nuntiate discipulis ejus et Petro quia surrexit Jesus.⟩

Cum Angeli ceperint cantare *Sed cito euntes,* Mulieres thurificent Sepul-chrum, et cito due redeant[4] in chorum cantantes:

Ad monumentum venimus ⟨gementes, angelum Domini sedentem vidimus et dicentem quia surrexit Jesus⟩.

Petrus et Johannes cantent:

Currebant duo simul, ⟨et ille alius discipulus præcucurrit citius Petro, et venit prior ad monumentum.⟩

Et currant versus Sepulchrum, Johanne precurrente, Petro sequente Venientes[5] ad monumentum auferant lintheamina et sudarium; ver-tentes se ad chorum ostendendo ea cantent antiphonam:

Cernitis, o socii, ecce lintheamina et sudarium, et corpus non est in sepulchro inventum.

Cantent versum:

Dic nobis, Maria, ⟨quid vidisti in via?⟩

[1] Herzogenburg, Stiftsbibl., MS 183, Brev. Pataviense sæc. xv, fol. 122^r–122^v, previously edited by Brooks, *New Texts,* pp. 487–8. Con-cerning associated texts see Notes, p. 650.
[2] monumento] monumentum (MS).
[3] Angeli . . . queritis] Inserted, no doubt, through a scribal error.
[4] redeant] reddant (MS).
[5] Venientes] venientibus (MS).

Maria versum:

Sepulchrum ⟨Christi viventis, et gloriam vidi resurgentis⟩.

Secunda versum:

Angelicos testes, ⟨sudarium et vestes.⟩|

Tertia versum:

Surrexit Christus, spes mea; ⟨præcedet suos in Galilæa.⟩

Apostoli:

Credendum est magis ⟨soli Mariæ veraci quam Judæorum turbæ fallaci⟩.

Versus:

Scimus Christum ⟨surrexisse a mortuis vere; tu nobis, victor rex, miserere⟩.
Populus: *Christ ist erstanden.* Sequitur *Te Deum laudamus.*

In this instance the song of the congregation is at least brought
into direct contact with the last utterances of those who participate in the dramatic action. The most arresting features of this
play, however, are associated with the scene of the two apostles.
In singing the antiphon *Currebant duo* they commit a mild
dramatic impropriety, but in addressing the question *Dic nobis?*
to Mary Magdalen and in singing the final sentences of the
sequence, they bring *Victimæ paschali* into the dramatic organism.
By this arrangement, however, the position of the sequence—
after the exhibiting of the *linteamina* by Peter and John—is made
to appear somewhat irrational. After their experience at the
tomb, the apostles scarcely need the testimony of *sola Maria
verax.* It is to be observed also that, in defiance of the opening
antiphon *Maria Magdalena,* the playwright has provided *three*
Marys, and that all three, rather than Mary Magdalen alone,
take part in the response to the apostles.

In a play from St Florian the singing of *Christ ist erstanden* is
followed by a special ceremonial:[1]

Post *Gloria Patri* responsorium[2] repetatur, et fiat processio ad monasterium, omnes portantes cereos accensos. Dyaconus qui legit ewangelium, uel alter qui aptam habet vocem, acturus officium Angeli precedat, sedeatque[3] in dextera parte ad caput, coopertus stola candida.
Ordinata stacione et finito responsorio, cantores incipiant antiphonam:

*Maria Magdalena et alia Maria ferebant diluculo aromata, Dominum
querentes in monumento,*

choro prosequente. Interim duo uel tres cum totidem thuribulis figuram

---

[1] St Florian, Stiftsbibl., MS XI.420,   22. For a similar version see Notes, p. 655.
Brev. Florianense anni 1482, fol. 319ʳ–319ᵛ,   [2] The third responsory *Dum transisset.*
previously edited by Lange, no. 193, pp.119–   [3] sedeatque] sedeantque (MS).

Mulierum tenentes procedant versus Sepulchrum, et stantes cantent antiphonam:

> *Quis reuoluit nobis ab hostio lapidem quem tegere[1] sanctum cernimus sepulchrum?*

Angelus sedens in dextera parte Sepulchri respondeat:[2]

> *Quem queritis, o tremule mulieres, in hoc tumulo gementes?*

Mulieres:

> *Ihesum Nazarenum crucifixum querimus.*

Angelus:

> *Non est hic quem queritis, sed cito euntes nuncciate discipulis eius et Petro quia surrexit Ihesus.*

Et cum ceperit cantare Angelus *Sed cito euntes,* Mulieres thurificent Sepulchrum, et festinanter redeant,[3] et versus chorum stantes cantent antiphonam:

> *Ad monumentum venimus gementes, angelum Domini sedentem[4] vidimus et dicentem quia surrexit Ihesus.*

Deinde chorus, uel duo, scilicet Petrus et Johannes, cantent antiphonam:

> *Currebant duo simul, et ille alius discipulus precucurrit cicius Petro, et venit prior ad monumentum, alleluia.*

Quo finito, Petrus et Iohannes aufferant lintheamina et sudarium, quibus involuta erat Ymago Domini, et vertant se ad chorum; ostendendo ea cantent antiphonam:

> *Cernitis, o socij, ecce lintheamina et sudarium, et corpus non est ⟨in sepulchro⟩ inventum.*

Post hoc chorus cantet hunc versum:

> *Dic nobis, Maria, quid vidisti ⟨in via⟩?|*

Tunc veniens in medium vnus loco Marie dicat versum:

> *Sepulchrum Christi viuentis, et gloriam vidi resurgentis.*

Iterum chorus:

> *Dic nobis, Maria, ⟨quid vidisti in via?⟩*

Maria:

> *Surrexit Christus, spes mea; precedet suos in Galilea.*

Chorus:

> *Credendum est magis soli Marie veraci quam Iudeorum turbe fallaci.*
> *Scimus Christum surrexisse ex mortuis vere; tu nobis, victor rex, miserere. Alleluia.*

Quo finito, populus cantet *Christ ist erstanden.* Postea incipiatur *Te Deum laudamus.* Quo finito, ascendant chorum cum antiphona *Christus resur-*

---

[1] tegere] tangere (MS).
[2] respondeat] respondeant (MS).
[3] redeant] reddeant (MS).
[4] sedentem] sedentes (MS).

gens.[1] Deinde cantores porrigant clero incensum dicentes tacita voce
Surrexit Christus. Clerus respondeat *Gaudeamus,* et inuicem se deosculentur.[2]

The censing, the giving of the kiss of peace, and the singing of
additional choral pieces contribute to this performance an
impressive and reverential conclusion. In the acting of the play
proper a considerable latitude is allowed, for the number of the
Marys may be either two or three, and *Currebant duo* may be
sung either by the chorus or by the two apostles.

Sometimes the singing of the congregation is found in the
very midst of the dramatic action, as in the following version
from Innsbruck:[3]

Visitacio Sepulchri

Mulieres:[4]

> *Quis reuoluet nobis ab hostio lapidem quem tegere sanctum cernimus sepul-*
> *chrum?*

Angelus:

> *Quem queritis, o tremule mulieres, in hoc tumulo gementes?*

Mulieres:

> *Ihesum Nazarenum crucifixum querimus.*

Angelus:

> *Non est hic quem queritis, sed cito euntes nunctiate discipulis eius et Petro*
> *quia surrexit Ihesus.*

Angelus:

> *Venite et videte locum vbi positus erat Dominus, alleluia, alleluia.*

Mulieres:

> *Ad monumentum venimus gementes, angelos[5] Domini sedentes uidimus et*
> *dicentes quia surrexit Ihesus.*

Chorus cantat:

> *Currebant duo simul, et ille alius discipulus precucurrit citius Petro, et venit*
> *prior ad monumentum, alleluia.*

Petrus et Iohannes:

> *Dicant nunc Iudei quomodo milites custodientes sepulchrum perdiderunt*

---

[1] For the text of this antiphon see above,
p. 246.

[2] Followed by the rubric: Quibus finitis et
finito *Te Deum laudamus,* sacerdos premittatur
versum *In resurrectione tua.*

[3] Innsbruck, Universitätsbibl., MS 610,
Brev. Œnipontanum sæc. xv, fol. 182ᵛ-183ʳ,
previously edited by Lange, no. 202, pp.
124-7. The text is preceded by the respon-

sory *Dum transisset.*

[4] Mulieres] Written twice (MS). The first
speech and its rubric were written twice. The
first writing of the speech is crossed out, but
not the first writing of *Mulieres.*

[5] angelos] angeles (MS). I leave uncor-
rected the inconsistency between the plural
of the speech and the singular *Angelus* of the
rubrics.

regem ⟨ad lapidis positionem⟩. Quare non seruabant petram iusticie? Aut sepultum reddant, aut resurgentem adorent, nobiscum dicentes.

Populus:

> *Crist ist erstanden.*

Item Petrus et Iohannes:

> *Cernitis, o socii, ecce lintheamina et sudarium, et corpus non est in sepulchro inventum, | alleluia.*

Chorus:

> *Surrexit enim sicut dixit Dominus; precedet vos in Galileam; ibi eum videbitis, alleluia, alleluia, alleluia.*

Item Petrus et Iohannes:

> *Dic nobis, Maria, quid uidisti in uia?*

Vna Maria:

> *Sepulchrum Christi viuentis, et gloriam uidi resurgentis.*

Secunda Maria:

> *Angelicos testes, sudarium et vestes.*

Tertia Maria:

> *Surrexit Christus, spes mea; precedet suos in Galilea.*

Chorus:

> *Credendum est ⟨magis⟩ soli Marie veraci quam Iudeorum turbe fallaci.*
> *Scimus Christum surrexisse ex mortuis vere; tu nobis, victor rex, miserere.*
> *Te Deum laudamus.*

According to the arrangement here, Peter and John, even before they have exhibited the grave-cloths, break forth with a taunt to the Jews, and this in turn leads directly into the congregational *Christ ist erstanden.* This procedure is so disturbing to the usual action of the play that one might be inclined to suspect the validity of the text before us.[1] A still more hearty participation of the people, however, appears in a *Visitatio* from Diessen:[2]

> Responsorium *Dum transisset* post *Gloria Patri* repetitur, et fiat cum responsorio processio ad Sepulchrum, et cantentur ibidem antiphone:
>
> > *Maria Magdalena ⟨et alia Maria ferebant diluculo aromata, Dominum quærentes in monumento⟩.*
>
> Mulieres:
>
> > *Quis reuoluet ⟨nobis ab ostio lapidem quem tegere sanctum cernimus sepulchrum⟩?*

---

[1] For an example of similarly intrusive singing by the *plebs* see the *Visitatio* from St Lambrecht below, p. 364.

[2] Munich, Staatsbibl., MS lat. 5545, Brev.

Diessense sæc. xv. fol. 21ʳ, previously edited by Brooks, *Neue Osterfeiern*, pp. 305–6. Concerning the related *Depositio* and *Elevatio* see below, p. 561.

Angeli:

Quem queritis?

et cetera. ⟨Chorus:⟩

Currebant duo ⟨simul, et ille alius discipulus præcucurrit citius Petro, et venit prior ad monumentum, alleluia⟩.

Deinde duo sacerdotes accedant ad Sepulchrum, et accipiant lintheum atque ostendendo cantent:

Cernitis, ⟨o socii, ecce lintheamina et sudarium, et corpus non est in sepulchro inventum, alleluia.⟩

Sequitur:

Surrexit enim ⟨sicut dixit Dominus, et præcedet vos in Galilæam, alleluia; ibi eum videbitis, alleluia, alleluia⟩.

Post hoc organista incipit:

Victime pascali ⟨laudes immolent Christiani⟩.

Completo versu, duo cantores eleuantes Ymaginem cantent:

Crist is erstanden.

Organista canit:

Agnus redemit ⟨oves, Christus innocens Patri reconciliavit peccatores⟩.

Chorus subiungat:

Mors et vita ⟨duello conflixere mirando; dux vitæ mortuus, regnat vivus⟩.

Populus cantet, cantore incipiente:

Alleluia, alleluia.

Organista:

Dic nobis, Maria, ⟨quid vidisti in via?⟩

Chorus:

Angelicos ⟨testes, sudarium et vestes⟩.

Populus:

Kirieleïson.

Organista:

Credendum ⟨est magis soli Mariæ veraci quam Judæorum turbæ fallaci⟩.

Chorus:

Scimus Christum ⟨surrexisse ex mortuis vere; tu nobis, victor rex, miserere⟩.

Populus:

Wär er nit erstanden, die welt di wär zergangen,

et cetera. Sequitur intrando per organistam *Te Deum laudamus,* cum quo redeunt ad chorum.[1]

The completeness of the speeches and the meagreness of the

---

[1] Followed immediately by this rubric: Quo finito, sequitur versiculus *In resurrectione tua, Christe, alleluia.* Ad Laudes.

rubrics in this text minimize one's hope of interpreting it correctly. It is clear, however, that after a verse of *Victimæ paschali*
by the organist, two cantors raise the *Imago Salvatoris*—which
was taken from the sepulchre at the *Elevatio* before Matins—and
sing the opening words of *Christ ist erstanden*.[1] Then the organist
and chorus respectively deliver the next two verses of the
sequence, which are followed by a congregational *Alleluia*. After
the dialogue beginning with *Dic nobis* has been said, and at the
end of the sequence, the congregation sing *Kyrie eleïson* and a
continuation of the vernacular *cantio* respectively. In this
ceremony the sequence is obviously detached from the dramatic
action and used as a purely liturgical conclusion.

IV

From the dramatic point of view, as we have seen, *Victimæ*
paschali is more effectual when used before, rather than after,
the scene of Peter and John.[2] This relatively infrequent arrangement is seen in a play from the monastery of St Lambrecht,
preserved in manuscripts of the sixteenth century:[3]

Ad processionem Sepulchri responsorium ad visitationem:[4]

> *Cum*[5] *transisset sabbatum, Maria Magdalena et Maria Jacobi et Salome*
> *emerunt aro|mata, vt venientes vngerent Jesum, alleluia, alleluia.* Versus:
> *Et valde mane vna sabathorum veniunt ad monumentum, orto iam sole.* Vt.[6]

Mulieres canunt:

> *Quis reuoluet nobis ab hostio lapidem | quem tegere sacrum cernimus sepul-*
> *chrum?*

Angelus respondet:

> *Quem queritis, o tremule mulieres, in hoc tumulo plorantes?*

Mulieres respondent:

> *Iesum Nazarenum crucifixum querimus.*

Angeli respondent:

> *Non est hic quem queritis, | sed cito euntes nunciate discipulis eius et Petro*
> *quia surrexit Iesus.*
> *Venite*[7] *et videte locum vbi positus erat Dominus, alleluia, alleluia.*

---

[1] Concerning the *Elevatio* from Diessen
see below, p. 561.

[2] See above, p. 338.

[3] Graz, Universitätsbibl., MS I.1459,
Process. monasterii Sancti Lamberti anni
1571, fol. 54ʳ–56ᵛ (A), previously edited by
Wonisch, pp. 16–7. I give the variants found
ibid., MS I.1537, Process. Sancti Lamberti
anni 1577, fol. 74ʳ–79ʳ (B), previously

edited by Wonisch, pp. 16–7. Both MSS
provide music. A seventeenth-century copy
of the latter MS is found *ibid.*, MS I.1551;
see Wonisch, p. 12.

[4] Ad processionem . . . visitationem] Ad
visitationem sepulchri responsorium (B).

[5] Cum] Dum (B).

[6] Vt] Vt ve. (B).

[7] Venite] Angeli respondent Venite (B).

Mulieres canunt:

Ad monumentum venimus gementes, angelos Domini se|dentes vidimus et dicentes quia surrexit Jesus.

Quo finito, conuentus canit:

Dic nobis, Maria, ⟨quid vidisti in via?⟩[1]

Prima persona:[2]

Sepulchrum Christi viuentis, ⟨et gloriam vidi resurgentis.⟩

Secunda persona:[2]

Angelicos testes, ⟨sudarium et vestes.⟩

Tertia persona:[2]

Surrexit Christus, spes ⟨mea; præcedet suos in Galilæa⟩.

Chorus:

Credendum est ⟨magis soli Mariæ veraci quam Judæorum turbæ fallaci⟩.
Scimus Christum surrexisse ⟨ex mortuis vere; tu nobis, victor rex, miserere⟩.

Iterum chorus can*it:*[3]

Currebant duo simul, et ille alius discipulus precucurrit[4] *citius Petro, et venit primus ad monumentum, alleluia.|*

Fratres:[5]

Cernitis, o socii, ecce lintheamina et sudarium, et corpus non est in sepulchro inuentum.

Antiphona finita, cantor incipit *Christ ist erstanden.* Chorus canit *Te Deum laudamus.*

Although the rubrics before us are not very generous, they disclose the careful composition of the piece in several particulars. In conformity with the processional responsory *Dum transisset,* for example, the number of the Marys is three; and the presence of more than one angel is recognized in the plurals of the speech *Ad monumentum venimus.* The dialogue from *Victimæ paschali,* however, is not directly united to the scene of the apostles, as it is in the following piece from Moosburg:[6]

Responsorium repetatur sollempni voce, et itur processionaliter ad Sepulchrum, cruce et candelis precedentibus; et statione facta in medio monasterio, Visitacio Sepulchri fiat in hunc modum. Duo canonici secundum nostram conswetudinem, vel tres secundum conswetudinem

---

[1] The speeches given incompletely in A, appear in full in B.

[2] persona] Maria (B).

[3] Iterum chorus canit] Iterum duo fratres Apostolorum Petri videlicet et Iohannis personas represensentantes et sepulchrum circuentes cappis induti canunt vt sequitur (B).

[4] precucurrit] precurrit (B).

[5] Fratres] Mulieres (A).

[6] Munich, Staatsbibl., MS lat. 9469, Brev. Mosburgense sæc. xv, fol. 59ʳ–59ᵛ, previously edited by Brooks, *Neue Osterfeiern,* pp. 307–8. The text is preceded by the responsory *Dum transisset.* The related *Depositio* and *Elevatio* are printed above, pp. 140–1.

aliorum, cum totidem thuribulis, induti vestibus quibus indui poterunt, vt rubeis casulis vel consimilibus, figuram sanctarum Mulierum tenentes; venientes a sacristia per ianuam prope altare Sancti Vdalrici procedant versus Sepulchrum, et stantes cantent:

> *Quis reuoluet ⟨nobis ab ostio lapidem quem tegere sanctum cernimus sepulchrum⟩?*

Deinde sint duo canonici pro Angelis deputati in dextera parte Sepulchri sedentes versus chorum decani, cooperti quasi stola[1] candida; querant a Mulieribus cantantes:

> *Quem queritis, o tremule ⟨mulieres, in hoc tumulo plorantes⟩?*

Mulieres:

> *Jhesum Nazarenum ⟨crucifixum quærimus⟩.*

Angeli:

> *Non est hic ⟨quem quæritis, sed cito euntes nuntiate discipulis ejus et Petro quia surrexit Jesus⟩.*

Quo finito, immediate subiungunt Angeli:

> *Venite et videte locum ⟨ubi positus erat Dominus, alleluia, alleluia⟩.*

Mulieres accedunt et thurificando Sepulchrum introspiciunt, et crucifixum non invenientes recedunt cantantes:

> *Ad monumentum venimus ⟨gementes, angelos Domini sedentes vidimus et dicentes quia surrexit Jesus⟩.*

Quibus duo pro Petro et Johanne deputati canonici dalmatica et subtili induti occurrant vt Apostoli. Venientes de latere ecclesie in quo situm est altare Sancti Johannis, transeundo gradus qui sunt|in ascensu chori prope altare Sancte Crucis cantent:

> *Dic nobis, Maria, ⟨quid vidisti in via?⟩*

Marie:

> *Sepulchrum Christi viuentis, ⟨et gloriam vidi resurgentis.⟩*

Apostoli:

> *Dic nobis, Maria, ⟨quid vidisti in via?⟩*

Marie:

> *Angelicos testes, ⟨sudarium et vestes.⟩*

Iterum Apostoli:

> *Dic nobis, Maria, ⟨quid vidisti in via?⟩*

Marie:

> *Surrexit Christus, spes mea; ⟨præcedet suos in Galilæa.⟩*

Chorus:

> *Credendum est magis ⟨soli Mariæ veraci quam Judæorum turbæ fallaci⟩.*

Et statim predicti duo Apostoli festinent ad Sepulchrum, precurratque

---

[1] stola] Before *a* a letter erased (MS).

Johannes, Petro sequenti et claudicanti.[1] Et interim eis currentibus chorus cantet antiphonam:

> Currebant duo simul, ⟨et ille alius discipulus præcucurrit citius Petro, et venit prior ad monumentum, alleluia.⟩

Veniantque ad Monumentum et auferant lintheamina et sudarium quibus involuta erat Ymago Domini, portantes ante altare Sancte Crucis, et vertentes se ad chorum ostendendo ea cantent:

> Cernitis, o socij, ⟨ecce lintheamina et sudarium, et corpus non est in sepulchro inventum, alleluia.⟩

Deinde chorus:

> Surrexit enim sicut dixit Dominus, ⟨et præcedet vos in Galilæam, alleluia; ibi eum videbitis, alleluia, alleluia.⟩

Populus: Christ ist erstanden;[2] vel obmittatur iste cantus vvlgaris vsque post Benedicamus post Matutinas Laudes, et imponatur statim Te Deum laudamus; et decantentur Laudes in eadem stacione in medio monasterio.

In this version the Marys, upon leaving the tomb, are made to meet the two apostles at the door of the choir, and to relate their experiences through the usual dialogue beginning Dic nobis. This conversation motivates the subsequent scene of Peter and John, which follows the course now familiar to us. The singing of the vernacular song at the end is optional.

A unique example of congregational singing is found in a relatively early play from the monastery of St Lambrecht:[3]

Interim autem, dum est circa finem tercie lectionis, distribuat custos singulas candelas singulis fratribus, et[4] diaconus reuestiat se stola candida, uadatque residere super lapidem iuxta Sepulchrum. Cum uero secundo tercium responsorium fuerit inceptum, candelis omnibus accensis quas habent in manibus, cantor processionem ordinet ita. Primo scolares cum pedagogo, deinde abbas, post illum seniores, dehinc iuniores et indocti; sed illi qui in personis sanctarum Feminarum uisitare debent Sepulchrum remaneant in choro et uelent capita sua humeralibus uel capitiis capparum quas habent in se. Reliquus uadat, ut predictum est, ad locum | Sepulchri conuentus, ibique silentio facit. Illi predicti tres remissa uoce canant:

> Quis reuoluet nobis ab hostio lapidem quem tegere sacrum cernimus sepulcrum?

---

[1] et claudicanti] et claudicant, partly erased (MS).

[2] erstanden] derstanden (MS).

[3] Graz, Universitätsbibl., MS II.798, Brev. monasterii Sancti Lamberti sæc. xii ex., fol. 52ʳ–53ʳ (A), with variants, except details of spelling, from ibid., MS II.193, Brev. Sancti Lamberti sæc. xiv. fol. 51ᵛ–52ʳ (B), and from ibid., MS III.722, Brev. Sancti Lamberti sæc. xiv, fol. 37ʳ–37ᵛ (C). Among the variants I do not indicate the length of the incipits of speeches. The texts from all three MSS have been previously edited by Wonisch, pp. 12–5. MS II.798 provides music for most of the speeches. In each MS the text is preceded by the responsory Dum transisset. For related versions of the Visitatio see Notes, p. 656. [4] et] Omitted (C).

Quibus respondeat leuita uice Angeli dicens:

Quem queritis, o tremule mulieres, in hoc tumulo plorantes?

Ad hec illi:

Iesum Nazarenum crucifixum querimus.

Quibus ille subiungat:

Non est hic quem queritis, sed cito euntes nunciate discipulis eius et Petro quia surrexit Iesvs.

Post hec illis accedentibus surgat et subleuet cortinam et Sepulchrum patefaciat, dicatque ad illos:

Venite et uidete locum ubi positus erat Dominus, alleluia, alleluia.

Qui uenientes inclinatis capitibus considerare debent intra Sepulchrum, et tollentes inde filacterium quo inuoluta[1] Crux fuerat et sudarium quod fuerat super Crucis caput, ac inde recedentes stent ante proximum altare et uersi contra conuentum canant[2] alta uoce:

Ad monumentum uenimus gementes, angelum Domini sedentem uidimus et dicentem quia surrexit Deus.

Quo dicto, totus conventu⟨s⟩ concinat dicens:

Dic nobis, Maria, quid uidisti in uia?

Et unus ex illis tribus qui uisitabant Sepulchrum dicat clara uoce:

Sepulchrum Christi uiuentis, et gloriam uidi resurgentis.

Alter uero dicat:

Angelicos testes, sudarium et uestes.

Et[3] tercius subiungat:

Surrexit Christus, spes mea; precedet suos in Galilea.

Post hec totus conuentus concinat ita:[4]

Credendum est magis soli Marie ueraci, quam ⟨Judæorum turbæ fallaci⟩.

Versus:

Scimus Christum ⟨surrexisse ex mortuis vere; tu autem, victor rex, miserere⟩.

Tunc incipiat ipsa plebs istum clamorem:[5]

Giengen dreie urovven[6] ce uronem grabe.|

Interim uero, dum plebs clamorem istum concrepat, cantor ordinet duos, unum senem et alterum iuuenem, qui, postquam finitus fuerit clamor populi, ueniant ad Sepulchrum, iuuenis primo et subsistat, senex uero subsequens prospiciat in Monumentum, et alter cum eo. Et illis factum incipientibus imponat cantor antiphonam:

Currebant duo simul, ⟨et ille alius discipulus præcucurrit citius Petro, et venit primus ad monumentum, alleluia.⟩

---

[1] inuoluta] inuolutum (B.C).
[2] canant] et canant (C).
[3] Et] Omitted (C).
[4] ita] Omitted (C).

[5] istum clamorem] clamorem istum (C).
[6] Giengen dreie urovven] Es giengen drei vravven (C).

Qua[1] finita, ueniant illi tres supradicti ante aram proximam subleuantes linteamina, ut ab omnibus uideantur, ita concinentes:

> *Cernitis, o socii, ecce linteamina et sudarium, et corpus non est in sepulchro inuentum.*

Atque mox extollant Crucem in altum sonora uoce conclamantes ita:

> *Surrexit Dominus de sepulchro.*

Quam simul cum eis concinat totus conuentus. Post hanc incipiat abbas uel prior *Te Deum laudamus*; et hunc ymnum canendo reuertantur in chorum, plebe conclamante[2] *Christ ist erstanden.*

The singing by the *plebs* here has the effect of dividing the action into two parts, the first ending with the cry *Giengen dreie urovven ce uronem grabe*,[3] and the second, with the usual *Christ ist erstanden.* The first of these vernacular passages appears in no other version of the *Visitatio*, and seems not to be well known, though a stanza of somewhat similar beginning is found in some texts of *Christ ist erstanden.*[4]

The chief dramatic interest of the present play, however, arises not from the participation of the congregation, but from the realism disclosed by the rubrics. The angel sits upon a *lapis* placed outside the sepulchre, and raises a curtain to reveal the interior of the burial-place. The grave-cloths are a fillet, or bandeau, in which the shaft and arms of the cross were wrapped, and a sudary which was placed over the head of the cross. The persons chosen to act the parts of the apostles are of different ages: an old man to represent Peter, and a youth for the part of John. It is to be observed, however, that after the visit of the apostles to the tomb it is not they, but the Marys, who display the grave-cloths and elevate the cross. This re-entering of the women into the action at the close gives to the composition a certain effect of unity.

A more original treatment of the sequence *Victimæ paschali* than any that we have observed hitherto is seen in the following from St Florian:[5]

[1] Qua] Omitted (B.C).

[2] conclamante] clamante (C).

[3] For a version beginning *Es giengen* see below, p. 657, note 1.

[4] See W. Bäumker, *Das katholische deutsche Kirchenlied*, iv, Freiburg, 1911, p. 317; Brooks, *Rheinau*, p. 234; Wonisch, p. 18. For other songs of similar *incipits* see L. Erk and F. M. Böhme, *Deutscher Liederhort*, iii, Leipzig, 1894, pp. 678, 682.

[5] St Florian, Stiftsbibl., MS XI.434, Liber Benedictionum Florianensis sæc. xv, fol. 165ʳ–170ʳ, previously edited by Lange, no. 203, pp. 127–9; Franz, *St Florian*, pp. 195–6; Schiffmann, *Drama*, pp. 12–4; Mühlbacher, pp. 387–90. The MS provides music. For the *Depositio* and *Elevatio* see below, p. 557. In regard to associated versions of the *Visitatio* see Notes, p. 657.

In uisitatione Sepulchri, iterato tertio responsorio, fit sollempnis processio cum luminibus | ad Sepulchrum. Responsorium:

> *Dvm transisset sabbatum, Maria Magdalena et Maria Iacobi et Salomee emerunt aromata, ut uenientes ungerent Ihesum, alleluia, alleluia.*

Sint parati sex in ornatu cuilibet competenti: vnus in persona Angeli, duo in figura Apostolorum, tres in specie Ma|rie. Stacione autem facta circa Sepulchrum, procedat Angelus ad caput Sepulchri, cantante choro antiphonam:

> *Sedit angelus ad sepulchrum Domini stola claritatis coopertus; uidentes eum mulieres nimio terrore perterrite astiterunt a longe.*[1]

Deinde procedunt Apostoli ad locum aptum, cantante choro:|

> *Virtute magna reddebant apostoli testimonium resurrectionis Ihesu Christi Domini nostri, alleluia, alleluia.*[2]

Tandem Marie tres procedunt cum thuribulis, cantante choro responsorium:

> *Maria Magdalene et altera Maria ibant diluculo ad monumen|tum. Ihesum quem queritis, non est hic, surrexit sicut locutus est; precedet uos in Galyleam; ibi eum uidebitis, alleluia, alleluia.*[3]

Quo finito, Marie uenientes ad Sepulchrum, stantes contra Angelum cantent antyphonam:

> *Qvis reuoluet nobis lapidem | ab hostio monumenti?*

Angelus respondit antiphonam:

> *Nolite expauescere; Ihesum queritis Nazarenum crucifixum; surrexit, non est hic.*[4]

Hic discooperiatur Sepulchrum:

> *Ecce locus ubi posuerunt eum; sed ite, dicite discipulis eius et Petro quia | precedet uos in Galyleam; ibi eum uidebitis sicut dixit uobis.*[5]

Tunc Marie redeuntes a Sepulchro ad Apostolos antiphonam:

> *Ad monumentum uenimus gementes, angelum Domini sedentem uidimus et dicentem*[6] *quia surrexit Ihesus.*

Tunc querent Apostoli cantando antiphonam:

> *Dic nobis, Maria, quid uidisti in uia?*

Respondent Marie antiphonam:

> *En angeli | aspectum uidimus,*
> *et responsum eius audiuimus,*
> *nam testatur Dominum uidere;*
> *sic oportet te, Symon, credere.*

---

[1] For this Easter processional antiphon see Hartker, pp. 231–2, and above, pp. 226, 227.
[2] The first part of an Easter responsory; see Hartker, pp. 234–5.
[3] Concerning this responsory see below, pp. 600–1.
[4] Mark xvi, 6.
[5] Mark xvi, 6–7.
[6] vidimus et dicentem] Written in lower margin (MS).

⟨Apostoli:⟩

> *Dic nobis, Maria, quid uidisti in uia?*

⟨Mariæ:⟩

> *Galyleam omnes adibitis;*
> *ibi Ihesum uiuum uidebitis.*
> *Quem post mortem ui|uum non uidimus,*
> *nos ibidem uisuros credimus.*

Iterum Apostoli:

> *Dic nobis, Maria, ⟨quid vidisti in via?⟩*

vt prius. Respondet versum:

> *Sepulchrum Christi uiuentis, et gloriam uidi resurgentis.*

Versus:

> *Angelicos testes, sudarium et uestes.*

Versus:

> *Surrexit Christus, spes mea; precedet suos in Galyleam.*

Tunc chorus subsequitur: |

> *Credendum est magis soli Marie uera⟨ci quam Judæorum turbæ fallaci⟩.*

Post Apostoli ibunt ad Sepulchrum, choro cantante antiphonam:

> *Currebant duo simul, et ille alius discipulus precucurrit cicius Petro, et venit prior ad monumentum, alleluia.*[1]

Sub qua antiphona uenientes ad Sepulchrum et diligenter intuentes, sudarium ex eo recipiunt et ad locum eminenciorem deferunt, et populo ostendentes cantent:

> *Cernitis, o socii, ecce lintheamina et sudarium, et corpus non est in sepulchro inuentum.* |

Respondet chorus:

> *Christus resurgens ex mor⟨tuis iam non moritur; mors illi ultra non dominabitur, quod enim vivit, vivit Deo, alleluia, alleluia⟩.*

Et populus: *Crist ist erstanden.* Sicque redibit clerus ad chorum.[2]

As the angel, three Marys, and two apostles proceed to their appointed places, according to this text, the chorus sings three narrative passages—all chosen appropriately, except the last, which mentions only *two* Marys. In the dialogue at the sepulchre the traditional dialogue *Quem quæritis* is supplanted by a single speech of the angel, taken from the Gospel of Mark. As the Marys withdraw from the tomb, they are interrogated by the apostles three times, in the usual way. The first two responses of the Marys are original compositions in the form of stanzas

---

[1] In its place on the page, only the first three words of this 'antiphon' are written. A slightly later hand, however, has written the complete text upon an attached slip.

[2] Followed by the rubric: In die sancto ad Aspersionem: *Vidi aquam egredientem.*

of four ten-syllable lines rhyming a a b b. The aptness of these speeches appears particularly in the direct address to Simon Peter in the first of them.[1] The third response, consisting of the usual sentences from *Victimæ paschali*, is appropriately spoken by Mary Magdalen alone.[2] The performance closes with the singing of *Christ ist erstanden*, no mention being made of the *Te Deum*

[1] For a similar address see below, p. 386.

[2] That a single Mary speaks here is indicated by the rubrics in St Florian MS XI.398, printed below, p. 657.

CHAPTER XIII

THE VISIT TO THE SEPULCHRE
THIRD STAGE

THE final stage in the development of the *Visitatio Sepulchri* is reached when the action includes a scene of which the centre is the risen Christ. Presumably this striking addition to the Easter play was not made before the latter part of the twelfth century. None of the manuscripts containing it is older than that; and, had the figure of Christ been generally familiar in Church plays before the period 1160–3, probably it would have been among the *vanitates et spectacula* denounced by Gerhoh of Reichersberg in his *De Investigatione Antichristi*.[1]

For a scene representing Christ's presence in close association with the visit of the Marys to the tomb the Gospels provide ample matter. St Matthew reports that as the two Marys were leaving the sepulchre they were met by Jesus, and were addressed in the words *Avete! . . . Nolite timere; ite, nuntiate fratribus meis ut eant in Galilæam; ibi me videbunt*.[2] According to St Mark, Christ appeared first of all to Mary Magdalen, early on the morning of the Resurrection.[3] In the twentieth chapter of the Gospel of St John we are told that this latter meeting occurred after Peter and John had left the sepulchre, and of the details we have the following circumstantial account:[4]

11. Maria autem stabat ad monumentum foris, plorans. Dum ergo fleret, inclinavit se, et prospexit in monumentum.

12. Et vidit duos angelos in albis sedentes, unum ad caput, et unum ad pedes, ubi positum fuerat corpus Jesu.

13. Dicunt ei illi: Mulier, quid ploras? Dicit eis: Quia tulerunt Dominum meum, et nescio ubi posuerunt eum.

14. Hæc cum dixisset, conversa est retrorsum, et vidit Jesum stantem; et non sciebat quia Jesus est.

15. Dicit ei Jesus: Mulier, quid ploras? quem quæris? Illa existimans quia hortulanus esset, dicit ei: Domine, si tu sustulisti eum, dicito mihi ubi posuisti eum, et ego eum tollam.

16. Dicit ei Jesus: Maria. Conversa illa dicit ei: Rabboni (quod dicitur, Magister).

---

[1] See Meyer, pp. 58, 88, 89; Chambers, ii, 98–9. For the relevant passage from Gerhoh of Reichersberg see Appendix C.

[2] Matt. xxviii, 9–10.

[3] See Mark xvi, 9: *Surgens autem mane, prima sabbati, apparuit primo Mariæ Magdalenæ, de qua ejecerat septem dæmonia.*

[4] John xx, 11–8.

17. Dicit ei Jesus: Noli me tangere, nondum enim ascendi ad Patrem meum; vade autem ad fratres meos, et dic eis: Ascendo ad Patrem meum, et Patrem vestrum, Deum meum, et Deum vestrum.

18. Venit Maria Magdalene annuntians discipulis: Quia vidi Dominum, et hæc dixit mihi.

It is this narrative which serves as the basis for the new dramatic development, and since the Gospel not only recounts the incident, but also records even the words of the participants, the playwright had the relatively simple task of adapting sentences of direct discourse to his own purpose.[1]

I

The simplest form of play containing the new scene is that from which the apostles, Peter and John, are absent, and in which the meeting of Christ and Mary Magdalen is simply an extension of the usual scene, or scenes, between the Marys and the angel, as in the following composition embodying the tradition of the cathedral of Rouen during the thirteenth, fourteenth, and fifteenth centuries:[2]

Finito tertio responsorio, Officium Sepulchri ita celebretur. Tres dyaconi canonici,[3] induti dalmaticis, et amictus habentes super capita sua ad similitudinem Mulierum, uascula tenentes in manibus, veniant per medium chori, et versus Se|pulchrum properantes uultibus submissis dicant pariter hunc versum:

Quis reuoluet nobis lapidem ⟨ab ostio monumenti⟩?

Hoc finito, quidam puer, quasi Angelus, indutus alba, et tenens spicam in manu, ante Sepulchrum dicat:

Quem queritis in sepulchro, ⟨o Christicolæ?⟩

Marie respondeant:

Ihesum Nazarenum crucifixum, ⟨o cœlicola.⟩

Tunc Angelus dicat:

Non est hic, surrexit enim ⟨sicut dixit; venite et videte locum ubi positus fuerat, et euntes dicite discipulis ejus et Petro quia surrexit⟩,

et locum digito ostendens. Hoc facto, Angelus citissime discedat, et

---

[1] For bibliography bearing upon the evolution of the scene see Notes, p. 659.

[2] Rouen, Bibl. de la Ville, MS 384 (*olim* Y.110), Ordin. Rothomagense sæc. xiv, fol. 82ᵛ–83ʳ, described by Lange, no. 220, pp. 155–7, and previously edited by Gasté, pp. 58–62. The play is preceded by the responsory *Dum transisset*. In my text I complete the speeches under the guidance of

the *Visitatio* in Paris, Bibl. Nat., MS lat. 904, Grad. Rothomagense sæc. xiii, fol. 101ᵛ–102ᵛ, printed in Notes, p. 659, where further bibliography is given. For the related *Depositio* see above, p. 135.

[3] canonici] After this word is a reference to a fifteenth-century marginal entry *de maiori sede* (MS).

duo presbyteri de maiori sede in tunicis, intus Sepulchrum residentes, dicant:

Mulier, quid ploras?

Medius trium Mulierum respondeat, ita dicens:

Quia tulerunt Dominum meum, ⟨et nescio ubi posuerunt eum.⟩

Duo residentes dicant:

Quem queritis, mulieres, ⟨viventem cum mortuis? Non est hic, sed surrexit. Recordamini qualiter locutus est vobis, dum adhuc in Galilæa esset, vobis dicens quia oportet filium hominis pati et crucifigi, et die tertia resurgere.⟩

Marie osculentur locum; postea exeant de Sepulchro. Interim quidam sacerdos canonicus in persona Domini, albatus cum stola, tenens crucem obuians eis in sinistro cornu altaris dicat:

Mulier, quid ploras? Quem queris?

Medius Mulierum dicat:

Domine, si tu sustulisti eum, dicito ⟨mihi, et ego eum tollam⟩.

Sacerdos crucem illi ostendens dicat:

Maria!

Quod cum audierit, pedibus eius citissime sese offerat, et alta uoce dicat:

Rabboni!

Sacerdos innuens manu dicat:

Noli me tangere, ⟨nondum enim ascendi ad Patrem meum; vade autem ad fratres meos, et dic eis: Ascendo ad Patrem meum, et Patrem vestrum, Deum meum, et Deum vestrum.⟩

Hoc finito, sacerdos in dextro cornu altaris iterum appareat, et illis transeuntibus ante altare dicat:

Auete, nolite timere; ⟨ite, nuntiate fratribus meis ut eant in Galilæam; ibi me videbunt.⟩

Hoc finito, se abscondat, et Mulieres, hoc audito, lete inclinent ad altare, et conuerse ad chorum hunc versum cantent:

Alleluia, resurrexit Dominus, alleluia.

Hoc finito, archiepiscopus vel sacerdos ante altare cum turibulo incip*iat* alte *Te Deum laudamus*, et sine neu*mpna* finiatur.[1]

Here the action begins with the familiar scene at the tomb between an angel, sitting outside the door, and the three Marys. The only noteworthy detail is the exceptionally appropriate position of the exhortation *Venite et videte*.[2] The single angel presently withdraws from the stage, making way for a second scene, within the sepulchre, between two angels and the Marys.

---

[1] For what follows see Notes, p. 661.   [2] See above, p. 247.

The angels first address Mary Magdalen, and she alone replies,[1] in accordance with the narrative of St John quoted above. For the second speech of the angels (*Quem quæritis, mulieres*), addressed to all three Marys, is used a passage from the Gospel of St Luke.[2] The Marys now leave the sepulchre, and, as we must infer, Mary Magdalen withdraws somewhat from her companions and approaches the main altar, at the *left* end of which appears a canon impersonating Christ. With him Mary Magdalen carries on the dialogue provided by the Gospel of John.[3] After his last speech to her, Christ withdraws behind the altar, it would seem, and at the *right* end of it appears again, this time to all three Marys, with the words *Avete, nolite timere*, recorded in the narrative of St Matthew.[4] Christ now leaves the stage, and the Marys turn towards the chorus, singing *Resurrexit Dominus*.

The free adaptation of Biblical passages here results in a smooth succession of scenes, and avoids dramatic improprieties. The recalling of the other two Marys into the action, after the scene between Christ and Mary Magdalen, discloses the playwright's desire to use all the appropriate matter present in the Bible, and gives a certain organic completeness to the performance.

Somewhat similar to the Rouen *Visitatio* in general scope, but very different in verbal content, is the following play of the fourteenth century from Mont-St-Michel:[5]

Ad Matutinum Pasche ante *Te Deum laudamus* frater qui erit Deus habebit habitum de alba tincta sicut in sanguine, cum dyademate et barba, nudis pedibus. Cum cruce transiet per chorum | in fine vltimi responsorii, et reuertatur in reuestiarium. Tres qui erunt Mulieres, post vltimum responsorium, vestiti de dalmaticis albis, habentes amicta[6] super capita ad modum matronarum, defferentes alabastra, venientes per inferiorem partem chori versus altare cantent:

Quis reuoluet ⟨nobis lapidem ab ostio monumenti⟩?

---

[1] In the text from the Rouen Gradual of the thirteenth century (Paris MS 904) the rubric runs *Una ex illis, loco Marie Magdalene*. See below, p. 660.
[2] Luke xxiv, 5–7.
[3] In the Rouen Gradual (Paris MS 904) the rubrics direct, inappropriately, that in the dialogue with Christ all the Marys take part in unison. See below, p. 660.
[4] Matt. xxviii, 9–10.

[5] Avranches, Bibl. de la Ville, MS 214, Ordin. Monasterii Sancti Michaëlis sæc. xiv, pp. 236–8. This text, now first printed, has been described by P. Gout, *Le Mont-Saint-Michel*, i, Paris, 1910, pp. 318–20. For a rubric concerning the text, and for the related *Depositio* and *Elevatio* see below, p. 575. For further bibliography see Notes, p. 662.
[6] amicta] admicta (MS).

Ille qui erit Angelus erit super altare inductus de capa alba, tenens palmam in manu et habens coronam in capite; cantet post:

 Venite, venite; ⟨*nolite timere vos.*

 Quem quæritis in sepulchro, o Christicolæ?⟩

Mulieres dicant:

 Ihesum Nazarenum ⟨*crucifixum, o cælicola*⟩.

Angelus iterum dicat:

 Non est hic, ⟨*surrexit enim sicut dixit; venite et videte locum ubi positus fuerat, et euntes dicite discipulis ejus et Petro quia surrexit.*⟩

Et dum dicitur *Venite et videte,* appropinquant se de Sepulcro et dicant:

 Iam cernere.

Duo fratres in Sepulcro, qui erunt duo Angeli inducti de capis rubeis, dicant:

 Mulieres,[1] *quid* ⟨*ploratis*⟩?

Mulieres dicant post:

 Quia tulerunt Dominum ⟨*meum, et nescio ubi posuerunt eum*⟩.

Angeli de Sepulcro dicant:

 Quid queritis ⟨*viventem cum mortuis? Non est hic, surrexit enim sicut dixit; venite et videte locum ubi positus fuerat, et euntes dicite discipulis ejus et Petro quia surrexit.*⟩

Et cum dixerint *Venite et videte,* intrant Mulieres in Sepulcro, et cum dixerint *Euntes,* exeant; et eant Mulieres circa altare et dicant:

 In sepulchro.

Deus veniat per aliam viam et ponat se ante altare; et cum reuerse fuerint[2] Mulieres ad altare, dicat Deus ad primam Mulierem:

 Mulier, ⟨*quid ploras? Quem quæris?*⟩

Mulier respondeat:

 Domine, si tu ⟨*sustulisti eum, dicito mihi, et ego eum tollam*⟩.

Deus dicat:

 Maria!

Mulier dicat:

 Rabb⟨*o*⟩*ni!*

Et prosternet se in terram sicut si vellet eum tangere, et maneat sic. Deinde Deus dicat:

 Noli me tangere, ⟨*nondum enim ascendi ad Patrem meum; vade autem ad fratres meos, et dic eis: Ascendo ad Patrem meum, et Patrem vestrum, Deum meum, et Deum vestrum.*⟩

---

[1] Mulieres] The plural here, and in the succeeding rubric, is probably, but not certainly, a scribal error.

[2] fuerint] The word is obscurely corrected in the MS, and the reading is doubtful.

Et dicat benedicionem. Et post benedicionem reuertatur in reuestiarium. Prima Mulier surgens dicat:

Christus viuens.

Secunda Mulier dicat:

Laniatur.

Tercia Mulier dicat:

Ergo clausa.

Angelus de altari dicat:

Resurrexit.

Angeli de Sepul|cro dicant:

Alleluia, resurrexit.

Deinde Mulieres reuertentes vnde primo venerint dicant:

Alleluia, resurrexit.

Et post dicatur *Te Deum laudamus.*[1]

This play, like that from Rouen, provides two scenes for the
Marys at the tomb: one with the single angel outside, and a
second with two angels within. Unusual, moreover, are several
of the speeches—the *Venite, venite* of the angel, and the sentences
of the Marys beginning *Iam cernere* and *In sepulchro.*[2] During
her dialogue with Christ, Mary Magdalen probably stands
apart from the other women; but after Christ has spoken his
benediction, and has withdrawn, she and the other Marys and
the angels, in succession, declare the Resurrection.

II

Most versions of the *Visitatio* which contain the scene between
Christ and Mary Magdalen are less simple in content than
those from Rouen and Mont-St-Michel. The greater part of
them, for example, incur the difficulties of dramatic arrangement entailed by the presence of the sequence *Victimæ paschali.*[3]
The first part of this poem is a lyrical expression of rejoicing;
hence it can precede only incongruously the inevitable lament
at the opening of the scene between Christ and Mary. In the
latter part of the poem, on the other hand, are mentioned
certain indirect evidences of the Resurrection, the *sudarium et
vestes* and the *angelicos testes*; hence if it is placed *after* Christ's

---

[1] Followed by the rubric *Infra octauam Pasche.*

[2] These last two, and also the three speeches of the Marys announcing the Resurrection (*Christus vivens, Laniatur,* and *Ergo clausa*), I have not found elsewhere.

[3] These difficulties are energetically discussed by Meyer, pp. 88–91. For the text of *Victimæ paschali* see above, p. 273.

actual appearance upon the stage, these secondary evidences produce a certain effect of anticlimax. In the forms of the *Visitatio* that follow, then, we may expect to observe not a few incongruities, some of them, no doubt, unconscious, and others the result of unsuccessful attempts to solve a small, but persistent, problem of composition.

A relatively harmless use of *Victimæ paschali*, along with a considerable amount of literary embellishment, may be seen in a fourteenth-century version of the play from the monastery of Engelberg:[1]

Antiphona. Omnes tres:[2]

> *Maria Magdalena et Maria Iacobi et Salomee sabbato quidem siluerunt secundum mandatum, alleluia. Cum autem transisset sabbatum, ementes aromata venerunt vngere Iesum, alleluia, alleluia.*

Antiphona. Sola:

> *Hev! nobis internas mentes　　qvanti pulsant gemitus*
> *Pro nostro consolatore,　　quo priuamur misere,*
> *Quem crudelis Iudeorum　　morti dedit populus.* |

Antiphona. Sola:

> *Iam percusso ceu pastore,　　oues errant misere;*
> *Sic magistro discedente,[3]　　turbantur discipuli,*
> *Atque nos, absente eo,　　dolor tenet nimius.[4]*

Antiphona. Sola, scilicet Maria Magdalena:

> *Sed eamus et ad eius　　properemus tumulum;*
> *Si dileximus viuentem,　　diligamus mortuum.*

Omnes tres:

> *Qvis reuoluet nobis ab hostio[5] lapidem quem tegere sanctum cernimus sepulchrum?*

Angeli:

> *Qvem queritis, o tremulæ mulieres, in hoc tumulo gementes?* |

Antiphona. Omnes tres:

> *Iesum Nazarenum crucifixum, o celicole.[6]*

---

[1] Engelberg, Stiftsbibl., MS 314 (*olim* I. 4/25), Collectio cantilenarum sæc. xiv, fol. 75ᵛ–78ᵛ, previously edited by Mone, *Schauspiele*, i, 23–7, and by Lange, no. 206, pp. 136–40. For other editions see Lange, p. 15. The text has musical notation on four lines. For observations on the text and the MS see Notes, p. 662.

[2] Apparently the text as originally written down had, for rubrics, merely the word *antiphona*, entered, or indicated, before a considerable proportion of the speeches. The other words of the rubrics are written, by a somewhat later hand, either in the margins or in blank spaces left at the ends of speeches. In some instances the reviser may have intended that the addition should precede the word *antiphona*.

[3] magistro discedente] Corrected by expunction from *magistero discendente* (MS).

[4] Here follows the word *Surrexit*, written in red, without music, as if it were part of the succeeding rubric.

[5] hostio] Corrected from *ostio* by a later hand (MS).

[6] celicole] celicola (MS).

Antiphona. Angeli:
Non est hic quem queritis, sed cito euntes dicite discipulis eius et Petro quia surrexit Ihesus.

Antiphona. Angeli alta voce:
Venite et videte locum vbi positus erat Dominus, alleluia, alleluia.

Antiphona. Omnes tres alta voce:
Surrexit Dominus de sepulchro, qui pro nobis pependit in ligno, alleluia.

Antiphona. Omnes tres:
Ad monumentum venimus gementes, angelum Domini sedentem vidimus et dicentem | quia surrexit Ihesus.

Antiphona. Omnes tres:
> *En angeli aspectum vidimus,*
> *et responsum eius audiuimus,*
> *qui testatur Dominum viuere;*
> *sic oportet te, Symon, credere.*

Antiphona. Maria Magdalena:
> *Cvm venissem vngere mortuum,*
> *monumentum inveni vacuum.*
> *Heu! nescio recte discernere*
> *vbi possum magistrum querere.*

Antiphona. Item Maria Magdalena:
> *Dolor crescit,[1] tremunt precordia*
> *de magistri | pii absencia,*
> *qui saluauit me plenam viciis,*
> *pulsis a me septem demoniis.*

Antiphona. Item Maria Magdalena:
> *En lapis est vere depositus,*
> *qui fuerat cum signo positus.*
> *Munierat locum militibus;*
> *locus vacat, illis absentibus.*

Antiphona. Dominica persona:
Mvlier, quid ploras? Quem queris?

Antiphona. Maria Magdalena:
Domine, si tu sustulisti eum, dicito michi vbi posuisti eum,[2] et ego eum tollam, alleluia, alleluia. |

Dominica persona:
Maria! Maria! Maria!

Maria:
Rabbi![3]

---

[1] crescit] cressit (MS).
[2] eum] Followed by *dicito*, crossed out (MS).
[3] Rabbi] In the lower margin a later hand adds *quod dicitur magister*.

Item Dominica persona:

Noli me tangere, nondum enim ascendi ad Patrem meum, alleluia, alleluia.
    Prima quidem suffragia
    stola tulit carnalia
    exhibendo communia
    se per nature munia.

Maria:
    Sancte Deus!

Dominica persona:
    Hec priori dissimilis,
    hec est incorruptibilis,
    que dum fuit passibilis,
    iam non erit solubilis. |

Maria Magdalena:
    Sancte fortis!

Dominica persona·
    Ergo noli me tangere,
    nec vltra velis plangere,
    que⟨m⟩ mox in puro sydere
    cernes ad Patrem scandere.

Maria Magdalena:
    Sancte et inmortalis, miserere nobis!

Dominica persona:
    Nam ignaros[1] *huius rei*
    fratres certos reddes mei;
    in Galyleam, dic, vt eant,
    et me viuentem videant.

Chorus:
    Victime paschali laudes.[2]

The play opens with a narrative prose passage adapted from the Gospels, spoken by the three Marys in unison.[3] After this each Mary in turn utters a lament in verses of fifteen syllables which now appear for the first time in this survey, but which will be seen frequently in the pages to follow. At the close of the usual scene at the sepulchre, the three women report the incident first in prose, and in four lines of ten-syllable iambic verse in which Simon Peter is addressed directly. Then follow three stanzas of lament from Mary Magdalen, which appropriately introduce the scene between her and Christ. This is

[1] ignaros] ignoras (MS).
[2] The last three words have no musical notation; and following them the last line on the page is left blank. At the top of fol. 79ʳ is the rubric *Tropus super primam lectionem de Natiuitate Domini.*
[3] See Luke xxiii, 56; Mark xvi, 1.

considerably more elaborate than the parallel scenes in the plays from Rouen and Mont-St-Michel. To the usual dialogue is added a succession of octosyllabic four-line stanzas in which Christ poetically amplifies the meaning of *Noli me tangere*; and after the first three of these Mary exclaims, in turn, *Sancte Deus*, *Sancte fortis* and *Sancte et immortalis*, thus reflecting the influence of the *Improperia* in the Adoration of the Cross of Good Friday.[1] The play appears to close, somewhat abruptly, with the singing of *Victimæ paschali* by the chorus. If the text before us is incomplete, the subsequent action may, possibly, be inferred from the play from Rheinau, considered below.[2]

To the metrical embellishments in the Engelberg play a few striking additions are made in a composition of the fourteenth century from the cathedral of Cividale:[3]

⟨Prima Maria:

> *Heu! nobis internas mentes   quanti pulsant gemitus*
> *Pro nostro consolatore,   quo privamur miseræ;*
> *Quem crudelis Judæorum   morti dedit populus.*

Secunda Maria:

> *Jam percusso ceu⟩ pastore,   oues er⟨r⟩ant misere;*
> *Sic magistro discedente,   turbantur discipuli,*
> *Atque nos, absente eo,   dolor tenet nimius.*

Dicat tunc tertia Maria:

> *Sed eamus et ad eius   properemus tumulum;*
> *Si dileximus uiuentem,   diligamus mortuum.*

Omnes tres Marie tunc simul dicant hunc versum stantes:

> *Qvis reuoluet nobis ab hostio lapidem quem tegere sacrum cernimus sepulchrum?*

Tunc respondet Angelus, et dicat:

> *Qvem queritis, o tremule mulieres, in hoc tumulo plorantes?*

Omnes Marie respondent simul:

> *Iesum Nazarenum crucifi|xum querimus.*[4]

---

[1] See above, pp. 118–20.
[2] See p. 385.
[3] Cividale, Reale Museo Archeologico, MS CI, Process. Cividalense sæc. xiv, fol. 77ʳ–79ᵛ, previously edited by Coussemaker, pp. 298–306, and reprinted from him by Milchsack, pp. 66–81; Lange, *Programm*, pp. 22–5; Lange, no. 207, pp. 136–40. The text of Lange is reprinted by Bartholomaeis, pp. 523–4. The music accompanying the text is published by Coussemaker. In regard to other matters relating to this text see Notes, p. 663.
[4] crucifixum querimus] crucifisum queritis (MS).

Statim Angelus dicat et hunc versum:

> *Nolite metuere*
> *uel ledi terrore.*
> *Scio quia queritis*
> *Iesum hic sepultum,*
> *cuius uos intenditis*
> *uenerari cultum.*
> *Iam surrexit, hic non est;*
> *ut non loquar multum,*
> *michi si non creditis,*
> *uidete sepulcrum.*

Angelus sequendo dicat hunc versum:

> *Venite et uidete locum ubi positus erat Dominus, alleluya, alleluya.*

Tunc omnes Marie vadant ad Sepulcrum et thurificent illud, et reuertantur ad locum suum; et tunc Angelus dicat hunc versum:

> *Ite ad discipulos,*
> *eisque nunciate*
> *quod Dominus a mortuis*
> *surrexit; festinate!*
> *In Galy|leam ibitis*
> *cum gaudio et pace;*
> *ibi eum uidebitis,*
> *nolite dubitare.*

Tunc omnes Marie stantes in loco suo simul dicant:

> *Ad monumentum uenimus gementes, angelum Domini sedentem uidimus et dicentem quia surrexit Yhesus.*

Tunc Magdalena se reuertatur uersus ortum Christi et dicat hunc versum:

> *Cvm uenissem ungere Dominum,*
> *monumentum inueni uacuum;*
> *et nescio recte discernere*
> *ubi possim magistrum querere.*

Statim dicat hunc versum ipsa Maria:

> *En lapis est uere depositus,*
> *qui fuerat cum signo positus; |*
> *comiserat locum militibus;*
> *locus uacat, eis absentibus.*

Statim dicat Maria:

> *Dolor crescit, tremunt precordia*
> *de magistri pij absentia,*
> *qui saluauit me plenam uicijs,*
> *pulsis a me septem demoniis.*

Yhesus admirans respondit ei dicendo:

> *Mvlier, quid ploras?*

Maria respondit ei dicens:

> *Quia tulerunt Dominum meum, et nescio ubi posuerunt eum. Domine, si tu sustulisti eum, dicito michi ubi posuisti eum, et ego | eum tollam.*

Ihesus dicit statim:

> *Maria!*

Maria currendo ad Yhesum dicit:

> *Raboni!*

Tunc Jesus[1] dicit:

> *O Maria, noli me tangere,*
> *sed fratribus nuntia propere:*
> *Ascendo ad Patrem meum,*
> *Deum meum, et uestrum Deum.*

Tunc Maria revertitur se ad locum suum, et dicat:

> *Vere uidi Dominum uiuere,*
> *nec dimisit me pedes tangere.*
> *Discipulos oportet credere,*
> *quod ad Patrem uelit ascendere.*

Tunc dicit chorus:

> *Dic nobis, Maria, quid uidisti in uia?* |

⟨Tunc Maria dicat hunc versum:⟩

> *Sepulchrum Christi uiuentis, et gloriam uidi resurgentis;*
> *Angelicos testes, sudarium et uestes.*
> *Surrexit Christus, spes mea; precedet uos in Galylea.*

Chorus cantorum moueat se uersus chorum dicens:[2]

> *Credendum est magis soli Marie ueraci quam Iudeorum turbe fallaci.*
> *Scimus Christum surrexisse a mortuis uere; tu nobis, uictor rex, miserere.*
> *Allelvia.*

Tunc exeant chorum.[3]

The laments with which this piece opens are similar to those in the play from Engelberg. The scene of the Marys at the sepulchre, however, shows significant elaboration, in that the traditional *Non est hic* of the angel is developed into verses of a goliardic structure, and the command *Ite, nuntiate* appears in still another metrical form.[4] Noteworthy also is the skill whereby the usual *Venite et videte* is motivated by the preceding sentence

---

[1] Jesus] Maria (MS).
[2] dicens] Reading uncertain.
[3] The reading of the last two words is uncertain. The text ends on the third line from the bottom of the page, the last two lines being blank.
[4] See Meyer, pp. 110, 116.

Michi si non creditis, videte sepulchrum—'If you doubt my word, you may believe the testimony of your own eyes!' The scene between Christ and Mary Magdalen is introduced by her lament in three stanzas of ten-syllable lines, after which the dialogue between the two is carried through somewhat more briefly than in the Engelberg play, though it includes a versifying of the prose speech *Noli me tangere*. Mary's announcement to the chorus also takes the form of four rhyming lines of ten syllables, which provide a transition to the dialogue from *Victimæ paschali*, but accentuate a certain ineptitude in general arrangement. After her declaration that she has actually seen the risen Christ, her enumeration of indirect evidences is, perhaps, somewhat anticlimactic. As a whole, however, the play shows unusual dramatic deftness and literary finish.

In interpreting the play from Cividale we may, if we wish, assume that in addressing to Mary Magdalen the question *Dic nobis?* the chorus represents the disciples; but this intention is not made explicit. For a definite indication of such an arrangement—and for several other novelties—we turn to the *Visitatio* which we owe to the reforming zeal of Katherine of Sutton, abbess of the nunnery of Barking, near London, from 1363 to 1376:[1]

Quibis peractis,[2] procedant tres sorores a Domina Abbatissa preᵣlecte, et nigris vestibus in capella Beate Marie Magdalene exute, nitidissimis superpellicijs induantur, niueis velis a Domina Abbatissa capitibus earum superpositis. Sic igitur preparate et in manibus ampullas tenentes argenteas dicant *Confiteor* ad abbatissam; et ab ea absolute, in loco statuto cum candelabris consistant. Tunc illa que speciem pretendit Marie Magdalene canat hunc versum:

Quondam Dei.[3]

Quo finito, secunda que Mariam Iacobi prefigurat alterum respondeat versum:

Appropinquans ergo sola.

Tercia Maria vicem optinens Salomee tercium canat versum:

Licet mihi vobiscum ire.

[1] Oxford, Univ. Coll., MS 169, Ordin. Berkingense sæc. xv, pp. 121–4, previously edited by Young, *Harrowing of Hell*, pp. 929–31; Tolhurst, i, 108–9. See also Tolhurst, ii, 378–9, and my plate x. For the related *Depositio* and *Elevatio* see above, pp. 164 sqq.

[2] The text printed here is immediately preceded in the MS by the *Elevatio* printed above, pp. 165–6.

[3] This and the succeeding two *versus* I have not found in the liturgy. They are not in the index to Hartker.

Post hec chorum incedentes flebili uoce et submissa hos pariter canant versus:

> *Heu! nobis internas men|tes   ⟨quanti pulsant gemitus*
> *Pro nostro consolatore,   quo privamur miseræ;*
> *Quem crudelis Judæorum   morti dedit populus⟩.*

Hijs versibus finitis, Magdalena sola dicat hunc versum:

> *Heu! misere, ⟨cur contigit*
> *videre mortem Salvatoris?⟩*

Jacobi respondeat:

> *Heu! consolacio nostra,*
> *⟨ut quid mortem sustinuit!⟩*

Salome:

> *Heu! redempcio Israel,*
> *⟨ut quid taliter agere voluit!⟩*

Quartum uero uersum omnes simul concinant, scilicet:

> *Jam iam, ecce, ⟨jam properemus ad tumulum,*
> *unguentes dilecti corpus sanctissimum.⟩*

Tunc Marie exeuntes a choro simul dicant:

> *Eya! Quis reuoluet ⟨nobis lapidem ab ostio monumenti⟩?*

Cum autem uenerint ad Sepulcrum, clericus alba stola indutus sedeat ante Sepulcrum, illius Angeli gerens figuram qui ab ostio monumenti lapidem reuoluit et super eum sedit, qui dicat illis:

> *Quem queritis in sepulcro, o Cristicole?*

Respondeant Mulieres:

> *Ihesum Nazarenum querimus.*

Angelus uero subinferat:

> *Non est hic, surrexit ⟨sicut prædixerat; ite, nuntiate quia surrexit de sepulchro.*
> *Venite et videte locum ubi positus erat Dominus, alleluia, alleluia⟩.*

Cumque dixerit *Venite et videte,* ingrediantur Sepulcrum et deosculentur locum vbi positus erat Crucifixus. Maria uero Magdalene interim accipiat sudarium quod fuerat super caput eius, et secum deferat. Tunc alius clericus in specie alterius Angeli in Sepulcro residens dicat ad Magdalenam:

> *Mulier, quid ploras?*

Illa autem subiungat:

> *Quia tulerunt Dominum meum, ⟨et nescio ubi posuerunt eum.⟩*

Deinde duo Angeli simul concinentes dicant Mulieribus:

> *Quid queritis viuentem cum mortuis?*

et cetera. Tunc ille de Resur⟨r⟩excione Domini adhuc dubitantes plangendo di*c*ant ad inuicem:
> *Heu, dolor,*[1]

et cetera. Postea Maria Magdalene suspirando concinat:[2]
> *Te suspiro,*[3]

et cetera. Tunc in sinistra parte altaris appareat Persona, dicens illi:
> *Mulier, quid ploras? Quem queris?*

Illa uero putans eum esse ortolanum respondeat:
> *Domine, si tu sustulisti eum,*

et cetera. Persona subiungat:
> *Maria!*

Tunc illa agnoscens eum pedibus eius prosternatur dicens:
> *Raboni!*

Persona | autem se subtrahens dicat:
> *Noli me tangere,*

et cetera. Cum Persona disparuerit, Maria gaudium suum consociabus communicet uoce letabunda hos concinendo versus:
> *Gratulari et letari,*[4]

et cetera. Quibus finitis, Persona in dextera parte altaris tribus simul occurrat Mulieribus dicens:
> *Auete, nolite timere,*

et cetera. Tunc ille humi prostrate teneant pedes eius et deosculentur. Quo facto, alternis modulacionibus hos versus decantent, Maria Magdalene incipiente:
> *Ihesus ille Nazarenus,*

et cetera. Finitis hijs versibus, tunc Marie stantes super gradus ante altare uertentes se ad populum canant hoc re*sponsum*:
> *Alleluia, surrexit Dominus de sepulcro,*

choro eis respondente. Finitis hijs, sacerdotes et clerici in figuram Discipulorum Christi procedant dicentes:
> *O gens dira.*

Tunc vnus illorum accedat et di*c*at Marie Magdalene:
> *Dic*[5] *nobis, Maria,*

et cetera. Illa autem respondeat:
> *Sepulcrum Christi ⟨viventis, et gloriam vidi resurgentis⟩.*
> *Angelicos testes, ⟨sudarium et vestes.⟩*

---

[1] See the version from Fleury below, p. 394.
[2] concinat] concinant (MS).
[3] This speech I have not found elsewhere.
[4] This speech, and the ones below beginning *Ihesus ille Nazarenus* and *O gens dira*, I have not found elsewhere.
[5] Dic] dixit (MS).

Digito indicet locum vbi Angelus sedebat, et sudarium prebeat illis ad deosculandum, hunc adicientes[1] versum:

Surrexit Christus, spes nostra; ⟨*præcedet suos in Galilæa.*⟩

Tunc subiunga⟨n⟩tur a Discipulis et a choro hij ultimi versus:

Credendum est ⟨*magis soli Mariæ veraci quam Judæorum turbæ fallaci*⟩,

et

Scimus Christum ⟨*surrexisse a mortuis vere; tu nobis, victor rex, miserere*⟩.

Postea incipiat Magdalena *Christus resurgens,* clero et choro pariter succinente. Hijs itaque peractis, solenniter decantetur a sacerdote incipiente ymnus *Te Deum laudamus.* Et interim predicti[2] sacerdotes in capellam proprijs vestibus reinduentes cum candelabris per chorum transeuntes orandi gratia Sepulcrum adeant, et ibi breuem orationem faciant. Tunc redeant in stacionem suam usque abbatissa | eas iubeat exire ad quiescendum.[3]

A particularly arresting feature of the Barking play is the impersonation of the Marys, not by the usual clerics, but by nuns. After these women have been costumed by the abbess herself, they make confession to her, receive absolution, and sing, in turn, three passages which do not appear in other versions of the *Visitatio.* The action proper begins as the Marys enter the choir singing stanzas of lament which we have already seen in other forms of the play. The first scene is the familiar one between the three women and one angel seated upon the stone beside the door of the sepulchre. Then, after the Marys have entered the tomb, Mary Magdalen takes up the sudary, and engages in a brief dialogue with a second angel. Still unconvinced of the Resurrection, she proceeds with her lament until Christ appears to her at the left side of the altar. After the usual dialogue between these two, Christ withdraws. As Mary Magdalen is reporting the incident to her companions, Christ re-appears at the right side of the altar, and speaks to all three women in a scene similar to one which we have already observed in the play from Rouen.[4] After Christ's second withdrawal, occurs a dialogue between the Marys and the clergy, in which the latter specifically represent, though they do not appear actually to impersonate, the disciples (*in figuram Discipulorum Christi*).[5] One of the clerics converses with Mary Magdalen in the usual form beginning with *Dic nobis*, and she

---

[1] adicientes] Possibly *adiciens* was originally intended.

[2] predicti] predicte (MS).

[3] Followed by the rubric *In Laudibus.*

[4] See above, p. 371.

[5] As to the representing of the disciples by the clergy, or chorus, see above, p. 290, and below, p. 401.

tes. Hijs ūsib; simus. magdalena sola dicat hūc ū̄u. heu
miser. Jacobi respondeat. Jeu consolacio mā. Salome
heu redimpm̄ israel. Q.uartū ū ūsū omis simul conduct
6. Jam iam ec̄c. Tunc marie exeuntes a choro: simul dicāt
Esa qnis reuoluet. Cum autē uenint ad sepulcrū. dic̄
alla stola induc̄. sedeat aūt sepulcrū illū angli generē
significātī qn ab ostio monumenti lapidem reuolūt.
et sup eum sedit. am dicat illis. Quē queritis ī sepulcro
o cristicole. Respondeant muliere̅s. Jhm nazarenū quen
m̄? anglē ū submiserat. non est hic surrexit. Cūq; dixit
venite et videte. ingrediant sepulcrū et deosculēt lo
cū ubi positus erat cruafixus. mana ū magdalene
nimi accipiat sudarū quod fuit sup caput ei? et secū
deferat. Tunc alius clerus in spe altius angeli ī sepul
cro residens: dicat ad magdalenā. a mulier qd ploras
illa aū subiungat. Q̄a tulerūt dn̄m meū. deinde duo
anglī simul cōnanentes dicant mulieribz. Q̄d queri
tis uiuente nī mortus et c̄. Tūc ille de resurrecōne cō
adhuc dubitantes: plangendo diit adinuic̄. Heu c̄
lor et c̄. pea maria magdalene suspirando cōnanant
te suspiro et c̄. Tūc in sinistra pte altaris appareat p
sona dicens illi. a mulier qd ploras. q̄m queris. illa ū
putans eū esse ortolanū respondeat. Dn̄e si tu sustu
listi eū et c̄. psona subiungat. maria. Tūc illa agnos
cens eum pedibz eius psternat dicēs raboni. psona

makes appropriate gestures and offers the *sudarium* to be kissed. The action closes with the antiphon *Christus resurgens*, sung by Mary Magdalen and the chorus. Apart from its unusual features of impersonation and dramatic action, the play is noteworthy for the considerable number of its speeches not found in other plays.[1]

III

Along with the dialogue from the sequence *Victimæ paschali* a good many versions of the play in the stage now before us contain also the familiar scene in which Peter and John visit the sepulchre, return rejoicing over the Resurrection and bringing, usually, the grave-cloths as evidence. It is obvious that as an accompaniment of the scene of Christ and Mary Magdalen the dramatic incident of Peter and John causes difficulties of arrangement similar to those mentioned in relation to this incident in the preceding chapter.[2] These appear in some measure, for example, even in the following highly meritorious play from the monastery of Rheinau:[3]

Quo[4] imposito, vii fratres exeunt: vnus diaconus, qui uestitus alba dalmatica Angelum Domini ad Sepulchrvm ueniendo lapidemque remouendo et super eum sedendo imitatur; tres sub sanctarum Mulierum persona cappis indute capita humeralibus cooperiunt; vnus alba casula indutus Dominicam Personam imitatur; reliqui duo cappis induti Apostolos imitantur, et in minori choro duarum Mulierum aduentum prestolantur. Sic autem fit ipsa uisitatio. In primis fit processio conuentus ad altare Sancte Crucis. Antiphona:

> *Maria Magdalena ⟨et alia Maria ferebant diluculo aromata, Dominum quærentes in monumento⟩.*

Qua finita, tres Mulieres figurantes prime ad Sepulcrvm procedentes singule singulos versus humili uoce decantant. Prima, *versum*:

> *Heu! nobis internas mentes   quanti pulsant gemitus*
> *Pro nostro consolatore,   quo priuamur misere,*
> *Quem crudelis Iudeorum   morti dedit populus.*

---

[1] See particularly the following *incipits:* *Quondam Dei; Appropinquans sola; Licet mihi vobiscum ire; Te suspiro; Gratulari et lætari; Jesus ille Nazarenus* ; and *O gens dira.*

[2] See above, p. 336; Meyer, pp. 88–91.

[3] Zurich, Zentralbibl., Rheinau MS XVIII, Lectionarium Rhenoviense sæc. xi–xiv, pp. 282–3 (sæc. xiii), previously edited by Brooks, *Easter Plays*, pp. 192–6. The speeches have musical notation. For a simpler version of the *Visitatio* containing both the scene of Christ and Mary and that of Peter and John see Notes, p. 664.

[4] In the margin is written: *Responsorium Dum transisset sabbatum.*

Secunda, *versum*:

> *Iam percusso cev pastore,   oues errant misere;*
> *Sic magistro discedente,   turbantur discipuli,*
> *Atque nos, absente eo,   dolor tenet nimius.*

Tercia, Marie Magdalene personam exprimens, *versum*:

> *Sed eamus et ad eius   properemus tumulum;*
> *Si dileximus viuentem,   diligamus mortuum.*

Deinde omnes tres:

> *Quis reuoluet nobis lapidem ab ostio monumenti?*

Hinc Angelus super lapidem Monumenti sedens hiis uerbis eas affatur:

> *Quem queritis in sepulcro, o Cristicole?*

Ille respondent:

> *Ihesum Nazarenum crucifixum, o celicola.*

Angelus:

> *Non est hic, surrexit sicut predixerat; ite, nunciate quia surrexit de sepulcro.*

Et eleuans pallam Monumenti ostendit eis dicens:

> *Venite et uidete locum ubi positus erat Dominus, alleluia, alleluia.*

Deinde, thurificato Sepulcro, aspiciunt intro, et redeuntes cantant antiphona⟨m⟩:[1]

> *Ad monumentum uenimus gementes, angelum Domini sedentem uidimus et dicentem quia surrexit Ihesus.*

Et conuerse ad Petrvm cantant versum:

> *En angeli aspectum vidimus,*
> *et responsum eius audiuimus,*
> *qui testatur Dominum viuere;*
> *sic oportet te, Symon, credere.*

Iterum redit Maria Magdalena ad Sepulcrvm querendo, et hos uersus cantando:

> Versus: *Cum uenissem vngere mortuum,*
> *monumentum inueni uacuum.*
> *Heu! nescio recte discernere*
> *ubi possim magistrum querere.*

> Versus: *Dolor crescit, tremunt precordia*
> *de magistri pii absentia,*
> *qui saluauit me plenam uiciis,*
> *pulsis a me septem demoniis.*

> Versus: *En lapis est uere depositus,*
> *qui fuerat cum signo positus.*
> *Munierat locum militibus;*
> *locus uacat, illis absentibus.*

---

[1] A mark over *antiphonam* refers to the following entry in the margin: *Hic euanescit angelus.*

Cui sic querenti Dominica Persona casula circumamicta qui moris ut
est dyaconi infra Quadragesimam, ei se manifestans interrogat dicens:

Mulier, quid ploras? Quem queris?

Illa respondit:

*Domine, si tu sustulisti eum, dicito michi ubi posuisti eum, et ego eum
tollam, alleluia, alleluia.*

Dominica Persona:

Maria! Maria! Maria!

Respondet:

Rabbi, quod dicitur magister.

Hec cantando currens procidit ad pedes eius et nititur eum tangere.
Ipse uero prohibet manu ne tangat eum dicens:

Noli me tangere, nondum enim ascendi ad Patrem meum, alleluia, alleluia.

Et infert versum:

*Prima quidem suffragia
stola tulit carnalia
exhibendo communia
se per nature munia.*

Quo finito, Maria procidendo ad pedes eius cantat:

Sancte Deus!

Dominica Persona:

*Hec priori dissimilis,
hec est incorruptibilis,
que dum fuit passibilis,
iam non erit solubilis.*

Maria secundo | ad pedes eius procidendo repetit:

Sancte fortis![1]

Dominus, *versum*:

*Ergo noli me tangere,
nec ultra uelis plangere,
quem mox in puro sydere
cernes ad Patrem scandere.*

Maria tertio repetit:

Sancte immortalis, miserere nobis!

Dominus:

Nunc[2] *ignaros huius rei
fratres certos reddes mei;
Galileam, dic, ut eant,
et me viuentem uideant.*

---

[1] fortis] Crossed out (MS).   [2] Nunc] Num (MS).

Hiis dictis, euanescit Dominus. Maria autem redeat a Sepulcro usque ad chorum cantando:

> *Victime paschali ⟨laudes immolent Christiani⟩.*
> *Agnus ⟨redemit oves; Christus innocens Patri reconciliavit peccatores⟩.*
> *Mors et uita ⟨duello conflixere mirando; dux vitæ mortuus, regnat vivus⟩.*

Chorus interrog*at*:

> *Dic nobis, Maria, ⟨quid vidisti in via?⟩*

Maria respondit:

> *Sepulchrum Christi uiuentis, ⟨et gloriam vidi resurgentis.⟩*
> *Angelicos testes, ⟨sudarium et vestes.⟩*
> *Surrexit Christus, ⟨spes mea; præcedet suos in Galilæa.⟩*

Hiis auditis, Apostoli Petrus et Iohannes festinant ad Sepulcrvm, iuniore seniorem precurrente; cantant hos uersus:[1]

> *Ihesu, nostra redemptio,*
> *⟨amor et desiderium,*
> *Deus, creator omnium,*
> *homo in fine temporum,⟩*
>
> *Que te uicit ⟨clementia,*
> *ut ferres nostra crimina*
> *crudelem mortem patiens,*
> *ut nos a morte tolleres⟩?*
>
> *Ipsa te cogat ⟨pietas,*
> *ut mala nostra superes*
> *parcendo et voti compotes*
> *nos tuo vultu saties⟩.*

Quibus finitis, chorus imponit antiphonam:

> *Currebant duo simul, et ille ⟨alius discipulus præcucurrit citius Petro, et venit prior ad monumentum, alleluia⟩.*

Interim Iohanne foris remanente, Petrus in Monumentum intrat, tollens inde sudarium. Hec illis ⟨a⟩gentibus, tres superueniunt Mulieres Sepulcrvm thurificantes simul inde cum Apostolis rediture. In ipso autem reditu omnes hee persone cantant versum:

> *Dicant nunc Iudei quomodo milites custodientes sepulcrum perdiderunt regem ad lapidis positionem. Quare non seruabant petram iusticie? Aut sepultum reddant, aut resurgentem adorent, nobiscum dicentes.*

Quousque ad gradus peruemant, chorus respond*et*:

> *Quod enim viuit, ⟨vivit Deo, alleluia, alleluia.⟩*

Illi autem uersa facie in chorum imponunt antiphonam:

> *Surrexit enim sicut ⟨dixit Dominus; ecce præcedet vos in Galilæam, alleluia; ibi eum videbitis, alleluia, alleluia⟩.*

---

[1] For the complete text of this hymn see below, p. 641.

Chorus:

> Credendum est magis ⟨soli Mariæ veraci quam Judæorum turbæ fallaci⟩.

Illi iterum imponunt:

> Scimus Christum surrexisse ⟨a mortuis vere⟩.

Chorus:

> Tu nobis, uictor ⟨rex, miserere⟩.

Cantor imponit Te Deum laudamus. Post hec benedicitur populus a custode.[1]

The action of the play begins with the approach of the Marys to the sepulchre, singing stanzas of lament with which we are now familiar. After the usual dialogue at the tomb, the three women carry their report to the disciples, singing a special stanza addressed to Peter. Then follows the scene between Christ and Mary Magdalen, in the admirable form which we have already seen in the play from Engelberg. After the withdrawal of Christ, Mary very appropriately sings the lyrical part of Victimæ paschali, and enters upon the familiar dialogue with the chorus. Inspired by what they hear, Peter and John hasten to the sepulchre singing three stanzas of the hymn Jesu, nostra redemptio. When Peter comes forth from the tomb bearing the sudary, the three Marys join the two apostles in singing a number of liturgical pieces antiphonally with the chorus.

The general arrangement and fluency of the action in this play are highly praiseworthy. The placing of the scene of Peter and John after that between Christ and Mary Magdalen reverses the Scriptural order of events, but entails no serious dramatic improprieties. The arrangement whereby Peter and John set out for the sepulchre directly after Mary Magdalen's disclosures to the chorus gives to the action a certain agreeable animation.[2] One is surprised to observe in so careful a composition the incongruity, all too frequent in other plays, between the mention of two Marys in the introductory antiphon and the actual appearance of three upon the stage.

Generally similar to the Rheinau play, but unique in some of its literary details, is the following composition from the neighbouring monastery of Einsiedeln:[3]

---

[1] Followed by the rubric Laudes.
[2] For a similar arrangement see the plays from Dublin and Moosburg above, pp. 350, 363.
[3] Einsiedeln, Stiftsbibl., MS 300, Lib. resp. Einsidlensis sæc. xii–xiii, pp. 93–4, previously

edited by Mone, Schauspiele, i, 15–9, and by Lange, no. 209, pp. 140–6. For references to other editions and reprints see Lange, p. 16; and for a later reprinting of Mone's text see Davidson, pp. 33–9. What precedes the present text in the MS is totally irrelevant. A

In Resvrrectione Domini

Ad uisitandam dominicam sepulturam, una de Mulieribus cantet sola:

Hev! nobis internas mentes   quanti pulsant gemitus
Pro nostro consolatore,   quo priuamur misere,
Quem crudelis Iudeorum   morti dedit populus.

Altera item sola:

Jam percusso ceu pastore,   oues errant misere;
Sic magistro decedente,   turbantur discipuli,
Atque nos, eo absente,   dolor tenet nimius.

Maria Magdalena:

Sed eamus et ad eius   properemus tumulum;
Si dileximus uiuentem,   diligamus mortuum.

Simul cantent:

Quis reuoluet nobis lapidem ab hostio monumenti?

Angelus:

Quem uos quem flentes?

Mulieres:

Nos Ihesum Christum.

Item Angelus:

Non est hic, uere.

Mulieres reuertentes cantent ad chorum;

Ad monumentum uenimus gementes, angelum Domini sedentem uidimus et
dicentem quia surrexit Ihesus.

Mulieres uertentes se ad personam Petri Apostoli omnes cantent:

En angeli aspectum uidimus,
et responsum eius audiuimus,
qui testatur Dominum uiuere;
sic oportet te, Symon, credere.

Maria Magdalena sola cantet hos tres versus:

Cum uenissem ungere mortuum,
monumentum inueni uacuum.
Heu! nescio locum discernere
ubi possim magistrum querere.

Dolor crescit, tremunt precordia
de magistri pii absentia,
qui sanauit me plenam uiciis,
pulsis a me septem demoniis.

photographic facsimile from p. 93 of the   Leipzig and Vienna, 1910, between pp. 70
manuscript is provided by F. Vogt and M.   and 71.
Koch, *Geschichte der deutschen Litteratur*, i,

En lapis est uere depositus,
qui fuerat in signum | positus.
Munierant locum militibus;
locus uacat, illis absentibus.

Chorvs:

Vna sabbati ⟨Maria Magdalena venit mane ad monumentum, et vidit
lapidem sublatum a monumento⟩.

Mulieres recurrentes iterum ad sepulturam nichil dicant; et Maria
Magdalena querendo circumquaque cantet:

Victime paschali, usque *Dic nobis.*

Dominica Persona subito Marie Magdalene apparens dicat:

Mulier, quid ploras? Quem queris?

Maria respondeat:

Domine, si tu sustulisti eum, dicito michi ubi posuisti eum, et ego eum
tollam, alleluia, alleluia.

Dominica Persona item ad eam:

Maria! Maria! Maria!

Illa procidens dicat:

Rabbi! quod dicitur magister.

Dominus ab ea paululum[1] diuertens dicat:

Noli me tangere, nondum enim ascendi ad Patrem meum, alleluia, alleluia.

Dominica Persona stans cantet:

Prima quidem suffragia
stola tulit carnalia
exhibendo conmunia
se per nature munia.

Maria adorans in terra cantet:

Sancte Deus!

Dominica Persona:

Hec priori dissimilis,
hec est incorruptibilis,
que dum fuit passibilis,
iam non erit solubilis.

Maria eodem modo quo prius:

Sancte fortis!

Dominus iterum ibidem stans dicat:

Ergo noli me tangere,
nec ultra uelis plangere,
quem mox in puro sydere
cernes ad Patrem scandere.

---

[1] paululum] paulolum (MS).

Maria ut supra:

> *Sancte inmortalis, miserere nobis!*

Item Dominus ad eam:

> *Nunc ignaros huius rei*
> *fratres certos reddes mei;*
> *Galileam, dic, ut eant,*
> *et me uiuentem uideant.*

Maria reliquis comitantibus, ad chorum sola dicat:

> *Surrexit enim sicut* ⟨*dixit Dominus; ecce præcedet vos in Galilæam; ibi eum*
> *videbitis, alleluia, alleluia*⟩.

Chorus ad eam:

> *Dic nobis, Maria,* ⟨*quid vidisti in via?*⟩

Ipsa ad chorum:

> *Sepulchrum Christi,*

cum r⟨eliquis⟩. Chorus:

> *Credendum est* ⟨*magis soli Mariæ veraci quam Judæorum turbæ fallaci*⟩.
> *Scimus Christum* ⟨*surrexisse a mortuis vere; tu nobis, victor rex, miserere*⟩.

Item chorus:

> *Currebant duo simul,* ⟨*et ille alius discipulus præcucurrit citius Petro, et*
> *venit prior ad monumentum, alleluia.*⟩

Interea cum Mulieribus Petrus et Iohannes currant, et Iohannes precurrens expectet Petrum; et nichil inuenientes reuertantur simul[1]
cantantes:

> *Ergo die ista exultemus.*
> *Astra, solum, mare.*

Chorus alta uoce: *Te Deum laudamus.*[2]

The most striking literary innovation is the transforming of
the sentences of *Quem quæritis* into hexameters. Since these
verses are not found elsewhere, however, one cannot expand
the *incipits* in the text before us.[3] Nor has any editor been able
to complete the verses introduced at the end of the play. Still
another novelty is the antiphon *Una sabbati*, sung by the chorus,
appropriately enough, after Mary Magdalen has reported that
the tomb is empty. In at least one point, however, the play
shows a defect in sequence. At the moment when Christ appears
to her, Mary Magdalen has just finished singing the first three
joyous sentences of *Victimæ paschali*; hence the question *Mulier,
quid ploras?* can hardly be addressed to her with dramatic
propriety.

---

[1] simul] Written by a later hand above
the abbreviation, mt.

[2] Followed by a trope of *Gloria in excelsis.*

[3] See Meyer, p. 110.

Among the versions of the *Visitatio Sepulchri* of the more highly developed form which we are now considering, the most finished and original, from the literary point of view, is the one preserved in the famous play-book from the monastery of St-Benoît-sur-Loire, at Fleury:[1]

Ad faciendam similitudinem Dominici Sepulcri primum procedant tres fratres preparati et uestiti in similitudinem trium Mariarum, pedetemtim et quasi tristes alternantes hos uersus cantantes. Prima earum dicat:

> *Heu! pius pastor occidit,*
> *quem culpa nulla infecit.*
> *O res plangenda!*

Secunda:

> *Heu! uerus pastor obiit,*
> *qui uitam functis contulit.*
> *O mors lugenda!*

Tercia:

> *Heu! nequam gens Iudaica,*
> *quam dira frendet uesania.*[2]
> *Plebs execranda!*

Prima:

> *Cur nece*[3] *pium impia*
> *dampnasti seua*[4] *inuida?*
> *O ira nefanda!*

Secunda:

> *Quid iustus hic promeruit*
> *quod crucifigi debuit?*
> *O gens dampnanda!*

Tercia:

> *Heu! quid agemus misere,*
> *dulci magistro orbate?*
> *Heu, sors lacrimanda!* |

Prima:

> *Eamus ergo propere,*
> *quod solum quimus facere*
> *mente deuota.*

[1] Orleans, Bibl. de la Ville, MS 201 (*olim* 178), Miscellanea Floriacensia sæc. xiii, pp. 220–5, previously edited by Monmerqué, in *Mélanges*, vii, 157–64; Wright, pp. 32–6; Du Méril, pp. 110–6; Coussemaker, pp. 178–94; Milchsack, pp. 67–81; Lange, no. 223, pp. 160–5. Wright's text is reprinted by Pollard, pp. 157–61; Davidson, pp. 33–9. Monmerqué's text is reprinted, with a French translation, by Barthélemy, iv, 460–3.

Lange's text is reprinted, with an English translation, by Adams, pp. 15–20. The music is included only by Coussemaker. The text before us is immediately preceded in the MS by the *Ordo Rachelis* printed below, ii, 110 sqq. For further bibliography see Notes, p. 665.

[2] frendet uesania] frendens uasania (MS).
[3] nece] nace (MS).
[4] seua] seuam (MS).

Secunda:

> *Condimentis aromatum*
> *ungamus corpus sanctissimum,*
> *quo preciosa.*

Tercia:

> *Nardi uetet commixcio,*
> *ne putrescat in tumulo*
> *caro beata.*

Cum autem uenerint in chorum, eant ad Monumentum et quasi querentes, et cantantes omnes simul hunc versum:

> *Sed nequimus hoc patrare   sine adiutorio;*
> *Quisnam saxum hoc reuoluet   ab monumenti hostio?*

Quibus respondeat Angelus sedens foris ad caput Sepulcri, uestitus alba deaurata, mitra tectus caput etsi deinfulatus,[1] palmam in sinistra, ramum candelarum plenum tenens in manu dextera, et dicat moderata et admodum graui uoce:

> *Quem queritis in sepulcro, o Christicole?*

Mulieres:

> *Ihesum Nazarenum crucifixum, o celicola.*[2]

Quibus respondeat Angelus:

> *Quid, Christicole, uiuentem queritis cum mortuis?*
> *Non est hic, sed surrexit, predixit ut discipulis.*
> *Mementote quid iam uobis locutus est in Galilea,*
> *Quia*[3] *Christum opportebat pati atque die tercia*
> *Resur|gere cum gloria.*[4]

Mulieres conuerse ad populum cantent:

> *Ad monumentum Domini uenimus gementes, angelum Dei sedentem uidimus*
> *et dicentem quia surrexit a morte.*

Post hec Maria Magdalene, relictis duabus aliis, accedat ad Sepulcrum, in quod sepe aspicie⟨n⟩s dicat:

> *Heu dolor, heu quam dira doloris angustia,*
> *Quod dilecti sum orbata magistri presencia!*
> *Heu, quis corpus tam dilectum sustulit e tumulo?*

Deinde pergat uelo⟨citer⟩ ad illos qui in similtu⟨di⟩ne Petri et Iohannis pr⟨e⟩stare debent ere⟨cti⟩, stansque ante eos quasi trist⟨is⟩ dicat:[5]

> *Tulerunt Dominum meum, et nescio ubi posuerunt eum,*
> *Et monumentum uacuum est inuentum,*
> *Et sudarium cum sindone intus est repositum.*[6]

---

[1] deinfulatus] The reading of the first syllable is uncertain.

[2] celicola] Corrected from *celicole* (MS).

[3] Quia] Corrected from *Quid* (MS).

[4] Cf. Luke xxiv, 5–7.

[5] The parts of this rubric (and of the suc- ceeding one) enclosed in pointed brackets have been lost through trimming of the parchment, and the restorations are not uniformly certain.

[6] intus est repositum] Corrected from *impositum* (MS).

Illi autem, h*ec* audientes, uel⟨ociter⟩ pergant ad Sepulcrum acsi curre⟨ntes⟩, sed iunior, scilicet Iohannes, preueniens st⟨et⟩ extra Sepulcrum; senior uero, scilicet Pe⟨trus⟩, sequens eum, statim intret; postquam et Ioh⟨annes in⟩tret. Cum inde exierint, Iohannes quasi ⟨ad⟩mirans[1] dicat:

> *Miranda sunt que uidimus!*
> *An furtim sublatus est Dominus?*

Cui Petrus:

> *Imo, ut predixit uiuus,*
> *surrexit, credo, Dominus.*

Iohannes:

> *Sed cur liquit[2] in sepulcro*
> *sudarium cum lintheo?*

⟨Petrus:⟩

> *Ista, quia resurgenti   non era⟨n⟩t necessaria,*
> *Imo Resurrectionis   restant hec indicia.*

Illis autem abeuntibus, acced⟨at⟩ Maria ad Sepulcrum, et prius dicat:[3] |
> *Heu dolor, heu quam dira!*

et cetera. Quam alloquantur duo Angeli sedentes infra Sepulcrum, dicentes:

> *Mulier, quid ploras?*

Maria:

> *Quia tulerunt Dominum meum, et nescio ubi posuerunt eum.*

Angelus:

> *Noli flere, Maria, resurrexit Dominus, alleluia.*

Maria:

> *Ardens est cor meum desiderio uidere Dominum meum; quero et non inuenio ubi posuerunt eum, alleluia.*

Interim ueniat quidam preparatus in similitudinem Hortolani, stansque ad caput Sepulcri et dicat:

> *Mulier, quid ploras? Quem queris?*

Maria:

> *Domine, si tu sustulisti eum, dicito mihi ubi posuisti eum, et ego[4] eum tollam.*

Et ille:

> *Maria!*

Que procidens ad pedes eius et dicat:

> *Raboni!*

---

[1] ⟨ad⟩mirans] Reading particularly doubtful.

[2] liquit] liquid (MS).

[3] This rubric is somewhat injured through trimming of the margin.

[4] ego] Written twice (MS).

At ille subtrahat se, et, quasi tactum eius deuitans, dicat:

Noli me tangere, nondum enim ascendi ad Patrem meum, et Patrem uestrum, Deum meum, et Deum uestrum.

Sic discedat Hortolanus. Maria uero conuersa ad populum dicat:

Congratulamini michi omnes qui diligitis Dominum, quia quem querebam ap⟨p⟩aruit mihi, et dum flerem ad mo|numentum, uidi Dominum meum, alleluia.[1]

Tunc duo Angeli exeant ad hostium Sepulcri, ita ut appareant foris, et dicant:

Venite et uidete locum ubi positus erat Dominus, alleluia.
Nolite timere uos.
Vultum tristem iam mutate;
Ihesum uiuum nunciate;
Galileam iam adite.
Si placet uidere, festinate.
Cito euntes dicite discipulis quia surrexit Dominus, alleluia.

Tunc Mulieres discedentes a Sepulcro dicant ad plebem:

Surrexit Dominus de sepulcro, qui pro nobis pependit in ligno, alleluia.

Hoc facto, expandant sindonem, dicentes ad plebem:

Cernite, uos socii, sunt corporis ista beati
Linthea, que uacuo iacuere relicta sepulcro.

Postea ponant sindonem super altare, *cum qua* reuertentes[2] alternent hos uersus. Prima dicat:

Resurrexit ⟨h⟩odie Deus deorum!

Secunda:

Frustra signas lapidem, plebs Iudeorum.

Tercia:

Iungere iam populo Christianorum.

Item prima dicat:

Resurrexit ⟨h⟩odie rex angelorum.

Secunda:

Ducitur de tenebris turba piorum.

Tercia:

Reseratur[3] aditus regni celorum!

Interea is[4] qui ante fuit Hortolanus in similitudinem Domini ueniat, dalmaticatus[5] candida dalmatica, candida infula infulatus, filacteria

---

[1] For this responsory of the Easter season see Hartker, p. 233. The melody is not that of Hartker.

[2] cum qua reuertentes] The scribe seems to have written ꝯ q̄ euertentes. Certainly *atque reuertentes*, printed by Du Méril, Cous-

semaker, Milchsack, and Lange, does not represent the MS.

[3] Reseratur] Reserator (MS).

[4] is] his (MS).

[5] dalmaticatus] dalmaticus (MS).

preciosa in capite, crucem cum labaro in dextra, textum auro paratum
in sinistra habens, et dicat mulieribus: |

> *Nolite timere uos; ite, nunciate fratribus meis ut eant in Galileam; ibi me*
> *uidebunt, sicut predixi eis.*

⟨Chorus:⟩

> *Alleluia, resurrexit hodie Dominus!*

Quo finito, dicant omnes insimul:

> *Leo fortis, Christus, filius Dei.*

Et chorus dicat *Te Deum laudamus.*[1]

The action of the Fleury play begins with the usual procession
of the grieving Marys to the tomb. Their lament consists of
some ten appealing stanzas, several of which have already been
seen in a less elaborate version of the *Visitatio.*[2] In the succeeding
scene at the tomb two of the speeches contain rhyming lines of
fifteen syllables. The angel's second speech is unique in its
tentative metrical paraphrasing of a passage in the Gospel of
Luke (xxiv, 5–7). Unique also, in the next three scenes, is the
fidelity of playwright to the order of events in the Gospel of
John: Mary Magdalen's meeting with Peter and John, the race
of the two apostles to the tomb, and Mary's meeting with Christ.
In freshly composed metrical forms are the lament of Mary
before meeting Peter and John, and the bewildered conversation
of the two apostles after leaving the sepulchre. After Mary
Magdalen has told the congregation of her meeting with Christ,
the two angels come forward from the tomb, invite the three
women to inspect it, and send them forth to inform the disciples. In exhibiting the grave-cloths, the Marys sing two
hexameters formed from the usual prose announcement
Cernitis, o socii, and as they depart from the altar, they use a
number of rhymed verses not found elsewhere. Finally Christ,
having removed his gardener's costume, re-appears and bids
the Marys prepare the disciples for seeing him in Galilee.
Whereupon the play ends with appropriate choral rejoicing.

IV

Of the same general content as the pieces just considered, but
less noteworthy for literary finish, is a type of play deserving
attention from the fact that it provides for the singing of the
congregation in the concluding part of the performance. Since

---

[1] For what follows in the MS see Notes, p. 666.
[2] See the play from Dublin above, pp. 347–8.

the versions of this sort are all from German territory, the vernacular song used is the well-known *Christ ist erstanden*,[1] as seen, for example, in the following play from Nuremberg:[2]

Rursus responsorium repetitur propter processionem ad Sepulchrum. Finito responsorio, chorus incipiat:

> *Maria Magdalena et alia Maria ferebant diluculo aromata, Dominum querentes in monumento.*

Tunc tres Marie simul egredientes de choro cum thuribulis et incenso, et una illarum cantet:

> *Hev! nobis internas mentes　　quanti pulsant gemitus*
> *Pro nostro consolatore,　　quo priuamur misere,*
> *Quem crudelis Iudeorum　　morti dedit populus.*

Alia Maria dicat:

> *Iam percusso ceu pastore,　　oues errant misere;*
> *Sic magistro discedente,　　turbantur discipuli,*
> *Atque nos, absente eo,　　dolor tenet nimius.*

Tercia Maria dicat:

> *Sed eamus et ad eius　　properemus tumulum;*
> *Quem dileximus uiuentem,　　diligamus mortuum.*

Appropinquantes autem Sepulchro simul cantent:

> *Quis reuoluet nobis ab ostio lapidem quem tegere sanctum cernimus sepulchrum?*

Angelus sedens in Sepulchro Mulieribus respondeat:

> *Quem queritis, o tre|mule mulieres, in hoc tumulo gementes?*

Mulieres econtra:

> *Ihesum Nazarenum crucifixum querimus.*

Angelus:

> *Non est hic quem queritis, sed cito euntes nunciate discipulis eius et Petro quia surrexit Ihesus.*

Tunc hoc modo certificate, quasi uolentes nunciare Apostolis, ad chorum conuerse sic decantent:

> *Ad monumentum uenimus gementes, angelum Domini sedentem uidimus et dicentem quia surrexit Ihesus.*

Maria Magdalena sola circa Sepulchrum de sublatione Corporis Domini flexis poblitibus ita cantet:

> *Heu! redemptio Israhel,*
> *ut quid mortem sustinuit.*

---

[1] Concerning this song see below, p. 636.

[2] Nuremberg, Germanisches National-Museum, MS 22923, Lib. resp. Noribergensis sæc. xiii, fol. 105ᵛ–107ᵛ, previously edited by Lange, in *Z.f.d.A.*, xxviii (1884), 125–8, and by Lange, no. 208, pp. 140–6. In the latter place Lange erroneously gives the shelf-number of the MS as 22933. In the MS music is provided, and the present text is preceded by the responsory *Dum transisset*. For observations on the MS, and for associated versions of the *Visitatio*, see Notes, p. 666.

Et chorus cantet responsorium:[1]

Maria plorans ad monumentum.

Finito respons*orio*, Maria secunda uice prospiciens in Monumentum repetat:

Heu! redemptio.

Chorus uersum:[2]

Non sufficiens sibi.

Quo finito, Maria tercia uice introspiciens Sepulchrum repetat:

Heu! redemptio Israhel.

Mox ex inprouiso Dominica Persona adueniens, que sit uestita dalmatica, casulamque complicatam super humeros habeat, coronamque capiti superimpositam, nudis pedibus incedat, et stans ex aduersa parte Sepulchri, et leni uoce dicat Ma|rie:

Mulier, quid ploras? Quem queris?

Maria mox conuersa ad Personam Dominicam, quam presentem uidens nec tamen adhuc cognoscens, ita prosequi debet cantando suppressa uoce:

Domine, si tu sustulisti eum, dicito michi ubi posuisti eum, et ego eum tollam.

Maria autem uolens abire, Dominica Persona ad eam dicat:

Maria!

Ad hanc uocem illa quasi cognito Domino procumbat ante ipsum, et uolens pedes amplexari dicat:

Rabbi, quod dicitur magister.

Post hec exhibeat se Maria cum reuerentia quasi auscultatura uerba ipsius, et Dominus ad eam auctorabili uoce dicat:[3]

Prima quidem suffragia
stola tulit carnalia
exhibendo communia
se per nature munia.

Hec priori dissimilis,
hec est incorruptibilis,
que tunc fuit passibilis,
iam non erit solubilis.

Ergo noli me tangere,
nec ultra uelis plangere,
quem mox in puro sydere
cernes ad Patrem scandere.

---

[1] responsorium] MS has r̄, and *responsorium* may not be the word intended. *Maria plorans ad monumentum* is not given by Hartker.
[2] uersum] uersum versum (MS).

[3] In the three stanzas that follow, several words are illegible through rubbing; but the text is familiar, and the scribe's intention is clear.

Tunc Maria tribus uicibus flexis genibus ita cantet:

> *Sancte Deus!*
> *Sancte fortis!*
> *Sancte immortalis, miserere nobis!*

Dominus ad eam:

> *Nunc ignaros huius rei*
> *fratres reddes certos mei;*
> *Galileam, dic, ut | eant,*
> *et me uiuentem uideant.*

Postea duo Discipuli aut tres in medio choro stantes cantent ymnum:

> *Ihesv, nostra redemptio.*
> *Que te uicit clementia,*
> *v⟨t⟩ n⟨ostra ferres crimina⟩?*
> *Inferni claustra penetrans.*
> *Ipsa te cogat pietas.*
> *Gloria tibi, Domine,*
> *qui surrexisti a mortuis.*[1]

Quo finito, Maria Magdalena procedat in occursum Discipulorum quasi gaudens nunciatura eis Resurrectionem Domini, ita cantando:

> *Victime paschali laudes im⟨molent Christiani⟩.*
> *Agnus redemit oues, Ch⟨ristus innocens Patri reconciliavit peccatores⟩.*
> *Mors et uita duello ⟨conflixere mirando; dux vitæ mortuus, regnat vivus⟩.*

Discipuli econtra:

> *Dic nobis, Maria, ⟨quid vidisti in via?⟩*

Et Maria:

> *Sepulchrum Christi uiuentis, ⟨et gloriam vidi resurgentis.⟩*
> *Angelicos testes, sudarium ⟨et vestes⟩.*
> *Surrexit Christus, spes mea; precedet et uos in Galileam.*

Et chorus communiter:

> *Credendum est magis ⟨soli Mariæ veraci quam Judæorum turbæ fallaci⟩.*

Rursus Maria:

> *Scio Christum surrexisse ex mortuis u⟨ere⟩.*

Chorus item:

> *Tu nobis, uictor rex, m⟨iserere⟩.*

Deinde duo ex suprascriptis Discipulis currant ad Sepulchrum in figura Petri et Iohannis. Iohannes quidem prior accurrat, nec ingrediatur. Petrus vero sequens eum protinus ingrediatur, et tunc Iohannes simul cum eo introeat; et accipientes linteamina egrediantur, choro interim canente antiphonam:

---

[1] The lines beginning with capitals open separate stanzas of the hymn, the complete text of which is found below, p. 641.

Currebant duo simul, et ille alius discipulus precu|currit cicius Petro, et uenit prior ad monumentum, alleluia.

Illi autem conuersi ad chorum, expansis lintheaminibus inter manus, ita cantent:

Cernitis, o socii, ecce linteamina et sudarium, et corpus non est in sepulchro inuentum.

Hic redeuntes a Sepulchro cum processione eant in chorum cantantes hanc antiphonam:

Surrexit enim sicut dixit Dominus, et precedet uos in Galileam, alleluia; ibi eum uidebitis, alleluia, alleluia, alleluia,

populo interim acclamante *Christ ist erstanden.* Et cantores imponant *Te Deum laudamus.*

Although the use of the vernacular song *Christ ist erstanden* is the particular reason for our examining the Nuremberg *Visitatio* here, this is not the most interesting feature of the play. Unique, for example, is the arrangement whereby, after the *Credendum est* of the chorus, Mary Magdalen sings the sentence *Scimus Christum surrexisse,* the first word of which has been appropriately altered to *Scio.* Striking also is the use of the so-called responsory *Maria plorans,* not found in other plays, and of the rubric assuring us, once more, that upon leaving the tomb the Marys are to regard themselves as carrying their message specifically to the disciples—*quasi volentes nuntiare discipulis.*[1] The rubrics, moreover, are generous in details concerning impersonation in the scene between Mary Magdalen and Christ—the bare feet, crown, and characteristic tones of voice of the latter, and the gestures of reverence of the former. Somewhat unexpected, perhaps, in a scene so carefully composed is Mary's speech *Rabbi, quod dicitur magister,* in which she herself is made to speak the gloss.

V

At the close of our review of the variety of ways in which the clerical playwrights represented the more important incidents in the Scriptural account of the Resurrection, we have still to notice the treatment occasionally accorded to one or two quite subsidiary elements in the narrative. One of these is the purchasing of spices and ointments by the Marys.[2] Of the Biblical statements that the Marys brought these things with them to the

[1] See above, pp. 282, 286, 290, 384.
[2] In regard to the development of this scene in the plays see Dürre, pp. 16–7, 19, 20; Rueff, p. 71; Sauer, p. 443; Meyer, pp. 58–9, 91–3.

sepulchre,[1] abundant recognition is given in the plays that we have examined. The rubrics concerning the thuribles, boxes or vessels borne by the women have been frequent and detailed. As yet, however, we have observed no specific representation of the acquiring of the *aromata*, although this transaction is mentioned by St Mark[2] and in the liturgical responsory *Dum transisset*, which usually precedes the *Visitatio* immediately. In several plays, to be sure, we have observed theatrical details from which such a scene might easily develop. In the *Visitatio* from Toul, for example, the Marys make a detour to receive their *vascula* from a special side-altar, and although we are given no information as to the action there, we can readily fancy something suggestive of a scene with a merchant.[3] In other versions of the play the Marys appear to receive their utensils from a special attendant, or custodian, whom we may regard, if we wish, as representing, though not impersonating, the *unguentarius* himself.[4] In a few instances we have found the Marys expressing their intention of anointing Christ's body, and hence implying that the necessaries had already been, or were about to be, bought;[5] and in some plays they actually speak of going to make the purchase.[6]

For an adequate or generous representation of the scene of the seller of spices and ointments we must, as a matter of fact, look to the longer Easter plays treated in the next chapter. In the versions of the *Visitatio* immediately before us the treatment of it is, at best, merely rudimentary. In its simplest stage, the *unguentarius* himself is not even assigned a speaking part, as is shown by a text such as the following of the thirteenth century from Prague:[7]

In sancta nocte, inposito responsorio *Dum transisset*, Domina Abbatissa precedet, Maria | Magdalena sequetur eam, tres Marie sequentur eas cum senioribus. Responsorium:

Dvm transisset sabbatum, Maria Magdalena et Maria Iacobi et Salome emerunt aromata, ut uenientes ungerent Ihesum, alleluia, alleluia. Versus: *Et valde ma|ne una sabbatorum ueniunt ad monumentum, orto iam sole. Vt ue⟨nientes⟩. Gloria Patri et Filio et Spiritui Sancto, alleluia.*

---

[1] See especially Luke xxiii, 56; xxiv, 1; Mark xvi, 1–2.   [2] See Mark xvi, 1.
[3] See above, pp. 265 sq.; Dürre, p. 16.
[4] See above, pp. 280, 340, and below, p. 630.
[5] See above, pp. 348, 394.
[6] See, for example, the play from Nar-

bonne above, p. 285.
[7] Prague, Veřejná a Universitní Knihovna, MS VI.G.3b, Process. Sancti Georgii Pragensis sæc. xiv, fol. 84ʳ–90ʳ, previously edited by Lange, no. 212, pp. 148–51. In regard to related versions of the *Visitatio* see Notes, p. 673.

Finito responsorio, tres Marie, cantantes *Aromata*, procedant ad Ungentarium pro accipiendis ungentis:

> *Aromata precio querimus;*
> *Christi corpus ungere uolumus.* |
> *Holocausta sunt odorifera*
> *sepulture Cristi memoriam.*

Quibus acceptis, accedant ad Sepulcrum, conuentu cantante antiphonam:

> *Maria Magdalena et alia Maria ferebant diluculo aromata, Dominum querentes in monumento.*

Qua finita, tres Marie cantent antiphonam stantes ante Sepulcrum:

> *Quis re|uoluet nobis ab hostio lapidem quem tegere sanctum cernimus sepulchrum?*

Angelus in Sepulchro:

> *Qvem queritis, o tremule mulieres, in hoc tumulo plorantes?*

Marie respondeant:

> *Ihesum Nazarenum crucifixum querimus.*

Angelus:

> *Non est | hic quem queritis, sed cito euntes nunciate discipulis eius et Petro quia surrexit Ihesus.*

Item Angelus, aperto Sepulchro:

> *Venite et uidete locum ubi positus erat Dominus, alleluia, alleluia.*

Deinde Marie uenientes ad chorum cantent antiphonam:

> *Ad monumentum venimus ge|mentes, angelum Domini sedentem uidimus et dicentem quia surrexit Ihesus.*

Postea procedente de loco Maria Magdalena, incipitur antiphona ista:

> *Alleluia, noli flere, Maria; alleluia, resurrexit Dominus, alleiuia, alleluia.*[1]

Stante Maria Magdalena ante Sepulchrum, conuentus cantet antiphonam istam:

> *Maria stabat ad monu|mentum foris plorans; dum ergo fleret, inclinauit se*
> (Hic inclinet se Maria, et inspiciat Sepulchrum) *et prospexit in monumentum.*[2]

Inspecto Sepulchro, conuertat se ad Ihesum, et dicat hanc antiphonam:

> *Tvlerunt Dominum meum, et nescio ubi posuerunt eum.*

Ihesus *respondeat*:

> *Mulier, quid ploras? Quem que|ris?*

Maria cantet antiphonam:

> *Domine, si tu sustulisti eum, dicito michi ubi posuisti eum, et ego eum tollam.*

---

[1] See Hartker, p. 241.
[2] The marks of parenthesis are editorial. A somewhat different antiphon beginning

Maria stabat ad monumentum is given by Hartker, p. 237.

Ihesus dicat:
> *Maria!*

Et illa inclinando se *respondeat*:
> *Raboni!*

At Ihesus retrocedens antiphonam cantet:
> *Noli me tangere, Maria; vade autem ad fratres meos et | dic eis: Ascendo ad Patrem meum, et Patrem uestrum.*

In reditu Marie ad chorum canitur antiphona:
> *Venit Maria annuncians discipulis: Quia uidi Dominum.*[1]

Cantrix incipit versum:
> *Dic nobis, Maria, quid uidisti in uia?*

At illa *respondeat*:
> *Sepulchrum Christi viuentis, et gloriam uidi resurgentis. |*
> *Angelicos testes, sudarium et uestes.*
> *Surrexit Cristus, spes mea; precedet suos in Galileam.*

Chorus dicat:
> *Credendum est magis soli Marie ueraci quam Iudeorum turbe fallaci.*

Mox unus sacerdos cum trina flexione inponit:
> *Christus Dominus resurrexit.*

Conuentus *respondeat*:
> *⟨D⟩eo gracias, gaudeamus. |*

Sequitur antiphona:
> *Currebant duo simul, et ille alius discipulus precucurrit cicius Petro, et uenit prior ad monumentum, alleluia.*

Duo presbyteri accipientes linteum vadunt ad gradum cantantes antiphonam:
> *Cernitis, o socij, ecce lintheamina et sudarium, et corpus non est in sepulchro inuen|tum.*

Qua finita, conuentus cantat antiphonam:
> *Surrexit Dominus de sepulchro, qui pro nobis pependit in ligno, alleluia, alleluia, alleluia.*

Sequitur *Te Deum laudamus.* Inde versus *In resurrectione tua, Christe, alleluia.* Statim sequitur evvangelium *Maria Magdalena.* In reditu responsorium *Christus resurgens.*[2]

The processional responsory *Dum transisset* is used here with striking effect, in that after it has narrated the purchase of the spices, the Marys actually enact the incident—presumably offering money to the *unguentarius*, and receiving incense-boats

---

[1] See Hartker, p. 238.
[2] Followed by the rubric *In die sancto ad Aspersionem Aque.*

in return. Since neither the Gospels nor the service-books provide the actors with anything to say, the playwright has composed for the Marys some ten-syllable verses which we now see
for the first time, and which we shall see again.[1] Having
acquired their ointments from the silent merchant, the three
Marys proceed to the sepulchre, while the convent sings the
antiphon *Maria Magdalena et alia Maria*. In its text this chant is
disturbingly inappropriate, for the preceding rubrics indicate
that the *aromata* are acquired not by Mary Magdalen and one
other Mary, but by the three Marys other than Mary Magdalen.
The subsequent action of the play is so familiar that one need
mention only the exceptional antiphons *Maria stabat* and *Venit
Maria*.

A similar play from Prague deserves cordial notice here from
the fact that in it the *unguentarius* is provided with a speaking
part:[2]

Finito responsorio, exeunt ante chorum, cantrice imponente, et
Domina Abbatissa precedente, responsorium *Dum transisset*. Maria
Magdalena sequetur eam, et postea tres Marie sequentur cum senioribus
et iunioribus subsequentibus eas. Intrabunt omnes ecclesiam, et
stabunt in medio ecclesie. Finito responsorio, tres Marie cantantes
antiphonam:

> *Aromata ⟨precio quærimus;*
> *Christi corpus ungere volumus.*
> *Holocausta sunt odorifera*
> *sepulturæ Christi memoria⟩,*

procedant ad Ungentarium pro accipiendis aromaticis ungentis. Qua
finita, Vngentarius cantans antiphonam:

> *Dabo vobis ungenta optima,*
> *⟨Salvatoris ungere vulnera,*
> *sepulturæ ejus ad memoriam,*
> *et nomini ejus ad gloriam,⟩*

deinde dat eis pixides. Quibus acceptis, ipse accedant ad Sepulcrum,
conuentu interim cantante antiphonam:

> *Maria Magdalena et alia Maria ⟨ferebant diluculo aromata, Dominum*
> *quærentes in monumento⟩.*

---

[1] Sauer (p. 443), mistaking the verses
Aromata precio for a traditional liturgical
antiphon, appears to regard them as the
germ from which the scene arose. The relationship is quite the other way round. The
verses were composed to meet the exigencies
of the scene itself.

[2] Prague, Veřejná a Universitní Knihovna,
MS XIII.E.14d, Ordin. Sancti Georgii
Pragensis sæc. xiv, fol. 77ʳ–78ʳ, mentioned
by Brooks, *Sepulchre*, pp. 104–5, and now first
printed. For related texts see Notes, p. 674.

Qua finita, tres Marie cantent antiphonam stantes ante Sepulcrum:

Quis reuoluet nobis ⟨ab ostio lapidem quem tegere sanctum cernimus sepulchrum⟩?

Angelus ad Sepulchrum sedens respondeat cantans:

Quem queritis, o tremule mulieres, ⟨in hoc tumulo plorantes?⟩

Marie tres cantent:

Ihesum Nazarenum ⟨crucifixum quærimus⟩.

Angelus respondeat:

Non est hic quem queritis, ⟨sed cito euntes nuntiate discipulis ejus et Petro quia surrexit Jesus.⟩

Item Angelus sedens aperto Sepulchro inuitat eas cantans hanc antiphonam:

Venite et uidete locum | ⟨ubi positus erat Dominus, alleluia, alleluia⟩.

Deinde Marie venientes ad chorum cantent antiphonam:

Ad monumentum venimus ⟨gementes, angelum Domini sedentem vidimus et dicentem quia surrexit Jesus⟩.

Postea, procedente Maria Magdalena de loco, incipitur antiphona:

Alleluia, noli flere, Maria; ⟨alleluia, resurrexit Dominus, alleluia, alleluia.⟩

Stante Maria Magdalena ante Sepulcrvm, cantant antiphonam:

Maria stabat ⟨ad monumentum foris plorans; dum ergo fleret, inclinavit se et prospexit in monumentum⟩.

Et dum ventum fuerit ad hoc verbum *inclinauit se et prospexit in monumentum,* Maria Magdalena inclinet se et, inspecto Sepulcro, conuertat se ad clerum et cantet antiphonam:

Tulerunt Dominum meum, ⟨et nescio ubi posuerunt eum.⟩

Ihesus respondeat:

Mulier, quid ploras? Quem queris?

Maria cantet:

Domine, si tu sustulisti eum, ⟨dicito mihi ubi posuisti eum, et ego eum tollam.⟩

Ihesus dicat:

Maria!

Et illa inclinando se respondeat:

Raboni!

At Ihesus paululum retrocedens cantet antiphonam:

Noli me tangere, ⟨Maria; vade autem ad fratres meos et dic eis: Ascendo ad Patrem meum, et Patrem vestrum, Deum meum, et Deum vestrum.⟩

In reditu Marie ad chorum canitur antiphona:

Venit Maria ⟨annuntians: Quia vidi Dominum⟩.

Cantrix incipit versum:

> Dic nobis, Maria, ⟨quid vidisti in via?⟩

At illa respondet:

> Sepulchrum Christi viuentis, et gloriam ⟨vidi resurgentis⟩.
> Angelicos testes, ⟨sudarium et vestes.⟩
> Surrexit Christus, ⟨spes mea; precedet suos in Galilæa.⟩

Chorus respondeat:

> Credendum est ⟨magis soli Mariæ veraci quam Judæorum turbæ fallaci.
> Scimus Christum surrexisse a mortuis vere; tu nobis, victor rex, miserere⟩.

Mox vnus sacerdos indutus dalmatica, tenens crucifixum, tribus uicibus flectit genua in medio ecclesie, cantans:

> Christus Dominus resurrexit.

Et conuentus totidem uicibus | flectens genua respondeat:

> Deo gracias, alleluia, siue Gaudeamus.

Item conuentus antiphonam:

> Currebant duo simul, ⟨et ille alius discipulus præcucurrit citius Petro, et venit prior ad monumentum, alleluia.⟩

Duo presbyteri accipientes lintheum vadunt ad gradus cantantes antiphonam:

> Cernitis, o socij, ⟨ecce lintheamina et sudarium, et corpus non est in sepulchro inventum.⟩

Qua finita, conuentus cantat antiphonam:

> Surrexit Dominus de sepulchro, ⟨qui pro nobis pependit in ligno, alleluia, alleluia, alleluia.⟩

Interim Domina Abbatissa deosculatur lintheum; deinde sorores et populus circumstans. Sequitur *Te Deum laudamus*. Inde versus *In resurreccione tua, Christe, alleluia*. Statim sequitur euuangelium *Maria Magdalena*. Ad reditum chori conuentus cantat antiphonam *Christus surgens*.

The reply of the merchant to the Marys in this play is in ten-syllable verses of appropriately reverent content. For the comic tendency which appeared in this scene in vernacular plays of the later Middle Ages there is no encouragement in the Latin plays of the Church.[1] For the representing of this little incident was required a *sedes* apart from the sepulchre itself— such a 'booth' for the *unguentarius* as could be provided by one of the side-altars, to which, as we have seen, the Marys could very appropriately go to obtain their ointment boxes or vessels.[2]

---

[1] As to the possibility of a relationship between the comic *mercator* of the vernacular plays and the quack doctor of the mummers'   play see Chambers, ii, 91, and above, p. 11.

[2] See above, p. 402.

Further consideration of this scene may be postponed until we encounter more extended versions of it in the plays reviewed in the next chapter.[1]

VI

In concluding our present examination of the versions of the *Visitatio* in which Christ appears, we must observe the dramatic use of one other subordinate element in the story of the Resurrection: the appointing of a group of Roman soldiers to watch the sepulchre. Of these persons we hear only through the Gospel of Matthew, which records that, in response to a request from the priests and Pharisees, Pilate stationed the required guard; that at the quaking of the earth during the visit of the two Marys to the tomb the soldiers were struck senseless; and that later, when the soldiers reported their experience to the chief priests, they were bribed to circulate a false report.[2] These occurrences are at least slightly reflected in a text of the fifteenth century from Coutances:[3]

Si Marie debeant representari, finito responsorio, quatuor clerici armati, accedentes ad Sepulcrum Domini pallis sericis decenter ornatum et factum, dicant personagia sua. Quo facto, duo pueri induti roquetis ueniant ad Monumentum ferentes duas virgas decorticatas, in quibus sint decem candelle ardentes; et statim cum appropinquauerint ad Sepulcrum, predicti Milites procidant quasi mortui, nec surgant donec incipi|atur *Te Deum*. Angeli vero intrent in Sepulcrum, et sedeant vnus ad capud et alter ad pedes. Tunc duo clerici capis sericis induti, quos tres Marie sequantur in habitu sanctimonialium tenentes pissides in manibus, et procedant ab introitu chori usque ad aquilam cantantes versus:

Adam nouus veterem,[4]

usque ibi dicentes.[5] Statim tres Marie euntes ad Sepulcrum dicant uoce lacrimabili:

Quis reuoluet ⟨nobis lapidem ab ostio monumenti⟩?

---

[1] For further observations on the origins of the scene of the *unguentarius* see Notes, p. 677.

[2] See Matt. xxvii, 62–6; xxviii, 2–4, 11–5; Meyer, pp. 93–4.

[3] Paris, Bibl. Nat., MS lat. 1301, Ordin. Constantiense sæc. xv, fol. 143ᵛ–145ᵛ, previously edited, with damaging omissions, by Lange, no. 222, pp. 157–60, and, in complete form, by Gasté, pp. 63–4.

[4] The complete text intended here may be that found in the *Peregrinus* from the Fleury play-book printed below, p. 473.

[5] Since the word *dicentes* lacks the under lining supplied for the rest of the rubric in the MS, this word may refer to a passage in the preceding verses beginning *Adam nouus veterem*. The text of these verses found in the Fleury *Peregrinus*, however, seems to contain no relevant passage.

Angeli voce moderata dicant:

> *Venite, venite; ⟨nolite timere vos.*
> *Quem quæritis in sepulchro, o Christicolæ?⟩*

Marie respicientes in eos quasi vereconde, uoce altiori quam prius dicant:

> *Ihesum Nazare|num ⟨crucifixum, o cælicolæ⟩.*

Angeli discooperientes Sepulcrum dicant:

> *Non est hic, ⟨surrexit sicut prædixerat; ite, nuntiate quia surrexit.⟩*

Tunc Angelis discedentibus et aliis Mulieribus paululum redeuntibus, Maria Magdalena crebro aspiciens in Monumentum, nec quem querit inueniens, fingat se flere et modicum recedat; et statim Angeli predicti, redeuntes ad Sepulcrum, sedeant sicut prius. Tunc Maria Magdalena, sedens in aliquo loco iuxta Sepulcrum, faciat lamentaciones suas dicens:

> *Me miseram.*[1]

Finita lamentacione, redeat ad Sepulcrum, stans et plorans; et dum | plorat, inclinet se et prospiciat in Monumentum. Tunc Angeli dicant ei:

> *Mulier, quid ploras?*

Illa autem quasi suspirans dicat:

> *Quia tulerunt Dominum ⟨meum, et nescio ubi posuerunt eum⟩.*

Tunc ueniat Christus in habitu Ortolani et dicat ei:

> *Mulier, quid ⟨ploras? Quem quæris⟩?*

Illa autem conuersa ad eum dicat:

> *Domine, si tu ⟨sustulisti eum, dicito mihi, et ego eum tollam⟩.*

Tunc ille recedat et satis cito redeat, indutus capa serica vel pallio serico, tenens crucem, et dicat ei:

> *Maria!*

Ipsa uero statim procidens ad pedes eius dicat:

> *Raboni!*

Ihesus autem sustrahat se, quasi tactum eius deuitans, et dicat:

> *Noli me tangere!* |

Quo finito, dispereat Ihesus. Maria vero statim ad alias Mulieres reuertatur, et venientes in chorum dicant simul voce iocunda hos versus:

> *Victime paschali ⟨laudes immolent Christiani⟩.*
> *Agnus redemit ⟨oves; Christus innocens Patri reconciliavit peccatores⟩.*
> *Mors et uita ⟨duello conflixere mirando; dux vitæ mortuus, regnat vivus⟩.*

Tunc cantor stans in choro dicat:

> *Dic nobis, ⟨Maria, quid vidisti in via?⟩*

---

[1] This lament I am unable to restore. Doubtless it resembled passages in the *Ludus* from *Tours*; see below, p. 443.

Maria Magdalena dicat sola:

Sepulchrum ⟨Christi viventis, et gloriam vidi resurgentis⟩.

Secunda Mulier sola dicat:

Angelicos ⟨testes, sudarium et vestes⟩.

Tercia Mulier dicat:

Surrexit Christus, ⟨spes mea; præcedet suos in Galilæa.⟩

Tunc cantor et archiepiscopus excelsa voce dicant:

Credendum ⟨est magis soli Mariæ veraci quam Judæorum turbæ fallaci⟩.

Chorus respondeat:

Scimus Christum ⟨surrexisse a mortuis vere; tu nobis, victor rex, miserere⟩.

Hiis peractis, incipiatur *Te Deum laudamus.*

In this performance the four soldiers are impersonated by appropriately costumed clerics. Concerning their stage-action at the opening of the play we have only the rubric *dicant personagia sua,* which may mean that they declare their own roles, or talk to one another, or merely engage in appropriate pantomime.[1] After the soldiers have taken their stations, two angels appear bringing lightning in their hands in the form of two candelabra, each holding ten candles.[2] At the sight of these, the soldiers fall down as if dead, and remain in that position until after the *Te Deum* at the end of the play. Outside the role of the soldiers the play is not highly remarkable. The processional *Adam novus veterem,* sung as the Marys enter, is found in no other version of the *Visitatio*; and possibly the same may be said of the lament of Mary Magdalen beginning *Me miseram.* The scene of Mary and Christ is noteworthy chiefly for Christ's sudden withdrawal and return in a changed costume after Mary's first speech.[3]

---

[1] Cf. the rubric *agat sua,* prescribing the stage-action of the *mercator,* in the play from Klosterneuburg below, p. 423.

[2] See the plays from Benediktbeuern and Klosterneuburg below, pp. 435, 639.

[3] Other texts bearing upon matters treated in this chapter are printed or mentioned in Notes, p. 683.

CHAPTER XIV

THE *LUDUS PASCHALIS*

THE four Easter plays reserved for consideration in the present chapter are not totally, or even essentially, different from certain of the pieces presented in the pages preceding. The compositions from Origny-Sainte-Benoîte, Klosterneuburg, Benediktbeuern, and Tours, to be treated here, introduce only slight additions in the way or theme or incident, and they maintain the devotional spirit which has characterized all the dramatic performances reviewed hitherto. They are, however, composed upon a distinctly more ample scale, showing a considerable increase in length, a notable advance in literary elaboration, and fresh intrusions of the vernacular. These enlargements, indeed, are so conspicuous as to raise the question whether such plays could still have been performed as genuine Church plays. Some modern writers emphatically maintain that the dramatic pieces about to be considered, along with some of those already reviewed, could not have been presented in close association with authorized worship within the church itself. These critics undertake to distinguish rather sharply between plays which are explicitly attached to the liturgy and are partly identical with it in content, and those which, through literary sophistication and amplitude, seem alien to Church worship. The former are sometimes called 'dramatic offices,' *officia*, or *Feiern*, and the latter, 'plays', *ludi*, or *Spiele*.[1] Among the *ludi*, Meyer, for example, would place not only the four plays below, but also such pieces as those from Fleury, Engelberg, Einsiedeln, Cividale, Nuremberg, and Coutances, treated in the preceding chapter.[2]

It may fairly be urged, however, that so sharp a distinction between 'plays' and 'dramatic offices' is hardly justified by the pieces now under consideration. It is not, in any case, completely supported by the terminology of the rubrics in the texts themselves. The play from Benediktbeuern, to be sure, bears the title *ludus*, but in spite of that designation it appears to have been performed in close association with the liturgy (*cantatis Matutinis*), and, possibly, in the very position assigned to the

---

[1] The advocates of these distinctions are mentioned in Notes, p. 684.
[2] See Meyer, pp. 80–1, 89.

ordinary type of *Visitatio Sepulchri*.[1] This is certainly the liturgical position of the plays from Coutances and Nuremberg,[2] and it may be also of those from Fleury, Engelberg, Einsiedeln, and Cividale. The play from Tours ends with the familiar *Te Deum*; the compositions from Klosterneuburg and Origny-Sainte-Benoîte bear no evidence of liturgical attachment. From these facts it would appear that so precise a distinction between liturgical *Feiern* and non-liturgical *Spiele* as that of Meyer is neither very safe nor very useful.

More genuine grounds for such a classification are found in the content and literary texture of the compositions themselves, without reference to their liturgical attachments. It has been held, for example, that a dramatic piece becomes a *Spiel* when it includes profane elements or pretentious *mise en scène* or metrical elaboration unbecoming to ecclesiastical surroundings.[3] It seems unlikely, however, that critics will agree as to what amount or kind of dramatic elaboration is ecclesiastically appropriate. At one moment, for example, Meyer places among the *Spiele* those versions of the *Visitatio* which include that 'worldly' personage, the *unguentarius*;[4] but at another time he can refer to these same plays as *Feiern*.[5]

It is to be understood, therefore, that in segregating four plays for treatment in the present chapter I am following the counsel of simple convenience rather than the dictates of formal definition. The general title *Ludus Paschalis*, moreover, has here no technical, but only a loosely descriptive, significance. We are, however, completely at liberty to emphasize the more ambitious literary qualities of these particular plays; and, in spite of their fragmentary state, to support their claim to be considered as 'de véritables créations dramatiques'.[6]

I

The play from the monastery for women at Origny-Sainte-Benoîte, near St Quentin, is found among the customs of that community recorded during the thirteenth and fourteenth centuries:[7]

[1] See below, pp. 432, 537.
[2] See above, pp. 398, 408.
[3] See Lange, *Programm*, p. 29; Milchsack, pp. 103, 115; Meyer, pp. 59, 92.
[4] See Meyer, pp. 59, 92; and above, pp. 401 sqq.
[5] See Meyer, p. 80.

[6] See Coussemaker, pp. ix–x.
[7] St Quentin, Bibl. de la Ville, MS 86 (*olim* 75), Miscellanea Oriniacensia sæc. xiv, pp. 609–25, previously edited, with the music, by Coussemaker, pp. 256–79. The text now printed begins on the fourth line of p. 609. The first three lines are occupied by the

⟨Ludus Paschalis⟩

Chascune des Maries doit auoir en se main un cierge alumeit, et
Marie Magdelainne doit auoir vnne boiste en se main, et les autres
deus nient, dusques adont quellez aient acate au Marchant. Et li
prestres doit aler deuant iceles, et doit auoir en se main vn encensier
atout lencens. Et li cuers ensiut iceles, et chascune diceles a I cierge
en se main alume.

> *Maria Magdalene et alia Maria ferebant diluculo*[1] *aromata, Dominum*
> *querentes in monumento.*

Li cuerz reprent:

> *Maria Madalene* ⟨*et alia Maria ferebant diluculo aromata*⟩.

Toutes les trois Maries dient *Jam percusso*:[2]

> ⟨*I*⟩*am percusso, heu,* | *pastore,*   *oues errant misere;*
> *Et magistro discedente,*   *turbantur discipuli;*   5
> *Ita nos, absente*[3] *eo,*   *dolor tenet nimius!*

Li cuers dist:

> *Dominum querentes* ⟨*in monumento*⟩.

Les trois Maries:

> *Sed eamus et ad eius*   *properemus tumulum,*
> *Et vnguento liniamus*   *corpus sacratissimum.*
> *Si dileximus uiuentem,*   *diligamus mortuum.*   10

Li cuers dist:

> *Dominum* ⟨*quærentes in monumento*⟩.

Les trois Maries:

> *Quis reuoluet ergo nobis*   *ab hostio lapidem,*
> *Ut condignum sepulture*   *agamus obsequium,*
> *Cuius mire bonita|tis*   *sensimus solatium?*

Li cuers dist:

> *Dominum* ⟨*quærentes in monumento*⟩.   15

Ci doit estre apparrillies li Ma⟨r⟩chans et lez trois Maries auoucques
leur oingnement:

> *Peres trestous puissans,*
> *hautismes rois des angles,*
> *gouureneres tres pitous,*
> *nostre cuer que feront malleuourous.*[4]
> *Heu las! nostre dolour con grans il est!*   20

incipits of four irrelevant responsories, and
by a line and a half of erasure immediately
preceding our text. For further observations
on the MS see Notes, p. 684.

   [1] diluculo] diliculo (MS).
   [2] In several instances, throughout the play,

the rubric ends with the *incipit* of the speech
that follows. These *incipits*, unlike the speeches
themselves, have no musical notation.
   [3] absente] abscente (MS).
   [4] malleuourous] malleuourons (MS).

Les trois Maries:

> *Nous auons perdu nostre confort,*
> *Ihesum Christum, trestout plain de doucour;*
> *il estoit biaus et*[1] *plains de bonne amour.*
> *He las! mout nous amoit li urais!*

Les ii Maries:

> *Mais ore alons longuement | acater*   25
> *duquel oindre puissons le cors tres bel;*
> *il estoit urais salus et uraie amours.*
> *He las! verrons le nous iamais!*

Ci doit remaner Marie Magdelainne, et les autres deus Maries doiuent
aproicher li Marchant. Li Marchans dist:

> *Ca aproi⟨ch⟩es vous, qui tant fort ames,*
> *cest vnguement sel uoles acater*   30
> *du quel oindre uostre Signeur porres*
> *son sainct cors qui tant par est sacres.*

En ce meesmes liu les deus Maries dient:

> *Di nous, marchans tres bons, urais et loiaus,*
> *cest vnguement se tu uendre le veus,*
> *di tost du pris que tu auoir en ueus. |*   35
> *He las! verrons le nous iamais!*

Li Marchans dist:

> *Cest oinguement se mout le conuoities,*
> *cinc besans dor donner vous en couuient,*
> *ne autrement ia ne lenporteres.*

Les ij Maries:

> *He las! ⟨verrons le nous iamais!⟩*   40

Li Marchans dist:

> *Jou ai vn autre mout*[2] *bon oinguement,*
> *pour mains lares, sil vous uient a talent;*
> *as autres est de mout plus chier piument.*

Les ij Maries:

> *Gentius marchans, du millour bien nous vent,*
> *tant que tu ueus de largent, plus em prent;*   45
> *no grant Signour du ciel oin|dre en volons.*
> *He las! ⟨verrons le nous iamais!⟩*

Li Marchans dist:

> *Vous aues bien palle, dames uaillans;*
> *iel vous donrai pour mainz bien deuz besans*
> *pour le Signeur cui vous parames tant.*   50

---

[1] et] Written twice (MS).
[2] mout] Followed by the word *tres*, virtually erased (MS).

Les ij Mariez:

> *Saiges marchans, pour Dieu nous te prions*
> *que tu nous liures asses du plus tres bon,*
> *que bonne odor en aient tout li bon.*
> *He las!* ⟨*verrons le nous iamais!*⟩

Li Marchans dist:

> *Tenes cestui, ou siecle na millor;*   55
> *oindre porres uostre tres grant Signeur.*
> *Merci queres a lui, dames, pour moi.*

Les ij Maries:

> *Merci te face li urais Diex glorious,*
> *et nous ossi trestous ensamble toi*[1] |
> *veus tu venir ou fu mis li sains cors?*   60
> *He las!* ⟨*verrons le nous iamais!*⟩

Li Marchans dist:

> *Douce dames, ne demandes mais ce;*
> *certes ie uoil aler apres Ihesu.*
> *Tout cil sont sot qui ne vont apres lui.*

Les ij Maries dient:

> *Amis, tu as mout tres bien dit le uoir;*   65
> *deceu sont cil qui naimment son sauoir.*
> *Il nous a trais trestous a son amour.*
> *He las!* ⟨*verrons le nous iamais!*⟩

Li Marchans dist:

> *Certes, ie uouel mout uolentiers aler,*
> *car il nous a mout uolentiers ames;*   70
> *il nous a de la mort denfer getes.*

Les ij Maries dient:

> *Jouenes marchans, ensamble o nous en vien;*
> *nous te merrons* | *ou le sains cors fu mis.*
> *Nostre Signour uolons veoir et tenir.*
> *He las!* ⟨*verrons le nous iamais!*⟩   75

Adont les deus Maries doiuent raler a Marie Magdelainne, et doiuent
aler au Sepucre entre elles trois, et doiuent chanter ensanle *Ille quippe*:

> *Ille quippe qui ferentem   suscitauit Lazarum,*
> *Eius et sorores*[2] *flentes   reduxit*[3] *ad gaudium,*
> *Poterit nobis*[4] *optatum   conferre solatium.*

Les iij Maries dient:

> *Eya! consolator,   Ihesu bone, respice.*
> *Eya! nunc vvltu sereno   mentes nostras refoue.*   80
> *Eya! sancte, laudes nostras,   uota, clemens, suscipe.*

---

[1] A rhyme might be effected by altering this line to the following: *et nous ossi ensamble toi trestous*.

[2] sorores] Corrected from *sororem* (MS).

[3] reduxit] Corrected from *reduxisti* (MS).

[4] nobis] *nobit* (MS).

En le fin de ceste anteuene doiuent estre les trois Maries a luis du Sepucre, et dire: |

Quis reuoluet nobis ab hostio lapidem quem tegere sanctum cernimus sepulcrum?

Ci doiuent estre li Angle apparrilliet au Sepuchre, li vns au chief, li autres as pies, vestus de blans aournemens; et doiuent chanter en seant:

O uos, Cristicole, quem queritis esse dolentes?
Unguentisque sacris ungere quem cupitis?

Les iij Maries dient:

Querimus, o superi ciues, Ihesum crucifixum;   85
Dicite quis nobis sustulit hunc miseris.

Ci doiuent li Angle descouurir le Sepuche un peu et demoustrer au doit en chantant ceste anteuene:

Non iacet hic, quia surrexit; uenite et uidete.[1] |

Ci doiuent li Angle haut descouurir le Sepuchre, et les trois Maries doiuent aproichier et si doiuent baisier le Sepuche, quant li Angle *En ecce locus:*

En ecce locus quo positus fuerat Dominus.

Ci doiuent li Angle recouurir le Sepucre, et les trois Maries sont ensanle et chantent:

Heu, infelices! quid agimus,
quia Dominum[2] *nostrum minime reperimus?*   90

Li Angle:

Recordamini qualiter loquutus sit nobis cum adhuc esset in Galileam, dicens
quia oportebat filium hominis pati et die tercia resurgere.[3]

Ci se departent les Maries, et Marie Magdelainne remaint seule au Sepucre, et chante:

Infelix ego misera! iure fleo quia Dominum meum, quem tam | diligebam,
non inuenio.

Li Angle dient:

Mulier, quid ploras?   95

Li Magdelainne dist:

Quia tulerunt Dominum meum, et nescio ubi posuerunt eum.

Li Angle dient:

Noli flere, Maria, alleluia; resurrexit Dominus, alleluia.

Li Magdelainne dist:

Ardens est cor meum; desidero uidere Dominum meum. Quero et non
inuenio ubi posuerunt eum, alleluia.

---

[1] This speech, and the next, Meyer (p. 92) emends to the following distich:
        Non iacet hic quia surrexit; venite, videte.
        Ecce locus, positus quo fuerat dominus.
[2] Dominum] domininum (MS).   [3] See Luke xxiv, 6–7.

Li Angle dient:

> *Douce dame, qui si ploures,*   100
> *dites nous ou uoles aler;*
> *ie croi mout bien, se Diex nous gart,*
> *de uraie amour li cuers vous art.*

Li Magdelainne dist: |

> *Lasse dolante, que ferai*
> *de mon Signour que perdu ai?*   105
> *Ie cuit de duel me tuerai.*
> > *Dolante!*
> *Ta mors au cuer grant duel me plante.*

Li Angle dient:

> *Douce dame, qui ci ueneis,*
> *qui si tres fort vous grame⟨n⟩tes,*   110
> *bien sai Ihesum ales querant*
> *pour cui souffres si grant torment.*

Li Madelainne dist:

> *Iai le cuer de duel abuure;*
> *tost mont de mon Signeur seure*
> *cil qui le mont a mort liure.*   115
> > *Dolante!*
> *Ta mors au cuer grant duel me plante.*

Li Angle dient:

> *Douce | dame, ne ploures plus;*
> *par tampz uerres le Roy Ihesu,*
> *proichainnement verra a toi,*   120
> *saligera ta grant dolour.*

Li Magdelainne dist:

> *Certes sor cui do⟨i⟩ ie trouuer*
> *celui qui tant fait a amer?*
> *Querroie le dela la mer?*
> > *Dolante!*   125
> ⟨*Ta mors au cuer grant duel me plante.*⟩

Li Angle dient:

> *Bonnes nouuelles vous aport,*
> *que releueis est de la mort*
> *Ihesus Cris, li dous fiex Marie.*
> *Ne ploures plus, ma douce amie.*   130

Li Magdelainne dist:

> *Nest pas merueille se ie pleur,*
> *car iai perdu mon douc Signour*
> *cauoit pitie de mes dolours.*
> > *Dolante!* |

⟨*Ta mors au cuer grant duel me plante.*⟩   135

Ci parole Nostre Sires a Marie Magdelainne en chantant, mais Marie ne uoit mie icelui:

Mulier, quid ploras? Quem queris?

Marie Magdelainne sencline, et dist:

Domine, si tu sustulisti eum, dicito michi ubi posuisti eum, alleluia, et ego eum tollam, alleluia!

Nostre Sires dist:

Maria!

Marie Magdelainne dist as pies Nostre Signeur:

Raboni!   140

Et gist enqui dusques adont que Nostres Sires a chante *Noli me tangere:*

Noli me tangere; nondum[1] *ascendi ad Patrem meum.*

Marie Magdelainne se drece toute seule deuant le Sepuchre, et Nostres Sires va as autres deus et dist *Auete*. Ces deus Maries gisent as pies Nostre Signeur dusques adont quil a parchante:

Auete uos michi dilecte,
et me de morte surrexisse
fideliter cer|tum habete.

Ci se dreccent les deus Maries et sont deuant Nostre Signeur dusques adont quil a parchanteit:

Ite, nuntiate fratribus meis, alleluia, ut eant in Galileam; ibi me videbunt, alleluya, alleluya, alleluya.   146

Apres ces chozes, Diex se part de Marie Magdelainne, et uient auocques les autres deus, et encomencent toutes trois a chanter ensanle:

Eya! nobis internas mentes pulsat gaudium pro nostro consolatore, quem gaudemus hodie cum triumpho victorie a mortuis resurgere.

Les iij Maries dient:

Ad monumentum uenimus plorantes, angelum Domini sedentem uidimus, et dicentem[2] *quia surrexit Ihesus.*   150

Li cuers dist *Deo gratias:*

Deo gratias! |

Et li doi Apostre vienent deuant les Maries, et prendent le manche le Magdelainne vn peu de lons, et dient:

Dic nobis, Maria,
quid uidisti in uia?

Et li Apostre laissent le manche le Magdelainne, et li Madelainne demoustre au doit le Sepuchre, et chante en haut en disant *Sepulc⟨rum⟩:*

Sepulcrum Cristi uiuentis,
et gloriam uidi resurgentis.   155

---

[1] nondum] nundum (MS).   [2] dicentem] dicenten (MS).

Les ij Maries dient, et Marie Magdelainne moustre le Sepuchre au doit:

> *Angelicos testes,*
> *sudarium et uestes.*
> *Surrexit Christus.*

Et Marie Magdelainne me⟨t⟩ se main a sen pis:

> *Spes nostra.*

Et Marie Magdelainne trestourne'sen doit dautre part, et dist *Prece⟨det⟩*:

> *Precedet uos in Galileam.*   160

Apres ces chozes, li doi Apostre queurent[1] au Sepuchre et dient:

> *Currebant duo simul.*

Li cuers chante:

> *Et ille alius discipulus pre|cucurrit cicius Petro, et uenit ad monumentum,*
> *alleluia.*

Endementiers que:[2]

> *Credendum est magis soli Marie ueraci*
> *quam Iudeorum turbe fallaci.*   165

Les trois Maries:

> *Scimus Cristum surrexisse ex mortuis uere;*
> *tu nobis, uictor rex, miserere!*

Li doi Apostre se dreccent et chantent en haut:

> *Cernitis, o socii!*[3]

Et maintenant les trois Maries sagenoillent et baisent le suaire, tant que li Apostre ont parchanteit:

> *Ecce linteamina et sudarium, et corpus non est in sepulchro inuentum.*

Ci reportent li doi Apostre le suaire ou Sepuchre, et les trois Maries chantent en haut ceste anteuene.[4]

Although the text before us is incomplete at the end, and also, probably, at the beginning, it appears that the amount lost is very slight. It provides that after the three Marys have entered the playing-space during the singing of the so-called antiphon *Maria Magdalena*, they utter a lament, of which the first two stanzas are already familiar,[5] but of which the third is a novel and skilful versification of the usual interrogation *Quis revolvet?* This lament is followed by a scene with the *unguentarius*, in French. The three stanzas sung by the three Marys as they

---

[1] queurent] q*u*eurent (MS).

[2] In the MS this fragmentary rubric is followed by several words erased, and by a considerable blank space.

[3] socii] socie (MS).

[4] Thus end the page and the fragment. On the next page appear only a few irre-

levant scribblings. Coussemaker assumes that the *Te Deum* was intended to follow immediately. I suggest an antiphon such as *Surrexit Dominus de sepulchro* or *Surrexit enim sicut dixit*, and then the *Te Deum*.

[5] See, for example, above pp. 386, 390.

approach the merchant's booth are a rather faithful rendering of Latin stanzas which we have already seen in the simpler *Visitatio* from Narbonne.[1] In the subsequent negotiation with the merchant Mary Magdalen has no part, since at the beginning of the play she is already provided with her traditional box of ointment. The dialogue between the other two Marys and the *unguentarius* is made especially touching through the latter's eagerness to join in honouring the 'tres grant Signeur'.

Provided with ointment, the three Marys depart together for the sepulchre singing two new stanzas of fifteen-syllable lines. At the door they repeat the question *Quis revolvet?*, this time in prose. The usual *Quem quæritis* and *Jesum Nazarenum* of the dialogue with the angels, however, they transform into distichs.[2] After the traditional disclosures have been made at the tomb, Mary Magdalen is left alone with the two angels, who comfort her in the course of an extended and moving dialogue, chiefly in stanzas of French.

Now occur the familiar scene between Christ and Mary Magdalen, and one in which Christ gives his charge also to the other two Marys. After his departure, the three women carry their report to the chorus, and in the dialogue from *Victimæ paschali* answer the inquiries of Peter and John. These two then visit the tomb, and bring forth the grave-cloths. Here the text breaks off abruptly. The previous editor conjectures that the antiphon referred to in the closing rubric is the *Te Deum*, with which Matins ends.[3] Since, however, the *Te Deum* is seldom, if ever, called an antiphon or sung by the Marys, we may surmise that the missing liturgical piece is *Surrexit Dominus, Christus resurgens* or some other of the forms frequently found at the end of the *Visitatio Sepulchri*.

In literary freedom this play shows a marked advance over the compositions reviewed in the preceding chapters. Of this the most striking evidence is the liberal use of the vernacular in the enlarged scene of the merchant, and the dialogue between Mary Magdalen and the angels. In each case the result is a closer approach to realism and an increase in human feeling. Notable also is the variety of literary forms employed: in Latin, prose, distichs, and lines of fifteen syllables; in French, lines of eight or ten syllables, and stanzas of varied arrangements. At one moment, indeed, the writer's metrical enthusiasm leads him into

---

[1] See above, p. 285.   [2] See Creizenach, i, 58.   [3] See Coussemaker, p. 279.

a mild incongruity: he inserts a versified form of *Quis revolvet* in a place where it has no direct connexion with the action (ll. 12–4). These displays of literary ambition, however, in no way detract from the devotional spirit of the play. Although we have no definite evidence showing that it was performed within the church in close attachment to the liturgy, there is no reason why it may not have been so used. The liturgical chorus participates, and passages from the service-books are not lacking.

II

Very different in its distribution of emphasis is the famous *Ordo Paschalis* from Klosterneuburg, brought to the attention of the modern world by Bernhard Pez in the early part of the eighteenth century, and then lost from view for about two centuries, until rediscovered by Hermann Pfeiffer, and published by him in 1908. The text is as follows:[1]

Incipit Ordo Paschalis

Primo producatur Pilatus cum responsorio *Ingressus Pilatus*,[2] et sedeat in locum sibi preordinatum. Post hec uenientes Pontiffices cantent:

> *O domine, recte meminimus,*
> *quod a turba sepe audiuimus,*
> *seductorem consuetum dicere:*
> *Post tres dies uolo resurgere.*

Respondeat Pylatus:

> *Sicut michi dictat discretio*   5
> *et ex uultu uestro conicio,*
> *michi crimen uultis inponere*
> *de Iesu, quem fecistis perdere.*

---

[1] Klosterneuburg, Stiftsbibl., MS 574, Miscellanea saec. xiii, fol. 142ᵛ–144ᵛ, first published by Pfeiffer, pp. 27–40, with complete photographic facsimiles. For most of the text the MS provides music. Corrections to Pfeiffer's text are offered by E. Schröder, in *Göttingische gelehrte Anzeigen*, clxxi (1909), 144; and of these some use is made in a new edition of the play by Pfeiffer, *Klosterneuburger Osterspiel*, pp. 161–7 (with photographic facsimile of one page, fol. 143ʳ). A history and description of the MS are given by Pfeiffer, pp. 3–10, 22–7. The play before us, which is the last piece in the manuscript, is written in two hands of the early thirteenth century, the second beginning at the top of fol. 144ʳ and continuing through fol. 144ᵛ.

[2] The only responsory with which this

processional can be identified is the following, from Lent (Hartker, p. 9): *Ingressus Pilatus cum Jesu in prætorium; tunc ait illi: Tu es rex Judæorum. Respondit: Tu dicis quia rex-sum. Exivit ergo Jesus de prætorio portans coronam et vestem purpuream; et cum indutus fuisset, exclamaverunt omnes: Crucifigatur, quia filium Dei se fecit. Versus: Tunc ait illis Pilatus: Regem vestrum crucifigam? Responderunt pontifices: Regem non habemus nisi Cæsarem.* In content, however, this responsory is alien to the context. As the ultimate source of the so-called responsory mentioned in the rubric above, Du Méril (pp. 126–7) cites a passage in the *Evangelium Nicodemi*, pt. ii, chap. xii (Tischendorf, *Evangelia*, p. 409). In the manuscript the words *Ingressus Pilatus* have no musical notation.

Respondeant Pontiffices:

> *Militibus ergo precipias*
> *custodire noctis uigilias,* 10
> *ne furentur illum discipuli,*
> *et credant eum uiuere populi.*

Pylatus permittit Milites ad custodiendum Sepulchrum:

> *En habetis ipsi custodias.*
> *Custodite noctis uigilias,*
> *ne furentur illum discipuli,* 15
> *et dicant plebi: Surrexit a mortuis.*

Tunc Pontiffices conducentes saxea pecunia Milites cantent:

> *Vestra uirtus et sapiencia*
> *nobis ualde est necessaria;*
> *seductores*[1] *namque discipuli*
> *machinantur ruinam populi.* 20

Milites promittentes Pontifficibus uigilias cantent:

> *Defensores erimus tumuli,*
> *ne furentur illum discipuli*
> *et fallendo dicant in populis:*
> *Resurrexit Christus a mortuis.*

Inde Milites circuientes Sepulchrum cantent:

> *Non credimus Christum resurgere,* 25
> *sed,* | *ne*[2] *corpus quis possit tollere,*
> *custodimus noctis uigilias.*
> *Schowa propter insidias.*

> *Non credimus ut quidquam conferat,*
> *sed et corpus eius quis aufferat,* 30
> *prouidemus per has uigilias.*
> *Schowa propter insidias.*

> *Schowa alumbe, ne fures ueniant,*
> *qui student ut plebem decipiant,*
> *obseruemus noctis uigilias.* 35
> *Schowa propter insidias.*

> *Non exigit humana racio*
> *ut resurgat uiuus*[3] *ex mortuo;*
> *seductores gerunt uersucias.*
> *Schowa propter insidias.* 40

---

[1] seductores] Emended to *seductoris* (Pfeiffer).
[2] ne] nec (MS).   [3] uiuus] uius (MS).

> *Si mortuus posset resurgere,*
> *potuisset profecto uiuere,*
> *quare tulit mortis angustias?*
> *Schowa propter insidias.*

Tunc silencio Angelus euaginato gladio ueniat cantans:

> *Alleluia!*   45
> *Resurrexit uictor ab inferis!*[1]

Hic percuciat unum gladio, et omnes ad terram proni cadant.

> *Pastor ouem reportans humeris.*
> *Alleluia!*
> *Reformator ruine ueteris*
> *causam egit humani generis.*   50
> *Vespertina migrauit hostia,*
> *matutina suscepta gloria.*
> *Alleluia!*
> *Non diuina tamen potencia*
> *est absor⟨p⟩ta carnis substancia.*   55
> *Cui perhennis est benedictio,*
> *summe laudis congratulatio.*
> *Alleluia!*
> *Benedicto Patre cum Filio,*
> *benedicat nostra deuocio.*   60

Custodes exterriti adhuc iaceant in terra, quasi mortui. Maria[2] cum ceteris uadat conparare aromata, et cantent:

> *Aromata precio querimus,*
> *Christi corpus ungere uolumus;*
> *holocausta sunt odoriffera*
> *sepulture Christi ad memoriam.*

Specionarivs respondeat et agat sua:

> *Dabo uobis ungenta optima,*   65
> *Saluatoris ungere uulnera,*
> *sepulture eius ad memoriam*
> *et nomini eius ad gloriam.*

Emptis aromatibus, procedunt ad Tumulum cantantes simul:

> *Quis reuoluet nobis lapidem ab ostio monumenti?*

Hoc ter repetito, surgat Angelus, qui et cantet:

> *Quem queritis uiuentem cum mortuis? Non est hic. Surrexit,[3] sicut dixit uobis cum esset in Galilea.*   71

---

[1] Concerning this composition see below, p. 619.
[2] Maria] Maria Maria (MS).

[3] Surrexit] Written in the right margin; preceded by *sed* crossed out.

Et ille perterrite parum retrocedant, et iterum Angelus cantet:

Nolite expauescere; Iesum queritis Nazarenum crucifixum. Surrexit;[1] *non est hic. Ecce locus ubi posuerunt eum; sed ite, dicite discipulis eius et Petro quia precedet uos in Galileam; ibi eum uidebitis sicut dixit uobis.*

Hiis dictis, Angeli redeunt sedentes ad Sepulchrum. Tunc[2] Marie ueniunt a⟨d⟩ Discipulos cantando:

> *En angeli aspectum uidimus,*   75
> *et responsum eius audiuimus,*
> *nam testatur Dominum uiuere;*
> *sic oportet te, Simon, credere.*

Apostoli cantent:

> *Ista sunt similia   deliramentorum,*
> *Nec persuasibilia   mentibus uirorum.*   80

Tunc Petrus et Iohannes properent ad Monumentum, et precurrens Iohannes inueniens sudarium cantet:

> *Monumentum inueni uacuum,*
> *nec in eo uidi mortuum;*
> *miror*[3] *quidem si resurrexerit,*
> *an aliquis eum abstulerit.* |

Postea ueniens Petrus tollat linteamina, et cantent ad ceteros Apostolos:

> *Monumentum uidimus uacuum,*   85
> *nec in eo uidimus mortuum;*
> *et nescimus si resurrexerit,*
> *an aliquis eum abstulerit.*

Tunc Maria Magdalena, que fuerat uestigio secuta Petrum et Iohannem, illis recedentibus, remanet sola plangens:

> *Cum uenissem ungere mortuum,*
> *monumentum inueni uacuum.*   90
> *Hev! nescio recte discernere*
> *ubi possim magistrum querere.*
>
> *En lapis est uere depositus,*
> *qui fuerat in signo positus.*
> *Munierat locum militibus;*   95
> *locus uacat, eis absentibus.*
>
> *Dolor crescit, tremunt precordia*
> *de magistri pii absencia,*
> *qui*[4] *saluauit me plenam uiciis,*
> *pulsis a me septem demoniis.*   100

Tunc Ihesus, quasi in specie Ortulani ei apparens, cante⟨t⟩:

> *Mulier, quid ploras?*

---

[1] Surrexit] Written in the right margin.
[2] Tunc] Preceded by a square bracket (MS).
[3] miror] mirror (MS).
[4] qui] quis (MS).

Tunc Maria:
>   *Quia tulerunt Dominum meum, et nescio ubi posuerunt illum.*

Cui iterum Ihesus:
>   *Mulier, quid ploras? Quem queris?*

It*erum* Maria:
>   *Domine, si tu sustulisti eum, dicito michi ubi posuisti eum, et ego eum tollam.*

Ihesus in specie Christi:
>   *Maria!*   105

Illa respond*et*:
>   *Rabboni!*

Illaque uolente tangere pedes eius, dic*it* ei Ihesus:
>   *Noli me tangere; nondum enim ascendi ad Patrem meum; uade autem ad fratres meos et dic eis: Ascendo ad Patrem meum et Patrem uestrum, Deum meum et Deum uestrum.*

Tunc duo Angeli precedentes Ihesum ad Infernum cantent:
>   *Cum rex glorie Christus.*[1]   110

Ihesus ueniens ad portas Inferni et inueniens eas clausas cantet:
>   *Tollite portas, principes, uestras, et e⟨levamini⟩ p⟨orte⟩ e⟨ternales⟩, et i⟨ntroibit⟩ r⟨ex⟩ glorie.*

Tunc Diabolus:
>   *Quis est iste rex glorie?*

Ihesus:
>   *Dominus fortis et p⟨otens⟩, d⟨ominus⟩ p⟨otens⟩ in prelio.*

Hoc ter repetito, Ihesus magno impetu confringat portas. Infernales uero intuentes uultum eius cantent:
>   *Aduenisti, desiderabilis!*[2]   115

Postea Maria inueniens alias duas Marias cantat:
>   *Vere uidi Dominum uiuere,*
>   *nec dimisit me pedes tangere;*
>   *discipulos oportet credere,*[3]
>   *quod ad Patrem uelit ascendere.*

Tunc ille tres iam certifficate de Resurrectione Domini nunciant eam Apostolis cantantes:
>   *Galileam omnes adibitis;*[4]   120
>   *ibi Iesum uiuum uidebitis;*
>   *quem post mortem uiuum non uidimus,*
>   *nos ibidem uisuros credimus.*[5]

[1] For the full text of this piece see above, p. 151. The theme of the Harrowing of Hell is treated in chap. v.

[2] For the complete text of this utterance see above, p. 151.

[3] credere] Written twice, second writing crossed out (MS).

[4] adibitis] Corrected from *adhibitis* (MS).

[5] credimus] Followed by a square bracket (MS).

Custodes redeunt ad Pontiffices, et reddunt collatam pecuniam cantantes:

> Nobis autem custodientibus
> et uigilias noctis seruantibus   125
> superuenit celestis nuncius,
> qui et dixit: Surrexit Dominus.
>
> Visionem grauem sustulimus,
> terribiles iuuenes uidimus;
> et in terre motu, quem sensimus,   130
> crucifixum surgere uidimus.

Hiis auditis, Pontiffices corrumpunt muneribus Custodes cantantes:

> Que refertis uerba subprimite;
> hanc mercedem ob hoc suscipite;
> et, ne rumor in turbam prodeat,
> fides uestra caute prouideat.   135
>
> Morem nobis in turba gerite,
> corpus furtim sublatum, dicite:
> Cum nos grauis sompnus obpresserit,
> fur de nocte eum abstulerit.

Milites, accepta pecunia, ad populum canta⟨n⟩t:

> Vigilie cunctos oppresserant,   140
> iam nos sparsim | dormire nouerant;[1]
> ad sepulchrum fures accelerant,
> ut magistrum alias transferant.
>
> In ruinam igitur populi
> furati sunt Ihesum discipuli,   145
> ut ualeant turbam seducere;
> mentiuntur, magistrum uiuere.

Tunc Marie redeunt ad Discipulos cantantes:

> En angeli aspectum uidimus,
> et responsum eius audiuimus,
> nam testatur Dominum uiuere;   150
> sic oportet te, Symon, credere.

Apostoli cantant:

> Ista sunt similia   deliramentorum,
> Nec persuasibilia   mentibus uirorum.

Petrus et Iohannes properant ad Monumentum, et precurrens Iohannes et inueniens sudarium cantat:

---

[1] Folios 144[r] and 144[v] are written in a different hand from that seen on the preceding pages.

> *Monumentum inueni uacuum,*
> *nec uideo in eo mortuum;*   155
> *miror quidem si resurrexerit,*
> *an aliquis eum abstulerit.*

Postea uenit Petrus,[1] tollens linteamina.[2] Reuertuntur ad omnes
Apostolos cantantes:

> *Monumentum uidimus uacuum,*
> *nec in eo uidimus mortuum;*
> *sed nescimus si resurrexerit,*   160
> *an aliquis eum abstulerit.*

Tunc Maria Magdalena, que fuerat[3] uestigio secuta P⟨etrum⟩ et
Jo⟨hannem⟩ ad Monumentum, illis redeuntibus, ipsa sola remanet
cantans:

> *Cvm uenissem ungere mortuum,*
> *monumentum inueni uacuum.*
> *Heu! nescio recte discernere*
> *ubi possim magistrum querere.*   165

> *En lapis est uere depositus,*
> *qui fuerat in signum positus.*
> *Munierant locum militibus;*
> *locus uacat, eis absentibus.*

> *Dolor crescit, tremunt precordia*   170
> *de magistri pii absencia,*
> *qui saluauit[4] me plenam uiciis,*
> *pulsis a me septem demoniis.*

> *Heu! redempcio Israel,*
> *ut quid mortem sustinuit!*   175

Tunc[5] Ihesus quasi in specie Ortulani apparens cantat:
> *Mvlier, quid ploras?*

Tunc Maria:
> *Quia tulerunt Dominum meum, et nescio ubi posuerunt illum.*

Cui iterum Iesus:
> *Mvlier, quid ploras? Quem queris?*

Iterum Maria:
> *Domine, si tu sustulisti eum, dicito michi ubi posuisti eum, et ego eum*
> *tollam.*   180

Iesus in specie Christi:
> *Maria!*

---

[1] Petrus] petens (MS).
[2] linteamina] linteamimina (MS).
[3] fuerat] fuerat eum (MS).
[4] qui saluauit] Quis saluabit (MS).
[5] Tunc] Cum (MS).

Maria respondit:

Rabboni!

Eaque[1] uolente iam tangere pedes eius, dic*it* ei Ihesus:

Noli me tangere; nondum enim ascendi ad Patrem meum; uade autem ad
fratres meos et dic eis: Ad patrem ascendo meum et Patrem uestrum, Deum
meum et Deum uestrum. 185

Tunc duo Angeli precedentes Iesum ad Infernum cantant:

Alleluia!
Surrexit Christus et illuxit populo suo,
quem redemit sanguine suo.

Ihesus ueniens ad portas Inferni et inueniens clausas cantat:

Tollite portas, principes, uestras, et eleuamini porte eternales, et introibit
rex glorie. 190

⟨Tunc Diabolus:

Quis est iste rex gloriæ?⟩

Ihesus:

Dominus fortis et potens, Dominus potens in prelio.

Hoc[2] ter repetito, Ihesus magno impetu tandem confringit portas
Inferni.[3] Infernales uero intuentes[4] uultum eius cantant:

Aduenisti, desiderabilis!

Postea Maria Magdalena inueniens alias duas Marias cantat:

Vere uidi Dominum uiuere,
nec dimisit me pedes tangere; 195
discipulos oportet credere,
quod ad Patrem uelit ascendere.

Tunc ille tres iam certificate de Resurrectione Domini nunciant eam
Apostolis | cantantes:

Galileam omnes adibitis;[5]
ibi Iesum uiuum uidebitis;
quem post mortem uiuum non uidimus, 200
nos ibidem uisuros credimus.

Apostoli sine cessatione murmurant ymnum istum plangentes Dominum:

Ihesu, nostra redemptio.[6]

Item Apostoli, uidentes eam eminus, in talem uocem prorumpunt
cantando:

Dic nobis, Maria
quid uidisti in uia?

---

[1] Eaque] Eoque (MS).   [2] Hoc] Hic (MS).   [5] adibitis] adhibitis (MS).
[3] Inferni] infernu (MS).   [6] For the text of this hymn see below,
[4] intuentes] intuentis (MS).   p. 641.

Maria respondit:

> *Sepulchrum Christi uiuentis,*   205
> *et gloriam uidi resurgentis.*
> *Angelicos testes,*
> *sudarium et uestes.*
> *Surrexit Christus, spes mea;*
> *precedet s⟨uos⟩ in G⟨alilæa⟩.*   210

Tunc Apostoli omnes:

> *Credendum est magis soli Marie ueraci,*
> *quam Iudeorum turbe fallaci.*
> *Scimus Christum surrexisse a mortuis uere;*
> *tu nobis, uictor rex, miserere.*

Deinde omnes Apostoli et Mulieres ueniunt ostendere linteamina populo; cantant:

> *Cernitis, o socii, ecce linteamina et sudarium, et corpus Iesu in sepulcro*
> *non est inuentum.*   216

Illis ostensis, chorus totus cantat:

> *Post pass⟨ionem⟩ Do⟨mini⟩.*[1]
> *Currebant duo simul, et ille alius discipulus precucurrit citius Petro, et*
> *prior uenit ad monumentum, alleluia.*

Et populus uniuersus iam certificatus de Domino, cantor sic inpon*it*:

> *Christ, der ist erstanden.*[2]   220

The most noticeable aspect of this composition, as it stands, is the confusion among its parts. Of this imperfection the most obvious example is the virtually complete repetition of lines 75–123 in lines 148–201, the repeated passage including the report of the Marys to the disciples, the episode of Peter and John at the sepulchre, the colloquy of Christ and Mary Magdalen, the Descent to Hell, and a second report of the Marys to the disciples. The readiest explanation of this repetition is that the later position of the passage is the correct one, and that the earlier occurrence of it was intended to be suppressed. This explanation may be supported by the fact that in its earlier position the passage is enclosed in what appear to be contemporary square brackets,[3] and by the additional fact that the second copying of the passage begins on the first page executed by the second scribe (fol. 144ʳ).

---

[1] This may be the following antiphon from Easter Lauds (Hartker, p. 230): *Post passionem Domini factus est conventus quia non est inventum corpus in monumento; lapis sustinuit perpetuam vitam, monumentum reddidit cælestem margaritam, alleluia.*

[2] The rest of the page is blank, except for the following inscription, in a later hand, at the very bottom: *Liber Sancte Marie in Niwenburga.*

[3] These brackets are not mentioned by Pfeiffer.

HARROWING

It may be inferred that after the first scribe had placed the passage in a wrong position, a second was set to work with a view to rectification. The placing of the excerpt in the later position, in any case, results in a sequence of events more nearly in conformity with what we find in the plays from Benediktbeuern and Tours, to be considered below. Through this revision the negotiations of the high priests and the soldiers are disposed of before the occurrence of more significant incidents in which the soldiers are not concerned.[1] The slight differences between the two copyings of the repeated passage can scarcely be considered significant. The blunder of the second scribe in omitting the speech of *Diabolus* (*Quis est iste rex gloriæ?*) is easily explained by the fact that this speech and the preceding one end with the same word. For his addition of a brief passage (ll. 174–5) to a speech of Mary Magdalen, and for the substitution of *Surrexit Christus* for *Cum rex gloriæ*, there is no apparent reason.

Even after the changes outlined above, the sequence of incidents and speeches leaves something to be desired. After Mary Magdalen has told her companions that she has seen Christ (l. 194), for example, she immediately joins them in reporting to the disciples as follows:

Galileam omnes adibitis;
ibi Iesum uiuum uidebitis;
quem post mortem uiuum *non* uidimus,
nos ibidem uisuros credimus.

At the very end of the play, moreover, is found the antiphon *Currebant duo*, which could be sung appropriately only when Peter and John race to the sepulchre, and which in its present position provides an uncommonly ineffectual ending for the performance.

But however defective the play may be in general construction, it is highly commendable for its vivid presentation of certain unusual scenes. Here for the first time we encounter in an Easter play a genuine dramatization of the Harrowing of Hell.[2] After his departure from Mary Magdalen, Christ is led by two angels to the infernal gates, where he sings the familiar command *Tollite portas*, and is challenged by Satan's *Quis est iste rex gloriæ?* After the third repetition of this dialogue, Christ breaks down the gates with a crash, and the imprisoned spirits acclaim him with

[1] Concerning the difficulty of placing appropriately the last scene in which the priests negotiate with the soldiers see Meyer, p. 94.
[2] On this scene see Schmidt, pp. 24–5.

the words *Advenisti, desiderabilis,* from the well-known antiphon *Cum rex gloriæ.* The speeches employed here are those which we have already seen repeatedly in certain versions of the *Elevatio,* but in the play before us we have a rare example of the actual participation in this scene of the impersonated Christ.[1]

Another role now before us for the first time in a fully developed form is that of the soldiers.[2] Of these personages we hear first in the opening scene, in which the Jewish high priests ask Pilate to set a guard at the sepulchre to prevent the disciples from removing Christ's body. To this request Pilate accedes, and the priests, giving bribes to the soldiers, lead them to their post. As they march round the tomb, the guard sing five stanzas having the Germanized refrain *Schowa propter insidias.* Then comes the angel with the flaming sword, singing *Resurrexit victor ab inferis,* and striking the soldiers to the earth. After the Marys depart from their scene with the angel at the sepulchre, the prostrated soldiers rise, report their experiences to the priests, receive further bribes, and report to the populace that the disciples have stolen Christ's body.

In these scenes all the details of the Gospel narrative are exhaustively employed, and the speeches of the participants, of which the Bible gives not a word, are amply and freely developed in stanzas of lines of ten syllables.[3] There is no cogent reason for rejecting Meyer's inference that these stanzas were composed by a German, and that, in adopting the ten-syllable line, he was under the influence of France, where this metrical form was indigenous and much esteemed.[4] Pfeiffer also may be right in conjecturing that this innovator was a monk of Klosterneuburg, who prepared the scenes before us for a performance of the Easter play on the occasion when Duke Leopold VI visited the monastery at Eastertide in 1204.[5]

The verse-form used in the scenes of the soldiers predominates throughout the play. Mary Magdalen and her companions employ stanzas of it which we have observed elsewhere,[6] and Peter and John speak new stanzas in the same form (ll. 81–8). Complete metrical monotony is avoided through the use of prose

[1] For treatments of the theme of the Harrowing of Hell in the *Elevatio* see above, chap. v.

[2] For a very rudimentary treatment of the theme see above, p. 408.

[3] See Matt. xxvii ,62–6; xxviii, 2–4, 11–5; Meyer, pp. 93–4.

[4] See Meyer, pp. 121–2, and below, pp. 677 sqq.

[5] See Pfeiffer, *Klosterneuburger Osterspiel,* pp. 175–6.

[6] Concerning their scene with the *specionarius* see Dürre, pp. 30–1.

in several scenes, of several liturgical pieces, and of a goliardic measure in one speech of Peter and John (ll. 79–80):

> Ista sunt similia   deliramentorum,
> Nec persuasibilia   mentibus virorum.

This disclosure of impatient scepticism is an unexpected and agreeable addition to the psychological traditions of the theme.

Although the play begins and ends in a liturgical manner, it may or may not have been performed in the choir or nave of the church. In the text there is, certainly, nothing prohibitive; and the church building could readily have provided the additional *sedes* required for Pilate, the *pontifices*, and the scene of the Harrowing of Hell.

III

Identical with the play of Klosterneuburg in considerable part,[1] and perhaps modelled upon it, is a composition belonging to the famous *Carmina Burana*. This varied collection of poems—joyous and sober, pious and licentious—is preserved in a manuscript of the late thirteenth century, found in the year 1803 at the Bavarian monastery of Benediktbeuern. It may have been the repertory of wandering scholars, or, more probably, the valued possession of a monastic community which desired to have its own anthology of the vivacious literary inventions of the *vagantes*. Among the six plays which formerly occupied the closing pages of the volume is the following:[2]

Incipit Ludus, immo Exemplum, Dominice Resurrectionis

Cantatis Matutinis in die Pasche, omnes persone ad ludum disposite sint parate in loco speciali secundum suum modum, et procedant ad locum ubi sit Sepulchrum. Primum ueniat Pilatus et Vxor sua cum magnis luminibus, Militibus precedentibus, Assessoribus sequentibus, deinde Pontificibus et Iudeis; post hec ueniant Angeli et Marie et Apostoli.

Ingressus Pilatus.[3]

---

[1] See Dürre, pp. 30–2.

[2] Munich, Staatsbibl. MS lat. 4660a, Carmina Burana sæc. xiii, fol. v^r–vi^v, published by Meyer, pp. 126–30, with complete photographic facsimiles, plates 8, 9, 10, and 11. The text of Hilka and Schumann will be no. 15*. For observations upon the MS see Notes, p. 686. For palaeographical remarks upon the text before us see Hilka and Schumann, ii, 57*, 58*. The MS provides musical notation.

[3] Ingressus Pilatus] These words are written in red, without music, as if they were part of the rubric. They appear to be intended, however, as the beginning of the responsory which we have already found used as a processional piece at the opening of the play from Klosterneuburg. See above, p. 421.

Primum cant*ent* Pontifices:

> *O domine, recte meminimus,*
> *quod a turba sepe audiuimus,*
> *seductorem consuetum dicere:*
> *Post tres dies uolo resurgere.*   5

Pilatus:

> *Sicut michi dictat discretio*
> *et astuta uestra cognitio,*
> *michi crimen uultis imponere*
> *de Iesu, quem fecistis perdere.*

Pontifices:

> *Vestra uirtus et sapientia*   10
> *nobis ualde est necessaria;*
> *seductores namque discipuli*
> *machinantur ruinam populi.*

Vxor Pilati:

> *Versutia horum non faciat,*[1]
> *ut sepulchrum preses custodiat;*   15
> *uestra namque perpendat gloria,*
> *quanta passa fui per sompnia.*

Assessores:

> *Militibus ergo precipias*
> *custodire noctis uigilias,*
> *ne furentur illum discipuli,*[2]   20
> *et dicant plebi:*[3] *Surrexit a mortuis.*

Judei stent ante Pilatum et cant*ent*:

> *Avdi, preses,   nostras preces,   ne sis deses;   nobis debes*
> *hos prestare milites*
> *Ad sepulchrum,   ut defunctus   obseruetur,   ne tollatur*
> *suis a discipulis.*   25

Respo*ndeat* Pilatus:

> *En habetis custodum copiam.*
> *Custodite noctis uigiliam,*
> *ne furentur illum discipuli,*
> *et dicant eum uiuere populi.*

Tunc Jvdei se uertant ad Milites parum:[4]

> *Militibus damus pecuniam,*   30
> *ut habeant semper | custodiam*
> *seductoris, qui dixit temere:*
> *Post tres dies uolo resurgere.*

---

[1] Versutia ... faciat] Versutias horum non fatiat (MS).

[2] After writing the line as printed here, the scribe altered it to the following defective form: *ne furetur a discipulis.*

[3] plebi] The first three letters crossed out (MS).

[4] parum] Meyer regards this as the correct reading, but, for intelligibility, emends to *pariter.*

Milites petant pecuniam:

> *Qvid mercedis ob hoc habebimus,*
> *si custodes uestri manserimus,*   35
> *ne tollant Iesum discipuli*
> *et credant eum uiuere populi?*

Judei ostendant illis pecuniam:

> *O viri fortes, uobis dabimus precium;*
> *custodite sepulchrum!*

Deinde exhibeant denarios in nvmero:

> *Nvmmos centum quiuis accipiat*   40
> *uel talentum, ut non decipiat,*
> *sed custodes existant tumuli,*
> *ne furentur illum discipuli.*

Demum in toto sine nvmero:

> *Pecunia militibus   habunde tradatur,*
> *ne seductor perfidus   furtim auferatur.*   45

Tunc Milites, accepta pecunia, evaginent enses et uadant ad Sepul-chrvm, et circueant illud ordinate cantando simul *Defensores*; deinde vnusquisque Militum suas vigilias solus si uelit.

> *Defensores erimus tumuli,*
> *ne furentur illum discipuli*
> *et fallendo dicant in populis:*
> *Resurrexit Christus a mortuis.*

Primus Miles:

> *Non credimus Iesum resurgere,*   50
> *sed, ne corpus quis possit tollere,*
> *prouidemus per has uigilias.*
> *Schăwe propter insidias!*

Secundus Miles:

> *Non credimus ut quidquam conferat,*
> *set ne corpus eius quis auferat*   55
> *custodimus noctis uigilias.*
> *Schăwe propter insidias!*

Tercius Miles:

> *Schăwe[1] alvmbe, ne fures ueniant*
> *et corpus Iesu furtim auferant,*
> *custodimus noctis uigilias.*   60
> *Schăwe propter insidias!*

Quartus Miles:

> *Non exigit humana ratio*
> *ut resurgat uiuus ex mortuo;*

---

[1] Schăwe] Shaw̆æ (MS).

               seductores ferunt uersutias.
               Schawe propter insidias!   65
Quintus Miles:

               Si mortuus posset re|surgere,
               potuisset profecto uiuere,
               quare tulit mortis angustias?
               Schǎwe propter insidias!

Tunc ueniant duo Angeli, unus ferens ensem flammeum et uestem
rubeam, alter uero uestem albam et crucem in manv. Angelus autem
ferens ensem percutiat unum ex Militibus ad galeam, et medio fiant
tonitrva magna, et Milites cadant quasi mortui. Et Angeli stantes ante
Sepulchrum et nuncient cantando Christum surrexisse:[1]

               Alleluia.   70
               Resurrexit uictor ab inferis,
               pastor ouem reportans humeris.
               Alleluia.
               Non diuina tamen potentia
               est absor⟨p⟩ta carnis substantia.   75
               Alleluia.
               Reformator ruine ueteris
               causam egit humani generis.[2]
               Alleluia.

Tunc ueniant Marie inquirendo aromata, et cantent simul:

               Aromata precio querimus,   80
               corpus Iesu ungere uolumus;
               aromata sunt odorifera
               sepulture Christi memoria.

Tunc Apotecarius audiens eas uocet:

               Hvc propius flentes accedite,
               et vngentum si uultis, emite;   85
               aliter nusquam portabitis.
                  Uere quantus est dolor uester![3]

Item Marie:

               Dic tu nobis, mercator iuuenis,
               hoc vngentum si tu uendideris,

---

[1] Relevant here are parts of the passages written by another hand at the very top of fol. vi[r]. See Hilka and Schumann, ii, 57*. These passages are partly lost through the wearing away of the parchment, but the following can still be read:

  Antequam canunt angeli *Alleluia* ad suscitandum Dominum (Jesum?)
  Surge uictor rex glorie qui . . .
  Et dominica persona: *Ego dor⟨miui⟩ qui*

    sompnum cepi
    Suscipe cum sceptro . . .
    Et induat uestem ortulani.

As a whole these passages cannot be inserted in the text as it stands.

[2] Concerning the verses beginning *Resurrexit uictor ab inferis* see below, p. 619.

[3] This speech is written by more than one hand, and the result is metrically imperfect. See Hilka and Schumann, ii, 57*.

> dic precium, pro quanto dederis.   90
> Hev, quantus est dolor noster!

Apotecarius:

> Dabo uobis ungenta optima,
> Saluatoris vngere vvlnera,
> sepulture eius in[1] memoriam
> et nomini eius ad gloriam.   95

Vxor Apotecarii leuet pixidem et cantet:

> Hoc vngentum si vvltis emere,
> auri talentum michi tradite;
> aliter nusquam portabitis.
> Uere quantus sit dolor uester!

Et sic ement aromata. | Apotecarius ostendat eis viam ad Sepulchrvm:

> Hec est uera[2] semita,   que recte, non per deuia   100
> uos ducet ad ortum.
> Ibi cum ueneritis,   illum, quem uos queritis,
> uidebitis Iesum,
> Saluatorem uestrum.

Marie, ostensa uia, uadunt ad Sepulchrum et cantant:

> Set eamus et ad eius   properemus tumulum;   105
> Si dileximus uiuentem,   diligamvs mortuum.

Marie lamentando cantent et uadant circa Sepulchrum:

> Hev! nobis internas mentes   quanti pulsant gemitus
> Pro nostro consolatore,   quo priuamur misere,
> Quem crudelis Iudeorum   morti dedit populus.

Item cantent:[3]

> Iam percusso cev pastore,   oues errant misere;   110
> Sic magistro discedente,   turbantur discipuli,
> Atque nos, absente eo,   dolor tenet nimius.

Item cantent:

> Iam iam, ecce iam properemus ad tumulum,
> vngentes corpus sanctissimum.

Vna sola cantet:

> O Deus!   115

Alia sola cantet:

> O Deus!

Tercia sola cantet:

> O Deus!

---

[1] eius in] eius eius im, with first *eius*
expunged (MS).

[2] Hec est uera] These words are repeated,
in a different hand, on the first line at the
top of the page—a line otherwise blank.

[3] In the right margin, opposite the line in
which this rubric occurs, are written, in
another hand, the words *awe wie*. See Hilka
and Schumann, ii, 57*.

Deinde simul:

> *Qvis reuolvet nobis lapidem ab hostio monumenti?*

Interea vadant Milites ad Pilatum et Pontifices et Judeos, et nuntient quod uiderunt et audierunt:

> *Visionem grauem sustulimus,*
> *terribiles iuuenes uidimus;*   120
> *et in terre motu, quem sensimus,*
> *crucifixum surgere nouimus.*

Item cant*ent:*

> *Nobis autem custodientibus*
> *et vigilias noctis seruantibus*
> *superuenit celestis nuntius,*   125
> *qui et dixit: Surrexit Dominus.*

Tunc Pontifices perterriti corrumpunt Milites muneribus ut taceant:

> *Qve refertis uerba supprimite;*
> *hanc mercedem ob hoc suscipite;*
> *et ne rumor in turba prodeat.*[1]

A scrutiny of this text discloses the fact that more than one-half of the lines in it are found also in the play from Klosterneuburg. In spite of this similarity, however, and in spite of brevity, the fragment from Benediktbeuern is conspicuously superior to the related play in several matters of dramatic elaboration. In the present play the action connected with the soldiery is not only more extended, but also more animated, through the presence of new personages. In appointing the guard for the sepulchre, Pilate has among his counsellors, for the first time, both his wife and certain additional advisers called *assessores*. These last may be imitations of the advisers in the Magi plays, to be considered in later chapters.[2] The scene between the Marys and the apothecary is enlarged by fresh speeches, and by the presence of the apothecary's wife.[3] It is she who names the price, and adds, in apparent irony, *Vere quantus sit dolor vester!* A touch of humanity is added also to the apothecary himself in that he courteously directs the Marys on their way from his shop to the sepulchre.

The manuscript bears also some evidence of a still more impressive innovation. In the upper margin of the third page (fol. vi[r]) are entries indicating that when the angels sing the passage *Alleluia, Resurrexit victor ab inferis*, Christ himself comes forth

---

[1] Here end the page and fragment.   [3] On this scene see Dürre, pp. 31–3, and
[2] See Meyer, p. 98, and chaps. xviii   below, ii, 504.
and xix below.

from the tomb, and takes a speaking part in the action.[1] The exact content of this scene, however, cannot be determined; nor are we certain that it was ever a genuine part of the play.

The Benediktbeuern version differs from that of Klosterneuburg, to a slight extent, also in its metrical tendencies. Even in the short fragment before us are evidences of a freer use of goliardic measures (ll. 44-5, 100-4), and the adoption of a species of *Stabat mater* stanza (ll. 22-5) which we have not encountered previously.

IV

The Easter play from the diocese of Tours, with which this chapter must conclude, is of still larger scope than the versions from Klosterneuburg and Benediktbeuern, since it contains not only the full range of scenes in which the guards are concerned, but also a somewhat generous dramatization of events which occurred during a period of a week or more after the Resurrection itself. Unfortunately, however, this elaborate composition is known to us only in the following fragmentary and disordered form:[2]

⟨LUDUS PASCHALIS⟩

Tunc erit error peior ⟨priore⟩.[3]

Hic Pilatus conuo⟨cet⟩ Milites ad se, et dicat eis:[4]

> *Uenite ad me, milites*
> *fortes atque incolumes;*
> *diligenter pergite.*
> *Quod uobis dico, facite:*   5
> *tres dies cum noctibus*
> *uigilate cum studio,*
> *ne fure⟨n⟩tur discipuli*
> *et dicant plebi:*

[1] These marginal entries are shown in the foot-notes to the text above, p. 435.

[2] Tours, Bibl. de la Ville, MS 927, Miscellanea Turonensia sæc. xiii, fol. 1ʳ-8ᵛ, previously edited by V. Luzarche, *Office de Pâques ou de la Résurrection*, Tours, 1856, pp. 1-26 (preceded, on unnumbered pages, by a complete, but defective, lithographic facsimile); Coussemaker, pp. 21-48; Milchsack, pp. 97-102; Lange, *Programm*, pp. 29-34; A. de Montaiglon, *Le Drame Paschal de la Résurrection*, Tours, 1895. For descriptions of the MS see *Catalogue général des Manuscrits des Bibliothèques publiques de France*, xxxvii (2 parts), ed. G. Collon, Paris, 1900, 1905,

pp. 667-70; L. Delisle, in *Romania*, ii (1873), 91-5. For textual observations see Meyer, pp. 86-8, 95-6. Obviously the text in the MS is uncommonly corrupt. Except in a few passages, the text is provided with musical notation on four lines.

[3] Although this line is not furnished with musical notation—as is most of the rest of the spoken text—it is certainly part of the dialogue. The word *priore*, representing a word illegible in the MS, is supplied from Matt. xxvii, 64.

[4] In this line the last syllable of *conuocet* is entirely illegible; but *eis*, overlooked by previous editors, can still be read.

　　　　　Surrexit a mortuis.　　　　　　　　　10
　　　　　Ite, uos milites, sollerti cura[1]
　　　　　uobis commissa sit sepultura.

Statim Milites eant insimul canendo hos uersus usquedum ueniant
ante[2] Sepulchrum:

　　　　　Ergo eamus,
　　　　　et quid dixit, faciamus;
　　　　　uigilando custodiamus,　　　　　　　15
　　　　　ne sepultum amittamus.
　　　　　Ne forte ueniant eius discipuli
　　　　　et furando transferant alibi,
　　　　　inuadamus eos cum | lanceis[3]
　　　　　et uerberemus eos cum gladiis.　　　　20

Modo ueniat Angelus et iniiciat eis fulgura; Milites cadant in
terra⟨m⟩ uelut mortui. Tunc tres parui uel clerici, qui debent esse
Marie: due uero deferant uas cum unguento pre manibus, tercia autem
turribulum. Tunc ueniant ante hostium ecclesie et dica⟨n⟩t hos uersus.
Maria Magdalene incipiat:

　　　　　⟨*O*⟩*mnipotens Pater altissime,*
　　　　　angelorum rector mitissime,
　　　　　quid faciunt iste miserrime?
　　　　　　　Heu! quantus est noster dolor!

Maria Iacobi:

　　　　　Amisimus enim solacium,　　　　　25
　　　　　Ihesum Christum, Marie filium;
　　　　　ipse erat nobis consilium.
　　　　　　　Heu! quantus,

et cetera. Maria Salome:

　　　　　Sed eamus unguentum emere,[4]
　　　　　ut hoc corpus possimus ungere,　　　　30
　　　　　quod numquam uermes possint commedere,
　　　　　　　Heu! ⟨*quantus est noster dolor!*⟩

Tunc Mercator dicat:

　　　　　Venite, si complacet emere
　　　　　hoc unguentum, quod uellem uendere,
　　　　　de quo bene potestis[5] *ungere*　　　　35
　　　　　　　corpus Domini sacratum.
　　　　　Quod, si corpus possetis ungere,
　　　　　non amplius posset putrescere,
　　　　　neque uermes possent commedere.

---

[1] cura] Corrected by a later hand from
cum (MS).
[2] ante] A corrector has attempted to alter
añ into, possibly, *ad.*

[3] lanceis] lanceas (MS).
[4] emere] o͞e (MS).
[5] potestis] pᵗ (MS).

Marie simul:

> *Heu! quantus ⟨est noster dolor⟩!*   40

Tunc Marie interrogent Mercatorem:

> *Dic nobis, tu mercator iuuenis,*
> *hoc unguentum si tu uendideris,*
> *dic precium quod tibi dederimus.*
> *Heu!*

et cetera. Respondeat Mercator:

> *Mulieres, michi intendite.*   45
> *Hoc unguentum si uultis emere,*
> *datur genus mire potencie.*

Marie simul:

> *Heu! ⟨quantus est noster dolor!⟩*

Mercator:

> *Hoc unguentum, si multum cupitis,*
> *unum auri talentum dabitis,*   50
> *non aliter unquam portabitis.*

Marie simul:

> *Heu!*

et cetera. Alius Mercator dicat eis: |

> *Quid queri⟨ti⟩s?*

Marie simul respondeant:

> *Aromata uenimus emere,*
> *o pigmentare, si habes*   55
> *illud quod nobis necesse est.*

Respondeat Mercator:

> *Dicite, quid uultis?*

Marie simul respondeant:

> *Balsamum, thus et mirram,*
> *silaloe et aloes.*

Respondeat Mercator:

> *Ecce, iam ante uobis sunt omnia;*   60
> *dicite, quantum uultis emere?*

Marie simul respondent:

> *Quasi centum libras satis habemus;*
> *dic nobis, quantum denos, domine?*

Respondet Mercator:

> *Mille solidos potestis habere.*

Marie simul respondent:

> *Libenter, domine.*   65

Tunc Marie dent munera, et accipiant unguentum, et pergant ad
Sepulcrum. Marie[1] simul primum:

> *O, summe rex e|terne,*
> *regem ostende nobis.*

Maria Iacobi:

> *Pilatus iussit militibus sepulcrum custodire.*

Maria Salome:

> *Nil timeamus;*[2] *Ihesum uenimus ungere.*

Maria Magdalene:

> *Heu! misera, cur contigit*   70
> *uidere mortem redemptoris?*

Maria Iacobi:

> *Heu! redemptio Israel,*
> *ut quid mortem sustinuit!*

Maria Salome:

> *Heu! consolatio nostra,*
> *ut quid taliter agere uoluit!*   75

Marie[3] simul respondent:

> *Iam iam, ecce, iam properemus ad tumulum,*
> *unguentes dilecti corpus sanctis⟨s⟩imum.*

Angelus respondet:

> *Non eget unguentum,*[4] *quia Christus de monu|mento sur⟨r⟩exit uere; locus*
> *ecce; uenite, uenite, videte!*

Tunc Maria Magdalene cum Maria Iacobi uadat uidere Sepulcrum;
non inuento corpore, redeat ad aliam, et dicat Maria Magdalene:

> *Lamentemus, tristis⟨s⟩ime*[5]   80
> *sorores, nunc karissime,*
> *nos de filio Marie*
> *sepulto tercia die.*

Maria Iacobi:

> *Tres uenimus iam hodie*
> *corpus ungere glorie,*   85
> *ut non posset*[6] *putrescere.*

Maria Salome:

> *Angelorum eloquio*
> *scientes sine dubio,*
> *quia sur⟨r⟩exit de tumulo,*
> *reuertamur cum gaudio.*   90

[1] Marie] Maria (MS).
[2] timeamus] Corrected, by a later hand, from *timeas* (MS).
[3] Marie] Maria (MS).
[4] unguentum] Meyer (p. 86) would emend to *unguento*, inferring that the speech is in verse.
[5] tristis⟨s⟩ime] cristisime (MS).
[6] posset] possed (MS).

Angelus respondit:

> *Ad uos dico, mulieres, nolite expauescere, neque timere; ego sum Michael arcangelus; dicite michi, quem queritis, aut[1] quem uultis | uidere?*

Maria Magdalene respond*et*:

> *O Deus! Quis reuoluet[2] nobis lapidem ab hostio monumenti?*

Marie simul dicant:

> *Ecce, lapis reuolutus, et iuuenis stola candida coopertus.*

Angelus alta uoce clamat Marias dicens:

> *Venite! venite! uenite! Nolite timere uos; dicite,*   95
> *Quem queritis in sepulcro, o Cristicole?*

Marie simul respondent:

> *Ihesum Nazarenum crucifixum querimus, o celicole!*

Angelus:

> *Non est hic, sur⟨r⟩exit sicut predixerat;[3] uenite et uidete locum ubi posuerunt eum, et euntes dicite di⟨s⟩cipulis eius et Petro quia | sur⟨r⟩exit.*
>> *Uultum tristem iam mutate,*   100
>> *Ihesum ui⟨u⟩um suis nunciate.*
>> *Galileam nu⟨n⟩c abite;*
>> *si placet uidere, festinate.[4]*

Tunc Milites surgant et redeant ad Pilatum tristi animo canendo:

>> *Heu! miseri, quid facimus,*
>> *quid dicimus,*   105
>> *quia perdidimus,*
>> *quem custodimus?*
>> *De celo uenit angelus,*
>> *qui dixit mulieribus*
>> *quia sur⟨r⟩exit Dominus.*   110

Deinde dicat Pilatus ad Milites:

>> *Vos, Romani milites,*
>> *precium accipite*
>> *et omnibus dicite*
>> *quod uobis sublatum est.*

Milites simul respondeant:

>> *Pro quo gentiles fuimus!*   115
>> *Sepulcrum custodiuimus,*
>> *magnum sonum audiuimus,*
>> *et in terram ce⟨ci⟩dimus. |*

---

[1] aut] aud (MS).
[2] reuoluet] Corrected from *reuoluit* (MS).
[3] predixerat] Though blurred, probably *predixerrat* (MS).
[4] uidere festinate] uidete festinare (MS).

Item dicat Pilatus:

> *Legem non habuistis,*
> *sed mentiri potestis,*   120
> *quod discipuli uenerunt*
> *et eum sustulerunt.*

Milites simul respondent:

> *Nos ueritatem dicimus:*
> *de celo uenit angelus,*
> *qui dixit mulieribus*   125
> *quia sur⟨r⟩exit Dominus*

Hoc audito, Pilatus dicat Militibus hos uersus:

> *Hec ergo uolo, ut sint uestra munera,*
> *ne uos credatis aliqua mendatia*
> *que uos seducant*
> *et perire faciant.*   130
> *Ad domos uestras ite nu⟨n⟩c cum gaudio,*
> *et que uidistis tegite silentio,*
> *ne ad auditum populi eueniat.*[1]

Milites simul respondea⟨n⟩t ad Pilatum:

> *Tu⟨n⟩c erit.*[2]

Et facto hoc, Maria Magdalene in sinistra parte ecclesie stans, et cetera;[3] exurgat inde et eat contra Sepulcrum et, plausis manibus, plorando dicat: |

> *Heu! me misera!*   135
> *Magnus labor,*   *magnus dolor,*   *magna est tristitia.*
> *Ihesu*[4] *Christe,*   *mundi tocius gloria,*
> *De te nasci*[5]   *teneo memoria,*
> *Quam emisti*   *tua misericordia;*
> *Qui condonasti*   *Magdalene grauia*   140
> *Peccamina;*   *per te uita*   *perfruar perpetua.*
> *O magister!*
> *Quare pie te si quando*   *his uidebo oculis,*
> *Quem*[6] *Iudei suspenderunt*   *crucis in patibulis*
> *Et audiui sur⟨r⟩exis⟨s⟩e*   *dictis nunc angelicis.*   145
> *Rex cun⟨c⟩torum*   *angelorum*   *pro nobis occisus est.*
> *Heu! michi tristi, dolenti*   *de morte altissimi.*
> *O quam magno dies* | *ista*   *celebranda*[7] *gaudio,*

[1] eueniat] eueniad (MS).

[2] This appears to be the *incipit* of the speech found at the opening of the play as preserved. The two words here have musical notation.

[3] et cetera] The MS has 7 c̄, ignored by all previous editors except Montaiglon, who reads *etc.* In the context this expression is hardly intelligible; nor is *et cantans* satisfactory.

[4] Ihesu] Iehu (MS).

[5] nasci] uascj (MS). Neither reading is satisfactory.

[6] quem] Inserted by a later hand (MS).

[7] magno . . . celebranda] magna . . . celebrando (MS). For a prose beginning *O quam magno dies ista* see above, p. 293.

Quam ingenti, tam deuoto,   recolenda[1] studio!
Angelus de celo uenit,   lapidem reuoluit; sedit.   150
Deus et homo! Deus et homo! Deus et homo!
Ihesu[2] Christe, tu spes mea,   salus uiua seculi,
Memorare Magdalene   tuique amici Lazari.
Te ui⟨u⟩um spero uidere   cum ⟨s⟩ceptro imperii.
Me misera! me misera! me misera!   155
Quid agam? Heu! tristis, quid dicam?

Stans Ihesus[3] iuxta Sepulcrum in horto[4] dicat Magdalene:
   Mulier, quid ploras?
Maria Magdalene respondit:
   Quia tulerunt Dominum meum, et nescio ubi posuerunt eum. |
Angelus dicat ad Marias:
   Quem queritis?
Maria Iacobi et Salome respondentes:
   Viuentem cum mortuis.   160
Angelus dicat:
   Non est hic, sed sur⟨r⟩exit; recordamini qualiter locutus est uobis dum
adhuc in Galilea esset,[5] uobis dicens[6] quia oportet filium hominis tradi et
crucifigi, et die tercia resurgere.   163
Et dicat Maria Magdalene; leuet manus ad celum:
   Tu Pater, qui es in celis, tunc sanctificatum[7] est nomen tuum in eternum.
Noli me derelinquere, sed demonstrare omnibus recordare, Domine, miserere
Magdalene, quando michi dimisisti peccata mea. Heu dolens! heu amara! |
hev misera! Quem interrogem, et ubi est Pater, nescio.   167
Deinde ueniat Maria Iacobi et sustentet brachium dextrum, et Maria
Salome per sinistrum et leuet de terra Maria⟨m⟩ Magdalenam; et
dicat ipsa:
   Cara soror,   nimis langor   insidet in animo
   De magistri   Ihesu Christi   morte sibi coacta.[8]
Maria Magdalene dicat:
   Ardens est cor meum; desidero uidere Dominum meum; quero et non inuenio
   ubi posuerunt eum.   171
Angelus interroget Marias:
   Quem queritis?
Marie simul respondent:
   Viuentem cum mortuis.

---

[1] ingenti . . . recolenda] ingentis . . . reco-
lendo (MS).   [2] Ihesu] Iehū (MS).
[3] Ihesus] Meyer (p. 86) emends to *angelus*
—which may well be right.
[4] horto] ordo (MS). I adopt the emendation of Meyer (p. 86).

[5] esset] essed (MS).
[6] dicens] diceret (MS).
[7] sanctificatum] sanctificatus (MS).
[8] coacta] The MS seems to read *coauta* or
coanta. Montaiglon emends to *coacta*, and
Meyer (p. 87), to *cognita*.

Angelus dicat hos versus:

   Nichil tibi est timendum,   sed gaudeto[1] pocius;
   Ihesus enim resurrexit,   uere Dei filius.   175
   Tu, Maria Magdalena, clama: Resur⟨r⟩exit uere Cristus, sur⟨r⟩exit Christus | . . .[2]

          . . . *uideam.*
   Hanc meam dolenti corde   tribue leticiam.

Et reuersus interroget Petrus:[3]

   Dic mihi, soror Maria,   quod iter incipiam?[4]   180

Et Maria ad Petrum dicat:

   Vade cito hanc per uiam,   unde nunc regressa sum;
   Set memento mei, Petre,   dum illum inueneris.[5]

Deinde ueniat Maria. Discipuli cantando dica⟨n⟩t:

   Tristes erant apostoli
   de nece ⟨sui Domini,
   quem pena mortis crudelis   185
   serui damnarant impii⟩.[6]

De alia parte ueniant alii[7] vi cantando[8] hymnum totum:

   Ihesu, nostra redempcio,
   ⟨amor et desiderium,
   Deus, creator omnium,
   homo in fine temporum.⟩[9]   190

Maria Magdalene ueniat ante eos; dicat hunc versum:

   Solutis iam gemitibus
   ⟨et inferni doloribus,
   quia surrexit Dominus,
   resplendens clamat angelus⟩.[10]

Statim Petrus uadat ad Discipulos et maneat cum eis. Deinde ueniat ⟨Jesus⟩, dalmatica indutus, ferens in manibus crucem; dicat:

   Pax uobis; ego sum; nolite timere. Uidete manus meas et pedes meos, quia ego ipse sum; palpate et uidete, quia spiritus carnem et ossa non ha|bet, sicut me uidetis habere, alleluia.   197

Discipuli uideant eum, et osculentur, et dicant:

   Ecce, Deus noster!
   Surrexit Dominus de sepulchro, qui pro nobis pependit in ligno, alleluia, alleluia, alleluia.   200

---

[1] gaudeto] gaudete (MS?). I adopt the suggestion of Meyer (p. 87).
[2] The lacuna arises from the loss of at least one leaf—possibly of several leaves.
[3] Petrus] Maria dicat (MS).
[4] This speech and the rubric which follows it are written in the lower margin.
[5] inueneris] inueniesris (MS).
[6] These four lines are the fifth stanza of the hymn *Aurora lucis rutilat*, printed in Notes, p. 687.
[7] alii] alnl (MS).
[8] cantando] Written twice (MS).
[9] For the text of the hymn *Jesu, nostra redemptio* see below, p. 641.
[10] The fourth stanza of *Aurora lucis rutilat*.

Thomas ueniat cantando:

Thomas dicor[1] Didimus.
Omnes fugam cepimus;
congreget[2] nos Dominus.
Post laudes in omnibus
Deo nostro dabimus. 205
O fallax Iuda, proditor,   magistrum tradidisti,
Quem pro paucis argenteis   Iudeis uendidisti.
Quod accepisti precium,   heu michi! quid fecisti?

Et duo Discipuli uadant et dicant ei:

Thomas, uidimus Dominum!

Thomas quasi indignatus dicat eis: |

Nisi uidero in manibus eius fixuram clauorum, et mittam manum meam in
latus eius, non credam. 211

Tunc ueniat Ihesus ad Discipulos, indutus sacerdotalibus uestimentis
candidis, et dicat eis item:

Pax uobis; ego sum, alleluia. Nolite timere, alleluia!

Deinde dicat ad Thomam:

Thomas, mitte manum tuam et cognosce loca clauorum, alleluia; et noli
esse incredulus, set fidelis, alleluia.

Tunc ostendat ei; et Thomas cadat ad pedes eius, et dicat tribus
uicibus:

Dominus meus et Deus meus, alleluia! 215

Dominus respondit:

Quia uidisti me, Thomas, credidisti; beati, qui non uiderunt et crediderunt,
alleluia.

Et Thomas, uersa facie contra populum, dicat alta uoce:

Misi digitum meum in fixuram clauorum, et manum | meam in latus eius,
et dixi: Dominus meus et Deus meus, alleluia.

Finito hoc, Maria[3] redeat ad Sepulcrum, et stans ante Sepulcrum cum
duobus Discipulis incipiant prosam *Victime paschali,* vsque *Dux uite*
mortuus, regnat uiuus. Tunc reliqui Discipuli ueniant ad Mariam et
interrogent dicendo ita:

Dic nobis, Maria, ⟨quid vidisti in via?⟩ 220

Et Maria ostendat eis Sepulchrum et dicat:

Sepulchrum Christi ⟨viventis, et gloriam vidi resurgentis⟩.

Hic ostendat eis Angelos:

Angelicos testes.

---

[1] dicor] dicet (MS). I adopt the suggestion of Meyer (p. 96).

[2] congreget] omnes congreget (MS).

[3] Maria] modo (MS).

Hic ostendat eis sudarium:
   Sudarium et uestes.

Hic ostendat eis crucem:
   Surrexit Christus, ⟨spes mea; præcedet suos in Galilæa.⟩   224

Et Discipuli incipiant antiphonam et compleant totam prosam:
   Credendum est magis soli ⟨Mariæ veraci quam Judæorum turbæ fallaci⟩.

Et chorus incipiat alta uoce *Te Deum laudamus.*[1]

The novelties, the blemishes, and the successful effects in this play may be most conveniently brought forward through a review of the scenes in order. We may infer that the part of the text lost at the beginning included a scene in which the Jews treat with Pilate for a guard of soldiers at the sepulchre. Although this lost part may have resembled, in general, the opening scene in the plays of Klosterneuburg and Benediktbeuern, it must have differed in some details. The words of the Jews seen in the first line of the text before us, for example, are not found in the other two plays; nor are the speeches of Pilate and the soldiers which follow.[2]

The scene in which the Marys buy their ointment and spices contains both familiar and unfamiliar passages. The stanzas which the Marys sing as they enter are already known to us,[3] as are also some of the lines spoken in the negotiation concerning the ointment. The play is original, however, in presenting two merchants, the first of whom, addressed as *mercator juvenis* (l. 41), may perhaps be regarded as the apprentice in the shop.[4] The lively dialogue between the Marys and the second merchant appears to have been invented for this play (ll. 53–65). Although it is entirely serious in tone, it obviously offers opportunities, or even temptations, in the direction of comedy.[5]

The scene of the visit of the Marys to the tomb contains a considerable number of new features, and is marred by a certain amount of confusion in the writing. The reference, in the opening speeches of the Marys, to Pilate's having set a guard at the sepulchre gives a laudable effect of unity to the composition.

---

[1] The hymn *Ave stella matutina*, which follows immediately in the MS, is not related to the play.

[2] Some nine lines from these two speeches occur in the fragmentary Passion play from Sulmona. See below, p. 707; Meyer, p. 95.

[3] See ll. 21–32, and the *Visitatio* from Narbonne above, p. 285.

[4] See Milchsack, p. 106. Dürre (p. 28), however, sees no evidence of differentiation between *mercator juvenis* and his associate.

[5] Dürre (pp. 28–9) is convinced of the complete seriousness of the scene before us. Pearson (ii, 302–3) discerns a comic intention.

The succeeding lament (ll. 70–7) is found in forms of the *Vistatio* treated above;[1] but the speech of the angel that immediately follows is new. If the rubrics can be trusted, the Marys actually encounter only one angel,[2] who speaks of himself as the Archangel Michael, declares the ointment to be of no avail, and shows the empty tomb to Mary Magdalen and Mary the mother of James. Then, after these two have rejoined their companion, all three approach the place again; and in spite of her having already seen the open sepulchre, Mary Magdalen inquires, *Quis revolvet nobis lapidem?*

The scene in which the soldiers report the Resurrection to Pilate is similar to the parallel part of the Klosterneuburg and Benediktbeuern plays in general content, but quite different in form.[3] The fact that the soldiers carry their misfortunes to Pilate rather than to the Jews is hardly significant.

The central part of the next scene, the appearance of Christ to Mary Magdalen, is lost from the manuscript, but the introductory section which is preserved shows the tendency towards confused amplification which we have observed in earlier scenes. In the long lament of Mary Magdalen is much that we now see for the first time. One is scarcely prepared to hear in it the joyous outburst *O quam magno dies ista.*[4] Her fainting and receiving support from her two companions are, of course, worthy dramatic additions. The writer's efforts towards extending the scene, however, lead to such ineptitudes as the repetition of the passage,

Quem quæritis?
Viventem cum mortuis.[5]

Although we cannot determine precisely how much has been lost in the lacuna in the manuscript after line 177, the fact that when the text is resumed Mary Magdalen is represented as in conversation with Peter suggests that the race of Peter and John to the tomb has probably occurred. Now follows a unique scene between Mary Magdalen and the disciples, which is far from clear in its arrangement (ll. 183–94). The speeches, in any case, are all supplied by stanzas from the celebrated hymns *Aurora lucis rutilat* and *Jesu, nostra redemptio.*

---

[1] See, for example, the play from Dublin above, p. 348.

[2] Salome, however, uses the plural *angelorum* (l. 87).

[3] It will be observed that the closing utterance of the soldiers here (*Tunc erit*, l. 134) appears to be similar to that at the end of the lost scene at the beginning of the play.

[4] Line 148. For the use of this composition in the *Visitatio* see above, p. 293.

[5] See ll. 159–60, 172–3.

Hereupon follow several scenes not represented in any other play centring in the Resurrection: the appearance of Christ to a group of disciples (ll. 195–200), a meeting of Thomas and two other disciples (ll. 201–11), and the appearance of Christ, eight days after the Resurrection, to all the disciples (ll. 212–19). The first scene rests upon the account by St Luke (xxiv, 36–40). The second, arising from the Gospel of St John (xx, 24–5), opens with an invented soliloquy sung by Thomas, which is note-worthy as containing an early example of the formula of self-announcement, 'I am' (*Thomas dicor Didymus*). The third scene follows closely the succeeding verses of St John (xx, 26–9). Since all three of these incidents will re-appear prominently in the next chapter, they require no further comment here.

The play is brought to a close, handsomely and conventionally enough, by the singing of *Victimæ paschali* and *Te Deum laudamus*. The opening lyrical part of the sequence is effective, as always; but, after the repeated appearances of Christ himself upon the stage, the dialogue of Mary and the disciples, beginning with *Dic nobis*, seems unusually ineffectual.

From our survey of scenes and sources it appears that, in its present state, the play from Tours is a very ambitious and de-fective composition. The nucleus is the usual scene of the Marys and the angel, and the dialogue from *Victimæ paschali*. But this is buried beneath an accumulation of repetitious inventions and bold amplifications. One gathers the impression that the writer, or compiler, had before him a considerable variety of dramatic material, some highly elaborated, and some very simple. These resources he seems to have used with avidity, in a desire to in-corporate everything that might enlarge and enliven his own composition. The result is a production very imperfectly articu-lated, but very generous in its range of scenes and its display of literary forms.

The number of liturgical pieces in the play is small, and its connexion with the church services is indicated only by the presence of the *Te Deum* at the end.[1] From the words *Veniant ante ostium ecclesiæ*, directing the first entrance of the Marys,[2] it might be inferred that the performance occurred outside the

---

[1] Sepet (*Drame*, p. 193) characterizes this play as 'semi-liturgique'; and A. Schönbach (*Anzeiger für deutsches Alterthum und deutsche Litteratur*, vi [1880], 309) speaks of it as being 'keine Osterfeier mehr, sondern ein Oster-schauspiel'. Pearson (ii, 302) appears to regard the *Te Deum* as sufficient evidence of the play's having been performed at Matins.

[2] See the rubric following l. 20.

church; but the rubric would apply aptly enough also to a position *within* the church, in front of one of the several doors.[1] We are told, in any case, that at one point in the action Mary Magdalen is standing *in sinistra parte ecclesiæ*,[2] and much of the action occurs about what seems to be the usual *sepulchrum*.

[1] See Chambers, ii, 39. Milchsack (p. 105) and Dürre (p. 25), however, understand the rubric to mean that the Marys enter the church from outside.

[2] See the rubric after l. 134; Chambers, ii, 39.

CHAPTER XV

OTHER PLAYS OF THE EASTER SEASON

THE JOURNEY TO EMMAUS—THE ASCENSION—PENTECOST

DURING the period immediately after the Resurrection the most conspicuous and significant events recorded in the Gospels are the several appearances of Christ to his followers, and the descending of the Holy Spirit upon them on the day of Pentecost. Of these occurrences several have been represented in one or another of the plays considered in the previous chapters. In the more highly developed versions of the *Visitatio Sepulchri*, for example, are dramatized Christ's appearances to Mary Magdalen and the other Marys;[1] and in the Easter play from Tours are found scenes showing also the meetings of Christ with some of his disciples on the day of the Resurrection, and with the whole apostolic group, including Thomas, eight days later.[2] The plays and dramatic ceremonies to be treated in the present chapter may be regarded as an appropriate sequel to the Easter plays in that they represent two further appearances of the Master to His disciples—one at Emmaus, and the other on the occasion of the Ascension—and also the culminating event of the period after the Resurrection: the descent of the Holy Ghost on the day of Pentecost.

THE JOURNEY TO EMMAUS

The play dramatizing the journey to Emmaus—conveniently termed *Peregrinus*—arises, directly or indirectly, from the following passage in the twenty-fourth chapter of the Gospel of St Luke:[3]

13. Et ecce duo ex illis ibant ipsa die in castellum, quod erat in spatio stadiorum sexaginta ab Jerusalem, nomine Emmaus.

14. Et ipsi loquebantur ad invicem de his omnibus quæ acciderant.

15. Et factum est, dum fabularentur, et secum quærerent, et ipse Jesus appropinquans ibat cum illis.

16. Oculi autem illorum tenebantur ne eum agnoscerent.

---

[1] See chap. xiii. [2] See pp. 445–6.
[3] Luke xxiv, 13–35. Cf. Mark xvi, 12. For bibliography, and observations upon the designation *Peregrinus*, see Notes, p. 688. The discussion by Schüttpelz (pp. 56–87) reached me too late for adequate use in this chapter.

17. Et ait ad illos: Qui sunt hi sermones quos confertis ad invicem ambulantes, et estis tristes?

18. Et respondens unus, cui nomen Cleophas, dixit ei: Tu solus peregrinus es in Jerusalem, et non cognovisti quæ facta sunt in illa his diebus?

19. Quibus ille dixit: Quæ? Et dixerunt: De Jesu Nazareno, qui fuit vir propheta, potens in opere et sermone coram Deo et omni populo;

20. Et quomodo eum tradiderunt summi sacerdotes et principes nostri in damnationem mortis, et crucifixerunt eum.

21. Nos autem sperabamus quia ipse esset redempturus Israel; et nunc super hæc omnia, tertia dies est hodie quod hæc facta sunt.

22. Sed et mulieres quædam ex nostris terruerunt nos, quæ ante lucem fuerunt ad monumentum,

23. Et, non invento corpore ejus, venerunt dicentes se etiam visionem angelorum vidisse, qui dicunt eum vivere.

24. Et abierunt quidam ex nostris ad monumentum; et ita invenerunt sicut mulieres dixerunt, ipsum vero non invenerunt.

25. Et ipse dixit ad eos: O stulti et tardi corde ad credendum in omnibus quæ locuti sunt Prophetæ!

26. Nonne hæc oportuit pati Christum, et ita intrare in gloriam suam?

27. Et incipiens a Moyse et omnibus Prophetis, interpretabatur illis in omnibus scripturis, quæ de ipso erant.

28. Et appropinquaverunt castello quo ibant; et ipse se finxit longius ire.

29. Et coegerunt illum, dicentes: Mane nobiscum, quoniam advesperascit, et inclinata est jam dies. Et intravit cum illis.

30. Et factum est, dum recumberet cum eis, accepit panem, et benedixit, ac fregit, et porrigebat illis.

31. Et aperti sunt oculi eorum, et cognoverunt eum; et ipse evanuit ex oculis eorum.

32. Et dixerunt ad invicem: Nonne cor nostrum ardens erat in nobis dum loqueretur in via, et aperiret nobis Scripturas?

33. Et surgentes eadem hora regressi sunt in Jerusalem; et invenerunt congregatos undecim, et eos qui cum illis erant,

34. Dicentes: Quod surrexit Dominus vere, et apparuit Simoni.

35. Et ipsi narrabant quæ gesta erant in via, et quomodo cognoverunt eum in fractione panis.

This narrative was appropriately used as the liturgical gospel for the Monday following Easter; hence the dramatic renderings of it were also commonly performed on that day.

I

Of these dramatizations the simplest type is well represented by the following play from a breviary of the fourteenth century used at Saintes, in France:[1]

Quando fiunt Peregrini, non di*citu*r prosa,[2] sed Peregrini deforis ueniunt canendo ista. Peregrini:

> Tercia dies est quo hec facta sunt.[3]

Dominus:

> Qui sunt hii sermones quos confertis ad inuicem ambulantes, et estis tristes? Alleluia.[4]

Peregrini:

> Tu solus peregrinus es in Iherusalem, et non cognouisti que facta sunt in illa hijs diebus? Alleluya!

Dominus:

> Que?

Peregrini:

> De Ihesu Nazareno, qui fuit uir propheta, potens in opere et sermone coram Deo et omni populo, alleluya.

Dominus:

> O stulti et tardi corde ad credendum in omnibus que loqu⟨u⟩ti sunt prophete, alleluya! Nonne sic oportuit pati Christum et intrare in gloriam suam? Alleluya![5]

Chorus:

> Cvm autem appropinquassent castello quo ibant, et ipse | se finxit longius ire, et coegerunt eum ut remaneret cum illis, alleluya.[6]

Modo Dominus fingit se longius ire; et Peregrini:

> Mane nobiscum, quoniam aduesperascit et inclinata est iam dies, alleluya, alleluya. Sol uergens ad occasum suadet ut nostrum uelis hospicium; placent enim nobis sermones tui, quos refers de resurrectione magistri nostri, alleluya.[7]

---

[1] Paris, Bibl. Nat., MS lat. 16309, Brev. Santonense sæc. xiv, fol. 604ʳ–605ʳ, published anonymously in *Bibliothèque de l'École des Chartes*, xxxiv (1873), 314–5. Fol. 603ᵛ ends in the midst of the eighth responsory of the *Officium Beatæ Mariæ Conceptionis*. The dramatic text before us begins at the very top of fol. 604ʳ, and is followed immediately, on fol. 605ʳ, by the rubric *Sancti Ausonii episcopi et martyris capitulum*. Clearly, then, the arrangement of the MS is disordered, and the play has no essential connexion with what immediately precedes and follows it. The MS provides music.

[2] This is presumed to be the prose, or sequence, often sung before the antiphon of the Magnificat in Vespers during the octave of Easter.   [3] See Luke xxiv, 21.

[4] For the words and music of this speech, and of the succeeding three speeches, see the antiphon *Qui sunt hi sermones*, Hartker, p. 233. For a list of antiphons relevant to the plays upon this theme see Notes, p. 688.

[5] Possibly this speech is extracted from the antiphon *Jesus junxit*, Hartker, p. 233.

[6] See Luke xxiv, 28–9.

[7] Of this speech the first sentence may be taken from the antiphon *Mane nobiscum*. Hartker, p. 234. The other two sentences are neither there nor in the Vulgate.

Chorus:

> *Et intrauit cum illis, et factum est cum recumberet*[1] *cum illis, accepit panem, benedixit ac fregit et porrigebat illis, alleluya.*[2]

Modo sedent et diuidit Dominus hostiam inter illos. Et postea euanescit ab occulis eorum, intrans opertum locum. Et assurgunt Peregrini dicentes: Peregrini:

> *Nonne cor nostrum ardens erat in nobis de Ihesu dum loqueretur nobis in uia, et aperiret | nobis scripturas? Heu! miseri, ubi erat sensus noster? Quo intellectus abierat? Alleluya!*[3]

Dominus:

> *Pax uobis. Ego sum. Nolite timere. Uidete manus meas et pedes meos, quia ego ipse sum. Palpate et uidete quia spiritus carnem et ossa non habet sicut me uidetis habere, alleluya.*[4]

Peregrini:

> *Surrexit Dominus de sepulcro, qui pro nobis pependit in ligno, alleluya, alleluya, alleluya.*[5]
>
> *Magnificat.*

Oratio: *Deus qui sollempnitate paschali.*

This play may be said to fall into three parts, or scenes, in the first of which Christ is represented as overtaking Cleophas and his companion on the road to Emmaus, and as carrying on with them the conversation recounted in the Gospel.[6] The second part is introduced by a narrative passage sung by the chorus, recounting the arrival of the three persons at the village in the evening.[7] The action shows how the two disciples succeed in persuading their guest to postpone his further journey, and to enter the dwelling, or inn, with them. The chorus introduces the third scene by recounting part of the action which occurs in dumb-show indoors. The pantomime represents Christ sitting at table, breaking bread with his hosts, and then suddenly vanishing. The disciples rise in astonishment, and as they are lamenting their failure to recognize their guest, Christ appears to them again, and displays evidences of his return to the flesh. The disciples sing a Resurrection antiphon, and the performance closes with the *Magnificat* and a liturgical prayer.

One particularly striking aspect of the dramatic arrangement

---

[1] recumberet] recumberent (MS).

[2] See Luke xxiv, 29–30; Hartker, p. 234. The melody differs from that of Hartker.

[3] For the first of these sentences see Luke xxiv, 32.

[4] See Luke xxiv, 36, 39.

[5] See Hartker, p. 241.

[6] See Luke xxiv, 17–29, quoted above.

[7] In regard to the meaning of the word *castellum* ('village') of the Vulgate see Cohen, *Pèlerins*, pp. 107–8.

is the re-appearance of Christ at Emmaus, for which the Gospel gives no warrant. According to St Luke (xxiv, 33–9), immediately after Christ had vanished from the table, the two disciples hastened to Jerusalem, and as they were recounting their experiences to the eleven disciples, the Master appeared in the midst of the gathering. This re-appearance the playwright seems to have transferred from Jerusalem to Emmaus.

The general content of most of the utterances in the play is found both in the Vulgate and in the *liber responsalis*, or choir-book for the Canonical Office. Since several speeches resemble traditional antiphons both in details of phraseology and in melody, these parts of the play are probably derived directly from the choir-book.[1] Such are the first speech of *Dominus*, and the four speeches that follow it, and part of the passage beginning *Mane nobiscum*.[2] From the Vulgate, with some modifications, appear to have been taken the opening words of the play, the passages *Cum autem* and *Et intravit*, sung by the chorus, the sentence beginning *Nonne cor nostrum*, and the last utterance of *Dominus*. Several sentences seem to have been invented by the playwright himself.[3]

As to *mise en scène* the text before us is relatively laconic. We cannot doubt that the personages are costumed with some attention to realism, and that the shelter at Emmaus is represented by some sort of structure within the playing-space.[4] We can only surmise that the meal is enacted at a table in front of the altar. The rubric *dividit Dominus hostiam inter illos* shows that during the supper Christ distributes a wafer among those present. It has been suggested that this wafer is the consecrated Host from Holy Thursday, previously used in a *Depositio* on Good Friday and in an *Elevatio* early Easter morning.[5] In weighing this suggestion, unfortunately, we have few facts to guide us. Since there is no extant text of a *Depositio* or *Elevatio* from Saintes, we do not know that the Eucharist was used in them. In general, the Host left after a performance of the *Elevatio* seems to have been

---

[1] For texts of the relevant liturgical pieces see below, p. 688.

[2] With the liturgical passages belongs also, of course, the familiar Easter antiphon *Surrexit Dominus*.

[3] The last two sentences of the speech beginning *Mane nobiscum*, and of that beginning *Nonne cor nostrum*. The dependence of the *Peregrinus* upon the liturgical pieces in the choir-books seems to be somewhat exaggerated by Meyer, pp. 133–4. See below, p. 689.

[4] I infer that the expression *deforis* of the opening rubric means 'outside' the dwelling represented on the stage.

[5] See Chambers, ii, 38. We have no text of a *Depositio* or *Elevatio* from Saintes. For the *Visitatio Sepulchri* from the MS before us see below, p. 599.

used in a subsequent Communion.[1] I infer, therefore, that in the dramatic text before us the *hostia* is merely some sort of unconsecrated wafer.

That the play from Saintes was closely attached to the liturgy is apparent from a mere glance at the opening and closing rubrics, which assure us that it was performed in the very midst of Vespers; and so, as we shall see, were other versions of the *Peregrinus*. Since the action is represented as occurring in the evening, this arrangement is distinctly appropriate. It happens, however, that the type of Vespers with which we are concerned here differs very strikingly from what has been outlined above as the normal form.[2] If, therefore, we are to have an accurate and vivid impression of the liturgical surroundings of the present play, and of similar ones, we must pause for a moment to consider the special form of Vespers used on Easter Day and during the octave.

According to the earliest Roman service-books, Vespers during this liturgical season assumed an enlarged form in three parts, each part being performed in a separate place within, or without, the church building. A service divided in this manner, and including the singing of the *Magnificat* in each division, may be regarded as a kind of triple Vespers, which, with its special ceremonials of procession and censing, produced an effect of unusual splendour.[3] Although during the later Middle Ages the details of this ceremony varied greatly from place to place, the triple arrangement and processional movement persisted, as we may see from the following outline of Vespers of Easter Monday at Rouen in the fourteenth century:[4]

The office opens with a procession, which, with crucifix, lights, and thuribles, passes from the sacristy to the west door of the nave, and through the nave to the choir. The processional chants are *Salve, festa dies* and *Kyrie eleïson*. In the choir are sung three psalms, *Dixit Dominus* (cx), *Confitebor* (cxi), and *Beatus vir* (cxii), the antiphon in each case being *Alleluia*. Then, at the lectern, three cantors sing the gradual *Hæc dies*, with its verse *Confitemini*;

---

[1] See the *Elevatio* from Augsburg below, p. 560.

[2] See above, p. 71.

[3] See especially A. Gastoué, *Les Origines du Chant romain*, Paris, 1907, pp. 286–99; Batiffol, pp. 97–8; G. M[orin], in *Le Messager des Fidèles*, vi (1889), 150–7; [P. L. Dionysius,]

Antiquissimi Vesperarum Paschalium Ritus Expositio, Rome, 1780.

[4] For the Latin texts, now first printed, see below, p. 692. These texts provide the full *ordo* for Vespers for Easter, and the slight exceptions, or *propria*, for Easter Monday.

and in the same place three others sing the *Alleluia*, with its verse *Nonne cor nostrum*. After a versicle and response are then sung the antiphon *Et coegerunt* and the *Magnificat*. At the *Magnificat* the altar and the choir are censed. Then follow a prayer and the *Benedicamus*.

The second part of the service is performed at the baptismal font, in the west end of the building. During the *Processio ad fontes* is sung the psalm *Laudate, pueri* (cxiii), the antiphon being *Alleluia*. At the font are sung the gradual *Hæc dies* and the *Alleluia*, each with its verse. Then follows a prayer.

At the beginning of the third part of the office the procession sets out upon its return to the choir singing the psalm *In exitu Israel* (cxiv), with the antiphon *Alleluia*. At the conclusion of this a halt is made in the nave, and the play of the *Peregrinus* is performed. Then are said a prayer, and commemorations of the Blessed Virgin Mary. Subsequently the procession advances to the portal of the choir, where commemorations of the saints are said. The service concludes with the singing of the *Benedicamus*.

In Vespers of Easter Monday at Rouen, then, the traditional three divisions are particularly clear, as is also the position of the *Peregrinus*, at a station of the procession on its way back from the font to the choir.

A halting of the procession for a special purpose on the way to or from the font was an established feature of Vespers in many churches, with or without the performance of a play. Thus in the office on Easter Monday at Bayeux, after a ceremony in the choir, including the singing of three psalms and the *Magnificat*, the procession moved to the Easter sepulchre, halting there to sing the *Magnificat* again, and say a collect. The next station occurred at the font, where the observance included the singing of one psalm and, once more, the *Magnificat*. Thence the procession advanced to the altar of St Nicholas, singing there a fifth psalm and, for the fourth time, the *Magnificat*. During the final return to the choir was sung an antiphon of the Blessed Virgin Mary.[1] The recognition of the *sepulchrum* in the ceremonial of Vespers, including sometimes a special censing,[2] is of some importance, since, as we shall see, at least one version of the *Peregrinus* includes the sepulchre in the dramatic action.[3]

---

[1] These details are found in a thirteenth-century *ordinarium* of Bayeux published by Chevalier, *Bayeux*, pp. 142–3, 390–1.

[2] See Frere, *Sarum*, i, 115.

[3] See below, pp. 478 sqq. For other examples of Vesper ceremonials at the sepulchre see Notes, p. 689.

The exact position of the *Peregrinus* in this elaborate form of Vespers was not the same in all communities. At Bayeux the play was performed during the procession to the font which followed the station at the sepulchre.[1] At Rouen, as we have seen, it was acted at a halt of the procession on the way back from the font to the choir.[2] As to the liturgical attachment of most of the other versions of the play we have only incomplete information.[3] In the case of the play from Saintes, with which we are immediately concerned, the data are somewhat confused. From the opening rubric, *Quando fiunt Peregrini, non dicitur prosa*, one infers that when the performance occurred, it supplanted the prose, or sequence, with which Vespers was embellished; and that the closing antiphon of the play, *Surrexit Dominus*, sung by the two disciples, was followed by the *Magnificat*, with its antiphon and a prayer. If we assume that the play was performed on Easter Monday, as were most of the other versions of the *Peregrinus*, and turn to Vespers for that day in the breviary which contains the dramatic text, we find liturgical conditions which meet our case fairly well.[4] Vespers here takes the following general form: a part sung in the choir, including three psalms and antiphons, the *Hæc dies* and two verses, the prose *Clara gaudia*, the *Magnificat* and its antiphon, and a prayer; a second part sung at the font, including another psalm; a third part sung at the cross; and finally a procession to the chapter-house. Although there is in the manuscript no indication that the text of the play is connected with this text of Vespers,[5] and although the two texts are written in different hands, we are probably not far wrong in assuming that this form of Vespers represents at least the general liturgical circumstances in which the dramatic performance occurred. The play, it appears, was given in the choir during the first part of the service. It took the place of the prose, and was followed by the *Magnificat*, with its antiphon, and the appropriate prayer.

II

Closely related to the play from Saintes in content is the following, which appears to represent Norman-French liturgical

[1] For the special rubric concerning this see Notes, p. 690. Of the Bayeux play itself we have no text.

[2] See also below, p. 693. Chambers (ii, 38) describes the *Peregrinus* of Rouen as 'a kind of dramatization of the procession itself'.

[3] For the facts concerning several versions see Notes, p. 690.

[4] For the text of Vespers of Easter Monday from Paris, Bibl. Nat., MS lat. 16309, fol. 147^v–148^r, see Notes, p. 690.

[5] In regard to the position of the text of the play in the MS see above, p. 453.

custom current in the kingdom of Sicily in the twelfth century:[1]

De Peregrino in Die Lune Pasche

Hoc dicat chorus:

> *Iesu, nostra redemptio,*
> *⟨amor et desiderium,*
> *Deus, creator omnium,*
> *homo in fine temporum,⟩*
>
> *Que te uicit clemencia,*
> *⟨ut ferres nostra crimina,*
> *crudelem mortem patiens,*
> *ut nos a morte tolleres?⟩*[2]

Duo clerici induti cappis dicant:

> *Tercia dies est quod hec facta sunt.*

Peregrinvs:

> *Qui sunt hii sermones quos comfertis ad inuicem ambulantes, et estis tristes? Alleluia! Alleluia!*

Discipvli:

> *Tu solus peregrinus es in Ierusalem, et non cognouisti que facta sunt in illa his diebus? Alleluia!*

Peregrinvs:

> *Que?*

Discipvli:

> *De Iesu Nazareno, qui fuit uir | propheta, potens in opere et sermone coram Deo et omni populo, alleluia, alleluia. Et quomodo tradiderunt eum summi sacerdotes in dampnatione mortis, alleluia.*

Peregrinvs:

> *O stulti et tardi corde ad credendum in omnibus his que locuti sunt prophete, alleluia! Nonne sic oportuit pati Christum, et ita intrare in gloriam suam? Alleluia!*

Chorvs:

> *Cum autem appropinquaret castello quo ibant, ipse se finxit longius ire, et coegerunt illum ut remaneret cum eis.*[3]

Discipuli:

> *Mane nobiscum, quoniam aduesperascit et inclinata est iam dies, alleluia.*

---

[1] Madrid, Biblioteca Nacional, MS 289 (*olim* C. 153), Trop. ad usum Ecclesiæ Siculorum sæc. xii, fol. 117ʳ–118ᵛ, previously edited by Young, *Some Texts*, pp. 329–31, and reprinted therefrom by Bartholomaeis, pp. 527–8; Beeson, pp. 205–6. The MS provides music. In the MS the text given here is immediately preceded by a troped, or 'farced,' epistle for Easter.

[2] For the complete text of this hymn see below, p. 641.

[3] Here follows a considerable blank space, left, no doubt, for a rubric.

Peregrinus:[1]

Michi longum iter restat, alleluia.

Discipuli: |

Sol uergens ad occasum suadet ut nostrum uelis[2] hospicium; placent enim nobis sermones tui, quos refers de resurrectione magistri nostri, alleluia.

Chorus:

Et intrauit cum illis, et factum est dum recumberet cum eis, accepit panem, benedixit ac fregit et porrigebat illis, et cognouerunt illum in fractione panis, et ipse euanuit ab oculis eorum, alleluia.

Et ita, tenendo in medio eorum Peregrinum, ueniant usque ad altare; ac ibi sit parata mensa cum pane et uino; et discumbant; et frangat panem eisque det; ac postea ab oculis eorum euanescat. Tunc dicant Discipuli:

Nonne cor nostrum ardens erat in nobis de Ihesu, dum loqueretur nobis in uia, et aperiret nobis scripturas? Heu! miseri, ubi erat sensus noster? Quo intellectus abierat? Alleluia!

Et iterum eis se ostendens dicat: |

Pax uobis. Ego sum. Nolite timere. Uidete manus meas et pedes meos, quia ego ipse sum. Palpate et uidete quia spiritus carnem et ossa non habet[3] sicut me uidetis habere, alleluia, alleluia.

Discipvli versvs chorvm dicant:

Surrexit Dominus de sepulchro, qui pro nobis pependit in ligno, alleluia, alleluia, alleluia.

Chorvs:

Deo gracias, alleluia, alleluia, alleluia.[4]

The Sicilian play, performed on Easter Monday, improves upon that from Saintes in several details. The two stanzas of the hymn *Jesu, nostra redemptio,* sung by the chorus, are a pleasing form of processional introduction. The longer form of choral piece introducing and accompanying the scene at the table provides a more complete exposition of the dumb-show. The dialogue is slightly enlarged through the invention of an additional speech for Christ, *Michi longum iter restat.*

As in the play from Saintes, impersonation here is merely implied. In regard to costuming we are told only that the two disciples wear copes. Concerning the setting of the stage we are given a few enlightening particulars. The table located *ad altare,* and set with bread and wine, may well be the altar-table itself.

---

[1] This rubric, the speech that follows, and the succeeding rubric are written by a somewhat later hand in the lower margin.

[2] uelis] uelit (MS).　[3] habet] habent (MS).
[4] Followed by the rubric *In Ascensione Domini.*

In the absence of information in the text, we must assume that the play was performed at Vespers.

III

In the *Peregrinus* from the cathedral of Rouen, the action is enlarged by the addition of a new scene:[1]

Post *Benedicamus* fiat processio ad fontes, ut in die Pasche, et processione stante in medio nauis ecclesie et cantante psalmum *In exitu*. Circa finem psalmi duo clerici de secunda sede induti tunicis et desuper capis in transuersum, portantes baculos et peras in similitudinem Peregrinorum, intrent ecclesiam per dextram portam occidentalem, et lento pede uenientes usque ad processionem. Cum finitus fuerit psalmus, subsistentes in capite processionis incipiant cantare hymnum:

Ihesu, nostra redemptio.[2]

Et cum cantauerint usque ad locum illum, *Nos tuo uultu sa⟨ties⟩*, tunc quidam sacerdos indutus alba et amictu, nudus pedes, crucem ferens in manibus, intret ecclesiam per sinistram portam occidentalem, et ueniens usque ad eos uultu demisso subito stet inter illos et dicat: |

Qui sunt hii sermones quos confertis ad inuicem ambulantes, et estis tristes?
Peregrini quasi admirantes et eum respicientes dicant:

Tu solus peregrinus es in Iherusalem, et non cognouisti que facta sunt in illa hiis diebus?
Sacerdos interroget:

Que?
Peregrini respondeant:

De Ihesu Nazareno, qui fuit uir propheta, potens in opere et sermone coram Deo et omni populo.
Sacerdos utrimque respiciens dicat:

O stulti et tardi[3] *corde ad credendum in omnibus que locuti sunt prophete! Nonne sic oportuit pati Christum, et ita intrare in gloriam | suam?*
Quibus dictis, statim recedat sacerdos fingens se longius ire, et Peregrini festinanter prosequentes eum detineant quasi ad hospicium inuitantes et trahentes baculum ostendentes castellum, et dicentes:

Mane nobiscum, quoniam aduesperascit et inclinata est iam dies. Sol uergens ad occasum suadet ut nostrum uelis hospicium; placent enim sermones tui, quos refers de resurrectione magistri nostri.
Et ita cantantes ducant eum usque ad tabernaculum in medio nauis

---

[1] Rouen, Bibl. de la Ville, MS 222 (*olim* A. 551), Process. Rothomagense sæc. xiii, fol. 43ᵛ–45ʳ, previously edited by Young, *Rouen*, pp. 213–4. The MS provides music. For the text of Vespers preceding this play, and for other texts from Rouen, see Notes, p. 691.

[2] For the complete text of this hymn see below, p. 641.

[3] tardi] tradi (MS).

ecclesie in similitudinem castelli Emaus preparatum. Quo cum ascenderint et ad mensam ibi paratam sederint, et Dominus inter eos sedens panem eis fregerit, in fractione panis agnitus ab illis subito recedens ab occulis eorum euanescat. Illi autem quasi stupefacti surgentes cantent uersus processionem *Alleluia,* cum versu *Nonne cor nostrum.* Quo reiterato, uertant se uersus pulpitum, et cantent hunc uersum sequentem:

> *Dic nobis, Maria, quid uidisti in uia?*

Tunc quidam de maiori sede indutus dalmatica et amictu, et uinctus in modum mulieris caput circumligatus respondeat:

> *Angelicos testes, suda|rium et uestes.*

Tun⟨c⟩ ostendat et explicet unum syndonem ex una parte loco sudarii, et alium ex altera parte loco uestium; deinde dicat:

> *Surrexit Christus, spes nostra; precedet uos in Galileam.*

Chorus cantet alios duos uersus sequentes, residuos, et interim recedant Maria et Peregrini, et processio, factis memoriis, redeat in choro, et ibi finiantur Vespere.[1]

Of this play the most arresting features are a scene representing the re-appearing of Christ to the two disciples after his repast with them, and a dialogue between these same two disciples and Mary Magdalen. This latter scene employs part of the sequence *Victimæ paschali,* and provides for a showing of the grave-cloths. For such a dialogue there is, of course, no suggestion in the Gospel. For his own purposes, then, the playwright is using here the Easter sequence which is very common in texts of the *Visitatio Sepulchri,* but which happens to be omitted from the version used at Rouen.[2] The dialogue appears to be spoken just outside the structure in the middle of the nave which represents the dwelling, or shelter, at Emmaus, the disciples standing before the door, and Mary appearing at the pulpit nearby. The presence of such a scene at the end of the *Peregrinus* would seem to result in anti-climax, for after the appearance of Christ himself in the action, the indirect evidences presented by Mary lose somewhat in impressiveness.

As has been shown above,[3] the play is performed in Vespers on Easter Monday, during a pause in the procession back from the font to the choir. The action centres in a special structure erected in the middle of the nave to represent the dwelling at

---

[1] Followed by the rubric *Feria tertia.*

[2] See above, p. 370. In a Nevers *Processionale* of 1535, the dialogue *Dic nobis* appears to have been sung on the return from the font in Vespers. See *Bulletin de la Société Nivernaise des Sciences, Lettres et Arts,* 2ᵉ série, viii (1877–80), 477–8.

[3] See p. 457, and below, pp. 691 sqq.

Emmaus, within which is a suitably prepared table.[1] The road to the village is represented by the space between this place and the west wall of the church, Christ entering by the north door in the western façade, and the two disciples by the south door.

The rubrics provide us with several details in regard to impersonation. The two disciples are dressed as pilgrims, with staffs and purses; Christ wears an alb and amice, carries a cross, and is bare-footed; and the cleric who represents Mary Magdalen is clad *in modum mulieris*. Even the gestures of the actors are prescribed with some care.

IV

In the versions of the *Peregrinus* considered thus far there seems to be no intention of including any disciples other than the two at Emmaus, or of shifting the scene from that place. An enlargement of the play in these respects is apparent in the following piece from the *Carmina Burana*:[2]

Incipit exemplum apparicionis Domini Discipulis suis iuxta[3] castellum Emaus, ubi illis apparuit in more[4] Peregrini, et tacuit uidens quid loquerentur et tractarent:[5]

> *Surrexit Christus et illuxit populo suo, quem redemit sanguine suo, alleluia.*[6]

Iesus audiens, se fingens Peregrinum, ad premissa r*espondet*:

> *Qui sunt hii sermones quos confertis ad inuicem ambulantes, et estis tristes? Alleluia! Alleluia!*[7]

Discipuli:

> *Tu solus peregrinus es*[8] *in Ierusalem, et non cognouisti que facta sunt in illa hiis diebus? Alleluia!*

Quibus Ihesus r*espondet*:

> *Que?*

Discipuli:

> *Nos loquimur de Iesu Nazareno, qui fuit uir propheta,*[9] *potens in opere et sermone coram Deo et omni populo, alleluia, alleluia.*

Iesus r*espondet*:

> *O stulti et tardi corde ad credendum in his que locuti sunt prophete, alleluia.*

[1] Concerning the presumable realism of this *tabernaculum* see Cohen, *Pèlerins*, p. 110.

[2] Munich, Staatsbibl., MS lat. 4660a, Carmina Burana sæc. xiii, fol. vii[r]–vii[v], previously edited by Meyer, pp. 136–8, with photographic facsimiles, plates 12 and 13. The text of Hilka and Schumann will be no. 26*. Concerning the MS see below, p. 686. For palaeographical observations upon the text before us see Hilka and Schumann, ii, 57*–58*, 60*–61*. The text is provided throughout with musical notation.

[3] iuxta] Partly illegible.

[4] more] morte (? MS).

[5] After this word a short entry seems to have been lost through rubbing.

[6] For this antiphon see Hartker, p. 240.

[7] The second *alleluia* (written *aevia*) is by another hand.

[8] es] Written above the line.

[9] propheta] Entered in the left margin.

Item Iesus:

Nonne sic oportuit pati Christum et intrare in[1] gloriam suam? Alleluia!

Clerus:

Et coegerunt eum dicentes:

Et Discipuli inuitabant eum:

Mane nobiscum, Domine,[2] quoniam aduesperascit et inclinata est iam dies, alleluia, alleluia.

Tunc uadat cum Discipulis et colloquatur de prophetis; et petat commestionem, et in fractione panis cognoscetur ab eis. Tunc euanescat Iesus ab oculis eorum. Tunc Discipuli cantent:

Nonne cor nostrum ardens erat in nobis de[3] Iesu, dum loqueretur nobis in uia? Alleluia!

Tunc Iesus appareat Discipulis cum uexillo, et cant*et*:

Pax uobis. Ego sum, alleluia. Nolite timere, alleluia.

Clerus cant*et*:

Thomas qui dicitur Didimus non erat cum eis quando venit Iesus. Dixerunt alii discipuli: Uidimus Dominum, alleluia.

Tunc Iesus monstret manus et pedes, et cantct:

Videte manus meas et pedes meos, quoniam ego ipse sum, alleluia, alleluia.[4]

Tunc iterum euanescat Icsus, et Discipuli cant*ent*:

Christus resurgens a mortuis iam | non moritur; mors illi ultra non dominabitur, quod enim uiuit, uiuit Deo, alleluia, alleluia.[4]

Tunc Apostoli conferentes inter se de Ihesu et dicunt Thome:

Vidimus Dominum, alleluia.

Thomas r*espondet* illis:

Nisi mittam digitos meos in fixuras clauorum et manus meas in latus eius,[5] non credam.

Tunc appareat Iesus secundo et dicat Discipulis:

Pax uobis. Ego sum,

et cetera. Et clerus cant*et*:

Post dies octo, ianuis clausis, ingressus Dominus et dixit eis.

Tercio appar*et*:

Pax uobis,

et cetera. Tunc dicit ad Thomam:

Mitte manum tuam et[6] cognosce loca clauorum, alleluia, et noli esse incredulus, set fidelis, alleluia.

---

[1] in] Written above the line.

[2] Domine] This may be the correct deciphering of an illegible word in the right margin.

[3] de] Preceded by *aevia*, crossed out.

[4] The second *alleluia* (written *aevia*) is by another hand.

[5] eius] Preceded by *suum*, crossed out.

[6] et] Preceded by what appears to be *in loca*, crossed out.

Et Thomas procidendo ad pedes Domini cantet:

> *Dominus meus et Deus meus, alleluia.*[1]

Jesus dicit:

> *Quia uidisti me, Thoma, credidisti; beati qui non uiderunt et crediderunt, alleluia.*

Tunc Apostoli simul cantent ymnum:

> *Jesu, nostra redemptio,*

et cetera.[2] Hoc finito, producatur Mater Domini; cum ea duo Angeli portantes sceptra, et cum ea Maria Iacobi et Maria Salome:

> *Egredimini et uidete, filie Syon, regem Salomonem in dyademate, quo coronauit eum mater sua in die desponsationis sue et in die leticie cordis eius, alleluia, alleluia.*[3]
>
> *Vox turturis audita est in turribus Ierusalem. Veni, amica mea. Surge, aquilo; et ueni, auster; perfla ortum meum et fluent aromata illius.*

Respondet Maria:

> *Veniat dilectus.*

Dominus:

> *Commedi.*

Maria:

> *Talis est dilectus.*

Dominus:

> *Tota pulcra.*[4]

The first two scenes in this play—on the road to Emmaus, and in the shelter there—do not differ substantially from the parallel parts of the versions previously considered, the only notable variation being the use of the antiphon *Surrexit Christus* by the disciples at the beginning. The remainder of the play, however, seems to show a somewhat disorderly use of antiphons and Biblical sentences for the purpose of creating additional situations on the stage. First occurs a scene representing the appearance of Christ to the group of disciples at Jerusalem,[5] in which he announces himself with the words *Pax vobis*, exhibits his wounded hands and feet, and disappears, leaving the disciples to sing the triumphal antiphon *Christus resurgens*. The action here is distinctly marred by the choral narrative *Thomas qui dicitur Didymus;*[6]

---

[1] alleluia] Written (as *aevia*) by another hand.

[2] For the text of this hymn see below, p. 641.

[3] From this point to the end, the text is written by another hand. Before *Vox turturis* is a blank space, left, no doubt, for a rubric.

The passage beginning *Vox turturis* will be printed by Hilka and Schumann as a separate piece, no. 26a*.

[4] After this speech the last four lines of the page are blank.

[5] See Luke xxiv, 36–9.

[6] See John xx, 24–5.

for if it was desirable that the audience be informed of Thomas's absence, the information could have been given more appropriately before Christ's first utterance. In any case, the concluding part of the narration, recounting the words of the disciples to Thomas on a later occasion, are entirely incongruous here. In the next brief scene the ten disciples report their experience to Thomas, repeating part of the passage previously narrated.

Then follows a representation of the appearing of Christ, eight days later, to all the apostles.[1] As on the occasion of his preceding appearance, he enters saying *Pax vobis*. By following this with a misplaced narrative passage, the chorus, as it were, forces Christ to repeat his words. The subsequent dialogue faithfully follows the Gospel account, and this part of the action is brought to a close by the disciples' singing the hymn *Jesu, nostra redemptio*.

Here, we may say, the play ends; for after the hymn follows a succession of utterances which are, in their present position, quite unintelligible. Upon the stage appear three Marys, and two angels bearing sceptres. The only speakers mentioned are one of the Marys and Christ; and the speeches consist of passages from the Song of Solomon and the *liber responsalis*.[2]

The dependence of the entire play upon this choir-book is, indeed, astonishing, for in the scenes properly belonging to the *Peregrinus*, virtually every utterance is, in whole or in part, a recognized antiphon.[3] This liturgical indebtedness is established by similarities in both the melodies and the words. The narrative passage beginning *Thomas qui dicitur Didymus*, for example, departs strikingly from the text of the Vulgate and adopts the exact wording of the antiphon, along with its music. From this close adherence to liturgical forms arises, no doubt, much of the awkwardness and crudeness of the play. Had the writer been following the fluent narrative of the Vulgate, he would almost certainly have achieved a more acceptable dramatic sequence and propriety.

V

Over the uncouth disorder of the *Peregrinus* from Benediktbeuern a marked advance in structure and literary form is shown in the play of the twelfth century from Beauvais:[4]

---

[1] See John xx, 26–9.

[2] Concerning these passages see Notes, p. 694.

[3] See below, p. 688. The sources in the

liber responsalis are very fully identified by Meyer, pp. 137–8.

[4] Paris, Bibl. Nat., Nouvelles Acquisitions, MS lat. 1064, Miscellanea liturgica sæc. xii,

BEAUVAIS

Ordo ad Peregrinum in Secunda Feria Pasche ad Uesperas

Duo Discipuli euntes dicant:

Ihesu, nostra redemptio,

vsque *Nos tuo uultu saties.*[1] Quibus appropinquans Peregrinus dicat:

Qui sunt hi sermones quos confertis ad inuicem ambulantes, et estis tristes?

Cleophas Discipulus solus respo*ndeat:*

Tu solus peregrinus es in Ierusalem, et non cognouisti que facta sunt in illa his diebus?

Et Peregrinus:

Que?

Et duo Discipuli:

De Ihesu Nazareno, qui fuit uir propheta, potens in opere et sermone coram Deo et omni populo.

Tunc unus:

Quem Iudei dampnauerunt
et in cruce occiderunt,
et nos quidem sperabamus
quod nos esset redempturus. |

Tunc alter dicat:

Iam tres dies abierunt,
facta ista quod fuerunt;
et nos quedam terruerunt,
que sepulchrum reuiserunt
uacuumque reppererunt.

Item alter:

Se uidisse narrauerunt
angelorum uisionem,
qui et eis indixerunt
eius resurrectionem;
sed ex nostris cucurrerunt,[2]
qui sic cuncta reppererunt,
sicut ille retulerunt,
sed ipsum non inuenerunt.

Tunc Peregrinus dicat:

O cum sitis eius discipuli,
cur tam stulti, tardi, increduli,
ignoratis ab ortu seculi
que prophete dixere singuli?

fol. 8ʳ–11ᵛ, previously edited by Dejardins, pp. 269–75; H. Omont, in *Bibliothèque de l'École des Chartes*, lxxiv (1913), 263–6 (with complete photographic facsimiles). The MS provides music. For additional comment see Grenier, p. 386; Meyer, pp. 133–6; Chambers, ii, 37.

[1] For the complete text of this hymn see below, p. 641.

[2] cucurrerunt] curcurrerunt (MS).

> *Nonne Christum pati oportuit*
> *et intrare | gloriam decuit?*

Sic in eundo dicat eis:

> *Hec Moyses significauerat,*
> *cum paschalem agnum occiderat;*
> *Isaias idem predixerat,*
> *cum ut agnum illum clamauerat*
> *flagellari et obmutescere,*
> *et occisum peccata tollere.*
> *Oblatus est, inquit, cum uoluit*
> *et peccata nostra sustinuit.*[1]
> *Sic et cunctis prophetis testibus,*
> *Christus, mortis solutis nexibus,*
> *quod sit uiuus, et hoc perhenniter,*
> *iam debetis credere firmiter.*

Tunc quasi recedere uolens Peregrinus dicat eis:

> *Ne moremur, fratres, diutius,*
> *iam oportet nos ire longius.*

Tunc retineant eum et dicat unus:

> *Declinante uespera,*
> *noctis instant tempora,*
> *nec patent itinera;*
> *subsiste. |*

Et alter dicat:

> *Mane nobiscum, quoniam aduesperascit et inclinata est iam dies.*

Tunc ambo eum ducant et, quasi cogentes eum ad hospitium, dicant:

> *Iam sol uergens ad occasum   suadet hospitium,*
> *Nostrum, Pater, obsecramus   intres habitaculum;*
> *Placent enim tui nobis   sermonis colloquia,*
> *Que de nostri referebas   magistri uictoria.*

Et ducant eum ad mensam, cantante interim choro:

> *Et coegerunt illum dicentes: Mane nobiscum, Domine, quia aduesperascit,*
> *alleluia.*

Tunc ipse Peregrinus solus ad mensam dicat:

> *Et intrauit cum illis, et factum est dum recumberet cum eis:*

Tunc accipiat panem | et dicat:

> *Accepit panem, benedixit* (faciat ✠), *ac fregit* (frangat), *et porrigebat eis.*[2]

Et det eis, et recedat. Duo illi se inuicem aspicientes surgant, et uadant per ecclesiam quasi querentes eum et cantantes:

> *Nonne cor nostrum ardens erat in nobis de Iesu, dum loqueretur nobis in*

---

[1] This line and the one preceding are written in the lower margin.
[2] The marks of parenthesis are editorial.

uia et aperiret nobis scripturas? Heu! miseri, heu! miseri, heu! miseri! ubi erat sensus noster? Quo intellectus abierat?

Tunc conuertant se ad chorum, et chorus cantet:

Surrexit Dominus et apparuit Petro, alleluia.

Mox ueniens Dominus in alia effigie dicat eis: |

Pax uobis. Ego sum. Nolite timere. Quid turbati estis, et cogitationes ascendunt in corda uestra?   JC⟹Disc.

Tunc ostendat eis manus et pedes dicens:

Videte manus meas et pedes meos, quia ego ipse sum. Palpate et uidete quia spiritus carnem et ossa non habet sicut me uidetis habere.

Et, sic recedente eo, cantet chorus:

Surrexit Dominus de sepulchro, qui pro nobis pependit in ligno, alleluia, alleluia, alleluia.

Tunc ueniat Thomas, qui defuerat, et stanti in medio dicant ei duo pro alijs:

> *Vere, Thoma, uidimus Dominum,*
> *qui destruxit mortis | imperium.*

Quibus Thomas:

> *Nisi fixuram clauorum uidero,*
> *et digito uulnus palpauero,*
> *atque manum in latus misero,*
> *hoc sciatis, nunquam credidero.*

Tunc in medio ueniens Dominus dicat omnibus:

Pax vobis. Ego sum, alleluia. Nolite timere, alleluia.

Deinde dicat Thome:

> *Thoma, nunc uulnera conspice corporis.*

Et ostendat ei:

> *Infer et digitum in locum uulneris,*
> *et iam incredulus in me ne fueris,*
> *exemplum fidei prebendo posteris.*

Et Thomas procidens ad pedes eius dicat:

> *O Ihesu Domine, celorum conditor,*
> *te credo | uiuere, credens et fateor.*
> *Quod fui dubius, ignosce, deprecor,*
> *Deus meus et Dominus meus.*

Cui Dominus:

Quia uidisti me, Thoma, credidisti; beati qui non uiderunt et crediderunt, alleluia.

Tunc cantor incipiat *Christus resurgens.* Versus *Gauisi sunt discipuli,* et oratio de Resurrectione.[1]

---

[1] The text of the play is complete in the MS. The lower half of fol. 11ᵛ is blank.

The play from Beauvais may be truly called a literary composition. In the scene on the road to Emmaus the Scriptural narrative is far more fully used than in the parallel part of any other play. After the introductory hymn sung by the two disciples, virtually the whole of St Luke's account is presented in dialogue, and a large proportion of it in verse.[1] The facility of the writer is shown both in his amplifying a single Biblical sentence into twelve verses,[2] and in the variety of his metrical forms: rhymed trochaic dimeters, iambic pentameters, and lines of fifteen syllables.

The prose scene in the dwelling at Emmaus seems to resemble the related part in the plays from Saintes and Sicily in representing Christ's re-appearance to the disciples. Somewhat inept, no doubt, is the use by the chorus of a narrative passage containing the words (*Mane nobiscum*) previously spoken by one of the actors; and particularly incongruous is Christ's singing the sentence beginning *Et intravit*, in which he refers to himself in the third person.

The remainder of the play consists in a scene dramatizing two separate incidents of the Scriptural account: the report of the disciples to Thomas,[3] and Christ's appearing, eight days later, to the complete apostolic group.[4] The text is formed in part by unaltered passages from the Vulgate, and in part by freely invented verses. The speech of Thomas to Christ beginning *O Jesu*, for example, contains three lines for which the Gospel offers no suggestion.

Although the rubrics are not generous in information concerning *mise en scène*, we may safely assume the use of appropriate costume and stage furnishings. From the text itself we know that the play was performed in the course of Vespers of Easter Monday; and from the liturgical formulæ at the end, I infer that the performance occurred in the choir, before the procession to the font.[5]

VI

Similar to the play from Beauvais in its mingling of verse and prose, but broader than any of the preceding versions in its use

[1] See Luke xxiv, 17–27, quoted above, p. 452.
[2] The lines beginning *Hec Moyses* are based on Luke xxiv, 27.
[3] See John xx, 25.   [4] See John xx, 26–8.
[5] I base this inference upon the form of
Vespers found at Soissons, as reported by Martene, iii, 179. In that church the *Processio ad fontes* began with virtually the same liturgical formulæ as those with which our play ends.

of Biblical matter, is the following composition from the monastery of St-Benoît-sur-Loire, at Fleury, designed for performance at Vespers on Tuesday of Easter Week:[1]

Ad faciendam similitudinem Dominice Ap⟨p⟩aricionis in specie Peregrini, que fit in tercia feria Pasce ad Uesperas, procedant duo a competenti loco, uestiti tunicis solummodo et cappis, capuciis absconsis ad modum clamidis, pilleos in capitibus habentes et baculos in manibus ferentes, et cantent modica uoce:

> ⟨J⟩esv, nostra redempcio,
> amor et desiderium,

et ceteros versus.[2] Illis hec cantantibus accedat quidam alius in similitudine Domini, pera⟨m⟩ cum longa palma gestans, bene ad modum Peregrini paratus, pilleum in capite habens, hacla uestitus et tunica, nudus pedes, latenterque eos retro sequatur,[3] finitisque uersibus, dicat eis:

> Qui sunt hii sermones quos offertis ad inuicem ambulantes, et estis tristes? Alleluia! |

Alter autem ex duobus, conuerso uultu ad eum, dicat:

> Tu solus peregrinus es in Ierusalem, et non cognouisti que facta sunt in illa his diebus? Alleluia!

Cui Peregrinus:

> Que?

Ambo Discipuli:

> De Iesu Nazareno, qui fuit uir propheta, potens in opere et sermone coram Deo et omni populo; quomodo tradiderunt eum summi sacerdotes et principes nostri in dampnacione mortis et crucifixerunt eum; et super omnia, tercia dies est quod hec facta sunt, alleluia.[4]

His dictis, Peregrinus graui uoce, quasi eos increpando, cantare incipiat:

> O stulti et tardi corde ad credendum in omnibus que locuti sunt prophete, alleluia! Nonne sic oportuit pati Christum et intrare in gloriam suam? Alleluia![5]

Quo facto, fingat se velle discedere; ipsi autem retineant eum et dicant:

> Sol occasum expetit,
> iam hospitari expedit;
> sane noli[6] deserere

---

[1] Orleans, Bibl. de la Ville, MS 201 (olim 178), Miscellanea Floriacensia sæc. xiii, pp. 225–30, previously edited by Monmerqué, in Mélanges, vii, 175–83; Wright, pp. 37–41; Du Méril, pp. 120–6; Coussemaker, pp. 195–209. Concerning the MS see below, p. 665. The MS provides music, included in the edition of Coussemaker.

[2] For the complete text of this hymn see below, p. 641.

[3] sequatur] After this word, eos is erased by underlining.

[4] See Luke xxiv, 19–21, quoted above, p. 452.

[5] See Luke xxiv, 25–6. The melodies are not those of Hartker's antiphons. See below, p. 688.

[6] sane noli] Mane nobis (MS). The emendation has been adopted by all previous editors.

nos, iam instante uespere;
sed mane nobiscum, Domine,
quo saciemur plenissime,
quo delectemur maxime
tui sermonis dulcedine.

Mane nobiscum, | quoniam aduesperascit et inclinata est iam dies, alleluia.
Sol uergens ad occasum suadet ut nostrum uelis hospicium; placent enim nobis
sermones tui,[1] *quos confers de resurrectione magistri nostri, alleluia.*

His dictis, eant sessum in sedibus ad hoc preparatis, et afferatur eis
aqua ad lauandum manus suas, deinde mensa bene parata, super quam
sit positus panis inscissus, et tres nebule, et calix cum uino. Accipiens
autem panem ⟨Peregrinus⟩, eleuatum in altum dextra benedicat,
frangatque singulis partibus cantando:

Pacem relinquo uobis; pacem meam do uobis.[2]

Deinde det uni eorum calicem et dicat:

Isti sunt sermones quos dicebam uobis, cum essem ⟨vobiscum⟩, alleluia,
alleluia.[3] *Sicut dilexit me Pater, et ego dilexi uos; manete in dilectione mea.*[4]

His dictis, illis manducantibus[5] de nebulis, ipse latenter discedat, quasi
illis nescientibus. Interuallo autem paruo facto, aspicientes ad inuicem,
et illo non inuento inter se, quasi tristes surgant, et eum, relicta mensa,
querere incipiant, et suauiter incedentes, hos uersus alta uoce dicant:

Nonne[6] *cor nostrum ardens erat in nobis de Ihesu, dum loqueretur nobis in*
uia et aperiret nobis scripturas? Heu! miseri, ubi erat sensus noster? Quo
intellectus abierat? Alleluia!

Uenientibus illis in chorum chorus dicat:

Surrexit Dominus et apparuit Petro, alleluia.

Interim ueniat Dominus, colobio candido uestitus, cappa rubea
superindutus,[7] ob signum Passionis[8] crucem auream in manu gestans,
infulatus candida infula cum aurifrisia; stansque in medio eorum dicat:

Pax uobis. Ego sum. Nolite timere.[9]

Et chorus dicat:

Quis est iste qui uenit de Edom, tinctis uestibus | de Bosra?[10]

Tunc Dominus:

Pax uobis.

Et chorus:

Iste formosus in stola sua, gradiens in multitudine fortitudinis sue.[11]

---

[1] placent . . . tui] placent . . . tuos (MS).
[2] See John xiv, 27, and below, p. 689.
[3] See Luke xxiv, 44: *Hæc sunt verba quæ locutus sum ad vos cum adhuc essem vobiscum.* See the antiphon below, p. 689.
[4] See John xv, 9, and the antiphon below, p. 689.
[5] manducantibus] manducandibus (MS).
[6] Nonne] Noone (MS).
[7] superindutus] After *super* the word *uestitus* is inserted, and erased by underlining.   [8] Passionis] passionem (MS).
[9] See the antiphon below, p. 689.
[10] See Isaiah lxiii, 1.   [11] See *ibid.*

Et tercio Dominus:

Pax uobis.

Et chorus:

Surrexit Dominus de sepulcro, qui pro nobis pependit in ligno, alleluia, alleluia, alleluia.[1]

Et Dominus:

Quid turbati estis, et cogitaciones ascendunt in corda uestra?[2] *Solus calcaui torcular, et de gentibus non est uir mecum.*[3]

Et monstret manus eius et pedes minio rubicatos dicens:

Videte manus meas et pedes meos, quia ego ipse sum, alleluia, alleluia.[4]

Et adiungat:

Palpate et uidete quia spiritus carnem et ossa non habet sicut uidetis me habere.[5] *Iam credite.*

Que dum cantauerit, accedant Discipuli et palpent eius manus et pedes. Hoc peracto, dicat Dominus extenta manu super illos:

Accipite Spiritum Sanctum; quorum remiseritis peccata, remittuntur eis, alleluia.[6]

Quo percantato, Dominus exiens[7] per hostium ex aduerso chori, Discipuli autem appropinquant, pedetentim incedentes, alternando hos uersus:

Adam nouus ueterem duxit ad astra; |
creatorem recolit iam creatura.

Sed Maria Iacobi cum Magdalena
et Maria Salome ferunt unguenta.

Quibus dixit angelus in ueste alba:
'Resurrexit Dominus, morte calcata.'

Fracta li⟨n⟩quens tartara et spoliata,
refert secum spolia uictor ad astra.

Se demonstrat postea forma preclara
dilectis discipulis in Galilea.

Comes factus increpat latens in uia;
scriptura[8] *reserat pius archana.*

Conuiuans agnoscitur propria forma;
panis reddit fractio lumina clara.
Sibi laus et gloria.[9]

---

[1] See above, p. 454.
[2] See Luke xxiv, 38.
[3] See Isaiah lxiii, 3.
[4] See Luke xxiv, 39, and the antiphon below, p. 689.
[5] See *ibid.*
[6] See John xx, 22–3, and the antiphon, Hartker, p. 271.
[7] exiens] Preceded by the same word, crudely written and erased by underlining.
[8] scriptura] Coussemaker's emendation *scripture* is highly acceptable, though not indispensable.
[9] The verses *Adam novus veterem* are not listed by Chevalier, *R.H.* For the use of them in the *Visitatio Sepulchri* from Coutances see above, p. 408.

Interea ueniat quidam in similitudine Thome, uestitus tunica et clamide serico,[1] baculum in manu habens et pilleum aptum in capite; cui Discipuli:

Thoma, uidimus Dominum.[2]

Thomas:

Nisi uidero in manibus eius fixuram clauorum et mittam manum meam in latus eius, non credam.[3]

Interim ueniat Dominus, colobio candido et cappa rubea uestitus, coronam gestans in capite ex amicto et philacteriis compositam, crucem auream cum uexillo in dextra, textum Evvangelii habens in sinistra; qui, dum chorum intrauerit, dicat:

Pax uobis.

Chorus:

Benedictus qui uenit in nomine Domini. Deus Dominus et illuxit nobis.[4]

Dominus:

Pax uobis.

Et chorus:

A Domino factum est mirabile istud in oculis nostris.[5]

Dominus:

Pax uobis.[6] *Ego sum. Nolite timere uos.*

Et chorus:

Hec est dies quam fecit Dominus; exultemus et letemur in ea.[7]

Deinde Dominus dicat ad Thomam:

Thoma, fer digitum tuum huc, et uide manus meas.

Et monstret uulnera, dicens:

Mitte manum tuam et cognosce loca clauorum, alleluia; et noli esse incredulus, sed fidelis, alleluia.[8]

Palpatis autem a Thoma cicatricibus Domini, procidat ad pedes Domini dicens:

Dominus meus, et Deus meus.[9]

Tunc Dominus:

Quia uidisti me, Thoma, credi⟨di⟩sti; beati qui non uiderunt et crediderunt, alleluia. Data est mihi omnis potestas in celo | et in terra, alleluia. Non uos relinquam orphanos, alleluia. Uado et uenio ad uos, alleluia. Et gaudebit cor uestrum, alleluia.[10]

[1] serico] gerico (? MS).
[2] See John xx, 25.
[3] See *ibid.*
[4] See Ps. cxvii, 26–7.
[5] See Ps. cxvii, 23.
[6] Here follow the words *nolite timere*, crossed out (MS).
[7] See Ps. cxvii, 24. The gradual of the

Mass of Easter. See above, p. 25.
[8] For the antiphon *Mitte manum*, see below, p. 689.
[9] For an antiphon containing this speech see below, p. 689.
[10] For the antiphons which may be the source of this passage see below, p. 689.

*Euntes in mundum uniuersum, et predicate Euangelium omni creature,
alleluia. Qui crediderit* [1] *et baptizatus fuerit, saluus erit, alleluia.* [2]
Sicque Discipuli accedentes, ducant eum per chorum ut uideatur a
populo, cantantes:

Salue, festa dies,

et cetera. [3] Sic finiatur.

Passing over the opening division of this play, as being sufficiently familiar to us from other versions, we observe that the
scene at Emmaus contains new elements. It is preceded by
verses not found elsewhere, and assigns to Christ utterances drawn
from parts of the Gospel employed in no other version. In the
third scene we have for the first time a separate and extended
representation of Christ's appearing to the apostolic group. At
his entrance Christ repeats *Pax vobis* three times, the chorus
responding with passages from Isaiah or from the *liber responsalis*.
For the subsequent dialogue are used appropriate passages from
various parts of the Vulgate.

In the final scene are combined the meeting between Thomas
and his brethren, and Christ's appearing to the united group. As
the disciples slowly approach the place they sing a *cantio*, or
hymn, *Adam novus veterem*, which appropriately recalls the Resurrection, the visit of the Marys to the tomb, the descent to hell,
and the occurrences at Emmaus. After the usual message has
been reported to Thomas, Christ enters saying *Pax vobis* three
times, the chorus responding with suitable sentences from the
Psalms. He convinces Thomas by showing his wounds, and then
charges the disciples to preach the Gospel throughout the world.
The play closes impressively with a procession of the disciples
singing *Salve, festa dies* as they accompany Christ through the
choir, in order that he may be seen by the whole congregation.

The arrangements for staging the play are somewhat ambitious.
The general arrangement of the action in the church seems to
resemble that at Rouen. Presumably the *locus competens* representing the road to Emmaus is in the western part of the building,
and the table for the supper, in the centre of the nave. Jerusalem,
where Christ appears to the ten disciples—and later, to the
eleven—is in the choir. The shelter at Emmaus is provided with
seats, and on the table are wine, an uncut loaf, and three thin

[1] crediderit] Fourth and fifth letters inserted by a later hand (MS).
[2] See Mark xvi, 15–6.

[3] For bibliography relating to these
famous Easter verses of Fortunatus see
Chevalier, *R.H.*, no. 17949.

wafers, or *nebulæ*. The realism of the supper-scene is augmented by the bringing of water for the washing of hands. The person who performs this service is, no doubt, the forerunner of the comic innkeeper of the later plays in the vernacular.[1]

The costumes are described with exceptional care. Cleophas and Luke arrange their vestments to look like cloaks, wear hats, and carry staffs. Thomas also has a cloak and a hat, and carries a staff. The costume of Christ is changed, very appropriately, from scene to scene. At Emmaus he is the typical pilgrim, with his palm-branch, wallet, and bare feet. When he appears to the eleven disciples he is clad in a white tunic and red cope, carries a golden cross, and has an embroidered woollen head-dress. The wounds in his hands and feet are represented by marks of vermilion. On the occasion of his final appearance he wears a crown, and carries the cross in his right hand and the gospel-book in his left.

In comparison with the play from Beauvais, the Fleury production can scarcely be considered remarkable as a literary composition. It contains a relatively small proportion of verse, drawing its speeches largely from the Vulgate or the choir-book.[2] Certain of the Biblical passages used, moreover, are of somewhat doubtful appropriateness.[3] As a whole the Fleury play adheres more closely to the conventional form of *Peregrinus* than we should expect after having observed the literary independence displayed in the *Visitatio Sepulchri* from this monastery.[4]

VII

Of all the extant versions of the *Peregrinus* the most comprehensive is the following from the Norman liturgical use current in the kingdom of Sicily in the twelfth century:[5]

---

[1] See Cohen, *Pèlerins*, pp. 109, 117 sqq.

[2] It should be recorded that in a number of passages of the play which resemble both the Vulgate and the *liber responsalis* verbally, the melodies are not those of Hartker. I infer, then, that the play draws largely from the Vulgate. Certain of these details are discussed by Meyer, pp. 133, 135.

[3] See Meyer, p. 133. The success of the two choral passages taken from Isaiah lxiii, 1, for example, might be questioned.

[4] See above, p. 393.

[5] Madrid, Biblioteca Nacional, MS C. 132, Grad. ad usum Ecclesiæ Siculorum sæc. xii, fol. 105ᵛ–108ʳ, previously edited by Young,

Peregrinus, pp. 120–4. Certain aspects of the MS are described by L. Delisle, *Un Livre de Chœur normano-sicilien conservé en Espagne*, in *Journal des Savants*, 1908, pp. 42–9. Delisle holds that it represents an adaptation of the liturgy of Normandy to the use of the kingdom of Sicily, and that it was written in the period 1130–9. He does not mention the *Peregrinus* now under consideration. Concerning this MS, and similar ones, see also Legris, p. 453. The text now before us is immediately preceded in the MS by the *communio* of the Mass of Easter, and is provided with music.

ICILY

Versus ad faciendum Peregrinum

Dicat unus ex Discipulis solus:

> *Ego, sodes, dum recordor,*
> *dum ad mentem redit odor,*
> *qualis erat noster doctor,*
> *ad momentum uix respiro.*

Dicat alivs:

> *Ecce quidam peregrinus*
> *appropinquat huc festinus;*
> *illum ergo prestolemur,*
> *et cum illo gradiamur.*

Pe⟨re⟩grinvs:

> *Qui sunt hii sermones?*

De Peregrino qui uult in die Pasche faciat. Si non die Pasce, fiat in
feria secunda ad Uesperas. Ita prius Uespere[1] di*cantu*r usque ad *Hec*
dies et *Alleluia.* Postea sic exeant de choro illi qui h*ec* agere debeant.
C⟨h⟩orvs incipit:[2]

> *Ihesu, nostra redemptio,*
> *⟨amor et desiderium,*
> *Deus, creator omnium,*
> *homo in fine temporum,⟩*
>
> *Que[3] te ⟨uicit clementia,*
> *ut ferres nostra crimina,*
> *crudelem mortem patiens,*
> *ut nos a morte tolleres⟩?*

⟨Discipuli:⟩

> *Tertia dies est quod hec[4] facta sunt.*

Peregrinvs:

> *Qvi sunt hi sermones quos confertis ad inuicem ambulantes, et estis tristes?*
> *Alleluia! Alleluia!*

Discipuli:

> *Tu solus peregrinus es in Iherusalem, et non cognouisti que facta sunt in*
> *illa his diebus? Alleluia!*

Peregrinvs:

> *Que?*

Discipuli:

> *De Ihesu Nazareno, qui fuit uir propheta, potens in opere et sermone |*
> *coram Deo et omni populo, alleluia, alleluia. Et quomodo tradiderunt eum*
> *summi sacerdotes in dampnatione mortis, alleluia.*

[1] Uespere] uesperas (MS).   [3] Que] Qui (MS).
[2] In the MS this rubric immediately pre-   [4] hec] e hec (MS).
cedes the speech *Tertia dies . . . sunt* below.

Peregrinvs:

> *O stulti et tardi corde ad credendum in omnibus his que locuti sunt prophete, alleluia! Nonne sic oportuit pati Christum et ita intrare in gloriam suam? Alleluia!*

Chorus:

> *Cum autem appropinquaret castello quo ibant, ipse se finxit longius ire, et coegerunt illum ut remaneret cum eis.*

Discipuli:

> *Mane nobiscum, quoniam aduesperascit et inclinata est iam dies, alleluia.*

Ihesus fingat se longius ire et precedat, et dicat:

> *Michi longum iter restat, alleluia.*

Discipuli tunc deteneant eum, et ostendant ei horam esse tardam:

> *Sol uergens ad hoccasum suadet ut nostrum uelis hospitium; placent enim nobis sermones tui, quos refers de resurrectione magistri nostri, alleluia.*

Chorus:

> *Et intrauit cum illis, et factum est | dum recumberet cum eis, accepit panem, benedixit, ac fregit, et porrigebat illis; et cognouerunt illum in fractione panis; et ipse euanuit ab oculis eorum, alleluia.*

Et ita tenendo in medio ⟨eorum Peregrinum, ueniant⟩[1] usque ad mensam, ac ibi sit panis[2] et uinum, et discumbant, et fra⟨n⟩gat panem, eisque[3] det, ac post ab oculi⟨s⟩ eorum euanescat. Tunc duo Discipuli:

> *Nonne cor nostrum ardens erat in nobis de Ihesu, dum loqueretur nobis in uia, et aperiret nobis scripturas? Heu! miseri, ubi erat sensus noster? Quo intellectus abierat? Alleluia!*

Tunc ueniat Ihesus iterum et his duobus Discipulis appareat dicatque:

> *Pax uobis. Ego sum. Nolite timere. Uidete manus meas et pedes meos, quia ego ipse sum. Palpate et uidete quia spiritus carnem et ossa non habet sicut me uidetis habere, alleluia, alleluia.*

Ex altera autem parte erit paratum Sepulchrum, ibique erit Ihesus et duo Angeli, unus ad caput et unus[4] ad pedes. Cum autem uenerit Maria Magdalena, dicent ei Angeli:

> *Mulier, quid ploras?*

Et illa:

> *Quia tulerunt Dominum meum, et nescio ubi posuerunt eum.*

Hec autem cum audierit, conuertat se retrorsum, uidensque Ihesum non cognouit eum, quia Ihesus esset. Qui dic*it* illi:

> *Mulier, quid ploras? Quem queris? |*

---

[1] For the passage supplied here see the other *Peregrinus* from Sicily above, p. 460.
[2] panis] panem (MS).
[3] eisque] eiusque (MS).
[4] unus] unum (MS).

Illa[1] putabat eum esse ortulanum, et dicit illi:

Domine, si tu sustulisti eum, dicito michi, alleluia, et ego eum tollam, alleluia.

Ihesus dic*it* illi:

Maria!

Et illa:

Raboni!

Et Ihesus:

Noli me tangere, nondum enim ascendi ad Patrem meum; sed uade, et dic fratribus meis ut eant in Galileam; ibi me uidebunt, alleluia, alleluia.

Item supradicti duo Discipuli dicent hos uersus in inuicem:

Victime paschali laudes[2] immolant Christiani.
Agnus redemit oues; Christus innocens Patri reconciliauit peccatores.
Mors et uita duello conflixere mirando; dux uite mortuus, regnat uiuus.

Postea redeat Maria ad illos duos Discipulos, dicatque:

Surrexit Dominus (tribus vicibus) *sicut predixerat; ecce precedet uos in Galileam.*[3]

Et illi duo Discipuli dicant:

Dic nobis, Maria, quid uidisti in uia?

Maria dicat hec:

Sepulchrum Christi uiuentis,
et gloriam uidi resurgentis.
Angelicos testes,
sudarium | et uestes.
Surrexit Christus, spes mea;
precedet suos in Galilea.

Discipuli:

Credendum est magis soli Marie ueraci,
quam Iudeorum turbe fallaci.
Scimus quidem surrexisse ex mortuis uere;
tu nobis, Christe rex, miserere.

Thomas autem non erat cum illis decem Discipuli⟨s⟩ qui sunt in medio choro; sed ueniens ex auerso ad illos decem Discipulos, et stabit. Qui surgentes, dicant ei tribus vicibus:

Vidimus Dominum.

Thomas respondit:

Nisi uidero in manibus eius fixuram clauorum et mittam digitum meum in locum clauorum, et mittam manum meam in latus eius, non credam, alleluia.

Tunc ueniat Ihesus et appareat omnibus Discipulis dicens:

Data est michi omnis potestas in celo et in terra, alleluia, alleluia.

---

[1] illa] ille (MS).   [3] The marks of parenthesis are editorial.
[2] paschali laudes] paschalis laude (MS).

Item dicat solummodo:

> *Pax uobis! O Thoma, infer digitum tuum huc, et uide manus meas et pedes meos, et affer manum tuam, et mitte in latus meum; et noli esse incredulus, sed fidelis, alleluia.*

Thomas uertat uultum suum ad populum; dicat:

> *Misi digitum | meum in fixuram clauorum, et manum meam in latus eius et dixi:*[1] *Dominus meus, et Deus meus, alleluia.*

Tribus uicibus dicat *Dominus meus*, adorans. Et hoc facto, dicat Ihesus Thome:

> *Quia uidisti me, Thomas, credidisti; beati qui non uiderunt et crediderunt, alleluia.*

Tunc omnes Discipuli uerta⟨n⟩t se ad populum; insimul dicant alta uoce:

> *Surrexit Dominus de sepulchro, qui pro nobis pependit in ligno, alleluia, alleluia, alleluia.*

Finitur[2] hec. Incipit cantor responsorium, et uadunt ⟨ad⟩ fontes: *Christus resurgens.*[3]

The representation here of the occurrences on the road to Emmaus shows no novel features except the alternative forms of introduction. When the play is performed on Easter Day— presumably at Vespers—Christ's first interrogation *Qui sunt?* is preceded by two four-line stanzas beginning *Ego, sodes,* sung by the disciples. These stanzas, of which the first is particularly touching, appear to have been composed especially for this play.[4] When the performance occurs at Vespers on Easter Monday, these verses are supplanted by two stanzas of the hymn *Jesu, nostra redemptio,* sung by the chorus, and a short prose speech of the disciples, *Tertia dies.*

Since the dramatizing of the meal at Emmaus takes a form now familiar, we may proceed to the succeeding scene, in which two angels, Mary Magdalen, and Christ appear in an action found in no other version of the *Peregrinus.* The presence of an episode centring in the Easter sepulchre is explained partly, no doubt, by the fact that the procession in Vespers during Easter week quite normally visited the *sepulchrum,*[5] and partly by a natural desire to enlarge the play through representing another appearance of Christ. The scene, in any case, is not a new composition, for, as we have observed in an earlier chapter,

---

[1] dixi] dixit (MS).

[2] Finitur] Fnitur (? MS).

[3] The MS proceeds thus: Ad crucem *Sedit angelus.*

[4] The stanzas have only a slight basis in Luke xxiv, 14–6.

[5] See above, p. 457, and below, p. 689.

it is a well established part of the *Visitatio Sepulchri* of Easter Day, in its more highly developed stages.[1] The form which it assumes in the play now before us is almost exactly that found, for example, in the *Visitatio* from Rouen.[2] Similarly adapted from the Easter play is the subsequent scene in which the two disciples converse with Mary Magdalen in the language of the sequence *Victimæ paschali*. The disciples of Emmaus merely replace Peter and John of the *Visitatio*.[3]

The final division of the play consists in a combination, once more, of a scene between the ten[4] apostles and Thomas, and a scene, historically eight days later, in which Christ appears to all the apostles together.

Concerning the details of the performance the text does not provide very ample information. The play is given in the midst of Vespers, after the responsory *Hæc dies* and before the procession to the font. Although costumes are not described, the characters are undoubtedly impersonated. A well furnished table is provided for the meal at Emmaus, and the Easter sepulchre serves for the intermediate scenes; but as to the setting for the occurrences at Jerusalem we know only that it was *in medio choro*.

As a dramatic composition this version of the *Peregrinus* can hardly be commended. After the pleasing introductory verses, originality is abandoned. According to Scriptural chronology the scenes in which Mary Magdalen appears are misplaced; and after having seen Christ himself, the two disciples can scarcely be expected to be greatly moved by her indirect evidences.

VIII

The records of other performances of the *Peregrinus* are not numerous. We know that such a play was performed at Lichfield after the twelfth century,[5] and at Lille in the thirteenth.[6] We have a crude fragment of one from the abbey of Ripoll, in Spain, from the twelfth century,[7] a fragment in a fifteenth-century manuscript at Shrewsbury,[8] and the following description of another, of the thirteenth century, from the cathedral of Padua:[9]

---

[1] See chap. xiii.
[2] See above, p. 371.
[3] See above, pp. 346 sqq.
[4] The number *decem* in the play recognizes the absence of Judas and Thomas.
[5] See Appendix B below, ii, 522.
[6] See Notes, p. 694.
[7] See below, p. 681.

[8] See Appendix B below, ii, 518.
[9] Padua, Bibl. Capit., MS S, Ordin. Patavinense sæc. xiii, fol. 103ʳ–104ʳ, described by Dondi Orologio, pp. 52–3; and described and printed by Bartholomaeis, pp. 149–50, 528. Concerning the MS see below, p. 552.

Sciendum est quod feria secunda cantatur Uesperum[1] ut in Pasca; et illi qui cantauerunt graduale et *Alleluia* ad Missam maiorem, cantant etiam in Uespero supra pergamum, cum sequentia *Victime pascali*, et ulterius non cantatur sequentia in Uespero. Ad *Magnificat* antiphona *Respondens unus*. Finito *Magnificat*, incipitur antiphona que cantata fuit in Matutinis ad *Benedictus*, scilicet, *Qui sunt hii sermones*, et dicitur etiam antiphona *Respondens unus*, et etiam alia *Quibus ille dixit.* Oratio diei. Finita oratione, incipit cantor antiphonam *Alleluia*, et tunc omnes descendunt cum processione ad fontem cantando duos psalmos ut in Pasca, scilicet, *Laudate pueri*, et *In exitu*. Antiphona ad *Magnificat* ad fontem *Mane nobiscum*. Et interim thurificantur altare, fons, et totus clerus, ut in Pascha. | Oratio *Concede, quesumus, omnipotens Deus*, ut festa Pascali. Finita oratione, incipitur antiphona *Dedit angelus*, et tunc extenditur chorus in corpore ecclesie, ut in Pasca, et cantantur antiphone ad altare Sancte Crucis et ad altare Sancti Danielis, ut in Pasca, scilicet, *Crucifixum*, et *Recordamini.*[2] Oratio *Deus qui populum tuum.* Tres scolares cantant *Benedicamus Domino*, *Alleluia*, in corpore ecclesie; et episcopus benedicit omnes, et ascendit cum clero ad altare Sancti Danielis.

Hic exeunt Peregrini de secrestia superiori, et associat se eis ipse Christus, ut hic dicitur. Et tunc exeunt de secrestia superiori duo ex Discipulis Christi, Cleophas et quidam alius, induti byrris et sclauinis cum burdonibus ad modum Peregrinorum; et magister scolarium uel cantor est cum eis, qui tuetur eos a pressura hominum. Et tunc associat se eis ipse Christus cum sclauina, burdone, et barisello uini ad modum Peregrini. Et Discipuli uolunt ire in castellum nomine Emaus, et ipsi non cognoscunt eum, et uadunt ad inuicem conferendo de facto et de morte Christi dolentes. Et ipse Christus dicit ad eos:

Qui sunt hii sermones quos confertis ad inuicem?

Et prosecuntur uerba Euangelii[3] quousque peruenunt | ad Sanctum Danielem. Et tunc ipse Christus fingit se longius ire. Et ipsi compellunt eum manere cum eis, quia iam declinata erat dies. Et ipse intrat et comedit et bibit cum eis supra discum ibi preparatum, et ipsi cognoscunt eum in fractione panis. Et ipse euanescit ab oculis eorum. Et tunc prohiciuntur nebule a tecto ecclesie, et omnes qui possunt capiunt eas.[4]

The play at Padua was performed at the end of Vespers of Easter Monday. Its most noteworthy features are the careful provision for costume, the use of the altar of St Daniel for the table at Emmaus, and the unique concluding ceremony in which

[1] Uesperum] This is the persistent spelling of the MS.

[2] Recordamini] Secordamini (MS).

[3] From the rubric here one fairly infers that the play is based upon the Vulgate rather than upon the *liber responsalis*.

[4] Followed by the rubric *Qualiter celebratur officium in Pasca. In Pasca annotino celebratur officium annotino Pasce cum omelia.*

a shower of wafers is precipitated from the roof of the church. Otherwise the play conforms to the simpler type reviewed in the earlier part of this chapter.

The general characteristic of all the versions of the *Peregrinus* is a relatively close adherence to the text of the Vulgate and of the service-books. This condition arises very largely, no doubt, from the generosity of these sources in providing not only the narrative facts, but a considerable amount of direct discourse as well. The result, in any case, is an occasional passage of pleasing verse, frequent awkwardness in dramatic arrangement, and a general lack of flexibility. Although we may safely assume that the *Peregrinus* arose after the risen Christ had already appeared as a figure in the Easter plays,[1] the later play did not achieve the vogue and literary variety of the earlier.

THE ASCENSION

To the several appearances of Christ represented in the various forms of the *Peregrinus* the recorded sequel is the Ascension, forty days after the Resurrection, celebrated on the Thursday following the fifth Sunday after Easter.[2] The liturgy of this day did not fail to recall the event vividly by special ceremonies, and in some communities it included the dramatic introit trope *Quem creditis super astra ascendisse?*[3] This latter composition, indeed, might well have evolved into a play, as did *Quem quæritis in sepulchro?* at Easter. So far as we know, however, no such development ever occurred. The really effectual efforts towards representing the Ascension seem to have been concerned not with literary embellishments of the liturgy, but merely with symbolic or mimetic acts accompanying the authorized forms of worship.

These ceremonials are sometimes associated with the procession before Mass. It is recorded that at Münster, for example, when the words *Ascendo ad Patrem* were sung, two priests raised a cross aloft.[4] At Essen, at the same place in the procession, certain clerics climbed stairs to a raised platform.[5] During the twelfth and thirteenth centuries at Soissons, one of the singers in the procession withdrew out of sight of the congregation, and sang alone the antiphon beginning *Non vos relinquam orphanos.*[6]

[1] See Chambers, ii, 37.
[2] For the Gospel record of the event see Acts i, 1–12. For bibliography concerning the history of the feast see Holweck, *Calendarium*, p. 170.

[3] See above, p. 196.
[4] See Stapper, *Feier*, pp. 156–7, quoting an ordinary of the thirteenth century.
[5] See Arens, pp. 88–9, 173–4.
[6] See *Soissons Ritual*, p. 158.

At Lille, somewhat more realistically, the presiding cleric, after the singing of the responsory *Non vos relinquam*, mounted a pulpit and made as if to ascend to heaven from the top of a mountain.[1]

A far more ambitious ceremony is described in a sixteenth-century ordinary from Bamberg.[2] It occurs after the office of None, and centres in the lifting up of an image of Christ. This *imago* is placed upon a *mensa*, or platform, in front of the choir, and after a short liturgical observance, including censing and sprinkling, the officiating priest and his ministers raise it aloft a short distance, singing *Ascendo ad Patrem*, and then lower it again, two choir-boys, stationed above, singing *Viri Galilæi*. After this raising and lowering has been done three times, the *imago* is slowly and finally drawn up through an opening in the roof, and bits of wafer and drops of water are flung down. Ceremonies of this sort seem to have been not uncommon in the fifteenth and sixteenth centuries, and perhaps earlier, in Germany. Very similar to the observance at Bamberg is that prescribed in an Augsburg service-book of 1487.[3] The still more elaborate form used in the cathedral of Berlin in the sixteenth century included effigies of the apostles and the Virgin Mary.[4]

Such observances, however, lack the element of genuine impersonation, and the enlivening effect of dialogue. For these dramatic features we must turn to a performance such as that prescribed in the following passage from an *ordinarium* of the fourteenth century from Moosburg:[5]

Finita Nona, Ascensio Domini nobiscum antiquo more sic peragitur. Preparetur tentorium sev domuncula de lignis, pannis pulchris circumdatis, et locetur in ipso medio monasterio infra ad pauimentum sub foramine alti tabulati | pro representacione montis Synay. Et in hac domuncula primo ponatur ymago Saluatoris, induta vestibus competentibus: videlicet, humerali, sarrocio precincto, vel alba, cum stola et cappa, sev alijs consimilibus secundum quod videtur competere, ferens vexillum in manu. Funiculus quoque subtilis descendat per foramen tabulati et sic innixus vertici ipsius ymaginis Saluatoris, vt

---

[1] See Du Cange, iii, 456–7. Du Cange does not give the date of the ordinary in which this bit of ceremonial is prescribed, nor does he indicate precisely the point in the liturgy at which the action occurred. For other evidences of dramatic Ascension observances at Lille see Lefebvre, i, 4.

[2] *Agenda Bambergensia*, Ingolstadt, 1587, pp. 627–35. For the text see Notes, p. 694.

[3] See Hoeynck, p. 227. Concerning a similar ceremony at Gloucester see T. Hannam-Clark, *Drama in Gloucestershire*, London [1928], p. 22.

[4] See Müller, *Statuten*, pp. 328–31; *Geschichte*, pp. 520–3. For text see Notes, p. 696.

[5] Munich, Staatsbibl., MS lat. 9469, Ordin. Mosburgense sæc. xiv, fol. 72ᵛ–73ᵛ, previously edited by Brooks, *Himmelfahrtsfeier*, pp. 91–6. For the text the MS provides no music.

eo mediante possit sursum eleuari. Sint eciam duo circuli, floribus inserti, in duobus alijs funiculis pendentes, ac in vno circulo sit ymago Columbe, in alio vero circulo ymago Angeli. Circulus quoque tercius, pannis sericeis circumductus, sit, qui pendeat inmobiliter in ore foraminis tabulati, per quem predicti funiculi transeant descendendo, et ymago Saluatoris quasi in celum transeat ascendendo. Hijs ita dispositis, sint xij de scola pro xij Apostolis, et vnus pro persona Beate Marie, et duo pro Angelis deputati, competenti apparatu vestium exornati: videlicet, Angeli sint induti togis, sev tunicis virgineis, alas habentes in lateribus, et serta sev crinalia de floribus in capitibus. Sed persona Marie vestibus sancte et honorabilis viduitatis induatur. Apostoli vero debent esse nudi pedes et superpelliciati casulis, sev cappis precincti, a sinistro humero in dextrum latus, sicut dyaconi solent se precingere, et habeant in suis capitibus scuta victorie, que nos dyademata appellamus, propriis suis nominibus inscripta. Et si non omnes, quidam tamen ex eis propria signa teneant in manibus: videlicet, Petrus clauem, Johannes librum, Andreas crucem, Bartholomeus cultrum, et Thomas lanceam, et sic de alijs. Et hij omnes de sacristia procedant, primo Angeli, deinde Maria inter manus duorum primorum Apostolorum, ceteris Apostolis binis et binis sequentibus, omnibusque insimul cantantibus responsorium:

> Post passionem suam ⟨per dies quadraginta apparens eis, loquens de regno Dei, alleluia, et videntibus illis elevatus est, alleluia, et nubes suscepit eum ab oculis eorum, alleluia⟩.[1]

Et cum pervenerint ad predictam domunculam, stacionem faciunt ab ipsa quantum ad tres passus, inter se et altare Sancte Crucis domunculam habentes, Mariaque posita in medio Apostolorum; Angeli stant in aliquo eminenti loco in latere domuncule, et cantant versum:

> Et conuescens ⟨præcepit eis ab Hierosolimis ne discederent, sed expectarent promissionem Patris. Et videntibus⟩.

Quo finito, Apostoli cantant repeticionem, et Angeli cantant:

> Silete, silete.

Deinde in domuncula sit vna persona pro persona Saluatoris, cantans antiphonam:

> Pater, manifestaui ⟨nomen tuum hominibus quos dedisti mihi; nunc autem pro eis rogo, non pro mundo, quia ad te vado, alleluia⟩.[2]

Et Apostoli Alleluia cantant eciam in omnibus antyphonis, siue ponatur in medio sev in fine. Deinde Angeli:

> Silete.

---

[1] This passage and the versus sung next constitute the Ascension responsory Post passionem. See Hartker, p. 262.

[2] Antiphon in First Vespers of Ascension. See Hartker, p. 261.

Saluator primo antiphonam:

Ascendo ad Patrem ⟨meum et Patrem vestrum, Deum meum et Deum vestrum, alleluia⟩.[1]

Et cum illa sic canitur, trahatur Ymago supra domunculam, quod ab omnibus possit videri. Quo facto, descendat Columba in circulo super caput Ymaginis, et Apostoli cantent:

Ecce spiritus in specie.[2]

Deinde descendat Angelus cum suo circulo, et it*er*um Apostoli:

Reliquit eum temptator, ⟨et accesserunt angeli et ministrabant ei.⟩[3]

Saluator antiphonam:

Exiui a Patre ⟨et veni in mundum, alleluia; iterum relinquo mundum et vado ad Patrem, alleluia, alleluia, alleluia⟩.[4]

Phylippus:

Domine ostende nobis Patrem, et sufficit nobis, alleluia,

cum richmo.[5] Saluator antiphonam:

Phylippe, | qui videt ⟨me, alleluia, videt et Patrem, alleluia, alleluia⟩,[6]

vel communionem:

Tanto tempore ⟨vobiscum sum, et non cognovistis me, Philippe? Qui videt me, videt et Patrem, alleluia; non credis quia ego in Patre et Pater in me est? Alleluia, alleluia⟩.[7]

Angeli:

Silete.

Saluator antiphonam:

Nisi ego abiero, ⟨paracletus non veniet; dum assumptus fuero, mittam vobis, alleluia.⟩[8]

Apostoli versum:

Presta hoc, genitor ⟨optime, maxime,
Hoc tu, nate Dei et bone Spiritus,
Regnans perpetuo fulgida Trinitas
Per cuncta pie secula⟩.[9]

Angeli:

Silete.

---

[1] Antiphon in Lauds of Ascension. See Hartker, p. 265.

[2] I have not found this passage in the liturgy. See Brooks, *op. cit.*, p. 94.

[3] Antiphon for the first Sunday in Lent; Hartker, p. 146.

[4] Antiphon for the fourth Sunday after Easter. See Hartker, p. 244.

[5] As Brooks explains (*op. cit.*, p. 92), the words *cum richmo* perhaps indicate that a vernacular rendering of the Latin is to follow.

[6] This speech and the preceding one constitute a single antiphon for the feast of St Philip and St James. See Hartker, p. 246.

[7] *Communio* for the Mass of St Philip and St James. See *Paléographie musicale*, i, 87.

[8] Antiphon for Ascension. See Hartker, p. 264.

[9] The last stanza of the Ascension hymn *Festum nunc celebre magnaque gaudia*. See Chevalier, *R.H.*, no. 6264, printed by Daniel, i. 217–8.

Saluator secundo *Ascendo ad,* et tunc Ymago trahatur vltra medium. Deinde veniat Maria, erectis manibus, et deuotis oculis Ymaginem intuens, cantet versum:

 Jhesu, nostra redempcio,[1]

cum richmo competenti. Apostoli antiphonam:

 O rex glorie, ⟨Domine virtutum, qui triumphator hodie super omnes cœlos ascendisti, ne derelinquas nos orphanos; sed mitte promissum Patris in nos, spiritum veritatis, alleluia.⟩[2]

Saluator antiphonam:

 Non vos relinquam ⟨orphanos, alleluia, vado et veniam ad vos, alleluia, et gaudebit cor vestrum, alleluia⟩.[3]

Angeli:

 Silete.

Saluator incipit responsorium:

 Ite in orbem ⟨universum, prædicate dicentes, alleluia: Qui crediderit et baptizatus fuerit, salvus erit, alleluia, alleluia, alleluia⟩.

Apostoli prosecuntur cantantes, circueundo domunculam. Deinde stant ad locum pristinum, et Saluator cantat versum:

 In nomine Patris ⟨et Filii et Spiritus Sancti. Qui crediderit⟩,[4]

Apostoli repeticionem. Saluator tercio *Ascendo,* et illa hora ymago Saluatoris totaliter trahitur intra tabulatum. Et, Apostolis intuentibus in celum, Angeli cantent antiphonam:

 ⟨Viri Galilæi, quid aspicitis in cœlum? Hic Jesus qui assumptus est a vobis in cœlum, sic veniet, alleluia⟩,[5]

vel offertorium:

 Viri Galylei, ⟨quid admiramini aspicientes in cœlum? Hic Jesus qui assumptus est a vobis in cœlum, sic veniet quemadmodum vidistis eum ascendentem in cœlum, alleluia.⟩[6]

Quibus finitis, Apostoli recedunt cum antiphona:

 Illi autem profecti ⟨prædicaverunt ubique, Deo cooperante et sermonem confirmante, sequentibus signis, alleluia, alleluia⟩.[7]

Et sic est finis. Et cauendum est ne strepitus[8] et turpitudo ymaginis Dyaboli cum abhominacionibus ignis sulphuris et picis sev aquarum coloribus permixtarum ceterisque irreuerencijs et parlamentis cuiuscumque condicionis per sanctam matrem ecclesiam prohibitis huic

---

[1] For the text of this hymn see below, p. 641.

[2] Antiphon for Ascension. See Hartker, p. 266.

[3] Antiphon for the first Sunday after Ascension. See Hartker, p. 267.

[4] This speech and the preceding one constitute a single responsory for Ascension day.

See Hartker, p. 264.

[5] Antiphon for Lauds of Ascension. See Hartker, p. 265.

[6] The offertory for the Mass of Ascension. See *Paléographie musicale,* i, 90.

[7] Antiphon for Lauds of Ascension. See Hartker, p. 266.

[8] strepitus] Followed by *pedum* crossed out.

deuocioni admisceantur, ex quibus loca sancta diuino cultui consecrata ac domus Dei quam decet sanctitudo in longitudine dierum non solum prophanantur, verum eciam populi deuocio in lasciuiam et ridiculum et aliquando in seditionem solet prouocari. Sed postquam ymago Saluatoris tabulatum intrauerit, tunc magne hostie, quemadmodum ad mandatum Domini in aliquibus ecclesijs solent distribui, si haberi poterunt, cum rosis, lilijs, et floribus diuersarum specierum mittuntur deorsum. Et paruuli pueri venientes de scola, vestibus abiectis, secundum nostram consvvetudinem hostias cum floribus colligunt, manibus in celum plaudentes, et cantantes *Sanctus, Sanctus, Sanctus*, vel *Veni, sancte ⟨spiritus⟩*. Per paruulos pueros, vestes abicientes, intelliguntur humiles, terrena non querentes, de quibus Dominus dicit: 'Nisi efficiamini sicut paruuli, non intrabitis in regnum celorum.' Illi colligunt flores diuersarum specierum, id est varia dona Spiritus Sancti. Per hostias intelligitur presencia Corporis Christi, quod nobiscum est sub specie panis vsque in consumacionem seculi.[1]

This dramatic ceremony occurs immediately before Vespers, about an enclosure, or *tentorium*, constructed in the middle of the nave, representing Mount Sinai.[2] Within the *tentorium* are an effigy of Christ[3] and a person who speaks the utterances of Christ, this person remaining concealed throughout the performance. Ropes are attached to the effigy, for drawing it up from the *tentorium* and through a ring of silk cloths under the roof. There is a ring of flowers enclosing a likeness of a dove, and another ring enclosing a likeness of an angel, both of which can be raised and lowered by cords. Concerned in the action also are fifteen persons outside the enclosure: twelve choristers representing the apostles, bearing appropriate symbols and their names written on their crowns; one representing the Virgin Mary, in the dress of a widow; and two representing angels, with wings and chaplets of flowers.

After these fifteen personages have advanced from the sacristy to the *tentorium* singing the responsory *Post passionem*, the concealed person, representing Christ, sings the antiphons *Pater*, *manifestavi*, and *Ascendo*. Then the effigy is raised sufficiently to be seen by all, and the dove and angel are lowered over it, the apostles singing appropriate liturgical passages. After a dialogue

---

[1] Followed immediately by the rubric *In secundis Vesperis*.

[2] According to the usual tradition, the Ascension occurred on Mount Olivet. See Acts i, 12.

[3] The Museum für Völkerkunde, at Basel, contains an Ascension effigy of this sort, from Kleinwangen, Switzerland, photographed by E. A. Stückelberg, in *Schweizerisches Archiv für Volkskunde*, xiii (1909), 150–1, along with references to other similar *imagines*. See plate xi.

XI. Ascension Image from Kleinwangen, Switzerland, in the
Museum für Völkerkunde, Basel

between Christ and Philip, the antiphon *Ascendo* is sung a second time, and the effigy is raised somewhat higher. Mary now sings a stanza of the hymn *Jesu, nostra redemptio*, and Christ and the apostles sing additional antiphons. After a third singing of *Ascendo*, the effigy is drawn through the opening in the roof, and disappears. Then the two angels sing *Viri Galilæi*, and the apostles withdraw.

The closing rubric forbids the horse-play of casting down the effigy of the devil, which seems to have been not uncommon on Ascension day, and recommends the dropping of wafers and flowers.[1]

Since this performance includes painstaking impersonation as well as genuine dialogue, it is unmistakably a play. In stark formalism, however, it exceeds all other examples of Church drama which we have encountered hitherto. This effect arises, obviously, from the use of an effigy for the central personage and from the complete dependence upon liturgical forms from the choir-books. It must be admitted, however, that under the limitation of using only liturgical texts for his dialogue, the writer —or compiler—has succeeded fairly well in attaining an orderly dramatic sequence and in avoiding incongruity.

PENTECOST

For the events of the Easter season surveyed in the preceding pages the fitting culmination is the descent of the Holy Ghost upon the disciples which occurred on the Jewish feast of Pentecost, fifty days after the Passover.[2] This occurrence was celebrated in the Christian calendar on the seventh Sunday after Easter, called *Dominica Pentecostes*, or, in English, Whitsunday. Although the Biblical account of the Pentecostal experience is not lacking in vividness and animation, the dramatizing of it in association with the liturgy did not proceed very far.

Some communities represented the descent of the Holy Spirit by filling the whole church with the smoke of incense.[3] In the cathedral of Nevers the gift of tongues was symbolized by the mingling of Greek and Hebrew words with the Latin of the official liturgy.[4] At St Paul's in London a censer swinging in a gigantic arc was suspended through a hole in the roof, through

---

[1] For the sixteenth-century testimony of Naogeorgus and George Gilpin see Appendix C below, ii, 531, 537, 538. See also Chambers, ii, 65, note 5; Stückelberg, *op. cit.*, p. 150; Rudwin, *Teufel*, p. 62.
[2] For the Gospel narrative see Acts ii.
[3] See Atchley, p. 303.
[4] See Boutillier, p. 486.

which issued also a dove. This ceremony is described by a sixteenth-century antiquary thus:[1]

The like Toye I my selfe (beinge then a Chyld) once saw in *Poules* Churche at *London*, at a Feast of *Whitsontyde*, wheare the comynge downe of the *Holy Gost* was set forthe by a white Pigion, that was let to fly out of a Hole, that yet is to be sene in the mydst of the Roofe of the great Ile, and by a longe Censer, which descendinge out of the same Place almost to the verie Grounde, was swinged up and downe at suche a Lengthe, that it reached with thone Swepe almost to the West Gate of the Churche, and with the other to the Quyre Staires of the same, breathinge out over the whole Churche and Companie a most pleasant Perfume of suche swete Thinges as burned thearin.

The hole in the roof was frequently used for ceremonials during the singing of the hymn *Veni creator* at Terce. Leaves, wafers, drops of water, burning tow, herbs, and flowers were among the objects dropped down into the church.[2] At various points in the liturgy, in different communities, a dove, real or artificial, was sent down through the same orifice.[3] A relatively full description of this last sort of ceremony is the following of the sixteenth century from the collegiate church at Halle:[4]

Nota ritum et modum missionis Sancti Spiritus. Peracto prandio, infra vndecimam et duodecimam cum duabus campanis maioribus competenti mora simpulsabitur ad Nonam, minor ad conuocandum, maior ad incipiendum. Interea subcustos et ecclesiastici accendent candelas totius ecclesie. Magister fabrice et scriniarius Columbam significantem Spiritum Sanctum de hiatu testudinis cum arcu et circulo suo pleno cereis suspendent, et tempore suo sensim demittent. Post pulsum Nona tarde et solenniter cantabitur. Hymnus *Hostem repellas. Per te sciamus.*[5] Nona finita, statim duo pueri bene vociferati super testudinem cantabunt antiphonam *Accipite Spiritum Sanctum*,[6] et non vltra. Statimque succentor incipiet solenniter hymnum *Veni creator*, et mox tubicines et fistulatores ciuitatis simul conflantes sonum edent. Et organista in or|gano complebit primum versum, chorus secundum.

[1] W. Lambarde, *Dictionarium Angliæ Topographicum et Historicum: An Alphabetical Description of the Chief Places in England and Wales*, London, 1730, p. 459. This work was written in the sixteenth century. See Atchley, pp. 303–4; Chambers, ii, 66.

[2] See Grenier, p. 388; Atchley, p. 301; Boutillier, p. 485; D'Ancona, i, 31–2; Chambers, ii, 66; Barbieri, p. 164; Lefebvre, i, 2; Hautcœur, *Histoire*, i, 426–7.

[3] See Boutillier, pp. 485–6; Cox, *Churchwardens' Accounts*, p. 265; Merimée, p. 5;

Tolhurst, i, 135; ii, 380; Hannam-Clark, *op. cit.*, p. 22.

[4] Bamberg, Staatsbibl., MS 119 (Ed. VI. 3), Ordin. Hallense anni 1532, fol. 114^r–114^v, previously edited by Müller, *Geschichte*, p. 524.

[5] *Hostem repellas longius* and *Per te sciamus, da, patrem* are the first lines, respectively, of the fifth and sixth stanzas of the famous hymn *Veni, creator, spiritus*, by Rabanus Maurus. See Chevalier, *R.H.*, no. 21204, and *A.H.*, l, 193.

[6] For this antiphon see Hartker, p. 271.

Iterum tubicines sonabunt, organista tertium versum, chorus quartum. Iterum tubicines modo predicto vsque in finem hymnum alternando. Interea paulatim demittetur Spiritus Sanctus, ita quod ad vltimum versum hymni perueniat ad summum altare. Hymno finito, cantabitur antiphona *Hodie completi sunt.*[1] Prepositus dicit versiculum *Emitte spiritum tuum,*[2] et collectam *Deus, qui hodierna die corda fidelium.* Deinde fiet sermo ad populum. Sub sermone subcustos et ecclesiastici deponent Spiritum Sanctum et remouebunt funes.[3]

The Holy Spirit is here represented by the figure of a dove surrounded by a circle of lighted candles. This contrivance is the centre of an independent liturgical ceremony after None. The dove is lowered slowly during the singing of the hymn *Veni creator*, and the observance includes the singing of an antiphon by two choir-boys on the roof, a prayer, and a sermon. During the preaching of the sermon the dove and ropes are removed.

Clearly such ceremonies are not lacking in theatrical effects, and one feels that they ought to have achieved something more positive in the way of impersonation and drama. The disciples, upon whom the Holy Spirit is assumed to be descending, could easily enough have been costumed realistically, and could have sung appropriate sentences, as in the Ascension play from Moosburg.[4] But of such developments the observances under review give no evidence. The impressive theme of Pentecost was not effectually dramatized.

[1] This antiphon does not appear in Hartker.

[2] See Hartker, p. 273.

[3] Followed by the rubric *Ad secundas Vesperas.*

[4] Slight evidences of such impersonation in Spain are referred to by Merimée, p. 5.

CHAPTER XVI

THE PASSION PLAY

IN comparison with the multitude of medieval Church plays treating events relating to the Resurrection, the number of dramatic representations of the Crucifixion is astonishingly small. We hear of no dramatization of the Passion earlier than the beginning of the thirteenth century, and even after that date evidences that such plays were promoted within the church are extremely rare.[1] We must infer, therefore, that the representation of the last occurrences in Christ's life was deliberately avoided. We may also surmise, if we wish, that for bringing vividly before the medieval worshipper the great Immolation, the Mass itself was felt to be sufficiently effective. Since by visible and audible means the celebrant could bring about daily an actual repetition of the great Sacrifice, what need was there of imitating it through the imperfect means of impersonation and stagecraft?

I

Had a writer wished to treat the Passion dramatically, he could have found ample points of departure in ceremonies mentioned in earlier parts of this treatise. Many of the liturgical observances of Holy Week, for example, were obviously devised for the express purpose of recalling vividly, through sensuous means, the closing events of Christ's earthly life. The processional entry into the city, or church, on Palm Sunday, the *Mandatum* on Holy Thursday, the singing of the four *Passiones*, the *Improperia* and Adoration of the Cross on Good Friday, and the *Depositio* on that day—any of these ceremonies was of such a nature that a mere touch of impersonation might have transformed it into a scene of a Passion play.[2] One or two of them, as we shall see, probably did exert a meagre influence upon the drama; but none of them can be regarded as the effectual source of the kind of play now under consideration.

When we turn from the traditional ceremonies of the Church and seek a source for the Passion play outside, we discern a

---

[1] For bibliographical observations see Notes, p. 697.

[2] In regard to the dramatic ceremonies of Holy Week, see above, pp. 90 sqq. Concerning the *Improperia* and the Adoration of the Cross see above, pp. 118 sqq., and below, pp. 504 sqq.

particularly promising nucleus in a form of extra-liturgical composition called the *planctus*, or lament, which undertakes to
express the emotions of one or another of the persons present at
the Crucifixion.[1] This sort of lament may not be the solitary
kernel from which the play developed, but it was probably
among the formative influences, and it certainly occupies a conspicuous place in the extant dramatic texts.

Although the *planctus* are sometimes found attached to parts of
the authorized liturgy, it seems probable that they did not origi-
nate as explicit embellishments of the official text, as did the
tropes, but were independent lyrical inventions. Sometimes the
chief person assumed to be uttering the lament is Christ himself.
In the one beginning *O vos omnes qui transitis*,[2] for example,
Christus, speaking from the cross, and *Homo* carry on a lyrical
dialogue. The great majority, and the earliest, of the *planctus*,
however, are assumed to be primarily the utterances of the
Virgin Mother as she stands near the cross, witnessing the agony
and death of her Son. Although she may address one or more
of the other persons assumed to be present, and may even evoke
replies from them, it is she who expresses the chief burden of
grief. It is with this type of *planctus Mariæ* that we are especially
concerned here.

For such laments the Gospels provide no direct encouragement,
as we may see from the only passage which mentions Mary's presence at the Crucifixion:[3]

Stabant autem juxta crucem Jesu mater ejus, et soror matris ejus,
Maria Cleophæ, et Maria Magdalene.

Cum vidisset ergo Jesus matrem, et discipulum stantem, quem
diligebat, dicit matri suæ: Mulier, ecce filius tuus.

Deinde dicit discipulo: Ecce mater tua. Et ex illa hora accepit eam
discipulus in sua.

These sentences convey a moving scene of the Blessed Virgin at
the foot of the cross, accompanied by other women and by John,
and surrounded by the hostile Jews. But Christ alone speaks;
His mother suffers in reserved silence. The conception of Mary
as suffering at the cross in stoical dignity seems to have domi-

---

[1] The *planctus* are briefly spoken of by
Chambers, ii, 39–40, and the Latin ones are
discussed, along with those in the vernacular,
by Schönbach, *Marienklagen*, pp. 10 sqq.;
Wechssler, pp. 12 sqq.; Thien, pp. 3 sqq.;
Lindner, pp. ii, cliv–clxxvi; Tanquerey, pp.
1 sqq.; Hirn, pp. 388–95; Meyer, pp. 66–7;
Brooks, *Lamentations*, pp. 415–6; Ermini,
pp. 57 sqq.
[2] Chevalier, *R.H.*, no. 31186, printed in
A.H., xxxi, 58–9.
[3] John xix, 25–7.

nated the fancy of the Western Church during the first ten centuries or so. Inevitably, however, arose the notion that as a human mother she could not possibly have concealed her grief entirely, but must have betrayed her suffering visibly and audibly. As early as the beginning of the fifth century, for example, St Augustine meditates freely upon her sobbing and tears as follows:[1]

Domina mea misericordissima, quos fontes dicam erupisse de pudicissimis oculis, cum attenderes unicum filium tuum innocentem coram te ligari, flagellari, mactari? Quos fletus credam perfudisse piissimum vultum, cum suspiceres eumdem et Deum et Dominum tuum in cruce sine culpa extendi, et carnem de carne tua ab impiis crudeliter dissecari? Quibus singultibus æstimabo purissimum pectus vexatum esse, cum tu audires: *Mulier, ecce filius tuus*; et discipulus, *Ecce mater tua*: cum acciperes discipulum pro Magistro, servum pro Domino?

The literary impulse prompting the invention of Mary's actual utterances of sorrow may have arisen from pious reflections such as these, or it may have come, directly or indirectly, from the Apocrypha. The Greek version of the Gospel of Nicodemus, often assigned to the fifth century, contains a very ample account of Mary's sorrowing.[2] This narrative includes John's bringing to Mary the news of the approaching Crucifixion, her swooning at the sight of Christ on the way to Golgotha, and her subsequent laments at the cross, in which she addresses Jesus, the bystanders, and the women who accompany her. Although the general resemblances between this passage and the lyrical poems under consideration are striking, it must be admitted that the initiating influence of the Greek composition is doubtful, for the Gospel of Nicodemus seems to have made its way into Western Europe through a Latin version which does not contain the lament of Mary.[3] Whatever their origin, sentences assumed to be spoken by Mary at the cross are found in the liturgy by the ninth or tenth century, as may be seen in the following responsory:[4]

Vadis propitiator ad immolandum pro omnibus; non tibi occurrit Petrus, qui dicebat: Pro te moriar. Reliquit te Thomas, qui clamabat

[1] *Meditationes*, cap. xli, Migne, *P.L.*, xl, 941.

[2] Tischendorf, *Evangelia*, Acta Pilati B, chap. x, pp. 302–6.

[3] See Wechssler, pp. 8–10, 12; Tanquerey, p. 7; Wülcker, pp. 3–4; Tischendorf, *Evangelia*, pp. liv sqq.

[4] *Paléographie musicale*, v, 243–4, from a facsimile of a MS of the twelfth century. This responsory was in the Roman *liber responsalis* of the ninth or tenth century, an incomplete text of it being found in the Gregorian service-book printed by Migne, *P.L.*, lxxviii, 768.

dicens: Omnes cum eo moriamur. Et nullus de illis, sed tu solus duceris, qui immaculatam me conservasti, filius et Deus meus. Versus: Venite et videte Deum et hominem pendentem in cruce.

For the immediate source of inspiration for the *planctus Mariæ* one is, of course, tempted to turn to the laments uttered by the three Marys in the more highly developed versions of the *Visitatio Sepulchri*. On their way to the sepulchre, as we have seen, one or another of the women pours forth her grief in such verses as the following:[1]

Heu! nobis internas mentes   quanti pulsant gemitus
Pro nostro consolatore,   quo privamur miseræ,
Quem crudelis Judæorum   morti dedit populus.

Jam percusso ceu pastore,   oves errant miseræ;
Sic magistro discedente,   turbantur discipuli,
Atque nos, absente eo,   dolor tenet nimius.

If it could be shown that 'complaints' like this were written for Easter plays before the twelfth century, we should inevitably infer that they had some bearing upon the invention, about that time, of laments of the Blessed Virgin. It happens, however, that the extant examples associated with the Resurrection do not antedate the earliest of those attached to the theme of the Passion; hence one infers that such influences as existed between the two groups might have flowed in either direction.[2]

Probably, however, there is no need of our supplying, or assuming, definite literary antecedents, for we shall be sufficiently near the truth if we regard the *planctus Mariæ* as merely one manifestation of the abundant cult of the Blessed Virgin which extended over Christendom from the twelfth century onwards.[3] As the great emotional moments in her life were increasingly contemplated, it was inevitable that prominence should be given to her role as Sorrowing Mother, and to her deepest suffering at the foot of the cross. What the Gospel failed to record was supplied by the imaginative impulses of the faithful. As St Augustine had already shown, earnest reflection upon the scene of the Crucifixion revealed the human necessity of her tears and sighs and open exclamation.

---

[1] For examples see above, pp. 375, 390.
[2] For versions of the *Visitatio Sepulchri* and *Ludus Paschalis* containing laments of the three Marys see above, chaps. xiii and xiv.

[3] The rise of this cult is sufficiently described by Beissel, pp. 379 sqq.; Lindner, pp. clx sqq.; Meyer, pp. 66–7.

II

Of the large number and variety of *planctus Mariæ* composed during the Middle Ages, we need consider here only the few which, in form or content, are most nearly related to the Passion play.[1] In a considerable proportion of these it is the Virgin alone who speaks, as in *Mœstæ parentis Christi*,[2] of Adam of St Victor (*circa* 1190), in which she addresses the cross, upbraids Gabriel, and recalls a threatening prophecy of Simeon; or in *Virgo plorans filium*,[3] which includes addresses to Christ and to Peter; or in *O filii ecclesiæ*,[4] addressed to Jews and Christians in general, and, in particular, to Judas. Most notable of all, in this group, are *Planctus ante nescia* and *Flete, fideles animæ*, to be considered below. A certain number of these pieces provide utterances for other persons, and thus become dialogues. The speakers may be, for example, the Virgin and Christ;[5] or the Virgin and the Cross;[6] or the Virgin and the bystanders;[7] or the Virgin, Christ, and John.[8] Because of their imitating the dialogue in the sequence *Victimæ paschali* one may draw special attention to the two laments *Surgit Christus cum trophæo*[9] and *Dic, Maria, quid vidisti contemplando crucem Christi*,[10] in each of which the Virgin, in response to interrogation, recalls successive moments in the Passion. It appears, however, that these two dramatic *planctus* are not directly related to the extant plays.

For its emotional power as well as for its direct relationship to the drama, the most notable of the laments of Mary is *Planctus ante nescia*, composed during the twelfth century:[11]

1a. Planctus ante nescia,
    planctu lassor anxia,
        crucior dolore.

1b. Orbat orbem radio,
    me Judæa filio,
        gaudio, dulcore.

[1] Concerning the *planctus Mariæ* specifically see Wechssler, pp. 12–8; Beissel, pp. 379–86; Thien, pp. 3–12; Ermini, pp. 57–87.

[2] Chevalier, *R.H.*, no. 11671, printed in *A.H.*, liv, 318–20.

[3] Chevalier, no. 34634, printed in *A.H.*, xxxi, 169.

[4] Chevalier, no. 12986, printed in *A.H.*, i, 78–9.

[5] See *Ante crucem virgo stabat*, Chevalier, no. 1169, printed in *A.H.*, xv, 76.

[6] See *Crux, de te volo conqueri*, Chevalier, no. 4014, printed in *A.H.*, xxi, 20–1.

[7] See *O perpulchra domina*, Chevalier, no. 30814, printed in *A.H.*, xxxi, 171.

[8] See *Qui per viam pergitis*, Chevalier, no.

16473, printed in *A.H.*, x, 79–81. See below, p. 500.

[9] See Chevalier, no. 19919, printed in *A.H.*, liv, 364–8. As the editors explain (pp. 365–6), there is an earlier sequence *Surgit Christus cum trophæo* in which the dominating personage in the dialogue is Mary Magdalen. A special form of this latter version is printed by Milchsack, pp. 92–4. See Chevalier, no. 19918.

[10] Chevalier, no. 4565, printed in *A.H.*, xxxi, 168–9.

[11] Chevalier, no. 14950, printed in *A.H.*, xx, 156–8. Chevalier ascribes the poem to Godefroy de St Victor.

2a. Fili, dulcor unice,
  singulare gaudium,
  matrem flentem respice,
  conferens solatium.

2b. Pectus, mentem, lumina
  torquent tua vulnera.
  Quæ mater, quæ femina,
  tam felix, tam misera!

3a. Flos florum,
  dux morum,
   veniæ vena,
  quam gravis
  in clavis
   est tibi pœna!

3b. Proh dolor,
  hinc color
   effugit oris,
  hinc ruit,
  hinc fluit
   unda cruoris.

4a. O quam sero deditus,
  quam cito me deseris,
  o quam digne genitus,
  quam abjecte moreris!

4b. O quis amor corporis
  tibi fecit spolia,
  o quam dulcis pignoris
  quam amara præmia!

5a. O pia gratia
  sic morientis,
  o zelus, o scelus
  invidæ gentis.

5b. O fera dextera
  crucifigentis,
  o lenis in pœnis
  mens patientis.

6a. O verum eloquium
  justi Simeonis;
  quem promisit, gladium
  sentio doloris.

6b. Gemitus, suspiria
  lacrimæque foris,
  vulneris indicia
  sunt interioris.

7a. Parcito proli,
  mors, mihi noli,
  tunc mihi soli
  sola mederis.

7b. Morte, beate,
  separer a te,
  dummodo, nate,
  non crucieris.

8a. Quod crimen, quæ scelera
  gens commisit effera!
  Vincla, virgas, vulnera,
  sputa, spinas, cetera
  sine culpa patitur.

8b. Nato, quæso, parcite,
  matrem crucifigite
  aut in crucis stipite
  nos simul affigite,
  male solus moritur.

9a. Reddite mœstissimæ
  corpus vel exanime,
  ut sic minoratus
  crescat cruciatus
  osculis, amplexibus.

9b. Utinam sic doleam,
  ut dolore peream,
  nam plus est dolori
  sine morte mori,
  quam perire citius.

10a. Quid stupes, gens misera,
  terram se movere,
  obscurari sidera,
  languidos lugere?

10b. Solem privas lumine,
  quomodo luceret?
  Ægrum medicamine,
  unde convaleret?

11a. Homicidam liberas,
　　　Jesum das supplicio;
　　　male pacem toleras,
　　　veniet seditio.

11b. Famis, cædis, pestium
　　　scies docta pondere
　　　Jesum tibi mortuum
　　　Barrabamque vivere.

12a. Gens cæca, gens flebilis,
　　　age pœnitentiam,
　　　dum tibi flexibilis
　　　Jesus est ad veniam.

12b. Quos fecisti, fontium
　　　prosint tibi flumina,
　　　sitim sedant omnium,
　　　cuncta lavant crimina.

13a. Flete, Sion filiæ,
　　　tantæ gratæ gratiæ
　　　muneris, angustiæ
　　　sibi sunt deliciæ
　　　pro vestris offensis.

13b. In amplexus ruite,
　　　dum pendet in stipite,
　　　mutuis amplexibus
　　　parat se amantibus
　　　manibus extensis.

14. In hoc solo gaudeo,
　　　quod pro vobis doleo,
　　　vicem, quæso, reddite,
　　　matris damnum plangite.

This is obviously a pure monologue. After announcing her grief in the opening stanza, Mary addresses two stanzas to Christ, describing their mutual suffering. Then follow three stanzas of sheer lament (4, 5 and 6), in the course of which she recalls Simeon's prophecy that a sword should pierce her spirit.[1] In the next three stanzas she appeals to death to spare her Son's life, and to take her in his place. Finally, after denouncing the Jews (10, 11 and 12), she closes with an appeal for sympathy addressed to the women of Jerusalem. The poem, then, is assumed to be spoken at the foot of the cross, during the last moments of Christ's agony. Were Mary actually impersonated, the composition would instantly become a play.

Another *planctus* with which we shall be intimately concerned is *Flete, fideles animæ*, an anonymous composition written at least as early as the thirteenth century: [2]

1a. Flete, fideles animæ,
　　　flete, sorores optimæ,
　　　ut sint multiplices
　　　doloris indices
　　　planctus et lacrimæ.

1b. Fleant materna viscera
　　　Mariæ matris vulnera.
　　　Materne doleo
　　　quæ dici soleo
　　　felix puerpera.

2a. Triste spectaculum
　　　crucis et lanceæ!

2b. Dum caput cernuum,
　　　dum spinas capitis,

---

[1] See Luke ii, 35.　　　[2] Chevalier, no. 26669, printed in *A.H.*, xx, 15.

Clausum signaculum
  matris virgineæ
    profunde vulnerat.
    Hoc est quod dixerat,
    quod prophetaverat
senex prænuntius;
hic ille gladius
  qui me transverberat.

3a. Ergo quare, fili care,
    pendes ita, cum sis vita
      vivens ante sæcula?
    Rex cœlestis, pro scelestis
    alienas solvis pœnas,
      agnus sine macula?

4a. O mentes perfidas
    et linguas duplices
  et testes subdolos
    ac falsos judices,
senes cum junioribus
solent majoribus
criminibus
  damnati
ferre stipendium
suspendium
  peccati.

5a. Mi Johannes, planctum move,
  plange mecum, fili nove,
    fili novo fœdere
    matris et materteræ.
    Tempus est lamenti;
immolemus intimas
lacrimarum victimas
    Christo morienti.

6a. Hac in vita sum invita,
  hoc in malo mori malo,
    fili mi, dum reprimi
    vel exprimi
    nequit æstus animi
      dolentis,
    tantis malis eximi
    volentis.

dum plagas manuum
  cruentis digitis
    supplex suspicio,
    sub hoc supplicio
    tota deficio,
dum vulnus lateris,
dum locus vulneris
  est in profluvio.

3b. Munda caro, mundo cara,
  cur in crucis ares ara
    pro peccatis hostia?
Cur in ara crucis ares,
caro, quæ peccato cares,
  caro culpæ nescia?

4b. A damnatis is
    damnatur innocens
explens, quod expedit,
  quod decet, edocens,
fremunt auctores criminum
et viri sanguinum
in Dominum
  salutis
zelo nequitiæ
sub specie
  virtutis.

5b. Salutaris noster Jesus,
captus, tractus, vinctus, cæsus
    et illusus alapis
    a gehennæ satrapis,
    auctor veræ lucis,
dies nocte clauditur,
vita mortem patitur,
    mortem autem crucis.

6b. Scelus terræ cœlum terret,
terræ motus terret motus
    impios nefarios,
    qui gladios
    in sanctorum filios
      allidunt
    et te, Christe hagios,
    occidunt.

Like the preceding poem, this one is assumed to be a monologue
spoken at the foot of the cross. It opens with Mary's appeal to

the women of Jerusalem, followed by a sorrowful address to Christ (stanza 3), a vehement condemnation of the Jews (4), an appeal to the apostle John (5), and a final cry to Christ (6). The most notable element in this composition is the direct address to John, to whom in *Planctus ante nescia* there is no reference.[1] The poem now before us resembles the one preceding in its suitability for dramatic use; but in literary quality it is somewhat less appealing. The sophisticated word-play in stanza 3b, for example, chills one's response to the avowed ardour of the speaker.

A third *planctus* related in some manner to the dramatic treatments of the Passion is the following:[2]

1a. 'Qui per viam pergitis,
    hic mecum sedete,
    Si est dolor similis
    ut meus, videte;
    Meum dulcem filium
    pariter lugete.

1b. Videte spectaculum
    in cruce pendentis
    More damnatitii
    crimina luentis,
    Pro peccato populi
    mortem patientis.

2a. Ordo juris vertitur,
    æquitas turbatur,
    Justitia læditur,
    ratio mutatur;
    Sine causa filius
    meus morti datur.

2b. Quare meus filius
    condemnatur ita?
    Sine causa moritur
    morientum vita,
    Et ego tam misera
    vivo jam invita.

3a. Quid commisit genitrix,
    cur orbatur prole?
    Me, Judæa, filio,
    mundum privas sole;
    Patre privas pauperes,
    ægros adjutore.

3b. Injustum judicium,
    judices, tractastis;
    Meum dulcem filium
    injuste damnastis,
    Quem crucis patibulo
    mori judicastis.

4a. Vertite judicium
    et videte jura;
    Creatorem perimit
    ejus creatura
    Et condemnat Dominum
    suum morte dura.
    Quod crimen, quæ scelera
    commisit, gens effera?

4b. Nato, quæso, parcite,
    matrem crucifigite,
    Aut in crucis stipite
    nos simul affigite,
    Male solus moritur.
    Sed quid prodest? misera
    loquor induratis;
    Non absolvunt penitus

---

[1] Although stanza 5 (*Mi Johannes*) sometimes follows the poem *Planctus ante nescia* in literary compositions, there is no evidence to show that this stanza was regarded as an enlargement of that poem. Wechssler (p. 16), however, appears to assume this relationship; Schönbach (*op. cit.*, p. 10) is non-committal.

[2] Chevalier, no. 16473, printed in *A.H.*, x, 79–81, from 'Miss. Praedicatorum imp. Venetiis, 1523.' The date of composition must be considerably earlier than the date of this printed book.

Vincla, virgas, vulnera,
sputa, spinas, cetera
sine causa patitur.

5a. Mi Johannes, proximos
tuos deprecare,
Ut me sinant vulnera
saltem alligare,
Quæ vides tam fortiter
sanguine manare.
Proh dolor!
jam color
exstinguitur oris.

6a. Fili, dulcor unice,
singulare gaudium,
matrem flentem respice
conferens solatium.

7a. Flos florum,
dux morum,
veniæ vena,

8a. O quam sero deditus,
quam cito me deseris,
o quam digne genitus,
quam abjecte moreris!

9a. Fili, dulcor animæ,
respice mœrentem,
Vide matrem miseram
pæne morientem,
Dum videt tam turpiter
te cruce pendentem.

10a. In sero recubuit
supra tuum pectus,
Et nunc ita remanet
miser et abjectus,
Patre, fratre, Domino
privatur dilectus.

11a. Ubi grex amabilis?
solus hic remansit
Atque tua vulnera
solus mecum planxit;
Tuus dolor potius
piam mentem transit.'

quem damnarunt gratis;
Meus Jesus moritur
mundi pro peccatis.

5b. Hinc ruit,
hinc fluit
unda nam cruoris.
Non sperabam misera
talia videre,
Sed credebam potius
de Jesu gaudere,
Quem crucis patibulo
video pendere.

6b. Pectus, mentem, lumina
torquent tua vulnera,
quæ mater, quæ femina,
tam infelix, tam misera!

7b. Quam gravis
in clavis
est tibi pœna!

8b. O quis amor corporis
tibi fecit spolia,
o quam dulcis pignoris
quam amara præmia!

9b. Fili, dulcor unice,
respice parentem
Et vide discipulum
jam deficientem,
Dum videt te Dominum
suum morientem.

10b. Ubi grex amabilis?
omnes ⟨au⟩fugerunt
Et timore maximo
furtim abierunt;
Te solum patibulo
crucis reliquerunt.

11b. 'Consolare, domina
magis et regina,
Cur mœrore deficis,
stella matutina?
Tuus levat filius
mundum a ruina.

12a. Consolare, genitrix,
　　　　et sileto, mei
　　Quem damnatum conspicis
　　　　nunc in forma rei,
　　Vere nosti filium
　　　　verum esse Dei.

12b. Dolet tuus filius
　　　　magis te dolente,
　　Sursum tollit lumina
　　　　te respiciente,
　　Et intendit gemitus
　　　　tantos te gemente.'

13a. 'Mi Johannes, qualiter
　　　　possum consolari,
　　Dum infelix orbitor
　　　　lumine solari
　　Et sic tantum Dominum
　　　　video necari?

13b. Si dolerem adeo,
　　　　quod deberem mori,
　　Nec sic meo penitus
　　　　parcerem sic ori,
　　Nec do, quanta debeo,
　　　　carmina dolori.

14a. Utinam sic doleam,
　　　　quod dolore peream,
　　　　nam plus est dolori
　　　　sine morte mori
　　　　quam perire citius.

14b. Detur nunc mœstissimæ
　　　　corpus vel exanime,
　　　　ut sic minoratus
　　　　cesset cruciatus
　　　　osculis, amplexibus.'

15a. Jesus matri loquitur
　　　　totus vulneratus:
　　'Cur tam doles, mulier?
　　　　ecce tuus natus,
　　Johannes discipulus,
　　　　tibi commendatus.'

15b. Postquam Jesus taliter
　　　　pia solvit ora,
　　Virgo matrem virginem
　　　　jam ex illa hora
　　Suscepit in propriam
　　　　omni pulsa mora.

16. Qui pro nobis voluit
　　　mortem sustinere,
　　Non sinat nos misere
　　　ignibus ardere;
　　Sed det suis famulis
　　　secum congaudere.

In this poem we encounter the element of dialogue. In a complaint which begins under the inspiration of the Lamentations of Jeremiah,[1] Mary appeals to the passers-by for sympathy (stanza 1), appeals to the judges for mercy (2–4), begs John to intervene (5), and pours out her grief to Christ himself (6–11a). John comforts and mildly reproves her for augmenting Christ's suffering by expressing her own (11b–12). By way of reply Mary merely continues her lament (13–14). A sentence of narrative now introduces Christ's response, in which he commits John to his mother as her new son (15a). The *planctus* closes with another brief passage of narrative. The composition as a

---

[1] See Lamentations i, 12: *O vos omnes, qui transitis per viam, attendite, et videte si est dolor sicut dolor meus.*

whole has the appearance of being a none too effectual expansion of the two poems which precede it in these pages. Substantial passages seem to have been borrowed literally from *Planctus ante nescia*,[1] and at least two utterances were probably inspired by the address to John in *Flete, fideles animæ*.[2] The result of these influences is a poem somewhat lacking in concentrated literary power.

III

For our immediate purpose, however, our curiosity concerning such *planctus* centres less in their content and form than in the manner and circumstances of their delivery. Upon this point, unfortunately, our information is not abundant. We have evidence of the thirteenth century from Toulouse which seems to show that in that metropolis a *planctus* was sung on Good Friday after Matins, presumably as part of the ceremony of *Tenebræ*.[3] The two singers stood on a platform surrounded by curtains, and in the course of their performance all the lights were extinguished except one, in token of the fact that, of all Christ's followers, only the Virgin Mary was steadfast in her devotion. We are not told what text was sung at Toulouse, or whether it was sung in dialogue.[4]

In the nature of the case, however, the liturgical ceremony to which the *planctus* could be most appropriately attached was the Adoration of the Cross.[5] In this observance, centred in the Crucifix, and vivified by the *Improperia*, which are conceived of as spoken by Christ himself, the setting for the lament of Mary is virtually complete. It would seem inevitable that the *planctus* should have occupied this position in many churches from the twelfth century onwards, and we have evidence for this arrangement in Northern Italy in the fourteenth century;[6] but the only adequate description of this use known to me is contained in the following passage in a manuscript of the fifteenth century from Regensburg:[7]

[1] See *Qui per viam*, stanzas 4b, 5 (in part), 5, 7, 8, 14.

[2] See stanzas 5a, 13a. That *Qui per viam* is of later date than the other two compositions is, of course, an unproved inference.

[3] In regard to *Tenebræ* see above, p. 101.

[4] For the evidence, from Du Cange, see Notes, p. 698.

[5] Concerning this ceremony see above, pp. 102, 117 sqq.

[6] According to Rubeis (p. 323), a missal of the fourteenth century from Friuli, after prescribing the singing of the *Passio*, adds the following: 'Postea fit planctus ad crucifixum, prout patet in cantuariis; et hoc si placet.' I infer that the *planctus* is connected here with the *Adoratio Crucis*, since this ceremonial normally follows the singing of the *Passio* almost immediately. See above, p. 118. For an elaborate vernacular *planctus* at this place in the liturgy see Schönemann, p. 129.

[7] Munich, Staatsbibl., MS lat. 26947.

Finitis orationibus,[1] sacerdos cum ministris et aliis[2] sacerdotibus ad minus xii canonicis Sancti Johannis, qui illo die presentes debent esse, indutis casulis, precedentibus duabus crucibus uelatis et duabus candelis extinctis et thuribulo et aspersorio, faciant processionem ad capellam Sancti Stephani; et ibi | sacerdos cum ministris et alijs sacerdotibus cum genufleccione in magna reuerencia dicat ante crucifixum velatum, quod presentari debet, psalmum *Domine, quid multiplicati.* Sequitur versus *Christus factus est obediens.* Deinde *Pater Noster.* Sacerdos dicat versum *Proprio filio.* Item versus *Foderunt manus.* Sequitur oratio *Respice, quesumus, Domine, super familiam.* Deinde aspergantur crucifixa et thurificentur. Deinde tollatur per sacerdotem et ministros et alios sacerdotes, et portant usque ante capellam Sancti Stephani. Ibi stent et cantent:

> *Popule meus,* et *Agios*[3] *o Theos.*

Et chorus respondeat:

> *Sanctus Deus.*

Interim cum chorus cantat *Sanctus,* procedant in medium claustri, et ibi cantent secundum versum:

> *Quia eduxi te,* et *Agios.*[3]

Chorus respondeat:

> *Sanctus Deus.*

Interim cum chorus cantat *Sanctus,* vadant usque sub ianuam monasterij,[4] et ibi stent et cantent tercium versum:

> *Quid ultra debui,* et *Agios*[3] *o Theos.*

Chorus respondeat:

> *Sanctus Deus.*

Interim intrent, cum chorus cantant *Sanctus,* ante altare Beate Uirginis aperte chori decani. Cum autem venerint ad gradum Beate Virginis, figant crucifixum uelatum in lapide forti. Et episcopus reuelet lignum[5] Sancte Crucis tollendo crucem magnam in qua lignum Sancte Crucis reconditum est. Deinde alij duo sacerdotes | reuelent crucifixum. Et tunc sacerdos alta voce incipiat antiphonam:

> *Ecce lignum.*

Psalmus:

> *Beati immaculati.*

Ordin. Ratisbonense sæc. xv, fol. 116^r– 117^v. This text is now printed for the first time, except part of the closing paragraph describing the *Depositio,* which has been published by Young, *Dramatic Associations,* p. 88. In the present text, in order to show adequately the liturgical position of the *planctus,* I give the whole *ordo* for the Adoration of the Cross, including the *Improperia.*

[1] As to the position of these *orationes solemnes* in the liturgy of Good Friday see above, p. 118.

[2] aliis] alij (MS).   [3] Agios] Ayos (MS).

[4] monasterij] monastarij (MS).

[5] lignum] lingnum (MS). This is the spelling throughout.

Repetitur antiphona:

Ecce lignum.

Deinde,[1] si placet, veniant duo scolares, indutis uestibus lamentabilibus, sub typus Beate Virginis et Sancti Johannis, et plangant ante crucifixum alternatim planctum:

Planctus ante nescia,

et alium:

Hew, hew! uirgineus ⟨flos⟩.

Quo debito modo peracto, reuertebantur ad sacrarium et exuant se. Deinde crucifixum adoretur cum summa reuerencia ab omni clero et populo. Canonici et clerici prostrati in longam veniam dicant has orationes:

Domine Ihesu Christe, Deus verus.

Oratio:

Deus, qui famulo tuo Moysi.

Oratio:

Domine Ihesu Christe qui nos per crucis passionem.

Sequitur antiphona:

Dum fabricator mundi.

Item alia:

O admirabile precium.

Deinde cantentur versus:

Crux fidelis.

Finito ympno, deferatur Corpus Domini per aliquem sacerdotem de sacrario cum magna reuerencia, precedentibus duabus crucibus uelatis et duabus candelis ardentibus et thuribulo et aspersorio. Et ille sacerdos qui fert det ad manus subdyaconi; deinde subdyaconus det ad manus dyaconi; et dyaconus conferat prespitero imponens illud in patena. Et sic deferat super altare simul cum calice, in quo fit solum vinum non conse|cratum. Et accipiens sacerdos patenam cum Hostia, et ponat ad locum suum. Et inclinet se ad altare et oret; post paululum eleuans se lenta uoce dicat *Oremus: Preceptis salutaribus moniti.* Sequitur *Pater Noster.* Cum autem dixerit *Sed libera nos a malo,* non dicit *Amen.* Sumat[2] Hostiam particulam, mittat in calicem silendo. *Pax Domini* non dicit, neque *Agnus Dei.* Et sic sanctificatur vinum non consecratum per panem sanctificatum. Deinde sacerdos communicet, et ceteri si placet. Aliud nichil oret nisi *Hoc corpus quod pro uobis.* Postea ueniat plebanus maioris ecclesie et porrigat omnibus communicantibus Evvkaristiam. Postquam omnes communicauerint, ueniat sacerdos cum ministris altaris et ceteris canonicis instantibus cum magna reuerencia, pre-

---

[1] Deinde] Preceded by *p* crossed out (MS).   [2] Sumat] Su*mm*at (MS).

cedentibus duabus crucibus uelatis, et vna candela extincta et aspersorio et thuribulo. Et tollant crucifixum quod ante fuit presentatum,
et deferant ad locum Sepulchri, et cantando lenta voce responsorium:

> *Recessit pastor.* Versus: *Ante cuius conspectum.*

Sequitur responsorium:

> *Ecce quomodo moritur iustus.* Versus: *In pace factus.*

Tunc locent crucifixum in Sepulchro, et stantes circa dicant Vesperas.

At Regensburg the laments, *Planctus ante nescia* and *Hew, hew, virgineus flos,* are placed in the very midst of the ceremony of the Adoration. This begins with the *Improperia,* sung before a veiled crucifix in front of the chapel of St Stephen. During this singing the procession moves by stages through the cloister into the church, up to the altar of the Blessed Virgin. Here the veiled processional crucifix is firmly fixed *in lapide forti.* After the bishop has disclosed a relic of the true Cross, two priests uncover the processional crucifix and the antiphon *Ecce lignum* is sung, along with the psalm *Beati immaculati.* At this stage are sung the *planctus,* by two *scolares* dressed in garments of mourning to represent the Blessed Virgin and St John. After they have completed their laments and have withdrawn, the Adoration is completed, and followed by the Communion of the Mass of the Presanctified, the Burial of the Crucifix,[1] and Vespers.

As to the exact nature of the laments sung *alternatim* by the two *scolares* impersonating the Blessed Mary and St John we cannot be certain. There is preserved, however, a composition from Regensburg which begins *Heu, heu! virgineus flos,* which includes a considerable number of stanzas from *Planctus ante nescia,* and which explicitly assigns at least one passage to St John.[2] This metrical piece must represent at least the general type of lament used in the ceremony before us. Whatever the precise content of the text, it was genuinely dramatized.[3]

A far more striking dramatic use of the *planctus* appears in the following from the cathedral of Cividale del Friuli: [4]

---

[1] In regard to the ceremony *Depositio Crucis* see above, pp. 132 sqq.

[2] For the text of this composition see Notes, p. 698.

[3] In regard to a ceremony at Padua which may have been somewhat similar see Notes, p. 700.

[4] Cividale, Reale Museo Archeologico, MS CI, Process. Cividalense sæc. xiv,

fol. 74^r–76^v, previously edited by Cousse-maker, pp. 285–97 (C), and reprinted therefrom by Bartholomaeis, pp. 532–5. The MS provides music. The marks of parenthesis are editorial, and they enclose passages which, in the MS, are written in a smaller hand above the spoken text. See plate xii. For further observations on the MS see below, p. 663.

XII. *Planctus Mariæ* from Cividale, in Cividale, Reale Museo Archeologico, MS CI, fol. 74ʳ

Hic incipit Planctus Marie et aliorum in die Parasceuen.

Magdalena:

(Hic uertat se ad homines cum brachijs extensis.)
O fratres!
(Hic ad mulieres.)
`       ` *et sorores!*
Ubi est spes mea?
(Hic percuciat sibi pectus.)
Ubi consolatio mea?
(Hic manus elleuet.)
Ubi tota salus,   5
(Hic, inclinato capite, sternat se ad pedes Christi.)
O magister mi?

Maria mai⟨or⟩:

(Hic percutiat manus.)
O dolor!
Proh [1] *dolor!*
Ergo quare,
(Hic ostendat Christum apertis manibus.)
fili chare, [2]   10
pendes ita,
cum sis uita
(Hic pectus percutiat suum.)
manens ante secula?

Iohannes:

(Hic, cum manibus extensis, ostendat Christum.)
Rex celestis,
pro scelestis   15
(Hic demonstret populum proiiciendo* [3] *se.)
alienas
soluis penas,
agnus sine macula.

Maria Iacobi: [4]

(Ostendat crucem apertis manibus.)
Munda caro, mundo cara,
cur in crucis ares ara,   20
(Hic sibi pectus percutiat.)
pro peccatis hostia?

---

[1] Proh] Last letter inserted by a later hand
(MS).
[2] chare] Second letter inserted by a later
hand (MS).
[3] proiiciendo] projiciendo (C); percucien-
do (? MS).
[4] Iacobi] Only partly legible (MS).

Iohannes:

(Hic uertat se ad Mariam, suas lacrimas ostendendo.)
Fleant materna uiscera
Marie ⟨matris⟩ uulnera.
(Hic se percuciat.)
Materne doleo
que dici soleo   25
(Hic salutet Mariam.)
felix puerpera.

Maria maior: [1]

(Hic amplectet vnam Mariam ad collum.)
Flete, fideles a|nime,
(Hic aliam.)
flete, sorores optime,
ut sint multiplices
(Hic se percutiat.)
doloris indices,   30
planctus et lacrime.

Ambe Marie:

(Hic ambe Marie erigant se cum manibus extensis ad Mariam
et ad Christum.)
Cur merore deficis,
mater crucifixi?
Cur dolore consumeris,
dulcis soror nostra?   35
Sic oportet fieri
(Hic se inclinant cum salute.)
ut predixit psalmista.

Maria maior:

(Hic se percuciat.)
Triste spectaculum
(Hic ostendat Christum.)
crucis et lancee!
(Hic ostendat latus Christi.)
Clausum signaculum   40
mentis uirginee
(Hic se percuciat.)
profunde [2] me uulnerat.
Hoc est quod dixerat,
quod prophetauerat

---

[1] maior] Only partly legible (MS).   and in the margin stands the rubric *Iohannes*
[2] profunde] The first letter is rubricated,   (MS).

(Hic ostendat angelum.)
> *ille prenuncius;*

45

(Hic se percutiat.)
> *hic ille gladius*
> *qui me trans|uerberat.*

Maria maior:

(Hic amplectet [1] Iohannem.)
> *Mi Iohannes, planctum moue,*
> *plange mecum, fili nove,*
> *fili,*

(Hic ostendat Christum.)
> *nouo federe*
> *matris et matertere.*

50

(Hic laxatis manibus.)
> *Tempus est lamenti;*

(Hic se percutiat.)
> *immolemus intimas*
> *lacrimarum uictimas*

(Hic laxet manus.)
> *Christo morienti.*

55

Iohannes:

(Hic uertat se ad Mariam cum manibus apertis.)
> *O Maria, mater mea,*
> *semper tu michi eris cara,*
> *et thesaurum conseruabo*

(Hic ostendat Christum.)
> *qui modo michi est commissus.*

Magdalena:

(Hic se flexis genibus ante crucem.)
> *O Pater benigne,*
> *o magister inclyte,*

60

(Hic se ipsam ostendat.)
> *noli me derelinquere;*

(Hic se percuciat.)
> *peccatricem respice,*
> *tu qui me saluasti.*

Maria maior:

> *O Maria |*

(Hic ostendat Magdalenam.)
> *Magdalena,*

65

(Hic ostendat Christum.) ·
> *filij mei dulcis discipula,*

      [1] amplectet] Not wholly legible (MS).

(Hic amplexetur Magdalenam ad collum cum duobus brachiis.)
plange mecum, soror mea,
(Hic uoluat ad aliam partem amplectendo Magdalenam.)
plange mecum cum dolore
(Hic ostendat Christum.)
mortem dulcis nati mei,
(Hic ostendat Magdalenam.)
et mortem magistri tui,   70
(Hic ostendat Christum.)
mortem illius qui
(Hic ostendat Magdalenam.)
te tantum amauit,
(Hic ostendat Magdalenam.)
qui omnia peccata tua
(Hic relaxet manus deorsum.)
tibi relaxauit,
(Hic amplectendo Magdalenam, ut primo fecit, finiat versum.)
dulcissima Magdalena.   75

Magdalena:
(Hic salutet Mariam cum manibus tantum.)
Mater Yhesu crucifixi,
(Hic tergat sibi lacrimas.)
tecum plangam mortem Christi, ·
(Hic se ipsam ostendat.)
et mortem mei magistri;
(Hic se percuciat ad pectus.)
et ex dolore cruciata,
(Hic manibus se percuciat.)
sum in corde uulnerata.   80

Maria maior:
(Hic se uertat ad homines manibus apertis.)
Ubi sunt discipuli
quos tu dilexisti?
(Hic se uertat ad mulieres manibus apertis.)
Ubi sunt apostoli
(Hic ostendat Christum.)
quos | tantum amasti?
(Hic se uertat ad populum.)
Qui timore ter⟨r⟩iti,   85
omnes fugierunt,
et te solum, fili mi,
(Hic ostendat crucem.)
in cruce dimiserunt.

(Hic se percuciet pectus.)
Heu me! heu me! misera Maria! [1]

Maria Iacobi:

(Hic ostendendo circumcircha et cum manibus ad oculos suos postea dicat.)

Quis est hic qui non fleret, 90
matrem Christi si uideret
(Hic se percuciat.)
in tanta tristicia?

Maria maior:

(Hic uertat se ad populum manibus apertis.)
O uos omnes qui transitis per uiam
(Hic ad oculos suos ponat manus.)
simul mecum flete,
(Hic ostendat Christum.)
et meum dulcem filium 95
pariter lugete, et uidete
(Hic se percuciat.)
si est dolor similis,
(Hic se percuciat.)
sicut dolor meus.
(Hic se percuciat.)
Heu me! heu me! misera Maria!

Maria sola: [2]

(Hic uersus Mariam maiorem.)
Consolare, Domina, 100
mater | et regina.
Cur merore deficis,
(Hic ostendat Mariam maiorem.)
stella matutina?
Tuus leuat filius
(Hic relaxet manus.)
mundum a ruina. 105

Maria maior:

(Hic ostendat Christum.)
Fili mi carissime,
(Hic ostendat se ipsam.)
dulcis amor meus,
cur te modo uideo
(Hic ostendat crucem.)
in cruce pendentem

---

[1] This line is written over an erasure, and is followed by a complete erasure of about the same length. [2] sola] Salome (C).

(Hic ostendat latrones.)
   inter latrones positum,   110
(Hic coronam spineam.)
   spinis coronatum,
(Hic latus ostendat.)
   latus tuum, fili mi,
   lancea perforatum?
(Hic se percuciat.)
   Heu me! heu me! misera Maria!

Iohannes:

(Hic ostendat Christum.)
   Cur in ara crucis ares,   115
   caro que peccato cares,
(Hic se percuciat.)
   caro culpe nescia?

Maria maior:

(Hic se uertat ad populum et stet usque ad uerbum *Fer⟨r⟩e stipendium,* et tunc se . . .)[1]
   O mentes perfidas,
   et linguas duplices,
   o testes subdolos   120
   et fal⟨sos⟩[1] judices
   senes cum junioribus
   solent majoribus
   criminibus
   damnati   125
   ferre stipendium
   ·suspendium
   peccati⟩.

The astonishing feature of this text is, of course, the unique rubrics prescribing the gestures of the actors. The care with which the rhetoric is here supported by realistic stage-movements could hardly be exceeded.

A considerable proportion of the spoken text is virtually identical with parts of two of the *planctus* considered above, and may have been derived from them. Some nine of the speeches [2] are found, in large part, in *Flete, fideles animæ,* and three [3] are more or less similar to passages in *Qui per viam.* In its relation to the first of these poems the Cividale text is probably the

---

[1] The rubric and the spoken text end defectively at the bottom of fol. 76ᵛ. Fol. 77ʳ begins with the text of the *Visitatio Sepulchri* printed above, p. 378.

[2] Ll. 7–13, 14–8, 19–21, 22–6, 27–31, 38–47, 48–55, 115–7, 118–28.

[3] Ll. 81–8, 93–8, 100–5.

borrower; but between it and the other poem the relationship may be the reverse. One speech of Maria Jacobi (ll. 90–2) is certainly derived from the renowned *Stabat Mater*, of the thirteenth century.[1] The resulting text is by no means uniformly fortunate in its arrangements.[2] The stanza *Fleant materna viscera* (ll. 22–6), for example, is hardly appropriate for John; and the third speech of Maria major (ll. 38–47) is by no means intelligible in all of its bearings. She points to an angel, and seems to attribute to him (*ille prenuncius*) the prophecy concerning the sword which should pierce her spirit. As we have observed above, however, this prophecy was made by Simeon, who in *Flete, fideles animæ*, is appropriately referred to as *senex prænuntius*.[3] The Cividale writer may be confusing the narrative concerning Simeon with that concerning the Annunciation.

Particularly noteworthy is the increase in the number of the speakers to five. Mary the Virgin, however, is still the dominating personage, uttering about half of the speeches in the part of the text preserved. As to the circumstances in which the piece was presented we have only the assurance of the introductory rubric, that it was sung on Good Friday.[4] By analogy from the *planctus* of Regensburg one may surmise that the performance occurred during the Adoration of the Cross. This arrangement would provide the cross and the inanimate figure of Christ which are clearly demanded by the dramatic action.

IV

Although the laments as sung at Regensburg and Cividale are, no doubt, true drama, such performances cannot undertake to represent the Passion comprehensively. From its very nature the *planctus* is confined to a single moment of the Gospel narrative, and although it may be amplified almost indefinitely through the addition of other interlocutors and through increase of rhetoric, it cannot conveniently treat events which precede and follow the Crucifixion itself. For this broader presentation of the theme it was necessary to resort to the Biblical account

---

[1] See Chevalier, no. 19416, now re-edited in *A.H.*, liv, 312–8. In regard to various aspects of this poem see Ermini, pp. 1–57, 85–6, 137–8.

[2] In one or two instances the scribe seems to have blundered in assigning the speakers. See, for example, the foot-note to l. 42.

[3] See above, pp. 497, 499. In regard to the tradition whereby the sword prophesied by Simeon became identified with the lance employed at the Crucifixion, see Hirn, pp. 380–1.

[4] I do not understand why Coussemaker (p. 346) assigns it to 'la veille de Pâques'.

without restriction, as is done, for example, in the following short play from *Carmina Burana*: [1]

LUDUS BREUITER DE PASSIONE

Primo inchoatur ita, quando Dominus cum Discipulis suis procedere vult ad locum deputatum, ubi Mandatum debet esse; et in processu dicant Apostoli[2] ad Dominum:

Vbi uis paremus tibi conmedere Pascha?[3]

Et Dominus respondet:

Ite in ciuitatem ad quendam, et dicite ei: Magister dicit: Tempus meum prope est; aput te facio Pascha cum discipulis meis.[4]

Et in deputato loco faciant mensam[5] parari cum mensale cum pane et vino. Et Dominus discumbat cum duodecim Apostolis suis, et edentibus illis dicat:

Amen dico uobis, quia unus vestrum me traditurus est in hac nocte.[6]

Et vnusquisque pro se *respondeat*:

Numquid ego sum, Domine?[7]

Et Dominus *respondeat*:

Qui intinguit mecum manum in parapside, hic me tradet. Filius quidem hominis vadit, sicut scriptum est de illo. Ve autem homini illi, per quem filius hominis tradetur; bonum erat illi si natus non fuisset homo ille.[8]

Respondeat Iudas:

Numquid ego sum, Rabbi?[9]

Et Dominus dicat:

Tu dixisti.[10]

Tunc medio tempore vadat Iudas ad Pontifices et ad Iudeos, et dicat:

Quid uultis michi dare, et ego uobis eum tradam?[11]

At illi constituant ei:

Triginta argenteos.[12]

Et ista hora accipiat Dominus panem, frangat, benedicat, et dicat:

Accipite et comedite, hoc est corpus meum.[13]

---

[1] Munich, Staatsbibl., MS lat. 4660a, Carmina Burana sæc. xiii, fol. iii^v–iv^v, published by Meyer, 123–4, with photographic facsimiles, plates 5, 6, and 7. The text of Hilka and Schumann will be no. 13*. Concerning the MS see below, p. 686. For palaeographical observations upon the text before us see Hilka and Schumann, ii, 57*. The MS provides no musical notation, except for *Planctus ante nescia*, as indicated below.

[2] Apostoli] Written above the line by another hand.
[3] Matt. xxvi, 17.
[4] See Matt. xxvi, 18.
[5] mensam] Preceded by *parari*, partly erased.
[6] Matt. xxvi, 21.
[7] Matt. xxvi, 22.
[8] Matt. xxvi, 23–4.
[9] Matt. xxvi, 25.
[10] Matt. xxvi, 25.
[11] Matt. xxvi, 15.
[12] Matt. xxvi, 15.
[13] Matt. xxvi, 26.

Similiter et calicem. Et postquam cenauit, Dominus dicat:

Surgite, eamus hinc; ecce appropinquabit qui me tradet.[1]

Et Iudas accedens ad Ihesum clamando dicat:

Aue Rabbi![2]

Et osculando irruant in eum. Tunc Dominus dicat:

Amice, ad quid uenisti?[3]

Judei et Milites accedant ad Dominum, et manus iaciant[4] in eum, et teneant eum. Et ita ducant eum ad Pilatum. Tunc Discipuli omnes, relicto eo, fugiant.[5] | Et accusent eum coram eo in tribus causis, et dicant:

Hic dixit: Possum destruere templum Dei, et post triduum reedificare illud.[6]

Secundo:

Hunc inuenimus subuertentem gentem nostram, et prohibentem tributa dari Cesari, et dicentem se Christum regem esse.[7]

Tertio:

Conmouit populum docens per uniuersam Iudeam, et incipiens a Galilea vsque huc.[8]

Tunc Pilatus *respondeat*:

Quid enim mali fecit?[9]

Dicant Iudei:

Si non esset malefactor, non tibi tradidissemus eum.[10]

Respondeat Pilatus:

Accipite eum uos, et secundum legem vestram iudicate eum. Ego nullam causam inuenio in hoc homine. Vultis ergo, dimittam regem Iudeorum?[11]

Iudei clamando dicant:

Non, sed crucifigatur.[12] |

Et clamando magis dica⟨n⟩t:

Crucifige, crucifige eum.[13]

Et Pilatus *respondeat*:

Accipite eum uos, et crucifigite.[14]

Dicant Iudei:

Non, nos legem habemus, et secundum legem debet mori, quia filium Dei se fecit.[15]

---

[1] Matt. xxvi, 46.
[2] Matt. xxvi, 49.   [3] Matt. xxvi, 50.
[4] iaciant] iaceant (MS).
[5] fugiant] After this word is written, and crossed out, the following rubric: Et ducant eum ad Pilatum. Thus ends fol. iii[v]. In the upper half of fol. iv[r] is written, with musical notation, an abbreviated version of *Planctus ante nescia*—obviously out of place. For the

text of this see Notes, p. 700. See also Hilka and Schumann, ii, 57*.
[6] Matt. xxvi, 61.   [7] Luke xxiii, 2.
[8] Luke xxiii, 5.   [9] Matt. xxvii, 23.
[10] John xviii, 30.
[11] John xviii, 31, 38, 39.
[12] See Matt. xxvii, 23.
[13] Luke xxiii, 21; John xix, 6.
[14] John xix, 6.   [15] John xix, 7.

Respondeat Pilatus:

> *Regem vestrum crucifigam?*[1]

Tunc dicant Pontifices:

> *Regem non habemus nisi Cesarem.*[2]

Et Pilatus accipiat aquam, et dicat:

> *Mundus sum a sanguine huius iusti; vos videritis.*[3]

Et baiolent sibi crucem, et ducant eum ubi crucifigitur. Tunc vnus ex Militibus ueniat; cum lancea tangat latus eius. Tunc ipse Dominus in cruce alta uoce[4] clamet:

> *Ely, Ely, lema sabactani: Deus ⟨meus⟩, Deus meus, vt ⟨quid dereliquisti me⟩?*[5]

Tunc Maria mater Domini veniat et due alie Marie et Iohannes. Et Maria planctum faciat quantum melius potest.[6] Et unus ex Iudeis dicat:

> *Si filius Dei es, descende nunc de cruce.*[7]

Alter Iudeus:

> *Confidit in Deo; liberet eum nunc si vult.*[8]

Item tertius:

> *Alios saluos fecit, seipsum autem non potest saluum facere.*[9]

Et Dominus dicat:

> *Consumatum est; et, In manus t⟨uas⟩ commendo spiritum m⟨eum⟩.*[10]

Et inclinato capite, emittat spiritum. Tunc ueniat Ioseph ab Arimathia et petat corpus Ihesu. Et permittat Pilatus. Et Ioseph honorifice sepeliat[11] eum.[12]

Although this brief play presents the story of the Passion comprehensively, from the account of the preparations for the Last Supper through the final act of burial, it is completely devoid of literary originality. To the metrical and rhetorical elaboration of the several *planctus* examined in the preceding pages, the unadorned prose of the composition now before us presents a marked contrast. The speeches, and a large part of the rubrics, are literal excerpts from the Vulgate, the selections being made from all four Gospels, as if the writer, or compiler, had before him some form of Gospel harmony.[13] The borrowings are chiefly

---

[1] John xix, 15.   [2] John xix, 15.
[3] See Matt. xxvii, 24.
[4] uoce] Preceded by the letter *u*, crossed out.
[5] Matt. xxvii, 46.
[6] The *planctus* which Mary sings is, presumably, the version of *Planctus ante nescia* written on the preceding page of the MS.

[7] Matt. xxvii, 40.   [8] Matt. xxvii, 43.
[9] Matt. xxvii, 42.
[10] John xix, 30; Luke xxiii, 46.
[11] sepeliat] sepelia*tur* (MS).
[12] Followed immediately by this passage: Et ita inchoatur ludus de Resurrectione. Pontifices: *O Domine, recte meminimus.* See above, pp. 432–3.   [13] See Meyer, p. 122.

from Matthew, supplemented freely from John, and, less amply, from Mark and Luke. The result is a Scriptural mosaic in which the joinings of the pieces are by no means completely concealed.

The most arresting feature of the play is the rubric *Et Maria planctum faciat quantum melius potest.* The lament which Mary is to sing during Christ's last expiring moments is, presumably, *Planctus ante nescia,* an abbreviated version of which is written, out of its appropriate place, upon the page preceding that containing the rubric. Whether the *planctus* was extended to include utterances also for the other two Marys and John, we do not know. Possibly the writer intended to incorporate here a somewhat extended scene of the sort found in the longer Passion play from Benediktbeuern.[1] It may be said, in any case, that the lyric, in whatever form, provides a gratifying interruption to the succession of prosaic speeches which form the body of the play.

The number of personages who appear is inevitably large, including Christ, the twelve disciples, the chief priests, other Jews, soldiers, Pilate, the Virgin Mary and her two companions, and Joseph of Arimathea. The playing-space, therefore, must have been generous. It may have been provided with separate *sedes* for the Last Supper, the station of the chief priests and Jews, the hall of Pilate, the garden of Gethsemane, and Golgotha; or some of these places may have been merely assumed as the characters moved about freely in an open place. Certainly the stage was set with a table arranged for the Last Supper, and with properties for representing the Crucifixion and the burial.

A considerable part of the action is pantomime. The preparation of the chamber for the Last Supper, the flight of the disciples, the journey to the hall of Pilate, the piercing of Christ's side with the lance, the burial—all these occurrences are represented without the accompaniment of speech. There appears to be at least one instance of the simultaneous representation of two scenes. While Judas withdraws and confers with the chief priests and Jews, the scene of the supper seems to be continued in silence.[2] It may be remarked, in passing, that according to the Gospel narrative Judas's negotiation with the Jews was concluded before the supper began.[3] The playwright's reason for altering this sequence of events is not obvious.

---

[1] See below, pp. 530 sqq.; Meyer, p. 68.   [2] See Creizenach, i, 85, 185.
[3] See Matt. xxvi, 14–6.

As to whether the play was performed in direct association with the liturgy we have no explicit information. In the manuscript the text is followed by the opening words of an Easter play, which seems to have been attached to Matins;[1] and from this attachment of the latter play we may, if we wish, infer some sort of liturgical association also for the former.[2]

V

In addition to the brief and rudimentary dramatic sketch just described, the *Carmina Burana* include a far more comprehensive and amply elaborated dramatization of the Passion, of which the text is as follows:[3]

⟨LUDUS DE PASSIONE⟩

Primitus producatur Pilatus et Uxor sua cum Militibus in locum suum; deinde Herodes cum Militibus suis; deinde Pontifices; tunc Mercator et Uxor sua; deinde Maria Magdalena.

> *Ingressus Pilatus ⟨cum Jesu in prætorium; tunc ait illi: Tu es rex Judæorum. Respondit: Tu dicis quia rex sum. Exivit ergo Jesus de prætorio portans coronam et vestem purpuream; et cum indutus fuisset, exclamaverunt omnes: Crucifigatur, quia filium Dei se fecit.* Versus: *Tunc ait illis Pilatus: Regem vestrum crucifigam? Responderunt pontifices: Regem non habemus nisi Cæsarem⟩.*[4] 6

Postea uadat Dominica Persona sola ad litus maris vocare Petrum et Andream, et inueniat eos piscantes; et Dominus dicat ad eos:

> *Venite post me, faciam vos piscatores hominum.*[5]

Illi dicunt:[6]

> *Domine, quid uis, hec faciemus,*
> *et ad tuam voluntatem protinus adimplemus.*

---

[1] See above, pp. 411, 432.

[2] The inference of Meyer (pp. 64, 122–3) and Creizenach (i, 85) as to this Passion play's being merely a prelude to the Easter play is considered below, pp. 537–8.

[3] Munich, Staatsbibl., MS lat. 4660, Carmina Burana, fol. 107ʳ–112ᵛ, previously edited by Schmeller, pp. 95–107 (S); Du Méril, pp. 126–47 (D); Froning, pp. 284–99 (F). The text of Hilka and Schumann will be no. 16*. For references to other editions, and for observations upon the MS see below, p. 686. For palaeographical remarks upon the text before us see Hilka and Schumann, ii, 57*–61*. The German passages in the play are edited by Lüers, pp. 27–30. For general bibliography see Rudwin, *Survey*, pp. 36–7. With the exceptions indicated in the foot-notes below, the spoken text is accompanied by musical notation. The play has no heading in the MS, and is totally unrelated to what precedes on the opposite page (fol. 106ᵛ). In the margin at the top of fol. 107ʳ one of the scribes who copied the play entered the following: *Sancta Maria virgo assit nostro principio. Amen.*

[4] In regard to this responsory see above, p. 421.

[5] Matt. iv, 19. See Mark i, 17.

[6] dicunt] dicant (S).

Postea uadat Dominica Persona ad Zacheum, et obuiet ei Cecus:

> *Domine Iesu, fili Dauid, miserere mei.*[1]　　　　　　　　　10

Iesus r*espondeat*:

> *Quid uis ut faciam tibi?*

Cecus:

> *Domine, tantum ut uideam.*

Iesus d*icat*:

> *Respice, fides enim tua saluum te fecit.*

Hiis factis, Iesus procedat ad Zacheum, et uocet illum de arbore:

> *Zachee, festinans descende, quia hodie in domo tua oportet me manere.*[2]

Zacheus d*icat*:

> *Domine, si quid aliquem defraudaui, reddo quadruplum.*　　　　　15

Iesus r*espondeat*:

> *Quia hodie huic domui salus facta est, eo quod et tu sis filius Abrahe.*

Iesus venit.

> *Cum appropinquaret Dominus*[3] ⟨*Jerosolymam, misit duos ex discipulis suis dicens: Ite in castellum quod contra vos est, et invenietis pullum asinæ alligatum, super quem nullus hominum sedit; solvite et adducite mihi. Si quis vos interrogaverit, dicite: Opus Domino est. Solventes adduxerunt ad Jesum et imposuerunt illi vestimenta sua, et sedit super eum. Alii expandebant vestimenta sua in via, alii ramos de arboribus externebant, et qui sequebantur clamabant: Hosanna, benedictus qui venit in nomine Domini; benedictum regnum Patris nostri David. Hosanna in excelsis. Miserere nobis, fili David⟩.*[4]　　24

Et:

> *Cum audisset* ⟨*populus quia Jesus venit Jerosolymam, acceperunt ramos palmarum, et exierunt ei obviam; et clamabant pueri dicentes: Hic est qui venturus est in salutem populi, hic est salus nostra et redemptio Israel; quantus est iste cui throni et dominationes occurrunt! Noli timere, filia Sion, ecce rex tuus venit tibi sedens super pullum asinæ sicut scriptum est. Salve, rex, fabricator mundi, qui venisti redimere nos⟩.*[5]　　　　　　30

Et Pueri prosternentes frondes et uestes:

> *Pueri Hebreorum* ⟨*tollentes ramos olivarum obviaverunt Domino clamantes et dicentes: Hosanna in excelsis⟩.*[6]

---

[1] For this speech and the three succeeding ones see Luke xviii, 38–42.

[2] For this speech, and the two succeeding ones see Luke xix, 5, 8, 9.

[3] Dominus] Omitted (S.D).

[4] An antiphon for the Palm Sunday procession. See *Paléographie musicale*, i, 63–4. In the MS of the play only the first word (*Cum*) has musical notation.

[5] An antiphon for the Palm Sunday procession. See *Paléographie musicale*, i, 63. The MS of the play provides no musical notation.

[6] An antiphon for the Palm Sunday procession. See Hartker, p. 175. The play has Hartker's melody.

Item Pueri:

⟨*Pueri Hebræorum vestimenta prosternebant in via, et clamabant dicentes:*
Hosanna filio David, benedictus qui venit in nomine Domini.⟩[1]

Item:

Gloria laus ⟨*et honor tibi sit, rex Christe, redemptor*⟩.[2]   35

Tunc ueniat Phariseus, et uocet Iesum ad cenam:

Rab⟨*b*⟩*i, quod interpretatur magister, peto ut mecum hodie velis manducare.*[3]

Iesus *respondeat*:

Fiat, ut petisti.

Phariseus dicat ad seruum:

Ite cicius,
preparate sedilia,
ad mense conuiuia,   40
ut sint placencia.

Maria Magdalena cantet:[4]

Mundi delectatio   dulcis est et grata;
Eius conuersatio   suavis et ornata.
Mundi sunt delicie,   quibus estuare
Volo, nec lasciuiam   eius deuitare.[5]   45
Pro mundano gaudio   uitam terminabo;
Bonis temporalibus   ego militabo.
Nil curans de ceteris   corpus procurabo,
Variis coloribus   illud perornabo.

Modo uadat Maria cum Puellis ad Mercatorem cantando:

Michi confer, venditor,   species emendas   50
Pro multa pecunia   tibi iam reddenda,
Si quid habes insuper   odoramentorum;
Nam volo perungere   corpus hoc decorum. |

Mercator can⟨tet⟩:

Ecce merces optime!   prospice nitorem!
Hee[6] *tibi conveniunt   ad vvltus decorem.*   55
Hee[7] *sunt odorifere;   quas si conprobaris,*[8]
Corporis flagrantiam   omnem[9] *superabis.*

---

[1] An antiphon for the Palm Sunday procession. See Hartker, p. 175. I follow Froning in supplying the antiphon here, although this arrangement is not demonstrably correct.

[2] Chevalier, *R.H.*, no. 7282, printed in *A.H.*, l, 160–2. How much of this Palm Sunday processional hymn of Theodulphus was sung in the play one cannot say.

[3] See Luke vii, 36.

[4] cantet] cantent (MS).

[5] deuitare] evitare (S.D).

[6] Hee] hec (MS. S).

[7] Hee] hec (S).

[8] conprobaris] conprobabis (emend. S); comparabis (emend. D).

[9] omnem] omnen (MS).

Maria Magdalena:

> *Chramer, gip die varwe mier,*
> *div min wengel roete,*
> *da mit ich di iungen man*   60
> *an ir danch der minnenliebe[1] noete.*

Item:[2]

> *Seht mich an,*
> *iungen man.*
> *Lat[3] mich ev gevallen.*

Item:[4]

> *Minnet, tugentliche man,*   65
> *minnekliche vråwen.*
> *Minne tuồt ev hoech gemůt*
> *vnde lat evch in hochen[5] eren schåuven.*

Item:[6]

> *Seht mich an,*
> *iunge man,*   70

et cetera. Item:[7]

> *Wol dir werlt, daz du bist*
> *also vreudenreiche.*
> *Ich wil dir sin vndertan*
> *durch dein liebe immer sicherlichen.*
> *Seht mich an,*   75

et cetera. Postea uadat dormitum, et Angelus cant*et*:

> *O Maria Magdalena,   noua tibi nuntio:[8]*
> *Symonis hospicio   hic sedens conuiuatur*
> *Iesus ille Nazarenus,*
> *gratia uirtute plenus,*
> *qui relaxat peccata populi.*   80
> *Hunc turbe confitentur   saluatorem seculi.*

Recedat Angelus, et surgat Maria cantando:

> *Mundi delectatio.*

Tunc accedat Amator, quem Maria salutet, et cum parum locuntur,
cantet Maria ad puellas:

> *Wol dan, minneklichev chint,*
> *schåwe wier chrame.*
> *Chauf wier di varwe da,*   85
> *di vns machen schoene vnde wolgetane.*

---

[1] minnenliebe] *minnen* in left margin (MS).
[2] Item] Omitted (S.D).
[3] Lat] Written twice, second writing expunged (MS).
[4] Item] Omitted (S.D).
[5] hochen] hoehen (F).
[6] Item] Ř (MS); omitted (S.D).
[7] Item] Omitted (S.D).
[8] With some readjusting of rubrics, S and D transfer ll. 76–81 to a position after l. 95.

Er muez sein sorgen vr̄i,
  der da minnet mier den leip.

Iterum cantet:
  Chramer, gip di varwe mier.

Mercator re*spondeat*:
  Ich gib ev varwe, deu ist guôt,   90
    dar zuoe lobelich.
  Dev eu machet reht schoene vnt dar zuoe
    uil reht wunechliche.[1]
  Nempt si hin, hab ir si;
    ir ist niht geleiche.   95

Accepto ungento, uadat dormitum. ⟨Angelus:⟩
  O Maria Magdalena.

Et evanescat.[2] Tunc surgat Maria et cant*et*:
  Mundi delectatio.

Et iterum postea obdormiat, et Angelus ueniat cantando ut supra, et
iterum euanescat. ⟨Maria Magdalena:⟩[3]
  Heu! uita preterita,   uita plena malis;
  Fluxus turpitudinis,   fons exsicialis.
  Heu! quid agam misera,   plena peccatorum,   100
  Que polluta polleo   sorde uiciorum.

Angelus dic*at* sibi:
  Dico tibi: gaudium est angelis Dei super vna pec⟨c⟩atrice penitentiam
  agente.[4]

Maria:
  Hinc ornatus | seculi,   vestium candores.
  Protinus a me fugite,   turpes amatores.   105
  Vt quid nasci volui,   que sum defedanda,
  Et ex omni genere   criminum[5] *notanda?*

Tunc deponat uestimenta secularia et induat nigrum pallium, et
Amator recedat, et Diabolus. ⟨Maria⟩ veniat ad Mercatorem:[6]
  Dic tu nobis, mercator iuvenis,
  hoc vngentum si tu vendideris,
  dic precium, pro quanto dederis.   110
    Hev! quantus est noster dolor!

---

[1] wunechliche] wnnechliche (MS).
[2] Et evanescat] *Et iterum evanescat*, with a line drawn through the last two words (MS). I infer that the corrector should have deleted only the second word.
[3] Maria Magdalena] S and D use here the rubric *Tunc surgat Maria et cantet.*

[4] See Luke xv, 7.
[5] genere criminum] *genere* faintly crossed out; *criminum* written in the margin. But both words are required by the metre.
[6] The last three words of this rubric are written in the margin.

Mercator *respondeat*:

> *Hoc vngentum si multum cupitis,*
> *vnum auri talentum dabitis;*
> *aliter nusquam portabitis.*
>   *Obtimum est.*   115

Et chorus cantet:

> *Accessit ad pedes.*[1]

Accepto ungento, uadat ad Dominicam Personam cantando, flendo:

> *Ibo nunc ad medicum*   *turpiter egrota*
> *Medicinam postulans;*   *lacrimarum vota*
> *Huic restat ut offeram,*   *et cordis plangores,*
> *Qui cunctos, ut audio,*   *sanat peccatores.*   120

Item:[2]

> *Iesus, troest der sele min,*
> *la mich dir enpholhen sin,*
> *vnde loese mich uon der missetat,*
> *da mich dev werlt zuoe hat braht.*

Item:

> *Ich chume niht uon den fůezzen dein,*   125
> *du erloesest mich uon den sunden mein,*
> *vnde uon der grôzzen missetat,*
> *da mich deu werlt zuô hat braht.*

Loquatur Phariseus intra se:

> *Si hic esset propheta, sciret utique que et qualis illa esset, que tangit eum,*
> *quia peccatrix est.*[3]   130

Et dicat Iudas:

> *Vt quid perditio hec? Potuit enim hoc venundari multo, et dari pauperibus.*[4]

Iesus cantet:

> *Quid molesti estis huic mulieri? Opus bonum operata est in me.*

Item statim:

> *Symon, habeo tibi aliquid dicere.*[5]

Symon Petrus:

> *Magister, dic.*

Dicit Iesus:

> *Debitores habuit*   *quidam creditorum*[6]   135
> *Duos, quibus credidit*   *spe denariorum:*
> *Hic quingentos debuit,*   *alter quinquagenos.*

---

[1] See Matt. xxvi, 7.
[2] The rubric is written twice. For the two four-line speeches that follow, no music is provided.
[3] See Luke vii, 39.
[4] For this speech and the next see Matt.
xxvi, 8–10.
[5] For this speech and the next see Luke vii, 40.
[6] creditorum] Preceded by *feneratorum*, expunged.

Sed eosdem penitus   fecerat egenos;
Cum nequirent reddere,   totum relaxauit.
Quis eorum igitur   ipsum[1] plus amauit?[2]   140

Symon *respondeat:*[3]

Estimo quod ille plus,   cui plus donauit.

Iesus dicat:[3]

Tua sic sententia   recte iudicauit.

Item Iesus cant*et* ad Mariam:

Mulier, remittuntur tibi peccata; fides tua saluam[4] te fecit; vade in pace.[5]

Tunc Maria surgat | et uadat lamentando, cantans:

PLANCTUS

Awe, auve, daz ich ie wart geborn.
Han ich uerdient gotes zorn,   145
der mier hat geben sele vnde leip.
Awe, ich uil vnseleich[6] wip.

Owe, awe, daz ich ie wart geborn,
suuenne mich erwechet gotes zorn.
Wol uf, ir gueten[7] man vnde wip,   150
got wil rihten sele vnde leip.

Interea cantent Disci⟨puli⟩:

Phariseus iste fontem misericordie conabatur obstruere.

Tunc uadat Iesus ad resuscitandum Lazarum, et ibi occurrant Maria
Magdalena et Martha plorantes pro Lazaro, et Iesus cant*et*:

Lazarus, amicus noster, dormit: eamus et a sompno resuscitemus eum.[8]

Tunc Maria Magdalena et Martha flendo cantent:

Domine, si fuisses hic, frater noster non fuisset mortuus.[9]

Et sic tacendo clerus cantet:

Videns Dominus flentes sorores Lazari, ad monumentum lacrimatus est
coram Iudeis, et clamabat.[10]   156

Et Iesus cantet:

Lazare, ueni foras.[11]

Et clerus cantet:

Et prodiit ligatus[12] m⟨anus⟩ et p⟨edes⟩, qui f⟨uerat⟩ q⟨uasi⟩[13] m⟨ortuus⟩.

---

[1] ipsum] Preceded by *plus*, expunged.
[2] See Luke vii, 41–3.
[3] A red line is drawn through each of these
two rubrics.   [4] saluam] saluum (MS).
[5] See Luke vii, 48, 50. For the first four
words of this speech there is no music.
[6] vnseleich] vnselaeich (? MS).
[7] gueten] guetem (MS).
[8] See John xi, 11. With this speech

another scribe assumes the copying. See
Hilka and Schumann, ii, 58*.
[9] See John xi, 21, 32. For this speech, and
the following one, there is no music.
[10] See John xi, 35, 43.
[11] See John xi, 43.
[12] ligatus] ligatis (MS). See John xi, 44.
[13] q⟨uasi⟩] Omitted (F). For this speech
there is no music.

Interim Judas ueniat festinando et querat oportunitatem tradendi, dicens:

> *O pontifices,*
> *o viri magni consilii,*   160
> *Iesum uolo uobis tradere.*

Cui Pontifices respondeant:

> *O Iuda, si nobis Iesum iam tradideris,*
> *triginta argenteis remuneraberis.*[1]

Iudas respondeat:[2]

> *Jesum tradam, credite;*[3]
> *rem promissam michi soluite;*   165
> *turbam mecum dirigite;*
> *Iesum caute deducite.*

Pontifices cantent:

> *Jesum tradas propere.*
> *Hanc turbam tecum accipe,*
> *et procede uiriliter;*   170
> *Iesum trade uelociter.*

Judas tunc det Iudeis signum ca*n*tans:

> *Quemcumque osculatus fuero, ipse est; tenete eum.*[4]

Tunc turba Iudeorum sequatur Iudam cum gladiis et fustibus et lucernis donec ad Ihesum. Interea Iesus faciat ut mos est in cena. Postea assumat quatuor Discipulos, et ceteris dicat, quos relinquit:

> *Dormite iam et requiescite.*[5]

Deinde uadat orare, et dicat quatuor Discipulis:

> *Tristis est anima mea usque ad mortem. Sustine⟨te⟩ hic et orate, ne*
> *intretis in temptationem.*[6]   175

Tunc ascendat in montem Oliueti, et flexis genibus respiciens celum plorat[7] dicendo:

> *Pater, si fieri potest, transeat a me | calix iste. Spiritus quidem promptus*
> *est, caro autem infirma. Fiat uoluntas tua.*[8]

Hoc facto, redeat ad quatuor Discipulos, et inueniat eos dormientes, et dicat Petro:

> *Symon, dormis? Non potuisti una hora uigilare mecum? Manete hic, donec*
> *uadam et orem.*[9]

---

[1] See Matt. xxvi, 15.
[2] Judas respondeat] Jesum R̄ ā (MS).
[3] credite] Preceded by *propere*, crossed out.
[4] See Matt. xxvi, 48.
[5] See Mark xiv, 41.

[6] hic . . . temptationem] Not provided with music. See Matt. xxvi, 38, 41.
[7] plorat] Hardly legible (orat?).
[8] See Mark xiv, 35; Matt. xxvi, 39, 41–2.
[9] See Mark xiv, 37; Matt. xxvi, 36.

Postea uadat iterum orare ut antea. Tunc iterato ueniat ad Discipulos
et inueniat eos dormientes, et dicat ad eos:

> *Manete hic.*[1]   180

Et it*eru*m dicat:

> *Pater, si non potest hic calix transire, nisi bibam illum, fiat uoluntas tua.*[2]

Tunc redeat ad Discipulos et cantet:

> *Vna hora non potuistis uigilare mecum, qui exhortabamini mori*[3] *pro me.*
> *Uel Iudam non uidetis, quomodo non dormit, set festinat tradere me Iudeis?*
> *Surgite, eamus. Ecce appropinquat, qui me traditurus est.*[4]

Veniat Iudas ad Iesum cum turba Iudeorum, quibus Ihesus dicat:

> *Quem queritis?*[5]   185

Qui r*espondea*nt:

> *Iesum Nazarenum.*

Iesus di*c*at:

> *Ego sum.*

Et turba retrocedat. It*em*[6] Iesus di*c*at:

> *Quem queritis?*

Iudei:

> *Jesum Nazarenum.*

Iesus r*espondea*t:

> *Dixi uobis quia ego sum.*   190

It*em*:

> *Si ergo me queritis, sinite hos abire.*

Tunc Apostoli dent fugam, excepto Petro, et Iudas dicat:

> *Aue, Rabbi.*[7]

Iesus illi r*espondea*t:

> *O Iuda, ad quid uenisti?*
> *Peccatum magnum tu fecisti.*
> *Me Iudeis traditum*   195
> *ducis ad patibulum*
> *cruciandum.*[8]

Et Petro sequente Ihesum, vna Ancilla di*c*at:

> *Vere tu ex illis es.*

Ipse di*c*at:

> *Non sum.*

[1] For this speech there is no music.
[2] See Matt. xxvi, 42.
[3] mori] Written in the margin.
[4] See Matt. xxvi, 46.
[5] For this speech, and the six succeeding

ones, see John xviii, 4–8.
[6] It*em*] Iterum (S.D).
[7] See Matt. xxvi, 49; Mark xiv, 45.
[8] For this speech, and the four succeeding
ones, there is no music.

Item Ancilla:

> *Vere tu ex illis es, nam et Galileus es, nam unus ex eis es. Nonne vidi te cum illo in horto? Nescis quid dicis.*[1] 201

Petrus:

> *Non noui hominem.*

Et Ihesus dicat:[2]

> *Tanquam ad latronem existis cum gladiis et fustibus comprehendere me,*[3]

et cetera. Et ducatur Ihesus ad Pontifices, et chorus ca*ntet*:

> *Collegerunt pontifices et,*[4]

⟨et⟩ cetera.[5] Et Pontifices cantent et cogitent quid faciant:

> *Quid facimus, quia hic homo multa signa facit? Si dimittimus eum sic, omnes credent in eum.* 206

Et Cayphas cantet:

> *Expedit uobis ut unus moriatur homo pro populo, et non tota gens pereat.*

Clerus cantet:

> *Ab ipso ergo die cogitauerunt,*

et cetera. Postea ducitur[6] ad Pilatum Iesus, et dicunt[7] Iudei:

> *Hic dixit: Soluite templum hoc, et post triduum reedificabo illud.*[8]

Pilatus re*spondeat*:

> *Quam accusa|cionem affertis aduersus hominem istum?*[9] 210

Iudei re*spondeant*:

> *Si non fuisset hic malefactor, non tibi*[10] *tradidissemus eum.*

Pilatus:

> *Accipite eum uos, et secundum legem uestram iudicate eum.*

---

[1] In this speech the words *Vere tu ex illis es nam et Galileus es* are an interlinear insertion, and the words *Nonne vidi te cum illo in horto? Nescis* (corrected from *nescio*) *quid dicis* are written in the right margin. Written by another hand, and partly obscured by *Nescis quid dicis*, are the words *Petrus (de Petro?) et ancill⟨a⟩*. Farther down in the margin are the words *Non noui tu cū ill*, crossed out. For a somewhat elaborate explanation of the palaeographical facts associated with the part of the play now before us see Hilka and Schumann, ii, 59*. Since the actual intention of the playwright cannot be recovered with certainty, the arrangement of the dialogue above must be regarded as a makeshift.

[2] Et Ihesus dicat] Written in the left margin; Iesus dicat (S); Jesus (D).

[3] See Matt. xxvi, 55. Neither in words nor in music does this speech conform to the responsory *Tamquam ad latronem* found in Hartker, p. 218.

[4] This passage and the three utterances that follow are taken, words and music, from the following processional antiphon of Palm Sunday: *Collegerunt pontifices et Pharisæi concilium et dicebant: Quid facimus, quia hic homo multa signa facit? Si dimittimus eum sic, omnes credent in eum, ne forte veniant Romani et tollant nostrum locum et gentem.* Versus: *Unus autem ex ipsis, Caiphas nomine, cum esset pontifex anni illius, prophetavit dicens: Expedit vobis ut unus moriatur homo pro populo, et non tota gens pereat. Ab illo ergo die cogitaverunt interficere eum dicentes. Ne forte veniant.* See *Paléographie musicale*, i, 64.

[5] Et ducatur Ihesus . . . cetera] Omitted (S.D).

[6] ducitur] ducatur (S.D).

[7] dicunt] dicant (S.D).

[8] See Matt. xxvi, 61; Mark xiv, 58; John ii, 19.

[9] For this speech, and the three succeeding ones, see John xviii, 29–31.

[10] tibi] Omitted (S.D).

Iudei:

Nobis non licet interficere quemquam.

Postea ducatur Iesus ad Herodem, qui dicat ei:[1]

Homo Galileus es?

Iesus uero tacebat, et Herodes iterum dicat:

Quem te ipsum facis? 215

Iesus non *respondeat* ei ad unum uerbum. Tunc Iesus induitur[2] ueste alba, et reducunt Ihesum[3] ad Pilatum. Tunc conueniunt[4] Pilatus et Herodes, et osculantur[5] inuicem. Et Ihesus ueniat ad Pilatum, et ipse dicit:[6]

Nullam causam mortis inuenio in homine isto.[7]

Iudei dic*ant*:

Reus est mortis.[8]

Tunc Pilatus dicat ad Ihesum:

Tu es rex Iudeorum?

Ihesus respondit:

Tu dicis, quia rex sum.

Pilatus dicat:

Gens tua et pontifices tui tradiderunt te michi. 220

Iesus paulatim dicat:

Regnum meum non est de hoc mundo.

Pilatus it*em* dicat:

Ergo quem te ipsum[9] facis?

Iesus vero taceat, et Pilatus dicat ad Pontifices:

Quid faciam de Iesu Nazareno?

Iudei:

Crucifigatur.

Pilatus:

Corripiam ergo illum et dimittam. 225

Tunc ducitur[10] Ihesus ad flagellandum. Postea Ihesus induatur ueste purpurea et spinea corona. Tunc dicant Iudei plasphemando ad Iesum:

Aue, rex Iudeorum.

---

[1] The scene before Herod arises from Luke xxiii, 7–12.

[2] induitur] inducitur (MS); induatur (S.D).

[3] reducunt Ihesum] reducant Iesum (S); reducant illum (D).

[4] conueniunt] conveniant (S.D).

[5] osculantur] osculentur (S.D).

[6] dicit] dicat (S.D). The last four words

of this rubric are written in the left margin.

[7] See Luke xxiii, 4, 22.

[8] See Matt. xxvi, 66. For the remaining scenes presenting the trial and condemnation of Jesus the familiar Biblical references need not be given here.

[9] ipsum] Written in the margin; omitted (S.D).

[10] ducitur] ducatur (S.D).

Et dent ei alapas:

Prophetiza, quis est, qui te percussit?

Et ducant eum ad Pilatum, cui[1] Pilatus dic*a*t:

Ecce homo.

Judei:

Crucifige, crucifige eum.

Pilatus:

Accipite eum uos, et crucifigite. Nullam causam inuenio in eo.   230

Judei:

Si hunc dimittis, non es amicus Cesaris.

Item:

Omnis qui se facit regem, contradicit Cesari.

Pilatus:

Vnde es tu?

Ihesus tacet. Pilatus:

Michi non loqueris?

Item:

Nescis quia[2] *potestatem habeo crucifigere te,[3] et potestatem dimittere te?* 235

Iesùs r*espondeat*:

Non haberes in me potestatem, nisi desuper tibi datum fuisset.

Pilatus ad Iudeos:

Regem vestrum crucifigam?

Judei r*espondeant*:

Crucifigatur, quia filium Dei se fecit.

Pilatus lauans manus suas cum aqua et dicat ad Iudeos:

Innocens ego sum a sanguine huius; uos uideritis. |

Tunc Iesus ducatur ad crucifigendum. Tunc Iudas ad Pontifices vadat
cantando, et reiectis denariis, dicat flendo:

Penitet me grauiter quod istis argenteis Christum uendiderim.   240

Item:

*Resumite uestra, resumite. Mori uolo et non uiuere. Suspendi supplicio
uolo perdere.*

Pontifices:

. *Quid ad nos, Iuda Scariotys? Tu uideris.*[4]

Statim veniat Diabolus, et ducat Iudam ad suspendium, et suspe*n*d*atur*.[5]

---

[1] cui] Omitted (S.D).
[2] quia] quod (S.D).   [3] te] Omitted (F).
[4] In the margin opposite this speech is
written, without musical notation: *Peccaui
tradens san⟨guinem⟩ iustum.* See Hilka and

Schumann, ii, 59*–6o*. Possibly this was
intended to supply for Judas another speech,
for which there is no rubric. See Matt.
xxvii, 4.
[5] suspendatur] suspendat (F).

Tunc ueniant Mulieres a longe plorantes flere Ihesum, quibus Ihesus dicat:

> *Filie Ierusalem, nolite flere super me, set super uos ipsas.*[1]

Tunc Iesus suspendatur in cruce, et titulus fiat:

> *Iesus Nazarenus, rex Iudeorum.*[2]   245

Tunc *re*spondeant Iudei Pilato cant*antes*:

> *Regem non habemus nisi Cesarem.*

Pilatus:

> *Quod scripsi, scripsi.*

Tunc ueniat Mater Domini lamentando cum Iohanne ewangelista, et ipsa accedens crucem respicit[3] crucifixum:

PLANCTUS
AT CROSS

> *Awe, awe mich hiût vnde immer we!*
> *Awe, wie sihe ich nv an*
> *daz liebiste chint, daz ie gewan*   250
> *ze dirre werlde ie dehain wip.*
> *Awe mines shoene chindes lip!*

I*tem*:

> *Den sihe ich iemerlichen an.*
> *Lat iuch erbarmen, wip vnde man.*
> *Lat iwer ovgen sehen dar*   255
> *vnde nemt der marter rehte war.*

I*tem*:

> *Wart marter ie so iemerlich*
> *vnte also rehte angestlich?*
> *Nv merchet marter, not vnde tot,*
> *vnde al den lip von blute rot.*   260

I*tem*:

> *Lat leben mir daz chindel min*
> *vnde toetet mich, die muter sin,*
> *Mariam, mich uil armez wip.*
> *Zwiv sol mir leben vnde lip.*

I*tem* Mater Domini omni ploratu exhibens multos planctus et clamat ad Mulieres flentes et conquerendo valde:

> *Flete, fideles anime,   flete sorores optime,*   265
> *ut sint multiplices   doloris[4] indices*
> *   planctus et lacrime.*
> *Fleant materna uiscera,   Marie matris volnera.*
> *Materne doleo,   que dici soleo*
> *   felix puerpera.*[5]   270

---

[1] For this speech there is no music.

[2] This inscription has musical notation, and the succeeding rubric seems to indicate that it may have been sung by Pilate.

[3] respicit] respiciat (S.D).

[4] doloris] doloros (MS).

[5] F reverses the order of the passages *Fleant materna . . . puerpera* and *Triste spectaculum . . . volnerat.*

Triste spectaculum   crucis et lancee!
Clausum signaculum   mentis virginee
　　profunde volnerat.
Hoc est quod dixerat,   quod prophetauerat
felix prenuntius;   hic ille gladius   275
　　qui me transuerberat.
Dvm caput cernu⟨um⟩.[1]

Tunc Maria amplexetur Iohannem et cantet, eum habens inter brachia:

Mi Iohannes, planctum moue,
plange mecum, fili noue,
fili nouo federe   280
matris et matertere.
Tempus est lamenti;
immolemus intimas
lacrimarum victimas
Christo morienti.   285

Et per horam quiescat sedendo, et it*eru*m surgat et cantet:[2]

Planctus ante[3] *nescia,*

et cetera. Tunc iterum amplexetur Iohannem et cantet:

Mi Iohannes,[4]

et cetera. Johannes ad hec:

O Maria, tantum noli
lamentare tuo proli;
sine me nunc plangere,   290
que uitam cupis cedere.

Et Iohannes teneat Mariam sub humeris, et dicat Iesus ad eam:

Mulier, ecce filius tuus.

Deinde dicat ad Johannem:

Ecce mater tua.

Postea uadant Maria et Johannes de cruce, et Jesus dicat:

Sitio.

Statim veniant Iudei prebentes spongiam cum acceto, et Iesus bibat:

Consummatum est.   295

[1] With these three words, not supplied with musical notation, ends the page (fol. 110^r). How much more of the sequence *Flete, fideles animæ* was to be sung we cannot tell. For the full text see above, p. 498. For the irrelevant German text occupying all of fol. 110^v see Hilka and Schumann, no. 17*. The rubric (*Tunc Maria*) which follows in the text printed here begins on the first line of fol. 111^r. In the margin at the top of fol. 111^r is written the following: *Domine miserere Christus Dominus factus est.*

[2] et cantet] What seems to be intended for *et* is written in by another hand. cantando (S.D); cantans (F).

[3] ante] Written above *est*, which is crossed out. For the complete text of the *planctus* see above, p. 496.

[4] This speech has no music.

Tunc Longinus ueniat cum lancea et perforet latus eius, et ille dicat
aperte:

> *Ich wil im stechen ab daz herze sin,*
> *daz sich ende siner marter pin.*

Jesus uidens finem dicit clamando:

> *Ely, Ely lama[1] sabactany. Deus,[2] Deus meus, ut quid dereliquisti me?*

Et inclinato capite, emittat spiritum. Longinus:

> *Vere filius Dei erat iste.*

Item:

> *Dirre ist des waren gotes sůn.*   300

Item:

> *Er hat zaichen an mir getan,*
> *wan ich min sehen wider han.*

Et unus ex Iudeis dicat ad Iudeos:

> *Elyam vocat iste; eamus et uideamus, si Elyas ueniens liberet eum an non.*

Alter Iudeus:

> *Si filius Dei es, descende de cruce.*

Item alter:

> *Alios saluos fecit, seipsum non potest saluum facere.[3]*   305

Cantus Ioseph ab Arimathia:

> *Iesus von gotlicher art,*
> *ein mensch an alle sunde,*
> *der an schuld gemartret wart,*
> *ob man den vurbaz vunde;[4]*
> *genaglet an dem chrivze stan,*   310
> *daz wer niht chuneges ere.*
> *Darumb sŏlt ir mich in lan*
> *bestaten, rihter herre.*

Pilatus:

> *Swer redelicher dinge gert,*
> *daz stet wol an der maze,*   315
> *daz er ir werde wol gewert.*
> *Du bitest, daz ich laze*

---

[1] lama] lema (MS).

[2] Deus] Preceded by *hoc est*, crossed out.
Music is lacking for the entire speech.

[3] The remainder of fol. 111ʳ, and all of fol.
111ᵛ and 112ʳ, are occupied by irrelevant
pieces (Hilka and Schumann, nos. 18*, 19*,
20*, 21*, 22*). The two speeches which
follow in the text as printed here are found,

with musical notation, at the top of fol. 112ᵛ,
and are in turn followed by irrelevant matter.
These last two speeches (Hilka and Schumann, no. 23*) are probably not part of the
play. See Meyer, pp. 74, 65; Hilka and
Schumann, ii, 60*.

[4] vurbaz vunde] furbaz funde (S.D); furbaz vunde (F).

dich bestaten Ihesum Christ:
daz main ich wol in gûte.
Seit er dir so ze herzen ist,   320
num in nach dinem mûte.

The play opens with the processional responsory *Ingressus Pilatus*, during the singing of which enter Pilate, with his wife and his military escort, Herod and his attendants, the high priests, the merchant and his wife, and Mary Magdalen. It is to be assumed that these several main personages take their places at separate *sedes* distributed about the playing-space.

The action itself begins with several brief scenes representing Christ's calling of Peter and Andrew, his healing of the blind Bartimæus, and his colloquy with Zacchæus outside Jericho.

Then, after the singing of several processional pieces from Palm Sunday, occurs a considerable dramatic passage centring in the meal at the house of Simon the Pharisee. First we witness Jesus' acceptance of Simon's invitation, and then significant parts of the career of Mary Magdalen. Under the influence of *Diabolus*, she buys her cosmetics and entices her lover. Presently, however, through the repeated appeals of an angel, she renounces her evil associations, clothes herself in the black of penitence, buys ointment, and proceeds to the house of Simon. Here are represented her anointing of Jesus' feet, the protest of Judas, Jesus' recital of the parable of the two debtors, his forgiving of Mary, and her departure in grief.

The short scenes that follow represent the raising of Lazarus, Judas's negotiation with the high priests, the Last Supper, the capture and trial of Christ, and the death of Judas.

The scene of the Crucifixion is occupied chiefly by laments of the Virgin Mary, in which John participates briefly. The play ends with the death of Christ, the piercing of his side by Longinus, and the mockery of the Jews. We may assume that a burial scene followed.

In considering the text of the play one observes that the number of liturgical pieces incorporated is relatively small, and that these are used chiefly as choral introductions to separate scenes.[1] Most conspicuous among them are the opening responsory *Ingressus Pilatus*, and the Palm Sunday processionals already referred to.[2] Another Palm Sunday antiphon *Colligerunt*

---

[1] See Meyer, p. 65.
[2] According to Scriptural chronology these

processionals referring to the entry into Jerusalem inappropriately precede here the

pontifices (l. 204) provides not only an introduction to the scene before Cayphas, but also the subsequent speeches. Several other choral passages appear to be non-liturgical pieces newly composed for the play before us.[1]

Most of the speeches in the shorter scenes are taken directly from the Vulgate. In some instances, however, the Scriptural text is ingeniously amplified through invention and rearrangement. The answer of Peter and Andrew (ll. 8–9), for example, is not in the Vulgate. One passage of dialogue from Luke is rendered in eight lines of verse,[2] and another passage of narrative is expanded into a brief dialogue.[3]

The most extensive amplification, however, is found in the two scenes in which the central personages are, respectively, Mary Magdalen and Mary the Virgin. The first of these constitutes virtually one-third of the whole play. In the Mary Magdalen of this play, and of medieval art generally, are fused at least two Biblical personalities. Historically she is the person who stood, with other women, at the foot of the cross,[4] who was the first to see Christ after the Resurrection,[5] and who, in earlier life, was purged of seven devils.[6] With this personality was merged, in the minds of medieval Christians, that of another person: namely, Mary of Bethany, the sister of Lazarus; and she, in the Gospel of John, seems to be identified with the unnamed sinner who anointed Christ's feet in the house of Simon.[7] It is with this latter personage that we are concerned in the scene now before us.[8]

The sinful life and later repentance of Mary Magdalen are here presented with an amplitude so marked as to suggest to one critic that this scene may originally have been an independent dramatic piece.[9] The portrayal of Mary's worldliness is, of course, inspired by the references to her sinfulness in the Bible; but the incident of her purchasing cosmetics may have been suggested by the scenes between the Marys and the *unguentarius*

scenes representing the supper at Bethany, and the raising of Lazarus.

[1] See *Accessit ad pedes*, *Videns Dominus*, and *Pharisæus iste*, ll. 116, 152, 155.

[2] Ll. 135 sqq., from Luke vii, 41–3.

[3] Ll. 36 sq., from Luke vii, 36. Similar rearrangements may be recognized through the Biblical references in the foot-notes to the text above.

[4] See John xix, 25.

[5] See John xx, 14–7.

[6] See Luke viii, 2.

[7] See John xi, 1–2; Luke vii, 37–50; Matt. xxvi, 6–13. For evidence that Mary Magdalen, the sister of Lazarus, and the sinner are the same person see Vigouroux, iv, 810 sqq.

[8] See Froning, p. 256; Sepet, *Origines*, pp. 53–4. For a scene presenting Mary Magdalen at the house of Simon in the play of Lazarus see below, ii, 200.

[9] See Meyer, p. 65.

in the Easter plays.[1] These latter scenes, in any case, are probably the source of Mary's second scene with *Mercator*, on her way
to Simon's house (ll. 108 sqq.). Particularly noteworthy are the
supernatural personages *Angelus* and *Diabolus*, representing the
forces of good and evil brought to bear upon Mary. These
figures, which, in their symbolical roles, now appear in our
survey for the first time, will be seen again in the Christmas play
from the Benediktbeuern manuscript.[2] They may be regarded
as precursors of the abstractions of virtue and vice which animate
the moral plays of the later Middle Ages.

The vernacular verses in the present scene seem to have been
freely invented for the purpose of making the play more intelligible and vivacious for a general audience. None of these passages
is a translation of any Latin speech preceding it. The last of
them (ll. 144 sqq.) appears to be unfortunately placed, for there
is no reason why Mary, after having been absolved from sin,
should depart singing the despairing lament *Awe, awe, daz ich ie
wart geborn*. Possibly the incongruity here lends further support
to the view that the scene as a whole was originally an independent piece, somewhat imperfectly fitted to its present surroundings.[3]

The other scene which elaborately amplifies a Biblical situation is that representing the Virgin Mary and her companions
at the foot of the cross. This takes the form essentially of a
planctus Mariæ. Mary first sings four stanzas in German (ll. 248
sqq.), addressed, very appropriately, to the bystanders. Although certain of the lines somewhat resemble passages in
Planctus ante nescia,[4] the stanzas as a whole seem to be an independent vernacular composition. Then follow some stanzas from
the lament *Flete, fideles animæ*.[5] As she sings the lines addressed
to John, *Mi Johannes*, Mary throws her arms about him. After
a pause, indicated by the rubric *Et per horam quiescat sedendo*,
Mary resumes her lament by singing part, or all, of *Planctus ante
nescia*, and follows this by a repetition of her address to John.
After being appealed to this second time, John brings the
planctus to a conclusion with a Latin stanza of four lines. This
scene, like the earlier one dominated by Mary Magdalen, may
have been originally an independent dramatic lament. To the

[1] See above, pp. 401, 435; Dürre, pp. 34–5.   [4] For the complete text see above, p. 496.
[2] See below, ii, 186.   [5] See above, p. 498. The stanzas used
[3] See Froning, p. 281.   here are 1, 2, and 5a.

writer of a comprehensive Passion play a separate literary unit of this sort may have seemed a fortunate resource for embellishing a text which might otherwise develop into a somewhat arid succession of prose sentences from the Vulgate.[1]

Viewed as a whole the play is obviously somewhat disordered. This lack of finish appears not only in details, such as the repetition of Mary's words to John, but also in certain violations of the Scriptural order of events. Peter's denial (ll. 198 sqq.), for example, is placed in the very midst of the scene of Christ's capture; and the Palm Sunday processionals (ll. 17 sqq.) referring to the entry into Jerusalem precede the scenes representing the supper at Bethany and the raising of Lazarus.[2] A dramatic piece so loosely and casually arranged may best be regarded not as an attempt towards a closely knit play, but as an episodic religious opera.

The direct attachment of so extended a play to a liturgical service is, of course, scarcely possible.[3] Presumably, however, it was designed for acting by clerics, and it could have been presented within the church building quite as well as outside.[4] It contains pieces borrowed from the liturgy, and the liturgical chorus participates in the performance. Wherever it was, the playing-space must have been very large, and must have contained several stations, or *sedes*, to represent such places as the houses of Simon, Pilate, and Herod, the room for the Last Supper, and Golgotha. The places for certain other scenes, such as the calling of Peter and Andrew, may have been unlocalized in the general *platea*.

The two compositions from Benediktbeuern are the only two extant Passion plays in Latin which are comprehensive and relatively complete. Other plays of a similar nature were un-

---

[1] See Meyer, p. 68.

[2] Concerning such misplacements see Michael, iv, 411; Schönbach, *Marienklagen*, p. 19. Wilken (pp. 82–6) is uncommonly severe, regarding all the text between the opening *Ingressus Pilatus* and l. 218 (*Tu es rex Judæorum*) as an interpolation. His grounds are that this part of the text is alien to the content of the introductory *Ingressus Pilatus*, and that the opening rubric mentions persons who do *not* speak in the play as it stands, and fails to mention others who *do* speak. Probably this critic demands of medieval playwrights and scribes a somewhat too exacting standard of explicitness and accuracy.

[3] From the rubric *Et per horam quiescat sedendo* (see above, p. 531) Wright (p. xi) infers that the Virgin Mary 'must sit down quietly for an hour', and that this period was probably 'occupied by the church service'. I interpret the phrase *per horam* less literally, in the sense of 'for a while'. I see no evidence that the period of her silence, however long, was occupied by a liturgical service.

[4] Without specific evidence, Golther (p. 165) infers that it was performed outside the church building, in some such place as the refectory.

doubtedly produced. Of one such we have a substantial fragment written in the fourteenth century and preserved in the
chapter library of the cathedral of Sulmona, in Italy.[1] The
passage preserved is a player's part, providing only the role of a
subordinate character, the 'fourth soldier', along with certain
cues. The providing of a separate and extensive text for a minor
personage indicates that the play itself was very long, and required careful rehearsals. The action certainly included the
sending of soldiers to seize Christ, the betrayal by Judas, the
trial before Pilate and Herod, the Crucifixion itself, the *planctus
Mariæ*, the burial, the stationing of soldiers to watch the tomb,
and some of their experiences there, before and after the
Resurrection. For the speeches themselves the writer employs
neither liturgical pieces nor Scriptural sentences, but in a variety
of metres versifies the Biblical account according to his own
rhetorical desire. Nor does he hesitate to indulge his romantic
fancy, naming one of the soldiers Tristan:[2]

> Vadat Tristaynus, miles nobilissimus,
> omnium nostrum armorum doctissimus;
> fuit scrimite hic inventor primitus.

The combining of dramatizations of the Passion and of the
Resurrection in such a play as that from Sulmona suggests the
possibility that the Passion play was conceived originally, not as
an independent invention, but as an enlargement of the Easter
play, composed by way of providing for the latter an appropriate
and impressive introduction. Just as the *Peregrinus* served as an
epilogue to the *Visitatio Sepulchri* or *Ludus Paschalis*, so the Passion
play might be regarded as an avowed prologue.[3] This view
would seem to be supported by the following passage, found at
the end of the shorter Passion play from Benediktbeuern: Et ita
inchoatur ludus de Resurrectione. Pontifices: *O Domine, recte
meminimus*.[4] From this rubric alone, one would infer that the
Passion play was to be followed immediately by the related
Easter play, in a continuous performance, for the opening speech
of the *pontifices* in the latter is *O domine, recte meminimus*. The
opening rubric of this Benediktbeuern Easter play, however,
seems to prescribe that it be performed immediately after Matins

---

[1] For text and bibliography see Notes, p. 701.
[2] See below, p. 707.
[3] See Meyer, p. 122; Coussemaker, p. 346;
Creizenach, i, 84–5; Brinkmann, p. 142;
Venzmer, pp. 14–5; Roy, p. 6*.
[4] See above, p. 516; Meyer, pp. 64, 122–3.

(cantatis Matutinis);[1] hence it could hardly be immediately preceded by the Passion play. The joining of the two types of play in a continuous performance has been thought to be shown also by the fact that the silent wife of *Mercator* in the longer Benediktbeuern Passion play has a speaking part, as *uxor apotecarii*, in the related Easter-play, the implication being that she is present in the former play as a silent figure because she is to speak in the latter play immediately afterwards.[2] Surely, however, there is no obstacle to her serving as a silent ornament in the first play, without reference to the second. The ornamental value of such a figure is clearly indicated by the treatment of the wife of Pilate, who is present in both plays without speaking. There appears, then, to be no proof that the Passion play was looked upon as a mere prefatory extension of the Easter play; but, on the other hand, it may sometimes have been so regarded.

A word remains to be said as to the source of the text of the Passion play, and as to the avenues through which it may have been derived. The view that the play is a straightforward development from the *planctus* appears to be supported by certain substantial facts.[3] We have observed, for example, that some of the laments of Mary are in a form fitted for dramatic use, that such compositions were sometimes uttered by impersonated speakers, and that the only comprehensive Passion plays now preserved contain laments of this sort. So far as we can tell, the composing of the *planctus Mariæ* was the first step taken towards the dramatizing of the Passion. At least one such lament, *Planctus ante nescia*, which was a notable feature of the thirteenth-century plays, arose as early as the twelfth century.

But although the *planctus* almost certainly preceded, and perhaps inspired, the composing of Passion plays, we can scarcely regard the two extant pieces from Benediktbeuern, and the lost play of Sulmona, as mere enlargements of dramatic lyrics. In large part these plays are dramatizations of substantial passages taken directly, or indirectly, from the Biblical narrative, in the midst of which the laments appear as important, but not indispensable, dramatic elements. At the outset the *planctus* itself may have provided the only dramatization of the Passion; but by the thirteenth century appeared plays which seem to be

---

[1] See above, p. 432.
[2] See Chambers, ii, 76; and above, pp. 436, 518.
[3] This is the position of Wechssler (p. 98)

and of Chambers (ii, 39–40). Brinkmann (p. 142) dismisses this view decisively, without proposing a substitute.

not mere accretions about a lyric poem, but rather, self-sustained compositions based upon the Biblical narrative; and in the midst of these the traditional lament occupies an important, but hardly a commanding, position.[1]

As to the process through which the Biblical text passed into dramatic form we cannot be entirely certain. In large part, the playwrights may have worked directly upon the Gospels as they stand in the Bible itself. If the modern custom of distributing the text of the Passions of Holy Week among three persons had prevailed during the early Middle Ages, the transformation of a *Passio* into a Passion play would have been relatively simple, through the addition of impersonation. But, as we have seen, this tripartite form of recital was unknown before the fifteenth century, or thereabouts. It should be remembered, however, that throughout the Middle Ages the single deacon who sang a *Passio* was required to signalize the element of dialogue in the text by changing the pitch of his voice and the tempo of his utterance, and that certain parts of the narration were accompanied by ceremonial acts of a somewhat realistic nature.[2] It is by no means improbable, therefore, that the singing of the *Passio* had some influence upon the formation of the plays.

As further intermediaries between the Vulgate and the dramatic texts should be mentioned, finally, two other possibilities. The fact that the speeches in the two plays from Benediktbeuern are mosaics of passages from the several Gospels suggests the likelihood that the playwrights used Gospel harmonies, in which each part of the narrative was composed of a compilation of passages from all four evangelists.[3] Much of the same narrative matter was available also, with vivacious accompaniments, in sermons upon the Passion. In such homilies the preacher necessarily quoted widely from the New Testament, and often undertook to bring persons and events vividly before his congregation through vocal emphasis, rhetorical question, and imitative gesture. The dramatic range of these animated discourses, it appears, has not yet been adequately investigated.[4]

[1] For the view that the extant Passion plays rest upon the Gospel narrative see Venzmer, p. 15.

[2] In regard to the medieval ceremony of singing the Passions see above, p. 100.

[3] See Meyer, p. 122; Cabrol and Leclercq, iv, 756–8; above, p. 516.

[4] See, for example, P. Keppler, *Zur Passionspredigt des Mittelalters*, in *Historisches Jahrbuch*, iii (1882), 285–315; iv (1883), 161–88; Tanquerey, p. 8; G. Mercati, *Antiche Omilie e sacre Rappresentazioni medievali*, in *Rassegna gregoriana*, iv (1905), 15–20.

NOTES

INTRODUCTION

Page 1, note 1. For the separate plays, or groups of plays, dealt with in the present treatise, bibliography will be given where they are discussed. I mention here only the more comprehensive treatments of the Church drama. As a guide to these, general bibliographies such as the following are not very useful: U. Chevalier, *Répertoire des Sources historiques du Moyen Âge: Topobibliographie*, i, Montbéliard, 1894, col. 924–5; E. C. Richardson, *An Alphabetical Subject Index and Index Encyclopaedia to Periodical Articles on Religion, 1890–9*, New York, [1907,] pp. 286–7; L. Duval, *Curiosités bibliographiques relatives au Drame chrétien*, in *Revue catholique de Normandie*, xxi (1911), 57–72. These add nothing of importance to the lists of Chambers, i, pp. xiii sqq.; ii, 1–2. The most convenient general collections of texts are those of E. Du Méril, *Origines latines du Théâtre moderne*, Paris, 1849; E. de Coussemaker, *Drames liturgiques du Moyen Âge*, Rennes, 1860; T. Wright, *Early Mysteries and other Latin Poems of the Twelfth and Thirteenth Centuries*, London, 1838; A. Gasté, *Les Drames liturgiques de la Cathédrale de Rouen*, Évreux, 1893. Several of the longer plays are edited by R. Froning, *Das Drama des Mittelalters*, Stuttgart [1891]; and selected texts are reprinted from previous editors by J. Q. Adams, *Chief Pre-Shakespearean Dramas*, Boston [1924]. A few examples are edited by Manly, *Specimens*, vol. i. A large proportion of the texts offered in the present volumes have never been assembled collectively before, and a certain number of them are now printed for the first time. The best general surveys of the subject are by Chambers, ii, 1–105; Creizenach, i, 43–99; Bartholomaeis, pp. 101–65. The Church drama is treated in brief outline by A. Vermeylen, *Le Théâtre dans l'Église*, Brussels, 1901. Incisive studies of special problems are presented by Meyer, pp. 31–144. For treatments of substantial parts of the subject see also Manitius, iii, 1041–56; D'Ancona, i, 18–71; F. Boutillier, *Drames liturgiques et Rites figurés ou Cérémonies symboliques dans l'Église de Nevers*, in *Bulletin de la Société Nivernaise des Sciences, Lettres et Arts*, 2ᵉ série, viii (1880), 441–521; A. Cahour, *Du Drame liturgique*, in *Études de Théologie, de Philosophie et d'Histoire*, nouv. sér., i (1859), 362–83; ii (1860), 37–63, 234–42; Madeleine Chasles, *Le Drame liturgique*, in *La Vie et les Arts liturgiques*, iii (1916–17), 65–70, 121–34, 169–81, 258–66, 297–307, 403–12; Clément, pp. 89–318; Cohen, *Théâtre*, pp. 16–8; Crosse, pp. 1–38; C. Cuissard, *Mystères joués à Fleury et à Orléans*, in *Lectures et Mémoires de l'Académie de Sainte-Croix d'Orléans*, iv (1880), 284–313; Davidson, pp. 6–65; L. Deschamps de Pas, *Les Cérémonies religieuses dans la Collégiale de Saint-Omer au xiiiᵉ Siècle: Examen d'un Rituel manuscrit de cette Église*, in *Mémoires de la Société des Antiquaires de la Morinie*, xx (1886–7), 97–211; Dondi Orologio, pp. 41–68; Gayley, *Forefathers*, pp. 14–69; Klein, iv, 1–15; Lintilhac, i, 9–55; Michael, iv, 400–48; G. Morel, *Das geistliche Drama vom 12. bis 19. Jahrhundert*, in *den fünf Orten und besonders in Einsiedeln*, in *Der Geschichtsfreund*, xvii (1861), 75–144,—*Zusätze und Nachträge*, xxiii (1868), 219–34; Schubiger, *Spicilegien*, pp. 7–76; Wilken, pp. 1–25, 63–87, 145–50, 190–208; Petit de Julleville, i, 18–80; Gröber, ii, i, 423–6; Mantzius, ii, 1–15; Stammler, pp. 5–19. Although the following treat limited topics, they have also a more general bearing: J. Schwietering, *Ueber den liturgischen Ursprung des mittelalterlichen geistlichen Spiels*, in *Z.f.d.A.*, lxii (1925), 1–20; H. Brinkmann, *Zum Ursprung des liturgischen Spieles*, in *Xenia Bonnensia: Festschrift zum fünfundsiebzigjährigen Bestehen des Philologischen Vereins und Bonner Kreises*, Bonn, 1929, pp. 106–43; P. Butler, *A Note on the Origin of the Liturgical Drama*, in *An English Miscellany presented to Dr. Furnivall*, Oxford, 1901, pp. 46–51; Wilmotte, pp. 1–47, 93–126. Negligible is the sketch of A. Salzer, *Die Anfänge des modernen Dramas: Die Osterfeiern*, in *Studien und Mitteilungen zur Geschichte des Benediktiner-Ordens*, xxxii (1911), 330–3. One hardly need revert, except incidentally, to the earlier accounts and bibliography of Du Méril, pp. 1–87; Coussemaker, pp. v–xix; Milchsack, pp. 3–22; C. Magnin, in *Journal général de l'Instruction publique*, iv (1835), 245–6, 370–2, 395–6, 418–9, 455–6, 478–80, 514–6; L. Gautier, in *Le Monde* (1872), Aug. 17, pp. 1–2; Aug. 28, p. 1; Aug. 30, pp. 1–2; Sept. 4, pp. 1–2. Of slight importance here is the chapter *Les Drames liturgiques*, by Auber, iv, 190–234; and that entitled *Les Origines du Théâtre religieux*, by Merimée, pp. 3–57. Jeanroy's treatment of the matter (pp. v–xi, 1–19) is avowedly informal and popular, as is the discourse of Ida del Valle de Paz, *Sulle Origini e lo Svolgimento del Teatro religioso in Italia*, Udine, 1924. The brief study by M. J. Rudwin, *Zum Verhältnis des religiösen Dramas zur Liturgie der Kirche*, in *M.L.N.*, xxix (1914), 108–9, does not bear very directly upon our subject. Rudwin's *A Historical and Bibliographical Survey of the German Religious Drama*, Pittsburgh, 1924, is important. Suggestive, but not pervasively lucid, is P. E. Kretzmann, *The Liturgical Element in the Earliest Forms of the Medieval Drama*, Minneapolis, 1916. See the review of Kretzmann by N. C. Brooks, in *J.E.G.P.*, xvi (1917), 609–14. Bibliography bearing upon the musical aspects of the plays is provided by F. Liuzzi, *L'Espressione musicale nel Dramma liturgico*, in *Studi medievali*, nuova serie, ii (1929), 74–109; L.-P. Thomas, in *Romania*, liii (1927), 43–4; lv (1929), 50 sqq.; Lintilhac, i, 49, note 2; Brinkmann, pp. 106–7. On the relations between Church drama and plastic art see, for example, P. Weber, *Geistliches Schauspiel und kirchliche Kunst*, Stuttgart, 1894; Mâle, *xiie Siècle*, pp. 121–50; R. Stumpfl, in *Zeitschrift für deutsche Philologie*, lv (1930), 245–50; Grace Frank, in *P.M.L.A.*, xlvi (1931), 333–40. Various topics in the present study are touched upon by O. Cargill, *Drama and Liturgy*, New York, 1930, pp. 1–92. I regret, however, that a considerable proportion of this part of Dr. Cargill's monograph is unintelligible to me, and that it contains misstatements and omissions for which I find it difficult to account. Unintelligible to me, for example, is the contention (pp. 29–33) that the *Visitatio Sepulchri* in the *Regularis Concordia* of St Ethelwold is not 'dramatic in its nature' (see the text above, p. 249). Plainly erroneous is the assertion (p. 77) that the medieval text of the Rouen *Festum Asinorum* 'no longer exists', and that 'Du Cange . . . alone saw the manuscript'. For the facts concerning *two* extant medieval MSS of the Rouen *Festum* used by recent editors see below, ii, 154. Similar unaccountable omissions and errors are abundantly indicated by reviewers such as Grace Frank, in *M.L.N.*, xlvi (1931), 62–4; N. C. Brooks, in *J.E.G.P.*, xxx (1931), 433–9; and G. R. Coffman, in *Speculum*, vi (1931),

610–7. Since the monograph cannot be said to contribute substantial fresh material to the subject, and since its peculiarities raise considerable doubt as to the author's scholarly seriousness, I shall not undertake to present its meanings in the course of the present treatise. I regret that Allardyce Nicoll's *Masks, Mimes, and Miracles: Studies in the Popular Theatre*, London [1931], appeared too late for use in appropriate parts of my Introduction.

Page 2, note 1. The Greek dramatic manifestations of the Middle Ages do not directly or essentially concern us in the present treatise. An able attempt to demonstrate that a Greek religious drama existed during the first eight or nine Christian centuries, and that it influenced the drama of Western Europe, is made by G. La Piana, *Le Rappresentazioni sacre nella Letteratura bizantina dalle Origini al Sec. IX*, Grottaferrata, 1912. La Piana surveys the earlier work of Sathas and Krumbacher, and renders superfluous the similar attempt of J. S. Tunison, *Dramatic Traditions of the Dark Ages*, Chicago, 1907. See the review of Tunison by J. M. Manly, in *The American Historical Review*, xiii (1907–8), 124–6. The hybrid Greek play Χριστὸς Πάσχων (ed. J. G. Brambs, Leipzig, 1885) is generally irrelevant to the present study. Concerning this play, and related abortive dramatic efforts, see La Piana, *op. cit.*, pp. 9–14; Chambers, ii, 206; A. Baumgartner, *Die lateinische und griechische Literatur der christlichen Völker*, Freiburg, 1905, pp. 540–6; K. Dieterich, *Geschichte der byzantinischen und neugriechischen Litteratur*, Leipzig, 1902, pp. 45–8; Hirn, p. 391. A fresh survey of Byzantine dramatic phenomena has been made by Vénétia Cottas, *Le Théâtre à Byzance*, Paris, 1931.

Page 2, note 3. For bibliography relating to Hrotsvitha see O. R. Kuehne, *A Study of the Thaïs Legend with Special Reference to Hrotsvitha's 'Paphnutius'*, Philadelphia, 1922, pp. 116–7; Manitius, i, 619–32; Paetow, pp. 396, 398; Schneiderhan, pp. v–vii; Raby, p. 475. Her plays are discussed in most histories of the drama in Western Europe, notably by Creizenach, i, 16–9. The standard editions are by P. de Winterfeld, *Hrotsvithæ Opera*, Berlin, 1902; K. Strecker, *Hrotsvithæ Opera*, Leipzig, 1906. In Cologne, Stadtarchiv, MS W101*, fol. 1ʳ–16ᵛ, are found twelfth-century copies of four of the plays, described by G. Frenken, in *Neues Archiv der Gesellschaft für ältere deutsche Geschichtskunde*, xliv (1922), 101–4. Concerning other recently discovered fragments see H. Menhardt, in *Z.f.d.A.*, lxii (1925), 233–6. For observations upon Hrotsvitha's style in her plays see B. I. Jarcho, in *Z.f.d.A.*, lxii (1925), 236–40; C. Weyman, in *Neophilologus*, vii (1922), 284–5. For English translations of the plays see *The Plays of Roswitha*, trans. by H. J. W. Tillyard, London, 1923; *The Plays of Roswitha*, trans. by Christopher St John, London, 1923.

Page 9, note 1. The history and activities of *mimi* and *jongleurs* are amply surveyed by Chambers, i, 1–86. Concurrently with Chambers's work appeared the first volume of Hermann Reich's *Der Mimus* (Berlin, 1903), in which the author contends, somewhat grandiosely, that the *mimus* is the basis of all drama of the last twenty-five or thirty centuries, except the ancient classical drama and the later imitations of it. For corrective reviews of Reich see W. Creizenach, in *Euphorion*, xiii (1906), 138–43; F. Skutsch, in *Studien zur vergleichenden Literaturgeschichte*, vii (1907), 122–33. In his view that the influence of the *mimus* upon the drama was continuous throughout the

Middle Ages, Reich is supported by Winterfeld, pp. 512–24 *passim*; E. Faral, *Les Jongleurs en France au Moyen Âge*, Paris, 1910. Creizenach (i, 386 sqq.) and Chambers (i, 83–4) are relatively non-committal. Reich's position is vigorously opposed by Allen, *Lyric*, pp. 250 sqq.

Page 10, note 3. A standard treatment of folk drama, and of the associated folk customs, is that of Chambers, i, 89–273—folk plays, in the strict sense, being discussed in chap. x, pp. 205–27. There are later studies by R. J. E. Tiddy, *The Mummers' Play*, Oxford, 1923; C. R. Baskervill, *Dramatic Aspects of Medieval Folk Festivals in England*, in *Studies in Philology* (University of North Carolina), xvii (1920), 19–87; Baskervill, *Mummers' Wooing Plays in England*, in *Modern Philology*, xxi (1923–4), 225–72; A. Beatty, *The St George, or Mummers', Plays: A Study in the Protology of the Drama*, in *Transactions of the Wisconsin Academy of Sciences, Arts and Letters*, xv, part 2 (1906), 273–324.

Page 12, note 1. The influence upon Church drama of the Roman literary tradition may be discerned, perhaps, in the verse-forms used in some of the more sophisticated Church plays. The popular productions of the minstrels may be reflected in the dramatic pieces composed, presumably, by *vagantes*, and found in *Carmina Burana*. See above, pp. 518 sqq., and below, ii, 172 sqq.; Jacobsen, pp. 87 sqq. The folk spirit of revelry seems to have invaded the church under cover of the Feast of Fools and the ceremonies of the Boy Bishop. See above, pp. 104 sqq.; Chambers, ii, 56. The Feast of Fools and the activities of the Boy Bishop, however, are hardly to be considered as genuine drama. For a suggestion that the *unguentarius* of the Easter play (see above, pp. 401 sqq.) and the devils in the dramatic *Sponsus* (see below, ii, 364, 367) may show the influence of folk plays and revelry see Chambers, ii, 91. Beatty (p. 324) inquires whether the striking fondness of the Church for the Easter play concerning the Resurrection may not reflect the influence of the ritualistic folk play dealing with death and revival. Of such influence I see no direct and explicit evidence. For the Easter play see above, chaps. ix–xiv.

CHAPTER I

THE ROMAN MASS

Page 15, note 2. From the vast bibliography of liturgiology applicable to the Church of Rome I mention here only a few representative works. A survey of the subject is given by F. Cabrol, *Introduction aux Études liturgiques*, Paris, 1907, and an orderly summary of the bibliography is provided by J. Braun, *Liturgisches Handlexikon*, Regensburg, 1924, pp. 378–99. Bibliographies are provided periodically in *Jahrbuch für Liturgiewissenschaft*, 1921 sqq., and in *Revue d'Histoire ecclésiastique*, 1900 sqq. A useful list of works which appeared during the first two decades of the twentieth century is found in the brochure of K. Mohlberg, *Ziele und Aufgaben der liturgiegeschichtlichen Forschung*, Münster, 1919. Of the innumerable liturgical manuals, the following are among the more serviceable: V. Thalhofer, *Handbuch der katholischen Liturgik*, 2 vols., Freiburg, 1912; G. Rietschel, *Lehrbuch der Liturgik*, 2 vols., Berlin, 1900–9. The manuals usually provide a certain amount of historical background. Additional historical comment may be conveniently found in the following: F. Cabrol, *Le Livre de la Prière antique*, Paris, 1903 (translated into English as *Liturgical Prayer: Its History and Spirit*, London, 1925); F. Cabrol, *Les Origines liturgiques*, Paris, 1906; P. Wagner, *Origine et Développement du Chant liturgique*, Tournai, 1904. Modern editions of medieval service-books have now become numerous, and many of these are cited in appropriate places in the present treatise. Important examples are listed in the bibliography of Braun mentioned above. Special attention may be called to the following series of liturgical publications: *Bibliothèque liturgique*, ed. U. Chevalier, Paris, 1893 sqq.; the publications of the Henry Bradshaw Society, London, 1891 sqq.; *Liturgische Bibliothek*, ed. A. Schönfelder, Paderborn, 1904–6. Numerous texts and treatises are found also in *Kleine Texte für theologische Vorlesungen und Uebungen*, ed. H. Lietzmann, Bonn, 1903 sqq.; *Liturgiegeschichtliche Forschungen*, ed. F. J. Dögler *et al.*, Münster, 1919 sqq.; *Liturgiegeschichtliche Quellen*, ed. K. Mohlberg *et al.*, Münster, 1918 sqq.; *Liturgiegeschichtliche Quellen und Forschungen*, ed. K. Mohlberg *et al.*, Münster, 1928 sqq. As to modern liturgical practice the basic guides are the *Rubricæ Generales* found at the beginning of the missal and the breviary. Authorized interpretations of questions arising under the rubrics are given in *Decreta authentica Congregationis Sacrorum Rituum*, 7 vols., Rome, 1898–1927. Later decisions of the Congregation of Sacred Rites may be found in the current volumes of *Acta Apostolicæ Sedis*, Rome, 1909 sqq. Many matters omitted by the authorities just mentioned are treated in approved commentaries such as the following: B. Gavantus and C. M. Merati, *Thesaurus Sacrorum Rituum*, 3 vols., Venice, 1762; P. Martinucci, *Manuale Sacrarum Cæremoniarum*, 2 parts, 4 vols., Regensburg and Rome, 1911–5; P. J. B. de Herdt, *Sacræ Liturgiæ Praxis juxta Ritum Romanum*, 3 vols., Louvain, 1894; I. Walpelhorst, *Compendium Sacræ Liturgiæ juxta Ritum Romanum*, 10th ed., New York, 1925. A large amount of lucid guidance is given by A. Fortescue, *The Ceremonies of the Roman Rite Described*, London, 1920. The language of the liturgy is treated, directly or indirectly, by H. P. V. Nunn, *An Introduction to Ecclesiastical Latin*, Cambridge, 1922; W. E. Plater and H. J. White, *A Grammar of the Vulgate*, Oxford, 1926. As to vocabulary, the *Glossarium* of Du Cange may be supplemented, for example, by the *Liturgisches Handlexikon* of Braun, mentioned above, by A. Sleumer, *Kirchenlateinisches Wörterbuch*, Limburg, 1926, and by A. Hoffmann, *Liturgical Dictionary*, Collegeville, 1928. Guidance for the study of medieval Latin in general is provided by K. Strecker, *Einführung in das Mittellatein*, Berlin, 1929; Paetow, pp. 485–7. Liturgical vestments are amply treated by J. Braun, *Die liturgische Gewandung im Occident und Orient*, Freiburg, 1907. For the purpose of this treatise one need not consider the Greek liturgy, the Ambrosian rite of Milan, or the Mozarabic rite of Spain. On the general absence of drama from the Mozarabic liturgy see Sturdevant, pp. 46–8, 78.

Page 16, note 1. The history of the Mass is summarized in the general manuals mentioned in the preceding note, and is treated in convenient amplitude and with appropriate documentation by A. Fortescue, *The Mass*, London, 1917. See also Duchesne, chaps. iii–vii; Wagner, chaps. i–vi. For the liturgical text of the modern Mass one may use any authorized edition of the

Missale Romanum. As to modern ceremonial and the duties of the officiating persons much information is supplied by the *Ordo Missæ* in the middle of the missal, and by the *Rubricæ Generales Missalis* and *Ritus servandus in Celebratione Missæ* in the introductory part of that volume. The duties of the liturgical chorus are prescribed in *Graduale Sacrosanctæ Romanæ Ecclesiæ*, Rome, 1908. The guidance given in these authorized texts may be supplemented from appropriate parts in Martinucci's *Manuale* and Fortescue's *Ceremonies*, mentioned in the preceding note.

Page 17, note 3. One might expect to find the required guidance in such treatises as the following: E. G. C. F. Atchley, *Ordo Romanus Primus*, London, 1905; O. J. Reichel, *Solemn Mass at Rome in the Ninth Century*, London, 1895; H. Netzer, *L'Introduction de la Messe romaine en France sous les Carolingiens*, Paris, 1910, chap. ix. But these treatments do not provide the elementary and orderly details needed for our present purpose. Similarly lacking in necessary detail are, for example, the descriptions of the Mass and the Canonical Office based upon Münster service-books of the thirteenth and fourteenth centuries given by Stapper, *Feier*, pp. 54 sqq., and the descriptions from Augsburg given by Hoeynck, pp. 39 sqq.

Page 21, note 3. Whatever its ultimate origin may have been, during the early Christian centuries the word *antiphona* commonly meant a musical piece, usually a psalm, in which the successive verses or sentences were sung in alternation by two choruses. This method of singing originated in the East, and was brought into Western Europe in the fourth century. Since about the sixth century, however, the term *antiphona* has been applied more especially to a separate, relatively short, text (with music) which introduces the psalm proper, and which is repeated at one time or another in the course of the singing of the psalm. During the Middle Ages the antiphon was sometimes repeated after each verse of the psalm. In modern times it is usually sung only before the first verse of the psalm and after the last verse. See Cabrol and Leclercq, i, 2282 sqq.; Wagner, pp. 13–48, 144–63.

CHAPTER II
THE CANONICAL OFFICE

Page 44, note 1. The history of the Canonical Office, summarized in the general manuals mentioned in the Notes to the preceding chapter, is treated with most amplitude and authority in the following works: S. Bäumer, *Histoire du Bréviaire*, trans. R. Biron, 2 vols., Paris, 1905; P. Batiffol, *History of the Roman Breviary*, London, 1912. The history of the choral parts is investigated especially by Wagner, pp. 126–86.

Page 49, note 1. For the liturgical text of the modern Canonical Office one may use any authorized edition of the *Breviarium Romanum*, which is commonly distributed into four volumes with the following sub-titles: *Pars Hiemalis*, *Pars Vernalis*, *Pars Æstivalis* and *Pars Autumnalis*. As to modern ceremonial and the duties of the officiating persons the breviary will supply a limited amount of information in the rubrics accompanying the text, and in the *Rubricæ Generales Breviarii* usually printed at the beginning of *Pars Hiemalis*. Concerning standard texts of the Roman Breviary see Lietzmann, pp. 2, 43–8. The duties of the chorus are prescribed in *Directorium Chori ad usum omnium Ecclesiarum in quibus Officium Divinum juxta Ritum S. Romanæ Ecclesiæ cantari solet*. I use the edition of Rome, 1889. The guidance purveyed in these official texts may be supplemented by that found in such works as the following: Fortescue, *Ceremonies*, pp. 199 sqq.; Martinucci, pt. i, vol. ii, 24–30; Hartmann, *Repertorium*, pp. 159–85, 226–36; Cabrol, *Prayer, passim*. The reform in the use of the breviary effected by the Apostolic Constitution *Divino afflatu* of Nov. 1, 1911, is explained in such authorized manuals as that of E. Burton and E. Myers, *The New Psalter and its Use*, London, 1912. This reform has no essential bearing upon the exposition offered in the present treatise.

Page 64, note 1. In modern practice, it happens that the *Te Deum* of Christmas is followed by a prayer, introduced by a verse and response, and followed by a response. With these we need not concern ourselves here. In medieval service-books the *Te Deum* is often followed by a verse and response, under the rubric *Versus sacerdotales*. These sometimes take the form of question and answer, as is observed by Meyer, pp. 35–6. Such formulæ, however, have no palpable bearing upon the development of drama. Among our observations upon liturgical details at the end of Matins should be mentioned the fact that after this office on Christmas Day follows the first of the three Masses of the day. Whereas each day of the liturgical year has, normally, a single form of Mass, sung between Terce and Sext, this particular feast has three such forms: one (*Missa in Nocte*, or *Missa in Gallicantu*) sung immediately after Matins, a second (*Missa in Aurora*) sung immediately after Prime, and a third (*Missa in Die*, or *Magna Missa*) sung between Terce and Sext. See above, p. 18; below, ii, 5, 16, 19. It will be observed that in the Middle Ages the second Christmas Mass could be sung immediately after Lauds.

Page 64, note 3. During the Middle Ages the Roman type of Easter Matins, consisting of only one Nocturn, not only prevailed in secular churches, but even supplanted the monastic form in the churches of some monasteries. The monastic form, however, is occasionally found in medieval breviaries, and it is established in the modern *Breviarium Monasticum*. It has three Nocturns, the first containing six psalms and four lessons, the second, six psalms and four lessons, and the third, a canticle and four more lessons. For an example from Oxford, Bibl. Bodl., MS Canonici Liturg. 325, Brev. monasticum sæc. xiii, fol. 82^r–82^v, see Young, *Some Texts*, pp. 311 sq.; and above, p. 312. For an example, along with the complete text of the *Cursus*, from Munich, Staatsbibl., MS lat. 23037, Brev. Pruveningense sæc. xii, fol. 175^v–178^r, see Young, *Harrowing of Hell*, pp. 936–46; and for a dramatic text associated with Matins in this MS see below, pp. 596–7.

CHAPTER III

THE DRAMATIC ELEMENT IN THE LITURGY

Page 79, note 1. The dramatic aspects of the Roman liturgy are summarized by Creizenach i, 50–1; Chambers, ii, 4–6; Alt, pp. 328–48. Frere (*Ceremonial*, pp. 103–61) makes suggestive distinctions among several kinds of liturgical ceremonial—utilitarian, interpretative, and symbolical. See also V. Valentin, *Tempel und Theater*, in *Die Grenzboten*, xlix (1890, 4th quarter), 66–78, 114–25; O. Casel, *Zur Idee der liturgischen Festfeier*, in *Jahrbuch für Liturgiewissenschaft*, iii (1923), 93–9; Mantzius, ii, 4; Davidson, pp. 130–43; Klein, iv, 2–8; Clément, pp. 92–285 *passim*; Boutillier, pp. 444–98; Du Méril, pp. 48–53; Ward, i, 29–35; Deschamps de Pas, pp. 103–86 *passim*; Thurston, pp. 26–404 *passim*.

Page 80, note 1. A tendency towards 'theatrical' gestures and vocalizations in the liturgy is thus censured by Ælred, abbot of Rievaulx (1150–66), in his *Speculum Charitatis*, ii, 33 (Migne, *P.L.*, cxcv, 571, cited by Chambers, i, 81; Waddell, pp. 72–3):

Sed quia aperte malos ab hac consideratione putavimus removendos, de his nunc sermo sit, qui sub specie religionis negotium voluptatis obpalliant: qui ea, quæ antiqui patres in typis futurorum salubriter exercebant, in usum suæ vanitatis usurpant. Unde, quæso, cessantibus jam typis et figuris, unde in Ecclesia tot organa, tot cymbala? Ad quid, rogo, terribilis ille follium flatus, tonitrui potius fragorem, quam vocis exprimens suavitatem? Ad quid illa vocis contractio et infractio? Hic succinit, ille discinit; alter medias quasdam notas dividit et incidit. Nunc vox stringitur, nunc frangitur, nunc impingitur, nunc diffusiori sonitu dilatatur. Aliquando, quod pudet dicere, in equinos hinnitus cogitur; aliquando virili vigore deposito, in femineæ vocis gracilitates acuitur, nonnunquam artificiosa quadam circumvolutione torquetur et retorquetur. Videas aliquando hominem aperto ore quasi intercluso halitu exspirare, non cantare, ac ridiculosa quadam vocis interceptione quasi minitari silentium; nunc agones morientium, vel exstasim patientium imitari. Interim histrionicis quibusdam gestibus totum corpus agitatur, torquentur labia, rotant, ludunt humeri; et ad singulas quasque notas digitorum flexus respondet. Et hæc ridiculosa dissolutio vocatur religio; et ubi hæc frequentius agitantur, ibi Deo honorabilius serviri clamatur. Stans interea vulgus sonitum follium, crepitum cymbalorum, harmoniam fistularum tremens attonitusque miratur; sed lascivas cantantium gesticulationes, meretricias vocum alternationes et infractiones non sine cachinno risuque intuetur, ut eos non ad oratorium, sed ad theatrum, nec ad orandum, sed ad spectandum æstimes convenisse. Nec timetur illa tremenda majestas, cui assistitur, nec defertur mystico illi præsepio, cui ministratur, ubi Christus mystice pannis involvitur, ubi sacratissimus ejus sanguis calice liberatur, ubi aperiuntur cœli; assistunt angeli; ubi terrena cœlestibus junguntur; ubi angelis homines sociantur.

Herrmann (pp. 201–5) infers that during the Middle Ages liturgical gestures were of a restrained sort, and hence gave small encouragement to drama.

Page 81, note 4. For assertions and assumptions, more or less explicit, that the Mass is a drama see Klein, iv, 2; Auber, iv, 196; Cohen, in *Revue de Belgique*, 2ᵉ série, xxxviii (1903), 29; Atchley, p. 294; I. S. Tucker, in *The Drama*, xiii (1922), 49; Du Méril, pp. 41–2; J. J. Jusserand, *A Literary History of the English People*, i, New York, 1895, pp. 456–7; Mantzius, ii, 4; Allen, *Institutions*, pp. 515, 532. Allen (p. 532) holds that 'the tendency to dramatize the Last Supper began at a very early period, when the congregations having become too large to sit down at the table, the bishop and his presbyters surrounded it after the example of Christ and His disciples'.

Page 82, note 4. The words of Honorius of Autun in regard to the dramatic role of the celebrant in the Mass are cited in the following passage from William Prynne, *Histrio-mastix*, London, 1633, pp. 112–4:

The historie of Christs death, and the celebration of his blessed Sacraments, are oft times prophaned in theatricall enterludes, especially by Popish Priests and Iesuites in forraigne parts: *Who, as they have turned the Sacrament of Christs body and blood into a Masse-play*; so they have likewise *trans-formed their Masse it-selfe, together with the whole story of Christs birth, his life, his Passion, and all other parts of their Ecclesiasticall service into Stage-playes* . . . *Honorius Augustodunensis*, an Author of some credit among the Romanists, in his Booke, *De Antiquo Ritu Missarum. lib.* I. *cap.* 83. the title of which chapter is, *De Tragœdijs*: to signifie to the world, that the Popish *Masse* is now no other but a *Tragicke Play*, writes thus, *Wee must know that those who rehearsed Tragedies on Theaters, did represent unto the people by their gestures, the acts of fighters. So our Tragedian* (thus hath he stiled the *Masse-Priest*, how aptly the ensuing words enforme us) *represents unto the Christian people by his gestures, the combate of Christ in the Theater of the Church, and inculcates into them the victory of his Redemption. Therefore when the Presbyter saith, (Pray ye,) he acteth or expresseth Christ, who was cast into an agony for us, when he admonished his Apostles to pray. By his secret silence, he signifieth Christ led to the slaughter as a Lambe without a voyce. By the stretching out of his hands, he denotes the extension of Christ upon the Crosse. By the Song of the Præface, he expresseth the cry of Christ, hanging vpon the Crosse, &c.* Loe here a Roman *Masse-priest* becomes a *Player*, and in stead of preaching, of reading, acts Christs Passion in the Masse; which this Author stiles, a *Tragedy*.

Page 94, note 1. In an ordinary of the twelfth century from Remiremont (Paris, Bibl. Nat., MS lat. 9486, fol. 9ʳ) the unpublished Palm Sunday procession contains the following passage, in which the speech of Caiphas is sung by a single cantor:

Duo cantores cantent antiphonam *Collegerunt pontifices et Pharisei consilium et dicebant.* Chorus: *Quid facimus, quia hic homo multa signa fecit? Si dimittimus eum sic, omnes credent in eum.* Item cantores respondent *Vnus autem ex illis, Cayphas nomine, cum esset pontifex anni illius prophetauit dicens.* Vnus de choro: *Expedit uobis ut unus moriatur homo pro populo, et non tota gens pereat.* Item cantores: *Ab illo ergo die cogitauerunt interficere eum dicentes.* Chorus respondet *Ne forte ueniant Romani et tollant nostrum locum et gentem.* Postea legitur evvangelium.

For a similar assignment of the part of Caiphas see Wonisch, pp. 21, 25, and above, p. 527. On the word *propheta* as meaning merely *cantor*, or 'singer', see C. Vivell, in *Rassegna Gregoriana*, xiii (1914), 277–80. For payments for the services of Palm Sunday 'prophets' in English churches, and for their 'dressing', see Cox, *Churchwardens' Accounts*, pp. 254–5. Cox (p. 268), speaks of the 'drama of Palm Sunday'—referring, presumably, more particularly to the procession and the 'prophet'. Feasey (*Ceremonial*, p. 75) regards the 'prophet' as 'a survival of the ancient liturgical drama'. I see no direct connexion between this personage and the dramatic procession of the prophets to be considered below, ii, 125 sqq. For further observations on the Palm Sunday procession see Creizenach, i, 50–1; Chambers, ii, 4–5, 20; Wonisch, pp. 20–31; Alt. pp. 346–8; Wilmart, pp. 23–5, 100–2; Feasey, *Ceremonial*, pp. 53–79; Deschamps de Pas, pp. 111–3; Thurston, pp. 191–232. Brooks (*Sepulchrum Christi*, p. 152) mentions a sixteenth-century symbolic scourging of Christ on Palm Sunday in the sculptural sepulchre outside the cathedral of Berlin.

Page 101, note 1. The manner in which the *Passiones* were sung during the Middle Ages is investigated by Young, *Observations on the Origin of the Mediaeval Passion-Play*, in *P.M.L.A.*, xxv (1910), 309–33. The matter is treated somewhat less comprehensively by H. M. Bannister, *Monumenti Vaticani di Paleografia musicale latina*, Leipzig, 1913, pp. 191–4. In the modern printed missals, in the texts of the Passions, the beginnings of the utterances of the narrator, of the Jews, and of Christ are marked respectively by the following symbols, printed in red: c, s,+. It is an astonishing fact that for generations these have been misinterpreted as indications of the three persons who have been assumed to sing the Passions. This misinterpretation has been sponsored by such representative writers as Thalhofer (i, 617) and Thurston (pp. 230–1). The explanations usually given are these: c=*cantor*, or *chronista*; s=*synagoga*; +=*Christus*. As a matter of fact, these symbols were originally designed for the musical guidance of the *single* person who sang the Passion, and the usual meanings were these: c=*celeriter*, or *cito*; s=*sursum*, or *susum*; t (for which the sign of the cross was, it appears, mistakenly substituted) =*trahere*, or *tenere*. In medieval MSS these symbols in red are usually written above the text to which they apply, and Notker calls them *litteræ in superscriptione*. See Young, p. 325. The three *litteræ* in modern missals are a mere remnant from the considerable number used during the Middle Ages. The following list is given by Young (p. 321) as having been used in various MSS to direct the singing of the passages of Christ, the narrator, and the Jews respectively:

Christ	Narrator	Jews
a	a	a
b	c	c
c	e	i
d	io	io
h	m	l
i	p̄t	m
l	s	mi
m	t	s
s		si
t		sl
+		sm
×		su

The musical significance of these letters is explained in a letter of Notker printed by Migne, *P.L.*, cxxxi, 1171–2; *Paléographie musicale*, iv, 10–1; Young, pp. 325–7; Van Doren, pp. 94–118. The evidence is overwhelming for the medieval singing of a *Passio* by a *single* deacon. The modern practice of employing three voices appears to have arisen during the fifteenth century. See Young, pp. 331–2. Feasey (*Ceremonial*, p. 80) remarks that the distribution of the parts of the Passions among three persons 'was in all probability a remnant of the Mystery Play'. It may well be that the custom reflects, in some measure, the influence of the Church drama; but it probably resulted chiefly from the general tendency towards ceremonial elaboration during the late Middle Ages and the Renaissance.

Page 102, note 5. The history of the ceremony of the Dedication of a Church is given, with ample bibliography, in Cabrol and Leclercq, iv, 374–405. See also Cabrol, *Prayer*, pp. 203–12; Duchesne, pp. 399–418; Chambers, ii, 4; Young, *Harrowing of Hell*, pp. 894–5.

Page 104, note 1. The most exhaustive study of the Feast of Fools, with extensive bibliography, is that of Chambers, i, 274–335. Since the date of Chambers's work the most important single publication upon the subject is the following edition of the office for the feast of the Circumcision, from Sens: H. Villetard, ed., *Office de Pierre de Corbeil* (*Bibliothèque musicologique*, iv), Paris, 1907. See also G. M. Dreves, *Zur Geschichte der Fête des fous*, in *Stimmen aus Maria-Laach*, xlvii (1894), 571–87; Baudrillart, ii, 1816–26; Gasté, pp. 20–4; Gayley, *Forefathers*, pp. 33–53; *Catholic Encyclopedia*, vi, 132–3; H. Villetard, *Remarques sur la Fête des Fous au Moyen Âge*, Paris, 1911.

Page 105, note 4. A text of the Prose of the Ass (Chevalier, *R.H.*, no. 14280) based upon several versions is printed by Chambers, ii, 280–2. The text from Sens MS 46, of the thirteenth century, is printed by Villetard (pp. 86–7; photographic facsimile on plate ii) as follows:

1. Orientis partibus
   aduentauit asinus,
   pulcher et fortissimus,
   sarcinis aptissimus.
   Hez, Sir Asne, Hez!

2. Hic in collibus Sichen
   enutritus sub Ruben,
   transiit per Iordanem,
   saliit in Bethleem.
   Hez, ⟨Sir Asne, Hez!⟩

3. Saltu uincit hinnulos,
   dagmas et capreolos,
   super dromedarios
   uelox Madianeos. Hez!

4. Aurum de Arabia,
   thus et myrram de Sabba
   tulit in ecclesia
   uirtus asinaria. Hez!

5. Dum trahit uehicula,
   multa cum sarcinula,
   illius mandibula
   dura terit pabula. Hez!

6. Cum aristis ordeum
   comedit et carduum;
   triticum a palea
   segregat in area. Hez!

7. Amen dicas, asine,
   iam satur ex gramine;
   Amen, amen itera,
   aspernare uetera. Hez!

I regret that the study of these verses by H. C. Greene (*Speculum*, vi [1931], 534–49) appeared too late for use here.

Page 105, note 6. To the ample study of the Boy Bishop by Chambers, i, 336–71, may be added that of J. M. J. Fletcher, *The Boy-Bishop at Salisbury and Elsewhere* Salisbury [1921]. See also Bartholomaeis, pp. 201–11; Clark, pp. 214–6; Meller, pp. 3–18; Gasté, pp. 35–48; Motter, pp. 6–8, 11–12, 31, 33, 49–50, 229, 252; Arens, p. 213; J. P. W. Crawford, *A Note on the Boy Bishop in Spain*, in *Romanic Review*, xii (1921), 146–54; Crawford, *Spanish Drama*, pp. 15–6; Gayley, *Forefathers*, pp. 54–61; Chasles, pp. 404–6.

Page 106, note 2. The thirteenth-century *ordinarium* in the Chapter Library of the cathedral of Padua is thus described by Dondi Orologio, p. 3: 'Il Codice, che illustriamo, vien conservato nell'Archivio capitolare di questa Cattedrale scritto in pergamena di CLI pagine in quarto grande con lo stemma della Sacristia, cioè una Croce con la lettera S attortigliata, sebbene in questo sia laterale, e le parole *Liber et signum Ecclesiæ Paduanæ.*' In the present treatise I shall refer to it as MS 'S'.

CHAPTER IV

THE BURIAL OF CROSS AND HOST

Page 112, note 1. The *Depositio* and *Elevatio* are the subject of a special study by the present writer, *The Dramatic Associations of the Easter Sepulchre* (*University of Wisconsin Studies in Language and Literature*, no. 10), Madison, 1920, which contains bibliography. Important additions are made by Brooks, *Sepulchre*, pp. 33–6, *et passim*. On the general subject see also Thiers, ii, 193–204; Chambers, ii, 16–25; A. Wilmart, *Le Samedi-Saint monastique*, in *Revue bénédictine*, xxxiv (1922), 159–63; Mühlbacher, pp. 385–7; Brinkmann, pp. 114 sqq.; Rock, iv, 103–17, 277–90. The more modern practices associated with the sepulchre are discussed by Brooks, *Sepulchrum Christi*, pp. 147–61. For the local uses of Breslau, Münster, and Paderborn to-day see *Rituale Wratislaviense ad normam Romani . . . editum*, Regensburg, 1891, pp. 397, 400–6; J. Jungnitz, *Die Breslauer Ritualien*, Breslau, 1892, pp. 18–9, 30; Stapper, *Agende*, pp. 43, 93; Hartmann, *Repertorium*, pp. 748, 764–5. The practices in Bohemia, medieval and modern, are considered by D. Orel-Prag, in *Kirchenmusikalisches Jahrbuch*, xxiii (1910), 59–72.

In connexion with the *Depositio* and *Elevatio* one may appropriately mention the ceremony called the 'Burial of the Alleluia', performed on the Saturday before Septuagesima Sunday. From 'Statuta Tullensis Ecclesiæ sæculo xv' Du Cange (i, 183) cites the following *ordo*:

Sabbato Septuagesimæ in Nona conveniant pueri chori feriati in magno vestiario, et ibi ordinent sepulturam *Alleluia*. Et expedito ultimo *Benedicamus*, procedant cum crucibus, tortiis, aqua benedicta et incenso, portantesque glebam ad modum funeris, transeant per chorum et vadant ad claustrum ululantes usque ad locum ubi sepelitur; ibique aspersa aqua et dato incenso ab eorum altero, redeunt eodem itinere.

This ceremony appears to have no direct relation to the dramatic traditions studied in the present treatise. Chambers (i, 186) refers to the 'funeral of Alleluia' as being analogous to the expulsion of winter or death in folk custom. See also C. Blume, *Des Alleluja Leben, Begräbniss und Auferstehung*, in *Stimmen aus Maria-Laach*, lii (1897), 429–43; Barthélemy, iii, 481–8; Wordsworth, *Notes*, p. 105; Stapper, *Münster*, pp. 72–3; Tolhurst, ii, 373; C. Blume, *Osterbotschaft des heimkehrenden Alleluja*, in *Die Kirchenmusik*, xi (1910), 20–2; Deschamps de Pas, pp. 108–9.

Page 121, note 6. In the *vita* of St Ulrich is found the following (*Acta Sanctorum*, Julii, ii, Paris and Rome, 1867, p. 103):

Die autem Parasceve . . . mane diluculo psalterium explere festinavit, et sacro Dei mysterio perpetrato, populoque sacro Christi Corpore saginato, et consuetudinario more, quod remanserat, sepulto, iterum inter ecclesias ambulando, psalterium explevit decantando. . . . Desideratissimo atque sanctissimo Paschali die adveniente, post primam intravit ecclesiam Sancti Ambrosii, ubi die Parasceve Corpus Christi superposito lapide collocavit, ibique cum paucis clericis Missam de sancta Trinitate explevit. Expleta autem Missa . . . secum portato Christi ⟨Corpore⟩ et Euangelio et cereis et incenso, et cum congrua salutatione versuum a pueris decantata per atrium perrexit ad ecclesiam Sancti Joannis Baptistæ.

This passage informs us that on Good Friday, after Communion at the close of the *Missa Præsanctificatorum* in the cathedral, the remains of the Sacrament were deposited in the church of St Ambrosius, in some sort of *sepulchrum* closed by a stone (*lapis*). Apparently the *Corpus Domini* thus buried remained in the sepulchre until Easter morning, and, as we may assume, was then taken up according to the ceremonial of the *Elevatio*. This latter ceremonial may be implied in the words *secum portato Christi Corpore*. Concerning the Augsburg observance see Brooks, *Sepulchre*, p. 32; *Decreta*, iv, 430; Brinkmann, pp. 125–6.

Page 123, note 3. With the texts from Gran may be associated the *Depositio* and *Elevatio* in a Salzburg Rituale of 1686 reprinted by Young, *Dramatic Associations*, pp. 36–8, from *Decreta*, iv, 429–30, 439.

Page 124, note 4. Another reason for excluding the general congregation from the *Elevatio* is recorded from the Synod of Worms of the year 1316 by J. F. Schannat and J. Hartzheim, *Concilia Germaniæ*, iv, Cologne, 1761, p. 258:

Cum a nostris antecessoribus ad nos usque pervenerit, ut in sacra nocte Dominicæ Resurrectionis ad sustollendam Crucifixi Imaginem de Sepulchro, ubi in Parasceve locata fuerat, nimia virorum et mulierum numerositas certatim sese comprimendo, ecclesiam simul cum canonicis et vicariis introire nitantur, opinantes erronee quod, si viderent Crucifixi Imaginem sustolli, evaderent hoc anno inevitabilem mortis horam, his itaque obviantes statuimus, ut Resurrectionis mysterium ante ingressum plebis in ecclesiam deinceps peragatur.

See Milchsack, p. 119; Brooks, *Sepulchre*, p. 42; Brinkmann, pp. 134–6; Chambers, ii, 20–1. See also the versions of the *Elevatio* from Raitenbuch and Regensburg published by Young, *Dramatic Associations*, pp. 82, 89.

Page 125, note 6. In regard to the several editions of Castellani's *Liber Sacerdotalis*, and its liturgical history, see R. Dörner, *Die Auferstehungsfeier am Charsamstag nach dem Sacerdotale Romanum*, in *Caecilien-Kalender*, x (1885), 27–36. Dörner (p. 32) briefly describes the *Depositio*, and, from an edition not precisely indicated, reprints (pp. 32–5) the combined *Elevatio* and *Visitatio Sepulchri*. Concerning this last text see below, p. 622. With the sepulchre ceremonies of Castellani may be associated those used at St Mark's in Venice in the eighteenth century, printed in *Officium Hebdomadæ Sanctæ secundum consuetudinem Ducalis Ecclesiæ Sancti Marci Venetiarum*, Venice, 1736, pp. 277–82, 345–9, and reprinted by Young, *op. cit.*, pp. 67–71. The *Elevatio* and *Visitatio* from this book are reprinted also by Lange, *Auferstehungsfeiern*, pp. 78–80.

Page 130, note 2. With the *Elevatio* from St Gall MS 387 may be associated versions from Lübeck, Erlau, Gran, and Barking mentioned by Brooks, *Sepulchre*, pp. 34, 35, 36, 41. For a combined version of *Elevatio* and *Visitatio Sepulchri* after Matins see above, pp. 304 sqq. Here may be given two special texts from Soissons and Sens, of which the primary sources are unknown, showing unusual forms of the *Elevatio* containing part of the sequence *Victimæ paschali*:[1]

⟨ELEVATIO HOSTIÆ⟩[2]

In Ecclesia Suessionensi hæc denuntiatio Resurrectionis fit quoque post tertium responsorium Matutini. Sed illic Sepulcrum adornatur in capella quadam, posito in altari sanctissimo Sacramento, quo procedit clerus cum episcopo, præeuntibus crucibus, cereis, et thymiamateriis, populo ciuitatis cum magistratibus subsequente. Et, cantata e superiore loco antiphona de Resurrectione, cantor festo habitu conspicuus interrogat tres vicarios, ante fores clausas stantes in albis: *Dic nobis, Maria, quid vidisti in via?*
Cui respondet unus ex iis: *Sepulcrum Christi viuentis, et gloriam vidi resurgentis.*
Alter: *Angelicos testes, sudarium et vestes.*
Tertius: *Scimus Christum surrexisse a mortuis vere.*
Tum cantor, conuersus ad chorum et populum: *Credendum est magis soli Mariæ veraci, quam Iudæorum turbæ fallaci.*
Hoc dicto, episcopus, apertis foribus, ingreditur capellam, et sanctissimum Sacramentum cum debito ornatu de altari tollens, duobus canonicis in albis latus tegentibus, incipit hymnum *Te Deum laudamus.*

⟨ELEVATIO HOSTIÆ⟩[3]

Aliter autem in Sennonensi Ecclesia in hac die observatur; nam in capella latis ornata, sanctissima Eucharistia exposita, ad quam solemnis processio dirigitur, et in ingressu ejusdem capellæ, ubi tres vicecurati assistunt, intonat cantor: *Dic nobis, Maria, quid vidisti in via?*
Tunc unus ex vicecuratis respondet: *Sepulcrum Christi viventis, et gloriam vidi resurgentis.*
Alius canit: *Angelicos testes, sudarium et vestes.*
Tertius vero concludit: *Scimus Christum surrexisse a mortuis vere.*
Ac cantor reassumit, et canit: *Credendum est magis soli Mariæ veraci quam Judæorum turbæ fallaci.*

---

[1] Concerning *Victimæ paschali* see above, pp. 273 sqq.
[2] Eveillon, pp. 179–80.   [3] Macri, ii, 175.

Deinde immediate ab episcopo intonatur *Te Deum*, qui ex capella proces-sionaliter ad majus altare defert Sacramentum, et genuflexus extremitatem pyxidis osculatur, et post episcopum idem facit clerus, magistratus, et populus.

Page 134, note 1. With the *Elevatio* from the *Regularis Concordia* may be associated the following text from Paris, Bibl. Nat., MS lat. 2402, fol. 83ʳ–83ʳ, previously edited by A. Wilmart, in *Revue bénédictine*, xxxiv (1922), 161–2:

DE VARIETATE DOMINICE NOCTIS

In ipsa nocte sancta ante Matut*inum* pulsetur maior nola semel, et conue-niant fratres in choro decantantes vii pentitentiales psalmos, *Domine ne in furore*, et al*ios* cum letan*ia*, inclinantes se ante Crucem. Hec illis facientibus nulli laicorum intersint. Deinde *Pater noster* cum precibus quas uoluer*int*. Tum eleuatur Crux atque constituitur in suo loco; sudaria autem remanent in Sepulchro usque *Te Deum laudamus*. | Deinde antiphona *Christus resurgens*. Versus *Dicant nunc Iudei*. Preces *Resurrexit Dominus. Surrexit Dominus de sepulchro. Crucem sanctam subiit. Dicite in nationibus. In resurrectione tua, Christe*. Collecta *Deus, qui hodierna die*. Alia *Gregem tuum*. Deinde pulsetur ad Matut*inum*. Interim paratur Sepulchrum. Visitatur post iii responsorium.

MS 2402, of the eleventh century, contains a confused version of the *De Divinis Officiis* of Amalarius, in the midst of which (fol. 82ᵛ–83ᵛ) is a monastic *ordo* for Holy Saturday and Easter morning. Wilmart infers that this *ordo* represents the custom of the ninth or tenth century.

Page 136, note 2. In the *Liber de Officiis Ecclesiasticis* of Jean d'Avranches the *Depositio* and *Elevatio* are described as follows:

⟨DEPOSITIO CRUCIS⟩[1]

Quo ⟨*i.e.* Adoratio Crucis⟩ peracto, Crucifixus, in commemoratione sanguinis et aquæ fluentis de latere Redemptoris, vino et aqua lavetur, de quo post sacram communionem chorus bibat et populus. Post responsorium *Sicut ovis ad occisionem*, cantando, ad ⟨locum⟩ aliquem deferant in modum Sepulcri compositum, ubi recondatur usque in diem Dominicum. Quo collocato, antiphona *In pace in idipsum*, et responsorium *Sepulto Domino*, cantetur.

⟨ELEVATIO CRUCIS⟩[2]

Decima hora noctis pauci clerici induti veniant, et Crucifixum cum incenso et thymiamate levantes, antiphonamque *Surrexit Dominus de sepulchro* ⟨cantantes⟩, loco suo honorifice constituant. Post cunctis campanis sonanti-bus, januas ecclesiæ aperiant, et Matutinas incipiant.

Page 136, note 4. With the *Depositio* from Durham may be associated the *Depositio* and *Elevatio* from Rouen, Bibl. de la Ville, MS 253, Ordin. Fiscannense sæc. xiv, fol. 44ʳ, 53–54ʳ, published by Young, *Harrowing of Hell*, pp. 902–3. The *Depositio* of Fécamp is attached directly to the *Adoratio Crucis*.

Page 140, note 1. The distinction between *Imago Crucifixi* and *Imago Resurrectionis* is well explained and illustrated by Brooks, *Sepulchre*, pp. 37–40.

---

[1] Migne, *P.L.*, cxlvii, 51–2.
[2] *Id.*, cxlvii, 53. For the parallel passages from Montpellier MS H. 304, see Delamare, pp. 34, 38–9.

See also Feasey, *Ceremonial*, pp. 164–5. Concerning the *Imago Resurrectionis* see also H. B. Walters, *The Churchwardens' Accounts of the Parish of Worfield* (no date or place of publication: British Museum 04705. bb. 1), p. 15, where is recorded a payment of 20 pence 'pro ymagine resurrectionis'. In regard to large effigies of this sort L. G. Bolingbroke writes as follows in *Norfolk Archaeology*, xi (1892), 335:

'We also meet with numerous entries relating to the setting up of the Easter Sepulchre. A wooden sepulchre or tomb would be brought into the church, and placed on the north side of the chancel on Good Friday, and watched until Easter Day, when, by means of pulleys, an image of the Saviour, which had been previously placed inside, was raised from the tomb, and set up, with great reverence, by the officiating priests in the chancel.'

See also *Bulletin archéologique du Comité des Travaux historiques*, 1886, p. 86, for the following entry from an inventory of 1557 from the Collegiate Church of St Omer: 'Une imaige de bois paincte, *Domini resurgentis*, couvert d'une toille.'

Page 140, note 2. With the texts from Moosburg may be associated the following *Depositio* from Munich, Staatsbibl., MS lat. 24882, Brev. Andecense sæc. xv, fol. 269^v, previously edited by Young, *Dramatic Associations*, pp. 80–1:

⟨Depositio Crucis⟩

Communione expleta, dicantur Uespere submissa uoce. Psalmi *Confitebor*, cum reliquis. Deinde sequitur psalmus *Magnificat*; quo finito, dicitur versus *Proprio filio suo non*. Si uero quis interfuerit sepulture, peracto officio sepulture Crucifixi, tunc sub silencio circa Sepulchrum leguntur Vespere, et claunduntur cum versu *In pace factus est locus eius, et in Syon habitacio eius*. Deinde Sepulchro preparato et decenter ornato, sint inprompto tria thuribula cum incensu, thure, mirra, et thimiamate, et quatuor candele ardentes. Et pontifex siue prespiter cum alijs ministris et sacerdotibus portent Ymaginem Crucifixi uersus Sepulchrum lugubri uoce cantantes responsorium *Ecce quomodo moritur iustus*. Versus *In pace factus*. Responsorio finito, collocetur in Sepulchro et lintheaminibus et sudario cooperiatur Deinde lapis superponatur. Quo facto, clerus inponat ista responsoria: *Sepulto Domino*. Versus *Ne forte*. Responsorium *Recessit pastor*. Versus *Ante cuius*. Quibus finitis, dicatur versus *In pace factus est locus eius*. Quo uersu omnes sequentes hore claunduntur.[1]

Here may be mentioned also the following texts of the *Depositio* and *Elevatio*: Oxford, Bodl., MS Canonici Liturg. 325, Ordin. Benedictinum sæc. xiii, fol. 78^r, published by Young, *Dramatic Associations*, pp. 78–9; Munich, Staatsbibl., MS lat. 23068, Brev. Mosburgense sæc. xiv, fol. 291^v, published by Young, p. 80; Munich, *ibid.*, MS lat. 12301, Brev. Raitenbuchense anni 1431, fol. 88^r, 90^r, published by Young, pp. 81–2; Prague, Veřejná a Universitní Knihovna, MS XIII. E. 14d, Ordin. Pragense sæc. xiv, fol. 73^r, published by Brooks, *Sepulchre*, p. 105. The following rubrics from Munich, Staatsbibl., MS lat. 14765, Consuetudines Sigiberti Abbatis sæc. xi-xii, fol. 89^v, 92^r–92^v have been previously edited by Albers, *Consuetudines*, ii, 99, 102:

---

[1] Followed by the rubric *Ad Completorium*. Concerning the *Visitatio Sepulchri* from this   MS see below, p. 637. The MS contains no *Elevatio*.

⟨Depositio Crucis⟩[1]

Vespera finita, exuentibusque ceteris ad lauandos pedes, secretarius accipiens crucem una cum sociis suis cum honore et tremore deferat ad locum sepulture. Peractisque omnibus secundum consuetudinem, eant lauare pedes, induantque nocturnales.

⟨Elevatio Crucis⟩[2]

Nocte sacra Resurrectionis Dominice appropinquante hora matutinali, custos, conuocatis adiutoribus suis, cum incenso reuerenter uisitans Sepulchrum eleuet Crucem, erigatque in locum vbi iugiter stare solet, dimisso lintheamine in loco Sepulchri. Dehinc accensis luminaribus, illuminataque ecclesia, sonetur classis sicut in die Natalis Domini. Post ternas orationes cantent quindecim psalmos sub silentio, et stent in choro sicut stant ad Missam: uidelicet, priores contra altare. Omnes vero qui in hac sanctissima nocte aliquid cantare uel legere aut antiphonas | debent pronuntiare sint vestiti. Ita autem pulsentur Matutine ut ad terciam lectionem incipiat dies apparere. Indutis illis, sonentur omnia signa.

The following are from St Florian, Stiftsbibl., MS XI. 434, Liber Benedictionum Florianensis sæc. xv. The *Depositio* (fol. 161ʳ–164ᵛ) is printed by Mühlbacher, pp. 385–6, from whom I reprint. The *Elevatio* (fol. 164ᵛ–165ʳ) is printed by Mühlbacher, pp. 386–7, and by Franz, *St Florian*, p. 195, from the latter of whom I reprint.

⟨Depositio Crucis⟩[3]

Deinde[4] portetur Crucifixus in Sepulchrum:

Ecce quomodo moritur iustus, et nemo percipit[5] corde; viri iusti tolluntur et nemo considerat; a facie iniquitatis ablatus est iustus, et erit in pace memoria eius. Versus: *In pace factus est locus eius, et in Syon habitacio eius. Et erit.*

Recessit pastor noster, fons aque vive, ad cuius transitum sol obscuratus est, nam et ille captus est qui captiuum tenebat primum hominem; hodie portas mortis et seras pariter Salvator noster disrupit. Versus: *Ante cuius conspectum mors fugit, ad cuius vocem mortui resurgunt; videntes autem eum porte mortis confracte sunt. Hodie.*
Psalmus: *Voce mea.*
Hic superponitur lapis cum responsorio:

Sepulto Domino, signatum est monumentum, volventes lapidem ad hostium monumenti, ponentes milites qui custodirent illud. Versus: *Ne forte veniant discipuli eius et furentur eum, et dicant plebi: Surrexit a mortuis.* ⟨Versus:⟩ *In pace factus est locus eius, et habitacio eius in ⟨Syon⟩.*

⟨Elevatio Crucis⟩[6]

In sancta nocte ante pulsacionem Matutinarum clam surgitur, et a senioribus summa reuerencia Crucifixus cum psalmis *Domine, quid multiplicati*, psalmo *Domini est terra*, psalmo *Domine, probasti me* ⟨uisitatur⟩.[7] Deinde excipitur de

---

[1] Munich MS lat. 14765, fol. 89ᵛ.

[2] Munich MS lat. 14765, fol. 92ʳ–92ᵛ. For the *Visitatio Sepulchri* from this manuscript see above, p. 263.

[3] St Florian MS XI. 434, fol. 161ʳ–164ᵛ.

[4] Vespers immediately precedes.

[5] percipit] pepercit (MS).

[6] St Florian MS XI. 434, fol. 164ᵛ–165ʳ.

[7] Franz supplies the word *uisitatur*.

Sepulcro cum responsorio *Surrexit pastor bonus, qui posuit animam suam pro ouibus suis, et pro suo grege mori dignatus est, alleluia, alleluia, alleluia.* Submissa uoce ad summum altare defertur, ibi dicta oracione *Deus qui hodierna die unigenitum.*[1]

The following are from Klosterneuburg, Stiftsbibl., MS 590, Brev. Claustroneoburgense sæc. xiv. The *Depositio* (fol. 296ᵛ) has, I think, not been published before. The *Elevatio* (fol. 299ᵛ) is represented in the variants of Pfeiffer, p. 16.

⟨DEPOSITIO CRUCIS⟩[2]

Illo die post communionem prelatus cum clero et ministris portantibus thuribula et candelas ardentes procedant ad locum aptum ubi positum est Sepulchrum, portantes Crucifixum et cantantes humili uoce hec responsoria: *Ecce quomodo moritur iustus.* Versus *In pace factus est.* Item responsorium *Recessit pastor.* Versus *Ante cuius conspectum.* Hec duo responsoria cantantes lignum Crucis mundis lintheis inuoluant, et in Sepulchrum ponant. In aliquibus ecclesiis corpus apponitur. Item cum hoc responsorio *Sepulto Domino*, lapidem benedictum superponant. Thurificant et aspergant et abeant. Et iuxta Sepulchrum sub silencio tantum psalmos ad Vesperas dicant.

⟨ELEVATIO CRUCIS⟩[3]

In sancta nocte, antequam sonentur Matutine, prelatus aliquibus sibi adiunctis Corpus Dominicum et Crucem de Sepulchro tollant, et ad summam aram deferant, adolentes et aspergentes ea, et cantantes sub silencio responsorium *Surrexit pastor.* Versus *Surrexit Dominus*; deinde hos psalmos dicentes: *Conserua me.* Psalmus *Domine, probasti.* Sequitur versus *Surrexit Dominus de sepulchro, alleluia, qui pro nobis. Dominus uobiscum.* Oratio *Deus, qui hodierna die per unigenitum tuum eternitatis.* Deinde antequam ad Matutinas pulsetur, omnes campane ter compulsentur.[4]

Here may be cited also the *Depositio* and *Elevatio* from a lost *ordinarium* of the thirteenth century recorded in vol. lvi of the Fonteneau MSS at Poitiers, and printed therefrom in *Revue Mabillon*, ix (1913–4), 392–4.

Page 142, note 6. In connexion with the texts from Treves may be mentioned the following: Clermont-Ferrand, Bibl. de la Ville, MS 63, Miss. Claromontense sæc. xiv, fol. 32ᵛ, published by Young, *Dramatic Associations*, p. 84; *Breuiarium Frisingense*, Venice, 1516, fol. 194ᵛ, 196ᵛ–197ʳ, reprinted by Young, *op. cit.*, pp. 84–5; Munich, Staatsbibl., MS lat. 11768, Brev. Frisingense sæc. xv, fol. 73ʳ, 75ᵛ–76ʳ, published by Brooks, *Sepulchre*, pp. 99–100; Munich, *ibid.*, MS lat. 12635, Ordin. Ranshofenense sæc. xiii, pp. 56, 59, published by Young, *op. cit.*, pp. 87–8; Munich, *ibid.*, MS lat. 26947, Ordin. Ratisbonense sæc. xv, fol. 117ᵛ, 120ᵛ–121ʳ, published by Young, *op. cit.*, pp. 88–9; Oxford, Bodl., MS Misc. Liturg. 202, Brev. monasticum sæc. xiii, fol. 71ᵛ–72ʳ, published by Young, *Harrowing of Hell*, p. 899; Munich *ibid.*, MS lat. 5546, Brev. Diessense sæc. xv, fol. 147ʳ, 150ᵛ–152ʳ, published by Young, *op. cit.*, pp. 906–9; Munich, *ibid.*, MS lat. 5349, Brev. Chiemense sæc. xv, fol. 195ʳ–195ᵛ, 197ᵛ–198ʳ, published by Young, *Observations*, pp. 343,

---

[1] Followed by the rubric *In uisitatione sepuleri*, introducing the *Visitatio Sepulchri* printed above, p. 366.

[2] Klosterneuburg MS 590, fol. 296ᵛ.

[3] *Id.*, fol. 299ᵛ.

[4] Followed by the rubric *Inuitatorium*.

351–4; *Breuiarium . . . secundum chorum Patauiensis ecclesie*, Venice, 1517, fol. 138ʳ, 140ʳ. Rome, Bibl. Vatic., MS lat. 9210, Brev. Passaviense sæc. xv, fol. 100ᵛ, published by Young, *Some Texts*, p. 313; Padua, Bibl. Capit., MS S, Ordin. Patavinense sæc. xiii, foꞌ. 94ᵛ, 98ʳ, printed below, p. 617. The following texts are from an Indersdorf breviary of the fifteenth century (Munich, Staatsbibl., MS lat. 7691):

⟨Depositio Crucis⟩[1]

Antequam populus recedat, duo sacerdotes induti casulis rubri coloris, qui et ante *Popule meus* cantauerunt, prelato immediate sequente similiter in casula sua, et ministris in albis portantibus reliquias sanctorum precedentibus, Ymaginem Saluatoris portent | ad sepeliendum, vna vice infra totam ecclesiam circueundo conuentu processionaliter cum accensis candelis precedente et cum depressa ac lugubri uoce cantante responsorium *Ecce quomodo moritur iustus*, cum responsorio *Recessit pastor*. Quibus finitis, locetur Ymago in Sepulchrum, et statim cantor imponit responsorium *Sepulto Domino*, absque versu, postea dicto versu ab omnibus, videlicet versu *In pace factus est locus eius*. Et percussa tabula ad Vesperas, conuentus per duos choros legat Vesperas circa Sepulchrum. Et sacrista aquam benedictam cum incensu procuret, et reliquias sanctorum accipiat a ministris, et ponat in Sepulchrum coram Ymagine Saluatoris. Sub *Magnificat* uero aepergatur Sepulchrum et thurificetur a prelato. Et psalmo *Miserere mei, Deus* a prostratis dicto, subiungant versum *In pace factus est locus*. Deinde dominus prelatus dicat *Domine uobiscum*. Oratio *Da nobis, quesumus, Domine, locum sepulture*. Completis omnibus, postquam fratres ad cellas redierint, sacrista per se uel per alium ob memoriam dominice exspirationis faciat fieri pulsum ad tabulas in loco quem superior deputauerit propter indulgentias ad hoc datas.

⟨Elevatio Crucis⟩[2]

In sancta nocte Pasce surgant fratres, et lotis manibus et accensis candelis, cum summa reverencia accedant ad Sepulchrum Domini et dicant ibi psalmum *Domine, quid multiplicati*, sine *Gloria Patri*, et psalmum *Miserere mei, Deus, miserere mei, quoniam in te confidit*. Et postea *Kyrie eleyson, Christe eleyson, Kyrie eleyson*. *Pater Noster*. Versus *Exurge, Domine, adiuua nos*. Versus *Domine, Deus uirtutum, conuerte nos*. Versus *Foderunt manus meas et pedes meos*. Versus *Domine, exaudi orationem*. Oratio *Da nobis, quesumus, Domine, locum sepulture*. Thurificata et aspersa Ymagine Crucifixi, dominus prelatus | sumat ipsam Ymaginem vna cum duobus senioribus cum summa reuerencia et portent ad chorum ante summum altare cantantes humili ac mediocri voce antiphonam *Christus resurgens ex mortuis*. Versus *In resurrecione tua, Christe*, cum oratione *Deus, qui nos resurreccionis dominice*, et cetera. Quibus finitis, dominus prelatus prior accedat ad Ymaginem Crucifixi eam osculando; deinde decanus et communiter secundum ordinem. Postea statim pulsentur terrores ad Mat*utinum*.

At the end of this version of the *Elevatio* occurs the interesting term *terrores*,

---

[1] Munich MS lat. 7691, pp. 113–4, now first printed.

[2] Munich MS lat. 7691, pp. 119–20, previously edited by Young, *Harrowing of Hell*, pp. 904–5.

meaning a somewhat complicated and animated ringing of church bells on a festal occasion.[1]

Page 143, note 5. With the texts from Aquileia may be associated the following from Paris, Bibl. Nat., MS lat. 9486, Rituale Romaricense sæc. xii, fol. 41ʳ–42ʳ, previously edited by Young, *Observations*, pp. 341–2, and Young, *Dramatic Associations*, p. 92:

⟨DEPOSITIO CRUCIS ET HOSTIÆ⟩

Postea[2] uadant cum candelis ardentibus et incensu | ad locum Sepulchri, et inponant Crucem cum Eucharistia. In eundo cantetur responsorium *Ecce quomodo moritur iustus, et nemo percipit corde; et uiri iusti tolluntur, et nemo considerat; a facie iniquitatis oblatus est iustus, et erit in pace memoria eius.* Versus *In pace factus est locus eius, et in Sion habitacio eius. Et erit.* Responsorium *Recessit pastor noster, fons aque uiue, ad cuius transitum sol obscuratus est, nam et ille captus est qui captiuum tenebat primum hominem; hodie portas mortis et seras pariter Saluator noster disrupit.* Versus *Ante cuius conspectum mors fugit, ad cuius uocem mortui resurgunt; uidentes autem eum porte mortis confracte sunt. Hodie.* Imposita autem Cruce, cantentur hee antiphone. Antiphona *In pace in idipsum dormiam et requiescam.* Antiphona *Caro | mea requiescet in spe.* Sudario superposito, cantetur responsorium *Sepulto Domino, signatum est monumentum, uoluentes lapidem ad hostium monumenti, ponentes milites qui custodirent eum.* Versus *Ne forte uenient discipuli eius et furentur eum, et dicant plebi: Surrexit a mortuis. Ponentes.* Sequuntur Uespere[3] sub silentio.

It will be convenient to have here also the following version of the *Elevatio* from Munich, Staatsbibl., MS lat. 226, Rationale Officiorum Divinorum Augustense sæc. xi–xii, fol. 10ʳ, previously edited by Young, *Dramatic Associations*, pp. 96–7:

⟨ELEVATIO CRUCIS ET HOSTIÆ⟩

In ipsa nocte, mattutina luce appropinquante, custodes ecclesie cum sacerdotibus maturius ante alios surgentes conueniant in ecclesiam. Et lotis manibus, cum cereis duobus et thuribulis et aqua benedicta reuerenter, quasi secreto, procedant ad locum vbi Crux et Corpus Domini in sexta feria fuerant tumulata. Aspersa autem et thurificata Cruce, maior inter sacerdotes reuerentissime tollat calicem cum Corpore Domini; ceteri uero Crucem portent. Sindone qua fuit cooperta in ipso loco relicta, et luminibus, ne locus despectus uideatur, precedentibus cereis et incenso portent illam ad altare ubi officium est peragendum submissa uoce cantantes responsorium *Surrexit pastor bonus qui posuit animam,* cum versu *Surrexit Dominus de sepulchro.* Sequitur oratio *Deus, qui unigenitum.* Et cooperiatur Crux de linteo mundo. Calix autem cum Corpore Domini reponatur in principali altare donec alicui detur ad consumendum. Quo facto, revertantur in chorum, et omnes mutua caritate se[4] invicem osculentur. Et dicat prior *Surrexit Christus.* Respondent *Gaudeamus omnes.* Et statim compulsentur omnia signa sollemnissime ad excitandum et conuocandum; et interuallo modico facto, bina et bina signa morosius pulsentur; et in fine illorum rursus compulsetur. Et imponat sacerdos tonali voce *Domine, labia mea aperies.*

---

[1] See N. C. Brooks, in *Modern Language Notes*, xl (1925), 76–9; Feasey, *Ceremonial*, p. 241.

[2] Preceded by the Adoration of the Cross.

[3] Uespere] uespera (MS).

[4] se] si (MS).

Of especial interest in this text is the rubric *Calix autem cum Corpore Domini reponatur in principali altare donec alicui detur ad consumendum.* This seems to answer the question—about which there has been some doubt—as to the final disposition of the Host used in the ceremonies of the sepulchre.[1] At Augsburg, at least, it appears to have been used for Communion. With the present series may be listed also the following texts: Harlem, Museum, MS 258, Grad. Harlemense (?) sæc. xiii, fol. 44^v, published by Young, *op. cit.*, p. 95; Klosterneuburg, Stiftsbibl., MS 629, Ordin. Claustroneoburgense sæc. xv, fol. 102^r– 103^r, published by Pfeiffer, p. 16, and reprinted by Young, *op. cit.*, pp. 95–6; Bayeux, MS 121 (bibliography and texts by Young, *op. cit.*, pp. 101–3); Paris, Bibl. de l'Arsenal, MS 279, Brev. Cadomense sæc. xiii, fol. 200^r–200^v, published by Young, *Harrowing of Hell*, p. 901; Cassel, Landesbibl., MS Theol. 2°.99, Ordin. Fredeslariense sæc. xv (texts unpaginated), published by Brooks, *Sepulchre*, p. 100.

Page 145, note 4. With the texts from Sarum may be listed the following: York versions printed from a *Manuale* of the year 1509, in *Surtees Society*, lxiii (1875), 163–4, 170–4, and reprinted by Young, *Dramatic Associations*, pp. 98–9; Exeter texts from a fourteenth-century *Ordinale* published by J. N. Dalton, in *Henry Bradshaw Society*, xxxvii, London, 1909, pp. 137, 138–9, and reprinted by Young, *op. cit.*, pp. 99–100; Munich, Staatsbibl., MS lat. 5545, Ordin. Diessense sæc. xv, fol. 19^v–20^v, published by Young, *op. cit.*, p. 124.

CHAPTER V

THE HARROWING OF HELL

Page 149, note 1. The subject of this chapter is treated in a special study by Young, *The Harrowing of Hell in Liturgical Drama*, in *Transactions of the Wisconsin Academy of Sciences, Arts, and Letters*, xvi, 2 (1909), 889–947, where bibliography is provided. Important additions are made in two monographs by Brooks: *Sepulchre*, pp. 42–3; *Sepulchrum Christi*, pp. 148–51. See also Kretzmann, pp. 116–33; Schmidt, pp. 18–25; Meyer, pp. 61–3, 99–104; Wilmart, pp. 36, 102–3; Stapper, *Feier*, pp. 87–8, 155; Pearson, ii, 295–7; Thiers, ii, 194, 201–2. Schmidt (p. 22) and Brinkmann (p. 139) are undoubtedly correct in their opinion that in its original form the *Elevatio* did not treat the Harrowing of Hell. Brinkmann feels sure that this theme did not enter the *Elevatio* until after it had been treated in the Easter plays which centre in the visit of the Marys to the empty tomb. For such plays see especially chapter xiv above. The place of the theme of the *Descensus* in the vernacular drama is treated by Wülcker, pp. 60–71.

Page 152, note 2. With the *Depositio* and *Elevatio* from Magdeburg (Berlin MS 113) may be associated the following: *Breuiarium Horarum Canonicarum secundum veram rubricam Archiepiscopatus Pragensis*, Venice, 1517,

---

[1] Chambers (ii, 38) suggests that it may have been consumed in the *Peregrinus* play of Easter Monday. See above, pp. 455–6.

fol. 199ᵛ, 270ᵛ, reprinted by Young, *Dramatic Associations*, p. 86; Munich, Staatsbibl., MS lat. 14183, Ordin. Sancti Emmerammi Ratisbonensis sæc. xv, fol. 47ᵛ–48ʳ, 50ᵛ, published by Young, *op. cit.*, pp. 109–10; Wolfenbüttel, Herzogliche Bibl., MS Aug. 84. 2, Ordin. Havelbergense sæc. xv, fol. 21ᵛ, 23ʳ, published by Brooks, *Sepulchre*, p. 102; Treves, Stadtbibl., MS 1635, Ordin. Sancti Maximini prope Treviris sæc. xv, fol. 78ʳ–78ᵛ, 79ʳ–79ᵛ, published by Brooks, *op. cit.*, pp. 107–8; Brussels, Bibl. Royale, MS 4860, Process. Romanum sæc. xvi, fol. 93ʳ, published by Brooks, *op. cit.*, pp. 96–7; Münster, Bibl. Capit., MS 4, Ordin. Monasteriense sæc. xiii, fol. 77ʳ, 78ʳ, published by Stapper, *Feier*, pp. 153, 155.

Page 155, note 2. With the *Depositio* and *Elevatio* from Eichstätt may be associated, for general convenience, the following: the several texts from Strassburg printed, with bibliography, by Young, *Dramatic Associations*, pp. 39–43; and by Wilmart, pp. 31, 102–3; the texts from Meissen reprinted, with bibliography, by Young, *op. cit.*, pp. 106–9; the *Depositio* and *Elevatio* of the fourteenth century from Essen published by Arens, pp. 57–8, 71–3, and reprinted, in part, by Brooks, *Sepulchre*, pp. 97–8; Bamberg, Staatsbibl., MS lit. 118 (Ed. I. 19) Ordin. Bambergense sæc. xvi, fol. 62ᵛ–63ʳ, 66ʳ–67ʳ, published by Brooks, *op. cit.*, pp. 92–3.

Page 157, note 3. With the texts from Munich MS lat. 12018 may be associated the following: Berlin, Staatsbibl., MS theol. lat. qu. 87ᵇ, Brev. Berolinense sæc. xvi, fol. 28ʳ–29ʳ, 33ʳ–34ʳ, published by Müller, *Statuten*, pp. 299–302, 312–4; Bamberg, Staatsbibl., MS lit. 119 (Ed. VI. 3), Brev. Ecclesiæ Collegiatæ Hallensis anni 1532, fol. 94ʳ–94ᵛ, 97ʳ–97ᵛ, published by Müller, *ibid.*, pp. 299–302, 312–4, and by Brooks, *Sepulchre*, pp. 101–2. For a summary of the relationship of these two manuscripts see Brooks, *Sepulchrum Christi*, pp. 151–3.

Page 160, note 2. The hymn *Ad cænam agni* (Chevalier, *R.H.*, no. 110) is printed as follows in *A.H.*, ii, 46:

1. Ad cœnam agni providi
   et stolis albis candidi,
   post transitum maris rubri
   Christo canamus principi.

2. Cujus corpus sanctissimum
   in ara crucis torridum,
   cruore ejus roseo
   gustando vivamus Deo.

3. Protecti Paschæ vespere
   a devastante angelo,
   erepti de durissimo
   Pharaonis imperio.

4. Jam Pascha nostrum Christus est,
   qui immolatus agnus est,
   sinceritatis azyma
   caro ejus oblata est.

5. O vere digna Hostia,
   per quem fracta sunt tartara,
   redempta plebs captivata
   redit ad vitæ præmia.

6. Cum surgit Christus tumulo,
   victor redit de barathro,
   tyrannum trudens vinculo,
   ⟨et reserans paradisum⟩.

7. Quæsumus, auctor omnium,
   in hoc paschali gaudio
   ab omni mortis impetu
   tuum defende populum.

8. Gloria tibi, Domine,
   qui surrexisti a mortuis,
   cum Patre et Sancto Spiritu
   in sempiterna sæcula.

Page 163, note 1. For its bearing upon the dramatic ceremonies in St Gall MS 448 may be quoted the following from Clark, pp. 208–9: 'In order to carry out the reformation of his monastery, ⟨Abbot⟩ Eglolf summoned six monks from Hersfeld (Hirschfeld) in Hessen. In 1432 these monks completed an *Ordinarium* for use at St Gall, copying it, with a few slight modifications, from a Hirschfeld original. The *Ordinarium* gives a version of the *Quem quæritis.* . . . As the Hirschfeld monks quarrelled with Abbot Eglolf and took their departure in 1440, many of their innovations disappeared with them.' See also I. von Arx, *Geschichten des Kantons St Gallen*, ii, St Gall, 1811, pp. 247–9; Brooks, *Neue Osterfeiern*, p. 310. Pages 50–139 of St Gall MS 448 contain a monastic *ordinarium* under this heading (p. 50): *In nomine Domini, Amen. Incipit registrum secundum ordinem et chorum monasterii Sancti Galli.* Over the words *Sancti Galli* a later hand, of the fifteenth century, has written *hirsfeldensium.* It is to be inferred that St Gall MS 448, pp. 50–139, is the *ordinarium* referred to by Clark; and that after the Hersfeld monks departed, the heading was changed to indicate that this book no longer represented the custom of St Gall, but was that of Hersfeld. Presumably, therefore, the sepulchre ceremonies printed above were in use at St Gall for only a short period during the first half of the fifteenth century. With respect to these matters the description of the manuscript by G. Scherer (*Verzeichniss der Handschriften der Stiftsbibliothek von St Gallen*, Halle, 1875, p. 147) is inadequate.

Page 168, note 1. The presence of two versions of the *Elevatio* in MS Rawlinson Liturg. d. iv. is quite exceptional. The *Depositio* (fol. 68ᵛ–70ʳ) and the first *Elevatio* (fol. 85ᵛ–86ᵛ) are found in the normal place in the sequence of ceremonies according to the liturgical seasons. In a supplement (of the same period, and probably by the same hand) are found a second *Elevatio* (fol. 127ᵛ–130ʳ) and a *Visitatio Sepulchri* (fol. 130ʳ–132ʳ). The same *Visitatio Sepulchri*, from the same church, is found in Archbishop Marsh's Library, Dublin, MS Z. 4. 2. 20 (*olim* v. 3. 2. 10). In regard to these texts of the *Visitatio Sepulchri* see above, pp. 347 sqq. With the texts from MS Rawlinson Liturg. d. iv, printed above, may be associated the printed *Elevatio* of the year 1505 from Hereford edited by W. H. Frere and L. E. G. Brown, *The Hereford Breviary (Henry Bradshaw Society*, xxvi), London, 1904, pp. 324–5, and reprinted by Young, *Dramatic Associations*, pp. 111–2; and the following texts from *Obsequiale siue Benedictionale secundum consuetudinem ecclesie . . . Ratisponensis*, Nuremberg, 1491, fol. 79ᵛ–81ᵛ, 108ʳ–110ᵛ, previously reprinted by Young, *op. cit.*, pp. 125–6, from defective copies in *Decreta*, iv, 432, 440, and now reprinted from the original:

⟨DEPOSITIO CRUCIS⟩[1]

Expleta autem communione fidelium, particule Corporis Christi, si que superfuerint, seruentur, et portentur in locum honestum, et cetera. Quibus omnibus peractis, sacerdos cum ministris tollat Crucifixum quod presentatum fuerat, et deferant ad Sepulchrum cantantes responsorium *Recessit pastor noster, fons aque viue ad cuius transitum sol obscuratus est, nam et ille captus est qui captiuum tenebat primum hominem; hodie portas mortis et seras pariter Saluator noster*

---

[1] *Obsequiale*, 1491, fol. 79ᵛ–81ᵛ.

disrupit. Versus: *Ante cuius conspectum mors fugit, ad cuius vocem mortui resurgent; videntes autem porte mortis confracte sunt. Hodie.* Vel loco illius canitur sequens responsorium: *Ecce quomodo moritur iustus, et nemo percipit corde; viri iusti tolluntur, et nemo considerat; a facie iniquitatis sublatus est iustus; et erit in pace memoria eius.* Versus: *In pace factus est locus eius, et in Syon habitatio eius. Et erit in pace.* Tunc locent Crucifixum in Sepulchrum, et flexis genibus legant Vesperas submissa voce.

⟨ELEVATIO CRUCIS⟩[1]

In sancta nocte Pasche poterit commemoratio Dominice Resurrectionis iuxta locorum consuetudinem obseruari. In ecclesia autem Ratisponensi sic obseruatur. Episcopus aut prepositus aut decanus siue senior canonicus indutus stola ante pulsum Matutinarum, congregato choro cum processione et duobus luminibus foribus ecclesie clausis, secretius tollat Sacramentum seu Crucifixum; et antequam tollat, dicantur psalmi flexis genibus et sine *Gloria patri,* videlicet: *O Domine quid multiplicati . . . benedictio tua.* Psalmus *Miserere mei, Deus . . . terram gloria tua.*[2] Psalmus *Domine, probasti me.* Queras feria sexta Paraceues in Vesperis. Sequitur *Kyrieleyson, Christeleyson, Kyrieleyson. Pater noster. Et ne nos.* Versus *Exurge, Domine, adiuua nos.* Versus *Foderunt manus meas et pedes meos. Dinumerauerunt omnia ossa mea. Domine exaudi.* Oratio *Da nobis, Domine, auxilium de tribulatione quod dedisti pro nobis precium magnum et quos mors Filii tui, Domini nostri, Ihesu Christi, redemit eorum vita te digne glorificet. Per eundem.* Finita collecta, aspergetur et thurificetur Crux, et portetur ad locum suum cum responsorio *Dum transisset*; media voce cantatur: *Dum transisset sabatum, Maria Magdalena et Maria Iacobi et Salome emerunt aromata, vt venientes ungerent Ihesum, alleluia, alleluia. Et valde mane vna sabatorum veniunt ad monumentum, orto iam sole. Ut.* Et antequam Crux in suum locum reponatur, tangatur porta ecclesie cum Cruce et dicatur versus[3] *Quis est iste rex glorie? Dominus fortis et potens, Dominus potens in prelio.* Finito responsorio, episcopus vel sacerdos dicat submissa voce versum *In resurrectione tua, Christe, alleluia, celum et terra letentur, alleluia.* Oratio *Deus, qui hodierna die per unigenitum tuum eternitatis nobis aditum, deuicta morte, reserasti, vota nostra que preueniendo aspiras etiam adiuando prosequere. Per eundem Christum.* Sequitur versus *Surrexit Dominus vere, alleluia; gaudeamus omnes, alleluia.* Finitis hys, incipiatur pulsus Matutinarum.

Page 176, note 1. The following from *Agenda Bambergensia,* Ingolstadt, 1587, pp. 489–90, has been previously reprinted by Young, *Dramatic Associations,* p. 114:

Quoniam Ecclesia Catholica in die sancto Parasceves Corpus Christi consecrare non solet, idcirco parochus sub sacro hodierno duas Hostias maiores consecret, quarum unam in Missa sumat, alteram vero in sequentem diem sumendam servet; eamque corporali involutam, peracto sacro, reverenter, præcedente lumine, et campanula tinniente, portet; atque recondat eo in loco ubi aliæ Hostiæ consecratæ asservari consueverunt. In ecclesiis porro maioribus, tertia quoque Hostia magna consecretur, quæ postridie in Sepul-

---

[1] *Obsequiale,* 1491, fol. 108ʳ–110ᵛ.
[2] These first two psalms are printed in full in the *Obsequiale.*
[3] For insertion here, the following is writ-

ten in ink at the bottom of the page: *Attolite portas, principes, vestras, et eleuamini porte eternales, et introibit rex glorie.*

chrum Domini posita, ibidem a populo Christiano usque ad tempus Dominicæ Resurrectionis adorari queat. Et hæc quoque Hostia cum prædicta
coniungatur et asservetur.

From this passage it appears that the Host placed in the sepulchre was
explicitly intended for adoration there. See Brooks, *Sepulchre*, pp. 45–6.

CHAPTER VI

LITERARY EMBELLISHMENTS OF THE LITURGY: TROPES

Page 178, note 1. The whole matter of the literary embellishment of the
authorized liturgy is treated by L. Gautier, *Histoire de la Poésie liturgique au
Moyen Âge: Les Tropes*, Paris, 1886. More recent treatments by G. M.
Dreves, or C. Blume, or Blume and H. M. Bannister in collaboration, are
found in *A.H.*, vii, 1–15; xx, 5–7; xlvii, 5–42; liii, pp. v–xxx; liv, pp. v–xix;
Catholic Encyclopedia, xii, 481–6; xv, 65–6. See also Blume, *Repertorium*,
pp. 26–31; Schubiger, *Sängerschule*, pp. 34–59; Moser, i, 101–26; Gröber,
ii, pt. i, 155–6, 325–9, 333–4; Wagner, pp. 247–312. As to the origin of the
word *trope* see Gautier, *Tropes*, pp. 49–60; Blume, in *A.H.*, xlvii, 18–20. The
word *tropus* derives from Greek τρόπος, and both words refer in some way
to the melody to which words are sung. Eventually *tropus* and *trope* came to
denote the words themselves, accompanied by the melody. The term *tropes*
is commonly used to designate both *the whole body* of unofficial embellishments
of the liturgy, and, more narrowly, all such embellishments *other than the ones
sung between the Alleluia and the gospel in the Mass*, these latter being called
sequences. Unless the context indicates the contrary, I use the term *trope*
always in the more inclusive sense. On this distinction and usage see Blume,
in *A.H.*, xlvii, 14–5. The use of the term *tropus*, or *trope*, in this chapter as
denoting *verbal additions to the liturgy*, is to be distinguished from the use of it
in the ninth century, and before, to denote a *mere melody* or a *figure of speech*.
See Gautier, *Tropes*, pp. 38–9, 141. With the controversy as to whether
sequences and tropes were derived ultimately from the Greek liturgy we
are not directly concerned. P. Wagner (pp. 251–2; and *Revue d'Histoire et de
Critique musicales*, ii [1902], 289–304) argues for a Greek origin; P. Aubry
(*id.*, ii [1902], 518–21) and Blume (*A.H.*, xlvii, 20; liii, p. xxvi) take the
opposing position. The particular body of tropes known as *sequences* have
been published in large numbers in *A.H.*, vii–x, xxxiv, xxxvii, xxxix, xl, xlii,
xliv, liii–lv. *Tropes*, in the narrower sense of the term, have been published
especially in *A.H.*, xlvii and xlix. For references to earlier publications in
this latter field see *A.H.*, xlvii, 27–37. For complete editions of two *troparia*
see W. H. Frere, ed., *The Winchester Troper (Henry Bradshaw Society*, viii),
London, 1894; C. Daux, ed., *Tropaire-Prosier de l'Abbaye Saint-Martin de
Montauriol (Bibliothèque liturgique*, ix), Paris, 1901.

Page 179, note 2. For general accounts (with bibliographies) of the Carolingian Renaissance, particularly in its effect upon arts and letters, see E. Lavisse, *Histoire de France*, ii, part i, Paris, 1903, pp. 342–55; Raby, pp. 154–201; Haskins, pp. 16–8; Paetow, pp. 392–4; Taylor, i, 207–38. For more detailed treatments see A. Hauch, *Kirchengeschichte Deutschlands*, ii, Leipzig, 1900, pp. 69–281; F. F. Leitschuh, *Geschichte der karolingischen Malerei*, Berlin, 1894; K. Künstle, *Die Kunst des Klosters Reichenau im ix. und x. Jahrhundert*, Freiburg, 1924; Maître, pp. 6–50; G. Kurth, *Les Origines de la Civilisation moderne*, ii, Paris, 1923, pp. 211–36, 282–303. In regard to Charlemagne's relations to the Church see J. de la Servière, *Charlemagne et l'Église*, Paris, 1904; Cabrol and Leclercq, i, 1072–92; iii, 807–25; Van Doren, pp. 39–69.

Page 182, note 1. In my brief sketch of the origin and development of sequences I follow chiefly the doctrine of C. Blume, *Vom Alleluja zur Sequenz*, in *Kirchenmusikalisches Jahrbuch*, xxiv (1911), 1–20. Blume's exposition here, and elsewhere (*A.H.*, xlvii, 12–5; liii, pp. v–xxx), is adequately and conveniently summarized by him in the article *Prose or Sequence*, in *Catholic Encyclopedia*, xii, 481–6, and is followed in the general sketches of Clark (pp. 173 sqq.) and Raby (pp. 210–19). Blume's treatment differs, in some details, from that of Gautier (*Tropes*, pp. 11–48, 61–7, 147–93) and Wagner (pp. 247–74). In regard to the sequences of Notker see J. Werner, *Notkers Sequenzen*, Aarau, 1901; Manitius, i, 355–6; Moser, i, 88–101. It must be admitted that those who expound the origin of the sequence are not very explicit as to the manner in which the *Alleluia* and its verse were sung.

Page 183, note 3. The authenticity of the Notkerian letter has been somewhat doubted by Blume (*A.H.*, liii, pp. xiii–xiv; liv, pp. xviii–xix; *Catholic Encyclopedia*, xii. 485–6). Most writers accept its genuineness. See especially W. Meyer, in *Abhandlungen der königlichen Gesellschaft der Wissenschaften zu Göttingen, Philologisch-Historische Klasse, Neue Folge*, xv, no. 3 (1914), 8; K. Strecker, *Neues Archiv der Gesellschaft für ältere deutsche Geschichtskunde*, xxxviii (1913), 60; P. von. Winterfeld, *id.*, xxv (1900), 386–9; P. von Winterfeld, in *Neue Jahrbücher für das klassische Altertum*, v (1900), 352; Gautier, *Tropes*, pp. 17–20; Wagner, p. 250; Clark, pp. 179–80; Meyer, *Fragmenta*, p. 171; Manitius, i. 355–6. In his earlier writing (*A.H.*, xlvii, 13–7) Blume himself speaks of it as genuine.

Page 188, note 1. The origin and nature of tropes—in the restricted meaning of this word—are fully discussed *passim* by Gautier, *Tropes*. Particularly useful is the account of Wagner, pp. 274–94. I am especially indebted to the treatment of C. Blume in *A.H.*, xlvii, 5–11, 15–27, which is adequately summarized in his article *Trope*, in *Catholic Encyclopedia*, xv, 65–6. Blume (*A.H.*, xlvii, 10) speaks of publishing a special study of tropes in a later volume of his *Hymnologische Beiträge*. See also Clark, pp. 192–5.

Page 197, note 4. I bring together here a few additional tropes and sequences which exhibit elements of dialogue. The following trope from Paris, Bibl. Nat., MS lat. 1139, fol. 62ʳ, has been previously printed by Gautier, *Tropes*, p. 172:

ALIUM

Benedicamus Domino. Deo gratias.

Benedicamus. *Angelus sedens ad sepulcrum et ecce tres mulieres qui querebant Dominum. Deo angelus dixit mulieribus: Quem queritis? Ihesum Nazarenum. Surrexit, non est hic* gracias.

Benedicamus Domino. Deo *dica⟨mus⟩*.

Benedicamus Domino. Deo *dicamus*.

Benedicamus Domino. Deo *⟨dicamus⟩*.

Benedicamus Domino.

Benedicamus Domino, *alleluia, alleluia*.

Benedicamus Domino.

The following sequence for Easter Week, from an eleventh-century source, is printed in *A.H.*, xl, 15, and, from other sources, by Young, *Easter Play*, pp. 55–6:

Quem quæritis, mulieres, ad sepulcrum Domini? Alleluia.
Iesum quærimus, et non invenimus ubi erat positus.
Si tu tuleris, hoc dicito mihi, ubi erat positus.
Cum fletu et stridore dentium ubi vadam? Eum tollam positum.
O quam gloriosus fuit ille mortuus!
O quam gloriosa erit vita ubi se revixerat!
Stabat angelus a dextris matris: 'Noli flere, regina cæli, quia mortuus fuerat et revixit?'
Si mihi non creditis, operibus credite et videte, in dextra Dei sedens.
Stella clara, lux magna, vitæ regem sedere Deo vidi.
Deo gratias, Deo gratias, quia surrexit leo fortis.
Deo gratias, Deo gratias, de magna tristitia revertimur in lætitia.
Deo gratias, Deo gratias; Amen dico vobis, Alleluia.

Another Easter sequence relevant here is the following, from a source of the eleventh or twelfth century, printed in *A.H.*, liii, 91–2, and in Young, *op. cit.*, pp. 56–7:

Ad sepulcri custodes descenderat angelus valde iam diluculo.
Mulieres veniunt invisendum sepulcrum, ad quas dixit angelus:
'Quem quæritis, mulieres, ad sepulcrum Domini?'
Responderunt et dixerunt cunctæ unanimiter:
'Iesum quærimus, et non invenimus ubi erat positus.
Si tu tuleris, dicito mihi ubi vadam; eum tollam Dominum.'
O quam gloriosus fuit ille mortuus!
O quam gloriosa erat vita ubi se revixerat!
Stabat angelus ad sepulcrum:
'Noli flere, Regina mundi, quia mortuus fuerat, et revixit.'
Deo gratias, Deo gratias, Deo gratias.
De magna tristitia vertit in lætitia.
Deo gratias, Deo gratias, Deo gratias.
Amen dico vobis, alleluia.

Dialogue is found also in the following sequence for the Annunciation printed, from sources of the tenth century and later, in *A.H.*, liii, 168–9:

1. Alleluia,

2a. Hac clara die turma
festiva dat præconia

2b. Mariam concrepando
symphonia nectarea,

3a. Mundi domina
quæ est sola
castissima virginum regina,

3b. Salutis causa,
vitæ porta
atque cæli referta gratia.

4a. Nam ad illam sic nuntia
olim facta angelica:

4b. 'Ave, Maria, gratia
Dei plena per sæcula,

5a. Mulierum pia
agmina intra
semper benedicta,

5b. Virgo et gravida,
mater intacta,
prole gloriosa.'

6a. Cui contra Maria
hæc reddit famina:

6b. 'In me quomodo tua
iam fient nuntia?

7a. Viri novi nullam
certe copulam,

7b. Ex quo atque nata
sum incorrupta.'

8a. Diva missus ita
reddit adfata:

8b. 'Flatu sacro plena
fies, Maria,

9a. Nova efferens gaudia
cælo, terræ nati per exordia;

9b. Intra tui uteri claustra
portas, qui gubernat æthera,

10. Omnia qui dat tempora
pacifica.'

CHAPTER VII

DRAMATIC TROPES OF THE MASS OF EASTER

Page 201, note 2. Some of those who have discussed the dramatic trope *Quem quæritis in sepulchro* have misapprehended its relation to the authorized liturgy. Lange, for example (p. 19), regards it not as an interpolation or addition, but as an original element in the liturgy itself. In this view he is followed by P. Butler, in *Furnivall Miscellany*, p. 49.

Page 201, note 3. Virtually identical with the text from St Gall MS 484 is the following found *ibid.*, MS 381, Trop. Sangallense sæc. xi, p. 247:

ALITER[1]

Interrogatio: Quem queritis in sepulchro, Christicolae?
Responsio: *Ihesum Nazarenum crucifixum, o celicole.*
Non est hic, surrexit sicut predixerat; ite, nuntiate quia surrexit de sepulchro. Resurrexi.

Chevalier (*R.H.*, no. 16321) erroneously regarded this general form of trope as a 'sequence', in verse. C. Blume (*Repertorium*, p. 268) corrects him, declaring such a composition to be 'ein Tropus in rein prosaischem Gewande'.

Page 206, note 3. Similar to the version from Modena MS O. I. 7. are

[1] This text is one of a series of introit tropes.

texts in Paris, Bibl. Nat., MS lat. 9508, Miscellanea Liturgica sæc. xvii, fol. 179ʳ, printed by Young, *Easter Play*, pp. 20–1; in Bamberg, Staatsbibl., MS lit. 6 (Ed. III. 7), Grad. Bambergense sæc. x, fol. 94ʳ, published by Brooks, *Osterfeiern*, p. 52; and in Paris, Bibl. de l'Arsenal, MS 1169, Trop. Æduense anni 996–1024, fol. 18ᵛ–19ʳ, printed by Young, *op. cit.*, p. 21 (facsimile by Gautier, *Tropes*, p. 217). With these may be associated the following from Vienna, Nationalbibl., MS lat. 1888, Miscellanea Moguntina (?) sæc. x, fol. 197ʳ, now printed, I think, for the first time:

IN RESURRECTIONE DOMINI

Quem queritis in sepulchro, Cristicole?
Responsio: *Ihesum Nazarenum crucifixum, o celicole.*
Responsio: *Non est hic, surrexit sicut locutus est; ite, nunciate quia surrexit.*
　　　Alleluia, resurrexit Dominus, hodie resurrexit leo fortis, Christus filius Dei.
Antiphona: *Surrexit Dominus de sepulchro, qui pro nobis.*

In the manuscript this text is followed immediately by the rubric *De sancta Trinitate*. Since the nature of its attachment to the liturgy is not indicated, we have no assurance that this is a trope of the introit.

Page 209, note 1. Texts differing in no significant way from the one in Paris MS 1119 are given in variants by Young, *Easter Play*, p. 24, from the following MSS: Paris, Bibl. Nat., MS lat. 1120, Trop. Sancti Martini Lemovicensis sæc. xi, fol. 20ᵛ–21ʳ; *ibid.*, MS lat. 1121, Trop. Sancti Martialis Lemovicensis sæc. xi, fol. 11ᵛ–12ʳ; *ibid.*, MS. lat. 1084, Trop. Sancti Martialis Lemovicensis sæc. xi, fol. 64ᵛ–65ʳ; Huesca, Bibl. Capit., MS 4, Trop. Oscense sæc. xi–xii, fol. 124ʳ–124ᵛ. Here should be listed the similar, but fragmentary, texts found in Paris, Bibl. Nat., MS lat. 909, Trop. Sancti Martialis Lemovicensis sæc. xi, fol. 21ᵛ–22ʳ, and *ibid.*, Nouv. Acq., MS lat. 1871, sæc. xi, fol. 13ᵛ, mentioned by Young, *loc. cit.* The latter is printed by C. Daux, ed., *Tropaire-Prosier de l'Abbaye Saint-Martin de Montauriol* (*Bibliothèque liturgique*, ix), Paris, 1901, p. 15. The texts in Paris MSS 909, 1084, 1120, and 1121 are mentioned by Lange, nos. 13, 14, 11, and 12 respectively. With the texts above may be listed that in Paris, Bibl. Nat., MS lat. 779, Grad. Arletense sæc. xiii, fol. 36ʳ–36ᵛ, printed by Young, *op. cit.*, p. 27. For the sake of a small variation I print the following from Paris, Bibl. Nat., MS lat. 887, Trop. S. Martini(?) Lemovicensis sæc. xi, fol. 19ʳ, previously edited by Young, *op. cit.*, p. 25:

IN PASCA AD MISSAM

Quem queritis in sepulcro, o Christicole?
Iesum Nazarenum crucifixum,[1] *o celicole.*
Non est hic, surrexit sicut predixerat; ite, nunciate in Galileam, dicentes:
Alleluia, ad sepulcrum residens angelus nunciat resurrexisse Christum.
　　　En ecce completum est illud quod olim ipse per prophetam dixerat, ad Patrem taliter inquiens: Resurrexi.

The passage *ite, nunciate in Galileam* may be a defective copying of a sentence composed under the influence of *ite, nuntiate fratribus meis ut eant in Galilæam* of the Vulgate (Matt. xxviii, 10).

　　　[1] crucifixum] crucifisum (MS).

Page 210, note 3. Tropes similar to that printed from Verona MS 107 are found in the following places: Vich, Museo, MS 111, Trop. Ripollense sæc. xi–xii, fol. 2ʳ, printed by Young, *Easter Play*, p. 17; Rome, Vittorio Emanuele, MS 1343 (Sessor. 62), Trop. Nonantulense sæc. xi, fol. 28ᵛ, printed by Young, *op. cit.*, p. 18, and by Bartholomaeis, p. 518; Rome, Bibl. Casanatense, MS. 1741 (C.IV.2), Trop. Nonantulense sæc. xi, fol. 75ʳ–75ᵛ, printed by Young, *op. cit.*, p. 18, and by Bartholomaeis, p. 518.

Page 212, note 5. With the text from Paris, Bibl. Nat., MS lat. 1139 may be associated the following from Vich, Museo, MS 111, Trop. Ripollense sæc. xi–xii, fol. 2ʳ, published by Young, *Some Texts*, p. 308:

Versos

Vbi est Cristus, meus Dominus et filius excelsi? Eamus uidere sepulcrum.
Alleluia, ad sepulcrum residens angelus nunciat resurrexisse Cristum.
    En ecce completum est illud quod olim ipse per prophetam dixerat,[1] ad Patrem taliter inquiens: Resurrexi.

The text is immediately preceded by the words *Cristi hodierna*, which may be the incipit of an Easter sequence. See *A.H.*, vii, 42.

CHAPTER VIII

THE EASTER INTROIT TROPE IN TRANSITION

Page 223, note 5. With the text from Ivrea MS 60 may be associated the following from Zurich, Zentralbibl., Rheinau MS 97, Trop. Rheno-viense (Sangallense?) sæc. xi, pp. 16–7, previously edited by Brooks, *Easter Plays*, pp. 191–2, and by Young, *Easter Play*, p. 15:

In die Paschae

Interrogatio: *Quem queritis in sepulchro, Christicole?*
Responsio: *Ihesum Nazarenum crucifixum, o celicole.*
Interrogantes: *Non est hic, surrexit sicut predixerat; ite, nuntiate quia surrexit de sepulchro.*
Ad Missam: *Hodie processit leo fortis sepulchro, ob cuius uictoriam gaudebant celestes ministri; ideo et nos letemur canentes.* Resurrexi. *Principe inferni deuicto, claustris ac reseratis.* Et adhuc ⟨tecum sum⟩, alleluia. *A quo numquam recessi, licet in carne paruerim.* Posuisti ⟨super⟩ me. *Quem tu solus et solum genuisti, Deus ante secula.* Manum ⟨tuam⟩, alleluia. *Quia iussu tuo mortem degustaui.* Mirabilis ⟨facta⟩ est. *Cui nulla sapientia mundi est equanda.* Scientia ⟨tua⟩, alleluia. *Quod tali uictoria uictorem tumidum strauisti, alleluia.* ⟨Psalmus:⟩ Domine probasti ⟨me, et cognovisti me; tu cognovisti sessionem meam, et resurrectionem⟩ meam. *Qui me de morte tur|pi assumptum sedere tecum in gloria facis.* ⟨Gloria Patri, et Filio, et Spiritui Sancto; sicut erat in principio, et nunc, et semper, et in

---

    [1] dixerat] dixerad (MS).

sæcula sæculorum, ⟩ Amen. *Que angelis est ueneranda cunctis atque mortalibus.*
Resurrexi.

The rubric *Ad Missam*, separating the dialogue *Quem quæritis* from the introit
trope which follows, may possibly indicate that *Quem quæritis* was here used as
some sort of processional, detached from the introit. On the other hand,
what follows the rubric *Ad Missam* may be regarded as merely a continuation
of the trope which precedes.

Page 227, note 3. Generally similar to the procession from St Gall MS
387 are the versions from St Gall MSS 391 (Hartker) and 339, printed by
Young, *op. cit.*, pp. 51–3. In regard to further versions of the same sort in
St Gall MSS 374 and 378 see Young, *op. cit.*, p. 53. With these may be
associated the following from Rome, Bibl. Angelica, MS 123 (B. III. 18),
Trop. Bononiense(?) sæc. xi, fol. 214ʳ–214ᵛ, printed by Young, *op. cit.*,
32–3; Bartholomaeis, pp. 518:

Incipit Trophus in Diem Sanctum Pasche ad Introitum

Quem queritis in sepulchro, Cristicole?
Hiesum Nazarenum crucifixum, o celicole.
Non est hic, surrexit sicut locutus est; ite, nuntiate quia surrexit, dicentes:
Alleluia, alleluia, resurrexit Dominus.
　　Surrexit Cristus, iam non moritur; mors illi ultra non dominabitur, alleluia,
alleluia.
　　Resurrexit.
　　Sedit angelus.
Prosa: *Crucifixum Dominum laudate.*
　　Nolite.
　　Recordamini qualiter.
　　Nolite, usque *Alleluia.*
Prosa: *Suggestione angelica nutantia mulierum corda nauiter solidantur.*
Trophus: *Surrexit leo de tribu Iuda, quem impii suspenderunt in ligno.*
　　　　Monumenta hodie aperta sunt, et multa corpora sanctorum surrexe|runt;
　　　　dicite eia! Resurrexi.

The aggregation of liturgical antiphons and bits of troping found here
defies precise explanation, and is chiefly significant, perhaps, as showing the
liberties taken in the way of liturgical decoration. From the rubrics alone,
one would assume that this is merely an uncommonly elaborate trope of
the introit; but from the general content I infer that it is a processional for
use before Mass begins.

Page 231, note 3. What appears to be a performance of the *Visitatio
Sepulchri* after Lauds is described in the following extract from P. de Monsa-
bert, *Documents inédits pour servir à l'Histoire de l'Abbaye de Sainte-Croix de
Poitiers,* in *Revue Mabillon,* ix (1913–4), 393–4:

Tunc¹ veniat sacerdos indutus dalmatica in choro, et cantet evangelium
Maria Magdalena. Et alius sacerdos induatur alba et capa, et deferat incensum, et Angelus sit revestitus de alba et amicto. Post evang⟨elium⟩ dicat
sacerdos collect⟨am⟩ *Deus qui hanc sacratissimam.* Et post incipiat sacerdos

　　　¹ *Tunc* refers to the end of Easter Matins, after the last responsory.

Deus in adjutorium,[1] et *Alleluya, Alleluya, Alleluya, Alleluya. Dominus regnavit.*
Ad *Benedictus,* antiphona *Et valde. Benedicamus.* Angelus et abbatissa eant
in medio choro, et duo servientes retro illam, et dicant *Deus in adjutorium* (ter).
Capiceria debet dare unicuique cereum vel candelam, et illuminentur
tamdiu quod dicant *Laudate Dominum de cœlis.* Sacerdos clanculo defert
crucem ad Sepulcrum expectando ibi completionem Matutinarum.[2] Quibus
expletis, hoc modo agetur processio a toto conventu. Una earum in loco
Marie Magdalene incipiente *Venite, omnes populi,*[3] accedunt ad Sepulcrum
portantes luminaria. Finito iterum incipit Maria:

> *Ubi est Christus meus?*

Et Angelus respondit:

> *Scio quod Jesum.*

Maria:

> *Et respicientes.*

Quo finito, exeuntes de Sepulcro, iterum incipit Maria:

> *Ubi est Christus meus?*

Et Angelus respondit:

> *Scio quod Jesum.*

Maria:

> *Et respicientes.*

Quo finito, exeuntes de Sepulcro, iterum incipit Maria:

> *Heu nobis!*

Et hoc cantantes exeuntes per majorem portam ecclesiæ venientes ad
fenestram Sepulcri, quæ clausa est, tunc dicit Maria antiphonam:

> *Ardens est cor meum.*

Angelus respondit:

> *Mulier, quid ploras?*

At illa:

> *Tulerunt Dominum.*

Et iterum Angelus:

> *Nihil vobis est mirandum.*

Quo finito, operta[4] fenestra ab ipsa Maria, incensatur crux Domini et adoratur
ab omni plebe. Et tunc incipiente *Congratulamini,* revertuntur per aliam
portam ad Sanctum Michaëlem; et finito cantu, interrogantur ab Angelo:

> *O vos Christicolæ?*

Et clauso ostio et responso ab omnibus:

> *Quærimus hoc superi,*

dicit Angelus:

> *Non jacet hic.*

Et tunc Maria aperiat ostium, et dicat publica voce:

> *Surrexit Christus.*

Et omnes respondeant:

> *Deo gratias.*

Quo finito, stantes in medio ecclesiæ cantent *Salve, rex Sabbaoth.*[5] Inde
adoretur crux ab omnibus. Sacerdotes revestiti teneant cruces.[6]

---

[1] *Deus in adjutorium* marks the beginning of
Lauds.

[2] *Matutinarum* means, I take it, Laudes
(*Laudes Matutinæ*).

[3] For this Easter hymn see *A.H.,* xii, 28.

[4] operta [For *aperta?*]

[5] For this Easter hymn see *A.H.,* xi, 20.

[6] Here follows the *ordo* for Prime.

This text is communicated from the copy in vol. lvi of the Fonteneau MSS at Poitiers, from a lost *ordinarium* of the thirteenth century which once belonged to the monastery of the Holy Cross in that city. One hesitates to draw conclusions from a text which is of secondary authority, and which may not be free from misprints. The *Visitatio Sepulchri* here is unusual in all respects, as may be seen by comparison with the texts in chapters ix and x. In a breviary of the eleventh century from Silos (London, Brit. Mus., Add. MS 30848, fol. 125ᵛ) the *Visitatio* is found at the end of the *Processio ad Fontem* of Easter Vespers. But this arrangement arises, I think, merely from exigences of space in the MS. The text is printed below, p. 577. A confused and fragmentary version of the *Visitatio* which may have been designed for performance at None on Holy Saturday is found in Karlsruhe, Landesbibl., MS Geo. 1, Lib. resp. Sancti Georgii Villingensis sæc. xv, fol. 189ʳ, printed by Brooks, *New Texts*, pp. 465–6. In regard to a special modern version printed at Venice in 1736 for performance before Prime see below, p. 625.

Page 231, note 7. A longer passage from Durandus, containing the quotation given above, is found below, p. 658. In asserting that the *Visitatio* should be placed at the *Te Deum* of Easter Matins because this chant marks symbolically the moment of the Resurrection, Durandus is repeating an explanation which had been given earlier by Honorius of Autun (see Migne, *P.L.*, clxxii, 677) and Sicardus of Cremona (see *id.*, ccxiii, 346). In an Augsburg *ordinarium* of the eleventh or twelfth century the following gloss is entered opposite the *Te Deum* of Easter: Per *Te Deum laudamus*, quod alte cantatur, hora Resurrectionis signatur (Munich, Staatsbibl., MS. lat. 226, fol. 11ʳ). The view presented by Durandus is discussed by Duriez, pp. 474–8, and by Brinkmann, p. 112.

Page 233, note 8. The following *ordo*, from a service-book of the twelfth or thirteenth century, is reprinted from *Soissons Ritual*, pp. 110–1, where it follows immediately after the *Elevatio* and *Visitatio Sepulchri* which are reprinted above, p. 304:

Notandum uero quod ad similitudinem trium Mariarum, incensum hodie ad Sepulchrum tantum defertur in initio lectionum sic: incepto euangelio, decanus et ebdomadarius exeant de sacrario cum capis de pallio, clericulis precedentibus cum thuribulis et igne; presententque se episcopo in igne mittentes incensum, episcopo dante benedictionem. Quo facto, eant simul ad altare. Episcopus autem, accipiens thuribulum, offerat incensum sacrosancto altari, et decanus cum illo. Interea clericuli, elevatis cereis suis, teneant illos ante altare. Quo facto, episcopo in sede sua regresso, offerant incensum decanus et ebdomadarius. Postea cum cereis eant ad Sepulchrum illud offerre, clerico custode cum capa de pallio acerram cum incenso perferente. Quo facto, reuersi in chorum, cantori et succentori, ceterisque in ordine suo defertur. Processione presenti peracta, uicem secundam impleuimus; in fine Matutinarum, tertiam exsoluemus. Versus post *Te Deum* Episcopus: *Surrexit Dominus uere*. Chorus: *Et apparuit Symoni, alleluya*.

From the somewhat obscure wording here I infer that in the course of Easter Matins at Soissons the altar and sepulchre were censed three times: at the first lesson, at the second lesson, and at the end of the office. Presumably the third censing was that performed in the combined *Elevatio* and *Visitatio Sepulchri* mentioned above.

Page 236, note 5. In regard to tropes of the Canonical Office in general see above, p. 191. Since very few tropes of the last responsory of Easter Matins have been printed, one or two unpublished examples may appropriately be given here. The following is from Paris, Bibl. Nat., MS lat. 1338, Trop. S. Martialis Lemovicensis sæc. xi, fol. 130^v:

Responsorium: Dum transisset.

Et ualde mane *euntes mulieres cum aromata,*
  Flentesque quidem die sab⟨b⟩atorum, *et cernunt illic esse angelum custodem uultu splendido* orto.

This text is immediately followed by the rubric *Marciale*. Although I do not pretend to understand this text, I give it as an early example of some sort of trope of the third responsory. The next example is from Paris, Bibl. Nat., Nouvelles Acquisitions, MS lat. 718, Brev. Vivariense sæc. xiv, fol. 276^r:

Responsorium:[1] Dum transisset sabbatum, Maria Magdalene et Maria Iacobi et Salome emerunt aromata, ut uenientes ungerent Ihesum, alleluia, alleluia. Versus: Et ualde mane una sabbatorum ueniunt ad monumentum, orto iam sole.

Prosellus.

  Et ualde deuote properantes[2] *mulieres unanime.*[3]
Versus: *Mane una sabbatorum ueniunt ad monumentum.*
Versus: *Unguento optimo ungerent sepultum Christum Deum.*
Versus: *Nouerant quem querebant; non uidebant fulgentem.*
  Sole. Ut.
  Gloria *lux uera Christus surrexit de petra* Patri, et Filio, et Spiritui Sancto.
Sicut *Deus altissimus in excelso in celis* erat in principio, et nunc et semper.
Responsorium: Dum transisset.[4]

Texts somewhat similar to this are found in Paris, Bibl. Nat., MS lat. 1033, fol. 92^v, and MS lat. 1057, fol. 87^r. The following is from Paris, Bibl. Nat., MS lat. 1309, Brev. Gerundense sæc. xv, fol. 84^r–84^v:

Responsorium:[5] Et ualde mane una sabbatorum, alleluia, ueniunt ad monumentum, alleluia, orto iam sole, alleluia, alleluia. Versus: Mulieres emerunt aromata; summo diluculo ueniunt ad monumentum. *Post* Or⟨to⟩, Gloria, et iteratur responsorium.

Verbeta.

  Christus hodie surrexit ex tumulo, |
  victo zabulo, expugnato baratro.
  Una sabbati ueniunt summo iam diluculo
  sancte femine unguento satis cum mirifico;
  redeunt sed Christo non inuento.

---

[1] This is the twelfth responsory of the monastic form of Easter Matins. See above, p. 547.

[2] properantes] prosperantes (MS).

[3] unanime] hunanimes (MS).

[4] Followed immediately by the rubric *In Laudibus.*

[5] The third responsory.

Post Orto, Te Deum.

The most notable of the non-dramatic tropes found in this part of the liturgy is the following somewhat fantastic piece from Paris, Bibl. Nat., MS lat. 750, Brev. Meldense sæc. xiv, fol. 4ᵛ:

Responsorium:[1] Et ualde mane una sabbatorum ueniunt ad monumentum, orto iam sole, alleluia. Versus: Maria Magdalene et Maria Iacobi et Salome uenerunt diluculo ad monumentum. Orto. Gloria.

Prosa.

Ortum predestinatio
paruo sabbati spatio
prouiderat in proximo
ciuitatis proastio,
ortum pomorum uario
non insignem edulio,
quantum uirtutis precio
coequalem Elisio.
In hoc magnus decurio
ac nobilis centurio
florem Marie proprio
sepeliuit in predio.
Flos autem die tercio
qui floret ab inicio,
refloruit e tumulo
valde mane diluculo.

Versus: Surrexit Dominus de sepulchro.
Oratio: Deus, qui hanc sacratissimam noctem.[2]

For other texts of *Hortum prædestinatio* see below, pp. 615, 616; ii, 460.

Page 238, note 2. The contrast, as to impersonation, between the *Visitatio* and the *Depositio-Elevatio* is emphasized by the following *ordo* from Avranches, Bibl. de la Ville, MS 214, Ordin. monasterii Sancti Michaëlis sæc. xiv, p. 236:

Die sabbati in vigilia Palmarum cantor precipiet fratribus ut dicant Passiones: scilicet succentori illam de Dominica, et aliis fratribus Passiones de feria tertia, quarta et sexta. Et precipiet vni qui faciat Deum ad misterium Matutini Pasche, et vni iuueni qui faciat[3] Angelum desuper altare, et tribus aliis iuuenibus vt faciant tres Mulieres, et duobus aliis fratribus vt faciant Angelos de Sepulcro. Et die Veneris in Parasceue in choro preparatur habitaculum ad modum Sepulcri. Et postquam Crux in illa die adorata fuerit, abbas dicat ad altare antiphonam *Super omnia*. Et post eat ad illud habitaculum et ponat ibi Crucem cantando antiphonam *In pace*. Et sit ibi Crux vsque ad duodecimam horam noctis ante Matutinum Pasche, in qua hora abbas veniet et fratres in albis, et leuabit eam et deferat super altare, et incipiet *Christus resurgens*.[4]

---

[1] The twelfth responsory.
[2] Followed by the rubric *In Laudibus*.
[3] Deum ad . . . faciat] Added in the left margin by another hand.

[4] Followed by the rubric *Ad Matutinum Pasche ante Te Deum laudamus*, which introduces the version of the *Visitatio* printed above, p. 372.

In this *ordo* the *Depositio* and *Elevatio* are treated as mere liturgical observances, whereas the *Visitatio* is regarded as a *misterium*, with impersonation. See below, ii, 409–10.

CHAPTER IX
THE VISIT TO THE SEPULCHRE: FIRST STAGE

Page 239, note 1. The term *Visitatio Sepulchri* is attached to the plays in some MSS and early printed service-books. See, for example, above, pp. 246, 248, 333. The largest single collection of texts printed hitherto is that of C. Lange, *Die lateinischen Osterfeiern*, Munich, 1887. This virtually supersedes Lange's earlier publication, *Die lateinischen Osterfeiern*, in *Jahresbericht über die Realschule erster Ordnung in Halberstadt*, Programm no. 223, Halberstadt, 1881, pp. 3–35, and that of G. Milchsack, *Die Oster- und Passionsspiele*: i. *Die lateinischen Osterfeiern*, Wolfenbüttel, 1880. Examples of the *Visitatio* are found in the anthologies of Du Méril and Coussemaker. A large number of additional texts have been published more recently in the studies of Brooks, Stapper, Stötzner, Windakiewicza, and Young, listed in the Bibliography. There are mentioned also the later publications of Lange. A few examples, mingled with introit tropes, appear in *A.H.*, xlix, 9–10. Isolated texts are referred to in relevant parts of the Notes below, or in the commentary above. The *Visitatio Sepulchri* has been surveyed in most of the general histories of the drama issued during the last forty or fifty years, and in numerous special studies. Reference may be made especially to the following: Creizenach, i, 43–50; Chambers, ii, 25–36; Bartholomaeis, 132–4, 139–46; Cahour, pp. 363–83; Clément, pp. 220–34; Brinkmann, pp. 111 sqq.; Butler, in *Furnivall Miscellany*, pp. 46–51; Clark, pp. 203–9; Duriez, pp. 460– 78; Meyer, pp. 32–131 *passim*; Salzer, *Osterfeiern*, pp. 330–3; Schwietering, pp. 1–20 *passim*; Van Mierlo, pp. 35–7, 41–75; Vale, col. 193–202; Wilmotte, pp. 13–47; Wirth, pp. 1–6; Vermeylen, pp. 6–8.

Page 240, note 4. The only text of the *Visitatio Sepulchri* at the end of Matins which I can cite as conforming to the simple type containing only three sentences is the following from Paris, Bibl. Nat., MS 1123, Processionale Navarrense sæc. xv, fol. 25ʳ, incompletely published by Lange, no. 17, p. 22:[1]

In die Pasche, post ultimum responsorium, ueniunt Mulieres ad Sepulcrum. Tunc Angelus ad eas dicit cantando quod sequitur: *Quem queritis in sepulcro, o Cristicole?*
Mulieres respondeant: *Ihesum Nazarenum crucifixum, o celicole.*
Angelus respondet: *Non est hic, surrexit sicut predixerat; ite, nunciate quia surrexit.*

This text may be incomplete in the MS. It ends at the bottom of fol. 25ʳ, and fol. 25ᵛ is blank. Folio 25 is out of place in the codex. One might cite

---

[1] Lange, p. 4, refers to the MS by the erroneous number 1223. In my references to versions of the *Visitatio Sepulchri* printed or mentioned in Lange's *Die lateinischen Osterfeiern*, Munich, 1887, I regularly give both the number of the version in his list (pp. 3–17), and the number of the later page on which the version is printed or mentioned.

here also the first version of *Quem quæritis* in Einsiedeln MS 366, if one were certain that it is really separate and complete. The facts concerning this version, and the text, are given below, p. 598.

Page 240, note 5. With the *Visitatio* from Tours belong several texts which may well be given in full. The following is from London, Brit. Mus., Add. MS 30848, Brev. Silense sæc. xi, fol. 125ᵛ, previously edited by Lange, no. 27, pp. 24–5:

Interrogatio: *Quem queritis in sepulcro hoc, Cristicole?*
Responsio: *Ihesum Nazarenum[1] crucifixum, o celicole.*
Interrogatio siue responsio, antiphona: *Non est hic, surrexit sicut loquutus est; ite, nuntiate quia surrexit Dominus, alleluia.*
    Surrexit.

This text is immediately preceded by the *Processio ad Fontem* of Easter Vespers, and is followed by these antiphons:

Antiphona ex Resurrectio⟨ne⟩: *In resurrectione tua, Criste, celum ac terra letantur; tu solus fulges per omnem mundum, et claritas tua replet orbem terrarum, alleluia.*
Antiphona: *Crucem sanctum subiit, qui infernum confregit, ac cinctus est potentia; surrexit die tertia, alleluia.*

Then follows the rubric *Feria secunda*. The same version, with fuller rubrics is found as follows in London, Brit. Mus., Add. MS 30850, Brev. Silense sæc. xi, fol. 106ᵛ, previously edited by Lange, no. 26, pp. 24–5:

Interrogat Angelus et dicat ad Discipulos: *Quem queritis in sepulcro hoc, Cristicole?*
Respondent Discipuli et dicant: *Ihesu⟨m⟩ Nazarenum[2] crucifixum, o celicole.*
Iterum respondet Angelus: *Non est hic, surrexit sicut loquutus est; ite, nuntiate quia surrexit, alleluia.*
Antiphona: *Surrexit. Te Deum laudamus.*

This text is written in the lower margin of the page, with an asterisk referring it to a position between the third responsory (*Dum transisset*) and the *Te Deum*. The following is from Besançon, Bibl. de la Ville, MS 97, Ordin. Bisuntinum sæc. xii (manu sæc. xviii), pp. 59–60, previously edited by Brooks, *Sepulchre*, p. 94:

Finito tertio responsorio, non statim incipitur Te Deum, sed fit quoddam intervallum. Et statim diaconi duo induti dalmaticis sedent juxta altare, et veniunt tres clerici e sacrario, induti capis albis, tenentes turibula; et venientibus illis statim illi duo incipiunt: Quem quæritis in sepulchro, o Christicolæ?
Et illi tres: | Jesum Nazarenum quærimus crucifixum, o cælicolæ.
Tunc illi duo:[3] Surrexit, non est hic, sicut prædixerat; ite, nunciate quia surrexit.
Et illi tres jungant se ad chorum, et dicant antifon⟨am⟩: Surrexit Dominus de sepulchro, qui pro nobis pependit in ligno, alleluia, alleluia, alleluia.
Tunc episcopus intonat Te Deum laudamus, et finiuntur Matutinæ ordine suo.

Page 241, note 4. With the text from Melk MS 1056 may be associated

---

[1] Nazarenum] nazareno (MS).
[2] Nazarenum] nazareno (MS).

[3] After *duo* are written, and crossed out, the words *non est hic.*

one from the *Consuetudines insignis monasterii Sancti Vitoni Verdunensis* of the tenth century, published by Martene (iv, 299), reprinted therefrom by Albers (*Consuetudines*, v, 123–4), and reprinted from Martene here:

Post tertium autem responsum erunt quatuor fratres albis vestiti in subterraneis specubus ad invicem quærentes: *Quem quæritis in sepulcro, Christicolæ?* Respondebunt alii duo clementer eos salutantes: *Jesum Nazarenum crucifixum, o celicolæ.*
Quibus vice Angeli primi respondebunt: *Non est hic, surrexit; ite, nunciate.*[1]
Hoc illi duo fratres audito, interim dum illi persolvunt versum, festinato chorum intrabunt cum thuribulis, et cruce vacua nuntiantes: *Surrexit Dominus de sepulcro.* Mox abbas, hoc audito, incipiet *Te Deum laudamus.* Et post, dato versu, subsequentur Matutinæ Laudes.

Here is to be recorded also the following from Metz, Bibl. Municipale, MS 452, Trop. Sancti Arnulphi Metensis sæc. xi–xii, fol. 25ʳ, now printed, I think, for the first time:

In Die Sancto Pasche

Quem queritis in sepulchro, o Cristicole?
Hiesum Nazarenum querimus crucifixum, o celicole.
Non est hic, surrexit sicut predixerat; ite, nuntiate quia surrexit a morte.
Surrexit Dominus de sepulchro.
Te Deum laudamus.

Page 242, note 5. With the texts from Utrecht MSS 406 and 407 should be associated the following from Cassel, Landesbibl., MS theol. 4⁰.25, Trop. Fredeslariense sæc. xi, fol. 114ᵛ, previously edited by Lange, no. 22, p. 23:

Ad Sepvlchrvm in Nocte

Interrogatio, versus: Quem queritis in sepulchro, Christicole?
Responsio, versus: Iesum Nazarenum crucifixum, o caelicole.
Versus:[2] Non est hic, surrexit sicut predixerat; ite, nuntiate quia surrexit, dicentes.
Antiphona: Surrexit.
Psalmus: Te Deum laudamus.

The following, from Paris, Bibl. Nat., MS lat. 10510, Trop. Epternacense sæc. xi, fol. 11ʳ, is mentioned by Lange (no. 21, p. 23) and by Gautier (*Tropes*, p. 221), and is now first printed:

Ad Visitandum Sepulchrum

Interrogatio: Quem queritis in sepulchro, o Christicole?
Responsio: Ihesum Nazarenum crucifixum, o celicole.
Item: Non est hic, surrexit sicut predixerat; ite, nuntiate quia surrexit, dicentes.
Antiphona: Surrexit Dominus.

This text is preceded by certain *Versus in Palmis* and followed by *Antiphone in Pascha* for the procession before Mass; hence it may not have been intended for use at the end of Matins. The following, from Paris, Bibl. Nat., MS lat. 9448, Trop. Prumiense sæc. x–xi, fol. 33ᵛ, is now printed, I think, for the first time:

---

[1] nunciate] nunciare (Martene).
[2] Versus] Preceded by a blank space once occupied, probably, by a rubric now erased.

DE SANCTO PASCHA

Quem queritis in sepulchro, o Christicole?
Ihesum Nazarenum querimus crucifixum, o celicole.
Non est hic, surrexit sicut predixerat; ite, nuntiate quia surrexit, dicentes.
Antiphona: *Surrexit Dominus.*
Te Deum laudamus.

Page 243, note 5. Similar to the *Visitatio* from Berlin MSS 11 and 15 is the following from Frauenfeld, Kantonsbibl., MS Y. 28, Brev. Crucelinense sæc. xiii, fol. 152ᵛ, mentioned by Brooks (*Neue Osterfeiern*, p. 298), and now first printed:

AD SEPULCHRUM

Quem queritis in sepulchro, o Christicole?
Hiesum Nazarenum crucifixum, o celicole.
Versus: *Non est hic, surrexit sicut predixerat; ite, nuntiate quia surrexit de sepulchro.*
Antiphona: *Surrexit enim sicut.*
Psalmus: *Te Deum laudamus.*

This text is preceded by the responsory *Dum transisset*, and followed by the rubric *Matutinæ Laudes.*

Page 245, note 1. With the text from Paris MS 1268 should be associated the following from Paris, Bibl. Nat., MS lat. 1269, Brev. Catalaunense sæc. xiv, fol. 279ʳ–279ᵛ, previously printed by Lange, no. 28, p. 25:

Angeli[1] ad Sepulchrum dicunt Mulieribus: *Quem queritis in sepulchro, o Christicole?*
Mulieres ad Angelos: *Ihesum Nazarenum querimus crucifixum, o celicole.*
Iterum Angeli Mulieribus: *Non est hic, surrexit sicut predixerat; | ite, nuntiate quia surrexit a morte.*
Mulieres ad[2] populum: *Alleluia, resurrexit Dominus, hodie resurrexit leo fortis, Christus, filius Dei.*
Deo gratias dicite.
Te Deum laudamus.

A few arresting textual details appear in the following from Paris, Bibl. Nat., MS lat. 9449, Trop. Nivernense sæc. xi, fol. 34ʳ, previously printed by Reiners (*Unbekannte Tropen-Gesänge*, p. 36), to which I append the single variant from Angers, Bibl. de la Ville, MS. 96, Grad. Andegavense sæc. xii, fol. 74ᵛ, not previously published:

Qvem queritis in sepulchrum Domini,[3] o Christicole?
Ihesum Nazarenum crucifixum, o celicole.
Non est hic, surrexit sicut predixerat; ite, nunciate quia surrexit.
Alleluia, resurrexit Dominus, hodie resurrexit leo fortis, Christus, filius Dei.
Deo gracias, dicite eya!
Te Deum laudamus.

The following from Clermont-Ferrand, Bibl. de la Ville, MS 67, Brev. Claromontense sæc. xv, fol. 120ʳ–120ᵛ, has been printed by R. Twigge, in *Dublin Review*, cxxi (1897), 362:

[1] Preceded by the responsory *Et valde mane.*
[2] ad] Preceded by *c* expunged (MS).
[3] Domini] Omitted (Angers).

Finito versu,[1] duo pueri cantent clara uoce versum: *Quem queritis in sepulcro, o Christicole?*

Tres presbiteri respondeant: *Ihesum Nazarenum crucifixum, o celicole.*

Duo[2] pueri alta | uoce respondeant: *Non est hic, surrexit sicut predixerat; ite, nunciate quia surrexit dicentes.*

Presbiteri respondeant: *Alleluia, resurrexit Dominus,* tribus uicibus.

Versus: *Alleluia, hodie resurrexit leo fortis, Christus, filius Dei.*

Psalmus: *Te Deum laudamus.*

The following, from Paris, Bibl. Nat., MS lat. 12044, Lib. Resp. Sancti Mauri Fossatensis sæc. xii, fol. 100^r–100^v, mentioned by Lange (no. 36, p. 28), is now first printed:

Post tertium responsorium[3] fiat a tribus processio ad Sepulchrum; et sint duo iuxta ita dicentes: *Quem queritis in sepulchro, o Christicole?*

Responsio: Hiesum Nazarenum crucifixum, o celicole.

Non est hic, surrexit sicut predixerat; ite, nunciate quia surrexit.

Alleluia, resurrexit Dominus, | *hodie resurrexit leo fortis, Christus, filius Dei.*

Chorus: *Deo gratias dicite, eya!*

Te Deum laudamus.

The following, from Paris, Bibl. Sainte-Geneviève, MS 117 (B.Bl. in fol. 26), Lib. resp. Bellovacensis sæc. xiii, fol. 101^r, is now first printed:

Duo presbyteri uel duo dyaconi dicant: *Quem queritis in sepulchro, o Christicole?*

Duo alij presbyteri respondeant: *Ihesum Nazarenum crucifixum, o celicole.*

Duo alii dyaconi: *Non est hic, surrexit sicut predixerat; ite, nuntiate quia surrexit a morte.*

Respondeant presbyteri alii: *Alleluia, resurrexit Dominus, hodie resurrexit leo fortis, Christus, filius Dei.*

Deo gratias.

Te Deum laudamus.

The following, from Paris, Bibl. Nat., Nouv. Acq., MS lat. 1235, Grad.-Trop. Nivernense sæc. xii, fol. 205^r, now first printed, is immediately preceded in the MS by an irrelevant sequence for the Annunciation:

Interrogacio: *Quem queritis in sepulchro Domini, o Cristicole?*

Responsio: *Ihesum Nazarenum crucifixum, o celicole.*

Non[4] est hic, surrexit sicut predixerat; ite, nunciate quia surrexit.

Alleluia, resurrexit Dominus, hodie resurrexit leo fortis, Cristus, filius Dei.

Deo gracias dicite, eya!

Te Deum laudamus.

The following, from Paris, Bibl. Nat., MS lat. 1206, Ordin. Senonense sæc. xiii, fol. 57^v, has been previously printed by Lange, no. 29, p. 25:

Post responsorium[5] tres Marie introducuntur querentes in Sepulcrum. Clerici uero procedunt tenentes cereos in manibus et cantantes, donec ueniant ante principale altare. Cantatis uersibus a clericulis, duo clericuli inducti albis stantes retro altare respondeant: *Quem queritis?*

---

[1] The reference is to the *versus* of the third responsory *Dum transisset.*

[2] Duo] Due (MS).

[3] The third responsory *Dum transisset.*

[4] Non] Preceded by a space for an un-written rubric.

[5] The third responsory *Et valde mane.*

Marie: *Ihesum Nazarenum.*

Clericuli: *Non est.*

Marie uertentes se ad chorum dicant: *Alleluia, resurrexit Dominus. Deo gratias dicite.*

Deinde pontifex incipiat *Te Deum laudamus.*

The *Visitatio* mentioned by Lange, no. 34, p. 27, as being in Paris, Bibl. Sainte-Geneviève, MS B.Bl.4°.14, cannot be found.

Page 247, note 2. With the text from Vienna MS 1882 may be associated the following from St Gall, Stiftsbibl., MS 392, Lib. resp. Sangallensis (?) sæc. xvi, pp. 109–10, previously printed by Brooks, *Neue Osterfeiern*, p. 299:

Antiphona: *Quem queritis, o tremule mulieres, in hoc tumulo plorantes?*

Antiphona: *Ihesum Nazarenum crucifixum querimus.*

Antiphona: *Non est hic quem queritis, sed cito euntes dicite discipulis quia surrexit Dominus.*

Antiphona: *Venite | et uidete locum ubi posuerunt eum, alleluia, alleluia.*

This succession of 'antiphons' cannot be assigned with precision to a place in the liturgy. In the MS the text before us is preceded by a choral piece ending *effundam super vos aquam mundam, alleluia,* and is followed by the responsory *Angelus Domini descendit.*

The following fragment, previously unpublished, is found in Rome, Bibl. Vaticana, MS Palat. lat. 619, Miscellanea sæc. xii–xv, fol. 25ᵛ:

Quem queritis in sepulchro, o Christicole?

Non est hic, surrexit sicut predixerat; ite, nunciate quia surrexit de sepulchro.

Venite et uidete locum ubi positus erat Dominus, alleluia, alleluia.

This passage, in a hand of the fifteenth century, probably had some connexion with the text on the rest of the page, now erased.

Page 249, note 1. The text of the *Visitatio Sepulchri* from British Museum, MS Cotton Faustina B. III, fol. 188ᵛ–189ᵛ (new pagination) is as follows:

⟨D⟩um tertia recitatur lectio, quattuor fratres induant se, quorum unus alba indutus acsi ad aliud agendum ingrediatur, atque latenter[1] Sepulchri locum adeat, ibique manu tenens palmam, quietus sedeat. Dumque tertium percelebratur responsorium, residui tres succedant, omnes quidem cappis induti, turribula cum incensu manibus gestantes, ac pedetemptim ad similitudinem querentium quid, ueniant ante locum Sepulchri. Aguntur enim haec ad imitationem Angeli sedentis in monumento, atque Mulierum cum aromatibus uenientium, ut ungerent corpus Ihesu. Cum ergo ille residens tres uelut erraneos, ac aliquid querentes, uiderit sibi approximare, incipiat mediocri uoce | dulcisone cantare: *Quem queritis?*

Quo decantato fine tenus, respondeant hy tres uno ore: *Ihesum* ⟨*Nazarenum*⟩.

Quibus ille: *Non est hic, surrexit sicut praedixerat; ite, nuntiate quia surrexit a mortuis.*

Cuius iussionis uoce uertant se illi tres ad chorum dicentes: *Alleluia, resurrexit Dominus.*

Dicto hoc, rursus ille residens uelut reuocans illos dicat antiphonam: *Venite et uidete locum.*

Hec uero dicens surgat, et erigat uelum, ostendatque eis locum cruce nuda-

---

[1] latenter] latentur (MS).

tum,[1] sed tantum linteamina posita, quibus crux inuoluta erat. Quo uiso, depona⟨n⟩t turribula, quae gestauerant, in eodem Sepulchro, suman⟨t⟩que linteum et extendant contra[2] clerum, ac ueluti ostendentes, quod surrexit Dominus, et iam non sit illo inuolutus, hanc canant antiphonam: *Surrexit Dominus de sepulchro.* Superponantque linteum altari. Finita antiphona, prior congaudens pro triumpho regis nostri, | quod deuicta morte surrexit, incipiat ymnum *Te Deum laudamus.* Quo incepto, una pulsantur omnia signa.

The early date and intrinsic importance of the *Visitatio Sepulchri* in the *Regularis Concordia* demand a special note on the MSS, editions, and historical relationships of the treatise. Such a note is provided by Chambers, ii, 306–7. To his bibliography may be added the following: B. Albers, *Untersuchungen zu den ältesten Mönchsgewohnheiten,* Munich, 1905, pp. 9–16; T. Symons, *The Monastic Reforms of King Edgar,* in *Downside Review,* xxxix (1921), 38–51; T. Symons, *The Regularis Concordia, id.,* xl (1922), 15–30; R. Graham, *The Intellectual Influence of English Monasticism between the Tenth and the Twelfth Centuries,* in *Transactions of the Royal Historical Society,* new series, xvii (1903), 23–65; U. Berlière, *Les Coutumiers monastiques,* in *Revue bénédictine,* xxiii (1906), 260–7; xxv (1908), 95–107; xxix (1912), 357–67; B. Albers, *Le plus grand Coutumier de Cluny,* in *Revue bénédictine,* xx (1903), 174–84. The *Regularis Concordia* is found in two medieval MSS: British Museum, Cotton MS Tiberius A. III, of the first half of the eleventh century, and Cotton MS Faustina B. III, of the end of the tenth (?) century. The text in MS Tiberius A. III has an Old English interlinear gloss. Two modern copies of the work are found in British Museum MS Harley 552 and Bodleian MS Junius 52. ii (fragmentary). For descriptions of one or another of the MSS see Symons, in *Downside Review,* xl (1922), 29–30; Logeman, in *Anglia,* xv (1893), 20–5. The most careful modern text is that of W. S. Logeman, in *Anglia,* xiii (1891), 365–448, from MS Tiberius A. III. From this text the *Visitatio Sepulchri* has been reprinted by Manly, i, pp. xix–xx, and all the dramatic ceremonies of the sepulchre, by Chambers, ii, 308–9. Earlier editions, or reprints, of the *Regularis Concordia* are found in C. Reyner, *Apostolatus Benedictorum in Anglia,* Douay, 1626, pp. 77–94; W. Dugdale, *Monasticon Anglicanum,* i, London, 1846, pp. xxvii–xlv; Migne, *Pat. Lat.,* cxxxvii, 475–502. A new edition is being prepared by Dom Thomas Symons.[3] The *Regularis Concordia* was drawn up, chiefly by Ethelwold, bishop of Winchester, probably within the period 965–75.[4] The sources appear to have been the rule of St Benedict, Continental monastic customs, and traditional English practices. Among these last Tupper would include the *Visitatio Sepulchri,* on the ground that he does not find this ceremony among the early *consuetudines* of Continental monasteries.[5] That the *Visitatio* existed in monasteries on the Continent in the tenth century, however, we have evidence from Toul, Verdun, and at least one German monastery.[6] Since the prologue of the *Regularis Concordia* informs us that the author, or

[1] nudatum] nudata (MS).
[2] contra] concra (MS).
[3] See *Downside Review,* xl, 26.
[4] See Chambers, ii, 307; J. Armitage Robinson, *The Times of Saint Dunstan,* Oxford,

1923, p. 146.
[5] See *M.L.N.,* viii (1893), 356.
[6] See Albers, *Consuetudines,* v, 40–1, 123–4; *Revue bénédictine,* xx (1903), 426–7.

authors, drew more or less upon the monastic customs of Fleury and Ghent, one is tempted to regard the *Visitatio* as a borrowing from one of these Continental communities. That appropriate persons in England were in communication with these two places we may be certain.[1] Unhappily, however, we have no *consuetudines* from Ghent, and those of an early date from Fleury do not mention the dramatic ceremonies of the sepulchre.[2] The general probability would seem to be that these ceremonies were brought into the *Regularis Concordia* from the Continent; but of this there is no proof. From the fact that St Evre de Toul and St Vannes de Verdun were closely related to Fleury in discipline, and that both had the *Visitatio Sepulchri*, Albers infers that Fleury also must have had this ceremony at an early date, and that it passed thence to England.[3] This, however, is a fragile argument.[4] On the *Visitatio* from the *Regularis Concordia* see also Chasles, pp. 69–70.

Page 252, note 1. The use of the unusual antiphon *Surrexit Christus et illuxit* may be seen in the following from Zurich, Zentralbibl., MS 65, Lib. resp. Augiensis sæc. xi–xii, p. 103, previously edited by Brooks, *Easter Plays*, p. 192:

Ad Visitandvm Sepvlchrvm

Antiphona: *Quem queritis in sepulchro, Christicole?*
Responsio: *Ihesum Nazarenum crucifixum, o celicole.*
Antiphona: *Non est hic, surrexit sicut predixerat; ite, nuntiate quia surrexit de sepulchro.*
Antiphona: *Venite et uidete locum ubi positus erat Dominus, alleluia, alleluia.*
Nvntia popvlo sic: *Surrexit Christus et inluxit populo suo, quem redemit sanguine suo, alleluia.*[5]
Te Deum laudamus.

Page 252, note 3. With the text from Treves MS 1635 may be associated the following from Munich, Staatsbibl., MS lat. 3205, Brev. Aspacense sæc. xiv, fol. 1 ᵛ, previously edited by Lange, no. 64, pp. 44–5:

Ad uisitandum Sepulchrum canitur responsorium *Dum transisset.* Questio Angelorum: *Quem queritis in sepulchro, o Christicole?*
Responsio: *Ihesum Nazarenum crucifixum, o celicole.*
Angeli: *Non est hic, surrexit sicut predixerat; ite, nunciate quia surrexit.*
Angeli: *Uenite et uidete locum ubi positus erat Dominus, alleluia, alleluia.*
Angeli: *Cito euntes dicite discipulis quia surrexit Dominus, alleluia.*
Tunc monstrant[6] lintheum populo, cantantes antiphonam *Surrexit Dominus de sepulchro, qui pro nobis pependit in ligno, alleluia.*
Deinde incipitur *Te Deum laudamus.*

The following is from Munich, Staatsbibl., MS lat. 2988, Lib. resp.

---

[1] See Symons, in *Downside Review*, xxxix (1921), 43, 47; Bateson, in *English Historical Review*, ix (1894), 690–1; F. Cabrol, *L'Angleterre chrétienne avant les Normands*, Paris, 1909, pp. 248–9; Cuissard-Gaucheron, in *Mémoires de la Société archéologique et historique de l'Orléanais*, xiv (1875), 589–602; A. de Foulques de Villaret, *id.*, pp. 350–2.

[2] See *Floriacensis Vetus Bibliotheca*, pp. 390–415; Albers, *Consuetudines*, v, 137–51. These *Consuetudines* of Fleury, of about the year 1000, are not to be confused with the Fleury playbook of the thirteenth century, with which we shall have much to do elsewhere. See below, p. 665.

[3] See *Revue bénédictine*, xx (1903), 427–9.

[4] See Symons, in *Downside Review*, xl, 21–2.

[5] For this Easter antiphon see Migne, *P.L.*, lxxviii, 775, 776; Hartker, p. 240.

[6] monstrant] monstratur (MS).

Ambergensis sæc. xv, fol. liv^v–lv^r, mentioned by Lange, no. 65, p. 45, and now first printed:

AD SEPULCHRUM

Quem queritis in sepulchro, o Christicole?
Versus: *Ihesum Nazarenum crucifixum, o celicole.*
Versus: *Non est hic, surrexit sicut predixerat; ite, nunciate quia surrexit.*
Versus: *Venite et videte locum vbi positus | erat Dominus, alleluia.*
Antiphona: *Cito euntes dicite discipulis quia surrexit Dominus, alleluia.*[1]
Antiphona: *Surrexit Dominus de sepulchro, qui pro nobis pependit in ligno, alleluia.*[2]

The following is from Wolfenbüttel, Herzog-August-Bibl., MS Helmst. 505, Brev. sæc. xiv, fol. 2^r, previously edited by Brooks, *Osterfeiern*, pp. 57–8:

AD[3] SEPULCHRUM

Antiphona: *Quem queritis in sepulcro, o Christicole?*
Antiphona: *Ihesum Nazarenum crucifixum, o celicole.*
Mulieres, antiphona: *Non est hic, surrexit sicut predixerat; ite, nunciate quia surrexit Dominus.*
Antiphona: *Venite et videte locum ubi positus erat Dominus, alleluia, alleluia.*
Antiphona: *Cito euntes dicite discipulis quia surrexit Dominus, alleluia.*
In ostencione crucis antiphona: *Surrexit Dominus de sepulchro, qui pro nobis pependit in ligno, alleluia.*
Sequitur laus populorum, et clerus alta uoce cantat *Te Deum.*

The noteworthy details here are the displaying of the cross instead of the sudary, and the singing of the congregation (*laus populorum*) at the end of the performance.

The following text is from Bamberg, Staatsbibl., MS 22 (Ed. III. 2), Grad. Bambergense sæc. xii–xiii, fol. 128^r (A), previously edited by Brooks, *Osterfeiern*, pp. 53–4, to which I attach the variants found *ibid.*, MS 27 (Ed. I. 13), Lib. resp. Bambergensis sæc. xv, fol. 170^r (B), mentioned by Brooks, *Osterfeiern*, p. 54, and *ibid.*, MS 26 (Ed. IV. 2), Lib. resp. Bambergensis sæc. xiii, fol. 50^v (C), previously edited by Lange, no. 63, pp. 44–5:

AD SEPULCHRVM[4]

Qvem queritis in sepulchro, o Christicole?
Ihesum[5] Nazarenum crucifixum, o celicole.
Responsio:[6] *Non est hic, surrexit sicut predixerat; ite, nuntiate quia surrexit de sepulchro.*
    Venite[7] et uidete.
Antiphona: *Cito euntes.*[8]
Antiphona: *Surrexit Dominus.*[9]

Immediately preceding this text, and immediately following the third

---

[1] Here follow the vowels *Euouae*, with musical notation. This is a familiar means for indicating the melody of the *Gloria Patri*, from the closing words of which (*seculorum, amen*) the vowels are taken. The intention of the scribe in entering this melody here is not clear.

[2] Followed by the rubric *Aa Laudes*.

[3] The responsory *Dum transisset* precedes.
[4] Ad sepulchrvm] Omitted (B).
[5] Ihesum] Antiphona Ihesum (C).
[6] Responsio] Omitted (B).
[7] Venite] Antiphona Venite (B.C).
[8] euntes] euntes dici (C).
[9] Followed by the rubric *Laudes* (A).

responsory *Dum transisset*, are found, in all three MSS, the following *versus*, which I print from MS 22, fol. 128ʳ:

> Ad tumulum uenere gementes. A.
> Et secum aromata portantes. A.
> Angelum Christi sedentem in uertice saxi. A.
> Vident et factum uacuum corpore locum. ⟨A.⟩
> Sed uirtute plenum. A.

Each *A* at the end of a line is provided with a separate melody. I do not know whether this is a mere *jubilus* to the vowel *a*, or the melody for *A*⟨*lleluia*⟩. In MS 27 the last *A* is followed by *Alleluia*, the melody of which is not that of the preceding *A*. A few rubrics concerning the performance of this *Visitatio* are given in the following from Bamberg, Staatsbibl., MS 116 (Ed. IV. 1), Ordin. Bambergense sæc. xiii, fol. 22ᵛ, previously edited by Brooks, *Osterfeiern*, p. 54:

Tercio responsorio dicto, dicantur versus *Ad tumulum uenere gementes*, cum sequentibus. Quibus finitis, ueniant tres sacerdotes cum thuribulis[1] ad uisitandum Sepulcrum; et assideant duo diaconi in albis dicentes ad sacerdotes:

> Quem queritis in sepulcro, o Cristicole?
> *Responsio*: Ihesum Nazarenum crucifixum,[2] o celicole.
> *Responsio*: Non est hic, surrexit sicut predixerat; ite, nuntiate quia surrexit de sepulcro.
> Antiphona: Venite et uidete l⟨ocum⟩.
> Antiphona: Cito euntes d⟨icite⟩.
> Ad[3] populum antiphona: Surrexit Dominus de sepulcro.
> Succinat populus. Item chorus *Te Deum laudamus*.

The two angels provided for here are reduced to one in the following text from Munich, National-Museum, MS 2494, Brev. Bambergense anni 1448, fol. 154ᵛ, mentioned by Brooks, *Neue Osterfeiern*, p. 299:

> Ad visitandum Sepulchrum Angelus dicit: *Quem queritis in sepulchro, o Christicole?*
> Marie: *Ihesum Nazarenum crucifixum, o celicole.*
> *Non est hic, surrexit sicut predixerat; ite, nuncciate quia surrexit de sepulchro.*
> *Venite et videte locum vbi positus erat Dominus, alleluia, alleluia.*
> Antiphona: *Cito euntes dicite discipulis quia surrexit Dominus, alleluia, alleluia.*
> *Surrexit Dominus de sepulchro, qui pro nobis pependit in ligno, alleluia.*[4]

The following text is found in Hildesheim, Dombibl. (Beverinische Bibl.), MS 684, Brev. Hildesiense sæc. xiii–xiv, fol. 245ᵛ (A), previously edited by Brooks, *New Texts*, pp. 468–9, to which I attach the variants found *ibid.*, MS 690, Brev. Hildesiense sæc. xv, fol. 7ʳ (B), and *ibid.*, MS 697, Lib. resp.

---

[1] thuribulis] thruribulis (MS).

[2] crucifixum] Followed by *querimus* expunged (MS).

[3] A reference-sign here indicates that, at a later date, before the antiphon *Surrexit Dominus* was to be inserted the following, written by a later hand in the left margin, and partly lost through trimming:

Presbyteris reversis de sepulcro ⟨a⟩d conuentum, primo chorarius ⟨in⟩cipiat *Dic*

nobis, Maria. Postea vnus sacerdos dicat *Sepulcrvm Christi*. Secundus, *Angelicos testes*. Tercius, *Surrexit Christus*. Totus chorus cantet(?) *Credendum est magis*, et cetera. Postea sacerdotes incipiant *Surrexit Dominus de sepulcro*. Hoc facto, conventus ad chorum revertatur, et perficiat Matutinum.

[4] Followed by the rubric *Laudes*. The text is preceded by the responsory *Dum transisset* and the verses *Ad tumulum venere gementes*.

Hildesiensis sæc. xvi, fol. 182 ᵛ (C), the last two texts having been mentioned by Brooks, *op. cit.*, p. 469:

¹Post *Gloria Patri*, tertium responsorium. Incipe responsorium *Dum transisset*, et statim descendatur. Nota: Duo canonici ad hoc deputati intrabunt Sepulchrum; tres sacerdotes induti casulis albis visitent Sepulchrum in parte aquilonari cum turribulis; et dicent qui sunt in Sepulchro: *Quem queritis?*¹

VISITATIO² SEPULCHRI

Quem queritis in sepulchro, o Christicole?
Versus:³ *Ihesum Nazarenum crucifixum, o celycole.*
Responsio:⁴ *Non est hic, surrexit sicut predixerat; ite, nuntiate quia surrexit Dominus.*
Versus:⁵ *Venite et uidete locum ubi positus erat Dominus, alleluia, alleluia.*
Responsio:⁶ *Cito euntes dicite discipulis quia surrexit Dominus, alleluia.*⁷
Et ascendentes pulpitum, ostenso sudario, cantent: *Surrexit.*⁸
Qua finita, dicatur *Te Deum laudamus.*⁹

Page 253, note 2. Similar to the version from Munich MS 12301 is the following from Munich, Staatsbibl., MS lat. 26947, Ordin. Ratisbonense sæc. xv, fol. 121ʳ–121ᵛ, previously edited by Brooks, *Neue Osterfeiern*, pp. 298–9:

Cantores imponant responsorium¹⁰ a capite, et de choro exeuntes cum magna reuerencia, portantes | manibus ardentes candelas, faciant processionem ad Sepulchrum. Illis ergo ordinatim stantibus, tres prespiteri maiores persone induti bonis cappis rubeis, cum tribus thuribulis fumigantibus, sub typo sanctarum Mulierum, vadunt ad Sepulchrum. Ibi sedent duo dyaconi dalmaticis albis uestiti, sub uice Angelorum, qui dicunt ad prespiteros: *Quem queritis?*
Respondent prespiteri: *Iesum Nazarenum.*
Angeli: *Non est hic quem queritis.*
Angeli: *Venite et videte.*
Angeli: *Cito euntes dicite.*
Tunc sacerdotes intrantes Sepulchrum linteamen inde tollant et portant ante se in monasterium ex oposito processionis; in gradu Sancte Marie omnibus ostendentes dicunt antiphonam: *Surrexit Dominus de sepulchro.*
Deinde cantores incipiant *Te Deum laudamus*; et populus, *Kyrie ⟨eleyson⟩, Christeleyson, Crist ist erstanden.* Et fit compulsacio cum omnibus campanis clare sonantibus.

This version is notable for the participation of the lay congregation in the singing at the conclusion of the performance.

Page 254, note 5. The following text of the *Visitatio* is found in Cambridge, Corpus Christi College, MS 473, Trop. Wintoniense sæc. xi, fol. 26ᵛ,

¹⁻¹ Omitted (B.C).
² Visitatio] In visitatione (C).
³ Versus] Mulieres (B); omitted (C).
⁴ Responsio] Angelus (B); omitted (C).
⁵ Versus] antiphona (B); omitted (C).
⁶ Responsio] antiphona (B); omitted (C).
⁷ alleluia] alleluia, alleluia (B).
⁸ Et ascendentes . . . Surrexit] Antiphona

Surrexit Dominus de sepulchro qui pro nobis pependit in ligno alleluia (B); Surrexit Dominus de sepulcro qui pro nobis pependit in ligno alleluia (C).
⁹ Qua . . . laudamus] Te Deum laudamus (B): Te Deum (C).
¹⁰ The third responsory *Dum transisset*.

previously edited by Frere, *Winchester Troper*, p. 17, with a facsimile (plate 26ª):

ANGELICA DE CHRISTI RESURRECTIONE

Quem queritis in sepulchro, Christicole?
Sanctarum Mulierum responsio:
　Ihesum Nazarenum crucifixum, o celicola.[1]
Angelice uocis consolatio:
　Non est hic, surrexit sicut predixerat; ite, nuntiate quia surrexit dicentes.
Sanctarum Mulierum ad omnem clerum modvlatio:
　Alleluia, resurrexit Dominus hodie, leo fortis, Christus, filius Dei. Deo gratias, dicite eia!
　Venite et uidete locum.
　Cito euntes.
　Surrexit Dominus de sepulchro, qui pro nobis pependit in ligno, alleluia.

Page 255, note 3. The text of the *Visitatio* from Bodl. MS 775 is preceded in the MS by tropes for Palm Sunday, and followed by the rubric *Sabbato Sancto primum Benedictio Cerei*. In Corpus Christi Coll. MS 473 (see preceding note) the text is preceded by tropes for Palm Sunday, and followed by the rubric *Tropi in die Christi Resurrectionis*. In the latter case the text occupies a sufficiently normal position in the MS; in the former, it is clearly out of place. Chambers probably takes this displacement too seriously when he writes the following (ii, 15, note 2): 'Why is the *Quem quaeritis* in the *Bodl. MS.* apparently on Good Friday? Perhaps this was an irregular use reformed by Bp. Ethelwold.' One may fairly say that the use of the *Quem quæritis* dialogue on Good Friday is inconceivable. The form of *Visitatio* in the two Winchester tropers differs slightly (chiefly in including *Cito euntes*) from that found in the *Regularis Concordia* drawn up at Winchester about the same date.[2] Although one would not expect such a discrepancy, it is, perhaps, no more surprising than are the verbal differences between the two tropers themselves.

Page 255, note 4. Concerning *Dicant nunc Judæi*, and other anti-Semitic liturgical compositions, see H. Villetard, *I Giudei nella Liturgia*, in *Rassegna Gregoriana*, ix (1910), 429–44; Weber, *Kunst*, pp. 62–8. *Dicant nunc Judæi* appears to have been originally a separate antiphon; then it became the *versus* of the responsory *Christus resurgens* (see Hartker, p. 203); and then, a separate antiphon again.

Page 255, note 5. The version of the *Visitatio* from Strassburg is seen in the following earlier text from London, Brit. Mus., Add. MS 23922, Lib. Resp. Argentoratensis sæc. xiii, fol. 41ᵛ–42ᵛ, previously published by Lange, no. 73, pp. 48–50, and by Wilmart, pp. 36–7:

AD CELEBRANDAM RESUR⟨R⟩ECTIONEM

Quem queritis in sepulchro, o Christicole?
Christicole, versus: *Iesum Nazarenum crucifixum, o celicole.*

---

[1] Celicola] Corrected by another hand from *celicole*.

[2] See above, pp. 249, 581; Chambers, ii, 13–4.

Responsio Celicolarum, versus: *Non est hic, surrexit sicut predixerat; ite, nunciate quia surrexit de se|pulchro.*

In ostensione Sepulcri antiphona: *Venite et uidete locum ubi positus erat Dominus, alleluia, alleluia.*

Hec antiphona cantetur a Sepulchro reuertendo, antiphona: *Dicant nunc Iudei quomodo milites custodientes sepulchrum perdiderunt regem ad lapidis positionem.*[1] *Quare non seruabant petram iusticie? Aut sepultum reddant, aut resurgentem adorent, nobiscum dicentes alleluia, alleluia.*

Christicole, antiphona: *Surrexit Dominus de sepulchro, qui pro nobis pependit in ligno, alleluia.*

Chorus, antiphona: *Surrexit Christus*[2] *et illuxit populo suo, quem redemit sanguine suo, alleluia.*

Christicole, antiphona; *Surrexit enim sicut dixit Dominus, et precedet uos | in Galileam, alleluia; ibi eum uidebitis, alleluia, alleluia, alleluia.*

Chorus: *Te Deum laudamus.*

To the details in this text and in the one printed above from the *Agenda* of 1590 no significant additions are found in the text printed by Lange (no. 74, pp. 48–50) from a Strassburg *Agenda* of 1513, or in the one published from an unidentified MS by Martene (iii, 181), and mentioned by Lange (no. 76, p. 50). For a text related to the last of these see Wilmart, p. 103.

Page 256, note 1. With the *Visitatio* from Munich MS 14741 may be associated the fragments from Bamberg, Staatsbibl., MS 10 (Ed. V. 10), Grad. Bambergense sæc. xii, fol. 90ʳ–91ʳ, published by Brooks, *Osterfeiern*, p. 53. For convenience I place here the following from Darmstadt, Landesbibl., MS 545, Cantuale Bumagense sæc. xiv, fol. 57ᵛ–58ʳ, previously edited by Lange, no. 72, p. 48:

VERSUS ANTE SEPULCRUM

Qvem queritis in sepulchro, o Christicole?
Ihesum Nazarenum crucifixum, o celicole.
Non est hic, surrexit sicut predixerat; ite, nunciate quia surrexit.
Venite et uidete locum ubi positus erat Dominus, alleluia, alleluia. |
Cito euntes dicite discipulis quia surrexit Dominus, alleluia.
Et recordate sunt uerborum eius, et regresse a monumento nunciauerunt hec omnia illis undecim et ceteris omnibus, alleluia.[3]
Surrexit Dominus de sepulchro, qui pro nobis pependit in ligno, alleluia.
Te Deum laudamus.

The antiphon *Et recordatæ sunt*, which appears here for the first time, will recur in numerous versions of the *Visitatio* to be considered later.

Page 257, note 1. With the text from Cassel MS 2°. 99 may be associated the following from Cassel, Landesbibl., MS theol. 2°. 129, Lib. resp. Fredeslariensis sæc. xiv, fol. 111ʳ, previously edited by Lange, no. 83, pp. 56–7:

Ad[4] *uisitandum Sepulcrum dyaconi duo cantent: Quem queritis, o tremule mulieres, in hoc tumulo plorantes?*

Tres accedentes cum thuribulis cantent: *Ihesum Nazarenum crucifixum querimus.*

---

[1] lapidis positionem] lapidem positionis (MS).

[2] Christus] Preceded by *dñs*, crossed out

[3] For this antiphon see Hartker, p. 232.

[4] The responsory *Dum transisset* precedes.

Dyaconi: *Non est hic quem queritis, sed cito euntes nunciate discipulis eius et Petro quia surrexit Ihesus.*

Antiphona: *Venite et uidete locum ubi positus erat Dominus, alleluia, alleluia.*

Mulieres: *Ad sepulchrum Domini gementes uenimus, angelos Dei in albis sedentes uidimus, qui Christum mortis triumphatorem uiuere atque in Galyleam dixerunt procedere.*

Antiphona: *Surrexit Dominus de sepulchro, qui pro nobis pependit in ligno, alleluia.*

Psalmus: *Te Deum laudamus.*

The particular interest of this text lies in the unusual form of the speech *Ad sepulchrum Domini.* A similar text is found in Darmstadt, Landesbibl., MS 3183, Rituale Burgholtense sæc. xiii, pp. 108–9, previously edited by Lange, no. 82, pp. 56–7:

In[1] mane, aliquibus loco Angelorum ad Sepulcrum residentibus, versus: *Qvem queritis in sepulchro, o Christicole?*

Quibus alij loco Mariarum r*espondeant: Ihesum Nazarenum crucifixum, o celicole.*

Adhuc prime: *Non est hic, surrexit sicut predixerat; ite, nunciate fratribus meis quia surrexit de | sepulchro.*

Antiphona: *Venite et uidete locum ubi positus erat Dominus, alleluia, alleluia.*

Antiphona: *Ad sepulcrum Domini gementes uenimus, angelos Dei in albis sedentes uidimus, qui Christum mortis triumphatorem uiuere atque in Galileam dixerunt precedere.*

Antiphona: *Surrexit Dominus de sepulchro, qui pro nobis pependit in ligno, alleluia. Te Deum laudamus.*

Page 260, note 2. With the *Visitatio* published by Gerbert may be associated the following from Andenne (Belgium), Bibl. Capit., MS II, Miss. Andennense sæc. xiii–xiv, fol. 125ʳ, now first printed:

Post tertium responsorium cant*ent* ad Sepulchrum Mulieres: *Quis reuoluet nobis lapidem ab ostio monumenti? Alleluia, alleluia.*

Angeli: *Quem queritis in sepulchro, o Christicole?*

Mulieres: *Ihesum Nazarenum crucifixum, o celicole.*

Angeli: *Non est hic, surrexit sicut predixerat; ite, nuntiate quia surrexit dicentes.*

Mulieres ad c⟨h⟩orum cum sudario revertentes dicant alta uoce: *Surrexit Dominus de sepulchro, qui pro nobis pependit in ligno, alleluia, alleluia, alleluia. Te Deum.*

The following is a reprint of Van Mierlo's text (p. 48) from an 'antiphonarium' of the fourteenth century from the monastery of Postel:

Visitantes: *Quis revolvet nobis lapidem ab ostio monumenti? Alleluia, alleluia.*

Sedentes: *Quem queritis in sepulchro, o Christicole?*

Querentes: *Iesum Nazarenum crucifixum, o celicole.*

Respondentes: *Non est hic, surrexit sicut predixerat; ite, nuntiate quia surrexit dicentes.*

Querentes: *Surrexit Dominus de sepulchro, qui pro nobis pependit in ligno, alleluia, alleluia, alleluia. Te Deum.*

Here may be mentioned also the *Visitatio* from Origny-Sainte-Benoîte printed below, p. 685. The following from Udine, Bibl. Arcivescovile, MS

[1] Preceded immediately by the words *Benedicamus Domino*, at the end of Compline on the eve of Easter.

F. 25, Lib. Resp. Tarvisinus (?) sæc. xii, fol. 94ᵛ–95ʳ, is now printed, I think, for the first time:

> *Quis revoluet nobis ab hostio lapidem quem sacrum cernimus tegere sepulchrum?*
> ⟨*Q*⟩*uem queritis, o tremule mulieres, in hoc tumulo plorantes?*
> ⟨*I*⟩*hesum querimus Nazarenum crucifixum.*
> ⟨*N*⟩*on est hic quem queritis, sed cito euntes | nunciate discipulis eius et Petro quia sur*⟨*r*⟩*exit Ihesus.*
> ⟨*A*⟩*d monumentum uenimus gementes, angelum Domini* ⟨*sedentem*⟩ *uidimus et dicentem quia sur*⟨*r*⟩*exit Ihesus.*
> ⟨*S*⟩*ur*⟨*r*⟩*exit Dominus.*
> ⟨*T*⟩*e Deum laudamus.*

This text is written over an erasure, without rubrics, immediately after the third responsory *Dum transisset*. The spaces left for initials are sufficiently large for short rubrics also. The text above is mentioned by G. Vale, in *Rassegna Gregoriana*, iv (1905), col. 197–8, and a text with substantial rubrics is incompletely printed by him (*id.*, col. 199) from a fifteenth-century MS of which he does not give the shelf-mark. See also Rubeis, p. 340. I have not seen the text of the *Visitatio* in MS 64 of the sixteenth century in the Stiftsbibliothek at Aachen, referred to by O. Gatzweiler, *Die liturgischen Handschriften des Aachener Münsterstifts*, Münster, 1926, pp. 177–8.

Page 261, note 1. With the text from Paris MS 990 is to be associated the following from Munich, Staatsbibl., MS lat. 14083, Trop. Emmeramense sæc. xi–xii, fol. 89ʳ–89ᵛ, previously printed by Lange, no. 40, p. 29:

AD SEPVLCHRVM

Interrog*ant* presbyteri, antiphona: *Qvis revolvet nobis lapidem?*
Diaconi, versus: *Quem queritis in sepulchro, Christicolae?* |
Respond*ent* presbyteri: *Iesum Nazarenum crucifixum, o celicole.*
Diaconi: *Non est hic, surrexit sicut predixerat; ite, nuntiate quia surrexit dicentes.*
Antiphona: *Surrexit Dominus de sepulchro.*
     Te Deum laudamvs.

Here may be offered also the following unpublished text from Munich, Staatsbibl., MS lat. 14845, Hymnarium-Prosarium Emmeramense sæc. xii, fol. 94ʳ–94ᵛ:

AD SEPULCHRUM DOMINI

Quis reuoluet nobis lapidem ab ostio ⟨*monumenti*⟩*?*
Quem queritis in sepulchro, Christicole? |
Ihesum Nazarenum crucifixum, o celicole.
Non est hic, surrexit sicut predixerat; ite, nunciate quia surrexit dicentes.
Antiphona: *Surrexit Dominus* ⟨*de sepulchro, qui pro nobis pependit in ligno, alleluia*⟩.
     Iam Dominus optatas reddit laudes Pascha, cum Christus adest; fauete cui canentes, alleluia.
     Confitemini.
Psalmus: *Laudate Dominum.*[1]

In this text the passages following the antiphon *Surrexit Dominus* are unique among versions of the *Visitatio*, and may not be intended as part of the

---

[1] The MS proceeds: Ad Processionem, antiphona: *Vidi aquam.*

dramatic composition. Here may be placed also the following from London, Brit. Mus., Add. MS 19415, Brev. Wormatense sæc. xv, fol. 327ʳ, previously printed by Lange, in *Z.f.d.A.*, xli (1897), 82:

Et[1] uadit processio ad Sepulchrum, ubi tres sacerdotes induti albis dicunt antiphonam: *Quis reuoluet nobis lapidem ab ostio monumenti? Alleluia, alleluia.*
Deinde dyaconi in Sepulchro existentes submissa uoce subiungunt antiphonam: *Quem queritis in sepulchro, o Cristicole?*
Sacerdotes autem respondentes dicunt antiphonam: *Ihesum Nazarenum ⟨crucifixum⟩, o celicole.*
Quibus respondent dyaconi antiphonam: *Non est hic, surrexit sicut predixerat; ite, nuncciate quia surrexit.*
Redeuntes autem sacerdotes cum sudario a monumento, alta uoce ostendendo sudarium cantant antiphonam: *Surrexit Dominus de sepulchro, qui pro nobis pependit in ligno, alleluia.*
Et in uulgari: *Crist ist erstanden.* Quibus finitis, cantor cum gaudio intonat *Te Deum laudamus.*

Page 262, note 1. Matters associated with the *Visitatio* from MS Barberini lat. 659 are discussed by Young, *Home of the Easter Play*, pp. 71–86. The monograph by J. B. Thibaut, *Ordre des Offices de la Semaine Sainte à Jérusalem du ive au xe Siècle*, Paris, 1926, appeared too late for notice in the article mentioned, and it bears only indirectly upon the subject in hand. MS Barberini 659 is described by B. Zimmerman, in Cabrol and Leclercq, ii, 2167. The version of the *Visitatio* printed above is found also, as follows, in Breslau, Universitätsbibl., MS I. Qu. 175, Ordin. ad usum Hierosolymitanum sæc. xiv, fol. 45ᵛ–46ʳ, previously edited by A. Schönfelder, in *Historisches Jahrbuch*, xxxii (1911), 588–9; J. Klapper, in *Zeitschrift für deutsche Philologie*, l (1923), 52; Young, *op. cit.*, p. 74:

Reiteratur *Dum transisset*, quod dum cantatur, preparantur tres clerici iuuenes retro altare in modum Mulierum iuxta consuetudinem antiquam. Finito responsorio, procedant inde contra Sepulcrum deferentes singuli vas aureum uel argenteum cum aliquo vngento, candelabris et turibulis preeuntibus, cantando ter: *O Deus! Quis reuoluet?*
Cumque ad portam Sepulcri venerint, duo alii clerici iuxta portam Sepulcri, albis uestiti et habentes amictus super capita et candelas in manibus, cantando respondeant sic: *Quem queritis?*
Mulieres: *Ihesum Nazare⟨num⟩.* |
Tunc illi duo: *Non est hic quem queritis.*
Interim Mulieres introeant in Sepulcrum, ibique facta oratione breui, exeant inde. Et uenientes in medium chori alta uoce nuncciabunt cantando: *Alleluia, resurrexit.*
Sed Uisitacionem hanc modo[2] non facimus propter astancium multitudinem. Quibus finitis, incipiat patriarcha *Te Deum laudamus.*

The text of a similar *Visitatio* from an unnumbered MS of the thirteenth century in the church of the Holy Sepulchre at Barletta, Italy, has been printed by C. Kohler in *Revue de l'Orient latin*, viii (1900–1), 423.

---

[1] Immediately preceded by the responsory *Dum transisset*.

[2] modo] Written twice, second writing crossed out (MS).

With the texts under consideration here belongs the following unpublished one from Rheims, Bibl. de la Ville, MS 265 (C. 206), Grad. Sancti Dionysii Remensis sæc. xii–xiii, fol. 22ᵛ:

> *O Deus, O Deus, O Deus!*
> *Quem queritis in sepulchro, o Christicole?*
> *Ihesum Nazarenum crucifixum, o celicole.*
> *Non est hic, surrexit sicut predixerat; ite, nuntiate quia surrexit dicentes.*
> *Alleluia, resurrexit Dominus, hodie resurrexit leo fortis, Christus, filius Dei.*
> *Deo gratias, dicite eia!*
> *Te Deum laudamus.*

This text begins, without heading, immediately after the pieces for Holy Saturday.

Page 263, note 2. Concerning the relationships of the *Visitatio* from Munich MS lat. 14765 see B. Albers, *Les 'Consuetudines Sigiberti Abbatis' dans CLM 14765*, in *Revue bénédictine*, xx (1903), 420–33. The MS formerly belonged to the monastery of St Emmeram at Regensburg, but Abbot Sigibert cannot be identified, and the *Consuetudines* may not have been used in this community. In the MS the *Visitatio* (printed above, p. 263) is preceded by the following passage (92ᵛ–93ʳ), the beginning of which follows immediately after the *Elevatio Crucis* (printed above, p. 557):

Et ueniat domnus abbas ante altare indutus cappa, incipiatque *Domine, labia mea aperies*, et respondeant omnes *Et os meum*. Subsequatur *Deus in adiutorium*, et dicant omnes *Domine, ad adiuuandum me festina*. Statimque veniant tres cantores induti cappis, qui cantent inuitatorium. Finito inuitatorio exuant se cappis et reuertantur in choro, sicut sunt in albis. Post inuitatorium non dicatur hymnus, sed statim incipiat ebdomadarius antiphonam *Ego sum qui sum*. . . . Si abbas presens fuerit, legat lectionem terciam indutus cappa; si autem alius legerit, non sit in cappa sed tantum in alba. Tres fratres cantent tercium responsorium. Ab inchoatione autem Matutini usque ad finem debet esse abbas indutus cappa, et habere ferulam in manu. Quod si abbas non fuerit presens, prior adimpleat omnia.

With the *Visitatio* from Munich MS 14765 should be associated that found in an unidentified MS in the 'Pfarrarchiv in der Oberstadt' at Cleves— Ordin. Clevense sæc. xv, fol. 10ʳ. I reprint the text of Stapper, *Kleve*, pp. 181–2:

MODUS ANTIQUUS VISITANDI SEPULCHRUM

Finito *Gloria Patri* tertii responsorii, iterabitur responsorium *Dum transisset sabbatum*. Decanus cum duobus canonicis senioribus tria thuribula secum cum incensu portantibus visitent Sepulchrum descendentes gradus chori, simul submissa voce cantantes: *Quis reuoluet nobis lapidem?* Et duo scholares albis induti sedeant in Sepulchro, vnus ad caput et vnus ad pedes; et ad pedes sedens respondeat cantans: *Quem queritis?* et cetera. Et surgens scholaris ad caput sedens respondeat: *Non est hic*, et cetera. Et tunc ambo scholares cantent: *Venite et videte*, digito indicantes locum in quo sudarium iacet, et decanus respiciens in Sepulchrum accipiat sudarium. Ascendentes celeriter gradus chori quasi fratribus Resurrectionem Dominicam nuntiantes, vertant se ad populum cantantes solempniter et lete: *Surrexit Dominus de sepulchro.* Qua finita, chori prouisores in signum leticie imponant alta voce *Te Deum laudamus.* Sed iste modus visitandi Sepulchrum per presbyteros deuenit extra usum, sed fit per scholares secundum tenorem libri qui dicitur *Agenda.*[1]

Similar to the *Visitatio* from Munich MS 14765, except for the closing antiphon, is the following from *Breuiarium secundum morem et consuetudinem sacrosancte Ecclesie Coloniensis*, Venice, 1498, fol. 233^r, now reprinted, I think, for the first time:

Finita repetitione responsorii, sequitur Visitatio Sepulchri hac die tantum hoc modo. Mulieres procedentes ad Sepulchrum submissa voce cantant responsorium *Dum transisset* usque ad versum. Deinde ante Sepulchrum cantant Mulieres: *Quis reuoluet nobis lapidem ab hostio monumenti?*
Angeli in Sepulchro respondent: *Quem queritis in sepulchro, o Christicole.*
Mulieres: *Jesum Nazarenum crucifixum, o celicole.*
Angeli: *Non est hic, surrexit sicut predixerat; ite, nunciate quia surrexit de sepulchro.*
Angeli: *Venite et videte locum ubi positus erat Dominus, alleluia, alleluia.*
Tunc Angeli ostendentes sudarium cantent: *Surrexit Dominus de sepulchro, qui pro nobis pependit in ligno, alleluia.*
Sequitur immediate *Te Deum.*

An unpublished text of the same version, from the same cathedral, is found in a fourteenth-century Cologne Breviary, fol. 280^v, said to be in the library of J. Meade Falkner, Esq., of Durham; and another text of the same version exists in a Cologne *Diurnale*, Paris, 1508, reprinted by Dankó, *Feier*, p. 183. In London, Brit. Mus., Add. MS 31913, Brev. Coloniense sæc. xiv, fol. 263^v–264^r, is found the following, previously edited by Lange, no. 52, p. 35:

AD SEPULCHRUM

Quis reuoluet nobis lapidem ab ostio monumenti? Alleluia, alleluia!
Angelus: *Quem queritis in sepulchro, o Cristicole?*
Marie: *Ihesum Nazarenum | crucifixum, o celicole.*
Versus: *Non est hic, surrexit sicut predixerat; ite, nuntiate quia surrexit de sepulchro.*
    Venite et uidete locum ubi positus erat Dominus, alleluia, alleluia.
Versus: *Surrexit Dominus de sepulchro, qui pro nobis pependit in ligno, alleluia.*
Psalmus: *Te Deum laudamus.*

Similar to the *Visitatio* from Cologne is the following from Paris, Bibl. Nat., MS lat. 1310, Brev. Wormatense sæc. xv, fol. 198^v–199^r, previously edited by Young, *Some Texts*, p. 317:

In Uisitacione Sepulchri cantatur predictum responsorium,[2] et tunc scolares cantant antiphonam: *Quis reuoluet nobis lapidem ab ostio monumenti? Alleluia!*
Tunc respondet quidam in forma Angeli: | *Quem queritis in sepulchro, o Christicole?*
Responde⟨n⟩t Uisitatores: *Ihesum Nazarenum crucifixum, o celicole.*
    Respondet Angelus: *Non est hic, surrexit sicut predixerat; ite, nunctiate quia surrexit de sepulchro.*

---

[1] Followed by the rubric *In die Pasche*, introducing an *ordo* for the procession before Mass.

[2] Referring to *Dum transisset.*

Item Angelus: *Venite et uidete locum ubi positus erat Dominus, alleluia, alleluia.*
Tunc conuertant se uisitantes ad populum, alta uoce cantantes hanc anti-
phonam:[1] *Surrexit Dominus de sepulchro, qui pro nobis pependit in ligno, alleluia.*
Deinde sequitur *Te Deum.*

Here belongs also the following from Cassel, Landesbibl., MS theol.
4°. 90, Brev. Fredeslariense saec. xiv, fol. 109ᵛ, previously edited by Lange,
no. 46, pp. 33–4:

Post tercium responsorium[2] ad visitandum Sepulcrum, sedentes in Sepulcro
cantent: *Quem queritis?*
Venientes ad Sepulcrum respondeant: *Ihesum Nazarenum.*
Iterum in Sepulcro: *Non est hic.*
   Venite et uidete.
Illi abeuntes cantent antiphonam: *Surrexit.*
Qua finita, *Te Deum laudamus.*

The same play, except for the closing antiphon (*Surrexit enim sicut dixit*),
is found in a Basel Breviary of 1515, fol. i. ba, published by Lange, no. 53,
p. 35. The following is found in Darmstadt, Landesbibl., MS 869, Brev.
Darmstadiense saec. xv, fol. 80ʳ, mentioned by Lange, no. 50, p. 35, and
now printed, I think, for the first time:

Et Mulieres ad Sepulchrum procedentes submissa voce cantant respon-
sorium *Dum transisset*, cum reliquis antiphonis sequentibus. Mulieres: *Quis
reuoluet nobis lapidem ab ostio monumenti? Alleluia, alleluia!*
Angelus: *Quem queritis in sepulchro, o Christicole?*
Mulieres: *Ihesum Nazarenum crucifixum, o celicole.*
Angelus: *Non est hic, surrexit sicut predixerat; ite, nunciate quia surrexit de sepulchro.*
Angelus: *Venite et videte locum vbi positus erat Dominus, alleluia, alleluia.*
Tunc Angeli ostendentes sudarium cantant: *Surrexit Dominus de sepulchro, qui
pro nobis pependit in ligno, alleluia.*
Sequitur *Te Deum.*

Lange (nos. 49 and 51) reports this same version from two other Darmstadt breviaries of the fourteenth century (Darmstadt MSS 977 and 1854),
but does not give the page-numbers. He also prints a text (pp. 34–5)
represented as coming from MS 977. Probably there is some confusion here,
for MSS 977 and 1854 appear not to contain the *Visitatio.*

Page 265, note 1. With the Toul version from Paris MS lat. 975 may be
associated the following text from Vienna, National-Bibl., MS lat. 1928,
Ordin. Ordinis Hospitalis Hierosolymitani saec. xiv, fol. 44ʳ–44ᵛ, previously
edited by Brooks, *New Texts*, p. 467:

Quod[3] dum cantatur, sint parati tres clerici iuuenes in modum Mulierum
retro altare. Finito responsorio, procedunt deferentes vasa aurea uel ar-
gentea, thuribulis et candelis precedentibus, cantando antiphonam: *O Deus!
Quis reuoluet?*
Respondentes in Sepulcro: *Quem queritis?*
Respondeant Mulieres: *Ihesum Nazarenum.*

---

[1] antiphonam] Written twice (MS).   [3] The third responsory *Dum transisset.*
[2] *Dum transisset.*

Tunc illi: *Non est hic quem queritis.*
   Venite | *et videte.*
Antiphona: *Cito euntes.*
Sacerdos ad populum in medio choro: *Surrexit Dominus de sepulchro.*
   Te Deum laudamus.

The unpublished *Depositio* (fol. 42ᵛ) and *Elevatio* (fol. 44ʳ) from Vienna
MS lat. 1928 are as follows:

⟨DEPOSITIO CRUCIS⟩

Deinde tollentes Crucifixum nuper adoratum, ferant ad Sepulchrum
cantantes responsorium *Ecçe quomodo moritur.* Reponentes et diligenter co-
operientes cantent responsorium *Sepulto Domino.* Versus *Ne forte.* Antiphona
In pace in idipsum. Antiphona *Caro mea.* Hiis completis, dicant Vesperas.[1]

⟨ELEVATIO CRUCIS⟩

In sancta nocte ante Matutinum presbyteri duo cum Eucharistia Crucem
de Sepulchro portent, et in loco suo ponant.

With the present group of texts of the *Visitatio* may be associated that from
Oxford, Bibl. Bodl., MS Misc. lit. 297, Brev. Benedictum Germanicum
sæc. xii, fol. 111ʳ, previously edited by Lange, no. 66, pp. 45–6:

VERSVS AD SEPVLCRVM[2]

Quis reuoluet nobis lapidem ab hostio monumenti? Alleluia, alleluia!
Quem queritis in sepulcro, o Christicole?
Ihesum Nazarenum crucifixum, o celicole.
Non est hic, surrexit sicut predixerat; ite, nunciate quia surrexit de sepulcro.
Venite et uidete locum.
Cito euntes dicite.
Antiphona: *Surrexit Dominus.*
   Te Deum laudamus.

The following is from Gotha, Herzogliche Bibl., MS II. 90, Brev. Gotha-
num (?) sæc. xiii, fol. 8ᵛ, previously edited by Lange, no. 67, pp. 45–6:

Responsorium[3] repetitur. Tunc[4] cantores procedunt ad Sepulchrum; per-
cantant ad ulterius.[5] Ecce tres clerici in albis ueniunt ad Sepulchrum cum
turribulis et incenso. In Sepulchro sedeant duo clerici in dalmaticis pro
Angelis. Sicque submissa uoce qui extra stant incipiant antiphonam istam:
Quis reuoluet nobis ab hostio lapidem, quem tegere sanctum cernimus sepulchrum?
Respondent Angeli: *Quem queritis, o tremule mulieres, in hoc tumulo plorantes?*
Item Mulieres:[6] *Ihesum Nazarenum crucifixum querimus.*
Tunc Angeli: *Non est hic quem queritis, sed cito euntes nunciate discipulis eius et*
   Petro quia surrexit Ihesus.

---

[1] As a matter of fact, the *ordo* for Vespers
has *preceded* the text of the *Depositio.*
[2] The text has musical notation and is preceded by the third responsory *Dum transisset.*
Before most of the speeches blank spaces are
left for rubrics.

[3] *Dum transisset.*
[4] Tunc] Reading uncertain. The rubrics
are faint throughout. I particularize only
the readings which are especially doubtful.
[5] ad ulterius] Reading uncertain.
[6] Mulieres] Reading uncertain.

Item Angeli: *Venite et uidete locum ubi positus erat Dominus, alleluia, alleluia.*
Tunc intrant et turificant locum. Item Angeli r*espondent: Cito euntes dicite discipulis quia surrexit Dominus, alleluia.*
Et tollunt Mulieres lintheamina et procedunt ad populum cantantes[1]
Surrexit Dominus de sepulchro, qui pro nobis pependit in ligno, alleluia.
Tunc cantor incipit[2] *Te Deum laudamus.*

Page 266, note 4. Similar to the *Visitatio* in Stuttgart MS 4°. 36, but furnished with different rubrics, is the following from Stuttgart, Landesbibl., MS theol. et phil. 4°. 249, Ordin. Hirsaviense sæc. xv, fol. 79ᵛ–80ʳ, previously edited by Lange, no, 77, pp. 51–2:

Quo[3] percantato, visitatur Sepulchrum Domini hoc ordine. Tres prespiteri siue diaconi, aibis et cappis induti, capita humeralibus uelata habentes, singulique singula cum incenso thuribula in manibus tenentes, pedetemptim procedunt ad Sepulchrum Domini cantantes summissa uoce antiphonam: *Quis reuoluet nobis ab ostio lapidem quem tegere sanctum cernimus sepulchrum?*
Quam antiphonam incipiunt ante altare Sancte Crucis et finiunt ante introitum Sepulchri. Duo diaconi induti dalmaticis, uelatis capitibus, sedent infra Sepulchrum, quique statim quasi uice Angelorum illos tres ad imitationem Mulierum venientes compellant: *Quem queritis in sepulchro, o Christicole?*
Inquisitores Sepulchri econtra antiphonam: *Ihesum Nazarenum crucifixum, o celicole.*
Item illi uice Angelorum: *Non est hic, surrexit sicut predixerat; ite, nunciate quia surrexit de sepulchro.*
Et subinferunt antiphonam: *Venite et uidete locum ubi positus erat Dominus, alleluia, alleluia.*
Mox ingressi inquisitores Sepulchri turificant locum vbi Crux posita erat; nam antequam ad Nocturnos[4] pulsaretur, a custodibus ecclesie sublata ˈest; sicque tollentes linteum illud inter se expansum et cantantes summissa uoce antiphonam: *Dicant nunc Iudei quomodo milites custodientes sepulchrum perdiderunt regem ad lapidis posicionem.[5] Quare non seruabant petram iusticie? Aut sepultum reddant, aut resurgentem adorent, nobiscum dicentes alleluia, alleluia.*
Regrediuntur eadem via qua venerunt. Finita antiphona ante introitum chori, intrant tacentes et super gradum sanctuarii consistentes, uersa facie in chorum et eleuato linteo, precelsa uoce intonant antiphonam: *Surrexit enim sicut ⟨dixit Dominus⟩.*
Qua ab ipsis percantata, imponitur *Te Deum laudamus.*

A similar version is found, as follows, in Munich, Staatsbibl., MS lat. 23037, Brev. Pruveningense sæc. xii, fol. 176ᵛ (A), previously edited by Young, *Harrowing of Hell*, pp. 943–4; to which I attach the variants from Zurich, Zentralbibl., MS Rheinau LIX, Ordin. Rhenoviense sæc. xiii, pp. 112–3 (B), previously edited by Lange, no. 78, pp. 51–2:

---

[1] cantantes] Reading uncertain.
[2] incipit] incipiat (? MS).
[3] The third responsory.
[4] The Nocturns of Matins. The reference

in this sentence is to the *Elevatio.*
[5] lapidis posicionem] lapidem posicionis (MS).

Ordo ad uisitandum Sepulchrum

Duodecimo[1] responsorio finito, uisitatur Sepulchrum; uisitatur hoc modo.[2] Tres presbyteri siue diaconi albis cappisque[3] induti, capita humeralibus uelata habentes, singulique singula cum incenso thuribula in manibus portantes,[4] pedetemptim procedunt ad Sepulchru⟨m⟩ Domini cantantes summissa uoce antiphonam: *Quis reuoluet nobis ab hostio lapidem quem tegere sanctum cernimus sepulchrum?*[5]

Qua finita, duo diaconi[6] induti dalmaticis uelatis similiter capitibus sedent infra Sepulchrum, quique statim quasi uice Angelorum illos tres ad imitationem Mulierum uenientes ita compellant antiphonam:[7] *Quem queritis in sepulchro, o Christicole?*[8]

Econtra isti: *Iesum Nazarenum crucifixum, o celicole.*[9]

Econtra[10] illi: *Non est hic, surrexit sicut predixerat; ite, nuntiate quia surrexit de sepulchro.*[11]

Tunc isti intrant Sepulchrum, illis cantantibus:[12] *Venite et uidete locum ubi positus erat Dominus, alleluia, alleluia.*[13]

Thurificant locum ubi Crux posita erat,[14] sicque tollentes pannum intra[15] se expansum, simul etiam gestantes thuribula et cantantes[16] mediocri uoce: *Dicant nunc Iudei quomodo milites custodientes sepulchrum perdiderunt regem ad lapidis positionem. Quare non seruabant petram iusticie? ⟨Aut sepultum reddant,⟩ aut resurgentem adorent, nobiscum dicentes alleluia, alleluia.*[17]

Regrediuntur per aliam uiam,[18] et finita antiphona ante introitum chori, intrant tacentes, et super gradum sanctuarii assistentes,[19] uersa facie in chorum et eleuato lintheo, precelsa uoce intonant antiphonam: *Surrexit enim sicut dixit Dominus; precedet uos in Galileam, alleluia; ibi eum uidebitis, alleluia, alleluia, alleluia.*[20]

A similar version, with negligible rubrics, is found in Admont, Stiftsbibl., MS 6, Brev. Benedictinum sæc. xv, fol. 143[r], published by Brooks, *New Texts*, p. 468. I have not seen the MS.

Page 267, note 4. In regard to performances of religious plays at Cividale

[1] This is one of the rare instances in which the *Visitatio* is attached to the monastic type of Easter Matins having three Nocturns and twelve lessons. The twelfth responsory is *Dum transisset*. Both A and B provide music for the *Visitatio*.

[2] Ordo ad . . . hoc modo] Tertio responsorio tercia uice percantato uisitatur sepulchrum hoc ordine (B).

[3] cappisque] cappis (B).

[4] portantes] tenentes (B).

[5] Quis . . . sepulchrum] Quis reuoluet (B).

[6] Qua finita, duo diaconi] Qua finita subsistunt non longe ab illis duobus fratribus qui (B).

[7] antiphonam] Omitted (B).

[8] Quem . . . Christicole] Quem queritis (B).

[9] Iesum . . . celicole] Ihesum nazarenum (B).

[10] Econtra] Item (B).

[11] Non est . . . sepulchro] Non est hic (B).

[12] illis cantantibus] et illis iterum canentibus (B).

[13] Venite . . . alleluia, alleluia] Venite et uidete locum (B).

[14] erat] erat nam antequam ad nocturnos pulsaretur sublata est a custodibvs ecclesie (B).

[15] pannum intra] linteum reportant illud inter (B).

[16] cantantes] Written in left margin (B).

[17] Dicant nunc . . . alleluia, alleluia] Dicant nunc iudei (B).

[18] per aliam uiam] alia uia quam uenerunt (B).   [19] assistentes] consistentes (B).

[20] Surrexit . . . alleluia, alleluia, alleluia] Surrexit (B). In A, the rubric *Ad Laudes* follows; in B, *Qua ab ipsis percantata inponitur Te deum laudamus. Statim omnia signa compulsantur.*

see Appendix D. In connexion with the *Visitatio* from Cividale MS T. VII I give the facts concerning the two versions of *Quem quæritis*—and the other dramatic texts—in Einsiedeln, Stiftsbibl., MS 366 (*olim* 179), Fragmenta liturgica sæc. xi–xii. The MS is described by P. G. Meier, *Catalogus Codicum manu scriptorum qui in Bibliotheca Monasterii Einsidlensis O.S.B. servantur*, i, Einsiedeln and Leipzig, 1899, pp. 331–2. The part of the manuscript containing dramatic pieces (pp. 53–6) is more fully described by Meyer, pp. 51–2, and by Young, *Ordo Prophetarum*, p. 72.· The dramatic pieces are found as follows:

(1) p. 53 (beginning on the first line and ending on the next to the last line): a fragment of the *Officium Stellæ*. See below, ii, 447.

(2) pp. 53 (last line) to 54 (last line): a fragment of the *Ordo Prophetarum*. See below, ii, 458.

(3) p. 55 (first three lines): a fragment (latter part) of the prose *Hortum prædestinatio*. See below, ii, 460. Between pp. 54 and 55 there has been a loss of one or more leaves, which contained at least a continuation of the *Ordo Prophetarum* and the beginning of *Hortum prædestinatio*.

(4) pp. 55 (line 3) to 56 (line 5): the following version (or versions) of the *Visitatio Sepulchri*:

In Resvrrectione

Angel*us* dicit: *Qvem qveritis in sepulchro, o Christicole?*

Mulieres respond*et*: *Ihesum Nazarenum crucifixum, o celicola.*

Angelvs dicit: *Non est hic, surrexit sicut predixerat; ite, nuntiate quia surrexit de sepulchro.*

Mulieres secum cant*ant*: *Quis reuoluet nobis ab hostio lapidem quem tegere sanctum cernimus sepulchrum?*

Angelvs inqvirit: *Quem queritis, o tremule mulieres, in hoc tumulo plorantes?*

Respond*ent* Mvlieres: *Ihesum Nazarenum crucifixum querimus.*

Angelvs dicit: *Non est hic, surrexit; sed cito euntes dicite discipulis eius et Petro quia surrexit Ihesus.*

Mulieres redeuntes secum cantant: *Dicant nunc Iudei quomodo milites custodientes sepulchrum perdiderunt regem ad lapidis positionem. Quare non seruabant petram iusticie? Aut sepultum | reddant aut resurgentem adorent, nobiscum dicentes alleluia.*

Venientes autem ad Discipulos dicunt: *Ad monumentum uenimus plorantes, angelum Domini sedentem uidimus ac dicentem quia surrexit Ihesus.*

Chorus: *Te Deum laudamus.*[1]

This text obviously presents two versions of the *Quem quæritis* dialogue, the second beginning with *Quis revolvet*. We cannot be certain whether the first was performed dramatically as a separate piece in the form before us. The text printed here is written continuously by one scribe. The two versions are treated separately by Lange, nos. 8 and 81, pp. 22, 55. In regard to earlier printings see Lange, pp. 3, 8.

Page 269, note 1. Similar to the *Visitatio* from Paris MS 1307, but incomplete, is the following from Paris, Bibl. Nat., MS lat. 1308, Brev. Xantense sæc. xv, fol. 101ʳ, previously edited by Lange, no. 41, pp. 29–30:

---

[1] Followed by the rubric *Incipiunt viii modi qui sunt in musica.*

Due[1] Marie: *Ardens est cor meum; desidero uidere Dominum meum; quero et non inuenio ubi posuerunt eum, alleluia.*

Quis reuoluet nobis lapidem ab ostio monumenti? Alleluia, alleluia!

Angeli: *Quem queritis in sepulcro, o Christicole?*

Due Marie: *Ihesum Nazarenum crucifixum, o celicole.*[2]

Angeli: *Non est hic, surrexit Dominus.*

Psalmus: *Te Deum laudamus.*

Here belongs also the following, now first printed, from Paris, Bibl. Nat., MS lat. 16309, Brev. Santonense sæc. xiv, fol. 143[r]:

Versus:[3] *Ardens est cor meum; desidero uidere Dominum meum; quero et non inuenio ubi posuerunt eum, alleluya.*

Quis reuoluet nobis lapidem ab hostio monumenti, alleluya, alleluya.

Versus: *Quem queritis in sepulcro, o Christicole.*

Versus: *Ihesum Nazarenum crucifixum, o celicole.*

Versus: *Non est hic, surrexit sicut predixerat; ite, nunciate quia surrexit.*

Alleluya,[4] *resurrexit Dominus.*

Psalmus: *Te Deum laudamus.*

Page 272, note 2. I exhibit here a few texts of the *Visitatio* which, because of irregularities or incompleteness, scarcely deserve a place in the discussion above. The following is from Madrid, Bibl. Nac., MS 289 (C. 153), Trop. ad usum ecclesiæ Siculorum sæc. xii, fol. 115[v]–116[r], previously edited by Young, *Some Texts*, p. 329, and reprinted therefrom by Beeson, pp. 204–5:

Mulieres: *Quis reuoluet nobis lapidem ab hostio monumenti?*

Pveri: *Venite.*

Clerici: *Quis re|uoluet?*

Pveri: *Venite.*

Clerici: *Quis reuoluet?*

Pveri: *Venite, nolite timere uos.*

Quem queritis in sepulchro, o Christicole?

Clerici: *Iesum Nazarenum crucifixum, o celicole.*

Pveri: *Non est hic, surrexit sicut predixerat; ite, nunciate quia surrexit.*

Clerici: *Alleluia, resurrexit Dominus, hodie resurrexit leo fortis, Christus, filius Dei.*

Chorus: *Deo gracias, dicite eia.*

Te Deum laudamus.

The text as printed here begins, without heading or introductory rubric, immediately after the *Benedictio Cerei*. This version of the *Visitatio* is especially noteworthy for the introductory summons *Venite*, and for the repetition of *Quis revolvet*.

The following is from Rouen, Bibl. de la Ville, MS 252 (A. 486), Lib. resp. S. Audoeni Rothomagensis sæc. xiv, fol. 101[v]–102[r], previously edited by Lange, no. 56, pp. 36–7:

PROSA

Ihesu, magne rex eterne,   *ad nos clemens respice.*

Tu de morte, morte tua,   *triumphasti hodie.*

[1] The responsory *Dum transisset* immediately precedes.

[2] celicole] Christicole (MS).

[3] Preceded by the third responsory *Dum*

transisset, without further rubric.

[4] Alleluya] Preceded by a blank space for
an unwritten rubric.

Te uictore mundus surgit,   qui iacebat misere;
Et ad astra tecum uadit   in splendore glorie,
Ubi leti mereamur   sine fine dicere,
Alleluya.

O Deus! Quis reuoluet nobis lapidem ab hostio monu|menti?
Quem queritis in sepulchro, o Christicole?
Ihesum Nazarenum crucifixum, o celicola.
Non est hic, surrexit sicut predixerat; ite, nunciate quia surrexit.
Alleluya, resurrexit Dominus hodie.
Alleluya, resurrexit Dominus, alleluya, sicut dixit[1] nobis, alleluya, alleluya.
Resurrexit Dominus, hodie surrexit leo fortis, Christus, filius Dei.
Venite et uidete locum ubi positus erat Dominus, alleluya, alleluya.
Ite, nunciate fratribus meis, alleluya, ut eant in Galileam; ibi me uidebunt,
alleluya, alleluya, alleluya.
Surrexit enim sicut dixit[2] Dominus, et precedet uos[3] in Galileam, alleluya; ibi
eum uidebitis, alleluya, alleluya, alleluya.
Deo gratias, alleluya, alleluya.
Te Deum.

This text is immediately preceded by the third responsory *Dum transisset.*
The prose *Jesu magne* (not found in Chevalier, *R.H.*) may be best regarded,
perhaps, as a trope of the responsory, rather than as an introduction to the
dramatic text. As an introduction it weakens the force of the first part of
the dialogue. The use of *meis* and *me* in the second dismissal, after *Venite et
videte*, seems to imply the presence of Christ (see Matt. xxviii, 10); but in the
absence of rubrics we may suspend speculation.

The following is from Prague, Veřejná a Universitní Knihovna, MS XIII.
C. 7. 4°, Lib. resp. Pragensis saec. xiv, fol. 2ᵛ–3ᵛ, previously edited by Lange,
no. 86, pp. 58–9:

Antiphona:[4] | *Maria Magdalena et alia Maria ferebant diluculo aromatum,*
Dominum querentes in monumento. Evovae.[5]

Quis reuoluet nobis ab hostio lapidem quem tegere sanctum cernimus sepulchrum?
Quem queritis, o tremule mulieres, in hoc tumulo plorantes?
Ihesum Nazarenum crucifixum querimus.
Non est hic quem queritis, sed cito euntes nunciate discipulis eius et Petro quia
surrexit Ihesus.
Venite et uidete locum ubi positus erat Dominus, alleluia. Evovae. |
Ad monumentum uenimus gementes, angelum Domini sedentem uidimus, et dicen-
tem quia surrexit Ihesus.
Cernitis, o socii, ecce lintheamina et sudarium, et corpus non est in sepulchro inuentum.[6]

The noteworthy element in this version is the introductory 'antiphon'
Maria Magdalena. This utterance, in which only *two* Marys are mentioned,
incongruously follows the responsory *Dum transisset*, in which are mentioned

---

[1] dixit] dicit (MS).
[2] dixit] dicit (MS).   [3] uos] nos (MS).
[4] Immediately preceded by the responsory
Dum transisset.
[5] Evovae] These are merely the vowels of
the words *seculorum Amen*, which conclude the

Gloria Patri. See above, pp. 21, 584. In the
present instance they seem totally irrelevant,
and may be an error for *alleluia*, which might
appear as *aevia.*
[6] Followed immediately by the first antiphon of Laudes, *Angelus autem.*

three women. Although the sentence *Maria Magdalena* is called *antiphona*, it appears not to be an authorized liturgical piece. More or less similar liturgical forms with this *incipit* are the following:[1]

Responsorium: *Maria Magdalena et altera Maria ibant diluculo ad monumentum. Jesum quem quæritis, non est hic, surrexit sicut locutus est; præcedet vos in Galilæam; ibi eum videbitis, alleluia, alleluia.* Versus: *Cito euntes dicite discipulis ejus et Petro quia surrexit Dominus. Præcedet* (Hartker, p. 232; Migne, *P.L.*, lxxviii, 771).

Antiphona: *Maria Magdalena et Martha cum uenissent ad monumentum, angeli splendentes apparuerunt dicentes: Quem queritis uiuentem cum mortuis; non est hic; uenite et uidete locum ubi iacuit; cito euntes dicite discipulis eius et Petro; surrexit Christus, quia creauit omnia et misertus est humano generi, alleluia* (Vienna, National-Bibl., MS lat. 1888, fol. 103ᵛ).

Antiphona: *Maria Magdalena et Maria Iacobi et Salome sabbato quidem siluerunt secundum mandatum, alleluia. Cum autem transisset sabbatum, ementes aromata uenerunt ungere Ihesum, alleluia, alleluia* (London, Brit. Mus., Add. MS 23922, fol. 41ᵛ).

It will be noticed that the third liturgical piece mentions *three* women, and thus accords with the responsory *Dum transisset*. *Maria Magdalena* will reappear in numerous versions of the *Visitatio* to be examined later; and when only the *incipit* of the 'antiphon' is given, it will hardly be possible to identify it exactly. The *incipit* is seen, for example, in the following from Berlin, Staatsbibl., MS theol. lat. 2°. 208, Brev. Berolinense (?) sæc. xvi, fol. 19ᵛ, previously edited by Lange, no. 84, p. 57:

In tercio Nocturno repetatur responsorium *Dum transisset*. Redeant ad Sepulcrum cum crucibus portantes singuli singulos cereos accensos. Et deinde duo sacerdotes visitant ad Sepulcrum cum incenso choro et interim cantata antiphona *Maria Magdalene*. Qua finita, predicti sacerdotes cantant antiphonam: *Quis reuoluet nobis?*
Duo dyaconi in Sepulcro cum dalmaticis residentes respondent antiphonam: *Quem queritis?*
Visitatores respondent antiphonam: *Ihesum Nazarenum.*
Angeli cantant: *Non est hic quem queritis.*
Et addant: *Venite et videte locum; non est hic.*
Tunc visitatores ingrediantur Sepulcrum, et thurificato Sepulcro, regredientur ante altare et cantant antiphonam: *Cernitis, o socij.*
Et tunc primi duo sacerdotes sint in ambone, et cantant solempniter *Surrexit Dominus de sepulcro*, in maiori nota. Postea cantor, qui incipiat *Te Deum laudamus.*

The sentence beginning *Maria Magdalena* is seen also in the following fragment, from St Gall, Stiftsbibl., MS 384, Brev. Sangallense (?) sæc. xiv, p. 240, mentioned by Lange, no. 6, p. 22:

Maria[2] *Magdalena.*

---

[1] The first of these shows particularly the influence of Matt. xxviii, 1–7. Of these Biblical verses the first is as follows: *Vespere autem sabbati, quæ lucescit in prima sabbati, venit Maria Magdalene et altera Maria videre sepulchrum.* In regard to an iconographic tradition that the *altera Maria* was the Blessed Virgin Mary see C. R. Morey, in *Clemen Festschrift*, p. 166.

[2] Immediately preceded in the MS by the words *Vidi aquam*, of the Easter procession.

Quem queritis in sepulchro, o Christicole?
Ihesum Nazarenum crucifixum, o celicole.
Non est hic.
Surrexit enim sicut dixit Dominus, et precedet uos in Galyleam; ibi eum uidebitis,
alleluia, alleluia.[1]

Here should be mentioned also a sixteenth-century text from Schonenberg, and two eighteenth-century texts from Cologne, published by Lange, nos. 45, 54, 55, pp. 33, 36. The three MSS were, in 1887, owned privately, and I have not seen them.

I record a series of texts showing the form of *Visitatio* used in the cathedral of Münster from the thirteenth century to the eighteenth. The first is found in the Chapter Library, MS 4, Ordin. Monasteriense sæc. xiii, fol. 78ᵛ, which I reprint from Stapper, *Feier*, p. 155 (see also pp. 88–9):

Dicto tercio responsorio, visitatores ad visitandum Sepulchrum[2] statim imponunt antiphonam:
   Maria Magdalena et altera Maria.
   Quis revolvet?
Et cum perventum fuerit, respondebunt duo scolares ex sepulchro: *Quem queritis?*
Visitatores respondent: *Jhesum Nazarenum.*
Scolares: *Non est hic.*
Item: *Venite et videte.*
Deinde statim visitatores reversi elevent crucem in altum cantantes: *Surrexit*
   Dominus de sepulchro.
Deinde reponetur crux, et offerant qui velint. Antiphona dicta, statim imponitur *Te Deum laudamus.*

The second text is from Münster, Domarchiv, MS (sine sig.) circa 1489, fol. 39ʳ–39ᵛ, reprinted from Stapper, *Münster*, p. 45:

Hic nota, quod infra tercium responsorium duo diaconi dalmaticis induantur ad faciendam representationem que eadem die fieri solet. Inter cantandum responsorium *Dum transisset* egredietur processio in nauim ecclesie ad stationem. Finito responsorio, et statione disposita, incipiunt hi qui prestant choro *Maria Magdalena.* Interim duo predicti diaconi portantes thuribula descendunt de choro, transeuntes per medium versus locum sepulture, et precedunt eos duo scholares cum luminaribus. Cum peruenerint ad locum, erunt in Sepulcro duo scholares cantantes loco Angeli: *Quem queritis?*
Diaconi respondent: *Ihesum Nazarenum.*
Et iterum Angeli: *Non est.*
Tunc diaconi dantes incensum redeunt cito per medium. Tenentes crucem versi ad populum incipiant alta voce *Surrexit Dominus de sepulchro,* quam antiphonam chorus percantat. Tunc qui presunt choro incipiunt *Te Deum,* et sic intramus chorum. Tunc tenetur crux ad gradum sanctuarij, et rursum offerunt singuli.

The third Münster text is from two MSS: one in the University Library,

---

[1] Followed by the words *Hec dies*, the *incipit* of the gradual of the Mass of Easter. Before each sentence in the text above is a blank space, for an unwritten rubric. The dramatic dialogue may be part of the procession at Vespers. See below, pp. 689 sqq.

[2] Sepulchrum] A later hand has added here: sacerdotalibus vestibus induti cum candelis et thuribulo (MS).

Cod. 354 (96), and the other, of the year 1696, preserved without shelf-number in the Domarchiv. I reprint the text of Stapper, *Münster*, pp. 48–9:

Ultima lectio quando legitur, duo leuitae retro altare vestiunt se albis et tunicis candidis. Quo peracto, duo pueri lumina ferentes praecedunt superplicijs induti, sed prius responsorium repetitur *Dum transisset sabbatum*. Tunc duo candelabra prope mensam propositionis cum luminibus deferuntur ad primum altare, choro sequente et infra in naui templi stationem faciente. Finito responsorio sine versu, illi qui praesunt choro, stantes retro altare S. Pauli intonant antiphonam *Maria Magdalena*. Tunc duo diaconi, praecedentibus cereis, exeunt choro per valuas prope altare decem millium martyrum; gerentes thuribulos singulos in manibus, pergunt ad Monumentum, in quo duo pueri cantabunt: *Quem quaeritis?*
Diaconi respondebunt: *Jesum Nazarenum.*
Rursum pueri: *Non est hic.*
Quod audientes diaconi faciunt suffitum thuribulis, festinantes ad locum ubi crux posita, et uterque eorum brachium arripiens crucis, alta et clara voce cantabunt *Surrexit Dominus de sepulchro*, quam chorus finit. Tunc domini choro praecinentes incipiunt *Te Deum*, et chorus alternatim prosequens ascendit. Aeditui vero tollent crucem, ponentes eam in gradibus circa mensam propositionis in latere decani, et domini offerent.

In the revision of the Münster *ordinarium* made in 1712 (*Agenda pastoralis dioecesis Monasteriensis*) the *Visitatio Sepulchri* was dropped, but the *Depositio* and *Elevatio* were continued. See Stapper, *Münster*, pp. 25, 39–44.

An *ordo* for the *Visitatio Sepulchri* as performed by the nuns and clergy of Notre Dame, in Troyes, is preserved in an ordinary written in French near the end of the thirteenth century. The text is in Troyes, Bibl. de la Ville, MS 792, fol. 301 ᵛ–302 ᵛ, previously edited by G. Baist in *Romanische Forschungen*, ed. K. Vollmöller, xxiii (1907), 752–3:

E doit la chantre proueo⟨i⟩r iij dames por estre les iij Maries, e ij enfans por estre Ange. E sont les iij dames en lor habiz e li enfant si sont toutes blanches e creuechie blanc sor lor testes. E doit auoir vne dame empres les enfans por enseignie la ou elle doiuent estre, e quele diront e doiuent estre appareillie tuit li preuoire e tuit li clerc e tuit li beneficie de leglise, nomement li prestes qui doit chanter la Messe, e li diacres e li sordiacres e li marreliers. E doit estre li prestes qui doit chanter la Messe doit estre reuestuz ausi appareilliez com por chanter la Messe fors la chasuble, e en leu de la chasuble vne chape de cuer. E li diacres e li sordiacres reuestu en damatiques e en tuniques. E doit auoir appareillie la tresoriere iij boites e iij cierges e iij touelletes. De rechief la trasoriere doit auoir appareillie des chandeles, e les doit baillier a la souprieusse, e por labbesse vn tortis, e doit la souprieusse baillier a chascune vne chandele, e a labbesse son tortis, e doit li couuens estre en cuer. E doit estre li prestes qui doit chanter la Messe deuant le | grant autel tout appareillie ausi com il est desus ordene. E li diacres e li sordiacres tout ausi com il est desus ordene, e doit a auoir le tieute e leau benoite e la croiz e les encensiers e les cierges. E viennent les iij Maries deuant le grant autel, la on a appareillie ces choses, e viennent e sagenoillent e dient *Confiteor*, e li prestes dist *Misereatur*. Quant il les a essolu, si done a une

chascune vn cierge e vne tuelle e vne boite. Li cierge si sont alume; si a
enqui vne nonain qui tient vn tortis alume e vn liure por elles conduire.
E li couuens sen uet ou grant moutier atout lor chandeles alumees. E son
enqui toute tornees deuers lautel sanz neant chanter. E sen uiennent li
preuoire auec le couuent ou grant motier, e li diacres e li sordiacres e leau
benoite, e li encencier e la crois e li teutes; e mennent les iij Mariez. E la
dame qui les conduit si uet de coste por elles alumer; e porte le liure en
quelles resgardent. E sen vont par mi cuer e vont par mi luis de la barroche
e sen uont par deuant lautel de la barroche, e puis par deuant lautel Saint
Nicholas. E sen uont par deuers le puis iusques deuant lautel Saint Michiel.
E quant elle mueuent de deuant lautel, premierement si preignent a chanter
Heu, nobis, e le uont chantant basset. E sont li Ange, la on les a ordenez cote
dou piler delez lautel de Saint Michiel, e enqui tot coj tant que les trois
Mariez uiennent e quele sont vn petit arriers daus, e li Ange sont torne
deuers elles. E quant elle dient *O Deus! O Deus! O Deus!* tot cest uer, e li
Ange respondent cest uer e chantent *O uos Christicole*, e dient tot cest uer,
e les Maries dient en chantant *Querimus* | quant elle ont cest uer chante.
E li Ange dient *Non iacet hic*, e le dient tout iusques a *Venite et uidete*. E quant
vient a *Venite*, si mueuent e chantent *Venite et uidete*[1] e les en moignent a lautel
Saint Tantoigne. E uiennent la crois e leau benoite e li teutes e li encensiers
e li cierges e li preuoire e li diacre e li sordiacre e la mestre descole e si
enfant e uont a lautel Saint Tantoigne e li couens demeure tout coj. E
chantent les iij Maries *Salue, rex Sabbaoth*, e chantent tot contreual iusques
a cest uer *Iam comcussa gemit*, e puis si preignent *Gloria, sancte, tibi*. E quant
cil[2] uers est diz, si uet li prestes a lautel e prent le calice ou Corpus Domini
est, e la veraie croiz sus e vn peile sus. Au leuer qui le fait si comence cest
respons[3] *Christus resurgens*, e sonne len les cloches,[4] e la chantre des ou elle
est auec le couuent si dist *Ex mortuis*, e sen uiennent au couuent la crois
deuant e leau benoite, et puis li sordiacres qui porte le tieute e li diacres e li
prestes qui porte Corpus Domini e dui preuoire qui uont encensant coste
dou preuoire qui porte Corpus Domini e li dui Ange qui portent chascun
vn sierge de coste le preuoire, e li autre apres e les iij Maries e la cele qui les
conuoie e puis la mestre descole e si enfant; e viennent la ou li couuens est,
e se tiennent enqui tot coj iusques len ait chante *Christus resurgens*. E quant
il est diz,[5] si dist la chantre *Dicant nunc*, e puis la reprise. Quant tot ce est
chantez, si comence li prestes *Te Deum laudamus*, e sen uont, e li couuens
apres chantant *Te Deum*, e sen uet li prestes au grant autel ausi com il sont
ordene e le met sus lautel vn biau paile sus. Quant *Te Deum* est finez, si
comence li diacres leuangile.

Since some of the speeches in this *Visitatio* appear to be unique, it is
unfortunate that the Latin passages are incomplete. *Salve, rex Sabbaoth* is
an Easter poem consisting of ten elegiac distichs, of which the second line
of the fifth distich is *Jam concussa gemit mors inimica tibi*. See Chevalier, *R.H.*,
no. 18157, printed in *A.H.*, xx, 20. The French rubrics describe the pro-

---

[1] et uidete] Inserted above the line (MS).
[2] cil] MS seems to have *cib*, the intention
of which may have been *cils*.
[3] repons] An erasure leaves the ending of

this word in doubt.
[4] et sonne . . . cloches] Entered in the
margin by a contemporary hand.
[5] E quant . . . diz] Written twice (MS).

cession in generous detail, and assure us that this is one of the rare instances in which the roles of the Marys are taken by women. See below, ii, 403.

CHAPTER X

THE VISIT TO THE SEPULCHRE: FIRST STAGE
(*Continued*)

Page 273, note 1. Among the many general discussions of *Victimæ paschali* are the following: Julian, pp. 1222–4; N. Gihr, *Die Sequenzen des römischen Messbuches*, Freiburg, 1887, pp. 131–70; A. Schubiger, *La Séquence de Pâques-'Victimæ pascali laudes' et son Auteur*, Paris, 1858; Clichtoveus, fol. 161 ᵛ–162 ᵛ; W. A. Merrill, *Latin Hymns*, Boston, 1904, pp. 45–6; Wagner, pp. 264–5; Meyer, pp. 49–50, 76–7; Raby, pp. 217–8; Moser, i, 118–20. Julian, *ibid.*, and Chevalier, *R.H.*, no. 21505, give further bibliography. The evidence for Wipo's authorship is summarized in *A.H.*, liv. 14; Julian, *ibid.* On Wipo's work as a whole see Manitius, ii, 318–28; H. Bresslau, *Die Werke Wipos*, Hannover and Leipzig, 1915.

Page 275, note 1. As to this sequence having been the original source of the *Visitatio* various more or less indiscreet observations have been made. Du Méril (p. 43) speaks of *Victimæ paschali* as 'un drame complet'. Luzarche (p. xviii) suggests that the sequence 'est peut-être la forme première, le plus ancien modèle du drame liturgique'. A. E. Schönbach (*Zeitschrift für deutsche Philologie*, iv [1873], 369) expresses a somewhat similar opinion, and attributes it also to F. K. Grieshaber. The latter, however, takes no such position in his study *Ueber die Ostersequenz* Victimæ paschali *und deren Beziehung zu den religiösen Schauspielen des Mittelalters*, Carlsruhe, 1844. In a passage quoted below (p. 658) Durandus says that the *Visitatio* was sometimes performed during Mass, at the place where the *Victimæ paschali* was sung. This assertion appears to be unfounded (see Duriez, p. 478). Durandus may have been misled by the fact that many versions of the *Visitatio* include the sequence, or by such a ceremony as that from Vienne considered above (p. 274).

Page 276, note 1. As we should expect, the number of extant texts of the *Visitatio* used in the cathedral (or diocese) of Paris is unusually large. All those treated below have been printed or mentioned by Lange, pp. 9, 60–2, by Brooks, *New Texts*, pp. 474–6, or by Young, *Some Texts*, pp. 298–301.

I print here the text from Paris, Bibl. Nat., MS lat. 1293, Brev. anni 1471, fol. 113 ʳ–113 ᵛ (A), with variants from the following: Bibl. Nat., MS lat. 1294, Brev. anni 1472, fol. 88 ᵛ (B); *ibid.*, MS lat. 1291, Brev. sæc. xv, fol. 175 ᵛ–176 ʳ (C); *ibid.*, MS lat. 1292, Brev. sæc. xv, fol. 124 ʳ–124 ᵛ (D); *ibid.*, MS lat. 746, Brev. sæc. xiv, fol. 151 ᵛ–152 ʳ (E); *ibid.*, MS lat. 1023, Brev. sæc. xiv, fol. 166 ʳ–166 ᵛ (F); *ibid.*, MS lat. 1025, Brev. sæc. xiv, fol. 219 ᵛ–220 ʳ (G); *ibid.*, MS lat. 746 A, Brev. sæc. xiv, fol. 78 ᵛ (H); *ibid.*, MS lat. 745, Brev. sæc. xv, fol. 80 ᵛ–81 ʳ (I); Paris, Bibl. Mazarine, MS 345, Brev. sæc. xv, fol. 296 ʳ–296 ᵛ (J); Paris, Bibl. de l'Arsenal, MS 660, Brev. sæc. xv, fol. 291 ᵛ (K); London, Brit. Mus.,

MS Harl. 2927, Brev. sæc. xv, fol. 285ᵛ–286ʳ (L); Paris, Bibl. Nat., MS lat. 10485, Brev. sæc. xv, fol. 190ʳ (M); *ibid.*, MS lat. 15613, Brev. sæc. xiv, fol. 239ʳ–240ʳ (N); *ibid.*, MS lat. 10482, Brev. sæc. xiv, fol. 176ʳ–177ʳ (O); *ibid.*, MS lat. 1263, Brev. sæc. xiv, fol. 97ᵛ (P):

1 Finito responsorio,[1] statim debet fieri representatio Sepulcri.
2 Angeli ad Mulieres:
3 *Quem queritis in sepulcro, o Christicole?*
4 Mulieres ad Angelum:
5 *Ihesum Nazarenum crucifixum, o celicole.*
6 Angeli:
7 *Non est hic, surrexit sicut predixerat;*
8 *ite, nunciate quia surrexit.*
9 Tunc uertant se Mulieres ad chorum et ueniant cantando prosam:
10 *Victime paschali lau|des immolant Christiani;*
11 *Agnus redemit oues;*
12 *Christus innocens Patri reconciliauit peccatores.*
13 *Mors et uita duello conflixere mirando;*
14 *Dux uite mortuus, regnat uiuus.*
15 Tunc cantor stet in medio chori et dicat versum:
16 *Dic nobis, Maria, quid uidisti in uia?*
17 Prima Mulier:
18 *Sepulcrum Christi uiuentis, et gloriam uidi resurgentis.*
19 Secunda Mulier:
20 *Angelicos testes, sudarium et uestes.*
21 Tercia Mulier:
22 *Surrexit Christus, spes nostra; precedet suos in Galileam.*
23 Cantor ad chorum:
24 *Credendum est magis soli Marie ueraci quam Iudeorum turbe fallaci.*
25 Chorus:
26 *Scimus Christum surrexisse a mortuis uere.*
27 *Tu nobis, uictor Rex, miserere.*
28 Psalmus *Te Deum.*

Variants:

1 Finito statim debet fieri presentacio sepulchri (B); Statim fit representatio sepulchri (C.H); Finito . . . fieri presentacio sepulchri (D); Versus ad sepulchrum (F.J); Prosa (I); Finito responsorio statim fit representatio sepulchri (N).
2 Et primo angeli ad mulieres cantando uersum sequentem (C.H.K); Angeli ad mulieres cantando (E); Angeli (F); *Omitted* (I); Angeli ad mulieres respondeant (L).
3 Quem angeli queritis . . . Christicole (I).
4 Mulieres uersus (B); Mulieres (C.E.F.H.J.N); Mulieres ad angelos versum (G.K.L); Mulier (I); Mulieres ad angelum versum (M.O).
5 Ihesum . . . o Christicole (D); crucifixum *omitted* (E).
6 Angeli versum (G.K.L.M.O).

[1] The *Visitatio* of Paris is regularly preceded by the responsory *Et valde mane.* See above, p. 232. The numerals accompanying the present text are, of course, merely editorial.

9 Tunc . . . chorum dicentes prosam (C.H); Tunc uertant se ad mulieres . . .
   prosa (D); Tunc . . . prosam sequentem simul Prosa (E); Tunc uertunt . . .
   et cantant sequentia (F); Tunc . . . mulieres et ueniant cantando istam
   prosam sequentem Prosa (G); Tunc . . . et cantant prosa (I); Tunc . . . et
   cantant (J); Tunc . . . cantando cantando prosam sequentem simul Prosa
   (K); Tunc . . . cantando prosam Prosa (L); Tunc reuertant se mulieres . . .
   cantando Prosa (M); Tunc . . . cantando simul (N); Hympnus Prima
   Maria (P).

10 Victime . . . immolent Christiani (C).

11 *Preceded by* Versus (E.F.G.H.I.O.P)

12 Christus innocens patris reconciliaui peccatores (G).

13 *Preceded by* Versus (E.F.G.H.I.O.P); duello *omitted* (K).

15 Tunc . . . dicat mulieribus (B.K.M.N); Cantor ad mulieres (C.F); Tunc
   cantor a dextris stet . . . dicat mulieribus versum (D); Tunc . . . dicat
   mulieribus versum (E.G.O); Tunc cantor ad mulieres (H); Versus (I);
   Tunc cantor stans in choro dicat mulieribus (J); Tunc . . . dicat dicat
   mulieribus versum (L); Cantor ad Mariam (P).

16 Dic . . . quid uidistis in uia (D.N).

17 *Omitted* (E); Prima mulier versum (G.L.O); Versus (I); Prima mulier
   sola dicat (J); Prima mulier respondeat cantori (K); Prima mulier sola
   (N); Prima Maria (P).

18 et *omitted* (B).

19 Secunda (C.H); Secunda mulier versum (D.G.L.O); *Omitted* (E); Versus
   (I); Secunda mulier dicat (J); Secunda mulier uero uertet se et cum manu
   ostendat sepulchrum dicens versum (K); Secunda mulier sola (N);
   Secunda Maria (P).

21 Tertia (C.H.P); Tercia mulier versum (D.G.O); *Omitted* (E.I); Tercia
   mulier sola dicat (J); Tercia mulier dicat versum (K); Tercia mulier sola
   (N).

22 Surrexit . . . uos in Galileam (C); Surrexit Christus spes mea precedet
   suos (*corrected to* uos) in Galileam (E); Surrexit . . . uos in Galylea (I);
   Surrexit . . . mea precedet suos in Galilea (K); Surrexit . . . mea . . .
   Galyleam (L); Surrexit . . . nostra (*corrected to* mea) precedit suos
   (*corrected to* vos) in Galilea (N); Surrexit . . . Galilea (P).

23 Cantor (B.P); Cantor a sinistris ad chorum versum (D); *Omitted* (E);
   Cantor ad chorum versum (G.L); Versus (I); Cantor cum duobus chorum
   tenentibus dicat ad chorum (J); Cantor versum (O).

24 *In margin* Non dicitur hic uersus (N).

25 Chorus versum (D.G.L.O); *Omitted* (E); Versus (I).

26 Scimus Christum surrexisse ex mortuis uere (G.H.I.J); Scimus Christum
   resurrexisse . . . uere (P).

27 Tu . . . miserere alleluia (B.D.I.M); uictor *omitted* (P).

28 Versus Surrexit dominus uere et apparuit Symoni Te Deum (B); Episcopus uel sacerdos psalmus Te deum (H.J); Et statim sequitur psalmus Te
   deum (K); *omitted* (M).

The same *Visitatio*, without significant variants, is found in printed Paris
breviaries of 1584 and 1474 mentioned by Lange, nos. 95 and 96, p. 62.
Lange (no. 92, p. 62) reports that this version is found also in a Léon breviary

of 1516, but I have not been able to inspect it. Textual irregularities suggest the separate printing of the following from Paris, Bibl. Mazarine, MS 342, Brev. Parisiense sæc. xiv, fol. 212 r–212 v:

Finito responsorio, statim debet fieri presentacio Sepulchri. Angeli ad Mulieres: *Quem queritis in sepulchro, o Christicole?*

Mulieres ad Angelum versum: *Ihesum Nazarenum crucifixum, o celicole.*

Angeli versum: *Non est hic, surrexit sicut predixerat; ite, nunciate quia surrexit.*

Tunc uertant se Mulieres ad chorum et ueniant cantando: *Alleluia! Resurrexit Dominus, hodie resurrexit leo fortis, Christus, filius Dei.*
    Deo gracias, dicite eya!

⟨Prima Maria:⟩ *Victime paschali laudes immolant Christiani.*

Secunda Maria dicit: *Agnus redemit oues, Christus innocens Patri reconciliauit peccatores.*

Tercia Maria versum: *Mors et uita duello conflixere mirando; dux uite mortuus, regnat uiuus.*

Tunc cantor a dextris stet in medio chori, et dicat Mulieribus versum: *Dic nobis, Maria, quid uidisti in uia?*

Prima Mulier versum: *Sepulchrum Christi uiuentis,[1] et gloriam uidi resurgentis.*

Secunda Mulier versum: *Angelicos testes, sudarium et uestes.*

Tercia Mulier versum: *Surrexit Christus, spes nostra; precedet suos in Galyleam.*

Cantor a[2] sinistris ad chorum versum: *Credendum est magis soli Marie ueraci quam Iudeorum turbe fallaci.*

Chorus: *Scimus | Christum surrexisse a mortuis uere; tu nobis, uictor rex, miserere.*

Psalmus[3] *Te Deum.*

This is unique among the Paris versions in introducing before *Victimæ paschali* the passage *Alleluia! Resurrexit Dominus.* For the sake of completeness I give also the abbreviated form of the Paris *Visitatio* from Bibl. Nat., MS lat. 978, Ordin. Parisiense sæc. xv, fol. 24 r (A), with the variants from Bibl. Nat., MS. lat. 16317, Ordin. Parisiense sæc. xiii, fol. 32 r–32 v (B):

AD SEPULCRUM

Angelus[4] ad Mulieres: *Quem queritis?*

Mulieres: *Ihesum.*

Angeli: *Non est hic.*

Tunc uertant se Mulieres ad chorum, et ueniant[5] cantando:
                Victime pascali.[6]
        Versus: *Agnus redemit.*
        Versus: *Mors et uita.*

Tunc cantor stans in choro dicat Mulieribus:[7] *Dic nobis, Maria.*

Prima Mulier sola dicat versum:[8] *Sepulcrum Christi.*

Secunda Mulier sola dicat versum:[9] *Angelicos testes.*

Tercia Mulier sola dicat versum:[9] *Surrexit Christus.*

---

[1] uiuentis] inuentis (MS).
[2] a] ad (MS).
[3] Psalmus] Versus Surrexit dominus uere et apparuit Symoni Psalmus (MS).
[4] Angelus] Angeli (B).

[5] et ueniant] Omitted (B).
[6] pascali] Omitted (B).
[7] Mulieribus] Mulieribus versum (B).
[8] versum] Omitted (B).
[9] sola dicat versum] Omitted (B).

Cantor cum duobus tenentibus chorum dicat ad chorum versum:[1] *Credendum est.*

Chorus versum:[2] *Scimus Christum.*

Episcopus uel sacerdos:[3] *Te Deum laudamus.*

Because of its rubrics in French a slight special interest attaches to the following from Paris, Bibl. Nat., MS lat. 13233, Brev. Parisiense sæc. xiv, fol. 189[r], previously edited by Lange, no. 87, pp. 60–2.

Les[4] angels deuant le Sepulcre: *Quem queritis in sepulchro, o Christicole?*

Et les Fames verse: *Ihesum Nazarenum crucifixum, o celicole.*

Angels: *Non est hic, surrexit sicut predixerat; ite, nunciate quia surrexit.*

Les Fames tornees uers le cuer dient ces uerses:

> *Victime paschali laudes immolant Christiani.*

Verse: *Agnus redemit oues, Christus innocens Patri reconciliauit peccatores.*

Verse: *Mors et uita duello conflixere mirando; dux uite mortuus, regnat uiuus.*

Le chantre au Fames: *Dic nobis, Maria, quid uidisti in uia?*

La i[e] Fame: *Sepulcrum Christi uiuentis, et gloriam uidi resurgentis.*

La ii[e] Fame: *Angelicos testes, sudarium et vestes.*

La iii[e] Fame verse: *Surrexit Christus, spes nostra; precedet suos in Galileam.*

Le chantre au cuer: *Credendum est magis soli Marie ueraci quam Iudeorum turbe fallaci.*

Chorus: *Scimus Christum surrexisse a mortuis uere; tu nobis, uictor rex, miserere.*

Psalmus: *Te Deum.*

A similar text, with French rubrics, is found in Paris, Bibl. Nat., MS lat. 1052, Brev. Parisiense sæc. xv, fol. 116[r]–116[v], mentioned by Lange, no. 93, p. 62. Towards the elucidation of the action the vernacular rubrics add nothing to what is contained in the Latin rubrics of the several texts printed in the commentary and notes above.

Related to the Paris *Visitatio* in content is the following unpublished text from Bari, Bibl. Capit., MS 7, Cantatorium Barense sæc. xiii, p. 83:

VERSUS[5] AD SEPULCRUM

Angeli ad Mulieres: ⟨*Q*⟩*uem queritis?*

Mulieres: *Iesum.*

Angeli: *Non est hic.*

Tunc vertant se Mulieres ad chorum, et ueniant cantando prosam:

> *Victime.*

Versus: *Agnus redemit.*

Versus: *Mors et vita.*

Tunc cantor stans in choro dicat Mulieribus: *Dic nobis, Maria.*

Prima Mulier sola dicat versum: *Sepulcrum Christi.*

Secunda Mulier sola dicat versum: *Angelicos testes.*

Tercia Mulier sola dicat versum: *Surrexit Christus.*

Cantor ad chorum: *Credendum est.*

---

[1] Cantor ... versum] Tunc cantor dicat ad chorum (B).

[2] versum] Omitted (B).

[3] sacerdos] sacerdos psalmum (B).

[4] Immediately preceded by the third responsory *Et valde mane.*

[5] Immediately preceded by the third responsory *Et valde mane.*

Chorus: *Scimus Christum.*

Episcopus: *Te Deum.*

For a closely similar text from a MS of the fourteenth or fifteenth century in the same library see Wilmotte, pp. 41–3. The editor does not identify the MS.

Page 277, note 1. The following *Visitatio* from London, Brit. Mus., Add. MS 37399, Brev. Parisiense sæc. xiii–xiv, fol. 236ᵛ–237ʳ, now first printed, is mentioned by Brooks, *New Texts*, p. 475.

Versus ad Sepulcrum

Angeli: *Qvem queritis in sepulcro, o Christicole?*

Mulieres: *Ihesum Nazarenum crucifixum, o celicole.*

Angeli: *Non est hic, surrexit sicut predixerat; ite, nunciate quia surrexit.*

Tunc uertunt simul et cantant:

> *Victime paschali laudes immolant Christiani.*
> *Agnus redemit oues; Christus innocens Patri reconciliauit peccatores.*
> *Mors et uita duello conflixere mirando; dux uite mortuus, regnat uiuus.*

Cantor ad Mulieres: *Dic nobis, Maria, quid uidisti in uia?*

Prima Mulier: *Sepul|crum Christi uiuentis, et gloriam uidi resurgentis.*

Secunda Mulier: *Angelicos testes, sudarium et uestes.*

Tercia Mulier: *Surrexit Christus, spes nostra; precedit suos in Galilea.*

Cantor ad chorum: *Credendum est magis soli Marie ueraci quam Iudeorum turbe fallaci.*

Chorus: *Scimus Christum surrexisse a mortuis uere; tu nobis, uictor rex, miserere.*

Psalmus: *Te Deum.*

Page 279, note 2. With the *Visitatio* from Paris MS 10579 should be associated another text from Châlons-sur-Marne found in Paris, Bibl. de l'Arsenal, MS 595, Brev.-Miss. Catalaunense sæc. xiv, fol. 164ᵛ, and now first printed:

Angeli[1] ad Mulieres dicunt: *Quem queritis in sepulchro, o Christicole?*

Mulieres ad Angelos: *Ihesum Nazarenum querimus crucifixum, o celicole.*

Angeli ad Mulieres: *Non est hic, surrexit sicut predixerat; ite, nuntiate quia surrexit a morte.*

Mulieres respondent vertentes se ad chorum: *Alleluya, resurrexit Dominus, hodie resurrexit leo fortis, Christus, filius Dei.*

> *Deo gracias dicite.*
> *Te Deum.*

The following passage, added in the lower margin (fol. 164ᵛ) by the same hand that wrote the rest of the page, appears to have been designed for insertion as a substituted continuation of the play after the last rubric in the text above (*Mulieres respondent vertentes se ad chorum*):

Et ipsis uenientibus versus chorum dicat prima hunc uersum: *Victime.* Secunda: *Agnus redemit.* Tercia: *Mors et uita.* Succentor ueniens eis obuiam ad primum gradum presbyterii interroget primam: *Dic nobis, Maria.* Cui illa: *Sepulchrum.* Secunda: *Angelicos te⟨stes⟩.* Tercia: *Surrexit Christus.* Tunc annun-

---

[1] Immediately preceded by the third responsory *Et valde mane.*

ciat succentor Resurrectionem cantans: *Credendum est.* Et omnes alii de choro: *Scimus Christum,* et cetera. Sequitur *Te Deum.*

The data before us may indicate merely that the scribe blundered, and then corrected himself, as best he could, in the lower margin. Possibly, however, the first passage above represents a simpler form of *Visitatio* once in use at Châlons, and the second passage is the expansion.

Page 280, note 3. With the *Visitatio* from Brit. Mus., MS Harl. 2958, should be associated the following from Treves, Stadtbibl., MS 1738, Ordin. Trevirense sæc. xv, fol. 54ᵛ, previously edited by Brooks, *New Texts,* pp. 470–1:

Post *Gloria Patri* resumatur ipsum responsorium, et egrediatur processio ante tumbam Sancti Symeonis, candelis accensis precedentibus tribus altaristis in cappis purpureis, qui stabunt simul ante ostium altaris. Finito responsorio, reperient duos scolares in Sepulchro tanquam Angelos cantantes sonora voce antiphonam: *Quem queritis?* Et prefati tres vicarii qui representant tres Mulieres simul cantando respondent antiphonam: *Ihesum Nazarenum.* Item Angeli respondent cantando antiphonam: *Non est hic.* Postea sine interuallo incipient idem Angeli antiphonam: *Venite et videte.* Qua finita, accedent dicte tres Mulieres accipientes sudarium de Sepulchro, et cantent Angeli: *Cito euntes.* Finito, cantor incipiet *Victime paschali laudes.* Procedat processio in medium ecclesie, et tres Marie ante chorum vertent se, et cum chorus cantauerit versum: *Dic nobis, Maria,* respondeat vna Maria cantando: *Sepulchrum Christi.* Item chorus: *Dic nobis, Maria.* Secunda Maria *respondeat* cantando: *Angelicos testes.* Item chorus: *Dic nobis, Maria.* Tertia Maria cantando *respondeat: Surrexit Christus.* Chorus: *Credendum est.* Intrando chorum postea cantor incipiet antiphonam: *Et recordate sunt. Te Deum laudamus.*

Here belongs also the *Visitatio* published 'ex ordin. Trevir.' by Würdtwein (pp. 187–8), whose text I reprint:

Et postquam ultimum responsorium fuerit cantatum, *Dum transisset sabbatum,* ut infra, idem resumitur, et egreditur processio ad medium ecclesiæ, prius egressis tribus vicariis cum tribus thuribulis, visitare Sepulchrum; et ibidem invenient duos sacerdotes in albis indutos tanquam Angelos alta voce cantantes ut sequitur: *Quem quæritis in sepulchro, o Christicolæ?*
Et respondeant alii tres: *Jesum Nazarenum crucifixum, o cœlicolæ.*
Angeli cantant: *Non est hic, surrexit.*
  Venite et videte locum ubi positus erat Dominus, alleluja, alleluja.
Et accedant dicti tres accipientes sudarium; Angeli canunt: *Cito euntes dicite discipulis quia surrexit Dominus, alleluja.*
Tunc tres cantent:
  Victimæ paschali laudes immolent Christiani;
  Agnus redemit oves, Christus innocens Patri reconciliavit peccatores;
  Mors et vita duello conflixere mirando; dux vitæ mortuus, regnat vivus.
Chorus tertio repetit: *Dic nobis, Maria, quid vidisti in via?*
Responsio 1: *Sepulchrum Christi viventis, et gloriam vidi resurgentis.*
Responsio 2: *Angelicos testes, sudarium et vestes.*
Responsio 3: *Surrexit Christus, spes mea; precedet suos in Galilæam.*
Chorus prosequitur:
  Credendum est magis soli Mariæ veraci quam Judæorum turbæ fallaci.

Scimus Christum surrexisse a mortuis vere; tu nobis, victor Rex, miserere, alleluja.
Intrando chorum: *Et recordatæ sunt verborum ejus, et regressæ a monumento nuntia-*
verunt hæc omnia illis undecim et cæteris omnibus, alleluja.
His finitis, canitur *Te Deum,* et cetera.

Page 282, note 1. With the *Visitatio* from the Würzburg *Directorium* of 1477
may be associated the following, from a *Directorium Marianum* of uncertain
date, from Mainz, published by Würdtwein, pp. 179–81, reprinted therefrom
by Rueff, pp. 72–3, and now reprinted again from Würdtwein:

Post *Gloria Patri* responsorium repetitur, et cum illa repetitione fit solempnis
processio usque ad Sepulchrum in capella Sancti Egidii, in qua processione
tres seniores ibidem presentes cappis sericis induti omnes alios antecedent,
precedentibus duabus candelis giratis; et interim duo cavernarii intrant
Sepulchrum sedentes ibidem absconditi, quo usque responsorium fuerit
finitum. Tunc pueri in Sepulchro cantent antiphonam: *Quem queritis in*
sepulchro, o Christicole? Tres seniores respondendo cantent: *Jhesum Nazarenum*
crucifixum, o celicole. Pueri iterum cantent: *Non est hic quem queritis,* et de post
surgentes aperiendo Sepulchrum et tenentes sudarium in manibus iterum
cantent: *Venite et videte locum.* Quo finito, tres seniores recipiunt sudarium
reverenter in manibus, et in alto tenentes cantent antiphonam: *Ad sepulchrum*
Domini gementes. Quo finito, recedunt cum processione in ordine sicut venerunt, et in recessu cantantur sequentia *Victime paschali laudes,* et circumeuntes
baptismum cum processione, in qua tres seniores iterum alios precedent,
revertuntur ad chorum, ubi tres seniores stabunt cum sudario in altum
extenso ante summum altare, et duo cavernarii ante pulpitum in medio
chori; et cavernarii primo cantent versum: *Dic nobis, Maria, quid vidisti in via?*
Quibus primus senior cantando respondet: *Sepulchrum Christi viventis.* Post hoc
alter senior cantet: *Angelicos testes.* De post tertius senior: *Surrexit Christus,*
spes mea. Deinde cavernarii cantent alium versum: *Credendum est magis soli*
Marie, choro respondente: *Scimus Christum surrexisse a mortuis vere.* Post hoc tres
seniores tenentes sudarium extensum apud summum altare incipient antiphonam cantando: *Surrexit Dominus de sepulchro,* quibus chorus respondet: *Qui*
pro nobis pependit in ligno, alleluja. Et seniores ponunt sudarium super altare.
Tunc cantor cum suis capellanis in medio chori incipiet solempniter *Te*
Deum laudamus, et cetera.

Page 283, note 1. Although the known texts of the Eichstätt *Visitatio*
offer, in general, no significant variants from the text in Munich MS 3918,
a slight interest attaches to the exceptional opening rubric in the following
from Bamberg, Staatsbibl., MS 101 (Ed.VII.53), Ordin. Eystettense sæc.
xv, fol. 103 ʳ–103 ᵛ, previously edited by Brooks, *Osterfeiern,* pp. 54–5:

In die Resurreccionis Domini ante Laudes fit processio in ecclesia kathe-
drali ad monasterium cum responsorio *Dum transisset sabbatum, Maria Mag-*
dalena et Maria Iacobi et | Salome emerunt aromata, vt venientes vngerent Ihesum,
alleluia, alleluia. Versus: *Et valde mane vna sabbatorum veniunt ad monumentum,*
orto iam sole. Vt venientes. Gloria Patri. Vt venientes. Post hoc precentores cum
cantore visitant Sepulchrum, et cantant antiphonam: *Quis reuoluet nobis ab*
ostio lapidem quem tegere sanctum cernimus sepulchrum?

Duo scolares in Sepulchro cantant antiphonam: *Quem queritis, o tremule mulieres, in hoc tumulo gementes?*

Precentores respondent: *Iesum Nazarenum crucifixum querimus.*

Scolares respondent: *Non est hic quem queritis, sed cito euntes nunciate discipulis eius et Petro quia surrexit Ihesus.*

Deinde scolares exeunt de Sepulchro cum lintheo, et cantant antiphonam: *Venite et videte locum vbi positus erat Dominus, alleluia, alleluia.*

Tunc cantor et precentores redeunt de Sepulchro; cantant antiphonam: *Ad monumentum venimus*, vt supra. Finita antiphona, chorus canit sequenciam: *Victime paschali laudes im⟨m⟩olent Christiani.*
Agnus redemit oues; Christus innocens Patri reconciliauit peccatores.
Mors et vita duello conflixere mirando; dux vite mortuus, regnat viuus.
Dic nobis, Maria, quid vidisti in via?

Vnus precentor respondet: *Sepulchrum Christi viuentis, et gloriam vidi resurgentis.*

Iterum chorus repetit versum: *Dic nobis, Maria.*

Alter precentor respondet: *Angelicos testes, sudarium et vestes.*

Chorus tercio repetit versum: *Dic nobis.*

Cantor respondet: *Surrexit Christus, spes mea; precedet suos in Galileam.*

Deinde finitur sequencia per chorum:
Credendum est magis soli Marie veraci quam Iudeorum turbe fallaci.
Scimus Christum surrexisse ex mortuis vere; tu nobis, victor rex, miserere.

In reditu canitur ad chorum *Te Deum laudamus.*

In this text the opening rubric shows very clearly the processional use of the full responsory *Dum transisset*, with its repeats and doxology. Without significant variants, the same version of the *Visitatio* is found in Munich, Staatsbibl., MS lat. 27233, Obsequiale Eystettense sæc. xvi, fol. 36ʳ, described by Brooks, *Neue Osterfeiern*, p. 303, and one is reprinted from an *Obsequiale* of 1539 by Lange, no. 106, pp. 71–4. See Brooks (*op. cit.*, p. 303) in regard to similar texts in Munich copies of printed Eichstätt breviaries of 1483, 1497, 1525, and 1589, and in an Eichstätt *Diurnale* of 1589.

Page 288, note 4. With the *Visitatio* from Le Mans MS 165 may be placed the same text found in two printed books: *Antiphonarius . . . secundum solennem Cenomanensis dioceseos ritum*, Paris, 1529, fol. 70ᵛ; and *Breviarium Cenomanense ad Romani formam expressum*, Paris, 1663, p. 460. Here belongs the following unpublished text from Paris, Bibl. de l'Arsenal, MS 275, Brev. Cenomanense sæc. xv, fol. 129ᵛ:

Hoc quod sequitur fit in ecclesia Cenomanense. Angelus ad Marias: *Quem queritis in sepulchro, o Christicole?*

Marie respondent: *Ihesum Nazarenum crucifixum, o celicole.*

Angelus: *Non est hic, surrexit sicut predixerat; ite, nunciate quia surrexit.*

Mulieres: *Alleluia, surrexit Dominus, hodie resurrexit leo fortis, Christus, filius Dei.*

Tunc se uertunt Mulieres uersus chorum, et cantor dicat Marie Magdalene:
Dic nobis, Maria, quid uidisti in uia?

Maria respondet: *Sepulchrum Christi uiuentis, et gloriam uidi resurgentis.*

Altera Maria: *Angelicos testes, sudarium et uestes.*

Tertia Maria: *Surrexit Christus, spes nostra; precedet suos in Galileam.*

Cantor ad chorum: *Credendum est magis soli Marie ueraci quam Iudeorum turbe fallaci.*

Totus chorus: *Scimus Christum surrexisse a mortuis uere; tu nobis, uictor rex, miserere, alleluia.*

Te Deum.

The following from an *Ordinarius . . . ecclesiæ Moguntinæ*, of the year 1547, is given by Rueff (p. 71), whose text I reprint:

Sub secundo responsorio duo juniores vicarii velud Angeli, induti rubeis albis, vadunt ad Sepulchrum, similiter sacrista ad tradendum tribus Mariis sudarium, quod idem sacrista secum portat ad Sepulchrum. Sub decantacione responsorii ultimi *Dum transisset sabbatum* tres prelati aut seniores induti cappis prioribus absque stolis habentes tres lucernas, quas campanator disponit, in manibus et tres libros, quos disponit sacrista, vadunt ad Sepulchrum ad ferendum sudarium. Tunc Angeli cantabunt: *Quem queritis*, ut in libris. Et hii tres prelati, accepto sudario ab Angelis, revertunt ad chorum. Et cum venerint ad gradus apud summum altare, vertunt facies suas ad chorum. Tunc succentor cum suo astanti incipiet: *Dic nobis, Maria, quid vidisti in via?*

Respondet primus: *Sepulchrum Cristi viventis, et gloriam vidi resurgentis.*

Statimque alter: *Angelicos testes, sudarium et vestes.*

Immediate tercius: *Surrexit Cristus, spes mea; precedet suos in Galilea.*

Chorus: *Credendum est magis soli Marie veraci.*

Tunc priores tres una voce cantent: *Surrexit Dominus de sepulchro, qui pro nobis pependit in ligno, alleluia.*

Sudario sic posito[1] supra summum altare, abeunt Marie. Tunc chorus, audita Resurrectione, prorumpit in vocem altisone cantans *Te Deum laudamus.*

The same version, from a source not precisely indicated, is printed by Würdtwein, pp. 174–5.

Page 290, note 2. Similar to the *Visitatio* from Besançon MS 99 is that in Besançon, Bibl. de la Ville, MS 98, Ordin. ecclesiæ Sancti Stephani Bisuntini sæc. xiii, fol. 40ʳ–40ᵛ, previously edited by Brooks, *Sepulchre*, pp. 94–5:

In die sancto Pasche ad Matutinas fit sicut est consuetum. Quando tercia lectio dicitur, debent esse parati tres canonici in sacrario ad | faciendum Marias, et in modum hunc ornari. Primo debent habere amictos paratos super capita ita quod cooperiant frontes, et dalmaticas albas, et in manibus portantes fialas aureas uel argenteas; et ita procedunt de sacrario post tertium responsorium, precedente cantore cum capa rubea et baculo, precedentibus cereis et turibulo, cantantes usque ad tympanarium et usque in choro bis aut ter: *Quis reuoluet?* Cum uenerint in medio choro, incipiunt ultimam uicem *Quis reuoluet nobis?* usque ante maius altare. A dextris et a sinistris altaris sunt duo pueri inducti admictis albis paratis, et super humeros alas habentes et capas plicatas rubeas super humeros circumdantes alas in modum quo ponunt diaconi stolas; respondent Mulieribus sic: *Quem queritis?* cantando. Et Mulieres: *Jhesum Nazarenum.* Et Angeli: *Non est hic, surrexit.* Et discooperiunt altare Angeli linteaminibus quibus erat altare uelatum. Et Mulieres statim offerunt super altare fialas suas genu flexo, cantantes: *Alleluia, surrexit Dominus hodie*, usque in choro in introitu. Tunc uenit cantor ad eas et dicit ad primam Mariam cantando: *Dic nobis, Maria, quid uidisti in uia?* Respondet prima:

---

[1] posito] posita (Rueff).

Sepulchrum Christi. Et altera que portat amictum sudarii sola dicit: *Angelicos testes,* ostendens sudarium et uestes et Angelos. Et tercia Maria dicit: *Surrexit Christus, spes nostra.* Et cantor respiciendo chorum cantat: *Credendum est magis soli Marie.* Et chorus alta uoce: *Scimus Christum.* Interim redeunt Marie per uiam per quam uenerunt in sacrario cum omnibus sibi adiunctis, et statim incipitur *Te Deum* alta uoce; et choriales deuestiunt rubeas capas et uestiunt albas capas. Et chorus deponit capas nigras usquequo cantatum fuerit *Te Deum.*

Page 291, note 1. With the *Visitatio* from Troyes MS 1150 is to be associated the following from the same library, MS 833, Ordin. Trecense sæc. xiv, fol. 49ʳ, previously edited by Brooks, *Sepulchre,* pp. 108–9:

Post tercium responsorium procedant ab aliqua parte ecclesie tres dyaconi, dalmaticis albis inducti, uelatis capitibus amictis, deferentes uasa aurea uel argentea cum thuribulis, pueris cum cereis et cruciculis ligneis precedentibus. Decantant versus istos: *Ortum predestinacio,* et cetera. Tunc unus de tribus dyaconis cantando dicit: *O Deus!* Respondent duo stantes ad altare: *Quem queritis?* Respondent primi: *Jhesum Nazarenum.* Dicunt stantes ante ad altare: *Non est hic.* Tunc tres primi, uerso uultu ad chorum, dicunt: *Alleluia! Resurrexit.* Succentor dicit: *Dic nobis.* Respondet unus de tribus dyaconis: *Sepulchrum Christi uiuentis.* Chorus cantando respondet: *Credendum est.* Sequitur *Te Deum laudamus,* quod incipitur ab episcopo uel decano tociens quociens faciunt officium; si non, a chorario.

An essentially similar version, from Sens, from an unspecified MS of the thirteenth century, was published in *Mélanges,* vii, 165–7, and reprinted by Lange no. 100, pp. 64–6. For references to earlier reprintings see Lange, p. 9. I give the text from *Mélanges,* vii, 165–7:

1. *Hortum¹ prædestinatio,*
   parvo sabbati spatio,
   providerat in proximo
   civitatis proastio;²

2. *Hortum pomorum vario,*
   non insignem edulio;
   quantum virtutis spatio
   coæqualem Elysio.

3. *In hoc magnus decurio*
   ac nobilis centurio
   florem Mariæ proprio
   sepelivit in tumulo.

4. *Flos autem die tertio,*
   qui floret ab initio,
   refloruit e tumulo
   summo mane diluculo.

Puer in vestitu angelico sedens super pulpitum a cornu altaris sinistro cantabat Angelus: *Quem quæritis in sepulcro, Christicolæ?*
Tres Mariæ simul respondent genua flectendo: *Jesum Nazarenum crucifixum, o cœlicolæ.*
Angelus autem sublevans tapetum altaris, tanquam respiciens in Sepulcrum, cantat: *Non est hic, surrexit sicut prædixerat; ite, nunciate quia surrexit.*
Mariæ revertentes ad chorum cantant: *Resurrexit Dominus, hodie resurrexit leo fortis, Christus, filius Dei.*

---

¹ In *Mélanges,* p. 165, the text, as I reprint it, is preceded by this passage, which is probably editorial: *Antiquitus in ecclesia Senonensi post ultimum responsum* Et valde, &c., *cantabatur prosa ut sequitur.* The numbering of stanzas here, and in the succeeding text, is mine.

² proastio] pro fascio (Print).

Duo vicarii, induti cappis sericis, in medio chori cantant: *Dic nobis, Maria, quid vidisti in via?*

Prima Maria stans a parte sinistra respondit: *Sepulcrum Christi viventis, et gloriam vidi resurgentis.*

Secunda Maria: *Angelicos testes, sudarium et vestes.*

Tertia Maria: *Surrexit Christus, spes nostra; præcedet suos in Galileam.*

Duo vicarii respondent: *Credendum est magis soli Mariæ veraci quam Judæorum turbæ fallaci.*

Totus chorus respondet: *Scimus Christum surrexisse a mortuis vere; tu nobis, victor rex, miserere.*

Deinde dicitur *Te Deum*, et cetera.

The usage of Sens may be further illustrated by the following text from Paris, Bibl. Nat., MS lat. 1028, Brev. Senonense sæc. xiv, fol. 120ʳ, previously edited by Young, *Ordo Prophetarum*, pp. 75–6:

Responsorium: *Et ualde mane una sabbatorum ueniunt ad monumentum, orto iam sole, alleluya.* Versus: *Et respicientes uiderunt reuolutum lapidem ab hostio monumenti. Orto. Gloria Patri et Filio et Spiritui Sancto. Et.* Prosa:

1. *Ortum predestinatio,*
   paruo sabbati spatio,
   prouiderat in proximo
   ciuitatis proastio;

2. *Ortum pomorum uario,*
   non insignem edulio;
   quantum uirtutis spatio
   coequalem Elisio.

3. *In hoc magnus decurio*
   ac nobilis centurio
   florem Marie proprio
   sepeliuit in tumulo.

4. *Flos autem die tercio,*
   qui floret ab initio,
   refloruit e tumulo
   summo mane diluculo.

Orto ⟨iam sole⟩. Post representationem Mariarum sequitur *Te Deum laudamus.*

This text shows clearly that, at Sens, the poem *Hortum prædestinatio* was regarded as a trope of the third responsory, and not as an essential part of the *Visitatio Sepulchri*.

Page 293, note 1. Similar to the play from Paris MS lat. 1255 is the following from *Breuiarium Sancte Patriarcalis et Metropolitane Bituricensis Ecclesie*, 1522, fol. lxxᵛ, previously reprinted, incompletely, by Lange no. 98, pp. 62–3:

PROSA[1]

O quam magno dies ista   celebranda gaudio!
Quam ingenti, quam deuoto   recolenda studio!
In qua Christus iam misertus   hominis exitio,
Morte victa, debellato   demonis imperio,
De tormentis traxit suos   in virtutis brachio.

Hac in die resurrexit   potestate deifica.
Angelus stat ad sepulchrum;   fugit plebs Iudaica.
Mulieres visione   pauentes angelica
Secum vasa cum unguentis   ferunt aromatica.

Duo Angeli: *Quem queritis in sepulchro, o Christicole?*
Mulieres: *Ihesum Nazarenum, o celicole.*

[1] Immediately preceded by the third responsory *Dum transisset.*

Angeli: *Non est hic, surrexit sicut predixerat; ite, nunciate quia surrexit.*
  Dic nobis, Maria, quid vidisti in via?
  Sepulchrum Christi viuentis, et gloriam vidi resurgentis.
  Angelicos testes, sudarium et vestes.
  Surrexit Christus, spes mea; precedet suos in Galileam, alleluia.
  Resurrexit Dominus.
Psalmus: *Te Deum.*

Page 294, note 1. From Padua MS S, of the thirteenth century, the *Depositio* (fol. 94 ᵛ) and *Elevatio* (fol. 98 ʳ) are here printed for the first time:

⟨DEPOSITIO CRUCIS⟩

Celebrato altaris officio,[1] episcopus accipiens Crucem, cum ministris altaris et aliis sacerdotibus incip*it* responsorium *Vadis propiciator.* Et deferunt Crucem ad altare Sancti Danielis, et deponunt eam in Sepulchro ante altare; et flexis genibus adorant et dicunt *Pater Noster* sub silentio.[2] Quo finito, leuant se, et tunc dic*it* sacrista episcopo *Domine, iube custodiri sepulcrum*; et episcopus respondet *Habetis custodiam; ite et custodite sicut scitis.* Et tunc magister scolarium confert episcopo responsorium *Sepulto Domino*, et reuertuntur cantando submissa uoce dictum responsorium. Et tunc exuit se episcopus, et uenit cum canonicis et aliis ecclesie clericis ad locum archipresbyteri, et ibi submissa uoce psalmos uespertinales cantant.

⟨ELEVATIO CRUCIS⟩

Custodes uadunt ad altare Sancti Danielis, et accipiunt Crucem de Sepulcro Christi, dimisso ibi pallio, et deferunt eam super altare Sancte Crucis. Et dum pulsantur campane, canonici uadunt et conducunt episcopum in ecclesiam, ut dictum et factum est supra in Natiuitate Domini.[3]

Here, for general convenience, may be placed the following from Bamberg, Staatsbibl., MS lit. 118 (Ed. I. 19), Ordin. Bambergense sæc. xvi, fol. 67 ᵛ–68 ʳ, previously edited by Brooks, *Osterfeiern*, pp. 55–6:

Responsorium tercium *Dum transisset sabbatum*, quod incipitur in organis. Quo finito, iterum in organis repetitur, sub quo fiet processio ad medium ecclesie cum sex candelis et tot candelabris ferreis, que portentur a choralibus; et quilibet chorus descendet per ianuam suam, et dicta candelabra locentur prope scampnum altaris Sancte Kunegundis ad medium ecclesie. Chorarii stabunt in medio ecclesie prope trunccum, et pueri kibiczen[4] maneant in choro Sancti Petri ante altare Sancte Michaëlis; finitoque responsorio in organis, pueri kibiczen incipiunt cantare versus *Ad tumulum venere gementes,* chorus notam ordine suo. Hiis finitis, tres sumissarii in cappis albis, cum thurribulis et stolis albis, venient ad Sepulchrum Saluatoris in choro Sancti Geor⟨g⟩ii; et assideant duo dyaconi in dalmaticis albis cantantes: *Quem queritis in sepulchro, o Cristicole?*
Sumissarii respondeant: *Ihesum Naza\renum crucifixum, o celicole.*

---

[1] The *Missa Præsanctificatorum* immediately precedes.

[2] silentio] scilentio (MS).

[3] Matins follows immediately.

[4] In explaining *Kibitz*, H. Fischer (*Schwä-bisches Wörterbuch*, iv, Tübingen, 1914, col. 361) refers to *Geifitz* (iii, 221), for meanings such as 'ungezogenes Kind', 'unruhige Person', and 'naseweiser junger Mensch'.

Dyaconi: *Non est hic, surrexit.*
Dyaconi: *Venite et videte locum.*
Dyaconi: *Cito[1] euntes.*
Dyaconi: *Surrexit Dominus de sepulchro.*
Summissarii redeant de Sepulchro sub eisdem versibus ad altare Sancti Stephani. Deinde[2] senior chorarius incipiet versum: *Dic nobis, Maria.*
Sumissarius senior respondet cantando versum: *Sepulchrum Christi viuentis.*
Secundus sumissarius versum: *Angelicos testes.*
Tercius sumissarius versum: *Surrexit Christus, spes mea.*
Chorus subsequitur alios versus: *Credendum est magis soli.*
Deinde succentor incipiet *Crist ist erstanden,* alta voce, et sic tota processio redeat ad chorum Sancti Petri. Deinde incipitur psalmus *Te Deum laudamus* in organis.

Concerning the processional *Ad tumulum venere gementes* used here see above, p. 585; and concerning the vernacular song *Christ ist erstanden* see below, p. 636.

Although its rubrics are laconic and its text is somewhat corrupt, one may offer here the exceptional version from Vienna, Nationalbibl., MS lat. 13427, Brev. Pragense sæc. xiv, fol. 129ʳ–129ᵛ, previously edited by Lange, no. 107, pp. 74–5:

Responsorium *Dum transisset sabbatum, Maria Magdalena et Maria Iacobi et Salomee emerunt aromata, ut uenientes vngerent Ihesum, alleluia.* Tres persone cantent istum versum, *Et ualde mane vna sabbatorum ueniunt ad monumentum, orto iam sole. Ut.* | Prima persona: *Omnipotens pater altissime.*
Secunda: *Amisimus enim solacium.*
Tercia: *Sed eamus.*
Stantes circa Sepulchrum ca*ntent: Quis reuoluet nobis?*
Angeli: *Quem queritis?*
Persone: *Ihesum Nazarenum.*
Angeli: *Non est hic.*
Et item ca*ntent: Venite et uidete.*
Tercia ibi manet. Due eundo ad chorum: *Ad monumentum uenimus.*
Tunc tercia transeundo cantat: *Cum uenissem,* cum aliis, usque ad illud: *Dic nobis, Maria.*
Tunc duo cantentes: *Dic nobis, Maria.*
Maria: *Sepulchrum Christi.*
Item illi: *Dic nobis, Maria.*
Maria: *Angelicos testes.*
Chorus: *Credendum est magis.*
Duo presbyteri cantent: *Christus Dominus resur⟨rexit⟩.*
Chorus: *Deo gracias.* Sequitur *Te Deum laudamus.*

The striking aspects of this version are the presence of certain ten-syllable verses,[3] and the apparent participation of the three Marys in the singing of the responsory *Dum transisset.*

Page 296, note 1. The text of the hymn *Aurora diem nuntiat* is printed as follows in *A.H.,* xix, 269–70:

---

[1] Cito] Scito (MS).
[2] Deinde] Preceded by *respicientes chorum,*   crossed out (MS).
[3] See below, p. 677.

1. Aurora diem nuntiat,
   et terram ros inebriat;
   nos verus sol justitiæ
   rore perfundat gratiæ.

2. Lux redit sine nubilo,
   lux festa digna jubilo,
   transcendens mundi nubila,
   Chorus, ex corde jubila.

3. Jesu, choro psallentium
   lucis infunde radium;
   Te lucem, lucis filium,
   vox una canit omnium.

4. Tibi nostra devotio
   clamat præ cordis gaudio,
   nec lingua potest exprimi,
   quod dictat ardor animi.

5. Prompti sumus et hilares,
   Victor, in tuis laudibus,
   sed laudi tamen impares
   tuis egemus precibus.

6. Pro Victoris victoria
   Patri prolique gloria,
   Patris prolisque nexui,
   laus sancto sit Spiritui.

Page 297, note 5. The fullest known form of the verses beginning *Resurrexit victor ab inferis* is found in the following version of the *Visitatio* from Melk, Stiftsbibl., MS 1094, Process. monasticum sæc. xv, fol. 35^r–38^v, previously edited by Brooks, *New Texts*, pp. 477–8:

Ad Visitandum Sepulchrum

Quis reuoluit nobis | lapidem ab hostio monumenti?
Angelus: *Quem queritis in sepulchro, o Christicole?*
Marie: *Ihesum Nazarenum crucifixum, o celicole.*
Angelus: *Alleluia.*
Resurrexit victor ab inferis,
pastor ovem reportans humeris. |
Alleluia.
Reformator ruine veteris
causam egit humani generis.
Vespertina migrauit hostia,
matutina suscepta gloria.
Alleluia.
Non di|uina tamen potencia
est absor⟨p⟩ta carnis substancia,
cui perhennis est benedictio,
summe carnis glorificacio.
Alleluia.
Benedicto Patre cum Filio
benedicat nostra devo|cio.
Angelus: *Nolite expauescere, Ihesum queritis Nazarenum crucifixum; surrexit, non est hic. Ecce locus vbi posuerunt eum. Sed ite, dicite discipulis eius et Petro quia precedet vos in Galilea; ibi eum videbitis sicut dixit | vobis.*
Angelus: *Venite et videte locum vbi positus erat Dominus, alleluia, alleluia.*
Marie: *Surrexit Dominus de sepulchro, qui pro nobis pependit in ligno, alleluia.*
Chorus: *Dic nobis, Maria, quid ⟨vidisti in via⟩?*
⟨Marie:⟩ *Sepulchrum Christi.*
Chorus: *Dic nobis.*

Marie: *Angelicos*.[1]

Marie: *Surrexit Christus*.

Chorus: *Cre|dendum est*, et sic per totum.

Mulieres: *Ad monumentum venimus gementes, angelum Domini sedentem vidimus et dicentem quia surrexit Ihesus.*

Ad chorum in processione: *Christus resurgens ex mortuis iam non moritur; mors illi vl|tra non dominabitur; quod enim viuit, viuit Deo, alleluia, alleluia.*[2]

In this play the ten-syllable couplets are used by the angel, in the place usually occupied by *Non est hic*, for announcing the Resurrection to the Marys. The full version of these verses is found also in the *Ludus paschalis* from Klosterneuburg, and some of them appear also in other plays.[3] Chevalier, *R.H.*, no. 32896, refers to the following lines from British Mus., MS Egerton 274 (sæc. xiii), fol. 2ᵛ, printed in *A.H.*, xx (1895), 17:

> Resurrexit victor ab inferis.
> Ecce locus infra quem jacuit,
> et se totum poscenti tribuit.
> Psallat ergo mundus in prosperis.

These are, it appears, not associated with a dramatic text.

Page 302, note 3. With the text from Laon MS 215 should be associated that from 'vetus ordinarium optimæ notæ, ante annos 400 scriptum', given by Martene (iii, 172), and reprinted from him by Young (*Dramatic Associations*, pp. 51–2), and, very incompletely, by Lange (no. 43, p. 30). A brief text of the same dramatic piece from Laon, Bibl. de la Ville, MS 263, Troparium-Hymnarium Laudunense sæc. xiii, fol. 145ʳ, was published by Young (*Joseph*, p. 33). Descriptions of the same dramatic ceremonial are given, without precise references to sources, by Bellotte (pp. 215–7, 819), and reprinted from him by Young (*Dramatic Associations*, pp. 52–5). In regard to the Laon ceremony and a similar one at Beauvais see Thiers, ii, 195–8.

Page 304, note 1. The Laon custom of bringing the Host to the altar of the sepulchre early Easter morning is thus described by Bellotte, p. 215 (reprinted by Young, *op. cit.*, p. 53):

Inter antiquissimas Ecclesiæ Christianæ consuetudines annumeratur processio, quæ solemni ritu, quotannis celebratur in Dominica Resurrectionis ante Matutinum, quo tam salutaris mysterij gaudium, aliquo lætitiæ signo, fidelibus populis nuntietur. Hinc est, quod in Ecclesia Laudunensi summo mane pulsantur campanæ hora post mediam noctem secunda in signum festiuæ exultationis, priusquam detur signum Matutini. Quo tempore custos sacrarij, vel alius sacerdos ad hoc deputatus, superpellicio et stola paratus, accedit ad locum pastophorij[4] præeuntibus duobus clericulis cum cereis

---

[1] Marie: Angelicos] Written in left margin. In the lower margin a later hand has written the following, without musical notation: 'Sepulchrum Christi viuentis et gloriam vidi resurgentis Angelicos testes sudarium et vestes Surrexit Christus spes mea precedet suos in Galilea.'

[2] Followed by the rubric *Ad visitandum sepulchrum post Matutinum in die sancto*, introducing the responsory *Cvm transisset sabbatum*. This rubric is clearly out of place.

[3] See above, pp. 423, 435, and below, pp. 648, 649.

[4] The *pastophorium* was a sort of sacristy, on the north side of the choir.

ardentibus, et inde sanctissimum Sacramentum reuerenter et cum debitis
genuflexionibus extrahit, vbi pridie fuerat ritu præscripto collocatum;
ipsumque ambabus manibus tenens ob oculos eleuatum, defert super altare
Sepulchri, vndique cereorum sufficienti numero collustratum, vt locus luci-
dior appareat, et nox ipsa quasi dies illuminetur; nullusque sæcularium illuc
accedit, nec vllus alius præter clericos qui dicti Sepulchri ritibus et ceremonijs
inseruire debent, ac qui proinde fuerint chorali veste parati.

Page 304, note 2. Among the *ordines* describing ceremonies in which the
Elevatio and *Quem quæritis* dialogue are combined should be included the
following from St Gall, Stiftsbibl., MS 1262, Ordin. Sangallense anni 1583,
pp. 142–3, previously published incompletely by Lange, no. 103, pp. 69–71:

In nocte Dominicæ Resurrectionis pulsantur Matutine circa vndecimam
more solito. Post compulsationem Dominus Reverendissimus, uel potius
Pater Decanus, cum ministris suis albis et cappis indutis, conuentus uero in
floccis, et totus chorus cum clero, procedunt processionaliter ad Sepulchrum
Domini in Sacello S. Sebastiani. Conuentus portat ardentes candelas in
manibus, item et scholastici et eorum rector. Procedendo ex choro orant
submissa uoce Domini Conuentuales psalmum *Miserere mei, Deus,* et cetera.
Peruenta processione | ad Sepulchrum, quatuor scholastici ordinati et induti
angelico habitu ad quatuor angulos Sepulchri incipiunt canere vt sequitur.
Primus canit solus versum: *Quem queritis?* et cetera. Secundus: *Jesum Nazarenum.* Tertius: *Non est hic.* Quartus: *Ite, nuntiate.* Deinde quatuor simul
inuicem canunt ultimum versum: *Venite et uidete locum,* et cetera, manibus
interim demonstrantes Sepulchrum. Statim diacono exeunte Sepulchrum cum
crucifixo discooperto, incipit ludi-magister, scilicet cum toto populo, *Christus
surrexit,* et cetera; *Christ ist erstanden,* et cetera; vnnd *Wer er nit erstanden,* et
cetera; *Erstanden ist,* et cetera; *Alleluia, alleluia, alleluia singen wir; Gott den
Herren loben wir; Kyrieleyson,* et cetera. Expletis thurificatione, aspersione, et
assumpto Sacramento, processio redit ad chorum[1] (demissa cruce ante altare
S. Onofry super tapetum);[2] cursorie canitur antiphona *Cum rex gloriæ,* siue[3]
Alle dei, et cetera. Qua finita, incipit chorus et canit sequentiam *Victime,* et
cetera (nihil fit in organis) siue[4] *Christus surrexit,* usque ad versum *Sepulchrum
Christi,* interim Patre Decano astante summo altari ostensuro populo insignia
Dominicæ Resurrectionis. Et prima uice a choro cantato versu: *Dic nobis,
Maria, quid uidisti in uia?* scholastici respondent (cereos in manibus habentes
coram Patre Decano) versum: *Sepulchrum Christi viuentis, et gloriam uidi resurgentis.* Deinde denuo canit chorus uersum: *Dic nobis,* et cetera. Respondent
scholastici: *Angelicos testes, sudarium et uestes.* Mox tertio chorus canit versum:
Dic nobis, Maria. Respondent ultimo scholastici: *Surrexit Christus, spes mea;
precedet suos in Galilæam.* Deinde residuum (scilicet *Credendum est,* et *Scimus
Christum surrexisse*) prosequitur chorus. Ad primum dictum puerorum versum,
ostendit Pater Decanus calicem vacuum; ad secundum, sudarium; ad tertium
versum, Corpus Christi, patena Corpori supposita. Quare ad hunc tertium

---

[1] A sign of omission here refers to the following entry, by another hand, in the upper
margin: *Nota, Dominus Decanus geht* ⟨*get?
gett?*⟩ *mit dem Sacrament zu letzt hernach.*
[2] The marks of parenthesis printed in this
text are in the MS.
[3] siue] The MS may read *sine.*
[4] siue] The MS may read *sine.* The relation of *Christus surrexit* to *Victimæ paschali,* in
any case, is not clear.

versum summe campanulæ pulsantur. His finitis, incipiunt pueri dicti supra versiculum *In resurrectione tua, Christe, alleluia.* *Respondet* chorus *Cælum et terra letentur, alleluia.* Mox Pater Decanus collectam desuper. Qua finita, statim ab ipso incipiuntur eodem loco preces matutinales his verbis: *Domine, labia mea aperies.*[1]

Particularly noteworthy in this text is the presence of four angels, who conduct the dialogue, undramatically, without the participation of the Marys. Striking also is the use of the title *ludimagister* for the director of the performance. With the text from St Gall MS 1262 may be associated the following: St Gall, Stiftsbibl., MS 1290, Lib. resp. Sangallensis anni 1582, fol. 22^r–24^r, published by Lange, no. 104, pp. 69–71; *ibid.*, MS 1296, Lib. resp. Sangallensis sæc. xvii, pp. 20–3, described by Brooks, *Neue Osterfeiern*, p. 302. Here should be mentioned also a dramatic text from Einsiedeln, Stiftsbibl., MS 757, Cantuarium Rhenoviense sæc. xvi, fol. 60^r–64^v, printed by Brooks, *Rheinau*, pp. 231–6, with references (p. 226) to earlier editions. This text presents alternative versions of the dialogue *Quem quæritis*, in German and in Latin, followed by the ceremony of the *Elevatio*, and the singing of *Christ ist erstanden* and *Victimæ paschali.* For further comment upon such combinations see Brooks, *Sepulchre*, pp. 43–4. As a last example of the ceremonies in which the *Elevatio* and *Visitatio* are brought into contact before Matins I bring forward the following elaborate ceremony from the *Liber Sacerdotalis*, Venice, 1523, fol. 275^r–278^v, edited, without complete Roman authorization, by Alberto Castellani, reprinted by Young, *Dramatic Associations*, pp. 61–4, and now reprinted with shortened forms of the psalms and introductory prayers:

De Processione in Nocte Pasche ante Matutinum ad Sepulchrum Christi

Die sancto Resurrectionis cum fuerit pulsatum ad Matutinum, antequam populus intret ecclesiam, sacerdos cum cruce et thuribulo apparatus superpelliceo, stolla, et pluuiali, precedentibus cereis accensis et sequente toto clero cum reuerentia, aperto Sepulchro, accipiat Corpus Domini et portet illud in loco sacrarii ubi sacrosanctum Sacramentum seruari consueuit. Et interim chorus cantet sequentes psalmos vel aliquem eorum:

Psalmus: *Domine, quid multiplicati sunt . . . benedictio tua. Gloria Patri, et Filio, et Spiritui Sancto.*

Psalmus: *Domine, probasti me et cognouisti me.* Supra fo. 160.

Psalmus: *Miserere mei, Deus, miserere . . . gloria tua. Gloria Patri, et Filio, et Spiritui Sancto.*

Finitis psalmis, sacerdos, precedentibus cereis et thurribulo, Corpus Domini portet ad sanctuarium suum, sequente clero et cantante responsorium *Surrexit pastor;* Sepulchrum patenter dimittatur apertum. Responsorium: *Surrexit pastor bonus, qui animam suam posuit pro ouibus suis, et pro suo grege mori dignatus est, alleluia, alleluia, alleluia.* Versus: *Surrexit Dominus de sepulchro, qui pro nobis pependit in ligno. Et pro suo grege.*[2]

Tunc sacerdos faciens officium stans cum sacerdotibus in choro dicit versum: *Surrexit Dominus vere, alleluia.*

Responsio: *Et apparuit Simoni, alleluia.*

---

[1] With these words Matins begins.
[2] For this responsory see Migne, *P.L.*, lxxviii, 773; Hartker, p. 237.

Oremus.

Oratio: *Omnipotens semipiterne Deus, qui hac sacratissima nocte cum potentia tue*
   maiestatis . . . in futura resurrectione beatorum spirituum cetibus facias aggregari.
   Qui cum patre, et cetera.
      In memoriam et laudem gloriose Resurrectionis tue hymnum dicat . . . nos a morte
   animarum nostrarum resuscitare digneris. Qui cum patre.
Oratio: *Domine Iesu Christe, propter hoc gaudium . . . cum omni affectu cordium et*
   corporum percipiamus. Qui cum patre et spiritu sancto viuis ac regnas in vnitate, et
   cetera.
Orationibus finitis, Sacerdos Corpus Domini reuerenter thurificet. Dum
predicte orationes dicuntur, duo diaconi parentur cum dalmaticis albis et in
ecclesia remaneant. Sacerdos autem paratus vt supra cum toto clero exeat
per portam ecclesie minorem, maiori porta clausa relicta, et veniant ad portam maiorem ecclesie cantando responsorium *Dum transisset sabbatum;* et cum
illuc peruenerint, sacerdos accedit ad portam clausam; clerus circumstat eum.
Responsorium: *Dum transisset sabbatum, Maria Magdalene, Maria Iacobi, et*
   Salome emerunt aromata, ut venientes vngerent Iesum, alleluia, alleluia. Versus: *Et*
   valde mane una sabbatorum veniunt ad monumentum, orto iam sole. Ut venientes.
   Gloria Patri, et Filio, et Spiritui Sancto, alleluia.
Et dum peruenerint ad fores ecclesie, completo responsorio cum versu et
replica, plebanus vel sacerdos paratus pulsat ad ostium manu vel cum cruce
dicens sonora voce in tono lectionis:
      Attollite portas, principes, vestras, et elleuamini porte eternales, et introibit rex
   glorie.
Et pro ista prima pulsatione illi deintus nihil respondent. Et facto modico
interuallo, sacerdos iterum vehementius pulsat ad ostium dicens voce altiori
in tono lectionis: *Attollite portas, principes,* et cetera. Et illi deintus nihil respondent. Et tunc sacerdos, modico interuallo facto, iterum in eodem tono sed
altius quam secundo pulsans fortiter ostium ecclesie dicit: *Attollite portas,*
   principes, et cetera.
Tunc illi dyaconi deintus statim cantando respondent:
      Quem queritis in sepulchro, Christicole?
Et illi de foris respondent:
      Iesum Nazarenum crucifixum, o celicole.
Et iterum illi deintus respondeant:
      Non est hic, surrexit sicut predixerat; ite, nuntiate quia surrexit a mortuis.
Hoc finito, qui deintus sunt aperiant portam ecclesiæ, et omnes ingrediantur.
Et iterum dicant qui deintus erant:
      Venite et videte locum vbi positus erat Dominus, alleluia, alleluia.
Et cum fuerint portam ingressi, firment se omnes et diuidant per choros.
Tunc plebanus vadat ad Sepulchrum et ponat caput in fenestra Sepulchri;
et postea conuersus ad populum dicat voce mediocri: *Surrexit Christus.* Chorus
respondeat: *Deo gratias.* Quo dicto, plebanus procedat aliquantulum versus
populum, et exaltet vocem altius quam primum et dicat: *Surrexit Christus.*
Chorus respondeat: *Deo gratias.* Iterum tertio plebanus procedat versus populum aliquantulum, et exaltata voce adhuc altius quam secundo fecerat et
dicat: *Surrexit Christus.* Chorus respondeat: *Deo gratias.* Quo facto, omnes
procedant ad Sepulchrum et faciant choros hinc et inde. Tunc plebanus vadit

ad ostium Sepulchri et statim retrocedat versus chorum et det pacem primo sacerdoti seu clerico vel Domino terre, si ibi fuerit, et dicat voce submissa: *Surrexit Dominus*. Et ille respondeat: *Deo gratias*. Deinde omnes sibi mutuo dent pacem dicentes: *Surrexit Dominus*. Et ille cui pax datur respondeat: *Deo gratias*. Postmodum vadant omnes ad altare Beate Virginis processionaliter, et coram altari genuflexi sacerdote incipiente antiphonam *Regina celi*, eam totam cantent pro gaudio Resurrectionis Filii sui, Domini Nostri. Antiphona:

> *Regina celi letare, alleluia,*
> *quia quem meruisti portare, alleluia,*
> *resurrexit sicut dixit, alleluia.*
> *Ora pro nobis Deum, alleluia.*

Versus: *Ora pro nobis, Sancta Dei Genitrix, alleluia.*
Responsio: *Ut digni efficiamur promissionibus Christi, alleluia.*

Oremus

Oratio: *Deus, qui per unigeniti Filii tui, Domini Nostri Iesu Christi, resurrectionem familiam tuam letificare dignatus es, presta, quesumus, vt per eius venerabilem genitricem virginem Mariam perpetue capiamus gaudia vite. Per eundem Christum.*

Oremus

Oratio: *Gratiam tuam, quesumus, Domine, mentibus nostris infunde, vt qui angelo nunciante Christi Filii tui incarnationem cognouimus, per passionem eius et crucem ad resurrectionis gloriam perducamur. Per eundem Christum Dominum.*

His finitis, reuertantur ad chorum et cantent Matutinas.

Part of the same ceremony from the edition of the *Liber Sacerdotalis* of 1560 is reprinted by Lange, no. 62, pp. 40–2. Concerning the editorship and editions of the *Liber Sacerdotalis* see above, pp. 125, 554. The most remarkable feature of this ceremony is the juxtaposition of the formula *Attollite portas*— commonly associated with the theme of the Harrowing of Hell—and the dialogue *Quem quæritis*. As Brooks observes (*Sepulchre*, p. 48; *Sepulchrum Christi*, p. 147), *Attollite portas* and the striking of the door are used here, probably, not to represent specifically the Harrowing of Hell, but merely for ceremonial effectiveness.

Page 305, note 2. From the *Soissons Ritual* I cite several passages describing the preparations for the combined *Elevatio* and *Visitatio* printed above. On Holy Thursday three Hosts are consecrated, as follows (*Soissons Ritual*, pp. 68–9, reprinted by Young, *Dramatic Associations*, pp. 45–6):

Sciendem autem quod die ista tres Hostie proponantur in altari: prima pro presenti Missa; secunda pro crastina; tertia reservetur usque ad diem Resurrectionis. Que deferantur a diacono ad sacrarium in uasculo quod dependet super altare, ut ibi reserventur, cereo ante accenso.

It will be observed that the third Host is reserved, not for burial in the *sepulchrum* on Good Friday, but for a later ceremony, on Easter. The object placed in the *sepulchrum* on Good Friday is not the Host, but the Gospel-book, as we learn from the following rubric (*Soissons Ritual*, p. 86):

Finito evangelio, subdiaconus accipiat illud et quasi in occulto sub infula sua velut in sinu suo deferat ad Sepulchrum, clericulo cum thure precedente; impositoque super altare quod est in Sepulchro, ambo reuertantur.

The placing of the Host on the altar of the sepulchre before Matins of Easter is described thus (*Soissons Ritual*, p. 108):

Summo diluculo pulsentur omnia signa; dein bina et bina. Ad ultimum uero tum simul iterum pulsentur. Pauimentum interea totius presbyterii et chori edera et alijs uiridibus folijs sternatur. Ecclesia preterea, cereis accensis, a capite usque ad pedes per circuitum uestiatur. Altare sacrosanctum amplificato numero cereorum lumine circumdetur. Numerus uero cereorum circa altare et ante sit lxxxxᵃ, et unus funiculus insuper a capite usque ad pedes pretendatur; in quo circulus quidam ferreus habens vii cereos super ostium Sepulchri in altum dependeat. Circulus autem iste qui et stella a nobis nuncupatur, uerum luciferum, qui mane resurrexit, designat. Adhuc autem x cerei ad crucifixum accendantur. In initio uero omnium istorum cunctus[1] clericus deferat cum summo honore ad Sepulchrum in superpellicio Corpus Dominicum in uasculo a die Cene reseruatum, ponens illud super altare. His peractis, duobus sacerdotibus antiquioribus ac duobus Diaconis in choro sedentibus cum capis de pallio, pontifex in sede sua cum capa de pallio mitratus stans incipit: *Domine, labia mea aperies.*[2]

Page 306, note 1. Some notice must be given here to a few remaining dramatic texts which do not require detailed discussion. The *Officium Hebdomadæ Sanctæ secundum consuetudinem Ducalis Ecclesiæ Sancti Marci Venetiarum*, Venice, 1736, pp. 345–9, contains an elaborate form of *Visitatio* reprinted by Young, *Dramatic Associations*, pp. 70–1, which, in the general sequence of its action, somewhat resembles the ceremony from the *Liber sacerdotalis* of 1523, printed above, p. 622. Concerning the *Depositio* from the *Officium Hebdomadæ Sanctæ*, pp. 277–82, see above, p. 554. Two other texts are exceptional in that, although they provide for a ceremony at a sepulchre, they do not contain the dialogue *Quem quæritis*. The first is from *Obsequiale . . . Ratisponense*, 1491, fol. 110ᵛ–111ʳ, previously reprinted in *Decreta*, iv, 440, and by Young, *op. cit.*, p. 126:

Quo[3] finito, incipiatur Matutinum. Et finito tertio responsorio, reincipiatur idem responsorium *Dum transisset sabbatum*, et fit processio cum toto choro ad Sepulchrum, ibique perficietur responsorium. Quo finito, duo presbiteri stantes ante Sepulchrum accepto[4] obumbrali loco sudarii, extendentesque illud cantent alta voce totam antiphonam *Surrexit Dominus de sepulchro, qui pro nobis pependit in ligno, alleluia.* Et cantata antiphona, episcopus, prepositus, vel decanus aut senior canonicus incipiat canticum leticie *Te Deum*, cum quo reditur ad chorum et completur Matutinum ibidem.

The second text shows an exceptional ceremony found in Prague, Veřejná a Universitní Knihovna, MS XIV. D. 21, Ordin. Pragense sæc. xiv, fol. 35ᵛ–38ʳ, previously edited by Lange, no. 205, pp. 130–1, and commented upon by Meyer, pp. 88–9:

In sacra nocte Resurreccionis Domini aguntur officia et cetera. Ebdomadaria imponat antiphonam: *Maria Magdalena et Maria Iacobi et Salomee*

---

[1] cunctus] cunctos (Print).
[2] With these words Matins begins.
[3] Preceded immediately by the *Elevatio*

Crucis printed above, p. 564.
[4] accepto] acceptis (Print).

sabbato quidem siluerunt secundum mandatum, alleluia. Cum autem transisset sabba|tum, ferentes aromata uenerunt vngere Ihesum, alleluia, alleluia.

Ebdo*madaria* incipiat antifonam: *Exquirebat Maria, quem non ̇invenerat, flebat inquirendo, et amoris sui igne succensa eius quem ablatum | credidit, ardebat desiderio: vnde contigit, ut Ihesum sola tunc videret, que remansit ut queret.*

Cum predicta persona steterit ante Sepulcrum, ebdo*madaria* imponat antiphonam: *Maria stabat ad monumentum foris plorans: dum ergo fleret, inclinauit se et prospexit | in monumentum et vidit duos angelos in albis sedentes, vnum ad caput et vnum ad pedes, ubi positum fuerat corpus Domini Ihesu.*

Ebdo*madaria* imponat versum: *Dic nobis, Maria, quid vidisti in via?*
Predicta persona: *Sepulcrum Christi viuentis, et gloriam vidi resurgentis.|*
Conuentus:

    Credendum est magis soli Marie ueraci quam Iudeorum turbe fallaci.
    Scimus Christum surrexisse a mortuis vere: tu nobis, victor rex, miserere.

Duo sacerdotes tenentes crucem inter se, stantes super gradum ter dicant: *Christus Dominus resurrexit.* Conuentus: *Deo gratias, alleluia.|* Sacerdos inponat antiphonam: *Surrexit Dominus de sepulchro, qui pro nobis pependit in ligno, alleluia.* Conuentus cantet cum populo circumstante *Buoh wssemohuczy.* Quibus finitis, abbatissa *imponat Te Deum laudamus.*

CHAPTER XI

THE VISIT TO THE SEPULCHRE: SECOND STAGE

Page 311, note 2. With trifling, or no, variants from the *Visitatio* in the Augsburg breviary of 1495 are the texts found in the following printed service-books of Augsburg: *Diurnale*, 1522, from which the *Visitatio* is printed by Lange, no. 137, pp. 90–1; *Diurnale*, 1508, from which the *Visitatio* is printed by Lange, no. 118, pp. 85–6; breviaries of 1504, 1479, and 1519, mentioned by Lange, nos. 119, 120, and 121, p. 86. Brooks (*Neue Osterfeiern*, p. 303) reports that the same *Visitatio* is found also in printed Augsburg breviaries of 1485, 1506, 1570, and 1584, and in a *Diurnale* of 1494. Briefer rubrics appear in the following from Munich, Staatsbibl., MS lat. 4117, Brev. Augustense sæc. xv, fol. 131ʳ, mentioned by Lange, no. 122, p. 86, and now first printed:

AD[1] UISITANDUM SEPULCHRUM

    Quis reuoluet nobis ab hostio lapidem quem tegere[2] sanctum cernimus sepulchrum ?
Angeli: *Quem queritis, o tremule mulieres, in hoc tumulo plorantes?*
Mulieres: *Ihesum Nazarenum crucifixum querimus.[3]*
Angeli: *Non est hic quem queritis, sed cito euntes nunciate discipulis eius et Petro quia surrexit Ihesus.*
Mulieres: *Ad monumentum uenimus gementes, angelum Domini sedentem uidimus et dicentem quia surrexit Ihesus.*
Cantor: *Currebant duo simul, et ille alius discipulus precucurrit citius Petro, et uenit prior ad monumentum, alleluia.*

---

[1] Preceded by the responsory *Dum transis-set.*

[2] tegere] tangere (MS).

[3] querimus] queritis (MS).

Apostoli: *Cernitis, o socii, ecce lintheamina et sudarium, et corpus non est in sepulchro inuentum, alleluia.*

Antiphona: *Surrexit Dominus de sepulchro, qui pro nobis pependit in ligno, alleluia.*
Te Deum laudamus.

The type of Augsburg *Visitatio* before us here may be seen also below, p. 645, where it appears as a possible alternative to the longer form of the play found in an Augsburg *Obsequiale* of 1499. Virtually the same text as that above from Munich MS 4117 is found in the following from Munich, Staatsbibl., MS lat. 11903a, Brev. Pollingense sæc. xv, fol. 253^v-254^r, previously edited by Lange, no. 123, pp. 86-7:

AD[1] UISITANDUM SEPULCHRUM

Mulieres: *Quis reuoluet nobis lapidem ab ostio monumenti quem tegere[2] sanctum cernimus sepulchrum?*

Angeli: *Quem queritis, o tremule mulieres, in hoc tumulo plorantes?*

Mulieres: *Ihesum Nazarenum crucifixum querimus.*

Angeli: *Non est hic quem queritis, sed cito euntes dicite discipulis eius et Petro quia surrexit Ihesus.* |

Mulieres antiphonam: *Ad monumentum venimus gementes, angelum Domini sedentem vidimus et dicentem quia surrexit Ihesus.*

Chorus: *Currebant duo simul, et ille alius discipulus precucurrit cicius Petro, et uenit prior ad monumentum, alleluia.*

Apostoli: *Cernitis, o socij, ecce lintheamina et sudarium, et corpus Ihesu in sepulchro non est inventum.*

Cantores: *Surrexit Dominus de sepulchro, qui pro nobis pependit in ligno, alleluia.*

Psalmus: *Te Deum laudamus.*

Slight variants are found in the following from Munich, Staatsbibl., MS lat. 19291, Brev. Tegirinsense anni 1432, fol. 119^r, previously edited by Lange no. 124, pp. 86-7:

Cantato[3] hoc, iterum fiat visita⟨tio⟩ Sepulcri. Et Mulier⟨es⟩: *Quis reuoluet nob⟨is⟩ ab hostio lapidem quem tegere sanctum cerni⟨mus⟩ sepulcrum?*

Angeli: *Quem queritis, o tremule mulieres, in hoc tumulo plorantes?*

Respondent: *Ihesum Nazarenum crucifixum querimus.*

Angeli: *Non est hic quem queritis, sed cito euntes nuntiate discipulis eius et Petro quia surrexit Ihesus, alleluia.*

Mulieres: *Ad monumentum venimus gementes, angelos Domini vidimus et dicentes quia surrexit Ihesus, alleluia.*

Petrus et Iohannes cantant: *Currebant duo simul, et ille alius discipulus precucurrit ci⟨tius⟩ Petro, et venit prior ad monumentum, alleluia.*

Accepto sudario, cantant: *Cernitis, o socij, ecce lintheamina et sudarium, et corpus Ihesu non est in sepul⟨cro⟩ inuentum.*

Simul canunt: *Surrexit enim sicut dixit nobis, alleluia: precedet nos in . . .*[4]

---

[1] Preceded by the responsory *Dum transisset.*

[2] tegere] tangere (MS).

[3] With a reference mark showing that it is intended for insertion between the third responsory *Dum transisset* and the *Te Deum*, the text before us is written, in a hand of the fifteenth century, in the lower and right-hand margins of fol. 119^r. The parts enclosed in pointed brackets have been cut away in the trimming of the margins. In the text above the reading of the first three words is doubtful.

[4] The rest is cut away.

Noteworthy in this text are the explicit rubric concerning the displaying of the sudary, the appropriate use of the plural *angelos* in the third speech of the Marys, and the less familiar closing antiphon *Surrexit enim*. With the text from Munich MS 19291 is to be associated the following from Stuttgart, Landesbibl., MS Ascet. 55. 4°, Lib. resp. Weingartensis sæc. xiii, fol. 81 ʳ–81 ᵛ, previously edited by Lange, no. 132, pp. 89–90:

Mvlieres: *Quis reuoluet nobis ab hostio lapidem quem tegere sanctum cernimus sepulcrum?*

Angeli: *Qvem queritis in sepulcro, o Christicole?*

Mvlieres: *Iesvm Nazarenum crucifixum, o celicole.*

Angeli: *Non est hic quem queritis, sed cito euntes dicite discipulis eius et Petro quia | surrexit Iesus.*

Mvlieres: *Ad monumentum uenimus gementes, angelum Domini sedentem uidimus et dicentem quia surrexit Iesus.*

    Currebant duo simul, et ille alius discipulus precucurrit cicius Petro, et venit prior ad monumentum, alleluia.

    Cernitis, o socii, ecce linteamina et sudarium, et corpus non est in sepulcro inuentum.

Antiphona: *Surrexit enim.*

    Hec est alma dies in qua spoliatur auernus,
    Et surrexit homo, Deus, exultate redempti.[1]

The following is found in Udine, Bibl. Arcivescovile, MS 234 (*olim* 38), Ordin. Aquilegiense (?) sæc. xi, fol. 1 ʳ–1 ᵛ, previously edited by Vale, col. 196–7:

Finito tertio responsorio, uisit*atur* Sepulchrum cum uersibus, duo fratres in uice Mulierum sanctarum dicentes: *Quis reuoluet nobis ab hostio lapidem quem tegere sacrum cernimus sepulchrum?*

Angeli dicant: *Quem queritis, o tremule mulieres, in hoc tumulo plorantes?*

Respondent fratres: *Iesum Nazarenum crucifixum querimus.*

Angeli: *Non est hic quem queritis, sed cito euntes dicite discipulis eius et Petro quia surrexit Iesus.|*

Fratres uice Mulierum uenientes conuertant se ad populum et ad chorum dicentes: *Ad monumentum uenimus gementes, angelum Domini sedentem uidimus et dicentem quia surrexit Iesus.*

Chorus cantet antiphonam: *Currebant duo simul.*

Deinde ostendunt linteamina duo fratres aliis dicentes: *Cernitis, o socii, ecce linteamina et sudarium, et corpus non est in sepulchro inuentum.*

Deinde *Surrexit.* Chorus: *Te Deum laudamus.* Populus: *Kyrieleison,* alta uoce.[2]

Page 312, note 1. Similar to the *Visitatio* from Oxford MS 325 is the following from Oxford, Bibl. Bodl., MS Misc. Liturg. 346, Brev. Benedictinum sæc. xiii, fol. 114ᵛ, previously edited by Lange, no. 140, pp. 91–2; Brooks, *New Texts*, pp. 478–9:

VERSVS AD MONUMENTUM

    Quis reuoluet nobis ab hostio lapidem quem tegere sacrum cernimus sepulchrum?

Angelus: *Quem queritis, o tremule mulieres, in hoc tumulo gementes?*

Mulieres, versus: *Ihesum Nazarenum crucifixum querimus.*

---

[1] Followed by the rubric *Maī Laus.*
[2] Followed by the rubric *In Matutinis Laudibus.*

Angelus: *Non est hic ⟨quem⟩ queritis, sed cito euntes nuntiate discipulis eius et Petro quia surrexit Ihesus.*

Versus: *Venite et uidete.*

Mulieres: *Ad monumentum uenimus gementes, angelum Domini sedentem uidimus et dicentem quia surrexit Ihesus.*

Chorus: *Currebant duo simul.*

Discipuli: *Cernitis, o socii,[1] ecce linteamina et sudarium, et corpus non est in sepulchro inuentum.*

Chorus: *Surrexit enim sicut.*

> *Te Deum laudamus.*

With this version belongs the following from Vienna, Nationalbibl., MS lat. 1890, Brev. sæc. xii, fol. 163ʳ–163ᵛ, previously edited by Lange, no. 109, pp. 81–2, with references to earlier editions, and most recently by Pfeiffer, pp. 13–4:[2]

In nocte sancta Mvlieres dicant antiphonam: *Et dicebant ad inuicem: Quis reuoluet nobis lapidem ab hostio ⟨monumenti⟩?*

Angeli antiphonam: *Qvem queritis in sepulchro, o Christicole?*

Mvlieres antiphonam: *Iesvm Nazarenvm crucifixum, o celicole.*

Angelus: *Non est hic, surrexit sicut predixerat; ite, nuntiate quia surrexit de sepulchro.*

Revertentur in chorum: *Et recordate sunt.*

Ad gradvm: *Ad monumentum uenimus gementes, angelos Domini sedentes uidimus et dicentes quia surrexit Iesus.*

Dvo Apostoli: *Cvrrebant duo simul, et ille.*

Apostoli et Mvlieres cantant in chorum antiphonam: *Dicant nunc Iudei quomodo milites custodientes sepulchrum perdiderunt regem ad lapidis positionem.| Quare non seruabant petram iusticie? Aut sepultum reddant, aut resurgentem adorent, nobiscum dicentes, alleluia, alleluia.*

Ewangelium: *Surrexit enim sicut dixit Dominus.*

> *Te Deum laudamus.*

In speaking of themselves in the third person here (*Et dicebant ad invicem*), the Marys are guilty of a mild impropriety which we have encountered in only one or two other versions.[3]

In this place should be exhibited also the special version from Würzburg found in London, Brit. Mus., MS Arundel 156, Grad. Wirceburgense sæc. xiii, fol. 35ʳ, previously edited by Lange, no. 144, pp. 95–8:

ORDO SEPULCHRI

Quis reuoluet nobis ab hostio lapidem quem tegere sanctum cernimus sepulchrum?

Angelus: *Quem queritis in sepulchro, o Christicole?*

Mulieres: *Ihesum Nazarenum crucifixum, o celicole.*

Angelus: *Non est hic, surrexit sicut predixerat; ite, nunciate quia surrexit de sepulchro.*

Angelus: *Non est hic quem queritis, sed cito euntes nunciate discipulis eius et Petro quia surrexit Ihesus.*

Antiphona: *Venite et uidete.*

Antiphona: *Cito euntes.*

---

[1] socii] sotii (MS).

[2] Lange assigns this service-book to the use of Vienna; Pfeiffer is non-committal.

[3] See above, p. 259.

Antiphona: *Ad monumentum uenimus gementes, angelum Domini sedentem uidimus, et dicentem quia surrexit Ihesus.*

Chorus: *Currebant duo simul.*

Angelus et Mulieres: *Dicant nunc Iudei quomodo milites custodientes sepulchrum perdiderunt regem ad lapidis positionem.*[1] *Quare non seruabant petram iusticie? Aut sepultum reddant, aut resurgentem adorent, nobiscum dicentes, alleluia, alleluia.*

Seniores duo: *Cernitis, o socij, ecce lintheamina et sudarium, et corpus non est in sepulchro inuentum.*

Antiphona: *Surrexit Dominus.*

Te Deum laudamus.

The presence here of two forms of the speech *Non est hic*, and the absence of music for the second form and for several other utterances,[2] seem to indicate that the writer, or scribe, is attempting an enlargement of a simpler version.[3] The additions appear to be the scene of the apostles, the second form of *Non est hic*, and the speech *Ad monumentum.*

Page 314, note 2. With the *Visitatio* from Zurich MS C. 8b. is to be associated the following from Berlin, Staatsbibl., MS 4°.113, Ordin. Cathedralis Magdeburgensis sæc. xv, fol. 89ʳ, mentioned by Lange, no. 134, p. 90, and previously edited by Brooks, *Sepulchre*, p. 103:[4]

Et[5] tunc processio cum candelis ardentibus exibit in monasterium, quam precedent primo cerei Pascales, deinde cruces cum vexillis. Hii stabunt circa baptismum hinc et inde. Conuentus vero stabit hoc modo, quo pueri versus occidentem et domini versus orientem, et chori stabunt versi contra se inuicem. Iuxta prepositum stabit archiepiscopus. Tunc duo canonici induentes cappas et accipientes duo thuribula que vtraque subcustos ibi parata habebit representabunt Mulieres, et visitabunt Sepulcrum ymaginarium. Interim chorus cantabit: *Maria Magdalena*, quod incipiet prepositus maior vel cui ipse commiserit. Ad Sepulcrum sedebunt dyaconi preparati, vnus ad dextram et alius ad sinistram, qui representabunt duos Angelos. Et Mulieres cantabunt non clamose: *Quis reuoluet?* Tunc Angeli cantando interrogabunt: *Quem queritis?* Et respondebunt Mulieres: *Ihesum Nazarenum.* Iterum Angeli: *Non est hic quem.* Tunc Mulieres, thurificato Sepulcro, reuertentur, et stantes inter locum baptismalem et conuentum cantabunt aperta voce: *Ad monumentum venimus.* Hoc cantato, parati erunt duo canonici induti cappis, qui representabunt Petrum et Iohannem, et peruenit vnus citius alio sicut Iohannes cucurrit citius Petro; nec tamen Iohannes introibit Sepulcrum nisi cum Petro. Interim chorus cantat: *Currebant duo.* Illi venientes ad Sepulcrum accipient duo linthea et cantabunt: *Cernitis, o socii.* Quo cantato, archiepiscopus incipiet alta voce: *Surrexit Dominus*, quod chorus prosequitur; et audita Christi Resurrectione, prorumpit in vocem alte cantans *Te Deum laudamus.* Et tunc solemniter compulsatur, et processio redibit ad chorum. Subcustos eciam ad inceptionem *Te Deum* deponet velamen de reliquijs in altari.

---

[1] ad lapidis positionem] aut lapidem positionis (MS).

[2] The text is written throughout by a single hand of the thirteenth century, but music is lacking for the following speeches: *Quis reuoluet, Non est hic quem queritis, Ad monumentum, Currebant duo*, and *Cernitis*.

[3] For simpler versions from Würzburg see above, pp. 257, 282.

[4] For the related *Depositio* and *Elevatio* see above, pp. 152–3.

[5] The responsory *Dum transisset* precedes.

The same version of the play, with briefer rubrics, is found in Halberstadt, Domschatz, MS XVIII, Lib. resp. Halberstadensis anni 1440, fol. 86ʳ–86ᵛ (A), previously edited by Lange, no. 111, pp. 85–6, to the re-edited text of which I attach the variants from a printed Magdeburg Breviary of 1491, sig. m 1 recto (B), mentioned by Lange, no. 115, p. 86, and from Wolfenbüttel, Landeshauptarchiv, Histor. Hs. vii. B. 167 (*olim* vii. B. 31), Agenda ecclesiæ sancti Blasii (?), fol. 1ʳ (C), previously edited by Milchsack, pp. 47 sqq., reprinted therefrom by Lange, *Programm*, pp. 21-2, and mentioned by Lange, no. 130, p. 89:

Ad uisitandum Sepulchrum[1]

Maria Magdalena et alia Maria ferebant diluculo aromata, Dominum querentes in monumento.

Due Mulieres cicius ad Sepulchrum cantent:[2] *Quis reuoluet nobis ab hostio lapidem quem tegere sanctum cernimus sepulchrum?*

Duo Angeli cantantes respondent eis:[3] *Quem queritis, o tremule mulieres, in hoc tumulo plorantes?*[4]

Mulieres: *Ihesum Nazarenum crucifixum querimus.*

Angeli:[5] *Non est hic quem queritis, sed cito euntes nuncciate discipulis eius et Petro quia surrexit Ihesus.*

Mulieres cantant:[6] *Ad monumentum uenimus gementes, angelum Domini sedentem vidimus et dicentem[7] quia surrexit Ihesus.*

Incipiunt cantores:[8] *Currebant duo simul, et ille alius discipulus precucurrit cicius Petro, et | uenit prior ad monumentum, alleluia.*[9]

Postea duo cantent alta uoce:[10] *Cernitis, o socij, ecce lyntheamina et sudarium, et corpus non est in sepulchro inuentum.*

Deinde autem hec antiphona:[11] *Surrexit Dominus de sepulchro,[12] qui pro nobis pependit in ligno, alleluia.*

Te Deum.[13]

The same version, with unimportant variants, is found in the following places: a printed Magdeburg *Rituale*, of 1513, mentioned by Lange, no. 116, p. 86; a printed Magdeburg *Breviarium*, of 1514, mentioned by Lange. no. 117, p. 86; Halberstadt, Domgymnasium, MS 164, Ordin. Halberstadense sæc. xiv, fol. 50ᵛ, mentioned by Lange, no. 133, p. 90; *ibid.*, Domschatz, MS XVII, Lib. resp. Halberstadensis sæc. xv, mentioned by Lange, no. 112, p. 86; *ibid.*, MS XX, Lib. resp. Halberstadensis sæc. xv, mentioned by Lange, no. 113, p. 86; *ibid.*, MS XXII, Lib. resp. Halberstadensis sæc. xv, mentioned by Lange, no. 114, p. 86, and printed by Lange, *Programm*, pp. 21-2. Longer rubrics are found in the following text from Cracow, Bibl. Capit., MS 83,

[1] uisitandum Sepulchrum] visitationem sepulchri (B); rubric omitted (C).
[2] Due . . . cantent] Mulieres (B.C).
[3] Duo . . . eis] Angeli (B); Angelus (C).
[4] plorantes] gementes (C).
[5] Angeli] Ang*elus* (C).
[6] Mulieres cantant] Ad mulieres cantant (A); Mulieres (B); Mulieres ueniunt et dic*unt* discipulis (C).
[7] ang*elum* . . . sedentem . . . dicentem] angelos . . . sedentes . . . dicentes (B).

[8] Incipiunt cantores] Chorus (B); Tunc ueniunt discipuli duo ad sepulchrum dum chorus *cantat* (C).
[9] prior ad monumentum, alleluia] prius ad monumentum (C).
[10] Postea . . . uoce] Petrus et Iohannes (B); Illi duo reuersi dicant (C).
[11] Deinde . . . antiphona] Chorus (B); rubric omitted (C).
[12] sepulchro] C ends here.
[13] Te] Sequitur Te.

Lib. resp. Cracoviensis sæc. xii, previously edited, with a photographic fac-simile, by Windakiewicza, pp. 348–9:[1]

Repetitur responsorium, quod canendo fratrum conuentus exit in medium ecclesie. Finito responsorio, cantor incipit antiphonam *Maria Magdalena*. Interim tres fratres albis induti, portantes aromata, procedunt de sacrario versus Sepulcrum. Postquam autem antiphona a conuentv dicta fuerit, fratres pre-dicti, quasi inter se colloquentes, uoce submissiori cantant hunc uersum: *Quis reuoluet nobis?* Quos interrogantes duo pueri iam antea intra Sepulcrum preor-dinati dicunt: *Quem queritis, o tremule?* Quibus illi respondent: *Ihesum Nazarenum.* Et illi: *Non est hic quem queritis.* Illis ita canentibus, fratres prenotati intrant Sepul-crum, et thurificato Sepulcro, exeuntes redeunt per chorum canendo versum: *Ad monumentum uenimus.* Sicque pertranseunt ad sacrarium. Tunc duo ex fratri-bus quasi cursum ostentantes properant ad Sepulchrum, choro interim can-tante antiphonam: *Currebant duo simul.* Acceptis igitur in Sepulchro linteamini-bus, redeunt ad chorum, et expansis coram omni populo cantant hunc versum: *Cernitis, o socij,* subiungentes antiphonam: *Surrexit Dominus de sepulchro.* Et hac ad finem usque per duos.[2] Episcopus si adest, si non, cantor, incipit *Te Deum laudamus.*

A different closing antiphon is found in the following from Graz, Univer-sitätsbibl., MS II. 208 (*olim* 42/13. 4°), Ordin. Sancti Lamberti sæc. xiii, fol. 29[r], previously edited by Schönbach, *Sanct Lambrecht,* p. 131:

Post *Gloria Patri* repetitur propter processionem responsorium,[3] duobus ceroferariis preeuntibus cum candelabris, et sic uisitatur Sepulchrum. Post responsorium, *Maria Magdalena*. Tunc duo presbyteri portantes thuribula cum incensu, et euntes ad Sepulchrum, apud se cantent antiphonam: *Quis reuoluet nobis?*
Angelus: *Quem queritis?*
Mulieres: *Iesum Nazarenum.*
Angelus: *Non est hic quem queritis.*
Mulieres: *Ad monumentum.*
Chorus: *Currebant duo.*
Tunc presbyteri, accepto sudario, redeunt cantantes antiphonam: *Cernitis, o socii.*
Chorus: *Surrexit enim.*
Qua finita, inponat cantor *Te Deum laudamus,* et sic redeant in chorum. Populus consonet *Khrist ist erstanden.*

Similar is the following from Nuremberg, Germanisches National-Museum, MS 22923, Lib. resp. Noribergensis sæc. xiii, fol. 107[v], mentioned by Lange (erroneously as 22933), no. 135, p. 90, and previously edited by him in *Z.f.d.A.,* xxviii (1884), 128–9:[4]

ALIUS ORDO MINOR AD UISITANDUM SEPULCHRUM

Finito responsorio *Dum transisset,* chorus incipit *Maria Magdalena.* Mulieres: *Quis reuoluet?*

---

[1] I am acquainted with this MS only through Windakiewicza's plate 1, which bears no folio-number. Since he does not mention a folio-number in his text, I infer that the MS is not so marked.

[2] duos] dominos (Windakiewicza). Neither reading is satisfactory, and the rubric is pro-bably defective.   [3] *Dum transisset.*
[4] For a longer *Visitatio,* immediately pre-ceding this one in the MS, see above, p. 398.

Angelus: *Quem queritis, o tre⟨mule⟩?*
Mulieres: *Ihesum[1] Nazarenum.*
Angelus: *Non est hic quem q⟨ueritis⟩.*
Mulieres: *Ad monumentum v⟨enimus⟩.*
Chorus: *Currebant duo si⟨mul⟩.*
Petrus et Iohannes reuersi a monumento, expansis linteaminibus, cantent: *Cernitis, o socii.*
Chorus antiphonam: *Surrexit enim.*
Cantores inci*piant Te Deum laudamus.*

The same version, with briefer rubrics, is found in Vienna, Nationalbibl., MS lat. 3824, Brev. Monseense sæc. xv, fol. 132ʳ (A), previously edited by Lange, no. 127, pp. 88–9, to the re-edited text of which I attach the variants from Munich, Staatsbibl., MS lat. 19932, Brev. Tegirinsense sæc. xv–xvi, fol. 294ʳ–294ᵛ (B), described by Brooks, *Neue Osterfeiern*, p. 303, and from Klosterneuburg, Stiftsbibl., MS 1185, Brev. Claustroneoburgense sæc. xiii, fol. 261ᵛ–262ʳ, previously edited by Pfeiffer, pp. 17–9 (C):

Antiphona eundo ad Sepulcrum:[2] *Maria Magdalena et alia Maria ferebant diluculo aromata,[3] Dominum querentes in monumento.*
Mulieres: *Qvis reuoluet nobis ab hostio lapidem quem tegere sanctum cernimus sepulchrum?*
Angelus: *Qvem queritis, o tremule mulieres, in hoc tumulo gementes?[4]*
Mulieres: *Ihesum Nazarenum crucifixum querimus.*
Angelus: *Non est hic quem queritis, sed cito euntes nuncciate discipulis eius et Petro quia surrexit Ihesus.*
Mulieres: *Ad monumentum venimus gementes, angelum Domini sedentem vidimus, et dicentem quia surrexit Ihesus.*
Chorus:[5] *Currebant duo simul, et ille alius discipulus precucurrit cicius Petro, et venit prior ad monumentum, alleluia.*
Prespiteri:[6] *Cernitis, o socij, ecce lintheamina et sudarium, et corpus non est in sepulchro inventum.[7]*
Chorus:[8] *Surrexit enim sicut dixit Dominus, precedet vos in Galileam, alleluia; ibi eum videbitis, alleluia, alleluia, alleluia.*
Psalmus:[9] *Te Deum laudamus.[10]*

An additional speech is seen in the following from Klosterneuburg, Stiftsbibl., MS 1193, Brev. Claustroneoburgense sæc. xv, fol. 240ᵛ–241ʳ, previously edited by Pfeiffer, pp. 17–9:

Sequitur Visitacio Sepulchri. Antiphona: *Maria Magdalena et altera Maria ferebant diluculo aromata, Dominum querentes in monumento, alleluia.*
Presbyteri in forma Mulierum dicant: *Quis reuoluet nobis lapidem ab hostio quem tegere sanctum cernimus sepulchrum?*
Antiphona: *Quem queritis, o tremule mulieres, in hoc tumulo gementes?*

---

[1] Ihesum] Ihc (MS).
[2] Antiphona... Sepulcrum] Cum visitatur sepulchrum (B); Ad uisitacionem sepulchri (C). [3] aromata] aromata ut venientes (C).
[4] gementes] plorantes (B).
[5] Chorus] Clerus (B); antiphona (C).
[6] Prespiteri] Petrus et Iohannes (B); antiphona (C).

[7] in ... inventum] inuentum in sepulchro (C). [8] Chorus] Clerus (B); antiphona (C).
[9] Psalmus] Sequitur (B).
[10] Psalmus ... laudamus] Omitted (C). Similar is the *Visitatio* in Vienna, Nationalbibl., MS lat. 4005, Brev. Monseense sæc. xv, fol. 452ʳ–452ᵛ, mentioned by Lange, no. 128, p. 89.

Antiphona: *Ihesum Nazarenum crucifixum querimus.*

Antiphona: *Non est hic quem queritis, sed cito euntes nunciate discipulis eius et Petro quia surrexit Ihesus.*

Antiphona: *Currebant duo simul, et ille alius discipulus precucurrit cicius Petro, et venit prior ad monumentum, alleluia.*

Antiphona: *Cernitis, o socii, ecce lintheamina et sudarium, et corpus non est inuentum in sepulcro, alleluia.*

Antiphona: *Surrexit enim sicut dixit Dominus, precedet vos in Galileam, alleluia; ibi eum videbitis, alleluia, alleluia, alleluia.*

Statim sequitur antiphona: *Dicant nunc Iudei quomodo milites custodientes sepulchrum perdiderunt regem ad lapidis posicionem.* *Quare non seruabant | petram iusticie?* *Aut sepultum reddant, aut resurgentem adorent, nobiscum dicentes.*

Et finita antiphona, dicitur *Te Deum laudamus.*[1]

Noteworthy merely for its German rubrics is the following from Graz, Universitätsbibl., MS I. 1549 (*olim* 40/6.8°), Brev. Sancti Lamberti sæc. xii, fol. 135^v–136^r, previously edited by Schönbach, *Sanct Lambrecht*, pp. 132–3, and mentioned by Lange, no. 129, p. 89:

Der chor singet: *Maria Magdalena et alia Maria ferebant diluculo aromata, Dominum querentes in monumento.*

Die Vrowen: *Quis reuoluet nobis ab ostio lapidem quem tegere sanctum cernimus sepulchrum?*

Der Engel: *Quem queritis, o tremule mulieres, in hoc tumulo gementes?*

Die Vrowen: *Iesum Nazarenum crucifixum querimus.*

Engel: *Non est hic quem queritis, sed cito euntes nunciate discipulis eius et Petro quia surrexit Ihesus.*

Die Vrowen ce dem chore: *Ad monumentum uenimus gementes, angelum Domini sedentem uidimus, et dicentem quia surrexit Ihesus.*

So lovfent zvene: | *Currebant duo simul, et ille alius discipulus precucurrit cicius Petro, et uenit prior ad monumentum, alleluia.*

Peter unde Iohannes: *Cernitis, o socii, ecce linteamina et sudarivm, et corpus non est in sepulchro inuentum.*

Der chor: *Surrexit enim sicut dixit Dominus, precedet uos in Galyleam, alleluia; ibi eum videbitis, alleluia, alleluia, alleluia.*

　　Te Deum laudamus.

A somewhat curtailed version is the following from Munich, Staatsbibl., MS lat. 16141, Lib. resp. Pataviensis sæc. xiv, fol. 76^v–77^r, mentioned by Lange, no. 131, p. 89:

Ad[2] visitandum Sepulchrum

Antiphona: *Maria Magdalena et alia Maria ferebant diluculo aromata, Dominum querentes in monumento.*

Versus: *Quis reuoluet nobis ab ostio lapidem quem tegere sanctum cernimus sepulchrum?*

Angelus: *Quem queritis, o tremule mulieres, in hoc tumulo gementes?*

Mulieres: *Ihesum Nazarenum crucifixum querimus.*

Angelus: *Non est hic quem queritis, sed cito euntes nunciate discipulis eius et Petro quia surrexit Ihesus.*

---

[1] Followed immediately by this passage: Deinde versus *In resurreccione tua, Christe,*　*alleluia. Deus in adiutorium. Laudes.*

[2] The responsory *Dum transisset* precedes.

Mulieres: | *Ad monumentum venimus gementes, angelum Domini sedentem uidimus, et dicentem quia surrexit Iesus.*

Scola: *Currebant duo simul, et ille alius discipulus precucurrit citius Petro, et venit prior ad monumentum, alleluia.*

Petrus et Iohannes: *Cernitis, o socij, ecce lintheamina et sudarium, et corpus non est inuentum in sepulchro.*[1]

A similar shortening appears in the following from Einsiedeln, Stiftsbibl., MS 614, Lib. resp. Freienbacensis sæc. xiv, fol. 17^r–17^v, previously edited by Lange, no. 138, pp. 90–1:

Antiphona:[2] *Maria Magdalena et alia Maria ferebant diluculo aromata.*

Antiphona: *Quis reuoluet nobis ab hostio lapidem quem tegere sanctum cernimus sepul|crum?*

Antiphona: *Quem queritis, o tremule mulieres, in hoc tumulo plorantes?*

Antiphona: *Ihesum Nazarenum crucifixum querimus.*

Antiphona: *Non est hic quem queritis, sed cito euntes nunciate discipulis eius et Petro quia surrexit Ihesus.*

Antiphona: *Currebant duo simul, et ille alius discipulus precucurrit cicius Petro, et uenit prior ad monumentum, alleluia.*

Antiphona: *Cernitis, o socij, ecce linteamina et sudarium, et corpus non est in sepulcro inuentum.*

Super nunc dicunt antiphonam: *Maria Magdalena et Maria Iacobi et Salomee sabbato quidem siluerunt secundum mandatum, alleluia. Cum autem transisset sabbatum, ementes aromata uenerunt ungere Ihesum, alleluia, alleluia, alleluia.*[3]

Page 315, note 3. Similar to the *Visitatio* from the Halberstadt breviary of 1515 is the following from Wolfenbüttel, Herzogliche Bibl., MS Helmst. 1156, Brev. anni 1465, fol. 2^v–3^r (A), described by Brooks, *Osterfeiern*, p. 59, and now first printed, with variants found *ibid.*, MS Helmst., 536 (583), Brev. sæc. xiv, fol. 76^r–76^v (B), described by Brooks, *ibid.*:

Antiphona:[4] *Maria Magdalena et alia Maria ferebant diluculo aromata, Dominum querentes in monumento.*

Antiphona: *Quis reuoluet nobis ab hostio lapidem quem tegere sanctum cernimus sepulchrum?*

Antiphona:[5] *Quem queritis, o tremule mulieres, in hoc tumulo plorantes?*

Antiphona:[5] *Ihesum Nazarenum crucifixum querimus.*

Antiphona:[5] *Non est hic quem queritis, sed cito euntes nunciate discipulis eius et Petro quia surrexit Ihesus.*

Antiphona: *Venite et videte locum vbi positus erat Dominus, alleluia, alleluia.*

Antiphona: *Ad monumentum ve|nimus gementes, angelos Domini sedentes*[6] *vidimus, et dicentes*[7] *quia surrexit Ihesus.*

[8]Antiphona: *Currebant duo simul, et ille alius discipulus precucurrit cicius Petro et venit prior ad monumentum, alleluia.*[8]

Antiphona: *Cernitis, o socii, ecce lintheamina et sudarium, et corpus non est in sepulchro inuentum.*

[1] Followed by the rubric *In Matutinas Laudes.*

[2] Preceded immediately by the responsory *Dum transisset.*

[3] Followed by the rubric *In Matutinis Laudibus.*

[4] Antiphona] Visitatio sepulcri (B).

[5] Antiphona] Omitted (B).

[6] angelos Domini sedentes] angelum domini sedentem (B).

[7] dicentes] dicentem (B). [8]–[8] Omitted (B).

Antiphona: *Surrexit Dominus de sepulchro,*[1] *qui pro nobis pependit in ligno, alleluia, alleluia, alleluia.*[1]

Tunc dicitur *Te Deum.*[2]

Page 316, note 2. The *Visitatio* edited from Cracow MS 85 is found also *ibid.*, MS 79, Lib. resp. Cracoviensis sæc. xv, fol. 244 ʳ–245 ʳ, edited by Windakiewicza, pp. 350–1. I have not seen MS 79, but in the edited text of the *Visitatio* the variants from the version in MS 85 are entirely negligible.

Page 323, note 2. Various songs beginning *Christ ist erstanden* are given by Wackernagel (ii, 726–33) and by W. Bäumker (*Das katholische deutsche Kirchenlied*, i, Freiburg, 1886, pp. 502–9). L. Erk and F. M. Böhme (*Deutscher Liederhort*, iii, Leipzig, 1894, pp. 676–7) infer that the song was composed in the twelfth century as a single stanza of four lines, and of these they give, from fifteenth-century sources, what they regard as the four oldest texts of it. Of these four the one which seems most likely to have been used in connexion with the plays runs as follows:

> Christ ist erstanden
> von der marter alle.
> Des sul wir alle fro sein,
> Crist wil vnser trost sein.
> Kyrieleyson.

This form is found in full at the end of a few texts of the *Visitatio* from Klosterneuburg. See p. 330, and below, p. 641. Which version, or how much of it, was usually sung at the end of the *Visitatio Sepulchri* cannot be determined. Probably usage varied from place to place. F. Scholz (in *Zeitschrift für deutsche Philologie*, liii [1928], 49–54) observes that the song was attached to the plays first in the thirteenth century, and suggests, very dubiously, that at that period only the three words *Christ ist erstanden* were used.

Page 325, note 1. Similar to the *Visitatio* from Vienna MS 1768, but negligible as to its rubrics, is the following from Herzogenburg, Stiftsbibl., MS 67, Brev. Ducumburgense anni 1451, fol. 1 ʳ (old pagination), previously edited by Brooks, *New Texts*, pp. 479–80:

Responsorium[3] repetatur, sicque ut mos habet, Sepulchrum visitatur.

Antiphona: *Maria Magdalena et alia Maria ferebant diluculo aromata, Dominum querentes in monumento.*

Alia antiphona: *Quis reuoluet nobis ab hostio lapidem quem tegere*[4] *sanctum cernimus sepulchrum?*

Antiphona: *Quem queritis, o tremule mulieres, in hoc tumulo gementes?*

Antiphona: *Ihesum Nazarenum crucifixum querimus.*

Antiphona: *Non est hic quem queritis, sed cito euntes nunciate discipulis eius et Petro quia surrexit Ihesus.*

Antiphona: *Ad monumentum venimus gementes, angelum Domini sedentem vidimus, et dicentem quia surrexit Ihesus.*

Antiphona: *Currebant duo simul, et ille alius discipulus precucurrit cicius Petro, et venit prior ad monumentum, alleluia.*

[1-1] Omitted (B).

[2] Tunc dicitur Te Deum] Te deum lauda-

mus (B).

[3] *Cum transisset.*

[4] tegere] tangere (MS).

Antiphona: *Cernitis, o socii, ecce lintheamina et sudarium, et corpus non est in sepul-*
chro inuentum.

Antiphona: *Surrexit enim sicut dixit Dominus, precedet vos in Galileam, alleluia;*
ibi eum videbitis, alleluia, alleluia, alleluia.

 Christ ist erstanden.[1]

Page 326, note 2. Extant texts of the *Visitatio* used in the diocese of
Salzburg are fairly numerous. Differing in no significant detail from the text
from Munich MS 24900, are the ones found in printed Salzburg service-
books of 1472, 1482, 1497, 1502, 1509, 1518, and of undetermined date,
mentioned, or printed, by Lange, no. 150, p. 101; Lange, no. 151, p. 101;
Lange, no. 147, pp. 99–101; Brooks, *Neue Osterfeiern*, p. 307; Lange, no. 152,
p. 102; Lange, no 149, p. 101; Lange, no. 148, p. 101. It should be noted
that the *Breviarium Salisburgense*, Nuremberg, 1497, mentioned, with erroneous
references, by Lange, no. 157, p. 101, is the same as that referred to above as
of the year 1497. The *Visitatio* is on fol. 116ᵛ. The same text, with no significant variants, is found also in the following MSS: St Florian, Stiftsbibl.,
MS XI. 417, Brev. Salisburgense anni 1439, fol. 294ʳ–294ᵛ, mentioned by
Lange, no. 156, p. 102; Munich, Staatsbibl., MS lat. 15914, Brev. Salisburgense sæc. xv, fol. 122ᵛ–123ʳ, mentioned (by the shelf-number 16914) by
Brooks, *Neue Osterfeiern*, p. 306; *ibid.*, MS lat. 23151, Brev. Salisburgense sæc.
xiv, fol. 242ᵛ–243ʳ, mentioned (by the shelf-number 24151) by Brooks, *loc.
cit.*; *ibid.*, MS lat. 24881, Brev. Salisburgense (?) anni 1481, fol. 175ʳ, mentioned by Brooks, *loc. cit.*

Plays differing in no significant detail from the *Visitatio* of Salzburg are
found as follows: Munich, Staatsbibl., MS lat. 5546, Brev. Diessense sæc. xv,
fol. 152ᵛ–153ʳ, printed by Lange, no. 146, pp. 99–101; *ibid.*, MS 5550, Brev.
Diessense sæc. xv, fol. 171ʳ–172ʳ, mentioned by Brooks, *Neue Osterfeiern*, p. 306;
Vienna, Nationalbibl., MS lat. 1863, Brev. Pataviense sæc. xv, fol. 179ᵛ–180ʳ,
mentioned by Lange, no. 154, p. 101; Munich, Staatsbibl., MS lat. 24882,
Brev. Andecense sæc. xv, fol. 274ʳ–274ᵛ, mentioned by Lange, no. 159, p. 101,
and by Brooks, *loc. cit.*; *ibid.*, MS lat. 23143, Brev. Sancti Zenonis sæc. xv,
fol. 291ʳ–291ᵛ, mentioned by Brooks, *loc. cit.*; *ibid.*, MS lat. 16404, Brev. Sancti
Zenonis sæc. xiv, fol. 230ʳ–230ᵛ, mentioned (by the shelf-number 16604) by
Lange, no. 158, p. 101.

A form of the Salzburg *Visitatio* with somewhat shorter rubrics is the
following from Vienna, Nationalbibl., MS lat. 1672, Brev. Salisburgense sæc.
xv, fol. 266ʳ–266ᵛ, previously edited by Brooks, *New Texts*, pp. 482–3:

Responsorium iteratur *Dum transisset.* Quo finito, omnis clerus portans
cereos accensos procedit ad visitandum Sepulchrum, et stantes cantant:
 Maria Magdalena et alia Maria ferebant diluculo aromata, Dominum querentes
 in monumento.

Mulieres: *Quis reuoluet nobis ab ho|stio lapidem quem tegere sanctum cernimus*
 sepulchrum?

Angelus respondit: *Quem queritis, o tremule mulieres, in hoc tumulo gementes?*

Mulieres: *Ihesum Nazarenum crucifixum querimus.*

Angelus: *Non est hic quem queritis, sed cito euntes nuncciate discipulis eius et Petro*
 quia surrexit Ihesus.

   [1] Followed by the rubric *Ad Laudes.*

Mulieres verse ad chorum: *Ad monumentum venimus gementes, angelum Domini sedentem vidimus, et dicentem quia surrexit Ihesus.*

Tunc chorus imponat: *Currebant duo simul, et ille alius discipulus precucurrit cicius Petro, et venit prior ad monumentum.*

Petrus et Iohannes veniunt ad monumentum et aufferant lintheamina et sudarium quibus involuta[1] erat Ymago Domini, et vertentes se ad chorum ostendendo ea cantant antiphonam: *Cernitis, o socij, ecce lintheamina et sudarium, et corpus non est in sepulchro inventum.*

Chorus: *Surrexit enim sicut dixit.*

Populus: *Crist ist er⟨s⟩tanden.*

Et ita clerus redeat ad chorum. Tunc sacerdos incipiat *Te Deum laudamus.*

Similar to this is the *Visitatio* from Herzogenburg, Stiftsbibl., MS 74, Brev. Salisburgense anni 1475 (unpaginated), printed by Brooks, *New Texts*, pp. 483–4. Still briefer rubrics appear in the following from Munich, Staatsbibl., MS lat. 11765, Brev. Pollingense sæc. xv, fol. 147^r, mentioned by Lange, no. 155, p. 101:

Post *Gloria Patri* responsorium a principio repetatur ad visitandum Sepulchrum. Post responsorium chorus cantat antiphonam: *Maria Magdalena et alia Maria ferebant diluculo aromata, Dominum querentes in monumento.*

Mulieres: *Quis reuoluet nobis ab hostio lapidem quem tegere sanctum cernimus sepulchrum?*

Angelus: *Quem queritis, o tremule mulieres, in hoc tumulo gementes?*

Mulieres: *Ihesum Nazarenum crucifixum querimus.*

Angelus respondet: *Non est hic quem queritis, sed cito euntes nuncciate discipulis eius et Petro quia surrexit Ihesus.*

Mulieres: *Ad monumentum venimus gementes, angelum Domini sedentem vidimus, et dicentem quia surrexit Ihesus.*

Chorus: *Currebant duo simul, et ille alius discipulus precucurrit cicius Petro, et venit prior ad monumentum, alleluia.*

Apostoli: *Cernitis, o socij, ecce lintheamina et sudarium, et corpus non est in sepulchro inventum.*

Chorus: *Surrexit enim sicut dixit Dominus, precedet vos in Galileam, alleluia; ibi eum videbitis, alleluia, alleluia, alleluia.*

Populus: *Crist ist erstanden.* Et ita clerus redeat in chorum. Tunc sacerdos incipiat *Te Deum laudamus.*

The briefest rubrics are found in the following from a Salzburg *Agenda* of 1511, fol. 58^v–60^v (A), mentioned by Lange, no. 164, p. 105, to which I append the variants from the text in a Salzburg *Agenda* of 1575, pp. 264–72 (B), previously edited by Lange, no. 163, pp. 104–5:[2]

Ad visitandum Sepulchrum responsorium: *Dvm transisset sabbatum, Maria Magdalena et Maria Iacobi et Salome emerunt aromata, vt venientes vngerent Iesum, alleluia, alleluia.*

Sequitur antiphona: *Maria Magdalena et altera Maria ferebant diluculo aromata, Dominum querentes in monumento.*

Mulieres cantent: *Quis reuoluet nobis ab ostio lapidem quem tegere sanctum cernimus[3] sepulchrum?*

---

[1] involuta] involutum (MS).   [2] These two printed books provide music.
[3] cernimus] credimus (B).

Angelus: *Quem queritis, o tremule mulieres, in hoc tumulo gementes?*

Mulieres: *Iesum Nazarenum crucifixum querimus.*[1]

Angelus: *Non est hic quem queritis, sed cito euntes nunciate discipulis eius et Petro quia surrexit Iesus.*

Mulieres: *Ad monumentum venimus gementes, angelum Domini sedentem vidimus, et dicentem quia surrexit Iesus.*

Chorus: *Currebant duo simul, et ille alius discipulus precucurrit citius Petro, et venit prior ad monumentum, alleluia.*

Petrus et Joannes: *Cernitis, o socij, ecce lintheamina et sudarium, et corpus non est in sepulchro inuentum.*

Populus: *Christ ist erstanden.*

Chorus:[2] *Surrexit enim sicut dixit Dominus, precedet vos in Galileam, alleluia; ibi eum videbitis, alleluia, alleluia, alleluia.*

Sequitur[3] *Te Deum laudamus.*

Related to the foregoing in general content is a version of the *Visitatio* in Latin and German edited by A. Schönbach, in *Z.f.d.A.*, xx (1876), 134, from Graz, Universitätsbibl., MS II. 763 (*olim* 40/81. 4°), Brev. Monasterii Sancti Lamberti sæc. xiii, fol. 187 ᵛ–188 ʳ.

Page 329, note 1. Similar to the version from Klosterneuburg MS 1213, with somewhat different rubrics, is the following from Herzogenburg, Stifts-bibl., MS 180, Brev. Claustroneoburgense anni 1570, fol. 33 ᵛ–34 ʳ, previously edited by Brooks, *New Texts*, pp. 481–2:

Iterum a choro repetatur responsorium *Dum transisset* usque ad versum, sicque ut mos habet, omnis clerus indutus cappis, et cereos in manibus accensos por-tans, Sepulchrum visitat. Ibique choro in duos ordines diviso, ut in choro fieri solet, cantores imponant antiphonam: *Maria Magdalena.* Tunc tres pres-biteri seniores ad hoc officium dispositi, portantes pixides alabastrinas, et eundo ad Sepulchrum ad invicem cantant antiphonam: *Quis revolvet nobis?* Et diaconus, solemni alba veste indutus, ex opposito sacristia veniens portans in manibus gladium multis luminibus circumscriptum circa Sepulchrum stans in persona Angeli humili | voce explicat: *Quem queritis, o tremule?* Iterum pres-biteri in persona Mulierum aromata ferentium respondeant: *Jhesum Nazare-num.* Et Angelus explicat: *Non est hic quem.* Item subiungat antiphonam: *Venite et videte.* Et abscedente Angelo, presbiteri ad clerum vertentes cantent: *Ad monumentum.* Et illis abeuntibus, chorus cantet antiphonam: *Currebant duo simul.* Interim dum canitur hec antiphona, duo presbiteri sub persona Johan-nis et Petri ad Sepulchrum venientes tollentes sudarium,[4] et ad populum clerumque conversi protendunt decantantes antiphonam: *Cernitis, o socii.* Tunc chorus subiungat antiphonam: *Surrexit enim sicut dixit.* Ac deinde predicti presbiteri seniores ascendant ad altare Sancte Crucis, et ibi cantent anti-phonam: *Dicant nunc Judei,* sub minori nota. Hac finita, intonent populo excelsa voce *Christ ist erstanden.* Populus succinat *Von der marter alle.* Deinde, clero ad chorum redeunte, imponatur *Te Deum laudamus.*

One is glad to visualize here the alabaster pyxes of the Marys and the flaming sword carried by the angel (*gladium multis luminibus circumscriptum*).

[1] querimus] queritis (A).
[2] Chorus] Chorus in redeundo (B).
[3] Sequitur] Quibus finitis cantetur (B).
[4] sudarium] Over this word a later hand has written: *est* mantille.

This last detail brings to mind the Biblical record of the blinding of the Roman soldiers by a flash of lightning, which we shall find included as an incident in certain more ambitious forms of the Easter play.[1] The variety allowed in the details of the *Visitatio* at Klosterneuburg is further shown by the following from Klosterneuburg, Stiftsbibl., MS 61, Brev. Claustroneoburgense sæc. xv, fol. 193^r–193^v (A), previously edited by Pfeiffer, pp. 17–9, to the new edition of which I append the variants from the text found *ibid.*, MS 590, Brev. Claustroneoburgense sæc. xv, fol. 300^v–301^r (B), previously edited by Pfeiffer, *ibid.*:

Responsorium *Dum transisset* repetitur, et cum eodem responsorio de choro ad monasterium itur, sicque, ut mos est,[2] Sepulchrum uisitatur. Ibique clero in duos ordines diuiso, ut fieri solet in choro, cantores incipiant[3] antiphonam:
> *Maria Magdalena et alia Maria ferebant diluculo aromata, Dominum querentes in monumento.*

Presbyteri in forma Mulierum dicant:[4] *Quis reuoluet nobis ab ostio lapidem quem tegere sanctum cernimus sepulchrum?*

Presbyter loco Angeli dicat:[5] | *Quem queritis, o tremule mulieres, in hoc tumulo gementes?*

Sacerdotes in persona Mulierum respondeant:[6] *Ihesum Nazarenum crucifixum querimus.*

Angelus:[7] *Non est hic quem queritis, sed cito euntes nuncciate discipulis eius et Petro quia surrexit Ihesus.*

Ad clerum reuertentes se presbyteri dicant:[8] *Ad monumentum venimus gementes, angelum Domini sedentem uidimus, et dicentem quia surrexit Ihesus.*

Recedentibus presbyteris, chorus subsequatur antiphonam:[9] *Currebant duo simul, et ille alius discipulus precucurrit cicius Petro, et uenit prior ad monumentum, alleluia.*

Interea duo presbyteri sub persona Petri et Iohannis[10] ad Sepulchrum uenientes tollant[11] sudarium, et ad clerum populumque conuersi procedant cantantes antiphonam:[12] *Cernitis, o socij, ecce linteamina et sudarium, et corpus non est in sepulchro inuentum.*

Deinde chorus cantet:[13] *Surrexit enim sicut dixit Dominus, precedet uos in Galileam, alleluia; ibi eum uidebitis, alleluia, alleluia, alleluia.*

Tunc rectores cantent:[14] *Dicant nunc Iudei quomodo milites custodientes sepulchrum*

---

[1] See above, for example, pp. 408, 423.

[2] est] habet (B).

[3] incipiant] inponant (B).

[4] Presbyteri . . . dicant] Tunc prelatus et duo presbyteri ad hoc officium dispositi portantes thuribula et incensum, et in eundo ad sepulchrum loco mulierum ad inuicem decantent antiphonam (B).

[5] Presbyter . . . dicat] Tunc dyaconus sollempni ac alba ueste uestitus, cooperto capite, intra sepulchrum residens in persona angeli gladium euaginatum et luminibus insitum manu tenens, humili uoce decantet (B).

[6] Sacerdotes . . . respondeant] Presbyteri in persona mulierum aromata ferencium respondeant (B).

[7] Angelus] Angelus ad hec (B).

[8] Ad . . . dicant] Abscedente angelo, presbyteri ad clerum se uertentes cantent (B).

[9] Recedentibus . . . antiphonam] Abeuntibus presbyteris chorus cantet antiphonam (B).

[10] Petri et Iohannis] Iohannis et Petri (B).

[11] tollant] tollunt (B).

[12] procedant . . . antiphonam] procedunt sic decantantes antiphonam (B).

[13] Deinde . . . cantet] Tunc clerus succinat omnis antiphonam (B).

[14] Tunc . . . cantent] Deinde rectores cantent antiphonam (B).

perdiderunt regem ad lapidis posicionem. Quare non seruabant petram iusticie? Aut sepultum reddant, aut resurgentem adorent, nobiscum dicentes.[1]
Sequitur *Te Deum laudamus.* Clero ad chorum redeunte, populus cantet:

> *Christ der ist erstanden*
> *von der marter alle.*
> *Des sull wir alle fro sein,*
> *Christ sol vnser trost sein.*
> *Kyrieleyson.*[2]

This text omits the sentence *Venite et videte*; and the antiphon *Dicant nunc Judæi* serves as a direct introduction to the *Te Deum.* Here may be exhibited also the following from Munich, Staatsbibl., MS lat. 11735, Brev. Pollingense sæc. xv–xvi, fol. 62ᵛ–63ʳ, previously edited by Brooks, *Neue Osterfeiern*, pp. 304–5:

Responsorium *Dum transisset*, quod iteratur post *Gloria Patri*; cum quo itur processionaliter ad altare Apostolorum. Et ibidem peragatur Visitatio Sepulchri secundum consuetudinem.[3] Chorus cantet antiphonam: *Maria Magdalena.* Nota: tres presbiteri induti cappis choralibus accedentes ad Sepulchrum cantando: *Quis reuoluet?*
Duo Angeli: *Quem queritis?*
Mulieres: *Jhesum Nazarenum.*
Angeli: *Non est hic.*
Mulieres verse ad chorum cantantes circa Sepulchrum antiphonam: *Ad monumentum.*
Chorus: *Currebant duo.*
Mulieres interim recipiant lintheum ostendentes choro et cantantes: *Cernitis, o socij.*
Chorus: *Surrexit enim.*
Deinde Mulieres cantantes: *Dicant nunc.*
Chorus: *Quod enim viuit.*
Cum quo itur[4] ad chorum. Tunc vnus ex sacerdotibus incipiat *Christ ist erstanden.* Finito cantu vulgari, *Te Deum laudamus* per Dominum Patrem incipiatur, sub quo campane compulsentur.[5]

The distinguishing aspect of this version is the singing of *Dicant nunc Judæi* by the Marys as their valedictory.

Page 332, note 1. The following text of the hymn, *Jesu, nostra redemptio* (Chevalier, *R.H.*, no. 9582), is from *A.H.*, li, 95–6:

1. Iesu, nostra redemptio,
   amor et desiderium,
   Deus, creator omnium,
   homo in fine temporum,

2. Quæ te vicit clementia,
   ut ferres nostra crimina,
   crudelem mortem patiens,
   ut nos a morte tolleres?

---

[1] Dicant . . . dicentes] Dicant nunc Iudei (B).
[2] Sequitur . . . Kyrieleyson] Finita antiphona, prelatus inponat Te Deum laudamus. Clero ad chorum redeunte, populus succinat Christ der ist erstanden (B). Followed in A by the rubric *Secuntur Laudes.*

[3] In the left margin, opposite this sentence, a somewhat later hand has written *Processio et Visitatio S. Sepulchri.*
[4] itur] iteratur (MS).
[5] compulsentur] Possibly *compulsantur* (MS).

3. Inferni claustra penetrans,
   tuos captivos redimens,
   victor triumpho nobili
   ad dextram patris residens,

4. Ipsa te cogat pietas,
   ut mala nostra superes
   parcendo et voti compotes
   nos tuo vultu saties.

5. Tu esto nostrum gaudium,
   qui es futurus præmium;
   sit nostra in te gloria
   per cuncta semper sæcula.

6. Gloria tibi, Domine,
   qui scandis super sidera,
   cum Patre et Sancto Spiritu
   in sempiterna sæcula.

CHAPTER XII

THE VISIT TO THE SEPULCHRE: SECOND STAGE
(Continued)

Page 337, note 1. With the *Visitatio* from Kremsmünster MS 274 is to be associated the following from St Florian, Stiftsbibl., MS XI. 403, Brev. Florianense sæc. xv, fol. 235ᵛ–236ʳ, previously edited by Lange, no. 185, pp. 116–8:

Quo[1] itur ad monasterium. Et finito responsorio, rectores incipiant *Maria Magdalena,* choro prosequente *et alia Maria ferebant diluculo aromata, Dominum querentes in monumento.* Duo prespiteri habentes figuram Mulierum cante⟨n⟩t: *Quis reuoluet nobis ab hostio monumenti lapidem quem tegere sanctum cernimus sepulchrum?*
Angelus: *Quem queritis, o tremule mulieres, in hoc tumulo gementes?*
Mulieres: *Ihesum Nazarenum crucifixum querimus.*
Angelus: *Non est hic quem queritis, sed cito euntes nuncciate discipulis eius et Petro quia surrexit Ihesus.*
Scolares cantent: *Currebant duo simul, et ille alius discipulus precucurrit cicius Petro, et uenit primus ad monumentum, alleluia.*
Petrus et Johannes currant ad Monumentum, et auferant linthiamina et ostendendo ea cantent: *Cernitis, o socij, ecce linteamina et sudarium, et corpus non est in sepulchro inuentum.*
Chorus: *Dic nobis, Maria, quid uidis|ti in uia?*
Vnus loco Marie Magdalene respondeat:
     Sepulchrum Christi uiuentis, et gloriam uidi resurgentis.
     Angelicos testes.
     Surrexit Christus.
Chorus: *Credendum est magis.*
Et unus respondeat antiphonam: *Surrexit enim sicut dixit Dominus, precedet uos in Galileam, alleluia; ibi eum uidebitis, alleluia, alleluia, alleluia.*
     Te Deum laudamus. Cum quo itur ad chorum.

This text differs from that from Kremsmünster MS 274 chiefly in including the antiphon *Surrexit enim* before the *Te Deum.*

[1] Preceded by the words *Dum transisset,* marking the repetition of the first sentence of the third responsory.

Page 340, note 6. Similar to the *Visitatio* from Bamberg MS 119 in general content is the following, of undetermined provenance, from Erlangen, Universitätsbibl., MS 417. 4°, Lib. resp. sæc. xvi, fol. 11^r–16^v, previously edited by Lange, no. 201, pp. 124–7:[1]

Ad visitationem Sepulchri cantabit chorus antiphonam: *Maria Magdalena et | alia Maria ferebant diluculo aromata, Dominum querentes in monumento.*

Mulieres cantant: *Quis reuoluet nobis ab hostio lapidem quem tegere sanctum | cernimus sepulchrum?*

Tunc Angeli cantabunt interrogando:[2] *Quem queritis, o tremule mulieres, in hoc tumulo plorantes?*

Respondebunt Mulieres: *Iesum Nazarenum crucifixum querimus. |*

Angeli iterum: *Non est hic quem queritis, sed cito euntes nunctiate discipulis eius et Petro quia surrexit Iesus.*

Et statim Angeli: *Venite et uidete locum | ubi positus erat Dominus, alleluia, alleluia.*

Mulieres reuertentes et stantes inter Sepulchrum et Altare S. Crucis aperta voce cantabunt: *Ad monumentum uenimus gementes, angelum Domini sedentem uidimus, et dicentem quia surrexit | Iesus.*

Chorus: *Currebant duo simul, et ille alius discipulus precucurrit citius Petro, et uenit prior ad monumentum, alleluia.*

Petrus et Iohannes portantes sudarium cantabunt: *| Cernitis, o socii, ecce lintheamina et sudarium, et corpus non est in sepulchro inuentum.*

Tunc processio intrabit chorum, cantando versum sequentem: *Dicant nunc Iudei | quomodo milites custodientes sepulchrum perdiderunt regem ad lapidis posicionem? Quare non seruabant petram iusticie? Aut se|pultum reddant, aut resurgentem adorent, nobiscum dicentes.*

Succentor incipit versum: *Dic nobis, Maria, quid uidisti in uia?*

Prepositus solus respondebit: *Sepulchrum Christi uiuentis, et glori|am uidi resurgentis.*

Tunc decanus cantet: *Angelicos testes, sudarium et uestes.*

Tunc cantor: *Surrexit Christus, spes mea; precedet suos in Galilea.*

Post hoc chorus cantabit: *| Credendum est magis soli Marie ueraci quam Iudeorum turbe fallaci.*

 Scimus Christum surrexisse a mortuis uere; tu nobis, uictor rex, miserere. |

Tunc tres illi iam nominati ante summum altare, cum ostensione crucis, ter simul cantabunt: *Surrexit Dominus de sepulchro.* Chorus: *Qui pro nobis pependit in ligno, alleluia.* Et tubicines fistulabunt bis optimum canticum quod nouerint, et interim tradunt crucem diuulgantibus Resurrectionem audita⟨m⟩. Postea cantor et regentes more solito incipiunt *Te Deum laudamus.*

Page 344, note 1. Differing in no significant detail from the *Visitatio* in Prague MS XV. A. 10, is the one found in a printed Prague breviary of 1517, mentioned by Lange, no. 196, p. 124, and the one reprinted by Lange, no. 194, pp. 122–4, from a Prague breviary of 1572. The same version, without significant variants, is found also in Prague, Veřejná a Universitní Knihovna, MS VI. G. 6. 4°, Brev. Pragense anni 1493, fol. 252^v–253^r, mentioned by Lange, no. 199, p. 124. Lange reports (no. 198, p. 124) the same version from Prague, Národni Museum, MS I. G. 5. 4°, Brev. Pragense

---

[1] The text is preceded by the responsory *Dum transisset.*   [2] interrogando] interrogendo (MS).

sæc. xiv; but this has not been found in the place indicated. A slightly different version is found in Vienna, Nationalbibl., MS lat. 1977, Brev. Pragense sæc. xiv, fol. 264ᵛ and 309ʳ. Lange (no. 200, p. 124) mentions this text; but not observing the continuation of it on fol. 309ʳ, he reports it as incomplete at the bottom of fol. 264ᵛ. The complete text is as follows:

Hoc responsorium cantantes secedunt in medium ecclesie, precedentibus candelis et vexillis. Canonici cappis uestiantur, et cereos in manibus baiulantes. Ibique responsorio cum versu et *Gloria Patri* debite finito, choro ad occidentem uerso, precedentibus duobus ad Sepulchrum more muliebri ornatis et habentibus duo thuribula et duos cereos, incipit prelatus hanc antiphonam: *Maria Magdalena et alia Maria ferebant diluculo aromata, Dominum querentes in monumento,* quam chorus finit. Tunc vice Mulieres stantes ante Sepulchrum cantant antiphonam: *Quis reuoluet nobis ab hostio lapidem quem tegere sanctum cernimus sepulchrum?*
Vice Angelus sedens ad Sepulchrum indutus, et stolam habens in capite, respondet: *Quem queritis, o tremule mulieres, in hoc tumulo plorantes?*
Vice Mulieres: *Ihesum Nazarenum crucifixum querimus.*
Uice Angelus: *Non est hic quem queritis, sed cito euntes nunciate discipulis eius et Petro quia surrexit Ihesus.*
Vice Angelus: *Venite et uidete locum ubi positus erat Dominus, alleluia, alleluia.*
Tunc vice Mulieres reuerse ad chorum, uersis vvltibus ad orientem cantant hanc antiphonam: *Ad monumentum uenimus gementes, angelum Domini sedentem uidimus, et dicentem quia surrexit Ihesus.*
Deinde senior incipit: *Dic nobis, Maria,*
quod chorus finit. Vna Mulierum respondet: *Sepulchrum Christi uiuentis,* et *Angelicos testes,* quod totum ipsa terminat. Chorus:

> *Credendum est magis.*
> *Scimus Christum.*

Deinde senior incip*it* antiphonam: *Currebant duo simul,* quam chorus finit. Interim duo de fratribus portantes cereos et induti cappis uadunt ⟨309ʳ⟩ ad Sepulchrum, et acceptis duobus linteaminibus, reuersi ad chorum, stantes ad orientem, cantant antiphonam: *Cernitis, o socij, ecce lintheamina et sudaria, et corpus non est in sepulchro inuentum.*
Hoc finito, incip*it* prelatus antiphonam: *Surrexit Dominus de,* quam chorus finit. Interim deponuntur lintheamina in altari Sancte Crucis. Tunc prelatus portans cereum progreditur in medium chori, versoque vvltu ad orientem cum trina genuflexione cantat solus *Christus Dominus resurrexit.* Chorus respondet *Deo gratias, gaudeamus,* eciam cum trina genuflexione, et sic ter dicantur. Post hec accedens prelatus deosculatur lintheamina, et dat pacem ad fratres et ad populum. Deinde incip*it* prelatus *Te Deum laudamus,* quod cantantes redeunt ad chorum.

The distinguishing feature of this version is the presence of the sentence *Venite et videte.* The same version, without significant variants, is found as follows: Prague, Veřejná a Universitní Knihovna, MS VI. E. 4. 4°, Brev. Pragense sæc. xiv, fol. 137ᵛ–138ʳ, printed by Lange, no. 195, pp. 122–4; Wolfenbüttel, Herzogliche Bibl., MS Helmst. 463, Brev. sæc. xv, fol. 153ʳ–153ᵛ, printed by Brooks, *Osterfeiern,* pp. 58–9.

Page 351, note 2. The text reprinted above from the Augsburg *Ritus* of 1580 is found also in an Augsburg *Agenda* of 1547, mentioned by Lange, no. 170, p. 14. The following form of the same version, with shortened rubrics, is found in *Obsequiale siue Benedictionale secundum ecclesiam Augustensem* [Augsburg, 1499], fol. xxxii ᵛ–xxxiv ᵛ, mentioned by Lange, p. 14:

AD VISITANDUM SEPULCRUM IN DIE SANCTO PASCE

Factis et cantatis Matutinis in choro, ad ultimum responsorium et cantando ipsum itur processionaliter, precedentibus duobus ceroferariis cum luminibus, ad locum Sepulchri, ubi fit statio per chorum. Duo sacerdotes induti simpliciter casulis super superliciis suis, representantes Mulieres que mane veniebant ad monumentum, remanent in choro, et hii, finito ultimo responsorio, cantent: *Quis reuoluet?* ut sequitur. Quibus respondent duo leuite induti dalmaticis super superliciis suis, qui sedere debent in Sepulchro, et representant Angelos, cantando: *Quem queritis?* Tunc iterum duo sacerdotes in choro cantant: *Ihesum crucifixum.* Iterum respondent Angeli, scilicet leuite, in Sepulchro cantantes: *Non est hic.* Tunc Mulieres, scilicet duo sacerdotes, in choro cantant: *Ad monumentum venimus.* Tunc duo cantores incipiunt antiphonam: *Currebant duo,* choro prosequente. Postquam statim duo seniores sacerdotes accedentes Sepulchrum et lintheum Sepulchri tollentes ad chorum se vertentes et ostendentes canunt: *Cernitis, o socii.* Quo finito, cantores ter cantant antiphonam: *Surrexit Dominus de sepulchro,* semper altius incipiendo, et choro prosequente: *Qui pro nobis.* Officiator accedit ad altare aspergendo et thurificando Crucifixum. Deinde Crucifixum reponitur ad locum suum solitum, et chorus cantat: *Victime pascali laudes* cum cantico *Crist ist erstanden,* et eetera.

Permittitur tamen aliis, qui forsan huiusmodi personas non habent, ut cum aliis personis et etiam moribus honestis tamen et discretis huiusmodi visitationem Sepulchri exequantur. Mulieres cantent: *Quis reuoluet nobis ab ostio lapidem quem tegere sanctum cernimus sepulcrum?*

Angeli cantent: *Quem queritis, o tremule mulieres, in hoc tumulo plorantes?*

Mulieres cantent: *Ihesum crucifixum Nazarenum querimus.*

Angeli cantent: *Non est hic quem queritis, sed cito euntes nunciate discipulis eius et Petro quia surrexit Ihesus.*

Mulieres cantent: *Ad monumentum venimus gementes, angelum Domini sedentem vidimus, et dicentem quia surrexit Ihesus.*

Cantores cantent antiphonam: *Currebant duo simul, et ille alius discipulus precucurrit citius Petro, et venit ꝓrior ad monumentum, alleluia.*

Apostoli cantent: *Cernitis, o socii, ecce lintheamina et sudarium, et corpus non est in sepulchro inuentum.*

Cantores ter cantent, semper altius incipiendo, antiphonam: *Surrexit Dominus de sepulchro, qui pro nobis pependit in ligno, alleluia.*

Sequitur *Te Deum laudamus,* et cetera.

This text is found also in an Augsburg *Obsequiale* of 1487, fol. xxxviii ʳ– xxxviii ᵛ, reprinted by Milchsack, p. 129; Lange, no. 169, pp. 108–10. It will be observed that, in the text above, the *Visitatio* particularly under discussion here is followed by an alternative version (fol. xxxiii ʳ–xxxiv ᵛ) without *Victimæ paschali* and *Christ ist erstanden.* This alternative version is

to be associated with the Augsburg *Visitatio* treated in the preceding chapter
See above, p. 626.

Page 352, note 2. Identical with the *Visitatio* from Melk MS 1671, except
for trifling scribal divergences, is that found *ibid.*, MS 1672, Brev. Pataviense
sæc. xv, fol. 259^v–260^r, mentioned by Lange, no. 184, p. 116. Somewhat
different rubrics appear in the following from Melk, Stiftsbibl., MS 1093,
Ordin. Pataviense sæc. xv, fol. 37^r, mentioned by Brooks, *New Texts*,
pp. 485–6:

Responsorium[1] repetatur, et fiat processio in monasterium, omnes portantes cer⟨e⟩os accensos. Dyaconus qui legit evvangelium, uel alter qui
aptam habeat uocem, acturus officium Angeli precedat, sedeatque[2] in
dextera parte ad caput Sepulchri coopertus stola candida. Ordinata stacione
et finito responsorio, cantores incipiant antiphonam: *Maria Magdalena*, choro
prosequente. Interim tres canonici cum totidem thuribulis figuram Mulierum
tenentes procedant uersus Sepulchrum, et stantes cantent: *Quis reuoluet?*
Angelus sedens in dextera parte Sepulchri coopertus stola respondeat: *Quem
queritis?* Mulieres: *Ihesum Nazarenum.* Angelus: *Non est hic.* Et cum ceperit
cantare *Sed cito euntes*, Mulieres thurificent[3] Sepulchrum, et festinanter
reddeant, et uersus chorum stantes cantent antiphonam: *Ad monumentum
venimus.* Qua finita, chorus imponat antiphonam: *Currebant duo.* Et duo
quasi Petrus et Iohannes currant, precurratque[4] Iohannes, sequente Petro,
et veniunt ad Monumentum. Auferant lintheamina et sudarium quibus
involuta erat Ymago Domini, et uertentes se ad chorum ostendentes ea et
cantent antiphonam: *Cernitis, o socij.* Post hec cantet chorus uersum hu⟨n⟩c:
Dic nobis, Maria. Tunc veniens vnus in medium, loco[5] Marie Magdalene,
dicat: *Sepulchrum Christi viuentis. Angelicos testes. Surrexit Christus, spes.* Chorus:
Credendum est. Scimus Christum surrexisse. Quo finito, cantor inponat *Te Deum
laudamus.* Populus cantet *Christ ist.* Finito *Te Deum laudamus*, sacerdos dicat
uersum *In resurrectione tua, Christe, alleluia.* Sacerdos: *Deus in adiutorium.*

Briefer rubrics are found in the following from Vienna, Nationalbibl.,
MS lat. 1919, Brev. Monseense sæc. xv, fol. 262^v–263^r, previously edited
by Lange, no. 182, pp. 114–6:

Responsorium[6] repetatur, et fiat processio ad Sepulchrum, et cantetur
antiphona: *Maria Magdalena et alia Maria ferebant diluculo aromata, Dominum
querentes in monumento.*

Postea veniunt tres Marie, et cantent: *Quis reuoluit nobis ab hostio lapidem quem
tegere sanctum cernimus sepulchrum?*

Angelus: *Quem queritis, o tremule mulieres, in hoc tumulo gementes?*

Marie: *Ihesum Nazarenum crucifixum querimus.*

Angelus: *Non est hic quem queritis, sed cito euntes nuncciate discipulis eius et Petro
quia surrexit Ihesus.*

Mulieres: *Ad monumentum venimus gementes, angelum Domini sedentem vidimus, et
dicentem quia surrexit Ihesus.*[7]

---

[1] *Dum transisset.*

[2] precedat sedeatque] precedant sedeantque (MS).

[3] thurificent] thurificens (MS).

[4] precurratque] precurrantque (MS).

[5] loco] locum (MS).

[6] The third responsory *Dum transisset.*

[7] Ihesus] Ihesum (MS).

Chorus: *Currebant duo simul, et ille alius discipulus precucurrit cicius Petro, et venit prior ad | monumentum.*

Petrus et Iohannes: *Cernitis, o socij, ecce lintheamina et sudarium, et corpus non est in sepulchro inuentum.*

Chorus cantet hunc versum: *Dic nobis, Maria.*

Maria respondeat: *Sepulchrum Christi.*

Chorus: *Dic nobis, Maria.*

Maria: *Angelicos.*

Chorus: *Dic nobis, Maria.*

Maria: *Surrexit Christus.*

Chorus: *Credendum est.* Versus: *Scimus Christum.*

Postea incipiatur *Te Deum laudamus*, et populus cantet *Christ ist erstanden.*[1]

Noticeable here is the repetition of the choral *Dic nobis, Maria.*

A special ceremonial appears at the end of the following from Vorau, Stiftsbibl., MS 90, Brev. Pataviense sæc. xiii, fol. 180ᵛ–181ʳ, now first printed:

Post *Gloria Patri* iteretur responsorium, et fiat processio in ecclesiam. Et qui acturus est officium Angeli precedat, sedeatque in dextra parte ad caput coopertus stola candida. Cantetque clerus uadens ad Sepulchrum: *Maria Magdalena.* Interim duo uel tres cum totidem thuribulis, figuram Mulierum tenentes, procedant uersus Sepulchrum, et stantes cantent: *Quis reuoluet nobis ab hostio lapidem quem tegere sanctum cernimus sepulchrum?*

Angelus re⟨s⟩pondeat: *Quem queritis, o tremule mulieres, in hoc tumulo gementes?*

Mulieres: *Iesum Nazarenum crucifixum querimus.*

Angelus: *Non est hic quem queritis, sed*[2] *cito euntes nunciate discipulis eius et Petro quia surrexit Ihesus.*

Et cum ceperit cantare Angelus *Sed cito euntes*, Mulieres thurificent Sepulchrum, et festinanter redeant, et uersus chorum stantes cantent: *Ad monumentum uenimus gementes, angelum Domini sedentem uidimus, et dicentem quia surrexit Ihesus.*

Qua fini|ta, chorus inponat antiphonam: *Currebant duo simul.* Et duo, quasi Petrus et Iohannes, currant precurratque Iohannes Petro; et ueniant ad Monumentum, et auferant linteamina et sudarium quibus inuoluta fuit Ymago Domini, et uertentes se ad chorum ostendendo ea cantent: *Cernitis, o socii, ecce linteamina et sudarium, et corpus non est in monumento inuentum.*

Post hec chorus cantet hunc uersum: *Dic nobis, Maria.*

Tunc ueniens in medium unus, loco Marie Magdalene, respondeat:

> *Sepulchrum Christi uiuentis.*
> *Angelicos testes.*
> *Surrexit Christus, spes.*

Chorus: *Credendum est magis. Scimus Christum surrexisse.*

Quo finito, cantores incipiant *Te Deum laudamus.* Populus cantet *Christ ist erstanden*, et ascendant chorum. Cantores porrigant clero incensum dicentes tacita uoce *Surrexit Christus.* Clerus respondeat *Gaudeamus*, et inuicem se deosculentur.

A concluding ceremonial similar to that in the *Visitatio* from Vorau MS 90 is found in the following texts, which differ in no significant detail from those printed above: Vienna, Nationalbibl., MS lat. 1874, Ordin. Pataviense anni 1364, fol. 58ʳ–58ᵛ, mentioned by Lange, no. 189, p. 119; *ibid.*, MS lat.

---

[1] Followed by the rubric *Ad incipiendas Laudes.*　　　　[2] sed] Written twice (MS).

4712, Ordin. Pataviense sæc. xv, fol. 47ʳ–47ᵛ, mentioned by Lange, no. 190, p. 119; St Florian, Stiftsbibl., MS XI. 430, Brev. Florianense sæc. xv, fol. 201ᵛ–202ʳ, mentioned by Lange, no. 191, p. 119; Melk, Stiftsbibl., MS 764, Ordin. Pataviense sæc. xiv, fol. 51ʳ–51ᵛ, mentioned by Brooks, *New Texts*, p. 486; Rome, Bibl. Vatic., MS lat. 9210, Brev. Pataviense sæc. xv, fol. 102ʳ–103ʳ, edited by Young, *Some Texts*, pp. 314–6.

Especially interesting are three texts in which is used some part of the poem *Resurrexit victor ab inferis* (see above, p. 619). The first is from Melk, Stiftsbibl., MS 992, Brev. Pataviense sæc. xv (not paginated), mentioned by Brooks, *New Texts*, p. 486, and now first printed:

Responsorium[1] repetatur. Deinde fiat processio in ecclesiam. Clericus qui habet sonoram vocem acturus officium Angeli precedat[2] cantando:

> *Alleluia!*
> *Resurrexit victor ⟨ab inferis⟩.*

Quo finito, sedeat[3] in dextram partem Sepulchri, ad caput coopertus stola candida. Ordinata stacione et finito responsorio, cantores incipiant antiphonam: *Maria Magdalena et alia Maria ferebant diluculo aromata, Dominum querentes in monumento.*

Hanc antiphonam chorus perficiat cantando. Deinde duo uel tres cum totidem thuribulis figuram Mulierum tenentes procedant ad Sepulchrum, et stantes cantent: *Quis reuoluit nobis lapidem ab hostio quem tegere sanctum cernimus sepulchrum?*

Angeli in dextera parte sedentes respondeant: *Quem queritis, o[4] tremule mulieres, in hoc tumulo gementes?*

Mulieres: *Ihesum Nazarenum crucifixum querimus.*

Angeli respondeant: *Non est hic quem queritis, sed cito euntes nunciate discipulis eius et Petro quia surrexit Ihesus.*

Mulieres thurificent Sepulchrum et festinanter reddeunt versus chorum; stantes cantent antiphonam: *Ad monumentum venimus gementes, angelum Domini sedentem vidimus, et dicentem quia surrexit Ihesus.*

Qua finit⟨a⟩, chorus cantet antiphonam: *Currebant duo simul, et ille alius discipulus precucurrit cicius Petro, et venit prior ad monumentum.*

Et duo, quasi | Petrus et Iohannes, currant ad Sepulchrum; precurrat Iohannes, sequente Petro; et veniant ad Monumentum auferentes linteamina et sudarium[5] quibus involuta Ymago Domini, et uertentes se ad chorum cantent:

> *Cernitis, o socij, ecce linteamina et sudarium, et corpus non est in sepulchro inuentum.*

Post hec chorus cantet versum: *Dic nobis.*

Tunc vnus veniet in medium loco Marie; dicit: *Sepulchrum Christi viuentis,* cum reliquis. Chorus: *Credendum est.* Versus *Scimus Christum.* Antiphona *Surrexit enim sicut dixit Dominus, precedet vos in Galileam, alleluia; ibi eum videbitis, alleluia, alleluia, alleluia.* Quo finito, ad incipiendas Laudes versus premittatur *In resurrectione tua, Christe, alleluia.* Psalmus *Te Deum laudamus.*

The concluding ceremonial of the Kiss of Peace is provided for in the following from Vienna, Nationalbibl., MS lat. 4942, Brev. Pataviense sæc. xv, fol. 394ᵛ–395ᵛ, defectively edited by Lange, no. 188, pp. 118–9:

---

[1] *Dum transisset.*
[2] precedat] precedant (MS).
[3] sedeat] sedeant (MS).
[4] o] V (MS).
[5] sudarium] sudaria (MS).

Responsorium repetatur, et fiat processio in monasterium. Angelus precedat[1] cantando:

Alleluia!
Resurrexit victor ⟨ab inferis⟩.

Quo finito, sedeat in dexteram partem Sepulchri ad caput coopertus stola candida. Ordinata stacione et finito responsorio, cantores inponant antiphonam: *Maria Magdalena et altera Maria | ferebant diluculo aromata, Dominum querentes in monumento.*

Hanc antiphonam chorus perficiat. Deinde duo uel tres cum totidem thuribulis figuram Mulierum tenentes procedant ad Sepulchrum, et stantes cantent antiphonam: *Quis reuoluet nobis ab ostio lapidem quem tegere sanctum cernimus sepulchrum?*

Angelus sedens in dextera parte Sepulchri respondeat: *Quem queritis, o tremule mulieres, in hoc tumulo gementes?*

Mulieres: *Ihesum Nazarenum crucifixum querimus.*

Angelus: *Non est hic quem queritis, sed cito euntes nuncciate discipulis eius et Petro quia surrexit Ihesus.*

Et cum Angelus inceperit cantare *Sed cito[2] euntes,* Mulieres thurificent Sepulchrum, et festinanter redeant, et versus chorum stantes cantent antiphonam: *Ad monumentum venimus gementes, angelum Domini sedentem vidimus, et dicentem quia surrexit Ihesus.*

Qua finita, chorus cantet antiphonam: *Currebant duo simul, et ille alius discipulus precucurrit cicius Petro, et venit prior ad monumentum, alleluia.*

Et duo, quasi Petrus et Iohannes, currant ad Sepulchrum. Precurrat Iohannes, sequente Petro, et veniat ad Monumentum. Auferentes lintheamina et sudaria quibus involuta erat Ymago Domini, et vertentes se ad chorum cantent antiphonam: *Cernitis, o socij, ecce lyntheamina et sudarium, et corpus non est in sepulchro[3] inventum.*

Post hec chorus cantet[4] versum: *Dic nobis, Maria, quid vidisti in via?*

Tunc veniens vnus in medium, loco Marie Magdalene | cantet versum: *Sepulchrum Christi viuentis, et gloriam vidi resurgentis.*

Versus: *Angelicos testes.* Versus: *Surrexit Christus, spes mea; precedet.* Quo finito, incipiatur *Te Deum laudamus.* Tunc populus cantet *Christ ist erstanden.* Clerici ascendant chorum. Sacerdos porrigat incensum clero dicens tacita voce *Surrexit Christus.* Clerus respondeat *Gaudeamus,* et se invicem deosculantes.

A somewhat shortened version is the following from Munich, Staatsbibl., MS lat. 2725, Ordin. Alderspacense sæc. xiv-xv, fol. 71ᵛ–72ʳ, mentioned by Brooks, *Neue Osterfeiern,* p. 309:

Post *Gloria Patri* responsorium[5] repetatur, et fiat processio in monasterium. Clericus qui habeat sonoram uocem acturus ⟨officium⟩ Angeli precedat[6] cantando:

Alleluia!
Resur⟨r⟩exit uictor ⟨ab inferis⟩.

---

[1] Angelus precedat] angeli precedant (MS).

[2] cito] scito (MS).

[3] sepulchro] sepulchrum (MS).

[4] cantet] cantent (MS).

[5] Third responsory *Dum transisset.*

[6] precedat] precedant (MS).

Quo finito, sedeat in dextram partem Sepulchri ad capud coopertus stola candida. Ordinata stac⟨i⟩one et finito responsorio, cantores incipiant: *Maria Magdalena.* Hanc antiphonam chorus perficiat. Deinde duo uel tres cum totidem thuribulis, figuram Mulierum tenentes, procedant ad Sepulchrum, et stantes cantent:[1] *Quem queritis, o tre⟨mulæ mulieres, in hoc tumulo plorantes⟩?*

Versus: *Ihesum Naza⟨renum crucifixum quærimus⟩.*

Angelus: *Non est hic quem queritis, ⟨sed cito euntes nuntiate discipulis ejus et Petro quia surrexit Jesus⟩.*

Et cum Angelus inceperit cantare *Sed cito euntes,* Mulieres thurificent Sepulchrum, et festinanter redeant, et versus stantes cantent: *Ad monumentum veni-⟨mus⟩ ge⟨mentes, angelum Domini sedentem vidimus, et dicentem quia surrexit Jesus⟩.*

Qua finita, chorus | cantet: *Currebant duo simul.* Et duo quasi Petrus et Iohannes currant ad Sepulchrum, precurratque Iohannes, sequente Petro; et venia⟨n⟩t ad Monumentum aufferentes linteamina et sudarium quibus inuoluta erat Ymago Domini, et cantent: *Cernitis, o socii.*

Post hec chorus cantet istum versum: *Dic nobis, Maria, quid uidisti in uia?*

Mulier: *Sepulchrum Christi.*

  Angelicos testes.

  Surrexit.

Chorus: *Credendum est magis.*

  Scimus Christum.

Quo finito, incipiatur *Te Deum laudamus.* Tunc populus: *Christ ist erstanden.* Clerici ascendant chorum. Sacerdos porrigat incensum clero. Finito *Te Deum laudamus,* sacerdos dicat versum *In resurrectione tua, Christe, alleluia. Celum et terra le⟨tantur⟩. Deus in adiutorium. Laudes.*

Page 354, note 1. A slight variation from the *Visitatio* in Herzogenburg MS 183 appears in the following from St Florian, Stiftsbibl., MS XI. 471. 4°, Brev. Florianense sæc. xv, fol. 152ʳ–152ᵛ, previously edited by Lange, no. 180, pp. 113–4:

AD VISITATIONEM SEPULchri

Chorus: *Maria Magdalena et alia Maria ferebant diluculo aromata, Dominum querentes in monumento.*

Mulieres: *Quis reuoluet nobis ab hostio lapidem quem tegere sanctum cernimus sepulchrum?*

Angelus: *Quem queritis, o tremule mulieres, in hoc tumulo plorantes?*

Mulieres: *Jhesum Nazarenum crucifixum querimus.*

Angeli: *Non est hic quem queritis, sed cito euntes nunciate discipulis eius et Petro quia surrexit Ihesus.*

Mulieres:[2] *Ad monumentum venimus gementes, angelum Domini sedentem uidimus, et dicentem quia surrexit Ihesus.*

Chorus: *Currebant duo simul, et ille alius discipulus precucurrit cicius Petro, et venit prior ad monumentum, alleluia.*

Apostoli: *Cernitis, o socij, ecce linteamina et sudarium, et corpus non est in sepulchro inventum, alleluia.*

---

[1] The text is obviously defective through the omission of *Quis revolvet.*
[2] Mulieres] Multi (MS).

Alia: *Surrexit enim sicut dixit.*
Apostoli: *Dic nobis, Maria.* |
Maria: *Sepulchrum Christi.*
　　　Angelicos testes.
　　　Surrexit Christus.
Apostoli: *Credendum est magis.*
　　　Scimus Christum.
Populus: *Christ ist erstanden.* Psalmus: *Te Deum laudamus.*

This version is expanded by the antiphon *Surrexit enim sicut dixit*, sung—by Peter and John or, possibly, by the chorus—immediately after the announcement *Cernitis, o socii.* A variation in the assignment of roles appears in the following from Munich, Staatsbibl., MS lat. 12635, Ordin. Ranshofense sæc. xiii, pp. 59–60, mentioned by Brooks, *Neue Osterfeiern*, p. 309, and now first printed:

Post *Gloria Patri* repetatur responsorium a principio, et omnis clerus portans cereos accensos procedit ad uisitandum Sepulcrum. Diaconus uero qui legerat euangelium acturus officium Angeli precedat, sedeatque in dextera parte coopertus stola candida. Ad ubi chorus cantare inceperit antiphonam *Maria Magdalena*, tres presbyteri induti cappis, cum totidem thuribulis, figuram Mulierum tenentes, et incenso, procedunt uersus Sepulchrum, et stantes cantant antiphonam: *Quis reuoluet nobis?*
Angelus antiphonam: *Quem queritis?*
Mulieres: *Iesum Nazarenum.*
Angelus antiphonam: *Non est hic.*
Et cum ceperit cantare Angelus *Sed cito euntes*, Mulieres thurificent Sepulchrum, et festinanter redeunt, et uersus chorum stantes cantant Mulieres antiphonam: *Ad monumentum uenimus.* Tunc chorus inponat antiphonam:[1] *Currebant duo simul.* Et cantores, quasi Petrus et Iohannes, currant, precurratque Iohannes, sequente Petro. Et ita ueniunt ad Monumentum, et auferant linteamina et sudarium, quibus inuoluta erat Ymago Domini, et uertentes se ad chorum ostendendo | ea cantant: *Cernitis, o socii, ecce linteamina.*
Post hec chorus cantet uersum hunc: *Dic nobis, Maria, quid uidisti in uia?*
Tunc ueniens in medium unus loco Marie Magdalene dicat:
　　　Sepulchrum Christi uiuentis, et gloriam uidi resurgentis.
　　　Angelicos testes, sudarium et uestes.
　　　Surrexit Christus, spes mea; precedet suos in Galilea.
Chorus: *Credendum est magis so⟨li⟩.*
Versus: *Scimus Christum.*
Deinde antiphonam:[2] *Surrexit enim sicut.*
Deinde populus: *Christ ist erstanden von der mar⟨ter⟩.* Et ita clerus redeat in chorum. Tunc pontifex siue presbyter incipiat *Te Deum laudamus.*

Here the antiphon *Surrexit enim* appears as part of the liturgical rejoicing at the end of the play. The reply to the interrogation *Dic nobis, Maria?* is made by Mary Magdalen alone. In the following text the angel, in addressing the Marys, includes the invitation *Venite et videte.* This text, from a breviary of the fifteenth century (without shelf-number) in the seminary at Brixen,

---

[1] antiphonam] Written twice (MS).　　　　　　[2] antiphonam] Written twice (MS)

is printed by G. M. Dreves, in *Stimmen aus Maria-Laach*, xxxiii (1887), 423.
Since I have not seen the original, I give the text of Dreves:

Deinde uisitatur Sepulchrum: *Maria Magdalena et altera Maria ferebant diluculo aromata, Dominum querentes in monumento.*

Mulieres: *Quis revolvet nobis ab hostio lapidem quem tegere sanctum cernimus sepulchrum?*

Angelus: *Quem quæritis, o tremulæ mulieres, in hoc tumulo gementes?*

Mulieres: *Jesum Nazarenum crucifixum querimus.*

Angelus: *Non est hic quem queritis, sed cito euntes nunciate discipulis eius et Petro quia surrexit Iesus.*

Angelus: *Venite et videte locum ubi positus erat Dominus, alleluja, alleluja.*

Mulieres: *Ad monumentum uenimus gementes, angelum Domini sedentem uidimus, et dicentem quia surrexit Iesus.*

Chorus: *Currebant duo simul, et ille alius discipulus precucurrit cicius Petro, et uenit prior ad monumentum, alleluya.*

Petrus et Johannes: *Cernitis, o socii, ecce lintheamina et sudarium, et corpus Iesu in sepulchro non est inventum.*

Et osculantes sudarium dent pacem choro et populo. Interim vadat Johannes ad sinistrum cornu altaris et dicat alta voce: *Dic nobis, Maria, quid uidisti in uia?*

Illa respondet: *Sepulchrum Christi.*
       Angelicos testes, s⟨udarium⟩.
       Surrexit Christus, spes.

Apostoli: *Credendum est magis soli.*[1]
       Scimus Christum.

Chorus: *Surrexit enim sicut dixit Dominus, precedet vos in Galileam, alleluja: ibi eum uidebitis, alleluia, alleluia, alleluia,* populo interim acclamante *Christ ist erstan⟨den⟩.* Chorus: *Te Deum l⟨audamus⟩.*

A certain number of service books from the diocese of Passau contain the following form of *Visitatio*, found in *Breuiarium . . . secundum chorum Patauiensis ecclesie*, Venice, 1517, fol. 140ᵛ, previously reprinted by Lange, no. 171, pp. 110–2, and referred to by Brooks, *Neue Osterfeiern*, p. 310:[2]

Responsorium repetatur, et fiat processio in monasterium, omnes portantes cereos accensos. Diaconus qui legit euangelium, vel alter, qui habet aptam vocem, acturus officium Angeli, precedat sedeatque in dextera parte ad caput coopertus stola candida. Ordinata statione et finito responsorio, obleiarii incipiant antiphonam: *Maria Magdalene et alia Maria ferebant diluculo aromata, Dominum querentes in monumento,* choro prosequente. Interim obleiarii cantent: *Quis reuoluet nobis ab ostio lapidem quem tegere sanctum cernimus sepulchrum?*

Angelus sedens in dextera parte Sepulchri respondeat: *Quem queritis, o tremule mulieres, in hoc tumulo gementes?*

Mulieres: *Jesum Nazarenum crucifixum querimus.*

Angelus: *Non est hic quem queritis, sed cito euntes nunciate discipulis eius et Petro quia surrexit Iesus.*

---

[1] soli] sin (Dreves).
[2] Lange prints his text from what he describes as a Melk 'Brevier', of 1517. The copy to which he refers as being in the library at Melk cannot be found there.

Et cum ceperit cantare Angelus *Sed cito euntes,* obleiarii thurificent Sepulchrum et festinanter redeant, et versus chorum stantes cantent antiphonam:
*Ad monumentum venimus gementes, angelum Domini sedentem vidimus, et dicentem
quia surrexit Dominus.*
Deinde Petrus et Ioannes antiphonam: *Currebant duo simul, et ille alius discipulus precucurrit citius Petro, et venit prior ad monumentum, alleluia.*
Et duo, quasi Petrus et Ioannes, currant, precurratque Ioannes, sequente
Petro, ad Monumentum, et auferant lintheamina et sudarium, quibus
inuoluta erat Imago Domini, et vertant se ad chorum, ostendendo ea cantent
antiphonam: *Cernitis, o socii, ecce lintheamina et sudarium, et corpus non est in
sepulchro inuentum.*
Post hoc chorus cantet hunc versum: *Dic nobis, Maria, quid vidisti in via?*
Tunc veniens in medio vnus loco Marie Magdalene dicat versum: *Sepulchrum
Christi viuentis, et gloriam vidi resurgentis.*
Chorus vt prius: *Dic nobis.*
Maria: *Angelicos testes, sudarium et vestes.*
Chorus: *Dic nobis.*
Maria: *Surrexit Christus, spes mea; precedet suos in Galilea.*
Chorus: *Credendum est magis soli Marie veraci quam Iudeorum turbe fallaci.*
    Scimus Christum surrexisse ex mortuis vere: tu nobis, victor rex, miserere.
Populus cantet *Krist ist erstanden,* et ascendant chorum sub cantu *Krist ist
erstanden.* Quo finito, cantores incipiant *Te Deum laudamus.*

A characteristic of this text is the triple repetition of *Dic nobis, Maria.*
Similar texts are found in two printed Passau breviaries of 1490 mentioned
respectively by Lange, no. 174, p. 112, and by Brooks, *Neue Osterfeiern,*
p. 310; in a printed Passau breviary of 1515, mentioned by Lange, no. 176,
p. 112; and in St Florian, Stiftsbibl., MS XI. 429, Brev. Florianense anni
1494, fol. 111ᵛ–112ʳ, mentioned by Lange, no. 117, p. 112. The same
version, with briefer rubrics, is found as follows in a Passau *Agenda* of 1490,
fol. xciiiiʳ–xcviʳ, previously reprinted by Lange, no. 172, pp. 110–2:

Deinde[1] fiat processio ad Sepulcrum. Adstatim subiungatur antiphona:
*Maria Magdalena et altera Maria ferebant diluculo aromata, Dominum querentes
in monumento.*
Tres Marie cantant: *Quis reuoluet nobis ab ostio lapidem quem tegere sanctum
cernimus sepulcrum?*
Angelus: *Quem queritis, o tremule mulieres, in hoc tumulo plorantes?*
Mulieres: *Iesum Nazarenum crucifixum querimus.*
Angelus: *Non est hic quem queritis, sed cito euntes nunciate discipulis eius et Petro
quia surrexit Iesus.*
Mulieres: *Ad monumentum venimus gementes, angelum Domini sedentem vidimus, et
dicentem quia surrexit Ihesus.*
Chorus: *Currebant duo simul, et ille alius discipulus precucurrit cicius Petro, et
uenit prior ad monumentum.*
Interea dum cantatur antiphona, Petrus et Iohannes reuertentes a monu-
mento ferentes sudarium cantent antiphonam, videlicet *Cernitis: Cernitis,
o socij, ecce lintheamina et sudarium, et corpus non est in sepulchro inuentum.*
Chorus: *Dic nobis, Maria, quid vidisti in via?*

    [1] Preceded by the responsory *Dum transisset.*

Mulieres: *Sepulcrum Christi viuentis, et gloriam vidi resurgentis.*
Chorus: *Dic nobis, Maria.*
⟨Mulieres:⟩ *Angelicos testes, sudarium et vestes.*
Chorus: *Dic nobis, Maria.*
⟨Mulieres:⟩ *Surrexit Christus, spes mea; precedet suos in Galilea.*
Chorus: *Credendum est magis soli Marie veraci quam Iudeorum turbe fallaci.*
    Scimus Cristum surrexisse ex mortuis vere; tu nobis, victor rex, miserere.
Deinde incipiatur *Crist ist erstanden.* Postea *Te Deum laudamus.*

The same form is found in printed copies of the Passau *Agenda* of 1498, 1514, and 1519 (circa), mentioned by Lange, nos. 175, 178, and 179, p. 112; in a printed Passau *Liber responsalis* of 1519, mentioned by Lange, no. 173, p. 112;[1] and in Munich, Staatsbibl., MS lat. 23198, Brev. Pataviense (?) sæc. xv, fol. 287^v–288^v, mentioned by Brooks, *Neue Osterfeiern*, p. 309. Virtually the same form is found as follows in Prague, Veřejná a Universitní Knihovna, MS I. D. 20, Lib. resp. Pragensis (?) sæc. xv, fol. 69^v, previously edited by Lange, no. 181, pp. 113–4:

Ad uisitationem Sepulchri cantet chorus antiphonam: *Maria Magdalena et altera Maria ferebant diluculo aromata, Dominum querentes ad monumentum.*[2]
Tres Marie cantent: *Quis reuoluet nobis ab hostio lapidem quem tegere sanctum cernimus sepulchrum?*
Angeli:[3] *Quem queritis, o tremule mulieres, in hoc tumulo plorantes?*
Mulieres: *Ihesum Nazarenum crucifixum querimus.*
Angelus: *Non est hic quem queritis, sed cito euntes dicite discipulis eius et Petro quia surrexit Ihesus.*
Mulieres: *Ad monumentum venimus gementes, angelum Domini sedentem vidimus, et dicentem quia surrexit Ihesus.*
Chorus: *Currebant duo simul, et ille alius discipulus precucurrit cicius Petro, et venit prior ad monumentum, alleluia.*
Petrus et Iohannes: *Cernitis, o socij, ecce lintheamina et sudarium, et corpus non est in sepulchro inuentum.*
Post hoc chorus ca⟨n⟩tet hunc versum: *Dic nobis, Maria.*
Maria respondet: *Sepulchrum christi viuentis.*
Iterum chorus: *Dic nobis, Maria.*
Maria: *Angelicos testes.*
Iterum chorus: *Dic nobis, Maria.*
Maria: *Surrexit Christus.*[4]
Chorus: *Credendum est magis.*
Populus cantet *Christ ist erstanden.*[5]

In the present series belongs the following text from Kremsmünster, Stiftsbibl., MS 100, Brev. Pataviense sæc. xv, fol. 168^v–169^r, mentioned by Brooks, *New Texts*, p. 487, and now first printed:

[1] Lange (p. 14) assigns to the *Agenda* of 1514 the erroneous date 1521; and the *Liber responsalis* of 1519 he assigns erroneously to Vienna, this being merely the place of printing.

[2] Followed by the vowels *Evovae*, accompanied by musical notation. See above, p. 600.

[3] *Angelus* may be intended.

[4] In the MS, the passage *Maria: Surrexit Christus* and the immediately preceding passage *Iterum chorus: Dic nobis, Maria* are in the reverse order.

[5] Followed by the rubric: Versus *In resurrectione tua, Christe, alleluia.* Laudes.

Responsorium iteratur, et fiat processio in ecclesiam, omnes portantes cereos accensos. Vnus qui habeat aptam vocem acturus officium[1] Angeli precedat, sedeatque in dextera parte ad caput; cooperiat se stola candida. | Ordinata[2] stacione et finito responsorio, cantores incipia⟨n⟩t antiphonam:

Maria Magdalena et alia Maria ferebant diluculo aromata, Dominum querentes in monumento.

Interim duo vel tres cum totidem thuribulis procedant versus Sepulchrum, et stantes cantent: *Quis reuoluet nobis ab hostio lapidem quem tegere[3] sanctum cernimus sepulchrum?*

Angelus respondeat: *Quem queritis, o tremule mulieres, in hoc tumulo plorantes?*

Mulieres: *Ihesum Nazarenum crucifixum querimus.*

Angelus: *Non est hic quem queritis, sed cito euntes nunciate discipulis eius et Petro quia surrexit Ihesus.*

Et cum ceperit Angelus cantare *Sed cito*, thurificetur Sepulchrum, et postea cantetur antiphona: *Ad monumentum venimus gementes, angelos Domini sedentes vidimus, et dicentes quia surrexit Ihesus.*

Chorus cantet: *Currebant duo simul, et ille alius discipulus precucurrit cicius Petro, et venit prior ad monumentum, alleluia.*

Petrus et Iohannes ostendentes sudarium cantent: *Cernitis, o socij, ecce lintheamina et sudarium, et corpus non est inuentum in sepulchro.*

Chorus: *Dic nobis, Maria, quid vidisti in via?*

Maria Magdalena respondeat: *Sepulchrum Christi.*

Chorus: *Dic nobis.*

Maria: *Angelicos testes.*

  Surrexit.

Chorus: *Credendum est magis.*

  Scimus Christum.

Deinde *Christ ist erstanden*; quo finito, incipiatur *Te Deum laudamus.*

Page 355, note 1. Similar in general content to the play from St Florian MS XI. 420, is the following from Vienna, Nationalbibl., MS lat. 3569, Brev. Monseense sæc. xv, fol. 276ᵛ–277ʳ, previously edited by Lange, no. 192, pp. 119–22:

Post *Gloria ⟨Patri⟩* responsorium repetatur, et fiat processio ad Sepulchrum.

Antiphona: *Maria Magdalena et alia Maria ferebant aromata, Dominum querentes in monumento.*

Mulieres veniunt ad Monumentum cantantes: *Quis reuoluet nobis ab hostio monumenti lapidem quem tegere sanctum cernimus sepulchrum?*

Angelus sedens in dextera parte respondit: *Quem queritis, o[4] tremule mulieres, in hoc tumulo gementes?*

Mulieres: *Jhesum Nazarenum crucifixum querimus.*

Angelus: *Non est hic quem queritis, sed cito euntes nunciate discipulis eius et Petro quia surrexit Ihesus.*

Mulieres recedendo: *Ad monumentum venimus gementes, angelum Domini ⟨sedentem⟩ vidimus, et dicentem quia surrexit Ihesus, alleluia.*

Deinde Petrus et Iohannes currunt simul ad Monumentum. Antiphona:

---

[1] officium] vocem (MS).

[2] Ordinata] With this word begins fol. 169ʳ, written in another fifteenth-century hand.

[3] tegere] tangere (MS).

[4] o] ob (MS).

Currebant duo simul, et ille alius discipulus precucurrit Petro, et venit prior ad monumentum, alleluia.

Deinde ostendendo sudarium et lintheamina populo antiphona: *Cernitis, o socij, ecce lintheamina et sudarium, et corpus non est in sepulchro inventum.*

Deinde vertunt se ad Mariam: *Dic nobis, Maria, quid vidisti in via?*

Maria respondet: *Sepulchrum Christi viuentis, et gloriam vidi resurgentis.*

Apostoli: *Dic nobis,* ut supra. Maria ut supra. Iterum Apostoli ut supra.

Maria respondet: *Angelicos testes, sudarium et vestes,* et cetera. Deinde Apostoli faciunt | finem sequentie, et populus cantat *Crist ist erstanden.* Quo finito, antiphona ascendendo ad chorum *Christus resurgens.* Deinde cantores porrigant clero incensum, dicentes tacita voce *Surrexit Christus.* Clerus respondet *Gaudeamus,* et invicem se osculantes. Deinde *Te Deum laudamus.*

Unlike the text from St Florian MS XI. 420., the one before us provides, very appropriately, that the interrogation *Dic nobis, Maria?* shall be spoken by the apostles.

Page 363, note 3. The version of the *Visitatio* from Graz MS II. 798 is found also, with·slight rubrics, in Graz, Universitätsbibl., MS III. 134, Brev. Sancti Lamberti sæc. xiii, fol. 247ʳ (A), and *ibid.,* MS III. 116, Lib. resp. Sancti Lamberti sæc. xv, fol. 66ʳ–67ʳ (B), both previously edited by Wonisch, pp. 15–6. Both MSS provide music. I re-edit A with variants from B:

Visitatio Sepulchri[1]

Quis reuoluet nobis ab hostio lapidem quem tegere sacrum cernimus sepulchrum?

Respondeat diaconus in figura Angeli:[2] *Quem queritis, o tremule mulieres, in hoc tumulo plorantes?*

Et illi tres respondeant:[3] *Ihesum Nazarenum crucifixum querimus.*

Dyaconus:[4] *Non est hic quem queritis, sed cito euntes nunciate discipulis eius et Petro quia surrexit Ihesus.*

Venite et uidete locum.[5]

Et illi uersi ad conuentum canant:[6] *Ad monumentum uenimus gementes, angelum Domini sedentem uidimus, et dicentem quia surrexit Ihesus.*

Quibus expletis, cantor imponat:[7] *Dic nobis, Maria.*

Unus vero ex illis tribus dicat cantando clara uoce:[8] *Sepulchrum Christi uiuentis.*

Alter:[9] *Angelicos testes.*

Tercius cantet:[10] *Surrexit Christus, spes.*[11]

Chorus: *Credendum est magis.*

Scimus Christum.[12]

Plebs conclamet: *Giengen dreie vrovven.*

---

[1] sepulchri] sepulchri mulieres can⟨tent⟩ (B).

[2] Respondeat . . . Angeli] Omitted (B).

[3] Et . . . respondeant] Omitted (B).

[4] Dyaconus] Omitted (B).

[5] locum] locum ubi positus erat dominus aeuia aeuia (B).

[6] Et . . . canant] Omitted (B).

[7] Quibus . . . imponat] Tunc inponat cantor (B).

[8] Unus . . . uoce] Tunc prima Maria (B).

[9] uiuentis. Alter] Secunda maria (B).

[10] Tercius cantet] Tercia (B).

[11] spes] Omitted (B).

[12] Credendum . . . Christum] Credendum Scimus (B).

Cantor imponat antiphonam:[1] *Currebant duo simul.*[2]

Qua finita, ueniant illi tres leuantes linteamina cum sudario ut ab omnibus uideantur et cantent:[3] *Cernitis, o socii, ecce linteamina et sudarium, et corpus non est in sepulchro inuentum.*

Et sustollant crucem in altum:[4] *Surrexit Dominus,*[5] quam antiphonam chorus cant*et*; et incip*iat*[6] *Te Deum laudamus*; et sic reuertantur in chorum, populo suo more acclamante *Christ ist erstanden.*[7]

Page 365, note 5. Similar to the *Visitatio* from St Florian MS XI. 434. is the following abbreviated and inferior version from St Florian, Stiftsbibl., MS XI. 398, Ordin. Florianense anni 1512, fol. 76ᵛ–77ʳ, previously edited by Lange, no. 204, pp. 127–9, and Mühlbacher, pp. 387–90, the rubrics of which aid the interpretation of the better text:[8]

In uisitacione Sepulchri, finito tercio ⟨responsorio⟩, fit solemnis processio cum luminibus ad Sepulchrum, iterato[9] responsorio *Dum transisset.* Sint parati sex in ornatu cuilibet competenti: vnus in persona Angeli, duo in figura Apostolorum, tres in specie Mariarum. Stacione autem facta circa Sepulchrum, procedat Angelus ad caput Sepulchri, cantante choro: *Sedit angelus*, vsque ad illum locum, *Tunc locutus est.* Deinde prodeunt Apostoli ad locum aptum, cantante choro responsorium: *Virtute magna.* Tandem Marie tres procedent cum thuribulis, cantante choro responsorium: *Maria Ma⟨g⟩dalene.*

Quo finito, Marie venientes ad Sepulchrum stantes contra Angelum cantent: *Quis reuoluet nobis lap⟨idem⟩?*

Respondet Angelus: *Nolite expauescere.*

Angelus discooperia⟨t⟩ Sepulchrum cantans: *Ecce locus ubi po⟨suerunt⟩.*

Tunc Marie redeuntes a Sepulchro ad Apostolos cantabunt: *Ad monumentum venimus.*

Tunc querent Apostoli cantando: *Dic nobis, Maria.*

Respondent Marie: *En angel⟨i⟩ aspectum.*

Item Apostoli: *Dic nobis, Maria.*

Item Marie respondent: | *Galileam omnes adibitis.*

Iterum Apostoli: *Dic nobis, Maria,*

ut prius. Respondet Maria sola versum vnum: *Sepulchrum Christi vi⟨ventis⟩.*[10]

Tunc chorus subsequitur: *Credendum est magis*, solum versum. Post Apostoli ibunt ad Sepulchrum, choro cantante antiphonam: *Currebant duo simul.* Sub qua antiphona Apostoli venientes ad Sepulchrum et diligenter intuentes, sudarium ex eo recipiunt, et ad locum eminenciorem deferunt, et populo ostendentes cantent: *Cernitis, o socij.*

Respondet chorus antiphonam: *Christus resurgens.* Et populus: *Christ ist erstanden.* Sicque redibit clerus ad chorum. Cantor inponat *Te Deum laudamus.* Laudes.

---

[1] conclamet . . . antiphonam] Es giengen (B).

[2] simul] simul et ille alius discipulus precucurrit cicius Petro et uenit primus ad monumentum aeuia (B).

[3] Qua . . . cantent] Omitted (B).

[4] altum] altum cantantes (B).

[5] Dominus] dominus de sepulchro (B).

[6] quam . . . incipiat] Chorus (B).

[7] et sic . . . erstanden] Omitted (B).

[8] For a facsimile of fol. 76ᵛ see Schiffmann, *Drama*, opposite p. 14.

[9] iterato] iterato cantetur (MS).

[10] Marginal signs indicate the omission of two verses of the sequence, but the text is not supplied.

As an addendum to the present chapter is to be recorded the following description of a *Visitatio* in the *Mitrale* of Sicardus of Cremona (†1215):[1]

Tertio responsorio cum *Gloria* decantato, cum cereis et solemnitate de choro ad aliquem locum tendimus ubi Sepulcrum imaginarium coaptamus, et ibi introducuntur personæ sub personis Mulierum et duorum Discipulorum, Joannis et Petri, qui ad Sepulcrum Domini quærentes eum venerunt, et quædam aliæ personæ in personis Angelorum, qui Christum a mortuis resurrexisse dixerunt, in personis quorum recte cantari potest illa secundi responsorii particula: *Nolite timere*, et cætera usque ad finem responsorii. Tunc redeunt ad chorum, quasi fratribus referentes quæ viderunt et audierunt, in personis quorum convenienter cantatur illud responsorium: *Congratulamini*, sine versu. Si quis autem habet versus de hac repræsentatione compositos, licet non authenticos, non improbamus. Tunc chorus, audita Christi resurrectione, prorumpit in vocem altisone cantans: *Te Deum laudamus*. Quidam hanc repræsentationem faciunt antequam inchoent Matutinas, sed hic est locus proprius, eo quod *Te Deum laudamus* exprimit horam qua Dominus resurrexit. Noster autem sacerdos crucem ante Matutinum incensat, et aspergit aqua benedicta, et ter alta voce dicit ante altare: *Christus, Dominus noster, resurrexit a mortuis*, et chorus respondet: *Deo gratias*. Postea sequitur antiphona: *Christus resurgens*; versiculus: *Dicite in nationibus*; oratio: *Respice*. Postea crux ponatur in loco suo, et interim cantetur antiphona: *Super omnia*. Deinde Laudes Matutinæ cantentur.

With only slight verbal changes this description of the *Visitatio* was included in the *Rationale Divinorum Officiorum* of Durandus, bishop of Mende (†1296), as follows:[2]

Sane tertio responsorio cum *Gloria Patri* decantato, cum cereis et solemni processione de choro ad aliquem locum tendimus vbi Sepulchrum imaginarium coaptatur, et vbi introducuntur persone sub forma et habitu Mulierum et duorum Discipulorum: scilicet Iohannis et Petri, qui ad Sepulcrum Christum querentes venerunt; et quedam alie persone in personis et forma Angelorum, qui Christum a mortuis resurrexisse dixerunt, in personis quorum recte cantari potest illa secunda responsorij primi particula: *Nolite timere*, et cetera, vsque in finem responsorij. Tunc redeunt ad chorum, quasi fratribus referentes que viderunt et audierunt. Et vnus redit citius alio, sicut Iohannes cucurrit citius Petro, in personis quorum conuenienter cantatur illud responsorium: *Congratulamini*, sine versu. Si qui autem habent versus de hac representatione compositos, licet non autenticos, non improbamus. Tunc chorus, audita Resurrectione Christi, prorumpit in vocem altissone cantans: *Te Deum laudamus*. Quidam vero hanc representationem faciunt antequam Matutinum inchoent; sed hic est proprior locus, eo quod *Te Deum laudamus* exprimit horam qua Dominus resurrexit. Quidam etiam

[1] *Mitrale*, vi, 15, in Migne, *P.L.*, ccxiii, 345–6. See Bartholomæis, pp. 143, 520. The *Depositio*, after Vespers on Good Friday, is described as follows (*P.L.*, ccxiii, 321): 'Hoc facto, crux reponatur in suo loco. Alicubi est consuetudo ut chorus dicat psalmos ante eam, episcopus etiam, aut ejus vicarius,

usque ad illam horam in qua Dominus resurrexit.'

[2] *Rationale Diuinorum Officiorum Guilhelmi Mimatensis Ecclesie Episcopi*, Strassburg, 1486, fol. ccxv. On this passage from Durandus see Duriez, pp. 474–8.

eam faciunt ad Missam cum dicitur sequentia illa: *Victime pascali laudes*, cum dicitur versus: *Dic nobis*, et sequentes.

The only noteworthy feature of the *Visitatio* described by these two writers is the use of the responsory *Congratulamini*, sung by the apostles. Other aspects of the passages quoted are mentioned above, pp. 231, 605. The monograph of Schüttpelz (pp. 2–31) reached me too late for adequate use in chapters xi and xii.

CHAPTER XIII

THE VISIT TO THE SEPULCHRE: THIRD STAGE

Page 370, note 1. In my general inference that the scene between Christ and Mary is primarily drawn directly from the Vulgate (John xx, 11–8) I am in general agreement with Milchsack (pp. 83–4, 87). Meyer (p. 80) appears to regard the Vulgate as the source, but hints at a possible use of sentences or melodies from the liturgical pieces in Hartker (pp. 232–41 *passim*). Lange (p. 167) dissents from Milchsack's view, and somewhat vaguely suggests that the dramatic speeches are derived from liturgical books. He appears to be influenced chiefly by the fact that many of the speeches in the *simpler* forms of the *Visitatio* are liturgical pieces. I have observed in the texts of the scene before us no demonstrable musical or textual dependence upon the liturgical pieces in Hartker, or in such MSS as Paris, Bibl. Nat., MSS lat. 17436, fol. 60ᵛ–61ʳ, and 14810, fol. 66ᵛ (see Lange, p. 32). The question as to a possible relationship between this dramatic scene and the music or text of the liturgical books can be settled only after a much more incisive study than has yet been made. Attempts are made by Milchsack (pp. 81 sqq.), Lange (pp. 165–7), and Meyer (pp. 80–9) to classify the plays of the present chapter into national, or other, groups, and to discuss their inter-relationships. Meyer's study of the matter is the most ambitious (see also below, pp. 677 sqq.). He concludes that the original play containing a scene between Mary Magdalen and Christ was written in France in the twelfth century, and that this was transported to Prague, where it was employed for several centuries. The plays from German territory containing this scene he does not regard as liturgical plays (*Feiern*), but as independent compositions (*Spiele*). Concerning this last distinction see chapter xiv.

Page 370, note 2. Bibliography concerning Rouen MS 384 and related MSS is given by Young, *Rouen*, pp. 224–7. In that place doubt is expressed as to the accuracy of texts of the Rouen *Visitatio* printed by Migne, *P.L.*, cxlvii, 139–42 (mentioned by Lange, no. 217, p. 157); by Du Cange, vii, 430; and by Du Méril, pp. 96–8. The text in Paris, Bibl. Nat., MS lat. 904, Grad. Rothomagense sæc. xiii, fol. 101ᵛ–102ᵛ, has been published by Coussemaker, pp. 250–5; Milchsack, p. 133; Lange, no. 216, pp. 155–7; and the entire MS is published in photographic facsimile by Loriquet, *Graduel*, vol. ii. I re-edit the *Visitatio* from Paris MS 904:

Deinceps[1] omnia festiue fiant in sancta nocte Pasche ante *Te Deum laudamus.* Tres Mulieres ad introitum chori hanc antiphonam cantantes usque
ad Sepulchrum:

> *Qvis reuoluet nobis lapidem ab hostio monumenti?*

Hoc finito, quidam puer loco Angeli, alba indutus, tenens palmam in manu,
ante Sepulchrum dicat:

> *Qvem queritis in sepulchro, o Christicole?*

Tunc Mulieres respondeant:

> *Ihesum Nazarenum crucifixum, o celicola.*

Iterum Angelus, aperiens Sepulchrum, dicat hoc Mulieribus:

> *Non est hic, surrexit enim sicut dixit; uenite et uidete locum ubi positus fuerat,
> et euntes dicite discipulis eius et Petro quia surrexit.*

Tunc, Angelo citissime discedente, Mulieres intrent Sepulchrum. Dum non
inuenerint, dicant duo residentes:

> *Mvlier, quid ploras?*

Tunc una ex illis, loco Marie Magdalene, respondeat:

> *Qvia tulerunt Dominum meum, et nescio ubi posuerunt eum.*

Duo Angeli, intus Sepulchrum sedentes, ita cantent:

> *Qvem queritis uiuentem cum mortuis? Non | est hic, sed surrexit. Recordamini
> qualiter locutus est uobis, dum adhuc in Galilea esset, uobis dicens quia oportet
> filium hominis pati et crucifigi, et die tercia resurgere.*

Hoc dicto, Marie exeant de Sepulchro. Post appareat Dominus in sinistro
cornu altaris, dulci uoce illis dicens:

> *Mvlier, quid ploras? Quem queris?*

Tunc conuerse ad eum dicant:

> *Domine, si sustulisti eum, dicito michi, et ego eum tollam.*

Hic ostendat crucem et dicat:

> *Maria!*

Que, ut audierint, cito se offerant pedibus eius clamando:

> *Raboni!*

Ipse uero retro trahens dicat illis hoc:

> *Noli me tangere, nondum enim ascendi ad Patrem meum; uade autem ad fratres
> meos et dic eis; Ascendo ad Patrem meum et Patrem uestrum, Deum meum et Deum
> uestrum.*

Iterum Dominus altaris appareat dicens:

> *Auete, nolite timere: ite, nunciate fratribus meis ut eant in Galileam; ibi me
> uidebunt.*

Tunc, Domino discedente, tres Marie ad chorum inclinent, dicentes hoc
alta uoce:

> *Alleluia, resurrexit Dominus,[2] surrexit leo fortis, Christus fili|us Dei.*

Psalmus: *Te Deum laudamus.*

This is the only Rouen text accompanied by musicaɪ notation. For the
music see the edition of Coussemaker, mentioned above. I re-edit also the
text in Paris, Bibl. Nat., MS 1213, Ordin. Rothomagense sæc. xv, p. 86 (A),
previously edited by Lange, no. 218, pp. 155–7, and by Young, *Rouen,*
pp. 221–2; with variants from Rouen, Bibl. de la Ville, MS 382 (*olim* Y. 108),

---

[1] In the MS the present text is immediately preceded by a rubric concerning First

Vespers of Easter: Et ita finiantur Uespere.
[2] Dominus] domine (MS).

Ordin. Rothomagense sæc. xv, fol. 70 bis^v–71^r (B), mentioned by Lange, no. 219, p. 157, and shown, in part, by Gasté's notes to his text from Rouen MS 384:

Finito tertio responsorio,[1] Officium Sepulcri ita cele*bretur*. Tres diaconi de maiori sede, induti dalmaticis et amictus habentes super capita sua ad similitudinem Mulierum, uascula tenentes in manibus, ueniant per medium chori, et uersus sepulcrum[2] properantes uultibus submissis cantent pariter hunc uersum: *Quis reuoluet nobis lapidem?*
Hoc finito, quidam puer quasi Angelus, indutus alba et amictu,[3] tenens spicam in manu, ante Sepulcrum dicat: *Quem queritis in sepulcro?*
Marie respondeant: *Ihesum Nazarenum crucifixum.*
Tunc Angelus dicat: *Non est hic, surrexit enim,*[4] et locum digito ostendens. Hoc finito,[5] Angelus citissime discedat, et duo presbyteri de maiori sede in tunicis intus Sepulchrum residentes dicant: *Mulier, quid ploras?*
Medius trium Mulierum respondeat, ita dicens: *Quia tulerunt Dominum meum.* Duo residentes dicant: *Quem queritis, mulieres?*[6]
Marie osculentur locum; postea exeant de Sepulcro. Interim quidam sacerdos de maiori sede in persona Domini, albatus cum stolla, tenens crucem obuians[7] eis, in sinistro cornu altaris dicat: *Mulier, quid ploras? Quem queris?*[8]
Medius Mulier[9] dicat: *Domine, si tu*[10] *sustulisti eum, dicito mihi.*[11]
Sacerdos illi crucem[12] ostendens dicat: *Maria!*
Quod cum audierit, pedibus eius citissime sese offerat, et alta uoce dicat: *Raboni!*
Sacerdos innuens manu dicat: *Noli me tangere.*
Hoc finito, sacerdos in dextro cornu altaris[13] iterum appareat, et illis transeuntibus ante altare dicat: *Auete, nolite*[14] *timere.*
Hoc finito, se abscondat, et Mulieres, hoc audito, lete inclinent ad altare, et conuerse ad chorum hunc versum cantent: *Alleluia! Resurrexit Dominus. Alleluia!*
Hoc finito, Dominus Archiepiscopus uel sacerdos ante altare cum turi*b*ulo incipiat alte *Te Deum laudamus.*

Page 371, note 1. The *Visitatio* from Rouen MS 384 as printed above is immediately followed in the MS (fol. 83^r–83^v) by the following *ordo* for Lauds, showing the participation of the Marys in this office:

Versus *Surrexit Dominus vere. Deus in adiutorium.* Antiphona de secunda sede *Angelus autem Domini.* Psalmus *Dominus regnauit.* Antiphona *Et ecce terre motus.* Psalmus *Jubilate.* Antiphona *Erat autem.* Psalmus *Deus, Deus.* Antiphona *Pre timore.* Psalmus *Benedicite.* Antiphona *Respondens autem.* Psalmus *Laudate.* Capitulum *Expurgate uetus fermentum.* Tres pueri, versus *Surrexit*

---

[1] *Dum transisset.*
[2] sepulcrum] sepulcri (A).
[3] et amictu] et amictus (A); amictu (B).
[4] hic surrexit enim] surrexit (B).
[5] finito] *facto* (B).
[6] mulieres] mulier (B).
[7] obuians] obuiens (B).
[8] queris] queritis (B).
[9] Mulier] mulierum (B).
[10] tu] Omitted (A).
[11] mihi] Omitted (B).
[12] illi crucem] autem illi (B).
[13] altaris] alter (B).
[14] nolite] noli (B).

Dominus de sepulchro. Antiphona *Et ualde mane.* Psalmus *Benedictus.* Antiphona ter repetatur. Oratio *Deus,* | *qui hodierna die per vnigenitum tuum.* Tres[1] Marie *Resurgente filio,* vel aliud *Benedicamus* ad placitum. Sequatur processio ante crucifixum cum cruce per totam ebdomadam. Vna de Mariis incipiat *Christus resurgens*; et tres Marie cantent versum in pulpito *Dicant nunc Iudei.* Versus *Dicite in nacionibus.* Oratio *Deus, qui pro nobis filium tuum.* Memorie in statione de Beata Maria. Antiphona *Paradisi porta.* Versus *Post partum uirgo.* Oratio *Gratiam tuam, quesumus, Domine.* In reditu de Omnibus Sanctis antiphona *Lux perpetua.* Alia antiphona per dies istos ad introitum chori quando necesse fuerit *Si diligeretis me, alleluia.*[2] Tres pueri *Benedicamus Domino, alleluia.* Hoc finito, benedicantur ab archiepiscopo, si presens fuerit, et osculetur omnes fratres, dicens ad singulos *Resurrexit Dominus.*

Page 372, note 5. A *Visitatio* very similar to that from Avranches MS 214 was published by Du Méril, pp. 94–6, from a manuscript which he describes as 'Bib. d'Avranches, no. intér. 14, et extér. 2524'; and Du Méril's text is reprinted by Milchsack, pp. 67–81, and by Lange, no. 221, pp. 157–60. This MS seems to be lost; see Lange, p. 17. L'Abbé Desroches, *Histoire du Mont Saint-Michel,* ii, Caen, 1838, pp. 105–7, describes a similar version from a 'Ms. 14'; and Le Héricher, in *Revue de l'Art chrétien,* xxviii (1885), 514, gives another description from 'un manuscrit du xiiie siècle, conservé à la Bibliothèque d'Avranches'. It appears that neither Du Méril's version nor any one of these descriptions conforms precisely to the text which I print from Avranches MS 214. For bibliography see also Gasté, p. 62.

Page 375, note 1. In view of the fragmentary appearance of the beginning of the text from Engelberg MS 314, I offer some notes concerning what precedes in the MS. The opening rubric of the play (*Antiphona. Omnes tres*) as printed above, begins fol. 75[v]. Folio 74[v] is blank. The complete content of fol. 75[r] is as follows:

Anno Domini M° CCC° lxxii in Vigilia Pasce factum est hoc opus per fratres, scilicet fratrem Waltherum Mirer et Johannem Grebler et Wernherum Stauffacher;[3] qui inveniat ipsum, reddat ipsis sub pena Iehenne ignis.

Antiphona: *Regina celi letare, alleluia,*
Quia quem meruisti portare, allelvia,
Resurrexit sicut dixit, allelvia.
Ora pro nobis Deum, allelvia, evou. Amen.

Versus super *Regina celi.*

Gaude, virgo gloriosa,
te iocunda laudis prosa
honorat ecclesia. Qvia.
Postquam suos releuabit
prothoplastum quos prostrauit,
mox in die tercia. Ora pro.

---

[1] Tres] Inserted by a somewhat later hand (MS).

[2] The following marginal entry is for insertion here: Versus *Vox leticie.* Oratio

Vide, Domine.

[3] et Wernherum Stauffacher] Crossed out (MS).

> *Ut nos secum resurgamus,*
> *et letanter concinamus .*
> *in celesti curia. Alle⟨luia⟩.*

Thus ends fol. 75 ʳ. My own inference is that what appears on this page of the MS has no connection with the play which begins at the top of fol. 75 ᵛ. Waltherus Mirer, Johannes Grebler, and Wernherus Stauffacher were monks of Engelberg, and Mirer became abbot (1398–1420). See Eberle, p. 166. They may have had a hand in the accompanying trope of the *Regina cœli* in the traditional style of such compositions. Any one who wishes may regard the troped *Regina cœli* as the festal introduction of the Easter play. This appears to be the view of the official cataloguer of the Engelberg MSS. See B. Gottwald, *Catalogus Codicum manu scriptorum qui asservantur in Bibliotheca Monasterii O.S.B. Engelbergensis*, Freiburg, 1891, p. 219. In any case, the three monks named above cannot have been the original *authors* of the *Visitatio* itself, for the play in a form sufficiently similar to that before us existed at least as early as the thirteenth century. See the version from Einsiedeln, MS 300, printed above, pp. 390 sqq.

Page 378, note 3. Cividale MS CI was formerly in the Chapter Library of the cathedral of Cividale, and Coussemaker (pp. 285, 344) refers to it as 'Processionale A'. The MS lacks some leaves, presumably two, between fol. 76 ᵛ and fol. 77 ʳ. Fol. 76 ᵛ ends with the fragmentary *planctus* printed above, p. 507. The *Visitatio* now under discussion begins fragmentarily at the top of fol. 77 ʳ.

Here, for general convenience, may be noticed a version of the *Visitatio* in a MS described as follows in *Ludwig Rosenthal's Antiquariat, Munich, Katalog 150, Bibliotheca Liturgica*, Pars I, p. 23, no. 215: 'Graduale cum sequentiis (ad usum ord. S. Augustini?). Manuscrit sur vélin en rouge et noir de la fin du xivᵉ ou du commencement du xvᵉ siècle, provenant d'un couvent de l'Allemagne septentrionale.' This *graduale* is probably from Münster. As to its present ownership I have no information. The *Visitatio*, fol. 64ᵛ–65ᵛ, is now printed, I think, for the first time:

AD SEPULCHRUM VISITANDUM

Ant*iphonæ*: *Christus resurgens.*
> *Angelus autem Domini.*
> *Maria Magdalena et alia Maria ferebant diluculo aromata, Dominum querentes in monumento.*

⟨Mariæ:⟩ *Quis reuoluet nobis | ab ostio lapidem quem tegere sanctum cernimus sepulchrum?*

Angeli: *Quem queritis, o tremule mulieres, in hoc tumulo plorantes?*

Marie: *Ihesum Nazarenum crucifixum querimus.*

Angeli: *Non est hic quem queritis, sed cito euntes nunciate discipulis eius et Petro quia surrexit Ihesus.*

Marie: *Ad monumentum venimus gementes, angelum Domini sedentem vidimus, et dicentem quia surrexit Ihesus.*

Interim Maria Magdalena ad Sepulchrum regreditur et conuersa retrorsum vidit Ihesum stantem pileatum. Dicit ei stando, *Heu:*

Heu, redempcio Israhel,
ut quid mortem sustinuit.

⟨Jesus:⟩ *Mulier, quid ploras? Quem queris?*

⟨Maria:⟩ *Tulerunt Dominum meum, et nescio vbi posuerunt eum. Si tu sustulisti eum, dicito michi, et ego eum tollam.*

⟨Jesus:⟩ *Maria!*

⟨Maria:⟩ *Tibi gloria in secula!*

⟨Jesus:⟩ *Maria!*

⟨Maria:⟩ *Raboni!*

⟨Jesus:⟩ *Prima quidem hec uaria*
   stola tulit mortalia.

   Hic pri|ori dissimilis
   iam est incorruptibilis:
   que tunc fuit passibilis,
   iam non erit solubilis.

   Ergo noli me tangere,
   nec ultra uelis plangere,
   quem mox in puro sydere
   cernes ad Patrem scandere.

Finito eo, illa flectens genua ante illum dicat: *Sancte Deus!*

Et ille cedat iterum retrorsum. Illa iterum flectens dicat: *Sancte fortis!*

Iterum cedet. Tercia uice stabit illa; tercia uice prostrabit se ante pedes eius et dicat: *Sancte et immortalis, ⟨miserere nobis⟩.*[1]

Ille inclinabit se et eriget eam, et faciet eam benedictionem. Postea incipiet:
 Uade ad fratres meos, et dic eis; Ascendo ad Patrem meum et Patrem vestrum, Deum meum et Deum vestrum.

Illa reuertente et in gradu stante, chorus incipiat: *Dic nobis, Maria.*

Illa respondet: *Sepulchrum Christi.*
   Angel⟨ic⟩os testes.
   Surrexit Christus, spes.

Chorus: *Credendum est magis.*[2]

Page 385, note 3. With the *Visitatio* from Rheinau MS XVIII at Zurich may be associated the following relatively simple version from Prague, Veřejná a Universitní Knihovna, MS VI. E. 13, Brev. Pragense sæc. xii, pp. 3–4, previously edited by Lange, no. 210, pp. 146–8:

ORDO[3] AD UISITANDUM SEPULCHRUM

⟨Chorus:⟩ *Maria Magdalena et alia Maria ferebant diluculo aromata, Dominum querentes in monumento.*

Sorores: *Quis reuoluet nobis ab ostio lapidem quem tegere sanctum cernimus sepulchrum?*

Econtra Angeli: *Quem queritis, o tremule mulieres, in hoc tumulo plorantes?*

---

[1] Here follow these words, accompanied by musical notation lacking to them in their previous occurrence: *Sancte Deus. Sancte fortis. Sancte et immortalis, miserere nobis.*

[2] Followed by the rubric *Ad processionem,* introducing a procession unrelated to the preceding *Visitatio.*

[3] Preceded by the responsory *Dum transisset.* The text of the play has no music.

Sorores: *Ihesum Nazarenum crucifixum querimus.*

Sedentes ad Sepulchrvm: *Non est hic quem queritis, sed cito euntes nunciate discipulis eius et Petro quia surrexit Ihesus.*

Item sedentes: *Venite et uidete locum ubi positvs erat Dominus, alleluia, alleluia.*

Deinde Sorores uenientes ad chorum cantent: *Ad monumentum uenimus gementes, angelum Domini sedentem uidimus, et dicentem quia surre|xit Ihesus.*

Chorus: *Alleluia, noli flere, Maria.*[1]

Accedente prima Sorore, chorus cantet: *Maria stabat ad monumentum foris plorans; dum ergo fleret, inclinauit se et prospexit in monumentum.*[2]

Predicta Soror, inspecto Sepulchro, conuertat se ad clerum et cantet: *Tulerunt Dominum meum, et nescio ubi posuerunt eum.*

Jesus:[3] *Mulier, quid ploras? Quem queris?*

Soror: *Domine, si tu sustulisti eum, dicito michi ubi posuisti eum, et ego eum tollam.*

Jesus:[4] *Maria!*

Et illa inclinando: *Rabboni!*

At ille paululum retrocedens: *Noli me tangere, Maria; uade autem ad fratres meos et dic eis; Ascendo ad Patrem meum et Patrem uestrum.*

Chorus: *Venit Maria annuncians discipulis.*

Soror: *Quia uidi Dominum, et hec dixit michi.*[5]

Chorus: *Alleluia, resurrexit Dominus.*

Post hec chorus: *Currebant duo simul.*

Deinde vero fratres accipientes lintheamina uadunt ad gradum et cantent: *Cernitis, o socii, ecce lintheamina et sudarium, et corpus non est in sepulchro inuentum.*

Chorus: *Surrexit enim.* Qua ab ipsis percantata, imponitur ymnus *Te Deum laudamus.*

Of particular interest here is the participation of the chorus through singing narrative passages. The text is in some disorder. The confusion in the assignment of roles (see Meyer, pp. 81–2) I have, in part, corrected.

Page 393, note 1. The collection of ten plays to which I shall refer as the Fleury play-book was produced at the monastery of St-Benoît-sur-Loire, at Fleury, and is preserved in Orleans, Bibl. de la Ville, MS 201 (*olim* 178), Miscellanea Floriacensia sæc. xiii, pp. 176–243 (right-hand pages being given even page-numbers). For a facsimile of p. 230 see below, plate xix. The official description of the MS is by C. Cuissard, *Catalogue général des Manuscrits des Bibliothèques publiques de France: Départements*, xii, Paris, 1889, pp. 108–9.[6] The MS contains 251 pages, pp. 1–175 being occupied by homilies and other religious pieces, and pp. 244–51, by a hymn and a prose. The play-book has no intrinsic relation to the other parts of the manuscript. The plays fill four gatherings easily separable from the rest of the volume, and are written, as a whole, by a single hand not seen in the other parts of the MS. The ten plays, with the editorial titles which I use generally in the present treatise, are found as follows:

(1) *Tres Filiæ* (Miracle play of St Nicholas), pp. 176–82;
(2) *Tres Clerici* (Miracle play of St Nicholas), pp. 183–7;

---

[1] Followed by *Vt supra*, crossed out (MS).
[2] See John xx, 11.
[3] Jesus] Angelus (MS).
[4] Jesus] Chorus (MS).
[5] See John xx, 18.
[6] See also Coussemaker, pp. 326–34.

(3) *Iconia Sancti Nicholai* (Miracle play of St Nicholas), pp. 188–96;

(4) *Filius Getronis* (Miracle play of St Nicholas), pp. 196–205;

(5) *Officium Stellæ* (Ordo ad repræsentandum Herodem), pp. 205–14;

(6) *Ordo Rachelis* (Ad Interfectionem Puerorum), pp. 214–20;

(7) *Visitatio Sepulchri* (Ad faciendam Similitudinem Dominici Sepulchri), pp. 220–5;

(8) *Peregrinus* (Ad faciendam Similitudinem Dominicæ Apparitionis in Specie Peregrini), pp. 225–30;

(9) *Conversio Sancti Pauli* (Ad repræsentandum Conversionem Beati Pauli Apostoli), pp. 230–3;

(10) *Resuscitatio Lazari* (Versus ad Resuscitationem Lazari), pp. 233–43.

These ten plays as a whole have been edited in *Melanges*, vii, 91–213; and by Wright, pp. 3–53; Du Méril, pp. 110–6, 120–6, 162–71, 175–9, 213–25, 237–41, 254–71, 276–84; and Coussemaker, pp. 83–234. Other editions of particular plays will be mentioned in appropriate places in this treatise. In regard to the precise circumstances under which the plays were written and performed at Fleury we have virtually no external information. See above, p. 583. Nothing substantial is contributed by C. Guissard, *Mystères joués à Fleury et à Orléans*, in *Lectures et Mémoires de l'Académie de Sainte-Croix d'Orléans*, iv (1880), 284–313. The general monastic background, without special reference to Fleury, is surveyed by U. Berlière, *Écoles claustrales au Moyen Âge*, in *Bulletins de l'Académie royale de Belgique; Classe des Lettres et des Sciences morales et politiques* (1921), pp. 550–72. Scholarship and letters at Fleury are studied by A. Foulques de Villaret, *L'Enseignement des Lettres et des Sciences dans l'Orléanais*, in *Mémoires de la Société archéologique et historique de l'Orléanais*, xiv (1875), 299–440—for the twelfth and thirteenth centuries, especially pp. 399–411. Observations of negligible value on the Fleury play-book are made by C. Cuissard, *id.*, xix (1883), 716. He refers to the 'dix tragédies' in the MS as being 'imitations des premiers drames grecs'.

Page 397, note 1. The text of the *Visitatio Sepulchri* from Fleury, as printed above, is immediately followed in Orleans MS 201, p. 225, by this passage:

Prima: ⟨*H*⟩*eu, misere cur contigit*
      uidere mortem Saluatoris!
Secunda: *Heu, redempcio Israel,*
      ut quid mortem sustinuit!
Tercia: *Heu, consolacio nostra*
      ut quid taliter agere uoluit.
Hos insimul: *Iam iam ecce, iam properemus ad tumulum,*
      unguentes corpus sanctissimum.

Then follows the opening rubric of the *Peregrinus*. See above, p. 471. This added passage may be intended to supply alternative speeches for the Marys at the opening of the *Visitatio*.

Page 398, note 2. Nuremberg MS 22923 contains two versions of the *Visitatio*, the second, and shorter, of which follows immediately after the text printed above, under the rubric *Alius ordo minor ad visitandum Sepulchrum.*

This shorter version is printed above, p. 632. Only the longer version has musical notation. With the longer *Visitatio* from Nuremberg MS 22923 are to be associated several more or less similar versions preserved in varying degrees of completeness. The following is from St Gall, Stiftsbibl., MS 448, Ordin. Sangallense sæc. xv, p. 106, previously edited by Brooks, *Neue Osterfeiern*, pp. 310–2; Young, *Some Texts*, pp. 322–4:[1]

Interim[2] preparant se tres honeste persone ordinati ad hoc, induentes se tribus cappis in signum Marie Magdalene, Iacobi et Salome. Et duo pueri portant duo lumina posita super baculos precedentes eos. Accedentes ante chorum, responsorio finito, prima Maria cantat versum: *Heu nobis*; altera Maria: *Iam percusso*, stantes ante chorum. Deinde intrantes chorum accedentes ad Sepulchrum, tercia Maria cantat: *Sed eamus*. Versu finito, chorus cantat antiphonam: *Maria Magdalena*. Interea procedunt ad Sepulcrum, ibique stantes cantent: *Quis reuoluet?*

Angeli sedentes in Sepulchro respondent: *Quem queritis?*

Marie: *Ihesum Nazarenum.*

Item Angeli: *Non est hic*, subiungentes antiphonam: *Venite et videte.*

Marie conuertunt se ad chorum incipientes et cantantes antiphonam: *Ad monumentum venimus.*

Respondent Peregrini stantes in medio chori ante primos gradus ympnum: *Ihesu, nostra redempcio*, primum versum cantantes. Chorus: *Que te vicit?*

Versus: *Gloria tibi, Domine, qui surrexit[3] a mortuis.*

Deinde chorus: *Currebant duo simul.*

Interea ascendunt Peregrini ad Sepulchrum accipientes sudarium, descendentes ad chorum ostendentes sudarium, et cantent: *Cernitis, o socij.*

Quo facto, conuertunt se Marie ad altare. Maria Magdalena cantat: *Dolor crescit*, et *Cum venissent*, et *En lapis.*

Interim ascendens Dominica Persona, rubea casula indutus, ad dextrum cornu altaris habens vexillum in manu, et conuertat se Maria Magdalena ad eum cantans tribus vicibus: *Heu, redempcio Israel*, flexis genibus.

Dominica Persona respondit: *Maria!*

Item illa: *Domine, si tu sustulisti.*

Dominica Persona: *Maria!*

Item Maria: *Rab⟨on⟩i!*

Deinde Dominica Persona: *Prima quidem.*

Item Maria: *Sanctus Deus*, cum genuflexionibus.

Dominica Persona: *Hec[4] priori.*

Maria: *Sancte fortis.*

Dominica Persona: *Ergo noli me.*

Maria: *Sancte et immortalis.*

Dominica Persona: *Nunc ignoras.*

Quibus finitis, chorus cantat sequenciam: *Victime.*

Versus: *Agnus rede⟨mit⟩.*

Versus: *Mors et vita.*

---

[1] For observations on the MS see above, p. 563.

[2] The third responsory *Dum transisset* im-mediately precedes.

[3] surrexit] surrect (MS).

[4] Hec] Hic (MS).

Deinde Peregrini stantes ante gradus in medio chori cantent versum: *Dic nobis, Maria.*

Marie respondent: *Sepulchrum Christi vi⟨ventis⟩.*

Angelicos testes.

Versus: *Scimus Christum,* et cetera.

Hijs finitis, Dominica Persona et Marie stantes ante altare cantent versum: *Dicant nunc,* choro respondente: *Quod enim viuit.*

Deinde Marie cantent antiphonam: *Surrexit Dominus de sepulchro.* Post hoc vniuersus populus cum magna leticia cantant *Crist ist erstanden,* postea cantor incipiens *Te Deum laudamus.*

Of the same general type is the following from Wolfenbüttel, Herzogliche Bibl., MS Aug. 84. 2, Ordin. Havelbergense sæc. xv, fol. 23^r–23^v, previously edited by Brooks, *Osterfeiern,* pp. 59–60:

Responsorium *Dum transisset* cum incipitur, intrent chorum in cappis albis tres persone visitantes, prima et secunda cum thuribulo, tercia cum pixide aurea, et cantant versum; post *Gloria Patri* responsorium reincipitur. Interim conuentus descendat in monasterium, singuli portantes cereos ardentes, preeuntibus vexillis. Finito responsorio, procedant visitantes a choro vna consequenter post aliam, singuli cum cantu suo.

Prima: *Heu, nobis.*

Secunda: *Iam percusso.*

Reliqua vero: *Sed eamus.*

Et conueniant usque ad medium altare, et subiungit chorus antiphonam: *Maria Magdalena.*

Interim visitantes procedant simul versus | Sepulcrum; et cum appropient cantant simul: *Quis reuoluet?*

Angeli in Sepulcro: *Quem queritis?*

At illi: *Ihesum Nazarenum.*

Angeli: *Non est hic.*

Et subdunt cantantes: *Venite.*

Persone inspicientes, thurificato Sepulcro, reuertentur, choro cantante: *Et recordate sunt.*

Reuersi de Sepulcro stantes cantant: *Ad monumentum.*

Tunc, duabus personis abeuntibus, tercia circuiens cantat:

Cum uenissem.

Heu, re⟨dempcio⟩.

Item: *En lapis.*

Heu, re⟨dempcio⟩.

Item: *Dolor cres⟨cit⟩.*

Heu, re⟨dempcio⟩.

Tunc in persona Saluatoris sacerdos cum vexillo submisse cantat: *Mulier, quid plo⟨ras⟩?*

Maria respondit: *Domine, si tu.*

Deinde Saluator: *Maria!*

At illa: *Rabi, quod.*

Saluator: *Prima quidem.*

At illa: *Sancte Deus.*

Saluator: *Hec priori.*

Illa iterum: *Sancte fortis.*

Saluator: *Ergo noli.*

Illa ad hoc: *Sancte et misericors*, et semper flectentes genua dum cantat *Deus, fortis, misericors.* Et iterum Saluator ad illam: *Nunc ignoras.*

Et post hec recedat. Tunc illa iterum circuiens cantat: *Vere vidi.*

Item: *Victime*, usque *Dic nobis.*

Tunc duo occurrentes, Pe⟨trus⟩ scilicet et Io⟨hannes⟩, cantant: *Dic nobis, Maria.*

At illa: *Sepulcrum Christi.*

Illi secundo: *Dic nobis.*

Ad quod illa: *Angelicos tes⟨tes⟩.*

Illi tercio: *Dic nobis.*

Illa vero: *Surrexit Christus.*

Et chorus prosequitur: *Credendum est magis*, usque ad finem.

Interim Maria recedat. Post hec, illis duobus currentibus ad Monumentum, chorus cantat: *Currebant duo.*

Et intrantes Sepulcrum tollant inde lintheum, et reuersi ante medium altare cantant: *Cernitis, o socij.*

Post hec in ambone leuantes crucem cantant: *Surrexit.* Chorus prosequitur. Deinde vulgus: *Crist is up ge⟨standen⟩.* Et redeat conuentus in chorum, et imponatur *Te Deum.* Versus *Surrexit Dominus de sepulcro.*[1]

This type of *Visitatio* is more completely preserved in the following text from Zwickau, Ratsschulbibl., MS XXXVI. I. 24, Visitationes Sepulchri sæc. xvi, fol. 1 ʳ–6 ʳ, previously edited by Stötzner, pp. 5–7:

In sacratissima nocte Resurrectionis Domini nostri,[2] Jesu Christi, Visitatio Sepulchri. Sub tercia lectione conuenient tres persone ad modum honestarum Mulierum vestite in sacristia, et finita tercia lectione, organo incipiente responsorium,[3] exeant, tribus pueris cum superpelliciis accensis luminibus precedentibus, ad medium chori, et finito responsorio, omnes tres simul concinne cantent versum dicti responsorii *Dum transisset*[4] *sabatum. Et valde mane vna sabatorum veniunt ad monumentum, orto iam sole. Gloria Patri, et Filio, et Spiritui Sancto.* Prima persona sola cantat eundo ad altare Sancte Crucis ante chorum:

> *Jhesu, nostra redempcio,*
> *amor et desiderium,*
> *Deus creator omnium,* |
> *homo in fine temporum.*

Post finem istius versus sequatur secunda persona cantans sequentem versum —secunda persona:

> *Que te vicit clemencia,*
> *ut ferres nostra crimina,*
> *crudelem mortem paciens,*
> *ut nos ab hoste tolleres?*

---

[1] Followed by the rubric *Ad Laudes.*
[2] nostri] Written twice (MS).
[3] responsorium] responsorio (MS).
[4] transisset] transissent (MS).

Tercia pe⟨r⟩sona similiter sequatur:

> *Inferni claustra penetrans,*
> *tuos captiuos redimens,*
> *victor triumpho nobili*
> *ad dextram patris residens.*

Statim iterum progrediatur prima persona ad medium ecclesie cantans sequentem antiphonam:

> *Omnipotens pater altissime,*
> *angelorum rector mitissime,*
> *quid faciemus nos miserrime?*
> *Hew, quantus est | noster dolor!*

Finita ista antiphona, immediate sequetur secunda persona cantans sequentem antiphonam:

> *Amisimus enim solacium,*
> *Jhesum Christum, Marie filium.*
> *Ipse erat nostra redempcio.*
> *Hew, quantus est noster dolor!*

Mox sequatur tercia persona cantans antiphonam sequentem:

> *Sed eamus vngentum emere,*
> *de quo bene possumus vngere*
> *corpus Domini sacratum.*
> *Hew, quantus est noster dolor!*

Tunc chorus cantet Antiphonam sequentem: *Maria Magdalena*, vt patet in anthiphonario. Et interim quod chorus cantet antiphonam, vadant predicte tres persone ad Sepulchrum. Et finita anthiphona, cantent omnes tres simul vt sequitur: |

> *Quis reuoluet nobis ab ostio lapidem quem tegere sanctum cernimus sepulchrum?*

Tunc quatuor iuuenes loco Angelorum in Sepulcro sedentes cantent antiphonam sequentem:

> *Quem queritis, o tremule mulieres, in hoc tumulo plorantes?*

Tunc tres Marie respondent sine interuallo ut sequitur:

> *Jhesum Nazarenum crucifixum querimus.*

Iterum Angeli:

> *Non est hic quem queritis, sed cito euntes nuntiate discipulis eius et Petro quia surrexit Ihesus.*

Et exeuntes detegunt Sepulchrum cantantes immediate antiphonam sequentem:

> *Venite et videte locum vbi positus erat | Dominus, alleluia, alleluia!*

Et sic reuertantur ad medium ecclesie, vbi prius steterant, cantantes:

> *Ad monumentem venimus gementes, angelum Domini sedentem vidimus, et dicentem quia surrexit Jhesus.*

Deinde tercia persona recedens ab aliis duabus, ceroferario precedente, facit circuitum per ecclesiam incipiens circa ambonem vsque ad altare Sancte Anne cantans antiphonas infra scriptas, incipiens: *Cum venissem*, et cetera:

> *Cum venissem vngere mortuum,*
> *monumentum inueni vacuum.*
> *Hew, nescio recte discernere,*
> *vbi possum magistrum querere.*

Dolor crescit, tremunt praecordia |
de magistri pii absencia,
qui saluavit me plenam viciis,
pulsis a me septem demoniis.

En lapis est vere depositus,
qui fuerat in signum positus.
Munierant locum militibus:
locus vacat, eis absentibus.

Circa altare Sancte Crucis ante chorum incipiat cantare sequentem anthi-
phonam, et cantet eam ter usque ad altare Sancte Anne, et cetera:

Hew, redempcio Israhel,
ut quid mortem | sustinuit, paciens.

Et cum ter cecinit, stans plebanus ante altare Sancte Anne sic cantans:

Mulier, quid ploras? Quem queris?

Respondit ipsa stans ante altare, dicens vt sequitur:

Domine, si tu sustulisti eum, dicito michi, et vbi posuisti eum, et ego eum
tollam.

Et tunc plebanus cantet illud vnum:

Maria!

Maria:

Rabi, quod dicitur magister.

Tunc iterum plebanus cantet *Prima*, et cetera, vt sequitur in propria cedula:

Prima quidem suffragia,

et cetera. Tunc geniculetur ipsa Maria ante altare Sancte Anne, vel alibi,
cantans:

Sancte Deus!

Tunc iterum respondit plebanus *Hec priori:*

Hec priori dissimilis,

et cetera, vt sequitur in propria cedula. | Iterum dicat Maria cantans:

Sancte fortis!

Iterum plebanus:

Ergo noli me tangere,

et cetera, vt sequitur. Iterum cantet Maria dicens:

Sancte et inmortalis, miserere nobis!

Tunc iterum plebanus vt sequitur:

Nunc ignaros[1] *huius rei,*

et cetera. Post finem huius antiphone recedit ipsa Maria a plebano, rediens
ad alias duas, cantans antiphonam ut sequitur:

        Vere vidi Dominum viuere,
        nec dimisit me pedes tangere.
        Discipulos oportet credere
        quod ad Patrem velit ascendere.

Post finem huius antiphone incipiat sola *Victime*, et cetera:

Victime pascali laudes ymmolant Christiani: |
Agnus redemit oues: Christus innocens Patri reconciliauit, et cetera.
Mors et vita duello conflixere mirando; dux vite,

---

[1] *ignaros*] ignoras (MS).

et cetera. Et ipsa sic cantans stabit sola aduersus alias duas Marias. Et ipse interrogant eam cantantes sub hac forma:

Dic nobis, Maria, quid vidisti in via?

Et sic eam interrogant trina vice; quibus ipsa respondet:

Sepulcrum Christi viuentis, et gloriam vidi resurgentis.

Post terciam responsionem subiungit illum versum:

Angelicos testes, sudarium et vestes:
Surrexit Christus,

et cetera. Post finem huius versus intrant chorum simul omnes tres cantantes sequentes versus, scilicet:

Credendum est, et
Scimus Christum surrexisse,

et cetera, vsque ad finem. Tunc chorus post finem illorum versuum in medio ecclesie stantes cantent antiphonam *Currebant duo simul,* et cetera. Tunc sub ista antiphona duo diaconi accipiant lintheamen ex Sepulchro, ostendentes illud omni populo et cantantes antiphonam *Cernitis, o socii,* et cetera, vt in antiphonario. Chorus subiungit *Surrexit enim sicut dixit,* et cetera. Post finem tunc plebanus superius in choro cantet tribus vicibus *Surrexit Dominus de sepulchro,* vt in anthiphonario. Et chorus respondit semper *Qui pro nobis pependit in ligno, alleluia!* Post terciam inchoacionem incipiet plebanus materna voce *Crist ist erstandenn,* et cetera. Et tunc chorus, scilicet scolares, intrant chorum. Et incipit organista *Te Deum laudamus,* et cetera. Sequentes anthiphonae omnes pertinent ad plebanum: |

Mulier, quid ploras? Quem queris?

Maria!
Prima quidem suffragia
stola tulit carnalia,
exhibendo communia
se per nature munia.

Hec priori dissimilis,
hec est incorruptibilis,
que nunc fuit passibilis,
iam non erit solubilis.

Ergo noli me tangere,
nec ultro venias plangere,
quem mox in puro sidere
cernes ad Patrem | scandere.

Nunc ignaros[1] huius rei
certos reddes fratres meos.
Gallileam dic ut eant,
et me viuentem videant, et cetera.

Among the noteworthy features of this version are the presence of the somewhat exceptional verses *Heu, redemptio Israhel* and *Vere vidi Dominum vivere,* the appearance of *four* angels at the tomb, and the assignment of *Victimæ paschali* to Mary Magdalen as part of her announcement to the remaining

---

[1] ignaros] ignoras (MS).

two Marys. Important also is the assignment of *Dic nobis* to the two Marys as the means whereby they interrogate Mary Magdalen after her scene with Christ.

Page 402, note 7. Similar to the *Visitatio* from Prague MS VI. G. 3b is the following found *ibid.*, MS XII. E. 15a, Lib. resp. Sancti Georgii Pragensis sæc. xiv, fol. 69ᵛ–74ᵛ (A), previously edited by Lange, no. 213, pp. 148–51, to the re-edited text of which I give the variants from the following MSS found *ibid.*: MS VI. G. 10b, Process. Sancti Georgii Pragensis sæc. xiv, fol. 72ᵛ–78ᵛ (B), previously edited by Lange, no. 214, pp. 151–4 (the number of the MS being given as VI. G. 10); MS VI. G. 5, Lib. resp. Pragensis sæc. xiv, fol. 243ᵛ–250ʳ (C), previously edited, incompletely, by Lange, no. 211, pp. 146–8:[1]

In sancta nocte, imposito responsorio *Dum transisset*, Domina Abbatissa precedet, Maria Magdalena sequetur[2] eam, tres Marie sequentur eam cum senioribus. Responsorium: *Dum transisset sabbatum, Maria Magdalena et Maria Iacobi et Salome emerunt aromata, ut uenientes ungerent Ihesum, alleluia, allel|uia. Versus: Et ualde mane una sabbatorum ueniunt ad monumentum, orto iam sole. Vt uenientes. Gloria Patri, et Filio, et Spiritui Sancto. Alleluia.*[3]

Finito responsorio, tres Marie cantantes *Aromata* procedant ad Ungentarium pro accipiendis ungentis:

> *Aromata precio querimus:*
> *Christi corpus ungere | uolumus:*
> *holocausta sunt odorifera*
> *sepulture Christi memoria.*[4]

Quibus acceptis, accedant ad Sepulchrum, conuentu cantante antiphonam:[5] *Maria Magdalena et alia Maria ferebant diluculo aromata, Dominum querentes in monumento.*[6]

Qua finita, tres Marie cantent antiphonam stantes ante Sepulchrum: *Quis reuoluet nobis | ab ostio lapidem quem tegere sanctum cernimus sepulchrum?*

Angelus in Sepulchro: *Quem queritis, o tremule mulieres, in hoc tumulo plorantes?*

Marie respondeant: *Ihesum Nazarenum crucifixum querimus.*

Angelus: *Non est hic quem queritis, sed cito euntes nunciate discipulis eius et Petro | quia surrexit Ihesus.*

Item Angelus, aperto Sepulchro:[7] *Venite et uidete locum ubi positus erat Dominus, alleluia, alleluia.*[8]

Deinde Marie uenientes ad chorum cantent antiphonam: *Ad monumentum uenimus gementes, angelum Domini sedentem uidimus, et dicentem quia surrexit Ihesus.*

Postea proceden|te de loco Maria Magdalena, antiphonam istam imponit cantrix: *Alleluia, noli flere, Maria; alleluia, resurrexit Dominus, alleluia, alleluia.*

Stante Maria Magdalena ante Sepulchrum, conuentus cantet antiphonam istam: *Maria stabat ad monumentum foris plorans; dum ergo fleret, inclinauit se*

---

[1] The *Visitatio* in MS VI. G. 5 has no rubrics whatever, a fact which I do not re-state in the foot-notes below.

[2] sequetur] sequentur (A).

[3] Versus: Et . . . Alleluia] Omitted (B.C).

[4] memoria] memoriam (A.B).

[5] conuentu . . . antiphonam] Omitted (B).

[6] monumento] monumento, alleluia (C).

[7] Rubric omitted (B).

[8] alleluia, alleluia] Omitted (C).

(Hic inclinet se Maria et inspiciat Sepulchrum), *et prospexit | in monumentum.*[1]

Inspecto Sepulchro, conuertat se ad Ihesum et dicat[2] hanc antiphonam: ⟨*Tulerunt Dominum meum, et nescio ubi posuerunt eum.*[3]

Ihesus respondeat:⟩ *Mulier, quid ploras? Quem queris?*[4]

Maria cantet antiphonam: *Domine, si tu sustulisti eum, dicito michi ubi posuisti eum, et ego eum tollam.*

Ihesus dicat:[5] *Maria!*

Et[6] illa inclinando se r*espondeat*:[5] *Raboni!*

At Ihesus retrocedens cantet antiphonam:[5] | *Noli me tangere, Maria; uade autem ad fratres meos et dic eis: Ascendo ad Patrem meum et Patrem uestrum.*

In reditu Marie ad chorum canitur antiphona:[7] *Venit Maria annuncians discipulis: Quia uidi Dominum.*

Cantrix incipit versum:[8] *Dic*[9] *nobis, Maria, quid uidisti in uia?* |

At illa respondit:

> *Sepulchrum Christi uiuentis, et gloriam uidi resurgentis.*
> *Angelicos testes, sudarium et uestes.*
> *Surrexit Christus, spes mea; precedet*[10] *suos in Galileam.*

Chorus dicat:

> *Credendum est magis soli Marie ueraci quam Iudeorum turbe fallaci.*
> *Scimus Christum surrexisse ex mortuis uere; tu nobis, uictor rex, miserere.*[11] |

Mox unus sacerdos cum trina flexione imponit: *Christus Dominus resurrexit.*

Conuentus respondit:[12] *Deo gratias, gaudeamus.*

Sequitur antiphona:[13] *Currebant*[14] *duo simul, et ille alius discipulus precucurrit cicius Petro, et uenit prior ad monumentum, alleluia.*

Duo presbyteri accipientes linteum uadunt ad gradum cantantes antiphonam: *Cernitis,*[15] *o socii, ecce | lintheamina et sudarium, et corpus non est in sepulchro inuentum.*[16]

Qua finita,[17] conuentus cantat antiphonam: *Surrexit Dominus de sepulchro, qui pro nobis pependit in ligno, alleluia, alleluia, alleluia.*

Sequitur ⟨*T*⟩*e Deum laudamus.* Inde uersus *In resurrectione tua, Christe, alleluia.* Statim sequitur euangelium *Maria Magdalena.*[18]

Page 405, note 2. Similar to the *Visitatio* from Prague MS XIII. E. 14d is the following found *ibid.*, MS VII. G. 16, Lib. resp. Sancti Georgii Pragensis sæc. xiv, fol. 96ʳ–101ᵛ, previously edited by Lange, no. 215, pp. 151–4:

[1] inclinauit . . . monumentum] inclinauit se et prospexit in monumentum Hic inclinet se Maria et inspiciat sepulchrum (B). The marks of parenthesis in the text above are editorial.

[2] dicat] dicant (A.B).

[3] Tulerunt . . . eum] Not omitted (C).

[4] Mulier . . . queris] Maria quid ploras quem (C).

[5] Rubrics omitted (B).

[6] Et] quia (A).

[7] antiphona] antiphonam (B).

[8] versum] antiphonam (B).

[9] Dic] Hic (A).

[10] precedet] precedens (B.C).

[11] Credendum . . . miserere] Credendum est magis soli marie. Scimus Christum surrexisse, alleluia (C). Then follow in C the words *Resurrexit Dominus*, and thus the text ends.

[12] Rubric omitted (B).

[13] Sequitur antiphona] antiphona (B).

[14] Currebant] Surrebant (B). In C *Currebant . . . monumentum, alleluia* supplants *Noli me . . . uestrum* after *Raboni*, above.

[15] Cernitis] Dernitis (B).

[16] inuentum] inueuentum (A).

[17] finita] finita antiphona (B).

[18] Sequitur Te . . . Magdalena] Omitted (B)

Tres¹ Marie: *Aromata precio querimus:*
                                Christi corpus vngere uolumus:
                                holocausta sunt odorifera
                                sepulture Christi memoria.
Vngentarius: *Dabo uobis vngenta optima,*
                                Saluatoris vngere vulnera,
                                sepultu|re eius ad memoriam,
                                et nomini eius ad gloriam.

Conuentus: *Maria Magdalena et alia Maria ferebant diluculo aromata, Dominum querentes in monumento.*

Tres Marie: *Quis reuoluet no|bis ab ostio lapidem quem tegere sanctum cernimus sepulchrum?*

Angelus: *Quem queritis, o tremule mulieres, in hoc tumulo plorantes?*

Tres Marie: *Ihesum Nazarenum crucifixum querimus.*

Angelus: *Non est hic quem | queritis, sed cito euntes nunciate discipulis eius et Petro quia surrexit Ihesus.*

Idem Angelus: *Venite et uidete locum ubi positus erat Dominus, alleluia, alleluia.*

Tres Marie: *Ad monumentum uenimus gementes, angelum | Domini sedentem uidimus, et dicentem quia surrexit Ihesus.*

⟨Conventus:⟩ *Alleluia, noli flere, Maria; alleluia, resurrexit Dominus, alleluia, alleluia.*

        Maria stabat ad monumentum foris plorans: dum ergo fleret, | inclinauit se (Hic inclinet se, et inspiciat Sepulchrum), *et prospexit in monumentum.*²

⟨Maria Magdalena:⟩ *Tulerunt Dominum meum, et nescio ubi posuerunt eum.*

Ihesus: *Mulier, quid ploras? Quem queris?*

Maria: *Domine, si tu sustulisti eum, | dicito michi ubi posuisti eum, et ego eum tollam.*

Ihesus: *Maria!*

Maria: *Raboni!*

Ihesus: *Noli me tangere, Maria; uade autem ad fratres meos et dic eis: Ascendo ad Patrem meum et Patrem uestrum, | Deum meum et Deum uestrum.*

Cantrix: *Venit Maria annuncians: Quia uidi Dominum.*

Cantrix: *Dic nobis, Maria, quid uidisti in uia?*

Maria: *Sepulchrum Christi uiuentis, et gloriam uidi resurgentis.*

Item: *| Angelicos testes, sudarium et uestes.*

Item: *Surrexit Christus, spes mea; precedet suos in Galileam.*

Chorus: *Credendum est magis soli Marie ueraci quam Iudeorum turbe fallaci.*

Item: *Scimus Christum surrexisse ex mortuis uere; | tu nobis, uictor rex, miserere.*

Mox vnus sacerdos, indutus dalmatica, tenens crucifixum, tribus vicibus flectat genua in medio ecclesie, cantans: *Christus Dominus resurrexit.*

Et conuentus totidem vicibus flectens genua respondeat: *Deo gracias, gaudeamus.*

Item conuentus: *Currebant duo simul, et ille alius discipulus precucurrit cicius Petro, et uenit | prior ad monumentum, alleluia.*

Duo presbyteri accipientes lintheum vadunt in medium ecclesie ante Sepulchrum ferreum cantantes: *Cernitis, o socij, ecce lintheamina et sudarium, et corpus non est in sepulchro inuentum.*

---

¹ The responsory *Dum transisset*, without rubric, immediately precedes, occupying all of fol. 95.ᵛ

² The marks of parenthesis are editorial.

Qua finita, conuentus cantat antiphonam: *Surrexit Dominus de sepulchro, qui pro nobis pependit | in ligno, alleluia, alleluia, alleluia, alleluia.*

Interim Domina Abbatissa deosculetur lintheum, et omnes. *Te Deum laudamus.* Versus *In resurrectione tua, Christe, alleluia.* ⟨Responsio⟩ *Celum et terra letentur, alleluia.* Sequitur Ewangelium *Maria Magdalena,* et cetera.[1]

An incomplete and disorderly text of the same version is found *ibid.,* MS VI. G. 10a, Process. Sancti Georgii Pragensis sæc. xiv–xv, fol. 149ʳ– 153ᵛ, mentioned by Meyer, p. 80, and now first printed:

Maria Magdalena et alia Maria ferebant diluculo aromata, Dominum querentes in monumento.

> *Aromata precio querimus;*
> *Christi corpus vngere | volumus;*
> *holocausta sunt odorifera*
> *sepulture Christi memoria.*

Maria Magdalena et alia Maria ferebant diluculo aromata, Dominum querentes in monumento.[2] |

> *Dabo uobis vnguenta optima,*
> *Saluatoris vngere uulnera,*
> *sepulture eius ad memoriam*
> *et nomini eius ad gloriam.*

Quis reuoluet nobis ab hostio lapidem quem tegere sanctum | cernimus sepulcrum?

Quem queritis, o tremule mulieres, in hoc tumulo plorantes?

Ihesum Nazarenum crucifixum querimus.[3]

Non est hic quem queritis, sed cito euntes | nunciate discipulis eius et Petro quia surrexit Ihesus.

Venite et uidete locum ubi positus erat Dominus.

Ad monumentum venimus gementes, angelum Domini seden|tem vidimus, et dicentem quia surrexit Ihesus.

Alleluia, noli flere, Maria; alleluia, resurrexit Dominus, alleluia, alleluia.

Maria stabat ad monumentum foris plorans; dum ergo fle|ret, inclinauit se et prospexit in monumentum.

Tulerunt Dominum meum, et nescio ubi posuerunt eum.

Mulier, quid ploras? Quem queris?

Domine, si tu sustulisti eum, | dicito michi ubi posuisti eum, et ego eum tollam.

Maria!

Raboni!

Noli me tangere, Maria; uade autem ad fratres meos | et dic eis: Ascendo ad Patrem meum et Patrem uestrum, Deum meum et Deum uestrum.

Dic nobis, Maria.

Sepulchrum Christi viuentis, per totum.

Surrexit.

Currebant duo. |

Cernitis, o socii.

Surrexit Dominus.[4]

---

[1] Here follows immediately, without introductory rubric, the antiphon *Christus resurgens.*

[2] Whereas the remainder of the text has musical notation, there is none for the repetition of the passage *Maria Magdalena . . . monumento,* which is clearly superfluous.

[3] querimus] Altered to *queritis* (MS).

[4] Followed by *In die resurrectionis mee.*

Page 408, note 1. A discussion of the merchant-scene from Prague must include some mention of Wilhelm Meyer's intricate inferences concerning the origin of this scene, and concerning the nature of a hypothetical *Zehn-silberspiel*, of which the action attached to the *unguentarius* is an important part.[1] By *Zehnsilberspiel* Meyer means an Easter play containing stanzas of four ten-syllable lines, typical examples being the forms of *Visitatio* from Engelberg, Cividale, Einsiedeln, and Nuremberg presented above.[2] In its full *theoretical* form this *Spiel* contains, principally, some six groups of stanzas, in varying metres, as follows:

A. A group of three stanzas, expressing the grief of the three Marys, in lines of fifteen syllables, the stanzas beginning *Heu nobis*, *Jam percusso*, and *Sed eamus* respectively, as seen, for example, in the plays from Engelberg and Rheinau.[3]

B. A group of three stanzas, expressing the intention of buying ointment, in rhyming lines of ten syllables, the stanzas beginning *Omnipotens pater*, *Amisimus enim*, and *Sed eamus unguentum* respectively, as seen, for example, in the plays from Narbonne, Zwickau, and Tours.[4]

C. A group of utterances accompanying the actual purchase of the ointment. Of these the most striking are the five stanzas of ten-syllable lines beginning respectively *Huc proprius*, *Dic tu nobis*, *Hoc unguentum*, *Aromata pretio*, and *Dabo vobis*. The last two stanzas may be seen in the play from Prague, and all five appear in the play from Benediktbeuern.[5]

D. A group of three stanzas of ten-syllable lines, in which Mary Magdalen expresses her grief. These stanzas begin *Cum venissem*, *En lapis*, and *Dolor crescit* respectively, and they may be seen, for example, in the plays from Engelberg and Cividale.[6]

E. A group of four stanzas in lines of eight syllables, in which Christ expounds the Resurrection to Mary Magdalen, and lays his command upon her. The stanzas begin respectively *Prima quidem*, *Hæc priori*, *Ergo noli*, and *Nunc ignaros*, and they may be seen, for example, in the plays from Engelberg and Einsiedeln.[7]

F. A single stanza of ten-syllable lines—either the one beginning *Vere vidi*[8] or that beginning *Galilæam omnes*[9]—in which Mary Magdalen makes her announcement to the disciples, or to others.

Meyer observes that, whereas groups A, B, and C—which are concerned with the merchant-scene—are found in plays from France, groups D, E,

---

[1] See Meyer, pp. 81, 106–20.

[2] See pp. 375, 378, 390, 398. I assume that Meyer would not have altered his hypothesis essentially if he had known the plays from Zurich (Rheinau) MS 18, Wolfenbüttel MS Aug. 84.2, St Gall MS 448, Zwickau MS XXXVI. i. 24, and Oxford (University Coll.) MS 169, concerning which see above, pp. 381, 385, 667, 668, 669.

[3] See above, pp. 375, 385; Meyer, pp. 106–7.

[4] See above, pp. 285, 439, 670; Meyer, pp. 107–8.

[5] See above, pp. 405, 435. See also the play from Tours, p. 440; and Meyer, pp. 108–9.

[6] See above, pp. 376, 379; Meyer, pp. 110–1.

[7] See above, pp. 377, 391 Meyer, pp. 111–5.

[8] See, for example, the plays from Cividale and Zwickau above, pp. 380, 671.

[9] See the plays of St Florian and Klosterneuburg above, pp. 367, 425; and Meyer, pp. 115–6.

and F—associated with the scene between Christ and Mary Magdalen—are not regularly found there. The combination of all three groups, A, B, and C, sometimes found in France, does not occur in Germany, a normal German arrangement being a combination of groups A, D, E, and F.[1] From these general facts Meyer infers the following:

(1) At the time when a French cleric added to the *Visitatio* a scene between Christ and Mary Magdalen, another French cleric invented a merchant-scene; and since neither the Bible nor the liturgy provided speeches for such a dramatic invention, the author used secular metrical forms, and composed group A for the entrance of the Marys, group B for their journey to the tomb, and group C for their dialogue with the merchant.[2]

(2) A play containing groups A, B, and C, along with the Christ-Magdalen scene, was carried from France to Germany; and upon the model of A, B, and C, a German writer embellished the Christ-Magdalen scene, the result being groups D, E, and F. For the sake of solemnity and contrast, this writer composed the four stanzas of Christ, group E, in lines of eight syllables. Thus the *Zehnsilberspiel* was brought to its theoretically complete form in Germany.[3]

Although certain of Meyer's ingenious *obiter dicta* cannot be taken very seriously, the general outline of his argument is theoretically acceptable.[4] There are good reasons for believing that the ten-syllable line arose first in France, and was used there dramatically before it was cultivated in Germany.[5] Meyer's general theory of the origin of the *Zehnsilberspiel* in France and of its completion in Germany accords well enough with the known facts and with the extant texts. His general view will, perhaps, be regarded by most students of the subject as an unproved possibility.

Certain modifications of Meyer's theory have been proposed by Dürre, pp. 11–25. These are based primarily upon passages in the following dis-ordered text from Vich, Museo, MS 111, Trop. Rivipullense sæc. xii, fol. 58ᵛ–62ʳ, previously edited by Young, *Some Texts*, pp. 303–8:[6]

VERSES PASCALES DE III Mariis[7]

Eamus mirram emere
cum liquido aromate,
vt ualeamus ungere
corpus datum sepulture.

Omnipotens Pater altissime,   5
angelorum rector mitissime,
quid facient iste miserime!

Dicunt Angelus:[8]

Heu, quantus est noster dolor!

---

[1] See Meyer, pp. 116–7.
[2] See Meyer, pp. 118–9.
[3] See Meyer, p. 119.
[4] For the sake of clarity, I have presented Meyer's extremely intricate argument only in its main outline.
[5] See Meyer, p. 118.
[6] In the MS this text is not only disordered, but also crudely written and seriously lacer-ated. The temptations to emend are nume-rous, and to a few of them I have yielded—not, of course, without presenting also the readings of the MS itself. Parts of the text are unintelligible.
[7] Mariis] The word intended may, of course, be *Mulieribus*.
[8] Obviously this rubric is out of place.

> Amisimus enim solatium,
> Ihesum Christum, Marie filium;   10
> iste nobis erat subsidium.
>   Heu, ⟨quantus est noster dolor!⟩

> Set eamus unguentum emere,
> quo possimus corpus inungere;
> non amplius posset putrescere.[1]   15
>   Heu, ⟨quantus est noster dolor!⟩

> Dic tu nobis, mercator iuuenis,
> hoc unguentum si tu uendide|ris;
> dic precium, nam iam habueris.
>   Heu, ⟨quantus est noster dolor!⟩   20

Respondet Mercator:

> Mulieres michi intendite.
> Hoc unguentum si uultis emere,
> datur genus mirre potencie,
> qvo si corpus possetis ungere,
> non amplius posset putrescere   25
> neque uermes possent comedere.

> Hoc unguentum si multum cupitis,
> unum auri talentum dabitis;
> nec aliter umquam portabitis.

Respondet Maria:

> O mercator, unguentum libera.   30
> Ecce tibi ⟨dabi⟩mus m⟨un⟩era.[2]
> Ibimus Christi ungere uulnera.
>   Heu, ⟨quantus est noster dolor!⟩ |

> ⟨Cuncta, sorores, gau⟩dia[3]
> deflorent in tristicia   35
> cum innocens opprobria[4]
> fert et crucis suspendia
> Iudeorum inuidia,
> et principum perfidia![5]
> Quid angemus et qualia!   40

> Licet, sorores, plangere,
> plangendo Christum querere,
> querendo corpus ungere,
> ungendo mente[6] pascere
> de[7] fletu, uiso uulnere,   45
> dilecto magno federe
> cor mo⟨n⟩stratur[8] in opere.

---

[1] posset putrescere] poscet putrescire (MS).

[2] In this line the parts within brackets are illegible.

[3] In this line the parts within brackets are obscured through laceration of the bottom of fol. 59ʳ. Fol. 59ᵛ begins with the letters *dia*.

[4] opprobria] obrobria (MS).

[5] perfidia] perfudia (MS).

[6] mente] With the first syllable of this word the musical notation ceases for the remainder of the page.

[7] De] Over this word is the letter *.a.* which I cannot explain.

[8] mo<n>stratur] Possibly the *s* is expunged (MS).

Cordis, sorores, creduli
simus et bene seduli,
vt nostri cerna⟨nt⟩ oculi   50
corpus Christi, uim seculi.
Quis uoluet petram cumuli
magnam sive uim populi?
virtus[1] celestis epuli.

Tanta, sorores, uisio   55
splendoris[2] et lustrascio
nulla sit stupefatio,
vobis sit exultatio.
Mors[1] et mortis occasio
moritur uita uicio.   60
Nostra, surge, surreccio.

Hoc, sorores, circuitu,
lecto, dicite, sonitu
illis[1] qui mesto spiritu
et proditio[3] transitu   65
dux uicto surgit obitu
querantur lecto strepitu
. . . scis . . . dux ortitu.[4]

Quid faciemus, sorores,
graues ferimus dolores?   70
Non est, nec erit seculis,
dolor doloris similis.

Iesum gentes perimere,
semper decet nos lugere,
set ut poscimus gaudere,   75
eamus tu⟨m⟩bam uidere.

Tumbam querimus non lento,
corpus ungamus unguento,
quod extinctum uulneribus
uiuis preualet omnibus.   80

Regis perempti premium[5]
plus ualet quam uiuencium,
cuius amor solacium
iuuamen et presidium
et perenne[6] subsidium   85
sit nunc et in perpetuum.

Vbi[7] est Christus, meus Dominus | et filius excelsi?
Eamus uidere sepulcrum.

---

[1] Over these words is the letter *.a.* which I cannot explain.
[2] Splendoris] Reading very doubtful.
[3] proditio] pr*odium* (MS?).
[4] Points represent illegible passages.

[5] perempti premium] perhempti pre-uium (MS).
[6] perenne] per homne (MS).
[7] The words *Ubi est Christus, meus Dominus* are repeated at the top of fol. 60[r].

Respondet Angel⟨us⟩:[1] *Qvem queritis in sepulcro, Christicole?*

Respondent Maria⟨e⟩: *Ihesum Nazarenum crucifixum, o celicole.*

Respondet Angel⟨us⟩:[1] *Non est hic, surrexit sicut predixerat; ite, nunciate quia surrexit dicentes.*

Respondent Mari⟨æ⟩:[1] *Alleluia, ad sepulcrum residens angelus nunciat resur⟨r⟩exisse Christum.*

Te Deum laudamus.

Versus de Pelegri⟨nis⟩[1]

Rex in acubitum iam se contulerat,
et mea redolens nardus spirauerat;
in ⟨hortum⟩[2] ue|neram in quem descenderat, ·
at ille transiens iam declinauerat.

Per noctem igitur hunc querens exeo;
huc illuc transiens nusquam reperio.

Angeli: *Mulier, quid ploras? Quem queris?*

Maria: *Occurrunt uigiles ardenti studio,*
Quos cum transierim, sponsum inuenio.

Ortolanus: *Mulier, quid ploras? ⟨Q⟩uem queris?*

Maria: *Tulerunt Dominum meum, et nescio ubi posuerunt eum. Si tu | sustulisti eum, dicito michi, et eum tollam.*

Ortolanus: *Maria, Maria, Maria!*

Respondet Maria:[3] *Raboni, Raboni, Raboni!*[4]

Maria rediens dic*a*t: *Dic, impie Zabule, quid ualet nunc fraus tua?*

Discipuli: *Dic nobis, Maria, quid uidisti in uia?*

Maria: *Sepulcrum Christi uiuentis, et gloriam uidi resurgentis;*
Angelicos testes, sudarium et uestes.

Angeli: *Non est hic, sur⟨r⟩exit sicut predixerat uobis.*

Discipuli: *Credendum est magis | soli Marie ueraci quam[5] Iudeorum turbe fallaci.*
Scimus Christum sur⟨r⟩exisse a mortuis uere: tu nobis, Christe, Rex, miserere.
Qvi sunt hij sermones quos confertis ad inuicem ambulantes, et estis tristes?
Alleluia.

Respondent du⟨o⟩:[6] *Respondens unus cui nomen Cleophas dixit ei: Tu solus peregrinus es in Iherusalem et non cognouisti que facta sunt in illa his diebus? Alleluia.*

Respondet:[6] *Quibus ille dixit: | Que?*

Respondet du⟨o⟩:[6] *Et dixerunt: De Ihesu Nazareno, qui fuit uir propheta, potens in opere et sermone coram Deo et omni populo, alleluia. Euouae.*[7]

Dürre concerns himself with the part of the text preceding the rubric *Versus de Pelegrinis*. The first 86 lines he regards as an introduction to the succeeding dialogue of the Angel and Marys. Among these 86 lines he distinguishes the following divisions:

(1) Lines 1–4: rhyming lines of eight syllables;

---

[1] Margin cut away.
[2] ⟨hortum⟩] Illegible (MS).
[3] Respondet Maria] Corrected, by a later hand, from *Item responde Maria*.
[4] Raboni] The third *Raboni* supplants, through erasure, *magister*.
[5] quam] quo*mo*do (MS).

[6] These rubrics are added above the line in a later hand.
[7] Euouae] These are, of course, the vowels of the closing formula *seculorum amen*. The rubric *Versus de Crismate in Cena Domini* follows immediately.

(2) lines 5–33: stanzas in lines of ten syllables;

(3) lines 34–86: rhyming groups of lines of eight syllables.

Dürre infers that the merchant-scene originated from the procession of the Marys to a side-altar to receive their vessels from an attendant, and that to accompany this act were composed, either in Spain or in France, the first four 8-syllable lines in the text before us.[1] These four lines, he thinks, are probably the original literary kernel of the merchant-scene, and had, at first, no connection with Meyer's *Zehnsilberspiel*. Later, some cleric composed the stanzas of 10-syllable lines (5–33). The first of these stanzas (ll. 5–8) was composed upon the model of 10-syllable prayer-formulas, such as *Omnipotens sempiterne Deus*.[2] The third stanza (ll. 13–6) was probably inspired by the original 8-line stanza (ll. 1–4).[3] The figure of the *mercator*, Dürre infers, may show the influence of the merchant who appears in the dramatic *Sponsus*; or, possibly, the Easter merchant-scene was the earlier, and is itself reflected in *Sponsus*.[4]

It does not appear that Dürre seriously invalidates Meyer's general theory. He merely points to what he considers an earlier form of the merchant-scene, in which were spoken only four 8-syllable lines. His indication may, or may not, be significant. Although I am complimented by Dürre's attaching so much importance to a text that I was the first to publish, I cannot regard his contentions as proved.

Professor Brook has considerably brought to my notice the following text on a sheet from an unidentified fifteenth-century (?) MS, which I reprint from K. C. Van Berckel, in *Bijdragen voor de Geschiedenis van het Bisdom van Haarlem*, xxviii (1904), 320:

Phisicus.

Heu! quantus est noster dolor!

Femine, quid gemitis?
Quid gementes queritis,
et sic hic preceditis,
et ex hiis non emitis
rebus aromaticis,
sepulture debitis?

Nostrum solatium. Heu!

Huc propius flentes accedite,
hoc vngentum si vultis, emite,
de quo bene potestis vngere
corpus Domini sacratum.

Ihesu, nostra redemptio.

Ista pixis nobile   continet vngentum
Ista cui simile   non est ad inuentum.
Si quis huius tercie   deferat vngentum,
Auri dabit integrum   marcam aut talentum.

Tibi dabimus. Heu!

Hoc vngentum si multum cupitis,
vnum auri talentum dabitis;
non aliter inde portabitis.

---

[1] See above, p. 402; Dürre, pp. 15–6, 24.

[2] This is an attractive and important suggestion.

[3] See Dürre, pp. 17–9.

[4] See Dürre, pp. 19–20, 24. For the text of *Sponsus* see below, ii, 362 sqq.

Page 410, note 3. The following text, without indication of date or provenance, is printed by Daniel, *Thesaurus*, ii, 366–7, and reprinted therefrom by Du Méril, p. 110:

DIALOGUS CHRISTI ET MAGDALENÆ

M⟨aria⟩: *Erumpe tandem iuste dolor,*
Quid me quærendo frustra solor?
Iesus evanuit,
Quis hunc mihi florem, amorem meum rapuit?
Eia, singultus locum date,
Per lacrymas evaporate.
Cor mihi finditur
Amore dolore in partes mille scinditur.

C⟨hristus⟩: *Quid mulier per sata ruis,*
Per hortos et per prata curris?
Quem quæris flosculum,
Cur lacrymis rigas, cur gressu vastas hortulum?

M⟨aria⟩: *Magistrum meum abstulerunt,*
Dic eum ubi posuerunt.
Quis mihi lilium,
Quis mihi dilectum ostendet Dei filium?
Hunc si tu florem abstulisti,
Dic, ubi eum posuisti,
Et ego repetam,
In gaudia matris sponsum repertum deferam.

C⟨hristus⟩: *Adsum, Maria! flos amœnus,*
Sum enim Iesus Nazarenus,
Tuus dilectus sum,
Qui solus electus ex millibus electus sum.

M⟨aria⟩: *O Jesu, mi magister bone,*
Quam tua lætor visione!
Des, ut affectibus
Et casti favoris constringam te complexibus.

C⟨hristus⟩: *Hic ab amplexu abstinebis,*
In cœlis, quando me videbis
Splendenti lumine
Tu propinquiore pasceris astri flumine.

Although this dialogue is inspired by the theme of the present chapter, it may not be intended for acting.

Here may be recorded also the following versions of the *Visitatio*, the large vernacular element in which excludes them from extended treatment at present: the Shrewsbury fragment, appendix B below, ii, 516; Munich, Staatsbibl., MS lat. 5249, fol. 57^r–57^v, printed by Meyer, p. 144, and plates 14 and 15; Zwickau, Ratsschulbibl., MS XXXVI. i. 24, Visitationes Sepulchri sæc. xvi, fol. 7^r–10^v, printed by Stötzner, pp. 7–12; *id.* fol. 10^v–16^r, printed by Stötzner, pp. 13–7. For further remarks on the vernacular in Church plays see below, ii, 423.

CHAPTER XIV

THE *LUDUS PASCHALIS*

Page 411, note 1. For attempts toward distinguishing between two types of dramatic performance represented by such terms as *Feier* and *Spiel* see Meyer, pp. 59, 79, 80–1, 89, 92; Creizenach, i, 84; Lange, *Programm*, p. 29; Milchsack, pp. 103, 115; Stötzner, p. 20; Coussemaker, pp. ix–x; Dürre, p. 25; Lange, p. 166. See also above, p. 449. Brooks (*New Texts*, p. 480) interprets the use of the word *ludus* in a Herzogenburg rubric of the sixteenth century as showing 'a recognized distinction between the liturgico-dramatic office of the *Visitatio* and the more fully developed *ludus*'. I see no clear evidence that the 'ludus' referred to in this rubric differs from numerous versions of the *Visitatio* which are unquestionably 'Feiern'.

Page 412, note 7. St Quentin MS 86 is described by E. de Coussemaker, in *Bulletin du Comité de la Langue, de l'Histoire et des Arts de la France*, iv (1857), 133–5; Coussemaker, pp. 337–44; *Catalogue général des Manuscrits des Bibliothèques publiques de France: Départements*, iii, Paris, 1885, pp. 238–40; H. Omont, in *Histoire littéraire de la France*, xxxv, Paris, 1921, pp. 640–1. This MS is the 'Livre du Trésor' of the abbey, put into French and revised under the direction of the abbess Isabelle d'Acy (1286–1324). See J. Poissonier, in *Société académique des Sciences, Arts, Belles-Lettres, Agriculture et Industrie de Saint-Quentin*, iii*e* série, ix, St Quentin, 1870, pp. 333–406. The translation into French seems to have been made in 1286, and additions to have been included in the fourteenth century. MS 86 contains also the following *Depositio* and *Elevatio*, now printed, I think, for the first time:

⟨Depositio Hostiæ⟩[1]

Quant on porte Nostre Signeur ou Sepuchre, on doit dire:

Sepulto Domino, signatum est monumentum: uoluentes lapidem ad hostium[2] monumenti, ponentes milites qui custo|dirent illud. Versus: *Ne forte uenient discipuli eius et furentur eum, et dicant plebi: Surrexit a mortuis.* Responsorium: *Ponentes milites qui custodirent illud.*

Responsorium:

Ecce quomodo moritur iustus, et nemo percepit corde; et uiri iusti ⟨tolluntur⟩, et nemo considerat; a facie iniquitatis oblatus est iustus, et erit in pace memoria eius. Versus: *In pace factus est locus eius, et in Syon habitatio eius. Et erit in pace memoria eius.*

⟨Elevatio Hostiæ⟩[3]

Le nuit de Pasques, quant li prestre uont querre Nostre Signeur ⟨i⟩n Sepulcre, on doit dire ce *respons*:

Christus resurgens ex mortuis, iam non moritur; mors illi ultra non dominabitur, quod enim uiuit, uiuit Deo, alleluia, alleluia. Versus: *Dicant nunc Iudei quomodo milites custodientes sepulcrum ad lapidis positionem. Quare non seruabant petram iusticie? Aut sepultum reddant, aut resurgentem adorent,[4] nobiscum di|centes. Quod enim uiuit, uiuit Deo, alleluia.*

---

[1] St Quentin MS 86, pp. 383–4.
[2] ad hostium] ab hostio (MS).

[3] St Quentin MS 86, pp. 384–5.
[4] adorent] adorant (MS).

Et le doit dire chascunne personne bas et a par li. Et quant on uient ou trone, on doit dire bas: *Laudate Dominum, omnes gentes*, et *Te Deum laudamus*, en lonneur de se benoicte Resurrection et de se benoite mort quil souffri pour nous, et de tous les biens qui sont en lui, et que il nous a fais.

From a source which I cannot identify, Coussemaker (pp. 340–1) prints the following *Elevatio* and *Visitatio Sepulchri* as coming from the same monastery:

⟨ELEVATIO HOSTIÆ⟩[1]

Le nuit de Pâques, le marliers doit aler querre li diacres et li sous diacres et se doit lever li trésorié et yaus faire revestir d'aubes. Quant ils sont venut tout ensiame sen deust chanter le grant Messe sans casure et sans tunique. Et doit alumer une torse et les deus candelabres et metre du feu en l'encensier. Li sousdiacres doit porter le torse, li diacres l'encensier et deus dames les deus candelabres. Et doit on ⟨aler⟩ au Sepucre et doit li prestres encenser le liu ou Nostre Sires est. Et puis si doit li prestres prendre le calice ou le Personne est et raporter du Sepucre sur le grant autel. Et quand on l'a aporteit, on doit avaler le ciboire et mettre le Personne ens. Et puis tantot si doist on sonner Matines et si doit on mettre le calice ou li Personne a esté es aumaires.

⟨VISITATIO SEPULCHRI⟩[2]

Et doit on faire les Maries le nuit de Paques, entre le derrain respons et le *Te Deum laudamus*. Et doivent estre aparilliés dès le derrainne Nocturne devant l'autelle Magdelainne et doivent estre dens leur blans chainses et leurs mantiaus et en blans cueurechies sans voil. Et devant chou qu'elles saroient, elles se doivent confesser et aler à me dame as cantiques des Matines, et doivent rendre leur propriété chascunne par li et mettre quanques elles ont le propre volunté et doivent dire *Confiteor* et me dame doit dire *Misereatur* et *Indulgentiam*. Après, les Maries se doivent aler atourner et venir devant l'autel de le Magdelaine et doivent estre en orisons dusques adonc est poins d'aler ou Sepucre. Et le trésoriere doit faire aporter les sanctuaires par un prestre et quatre candelabres et l'encensier par les jouenes demiseles et les doit on aporter devant l'autel de le Magdelainne quant on a chanté le derrain respons. Les Maries se lievent et prent chascune sen sanctuaire parmi une touaille bénite et s'en vont parmi le cuer et parmi le ves dou moustier, et vont droit à l'uis dou Sepucre et sarestent la et doit estre li huis dou Sepucre clos, et doit on porter devant les Maries deus candelabres et derrière elles deus. Et li prestres se doivent revestir en aubes par coi il soient aparilliet ou Sepucre ancors que les Maries maingnent et i doivent aler quant on chante le derrain respons. Et doit estre li chantre avocques yaus qui leur doit ensaingnier ce que il doivent dire. Et quant les Maries sont devant l'uis dou Sepucre, elles doivent chanter bien bas à fausset: *Quis revolvet?* Et li prestre doivent dire bien bas: *Quem queritis?* Et les Maries doivent dire un peu plus haut: *Jhesum Nazarenum*. Et li prestre doivent dire à haute vois: *Non est hic*. Et quant ils ont pardit coula, les Maries doivent entrer ou Sepucre, et quant elles sont ens, nul ne doit entrer, fors que les deus dames qui portent les deus candelabres devant elles, et doit on clore l'uis. Et ne doivent mie li prestre issir hors dusques adonc c'on chante: *Te Deum laudamus*. Et quant les Maries sont

---

[1] Coussemaker, p. 340.　　　　　　　　[2] *Id.*, pp. 340–1.

entrés ens, elles doivent primiers aler à l'autel du Sepucre et là mettre leurs sanctuaires et baisier l'autel et revenir au linsel où Nostre Sires fu mis et là dire leur orison. Et quant elles ont dit leurs orisons, elles se doivent lever et doivent prendre un drap qui est croisés sus le linsel et le doivent aporter et doivent issir hors du Sepucre et venir ou li couvens est et se doivent arrester là et canter: *Surrexit Dominus de sepulcro*. Et quant elles ont dit coula, me dame commence: *Te Deum laudamus*. Li prestre doivent dire ou trone: *Dicant nunc*, et après lire l'évangile. Quant les Maries s'en vont, li trésoriere doit desmourer ou Sepucre et doit on donner les bonnes gens à baisier les saintuaires qui sunt ou Sepucre. Et quant les gens ont baisié, on doit rapporter les saintuaires. Les saintuaires que on aporte, ce sont li Crois que saint Éloi fist; et les cheviaus de le Magdelainne et un autre saintuaire qui est ensi comme une lanterne.

Page 432, note 2. The seven leaves of parchment published (with photographic facsimiles and commentary) by W. Meyer, *Fragmenta Burana*, Berlin, 1901, and now constituting MS lat. 4660a, in the Staatsbibliothek at Munich, were at one time incorporated in another separate MS in that library: the celebrated MS lat. 4660, known as *Carmina Burana*. The latter MS was published by J. A. Schmeller, *Carmina Burana*, Stuttgart, 1847, and this edition has been anastatically reproduced several times. I use the print of Breslau, 1894. A new comprehensive and critical edition of MSS 4660 and 4660a is being issued by A. Hilka and O. Schumann, *Carmina Burana*, the first two volumes of which have appeared (Heidelberg, 1930). The dramatic texts will be edited in later volumes. For their extraordinary generosity to me I have expressed gratitude to Professors Hilka and Schumann in my Preface. Meyer's description of the two MSS and their interrelationships (*Fragmenta Buruana*, pp. 4–21) is superseded by that of Schumann (Hilka and Schumann, ii, 3*–91*). Meyer (pp. 17, 32) assigns the writing of the MSS to a period about the year 1225; Schumann (ii, 71*–72*) infers that they were produced toward the end of the thirteenth century. The latter editor holds that they were written in Bavaria (ii, 81*), and that their original home *may* have been the Bavarian monastery of Benediktbeuern, whence MS 4660 was transported to Munich in 1803 (ii, 70*–71*). As to ultimate provenance there is no positive proof. Concerning the literary content of *Carmina Burana* as a whole see, for example, Waddell, pp. 200–21; Hilka and Schumann, ii, 77*–91*.

The latter part of MS 4660 (fol. 99^r–112^v) and the seven leaves (I-VII) of MS 4660a contain, together, the texts of six plays. The correct position of the seven leaves of MS 4660a within MS 4660 may be indicated thus: fol. 99–106 +I–VI+107–112+VII.[1] The six plays are found in the following order:

(1) Christmas Play, MS lat. 4660, fol. 99^r–104^v, printed by Schmeller, no. CCII (to section 45, p. 91); Du Méril, pp. 187–206; Froning, pp. 877–96: and below, ii, 172 sqq. The text to be given by Hilka and Schumann will be no. 227.

(2) Ludus de Rege Ægypti, MS 4660, fol. 105^r–106^v, printed by Schmeller, no. CCII (from section 45, p. 91, to the end); Du Méril, pp. 206–13; Froning,

---

[1] I follow the conclusions of Schumann (ii, 31*–39*, 62*), which differ slightly from those of Meyer (pp. 4–17). For the folio-numbers in MS 4660a I use Roman numerals.

pp. 896–901; and below, ii, 463 sqq. The text of Hilka and Schumann will be no. 228.

(3) Ludus breviter de Passione, MS 4660a, fol. III^v–IV^v, printed by Meyer, pp. 123–5 (see his plates 5–7); and above, pp. 514 sqq. The text of Hilka and Schumann will be no. 13*.

(4) Ludus Paschalis, MS lat. 4660a, fol. V^r–VI^v, printed by Meyer, pp. 126–30 (see his plates 8–11); and above, pp. 432 sqq. The text of Hilka and Schumann will be no. 15*.

(5) Passion Play, MS lat. 4660, fol. 107^r–112^v, printed by B. I. Docen, in *Beyträge zur Geschichte und Literatur* (ed. C. von Aretin), vii (1806), 497–508; H. Hoffman, *Fundgruben für Geschichte deutscher Sprache und Litteratur*, ii, Breslau, 1837, pp. 239–58; Schmeller, no. CCIII; Du Méril, pp. 126–47; Wackernagel, ii, 341–5; Froning, 284–301; and above, pp. 518 sqq. The text of Hilka and Schumann will be no. 16*.

(6) Peregrinus, MS lat. 4660a, fol. VII^r–VII^v, printed by Meyer, pp. 136–7 (see his plates 12–13); and above, pp. 463 sqq. The text of Hilka and Schumann will be no. 26*.

Page 445, note 6. The following text of the hymn *Aurora lucis rutilat* (Chevalier, *R. H.*, no. 1644) is from *A.H.* li, 89:

1. Aurora lucis rutilat,
caelum laudibus intonat,
mundus exsultans iubilat,
gemens infernus ululat,

2. Cum rex ille fortissimus
mortis confractis viribus
pede conculcans tartara
solvit catena miseros.

3. Ille, qui clausus lapide
custoditur sub milite,
triumphans pompa nobili
victor surgit de funere.

4. Solutis iam gemitibus
et inferni doloribus,
'Quia surrexit Dominus,'
splendens clamat angelus.

5. Tristes erant apostoli
de nece sui Domini,
quem poena mortis crudeli
saevi damnarunt impii.

6. Sermone blando angelus
praedixit mulieribus:
'In Galilaea Dominus
videndus est quantocius.'

7. Illae dum pergunt concite
apostolis hoc dicere,
videntes eum vivere,
osculant pedes Domini.

8. Quo agnito, discipuli
in Galilaea propere
pergunt videre faciem
desideratam Domini.

9. Claro paschali gaudio
sol mundo nitet radio,
cum Christum iam apostoli
visu cernunt corporeo.

10. Ostensa sibi vulnera
in Christi carne fulgida
resurrexisse Dominum
voce fatentur publica.

11. Rex, Christe, clementissime,
tu corda nostra posside,
ut tibi laudes debitas
reddamus omni tempore.

CHAPTER XV

OTHER PLAYS OF THE EASTER SEASON: THE
JOURNEY TO EMMAUS—THE ASCENSION—PENTECOST

Page 451, note 3. A summary account of the known versions of the *Peregrinus* is given by Young, *A New Version of the Peregrinus*, in *P.M.L.A.*, xxxiv (1919), 114–29. See also Chambers, ii, 36–8, 107; Meyer, pp. 131–8; Cohen, *Pèlerins*, pp. 106–10. The companion of Cleophas at Emmaus is traditionally assumed to be Luke himself; and this tradition is explicitly followed in vernacular plays such as the fifteenth-century *rappresentazione* published by V. Bartholomaeis in *Rendiconti della Reale Accademia dei Lincei, Classe di Scienze morali, storiche e filologiche*, serie 5, i (1892), 769–82. The designation *Peregrinus* is supported by the Vulgate (Luke xxiv, 18), and by a fair proportion of the MSS. The versions from Sicily are introduced, respectively, by the rubrics *De Peregrino* (see above, p. 459) and *Versus ad faciendum Peregrinum* (p. 477). The Fleury play is introduced by the words *Ad faciendam similitudinem dominice ap⟨p⟩aricionis in specie Peregrini* (p. 471), and in subsequent rubrics Christ is referred to as *Perigrinus* or *Dominus*. The version from Beauvais is headed *Ordo ad Peregrinum* (p. 467). The play from Benediktbeuern is introduced by the words *Incipit exemplum apparicionis Domini . . . ubi illis in more Peregrini* (p. 463). In the version from Saintes the disciples at Emmaus are called *Peregrini*, and Christ is called *Dominus* (p. 453). The Rouen play is referred to as *Officium Peregrinorum* (see below, p. 693). It appears, then, that *Peregrinus, Peregrini, Officium Peregrini* (see Du Méril, p. 118, note), and *Officium Peregrinorum* are all permissible designations.

Page 453, note 4. The following antiphons are among those provided in Hartker's *Liber responsalis* for Easter Monday, and other days of the Easter season:

Ihesus iunxit se discipulis suis in uia et ibat cum illis; oculi eorum tenebantur ne eum agnoscerent, et increpabat eos dicens: O stulti et tardi corde ad credendum in his que locuti sunt prophete, alleluia (Hartker, p. 233).

Qui sunt hi sermones quos confertis ad inuicem ambulantes, et estis tristes? Alleluia, alleluia. Respondens unus cui nomen Cleopas dixit ei: Tu solus peregrinus es in Hierusalem et non cognouisti que facta sunt in illa his diebus? Alleluia. Quibus ille dixit: Que? Et dixerunt: De Ihesu Nazareno, qui fuit vir propheta, potens in opere et sermone coram Deo et omni populo, alleluia, alleluia (*id.*, p. 233).

Tu solus peregrinus es, et non audisti de Ihesu quomodo tradiderunt eum in damnationem mortis? Alleluia (*id.*, p. 233).

Et incipiens a Moyse et omnibus prophetis interpretabatur illis scripturas de omnibus que de ipso erant, alleluia (*id.*, p. 234).

Nonne sic oportuit pati Christum, et intrare in gloriam suam? Alleluia (*id.*, p. 234).

Et coegerunt illum dicentes: Mane nobiscum, Domine, quia aduesperascit, alleluia (*id.*, p. 234).

Mane nobiscum quoniam aduesperascit, et inclinata est iam dies, alleluia, alleluia (*id.*, p. 234).

Et intrauit cum illis, et factum est dum recumberet cum illis, accepit panem et benedixit, fregit ac porrigebat illis, alleluia (*id.*, p. 234).

Cognouerunt Dominum, alleluia, in fractione panis, alleluia (*id.*, p. 234).

Nonne cor nostrum ardens erat in nobis de Ihesu dum loqueretur nobis in uia? Alleluia (*id.*, p. 234).

Videte manus meas et pedes meos, quia ego ipse sum, alleluia, alleluia (*id.*, p. 235).

Spiritus carnem et ossa non habet sicut me videtis habere; iam credite, alleluia (*id.*, p. 235).

Isti sunt sermones quos dicebam vobis cum essem vobiscum, alleluia, alleluia (*id.*, p. 235).

Sicut dilexit me Pater, alleluia, et ego dilexi vos, alleluia (*id.*, p. 272).

Pacem meam do uobis, alleluia; pacem relinquo vobis, alleluia (*id.*, p. 266).

Pax vobis, ego sum, alleluia; nolite timere, alleluia (*id.*, p. 235).

Post dies octo, ianuis clausis, ingressus Dominus et dixit eis: Pax uobis, alleluia, alleluia (*id.*, p. 239).

Thomas, qui dicitur Didimus, non erat cum eis quando uenit Ihesus; dixerunt alii discipuli: Uidimus Dominum, alleluia (*id.*, p. 239).

Mitte manum tuam, et cognosce loca clauorum, alleluia, et noli esse incredulus, sed fidelis, alleluia (*id.*, p. 240).

Misi digitos meos in fixuras clauorum, et manus meas in latus eius, et dixi: Dominus meus et Deus meus, alleluia (*id.*, p. 240).

Quia uidisti me, Thoma, credidisti; beati qui non uiderunt et crediderunt, alleluia (*id.*, p. 240).

Data est mihi omnis potestas in celo et in terra, alleluia (*id.*, p. 238).

Non uos relinquam orphanos, alleluia; vado et ueniam ad uos, alleluia; et gaudebit cor vestrum, alleluia (*id.*, p. 267).

In his discussion of the several versions of the *Peregrinus* known to him, Meyer (pp. 131–8) somewhat overemphasizes their direct dependence upon the liturgical text when he writes the following (p. 134): 'So gewinnt dieses liturgische Spiel von den drei Erscheinungen Christi ⟨*i.e.* the *Peregrinus*⟩ ein hohes Interesse: es ist nicht, wie das kleine benediktbeurer Passionsspiel, aus Bibelstellen zusammengesetzt, sondern ganz und gar aus sehr alten Antiphonen und Responsorien der Liturgie.' It is fair to say, however, that, although Meyer appears to be generalizing, he has particularly in mind the *Peregrinus* from Benediktbeuern, to which his assertion applies with substantial accuracy. From a rubric describing the *Peregrinus* at Padua in the thirteenth century we may fairly infer that the play there drew directly upon the Vulgate. See above, p. 482.

Page 457, note 3. Vespers of Easter, and of certain other days, at the monastery for women at Origny-Sainte-Benoîte seems to have included a special ceremony at the *sepulchrum*. From an unidentified *ordinarium* of the thirteenth or fourteenth century Coussemaker (p. 341) quotes the following:

Le diemainche, le jour de Paques, le lundi et le mardi, le mercredi que on doit aler ou sepucre après Vespres de Nostre-Dame et chanter *Christus resurgens*. Trois dames doivent chanter *Dicant nunc*; et celle qui fait Deus doit dire le colloite *Repelle*.

A visit to the sepulchre during Vespers of Easter Week is prescribed in the following *ordo* from a German monastic breviary of the thirteenth century (Oxford, Bibl. Bodl., MS Misc. Liturg. 202, fol. 73ʳ–73ᵛ):

Vespere incipiantur ista septimana per Kyrieleison. In tota ista septimana super psalmos antiphona *Alleluia, alleluia, alleluia.* Psalmus *Dixit Dominus.* Nec lectio nec uersus his diebus recitetur, sed responsum graduale et *Alleluia.* Antiphona super *Magnificat: Et respicientes uiderunt reuolutum lapidem, erat quippe magnvs | ualde, alleluia.* Postea ad fontem eundo cantent antiphonam *Vidi aquam egredientem de templo a latere dextro, alleluia, et omnes ad quos peruenit aqua ista salui facti sunt, et dicent alleluia, alleluia.* Psalmus *Laudate pueri.* Deinde ad Sepulchrum antiphona *Venite et uidete locum.* Psalmus *In exitu.* Redeundo antiphona *Christus resurgens ex mortuis, iam non moritur; mors illi ultra non dominabitur, quod enim uiuit, uiuit Deo, alleluia, alleluia.*[1]

In regard to liturgical processions in Vespers at Eastertide at Strassburg and Münster see Wilmart, pp. 40–3; Stapper, *Feier*, pp. 90–1.

Page 458, note 1. The following rubrics concerning the *Peregrinus* at Bayeux in the thirteenth century are given by Chevalier, *Bayeux*, p. 143:

Ad Vesperas, antiphone et psalmi et responsum sicut in die precedenti. ⟨*Alleluia.*⟩ Versus *Nonne cor.* Versus *Mane nobiscum, Domine.* Antiphona *Et incipiens.* Psalmus *Magnificat.* Oratio *Deus qui sollennitate.* Ad Sepulchrum oratio *Concede quesumus.* In regrediendo ad fontes fit statio in medio ecclesie, et omnibus ibidem considentibus, fit representatio qualiter apparuit Dominus duobus discipulis euntibus in Emaus, qui dicuntur Peregrini. Qua facta, reincipitur quarta antiphona ut prius, et psalmus dicitur. Ad fontes antiphona *Et coegerunt.* Psalmus *Magnificat.* Oratio *Concede, quesumus.* Ad Sanctum Nicholaum antiphona *Mane nobiscum.* Psalmus *Magnificat.* Oratio *Deus qui populum. Benedicamus. Exultemus et letemur hodie,* et cetera.

The complete form of Vespers for Easter Monday, and the position of the *Peregrinus* therein, can be determined by relating the passage quoted here with the *ordo* for Easter Vespers given by Chevalier, p. 142.

Page 458, note 3. As to the liturgical attachment of the *Peregrinus* from Benediktbeuern we have no information at all. Of the attachment of four other plays we know only the following facts: the Fleury play was performed at Vespers on Tuesday after Easter; that from Beauvais, at Vespers on Easter Monday; one Sicilian play (Madrid MS 289), on Easter Monday; and a second Sicilian version (Madrid MS C. 132) at Vespers either on Easter or on the next day. See above, pp. 459, 463, 467, 471, 477.

Page 458, note 4. In Paris, Bibl. Nat., MS lat. 16309, fol. 147ᵛ–148ʳ, the text of Vespers for Easter Monday is given, without introductory rubric, as follows:

⟨In Vesperis⟩

Antiphona *Angelus.* Psalmus *Dixit Dominus.* Antiphona *Erat autem.* Psalmus *Confitebor.* Antiphona *Pre timore.* Psalmus *Beatus*[2] *uir.* Responsum *Hec dies.* Versus *Dicant nunc Israhel, quoniam bonus, quoniam in seculum misericordia eius.*

---

[1] Followed by the rubric *Ad Completorium.*   [2] Beatus] Deus (MS).

Alleluia. Versus *Nonne cor nostrum*[1] *ardens erat in nobis de Ihesu dum loqueretur nobis in uia? Alleluia.* Prosa:[2]

> *Clara gaudia festa paschalia.*

Versus: *Congaudet cetus per omnia dulce decantans alleluya,*
> *In qua Christus per crucem redemit animas inferno deditas,*
> *A prothoplausto, quodquod in hoc seculo progenite fuerant,*
> *Patriarcharum omniumque simul prophetarum, regum, pontificum*
> *Detinebantur claustris tarthareis mortis cruore retruse,*
> *Donec uictor mortis, Dominus omnium atque sanctus sanctorum,*
> *Cum crucis tropheo infernum penetrans abegit claustra seua.*
> *'Quis est'*[3] *demones ululant, 'crucifer qui Deus ut | nostra soluat uincula cuncta?*
> *Fugans tenebras fugerat teatralis horror*[4] *rutilans lumine perlustrata.*
> *Clamabant sancti; 'Aduenisti, o iam Domine, regnum rex; ades quem olim uates precinere; iam nos habes redemptos,*[5] *rex Christe.'*
> *Tunc Ihesus cum leta sanctorum gloria processit nostra*[6] *uita.*
> *Cui psallere laudes sub omni cardine non cessat omnis etas decantans alleluya.*
> *Amen.*

Versus *Resurrexit Dominus.* Antiphona *Mane nobiscum quoniam aduesperascit, et inclinata est iam dies, alleluya, alleluya.* Psalmus *Magnificat.* Oratio *Deus qui sollempnitatem.* Ad fontes antiphona *Cito euntes.* Psalmus *Laudate pueri.* Psalmus *In exitu. Alleluya.* Versus *In die resurrectionis.* Antiphona *Et respicientes.* Psalmus *Magnificat.* Oratio *Concede, quesumus, omnipotens Deus, ut qui festa*[7] *paschalia, que uenerando colimus, etiam uiuendo teneamus. Per.* Ante crucifixum responsorium *Christus resurgens.* Versus *Dicant nunc.* Quatuor presbyteri: *Dicite in nationibus.* Oratio *Solita, quesumus, Domine.* Deinde procedit processio in capitulo cum duobus presbyteris, clericis cantantibus versum *Hec est clara dies.* Quibus finitis, cappellanus[8] Domini Episcopi dicit ibi versiculum *Surrexit Christus.* Postea redit conuentus ad cantandum Conpletorium.

Page 461, note 1. The text of the *Peregrinus* from Rouen MS 222 is immediately preceded by the following *ordo* (fol. 43ʳ-43ᵛ) concerning Vespers of Easter Monday, previously printed by Young, *Rouen,* p. 212:

Feria secunda in Matutinis, processio ut in die Pasche. In Vesperis similiter, excepto quod duo tantum de maiori sede regant chorum, et duo similiter de maiori sede cantent *Alleluia. Redemptionem.* Ad Vesperas post tres psalmos, finita antiphona, duo de secunda sede cantent hoc responsum *Hec dies.* Versus *Dicant nunc Israhel, quoniam bonus, quoniam in seculum | misericordia eius.* Duo regentes chorum: *Alleluya.* Versus *Nonne cor nostrum ardens erat in nobis de Ihesu dum loqueretur nobis in uia?* Versus *Resurrexit Dominus.* Antiphona *Et coegerunt illum dicentes: Mane nobiscum quia aduesperascit, alleluya.* Psalmus *Magnificat.*

Here follow the words *Post Benedicamus,* at the beginning of the *Peregrinus* above, p 461. The other extant versions of the Rouen *Peregrinus* differ in no

---

[1] nostrum] uestrum (MS).
[2] For the text of the prose *Clara gaudia festa paschalia* see *A.H.,* liii, 71–2.
[3] Quis est] Quod et (MS).
[4] horror] hortor (MS).
[5] habes redemptos] aue redemptor (MS).
[6] nostra] uestra (MS).
[7] festa] festo (MS).
[8] cappellanus] Capplle (MS).

substantial way from the play in Rouen MS 222. For the sake of certain details in the rubrics, however, I present the text from a fourteenth-century *ordinarium* of the cathedral (Rouen, Bibl. de la Ville, MS 384), along with the complete *ordo* for Easter Vespers. The *ordo* for Easter Vespers is as follows:[1]

Ad Vesperas tres de maioribus in cappis cantent ad processionem *Salue, festa dies*. Cum dyaconis et subdiaconis reuestitis, cruce, candelis, et thuribulis et signis descendat processio per alam ecclesie usque ad occidentalem portam; et processione ordinata in naui ecclesie, vnus de cantoribus incipiat *Kyrieleyson*, et processio ad chorum redeat cantando *Christeleyson*. Et finito *Kyrieleyson*, incipiatur in maiori sede antiphona *Alleluia*. Illi qui cantauerunt *Salue, festa dies*, regant chorum, et vnus ex illis incip*iat* in dextro choro psalmum *Dixit Dominus*; psalmum *Confitebor*; psalmum *Beatus uir*. *Alleluia, alleluia, alleluia, alleluia*. Tres de secunda sede,[2] finita antiphona, ante aquilam cantent responsum *Hec dies*. Versus *Confitemini Domino*. Tres de maioribus ibidem cantent sine cappis *Alleluia*. Versus *Pascha nostrum*. Hoc finito, tres pueri versum *Resurrexit Dominus*. Antiphona *Et respicientes* bis repetatur. Psalmus *Magnificat*. Interim altaria incensentur, et postea chorus. Oratio *Deus qui hodierna die*. Tres de secunda sede *Benedicamus Domino*. *Alleluia*. Vnus de maioribus incipiat *Alleluia*; et vnus de regentibus chorum incipiat psalmum *Laudate, pueri, Dominum, laudate nomen Domini*. *Alleluia*. Versus *Sit nomen Domini beatum*. *Alleluia*. Et sic cantando psalmum eat processio ad fontes cum dyaconis et subdyaconis et ampullis a duobus presbyteris albatis et cereo benedicto, quem ferat vnus dyaconus de secunda sede. Et chorus psalmum finiat, et dicatur *Alleluia* iiij, et *Hec dies*. Finito versu a choro,[3] cantetur ante altare Sancti Iohannis *Alleluia*. Versus *Laudate pueri*. Et reiteretur *Alleluia*. Quo finito, sacerdos dicat *Oremus: Deus qui ecclesiam tuam*. *Per Christum Dominum*. Qua finita, vnus de maioribus incipiat *Alleluia*, et vnus de regentibus chorum psalmum *In exitu Israel de Egypto*. *Alleluia*. Versus *Facta est Iudea sanctificatio*. *Alleluia, alleluia*. Versus *Mare uidit et fugit*. *Alleluia, alleluia, alleluia*. Et sic ad finem ordinate perducatur, et in fine psalmi dicatur *Gloria Patri*. *Alleluia*. *Sicut erat in principio*. *Alleluia, alleluia*. Versus *Surrexit Dominus de sepulchro, alleluia, alleluia, alleluia*. Et sic cantando psalmum descendat processio per aliam alam ecclesie ad oc|cidentalem portam ecclesie. Et processione in naui ecclesie statuta, et vltimo versu psalmi finito, tres de maiori sede in pulpito cantent *Alleluia*. Versus *Redemptionem* non reiteretur. Quo finito, sacerdos dicat versum *Dicite in nationibus*. *Oremus: Deus qui pro nobis Filium tuum*. Sequatur ibidem memoria Beate Marie. Antiphona *Paradisi porta*. Versus *Post partum uirgo*. Oratio *Gratiam tuam, quesumus, Domine*. Ante introitum chori memoria omnium Sanctorum. Antiphona *Lux perpetua lucebit*. *Si diligeretis me*. Versus *Vox leticie et exultationis*. *Oremus: Vide, Domine, infirmitates nostras*. Tres pueri: *Benedicamus Domino*. *Alleluia*.[4]

In the same MS the *ordo* for Vespers of Easter Monday and for the *Peregrinus* are written continuously as follows:[5]

[1] Rouen MS 384, fol. 84v–85r.

[2] sede] After this word is a marginal insertion by a late hand: in superlicijs.

[3] Finito . . . choro] This passage has been crossed out, and a later hand has written in

the margin: sine alleluia et versu et post.

[4] Followed by the rubric *Ad Completorium*.

[5] Rouen MS 384, fol. 86r–86v (A). The *Peregrinus* from this MS has been edited by Gasté, pp. 65–8, and reprinted from him by

Ad Vesperas sicut in die Pasche. Duo de maiori sede in cappis: *Salue, festa dies*, cum processione ut supra, et *Kyrieleison* ut supra. *Alleluia*. Psalmus *Dixit Dominus*. Psalmus *Confitebor*, et cetera. Duo de secunda sede responsum: *Hec dies*. Duo de maiori sede *Alleluia*. Versus *Nonne cor nostrum*. Versus *Resurrexit Dominus*. Antiphona *Et coegerunt*. Psalmus *Magnificat*. Oratio *Deus qui hodierna die*. Benedicamus Domino. *Alleluia*. Processio ad fontes ut supra. Oratio *Concede, quesumus, omnipotens Deus*. In reditu: *Alleluia*. Psalmus *In exitu*, et cetera, ut supradictum est.

Nota, fili: Officium Peregrinorum debet hic fieri hoc modo. Duo de secunda sede, qui sint scripti in tabula ad placitum scriptoris, induti tunicis[1] et desuper cappis transuersum,[2] portantes baculos et peras in similitudinem Peregrinorum, et habeant capellos super capita, et sint barbati. Exeant a[3] vestiario, cantantes hymnum *Jhesu, nostra redempcio*, venientes lento pede per dextram alam ecclesie usque ad portas occidentales, et subsistentes in capite processionis. Et cum cantauerint[4] hymnum usque ad eum locum: *Nos tuo vvltu sacies*, tunc quidam[5] sacerdos de maiori sede, scriptus in tabula, indutus alba et amictu, nudus[6] pedes, ferens crucem super dextrum humerum, vvltu demisso, ueniens usque ad eos per dextram alam ecclesie, et subito stet inter illos et dicat: *Qui sunt hij sermones?* Peregrini quasi admirantes, et eum respicientes dicant:[7] *Tu solus peregrinus*.[8] Sacerdos interroget: *Que?* Peregrini | respondeant: *De Ihesu Nazareno*. Sacerdos, utrumque respiciens, dicat: *O stulti et tardi corde*. Quibus dictis, statim recedens sacerdos, fingens se longius ire, et Peregrini, festinantes, prosequentes, eum detineant quasi ad hospicium inuitantes et trahentes, baculis ostendentes castellum, et dicentes: *Mane nobiscum*. Et ita cantantes ducant eum usque ad tabernaculum, in medio nauis ecclesie, in similitudinem castelli Emaux preparatum. Quo cum ascenderint, et ad mensam ibi paratam sederint, et Dominus inter eos sedens panem eis fregerit, et fractione panis agnitus ab[9] illis, subito recedens ab oculis eorum euanescat. Illi autem, quasi stupefacti surgentes, versis uultibus inter ipsos, cantent lamentabiliter: *Alleluia*, cum versu *Nonne cor nostrum*. Quo reiterato, vertent se versus pu⟨l⟩pitum, et cantent hunc versum: *Dic nobis, Maria*. Tunc quidam de maiori sede, indutus dalmatica et amictu, in modum Mulieris caput circumligatus, respondeat: *Sepulchrum Christi. Angelicos testes*. Tunc ostendat et explicet vnam syndonem,[10] ex vna parte, loco sudarij, et aliam, ex alia parte, loco[11] uestium, et proiiciat[12] ante magnu⟨m⟩ hostium chori. Deinde dicat: *Surrexit Christus*. Chorus cantet alios duos versus sequentes residuos. Et interim recedant[13] Maria et Peregrini. Et processio, factis memoriis,[14] redeat in choro, et ibi finiantur Vespere.[15]

Adams, pp. 21–4. I give the variants for the *Peregrinus* (beginning *Nota, fili*) from Rouen, ibid., MS 382 (*olim* Y. 108), Ordin. Rothomagense sæc. xv, fol. 73ʳ–73ᵛ (B), and from Paris, Bibl. Nat., MS lat. 1213, Ordin. Rothomagense sæc. xv, p. 90 (C).

[1] tunicis] amictis (B).
[2] transuersum] Omitted (B).
[3] a] de (C).
[4] cantauerint] cantaueris (B).
[5] quidam] quidem (A).

[6] amictu nudus] amictus nudis (C).
[7] dicant] dicat (C).
[8] peregrinus] peregrinus es (C).
[9] ab] uel (C).
[10] et explicet vnam syndonem] vnam sindonem et explicet (C).
[11] loco] locum (B).
[12] proiiciat] proficiat (B).
[13] recedant] recedat (C).
[14] factis memoriis] memoriis factis (C).
[15] Followed by the rubric *Ad Completorium*.

Further bibliography concerning Rouen MSS and the dramatic texts therein is given by Young, *Rouen*, pp. 224 sqq.

Page 466, note 2. As ultimate sources for the greater part of the last five speeches, beginning with *Egredimini*, one may cite the following from the *Canticum Canticorum*:

En dilectus meus loquitur mihi: Surge, propera, amica mea, columba mea, formosa mea, et veni. (ii, 10).

Flores apparuerunt in terra nostra, tempus putationis advenit; vox turturis audita est in terra nostra. (ii, 12).

Egredimini et videte, filiæ Sion, regem Salomonem in diademate, quo coronavit illum mater sua in die desponsationis illius, et in die lætitiæ cordis ejus (iii, 11).

Surge, Aquilo, et veni, Auster, perfla hortum meum, et fluant aromata illius (iv. 16).

Hartker's *Liber responsalis* (pp. 309–10) has the following relevant antiphons for the Nativity of the Blessed Virgin Mary:

Veniat dilectus meus in ortum suum, ut comedat fructus pomorum suorum. Comedi fauum cum melle meo, bibi uinum meum cum lacte meo.

Talis est dilectus meus et ipse est amicus meus, filie Ierusalem.

Tota pulchra es, amica mea, et macula non est in te; fauus distillans labia tua; mel et lac sub lingua tua; odor unguentorum tuorum super omnia aromata; iam enim hiemps transiit, ymber abiit et recessit; flores apparuerunt, uinee florentes odorem dederunt, et uox turturis audita est in terra nostra. Surge, propera, amica mea; ueni de Libano; ueni, coronaberis.

Meyer has observed (p. 138) that when the play and these antiphons agree verbally, they agree also in their melodies.

Page 481, note 6. The following passage is found in a thirteenth-century *ordinarium* from the collegiate church of St Peter at Lille, printed by E. Hautcœur, *Documents*, p. 55:

In Vesperis, sequentia *O Maria*. Ad fontes: *Alleluia. Gavisi sunt.* Ad crucem: *Alleluia. Surgens Jhesus*. Post collectam fit representatio Peregrinorum. Qua facta, cantatur *Christus resurgens*, et itur in chorum.

Concerning the *Peregrinus* at Lille see also Lefebvre, i, 4; Hautcœur, *Histoire*, i, 425–6. For a reference to a *Peregrinus* at Gerona, in Spain, see below, ii, 504.

Page 484, note 2. The following is from *Agenda Bambergensia*, Ingolstadt, 1587, pp. 627–35, not, I think, reprinted elsewhere:

ORDO SERVANDUS IN FESTO ASCENSIONIS DOMINI

Hoc festo in ecclesiis celebrioribus post prandium, circa horam vndecimam, vel duodecimam, cantanda est Nona, idque in choro. Extra chorum vero eo in loco, vbi Christi Ascensio repræsentanda est, sternatur mensa, Christique in cœlum ascendentis Imago[1] super eam collocetur, ardentibus ex vtraque parte cereis. Sit etiam scabellum ante mensam illam, cui sacerdos et ministri

---

[1] See plate xi.

paulo post genibus innitantur. Cantata Nona, descendat processio ad locum aliquem, non ita longe a prædicta mensa remotum, facie ad mensam, et chorum templi versa, cantetque hymnum de Ascensione Dei: *Festum nunc celebre*, &c. Postea sacerdos cum duobus ministris vadat ad mensam, ibique flexis supra prædictum scabellum genibus, recitent deuote sequentia:

Psalmus 122.

Ad te levavi oculos meos, qui habitas in cœlis.

Ecce sicut oculi servorum in manibus Dominorum suorum.

Sicut oculi ancillæ in manibus dominæ sue, ita oculi nostri ad Dominum Deum nostrum donec misereatur nostri.

Miserere nostri, Domine, miserere nostri, quia multum repleti sumus despectione.

Quia multum repleta est anima nostra: opprobrium abundantibus, et despectio superbis.

Gloria Patri, et Filio, &c.

Kyrie eleïson, Christi eleïson, Kyrie eleïson.

Pater noster. Et ne nos inducas, &c.

Oremus: Deus qui ad æternam vitam in Christi resurrectione nos reparas, erige nos ad considentem in dextera tua nostræ salutis auctorem: vt qui propter nos iudicandus advenit, pro nobis iudicaturus adveniat Iesus Christus, Dominus noster; Qui tecum vivit, &c.

His dictis, thurificetur et aqua lustrali aspergatur Imago Christi ascendentis. Postea sacerdos et ministrantes apprehensa in manus Imagine, eaque eleuata cantent simul:

Ascendo ad Patrem meum, et ad Patrem vestrum.

Tunc dimittant iterum Imaginem Christi, et supra mensem sistant. Chorus vero ad cantum prædictum finitum immediate quod sequitur canat:

Deum meum, et Deum vestrum, alleluia.

Sint deinde duo pueri supra fornicem, vel tabulatum templi, qui ex foramine, in quod Imago Christi paulo post recipienda erit, deorsum clara voce cantent:

Viri Galilæi, quid aspicitis in cœlum?

Chorus postea:

Hic Iesus qui assumptus est, a vobis in cœlum sic veniet, alleluia.

Deinde sacerdotes aliquantulum altius incipiant: *Ascendo ad Patrem meum,* &c. Et habeant se vt antea; similiter et pueri cum choro. Et idipsum etiam tertio fiat. Posthæc Imago Christi funi alligata lente trahata sursum, inque foramen prædictum recipiatur. Quod vbi factum fuerit, particulæ hostiarum cum pauxillo aquæ deiiciantur, per quod admonentur fideles: Christum, licet in propria specie humana in cœlum abierit, manere tamen adhuc nobiscum in specie aliena, videlicet in Sacramento Eucharistiæ sub Hostiis consecratis. Manere item secundum gratiam in Sacramento Baptismi, quod per aquam administrari, et hodierna die per apostolos suos omnibus gentibus offerre voluit, dicens *Euntes docete omnes gentes, baptizantes eos in nomine Patris, et Filii, et Spiritus Sancti.* Dum vero Imago Christi sursum fertur, processio redeat ad chorum cum sequente responsorio: *Ite in orbem,* vti sequitur. *Ite in orbem uniuersum et prædicate dicentes, alleluia: Qui crediderit et baptisatus fuerit, salvvs erit, alleluia, alleluia, alleluia* ⟨Versus:⟩ *In nomine Patris, et Filii, et Spiritus Sancti. Qui cre⟨diderit⟩.*[1] Postremo præcinatur populo cantus germanicus de Ascensione: *Christ fuhr gen Himmel,* et cetera, vt habetur in fine libri, et cetera.

[1] See Hartker, p. 264.

Page 484, note 4. The following is the *ordo* for a dramatic ceremony of the Ascension from Berlin, Staatsbibl., MS theol. lat. qu. 87ᵇ, Ordin. Berolinense sæc. xvi, fol. 44ᵛ–46ᵛ, previously edited by Müller, *Statuten*, pp. 328–31:

Post Nonam fiet processio per ecclesiam et ambitum, et cantabitur responsorium *Post passionem suam*, et, quando processio exibit, compulsabitur cum omnibus campanis. Erit autem ita ordinata processio. Primo preibunt camerarij, duo minima viridia vexilla; postea chorales, vicarii et domini, qui non habent cappas nec portant reliquias; post hos iterum duo viridia vexilla, et sequentur vicarij et domini in cappis cum reliquijs. Postea portabuntur iterum duo viridia vexilla et duo cerei. Decanus cum cantore portabit Imaginem Saluatoris.[1] Deinde sequetur prepositus cum Imagine Beate Virginis post Saluatorem. Quando vero processio redierit in ecclesiam, habebitur stacio ante chorum, et cantabitur responsorium *Tempus est, vt reuertar*[2] in organo et choro. Ordinabitur autem ita stacio, quod camerarij et chorales, vicarij et domini sine cappis cum duobus vexillis prope baptisterium stantes manebunt, diuisi tamen vtrinque pro more, et in medio ecclesie imponetur Saluator super scamnum cum rubeo sammitto tectum et stabit inter manus decani et cantoris. Interim succustos accipiet Apostolos a canonicis et vicariis, et ponet eos in mensa apud scamna in modum dimidij circuli, et in medio Imaginem Beate Virginis locabit et ex aduerso Imaginem Saluatoris. |

Prepositus autem, canonici et vicarij in cappis eciam se ordinabunt in medium circulum ante mensam, et ex vno quoque latere scamni vel mense erit vna candela, vnum vexillum, et vnum turribulum. Finito responsorio, solenniter in choro et organo cantabitur hymnus *Festum nunc celebre*, per totum. Quo eciam finito, decanus et cantor incipient antiphonam *Ascendo ad Patrem meum*, et non vltra. Tunc statim succentor solenniter incipiet *Benedictus*, quod in organo et choro vsque ad finem alternatim cantabitur. Interim prepositus thurificabit cum maiori turribulo Imaginem Saluatoris, altare Sancte Crucis, et mensam reliquiarum, et personas stantes in circulo.

Post *Benedictus* decanus et cantor eleuabunt pariter Imaginem Saluatoris ad altitudinem capitum suorum cantantes *Ascendo ad Patrem meum, et Patrem vestrum*. Et respondebit chorus *Deum meum, et Deum vestrum, alleluia*. Et mox tubicines super testudinem personabunt canticum aliquod artificialiter compositum. Interea predicti prelati circumportabunt Imaginem Saluatoris in dimidio circulo, quam | singuli aspicient et ante eam genuflectent. Et ipsi deferentes Imaginem Saluatoris similiter paulisper Imaginem inclinabunt, et hoc debet ter fieri modo prescripto. Deinde iterum predicti prelati cantabunt *Ascendo ad Patrem meum*, respondente choro *Deum meum*, et cetera. Interim tubicines ⟨ludent⟩, dum circumfertur secunda vice Imago Saluatoris. Deinde iterum predicti prelati tercio cantabunt *Ascendo*, respondente choro *Deum meum*. Tubicines iterum ludent interim, dum circumfertur tercia vice Imago Saluatoris. Quo facto, debent modulari, donec prelati, canonici et vicarij in cappis Imaginem Saluatoris fuerint osculati. Et tunc Angeli cum cereis debebunt de testudine sensim demitti. Interim prepositus turificabit solam Imaginem Saluatoris, et tradet turribulum a se et genuflectet coram Imagine, et surgens cum vnius genu flexione vsque ad tapetum. Osculabitur

---

[1] See plate xi.   [2] See Hartker, p. 408.

cicatricem dextri pedis Saluatoris. Et hoc similiter facient omnes prelati, canonici et vicarij in cappis secundum ordinem in memoriam valedictionis Ihesu, apostolorum et discipulorum suorum. Postea duo dicti prelati prudenter et diligenter alligabunt Imaginem cum funibus, versa facie Imaginis ad orientem, et permittent euehi in altum cum Angelis, vno in capite,| alio in pedibus circumuolantibus. Interim tubicines cum instrumentis debent modulari. Et omnes persone in circulo sursum aspicient, versis vultibus ad Imaginem contra occidentem. Tunc prepositus, decanus, cantor, scolasticus pro reuerencia Ascensionis Dominice, et ad prouidendum periculum in casu Imaginis (quod auertat Dominus), tenebunt in manibus firmiter aureum tapete directe sub Imagine et hiatu testudinis, donec Imago videtur. Imagine autem euecta, super testudinem Hostie sunt deijciende, et timpanum est percuciendum in representacionem tonitrui. Magister fabrice accipiet illam et occultatam reportabit ad sacrarium. Et mox duo pueri altis vocibus super testudinem cantabunt soli totam antiphonam *Viri galilei, quid aspicitis in celum?* et cetera. Post hanc antiphonam incipient iterum pueri solenniter responsorium *Ite in orbem,* quod cantabitur in organo et choro. Interim processio redibit ad chorum eo ordine quo exiuit, cum reliquijs et vexillis, et compulsabitur cum omnibus campanis. Post responsorium, *Te Deum laudamus.* | Deinde *Regina celi* etiam in organo et choro, et pro *Resurrexit* cantabitur *Iam ascendit.* Versus *Gaude, Dei genitrix, quia ascendit in altum.* Collecta *Deus, qui per ascensionem,* et cetera.[1] Similiter in versiculo et collecta fiet mencio de Ascensione et non de Resurrectione. Vicarij et canonici ascendent cum preposito ad sanctuarium, et reponent reliquias in summo altari; quo facto, redeunt ad sedes suas et ibidem exuent cappas. Seniores autem et alij prelati, qui cum preposito prius induebantur in sacristia, cum eodem istuc redibunt.

For a discussion of such ceremonies in Berlin and Halle see Müller, *Geschichte,* pp. 520–3. For references to Ascension ceremonies elsewhere see Chambers, ii, 65; Petit de Julleville, ii, 9.

CHAPTER XVI

THE PASSION PLAY

Page 492, note 1. In regard to the Passion play, and related matters, see Chambers, ii, 39–40, 75–6; Brooks, *Lamentations,* pp. 415–6; Meyer, pp. 64–76, 122–5; Creizenach, i, 84–9; Beissel, pp. 379–86; Lindner, pp. ii, cliv sqq.; Roy, pp. 4*–7*; Sepet, *Origines,* pp. 21–30; Tanquerey, pp. 7–13; Wechssler, pp. 3–29; Hirn, pp. 380–96; Wirth, pp. 35–9. One is disappointed in observing that the study by R. Molitor, *Passionspiel und Passionsliturgie,* in *Benediktinische Monatschrift,* v (1923), 105–16, has virtually no direct bearing upon the subject of this chapter. One aspect of the subject is treated by Young, *Observations on the Origin of the Mediaeval Passion-Play,* in *P.M.L.A.,* xxv (1910), 309–54. Concerning a representation of the Passion at Siena about the year 1200 we have the following information, from D'Ancona, i, 90:

[1] Versus Gaude . . . et cetera] Written in the left margin (MS).

Che anche a Siena si facessero simili spettacoli, attesta l'erudito Uberto Benvoglienti, scrivendo che 'intorno al 1200 era per decreto del Comune nel Venerdì santo rappresentata la Passione di Nostro Signore, e si pagavano dal pubblico coloro che facevano tali figure'; ma qui come ognuno vede si stà troppo sulle generali, sia pel tempo, sia pel genere e la lingua del sacro spettacolo.

D'Ancona is quoting from an unpublished treatise on the *Commedia italiana* by Uberto Benvoglienti, and does not mention the primary evidence. For records of a *Repræsentatio Passionis et Mortis Christi*, or of a combined Passion and Resurrection play, at Padua in 1243 or 1244, see D'Ancona, i, 87–8. As to the nature of the plays at Siena and Padua, and as to the language used, we lack precise information. For references to Passion plays in Friuli in 1298 and 1303–4 see Dondi Orologio, p. 64; Bartholomaeis, pp. 159, 160; below, ii, 540.

Page 503, note 4. Du Cange (vi, 353) quotes the following from a Toulouse service-book of the thirteenth century from 'ecclesia B. M. Deauratæ Tolos.':

Officium Matutinorum incipitur hora meliori propter solempnitatem diei (feria v in Cœna Domini) et propter gentium multitudinem et etiam propter Planctum Beatissimæ Virginis Mariæ, quæ dicitur a duobus puerulis post Matutinum, et debent esse monachi, si possunt reperiri, ad hoc apti, sin autem dicetur a secularibus ad hoc fundati, monachisque deficientibus. Et omnes candelæ extinguntur post Matutinum, scilicet post *Kyrie eleyson* quod dicitur super altare cum versibus, excepta una candela quæ remanet accensa usque Planctus finiatur; ad denotandum quod in ista die tota fides remanserit in sola Virgine Maria, quia omnes discipuli erraverunt seu dubitaverunt secundum magis et minus, excepta Virgine Maria. Ita Planctus dicitur in cathedra predicatorii, et debet esse cooperta et circumcincta de cortinis albis prædicta cathedra ad finem, quod dicentes sive cantantes prædictum Planctum non possint videri a gentibus, nec ipsi videant gentes, ut securius possint cantare sine timore, quia forte videndo gentes turbarentur.

There is no support for Du Cange's assumption that the *planctus* sung at Toulouse was the *Stabat mater*. See R. Otto, in *M.L.N.*, iv. (1889), 211–3. According to Dondi Orologio (pp. 60–1), in the cathedral of Padua, in the thirteenth century, two clerics sang a *planctus* on Good Friday at the *sepulchrum*; but we do not know at what point in the liturgy. See below, p. 700. The long vernacular *planctus* of Bordesholm was to occupy two hours and a half, 'sexta feria ⟨Good Friday⟩ ante prandium in ecclesia ante chorum in loco aliquantum elevato vel extra ecclesiam si bona est aura'. If necessary it could be placed 'ante prandium' on Monday of Holy Week. See *Z.f.d.A.*, xiii (1867), 288.

Page 506, note 2. The following text is found in Munich, Staatsbibl., MS lat. 14094, Miscellanea Ratisbonensia sæc. xiv, fol. 44ᵛ–45ʳ:[1]

---

[1] This text—not printed elsewhere, so far as I know—was generously pointed out to me by Dom André Wilmart, O.S.B. The text follows immediately after the well-known *Sancti Anselmi cum Beata Maria Dialogus de Passione Domini*, which, in the present MS,

Planctus.[1]

1. *Hev, hev! virgineus flos!*
   Hev! nature pulcherrima dos!
   Hev! vix cepit esse,
   et trahitur ecce ad non esse!

2a. *Planctus ante nescia,*
    planctu lassor anxia
    crucior dolore;

2b. *Orbat orbem radio,*
    me Iudea filio,
    gaudio, dulcore.[2]

Iohannes:

3. *O quanta est miseria*[3]
   et doloris tristicia,
       quo si patris gladius
       transit et non alius
   in filie viscera,
   que nunc habent vbera!

Maria:

4a. *Fili, dul|cor vnice,*
       singulare gaudium,
    matrem flentem respice,
       conferens[4] *solacium.*

4b. *Pectus, mentem, lumina*
       tua torquent vvlnera.
    Que mater, que femiña,
       tam felix, tam misera!

5a. *Flos florum,*
    dux morum,
       venie vena;
    quam grauis
    in clauis
       est tibi pena!

5b. *Proth dolor,*
    hinc color
       effugit oris!
    Hinc ruit,
    hinc fluit,
       vnda cruoris!

6a. *O quam sero deditus,*
       quam cito[5] *me deseris!*
    O quam digne genitus,[6]
       quam abiecte moreris!

6b. *O quis amor corporis*
       tibi fecit spolia!
    O quam dulcis pigneris,
       quam amara premia!

7a. *O fera dextera*[7]
       crucifigentis!
    O zelus, o scelus,[8]
       invide gentis!

7b. *O pia gratia*
       sic morientis!

8a. *O verum eloq⟨u⟩ium*
       iusti Symeonis:
    quem promisit gladium
       sencio doloris.

8b. *Gemitus, suspiria*[9]
       lacrimeque foris,
    doloris indicia
       sunt interioris.

ends as follows: 'O quanta iniuria facta est hodie in Ierusalem in ista pulcherrima domina, et filio eius. Et ei compaciebantur. Hec dicta manifesta facta sunt Beato Anshelmo a Beata Virgine.' The numbering of stanzas is editorial.

[1] Planctus] Planctum (MS).
[2] dulcore] culcore (MS).

[3] miseria] Corrected from *misera* (MS).
[4] conferens] Corrected from *referens* (MS).
[5] cito] scito (MS).
[6] genitus] Corrected from *gemitus* (MS).
[7] dextera] texdera (MS).
[8] scelus] zelus (MS).
[9] suspiria] susperia (MS).

9a. *Parcito proli,*
   mors, michi noli
   tu michi soli
    sola mederis.

9b. *Morte, beate,*
   separor[1] a te:
   tu michi, nate,
    non mor⟨i⟩eris

10. *Nato, queso, parcite,*
   matrem crucifigite
   aut in crucis stipite
   ambos nos affigite:
    male solus moritur.

11. *Vtinam sic doleam*
   ut dolore peream,
    nam plus est dolori
    sine morte mori
     quam perire citius.[2]

Of this composition all the stanzas except 1 and 3 are from *Planctus ante nescia* (see above, p. 496). Since the text seems to come from Regensburg, it probably represents what the Blessed Virgin and St John sang *alternatim* in the dramatic ceremony printed above from Munich MS 26947. Possibly stanza 1 was spoken by St John, as well as stanza 3.

Page 506, note 3. From evidences in a MS not precisely indicated, Dondi Orologio (pp. 60–1) writes as follows concerning a ceremony on Good Friday at Padua: 'Nel Venerdì santo doveano due chierici stare al sepolcro, e piangere la morte di G. C. ed il camerlengo darà loro mercede.' He also cites the following payment: 'Item: dedi duobus pueris, qui fecerunt plan⟨c⟩tum in die Veneris S., solidos decem.' In regard to the dramatic singing of *planctus* in Vienna and in southern Bavaria since the Middle Ages see Brooks, *Sepulchrum Christi*, pp. 153, 154, 157.

Page 515, note 5. The text of *Planctus ante nescia* from Munich MS 4660a, fol. iv[r], is as follows:[3]

1a. Planctus ante nescia,
   planctu lassor[4] anxia,
    crucior dolore.

1b. Orbat orbem radio,
   me Iudea filio,
    mentibus dulcore.

2a. Fili, dulcor unice,
    singulare gaudium,
   matrem flentem respice,
    conferens solatium.

2b. Mentem, pectus, lumina
    tua torquent uulnera.
   Que mater, que femina,
    tam[5] felix, tam misera!

[1] separor] separator (MS).
[2] citius] scicius (MS). Followed immediately by the rubric *Item alius tractatus bonus de Passione Domini*, introducing a treatise on the *Planctus Mariæ*.
[3] Previously edited by Meyer, p. 125. The

numbering of stanzas is editorial.
[4] Planctu lassor] plantula solor—with *lassor* written above *solor* (MS).
[5] Tam] Corrected by a later hand from *quam*.

3a. Flos florum,
    dux morum,
        venie uena.[1]

3b. Hinc ruit,
    hinc fluit
        unda cruoris.
    Proh dolor,
    hinc color
        effugit oris.

4a. O uerum eloquium
      iusti Symeonis;
    quem promisit gladium
      sentio doloris.

4b. Gemitus, suspiria
      lacrimeque foris,
    uulneris indicia
      sunt interioris.

5a. Parcite proli,
    mors, mihi noli,
    tu quid tibi soli
        sola mederis.

5b. Morte, beate,
    separor a te,
    ut dum, nate,
        sic cruciaris.

6a. Quod[2] crimen, que scelera
    gens promisit effera!
    Virgam, uincla, uulnera,
    sputa, clauos, cetera
        sine culpa patitur.

6b. Nato, queso, parcite,
    matrem crucifigite,
    uel in crucis stipite
    nos simul affigite;
        male solus moritur.

Page 537, note 1. The Sulmona fragment is found in that town, in the Archivio capitolare di S. Panfilo, in a MS roll marked 'Fascicolo 47, n. 9.' This parchment roll is formed by uniting two notarial documents of the fourteenth century, the dramatic fragment being written on the back, in a book hand of the fourteenth century. The dramatic text has been published by G. Pansa, *Noterelle di varia Erudizione*, Lanciano, 1887, pp. 192–200; by Bartholomaeis, in *Bullettino dell'Istituto storico italiano*, no. 8 (1889), 162–5; and, with improvements, by Bartholomaeis, *Teatro*, pp. 3–8. In making the present text I have used a photograph of the MS. For the first fifteen lines, which are only partly legible, and for the accompanying rubrics, I have drawn largely upon the later text of Bartholomaeis. The remainder of the text I have re-edited independently, mentioning (B) the significant readings in which I differ from him. The fragment is as follows:

. . . Voce Preconis Pylati veniunt duo Milites, unus ab una parte et alter ab alia, o⟨b⟩viantes sibi ad invicem. Postea veniant tertius et quartus Miles, et pugnent cum primo et secundo et dicant:

> Tertius et quartus:[3] *Qui sunt isti lori⟨ca⟩ti?*[4]
>   *Ne sint hostes predam rati*
>   *nos et nostri querimus.*
>   *Ne hostili sint aspectu,*
>   *puro corde set affectu,*   5
>   *si libet, diligimus.*

---

[1] uena] uenia (MS).
[2] Quod] Que (MS).
[3] Short rubrics, such as *Tertius et quartus* and *Omnes*, printed in this position in the text, are written in the left margin of the MS.
[4] loricati] Partly lost through perforation of the MS.

Primus et secundus respondeant:[1] *Nobis ergo.* Secundus, tercius et quartus:

Omnes: .   .   .

et secunda feliciter
. . . testes homine.
. . . unum simus   10
uel districte non uelimus
actu sive facie.

Omnes Milites insimul dicant, iunctis manibus ad celum:

Omnes: . . .

. . . grate famulemur
. . .   quam splendide   15

Post hec eant omnes coram Pylato, et dicant:

Omnes: *Preses magne probitatis,*
gloria nobilitatis,
salue, salue iugiter!

Pylatus respondeat ad eos: *Salus uobis.* Milites respondeant:

Omnes: *Fama nunctiauit nobis*
quod prepositum[2] est uobis   20
retinere milites.
Ideoque famulari
cupientes uoto pari
uenimus nos desides.

Pylatus ad Milites: *Est accessus uester.* Milites ad Pilatum:

Omnes: *Ergo iube quid agamus;*   25
nil laboris recusamus
pro te, uir egregie.
Orbem totum circuire,
uel quocumque libet ire
cupimus cotidie.   30

Cum ueniunt[3] ad Personam, et Persona dic*it: O amice, quid,* Milites et Turba respondeant:

Omnes: *Ihesum, uirum Nazarenum,*
uirum multa fraude plenum,
et horrendum[4] meritis.

Persona respondeat: *Ego sum.* Quo dicto, cadant omnes in terra, et Persona dic*at:*[5] *Quem queritis?* Respondeat Turba: *Ihesum, uirum Nazarenum.* Persona dic*at:*[5] *Si me queritis, surgatis.* Et statim surgant, et Iudas osculetur Personam, et dicat: *Aue, Rabi ueri.* Et ex magno tremore cadant omnes in terra, et Persona dicat: *Si me queritis.* Et Milites et Iudei capiant Ihesum, et dicant:

---

[1] *Respondeat* and *respondeant* printed in the rubrics of this text virtually always represent R of the MS. The forms intended may, of course, be *respondet* and *respondent*, or other forms of the verb.

[2] prepositum] propositum (B).
[3] ueniunt] ueniant (B).
[4] horrendum] orredum (MS).
[5] dicat] dicit (B).

         Omnes: *Ecce Ihesum teneamus,*
              quem ligatum perducamus   35
                Cayphe in atrium,
            vbi populi maiores
            scribe necnon seniores
              faciunt consilium.

Coram Principibus percuciant Christum et dicant:
         Omnes: *Reus mortis puniatur;*   40
              collum colaphis cedatur,
                quod est hoc quod protulit!
              Prophetiza nobis, Christe;
              dicas nobis, quis est iste
              qui te modo percutit?[1]   45

Et Milites uerberant Christum ad columnam, et dicant:
         Omnes: *Religemus ad columnam*
              demergentes in erumnam[2]
              Ihesum nobis obsidem.

Postea ducant eum ad Pylatum dicentes:
         Omnes: *Ihesum fortiter ligatum*
              perducamus ad Pylatum,   50
              Iudeorum presidem.

Coram Pylato dicant:

              Preses inclite, saluete,
              semper prosperis[3] *gaudete,*
              preses benignissime.

Pylatus respondeat: *Fratres bene.* Milites respondeant:
         Omnes: *Ecce uobis seductorem,*   55
              nostre gentis peruersorem,
              sacerdotes dirigunt.
              Vt in ligno suspendatur
              atque clauis[4] *configatur*
              postulant et cupiunt.   60

Pylatus dicit Militibus: *O uos milites.* Milites respondeant:
         Omnes: *Ecce uiri seruientes,*
              pronti semper assistentes
              ad uestrum seruitium.
              Quod iubetis est peractum;
              nulla mora, preses, factum   65
              tenet ad distribuum.

Hoc dicto, ducant Christum coram Herode, et dicant:
         Omnes: *O archana Galilee,*
              gentis speculum Iudee,
              salue, salue iugiter.

---

[1] percutit] percutis (MS).   [3] prosperis] prosperijs (MS).
[2] erumnam] erumdam (MS).   [4] clauis] clouis (MS).

Herodes respondeat: *Vobis, fratres.* Milites respondeant:

Omnes: *Galilee dominator,*   70
    ad te mittit[1] procurator
    nunc Iudee Pontius
    istum Ihesum Galileum,
    ut uos puniatis eum
    sicut est decentius.   75

Herodes ad eos: *Grates ualde.* Milites respondeant:

Omnes: *Iste dicit quod tributum*
    non sit Cesari solutum,
    principi contrarius.
    Hic peruertit nostram legem,
    se dicendo fore regem,   80
    homo temerarius!

Herodes ad Christum: *O tu, Ihesu.* Milites ad Ihesum:

Omnes: *Non respondes ad Herodem,*
    cum te scias sub eodem
    potestati subditum?

Herodes dicit: *Sit uerberibus.* Et Milites induant Ihesum ueste alba, et dicant:

Omnes: *Quare tempus deuastamus?*   85
    Istum Ihesum reducamus
    ad Pilatum presidem.

Ducto coram Pilato, dicant:

Omnes: *O Pilate gloriose,*
    uir illustris et formose,
    preses benignixime,   90
    et emittit[2] hunc Herod⟨es⟩,
    nam remisit per custodes,
    uir excellentixime.

Pilatus dicit: *Quem dimitti.[3]* Milites respondeant:

Omnes: *Ihesus nobis non red⟨d⟩atur,*
    Barabbas sed dimittatur,[4]   95
    populis[5] petentibus.

Pilatus dicit: *De Ihesu quid sum.* Milites respondeant:

Omnes: *Crucifige, preses bone!*
    Mori debet ratione
    qui sic peccat grauiter.

Pylatus dicit: *Hunc non cerno.* Milites respondeant:

Omnes: *Si non esset hic malefactor*   100
    neque populi detractor,
    non foret hic[6] traditus.
    Crucifige, crucifige!
    Penis uarijs afflige
    hunc uirum nequissimum.   105

---

[1] mittit] mictit (MS).
[2] emittit] emictit (MS).
[3] dimitti] dimicti (MS).
[4] Barabbas sed dimittatur] Baran sed

dimictatur (MS).
[5] populis] ipsis (B).
[6] hic] tibi (B)—which may represent the scribe's intention.

Pylatus dicit: *Non me tangat.* Milites respondeant:

> Omnes: *Sanguis hic in nos fundatur;*
> *nobis crimen non parcatur,*[1]
> *nostris quoque filijs.*
> *Si seruatur hic iniquus,*
> *non es Cesaris amicus;*   110
> *preses esto prescius.*[2]
> *Esse regem qui se dicit,*
> *hic A⟨u⟩gusto contradicit,*
> *quod egit hic fatus.*

Pylatus dicit: *O uos milites.* Milites respondeant:

> Omnes: *Cito, cito properemus,*   115
> *et Ihesum non dubitemus*
> *alte crucifigere.*
> *Vestimentis sit exutus*
> *iste Ihesus, et indutus*
> *de nuda coccinea.*   120

Hic inclinent se in terra dicentes:

> Omnes:[3] *Genuflexo salutemus,*
> *atque ipsum coronemus*
> *de corona spinea.*
> *Illudamus sibi multum:*
> *conspuamus eius uultum*   125
> *ad maius obprobrium.*

Primus Milex dicit: *Aue, rex tu Iudeorum.* Omnes Milites dicant:

> Omnes: *Eya, eya! quid tardamus?*
> *Et Ihesum crucifigamus*
> *ad Montem Caluarium.*

Et tollant crucem, et ponant in humeris Ihesu, et dicant:

> Omnes: *Tollat crucem Cironeus,*   130
> *qui deponens homo reus*
> *sufferat patibulum.*

Et mittentes[4] sortes super uestes primus Milex dic*it: Vestem sorte.* Quartus respondeat:

> Solus: *Ecce sortes ceciderunt*
> *super hunc cuius fuerunt*[5]
> *primitus eximie!*   135

Omnes Milites:

> Omnes: *Iam non ergo diuidamus*
> *uestem, illi sed red⟨d⟩amus*
> *cuius absit pro⟨p⟩rie.*

---

[1] parcatur] peccatur (B).
[2] prescius] prestius (B).
[3] Omnes] Solus (B).
[4] mittentes] mictentes (MS).

[5] fuerunt] Although he recognizes this as the reading of the MS, B prints *fuere*, and in the preceding line, *cecidere*.

Quo facto, crucifigant eum inter duos latrones. Hoc facto, dicant:

> Omnes: *Vath, qui templum dest⟨r⟩uebas,*
> *et destructum[1] construebas* 140
> *illud die tercia.*

Quando Persona dicit: *Sitio,* unus Militum,[2] ac⟨c⟩epta spongia, ponat ori eius dicens:

> Omnes: *Siciatum fore Christum*
> *detur uinum felle mistum*
> *et acetum spongia.*

Cum uero dixerit: *Heli,* Milites dicant:

> Omnes: *Ecce uocat nunc Heliam;* 145
> *dixit se esse Mexiam*
> *falso testimonio.*
> *Multos potuit saluare,*
> *se non potuit adiuuare*
> *pro⟨p⟩rio auxilio.* 150
> *Iam descendat hic de cruce*
> *si est uera lux de luce,*
> *uerus Dei filius.*
> *Salluum faciat seipsum*
> *quem uidemus crucifixum* 155
> *et suspensum altius.*

Quando uenit Maria ad crucem, quartus Milex dicat:

> Solus: *Que est mulier que plorat*
> *et plorando semper orat*
> *ut red⟨d⟩atur filius?*

Quando uenit Iosep dicens: *O uos uiri curiosi,* Milites dicant:

> Omnes: *Stulte senex, hinc recede,* 160
> *statim morieris, crede;*
> *uade, senex perfide!*
> *Vade, impie crudelis;*
> *uade, senex infidelis,*
> *O tirande[3] perfide!* 165

Quando uenit Centurio dicens: *O uos Milites preclari,* Milites respondeant:

> Omnes: *Ecce cor⟨p⟩us capiatis:*
> *cui placet uos tradatis:*
> *sit ad uestrum libitum.*

Quando uenit Seruus Pontificum dicens: *Clari milites,* Milites dicant:

> Omnes: *Imus libenter coram illo preside;*
> *grates millenas episcopis red⟨d⟩ite;* 170
> *sumus parati ad Pilatum pergere.*

---

[1] destructum] distructum (B).　　　　[2] Militum] mlū (MS); Miles (B).
[3] tirande] For *tyranne?*

Seruo eunte, secundus Miles dicat: *Prius mittamus.*[1] Quartus Miles dicat primo:

> Quartus solus: *Vadat Tristaynus, milex nobiliximus,*
> *omnium nostrum armorum doctiximus;*
> *fuit scrimite hic inuentor primitus.*

Et ille respondeat dicens: *Promptus esisto.* Quo dicto, uadat ad Pylatum. Cum uero redierit socios dicat: *Parata uobis nunctio.* Omnes Milites dicant insimul:

> Omnes: *Ergo eamus ad illa regalia*   175
> *et cum Pilato habeamus consilia*
> *que ualde nobis sunt modo utilia.*

Cum fuerint coram Pilato dicant:

> Omnes: *O Pilate, magne uir egregie,*
> *audi nunc uerba deprecatorie*
> *que modo tibi uenimus dicere.*   180
> *Cum adhuc ille seductor uiueret,* ·
> *nobis et multis ausus fuit dicere:*
> *'Post mortem istam debeo resurgere.'*
> *Ne si qua arte ualeat surripere,*
> *nos tamen omnes mittat*[2] *tunc in crimine*   185
> *et dicant illum a morte resurgere.*
> *Tunc esset error uere hic nouiximus*
> *sat peior primo et cun⟨c⟩torum peximus*
> *si raperetur uelud uobis diximus.*

Pylatus respondeat: *O Ebreorum fortiximi.* Qui singulariter respondeant, et quartus Miles dicat:

> Solus:[3] *Ense uibrato ad sepulcrum ueniam;*   190
> *si rapientes aliquos reperiam,*
> *capud eorum meo ense feriam.*

Pylatus dicit: *Ite uo⟨s⟩ ergo.* Milites eant ad Sepulcrum dicendo:

> Omnes: *Ergo eamus,*
> *et quod dixit faciamus,*
> *uigilando custodiamus*   195
> *ne sepulcrum admittamus;*[4]
> *ne forte ueniant eius discipuli*
> *rapturi cor⟨p⟩us capiantur si⟨n⟩guli,*
> *ne sint immunes a pena patibuli.*

Cum uenerit Pilatus ad Sepulcrum dicens: *Milites clari*, Milites circumdent Sepulcrum dicentes:

> Omnes: *Ne forte ueniant eius discipuli,* ·   200
> *et furando transferant alibi,*
> *inuadamus eos cum lanceis,*
> *et uerberemus eos gladiis.*

---

[1] mittamus] mictamus (MS).
[2] mittat] mictat (MS).
[3] Solus] Omnes (B).
[4] admittamus] admictamus (MS).

Cum fuerint excitati ad Sepulcrum, quilibet eorum dicat:

Omnes: *Heu, misereri!*
Heu, misereri! 205
Heu, misereri dolentes!
Heu, misereri plangentes!
Eamus ad principem.

Primus et secundus Milites dicunt:[1] *Dira tellus.* Tertius et quartus respondeant:

Tertius et quartus:[2] *Prosperitas, in quam donis*
a Pilato ualde bonis 210
sequimur iniuriam,
dedecus est et iactura
plurima in hac futura
si⟨n⟩gulis obprobria.

Quando Pylatus dicit: *Nicil est quod enarratis,* quartus respondeat:

Solus:[3] *Cur nos cruciat Pilatus?* 215
Ecce nostrum patet latus
ad queque[4] flagitia.
Quicquid agat, quicquid dicat,
mentes nostras numquam plicat
ut dicamus alia. 220

Primus et secundus dicant: *Ihesus lancea.* Tertius et quartus respondeant:

Tertius et quartus:[5] *Hoc testamur, hoc fatemur,*
neque uerum diffidemur.
O Iudei, credite.
Ihesus tectus uase pulcro
resurrexit de sepulcro. 225
Alleluya canite![6]

The content of this fragment is discussed by Bartholomaeis, *Le Origini,* 161–5. The attachment of the play to the liturgy is nowhere indicated.

[1] Milites dicunt] Miles dicant (B).
[2] Tertius et quartus] Omnes (B).
[3] Solus] Omnes (B).
[4] queque] quodque (B).
[5] Tertius et quartus] Omnes (B).

[6] Since blank space remains at the bottom of the sheet of parchment, we may assume that the part in which the fourth Soldier is concerned is complete at the end.

PRINTED IN GREAT BRITAIN AT THE UNIVERSITY PRESS, OXFORD
BY VIVIAN RIDLER, PRINTER TO THE UNIVERSITY